FINANCIAL MARKETS

FINANCIAL MARKETS

JOHN H. WOOD
Northwestern University

NORMA L. WOOD

Harcourt Brace Jovanovich, Publishers

San Diego   New York   Chicago   Atlanta   Washington, D.C.
London   Sydney   Toronto

FOR SUE, JIM, AND ANN

Copyrights and Acknowledgments

The authors are grateful to the following publishers and copyright holders for permission to use the material reprinted in this book:

THE AMERICAN FINANCE ASSOCIATION: Data for **Table 15.1** from *Journal of Finance* used by permission of publisher.

CRC PRESS, INC.: **Table 6.3** reprinted with permission from *C.R.C. Standard Mathematical Tables,* Chemical Rubber Publishing, Cleveland, 1963, page 435. Copyright CRC Press, Inc., Boca Raton, FL.

CHICAGO MERCANTILE EXCHANGE: **Tables 12.6** and **12.7** reprinted by permission.

DOW JONES & COMPANY, INC.: **Tables 6.2, 8.1, 8.3, 9.9, 10.4, 10.5, 10.12, 11.4, 12.2, 12.10** and **table on page 653**; data for **Tables 6.7, 8.4, 8.5,** and **19.1** Reprinted by permission of *The Wall Street Journal,* © Dow Jones & Company, Inc. (1980, 1981, 1982, 1983, 1984) All rights reserved.

DOW JONES-IRWIN: Data for **Table 8.2** used by permission of publisher.

FEDERAL RESERVE BANK OF CHICAGO: Data for **Table 9.10** used by permission.

FEDERAL RESERVE BANK OF NEW YORK: Data for **Table 7.7** used by permission.

FEDERAL RESERVE BANK OF ST. LOUIS: Data for **Tables 9.2** and **9.6** used by permission.

FINANCIAL ANALYSTS FEDERATION: Data for **Table 10.9** used by permission of Gordon Pye and publisher.

FINANCIAL PUBLISHING COMPANY: Data for **Table 6.5** used by permission.

FINANCIAL TIMES WORLD BUSINESS WEEKLY OF LONDON: **Table 12.1** used by permission.

MOODY'S INVESTORS SERVICE: Data for **Tables 10.1, 10.2,** and **10.3** adapted from *Moody's Industrial Manual, 1982* and used by permission of Moody's Investors Service, a company of The Dun & Bradstreet Corporation.

NEW YORK STOCK EXCHANGE, INC.: Data for **Tables 7.1, 7.8, 11.3, 11.8** used by permission of NYSE *Fact Book* and publisher.

NORTH-HOLLAND PUBLISHING COMPANY: Data for **Table 7.3** from *Journal of Financial Economics* used by permission of authors Eugene F. Fama and G. William Schwert and the publisher, North-Holland Publishing Company, Amsterdam.

Continued on page 704

Intelligent financial management requires not only a knowledge of your own or your firm's financial needs but an awareness of the financial opportunities and constraints offered and imposed by your environment. Such awareness results from familiarity with a wide and expanding variety of financial instruments. This book's first goal is to acquaint students with existing instruments, institutions, and markets so that future managers and other borrowers and lenders will be informed of the financial environment within which businesses and other decision-making units are presently required to operate.

The book's second goal is to give students an understanding of the directions and causes of financial innovation. Students need to develop a framework of analysis that will help them understand financial markets 5 or 10 years from now. The story of the financial markets during the past 20 years has been one of change; in 5 years the financial markets will differ significantly from those of today, but this book's approach will continue to apply because it focuses on the causes of financial change, because it views firms and individuals as profit and wealth seekers (not merely as sets of balance sheets and income statements), and because it views markets as arrangements that are constantly subject to modification to fit the evolving needs of traders.

These goals are pursued in the following ways:
- Theories are introduced in relation to events. Theories are attempts to explain events, so discussions of the data to be explained are integrated with explanations and illustrations of the theories.
- Financial instruments and institutions are discussed in relation to events. Institutions, instruments, and their markets can be understood only in the process of change, which means that we must consider the technological developments, regulations, and price fluctuations that have produced today's financial environment.
- The application of general principles to important problems has been chosen rather than an encyclopedic approach. Instead of touching more or less equally—and superficially—on all competing theories or on all existing financial arrangements, we focus on a limited number of problems that are not only interesting in themselves but capable of demonstrating general principles.
- Institutional detail is not neglected. Our interest in the fundamental causes of change does not mean that we can ignore the details concerning how portfolios are arranged and trading is actually conducted. Such ignorance would prevent us from recognizing, much less understanding, change. Students of the financial markets must be able to understand and modify theories of finance in light of the actual operation of the financial markets as reported in the financial press.
- Theories are presented in their simplest forms. Many well-known theories of finance that have been reserved to the mathematically

sophisticated are made accessible to students by means of illustrations and simple derivations. The main text requires no mathematical training beyond the basic rules of arithmetic. Proofs and further results that depend on calculus have been placed in appendixes at the ends of chapters.
- A consistent theoretical framework is maintained. Prices and interest rates are determined by profit and wealth seekers whose choices drive markets toward efficiency, although in most cases government interference and the costs of information and transactions prevent the attainment of perfectly efficient markets.
- Numerical examples and exercises are integrated with discussions of theories and events. General principles are reinforced by numerical illustrations in the text and problems at the ends of chapters. A Solutions Manual for these problems is available.

Financial Markets was developed over a period of 6 years in response to the needs of a money markets course at Northwestern University; portions of the manuscript have been used at Oklahoma State University, Dartmouth College, and the Universities of Minnesota, Chicago, and Rochester. The book has been designed with three or four courses in mind, and the chapters that correspond to these courses may be listed as follows: **All courses** would include Chapters 1 to 7 and 9, which provide (i) an overview of the financial markets and the changing environment within which financial institutions operate, (ii) the elements of the supplies and demands for money and other financial instruments, and (iii) the basic arithmetic of present value and security prices, yields, and rates of return. **Financial markets courses** that emphasize financial instruments and their markets, rather than financial institutions, would also include Chapters 8 and 10 through 12. **Financial institutions courses** would include Chapters 13 through 17. (Of course distinctions between courses in financial markets and financial institutions are largely arbitrary. Differences must be almost entirely those of emphasis—either on the institutions trading the instruments or on the instruments themselves.) **Courses concerned with the determination of interest rates** in a macroeconomic context would include Chapters 18 through 20. The term structure of interest rates is a popular subject, and so is the relationship between interest rates and inflation, so that Chapters 18 and 19 are likely to be included in a variety of courses.

Scores of generous people have contributed to the production of this book. We are especially thankful to Dale and Peggy Osborne (University of Texas at Dallas). Dale read the entire manuscript with understanding and insight, and suggested many improvements in substance and exposition, most of which we adopted and the rest of which, perhaps, we should have. And many delightful hours spent with Peggy and Dale greatly lightened the burdens associated with bringing the book to completion.

The book was finished during a 2-year visit at the Federal Reserve Bank of Dallas, and we are grateful to Joe Burns and Jim Pearce for ensuring that we were able to take full advantage of the bank's excellent research environment. We are also grateful to Karl A. Scheld and Harvey Rosenblum for making the facilities of the Federal Reserve Bank of Chicago's Research Department available to us. Much of the book was researched or written on Federal Reserve premises, which would not have been possible without the competent and cheerful support of Jane Freeman and Dorothy Phillips and their colleagues in the Research Libraries of the Federal Reserve Banks of Dallas and Chicago. Invaluable support, suggestions, and information have also been provided by a great many other Fed workers, including Gerald P. O'Driscoll, Jr., Robert T. Clair, Dean Pankonien, Stephen P. A. Brown, John Loney, Dan Keys, Robert Feil, Steve Prue, Pat Lawler, Franklin D. Berger, Eugenie D. Short, Bill Gruben, Leroy Laney, and Tom Fomby of the Dallas Fed, Robert Laurent, Dorothy M. Nichols, Randy Merris, Larry R. Mote, Paul L. Kasriel, Alan K. Reichert (now at Illinois State University), and Jack Hervey of the Chicago Fed, Christopher McCurdy of the New York Fed, Jack Tatom of the St. Louis Fed, and our long-ago colleagues at the Federal Reserve Board, Steve Taylor, Neva Van Peski, and Leigh Ribble. We clearly owe much to the Federal Reserve System, but nothing in this book should be interpreted as representing the official views of the system or of any of its parts. In fact, biting the hand that has fed us, the opposite is more likely to be the case.

We are also indebted for much valuable information and advice to Scott Ulman (University of Minnesota), Ruth Heisler and Edd D. Villani (Scudder, Stevens and Clark), Patric H. Hendershott (Ohio State University), Richard Marchisotto (Mabon Nugent), Stephen Smith (University of Texas at Austin), Paul Burik and Leslie Wurman (Chicago Mercantile Exchange), Alan Hess (University of Washington), Tony Marcussen (First Chicago), Allan Kleidon (Stanford University), Dwight Grant (North Carolina State University), Ron Masulis (UCLA), Dan White (Georgia State University), John M. Finkelstein (University of New Mexico), Jonathan Scott (Federal Home Loan Bank of Dallas), Douglas N. Diamond (University of Chicago), Roger D. Rutz (Chicago Board of Trade), C. Herman Lin (Oklahoma State University), Veronica Cook (Northern Trust), Robert A. Taggart (Boston University), Scott A. Baily (Smith Barney), and Daniel E. Schmidt (The Chicago Corporation).

We have also benefited from active contributions by students. An important part of our money markets course is a term paper in which the student is asked to select, examine, and explain one or more empirical relationships. The objects of this exercise are to encourage students to become acquainted with data sources and to learn to apply financial theories to the data that they have uncovered. The ideal university is a community of scholars in which students as well as professors are expected to advance knowledge, and we have learned much from students' term papers, especially those of Bernard Casties, Dan Chapman, Michael Hogan, Elizabeth Metcalf Atkin, Michael Boehm, Larry Farrell, Philip Friedman, David Hays, Barbara Carroll, Sidonie Walters, Paul E. Misniak, Phyllis Hynes, Mitch Cohen, Kevin Buchi, Brad Ihlenfeld, David Greenberg, Margaret Nelson, Scott Huff, Fred Kiehne, George Yanku, Bart Naughton, Steve Loeb, James Benson, Joel Carlson, Peter Tam, Gidon Cohen, Rafel Javellana,

Jakob Stott, Dennis Svoronos, Susan Hatch, Sheila Lynch, Phil Gong, Carole Munro, and Mitch Rasky.

The book was a long time in preparation, and we were fortunate in obtaining the skillful services of Susan McMahon, Helen Maibenco, Diane Pierce, Darlene Pierce, Ellah Pina, Patricia Warring, and Ann Wood, who typed successive versions of the manuscript.

We are also grateful to our manuscript editor, David Esner, for improving our English, and to the people at Harcourt Brace Jovanovich for their patience and forbearance in allowing us to write the book that we wanted to write in (almost) the amount of time that we wanted to take. Our acquisitions editors, Brian Hinshaw and Johannah McHugh, smoothed the way during every stage of the book's preparation. It has been a pleasure to work with them and the excellent editorial and production staff, including Marji James, Cathy Fauver, Diane Pella, Don Fujimoto, Schamber Richardson, and Avery Hallowell.

CONTENTS

ONE

An Introduction to the Changing Financial System

"How puzzling all these changes are!
I'm never sure what I'm going to be,
from one minute to another!" . . .
For, you see, so many out-of-the-way
things had happened lately, that Alice
had begun to think that very few things
indeed were really impossible.

Lewis Carroll, *Alice's Adventures in Wonderland*, chs. 1, 5

A ROADMAP (OF REGULATION, INFLATION, AND INNOVATION) AND A VEHICLE (RATIONAL SELF-INTEREST) THROUGH THE FINANCIAL MARKETS

Every individual is continually exerting himself to find out the most advantageous employment for whatever capital he can command. It is his own advantage, indeed, and not that of the society, which he has in view. But the study of his own advantage naturally, or rather necessarily leads him to prefer that employment which is most advantageous to the society.

. . . He generally indeed neither intends to promote the public interest, nor knows how much he is promoting it. . . . [H]e intends only his own gain, and he is in this, as in many other cases, led by an invisible hand to promote an end which was no part of his intention. Nor is it always the worse for the society that he was no part of it. By pursuing his own interest he frequently promotes that of the society more effectually than when he really intends to promote it. I have never known much good done by those who affected to trade for the public good. It is an affectation, indeed, not very common among merchants, and very few words need be employed in dissuading them from it.

Adam Smith, *An Inquiry into the Nature and Causes of the Wealth of Nations*, bk. 4, ch. 2, 1776

MODELS OF THE FINANCIAL MARKETS

This book is about the workings of the financial markets. We begin by discharging our first obligation to the reader: explaining the framework and viewpoint that have formed our analysis of these markets. The range of available market models is bounded by two extremes. One extreme, model A, is especially popular along the banks of the Potomac and views people as rather dull, imperfectly aware of "what's good for them," and incapable of achieving their dimly perceived goals without large measures of protection and direction. The advocates of this model do not believe that economic exchanges in the absence of government involvement can be to the mutual advantage of the parties concerned. The opposite extreme, model Z, is often associated with the University of Chicago and sees people as aware of their own interests and ingenious in devising means of achieving their goals without assistance from Washington or state capitals. This model assumes perfect markets that allocate resources toward their most valuable uses.

These models are not straw men set up by us especially for the occasion. They dominate newspaper columns, the six o'clock news, and political speeches. Federal, state, and local governments are under continuous attack for making a mess of things by doing too much (that is, for violating model Z) or for allowing the public to make a mess of things by not doing enough (that is, for violating model A). Nowhere is the controversy carried on with greater intensity than in the highly regulated American financial markets.

Of course the "true" model lies somewhere between A and Z and differs between markets. Some markets are more imperfect than others. But this is not to say that the correct financial model typically lies midway between A and Z. There is a large and growing body of evidence that suggests that financial markets are highly efficient in achieving the goals of borrowers and lenders.[1] This evidence supports the view that the appropriate model is much closer to Z than it is to A. It might even be Y. Much of this book will be devoted to the systematic exploration of the efficient-markets literature. But we shall also present the case for the other side, usually by calling attention to those areas in which the case for perfect markets is weakest.

The above market models suggest companion explanations of regulation: Model A explains regulation as high-minded, disinterested attempts to discourage fraud, encourage competition, and otherwise improve markets in ways that in some sense benefit society. Even the regulations that interfere with competition, such as limitations on entry into banking and ceilings on interest rates, are pursued in the public's interest by ensuring a profitable and therefore a sound and stable financial system. Model Z, on the other hand, explains regula-

---

1 Market efficiency will later be given a more precise meaning.

tion as an extension of the pursuit of economic self-interest to the political arena. No one, after all, favors competition and perfect markets in the areas in which he does business. All seek advantages over other traders, and many attempt to induce governments to secure or preserve those advantages. That is, model Z explains regulation as a series of impediments to competition adopted in response to political pressures by special-interest groups. This model sees governments in general and regulations in particular as instruments by which people pick the pockets of their fellow citizens. As with market models, we shall find that the appropriate regulatory model is much closer to Z than it is to A.

The following sections outline the interactions between the private forces that drive markets toward efficiency and the regulatory forces that impede efficiency. Much of this book is devoted to the workings of specific markets in terms of these interactions—with emphasis on the problems confronted by managers and other decision makers in efficient and inefficient markets. The roadmap at the end of this chapter highlights the problems and some of their solutions and shows how the different parts of the book—markets and decision makers— are connected.

EFFICIENT MARKETS
Markets
Dictionaries define markets as places where things are traded. Markets come in all shapes and sizes: The place where trades occur might be the large room that contains the New York Stock Exchange or the wheat pit of the Chicago Board of Trade; it might cover a somewhat larger area, like that of a medieval fair or a modern shopping center; it might be spread over an entire region, like the California wine district; it might consist of hundreds of offices closely linked by sophisticated communications networks from Boston to San Diego or from London to Tokyo, such as the markets for commercial paper and foreign exchange; or like the market for tacos, it might be widely diffused and lack any apparent system.

But in a larger sense all these markets are much more widely spread over area and people than might at first be thought by someone on the balcony overlooking a stock exchange or a wheat pit. These gatherings of frantic, running, gesticulating, shouting people are executing trades on the order, or in anticipation of the order, of the woman on the 8:05 quietly intent on the stock-market reports in the *Wall Street Journal*, the insurance-company financial officer in search of the highest and safest return on the millions of which he is custodian, the farmer who wants to hedge against the possibility of a fall in the price of wheat, and the worried corporate treasurer who still does not have the money to pay for the afternoon shipment. All these people affect the financial and commodity markets. All of them influence the quantities traded and the prices at which trades occur. Most of the markets described in this book are national or international markets in the most complete senses of these terms even though in some cases the actual trading, the exchange of things, takes place in a few rooms or over a few telephone lines.

Markets consist of traders and things traded. We are all traders, and most of us are traders in the financial markets. This is true, for example, of the owner of a bank account who has traded $500 in currency for a checkbook and a deposit slip that together entitle her to write checks in the amount of $495 (we assume that service charges and the cost of the checks amount to $5). The more important trader–decision makers are discussed in Part 5. The things traded in the financial markets are usually called either "securities" or "financial instruments." An instrument is defined as "a thing by means of which something is done," and this definition perfectly fits a financial instrument, including your checks, by means of which you may effect exchanges of the money in your checking account for goods that you desire. Other, more esoteric-sounding but really quite simple financial instruments are described in Parts 2 to 4.

Efficiency

So far we have learned that traders in the financial markets exchange financial instruments as means to their various ends. (This may not seem like much, but isn't it nice to know that, notwithstanding the complicated technical terms thrown around by practitioners and theorists, finance is such a simple, straightforward subject?) The most common end is "making money," ponderously referred to by economists as "the accumulation of wealth," in a form that can easily be translated into the ultimate economic goals of food, clothes, shelter, and all the other things that money can buy (maybe even happiness).

Money is made in the financial markets by buying low and selling high or, equivalently, by borrowing at low rates of interest and lending at high rates. Nearly all traders try to do this; but all fall short of their goals. They are seldom able to borrow or lend on the terms that they would like and must settle for the best rates available. This book is a study of the forces that determine the rates of interest at which people and organizations actually borrow and lend. Such a study requires us to take account of the goals and resources of those people and organizations and of the legal and institutional environments in which they operate. To keep the study within manageable limits and to focus on the most fundamental and important determinants of interest rates, we make some simplifying assumptions. But we will try not to get far away from the actual behavior of borrowers and lenders and the day-to-day workings of the financial markets.

Notice that we do not promise to be "realistic." This is impossible in any general sense because different people have different perceptions of reality. This is not a subtle philosophical point but a recognition that, for example, the workings of the stock market seen by a trader at the New York Stock Exchange are not the same as those seen by the corporate treasurer contemplating a new stock issue. Each views the market in terms of his own ends and as part of an environment specific to himself; his vision of the financial markets is not general and benevolent but narrow and selfish. He neither knows nor cares about Adam Smith's "invisible hand." We, on the other hand, are students of the financial markets and therefore must try to take a general view of those markets although along the way we shall have to consider the specific viewpoint and role of each of the important groups of borrowers and lenders. Only then will we be able to understand how they interact to determine market rates of interest. We shall find that the effects of their actions are remarkably efficient, in the sense defined next:

DEFINITION 1.1   An *efficient market* is one in which prices equal values.

That is, in efficient markets the prices of production inputs, securities, and consumption goods reflect the profits and enjoyments expected by their purchasers and forgone by their sellers.[2] People are not taken advantage of in efficient markets; there are no "sure things," no "easy pickings," no matter what your real estate agent, stockbroker, or college recruiter says—if the house, stock, and education markets are efficient. This is because prices reflect all available information in efficient markets. Otherwise, some people with superior information or legal advantages could take advantage of others. They could systematically beat the market by buying goods for less or selling goods for more than they are worth.

Would you believe that not all markets, even all financial markets, are perfectly efficient? Economists often show a tendency to damage their credibility by excessive claims for the explanatory power of their theories and by the extreme nature of their assumptions. This is too bad; for some of their theories are reasonably consistent with what is observed in the financial markets. Contrary to an opinion held in some circles, however, no financial market has been proved (and probably cannot be proved) to be perfectly efficient. Some are highly inefficient, and in view of the costs of acquiring and using information, this is hardly remarkable. What *is* remarkable is the closeness with which most financial markets approximate the efficient-markets ideal when

---

2 Richard West (1981; page 20) has called this *allocational efficiency*. An allocationally efficient capital market is one that establishes securities prices that "encourage the economy's capital resources to flow [to] the most promising investment opportunities." On the other hand West defines an *operationally efficient* market as one in which traders are able to perform transactions as cheaply as possible. A high degree of operational efficiency is a necessary condition for allocational efficiency because large transaction costs discourage the flows of goods and credit toward their most valued uses.

allowed to operate free of government interference. Numerous statistical studies have demonstrated that one cannot systematically beat these markets with simple rules—for example with rules based on charts of historical price movements—that are also available to other investors.[3] The studies do not imply that you cannot, as in other spheres of life, achieve above-average results if you are smarter and work harder than others. On the other hand you are unlikely to get rich on tips from your stockbroker, who like his colleagues acts on the information before passing it on to you.[4] The little old television professor tells us that "Smith Barney makes money the old-fashioned way. They *earn* it." We daresay they do—for themselves. You will have to follow their example if you hope to make money also, which is probably not the message intended by this commercial.

Some modest assumptions

The most important prerequisite of market efficiency is competition. Since it is not the purpose of this book to sell the student on perfect market efficiency, it will not always be necessary to make the extreme assumptions usually associated with perfect competition: a large number of perfectly informed, utility-maximizing traders dealing free of transaction costs in an infinitely divisible, homogeneous good such that everyone pays or receives the same price, which no one alone is substantial enough to influence. Sometimes we shall make use of these assumptions, either for expositional convenience or because the perfectly competitive model implies results much like those observed in the financial markets. But we shall usually find a weaker set of assumptions sufficient for our purposes. The only assumption that we take in unalloyed form from the perfectly competitive model is that of utility maximization. Essentially all that we assume is that people are, in the main, selfish and smart. In particular we assume that people have a pretty good idea of what they want, are reasonably knowledgeable about the opportunities available to them, and are fairly ingenious in devising means to their ends, subject to the constraints imposed by their environment and by their personal and resource limitations.

Understanding markets

All of these human and environmental characteristics are brought together in financial markets to determine financial flows and interest rates. The exact process by which these factors combine to produce the results that we see reported in the financial press is impossible to

---

3 Some of these studies are listed below in item 1 of the subsection entitled "Freeways: almost-efficient markets."

4 But such tips are not always useless: You will not be the *first* to acquire the information, but neither, if your source is timely and reliable, will you be the *last*.

describe or even to understand in all its complexity. *Market* is an abstract concept. Each of us, participants and observers, sees and comprehends only bits and pieces of markets. Each person's view of a market must therefore be a simplified version, a model, of the "real thing." Each model must be judged in terms of its usefulness in explaining observed phenomena; that is, are the predictions of the model consistent with our observations of the financial flows and interest rates that have been generated by the actual market process? The standard tools of economic analysis, especially supply and demand (which are founded on the assumptions listed above at the end of the last subsection), are important components of most models. Many financial models constructed in this way, when modified in light of the institutional arrangements peculiar to the markets under study, have increased our understanding of events.

We have referred to the persuasive evidence in support of the thesis that, when free of regulation, financial markets *work*. By this we mean that they are almost efficient in the sense that funds are transmitted from lenders to borrowers on terms that closely reflect the expected costs of saving and the expected returns to consumption and investment. But the idea of a market that actually performs this function has proved to be too difficult, too abstract, to earn general acceptance. To the bureaucrat such a concept is worse than "unrealistic"—it is anathema. His reasoning is partly self-serving: His job depends on regulation, which in turn depends on the belief that markets do not work or, at least, do not produce desired results. But there is also an element of sincerity in his argument. He simply cannot believe that the market jungle, with its unbridled competition and antagonistic behavior by traders with directly opposing goals, can yield outcomes that are in any sense desirable or even bearable. The idea that money or goods can be moved from suppliers to demanders on socially acceptable terms without some kind of central control is beyond his or her comprehension.

Even the businessman and the housewife, the two who contribute most to market efficiency, cannot believe what they have accomplished. One wants to get as much money from the other, while supplying as few goods, as possible; the other wants as many goods, for as little money, as possible, and by shopping around, she forces suppliers to provide goods at prices that approach their competitive (efficient) levels. Some markets are less efficient than others, and because of imperfect information and the costs of moving people and goods, none functions perfectly; yet despite all of its obvious and deplorable imperfections, it is difficult to conceive of another game as fair, or as likely to direct resources to the ends most highly valued by the public, as an unregulated (that is, free) market. Nevertheless, the people who make markets work often deny what they have done. As in the case of the regulator, part of their reasoning is self-serving: They are not satisfied with the terms on which they are able to buy and sell, and by arguments that invent or exaggerate market imperfections[5] they hope to bring government on the scene in a way that gives them advantages over other traders. But they also experience genuine difficulty in comprehending all the complex and often unseen operations of markets. Few businessmen show any interest in how or why they contribute to the efficiency of markets through their efforts to maximize profits by taking advantage of perceived market imperfections. We might as well ask Julius Erving for a scientific discourse on the principles of anatomy and physics that enable him to fly around and over his earthbound opponents. Yet like the businessman and the housewife he knows what to do and how to do it.

Budget constraints and printing presses

Although market processes may be complex and, in their entirety, abstract, they are based on a few simple, concrete elements. One of these was described above as the awareness of opportunities. Economists refer to this concept as the *budget constraint,* which is merely a calculation of what we can buy, given our resources. Not every item in the budget constraint (which, unlike the Economics 101 textbook example, usually extends over several periods) is foreknown with certainty. The student may have to make a decision about whether to take her boyfriend out for a Big Mac or to La Rotisserie Française before knowing for sure whether the tax refund or the check from home is going to arrive on time. A banker may have to say yes or no to a loan request by a valued customer without full knowledge of the bank's vacillating available funds. However, although these decisions are made under conditions of uncertainty, they are usually made with a pretty good notion of the consequences involved. They are calculated risks similar to bets on the stock market or the toss of a coin. If our guess (prediction) is correct, our enjoyment and/or profits are increased. If we guess incorrectly, we live on popcorn for a week or are left behind in the next round of promotions.

We are all familiar with people, firms, and cities that apparently live in innocence of budget constraints. But most of the households, firms, and governments whose behavior is important to the workings of the financial markets manage, particularly when considered as groups, to live within their incomes.[6] And they do this in a fairly predictable manner. Their spending/income ratios are not among life's constants, but we shall see that the highly publicized variations in consumer spending patterns (for example) are much exaggerated. This relative steadiness of behavior makes the job of those who would understand and forecast interest-rate movements much easier than would be the

---

5 For a seller a market imperfection is a low price; for a buyer it is a high price.

6 The steadiness of private and state and local-government spending behavior and the unsteadiness of federal-government spending are described in Chapters 13 and 20.

case if all groups were susceptible to wide fluctuations in their attitudes toward spending, saving, borrowing, and lending.

However, the task of explaining and, to an even greater extent, forecasting interest rates is still not an easy one. For the steadiness of households, firms, and state and local governments (taken as groups) is more than offset by what can be described only as the wild fluctuations of the federal government and the Federal Reserve System (the Fed). But even the wildness of these two groups, although impossible to predict, is not difficult to understand. Other groups, even those with powers of taxation, cannot avoid eventually facing up to Mr. Micawber's dictum:

> Annual income twenty pounds, annual expenditure nineteen nineteen six, result happiness. Annual income twenty pounds, annual expenditure twenty pounds ought and six, result misery.[7]

But the everyday, commonsense notions of finance (which we hope this book will do nothing to dispel), of which this quotation is one example, do not apply to the federal government or to the Fed. They can print money. We are sure the student will have no difficulty comprehending what a liberating influence is conferred on spending patterns by the possession of printing presses. The limitations on, and predictability of, your behavior and ours are not shared by the owners of these machines. We shall see that the unprecedented inflation of the past 50 years may be explained by the unique financial freedoms enjoyed by the federal government and the central bank.

Examples of efficient and inefficient markets

A better understanding of the factors that contribute to efficiency in financial markets may be gained by considering some inefficient markets. The most common cause of inefficiency is lack of information. A good example is the market for used cars. The typical buyer in this market is unsure of the mechanical condition of the car that he or she buys and must rely at least partly on guesswork. Sellers know more (although not everything). Consequently there is a tendency for buyers to suspect the worst—"If the car is in such great shape, why are you getting rid of it?"—so that good cars commonly cannot be sold for their true worth.[8]

College students are also familiar with other inefficient markets. They frequently complain of being ripped off by the college food

---

7 Charles Dickens, *David Copperfield*. For those unfamiliar with pre-1971 British currency "nineteen nineteen six" means 19 pounds, 19 shillings, 6 pence. There were 20 shillings in a pound and 12 pence in a shilling. Mr. Micawber, by the way, was himself neglectful of the advice implicit in this dictum—as is usual with givers of advice.

8 In an article entitled "The Market for 'Lemons'," George Akerlof (1970) has argued persuasively that, in markets for goods where buyers are unable to judge quality accurately, there is a tendency for bad products to drive out good products.

service and bookstore and by local merchants, and they are right. But it is their own fault for being so *ignorant*—not in the sense of being stupid but rather in the sense of being uninformed. Most students either are inexperienced shoppers or find their work and social lives too full to allow the time to search for alternatives. When you have an hour to spare and can borrow a car, compare the prices of stationery and sweatshirts at the stores on and near campus with those at the Sears or K-Mart across town. Also check the prices of tennis shoes, racquets, and balls away from campus, preferably at a discount store. The usually very substantial differences between the prices paid by students and by others almost constitute a definition of inefficient markets.

There is no villain in this story. Each seller is charging "all the traffic will bear," and why not? So will you when after college it comes time to sell your labor in the "real world." The only remedy for the inefficiencies described above is effort in the acquisition and use of information. Consumer groups and government regulations are unlikely to help the buyer as much as she can help herself by shopping around, comparing prices, and buying goods where they are cheapest. Comparison shopping by students would soon have the effect of bringing prices closer together although transportation costs and the value of time would continue to produce different prices for tennis balls on and off campus.

Many—perhaps most—markets are more efficient than are those for used cars or college sweatshirts. The main reason for this difference is that many markets are composed of skilled and experienced traders, who spend much time and effort in shopping around for the best deals. Probably the most efficient of all are those national and international financial markets that have remained relatively free of regulation. Careful consumers check newspapers, compare notes with other shoppers, and drive from store to store in search of good hamburger at a good price, but securities dealers and corporate treasurers devote nearly all their working hours to searches for the best yields. Their information is far better than that of consumers because their search is conducted in a more efficient and thorough fashion than is possible for the overworked housewife. The telephone, the teletype, and communications satellites keep them up to the minute on developments in major trading locations throughout the world. Their information is not only timely but also usually clear and in a form that is easily interpreted. For example such homogeneous goods as a bond issue of the U.S. government do not present the problems of quality evaluation that are inherent in choices between used cars or even between packages of hamburger. Different investors have different needs and expectations, but all know the meaning of a price quotation on an 8 percent U.S. security maturing on August 15, 1990. Judgments of the quality (riskiness) of privately issued debt are not so easy as those for U.S. securities. However, especially in the case of the short-term debt of large firms with high credit ratings, information is as readily available and almost as clear as that for U.S. securities. Temporary price advantages that are sometimes gained by traders even in the financial markets are quickly closed by their competitors—unless those advantages are perpetuated by government intervention.

REGULATION + INFLATION + SELF-INTEREST ⇒ INNOVATION

The promotion of efficiency by financial intermediaries

Of Lincoln it was said:

> It did not seem to be one of the purposes of his life to accumulate a fortune. In fact, outside of his profession, he had no knowledge of the way to make money, and he never even attempted it.[9]

Lincoln was unique, but in his attitudes toward work and wealth he has, even today, many kindred spirits. These ordinary people stand to benefit from efficient financial markets at least as much as, and probably more than, sharp traders constantly on the lookout for a profitable deal. Few societies would not rather be judged by their rail splitters than by their bankers. But notwithstanding the shady reputation of moneylenders, which is at least as old as history, financial intermediaries have a valuable, even noble, role to play in the economic life of society. The claims of the New York Stock Exchange and other financial groups that they "make America grow" are noteworthy in the field of advertising for their accuracy. They really do facilitate saving, productivity, and the accumulation of wealth by offering the means by which funds can be transferred from savings to productive investments. And they have demonstrated that they are able to perform this service efficiently, even for the small investor.

For example the difference between the buying and selling prices bid and asked by securities dealers is about $2 for a $10,000, 3-month Treasury bill (T bill). That is, the dealer takes one-fiftieth of 1 percent of the value of the security. He takes about one-half of 1 percent of the value of long-term U.S. securities. For small quantities odd-lot charges may amount to an additional one-half of 1 percent. In the stock market the average discount broker charges a commission of about $35 for the purchase or sale of 100 shares of stock selling for $40 a share. Her commission is thus less than 1 percent of the value of the stock. Many large transactions are handled even more cheaply. Brokers charge a fee of $1 for each $1 million exchange of federal funds (overnight borrowing and lending between banks). These low transaction costs contribute greatly to the efficiency of the financial markets and may be

---

9 From a eulogy delivered in Indianapolis in May 1865 by David Davis, for many years a fellow rider on the Eighth Illinois Circuit.

contrasted with the 10 percent take by real estate brokers and lawyers from the sale of houses.

Banks, bond dealers, and other financial intermediaries have contributed to market efficiency in many ways. The potential gains to the average rail splitter in New Salem, who during the course of his life sometimes saves a bit of money and sometimes borrows to buy a house or horseless carriage, are substantial. Without diverting very much time and effort from his trade or his leisure pursuits, he benefits from technological advances in distant locations. Increases in productivity in Miami or Seattle, which induce entrepreneurs to increase their borrowing for the purpose of investment, cause bank loan rates to rise. Banks in turn compete for these increasingly profitable funds by paying higher rates of interest on deposits. Empirical evidence presented in the following chapters shows that this process tends to operate quickly and effectively. In fact, it is too quick and effective to suit some market participants. Financial intermediaries have wrought better than they wanted and have induced governments to interfere with market processes in their favor.

Regulation, inflation, and the destruction of efficiency

The regulations that have had the greatest impact on financial flows and have given the greatest stimulus to financial innovation during the past 20 years are ceilings on interest rates. After the near collapse of the banking system during the Great Depression[10] Congress enacted a series of restrictive measures designed to enhance the profitability of banks by insulating them from the rigors of competition. These measures, which were extended to savings and loan associations (S&Ls) in 1966,[11] included the prohibition of interest on checking accounts and low ceilings (under Regulation Q) on interest on savings accounts. In recent years, however, under pressure from high interest rates caused by the federal government's inflationary monetary and fiscal policies, these restrictions have been relaxed or evaded until they are applicable only to small savers.[12] During the early 1980s households lent money to banks in the form of checking accounts at zero interest and in the form of savings accounts at a maximum of $5\frac{1}{4}$ percent. They lent money to S&Ls at a maximum of $5\frac{1}{2}$ percent. During the same period bank loan rates were sometimes 20 percent and many S&Ls charged mortgage rates above 15 percent. These extortionate differentials between the borrowing and lending rates of banks and S&Ls in their dealings with small savers reflect the gross inefficiencies caused by government interference: The rates earned by

---

10 Of 26,000 banks existing in 1929 over 9,000 had failed by 1933. This contrasts with 272 failures between 1941 and 1981 (*Statistical Abstract of the United States, 1982–83*).

11 And also to credit unions and mutual savings banks.

12 The main themes of Chapters 2 and 3 are the incentives to evade interest-rate ceilings provided by high interest rates and the forms taken by those evasions.

small depositors bore no relation to the value of the deposits in bank and S&L loan markets. These differentials rendered those institutions virtually useless to the average citizen in search of a way to protect the purchasing power of his savings. Of course, if he had been able to lay his hands on $100,000, he could have earned as much as 17 percent by investing in a bank time deposit. There are no maximum rates on time deposits in denominations of $100,000 or more.

A short sermon on the student's responsibilities

The long-suffering taxpayer, whether formally educated or not, is conscious of his or her financial contribution to your education[13] and she approves of it. Americans still associate education with "progress," often are proud of their local colleges and universities, and complain less about taxes for the support of these institutions than they do about taxes for most other purposes. They see higher education as the principal means of advancement of both knowledge and the economic and social status of their children.

Students owe a large debt to taxpayers, and merely incurring similar burdens for their own children is not sufficient repayment. Those who go to work for financial institutions will be especially well placed to made restitution. Risking more than a few snickers, we assert that the best way of paying your debt is by *doing your job* to make the financial markets as efficient as possible. Lend at the highest rate of interest you can get and borrow at the lowest rate available—without injuring your fellow citizens by soliciting the interference of government on your behalf.[14] This debt is all the more binding for being legally unenforceable.[15]

Regulation begets innovation begets regulation begets . . .

The honest burglar takes his chances with the law. The lobbying banker not only operates on a larger scale than the burglar,[16] he turns

---

13 This applies not only to state universities but also to so-called private colleges and universities, which receive public funds in a variety of ways.

14 This plea permeates Adam Smith's *Wealth of Nations.* Smith raged against the destructive effects of tariffs, monopolistic privileges granted by government to "exclusive companies," and the regulation of wages, prices, and interest rates. Most of his illustrations of the damage done by licenses and restrictions are of injuries to unprotected workers and consumers.

15 One of our romantic Southern friends, who believes the Confederacy still lives or ought to, illustrates what he takes to be the tradition of honor in the Old South with the following story: One day, after an impecunious "gentleman" had again declared his inability to redeem the IOUs held by his tailor, the tailor complained that the gentleman always paid his gambling debts promptly and fully. "But sir," responded the latter, "those are debts of honor to those who have no legally binding claim upon me. You, on the other hand, have by your possession of my notes recourse to the law." Hearing this, the exasperated (but shrewd) tailor tore up the IOUs and declared, "Now I am in the same position as the others," whereupon the gentleman paid him immediately.

16 David Pyle (1974) has estimated that losses to depositors caused by ceilings on savings-deposit rates exceeded $5 billion during the period 1968 to 1970. Robert Taggart's (1978) estimate for Massachusetts mutual savings banks during 1970 to 1975 exceeded $500 million. In comparison the President's Commission on Law Enforcement and Administration of Justice (*The Challenge of Crime in a Free Society*) estimated that, in the United States in 1965, losses due to

the law on the small saver, who becomes criminal as well as victim if she breaks the law in an attempt to earn a good rate of return. But this does not deter investors from making the attempt. We have noted the ingenuity displayed by people in evading constraints as they strive for their goals. This is true of small and large investors. It is also true of the borrowers at whose behest many of those constraints have been imposed. The purpose of many regulations is to limit competition by agreement among competitors to submit to a government-imposed high selling price or low buying price. Having thus maneuvered its rivals into an uncompetitive position, each firm then attempts to increase its profits by cheating on the regulations. There is no better example of this behavior than that stemming from Regulation Q. The large differentials between borrowing and lending rates that have characterized the past 20 years have been strong inducements to violate the spirit and sometimes the letter of the regulations. Banks, S&Ls, and other borrowers have actively competed for the funds of small savers and other lenders, and they have shown substantial talents for innovation in the process. They have promoted new financial instruments and have found ways of paying above-ceiling rates on old instruments. But they have at the same time urged the regulators to interfere with their competitors, giving the latter new incentives to evade new regulations. The continuing evolution of the financial markets is largely a story of this interaction between regulation and innovation, which may best be told in terms of regulatory roadblocks, innovative detours, and the construction of efficient freeways.

HIGHWAYS AND BYWAYS

Financial markets have changed a great deal in recent years. Many current financial institutions and instruments would not be recognized by a Rip van Winkle born in 1930, gone to sleep in 1960, and awakened in 1980. But they would be familiar to his parents and grandparents. For the financial markets have been set on a course toward the sophisticated and competitive environment of the 1920s. These changes have been accompanied by significant (though still far from triumphant) pressures to jettison the regulations of the 1930s and by increasingly erratic official monetary actions that have revived the price and interest-rate volatility of the pre-1914 era.

Strangely, perhaps, our understanding of financial markets has been strengthened by these changes. Marble columns do not a bank make, and dormant, unchanging institutions in a pacific environment are less susceptible to analysis than are those in the process of

---

robbery, burglary, and larceny (including car theft) amounted to $600 million (reported in the *Statistical Abstract of the United States, 1970*). Studies by Charles Clotfelter and Charles Lieberman (1978) and by Edward Lawrence and Gregory Elliehausen (1981) have shown that the adverse effects of rate ceilings weigh most heavily on low-income families.

adaptation to a volatile environment. We cannot know what a bank *really is* until it is subjected to a few shocks—by courtesy of Congress and the Fed. To understand the changing financial institutions and markets of the 1980s, we must know where they have been and where they appear to be headed. We must also be aware of the forces causing them to change. This book is meant to be a guide to those forces and their directions, and this section presents a roadmap of the remaining chapters, with emphasis on the forces of regulation and innovation described above.

Roadblocks: government interferences with market efficiency

Congress and the regulators have attempted to impede market processes in the following ways:

1. The most dramatic of these attempts has been the prohibition of interest on demand deposits and the severe administration of interest ceilings by the Fed (for commercial banks) and the Federal Home Loan Bank Board (for S&Ls) (Chapters 1 to 3 and 17).

2. The federal and state governments have long sought to discourage interregional flows of funds by imposing severe limits on branch banking. The reinforcement of this objective was among the stated purposes of the Federal Reserve Act of 1913 (which required banks to keep specified amounts of funds with Fed Banks instead of sending them to Chicago, New York, and other money centers) and the Banking Act of 1933 (which prohibited interest payments on deposits when it was seen that banks continued to send funds to their most valued uses) (Chapters 2 and 9).

3. Restrictive laws and their severe application by regulators have prevented financial institutions from extending loans with rates and other terms that reflect interest-rate and inflation uncertainty. Attempts by federally chartered S&Ls to reduce uncertainty in a volatile environment by offering variable-rate mortgages were for a time prevented and are still restricted by the Federal Home Loan Bank Board (Chapter 17).

4. The Securities Exchange Acts of 1933 and 1934, as administered by the Securities and Exchange Commission (SEC), have placed heavy burdens on capital market issues, especially by small firms (Chapter 11).

5. The SEC has promoted monopoly in the capital markets by increasing the cost of entry into the securities business, discouraging the growth of rivals to the New York Stock Exchange, and overseeing commission-fixing arrangements by securities brokers and dealers. Congress and the SEC are now trying to force stock trading into a single, narrow "National Market System," to be regulated as a public utility (Chapter 11).

6. The last item in this category is a wrong signal rather than a roadblock. The recent growth of government insurance obligations, by which the taxpayer has been obligated to bear the burdens of failed pension funds, securities dealers, and deposit-insurance agencies (in addition to Chrysler, New York City, and Lockheed), reduces or eliminates the costs of risky actions. For example banks may extend risky loans without paying higher deposit rates or fear of losing depositors because deposits are guaranteed by the taxpayer.[17] Loan and deposit rates thus reflect the direct opportunity costs of banks and depositors but not of society (Chapters 11 and 17).

Detours: innovative evasions of regulations

The increasing burdens of regulation caused by accelerating inflation and rising interest rates have led to the following more or less successful innovations by private profit seekers and risk averters.

1. Interest ceilings on deposits and inflationary increases in free-market interest rates have combined to produce increased demands for existing deposit substitutes, the development of new money market instruments, and roundabout ways of paying interest on checking accounts (Chapters 2, 3, and 9).

2. Restrictions on branch banking encouraged bank correspondent relations and interbank lending throughout the nineteenth century, activities that in recent years have begun to resume their former importance (Chapter 9).

3. State-chartered S&Ls have offered variable-rate mortgages for several years, but Federal Home Loan Bank Board constraints on other S&Ls were, until too late, unyielding (Chapter 17).

4. Corporations have evaded the regulatory costs imposed on stocks and bonds by increasing their reliance on retained earnings and short-term debt as sources of finance. However, to the extent that securities regulations have encouraged the finance of long-term projects by short-term borrowing, those regulations have increased the riskiness of entrepreneurial activities (Chapters 8 and 16).

5. During the 1960s, under pressure from their large institutional customers, member brokers of the New York Stock Exchange and other exchanges developed many ways of evading collusive commissions until the SEC and exchange governing boards had to give up their attempts to fix commissions (Chapter 11).

Freeways: almost-efficient markets

The detours listed above illustrate the tendencies of markets toward efficiency in spite of official interference, although that interference has remained a source of significant inefficiencies. But some markets, including those listed below, have remained relatively free of regula-

---

17 Deposit insurance is limited to $100,000 per account, but funds are so easily allocated to multiple accounts within and among institutions that effectively unlimited coverage has become routine. See Gerald O'Driscoll and Eugenie Short (1983) for a discussion of these issues.

tion and as a consequence are quite efficient, sometimes almost textbook efficient.[18]

1. The best-known studies of market efficiency have concerned the stock market. But many other financial markets also appear to have functioned efficiently—including the Treasury bill market except during periods of volatile inflation and/or Fed interference with interest-rate adjustments. Studies of the efficiency of this market have been carried out in the context of choices between goods and claims on money (Chapter 18), securities of different terms to maturity (Chapter 19), domestic and foreign currencies (Chapter 12), and spot and forward contracts (Chapter 12).

2. The markets for other relatively unregulated money-market instruments, especially commercial paper, bankers' acceptances, and money market funds, are quite efficient. These instruments pay yields that vary closely in line with T bill yields (Chapter 8).

3. Bank loans, unlike bank deposits or the loans of S&Ls, have largely, except in wartime, been left alone by Congress and the regulators.[19] The competitiveness of bank loan markets has increased until these markets rival the money markets in efficiency[20] and bank loan rates vary with money market rates (Chapter 16).

4. Foreign exchange markets have apparently been quite efficient except when governments, particularly during periods of fixed (pegged) exchange rates, have prevented adjustments (Chapter 12).

5. The new and rapidly growing financial futures exchanges represent great tours de force of a naturally competitive financial environment. The efficiency of these markets is a dramatic illustration of the ingenuity of financial entrepreneurs in the development of new instruments and markets in response to new needs, specifically in the provision of means by which investors may avoid a few of the consequences of volatile government monetary and fiscal policies (Chapter 12).

Going home. Say hello to Grover Cleveland.

The catastrophic depression of the 1930s, the extensive government demands on the economy during World War II, and the steadiness of prices and economic growth between 1945 and 1970 have had no parallels in American history. The country may be too young to allow

---

18 All these markets are subject to reporting costs and other regulatory burdens that reduce efficiency by increasing transaction costs. But these impediments are small compared with those borne by markets in which prices or yields are directly regulated, such as bank-deposit markets.

19 Despite attempts by some members of Congress to achieve government direction of credit, as in the case of a bill introduced in 1975 by Chairman Reuss of the House Banking Committee that would have required the Fed to determine national priorities and direct credit toward those priorities. See Michael Laub (1979) for further examples of attempts to control credit flows by political criteria.

20 As indicated in item 6 under Roadblocks, this market may be efficient in a narrow private sense, but the existence of government-subsidized deposit insurance induces inefficient actions from society's viewpoint.

us to say what is typical of American experience. However, with respect to the financial markets, a strong case exists for the contention that after four unusual decades the 1970s and 1980s have seen a restoration of normal conditions—if by normal we mean the competitive, sophisticated, and volatile financial environment that prevailed between the Civil War and 1930. At any rate the current financial environment bears a greater similarity to that of the 1920s and even to that of the nineteenth century than it does to that of any period between 1930 and 1970.

The American financial system as we know it today was essentially in place by 1880. Nearly all the financial instruments, institutions, and markets that are important now were familiar to J. P. Morgan, including stocks, bonds, mutual funds, commercial paper, banks, insurance companies, brokers, dealers, and organized stock, bond, and commodity exchanges. Possibly the most important advances since 1880 have been the increased speeds with which information (especially prices) and financial instruments (especially money) are moved. But even these improvements have been small relative to those of the quarter century preceding 1880, which saw the near-completion of nationwide rail and telegraph networks, the laying of the Atlantic cable, and an already rapidly spreading telephone system. Developments in the movement of money and information during the past 100 years have just about kept up with the volume and geographical dispersion of the financial business of the country.

The most important changes in the financial markets between 1880 and 1970 occurred between 1930 and 1950 and were highly destructive of market efficiency. We have already described some of the effects of the restrictive legislation of the 1930s. But more important to the disappearance or decline of numerous financial instruments and procedures for managing money were the extremely low interest rates caused by the depressed economic conditions of the 1930s and the government's easy-money policies of the 1940s. Only recently, under the pressure of high and volatile interest rates resembling those of the pre-1930 era, have the financial markets regained their former variety and sophistication. The principal forms taken by this resurgence, the most important ways in which the financial markets of the 1980s have become more like those of 1880 to 1930 than like those of 1930 to 1970, are listed below.

Our list begins with new (and old) commercial banking practices. The restoration of nineteenth-century competition has nowhere been more dramatic than in this industry, which in its role as creator and manager of the nation's money exerts unequaled influence in the financial markets. Some of these developments have already appeared as efficiency-promoting regulatory evasions.

1. Bank competition for funds before the 1930s often took the form of interest payments on checking accounts. These payments were made illegal in 1933 and, because of low interest rates, would have been unimportant in any case until the 1960s. Partly because of changes in the law but mainly through evasions of the law, banks have returned to their former practice (Chapters 2, 3, 9, and 16).

2. Interbank borrowing, which fell radically during the period 1930 to 1950, has again become an important means by which the nation's funds are directed toward their most profitable uses (Chapters 9 and 16).

3. The bank loan market has also shown strong signs of returning to its nineteenth-century competitiveness. The end of a meaningful prime-rate cartel, the deterioration of customer relationships, the increase in shared and brokered loans, and the tying of loan rates to market rates have all been aspects of the return to the impersonal, competitive conditions of the nineteenth century. The most obvious reflection of these changes has been an increase in the volatility of loan rates until, as before 1929, they now move as much as "market" rates. For now they *are* market rates (Chapter 16).

4. With the assistance of the Fed and against the opposition of the SEC in its role as advocate for security firms, banks have defied the Banking Acts of the 1930s by reentering the underwriting business (Chapter 8).

Some other ways in which the financial markets have returned to pre-1929 conditions include the following:

5. Private short-term financial instruments, especially bankers' acceptances and commercial paper, have resumed the importance they had in the 1920s (Chapter 8).

6. Rising interest rates have reversed the decline in money-management procedures, which may now be as sophisticated as in the 1920s (Chapter 3).

7. After the tranquil 1953 to 1971 period, in which interest rates managed to keep up with inflation, we have seen a return to "normal" conditions, in which interest rates trail inflation (Chapter 18).

8. The slopes of yield curves have seen three distinct phases: about equally numerous positive and negative slopes between the Civil War and 1930, almost continuously upward-sloping yield curves between 1930 and 1965, and about equally numerous positive and negative slopes since 1965 (Chapter 19).

There's a muddy road ahead: deregulation?

Much has been made recently of deregulation, especially by regulators. However, while a few restrictions have been loosened, others have been tightened, and some new constraints on private actions have been introduced. American financial markets have always been heavily regulated, and business actions in general have come under increasingly severe regulatory burdens at least since the 1880s. It would have been a remarkable thing if society had suddenly seen the competitive light in 1980 and begun to dismantle the work of a hundred years. It would have been even more remarkable given the fact that the imposition and dismantling of economic regulations are the outcomes not of ideological conflicts but of pragmatic conflicts between profit-seeking groups either soliciting the government's support for themselves or attempting to remove government-supported advantages for others. Evasions that have been tacitly or explicitly accepted by Congress or the regulators because restrictions have proved politically or practically unenforceable should not be interpreted as changes in official policy.[21] In view of the rapid pace of effective deregulation as people and firms evaded existing regulations, the SEC's acceptance of competitive commissions (while continuing to support other collusive practices), the abandonment by Congress and the Federal Home Loan Bank Board of the requirement that *all* S&L loans be at fixed rates for long terms, and a literally slower-than-molasses-in-January implementation of Congress's hesitant expression that ceilings on deposit rates be lifted must all be seen as official attempts to administer the pace of (that is, to slow) deregulation. In fact a strong case can be made that the long-term tendency toward greater financial regulation has accelerated in recent years, as evidenced by the increasing regulation of pension funds, the growing interference with private loan contracts and lender remedies in the event of default,[22] restrictions on insurance contracts that prevent premiums from reflecting the riskiness of various groups,[23] the attempt by Congress and the SEC to impose the National Market System on securities traders, and the massive expansion of Fed control from member commercial banks to all depository institutions.

As we have stressed, it is inevitable that private citizens attempt to use government for their own ends at the expense of their fellows. But an additional proregulatory force has greatly increased in importance: regulation that has not been sought by the parties affected and serves no one except the regulator, unless one accepts the view that ignorant

---

21 This point is made by Lewis Spellman (1982, Chapter 15) and by many of the papers in Lawrence Goldberg and Lawrence White (1979).

22 Recent and possible future examples are the increasingly severe application of the Consumer Credit Protection Act of 1968, which limits the information available to lenders, and the Bankruptcy Reform Act of 1978, which limits the security that borrowers may offer for loans (by expanding the list of personal-property exemptions and delaying creditor recovery of collateral). The Federal Trade Commission's Bureau of Consumer Protection (BCP) has proposed further restrictions. Clifford Smith (1981) and others have argued and Jonathan Scott (1983) has provided evidence that these interferences with private loan contracts must raise borrowing costs to all borrowers and reduce the funds available to low-income and other high-risk borrowers— to which the BCP has replied that these people would be better off if they did not borrow: Consumers ought to be protected against creditor default remedies "even if some high-risk debtors will have to acquire less expensive cars than they now do while others, at least for a time, will have to purchase none" [BCP memorandum quoted by Richard Peterson (1981, page 186)].

23 The Credit Rationing section of Chapter 16 discusses government creation and reinforcement of "adverse-selection" problems in loan and insurance markets.

and/or irrational people need to be protected against themselves (model *A*). The growing interference with the freedom of borrowers and lenders to construct mutually beneficial contracts and the SEC's National Market System, which has been sought by neither investors nor securities firms, are examples of this proregulatory bias that will continue to impede tendencies toward efficiency.

THE VEHICLE: RATIONAL SELF-INTEREST
Understanding decision makers and their environment

The guiding principle in our travels through the financial markets is the pursuit of self-interest by rational decision makers subject to the constraints imposed by their environment and their own resources. By *rational* we mean the expression of preferences and the use of information in an intelligent, consistent manner. The rational decision maker does not pursue inconsistent goals or hold contradictory beliefs.

To understand the behavior of these decision makers, we must be familiar with both their environment, especially the markets in which they operate, and the principles of choice in a world of scarcity. Chapters 2 to 12 describe the financial instruments, regulations, methods of payment, and other aspects of the financial environment, with frequent references to actions by decision makers because those actions determine, as well as depend on, their environment. We begin with the market for bank deposits (Chapter 2) because of its close relation to money and also because it provides a particularly clear example of the regulatory roadblocks that our decision makers encounter in other markets later in the book. Chapters 3 and 4 illustrate within the context of the all-important money market and payments system how innovative detours are found around those roadblocks. Chapters 5 and 6 describe important parts of the investor's environment: the principles of present value (Chapter 5) and the application of those principles to financial-market reporting. The principal financial instruments (except those previously introduced in Chapters 2 and 3 as recently developed substitutes for money) are discussed in Chapters 7 to 12, with emphasis on changes in the instruments and in the ways they are traded. The goals, constraints, and decisions of the principal decision makers in this environment are described in Chapters 13 to 17.[24] Finally, instruments and decision makers are combined in Chapters 18 to 20 to determine inflation, interest rates, and stock prices.

Management in a changing financial environment

Management is the application of rational decision making to the goals of firms—most importantly the maximization of owner wealth

---

24 No penalty is imposed on the reader who wishes to deal with decision makers before financial instruments.

through profits. The manager must of course be familiar with both the internal operations of the firm and the firm's environment. Two goals of this book are to acquaint present and future managers with their financial environment, as it exists today and as it is likely to evolve in the near future, and with the implications of that environment for management decisions.

The achievement of these goals requires liberal doses of institutional description, including descriptions in Parts 2 to 4 of new and old financial instruments and how they are traded and in Part 5 of financial and nonfinancial firms and their problems. These descriptions are accompanied by statements of problems that have been encountered by managers in the past and are likely to be encountered in the future, along with some actual past and possible future solutions. In fact all our discussions of financial innovation are of management responses to avoidable restraints, regulatory and otherwise, imposed by their environment. We hope that this book will contribute to the understanding of that environment and therefore to greater efficiency through innovative evasions of the roadblocks raised by government and nature.

QUESTIONS

The following leading questions are intended to encourage you to think about the operations of financial markets and in particular about how decision makers respond to prices, interest rates, and regulations:

1. The maximum rate of interest payable on savings deposits at commercial banks, under Regulation Q, was raised in steps from 2½ percent in 1936 to 5¼ percent in 1980 while the maximum rate of interest on checking accounts stayed at zero. What do you think happened to the public's allocation of funds between savings deposits and demand deposits during that time?

2. (a) Many firms and individuals hold bank deposits in several countries.

   (b) Inflation and high interest rates have been worldwide phenomena in recent years.

   (c) Although the British economy is in many spheres even more highly regulated than the U.S. economy, Britain's financial markets are much freer than are those in the U.S.; for example there are no legally enforced interest ceilings in Britain. Do you think Americans during the last 20 years have increased or decreased their holdings of deposits in London banks relative to New York banks?

3. Prices of foreign exchange are determined, like other prices, by supply and demand. For example people demand German marks in order to buy German goods. The lower the prices of German

goods, the greater will be the demands for those goods and, therefore, for marks. Between 1967 and 1980 the mark rose in value relative to the U.S. dollar from $0.25 to $0.55. Does this tell you anything about the relative rates of inflation in the United States and West Germany between 1967 and 1980?

4. During periods of inflation people seek investments that protect the purchasing power of their savings. In view of this, what prices (other than oil prices and doctors' and hospital fees) do you think have risen most in recent years?

5. Based on your knowledge that the federal government can print money, whereas state and local governments, firms, and households cannot print money, guess which of these sectors (a) tends to spend the most relative to its income and (b) exhibits the most volatile and least predictable spending patterns.

6. Suppose interest rates fall drastically as the result of another Great Depression. What is likely to happen to financial innovations such as those discussed in Chapter 1?

7. Why is the food better on Parents' Day?

8. Do you think the NCAA's limits on aid to athletes stem from an idealistic concern for the preservation of amateurism? Do you see any similarities between the causes and effects of the NCAA's rules and the causes and effects of Regulation Q?

9. Suppose the government announces today that in 30 days it will stop delivering the mail and will not in any way after that date, either as regulator or as active participant, be involved with the postal service or any other activity concerned with mail delivery. Will you receive punctual mail deliveries in 30 days and afterwards, assuming someone writes to you? (*Hint.* As early as 1792 to protect the Post Office's monopoly, Congress found it necessary to make the private carriage of letters illegal. That law, amended only in detail, is still on the books and has been the subject of much litigation between the government and private citizens concerning alleged infringements by the latter of the former's monopoly.[25])

10. The primary objective of the Securities Exchange Act of 1933 was to improve the quality of corporate stocks and bonds by requiring extensive disclosures of company affairs, the submission of new issues to official inspection, and other investor protections from fraud. So why have stocks and bonds become much less important sources of corporate finance since 1933?

11. Consider the following observations: Most of the 5,900 bank failures in the United States during the 1920s occurred in rural areas and were due to loans made bad by falling agricultural

---

25 See Lindsay Rogers (1916) and the *Code of Federal Regulations,* 39 CFR 310.

prices.[26] Bank failures in England greatly declined after effective limits on branching were removed in the 1830s. Failures had not been a problem in the unregulated Scottish system of branch banks.[27] Failures were almost unknown in the national branch-banking systems of Great Britain and Canada during the 1920s and 1930s, when about 15,000 of 30,000 U.S. banks failed.

What do these observations suggest regarding the effects of American regulations on the riskiness of banking? Discuss possible reasons for existing American policies toward branch banking.

REFERENCES

George A. Akerlof, "The Market for 'Lemons': Quality Uncertainty and the Market Mechanism," *Quarterly Journal of Economics,* August 1970, pages 488–500.

S. G. Checkland, *Scottish Banking: A History, 1695–1973,* Collins, Glasgow, 1975.

Charles P. Clotfelter and Charles Lieberman, "On the Distributional Impact of Federal Interest Rate Restrictions," *Journal of Finance,* March 1978, pages 199–213.

James W. Gilbart, *The History of Banking in America: With an Inquiry How Far the Banking Institutions of America Are Adapted to This Country,* Longman, Rees, Orme, Brown, Green, and Longman, London, 1837. Reprint Kelley, New York, 1967.

Lawrence G. Goldberg and Lawrence J. White (eds.), *The Deregulation of the Banking and Securities Industries,* Heath, Lexington, MA, 1979.

P. Michael Laub, "The Deregulation of Banking," in Lawrence G. Goldberg and Lawrence J. White (eds.), *The Deregulation of the Banking and Securities Industries,* Heath, Lexington, MA, 1979.

Edward C. Lawrence and Gregory E. Elliehausen, "The Impact of Federal Interest Rate Regulations on the Small Saver: Further Evidence," *Journal of Finance,* June 1981, pages 677–684.

Gerald P. O'Driscoll and Eugenie D. Short, "Competitive Deposit Insurance: Pricing Risk in a Deregulated Environment," Federal Reserve Bank of Dallas *Economic Review,* September 1983, pages 11–23.

Richard L. Peterson, "Rewriting Consumer Contracts: Creditors' Remedies," in Kenneth W. Clarkson and Timothy J. Muris (eds.), *The Federal Trade Commission since 1970: Economic Regulation and Bureaucratic Behavior,* Cambridge University Press, Cambridge, 1981.

David H. Pyle, "The Losses on Savings Deposits from Interest Rate Regulation," *Bell Journal of Economics and Management Science,* Autumn 1974, pages 614–622.

Lindsay Rogers, *The Postal Power of Congress: A Study in Constitutional Expansion,* Johns Hopkins, Baltimore, 1916.

Jonathan A. Scott, "The Effect of the Bankruptcy Reform Act of 1978 on Small Business Loan Pricing," Southern Methodist University unpublished paper, June 1983.

Adam Smith, *An Inquiry into the Nature and Causes of the Wealth of Nations,* Strahan and Cadell, London, 1776.

Clifford W. Smith, "On the Theory of Financial Contracting: The Personal Loan Market," *Journal of Monetary Economics,* January 1981, pages 333–358.

Lewis J. Spellman, *The Depository Firm and Industry: Theory, History, and Regulation,* Academic, New York, 1982.

Robert A. Taggart, "Effects of Deposit Rate Ceilings: The Evidence from Massachusetts Savings Banks," *Journal of Money, Credit and Banking,* May 1978, pages 139–157.

Richard R. West, "Efficiency of the Securities Markets," in Frank J. Fabozzi and Frank G. Zarb (eds.), *Handbook of Financial Markets,* Dow Jones-Irwin, Homewood, IL, 1981.

Ray B. Westerfield, *Money, Credit and Banking,* Ronald, New York, 1938.

---

26 See the data and discussion in Ray Westerfield (1938, Chapter 46).

27 See James Gilbart (1837) and S. Checkland (1975).

TWO

Innovations in Money and the Payments System

*"What do you mean by that?" said the
Caterpillar sternly. "Explain yourself!"
"I can't explain myself, I'm afraid,
Sir," said Alice, "because
I'm not myself, you see."
"I don't see," said the Caterpillar.
"I'm afraid I can't put it more clearly,"
Alice replied very politely. . . .*

Lewis Carroll, *Alice's Adventures in Wonderland*, ch. 5

REGULATION, INFLATION, AND INCENTIVES FOR FINANCIAL INNOVATION

If the term "invention" is to be broadly defined as an act of the creative imagination, it is easy to understand why the French patent act of 1791, based on the Declaration of the Rights of Man (1789), placed economic or social inventions on the same footing as mechanical and scientific inventions. Patents were therefore granted for tontine life annuities, tariff systems, credit plans, types of mortgages, banking systems, exchange controls and methods for guaranteeing the value of assignats. When it became apparent that there would be an avalanche of such schemes the national assembly on Sept. 20, 1792 decreed that the executive power should not only cease to grant patents for financial inventions but also counteract the effect of those already granted.

W. B. Kaempffert, "Inventions and Discoveries," *Encyclopaedia Britannica,* **1957**

THE DEMAND FOR REGULATION

There has never been a shortage of financial schemes although they have been more numerous than usual since 1960. The increase in financial innovation has had several causes, but the discussion in this chapter is limited to the most important cause: the interaction of interest-rate regulation and inflation.[1]

Business firms attempt to earn profits by buying inputs as cheaply as possible, transforming those inputs into outputs as efficiently as they can, and then selling the outputs for all the market will bear. Financial intermediaries are special kinds of firms that deal almost

---

1 For more general discussions of the causes of financial innovation see S. Greenbaum and C. Haywood (1974) and William Silber (1975, 1983).

exclusively in financial instruments. They borrow as cheaply as they can (that is, issue debt at the lowest possible interest rates) and lend at the highest rates obtainable. Most firms, especially small firms, are required to pay and accept competitive, market-determined prices for their inputs and outputs. The major exceptions have been farmers, who have profited from government price supports for their outputs, and commercial banks,[2] which have benefited from government-imposed ceilings on the prices of their inputs.

Commercial banking is an excellent example of the *capture theory* of regulation, which maintains that regulation is demanded: That is, "as a rule, regulation is acquired by the industry and is designed and operated primarily for its benefit."[3] There is a regulatory bias in favor of producers because their incentives to secure protection exceed consumer incentives to resist producer protection. Legal ceilings on the interest rates payable on bank deposits are examples of the political dominance of a small group with a large per capita interest in a narrow issue over a large group with more diffuse interests.[4]

But Congress and the regulators must not push producer protection too far. They must not impose costs on the larger groups so great that those groups are induced to remove regulatory agencies and their Congressional patrons.[5] The losers must be appeased.[6] This modified capture theory is consistent with the granting of price-fixing and other monopolistic privileges to banks and then the withdrawal of some of those privileges when they become too burdensome.

By the 1860s the banking industry had obtained a monopoly of checking accounts (demand deposits) and the establishment of state and federal regulatory agencies that protected existing firms by

---

2 We use the terms "banks" and "commercial banks" interchangeably. Banks are described in detail in Chapter 4. For our present purposes it is sufficient to understand banks as those financial intermediaries that historically have borrowed mainly in the form of demand deposits.

3 George Stigler (1971, page 3).

4 Examples of successful producer lobbying of the Depository Institutions Deregulation Committee (created by Congress to control the pace of deposit-rate increases) were the decisions of that committee on, among other occasions, November 17, 1981, December 16, 1981, and March 1, 1983, to postpone ceiling increases because of letters and phone calls from financial institutions and their Congressmen (see the *Wall Street Journal* and the *Wall Street Journal Index*). Other examples are given by Gary Becker (1983), who also quotes Simon Newcomb (1886, page 457) as follows:

   If Congress can be induced to adopt a certain policy [a company] can collect an extra profit of one cent per annum out of each inhabitant of the country. Not one person in a thousand would give a moment's attention to the wrong, or indeed even find it out . . . or call a meeting of his neighbors without spending more time than the question was worth.

5 See Sam Peltzman (1976) for a generalization of the capture theory to include regulatory accommodations of more than one group.

6 Though not always promptly. "In spite of the opposition of two of the nation's largest lobbying groups for retired people, the Depository Institutions Deregulation Committee voted [November 17, 1981] to delay a scheduled increase in the maximum interest payable on passbook savings accounts. A spokesman for the American Association of Retired Persons and the National Retired Teachers Association said that 'interest rates should be allowed to rise to whatever level the market sets . . . which would provide the elderly . . . with a means of conserving the value of their assets and the purchasing power of their income'" (*Chicago Tribune*, October 25, 1981, section 5, page 5).

restricting entry. But it took a long time to persuade government to regulate deposit rates. Banks in most localities promoted agreements on rates, and in fact the supervision of rate agreements and other forms of "equitable" competition was considered a normal function of Clearing House Associations.[7] Many of these price-fixing arrangements were successful, but many failed because of "the ignorance, selfishness, or immoral conduct"[8] of a few banks, particularly the more aggressive banks in New York and Chicago that competed for the deposits of banks in smaller cities and towns. A major objective of the Federal Reserve Act of 1913 was to end interbank competition for deposits by requiring banks to hold their reserves with a government agency (the Federal Reserve) instead of with other banks. This effort was only partially successful. But the demand for ceilings on deposit rates grew stronger as those rates rose during the inflation of World War I and then in response to the increase in bank failures, especially in depressed agricultural areas, during the 1920s. The massive bank failures during the Great Depression of 1929 to 1933 clinched the issue.[9]

The Banking (Glass-Steagall) Act of 1933 contained many restrictive provisions. But those which eventually had the greatest impact on the financial markets and which concern us here were contained in Section 11:

> No member bank shall directly or indirectly, by any device whatsoever, pay any interest on any deposit which is payable on demand. . . .
> The Federal Reserve Board shall from time to time limit by regulation the rate of interest which may be paid by member banks on time deposits, and may prescribe different rates for such payment on time and savings deposits having different maturities or subject to different conditions respecting withdrawal or repayment or subject to different conditions by reason of different locations.[10]

Senator Glass defended the first provision by calling the payment of interest on demand deposits "a system viciously and partially admin-

---

7 See James Cannon (1908).

8 From an address by George S. Coe, president of the American Exchange National Bank, in presenting a resolution to the New York Clearing House Association on June 4, 1884, "to make common cause" by inquiring "whether the methods of business, as conducted by the several members of this association, are uniform and correct in their operation with the public, and equitable to all the banks which are thus bound together in the Clearing House Association" [published in *Bankers Magazine,* July 1884, and reprinted in O. Sprague (1910, pages 371–380)].

9 See Albert Cox (1964) and Charles Linke (1966) for histories of the demand for deposit-rate regulation.

10 These restrictions were extended to all banks in 1935 and to savings and loan associations in 1966.

istered [which has] resulted in withdrawing from the interior country banks . . . millions of dollars to the money centers, to be cast into the maelstrom of stock gambling" (and which, by the way, in 1929 meant interest costs of $259 million to Federal Reserve member banks). The latter provision, which was implemented by the Federal Reserve Board's Regulation Q, was explained by the senator as follows:

> We confide to the Federal Reserve Board authority which it does not now possess in this connection to regulate interest on time deposits in order to put a stop to the competition between banks in payment of interest, which frequently induces banks to pay excessive interest on time deposits and has many times over again brought banks into serious trouble.[11]

So banks were awarded a government-supervised price-fixing scheme, and the first part of our story of regulation and innovation comes to an end. The rest of the story is about how banks and their customers proceeded to destroy the scheme as soon as it became operative. The rest of the story has three themes: (1) The next section of the present chapter discusses *incentives to evade the regulations,* even by those who had sought them; (2) the remainder of this chapter and most of Chapters 3 and 4 discuss the *evasive innovations* that resulted from these incentives; (3) the final theme, which runs throughout Chapters 2 to 4, concerns the chaotic *mixture of official accommodations and obstructions of effective deregulation* until in the 1980s Congress finally rubber-stamped part of the public's de facto repeal of the Glass-Steagall Act.[12]

INTEREST CEILINGS AND BANK PROFITS
The course of deposit and market rates, 1933 to 1984

The ceilings imposed by the Federal Reserve (the Fed) on two categories of time deposits are shown in Figure 2.1. The maximum rate payable on ordinary passbook savings was 3 percent between November 1933 and January 1935, when it was reduced to 2.5 percent until January 1962, after which it has been raised slightly on several occasions. The number of categories of time deposits, with different interest ceilings, has grown since the early 1960s. The category with

---

11 *Congressional Record,* 73rd Cong., 1st Sess., May 19, 1933. Reprinted in "Legislative History of Provision of Banking Act of 1933 Prohibiting Payment of Interest by Banks on Demand Deposits," in *To Eliminate Unsound Competition for Savings and Time Deposits,* Hearings before the House Committee on Banking and Currency on "A Bill to Prohibit Insured Banks from Issuing Negotiable Interest-bearing or Discounted Notes, Certificates of Deposit, or Other Evidences of Indebtedness," May and June 1966, pages 651–653.

12 The public's rejection of the Act has extended to nearly all its sections, including those intended to separate investment and commercial banking. But we are concerned here with interest ceilings. An important exception to Congress's abandonment of these ceilings is its determination to maintain the zero ceiling on corporate checking accounts, including the interbank demand deposits that Glass was most eager to control.

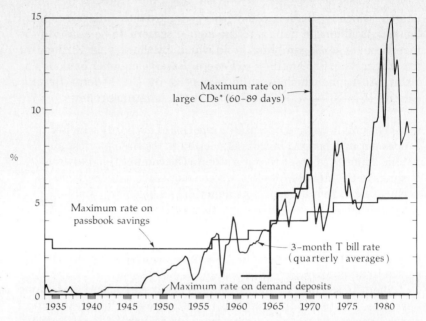

* Ceiling rates on time deposits with maturities exceeding 90 days were raised earlier than those on
time deposits maturing in less than 90 days. For example ceilings on time deposits payable in 6
months to 1 year were raised (from 3.00 percent as shown in Table 2.1) to 3.50, 4.00, 4.50, and
5.50 percent in January 1962, July 1963, November 1964, and December 1965, respectively.

Sources: *Banking and Monetary Statistics, 1941–70, Annual Statistical Digest, 1970–79,* and *Federal Reserve Bulletins.*

Figure 2.1   T bill rates and maximum rates payable on demand deposits,
passbook savings, and large certificates of deposit.

the highest ceiling has been 60- to 89-day certificates of deposit (CDs)
in minimum denominations of $100,000. The ceiling on these large
CDs was suspended in June 1970, as indicated by the dark line rising
to the top of the chart. The most important interest ceiling is the zero
ceiling on demand deposits, indicated by the dark line along the
bottom of the chart. The rate on 3-month Treasury bills (T bills) is
shown so that maximum rates payable on deposits may be compared
with free-market rates.

A simple model of bank profit maximization without regulatory constraints

We will now examine the impact of deposit-rate ceilings on bank
behavior and profits within a framework that is simple but captures
the most important effects of those ceilings. Our bank has only one
source of funds: demand deposits (D) that are attracted to the bank as
an increasing function of the deposit rate (R_D) paid by the bank. The
deposit-supply function is indicated by the solid line D in the right-
hand portion of Figure 2.2. The height of D is the average cost of
deposits, that is, the deposit rate, R_D. Since higher deposit rates must
be paid in order to attract additional deposits, the marginal cost of

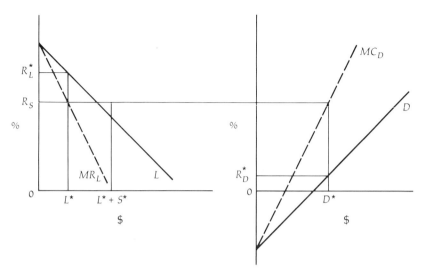

Figure 2.2   An unconstrained profit maximum ($R_D^* > 0$).

Numerical example

If $L = 20 - 100R_L$,   then $R_L^* = 0.16$, $L^* = 4$
$D = 8 + 100R_D$ $R_D^* = 0.02$, $D^* = 10$
$R_S = 0.12$ $S^* = 6$

$$\Pi^* = R_L^* L^* + R_S S^* - R_D^* D^* = 1.16$$

These results are derived in Appendix 2.A.

deposits (MC_D) lies above the average cost function (D), as indicated by the dashed line.

We have drawn the deposit-supply function so that D is positive even at negative deposit rates. Demand deposits are useful and, if no convenient substitute is available, will be demanded in some quantities even at negative rates, that is, at positive service charges.

The bank invests the funds obtained from depositors in two ways: (1) Loans (L) are demanded from the bank as a decreasing function of the loan rate (R_L) charged by the bank. The loan-demand function is the solid line L in the left-hand portion of Figure 2.2. The height of L is the average revenue from loans, that is, the loan rate R_L. Since lower loan rates must be offered in order to attract additional borrowers, the marginal revenue from loans (MR_L) lies below the average revenue function (L), as indicated by the dashed line on the left side of the figure. (2) Government securities (S) pay the perfectly competitive rate R_S indicated by the horizontal solid line drawn at the height R_S. Since the bank may buy as many of these securities as it wishes without affecting their rate of return, R_S is both marginal and average revenue.

The bank wishes to maximize profit (Π), which is revenue from loans and securities less the cost of deposits,

(2.1) $\Pi = R_L L + R_S S - R_D D$

subject to the balance-sheet constraint

(2.2) $L + S = D$

and the market constraints

(2.3) $L = L(R_L)$

(2.4) $D = D(R_D)$

and the rate on securities R_S. The bank's decision variables are the deposit rate (R_D), the quantity of deposits (D), the loan rate (R_L), the quantity of loans (L), and its purchases of securities (S). Of course these decisions are not independent. We see from the constraints (2.2) to (2.4) that assets (L and S) must sum to liabilities (D), and choices of R_L and R_D imply choices of L and D.

The bank's optimal decision is to set the deposit rate at R_D^* and the loan rate at R_L^* (in order to attract D^* deposits and to make L^* loans) and buy $S^* = D^* - L^*$ securities. This decision may be explained as follows: The bank maximizes the total revenue from a given quantity of deposits by extending loans up to the point at which the marginal revenues from loans and securities are equal, that is, $MR_L = R_S$. This occurs at $R_L = R_L^*$ and $L = L^*$. If $R_L > R_L^*$ so that $L < L^*$, we have $MR_L > R_S$, and the bank is in a position to increase total revenue by shifting from securities to loans. On the other hand, if $R_L < R_L^*$ so that $L > L^*$, we have $MR_L < R_S$, and the bank can increase total revenue by shifting from loans to securities. So the bank's optimal choice is L^* loans, and its remaining funds are invested in securities, S^*, such that $L^* + S^* = D^*$.

The optimal quantity of deposits is that for which the marginal cost of deposits equals the marginal revenues from loans and securities, that is, $MC_D = MR_L = R_S$. This is achieved by setting $R_D = R_D^*$. Lower values of R_D and D mean $MC_D < MR_L = R_S$ so that profit can be increased by raising R_D and D. On the other hand, values of $R_D > R_D^*$ and $D > D^*$ mean that the bank is attracting more funds than it can profitably employ. A numerical example of the bank's optimal choice and resulting maximum profit, Π^*, is given in the caption to Figure 2.2.[13]

---

13 This model is easily extended in many ways. For example: (1) There could be any number of loan-demand functions, each representing a different category of borrowers, but a loan rate would be set for each category such that the marginal revenue from each category equaled R_S; (2) similarly there could be any number of deposit supplies, but a deposit-rate would be set for each category such that marginal costs equaled R_S; (3) the addition of a fixed amount of bank capital (equity) would merely mean more funds invested in S without affecting the loan and deposit decisions; (4) the addition of reserve-requirement ratios such that noninterest-earning cash reserves equaled kD would mean that deposits would be attracted only up to the point at which $MC_D = (1 - k)MR_L = (1 - k)R_S$ because the profitability of deposits would be reduced by the proportion of funds $(1 - k)$ that earn no interest (this would apply with a different k for each category of deposits subject to a different reserve requirement).

Figure 2.2 depicts the bank's behavior when there are no binding regulatory constraints on its behavior. If there is a deposit-rate ceiling, it is above R_D^*. Figure 2.3 is like Figure 2.2 except for the lower rate on securities. The fall in R_S from 0.12 to 0.065 induces the bank to move from securities to loans by reducing R_L and increasing L until $MR_L = R_S = 0.065$. The fall in marginal revenues reduces the bank's willingness to pay high rates for deposits to such an extent that, instead of paying interest on deposits, it imposes a service charge; that is, $R_D^* < 0$.

A binding deposit-rate ceiling

Now suppose the regulator imposes a deposit-rate ceiling of zero. That is, the actual deposit rate must be set such that $R_D \leq R_D^r = 0$, where R_D^r is the regulatory ceiling. This has no influence on the bank's decision in the case in Figure 2.3 since the optimal R_D^* is already below zero. The regulation is not binding. This corresponds to the situation between 1933 and the late 1950s, when market rates began to exceed regulated deposit rates by substantial amounts. Deposit-rate ceilings that had been irrelevant from their inception began to bite.

The effects of a binding ceiling are illustrated in Figure 2.4, which is like Figure 2.2 except for the added constraint $R_D \leq R_D^r = 0$. The bank would like to pay $R_D^* > 0$ on deposits but, being unable to do so, pays the highest rate allowable, $R_D^r = 0$. This attracts deposits $D^r < D^*$, and

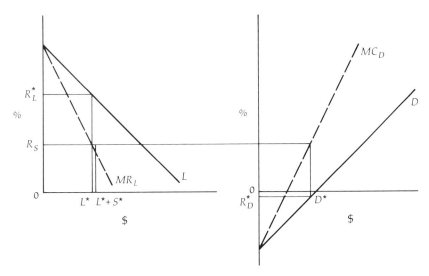

Figure 2.3   Another unconstrained profit maximum ($R_D^* < 0$).

Numerical example
If $L = 20 - 100R_L$, then $R_L^* = 0.1325$, $L^* = 6.75$
    $D = 8 + 100R_D$ $R_D^* = -0.0075$, $D^* = 7.25$
    $R_S = 0.065$ $S^* = 0.50$

$$\Pi^* = 0.98125$$

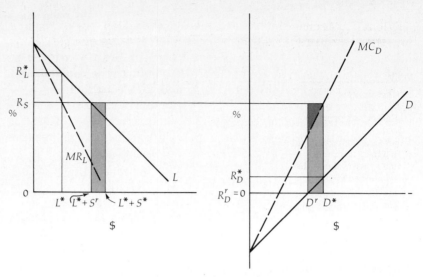

Figure 2.4   A profit maximum when $R_D^* \geq R_D^r = 0$.

Numerical example
If $L = 20 - 100R_L$,   then $R_L^* = 0.16$, $L^* = 4$
     $D = 8 + 100R_D$ $D^r = 8$, $S^r = 4$
     $R_S = 0.12$
     $R_D = R_D^r = 0$

$$\Pi^r = R_L^* L^* + R_S S^r - R_D^r D^r = 1.12 < 1.16 = \Pi^*$$

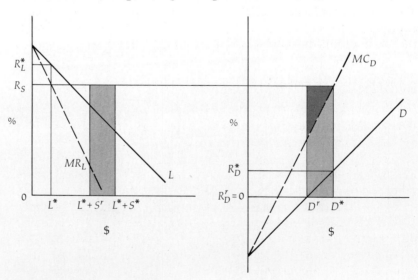

Figure 2.5   Another profit maximum when $R_D^* \geq R_D^r = 0$.

Numerical example
If $L = 20 - 100R_L$,   then $R_L^* = 0.175$, $L^* = 2.5$
     $D = 8 + 100R_D$ $R_D^* = 0.035$, $D^* = 11.5$, $D^r = 8$
     $R_S = 0.15$ $S^* = 9$, $S^r = 5.5$
     $R_D^r = 0$

$$\Pi^r = 1.2625 < 1.3850 = \Pi^*$$

Table 2.1   Maximum Interest Rates Payable on Time Deposits (%/year)

Type	11/1/33–1/31/35	2/1/35–12/31/35	1/1/36–12/31/56	1/1/57–12/31/61
Savings deposits	3	2½	2½	3
Postal savings deposits	3	2½	2½	3
Other time deposits payable:				
In 6 months or more	3	2½	2½	3
In 90 days to 6 months	3	2½	2	2½
In less than 90 days	3	2½	1	1

Source: *Federal Reserve Bulletin*, December 1961, page 1424.

as a consequence the bank reduces its security purchases from S^* to S^r, a reduction equal to that in D (from D^* to D^r).

The binding deposit-rate ceiling reduces bank costs by the area under the marginal-cost line between D^* and D^r, which is indicated by the lightly shaded area under MC_D. But bank revenue is reduced by the area under R_S (the marginal revenue from securities) between $L^* + S^*$ and $L^* + S^r$. This is the lightly shaded area under R_S on the left-hand side of Figure 2.4, which is equal to the area of the rectangle under R_S between D^r and D^* on the right-hand side of the figure. Therefore the reduction in revenue exceeds that in cost by an amount equal to the area of the darkly shaded triangle in Figure 2.4.[14] This is the loss in profits due to the regulation. It is also the incentive to evade the regulation.

SOME EFFECTS OF BINDING CEILINGS
Market rates, ceiling rates, and bank deposits in the 1960s

Rising market interest rates in the late 1950s and early 1960s—and the consequent increased competition for deposits—led the more competitive banks to lobby the Fed for increases in deposit-rate ceilings. The Fed responded, but only slightly, as indicated by the increases in the ceiling on passbook savings in Figure 2.1. The zero ceiling on the rate payable on demand deposits was outside the Fed's control. Figure 2.5 is like Figure 2.4, only more so. Higher interest rates mean higher bank profits. But they also mean more profits perceived lost because of deposit-rate ceilings.[15] Some of the responses by banks and their "regulator," the Fed, are shown in Tables 2.1 and 2.2.

The legal ceilings payable on time deposits are listed in *Federal Reserve Bulletins*. Table 2.1 reproduces the list applicable at the end of 1961. See how simple it was. One number, 3 percent during 1957 to

14 Comparing the numbers below Figures 2.2 and 2.4, we see that the darkly shaded area is 1.16 − 1.12 = 0.04.

15 Compare the numerical examples below Figures 2.4 and 2.5.

Table 2.2 Maximum Interest Rates on Commercial Bank Time and Savings Deposits in May 1983[a]

	Type and Maturity of Deposit	In Effect 5/31/83		Previous Maximum	
		%	Effective Date	%	Effective Date
1	Savings	5¼[a]	7/1/79	5	7/1/73
2	Negotiable order-of-withdrawal accounts	5¼	12/31/80	5	1/1/74
	Time accounts, fixed ceiling rates by maturity				
3	14–89 days[b]	5¼	8/1/79	5	7/1/73
4	90 days–1 year[b]	5¾	1/1/80	5½	7/1/73
5	1–2 years[b]	6	7/1/73	5½	1/21/70
6	2–2½ years[b]			5¾	1/21/70
7	2½–4 years[b]	6½	7/1/73	5¾	1/21/70
8	4–6 years[b]	7¼	11/1/73	c	—
9	6–8 years[b]	7½	12/23/74	7¼	11/1/73
10	8 years or more[b]	7¾	6/1/78	d	—
11	Issued to governmental units (all maturities)[b]	8	6/1/78	7¾	12/23/74

			Requirements in Effect 5/31/83		
Time Deposits with Variable Ceiling Rates	Date Introduced and Initial Minimum Denomination	Minimum Denomination	Minimum Maturity	Ceiling Rate[e]
12 91-day accounts	5/1/82	$7,500	$2,500	91 days	Rate on 91-day T bills
13 6-month money market certificates	6/1/78	$10,000	$2,500	6 months	Rate on 6-month T bills
14 2½- to 4-year deposits	8/1/81	None	None	1½ years	Maximum of 9¼ percent or the yield on 1½-year Treasury securities
Time Deposits without Interest Rate Ceilings					
15 Money market deposit accounts	12/14/82	$2,500	$2,500	None	
16 IRAs and Keogh accounts	12/1/81	f	f	18 months	
17 7- to 31-day accounts	9/1/82	$20,000	$2,500	7 days	
18 Deposits of 3½ years or more	5/1/82	None	None	2½ years	
19 Large CDs	5/16/73[g]	$100,000	$100,000	30 days	

a Maximum rates payable by savings and loan associations (S&Ls) and mutual savings banks, most of which were ¼ percent above the maximum rates payable by commercial banks, are not shown. The Garn-St Germain Depository Institutions Amendments of 1982 provided that differentials between maximum rates paid by different institutions be eliminated by January 1, 1984.

b These accounts had $1,000 minimum-balance requirements until various dates between 1973 and 1979.

c No ceiling during July to October 1973 on amounts up to 5 percent of a bank's total time and savings deposits.

d Not a separate category before June 1978.

e Descriptions of the sometimes complicated procedures for calculating these rates may be found in *Federal Reserve Bulletins*.

f Allows taxable income to be deferred by the amount of the annual deposit up to $2,000 for individual retirement accounts (IRAs) and the minimum of $15,000 or 15 percent of gross income for Keogh accounts. There are substantial early-withdrawal penalties.

g Date of suspension of rate ceilings on all large CDs with maturities of 30 days or more.

Source: *Federal Reserve Bulletin*, June 1983, Table 1.16.

1961, would have been sufficient if the Fed had not, consistent with banking practice, set lower ceilings on time deposits available to businesses. Savings and postal savings deposits were limited to individuals and not-for-profit organizations.

Now look at Table 2.2, which shows the complexity of interest ceilings 22 years later, in May 1983. The differences between Tables 2.1 and 2.2 are in effect a partial list of Fed responses to evasions of interest ceilings and to pressures from some banks for higher ceilings, especially the money center banks that wanted deposit rates competitive with the money market rates available to their large customers.[16]

In 1961 several large New York City banks terminated their agreement, dating from the 1930s, not to accept business time deposits. They began to issue time CDs, principally with maturities between 30 days and 6 months, in denominations ranging upward from $1 million although smaller denominations soon became available. These CDs were designed to compete with T bills, which are short-term obligations of the U.S. government issued with original maturities of 13, 26, and 52 weeks but available in an active secondary market in maturities from 1 day to 1 year. Holders of T bills can easily convert them into cash at market prices before maturity because bill dealers stand ready to buy and sell T bills at quoted bid and asked prices. By thus "making a market" in T bills, these dealers make it possible for corporate cash managers and other short-term investors to invest surplus funds for short periods with little risk of loss and the knowledge that, in the event of unforeseen cash needs, the T bills can be converted into cash. Effective competition with T bills required a similar market in large CDs, which several securities dealers agreed to provide.[17]

The Fed cooperated by raising ceilings on time deposits in several stages until, by December 1965, all time deposits could legally earn 5½ percent, 1½ percent more than passbook savings[18] (see Figure 2.1). However, rising inflation kept market rates hard on the heels of these ceilings, and the sharp rise in T bill rates during the "credit crunch" of 1966 caused investments in large CDs to fall by one-tenth between

16 These pressures were evident in many official statements, including some that may be found in *Federal Reserve Bulletin*, December 1965, pages 1667–1674.

17 See Gilbert Heebner (1969) for a discussion of these and other developments in the CD market. CDs had also been a source of funds to New York City and other banks before the 1930s—described, for example, by Albert Bolles (1903, pages 73–76)—and had begun to resume their former importance outside New York City during the 1950s. Large negotiable CDs played an important part in the temporary reversal of the long-term decline of New York City's role in the American financial system. This decline had accelerated during the 1950s, when the assets of large New York City banks as a proportion of the assets of all U.S. banks fell from 0.17 in 1951 to 0.14 in 1959. This proportion rose to 0.17 in 1967 but again fell to 0.14 by 1975 and to 0.13 in the early 1980s. (Based on data for "all domestically chartered banks" and "large weekly reporting New York City banks" in *Federal Reserve Bulletins*.)

18 As indicated by the title to Table 2.1, "time deposits" used to refer to all deposits except demand deposits. But in the 1960s time deposits began to be reserved for those deposits with enforced minimum maturities while "savings deposits" referred to (and continue to refer to) passbook accounts from which withdrawals may be made without penalty at any time (subject to seldom-exercised notice periods).

July and November 1966. Ceilings on large CDs were raised slightly in 1968, but the rapid rise in the 3-month T bill rate from 5½ percent in late 1968 to 8 percent in January 1970 caused large CDs to fall by one-half. The instability of large CDs due to the recurrent inability of banks to offer competitive rates finally led the Fed to suspend rate ceilings on time deposits of $100,000 or more and maturities of 30 days or more.

Interest ceilings as a discriminatory price list

Firms with monopoly power often charge different prices to different customers for the same product. In the realm of banking, for example, individuals with impeccable credit records typically pay higher loan rates than large firms do, even large firms with low credit ratings. The explanation for this difference in rates may be found in differences in elasticities of demand for funds, which are in turn due to differences in alternatives. Because large firms are well known and because they deal in sums that make it worth their while to employ staffs to search for the cheapest sources of funds, they can borrow at lower interest rates than can equally creditworthy individuals.

These considerations also apply to bank creditors. A young working couple with $1,000 in savings will not devote much time and expense looking for the best rate of return on those savings. This is not because they are less sophisticated than large investors but rather because, in the midst of a busy life with many claims on their time and budget, the prospective returns do not justify an extensive search, especially when interest rates are low and interest differentials are small. Banks did not have to worry very much about losing these deposits in the 1950s or early 1960s.

But rising interest rates made life in the money markets more interesting as borrowers began to compete for funds, even the piggy-bank savings of our young couple. High mortgage rates in California led to nationally advertised offers of high rates for savings deposits by California S&Ls. Complaints by other S&Ls and by banks led Congress to extend interest ceilings to S&L deposits in 1966. Then, when small investors began to shift from savings deposits to T bills in the late 1960s, the minimum denomination in which bills could be bought was raised from $1,000 to $10,000.

Not all small investors could forever be forcibly restrained from attractive nonbank investments. This was particularly true of investors with a few thousand dollars to invest for a few years, for whom some time and expense of a search and then the transaction cost of a purchase of private or government bonds were worthwhile, especially as interest rates rose to record highs in the 1970s. The banks competing most actively for funds responded by offering higher rates on large and/or long-term deposits—after getting the Fed to legalize those rates. Lines 1 to 19 of Table 2.2 constituted a list of increasing rates paid to investors in order of their elasticities of demand as perceived by banks and their regulators in 1983.

By and large, longer maturities and greater minimum balances earned higher rates. Effective price discrimination requires the separation of customers with different demand elasticities. Depository institutions attempt to separate customers by differentiating deposit rates according to the maturities and sizes of deposits.[19] Table 2.2 shows the Fed's legal support of these industry goals until political pressure from aggrieved depositors forced the abandonment of most interest ceilings under the Depository Institutions Deregulation and Monetary Control Act of 1980, which required ceilings on time and savings accounts to be phased out by 1986.

CONCLUSION: INCOMPLETE CARTELS AND INEFFECTIVE COLLUSION

The combination of interest ceilings and limited entry no doubt enables banks with local monopolies to exploit their smaller customers. Noninterest forms of competition for small accounts, such as giveaways and favorable loan terms, are costly and difficult to arrange from afar. But it is unlikely that interest ceilings have enabled banks to profit significantly from large investors, for whom the search for high-yielding deposit substitutes is worthwhile, or even from most small investors, who live in communities with several banks. Banks have had to compete for the funds of both these groups—if not by competitive interest rates, then by other means.[20]

Nonprice competition is common in industries in which price collusion is prevalent, whether legally enforced or not. This is especially true when collusive arrangements to fix prices are not extended to agreements on quantities. A group of firms that wishes to maximize the sum of its profits must, after predicting costs and total demand, agree on price and the output to be produced by each firm. If the second part of the arrangement is neglected (and often even if it is not neglected), firms will violate the spirit of the agreement by attempting

---

19 See Scott Winningham and Donald Hagan (1980) for a history of the application of Regulation Q.

20 We saw above that the Banking Act of 1933 prohibited banks "directly or indirectly, by any device whatsoever" from paying interest on demand deposits. The Fed took the Act at face value and after "exhaustive consideration" interpreted "interest" to mean, effective February 1, 1937, "a payment, credit, service or other thing of value which is made or furnished by a bank as consideration for the use of the funds constituting a deposit and which involves the payment or absorption by the bank of out-of-pocket expenses. . . , regardless of whether such payment, credit, service or other thing of value varies with or bears a substantially direct relation to the amount of the depositor's balance" (*Federal Reserve Bulletin*, January 1937, page 11).

Bankers complained to their Congressmen, and the Chairmen of the House and Senate Banking and Currency Committees complained to the Fed that this definition violated "certain banking practices" and requested a delay of the definition's implementation until the Act could be amended. The Fed complied, and in February 1937 the Act was amended to define interest as "any payment to or for the account of any depositor as compensation for the use of funds constituting a deposit" (*Federal Reserve Bulletin*, March 1937, pages 186–187).

to increase their sales and profits at the expense of others. This is a familiar story in the airline industry, and the same considerations apply to incomplete collusive agreements regarding purchases of inputs such as bank deposits.

In the extreme the effect of binding deposit-rate ceilings without quantity agreements is that banks compete by raising effective deposit rates (including noninterest terms) until the darkly shaded areas in Figures 2.4 and 2.5 are bid away.[21] For these areas represent the opportunity costs of ceilings *as perceived by an individual bank, assuming that other banks abide by the regulations.* So in the end, except for the regulators and small banks in protected rural situations, no one wins. Large depositors suffer a little by having to incur the costs of searching for alternative investments, small depositors suffer a lot from reimbursements in forms inferior to cash, the taxpayers must pay the regulators, and bank profits are no more than in the absence of regulation.[22]

Chapters 3 and 4 describe the principal innovations in financial instruments and means of payment that have been devised by banks and their customers to avoid the burdens of interest ceilings. Some of these innovations may soon be reversed because of the partial deregulation of deposit rates. But several will continue to be important at least as long as the zero ceiling on interbank and other corporate demand deposits remains on the books.

QUESTIONS

1. Is there a "demand for regulation"? What would *you* like to see regulated and why? (Surely you can think of *something*.)
2. Not all bankers favor regulation. What do you think are the characteristics of banks most opposed to regulation? What do you think are the characteristics of banks most in favor of regulation?

Figures 2.4 and 2.5 considered a situation in which R_S rose but the loan-demand (L) and deposit-supply (D) functions remained the same. This was a simplification because normally R_S, L, and D rise and fall together. The next question asks you to consider what happens

---

21 Edward Kane (1981) has referred to these activities as "arbitrage by innovation."

22 These arguments also apply to S&Ls. In a study of S&L profitability during the period 1951 to 1979, Alan Hess and Daniel Vrabac (1983) found the rate of return on assets to depend on the spread between the mortgage rate and the T bill rate and on the mismatch between the durations of assets and liabilities but not to be affected by the extension of Regulation Q to S&Ls in 1966. (Duration is a weighted average of the maturities of a security's payments and is discussed in Appendix 6.A.)

On the other hand Larry Dann and Christopher James (1982) found S&L stock values to be adversely affected by the relaxation of deposit-rate ceilings in the forms of two of the new long-term, minimum-balance accounts introduced in 1973 and 1978 (like some of those in Table 2.2). This suggests that not all the advantages of deposit ceilings had been bid away by nonprice competition. It is also consistent with Peltzman's modified capture-theory hypothesis because the regulator's appeasements of the majority consumer (depositor) group apparently reduced the subsidy to the producer (S&L) group.

when our simplifying assumptions are relaxed. (Problem 1 at the end of Appendix 2.A is a numerical version of question 3.)

3. Consider the differences between Figures 2.4 and 2.5:
   (a) Suppose that, instead of a rise in R_S, there had been an increase in loan demand. How would the optimal values of R_L, L, and S and the opportunity cost of the regulation (that is, the darkly shaded area) have been affected?
   (b) Suppose both loan demand and R_S had increased. How would the optimal values of R_L, L, and S and the opportunity cost of the regulation have been affected?
   (c) Suppose loan demand, deposit supply, and R_S had increased. How would the optimal values of R_L, L, and S and the opportunity cost of the regulation have been affected?
   Illustrate your answers with diagrams.
4. If interest ceilings reduce bank profits as shown in Figures 2.4 and 2.5, why do so many bankers favor ceilings?
5. Suppose the bank in Figure 2.5 finds a way of attracting D by evading R_D^r (for example, by gifts). What will be its new optimal loans, deposits, and profits?
6. What if all banks follow the example of the bank in question 5? What will be the new optimal loans, deposits, and profits of the bank in question 5?
7. Find and discuss exceptions to the rule of higher ceilings for more highly interest-elastic deposits in Table 2.2.
8. Which of the deposits in Table 2.2 would be preferred by
   (a) managers of short-term corporate investments,
   (b) young households saving for old age, and
   (c) poor (but not quite destitute) college students?
   Explain your answers.
9. Please look in the statistical section of a recent *Federal Reserve Bulletin* at the table dealing with maximum interest rates payable on deposits, and discuss the differences between that table and Table 2.2.

REFERENCES

Gary S. Becker, "A Theory of Competition among Pressure Groups for Political Influence," *Quarterly Journal of Economics*, August 1983, pages 371–400.

Albert S. Bolles, *Money, Banking, and Finance*, American Book, New York, 1903.

James G. Cannon, *Clearing Houses and the Currency*, Columbia University Press, New York, 1908.

Albert H. Cox, *Regulation of Interest Rates on Bank Deposits*, University of Michigan Bureau of Business Research, Ann Arbor, 1964.

Larry Y. Dann and Christopher M. James, "An Analysis of the Impact of Deposit Rate Ceilings on the Market Values of Thrift Institutions," *Journal of Finance*, December 1982, pages 1259–1275.

S. I. Greenbaum and C. F. Haywood, "Secular Change in the Financial Services Industry," *Journal of Money, Credit and Banking*, May 1974, pages 571–589.

A. Gilbert Heebner, *Negotiable Certificates of Deposit: The Development of a Money Market Instrument*, New York University Graduate

School of Business Administration, New York, 1969.

Alan C. Hess and Daniel J. Vrabac, "Regulation Q and the Profitability of Savings Associations," Federal Reserve Bank of Kansas City Research Working Paper 83-03, March 1983.

Edward J. Kane, "Accelerating Inflation, Technological Innovation, and the Decreasing Effectiveness of Banking Regulation," *Journal of Finance,* May 1981, pages 355–367.

Charles M. Linke, "The Evolution of Interest Rate Regulation on Commercial Bank Deposits in the United States," *National Banking Review,* June 1966, pages 449–469.

Simon Newcomb, *Principles of Political Economy,* Harper, New York, 1886.

Sam Peltzman, "Toward a More General Theory of Regulation," *Journal of Law and Economics,* August 1976, pages 211–240.

William L. Silber, "Towards a Theory of Financial Innovation," in William L. Silber (ed.), *Financial Innovation,* Heath, Lexington, MA, 1975.

William L. Silber, "The Process of Financial Innovation," *American Economic Review,* May 1983, pages 89–95.

O. M. W. Sprague, *History of Crises under the National Banking System,* National Monetary Commission of the U.S. Senate, U.S. Government Printing Office, Washington, 1910.

George J. Stigler, "The Theory of Economic Regulation," *Bell Journal of Economics and Management Science,* Spring 1971, pages 3–21.

Scott Winningham and Donald G. Hagan, "Regulation Q: An Historical Perspective," Federal Reserve Bank of Kansas City *Economic Review,* April 1980, pages 3–17.

APPENDIX
2.A
DERIVATION OF THE RESULTS IN FIGURES 2.2 TO 2.5

We begin with a slightly more general model than that in Chapter 2 by taking account of (1) bank capital K, (2) a reserve-requirement ratio k, and (3) general linear forms of the loan-demand and deposit-supply functions so that Equations (2.1) to (2.4) may be written

(2.A.1) $$\Pi = R_L L + R_S S - R_D D$$

(2.A.2) $$R + L + S = kD + L + S = D + K$$

(2.A.3) $$L = L(R_L) = a - bR_L = 20 - 100R_L$$

(2.A.4) $$D = D(R_D) = c + fR_D = 8 + 100R_D$$

Equation (2.A.1) is identical with Equation (2.1), but Equation (2.A.2) differs from Equation (2.2) by including K as a source of funds and $R = kD$ as a noninterest-earning required-reserve use of funds. Equations (2.A.3) and (2.A.4) include more general forms of Equations (2.3) and (2.4). We first solve the problem in general form and then for the specific form used in Figures 2.2 to 2.5.

The problem is to choose R_L, L, R_D, D, and S so as to maximize Π, subject to the constraints (2.A.2) to (2.A.4) and the given value of R_S. We start by substituting the constraints into the objective function, specifically by substituting $L(R_L)$ for L, $D(R_D)$ for D, and the solution of Equation (2.A.2) for S into Equation (2.A.1) and rearranging to get

(2.A.1)′ $$\Pi = R_L L(R_L) - R_D D(R_D) + R_S[(1 - k)D(R_D) + K - L(R_L)]$$

With L, D, and S substituted out of Equation (2.A.1) the problem is reduced to maximizing Equation (2.A.1)′ with respect to R_L and R_D, which we do by setting the derivatives of Equation (2.A.1)′ with respect to R_L and R_D equal to zero:

(2.A.5) $$\frac{\partial \Pi}{\partial R_L} = R_L L' + L - R_S L' = 0$$

(2.A.6) $$\frac{\partial \Pi}{\partial R_D} = -(R_D D' + D) + R_S(1 - k)D' = 0$$

where $L' = dL/dR_L$ and $D' = dD/dR_D$.

For conformity with Figures 2.2 to 2.5, let us express Equations (2.A.5) and (2.A.6) in terms of the marginal revenue from loans, MR_L, and the marginal cost of deposits, MC_D. The marginal revenue from loans is the change in total loan revenue relative to a change in loans:

$$(2.A.7) \quad MR_L = \frac{dR_L L(R_L)}{dL} = R_L + L(R_L)\frac{dR_L}{dL} = R_L + \frac{L}{dL/dR_L}$$

$$= R_L + \frac{L}{L'} = \frac{1}{L'}(R_L L' + L)$$

since dR_L/dL is the inverse of dL/dR_L. The marginal cost of deposits is the change in total deposit cost relative to a change in deposits:

$$(2.A.8) \quad MC_D = \frac{dR_D D(R_D)}{dD} = R_D + D(R_D)\frac{dR_D}{dD}$$

$$= R_D + \frac{D}{dD/dR_D} = R_D + \frac{D}{D'} = \frac{1}{D'}(R_D D' + D)$$

since dR_D/dD is the inverse of dD/dR_D.

Substituting Equations (2.A.7) and (2.A.8) into Equations (2.A.5) and (2.A.6) gives

$$(2.A.5)' \quad \frac{\partial \Pi}{\partial R_L} = L'MR_L - R_S L' = 0 \quad \text{or} \quad MR_L = R_S$$

$$(2.A.6)' \quad \frac{\partial \Pi}{\partial R_D} = -D'MC_D + R_S(1-k)D' = 0 \quad \text{or} \quad MC_D = (1-k)R_S$$

These results, which together state that profit is maximized when $(1-k)MR_L = (1-k)R_S = MC_D$, are identical with those depicted in Figures 2.2 to 2.5, except that here deposits are attracted only up to the point such that MC_D is $(1-k)$ times the marginal revenues from loans and securities because only $(1-k)D$ can be invested; kD must be held as noninterest-earning reserves.

Substituting the linear forms of Equations (2.A.3) and (2.A.4) into the maximum conditions (2.A.5) and (2.A.6) gives

$$(2.A.9) \quad R_L(-b) + a - bR_L - R_S(-b) = 0 \quad \text{or} \quad R_L^* = \frac{a + bR_S}{2b}$$

$$(2.A.10) \quad -R_D(f) - (c + fR_D) + R_S(1-k)(f) = 0$$

$$\text{or} \quad R_D^* = \frac{-c + f(1-k)R_S}{2f}$$

Substituting the optimal loan and deposit rates, R_L^* and R_D^*, into Equations (2.A.3) and (2.A.4) gives

$$(2.A.11) \qquad L^* = a - bR_L^* = \frac{a - bR_S}{2}$$

(2.A.12) $$D^* = c + fR_D^* = \frac{c + f(1 - k)R_S}{2}$$

We see from Equation (2.A.2) that

(2.A.13) $$S^* = (1 - k)D^* - L^* + K$$

Using the numerical values $a = 20$, $b = 100$, $c = 8$, and $f = 100$ shown on the right-hand sides of Equations (2.A.3) and (2.A.4) and assuming $R_S = 0.12$ and $k = K = 0$, we find that the optimal rates and dollar values in Equations (2.A.9) to (2.A.13) become $R_L^* = 0.16$, $R_D^* = 0.02$, $L^* = 4$, $D^* = 10$, and $S^* = 6$, as shown in Figure 2.2.

PROBLEMS

Problem 1 presents variations on Figures 2.4 and 2.5 and asks for numerical examples of question 3 at the end of Chapter 2.

1. With the values of a, b, c, f, R_S, k, and K given above what happens to the bank's decision (that is, its choice of R_L, L, R_D, D, and S) **(a)** when the loan-demand function increases such that $a = 28$, **(b)** when both loan demand and R_S increase such that $a = 28$ and $R_S = 0.15$, and **(c)** when loan demand, R_S, and deposit supply increase such that $a = 28$, $R_S = 0.15$, and $c = 11$? If you have not already done question 3, illustrate your results with diagrams.
2. Again with $a = 20$, $b = 100$, $c = 8$, $f = 100$, and $k = K = 0$ how is the bank's decision changed when **(a)** k rises to 0.10 and **(b)** k rises to 0.10 and K to 3?

FINANCIAL INNOVATION AND THE DEMAND FOR MONEY

A feast is made for laughter, and wine maketh merry:
but money answereth all things.
Ecclesiastes, 10:19

The stock market used to dominate the financial press, and more space is still allocated to stock price quotations than to any other aspect of financial news. But transactions in stocks and other capital market instruments are dwarfed by those in money market instruments, by which we mean money and short-term marketable securities that are easily converted into money. For example on a typical day shares valued at about $4 billion are traded on the New York and American Stock Exchanges. In contrast daily transactions in overnight federal funds and repurchase agreements usually surpass $100 billion.[1] Moving to U.S. government securities, dealers typically execute daily trades valued at $25 billion in Treasury bills (T bills) and other U.S. securities maturing in less than a year, compared with $15 billion worth of trades in longer-term U.S. securities.[2] The list could go on, but the point would remain: The greatest part of the value of financial market transactions involves exchanges of money and securities for short periods—most often for 1 day. These "money markets" have grown more rapidly than most other markets in recent years. This chapter is concerned with the causes of that growth.

Our analysis of the demands and supplies of money market instruments is centered on the demand for money. That demand function describes household, business, and government choices between money and other money market instruments and is therefore essential to an understanding of the evolution of the money markets. The demand-for-money function (3.1) presented below will be familiar

---

1 Federal funds and repurchase agreements have become the most important money market instruments in values traded. Briefly, they are short-term (usually 1-day) loans between banks, large corporations, and state and local governments.

2 These data are from *Federal Reserve Bulletins*.

to those who remember their introductory courses in economics and finance. In this course we take the analysis a step further by applying the traditional statement of money demand to the analysis of recent developments and the prediction of possible future developments in the money markets. But first things first. We begin simply by discussing what money is and what functions it performs.

THE FUNCTIONS OF MONEY

DEFINITION 3.1.   *Money* is the "medium of exchange," the "means of payment." It is whatever is generally accepted as payment for goods and the settlement of debts.

In modern economies money consists of currency, coin, and checking accounts and will continue to do so even after the advent of the checkless society although money deposits in banks will have a different name. Nowadays you may obtain goods from a store with currency or a check—often in the latter case only after a suspicious look and proof of identification. The store has extended a loan to you in the amount of the check, which it intends to redeem through its bank. The store hopes that its bank will be able to collect the promised funds from your bank, thereby transferring money from your checking account to its own. In the checkless, electronic-funds-transfer society of the future the store will be able to arrange this transfer immediately (with no risk of bad checks) by means of checkout-counter computer terminals linked to its bank and yours.

In addition to being characterized as the medium of exchange, money has been described as a "store of value," a "standard of value," and a "unit of account."[3] Money may be all these things, but only the first is an essential property of money. Any storable good may serve as a store of value; but in an inflationary economy in which it earns little or no interest money is inferior as a store of value to most other goods. Money is also an inferior standard of value in such an economy, the term "millionaire" being less meaningful than the description of Job's "substance" as "seven thousand sheep, and three thousand camels, and five hundred yoke of oxen, and five hundred she asses, and a very great household; so that this man was the greatest of all the men of the east."[4] Finally, a specific denomination of money (the dollar) is the

---

3 These descriptions of money, which date at least from Aristotle (see *Ethica Nicomachea*), were in fact descriptions of the metals that, in addition to their other uses, also served as money, that is, as the medium of exchange. See Dale Osborne (1984) for a thorough analysis of alternative definitions of money.

4 Alfred Marshall wrote in 1887 that the "second function of money [in addition to serving as the medium of exchange] is to act as a *standard of value,* or *standard for deferred payments*—that is, to indicate the amount of general purchasing power, the payment of which is sufficient to discharge a contract, or other commercial obligation, that extends over a considerable period of time. For this purpose stability of value is the one essential condition." The failure of this function in our paper-money economy has led to the increasing use of indexed contracts, by which

most common unit of account. But many other goods could perform
this function just as well as money, and some of them are in fact being
called upon to do so under the name of "inflation accounting."[5]

So we come back to the definition of money as simply the medium of
exchange:

> For any commodity may serve as a unit of account and stan-
> dard of deferred payments: and every asset is, by its very nature,
> a potential store of value. If money is to be distinguished by the
> functions it performs, therefore, it is to the medium of exchange
> function that we must address our attention.[6]

> Although money has many close substitutes as a store of value,
> not even the nearest of near-money shares with it the mo-
> mentous characteristic of routine exchange and circulation.[7]

The distinct character of money (coin, currency, and checking
accounts) continues in the 1980s, even with the reduced expense and
increased ease with which money and other assets can be exchanged. It
is still true that the distinguishing feature of a monetary economy—as
opposed to a barter system—is that in a monetary economy there is a
distinct good (money) that is one side of every transaction.[8]

THE DEMAND FOR MONEY

The inadequacy of money as a store of value—especially during
periods of inflation and high rates of return on other forms of
wealth—is especially important to our analysis. It means that households and firms have strong incentives not to hold money. But there
are also strong incentives operating in the other direction: Economic
units must hold money (at least for short periods) because money is
the medium of exchange; they must have money if they want to buy
goods or pay their debts. If transaction costs were zero and trades were
executed instantaneously, no one would hold money as long as the
twinkling of an eye, not long enough to be observed. The velocity of
money would approach infinity as people held their wealth in interest-
earning assets as long as possible, which means until the moment
payments were due, when they would instantly and costlessly transfer
other assets to currency or checking accounts and, in the same instant,
reduce their money holdings again to zero by making the required

---

payments are tied to the values of specific goods (such as gold) or groups of goods (such as the
"market basket" used for the Consumer Price Index).

5 "Constant-dollar (indexed) accounting" has developed for the same reasons as (and is formally
identical to) indexed contracts. For obvious reasons, both inflation accounting and indexed contracts are used more widely in Argentina and Brazil than in the United States. See Robert
McGee (1981).

6 Robert Clower (1967, page 3).

7 Leland Yeager (1968, page 64).

8 This point was stressed by Robert Clower (1967).

payments. This is why Superman has no pockets in his suit. He is able to transfer his wealth between money and other assets at the speed of light and to make payments at the same speed. He is thus spared the inconvenience of carrying money.

To describe the conditions under which money will not be held is to explain why money is held. Transactions are neither costless nor instantaneous, even for those with access to electronic transfer facilities. Firms and consumers who try to emulate Superman incur large transaction costs (both internally and in bank charges and brokers' commissions) and are frequently embarrassed by their inability to meet obligations on time. Optimal money balances are those that minimize the sum of two costs: the forgone interest cost of not holding other assets and the transaction costs involved in shifting back and forth between money and other assets. The following demand for money is the result of such a cost-minimization problem:[9]

$$(3.1) \qquad\qquad \frac{M_c}{P} = \sqrt{\frac{bz}{2(R_s - R_m)}}$$

Equation (3.1) shows the per capita demand for average real money balances, M_c/P, during some period: M_c is the average number of dollars held as currency or in checking accounts by the typical money holder; P is an index of the prices of goods paid by money holders so that M_c/P is the real value (that is, purchasing power) of M_c; R_s is the rate of interest earned on money substitutes, for example, T bills; R_m is the rate of interest earned on money balances; b is the real cost in terms of time, phone bills, and bank charges or brokerage fees of switching between money and money substitutes; and z is per capita real expenditures.

Notice that the demand for real money balances is positively related to the quantity of purchases, z. But M_c/P rises less than proportionally to z because there are economies of scale in managing money. The demand for money is also positively related to the costs, b, of transfers between money and other assets. If these costs are high relative to the returns on money substitutes, money managers will choose to hold large amounts of money. This will be less costly than holding funds in other forms and then switching into money as payments come due. Finally, the demand for money is an inverse function of the difference, $R_s - R_m$, between the rates of return on money and other assets.[10]

---

9 Equation (3.1) is derived in Appendix 3.A and is based on W. Baumol's (1952) model, in which receipts occur periodically in lump sums and expenditures occur in a certain and continuous steady stream. Baumol's model has been extended by James Tobin (1956), Merton Miller and Daniel Orr (1966), and Robert Clower and Peter Howitt (1978) to take account of uncertainty in the timing of receipts and expenditures and to allow the frequency of transactions to be a decision variable. But we shall see below that Baumol's simple framework provides a robust description of the demand for money at least from 1915 to the 1980s.

10 Examples of the effects of changes in these variables on the demand for money may be obtained by doing problems 1 and 2 at the end of the chapter.

The importance of transaction costs to the demand for money is illustrated in Table 3.1. This table shows, for the presently zero interest ceiling on corporate demand deposits ($R_m = 0$) and for various T bill yields and transaction costs, the number of days (n) that a T bill must be held to recoup transaction costs. The dealer bid-ask spread (that is, the difference between quoted purchase and selling prices) on large T bill transactions is normally about 0.015 percent of the purchase price, for example, 0.00015 ($1,000,000) = $150 on bills selling for $1,000,000. If the simple annual yield is 0.0250 so that the daily yield is 0.0250/365 = 0.0000685, the firm must hold the bill 3 days in order to break even. We see in the table that the break-even point is 2.19 days and, since calculated yields depend on the number of full days to maturity, this means 3 days. For annual yields exceeding about 5.5 percent the firm breaks even on bills held only 1 day. Of course these calculations take no account either of risk arising from possible fluctuations in yields or of transaction costs other than bid-ask spreads. Inclusion of these factors would tend to increase the break-even holding period and therefore to increase the demand for money.

The last column in Table 3.1 shows the holding period that would be necessary to break even if the bid-ask spread as a proportion of the bill's price were 0.00030 instead of 0.00015. In summary the table implies a high demand for money when transaction costs are high and interest rates are low. For example, if a firm acquires money on which it expects no claim for 3 or 4 days, it will leave that money in its checking account, earning no interest, if $S/P = 0.00030$ and the best yield on money substitutes is 0.0250. In terms of Equation (3.1) its

Table 3.1   Break-even Holding Periods for 3-month T Bills

Simple Annual Yield[a]	Daily Yield	n[a] If S/P[a] Is 0.00015	If S/P Is 0.00030
0.0250	0.0000685	2.19	4.38
0.0500	0.0001370	1.09	2.19
0.0750	0.0002055	0.73	1.46
0.1000	0.0002740	0.55	1.09
0.1250	0.0003425	0.44	0.88
0.1500	0.0004110	0.36	0.73

a n = number of days the bill must be held to break even; S/P = bid-ask spread as a proportion of the purchase price; simple annual yield = 365 × (daily yield).

Based on P. A. Tinsley, B. Garrett, and M. E. Friar, *The Measurement of Money Demand*, tab. II.1, Federal Reserve Board of Governors, Washington, 1978.

demand for money is high because b is high and R_s is low. In recent years real transaction costs have fallen and interest rates have risen so that, for money managers handling large sums, the break-even holding period for money substitutes has often been 1 day.

These determinants of the demand for money are illustrated in Figure 3.1. Below the figure, the real per capita demand for money is written in general form in Equation (3.1)′ as a function of real expenditures, z, and transaction costs relative to the difference between the rates of return on money substitutes and money, $b/(R_s - R_m)$. We have followed common practice in using the functional notation L (for "liquidity"). Each of the real demands for money in Figure 3.1 is pictured as a function of only R_s; b, z, and R_m are held constant. The values assumed for the functions L'' and L''' are shown to the right of Equations (3.1)″ and (3.1)‴. L''' lies to the right of L'' because, other things being equal, the demand for money is greater when the return on money is 3.6 percent than when R_m is zero. The

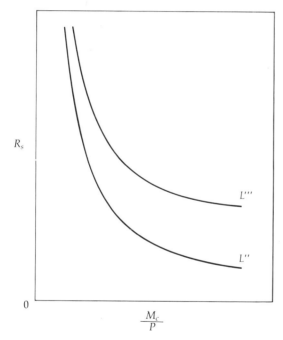

Figure 3.1   The demand for money.

(3.1)′ $\dfrac{M_c}{P} = L\left(z, \dfrac{b}{R_s - R_m}\right)$

(3.1)″ $\dfrac{M_c}{P} = L''(R_s) = \sqrt{\dfrac{100(32{,}000)}{2(R_s - 0)}}$ $b = 100,\ z = 32{,}000,\ R_m = 0$

(3.1)‴ $\dfrac{M_c}{P} = L'''(R_s) = \sqrt{\dfrac{100(32{,}000)}{2(R_s - 0.036)}}$ $b = 100,\ z = 32{,}000,\ R_m = 0.036$

same effect (that is, an increase in the real demand for money) would be produced by either an increase in the quantity of real transactions, z, to be performed or an increase in the real cost, b, of switching between money and money substitutes.[11]

THE VELOCITY OF MONEY

We are interested in the effects of recent developments on the demand for money. An informative way of studying these developments is to examine the *velocity* of money, the velocity of money being the demand for money turned upside down. To say that people economize on their money balances, that is, demand less money relative to their purchases, is to say that they spend or turn over those money balances at a faster rate. The velocity of money during some period is the number of times the average dollar is spent. Velocity is best understood as part of the *equation of exchange,* which is usually written as

$$(3.2) \qquad MV_T = P_T T$$

where P_T is the average price of transactions and T is the number of transactions. If $P_T = \$1.50$ and $T = 2,000$, people spend $3,000 during the period. If M is $1,000, the equation tells us that $V_T = \$3,000/\$1,000 = 3$. That is, the *transactions velocity of money* during the period is 3. If the period in our example is 1 month and if this month is typical, the *annual* transactions velocity of money is $12(3) = 36$.

Economists usually prefer to discuss the *income velocity of money,* which we denote simply as V to distinguish it from transactions velocity, V_T. Using V instead of V_T, real income (Y) instead of transactions (T), and the price index (P) appropriate to income, we may rewrite the equation of exchange as

$$(3.3) \qquad MV = PY$$

For convenience Y and P are often approximated by the real gross national product (GNP) and the GNP deflator, respectively.[12] The latter term is the Department of Commerce's name for its index of the prices of all the goods and services that make up the GNP. The dollar, or nominal, value of the GNP is therefore PY. Income velocity is the number of times the average dollar is spent on final goods and services. Now let us apply the money-demand function (3.1) to the analysis of velocity as defined in Equation (3.3). Since Equation (3.1) described individual money demands, we must convert Equation (3.3) to per

---

11 Illustrations of these effects are requested in problem 2 at the end of the chapter.

12 Since the GNP is the value of final goods and services sold in a year, our V might better be called "final expenditure velocity." But we follow others in calling it "income velocity."

capita values. We can write

(3.4) $Y = Nz$ and $M = NM_c$

where Y = real GNP; z = per capita GNP; N = population; M = aggregate money balances; M_c = per capita money balances.

Solving Equation (3.3) for V and substituting Equations (3.1) and (3.4) into the result gives

(3.5) $$V = \frac{Y}{M/P} = \frac{Nz}{NM_c/P} = \frac{z}{M_c/P} = \sqrt{\frac{2(R_s - R_m)z}{b}}$$

In view of our discussion of the demand for money, it comes as no surprise that the turnover rate (velocity) of money is a positive function of the opportunity cost of holding money ($R_s - R_m$) and an inverse function of the cost of switching between money and money substitutes (b). Velocity is a positive function of per capita GNP (z) because the demand for money responds less than proportionally to expenditures. Real money balances as a proportion of real expenditures decline (that is, velocity rises) as real expenditures increase.[13] The next section examines the actual behavior of velocity and some of its determinants during the past 70 years.

THE BEHAVIOR OF VELOCITY AND AN EXPLANATION: MARKET INTEREST RATES AND INNOVATIONS IN TRADING COSTS

The data in Figure 3.2 are broadly consistent with Equation (3.5). The upper curve is velocity as defined in that equation; the bottom curve is the 4- to 6-month prime commercial paper rate[14] and corresponds to R_s. Other money market rates could have been used, but they would not have changed our story because variations in short-term rates are similar in timing and magnitude. The chart begins with 1915 because M first began to be reported on a regular basis in that year.[15]

Long-term movements in V have been positively associated with long-term movements in R_s. The largest changes in V were the fall from 3.90 in 1929 to 1.97 in 1946 and the rise to 6.83 in 1981. R_s was 5.85 percent in 1929, 0.81 in 1946, and 15.04 in 1981. V also responded to short-term variations in R_s in a fairly regular, positive manner before World War II. These movements are consistent with Equation

---

13 The relationships between velocity and the demand for money may be illustrated by doing problem 5 at the end of the chapter.

14 R_s is the average of the 3- and 6-month commercial paper rates beginning in 1979, when the 4- to 6-month rate series was discontinued.

15 We shall see below in Table 3.2 that an estimate of M is reported by the Federal Reserve (the Fed) as $M1$.

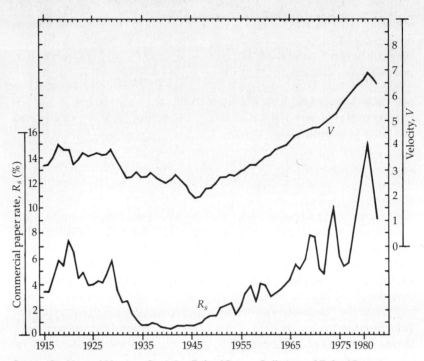

Sources: *Banking and Monetary Statistics, Federal Reserve Bulletins,* and Federal Reserve
money-supply releases.

Figure 3.2   The 4- to 6-month prime commercial paper rate and the
velocity of money, 1915 to 1983 (annual data).

(3.5) if b is not volatile and R_m varies less than R_s. The relationship
between R_s and R_m will be considered later in this chapter. This section
is concerned with the forces that have operated to change the costs (b)
of switching between money and money substitutes. We first notice
something unusual in Figure 3.2 in the continued decline of V between
1941 and 1946 even though R_s had stopped falling and even rose
slightly during that period. But before considering alternative explanations of this decline in V, we take a closer look at the postwar
period.

The two most notable characteristics of interest rates since World
War II have been their strong upward trend and, since the 1960s, their
increasing volatility. V possesses only the first of these characteristics,
which has meant frequent short-term deviations from the longer-term
positive relationship between R_s and V. Specifically, cyclical declines
in R_s between 1946 and 1981 were not accompanied by declines in V.

We shall consider two possible explanations of the strong and
almost continuous postwar rise in V. One possible explanation is based
on large increases in per capita income and expenditures, which,
because of economies of scale in handling money, may have induced
increases in velocity, as indicated in Equation (3.5) by the positive

effect of z on V. But this effect cannot explain why V did not fall during postwar recessions. Nor can it explain the decline in V in the face of constant or slightly rising interest rates during World War II because per capita real expenditures did not fall during that period.[16]

A more promising explanation of the persistency of the postwar rise in V, which has the added virtue of helping to explain the decline in V between 1941 and 1946, is in terms of long-term responses of the financial structure to short-term variations in interest rates. One's ability to switch into and out of money depends on the presence of people and firms willing to take the other sides of these transactions. The magnitudes of the costs of executing trades depend, for a given state of technology, on (1) the quality and quantity of staff and equipment devoted by financial firms to the performance of transactions and (2) the number of firms involved. Item (1) refers to firm efficiency and (2) refers to competition. Increases in both tend to reduce b and therefore to reduce the demand for money and increase its velocity. New firms are attracted to the financial markets and existing firms add to their capacity in response to perceived profit opportunities. In the financial markets this means high interest rates. When interest rates are high, you want to economize on cash balances. If rates are high enough, financial firms will be there to help you do it quickly and efficiently. These firms compete for your money by offering good rates of return and low transaction costs—in the forms of time deposits, shares in money market mutual funds, and other convenient money substitutes, as well as conveniently located 24-hour remote teller machines and automatic transfer services. They are willing to do this because of the high rates of return they expect to earn when they relend your money.

Markets and services have *start-up costs*. When interest rates are low, firms will not find it worth their while to expand their capacities for the purpose of competing for your money in order to relend it at, say, 2 percent. But 8 percent is a different ballgame. Apparently, even 4 percent is enough to induce significant financial innovation and the expansion of financial trading facilities. Suppose, after a period of rapidly rising interest rates, we observe financial markets made more sophisticated by the addition of markets for repurchase agreements and money market funds as well as extensive facilities for electronic funds transfers. When interest rates fall back from 8 percent to their

---

16 This is true of both total final expenditures (GNP) and private final expenditures (GNP less federal government expenditures). World War II ended the American depression and, despite rationing and a tremendous increase in government expenditures, the rise in output permitted per capita real private expenditures to be about the same at the end as at the beginning of the war.

 A case can be made that the calculation of V should be based on private (including state and local government) expenditures because the reported money supply excludes federal government checking accounts and currency holdings. But we have followed general usage in defining V as the ratio of GNP to private money holdings. Both definitions are consistent with the velocity patterns in Figure 3.2.

previous level of 2 percent, the commitments to these markets by financial firms may not be reversed. The start-up period is over and profits can, perhaps, continue to be made at interest rates of 3 percent. More persuasively, these firms will stick around for a while just in case interest rates rise again. But suppose interest rates fall below 1 percent and stay there for a dozen years, as in the case of short-term rates between 1934 and 1946. Financial firms may take some time to withdraw their services. Instead of firing people and selling specialized equipment, they merely do not replace them. Gradually, costs rise and velocity falls—even after interest rates have ended their decline.[17]

NEW WAYS OF PAYING INTEREST ON MONEY

The remainder of this chapter completes our analysis of the demand for money by considering the response of R_m to R_s. The preceding section emphasized the impact of R_s on b, that is, on the development of inexpensive ways of switching into and out of money. The other major money market response to the combination of high market interest rates and the prohibition of interest on demand deposits has been simply to evade the prohibition.[18]

Two of the most interesting and important ways of paying interest on demand deposits use *overnight repurchase agreements and "Eurodollars."*[19] A repurchase agreement (RP) is a contract between two parties, A and B, such that B sells a security to A with an agreement to buy it back on a specified date at a specified price. RPs are a simple form of secured loan. B has borrowed money from A and has given him possession of a security as collateral for the loan. The securities involved are usually those of the U.S. government. Suppose A and B enter into a 1-day (overnight) RP agreement for $15 million at the going RP rate of 12 percent per annum. On Monday B receives $15 million in cash from A and delivers U.S. securities worth approximately $15 million to A. On Tuesday B gets the securities back and pays A the principal plus interest, or $15,005,000.[20] Banks have borrowed large sums from corporations and state and local governments overnight and for longer terms in this way, using RPs as a means

---

17 See Hyman Minsky (1957) and P. Tinsley, B. Garrett, and M. Friar (1978) for statements of the thesis that long-run movements in velocity are responses to short-run fluctuations in interest rates.

18 The incentives for violating this prohibition in the presence of high market rates was the principal subject of Chapter 2.

   There is no reason (in an unregulated system) why interest should not also be paid on currency, which would probably occur in the presence of high market rates if the "circulating notes" of commercial banks had not been taxed out of existence by Congress in order to monopolize this form of money as a source of interest-free borrowing (although ostensibly to exercise its constitutional obligation to control money—as if bank notes were money and checking accounts were not money).

19 The role of RPs in the management of bank reserves is discussed in Chapter 9. For more about Eurodollars see Gunter Dufey and Ian Giddy (1978).

20 These rates are quoted on a 360-day basis.

of effectively paying interest on demand deposits. This is done as follows. Suppose corporation A maintains demand deposits with bank B. At 11:00 A.M. on Monday A agrees to buy securities from B with an understanding that the transaction (plus interest) will be reversed on Tuesday morning. But the first transaction does not actually take place until the end of the day on Monday (3:00 bankers' hours). This means that A has use of the money throughout the day and, in addition, earns the RP rate of interest on that money. Banks would rather have the money for nothing, that is, at the zero rate of interest allowed on demand deposits. But competition for funds has forced them, like other borrowers, to pay high interest rates.

By Eurodollars we used to mean exclusively dollars in European banks. The British, for example, see no reason why you or anyone else should not be able to deposit dollars, rather than pounds, in a London bank with the understanding that the bank will repay you dollars whenever you and the bank have agreed. They also see no reason why you should not be able to earn whatever rate of interest the market will bear. Neither of these practices is permitted, without harassment, in the United States. Restrictive American regulations, especially interest-rate ceilings, have caused many Americans and others to hold dollars in banks outside the United States. All these deposits are now commonly called Eurodollars, whether held in European banks or not. Because of the time factor, most overnight Eurodollars owned by Americans are in Caribbean branches of U.S. banks, which have been established for this purpose and are in the same time zone as New York. These overnight Eurodollars, like overnight RPs, are a means by which U.S. banks effectively pay interest on demand deposits. Instead of bank B's entering into a repurchase agreement with corporation A, B transfers A's funds to its Caribbean branch overnight. Just a few punches on a computer terminal are involved.

In most cases it is not necessary for the bank and the depositor to make new RP or Eurodollar arrangements each day. They usually have a continuing arrangement whereby the bank automatically *sweeps* the customer's demand deposits (either the entire account or the portion in excess of a specified minimum overnight balance) into RPs, Eurodollars, or other investments that earn interest. By the end of 1983, the total volume of overnight RPs issued by U.S. banks and overnight Eurodollars issued by foreign branches of U.S. banks to U.S. residents (excluding financial institutions) was 22 percent as large as reported demand deposits.[21]

The most dramatic financial contribution to consumer welfare during the 1970s was the *money market mutual fund (MMMF)*. A

---

21 See Table 3.2, below. Money-supply figures apply to the end of the day, and the reporting of what are effectively demand deposits as RPs and Eurodollars has caused M to be underestimated (and V to be overestimated) by unknown amounts because we do not know what proportions of these funds in fact also serve as demand deposits.

stock mutual fund is an investment company that provides share-holders with a rate of return that varies with the prices and dividends of the stocks held by the fund. Money market funds operate on the same principle. But their investments are money market instruments such as T bills, certificates of deposit, bankers' acceptances, and commercial paper. Shares in MMMFs are available in small denominations, often as little as $500. Dividends are calculated and paid on a daily basis, and shares can be redeemed by check. Shareholders receive books of checks from the fund's bank and can write checks on their shares in the fund just as on ordinary demand deposits. At its peak, in November 1982, the volume of MMMFs exceeded demand deposits and was 70 percent as large as all checking accounts in depository institutions.

A Massachusetts mutual savings bank found a different way of paying interest on checking accounts. This required some ingenuity because mutual savings banks were not allowed even to issue checking accounts (much less pay interest on them). But in June 1972 the Consumers Savings Bank of Worcester offered its savings depositors the privilege of withdrawing funds from their accounts by writing *negotiable orders of withdrawal* that directed Consumers Savings to make payments to third parties. This is merely the definition of a check so that these NOW accounts were effectively demand deposits.

Consumers Savings had sought permission for NOW accounts from the Massachusetts Commissioner of Banks in 1970 but was denied. However, the bank brought suit against the Commissioner, and in 1972 the state Supreme Court ruled that the charters of mutual savings banks did not prohibit withdrawals from savings accounts by means of the proposed negotiable orders. So Consumers Savings was free and clear of the regulations as long as it did not call the accounts demand deposits or refer to the orders as checks.[22]

As more state-chartered mutual savings banks in Massachusetts and then New Hampshire began to offer NOW accounts, other depository institutions complained that they had been placed at a competitive disadvantage. Congress corrected this imbalance in 1973 by authorizing all depository institutions in Massachusetts and New Hampshire, except credit unions, to offer NOW accounts—a privilege extended to the rest of New England in 1976.

Credit unions were not left behind. Several began to offer *share draft accounts* in the early 1970s, and in 1974 the National Credit Union Administration authorized all federally chartered credit unions to offer them. Share drafts are to credit union savings accounts what NOWs are to savings accounts in other depository institutions. They enable depositors to write checks on their savings and thus effectively convert savings accounts into interest-earning checking accounts.

Banks had begun to transfer funds between savings and checking

---

22 See Katherine Gibson (1975) for the early history of NOW accounts.

accounts upon phone requests from depositors and in 1978 secured Fed approval of *automatic transfer services*.[23] ATS accounts are arrangements whereby the bank transfers funds from savings to checking accounts whenever balances in the latter fall below agreed levels. Thus ATS accounts are also, in effect, interest-earning checking accounts.

THE DEPOSITORY INSTITUTIONS DEREGULATION AND MONETARY CONTROL ACT OF 1980 AND THE GARN–ST GERMAIN DEPOSITORY INSTITUTIONS AMENDMENTS OF 1982

NOW accounts, ATS accounts, and other regulator-approved violations of the Banking Act of 1933 were endangered when in April 1979 the U.S. Court of Appeals for the District of Columbia directed the regulators to enforce the law. The case before the Court was part of the usual game in which financial institutions seek to gain competitive advantages by persuading their own regulator-patrons to allow them to evade legal restrictions while filing suits against other agencies similarly accommodating the desires of their clients. The Court expressed the following views in its ruling on suits filed by the American Bankers Association (with the Tioga State Bank) against the National Credit Union Administration, the Independent Bankers Association against the Federal Home Loan Bank Board, and the U.S. League of Savings Associations against the Federal Reserve Board:

> It appears to the court that the development of fund transfers . . . utilized by . . . commercial banks with "Automatic Fund Transfers," savings and loan associations with "Remote Service Units," and federal credit unions with "Share Drafts," in each instance represents the use of a device or technique which was not and is not authorized by the relevant statutes, although permitted by regulations of the respective institutions' regulatory agencies.[24]

The Court pointed out that these procedures amounted to "the practical equivalent of checks drawn on . . . interest-bearing time deposits" in violation of laws governing the institutions concerned.

23 The Fed "acted after extensive review of the record number of comments—1380—received on the proposal. . . . Surprisingly . . . the largest number, 517, came from individuals. Many of the letters were handwritten, and almost all were in favor of the proposal. . . . Most banking regulations published by the Board for comment generate very little consumer response." Most of the 382 commercial bank responses supported ATS and all 370 S&L (savings and loan) comments opposed it. Of the comments from the Federal Reserve Bank of Dallas district 63 percent of banks opposed ATS, 97 percent of individuals were in favor, and all 34 responses from S&Ls and 5 from members of Congress were opposed (Federal Reserve Bank of Dallas *Voice*, May 1978, page 21).

24 This and the following quotations are from *United States Court of Appeals for the District of Columbia Circuit*, September term, 1978, nos. 78-1337, 78-1849, 78-2206.

The history of the development of these modern transfer techniques reveals each type of financial institution securing the permission of its appropriate regulatory agency to install these devices in order to gain a competitive advantage, or at least competitive equality, with financial institutions of a different type in its services offered the public. The net result has been that three separate and distinct types of financial institutions created by Congressional enactment to serve different public needs have now become, or are rapidly becoming, three separate but homogeneous types of financial institutions offering virtually identical services to the public, all without the benefit of Congressional consideration and statutory enactment.

The judges were sympathetic. They recognized that the statutes had been rendered obsolete by events and also appreciated that "enormous investments" had been made in the new technology. But this did not mean that the regulators should rewrite the law even though Congress had "at some times and in some measure, tacitly approved part of these regulatory authorizations. . . ." However, because of the disruptions likely to result from the withdrawal of these services, upon which the financial community had "rapidly grown to rely," and to give Congress time to decide whether it wanted to override the Court by changing the law, about 7 months, until January 1, 1980, were allowed for compliance with the Court's ruling.

Twice before, in 1975 and 1977, the Senate had shown a willingness to accommodate the new financial innovations.[25] But the House had rejected the Senate's bills because conflicting groups had been unable to compromise. As observed by the Court of Appeals, Congress (at least the House) appeared to be content with a state of affairs in which it had abandoned its legislative responsibilities to the regulators. But Congress was now spurred to action and, after beginning hearings in June 1979 and enacting legislation in December that temporarily authorized the devices found illegal by the Court, granted them permanent approval in the Act of 1980 named in the title of this section.

The Act of 1980 (as we shall call it) was called (by its authors) "the most significant banking legislation since the 1930s." So was the Act of 1982.[26] This sounds like the annual pronouncement of New York sports writers that the latest rookie prospect "is the next Mickey Mantle." But the exaggerations of the former group greatly exceed those of the latter; for the field of banking legislation has not produced even a Bobby Murcer. These Acts provided for slightly relaxed restrictions on S&L portfolios, but otherwise their only significant

25 For discussions of these and other more ambitious Congressional deregulatory efforts that failed during the 1970s see Thomas Cargill and Gillian Garcia (1982).

26 See Elijah Brewer (1980) and Gillian Garcia (1983) for summaries of these Acts and their supposed importance.

provisions that might be called "deregulatory" were those which legalized the methods of paying interest described above, permitted all depository institutions throughout the country to offer NOW accounts, and ordered interest ceilings on time and savings deposits to be phased out by 1986. In view of the multitude of ways that had been devised to evade interest ceilings and the replacements that would certainly have been devised if the Court's decision had been allowed to take effect, these Acts should be regarded primarily as partial rubber stamps of the public's effective repeal of the Banking Act of 1933. Their real contribution was not the elimination of interest ceilings, which banks and their customers had already accomplished, but the elimination of some of the costs of avoiding those ceilings. A large part of those costs must still be incurred, however, for the Acts preserved the legal zero interest ceiling on corporate checking accounts.

These Acts probably had the effect of slowing deregulation because the Depository Institutions Deregulation Committee,[27] established by the Act of 1980 to control the pace at which deposit interest ceilings would be phased out, saw to it that those ceilings rose more slowly after the Committee's formation than before, even though market interest rates attained record levels during its tenure (see Figure 2.1). The Committee's first action, in May 1980, was an attempt to eliminate competition for deposits through "gifts." Later, in 1982, the Committee denied requests from three states that individual states be allowed to proceed with interest deregulation. Most of the Committee's actions and inactions during the first 3 years of its existence (the first half of the ceiling-phase-out period) appear in the discriminatory price list of Table 2.2 and must be understood merely as a continuation of industry-regulator rate agreements that attempt to maximize industry profits by adjusting rates to reflect the elasticities of demand of different groups of depositors. The phase out did not begin in earnest until October 1983, and the Committee took no action on the 5¼ percent ceiling on passbook savings until January 1984[28] even though the 3-month T bill rate averaged 12 percent during 1980 to 1982 and at times exceeded 16 percent. By comparison the passbook ceiling rate had been raised from 2½ percent in 1956 to 5¼ percent in 1979, almost keeping up with average T bill rates during that period (see Figure 2.1).

FEDERAL RESERVE DEFINITIONS OF MONEY AND NEAR MONIES

Table 3.2 summarizes the growth of money and money substitutes since 1971. First note the distinction between "demand deposits" and

---

27 Composed of the Secretary of the Treasury and the Chairmen of the Federal Reserve Board, the Federal Deposit Insurance Corporation, the Federal Home Loan Bank Board, and the National Credit Union Administration.

28 And even then raised the commercial bank passbook rate only to the 5½ percent level applicable to S&Ls and left the S&L passbook ceiling unchanged.

Table 3.2   Federal Reserve Definitions of Money and Liquid Assets
(Averages of Daily Figures, Not Seasonally Adjusted)

Monetary Aggregates and Components	December, Billion Dollars				
	1971	1974	1977	1980	1983
M1	236.9	285.1	344.3	424.7	537.8
Currency	53.5	69.0	90.3	118.3	150.5
Nonbank traveler's checks[a]	1.1	1.7	2.9	3.9	4.6
Demand deposits at commercial banks	182.1	213.9	246.9	275.2	251.6
Other checkable deposits	0.2	0.4	4.2	27.2	131.2
M2	713.5	909.5	1,288.9	1,635.0	2,197.9
M1	236.9	285.1	344.3	424.7	537.8
Overnight RPs	2.3	5.6	13.7	23.4	44.8
Overnight Eurodollars	0.0	0.0	1.0	5.0	11.3
Savings deposits	289.9	335.4	488.1	398.3	308.5
Small time deposits	186.8	284.8	443.3	728.3	788.6
Money-market deposit accounts	0.0	0.0	0.0	0.0	376.0
MMMFs: general-purpose and broker-dealer	0.0	1.7	2.4	61.4	138.2
M2 consolidation component[b]	−2.4	−3.1	−3.9	−6.1	−7.3
M3	776.6	1,070.9	1,475.6	1,992.9	2,712.8
M2	713.5	909.5	1,288.9	1,635.0	2,197.9
Term RPs	2.7	8.1	19.5	34.8	56.0
Term Eurodollars	2.7	8.0	18.4	48.0	92.3
Large time deposits	57.7	145.2	148.0	262.4	329.7
MMMFs: institutions only	0.0	0.2	0.9	14.9	40.3
M3 consolidation component[c]	0.0	0.0	0.0	−2.2	−3.4
L	903.3	1,248.5	1,715.9	2,350.8	3,184.7
M3	776.6	1,070.9	1,475.6	1,992.9	2,712.8
U.S. savings bonds	54.3	63.2	76.6	72.7	71.3
Short-term Treasury securities	36.3	53.9	89.3	155.3	222.8
Commercial paper	32.6	50.2	63.1	98.5	132.9
Bankers acceptances	3.5	10.2	11.4	31.4	44.8

a Bank traveler's checks are included in "demand deposits at commercial banks."

b Estimated amount of demand deposits and vault cash held by thrift institutions to service time and savings deposits.

c Estimated amount of overnight RPs held by institution-only MMMFs.

Source: "Federal Reserve Statistical Release" H.6. Most of these data also appear in *Federal Reserve Bulletins.*

other checking accounts, called "other checkable deposits" by the Fed. The law still prohibits depository institutions from paying interest on demand deposits and permits interest on checking accounts only if they are called "NOW accounts," "share draft accounts," or (since December 1982) "money market deposit accounts." The demand deposit component of money is held by corporations, which are still by law denied interest on checking accounts, and by individuals who cannot or do not wish to maintain the minimum or average balances required by most interest-earning checking accounts.

The Fed's $M1$ includes most of money (M) as we have defined it. $M2$ is a motley collection of partial and near monies. By a "partial money" we mean something like overnight RPs, which in an unknown proportion represent demand deposits reported as investments in U.S. securities. Eurodollars are another partial money. So are the money market deposit accounts allowed to depository institutions by the Act of 1982. The ability to write checks on these accounts is so hedged by official restrictions (no more than six preauthorized, automatic, or other third-party transfers per month, of which no more than three can be checks) that there is some question of whether they should be considered checking accounts at all—which may be why the Fed has not included them in its definition of money ($M1$).[29]

The other components of $M2$ are near monies, that is, close substitutes for money; but they are not money. This is obviously true of savings and time deposits, which are easily and cheaply transferred to checking accounts but cannot themselves be used directly as means of payment. Nor are MMMFs additions to the stock of money because checks written by fund shareholders are against fund checking accounts, which are already included in $M1$.

$M3$ includes $M2$ plus some more items thought to be less closely substitutable for money, including institution-only MMMFs, which do not offer accounts to individuals and are used almost exclusively as nonchecking-account investments.[30] Finally, L includes nearly all the money market instruments (that is, money and money substitutes, or "liquid assets") for which the Fed has reliable data on a continuing basis.

The growth and decline of the instruments in Table 3.2 have largely been responses to rising market interest rates in the presence of ceilings on deposits in financial institutions. The greatest proportional increases during the 1970s occurred in RPs, Eurodollars, and MMMFs. Time deposits also grew rapidly as ceilings were raised and maturity and size restrictions were relaxed. The largest changes since 1980 have been due to the extension of NOW accounts and share drafts (that is, "other checkable deposits") to the entire country in January 1981 and permission in December 1982 for depository institutions to offer government insured money market deposit accounts in competition with MMMFs—changes that have caused declines or slower growth in demand, savings, and small time deposits.

---

29 This decision is supported by evidence that their growth has been almost entirely at the expense of money substitutes (principally time and savings deposits), with little or no effect on checking accounts.

30 For more detailed descriptions of the items in Table 3.2 and reasons for their inclusion in particular categories, see *Federal Reserve Bulletin,* February 1980, pages 97–114, March 1982, pages 185–187, March 1983, pages 199–202, March 1984, pages 214–217.

THE DEMAND FOR MONEY
IN THE NEW ENVIRONMENT

Now let us look at the evolution and present state of the demand for money. The decline in money substitutes (and in the velocity of money) during the 1940s and the rapid increase in money substitutes (and in velocity) during the 1970s suggest an increase in the demand for money during the earlier period and a reduction in money demand more recently. These shifts may be seen in Figure 3.3.

Shifts in the demand for money may be examined within the framework of Equation (3.1) once we have taken account of the response of the rate of interest on money to the rate of interest on money substitutes. If we abstract from the government monopoly of currency and assume that competition forces banks to pay rates of return on checking accounts that approximate their investment values to banks, the rate of interest on money is[31]

$$(3.6) \qquad R_m = (1 - k)R_s - (1 + 0.5R_s)c$$

where k denotes the proportion of checking accounts held by banks in noninterest-earning reserves (till money and deposits with the Fed) so that the proportion $(1 - k)$ of checking accounts is invested in assets earning the rate R_s, and c is the cost per dollar of checking accounts incurred by the bank in handling those accounts. We assume that these costs occur in a steady stream so that their interest burden is $0.5cR_s$. For example, if $c = 0.01$, $k = 0.12$, and $R_s = 0.10$, then[32]

$$R_m = 0.88(0.10) - (1.05)(0.01) = 0.0775$$

In the present environment of high market rates and legal ceilings on *direct* payments of interest on money much of R_m takes the forms of gifts, free services, favorable loan rates, and overnight investments in RPs and Eurodollars.

---

31 The rate R_m will be less than this under imperfectly competitive conditions (such as those in Chapter 2). However, Benjamin Klein (1974) has found that a rate of interest on money similar to R_m (or correlated with R_m) explains the demand for money better than does the opposite hypothesis that interest ceilings have been effective, that is, that interest rates on checking accounts between 1933 and the 1970s were zero or the negative of service charges and expected losses on deposits.

32 The costs associated with checking accounts are normally much more than 1 percent per annum of average balances; Dale Osborne's (1982) work suggests that 5 percent (or more) may be more reasonable although the correct figure varies with the average balance and activity of accounts. Most checking-account costs arise from processing checks and are due to the *number of expenditures* (i.e., to the number of checks processed) and not to the *average balances held* and are therefore independent of the demand-for-money decision with which we are concerned. (The costs of processing deposits to accounts are already included in *b*.) In fact, apart from the one-twelfth of 1 percent per annum cost of deposit insurance, most of the costs of keeping a checking account are small fixed charges (for monthly statements and the like), which are also irrelevant to the decision of *how much* money to hold, so that 1 percent may be an overstatement of the marginal cost of holding money.

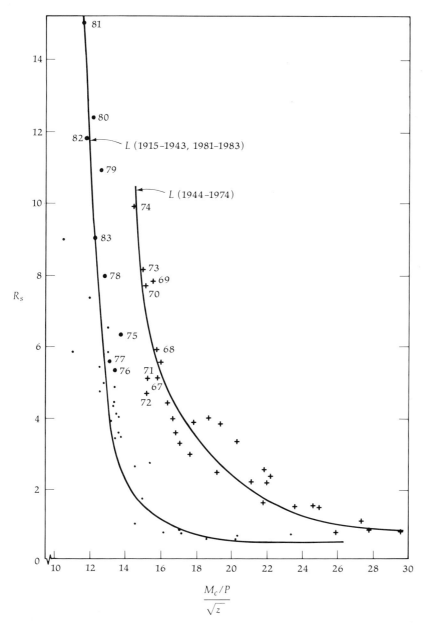

Sources: *Banking and Monetary Statistics, Federal Reserve Bulletins,* and Federal Reserve money-supply releases.

Figure 3.3   The demand for money, 1915 to 1983 (annual data).

Substituting Equation (3.6) into the money demand function (3.1) and rearranging give

(3.7)
$$\frac{M_c/P}{\sqrt{z}} = \sqrt{\frac{b}{(2k + c)R_s + 2c}}$$

Equation (3.7) expresses the per capita real demand for money as a proportion of the square root of per capita real expenditures and (given k, b, and c) varies inversely with R_s very much in the manner shown in Figure 3.1. We see that the two curved lines in Figure 3.3 are in fact reasonable approximations to the theoretical demand curves in Figure 3.1. The left-hand demand curve has been drawn through the dots generated by annual data from 1915 to 1943 and 1981 to 1983. The right-hand curve corresponds to the crosses of 1944 to 1974. Points are identified by year beginning with 1967. Figure 3.3 lends support to the widespread view that the rapid introduction of money substitutes during the mid-to-late 1970s caused a decline in the demand for money by reducing the costs (b) of switching into and out of money.[33] Apparently, the effects of the fall in b were not offset by reductions in the costs (c) of servicing checking accounts or the declines in legal and excess reserve ratios (k).

We cannot know what the future holds, but Figure 3.3 suggests that the demand for money may have returned in the 1980s to a "normal," long-run position. The leftward shift appears to have ended (at least temporarily), and the increase in money demanded (and the consequent decline in velocity seen in Figure 3.2) during 1982 to 1983 can be interpreted as a movement along such a long-run demand curve.[34] Furthermore, we should not expect significant rightward shifts in L because of any future deregulations of interest ceilings on checking accounts, which would merely be official acknowledgments of effective deregulations already arranged between banks and their customers.

CONCLUSION: HOW TO SIMPLIFY MONEY, SLOW FINANCIAL INNOVATION, AND SHORTEN TEXTBOOKS

The money substitutes that have been introduced in recent years have resulted from growing desires either to economize on money holdings or to find ways to pay interest on money. These desires have been responses to the failure of currency and checking accounts to pay interest and the dramatic rise in interest rates on other financial instruments. Many of the instruments that are discussed in this chapter and that will also play important parts in later chapters did not exist or were unimportant between the 1930s and the 1960s or 1970s. These include federal funds, RPs, CDs, Eurodollars, MMMFs, and NOW accounts. Just think: If you had not been born 30 years too

33 See Stephen Goldfeld (1976) and Michael Hamburger (1977) for discussions of the overprediction of the demand for money in the mid-1970s by previously estimated demand functions. See R. Hafer and Scott Hein (1982) and John Judd and John Scadding (1982) for arguments that the observed instability of money demand in this period was due to an abrupt downward shift in demand caused by a rapid acceleration of financial innovation. Charles Lieberman (1977) offers evidence that money demand had been declining for some time, possibly in response to a fairly steady process of innovation.

34 See John Judd (1983) for further evidence in support of this interpretation.

late, you would have been saddled with a shorter textbook, fewer financial instruments, and a simpler money stock. On the other hand, although life in the financial markets was simpler in the 1950s, it was also less interesting.

The important thing to remember about this chapter is not the list of money substitutes and components of money that exist on some date in the 1980s. For the list is constantly changing. At this moment corporate money managers are implementing or searching for new ways of economizing on cash balances and of effectively earning more than is legally allowed on their checking accounts. The important idea of this chapter is that developments in the financial markets, as elsewhere, are responses to profit opportunities. Instruments and institutions come and go. But the forces operating in the direction of economic freedom, the incentives to construct arrangements conducive to mutually beneficial transactions, are almost irresistible. We seldom have any way of knowing what forms financial innovation will take. But as long as rates on loans and marketable securities are high while the legislators and regulators try to keep some deposit rates low, both bankers and depositors have strong incentives to circumvent the laws and regulations.

The short response to the title of this section is: Abandon regulations and/or inflationary monetary and fiscal policies. Excessive monetary expansion causes inflation, which in turn causes high interest rates. Any attempt to keep rates of return on checking accounts artificially low under these conditions leads to a myriad of supporting regulations and produces active trading in MMMFs, RPs, and Eurodollars. If all deposits were permitted to pay competitive rates directly, investors would be able to keep their funds in a few convenient forms, and the resources devoted to new instruments, institutions, and trading procedures designed to circumvent interest rate ceilings would be freed for other uses.

QUESTIONS

1. In what ways might technological advances increase the demand for money? In what ways might these advances reduce the demand for money? Do you expect the demand for money to increase or to decrease in the near future? Why?

2. Money has been said to perform the functions of store of value, standard of value, unit of account, and medium of exchange. Give examples (if you can) of goods that perform or could perform these functions as well as money.

3. Why is the balance of your checking account money but your check is not money? (*Hints.* See Definition 3.1. Also, when you write a check for goods, have you paid for them or have you obtained them on credit?)

4. Referring to Table 3.2, give the reasons (private incentives, regula-

tory accommodations, and other reasons, if any) for the relative changes since 1971 in (a) demand deposits at commercial banks and other checkable deposits, (b) demand deposits and overnight RPs, (c) savings deposits and small time deposits, and (d) demand deposits and MMMFs.

5. Please forecast (and explain) possible values of the instruments in Table 3.2 in 1986 in each of the following circumstances:
   (a) Inflation and expectations of inflation are ended so that interest rates fall to a low level, say, 3 percent.
   (b) All interest ceilings and other restrictions on bank deposits are eliminated.
   (c) (Most likely.) (i) The Fed monetizes increasing amounts of the federal deficit, which is consistent with an acceleration of monetary expansion in 1984, as in every other election year since World War II, so that inflation, expectations of inflation, and interest rates rise in 1985 and 1986; (ii) Interest ceilings on demand deposits are retained.

6. What will happen to the demand for money (in Figure 3.3) under the conditions described in question 5?

7. What will happen to the velocity of money (in Figure 3.2) under the conditions described in question 5?

PROBLEMS

1. A firm's planned expenditures during the coming month are $64,000, each unit of goods costs $2, and the transaction costs involved in each sale of T bills are $20. In terms of the notation of Equation (3.1), $P = \$2$, $z = \$64,000/\$2 = 32,000$ is the number of units purchased, and $b = \$20/\$2$ is the real cost of each securities transaction. Finally, let $R_s = 1$ percent per month and $R_m = 0$.
   (a) What is the demand for average real money balances?
   (b) What is the effect of an increase in R_m from 0 to 0.36 percent per month on the demand for average real money balances?
   (c) Suppose that next month z will be 128,000 units whereas b, R_s, and R_m continue to be 10, 0.01, and 0.0036, respectively. What will be optimal average real money balances?

2. (a) A firm's planned expenditures during the coming month are $3,000, each unit of goods costs $3, the transaction costs of each sale of T bills is $60, and the rate of return on money is zero. Draw its real demand for money.
   (b) What is the real demand for money when the monthly rate of return on T bills is 1 percent?
   (c) Starting from the values in (a) and (b), what are the real and nominal demands for money when the following values are changed, one at a time: (i) Planned expenditures to $12,000, (ii) transaction costs to $240 per sale of Treasury bills, (iii) the monthly rate of return on T bills to one-quarter of 1 percent,

and (iv) the monthly rate of return on money to three-quarters of 1 percent?

3. **(a)** It was stated in the discussion of Table 3.1 that for a bid-ask spread of 0.015 percent of the cost of a bill the 1-day break-even yield on T bills is *about* 5.5 percent. What is the exact break-even yield?

   (b) What is the exact 1-day break-even yield when the spread is 0.030 percent of the bill's cost?

4. Using Equation (3.5), calculate the income velocities of money for the values of R_s, R_m, z, and b in problems 1(a) to 1(c).

5. **(a)** Given the values in problem 2(a), draw velocity as a function of R_s.

   (b) Given the values in (a), what is monthly velocity when R_s is 1 percent per month? What is annual velocity?

   (c) Calculate V for the data in problem 2(c).

6. Assuming $b = 6.48$, $k = 0.12$, and $c = 0.01$, compare Equation (3.7) with the demand functions in Figure 3.3.

REFERENCES

William J. Baumol, "The Transactions Demand for Cash: An Inventory Theoretic Approach," *Quarterly Journal of Economics,* November 1952, pages 545–556.

Elijah Brewer et al., "The Depository Institutions Deregulation and Monetary Control Act of 1980," Federal Reserve Bank of Chicago *Economic Perspectives,* September/October 1980, pages 2–23.

Thomas F. Cargill and Gillian Garcia, *Financial Deregulation and Monetary Control: Historical Perspective and Impact of the 1980 Act,* Hoover Institution Press, Stanford, CA, 1982.

Robert W. Clower, "A Reconsideration of the Microfoundations of Monetary Theory," *Western Economic Journal,* December 1967, pages 1–8.

Robert W. Clower and Peter W. Howitt, "The Transactions Theory of the Demand for Money: A Reconsideration," *Journal of Political Economy,* June 1978, pages 449–466.

Gunter Dufey and Ian H. Giddy, *The International Money Market,* Prentice-Hall, Englewood Cliffs, NJ, 1978.

Gillian Garcia et al., "The Garn–St Germain Depository Institutions Act of 1982," Federal Reserve Bank of Chicago *Economic Perspectives,* March/April 1983, pages 2–31.

Katherine Gibson, "The Early History and Initial Impact of NOW Accounts," Federal Reserve Bank of Boston *New England Economic Review,* January/February 1975, pages 17–26. Reprint Robert W. Eisenmenger et al., *The NOW Account Experience in New England,* Federal Reserve Bank of Boston, Boston, 1981.

Stephen Goldfeld, "The Case of the Missing Money," *Brookings Papers* 3, 1976, pages 683–730.

R. W. Hafer and Scott E. Hein, "The Shift in Money Demand: What Really Happened?," Federal Reserve Bank of St. Louis *Review,* February 1982, pages 11–16.

Michael J. Hamburger, "Behavior of the Money Stock: Is There a Puzzle?," *Journal of Monetary Economics,* July 1977, pages 265–288.

John P. Judd, "The Recent Decline in Velocity: Instability in Money Demand or Inflation?," Federal Reserve Bank of San Francisco *Economic Review,* Spring 1983, pages 12–19.

John P. Judd and John L. Scadding, "The Search for a Stable Money Demand Function: A Survey of the Post-1973 Literature," *Journal of Economic Literature,* September 1982, pages 993–1023.

Benjamin Klein, "Competitive Interest Payments on Bank Deposits and the Long-run Demand for Money," *American Economic Review,* December 1974, pages 931–949.

Charles Lieberman, "The Transactions Demand for Money and Technological Change," *Review of Economics and Statistics,* August 1977, pages 307–317.

Alfred Marshall, "Remedies for Fluctuations of

General Prices," *Contemporary Review,* March 1887. Reprint A. C. Pigou (ed.), *Memorials of Alfred Marshall,* Macmillan, London, 1925.

Robert W. McGee, *Accounting for Inflation,* Prentice-Hall, Englewood Cliffs, NJ, 1981.

Merton H. Miller and Daniel Orr, "A Model of the Demand for Money by Firms," *Quarterly Journal of Economics,* August 1966, pages 413–435.

Hyman P. Minsky, "Central Banking and Money Market Changes," *Quarterly Journal of Economics,* May 1957, pages 171–187.

Dale K. Osborne, "The Cost of Servicing Demand Deposits," *Journal of Money, Credit and Banking,* November 1982, pt. 1, pages 479–493.

Dale K. Osborne, "Ten Approaches to the Definition of Money," Federal Reserve Bank of Dallas *Economic Review,* March 1984, pages 1–23.

P. A. Tinsley, B. Garrett, and M. E. Friar, *The Measurement of Money Demand,* Staff Study, Federal Reserve Board of Governors, Washington, 1978.

James Tobin, "The Interest-elasticity of Transactions Demand for Cash," *Review of Economics and Statistics,* August 1956, pages 241–247.

Leland B. Yeager, "Essential Properties of the Medium of Exchange," *Kyklos,* 1968, no. 1, pages 45–69.

3.A

THE TRANSACTIONS DEMAND FOR MONEY

This appendix derives Equation (3.1), which is a slightly modified version of William Baumol's still-influential model of the transactions demand for money. Baumol's most important assumptions were that a household or firm receives income periodically in discrete amounts but makes disbursements continuously. The following decision must be made: How much of the economic unit's stock of financial assets should be kept in the form of money, which is convenient but earns a low rate of interest or none at all, and how much in marketable securities or time deposits, which are less convenient than money (because they must be converted to money before they can be spent) but earn higher rates of interest? Baumol pointed out that this is an inventory problem: "A stock of cash is its holder's inventory of the medium of exchange, and like an inventory of a commodity, cash is held because it can be given up at the appropriate moment, serving then as its possessor's part of the bargain in an exchange." It is therefore not surprising that the optimal inventory of money, that is, the optimal demand for money, derived below is formally identical with the square-root formula familiar to students of inventory theory.

The terms in our analysis are defined as follows, where we conform to Baumol in using "money" and "cash" interchangeably:

C = the fixed cash withdrawal. It is assumed that all withdrawals are identical amounts. Cash is obtained, for example, by selling T bills or by asking the bank to switch funds from time to demand deposits.

z = the number of goods purchased during the period in question.

P = the price per unit of goods, z. We can think of P as an index of prices of the goods purchased by the firm or household.

$Z = Pz$ = total expenditures during the period.

B = the cost (in dollars) of each cash withdrawal, for example, the bank's charge for a transfer between deposits or the broker's fees associated with a sale of T bills.

$b = B/P$ = the "real" cost of each cash withdrawal.

R_s = the rate of interest earned on nonmonetary assets, for example, on T bills or time deposits.

R_m = the rate of interest on money holdings. In 1983 this was $5\frac{1}{4}$ percent on NOW accounts but zero for corporate demand deposits.

$M = C/2$ = average money holdings (that is, the average stock or inventory of money) during the period.

Figure 3.A.1 shows money holdings during the interval between receipts. These receipts occur on dates 0 and 1. Of the funds received on date 0, Pz dollars are allocated to cash and assets that are easily

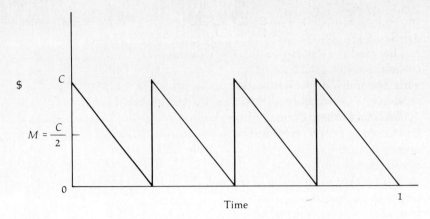

Figure 3.A.1   Cash withdrawals, disbursements, and average money balances.

converted to cash. For example, if total expenditures during a year are $Z = \$100$, which we have assumed to be disbursed continuously, the consumer or money manager can meet her obligations by withdrawing $50 every 6 months or $25 quarterly or in any other sequence such that the number of withdrawals times C equals Z. If money is withdrawn quarterly, as shown in Figure 3.A.1, $C = \$25$ and average money holdings are $M = C/2 = \$12.50$. The number of withdrawals is $Z/C = Z/2M$.

Assuming all money to be held in the form of demand deposits that pay a rate of interest, R_m, the annual interest cost of holding money is

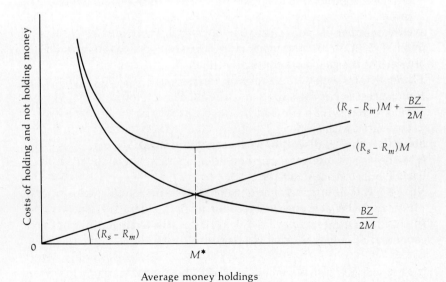

Figure 3.A.2   The optimal inventory of money.

$(R_s - R_m)M$, as indicated by the line with slope $(R_s - R_m)$ in Figure 3.A.2.

The total cost of making withdrawals is the cost per withdrawal times the number of withdrawals, $BZ/2M$. This cost, which decreases with the size of withdrawals and therefore with average money balances, is shown in Figure 3.A.2 as a declining function of M.

The sum of these costs is

$$(R_s - R_m)M + \frac{BZ}{2M}$$

which is depicted as the U-shaped function of M in Figure 3.A.2. Differentiating with respect to M, this sum is minimized when

(3.A.1) $$(R_s - R_m) - \frac{BZ}{2M^2} = 0$$

The optimal (cost-minimizing) value of M is thus

(3.A.2) $$M^* = \sqrt{\frac{BZ}{2(R_s - R_m)}} = \sqrt{\frac{(Pb)(Pz)}{2(R_s - R_m)}}$$

or

(3.A.3) $$\frac{M^*}{P} = \sqrt{\frac{bz}{2(R_s - R_m)}}$$

Since people hold money in order to buy goods, it is useful to express average money balances in "real" terms, that is, in terms of the purchasing power of those balances. For example, suppose that each unit of goods costs $P = \$1$, $z = 320$, $R_s = 0.10$, $R_m = 0.05$, and $b = 0.50$. The last value means that the bank's or broker's services purchased in connection with a cash withdrawal cost half as much as one unit of other goods.

Using these data, we see from Equation (3.A.3) that optimal money holdings are $M^* = \$40$. The optimal cash withdrawal is therefore $C^* = 2M^* = \$80$. Now suppose that all prices, including the prices of bank and brokerage services, are doubled. If other data have not changed, the optimal cash withdrawal and demand for money are now $\$160$ and $\$80$, respectively. But the real cash withdrawal, C^*/P, and the real demand for money, M^*/P, are unaltered. Since the number of goods purchased, z, the real cost of withdrawals, b, and interest rates, R_s and R_m, are the same as before, the real demand for money is also the same.

In an aggregate sense, Equation (3.A.3) may be thought of as the per capita demand for real money balances and z as per capita real GNP.

Such an aggregate demand for money is the basis of the monetary analysis in Chapter 3.

PROBLEMS

1. Suppose a household makes 100 purchases, at $10 each, between income receipts. Cash withdrawals cost $2 each, the return on interest-earning assets is 5 percent, and money earns no interest. What is the optimal cash withdrawal, and what are optimal real and nominal money balances?

2. What are optimal real money balances when (a) the data are the same as in problem 1 except that $R_s = 10$ percent, (b) when the data are the same as in problem 1 except that $B = \$1.50$, and (c) when the data are the same as in problem 1 except that $R_m = 2$ percent?

REFERENCE

William J. Baumol, "The Transactions Demand for Cash: An Inventory Theoretic Approach," *Quarterly Journal of Economics*, November 1952, pages 545–556.

COMMERCIAL BANKS AND THE PAYMENTS SYSTEM

When asked why he robbed banks, Willie Sutton answered,
"Because that's where the money is."[1]

A good understanding of the financial markets requires that we know how money and other financial instruments are exchanged. Households, firms, and governments do not acquire assets and liabilities by magic. Financial instruments are traded in a varied, often sophisticated information and exchange network that to an important extent defines the nature of the things traded. Credit checks, title searches, and other paper-intensive verification procedures often require a month before the buyers and sellers of mortgages (S&Ls and house owners) can consummate a transaction even after terms have been settled. Small traders in stocks and bonds must accept a week's delay. Because these securities are convertible into their quoted market values only after substantial delays and by incurring high transaction costs, they are said to possess low "liquidity" and "reversibility."[2] But a money market instrument, that is, a close substitute for money, does not deserve its name if it cannot be exchanged for money almost immediately at little cost—as in a completed exchange of millions of dollars of money and securities between New York and San Francisco within minutes after the idea first occurs to a money manager, at a cost of less than $100 in clerical, telephone, wire, and brokers' charges. Such transactions are made possible by several systems of electronic links between computer terminals in the offices of commercial banks and other money traders throughout the country. Most transactions, especially small transactions, still rely on currency and checks in ways that were old 100 years ago. But rising interest rates and technological

---

1 William Sutton (1976, page 119).

2 These and other characteristics of securities, which depend both upon their underlying contractual terms and upon the procedures by which they are exchanged, are discussed in greater detail in Chapter 7.

developments have provided the incentives and means to speed up and reduce the costs of small as well as large transactions.

Chapter 3 dealt with the causes and consequences of innovations in money and substitutes for money. This chapter is concerned with innovations in the payments system. The two subjects are inseparable. Both stem from desires by wealth holders to earn as much as possible on their assets for as long as possible, which means that they are willing to pay for services that speed up the collection, or delay the delivery, of money and other financial instruments. This chapter describes the evolution and current state of these services, with an unavoidable emphasis on the parts played by commercial banks and the Federal Reserve System (the Fed).

A PRIMER ON COMMERCIAL BANKS
The roles of commercial banks

We cannot discuss money and the payments system without dwelling on commercial banks. Three chapters of this book are devoted to the four main roles of commercial banks: as handlers of money (in the present chapter), as financial intermediaries (in Chapter 16), and as creators of money and handlers of money substitutes (in Chapter 9). It is natural that since banks manage money they also manage the things most like money and for which money is most often exchanged.

Financial and nonfinancial firms

Our story of commercial banks will be told in terms of balance sheets, which are snapshots of economic units at points in time. We begin by distinguishing banks from other businesses. The balance sheet in Table 4.1 is completely general. The balance sheet of every firm, financial or nonfinancial, bank or nonbank, looks like that in the table. The owners of firms raise money in two ways: (1) They put up some of their own money. This is called the owners' equity (E) and in the case of corporations takes the form of common stock. (2) They may borrow in the form of loans from friends (soon to become former friends) or from banks or other financial institutions or by selling bonds. This is debt (D). The money raised in these two ways is used to buy assets (A).

The main distinction between financial and nonfinancial firms lies in the form of their assets. Most of U.S. Steel's assets are plant, equipment, and materials: blast furnaces, rolling mills, and inventories of iron ore. The same is true of the corner grocery: the building, shopping carts, and goods on the shelf. Most of the assets of financial

Table 4.1   The Balance Sheet of Any Firm

A	D
	E

firms, on the other hand, are pieces of paper—stocks, bonds, and loans—that are evidences of obligations of others to pay money to these firms in the future. The corner grocer raises money, either debt or equity, in order to buy more meat, which he hopes to sell at a profit. The financial firm raises money, either debt or equity, in order to lend it—perhaps to the grocer—at a profit. Of course nearly all nonfinancial firms also lend money by buying securities or in the form of credit extended to customers; and financial firms also own real assets. In practice the distinction between financial and nonfinancial firms is therefore one of degree. However, we shall avoid classification problems by discussing only those firms whose assets are predominantly the pieces of paper or, increasingly, the computer entries called financial instruments.

Depository institutions

Depository institutions (DIs) are financial firms. But they differ from other financial firms in their reliance on demand and savings deposits as important forms of debt. Demand deposits,[3] of course, are payable on demand, a property that in practice also applies to savings deposits. A third and increasingly important form of deposits, time deposits, cannot be called a distinct feature of DIs because of their close similarity to the debt of other firms. Time deposits, like the bonds, Treasury bills, and commercial paper issued by governments and nonfinancial firms, are promises to pay specific amounts on specific dates. We saw in Table 3.2 that time deposits have grown much more rapidly than demand and savings deposits in recent years. The distinction between DIs and other firms has eroded as rising interest rates have forced DIs into new and more active forms of competition for funds instead of being able to rely on their old standbys, demand and savings deposits. The active competition by banks for varied sources of funds has been called *liability management*, which is the name recently given by bankers to what everyone else has always known. It is no longer possible to run a growing or profitable operation merely by sitting back and waiting for funds.

Commercial banks

Our discussion has narrowed from firms to financial firms to DIs and now, finally, to commercial banks. Historically banks have differed from other DIs in several respects. But their most important distinguishing feature has been a monopoly of checking accounts, and as a result, an almost complete control of the payments system. Chapter 3 described the infringement of this monopoly by mutual savings banks, savings and loan associations, credit unions, and money market funds. Nevertheless, banks remain by far the most important creators and

---

3 Many of which must now, by law, be called something else, such as NOW accounts or share drafts.

Table 4.2 Large Weekly Reporting Commercial Banks, December 29, 1982

Assets, Million Dollars		Liabilities, Million Dollars	
1 Cash items in process of collection	51,767	*Deposits*	
2 Demand deposits due from banks in the United States	8,577	45 Demand deposits	176,773
		46 Mutual savings banks	610
3 All other cash and due from depository institutions	35,695	47 Individuals, partnerships, and corporations	129,320
4 Total loans and securities	611,936	48 States and political subdivisions	4,870
		49 U.S. government	1,619
Securities		50 Commercial banks in the United States	22,003
5 U.S. Treasury securities	40,746	51 Banks in foreign countries	6,604
6 Trading account	7,782	52 Foreign governments and official institutions	1,309
7 Investment account, by maturity	32,964	53 Certified and officers' checks	10,439
8 1 year or less	10,701	54 Time and savings deposits	380,614
9 Over 1 through 5 years	20,399	55 Savings	102,276
10 Over 5 years	1,863	56 Individuals and nonprofit organizations	95,414
11 Other securities	74,538		
12 Trading account	5,649	57 Partnerships and corporations operated for profit	6,102
13 Investment account	68,889	58 Domestic governmental units	730
14 U.S. government agencies	14,148	59 All other	30
15 States and political subdivisions, by maturity	51,996	60 Time	278,338
16 1 year or less	6,452	61 Individuals, partnerships, and corporations	242,564
17 Over 1 year	45,544	62 States and political subdivisions	18,678
18 Other bonds, corporate stocks and securities	2,745	63 U.S. government	576
		64 Commercial banks in the United States	11,862
Loans		65 Foreign governments, official institutions, and banks	4,658
19 Federal funds sold[a]	36,373		
20 To commercial banks	24,889		
21 To nonbank brokers and dealers in securities	8,656	*Liabilities for borrowed money*	
22 To others	2,828	66 Borrowings from Federal Reserve Banks	1,025
23 Other loans, gross	472,254	67 Treasury tax-and-loan notes	7,391
24 Commercial and industrial	205,698	68 All other liabilities for borrowed money[c]	148,841
25 Bankers acceptances and commercial paper	5,728	69 Other liabilities and subordinated notes and debentures	87,138
26 All other	199,970	70 Total liabilities	801,782
27 U.S. addressees	193,273	71 Residual (total assets minus total liabilities)[d]	53,824
28 Non-U.S. addressees	6,697		
29 Real estate	124,931		
30 To individuals for personal expenditures	67,454		
To financial institutions			
31 Commercial banks in the United States	7,621		
32 Banks in foreign countries	7,440		
33 Sales finance, personal finance companies, etc.	10,503		
34 Other financial institutions	15,763		
35 To nonbank brokers and dealers in securities	8,268		
36 To others for purchasing and carrying securities[b]	2,681		
37 To finance agricultural production	6,125		
38 All other	15,770		
39 Less: Unearned income	4,836		
40 Loan loss reserve	7,138		
41 Other loans, net	460,280		
42 Lease financing receivables	10,743		
43 All other assets	136,889		
44 Total assets	855,606		

a Includes securities purchased under agreements to resell.

b Other than financial institutions and brokers and dealers.

c Includes federal funds purchased and securities sold under agreement to repurchase; for information on these liabilities at banks with assets of $1 billion or more on December 31, 1977, see Table 9.4.

d Not a measure of equity capital for use in capital adequacy analysis or for other analytic uses.

Source: *Federal Reserve Bulletin*, March 1983, page A20.

handlers of money so that discussions of money and the payments system must still emphasize banks.

We are interested primarily in the large money market banks. So is the Fed, which requires the 134 largest banks to submit detailed balance sheets each week. These are aggregated and reported in the *Federal Reserve Bulletin,* as shown in Table 4.2. In addition to demand deposits and their time and savings deposit substitutes, the following items (numbered as in the table) are especially important to the payments system:[4]

CASH ITEMS IN PROCESS OF COLLECTION (1) is the value of checks written on accounts in other banks that have been received by our bank but have not yet been redeemed. Suppose you receive a check payable to you and drawn on an account at bank A in another town. You deposit that check in your bank, B, which may credit your account immediately or after the check clears. In either case bank B has incurred a liability to you, payable now or in the future. But B has also acquired an asset: your endorsed check, which is a claim on bank A. B sends the check to A and, in a few days, receives payment. In most cases, payment takes the form of an exchange of deposits at the Fed. The steps in this process are discussed in connection with check clearing later in this chapter.

DEMAND DEPOSITS DUE FROM BANKS IN THE UNITED STATES (2) is self-explanatory. Correspondent banks maintain demand deposits with each other as payment for services and to facilitate the clearing of checks.[5] Notice that our large banks have borrowed more funds in the form of demand deposits from other banks ($22,003 million) than they have lent to other banks ($8,577 million) in that form. This is a continuation of the 200-year-old tendency for money-center banks to be net borrowers from other banks,[6] a practice that was continued even after the 1933 prohibition of interest on demand deposits, the debtor banks paying for those deposits by rendering check clearing and other services for their creditor correspondents.

ALL OTHER CASH AND DUE FROM DEPOSITORY INSTITUTIONS (3) includes metal and paper pictures of Washington, Lincoln, and company (still no insignificant part of the payments system), time deposits with

---

4 See David Friedman (1975), Paul Jessup (1980), and Arthur Samansky (1981) for more detail.

5 Banks that deal with each other on a regular basis are called "correspondents." See Katherine Finney (1958) for a discussion of the continued importance of correspondent banking and interbank demand deposits even after the Banking Act of 1933. See Robert Knight (1976) for a description of attempts by debtor banks to assess the profitability of their correspondent relations based on estimates of the interest earned by lending borrowed funds and the costs of providing services to creditor banks.

6 The earliest documented interbank deposit in the United States was opened by the Bank of New York in a Philadelphia bank in 1784 [Katherine Finney (1958, page 1)].

banks and other depository institutions, and reserves with Federal Reserve Banks. The last item makes up the largest part of this category and plays an important role in the payments system because most interbank transfers take the form of debits and credits to Fed accounts.

FEDERAL FUNDS (FED FUNDS) SOLD TO (AND BORROWED FROM) COMMERCIAL BANKS (19, 68). Commercial banks are required to hold noninterest-earning reserves in the forms of currency, coin, or deposits with the Fed as specified proportions of their deposit liabilities. Banks borrow and lend these reserves, usually overnight but often for longer periods. Suppose A wants to borrow reserves from B. After arranging the conditions of the loan (interest rate, maturity, and collateral), B phones or wires the Fed to transfer, say, $50 million from B's account at the Fed to A's account. The aggressive money market banks tend to be net borrowers of fed funds, whereas smaller banks with fewer local profitable loan opportunities tend to be net lenders of fed funds, that is, suppliers of reserves to the large banks. Specifically, the large banks in Table 4.2 were fed funds creditors of other banks to the extent of about $25 billion at the end of 1982 but had borrowed about $64 billion[7] in fed funds from other banks.

FED FUNDS SOLD TO (AND BORROWED FROM) NONBANK BROKERS AND DEALERS IN SECURITIES AND OTHERS (21, 22, 68). These lines actually refer to repurchase agreements (RPs), which were discussed in Chapter 3 and are arrangements whereby the lender purchases a security from the borrower, who agrees to repurchase the security at an agreed higher price (determined by the rate of interest on the loan) on a specified future date, often the next day. RPs are in effect secured fed funds, and the two are often lumped together, as in Table 4.2, in Fed reports. RP transactions involving nonbanks are executed almost as quickly as fed funds transactions between banks. A state or local government, corporation, or securities dealer with an account in bank A in Atlanta may borrow from bank B in Boston by arranging a wire transfer of funds from B's account at the Federal Reserve Bank of Boston to A's account at the Federal Reserve Bank of Atlanta, with the security collateral (which exists only in bookkeeping form, that is, as a computer entry) wired in the opposite direction. These transactions are reversed when the loan is repaid.

BORROWING FROM THE FED (66). Banks also borrow from the Fed. If a bank needs reserves, is willing to pay the below-market rate of interest usually charged by the Fed (the "discount rate"), pretends that its reserve deficiency is due to circumstances beyond its control, and says

---

7 This value, which is part of line 68 in Table 4.2, was obtained from Table 9.4.

"pretty please," the Fed will add something to the bank's reserve account (line 3).

TREASURY TAX-AND-LOAN NOTES (67) represent a government evasion of the government's interest ceilings. Commercial banks help the U.S. Treasury collect taxes. Most banks maintain Treasury Tax and Loan (TTL) accounts into which certain taxes can be paid, principally corporate income taxes and income taxes withheld from wages and salaries. Banks also act as sellers of certain Treasury securities, such as savings bonds. For many years banks paid no interest on funds received and maintained on behalf of the Treasury—which began to bother Treasury officials as interest rates rose during the 1970s. They obtained legislation that, beginning in 1978, required banks either to forward TTL receipts to the Treasury's account at their district Federal Reserve Banks within 1 day or to pay interest on those funds. Congress did not explicitly exclude Treasury accounts from the legal prohibition against interest on demand deposits. But the effect was the same. If banks wanted Treasury deposits, they had to transfer Treasury receipts to so-called note accounts, which earned the same rate of interest as RPs and which, like demand deposits, were payable on demand.[8] These notes have not been necessary to their original purpose since governments began to be allowed to earn interest on checking accounts in 1982. But banks prefer them to ordinary checking accounts because they are not subject to reserve requirements.

After a discussion of the Federal Reserve System, we shall describe how commercial banks, with some help from the Fed, manage the payments system.

THE FEDERAL RESERVE SYSTEM

The Federal Reserve System is America's central bank. Its activities may be separated into three categories: (1) regulation, (2) transfers of funds, and (3) monetary policy.[9] The first, especially in the form of enforcing ceilings on interest rates (Regulation Q), was discussed in Chapters 1 to 3. The second is considered later in this chapter in connection with the payments system. Our concern in this section is with the effects of monetary policy on bank reserves and therefore on the most important component of the payments system. The Board of Governors in Washington and the presidents of the district Federal Reserve Banks share responsibilities for the three tools of monetary policy as follows:

1. RESERVE REQUIREMENTS. Banks and other DIs are required to hold reserves of cash or deposits with the Fed. These reserve requirements

---

8 See Richard Lang (1979) for further discussion of TTL accounts.

9 See the Fed's *Purposes and Functions* (1974) for more detail.

have in the past been determined by the Board of Governors within broad legal limits. The Monetary Control Act of 1980 provides that by 1987 most DIs will be required to hold reserves of about 12 percent against checking accounts and 3 percent against business and government time deposits—except when the Fed, in consultation with Congress, decides otherwise.[10]

2. OPEN MARKET OPERATIONS. Most bank reserves are supplied by Fed purchases of U.S. government securities. The Fed buys securities with checks written on itself. The sellers of these securities deposit the Fed's checks in their banks, which pass those checks on to their Fed district banks for credit to their reserve accounts.[11] Initially, most of the reserves are credited to accounts of commercial banks in the New York Federal Reserve District because open market operations are conducted by the Federal Reserve Bank of New York. Decisions regarding open market operations are made by the Federal Open Market Committee, which has twelve members: the seven governors of the Federal Reserve Board, the president of the Federal Reserve Bank of New York, and four of the other eleven Federal Reserve bank presidents on a rotating basis.

3. LENDING TO BANKS AND OTHER DIs takes place at the "discount windows" of the twelve Federal Reserve Banks. Although originally intended as the principal tool of monetary policy, discount windows are no longer major sources of bank reserves. Of total Fed credit about 90 percent takes the form of open market operations and only about 1 percent comes from discount windows. Thus the function of supplying bank reserves has shifted from the district Federal Reserve Banks to the Federal Open Market Committee, which is dominated by the Board of Governors in Washington.

In summary the Fed provides reserves to the financial system and specifies the quantities of reserves that banks must hold as fractions of their deposit liabilities. In exercising these functions as supplier and regulator of bank reserves, the Fed determines much of the environment within which the payments process is enacted.

THE PAYMENTS SYSTEM

Bank reserves

Most payments are effected through exchanges of bank reserves. It is therefore appropriate that our discussion of the payments system begins with a description of the functions of those reserves. Bank reserves are required by law; but some reserves would be held even in

---

10 See "Reserve Requirements of Depository Institutions," reported monthly in the *Federal Reserve Bulletin*.

11 In every case a reference simply to "banks" means commercial banks as described in previous sections. When we mean "Federal Reserve Banks" we say so.

the absence of legal requirements. We keep money, in the forms of currency and bank accounts, as a reserve for the settlement of immediate and often unanticipated claims. So do commercial banks. Like us, banks keep some currency on hand but keep most of their funds with other banks, both commercial banks and (unlike us) Federal Reserve Banks. Bank needs for immediately available funds are greater than ours because of the nature of bank liabilities. Since demand deposits are payable on demand, banks must keep some currency in the till in order to redeem checks drawn against it and personally presented to its tellers.

But relatively few checks are presented to tellers. Most checks are presented to banks by other banks. The following is a typical sequence of events in a two-bank town: Abel writes a check, on his account at bank A, to Baker, who endorses the check and deposits it to the credit of her account in bank B. Bank B now owns a check written against bank A and is therefore A's creditor. The two banks accumulate many claims against each other in this way and every so often, usually at the end of each business day, settle their accounts. Suppose that during the course of a day A acquires $2,000,000 in checks written on B, and B acquires $1,800,000 in checks written on A. At the end of the day the banks exchange checks and agree on the way in which B will pay A the $200,000 difference. B might settle its debt by sending currency and coin across the street to A. Although this is sometimes done, it may be wasteful and is usually avoided because tomorrow the settlement may go the other way. A more convenient method of settlement is for the banks to keep deposits with each other. The $200,000 debt of bank B to bank A can then be settled by a couple of bookkeeping entries, in which B's account with A is reduced or A's account with B is increased.

Another and more common means of settlement between A and B is through a third bank in which they both hold deposits. The third bank might be a correspondent commercial bank or a Federal Reserve Bank. In either case B phones or wires directions to the third bank to transfer $200,000 from its account to A's account at that bank.

Many interbank settlements are made in the direct ways described above. But most are made by more roundabout routes that require the use of clearinghouses. In every case banks must pay special attention to their deposits (reserves) with Federal Reserve Banks.

Clearinghouses

During the course of each business day a bank comes into possession of checks on hundreds of other banks. It would be too costly and time consuming to exchange checks and settle with each of those banks individually. Instead most check collections and settlements are executed through clearinghouses. The advantages of clearinghouses are illustrated in Table 4.3, which gives an example of settlements through a local clearinghouse in a three-bank city. A has received

Table 4.3   Settlements in a Three-bank Clearinghouse

Bank A, $	Bank B, $	Bank C, $
Receives	Receives	Receives
200 from B	300 from A	100 from A
400 from C	500 from C	900 from B
600	800	1,000
Pays	Pays	Pays
300 to B	200 to A	400 to A
100 to C	900 to C	500 to B
400	1,100	900
Net settlement + 200	Net settlement − 300	Net settlement + 100

checks on B and C worth $200 and $400, respectively, while B and C have received checks on A worth $300 and $100. Instead of each bank's sending messengers to the other two banks, all three banks deliver checks drawn on the other banks to the clearinghouse and collect the checks drawn on themselves. Instead of six roundtrips (two for each of the three banks to the other two banks) there are only three (between each bank and the clearinghouse). And instead of the banks settling their net claims individually with each other, the clearinghouse simply informs each bank of its net balance with all the other members of the clearinghouse and instructs the district Federal Reserve Bank to add $200 and $100 to the accounts of A and C and to deduct $300 from B's account.

Float

We have so far considered only local checks. But intercity checks are collected (that is, redeemed) in similar, although more time-consuming, ways. An Atlanta bank that has come into possession of a check on a Boston bank may collect payment on that check by sending it to Boston directly (to its Boston correspondent, the bank on which the check is drawn, the Boston Clearing House, or the Federal Reserve Bank of Boston) or through the Atlanta Clearing House or the Federal Reserve Bank of Atlanta. All these procedures take time, often several days. These delays in delivering checks and transferring funds gives rise to *float,* which is the amount of money represented by checks outstanding and in the process of collection.[12]

We see from lines 1 and 44 of Table 4.2 that unredeemed checks represented about 6 percent of the total assets of large banks at the end of 1982. Those checks are in effect noninterest-earning loans. It is

---

12 More generally, float refers to all "cash items" (including checks, food stamps, bond coupons, and matured savings bonds) in the process of collection. But our concern here is with checks, which are the largest source of float. See Bank Administration Institute (1982) for definitions and discussions of float.

not surprising, therefore, that banks want them to be processed as quickly as possible, both on their own premises and by their clearing agents. The procedures of the largest intercity clearing agent, the Fed, are described next.

Fed float

The Fed's check-collection and settlement facilities are illustrated in Figure 4.1. The figure is self-explanatory except for the time intervals

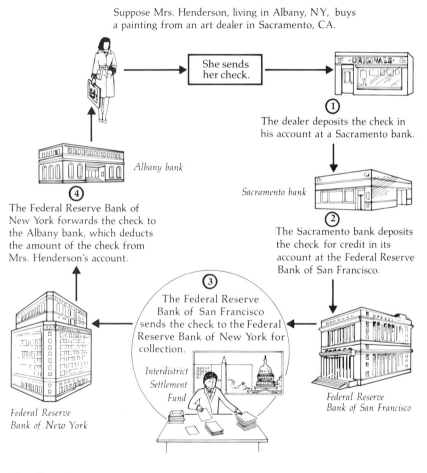

Suppose Mrs. Henderson, living in Albany, NY, buys a painting from an art dealer in Sacramento, CA.

She sends her check.

① The dealer deposits the check in his account at a Sacramento bank.

Albany bank

④ The Federal Reserve Bank of New York forwards the check to the Albany bank, which deducts the amount of the check from Mrs. Henderson's account.

Sacramento bank

② The Sacramento bank deposits the check for credit in its account at the Federal Reserve Bank of San Francisco.

③ The Federal Reserve Bank of San Francisco sends the check to the Federal Reserve Bank of New York for collection.

Interdistrict Settlement Fund

Federal Reserve Bank of New York

Federal Reserve Bank of San Francisco

The Albany bank authorizes the Federal Reserve Bank of New York to deduct the amount of the check from its deposit account with the Reserve Bank.	The Federal Reserve Bank of New York pays the Federal Reserve Bank of San Francisco by payment from its share in the Interdistrict Settlement Fund.	The Federal Reserve Bank of San Francisco credits the Sacramento bank's deposit account, and the Sacramento bank credits the art dealer's account.

Source: Federal Reserve Bank of New York, *The Story of Checks*, 7th ed., 1979.

Figure 4.1   Check clearing and collection by the Federal Reserve.

involved. When the Federal Reserve Bank of San Francisco receives Mrs. Henderson's check for, say, $100, it does not credit the Sacramento bank's reserve account at the Fed immediately. Each Federal Reserve Bank publishes an *availability schedule,* which states when checks will be credited to the accounts of depositing banks. Total commercial bank reserves at Federal Reserve Banks would be unaffected by the check-clearing process if the Sacramento bank's reserves at the San Francisco Fed were credited at the same time that the Albany bank's reserves at the New York Fed were debited. But synchronized reserve accounting would place a heavy burden on the communications system. Furthermore, the Fed wants to minimize the Sacramento bank's uncertainty about its future reserve position. The check has to be delivered physically, usually by air freight. Fog at the San Francisco airport, airline strikes, inattentive handlers, and New York City traffic jams combine to make it impossible to predict exactly when the New York Fed will receive the check and credit it to the Albany bank's account. But this is immaterial to the Sacramento bank because the San Francisco Fed's availability schedule tells it that $100 will be credited to its reserve account on a specific date, say, 3 days after Mrs. Henderson's check is delivered to the San Francisco Fed. Checks on banks in Sacramento might be credited to the reserve accounts of depositing banks with only 1 day's delay. Checks on banks in San Francisco would be credited on the day of receipt by the San Francisco Fed.

Fed availability schedules were in the past unrealistically short so that, for example, the Sacramento bank's reserve account was often credited before the Albany bank's reserve account was debited. This free credit extended by the Federal Reserve System to the banking system is called *Federal Reserve float.*

Fed float has received the attention of Congress because it represents a loss of revenue. In its conduct of monetary policy the Fed supplies reserves to commercial banks by buying securities of the U.S. government. The Fed buys these securities with checks written on itself (on previously nonexistent funds, not with borrowed money) and thereby earns profits close to the yields on U.S. securities. In short the Fed is a money maker for the federal government. It receives no appropriation from Congress but rather is in a position to pay profits into the Treasury.[13] Not enough to suit Congress, however. Fed float reduces federal revenue because, for a given level of bank reserves (as dictated by monetary policy), the more reserves that are provided by Fed float (on which the Fed used to earn nothing), the less can be provided by Fed security purchases (on which the Fed earns market yields to be returned to the Treasury).

---

13 For example, Fed income in 1982 was $16.5 billion, of which $15.5 was derived from U.S. securities. Expenses were $1.1 billion, and $15.2 billion was paid to the U.S. Treasury (*Annual Report,* Federal Reserve Board of Governors, Washington, 1983, pages 218–220).

The inflationary fiscal and monetary policies of Congress and the Fed during the 1970s caused record-high interest rates—and therefore record-high float as money managers found it increasingly profitable to delay check collection. A common delay tactic was *remote disbursement,* by which, for example, an Albany firm might pay local bills with checks drawn on a Sacramento bank. The rise in Fed float from an average of $2.1 billion in 1975 to an average of $6.5 billion in 1979 did not encourage Congress to reduce the incentive to maximize float by pursuing less inflationary fiscal policies, but instead led to a provision in the Monetary Control Act of 1980 that directed the Fed to charge "interest on items credited prior to actual collection . . . at the current rate applicable in the market for Federal funds." The Fed has responded by trying to reduce float as much as possible and adding the interest lost on remaining float to its check-collection fees. By 1983 Fed float had been reduced to $2 billion by means of improved check-processing facilities, longer availability schedules, and the growing substitution of wire transfers for paper checks.[14]

Fun and games in the payments system

But float is not dead. It's a game that can still be played by anyone, even you: The time is 6 P.M. on Friday. Your wallet is empty, your checking account has a balance of $0.36, and you won't be paid until Monday morning. But you have an important and costly engagement this evening and, in addition, must get in a supply of groceries for the weekend. No problem. You merely take yourself and your A&P "check card" to the local A&P and cash a check for the $100 limit allowed by the store. You do not have to worry about your checking account's being overdrawn because the A&P cannot deliver the check to the bank until Monday morning, by which time you will have taken advantage of your coffee break to deposit your paycheck in the bank. You have been the beneficiary of a 3-day interest-free loan from the A&P.

You will not be surprised to learn that professional money managers also play the float game. The two guiding principles of cash management are to collect from your debtors as soon as possible and to delay paying your creditors for as long as possible. Not all firms apply these principles fully for fear of damaging customer and supplier relationships. But many take elaborate steps to maximize the delays involved

---

14 See Benjamin Wolkowitz and Peter Lloyd-Davies (1979) for a discussion of the costs and benefits of various methods of reducing Fed float. Some of these methods may involve net losses to society. Float is not a true social cost but is primarily a transfer from taxpayers to banks in the form of interest-free loans, the benefits of which accrue to the owners of banks in the form of profits and to others in the form of reduced costs of financial services. The reduction of float by means of improved check-processing facilities by the Fed, on the other hand, represents substantial resource costs. And the reduction of float by the lengthening of Fed availability schedules (that is, longer delays in crediting checks to reserve accounts) leads to private investment in alternative check-collection systems. [For example see the cost-benefit analysis of float-reduction systems in Bank Administration Institute (1982).]

in the collection of their checks.[15] One of the most common procedures by which firms maximize float used to be called "remote disbursement" but is now, with other delay tactics, called *controlled disbursement* because the Federal Reserve Board disapproves of this "abuse of the check collection system."[16] For example suppose that a San Diego firm delivers a check for $1 million to one of its suppliers, also in San Diego, on a bill's due date. But the check is drawn on the firm's controlled-disbursement bank in Helena, Montana.[17] The supplier has no cause for complaint if it receives immediate credit when the check is deposited in its own bank in San Diego. The supplier's bank is not so content; for it must wait 2 days before receiving credit to its reserve account with the Fed after delivering the check to the Los Angeles branch of the Federal Reserve Bank of San Francisco. The paying firm's account in Helena will not be debited for at least 2 days. Sometimes the delay will be as long as 5 days. Every day that the firm can delay collection of the $1 million is another day that it can keep those funds invested in interest-earning assets.

Our San Diego firm is merely a casual float player. Some of the more serious players "use a Troy printer, a computer-controlled machine that turns out checks bearing the names of various banks. These companies maintain several bank accounts in different parts of the country, and the printer dutifully produces a check drawn on the bank that is most remote from the payee's zip code."[18] A less sophisticated procedure, popular among securities brokers, is simply to pay customers east of the Mississippi with checks drawn on West Coast banks and to pay western customers with checks on East Coast banks. It was estimated that between September 1976 and December 1978, when it disbursed to New York State customers alone about $1.25 billion, with an average daily float of about $1.5 million, Merrill Lynch made $418,000 on the basis of 1½ days' extra float generated by such a west-to-east disbursement policy and an average interest rate of 8 percent.[19]

The float game is not limited to the writers of checks. Those to whom payment is due have an interest in minimizing float. So the float game is a true contest. San Diego firms and their banks have been known to fly their customers' checks to Helena by courier and demand payment on the spot. This can be an awkward situation for a small

---

15 See Lawrence Gitman, Keith Forrester, and John Forrester (1976) for an analysis of methods of maximizing float.

16 *Federal Reserve Bulletin,* February 1979, pages 140–141.

17 Apparently the most popular remote-disbursement points are Helena, Montana; Midland, Texas; and Grand Junction, Colorado—with an average collection time to all locations in the United States of about 3½ days [Irwin Ross (1983, page 79)].

18 Irwin Ross (1983).

19 These are the estimates of the plaintiff's lawyer in a class-action suit. "Merrill Lynch claimed that the additional float time was one day and that its profit was $278,000" [Irwin Ross (1983)].

bank and might reduce its appetite for service as a remote-disbursement point.

Some large banks keep helicopters for the purpose of speeding the delivery of large checks to local airports. If a Chicago bank can deliver checks on New York banks to New York before the close of business, it can get the value of those checks credited to its account at the Chicago Fed, by wire from the New York Fed, faster than is permitted by the Chicago Fed's availability schedule. One day makes a difference when interest rates are high. One day's interest on $100 million (not a large sum in the money markets) at 9 percent per annum is about $25,000— enough to maintain a helicopter for a day.

But the most effective ways to discourage controlled-disbursement float are either to refuse to accept it (which most banks do by refusing to credit customer accounts until deposited checks have cleared and payments have been received and which brokers' customers may do by conducting business with the firms that offer the fastest payments) or for San Diego suppliers and other creditors to charge for it by adding the interest cost of float to outstanding accounts.

Wire, Fed Wire, and BankWire

Coin and currency are the principal forms of payment in terms of the *number* of transactions, being used in about 88 percent of about 300 billion transactions per year; checks are used in about 12 percent of all transactions; and wire transfers are used in only about 0.1 percent of all transactions. In terms of the *value* of transactions, however, coin and currency, checks, and wire transfers, respectively, account for less than 1 percent, about 25 percent, and about 75 percent of all transactions.[20] The value of wire transfers has grown much more rapidly than other means of payment. But the value of checks handled by the Fed has increased at about the same rate as nominal GNP during the postwar period, which suggests that wire transfers have not displaced other means of payment.[21] Their increasing use has been an accompaniment of the growing importance of the money markets, particularly the markets for fed funds and RPs, in which payments are effected by wire transfers between commercial bank accounts at Federal Reserve Banks.

Wire transfers of securities and bank reserves have been common since the development of a national telegraph system during the 15 years preceding the Civil War. Private, leased, wire systems were first used by Wall Street "wire-house" brokers for transactions within New York City in 1873 and were extended to Boston and Philadelphia in 1879, Chicago in 1881, and San Francisco in 1901.[22] The situation in

---

20 These are rough midpoints of the ranges estimated by Ralph Kimball (1980, pages 7–8).

21 See Ralph Kimball (1980, pages 9–10).

22 Edward Meeker (1930, pages 434–435).

1921 has been described as follows:

> Now there are about a thousand private wires in operation, tap-
> ping every city or locality of any importance in the United States
> and Canada. It is estimated that they are more than 500,000
> miles in length. . . .
>
> Between New York and Chicago it is estimated that there are
> 100 leased wires; eight between Chicago and the Pacific coast;
> 100 between New York and Boston; 75 between New York and
> Philadelphia, Baltimore and Washington; 10 between New York
> and points south of Washington; 15 between New York and
> Montreal; 25 between New York, Pittsburgh and Buffalo; and
> about 25 from New York to other nearby cities. . . .
>
> The private wires now in operation are mainly employed by
> those who are engaged in business on the great speculative ex-
> changes of the country, the New York Stock Exchange, the Chi-
> cago Board of Trade, the New York Cotton Exchange, and the
> smaller stock and commodity exchanges of the country, of which
> there are about fifty. . . .
>
> Then there are many large industrial and financial concerns
> that operate private wires in handling their business. The Fed-
> eral Reserve Banks have a private wire system connecting them
> and their branches with each other and the Federal Reserve
> Board in Washington. The United States Steel Corporation and
> most of the big packers have their own private wire systems.
> Many of the large banks and banking firms lease private tele-
> phone circuits between New York and their home offices.[23]

The Fed's leased wire system ("Fed Wire") has played an important
role in the payments system since its inception in 1918. This is because
the Federal Reserve Act of 1913 provided that all national banks[24] had
to keep their required reserves at the newly created Federal Reserve
Banks instead of with correspondent banks.[25] Since most large banks
in large cities were nationally chartered[26] and since reserve requirements were 10 to 13 percent of demand deposits in those cities, the Fed
necessarily became involved in interbank funds transfers in a big way.
Transfers through the Federal Reserve System were further encouraged by the Fed's willingness to perform these transactions free of

---

23 "The Nerves of Wall Street," *Commerce and Finance,* June 22, 1921, page 879; quoted by Edward Meeker (1930, pages 435–436).

24 These were (and are) "national" banks only in the sense of being chartered by an agency of the
   federal government (the Comptroller of the Currency) instead of in the more usual sense of
   operating throughout the country, which was (and is) severely restricted by antibranching laws.

25 State-chartered banks could also hold their reserves with Federal Reserve Banks if they chose
   to become members of the Federal Reserve System. National banks were not given a choice, nor
   was anyone else after 1980.

26 About 30 percent of all banks, with about 50 percent of total deposits, were national banks during the early years of the Federal Reserve System.

charge. "Immediate funds" (or "good funds") became synonymous with "fed funds." Other interbank transfers and the confirmation of fed funds transfers continued to rely on other commercial and private wire services, including the BankWire network, which was established in the early 1950s and now links about 225 banks.

The capacity and speed of the Fed and BankWire systems have increased substantially in recent years, although the Fed Wire has been unable to keep up with message volume during peak trading periods. During 1981 BankWire carried 4.5 million messages; about two-thirds were funds-transfer messages, averaging about $1 million, and the remaining one-third were confirmations of funds transfers and other administrative messages. During the same year, Fed Wire carried about 50 million transfers, averaging $1.9 million.[27]

CONCLUSION: THE FUTURE OF THE PAYMENTS SYSTEM

We hear little these days of "the checkless society." Wire connections between banks and the corner grocery have been slow to develop.[28] It is possible that high interest rates and reductions in the costs of operating point-of-sale (POS) computer terminals will eventually bring immediate funds transfers to consumers and small businesses. Buyers will then be able to transfer funds from their bank accounts to those of sellers immediately through POS terminals. Electronic cash registers have brought us closer to that day. So have home computers, which should eventually enable us to order goods and pay for them immediately from home. But the wide application of these procedures is still a few years in the future. Of course we know from our discussion of float that many buyers will be less than enthusiastic about POS terminals and immediate payments and may delay their implementation by patronizing stores with slower collection methods—unless the fast-collection stores offer something to compete with interest-free loans (float).

But the electronic-funds-transfer revolution that was so widely heralded in the early 1970s for retail transactions had already occurred for large financial transactions. Wire transfer facilities have made immediately available funds (IAF) available to large investors for many decades. The speed with which wire networks will be extended to the rest of the economy depends upon the costs of IAF, that is, the costs of wire transfers, and the returns from IAF, that is, the interest earned on funds received today instead of tomorrow. The Fed has stimulated much of the demand for IAF by the high interest rates resulting from its inflationary monetary policies. Offsetting this stimulus to demand is the provision of the Depository Institutions Deregu-

---

27 These data are from Edwin Cox (1983, pages 191, 204).

28 See the discussion by Sue Ford (1980).

lation and Monetary Control Act of 1980 that requires the Fed to stop giving things away. Instead of providing free check clearing, wire transfers, securities safekeeping, and other services, the Fed is now required to charge fees that cover its costs of providing these services plus the interest and tax costs that would be incurred by a private firm supplying the same services. These new requirements that banks and check writers pay their own ways instead of being subsidized by taxpayers are likely to have several effects on the financial markets. Two of the most important effects may be described as follows:

1. As service charges on checks and wire transfers grow larger, investors will shift between money and money substitutes less often.[29] Average money balances may increase and the rate of growth of money substitutes may be reduced.

2. Even when investors move into and out of money, they may sometimes settle for a means of payment and delivery slower and cheaper than the Fed Wire.

However, these two effects tending to slow financial innovation may be more than offset by future developments in technology and by continued high interest rates. The latter are likely to be especially important. Movements in interest rates have in the past been closely associated with advances and declines in financial innovation (with respect to both money substitutes and means of payment) and will probably continue to be the dominant influence on innovation in the future. If the high interest rates of the 1970s and early 1980s continue, the incentives to economize on money holdings and to speed exchanges between money and other assets will be strong. These incentives may overwhelm the effects of Fed fees so that we may observe continued improvements in money management and the payments system. On the other hand, a prolonged recurrence of low interest rates, such as in the 1930s and 1940s, would be likely to slow and perhaps even reverse financial innovation.

QUESTIONS

1. Discuss the differences between the balance sheet of a small bank in Helena and that of the large banks in Table 4.2. Give an example of the balance sheet of the former.
2. Discuss the principal differences between the balance sheet in Table 4.2 and that of International Telephone and Telegraph in Table 10.1.
3. Suppose the National Banking Act of 1863, the Federal Reserve

---

29 The elimination of already low fees in 1918 naturally led to many frivolous "$2" transfers over the Fed Wire, which were speedy and efficient for senders and receivers but costly for taxpayers. See Walter Spahr (1926, Chapter 6).

Act of 1913, and the Banking Act of 1933 had been successful in preventing funds from flowing between and even within regions. How would this have affected the growth and distribution of American population and industry?

4. Please look up the volume of TTL notes in a recent *Federal Reserve Bulletin.* Is the volume larger or smaller than line 67 of Table 4.2? Why?

5. What proportion of check-collection and settlement roundtrips are saved by a clearinghouse in a four-bank town? A five-bank town? An *n*-bank town?

6. What was the cost of Fed float to the U.S. Treasury in 1979 assuming an average fed funds rate of 10 percent and (a) no taxes on earnings from securities or (b) 20 percent federal taxes on securities earnings?

7. Suppose you were made dictator in charge of reducing float. What would you do?

8. How have Samuel F. B. Morse, Alexander Graham Bell, Carter Glass, and Tom Watson affected the demand for money as discussed in Chapter 3?

REFERENCES

Bank Administration Institute, *An Analysis of Float in the Commercial Banking Industry,* Rolling Meadows, IL, 1982.

Edwin B. Cox (ed.), *Bankers Desk Reference,* Warren, Gorham and Lamont, Boston, 1983.

Federal Reserve Bank of New York, *The Story of Checks,* 7th ed., New York, 1979.

Federal Reserve Board of Governors, *Purposes and Functions,* 6th ed., Washington, 1974.

Katherine Finney, *Interbank Deposits: The Purpose and Effects of Domestic Balances, 1934–54,* Columbia University Press, New York, 1958.

N. Sue Ford, "Electronic Funds Transfer: Revolution Postponed," Federal Reserve Bank of Chicago *Economic Perspectives,* November/December 1980, pages 16–23.

David Friedman, *Glossary: Weekly Federal Reserve Statements,* Federal Reserve Bank of New York, New York, 1975.

Lawrence J. Gitman, D. Keith Forrester, and John R. Forrester, "Maximizing Cash Disbursement Float," *Financial Management,* Summer 1976, pages 15–24.

Paul F. Jessup, *Modern Bank Management,* West, St. Paul, MN, 1980.

Ralph C. Kimball, "Wire Transfer and the Demand for Money," Federal Reserve Bank of Boston *New England Economic Review,* March/April 1980, pages 5–20.

Robert E. Knight, "Account Analysis in Correspondent Banking," Federal Reserve Bank of Kansas City *Monthly Review,* March 1976, pages 11–20.

Richard W. Lang, "TTL Note Accounts and the Money Supply Process," Federal Reserve Bank of St. Louis *Review,* October 1979, pages 3–14.

J. Edward Meeker, *The Work of the Stock Exchange,* Ronald Press, New York, 1930.

Irwin Ross, "Cash Management: The Race Is to the Slow Payer," *Fortune,* April 18, 1983, pages 75–80.

Arthur W. Samansky, *Statfacts: Understanding Federal Reserve Statistical Reports,* Federal Reserve Bank of New York, New York, 1981.

Walter E. Spahr, *The Clearing and Collection of Checks,* Bankers, New York, 1926.

William Francis Sutton (with Edward Linn), *Where the Money Was,* Viking, New York, 1976.

Benjamin Wolkowitz and Peter R. Lloyd-Davies, "Reducing Federal Reserve Float," *Federal Reserve Bulletin,* December 1979, pages 945–950.

THREE

The Valuation of Securities under Certainty

"I only took the regular course."
"What was that?" inquired Alice.
"Reeling and Writhing, of course, to begin with,"
the Mock Turtle replied;
"and then the different branches of Arithmetic—
Ambition, Distraction, Uglification, and Derision."

Lewis Carroll, *Alice's Adventures in Wonderland***, ch. 9**

THE ARITHMETIC OF SECURITY PRICES AND INTEREST RATES

Remember that money is of the prolific, generating nature. Money
can beget money, and its offspring can beget more, and so on.
Five shillings turned is six; turned again it becomes a hundred
pounds. The more there is of it the more it produces every turning,
so that the profits rise quicker and quicker. He that kills a breeding
sow destroys all her offspring to the thousandth generation.
He that murders a crown [five shillings] destroys all that
might have produced even scores of pounds.

Benjamin Franklin, *Advice to a Young Tradesman,* **1748**

Chapters 5 and 6 are concerned with the mathematical relationships
among the *present values, prices, yields to maturity* (or *yields*), and
rates of return on fixed-income securities, that is, on securities such as
bonds, bills, notes, and mortgages, which represent promises to pay
specific amounts on specific dates.[1] These relationships are introduced
early in the book because a firm grasp of them is essential to an
understanding of the financial market events, mostly fluctuations in
security prices and yields, that fill most of the later chapters. Many
readers will already be familiar with the concept of present value, but
many will not be familiar with the connections between that concept
and security prices, yields, and rates of return. This chapter presents
general statements, with hypothetical examples, of these connections.
Chapter 6 will present examples drawn from actual market events
affecting U.S. Treasury securities.

SECURITY PRICES ARE PRESENT VALUES. YIELDS TO MATURITY ARE DISCOUNT RATES.

Present value

Money now is worth more than money later. This statement is both
the cause and an effect of interest rates. First consider the *effect*.

---

1 The most important nonfixed-income security, common stock, is discussed in Chapter 10.

Suppose the highest interest rate available to you today—October 1, 1985—is 5 percent per annum on a savings account at the friendly neighborhood bank. This means that a deposit of $100 now earns $5 over the next year so that, on October 1, 1986, your deposit will have grown to a sum of $105 in principal and interest. Now suppose that another borrower, B, whose financial soundness is known to be as good as the bank's, offers to sell you a security, which is simply a piece of paper on which is written his promise to pay $105 on October 1, 1986. The *most* that you would be willing to pay for this security is $100: If the bank will give you $105 next year for $100 now, you will not pay more than $100 for an identical promise from B; on the other hand the least that B would accept for his promise is $100.

B's ability to sell his security for a price as high as $100, that is, his ability to borrow at a rate of interest as low as 5 percent, depends on the credibility of his promise to pay the $105 in full and on time. If investors are suspicious of B's ability to fulfill that promise, they will buy his security only at a price less than $100, possibly $96. In such a case investors earn a rate of return of $(105 - 96)/96 = 9.375$ percent if B pays in full and on time. If he defaults completely, the rate of return will be $(0 - 96)/96 = -100$ percent. On the other hand, if B's credit rating is superior to the bank's (banks sometimes fail), he might be able to borrow for less than 5 percent, that is, to sell his security for more than $100. We shall examine problems of default risk later.[2] The remainder of this chapter is limited to securities for which payment is certain so that identical promises by different people sell for identical prices.

A riskless 5 percent rate of interest means that the market places the same value on $100 now and $105 a year from now. If you have $100 but prefer to save for a rainy day, you can buy a security now that will be worth $105 in a year. On the other hand, if you own that security but would rather have a good time today, you can sell it immediately for $100. Briefly, the *present value* on October 1, 1985, of $105 to be paid on October 1, 1986, is $100.[3]

Present values, prices, discount rates, and yields

The price (P_1) of a security that promises a single payment (C_1) in 1 year may be expressed as

(5.1)
$$P_1 = \frac{C_1}{1 + Y}$$

where Y is the discount rate that reduces the future payment C_1 to the present value, or price, P_1. In the example presented above $C_1 = \$105$

---

2 In Chapter 10.

3 We abstract from transaction costs throughout this chapter.

and $Y = 0.05$ so that $P_1 = \$100$. The discount rate, Y, was 5 percent because that was the rate of interest investors could earn elsewhere. Consequently, they discounted B's promise by $1 + Y = 1.05$. Notice that Equation (5.1) may be rearranged to give $P_1 (1 + Y) = C_1$. In our example this becomes $\$100(1.05) = \$105$. That is, the discount rate is the yield that causes an investment equal to the present value, P_1, to accumulate to the maturity value, C_1.

Question: How do we know the present value of a security? Answer: By looking at its price, which is the market's determination of the present value of the security's future payments. Relationships like Equation (5.1) enable us to infer yields from the security prices quoted in the financial markets and reported in newspapers. For example, returning to the 1-year security issued by B, we see from the face of the security that $C_1 = \$105$ and learn from security traders that it has just changed hands at a price of $P_1 = \$100$. Equation (5.1) tells us that $Y = 0.05$.

We have seen that people's preference for money today over money later is an *effect* of interest rates. But it is equally true to say that this preference is the *cause* of interest rates. (As in so many questions of economics and finance, cause and effect operate in both directions.) In general, people wish to borrow and pay interest for one or both of two reasons: to consume beyond the limits of current income and to invest in potentially profitable enterprises. For example, if a society consists mainly of households and businesses that are impatient to consume and optimistic about the profitability of investment projects, the desire to borrow will be great and interest rates will be bid to high levels. On the other hand in a stagnant, zero-profit society of people content to consume their current incomes interest rates will be low. In the extreme case interest rates might be zero, a situation nearly achieved in the United States during the 1930s.[4] Under these conditions, money now is worth no more, or not much more, than money later.

Later chapters, especially Chapter 20, will be concerned with how, in a macroeconomic context, the impatience to consume and the expectation of profits interact to determine interest rates. The present chapter takes interest rates, whatever values they may assume, as given and shows how they may be applied to the present valuation of future cash flows, that is, to the pricing of securities.

COMPOUND INTEREST

This section extends the one-period relationships of the preceding section to single-payment securities with two or more periods until maturity. Continuing the previous example, assume that you can still

---

4 Most money market (short-term) rates were below 1 percent during most of the 1930s, and Treasury bill yields were actually zero on occasion.

earn 5 percent per annum on a savings account but that B now wants to sell you a promise to pay \$105 in 2 years—on October 1, 1987. For this security you will pay no more than

$$\textbf{(5.2)} \qquad P_2 = \frac{C_2}{(1 + Y)^2} = \frac{\$105}{(1.05)^2} = \frac{\$105}{1.1025} = \$95.24$$

If you were to deposit \$95.24 in a savings account at 5 percent per annum, that investment would be worth $\$95.24(1.05) = \$100$ after 1 year and $\$95.24(1.05)^2 = \$105$ after 2 years. Therefore, with an interest rate of 5 percent, the present or discounted value of \$105 payable in 2 years is \$95.24.

This is an example of *compound interest,* which means earning interest on interest as well as on principal. If you leave an initial savings deposit of \$95.24 plus interest of \$4.76 in the bank after 1 year, then during the second year, if the interest rate remains 5 percent, you will earn \$5 interest (\$4.76 on the initial investment plus \$0.24 on the first year's interest, that is, interest on interest).

The only difference between Equations (5.1) and (5.2) is the term to maturity of the security, that is, the length of time that elapses before the payment, C_2, is due. We can rearrange Equation (5.2), as we did Equation (5.1), to obtain $P_2(1 + Y)^2 = C_2$, or $\$95.24(1.05)^2 = \$105$. We again see that, if the present value (price) is invested at the discount rate (yield), the promised future value is achieved.

Consider another example, that of a security maturing in the year 2085. If Y is 5 percent per annum, a riskless promise to pay \$105 in 100 years is worth

$$\textbf{(5.3)} \qquad P_{100} = \frac{\$105}{(1.05)^{100}} = \$0.80$$

Eighty cents isn't much. But neither is a promise to pay \$105 in 100 years. Still, that promise is worth something, either to your great-grandson, who may be around to collect the \$105, or to you or one of your more immediate descendants if one of you should decide to sell the security and take cash some time before 2085.

The power of compound interest is impressive. It has led many states, for the protection of depository institutions, to put time limits on the liability of those institutions for inactive accounts. Consequently, even though in the midst of your rummaging in the attic you find a dusty passbook showing that your Revolutionary War ancestor deposited \$1,000 at 5 percent per annum in the local savings society in 1785, you may not be able to collect the $\$1,000(1.05)^{200} = \$17,292,581$ that ought to be due to you as her heir.[5]

---

5 If interest had not been compounded, the initial \$1,000 would have accumulated to only
   $\$1,000(0.05) \, (200) + \$1,000 = \$1,000 \, [1 + 0.05(200)] = \$11,000$.

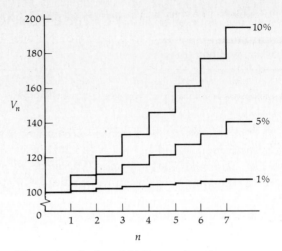

Figure 5.1   The accumulation of $100 at various interest rates.

The Brooklyn Indians have been ridiculed for selling Manhattan in 1626 for $24 (the equivalent of 60 guilders) worth of trinkets. But if they had sold the trinkets and invested and reinvested the money in securities at prevailing interest rates averaging about 6 percent per annum during the last 3.5 centuries, their descendants would in 1984 have been the happy possessors of $27.5 billion, more than the assessed value of taxable real estate in Manhattan, which amounted to $23.4 billion.

Figure 5.1 depicts the accumulation of a $100 investment. The figure shows that the rate of accumulation is very sensitive to the yield on the investment. For example after seven periods $100 has increased to approximately $195 at 10 percent, $141 at 5 percent, and $107 at 1 percent.

Table 5.1 shows how long it takes to double your money at a variety of yields. When the yield is 1 percent per annum, a 20-year-old person has to wait until she is 90 before her $100 investment has increased to $200. She can have the $200 before she is 22, while she is young enough to enjoy it, if the yield is 50 percent. She can double her money in 8.5 years at a yield of 8.5 percent.[6]

Present values are reciprocals of accumulated, or future, values. Therefore present values must also be sensitive to changes in yields. This is shown in Figure 5.2, which is the inverse of Figure 5.1. The accumulated values, V_n, in Figure 5.1 are given by the equation

(5.4) $$V_n = \$100(1 + Y)^n$$

---

6 A handy formula for computing the number of periods (n) necessary to double your money (M) as a function of the yield per period (Y) is $M(1 + Y)^n = 2M$, or $n \ln (1 + Y) = \ln 2$, or $n \doteq 0.69/Y$, where Y is a close approximation of the natural logarithm ($\ln$) of $1 + Y$ for small Y.

Table 5.1   Double Your Money in n Periods at a Yield of Y Percent per Period

Y	1	2	5	8.5	10	15	25	50
n	69.7	35.0	14.2	8.5	7.3	5.0	3.1	1.7

where $100 is the initial investment. The present values, V_0, in Figure 5.2 are given by

(5.5)
$$V_0 = \frac{\$100}{(1 + Y)^n}$$

where now $100 is the future payment to be made after n periods.

Figure 5.2 shows that the sensitivity of present values to yields is especially pronounced for payments to be made in the distant future. This point is further illustrated by Table 5.2, which shows the present values of $100 payable after 1, 2, 10, 49, 50, and 100 periods for discount rates of 1, 5, 10, and 25 percent per period. Suppose that the length of a period is 1 year and that we are interested in the effects of an increase in the discount rate from 5 to 10 percent. The price (present value) of a 1-year security falls $4.33 (from $95.24 to $90.91), whereas the price of a 10-year security falls $22.84 (from $61.39 to $38.55).

Other present values may be obtained from Table C.1 in Appendix C near the end of the book. For example, the present value of $1 payable at the end of 10 years is $0.10737 if the discount rate is 25 percent per annum. Multiplying this number by 100 gives the present value, at 25 percent, of $100 payable in 10 years. This checks with the value shown in Table 5.2, which is rounded to the nearest penny. The uses of Tables 5.2 and C.1 are further illustrated by Exercise 5.1.

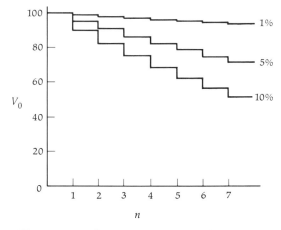

Figure 5.2   The present value of $100 at various interest rates.

Table 5.2   Present Values (Dollars) of $100 Payable after n Periods When the Discount Rate Is Y Percent per Period

	Y			
n	1	5	10	25
1	99.01	95.24	90.91	80.00
2	98.03	90.70	82.64	64.00
10	90.53	61.39	38.55	10.74
49	61.41	9.16	0.94	0.002
50	60.80	8.72	0.85	0.001
100	36.97	0.76	0.01	0.00000002

EXERCISE 5.1.   Show that the price (present value) of a 50-year security that promises $100 is more responsive to an increase in the discount rate from 1 to 5 percent per annum than is the price of a similar 10-year security.

Using Table 5.2, we see that the stated rate increase causes the price of the 50-year security to fall from $60.80 to $8.72, compared with the decline in price of the 10-year security from $90.53 to $61.39. Using Table C.1, we see that the present values of $1 payable in 10 and 50 years are $0.90529 and $0.60804 when the discount rate is 1 percent and are $0.61391 and $0.08720 when the discount rate is 5 percent. Multiplying these results by 100 gives the results in Table 5.2.

The greater sensitivity of long-term security prices to discount-rate variations may be explained in terms of either arithmetic or finance. As a matter of arithmetic, higher powers of numbers magnify their proportional differences. For example the price of the 10-year security after the rate increase in Exercise 5.1 was about 68 percent of the original price. The ratio of these prices is

$$(5.6) \qquad \frac{\$61.39}{\$90.53} = \frac{\$100/(1.05)^{10}}{\$100/(1.01)^{10}} = \left(\frac{1.01}{1.05}\right)^{10} = 0.678$$

The ratio of the after and before prices of the 50-year security is

$$(5.7) \qquad \frac{\$8.72}{\$60.80} = \frac{\$100/(1.05)^{50}}{\$100/(1.01)^{50}} = \left(\frac{1.01}{1.05}\right)^{50} = 0.143$$

As a matter of finance, the greater proportional sensitivity of the present values of long-term payments to discount-rate changes is due to the fact that interest on interest, even over a long period, does not amount to much if interest is low. This is why a $36.97 investment is required in 1985 for an accumulated value of $100 in 2085 if the interest rate is 1 percent. But compound interest greatly magnifies the impact of a change in the rate on the required investment, reducing that investment to $0.76 if the rate rises to 5 percent. Compound interest has more time to work and will have a greater effect, the longer the term to maturity of the investment.

The practical implication of these results for investors is that they can expect given changes in discount rates (yields) to cause greater changes in the prices of long-term than of short-term single-payment securities. We shall see in a later section that this comparison also holds for annuities—after developing its implications for rates of return on single-payment securities in the next section.

YIELDS TO MATURITY AND RATES OF RETURN

Consider the fortunes of an investor who on October 1, 1985, holds a 2-year security with maturity value of $100. The security's yield to maturity on that date is 5 percent per annum but rises to 10 percent on October 1, 1986. Using Table 5.2, we see that in 1985 the security is worth $90.70 and that in 1986, with 1 year until maturity, it is worth $90.91. The investor's annual *rate of return,* that is, the change in the value of the investment relative to its initial value, is

(5.8) $$R = \frac{\$90.91 - \$90.70}{\$90.70} - 0.0023 - 0.23 \text{ percent}$$

In the calculation of rate of return it makes no difference whether or not the investment was initiated at the beginning of the period. Nor does it matter whether it is liquidated at the end of the period. In our example the investor earned $0.21 on the security. She might have bought it either last year or when it was a newly issued 20-year security. She might or might not sell it at the end of the present year. In all these cases her rate of return is 0.23 percent. Consider another example: When someone tells you that his investment in Xerox rose from $50 to $52 per share yesterday, giving him a daily return of 4 percent, he is using the concept of rate of return in precisely the way that we are using it. He may or may not realize that return (take his profits) by selling the stock.

EXERCISE 5.2. Consider another example based on the investment used in Equation (5.8). As before, suppose the investor buys the 2-year security for $90.70. But this time suppose *Y falls* from 5 percent in 1985 to 1 percent in 1986. The rate of return in this case is

$$R = \frac{\$99.01 - \$90.70}{\$90.70} = 9.16 \text{ percent}$$

Equation (5.8) and Exercise 5.2 are illustrations of the following general relationships:

RELATIONSHIP 5.1.   The rate of return on a single-payment security during some period equals its yield to maturity at the time of purchase if and only if either (a) the security is held until maturity or (b) the yield at the time of sale equals the purchase yield.

RELATIONSHIP 5.2.   The rate of return on a single-payment security that is sold before maturity exceeds, equals, or is less than its yield at the time of purchase if and only if its yield at the time of sale is less than, equal to, or greater than its purchase yield. (Notice that Relationship 5.2 includes Relationship 5.1(b).)

The rates of return in Equation (5.8) and Exercise 5.2, 0.0023 and 0.0916, were caused by 1986 yields of 0.10 and 0.01, respectively. Only if the 1986 yield had been the same as the 1985 purchase yield of 0.05, would the 1985–1986 rate of return have been 0.05. The latter assertion is supported by the following equation, which uses Table 5.2 to derive the 1-year rate of return on a 2-year security bought at a yield of 0.05 and sold after 1 year at the same yield:

(5.9) $$R = \frac{\$95.24 - \$90.70}{\$90.70} = 5 \text{ percent}$$

So far we have had examples. But a proof of Relationships 5.1 and 5.2 will be presented as soon as we define *average multiperiod rates of return*. First notice that the annual rate of return from the purchase of a 2-year single-payment (\$100)[7] security (for price P_2 and yield Y_2) that is sold after 1 year as a 1-year security (for price P_1 and yield Y_1) may be written (using R_{21} instead of R)

$$R_{21} = \frac{P_1 - P_2}{P_2} \quad \text{or}$$

(5.10)

$$1 + R_{21} = \frac{P_1}{P_2} = \frac{\$100/(1 + Y_1)}{\$100/(1 + Y_2)^2} = (1 + Y_2) \frac{1 + Y_2}{1 + Y_1}$$

---

7 The maturity value of the security may be any nonzero number (for example, \$100, \$1, or \$3.18) without affecting the rate of return.

If we extend Equation (5.10) to any number of periods, the average annual rate of return (R_{nm}) from the purchase of an n-year single-payment ($\$100$) security (for price P_n and yield Y_n) that is sold after m years as an $(n - m)$-year security (for price P_{n-m} and yield Y_{n-m}) is such that[8]

(5.11)

$$(1 + R_{nm})^m = \frac{P_{n-m}}{P_n} = \frac{\$100/(1 + Y_{n-m})^{n-m}}{\$100/(1 + Y_n)^n}$$

$$= (1 + Y_n)^m \left(\frac{1 + Y_n}{1 + Y_{n-m}}\right)^{n-m}$$

Therefore

(5.12) $R_{nm} \gtreqless Y_n$ as $Y_{n-m} \lesseqgtr Y_n$

which proves Relationship 5.2. Further notice that, if the n-year security is held to maturity, that is, if $m = n$, Equation (5.11) reduces to $R_{nn} = Y_n$, which proves Relationship 5.1(a). Relationship 5.2 is illustrated for $n = 10$ and $m = 8$ in Exercise 5.3.

EXERCISE 5.3.   Check Relationship 5.2 for the three cases in which an investor buys a 10-year single-payment security at a yield of $Y_n = 0.10$ and sells it after 8 years at yields of **(a)** 0.05, **(b)** 0.10, and **(c)** 0.25.
   (a) Using Equation (5.11) and Table 5.2,

$$(1 + R_{10,8})^8 = \frac{P_2}{P_{10}} = \frac{\$100/(1.05)^2}{\$100/(1.10)^{10}} = \frac{\$90.70}{\$38.55} = 2.3528$$

Taking the eighth root of this result gives $1 + R_{10,8} = 1.11288$ so that $R_{10,8} = 0.11288 > 0.10 = Y_{10}$ because $Y_2 = 0.05 < 0.10 = Y_{10}$.
   Notice that an investment in the 10-year security is worth

$$\$38.55(1.11288)^8 = \$90.70$$

after 8 years; that is, the average annual rate of return is 11.288 percent.

(b) $(1 + R_{10,8})^8 = \dfrac{P_2}{P_{10}} = \dfrac{\$100/(1.10)^2}{\$100/(1.10)^{10}} = \dfrac{\$82.64}{\$38.55} = 2.1437$

so that $R_{10,8} = 0.10 = Y_{10}$ because $Y_2 = 0.10 = Y_{10}$.

---

8 Equation (5.11) reduces to Equation (5.10) when $n = 2$ and $m = 1$.

(c) $(1 + R_{10,8})^8 = \dfrac{P_2}{P_{10}} = \dfrac{\$100/(1.25)^2}{\$100/(1.10)^{10}} = \dfrac{\$64.00}{\$38.55} = 1.6602$

so that $R_{10,8} = 0.0654 < 0.10 = Y_{10}$ because $Y_2 = 0.25 > Y_{10}$.

As an illustration of Relationship 5.1(a), if an investor in the 2-year security in Equation (5.8) had held it until maturity, she would have received the maturity value of \$100. Notice that $\$100/90.70 = (1.05)^2$. This means an average annual rate of return of 5 percent during the 2-year period of the investment. This is independent of anything that might have happened to the price and yield of the security between the purchase and maturity dates. Her rate of return in the first year is 0.0023, as shown in Equation (5.8), and in the second year is ($\$100 - \$90.91)/\$90.91 = 0.10$. Given these rates of return, the total value of the investment after 2 years must be

$$\$90.70(1.0023)(1.10) = \$90.70(1.1025) = \$100$$

and since $1.1025 = (1.05)^2$, we see again that the average rate of return is 5 percent.

Relationship 5.1(a) follows directly from the relationship between a security's price and discount rate (yield). If $P_n = \$100/(1 + Y_n)^n$ is the price of an n-period security at the time of purchase, Y_n must be its average rate of return (R_{nn}) if it is held to maturity because, using the notation of Equation (5.11),

(5.13) $\qquad (1 + R_{nn})^n = \dfrac{P_{n-n}}{P_n} = \dfrac{\$100}{\$100/(1 + Y_n)^n}$

where $P_{n-n} = P_0$ is the price (which is also in this case its maturity value) of the security on its maturity date.

The object of any investment is a high rate of return, R. But securities are reported in terms of yields to maturity, Y. Two points should be carried away from this section: (1) Except in special circumstances Y does not equal R and often is not even a good indicator of R; (2) Since security prices fall as their yields rise, rates of return on single-payment securities that are sold before maturity are inversely related to yield movements between their purchase and sale dates, and this relationship is strongest for long-term securities.

CONTINUOUS COMPOUNDING

Suppose we are interested in the *effective yield*[9] on an investment during a period in which interest is paid, and compounded, two or

---

9 The terms *effective yield* and *effective rate* are used in a variety of ways: sometimes, as in this chapter, to distinguish the annual compounded yield actually earned from a stated simple (that

more times during the period. For example assume that a savings and loan association (S&L) pays 2.5 percent semiannually on savings accounts. If you deposit $100 on October 1, 1985, you will own a deposit worth $100(1.025) = $102.50 on April 1, 1986, and worth $102.50(1.025) = $105.0625 on October 1, 1986. The effective annual yield on your account is $(1.025)^2 - 1 = 5.0625$ percent. In general, with semiannual compounding, the sum accumulated at the end of one year, V_1, from an initial investment of V_0 is

$$(5.14) \qquad V_1 = V_0 \left(1 + \frac{Y}{2} \right)^2$$

where $Y/2$ is the semiannual yield and Y is the simple (uncompounded) annual yield.

The present value of V_1 to be paid in 1 year is

$$(5.15) \qquad V_0 = \frac{V_1}{\left(1 + \dfrac{Y}{2} \right)^2} \equiv \frac{V_1}{1 + Y_e}$$

That is, the effective (compounded) annual yield, or effective annual discount rate, is defined in the case of semiannual compounding as

$$(5.16) \qquad Y_e = \left(1 + \frac{Y}{2} \right)^2 - 1$$

After n years the investment is worth

$$(5.17) \qquad V_n = V_0 \left(1 + \frac{Y}{2} \right)^{2n} = V_0 (1 + Y_e)^n$$

EXERCISE 5.4.   Find the value of an investment of $100 at 6 percent per annum, compounded semiannually, after **(a)** 1 year and **(b)** 2 years.

---

is, uncompounded) annual yield; sometimes to distinguish after-tax yields or rates from before-tax yields or rates; and sometimes to indicate yields or rates net of transaction costs.

(a) After 1 year the investment is worth

$$V_1 = V_0 \left(1 + \frac{Y}{2}\right)^2 = \$100(1.03)^2 = \$106.09$$

(b) After 2 years it is worth

$$V_2 = \$100(1.03)^4 = \$100(1.0609)^2 = \$112.55$$

Interest may be compounded as many times in a period as we like. If it is compounded a times per period, an investment of V_0 accumulates after n periods to

(5.18)
$$V_n = V_0 \left(1 + \frac{Y}{a}\right)^{an}$$

where, as before, Y is the simple (uncompounded) periodic yield.

For example, if a 5 percent simple annual yield is compounded daily, a \$100 investment grows in 2 years to

(5.19)
$$V_n = \$100 \left(1 + \frac{0.05}{365}\right)^{365(2)}$$
$$= \$100(1.051268)^2 = \$110.5163$$

We see that the effective annual yield is

$$\left(1 + \frac{0.05}{365}\right)^{365} - 1 = 0.051268$$

for daily compounding. An S&L that advertises an "annual yield" of 5 percent and an "effective annual yield" of 5.13 percent compounds interest daily.[10] Table 5.3 shows effective annual yields when interest is compounded annually, semiannually, quarterly, monthly, daily, and continuously. It is not surprising that frequent compounding (frequent interest on interest) increases the effective annual yield more for high than for low yields.

When the number of times per period (a) that interest is com-

---

10 Section 3(a) of the Federal Reserve Board's Regulation Q states that "in ascertaining the rate of
   interest paid, the effects of compounding of interest may be disregarded." This means that the
   5½ percent maximum on savings deposits at S&Ls and banks may, if the institutions choose, be
   raised to an effective annual yield of 5.65 percent by continuous compounding.
   However, according to Section 6, the advertisement of these effective yields must be circum-
   spect: (1) "Interest rates shall be stated in terms of the annual rate of simple interest. In no case
   shall a rate be advertised that is in excess of the applicable maximum rate for the particular deposit." (2) "Where a percentage yield achieved by compounding interest during one year is advertised, the annual rate of simple interest shall be stated with equal prominence, together with
   a reference to the basis of compounding."

Table 5.3   Effective Annual Yields When Interest Is Compounded at Y Percent per Annum a Times per Annum

		Y		
a	1	5	10	25
1	1.00000	5.0000	10.0000	25.0000
2	1.00250	5.0625	10.2500	26.5625
4	1.00376	5.0945	10.3813	27.4429
12	1.00460	5.1162	10.4713	28.0732
365	1.00500	5.1268	10.5156	28.3916
∞	1.00502	5.1271	10.5171	28.4025

pounded goes to infinity, that is, when compounding is continuous, Equation (5.18) becomes[11]

(5.20) $V_n = V_0 e^{Yn}$

where e is approximately 2.71828, Y as before is simple interest per period, and n is the number of periods that interest is allowed to accumulate. For example, suppose that $100 is invested at 5 percent simple interest compounded continuously. After two periods the investor has $V_2 = \$100e^{0.10} = \$110.52$.

EXERCISE 5.5.   Find the value of an investment of $100 at 12 percent per annum after 1 year and after 2 years when interest is compounded **(a)** quarterly, **(b)** monthly, and **(c)** continuously.

(a) $V_1 = \$100(1.03)^4 = \$112.55$

$V_2 = \$100(1.03)^8 = \$126.68$

Notice the similarity to Exercise 5.4: 6 percent per annum compounded semiannually for 2 years, that is, 3 percent per period for four periods, is equivalent to 12 percent per annum compounded quarterly for 1 year.

If you can't find your hand calculator but the professor has been kind enough to give a problem with an annual rate that is evenly divisible by the annual frequency of compounding, Table C.3 can be applied to problems like this. Since 12 percent per annum compounded quarterly is 3 percent per quarter, the 3 percent column in Table C.3 provides answers to part (a) of this ex-

---

11 Equation (5.20) is derived in Appendix 5.A.

ercise for $n = 4$ and $n = 8$. The 1 percent column in Table C.3 gives answers to part (b) for $n = 12$ and $n = 24$.

$$\textbf{(b)} \ V_1 = \$100(1.01)^{12} = \$112.68$$

$$V_2 = \$100(1.01)^{24} = \$126.97$$

Applying Equation (5.20) gives

$$\textbf{(c)} \ V_1 = \$100e^{0.12} = \$112.75$$

$$V_2 = \$100e^{0.24} = \$127.12$$

If you still can't find your hand calculator, you can use the table of logarithms to the base e in Appendix B to solve this problem. Notice that $\ln e^{0.12} = 0.12$. The antilogarithm of 0.12, which in this case is the value of \$1 after 1 year, is found by interpolation between $\ln 1.12 = 0.11333$ and $\ln 1.13 = 0.12222$. Since 0.12 is $(0.00667/0.00889) = 0.750$ of the distance between 0.11333 and 0.12222, we can say that 0.12 is approximately the natural logarithm of 1.1275. (We say "approximately" because logarithms do not rise linearly with N, and we have used the "straight-line" method of interpolation.) Multiplying this by \$100 gives V_1. (We have been lucky. Our method of approximation gives an answer that is "exact" to two decimal places.)

ANNUITIES

An *annuity* is the payment of a fixed sum of money at uniform intervals of time. Life insurance premiums and mortgages are examples of annuities. The present value of an n-period annuity is the sum of the present values of the n payments:

$$(5.21) \qquad A_n = \frac{C_1}{1 + Y} + \frac{C_2}{(1 + Y)^2} + \cdots + \frac{C_n}{(1 + Y)^n}$$

If the discount rate is 5 percent, the present value of a two-period annuity of \$100 per period is

$$(5.22) \qquad A_2 = \frac{\$100}{1.05} + \frac{\$100}{(1.05)^2} = \$95.24 + \$90.70 = \$185.94$$

This result may also be obtained either from Table 5.2 or, more directly, from Table C.2.

Payments on annuities are just sufficient to repay the loan at the rate of interest implied by the discount rate. For example suppose you borrow $185.94 at a yield of 5 percent on October 1, 1985, and promise to repay the loan in two equal annual installments. These installments are $100, as shown in the following equation:

(5.23) $[\$185.94(1.05) - \$100](1.05) - \$100 = 0$

That is, a loan of $185.94 at 5 percent becomes a debt of $185.94(1.05) = $195.24 at the end of a year, which is immediately reduced to $95.24 by the first payment of $100. This debt becomes $95.24(1.05) = $100 at the end of the second year and is extinguished by the second (and last) payment. The following exercise gives another example of this principle.

EXERCISE 5.6.   Show that the payments on a $100 two-period annuity are just sufficient to repay a loan equal to the present value of that annuity when the yield is 10 percent.
   Using Equation (5.21) or Table C.2, the present value of the annuity is

$$\frac{\$100}{1.10} + \frac{\$100}{(1.10)^2} = \$90.91 + \$82.64 = \$173.55$$

If you borrow $173.55 at 10 percent and repay $100 per period, the balance outstanding after two periods is

$$[\$173.55(1.10) - \$100](1.10) - \$100 = 0$$

and the loan is repaid.

The present value of an n-period annuity may be stated in a more concise form than Equation (5.21) as follows for uniform Cs and a nonzero Y:[12]

(5.24) $$A_n = \frac{C}{Y}\left[1 - \left(\frac{1}{1 + Y}\right)^n\right]$$

---

12 Equation (5.24) is undefined for $Y = 0$, in which case A_n is simply $C_1 + C_2 + \cdots + C_n = nC$ if the Cs are uniform. The derivation of Equation (5.24) from Equation (5.21) is shown in Appendix A.

As a check it can be shown that, when $C = \$100$, $Y = 0.05$, and $n = 2$, Equation (5.24) gives the same result as Equation (5.22):

$$\textbf{(5.25)} \qquad A_2 = \frac{\$100}{0.05}\left[1 - \left(\frac{1}{1.05}\right)^2\right]$$

$$= \$2,000[1 - 0.90703] = \$185.94$$

A *perpetuity* is an annuity whose payments continue without end. Payments from endowment funds and British government consols[13] are examples of perpetuities. The present value of a perpetuity is easily obtained. Letting n go to infinity, the term $1/(1 + Y)^n$ in Equation (5.24) goes to zero for all positive yields so that the perpetuity's price is

$$\textbf{(5.26)} \qquad A_\infty = \frac{C}{Y}$$

Table 5.4 illustrates the sensitivity of annuity prices to yield changes. As with single-payment securities this sensitivity is greater for long-term than for short-term annuities. For example an increase in Y from 5 to 10 percent reduces the prices of a one-period annuity by $4.33/95.24 = 4.5$ percent, a ten-period annuity by $157.71/772.17 = 20.4$ percent, and a perpetuity by $1,000/2,000 = 50$ percent.

Rates of return on annuities are calculated like those on the single-payment securities considered previously. For example suppose that you own a 2-year annuity on October 1, 1985, when its yield is 5 percent per annum so that its price is $185.94. If the yield is still 5 percent on October 1, 1986, the 1-year rate of return is

$$\textbf{(5.27)} \qquad R = \frac{\$95.24 + \$100 - \$185.94}{\$185.94} = 0.05$$

The rate of return is the end-of-year value of the investment (which is the price of the annuity at the time, $95.24, plus the $100 payable to the owner of the annuity) less the beginning-of-year value of the investment, all divided by the beginning-of-year value.

But suppose the yield in 1986 on 1-year annuities is 1 percent. In

---

13 Consols, or "consolidated annuities," are so called because in the 1750s Chancellor of the Exchequer Henry Pelham consolidated several existing government debt issues into a single annuity with no maturity date although they were redeemable at the government's option (that is, were "callable"). These consols constituted most of the national debt until World War I but are now less than 1 percent of the debt.

In 1900 the U.S. government issued the "2% consols of 1930," which paid an annual annuity equal to 2 percent of their initial sale price ("par value") and were redeemable at par at the government's option beginning in 1930. They were redeemed in 1935.

The Canadian Pacific Railroad's 4 percent bonds are also perpetuities.

Table 5.4   Present Values (Dollars) of $100 Annuities Payable for n Periods When the Discount Rate Is Y Percent per Period

			Y	
n	1	5	10	25
1	99.01	95.24	90.91	80.00
2	197.04	185.94	173.55	144.00
10	947.13	772.17	614.46	357.05
49	3,858.81	1,816.87	990.63	399.993
50	3,919.61	1,825.59	991.48	399.994
100	6,302.89	1,984.79	999.93	399.999$^+$
∞	10,000.00	2,000.00	1,000.00	400.00

+ This number, to seven decimal places, is 399.9999992

this case, again using either Table 5.4 or Table C.2, the 1-year rate of return is

$$(5.28) \qquad R = \frac{\$99.01 + \$100 - \$185.94}{\$185.94} = 7.03 \text{ percent}$$

If the yield on 1-year securities had been 10 percent, the rate of return would have been

$$(5.29) \qquad R = \frac{\$90.91 + \$100 - \$185.94}{\$185.94} = 2.67 \text{ percent}$$

Equations (5.27) to (5.29) are examples of a general relationship, according to which the one-period rate of return on an annuity equals its yield if and only if the end-of-period and beginning-of-period yields are the same. This is reminiscent of Relationship 5.1(a) for single-payment securities, which is not surprising since an annuity that is held for one period is in effect a single-payment security. But the conditions necessary for the equality of R and Y for annuities that are held for more than one period are more stringent than are those for single-payment securities. They may be stated as follows:

RELATIONSHIP 5.3.   The rate of return on an annuity that is held for more than one period equals its yield to maturity at the time of purchase if (a) all payments are reinvested at the purchase yield and *either* (b) the annuity is held until maturity *or* (c) the yield at the time of sale equals the purchase yield.

The first part of Exercise 5.7 proves Relationship 5.3 for the simplest possible case, in which a two-period annuity is held to maturity.

EXERCISE 5.7. **(a)** Prove Relationship 5.3 for a 2-year annuity that is held to maturity. Then **(b)** derive the rate of return on this investment when the purchase yield is 10 percent and the yield after 1 year is 15 percent.

(a) Our proof will be assisted by the introduction of a t subscript that indicates the dates of transactions. Let C_t denote the constant annual annuity payment received at time t and P_{nt} and Y_{nt} denote the price and yield on an n-period annuity at time t. Then the purchase price of the annuity on the date of the initial investment ($t = 0$) is

$$P_{20} = \frac{C_1}{1 + Y_{20}} + \frac{C_2}{(1 + Y_{20})^2}$$

and the value of this investment after two years is

$$C_1(1 + Y_{11}) + C_2$$

where $C_1(1 + Y_{11})$ is the reinvestment value of the first payment. Now let R_{nmt} be the rate of return on an m-year investment in an n-year annuity purchased at time t. The rate of return on the purchase of a 2-year annuity at time 0 that is held to maturity may therefore be written such that

$$(1 + R_{220})^2 = \frac{C_1(1 + Y_{11}) + C_2}{[C_1/(1 + Y_{20})] + [C_2/(1 + Y_{20})^2]}$$

$$= (1 + Y_{20})^2 \frac{2 + Y_{11}}{2 + Y_{20}}$$

and we see that the rate of return equals the purchase yield Y_{20} if condition (a) of Relationship 5.3 is satisfied, that is, if $Y_{11} = Y_{20}$ so that the first payment is reinvested at the purchase yield.

(b) If $Y_{20} = 0.10$ and $Y_{11} = 0.15$,

$$(1 + R_{220})^2 = (1.10)^2 \frac{2.15}{2.10} = 1.2388$$

so that $R_{220} = 0.1130$.

Exercise 5.7 is a simple illustration of the general result that investors in long-term annuities (and other multipayment securities, such as the bonds to be introduced in Chapter 6) are happy when yields rise—if they had planned to hold those securities until maturity. This is because the higher yields mean higher returns on reinvested annuity payments although this result is guaranteed only if the payments are invested in securities that mature at the same time as the original annuity investment.[14] It can also be shown that investors in long-term annuities *may* be happy when yields rise even if they had planned to sell their annuity holdings before maturity. On the other hand a rise in yields may make them sad. The effect on their rate of return depends upon the net effect of the rise in yields on (1) the sale price of the annuity, which is adversely affected, and (2) the reinvestment values of the annuity payments, which are favorably affected.[15] These two effects are illustrated for the simplest possible case in Exercise 5.8, which is also a further illustration of Relationship 5.3.

EXERCISE 5.8.   **(a)** Prove Relationship 5.3 for a 3-year annuity that is held for 2 years. Then **(b)** derive the rate of return on this investment when the purchase yield is 10 percent and all yields thereafter are 15 percent.

(**a**) Using the notation of Exercise 5.7, the purchase price of the annuity is

$$P_{30} = \frac{C_1}{1 + Y_{30}} + \frac{C_2}{(1 + Y_{30})^2} + \frac{C_3}{(1 + Y_{30})^3}$$

and the value of the investment after 2 years is

$$C_1(1 + Y_{11}) + C_2 + \frac{C_3}{1 + Y_{12}}$$

where $C_3/(1 + Y_{12}) = P_{12}$ is the sale price of the annuity. Rearranging the ratio of the terminal and initial values of the investment gives

$$(1 + R_{320})^2 = (1 + Y_{30})^2 \frac{[1/(1 + Y_{12})] + 2 + Y_{11}}{[1/(1 + Y_{30})] + 2 + Y_{30}}$$

and we see that $R_{320} = Y_{30}$ if $Y_{30} = Y_{11} = Y_{12}$; that is, the rate of return equals the purchase yield if conditions (a) and (c) of Relationship 5.3 are satisfied.

(**b**) If $Y_{30} = 0.10$ and $Y_{11} = Y_{12} = 0.15$,

$$(1 + R_{320})^2 = (1.10)^2 \frac{3.0196}{3.0091} = 1.2142$$

---

14 Otherwise losses may be incurred due to price declines.

15 This statement means that the simple Relationship 5.2, which depends only on (1), cannot be applied directly to annuities. It also explains why the "only if" condition in Relationship 5.1 is omitted from 5.3; for the two effects might be exactly offsetting, in which case the investment is said to be "immunized," a concept that is developed in Appendix 6.A.

so that $R_{320} = 0.1019 > Y_{30}$. The rise in yields (from 0.10 to 0.15) has led to an increased rate of return in this case (from 0.10 to 0.1019) because the sale price P_{12} is only \$3.95 = \$90.91 − \$86.96 less when $Y_{12} = 0.15$ than when $Y_{12} = 0.10$, compared with the increased reinvestment value of the annuity payments amounting to \$5 = \$215 − \$210.

SUMMARY

The concepts presented in this chapter may be summarized as follows:

1. The *present value* of the future payments promised by a security is its *price* (*P*), that is, what you can sell it for.

2. A security's *yield to maturity* (*Y*) is the rate at which its future payments must be discounted to give its present value, for example, as in Equations (5.1) to (5.3), (5.21), and (5.22). This is equivalent to the demonstrations in Equation (5.23) and Exercise 5.6 that the payments on annuities are just sufficient to repay the loan at the rate of interest implied by the discount rate.

3. *Compound interest* is interest computed on the sum of an initial principal investment and accrued interest.

4. The *effective yield* on a security in which interest is paid more than once per period includes interest on interest during the period, for example, as shown in Equations (5.14) to (5.17).

5. The *rate of return* on an investment during some period is the change in its value as a proportion of its value at the beginning of the period.

6. Rates of return equal yields only under very special conditions, most simply when purchase and sale yields are the same and, in the case of annuities, when payments are invested at the purchase yield (as indicated in Relationships 5.1 to 5.3).

PROBLEMS

1. Suppose the best interest rate available to you is on a commercial bank savings account. The current 8 percent per annum rate on that account is expected to continue unchanged for at least 10 years. What would you pay for the following riskless securities: **(a)** a single-payment security that promises \$100 at the end of 1 year, **(b)** a single-payment security that promises \$100 after 10 years, and **(c)** an annuity that promises \$10 at the end of each of the next 10 years?

2. How long would it take to double your money at a yield of 7 percent per annum?

3. In 1797 Peter Thellusson, an English merchant, left a will directing that the income from his estate (worth about £600,000) be accumulated during the lives of his children, grandchildren, and great-grandchildren living at the time of his death and their immediate survivors. Assume that his youngest and longest-lived great-grandchild, born on the day of Thellusson's death, died at 70 and that the youngest and longest-lived child of that great-grandchild survived her mother by 30 years. What was the value of the estate when it was finally inherited? Also assume that the estate earned a steady 5 percent per annum rate of return after Thellusson's death. (Thellusson's will was held valid by the courts. However, to prevent such a disposition of property in the future, the Accumulations Act of 1800 provided that no property should be accumulated for any longer term than 21 years after the death of the settlor.)

4. Suppose you buy a 2-year single-payment security that promises $100 and yields 7 percent. What will be your annual rate of return on that investment if you sell it after 1 year at a yield of (a) 5 percent, (b) 7 percent, or (c) 9 percent?

5. What are the percentage changes in the prices of the following securities due to an increase in Y from 9 to 10 percent (use Tables C.1 and C.2): (a) a single-payment 20-year security, (b) a single-payment 5-year security, (c) a 20-year annuity, and (d) a 5-year annuity?

6. On the morning of October 1, 1985, the postal "service" finally delivers your income-tax refund. Resisting the Devil's temptations to blow it all on riotous living immediately, you decide to blow a greater amount on riotous living later and so buy a security that promises $100 on October 1, 1987, and yields 5 percent.

   (a) What will be your 1-year rate of return on this investment if the yield on 1-year securities is 1 percent on October 1, 1986?

   (b) What will be your rate of return between October 1, 1986, and October 1, 1987, under the conditions stated in (a) if you hold the security until maturity?

   (c) What is your average annual rate of return during these 2 years?

7. Explain how your answers to problems 4 and 6 have illustrated Relationships 5.1 and 5.2.

8. Do Exercise 5.3 for $n = 5$ and $m = 3$.

9. (a) Suppose the local S&L advertises an 8 percent simple annual yield, compounded quarterly. What is the effective annual yield?

   (b) What is the effective annual yield if the simple yield is compounded continuously?

10. Do Exercise 5.5 when Y is 8 percent instead of 12 percent.

11. Derive in three different ways—using Equations (5.21) and (5.24) and Table C.2—the price of a $100 three-period annuity yielding 10 percent.

12. Show that the payments on a $100 three-period annuity are just sufficient to repay a loan equal to the present value of that annuity when the yield is 10 percent.
13. What are the rates of return on an investment in a 50-year annuity bought at 5 percent and sold a year later at yields of 1, 5, and 10 percent?
14. Do Exercise 5.7(b) when the purchase yield is 10 percent and the yield after 1 year is 5 percent.
15. Do Exercise 5.8(b) when the purchase yield is 10 percent and all yields thereafter are 5 percent.

APPENDIX
5.A
THE CONTINUOUS RATE OF INTEREST

This appendix derives Equation (5.20), which states the value of an investment when interest is compounded continuously. We begin with the definition of the base of natural logarithms as the limit

(5.A.1)
$$e = \lim_{m \to \infty} \left(1 + \frac{1}{m}\right)^m = 2.71828 \ldots$$

The value of an investment after n periods when interest Y is compounded a times per period was seen from Equation (5.18) to be

(5.A.2)
$$V_n = V_0 \left(1 + \frac{Y}{a}\right)^{an} = V_0 \left[\left(1 + \frac{Y}{a}\right)^{a/Y}\right]^{Yn}$$

If we let $m = a/Y$, then

(5.A.3)
$$\lim_{m \to \infty} V_n = \lim_{m \to \infty} V_0 \left[\left(1 + \frac{1}{m}\right)^m\right]^{Yn} = V_0 e^{Yn}$$

so that Equation (5.20) is seen to be a limit.

THE VALUATION OF FIXED-INCOME SECURITIES

*Creditors are a superstitious sect, great observers
of set days and times.*

Benjamin Franklin, *Poor Richard's Almanack*, 1757

The relations between prices and yields defined in Chapter 5 are correct for the purposes for which they were designed. But they must be modified for use in the financial markets. The present chapter shows how traders have adapted the standard equations of Chapter 5 to their needs—to the daily calculation of prices, yields, and discount rates. Those who wish to read the financial press with understanding must be familiar with the relationships presented below.

The first section shows the extent to which market participants use the concepts of Chapter 5 in calculating and quoting the prices and yields of single-payment securities. The next section shows the connection between the prices and yields of bonds, which are combinations of single-payment securities and annuities. The main reason for the differences between Chapters 5 and 6 is that securities are priced and their yields are calculated every business day whereas the expressions in Chapter 5 do not take account of fractional interest periods. For example consider a 10-year bond that pays interest twice a year. The standard textbook equations define the price-yield relation for this bond on only twenty dates, that is, with $20, 19, 18, \ldots,$ 1 full 6-month interest periods to go until maturity. Even a stopped clock is right twice a day. But the standard bond-valuation equations are right only twice a year.

The final section considers empirical relationships between yields and rates of return on short-term and long-term U.S. securities, with examples drawn from one of the most volatile years in the history of American financial markets.

TREASURY BILLS

Single-payment securities are often called *pure discount securities* because they are always (for yields greater than zero) sold at discounts from their *face values*. The face value of a security is the payment promised at maturity. Treasury bills (T bills) are probably the most important discount securities. The role of T bills in the money markets and the conditions under which they are issued and traded will be considered in detail in Chapter 8. For purposes of the present discussion it is sufficient to know that they are issued by the U.S. Treasury in maturities of 13, 26, and 52 weeks in denominations that are multiples of $5,000 but no smaller than $10,000. Since reported yields on short-term bills (those maturing in 6 months or less) are calculated differently from those on long-term bills, we shall discuss short and long bills under separate headings.

Short bills

T bill yields are not quoted by dealers or reported in the financial press precisely according to the procedures used in Chapter 5 but are expressed in terms of percentage discounts from face values. For example consider a 90-day bill currently selling for $98 per $100 face value. That is, the bill is selling at a 2 percent discount from its face value. Dealers quote this rate in simple annual terms (assuming 360-day years) so that the reported discount rate is 0.02 (360/90) = 8 percent.[1] This procedure is shown for dealer bid and asked discount rates in Relationships 6.1 and 6.2 in Table 6.1. Actual market rates are listed in Table 6.2. For example "representative"[2] dealers' bid and asked discounts in the afternoon of Thursday, August 11, 1983, for a bill maturing September 8, 1983, were 8.93 percent and 8.87 percent, respectively. A complete understanding of these quotations requires a knowledge of payment and delivery practices in the financial markets, which may be described in terms that are defined as follows:

> **DEFINITION 6.1.** The *trade date* is the date on which a transaction is agreed. The *settlement date* is the date on which a transaction is effected, that is, on which the seller delivers the security to the buyer and receives payment.[3] The Uniform Practice Code of the National Association of Securities Dealers provides that,

---

1 Dealer quotations are less than the true discount rates (yields to maturity) discussed in Chapter 5 for three reasons: (1) Dealers divide gains by face values instead of by prices. For example the true 90-day discount rate (Y) in the above case is such that $98 = 100/(1 + Y)$, or $Y = (100 - 98)/98 = 0.0204$, instead of 2 percent. (2) Dealers assume 360-day years. And (3) dealers ignore compounding. The "yields" reported in newspapers adjust for (1) and (2) but not for (3), as will be seen in Relationship 6.3 and Equation (6.2) below.

2 As selected by someone at the Federal Reserve Bank of New York and reported to the financial press.

3 Usually in "immediately available funds" or "federal funds" as described in the discussion of the Fed Wire in Chapter 4. For further details of settlement practices, see the *National Association of Securities Dealers Manual* or the discussion of the Uniform Practice Code in Leo Loll and Julian Buckley (1981, Chapter 11). Additional information regarding U.S. securities and their markets is given in Kenneth Garbade (1982) and the First Boston Corporation's *Handbook of Securities of the U.S. Government and Federal Agencies and Related Money Market Instruments* (published biennially).

Table 6.1 Relationships between Treasury Bill Prices and Their Quoted Discount Rates and Yields

Notation

P_b, P_a = dealer bid and asked prices per $100 face value

d_b, d_a = bid and asked discount rates quoted by dealers

D = number of days from *settlement*[a] to maturity

Y_s, Y_L = approximate yields to maturity on short (maturing in 6 months or less) and long (maturing in 6 months or more) bills reported in the financial press

$$s = \frac{D}{0.5(365)} = \frac{2D}{365} = \text{maturity of a short bill as a proportion of 6 months}^{b}$$

$$u = \frac{D - 0.5(365)}{0.5(365)} = \frac{2D}{365} - 1 = \begin{array}{l} \text{proportion of the interval between 6 months} \\ \text{and a year that a long bill will mature}^{b} \end{array}$$

Relationships

6.1 $\quad d_b = \dfrac{\$100 - P_b}{\$100} \times \dfrac{360}{D} \quad$ or $\quad P_b = \$100 \left(1 - \dfrac{Dd_b}{360}\right)$

6.2 $\quad d_a = \dfrac{\$100 - P_a}{\$100} \times \dfrac{360}{D} \quad$ or $\quad P_a = \$100 \left(1 - \dfrac{Dd_a}{360}\right)$

6.3[b] $\quad P_a = \dfrac{\$100}{1 + s\,\dfrac{Y_s}{2}} \quad$ or $\quad Y_s = \dfrac{\$100 - P_a}{P_a} \times \dfrac{365}{D} = \dfrac{365 d_a}{360 - D d_a}$

6.4[b] $\quad P_a = \dfrac{\$100}{\left(1 + \dfrac{Y_L}{2}\right)\left(1 + u\,\dfrac{Y_L}{2}\right)}$

a See Definition 6.1.

b Replace 365 by 366 when the 12 months following settlement include February 29. Notice that Relationships 6.3 and 6.4 are identical and that $Y_s = Y_L$ when maturity is exactly 6 months, that is, when $D = 0.5$ (365 or 366), so that $s = 1$ and $u = 0$.

---

unless otherwise specified, settlement for U.S. Treasury securities takes place *in the regular way* on the business day following the trade date. Regular-way settlement for corporate, municipal, and most federal-agency securities takes place on the fifth business day following the trade date. A *cash sale* is one in which settlement takes place on the trade date. *Skip-day settlement* is one that takes place 2 business days following the trade date.

Buyers and sellers alter these settlement practices to suit their convenience. In fact most transactions in U.S. securities and an increasing proportion of transactions in other securities are "for cash." However, the U.S. Treasury yields reported in the financial press have long been calculated on the assumption of skip-day settlement, and that is what we assume in most of the following discussion. For example, since the quotations for Thursday, August 11, in Table 6.2 assume settlement on Monday, August 15, we use a value of $D = 24$ in calculating the bid and asked prices of the bill maturing September 8.[4] Substituting 24 for D and the values of d_b and d_a from Table 6.2 into the right-hand expressions of Relationships 6.1 and 6.2 in Table 6.1 gives

(6.1)

$$P_b = \$100\left[1 - \frac{24(0.0893)}{360}\right] = \$99.4047$$

$$P_a = \$100\left[1 - \frac{24(0.0887)}{360}\right] = \$99.4087$$

If you had been paying attention on August 11, 1983, you could have bought a $1,000,000 T bill maturing on September 8 for the dealer's asked price of $994,087. If you had already owned the bill, the dealer would have taken it off your hands for $994,047—cash and security to be exchanged on August 15.

In addition to discount rates, newspapers also report simple annual yields based on dealers' asked prices, which are calculated for short bills according to Relationship 6.3 in Table 6.1. In the case of the 24-day bill quoted for settlement on August 15, 1983,

(6.2)
$$Y_s = \frac{\$100 - \$99.4087}{\$99.4087} \times \frac{366}{24} = 0.09071$$

which conforms to the value reported in Table 6.2 to the nearest basis point, that is, to the nearest one-hundredth of 1 percent. (Notice that the year beginning August 15, 1983, had 366 days.)

If a bill matures in exactly half a year so that $s = 1$, Relationship 6.3 reduces to a form precisely like that for the one-period single-payment security considered in Chapter 5 except that the yield per period (6 months) is now written $Y/2$. We know that the correct annual yield under these conditions must take compounding into account. For example consider a 6-month bill that sells for $95.24. Following market practice by referring to annual yields as Y and semiannual yields as $Y/2$, the 6-month yield on this bill is

(6.3)
$$\frac{Y}{2} = \frac{\$100 - \$95.24}{\$95.24} = 0.05$$

---

4 Table 6.3 may speed your calculation of D.

Table 6.2

Treasury Issues

* * *

Bonds, Notes & Bills

Thursday, August 11, 1983

Mid-afternoon Over-the-Counter quotations supplied by the Federal Reserve Bank of New York City.

Decimals in bid-and-asked and bid changes represent 32nds; 101.1 means 101 1/32. a-Plus 1/64. b-Yield to call date. d-Minus 1/64. n-Treasury notes.

U.S. TREASURY BONDS

Rate	Mat. Date		Bid	Asked	Bid Chg.	Yld.
9 1/4s,	1983	Aug n	99.31	100.3	+ .1	0.00
11 7/8s,	1983	Aug n	100	100.4	....	0.00
16 1/4s,	1983	Aug n	100.10	100.12	....	7.07
9 3/4s,	1983	Sep n	99.31	100.3	....	8.68
16s,	1983	Sep n	100.25	100.29	− .1	8.22
15 1/2s,	1983	Oct n	101.3	101.7	− .1	9.15
7s,	1983	Nov n	99.7	99.11	....	9.52
9 7/8s,	1983	Nov n	99.30	100.2	....	9.39
12 1/8s,	1983	Nov n	100.18	100.22	....	9.47
10 1/2s,	1983	Dec n	100.2	100.6	+ .1	9.85
13s,	1983	Dec n	100.29	101.1	− .1	9.98
15s,	1984	Jan n	102.1	102.5	− .2	10.03
7 1/4s,	1984	Feb n	98.15	98.19	+ .1	10.21
15 1/8s,	1984	Feb n	102.14	102.18	− .2	10.17
14 1/8s,	1984	Mar n	102.5	102.9	....	10.28
14 1/4s,	1984	Mar n	102.7	102.11	....	10.30
13 7/8s,	1984	Apr n	102.6	102.10	....	10.42
9 1/4s,	1984	May n	99	99.8	....	10.31
13 1/4s,	1984	May n	101.25	102.1	− .1	10.37
13 3/4s,	1984	May n	102.8	102.12	− .1	10.56
15 3/4s,	1984	May n	103.17	103.21	− .2	10.57
8 7/8s,	1984	Jun n	98.18	98.26	....	10.33
14 3/8s,	1984	Jun n	102.30	103.2	....	10.66
13 1/8s,	1984	Jul	102.1	102.5	− .2	10.70
6 3/8s,	1984	Aug	96.11	96.27	+ .2	9.77
7 1/4s,	1984	Aug n	96.30	97.6		10.28
11 5/8s,	1984	Aug n	100.21	100.25	+ .1	10.81
13 1/4s,	1984	Aug n	102.4	102.12	− .1	10.68
12 1/8s,	1984	Sep n	101.3	101.11	− .1	10.83
9 3/4s,	1984	Oct	98.18	98.22	....	10.93
9 7/8s,	1984	Nov n	98.18	98.22	....	10.99
14 3/8s,	1984	Nov n	103.19	103.23	− .3	11.11
16s,	1984	Nov n	105.15	105.19	− .3	11.10
9 3/8s,	1984	Dec n	97.24	97.28	− .1	11.08
14s,	1984	Dec n	103.16	103.24	− .2	10.99
9 1/4s,	1985	Jan n	97.15	97.23	+ .3	10.98
8s,	1985	Feb n	96.3	96.11	+ .5	10.71
9 5/8s,	1985	Feb n	97.27	97.31	+ .4	11.09
14 5/8s,	1985	Feb n	104.19	104.27	+ .2	11.04
9 5/8s,	1985	Mar	97.20	97.24	+ .2	11.17
13 3/8s,	1985	Mar n	103.1	103.9	+ .1	11.12
9 1/2s,	1985	Apr n	97.12	97.16	+ .3	11.14
3 1/4s,	1985	May	91.26	92.26	− .6	7.71
4 1/4s,	1975-85	May	92.12	93.12	− .3	8.39
9 7/8s,	1985	May n	97.25	97.27	+ .4	11.23
10 3/8s,	1985	May n	98.28	99.4	+ .6	10.94
14 1/8s,	1985	May n	104.11	104.15	+ .3	11.25
14 3/8s,	1985	May n	104.23	104.31	− .3	11.18
14s,	1985	Jun n	104.16	104.20	+ .4	11.20
10s,	1985	Jun n	97.27	97.31	+ .4	11.23
10 5/8s,	1985	Jul n	98.27	98.31	+ .5	11.23
8 1/4s,	1985	Aug n	94.30	95.6	+ .4	10.99
9 5/8s,	1985	Aug n	97.3	97.11	+ .3	11.14
13 1/8s,	1985	Aug n	103	103.8	+ .4	11.26
15 7/8s,	1985	Sep n	108.8	108.16	+ .2	11.27
9 3/4s,	1985	Nov n	96.26	97.2	+ .3	11.26
11 3/4s,	1985	Nov n	100.23	100.31	+ .3	11.25
14 1/8s,	1985	Dec n	105.16	105.24	+ .4	11.29
13 1/2s,	1986	Feb n	104.8	104.16	+ .6	11.39
9 7/8s,	1986	Feb n	96.22	96.26	+ .5	11.37
14s,	1986	Mar n	105.13	105.17	+ .2	11.50
7 7/8s,	1986	May n	91.25	91.29	+ .6	11.38
9 3/8s,	1986	May n	95.9	95.13	+ .6	11.37
13 3/4s,	1986	May n	104.24	105	+ .3	11.58
14 7/8s,	1986	Jun n	107.23	107.31	+ .4	11.54
8s,	1986	Aug n	91.14	91.22	+ .10	11.35
11 3/8s,	1986	Aug n	99.20	99.24	+ .10	11.48
12 1/4s,	1986	Sep n	101.17	101.21	+ .8	11.60
6 1/8s,	1986	Nov	90.8	92.8	+ .1	8.92
13 7/8s,	1986	Nov n	105.24	106	+ .7	11.61
16 1/8s,	1986	Nov n	111.22	111.30	+ .6	11.62
10s,	1986	Dec n	95.20	95.24	+ .7	11.56
9s,	1987	Feb n	92.19	92.27	+ .8	11.54
12 3/4s,	1987	Feb n	102.18	102.26	+ .9	11.75
10 1/4s,	1987	Mar n	95.22	95.26	+ .8	11.70
12s,	1987	May n	100.24	101	+ .8	11.66
14s,	1987	May n	106.7	106.15	+ .10	11.82
10 1/2s,	1987	Jun n	96.8	96.12	+ .10	11.69
13 3/4s,	1987	Aug n	105.18	105.26	+ .8	11.88
7 5/8s,	1987	Nov n	87	87.8	+ .8	11.50
12 5/8s,	1987	Nov n	102.7	102.15	+ .9	11.87
12 3/8s,	1988	Jan n	101.14	101.22	+ .10	11.87
10 1/8s,	1988	Feb n	94.2	94.10	+ .12	11.79
13 1/4s,	1988	Apr n	104.14	104.22	+ .10	11.91
8 1/4s,	1988	May n	87.20	87.28	+ .12	11.64
9 7/8s,	1988	May n	93.2	93.6	+ .10	11.79
14s,	1988	Jul n	107.6	107.14	+ .12	11.96
10 1/2s,	1988	Aug n	94.30	95.2	+ .12	11.83
15 3/8s,	1988	Oct n	112.4	112.12	+ .13	12.08
8 3/4s,	1988	Nov n	88.9	88.17	+ .11	11.74
14 5/8s,	1989	Jan n	109.20	109.28	+ .11	12.10
14 3/8s,	1989	Apr n	108.24	109	+ .9	12.13
9 1/4s,	1989	May n	89.12	89.20	+ .12	11.78
14 1/2s,	1989	Jul	109.17	109.25	+ .8	12.15
11 7/8s,	1989	Oct n	99.5	99.13	+ .12	12.01
10 3/4s,	1989	Nov n	94.19	94.27	+ .16	11.95
10 1/2s,	1990	Jan n	93.9	93.17	+ .17	11.97
3 1/2s,	1990	Feb	89.10	90.10	+ .4	5.28
10 1/2s,	1990	Apr n	93.3	93.7	+ .17	12.01
8 1/4s,	1990	May	83.20	83.28	+ .13	11.78
10 3/4s,	1990	Jul n	94.3	94.12	+ .14	11.97
10 3/4s,	1990	Aug n	93.28	94.4	+ .8	12.01
13s,	1990	Nov n	103.26	104.2	+ .15	12.14
14 1/2s,	1991	May n	110.28	111.4	+ .18	12.24
14 7/8s,	1991	Aug n	113	113.8	+ .17	12.23
14 1/4s,	1991	Nov n	109.31	110.7	+ .17	12.25
14 5/8s,	1992	Feb n	112.6	112.14	+ .16	12.23
13 3/4s,	1992	May n	107.24	108	+ 19	12.23
4 1/4s,	1987-92	Aug	90.15	91.15	+ .25	5.45
7 1/4s,	1992	Aug	75.2	75.18	+ .14	11.72
10 1/2s,	1992	Nov n	91.16	91.24	+ .16	12.00
4s,	1988-93	Feb	89.28	90.28	+ .8	5.22
6 3/4s,	1993	Feb	71.23	72.7	+ .8	11.66
7 7/8s,	1993	Feb	77.10	77.26	+ .17	11.82
10 7/8s,	1993	Feb n	93.24	94	+ .17	11.95
10 1/8s,	1993	May n	89.30	90.2	+ .28	11.87
7 1/2s,	1988-93	Aug	74.28	75.12	+ .4	11.75
8 5/8s,	1993	Aug	80.28	81.4	+ .17	11.91
11 7/8s,	1993	Aug n	99.3	99.7	+ .25	12.01
8 5/8s,	1993	Nov	80.19	80.27	+ .11	11.91
9s,	1994	Feb	82.16	82.24	+ .19	11.93
4 1/8s,	1989-94	May	89.22	90.22	+ .12	5.27
8 3/4s,	1994	Aug	80.20	80.28	+ .19	11.92
10 1/8s,	1994	Nov	88.25	89.1	+ .20	11.92
3s,	1995	Feb	89.16	90.16	+ .8	4.04
10 1/2s,	1995	Feb	90.13	90.21	+ .17	12.02
10 3/8s,	1995	May	89.14	89.22	+ .14	12.06
12 5/8s,	1995	May	103.2	103.10	+ .18	12.09
11 1/2s,	1995	Nov	96.8	96.16	+ 1	12.05
7s,	1993-98	May	66.28	67.12	+ .16	11.69
3 1/2s,	1998	Nov	90.4	91.4	+ .28	4.30
8 1/2s,	1994-99	May	75.22	76.6	+ .20	11.88
7 7/8s,	1995-00	Feb	70.27	71.3	+ .12	11.92
8 3/8s,	1995-00	Aug	73.29	74.5	+ .23	11.97
11 3/4s,	2001	Feb	96.16	96.24	+ .18	12.20
13 1/8s,	2001	May	106.14	106.22	+ .26	12.20
8s,	1996-01	Aug	70.29	71.5	+ .18	11.93
13 3/8s,	2001	Aug	108.13	108.21	+ .21	12.18
15 3/4s,	2001	Nov	125.20	125.28	+ .22	12.18
14 1/4s,	2002	Feb	114.28	115.4	+ .26	12.17
11 5/8s,	2002	Nov	95.30	96.6	+ .27	12.14
10 3/4s,	2003	Feb	89.26	90.2	+ .27	12.08
10 3/4s,	2003	May	89.26	90.2	+ .27	12.08
11 1/8s,	2003	Aug	92.14	92.22	+ .28	12.11
8 1/4s,	2000-05	May	72.16	72.24	+ .28	11.74
7 5/8s,	2002-07	Feb	67.18	67.26	+ .30	11.65
7 7/8s,	2002-07	Nov	69.9	69.17	+ .25	11.67
8 3/8s,	2003-08	Aug	72.21	72.29	+ .26	11.75
8 3/4s,	2003-08	Nov	74.30	75.6	+ .23	11.86
9 1/8s,	2004-09	May	77.28	78.4	+ .26	11.85
10 3/8s,	2004-09	Nov	87.7	87.15	+ .29	11.95
11 3/4s,	2005-10	Feb	97.7	97.15	+ .29	12.07
10s,	2005-10	May	84.16	84.24	+ .29	11.89
12 3/4s,	2005-10	Nov	104.8	104.16	+ .29	12.16
13 7/8s,	2006-11	May	112.22	112.30	+ .31	12.18
14s,	2006-11	Nov	113.29	114.5	+ .29	12.16
10 3/8s,	2007-12	Nov	87.19	87.27	+ 1	11.88
12s,	2008-13	Aug	99.29	100.1	+ 1.3	12.00

U.S. Treas. Bills

Mat. date	Bid (Discount)	Asked (Discount)	Yield
-1983-			
8-18	8.94	8.78	8.93
8-25	8.98	8.88	9.05
9- 1	8.92	8.86	9.05
9- 8	8.93	8.87	9.07
9-15	8.73	8.61	8.82
9-22	8.94	8.90	9.13
9-29	8.95	8.83	9.08
10- 6	9.24	9.18	9.46
10-13	9.30	9.22	9.52
10-20	9.36	9.28	9.60
10-27	9.44	9.38	9.72
11- 3	9.52	9.44	9.80
11-10	9.52	9.50	9.89
11-17	9.57	9.49	9.89
11-25	9.57	9.49	9.91
12- 1	9.59	9.49	9.93
12- 8	9.55	9.47	9.93
12-15	9.54	9.46	9.94
12-23	9.53	9.45	9.94
12-29	9.52	9.44	9.95
-1984-			
1- 5	9.49	9.43	9.96
1-12	9.51	9.43	9.96
1-19	9.56	9.48	10.05
1-26	9.61	9.53	10.13
2- 2	9.63	9.55	10.17
2- 9	9.67	9.63	10.28
2-23	9.70	9.62	10.28
3-22	9.70	9.62	10.30
4-19	9.73	9.65	10.37
5-17	9.75	9.67	10.44
6-14	9.78	9.70	10.52
7-12	9.79	9.71	10.59
8- 9	9.78	9.75	10.70

Source: *Wall Street Journal*, August 12, 1983.

Table 6.3   The Number of Each Day of the Year

Day of Mo.	Jan.	Feb.	Mar.	Apr.	May	Jun.	Jul.	Aug.	Sep.	Oct.	Nov.	Dec.
1	1	32	60	91	121	152	182	213	244	274	305	335
2	2	33	61	92	122	153	183	214	245	275	306	336
3	3	34	62	93	123	154	184	215	246	276	307	337
4	4	35	63	94	124	155	185	216	247	277	308	338
5	5	36	64	95	125	156	186	217	248	278	309	339
6	6	37	65	96	126	157	187	218	249	279	310	340
7	7	38	66	97	127	158	188	219	250	280	311	341
8	8	39	67	98	128	159	189	220	251	281	312	342
9	9	40	68	99	129	160	190	221	252	282	313	343
10	10	41	69	100	130	161	191	222	253	283	314	344
11	11	42	70	101	131	162	192	223	254	284	315	345
12	12	43	71	102	132	163	193	224	255	285	316	346
13	13	44	72	103	133	164	194	225	256	286	317	347
14	14	45	73	104	134	165	195	226	257	287	318	348
15	15	46	74	105	135	166	196	227	258	288	319	349
16	16	47	75	106	136	167	197	228	259	289	320	350
17	17	48	76	107	137	168	198	229	260	290	321	351
18	18	49	77	108	138	169	199	230	261	291	322	352
19	19	50	78	109	139	170	200	231	262	292	323	353
20	20	51	79	110	140	171	201	232	263	293	324	354
21	21	52	80	111	141	172	202	233	264	294	325	355
22	22	53	81	112	142	173	203	234	265	295	326	356
23	23	54	82	113	143	174	204	235	266	296	327	357
24	24	55	83	114	144	175	205	236	267	297	328	358
25	25	56	84	115	145	176	206	237	268	298	329	359
26	26	57	85	116	146	177	207	238	269	299	330	360
27	27	58	86	117	147	178	208	239	270	300	331	361
28	28	59	87	118	148	179	209	240	271	301	332	362
29	29	a	88	119	149	180	210	241	272	302	333	363
30	30		89	120	150	181	211	242	273	303	334	364
31	31		90		151		212	243		304		365

a In leap years, after February 28, add 1 to the tabulated number.

Source: *C.R.C. Standard Mathematical Tables*, Chemical Rubber Publishing, Cleveland, 1963, page 435.

and the annual yield is reported as 0.10 even though the annual yield from two successive investments on these terms is actually $(1.05)^2 - 1 = 0.1025$. The use of simple annual yields by dealers and newspapers means that reported yields are not comparable so that the investor must perform some calculations of her own in order to obtain meaningful comparisons between true (or "effective" or "compounded") yields. For example a 3-month bill with a reported (simple annual) yield of 10 percent has an effective (compounded annual) yield of $(1.025)^4 - 1 = 0.1038$, greater than the effective yield of 0.1025 on the

6-month bill in Equation (6.3), for which the reported yield is also 10 percent.[5]

Long bills

The Relationships 6.1 and 6.2 between prices and quoted discount rates apply to both long and short bills. But reported yields are calculated differently. Yields on long bills are calculated according to Relationship 6.4 in a manner similar to those on bonds with maturities exceeding 6 months and are called "bond-equivalent yields."[6] If a bill matures in exactly 1 year ($D = 365$) so that $u = 1$, 6.4 gives an exact statement of the semiannual yield. For example, if the dealers' asked price is \$90.70, the semiannual yield is found from Relationship 6.4 to be $Y_L/2 = 0.05$. As with the short bill in Equation (6.3), the effective annual yield here is $(1.05)^2 - 1 = 0.1025$, but again newspapers report the yield simply as 0.10. A further illustration of Relationship 6.4 is given in Exercise 6.1.

EXERCISE 6.1.   Derive the simple annual yield to maturity reported on August 11, 1983, for the bill maturing February 23, 1984. The procedure begins by using Relationship 6.2 to find

$$P_a = \$100 \left[1 - \frac{(192)(0.0962)}{360} \right] = \$94.8693$$

The next step uses Relationship 6.4. Since Y_L enters 6.4 in a quadratic fashion, we may solve for Y_L either by the quadratic formula or by iteration. It will help get us in shape for later sections of this chapter if we adopt the iterative procedure, which is merely a fancy name for trying different values of Y_L until we find the one that comes closest to satisfying the equation

$$P = \$94.8693 = \frac{\$100}{\left(1 + \dfrac{Y_L}{2}\right)\left(1 + u\,\dfrac{Y_L}{2}\right)}$$

where $u = 2(192)/366 - 1 = 3/61$.

Normally in iteration the most important step is the selection of the first trial Y_L. But in the present case we are given a strong hint: $Y_L = 0.1028$. Trying this value of Y_L, we get

---

5 For the further development of this point see Bruce Fielitz (1983). Also see the entries in Table 5.3 corresponding to the compounding of interest two and four times per annum when the simple annual yield is 10 percent.

6 We are grateful to Chris McCurdy of the Federal Reserve Bank of New York for supplying the yield formulas upon which the relationships in Tables 6.1 and 6.2 are based.

$$\frac{\$100}{(1.0514)(1 + 0.0514u)} = \$94.8715$$

Since this is above the actual price, $94.8693, we try the next higher value of Y_L, 0.1029, which gives

$$\frac{\$100}{(1.05145)(1 + 0.05145u)} = \$94.8667$$

Since these trial prices span the actual price and since the trial price corresponding to $Y_L = 0.1028$ is closer to the actual price, this is the simple annual yield chosen according to Relationship 6.4 and reported in Table 6.2.

TREASURY NOTES AND BONDS

Most notes and bonds promise two kinds of payment: an annuity and the "face," "par," or "maturity" value on the maturity date that marks the end of a security's life. The price (present value) of such a note or bond may be written

$$
P = \frac{C/2}{1 + \dfrac{Y}{2}} + \frac{C/2}{\left(1 + \dfrac{Y}{2}\right)^2} + \cdots + \frac{C/2}{\left(1 + \dfrac{Y}{2}\right)^n} + \frac{F}{\left(1 + \dfrac{Y}{2}\right)^n}
$$

(6.4)

$$
= \frac{C}{Y}\left[1 - \frac{1}{\left(1 + \dfrac{Y}{2}\right)^n}\right] + \frac{F}{\left(1 + \dfrac{Y}{2}\right)^n} = \frac{C}{Y} + \left(F - \frac{C}{Y}\right)\frac{1}{\left(1 + \dfrac{Y}{2}\right)^n}
$$

where n is the number of semiannual periods remaining in the life of the security, F is its face value, C is the annual coupon, $Y/2$ is the true compound semiannual yield to maturity, and Y is the simple annual yield reported in the financial press. Coupons are often called "interest," and these securities are referred to as "coupon" or "interest-bearing" issues. An example is shown in Figure 6.1.[7]

The coupons, prices, and yields of Treasury notes and bonds outstanding on August 11, 1983, are listed in Table 6.2 along with the

---

7 The note in Figure 6.1 is a *bearer security*, meaning that payments are made upon presentation of the coupons or the security by the bearer. Payments due to *registered securities* are automatically paid to the parties whose names appear on the face and have been recorded on the books of the issuer. Registered securities are more costly to trade and consequently often sell for lower prices because ownership changes must be reported and recorded. Bearer securities are easier to trade but harder to recover if lost.

The note in Figure 6.1 is also a *definitive security*, meaning that it is represented by a piece of paper. Most Treasury securities, including nearly all bills, are *book-entry securities*, that is, are represented only by computer entries.

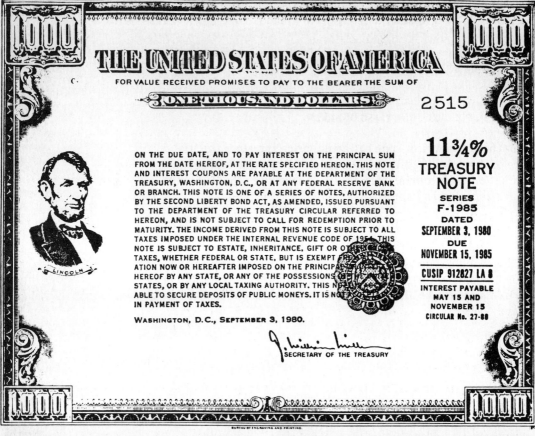

Figure 6.1

months in which they mature. Exact maturity dates are given in Table 6.4. The Treasury refers to its shorter-term (usually 10 years and less) coupon issues as notes and its longer-term coupon issues as bonds. Term to maturity is the only difference and we shall often include both notes and bonds under the heading of "bonds."[8]

Bond quotations differ from those on bills. Instead of making us calculate prices from discount rates, as in Table 6.1, dealers are nice enough to quote bond prices directly. For example the dealer bid and asked prices on August 11, 1983, for the 8 percent bonds of August 1996 to 2001 were $70^{29}/_{32}$ and $71^{5}/_{32}$ per $100 face value, respectively. This issue is "callable," which means that the Treasury has the option of calling (redeeming) these bonds at par on any coupon date beginning August 15, 1996. Yields are normally calculated to first call (8/15/96) when prices exceed par but to final maturity (8/15/01) when, as in this case, prices are less than par. The bonds in our example are called the "8s of 2001" and pay coupons of $4 per $100 face value each February 15 and August 15. The next-to-last column in Table 6.2 shows the change in the bid price from the day before. For example, the representative price bid by dealers in the midafternoon of August 10, 1983, for the 8s of 2001 was $70^{11}/_{32}$. The last column reports yields to maturity that are calculated almost, but not exactly, according to the procedures discussed in Chapter 5.

Bond yields on coupon dates

The yields in Table 6.2 have been calculated on the assumption that prices quoted on Thursday, August 11, 1983, were for delivery 2 business days later. Since August 15 is a coupon date for the 8s of 2001, the yield of 0.1193 was for thirty-six full semiannual coupon periods. All the price-yield relationships for annuities and bonds stated so far in this book, including Equation (6.4), have been restricted to full coupon periods. Price-yield relationships between coupon dates will be considered later. For now let us use Equation (6.4) to ascertain the relation between Y, on the one hand, and the value of P relative to F, on the other hand. We are interested in those yields for which bonds sell below, at, or above par on coupon dates. Dividing through by F, Equation (6.4) may be written as

(6.5)
$$\frac{P}{F} = \frac{C/F}{Y} + \left(1 - \frac{C/F}{Y}\right)\frac{1}{\left(1 + \frac{Y}{2}\right)^n}$$

---

8 Treasury bonds may have any maturity but since 1918 have been subject to a 4.25 interest (coupon rate) ceiling—except when Congress grants the Treasury special authority (which in recent years has become almost routine) to issue limited amounts without regard to the ceiling. Treasury notes are not subject to an interest ceiling but have a maximum maturity of 10 years (raised from 7 in 1976 and from 5 in 1967). (See the *Annual Report of the Secretary of the Treasury*, Washington, 1977, pages 275–276, and 1980, pages 368–369.)

Table 6.4   U.S. Treasury Notes and Bonds Outstanding on March 31, 1983

PUBLIC DEBT OPERATIONS

Table PDO-1. — Maturity Schedule of Interest-Bearing Marketable Public Debt Securities Other than Regular
Weekly and 52-Week Treasury Bills Outstanding, Mar. 31, 1983

[In millions of dollars. Source: Monthly Statement of the Public Debt of the United States,
and Office of Government Finance and Market Analysis in the Office of the Secretary]

Date of final maturity	Description	Issue date	Total	U.S. Gov't accounts and Federal Reserve banks	All other Investors	Date of final maturity	Description	Issue date	Total	U.S. Gov't accounts and Federal Reserve banks	All other Investors
1983						**1989**					
Apr. 1...	1-1/2%-EA Note	4/01/78	*	-	*	Jan. 15...	14-5/8%-C Note	1/13/82	3,508	13	3,495
Apr. 30...	14-1/2%-Q Note	4/30/81	4,586	342	4,244	Apr. 15...	14-3/8%-D Note	4/07/82	3,348	2	3,346
May 15...	7-7/8%-C Note	4/05/78	2,573	113	2,460	May 15...	9-1/4%-A Note	5/15/79	2,628	459	2,169
May 15...	11-5/8%-G Note	11/15/79	3,618	862	2,756	July 15...	14-1/2%-E Note	7/08/82	4,723	51	4,672
May 15...	15-5/8%-R Note	6/01/81	4,763	525	4,238	Oct. 15...	11-7/8%-F Note	9/29/82	4,237	n.a.	n.a.
June15,78-83	3-1/4% Bond	5/01/53	979	157	822	Nov. 15...	10-3/4%-B Note	11/15/79	5,779	1,942	3,837
June 30...	8-7/8%-E Note	7/02/79	3,123	426	2,697	Total.......			24,223	2,467	17,519
June 30...	14-5/8%-S Note	6/30/81	4,607	490	4,117	**1990**					
July 15...	15-7/8%-T Note	7/31/81	4,974	387	4,587	Jan. 15...	10-1/2%-C Note	1/04/83	4,842	n.a.	n.a.
Aug. 15...	11-7/8%-J Note	2/15/80	4,285	1,086	3,199	Feb. 15...	3-1/2% Bond	2/14/58	1,114	307	807
Aug. 15...	9-1/4%-K Note	5/15/80	6,670	3,214	3,456	May 15...	8-1/4% Bond	4/07/75	1,203	342	861
Aug. 31...	16-1/4%-U Note	8/31/81	5,431	643	4,788	Aug. 15...	10-3/4%-A Note	8/15/80	3,762	1,186	2,576
Sept. 30...	9-3/4%-F Note	10/10/79	2,802	284	2,518	Nov. 15...	13%-B Note	11/17/80	5,701	644	5,057
Sept. 30...	16%-Y Note	9/30/81	5,268	459	4,809	Total.......			16,622	2,479	9,301
Oct. 1...	1-1/2%-EO Note	10/01/78	1		1	**1991**					
Oct. 31...	15-1/2%-W Note	11/02/81	5,470	636	4,834	May 15...	14-1/2%-A Not	5/15/81	2,047	324	1,723
Nov. 15...	7%-8 Note	11/15/76	2,309	105	2,204	Aug. 15...	14-7/8%-B Note	8/17/81	2,812	456	2,356
Nov. 15...	9-7/8%-L Note	8/15/80	5,832	2,025	3,807	Nov. 15...	14-1/4%-C Note	11/16/81	2,886	405	2,481
Nov. 30...	12-1/8%-X Note	11/30/81	5,493	694	4,799	Total.......			7,745	1,185	6,560
Dec. 31...	10-1/2%-H Note	12/31/79	2,701	271	2,430	**1992**					
Dec. 31...	13%-Y Note	12/31/81	5,427	635	4,792	Feb. 15...	14-5/8%-A Note	2/16/82	2,813	182	2,631
Total.......			80,912	13,354	67,558	May 15...	13-3/4%-B Note	5/17/82	10,798	1,853	8,945
1984						Aug.15,87-92	4-1/4% Bond	8/15/62	2,003	1,056	947
Jan. 31...	15%-N Note	2/01/82	6,208	558	5,650	Aug. 15...	7-1/4% Bond	7/08/77	1,504	92	1,412
Feb. 15...	7-1/4%-A Note	2/15/77	8,438	3,913	4,525	Nov. 15...	10-1/2%-C Note	11/15/82	4,331	250	4,081
Feb. 29...	15-1/8%-P Note	3/01/82	5,950	651	5,299	Total.......			21,449	3,433	18,016
Mar. 31...	14-1/4%-D Note	3/31/80	2,914	573	2,341	**1993**					
Mar. 31...	14-1/8%-Q Note	3/31/82	6,219	625	5,594	Feb. 15...	10-7/8%-A Note	2/15/83	5,171	650	4,521
Apr. 1...	1-1/2%-EA Note	4/01/79	*		*	Feb.15,88-93	4% Bond	1/17/63	111	42	69
Apr. 30...	13-7/8%-R Note	4/30/82	5,877	826	5,051	Feb. 15...	6-3/4% Bond	1/10/73	627	209	418
May 15...	9-1/4%-C Note	9/05/79	2,587	69	2,518	Feb. 15...	7-7/8% Bond	1/06/78	1,501	136	1,365
May 15...	13-1/4%-G Note	11/17/80	4,315	510	3,805	Aug.15,88-93	7-1/2% Bond	8/15/73	1,814	1,221	593
May 15...	15-3/4%-K Note	5/15/81	3,776	776	3,000	Aug. 15...	8-5/8% Bond	7/11/78	1,768	132	1,636
May 31...	13-3/4%-S Note	6/01/82	6,018	430	5,588	Aug. 15...	8-5/8% Bond	10/10/78	1,509	159	1,350
June 30...	8-7/8%-E Note	6/30/80	3,726	510	3,216	Total.......			12,501	2,549	9,952
June 30...	14-3/8%-T Note	6/30/82	6,232	837	5,395	**1994**					
July 31...	13-1/8%-U Note	8/02/82	7,177	1,152	6,025	Feb. 15...	9% Bond	1/11/79	3,010	97	2,913
Aug. 15...	6-3/8% Bond	8/15/72	2,171	1,205	966	May 15,89-94	4-1/8% Bond	4/18/63	670	330	340
Aug. 15...	7-1/4%-B Note	8/15/77	2,863	385	2,478	Aug. 15...	8-3/4% Bond	7/09/79	1,506	52	1,454
Aug. 15...	13-1/4%-J Note	2/17/81	4,662	860	3,802	Nov. 15...	10-1/8% Bond	10/18/79	1,502	49	1,453
Aug. 31...	11-5/8%-V Note	8/31/82	7,492	596	6,896	Total.......			6,688	528	6,160
Sept. 30...	12-1/8%-F Note	9/30/80	11,012	889	10,123	**1995**					
Oct. 31...	9-3/4%-X Note	11/01/82	7,890	478	7,412	Feb. 15...	3% Bond	2/15/55	255	57	198
Nov. 15...	16%-L Note	8/17/81	5,780	1,189	4,591	Feb. 15...	10-1/2% Bond	1/10/80	1,502	28	1,474
Nov. 15...	14-3/8%-M Note	11/16/81	6,213	1,087	5,126	Feb. 15...	12-5/8% Bond	4/08/80	1,503	330	1,173
Nov. 15...	9-7/8%-Y Note	11/30/82	7,571	437	7,134	May 15...	10-3/8% Bond	7/09/80	1,504	12	1,492
Dec. 31...	14%-H Note	12/31/80	3,620	309	3,311	Nov. 15...	11-1/2% Bond	10/14/80	1,482	32	1,450
Dec. 31...	9-3/8%-Z Note	12/31/82	8,009	600	7,409	Total.......			6,246	459	5,787
Total.......			136,720	19,465	117,255	**1998**					
1985						May 5,93-98	7% Bond	5/15/73	692	228	464
Jan. 31...	9-1/4%-Q Note	1/31/83	8,298	544	7,754	Nov. 15...	3-1/2% Bond	10/03/60	733	162	571
Feb. 15...	8%-A Note	2/15/78	4,203	1,448	2,755	Total.......			1,425	390	1,035
Feb. 15...	14-5/8%-L Note	2/16/82	5,888	355	5,533	**1999**					
Feb. 28...	9-5/8%-R Note	2/28/83	8,434	499	7,935	May 15,94-99	8-1/2% Bond	5/15/74	2,378	1,614	764
Mar. 31...	13-3/8%-G Note	3/31/81	3,786	389	3,397	**2000**					
Mar. 31...	9-5/8%-S Note	3/31/83	9,170	40	9,130	Feb.15,95-00	7-7/8% Bond	2/18/75	2,749	595	2,154
May 15...	14-3/8%-D Note	3/03/80	2,719	600	2,119	Aug.15,95-00	8-3/8% Bond	8/15/75	4,612	2,067	2,545
May 15...	10-3/8%-C Note	12/04/79	2,539	264	2,275	Total.......			7,361	2,662	4,699
May 15...	3-1/4% Bond	6/03/58	445	147	298	**2001**					
May 15...	14-1/8%-M Bond	5/17/82	6,952	1,627	5,325	Feb. 15...	11-3/4% Bond	1/12/81	1,501	n.a.	n.a.
May 15,75-85	4-1/4% Bond	4/05/60	708	268	440	May 15...	13-1/8% Bond	4/02/81	1,750	16	1,734
June 30...	14%-H Note	6/30/81	3,393	250	3,143	Aug.15,96-01	8% Bond	8/16/76	1,485	741	744
Aug. 15...	8-1/4%-B Note	8/15/78	4,837	1,624	3,213	Aug. 15...	13-3/8% Bond	7/02/81	1,753	44	1,709
Aug. 15...	9-5/8%-E Note	6/05/80	3,293	84	3,209	Nov. 15...	15-3/4% Bond	10/07/81	1,753	107	1,646
Aug. 15...	13-1/8%-N Note	8/16/82	7,487	1,400	6,087	Total.......			8,242	908	5,833
Sept. 30...	7-7/8%-J Note	9/30/81	3,961	385	3,576	**2002**					
Nov. 15...	11-3/4%-P Note	9/03/80	3,087	5	3,082	Feb. 15...	14-1/4% Bond	1/06/82	1,759	40	1,719
Nov. 15...	9-3/4%-P Note	11/15/82	6,986	600	6,386	Nov. 15...	11-5/8% Bond	9/29/82	2,753	n.a.	n.a.
Dec. 31...	11-1/4%-K Note	12/31/81	3,430	171	3,259	Total.......			4,512	40	1,719
Total.......			89,616	10,700	78,916	**2003**					
1986						Feb. 15...	10-3/4% Bond	1/04/83	3,007	n.a.	n.a.
Feb. 15...	13-1/2%-C Note	12/08/80	3,188	43	3,145	**2005**					
Feb. 15...	9-7/8%-L Note	2/15/83	8,107	1,100	7,007	May 15,00-05	8-1/4% Bond	5/15/75	4,224	2,156	2,068
Mar. 15...	14%-G Note	3/31/82	4,215	295	3,920	**2007**					
May 15...	13-3/4%-D Note	3/04/81	3,460	27	3,433	Feb.15,02-07	7-5/8% Bond	2/15/77	4,234	1,568	2,666
May 15...	7-7/8%-A Note	5/17/76	5,219	1,158	4,061	Nov.15,02-07	7-7/8% Bond	11/15/77	1,495	265	1,230
June 30...	14-7/8%-H Note	7/06/82	4,758	349	4,409	Total.......			5,729	1,833	3,896
Aug. 15...	8%-B Note	8/16/76	9,515	2,000	7,515	**2008**					
Sept. 30...	12-1/4%-J Note	9/30/82	5,813	100	5,713	Aug.15,03-08	8-3/8% Bond	8/15/78	2,103	749	1,354
Nov. 15...	16-1/8%-F Note	9/08/81	3,469	214	3,255	Nov.15,03-08	8-3/4% Bond	11/15/78	5,230	1,611	3,619
Nov. 15...	6-1/8% Note	11/15/71	1,196	864	332	Total.......			7,333	2,360	4,973
Nov. 15...	13-7/8%-E Note	6/03/81	3,206	22	3,184	**2009**					
Dec. 31...	10%-K Note	12/31/82	5,908	343	5,565	May 15,04-09	9-1/8% Bond	5/15/79	4,606	725	3,881
Total.......			58,054	6,515	51,539	Nov. 15,04-09	10-3/8% Bond	11/15/79	4,201	820	3,381
1987						Total.......			8,807	1,545	7,262
Feb. 15...	9%-B Note	2/15/79	6,238	1,659	4,579	**2010**					
Feb. 15...	12-3/4%-D Note	12/02/81	3,437	n.a.	n.a.	Feb.15,05-10	11-3/4% Bond	2/15/80	2,494	662	1,832
Mar. 15...	10-1/4%-H Note	3/31/83	6,522	300	6,222	May 15,05-10	10% Bond	5/15/80	2,987	1,070	1,917
May 15...	12%-C Note	2/15/80	2,472	498	1,974	Nov. 15,05-10	12-3/4% Bond	11/17/80	4,736	529	4,207
May 15...	14%-E Note	3/03/82	3,519	17	3,502	Total.......			10,217	2,261	7,956
Aug. 15...	13-3/4%-F Note	6/02/82	4,078	7	4,071	**2011**					
Nov. 15...	7-5/8%-A Note	11/15/77	2,387	616	1,771	May 15,06-11	13-7/8% Bond	5/15/81	4,609	821	3,788
Nov. 15...	12-5/8%-G Note	9/07/82	5,384	n.a.	n.a.	Nov.15,06-11	14% Bond	11/16/81	4,901	481	4,420
Total.......			34,037	3,097	22,119	Total.......			9,510	1,302	8,208
1988						**2012**					
Jan. 15...	12-3/8%-C Note	1/05/81	2,710	5	2,705	Nov.15,07-12	10-3/8% Bond	11/15/82	7,104	598	6,506
Feb. 15...	10-1/8%-G Note	12/02/82	5,040	n.a.	n.a.						
Apr. 15...	13-1/4%-D Note	4/06/81	2,972	142	2,830						
May 15...	9-7/8%-H Note	3/01/83	5,955	n.a.	n.a.						
May 15...	8-1/4%-A Note	5/15/78	4,148	1,754	2,394						
July 15...	14%-E Note	7/07/81	3,469	23	3,446						
Oct. 15...	15-3/8%-F Note	10/14/81	3,474	238	3,236						
Nov. 15...	8-3/4%-B Note	11/15/78	3,445	1,139	2,306						
Total.......			31,213	3,301	16,917						

* Less than $500,000.

Source: *Treasury Bulletin*, Spring 1983, Table PDO-1.

where C/F is the annual coupon rate and P/F is the bond's price as a proportion of its face value. For the 8s of 2001, C/F is always $8/100 = 0.08$. On August 11, 1983, the asked price as a proportion of face value was $(71^5/_{32})/100 = 0.7115625$. We see from Equation (6.5) that bonds sell at par when yields equal coupon rates. That is, if $C/F = Y$ so that $(C/F)/Y = 1$, then $P/F = 1$ and $P = F$.

But we can get more information than this from Equation (6.5). Among other things it tells us that

$$P \gtreqless F \qquad \text{as} \qquad \frac{C/F}{Y} + \left(1 - \frac{C/F}{Y}\right)\frac{1}{\left(1 + \dfrac{Y}{2}\right)^n} \gtreqless 1$$

or, subtracting $(C/F)/Y$ from both sides of the second expression,

$$P \gtreqless F \qquad \text{as} \qquad \left(1 - \frac{C/F}{Y}\right)\frac{1}{\left(1 + \dfrac{Y}{2}\right)^n} \gtreqless 1 - \frac{C/F}{Y}$$

If $Y > C/F$, the right-hand side of the second expression exceeds the left-hand side (for positive yields) and $P < F$. If $Y < C/F$, the right-hand side is less (more negative) than the left-hand side and $P > F$. As a check on our earlier result, we see that the two sides are equal (both are zero) when $Y = C/F$, in which case $P = F$. Summarizing, we have shown that

(6.6) $$P \gtreqless F \qquad \text{as} \qquad Y \lesseqgtr \frac{C}{F}$$

That is, on coupon dates bonds sell above, at, or below par as their yields are less than, equal to, or greater than their coupon rates. The prices in Table 6.5 are consistent with expression (6.6). That table lists prices and yields of an 8 percent bond for selected maturities. Notice that on all coupon dates (that is, for maturities of 6, 12, 18, . . . months) $P = F = \$100$ when $Y = C/F = 8$ percent. Furthermore, P exceeds $\$100$ when Y is less than 8 percent, and P is less than $\$100$ when Y exceeds 8 percent.

If the coupon, face value, maturity, and price of a bond are known, its yield may be calculated by any of the three methods shown below. We follow market practice by using asked prices and will illustrate the three methods by applying them to the 8s of 2001.

1. The first (and only exact) method of calculating bond prices uses Equation (6.4). Specifically, we try a variety of yields until we find the one that comes closest to satisfying that equation. But which Y do we try first? One approach is to begin with the approximation.

Table 6.5 Prices of 8 Percent Bonds for Selected Yields and Maturities

						Years–Months							
Yield	1–0	1–3	1–6	1–9	2–0	2–3	2–6	2–9	3–0	16–0	16–6	17–0	17–6	18–0
4.00	103.88	104.82	105.77	106.69	107.62	108.52	109.43	110.31	111.20	146.94	147.98	149.00	150.00	150.98
4.20	103.68	104.57	105.47	106.34	107.22	108.07	108.93	109.76	110.61	143.95	144.91	145.84	146.76	147.66
4.40	103.48	104.32	105.17	105.99	106.82	107.62	108.44	109.22	110.01	141.04	141.92	142.78	143.62	144.44
4.60	103.29	104.07	104.87	105.64	106.43	107.18	107.94	108.68	109.43	138.21	139.01	139.80	140.56	141.31
4.80	103.09	103.83	104.58	105.30	106.03	106.74	107.45	108.14	108.84	135.46	136.19	136.90	137.60	138.28
5.00	102.89	103.58	104.28	104.96	105.64	106.30	106.97	107.61	108.26	132.77	133.44	134.09	134.72	135.33
5.20	102.69	103.33	103.99	104.61	105.25	105.86	106.49	107.08	107.69	130.16	130.76	131.35	131.92	132.47
5.40	102.50	103.09	103.70	104.27	104.87	105.43	106.00	106.55	107.11	127.62	128.16	128.69	129.20	129.70
5.60	102.30	102.85	103.41	103.93	104.48	104.99	105.53	106.03	106.54	125.15	125.63	126.10	126.55	127.00
5.80	102.11	102.60	103.12	103.60	104.10	104.56	105.05	105.50	105.98	122.74	123.16	123.58	123.98	124.38
6.00	101.91	102.36	102.83	103.26	103.72	104.14	104.58	104.99	105.42	120.39	120.77	121.13	121.49	121.83
6.10	101.82	102.24	102.68	103.09	103.53	103.92	104.34	104.73	105.14	119.24	119.59	119.93	120.26	120.59
6.20	101.72	102.12	102.54	102.93	103.34	103.71	104.11	104.47	104.86	118.10	118.43	118.75	119.06	119.36
6.30	101.62	102.00	102.40	102.76	103.15	103.50	103.88	104.22	104.58	116.98	117.29	117.58	117.87	118.15
6.40	101.53	101.88	102.25	102.59	102.96	103.29	103.64	103.96	104.31	115.88	116.16	116.43	116.70	116.96
6.50	101.43	101.76	102.11	102.43	102.77	103.08	103.41	103.71	104.03	114.78	115.05	115.30	115.54	115.78
6.60	101.33	101.64	101.97	102.26	102.58	102.87	103.18	103.45	103.75	113.71	113.95	114.18	114.40	114.62
6.70	101.24	101.52	101.83	102.10	102.40	102.66	102.95	103.20	103.48	112.64	112.86	113.07	113.28	113.48
6.80	101.14	101.40	101.68	101.93	102.21	102.45	102.72	102.95	103.21	111.59	111.79	111.99	112.17	112.35
6.90	101.05	101.28	101.54	101.77	102.02	102.24	102.49	102.70	102.94	110.56	110.74	110.91	111.08	111.24
7.00	100.95	101.16	101.40	101.60	101.84	102.03	102.26	102.45	102.66	109.53	109.70	109.85	110.00	110.15
7.10	100.85	101.04	101.26	101.44	101.65	101.82	102.03	102.20	102.39	108.52	108.67	108.80	108.94	109.07
7.20	100.76	100.92	101.12	101.28	101.47	101.62	101.80	101.95	102.12	107.53	107.65	107.77	107.89	108.00
7.30	100.66	100.80	100.98	101.11	101.28	101.41	101.57	101.70	101.86	106.54	106.65	106.75	106.85	106.95
7.40	100.57	100.69	100.84	100.95	101.10	101.20	101.35	101.45	101.59	105.57	105.66	105.75	105.83	105.92
7.50	100.47	100.57	100.70	100.79	100.91	101.00	101.12	101.20	101.32	104.61	104.69	104.76	104.83	104.90
7.60	100.38	100.45	100.56	100.63	100.73	100.79	100.90	100.96	101.06	103.67	103.73	103.78	103.84	103.89
7.70	100.28	100.33	100.42	100.46	100.55	100.59	100.67	100.71	100.79	102.73	102.78	102.82	102.86	102.90
7.80	100.19	100.21	100.28	100.30	100.36	100.39	100.45	100.47	100.53	101.81	101.84	101.87	101.89	101.92
7.90	100.09	100.10	100.14	100.14	100.18	100.18	100.22	100.22	100.26	100.90	100.91	100.93	100.94	100.95
8.00	100.00	99.98	100.00	99.98	100.00	99.98	100.00	99.98	100.00	100.00	100.00	100.00	100.00	100.00
8.10	99.91	99.86	99.86	99.82	99.82	99.78	99.78	99.74	99.74	99.11	99.10	99.09	99.07	99.06
8.20	99.81	99.75	99.72	99.66	99.64	99.58	99.56	99.50	99.48	98.24	98.21	98.18	98.16	98.14
8.30	99.72	99.63	99.58	99.50	99.46	99.38	99.34	99.26	99.22	97.37	97.33	97.29	97.26	97.22
8.40	99.62	99.51	99.45	99.34	99.28	99.17	99.11	99.02	98.96	96.51	96.46	96.41	96.37	96.32
8.50	99.53	99.40	99.31	99.18	99.10	98.97	98.89	98.78	98.70	95.67	95.61	95.55	95.49	95.43
8.60	99.44	99.28	99.17	99.02	98.92	98.77	98.68	98.54	98.44	94.84	94.76	94.69	94.62	94.56
8.70	99.34	99.17	99.04	98.86	98.74	98.58	98.46	98.30	98.19	94.01	93.93	93.85	93.77	93.69
8.80	99.25	99.05	98.90	98.71	98.56	98.38	98.24	98.06	97.93	93.20	93.10	93.01	92.92	92.84
8.90	99.16	98.94	98.76	98.55	98.38	98.18	98.02	97.82	97.68	92.40	92.29	92.19	92.09	92.00
9.00	99.06	98.82	98.63	98.39	98.21	97.98	97.81	97.59	97.42	91.61	91.49	91.38	91.27	91.17
9.10	98.97	98.71	98.49	98.23	98.03	97.78	97.59	97.35	97.17	90.82	90.70	90.57	90.46	90.35
9.20	98.88	98.59	98.35	98.08	97.85	97.59	97.37	97.12	96.92	90.05	89.91	89.78	89.66	89.54
9.30	98.79	98.48	98.22	97.92	97.68	97.39	97.16	96.89	96.66	89.29	89.14	89.00	88.87	88.74
9.40	98.69	98.36	98.08	97.77	97.50	97.20	96.94	96.65	96.41	88.53	88.38	88.23	88.09	87.96
9.50	98.60	98.25	97.95	97.61	97.33	97.00	96.73	96.42	96.16	87.79	87.62	87.47	87.32	87.18
9.60	98.51	98.13	97.81	97.45	97.15	96.81	96.52	96.19	95.91	87.05	86.88	86.72	86.56	86.42
9.70	98.42	98.02	97.68	97.30	96.98	96.61	96.30	95.96	95.66	86.32	86.15	85.98	85.81	85.66
9.80	98.32	97.91	97.54	97.14	96.80	96.42	96.09	95.73	95.42	85.61	85.42	85.24	85.08	84.91
9.90	98.23	97.79	97.41	96.99	96.63	96.23	95.88	95.50	95.17	84.90	84.70	84.52	84.35	84.18
10.00	98.14	97.68	97.28	96.84	96.45	96.03	95.67	95.27	94.92	84.20	84.00	83.81	83.63	83.45
10.20	97.96	97.45	97.01	96.53	96.11	95.65	95.25	94.81	94.43	82.82	82.61	82.41	82.21	82.03
10.40	97.78	97.23	96.74	96.22	95.76	95.27	94.83	94.36	93.95	81.48	81.25	81.04	80.84	80.64
10.60	97.59	97.00	96.48	95.92	95.42	94.89	94.42	93.91	93.46	80.17	79.93	79.71	79.50	79.29
10.80	97.41	96.78	96.22	95.61	95.08	94.51	94.01	93.46	92.98	78.89	78.64	78.41	78.19	77.98
11.00	97.23	96.56	95.95	95.31	94.74	94.13	93.59	93.02	92.51	77.64	77.39	77.14	76.91	76.70
11.20	97.05	96.33	95.69	95.01	94.40	93.76	93.19	92.57	92.03	76.43	76.16	75.91	75.67	75.45
11.40	96.87	96.11	95.43	94.71	94.07	93.39	92.78	92.13	91.56	75.24	74.96	74.70	74.46	74.23
11.60	96.69	95.89	95.17	94.41	93.73	93.02	92.38	91.70	91.09	74.07	73.79	73.53	73.28	73.04
11.80	96.51	95.67	94.91	94.12	93.40	92.65	91.97	91.26	90.63	72.94	72.65	72.38	72.13	71.89
12.00	96.33	95.45	94.65	93.82	93.07	92.28	91.58	90.83	90.17	71.83	71.54	71.26	71.00	70.76

Source: Reproduced from *Bond Values Tables,* Publication No. 183, Financial Publishing Co., Boston, MA, 1981.

$$(6.7) \quad \frac{Y_a}{2} = \frac{(F - P)/n + C/2}{(F + P)/2} = \frac{(100 - 71.15625)/36 + 8/2}{(100 + 71.15625)/2} = 0.0561$$

The numerator is the simple average semiannual capital gain or loss plus the semiannual coupon; the denominator is the simple average investment (that is, value of the bond) from the date of purchase until maturity. The approximation is exact when bonds are selling at par, in which case $Y_a = Y = C/F$, but deteriorates as P diverges from F.

Pretending ignorance of the yield reported in Table 6.2, we plug $Y = 0.1122$ into Equation (6.4) to get

$$(6.8) \quad P = \frac{8}{0.1122} + \left(100 - \frac{8}{0.1122}\right) \frac{1}{(1.0561)^{36}} = 75.3236$$

Since this price exceeds the quoted price of 71.15625, we try higher yields until we find $P = 71.20575$ for $Y = 0.1192$ and $P = 71.14954$ for $Y = 0.1193$. The quoted price falls between these two calculated prices so that the correct yield lies between 0.1192 and 0.1193. Since 71.15625 lies closer to 71.14954 than to 71.20575, the correct yield to the nearest basis point is 0.1193, as reported in Table 6.2.

2. Bond tables provide another means by which yields may be calculated. Selections from the Financial Publishing Company's tables of prices and yields on 8 percent bonds are presented in Table 6.5. Looking at the column of prices for an 18-year bond, we see that, since the quoted price 71.15625 falls between 70.76 and 71.89, the yield lies between 0.1200 and 0.1180. Using straight-line interpolation and noting that 71.15625 is $0.39625/1.13 = 0.351$ of the distance between 70.76 and 71.89, we estimate Y as $0.1200 - 0.351(0.0020) = 0.119298$, or 0.1193 to the nearest basis point, which agrees with our first method. We will not always be so fortunate because interpolation often involves some error.

3. Finally, since the price of a bond is the sum of the present values of the face value and an annuity, we can use the present-value Tables C.1 and C.2. Letting $n = 36$, the number of semiannual periods to maturity, the bond's price when the semiannual yield is 5 percent ($Y = 0.10$) is $P = 100(0.17266) + 4(16.547) = 83.454$. When the semiannual yield is 6 percent ($Y = 0.12$), the bond's price is $P = 100(0.12274) + 4(14.621) = 70.758$. Interpolating, since the quoted price 71.15625 falls $0.39825/12.696 = 0.031$ of the distance between the two calculated prices, we estimate Y to be this proportion of the distance between 0.12 and 0.10, that is, to be $0.12 - 0.031(0.02) = 0.11938$, or 0.1194 to the nearest basis point. This misses the correct yield by one basis point.

Yields between coupon dates

Most transactions occur between coupon dates. At those times it is normal practice for "accrued interest to settlement" to be added to the cost of bonds. For example consider the purchase of some 13s of November 1990 on August 11, 1983, for settlement on August 15. We see in Table 6.4 that this issue matures on November 15 so that its coupons are paid on May 15 and November 15. There were $D_c = 184$ days (May 15 to November 15) in the coupon period during which the trade took place. The seller was entitled to that portion of the interest or coupon that had accrued between the last coupon date and settlement, that is, between May 15 and August 15, or $D_a = 92$ days. Since the coupon due on November 15 was $6.50 per $100 face value, the total cost of the note was

$$\$104.0625 + \frac{92}{184}\,(\$6.50) = \$107.3125$$

The relationship between the quoted prices and yields of Treasury notes and bonds with more than one coupon remaining is shown in Relationship 6.5 of Table 6.6. Notice that, when settlement occurs on coupon dates, so that $D_a = m = 0$, Relationship 6.5 reduces to Equation (6.5). Now let's examine the meaning of Relationship 6.5 between coupon dates. There are two differences between Relationship 6.5 and Equation (6.5): The $-m$ exponent takes account of the fact that the security's term to maturity is $n - m$ coupon periods, where m is the proportion of the current period that has expired, and the second term on the left-hand side of the relationship is the interest that has accrued by the settlement date and is added to the cost of the security. Exercises 6.2 and 6.3 apply Relationship 6.5 first to a simple hypothetical case and then to a more complicated actual case.

EXERCISE 6.2.   Consider an 8 percent bond that sells at a yield of 8 percent for delivery midway between coupon dates; that is, $C = 8$, $Y = C/F = 0.08$, and $m = 0.50$. Substituting these values into Relationship 6.5 gives

$$P + \frac{8}{2}(0.50) = \frac{100}{(1.04)^{-0.50}}\,(1 + 0)$$

or $P = 100(1.04)^{0.50} - 2 = 99.98$

This result checks with Table 6.5, which shows that 8 percent bonds yielding 8 percent midway between coupons (that is, with maturities of x years and 3 or 9 months) sell for $99.98 per $100 face value.

Table 6.6 Relationships between Quoted Treasury Bond Prices and Yields

Notation

P = dealer asked price
C = annual coupon
F = face value = 100
$Y/2$ = semiannual yield to maturity
D_c = number of days in coupon period in which settlement occurs
D_a = number of days accrued from beginning of coupon period to settlement
D_s = number of days from settlement to next coupon
n = number of coupons to be paid
$m = D_a/D_c$

The total cost of the security is $P + AC$, where

$$AC = \frac{C\,D_a}{2\,D_c} = \text{accrued interest}$$

Relationships

For issues with more than one coupon to be paid

6.5 $\quad P + \dfrac{C\,D_a}{2\,D_c} = \dfrac{100}{\left(1 + \dfrac{Y}{2}\right)^{-m}}\left[\dfrac{C/F}{Y} + \left(1 - \dfrac{C/F}{Y}\right)\dfrac{1}{\left(1 + \dfrac{Y}{2}\right)^{n}}\right]$

For issues with one coupon to be paid

6.6 $\quad P + \dfrac{C\,D_a}{2\,D_c} = \dfrac{F + \dfrac{C}{2}}{1 + \dfrac{Y\,D_s}{2\,D_c}}$ or $Y = \dfrac{\left(F + \dfrac{C}{2}\right) - \left(P + \dfrac{C\,D_a}{2\,D_c}\right)}{P + \dfrac{C\,D_a}{2\,D_c}} \times 2\dfrac{D_c}{D_s}$

Exercise 6.3 applies Relationship 6.5 to the 13s of November 1990.

EXERCISE 6.3. We want to find the simple annual yield prevailing on the 13s of November 1990 in the afternoon of August 11, 1983. Using the notation of Table 6.6, we know from Tables 6.2 and 6.4 that $P = 104.0625$, $C = 13$, $D_a/D_c = m = 0.50$, and $n = 15$. Therefore,

$P + AC = 107.3125$

$\qquad = 100\left(1 + \dfrac{Y}{2}\right)^{0.5}\left[\dfrac{0.13}{Y} + \dfrac{1}{\left(1 + \dfrac{Y}{2}\right)^{15}}\left(1 - \dfrac{0.13}{Y}\right)\right]$

Trying different values of Y, we find that

$$P + AC = 107.2718 \quad \text{for} \quad Y = 0.1214$$
$$= 107.3205 \quad \text{for} \quad = 0.1213$$

Since the actual $P + AC = 107.3125$, the correct simple annual yield to the nearest basis point is 12.13 percent. The newspaper's report of 12.14 percent is slightly erroneous (a common occurrence).

Yields with one coupon remaining

Relationship 6.5 shows how to calculate yields on Treasury bonds with two or more coupons remaining. A simpler formula for issues with only one coupon remaining is described by Relationship 6.6 at the bottom of Table 6.6. Notice the term $2D_c/D_s$ on the right-hand side of Relationship 6.6, which converts the yield for the period between settlement and maturity to the simple annual yield, Y, reported in the financial press. Relationship 6.6 is applied in Exercises 6.4 and 6.5 to two securities found in Table 6.2: first for a note with one full coupon period remaining until maturity and then for a note with maturity less than 6 months.

EXERCISE 6.4.   Consider the 7¼s of February 15, 1984. The price 98.59375 was quoted on August 11, 1983, for settlement on August 15 so that $D_a = 0$ and $D_c = D_s = 184$. Therefore, using Relationship 6.6,

$$Y = \frac{103.625 - 98.59375}{98.59375} \times 2 = 0.1021$$

which is the yield reported in Table 6.2.

EXERCISE 6.5.   The 16s of September 30, 1983, pay coupons on the last days of March and September. Therefore, when settlement is August 15, we have $D_c = 183$, $D_a = 137$, $D_s = 46$, and

$$Y = \frac{108 - \left(100.90625 + \dfrac{16}{2}\dfrac{137}{183}\right)}{106.89532} \times 2\frac{183}{46} = 0.0822$$

which is the yield reported in Table 6.2.

FLUCTUATIONS IN YIELDS, PRICES,
AND RATES OF RETURN
ON U.S. SECURITIES

By these forced expansions and contractions of the currency during the last three years, some of the most prudent and wealthy of our merchants and manufacturers have incurred that ruin which, in a more wholesome and natural state of the circulating medium, could befall only the reckless adventurer or gambler. Under such a state of things as has been described, calculations, based upon the most enlarged experience, afford no security against loss and failure. The trader learns the fate of his undertakings, not in the markets of the world, as influenced by the law of supply and demand, but in the acts of twenty-six irresponsible individuals [the Directors of the Bank of England] conducting a joint-stock banking association in the city of London.

> "Report from the Board of Directors of the Manchester Chamber of Commerce and Manufactures on the Effects of the Administration of the Bank of England on the Commercial and Manufacturing Interests of the Country," *Manchester Chronicle and Salford Standard,* December 28, 1839

An introduction: some empirical tendencies

The yields, prices, and rates of return that have been discussed in such a cold, abstract manner in Chapter 5 and this chapter are in fact the life of the financial markets. They are causes of excitement, anxiety, disappointment, and satisfaction—never more than in recent years. The 1970s and 1980s, particularly the period since October 1979, have been more than usually anxious for investors. But it has been a fascinating time for students of the financial markets because the following empirical tendencies have occurred with unusual force:

EMPIRICAL TENDENCY 6.1.   A given change in yield to maturity affects the prices and rates of return of long-term more than short-term securities.[9]

EMPIRICAL TENDENCY 6.2.   Short-term yields normally fluctuate more widely than long-term yields.

The third tendency is the net effect of the first two tendencies.

---

9 This statement is a simplification in two respects: First, it is generally true for rates of return only for short holding periods in which, for example, an increase in yield causes the price to fall but does not have time to contribute to increased reinvestment values. (The net result of these two effects of yield changes is considered in connection with "immunization" in Appendix 6.A.)

Second, the statement is generally true for prices only if term to maturity is replaced by duration (which is also discussed in Appendix 6.A) although duration and term to maturity tend to be closely related.

EMPIRICAL TENDENCY 6.3.   Although long-term yields tend to vary less than short-term yields, the greater sensitivity of long-term prices to yield changes normally dominates relative price movements. That is, the prices of long terms normally undergo much greater changes than the prices of short terms so that investors in long-term securities enjoy greater gains when yields fall and suffer greater losses when yields rise than do the holders of short-term securities.

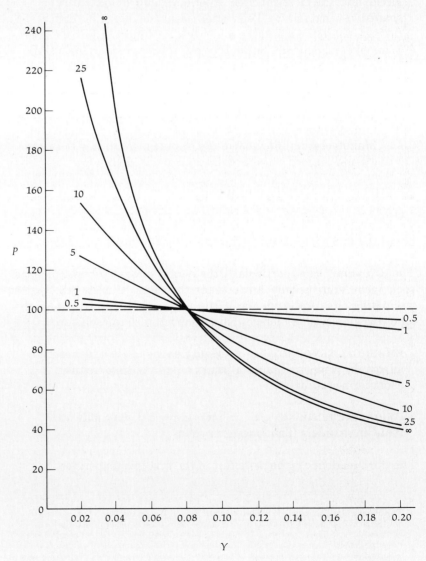

Figure 6.2   Yields to maturity and prices on 8 percent bonds of various terms to maturity (in years).

Table 6.7   Prices, Discount Rates, and Yields of Selected U.S. Securities on Selected Dates, 6/26/79 to 6/24/80

	52-Week Bill of 6/24/80			8% Note of 2/15/85			8% Bond of 8/15/96–01			13-Week Bills		
	Bid	Asked	Yield	Bid	Asked	Yield	Bid	Asked	Yield	Bid	Asked	Yield
1979												
											(9/20/79)	
6/26	(8.829)[a]		9.86	97	97.4	8.65	92.8	92.16	8.77	8.80	8.70	9.01
8/15	9.25	9.15	10.08	96.10	96.18	8.80	91.10	91.18	8.88	9.32	9.08	9.29
											(12/20/79)	
9/20	10.15	10.05	10.87	94.18	94.26	9.25	89.7	89.15	9.12	(10.353)[a]		10.78
10/ 5	10.44	10.32	11.15	93	93.22	9.54	86.28	87.4	9.39	10.60	10.42	10.79
10/ 9	11.36	11.16	12.12	91.26	92.2	9.94	84.22	84.30	9.67	11.68	11.44	11.90
11/16	11.76	11.60	12.56	89.11	89.15	10.68	79.18	80.2	10.31	11.64	11.06	11.32
											(3/20/80)	
12/20	11.62	11.50	12.42	90.16	90.24	10.36	81.13	81.29	10.07	(12.228)[a]		12.79
1980												
2/15	12.85	12.67	13.47	85.1	85.9	12.01	68.19	68.27	12.10	11.82	11.26	11.55
											(6/19/80)	
3/20	15.10	14.82	15.62	82.28	83.4	12.74	67.23	68.7	12.22	(15.049)[a]		15.86
3/24	16.03	15.49	16.31	80.22	80.30	13.44	64.24	65.8	12.78	15.93	15.81	16.65
6/19	7.62	7.00	7.10	96.27	97.3	8.78	85.26	86.10	9.52	—	—	—
6/24	—	—	—	96.13	96.21	8.91	84.16	85	9.68	—	—	—

a Average auction discount rates of bills.

Source: *Wall Street Journal.*

Empirical Tendency 6.1 is illustrated in Figure 6.2, which shows the sensitivity of bond prices to variations in yields between 2 and 20 percent. The six bonds in the figure include five 8 percent bonds with maturities ranging from 6 months (0.5 year) to 25 years and a perpetuity (∞) that pays $8 a year. Similar data for maturities from 1 to 18 years and yields from 4 to 12 percent are shown in Table 6.5.[10]

Several illustrations of Empirical Tendency 6.2 will be found in later chapters, especially in connection with the term structure of interest rates in Chapter 19.[11] All of these empirical tendencies were vividly illustrated by the events of 1979 and 1980 described below.

Some unfortunate examples, 1979 to 1980

SEVEN SECURITIES. Empirical Tendencies 6.1 to 6.3 are illustrated by a group of investment plans that are based on the securities for which selected bid and asked prices (discount rates for bills) and yields are reported in Table 6.7.

10 Empirical Tendency 6.1 was also illustrated for single-payment securities and annuities by Tables 5.2 and 5.4 and Exercise 5.1.

11 See Table 19.5 and the discussions of Figures 19.2, 19.3, and 19.5.

Table 6.8   Returns on Four Investment Plans, 6/26/79 to 6/24/80

	52-Week Bill			8s of 1985				8s of 1996 to 2001				13-Week Bills		
	P	V/V_0	R	P	C	V/V_0	R	P	C	V/V_0	R	P	V/V_0	R
1979														
6/26	(91.07)[a]	100		97.13[b]	2.90	100		92.50[b]	2.90	100		97.92[b]	100	
8/15	91.93	100.94	6.88	96.31	4.00	100.28	2.05	91.31	4.00	99.91	− 0.66	99.07	101.17	8.56
9/20	92.16	101.20	5.11	94.56	4.78	99.31	− 2.94	89.22	4.78	98.53	− 6.26	(97.38)[a]	102.12	9.02
10/ 5	92.37	101.43	5.18	93.00	5.11	98.08	− 6.96	86.88	5.11	96.43	−12.94	97.76	102.52	9.13
10/ 9	91.83	100.83	2.89	91.81	5.20	96.98	−10.53	84.69	5.20	94.22	−20.15	97.66	102.42	8.44
11/16	92.78	101.88	4.81	89.34	6.06	95.37	−11.85	79.56	6.06	89.75	−26.23	98.90	103.71	9.50
12/20	93.96	103.17	6.55	90.50	6.84	97.31	− 5.56	81.41	6.84	92.51	−15.49	(96.91)[a]	104.87	10.07
1980														
2/15	95.36	104.71	7.37	85.03	8.16	93.16	−10.70	68.59	8.16	80.45	−30.58	98.88	107.00	10.95
3/20	95.97	105.38	7.35	82.88	8.95	91.80	−11.20	67.72	8.95	80.37	−26.81	(96.20)[a]	108.22	11.23
3/24	95.90	105.30	7.13	80.69	9.04	89.70	−13.86	64.75	9.04	77.35	−30.48	96.15	108.16	10.98
6/19	99.89	109.68	9.87	96.84	11.31	108.12	8.28	85.81	11.31	101.80	1.84	99.90[c]	112.49	12.73
6/24	100	109.81	9.86	96.41	11.42	107.80	7.84	84.50	11.42	100.97	0.98	100	112.60	12.67

P = price to the nearest penny per \$100 face value
C = value of invested coupons to the nearest penny per \$100 face value (see Table 6.9)
V/V_0 = value of investment as a percentage of initial cost on June 26, 1979
R = simple annual rate of return, based on 366 days and assuming "cash" settlement

a Auction prices.

b Asked prices for the securities indicated.

c Asked price for the 52-week bill maturing 6/24/80.

Other prices are bid prices.
Sources: Tables 6.7 and 6.9.

    1. A 52-week T bill issued on 6/26/79 and maturing on 6/24/80. Discount rates in parentheses pertain to bills purchased on issue dates at average auction prices.[12]

    2. A U.S. note with coupon rate of 8 percent, paying coupons on February 15 and August 15 and maturing February 15, 1985.

    3. A U.S. 8 percent bond paying coupons on February 15 and August 15 and maturing August 15, 2001.

    4 to 7. Four 13-week T bills maturing on the parenthetical dates.

FOUR INVESTMENT PLANS. These securities are used in the following investment plans, whose fluctuating fortunes are described in Table 6.8:

    1. The simplest plan is the purchase of a 52-week bill on its date of issue (6/26/79), to be held until maturity (6/24/80). These dates bound both the period of our analysis and the life of this bill. The secondary-market (that is, nonauction) prices in Table 6.8, except those with a "b" superscript, are bid prices. In the case of bills the

---

12 Newly issued U.S. securities are sold by an auction procedure described in Chapter 8.

prices in Table 6.8 are derived from the quotations in Table 6.7, using Relationships 6.1 and 6.2 in Table 6.1. The V/V_0 column indicates the value of the investment (if sold) as a percentage of the initial investment. The R column shows the rate of return on the investment, converted to a simple annual basis, from 6/26/79 to the date indicated.[13] For example, the ratio of the 8/15/79 sale price of 91.93 to the 6/26/79 purchase price of 91.07 gives the value of the investment on 8/15/79 as a proportion of the initial cost: 91.93/91.07 = 100.94 percent. Conversion of the 0.94 percent rate of return over this 50-day period to a simple annual basis gives 0.94(366/50) = 6.88 percent. The last row shows that the bill was redeemed on its maturity date at par, the value of the investment increased 9.81 percent during the 364-day investment period, and the rate of return on an annual basis was 9.86 percent. Notice from Table 6.7 that the yield to maturity on the purchase date was also 9.86 percent, an equality that must hold because the bill was a single-payment security that was held to maturity.

2 and 3. The next two plans involve the purchase of the 8s of 1985 or the 8s of 1996 to 2001 on 6/26/79 at the dealer asked price plus accrued interest for delivery on the same day, investment of coupons in the 52-week bill discussed above, and sale of the bill investments and the note or bond at prevailing bid prices. The value of each of these plans as a proportion of the initial investment is shown for selected dates in Table 6.8. The total value of each investment is the sum of the security's bid price and coupon values. The columns headed by C show the accrual of coupons plus the value of investments of coupons in the 52-week bill. For example, on 8/15/79 the value of an investment in the 8s of 1985 was (96.31 + 4.00)/(97.13 + 2.90) = 100.28 percent of the original investment.

Table 6.9 gives a precise accounting of V for the 8s of 1985. As before, P denotes the asked or bid price of the bond. D_a/D_c is the proportion of time expired in the coupon period; for example, on 6/26/79, 131 of the 181 days between the 2/15/79 and 8/15/79 coupons had expired. This meant accrued interest of $AC = \$4(131/181) = \$2.90$, which was part of the investment cost on 6/26/79. The investor received a coupon on 8/15/79, which we have assumed to be invested immediately in the bill of 6/24/80.[14] We can use the last two columns to find that a \$4 bill investment on 8/15/79 at the asked price prevailing on that date had increased to \$4(93.96/92.02) = \$4.08 = IC(Aug) on 12/20/79. Columns 6 and 7 show for the coupon of 2/15/80 what columns 4 and 5 show for the coupon of 8/15/79. Column 8 gives the

---

13 We use 366 days because our period includes February 29. The yields in Table 6.7 are taken from newspapers and therefore assume skip-day settlement. But the value and return calculations in Tables 6.8 and 6.9 are based on cash settlement.

14 We assume the initial investment to be on a sufficiently large scale that the coupons can buy integer numbers of 52-week bills. All security prices and coupons are expressed as percentages of the face values of those securities.

Table 6.9   Calculations for Returns on the 8s of 1985

		(1)	(2)	(3)	(4) $\dfrac{p}{p(\text{Aug.})}$	(5) IC (Aug.)	(6) $\dfrac{p}{p(\text{Feb.})}$	(7) IC (Feb.)	(8)	(9)	(10) $\dfrac{p}{}$
		P	D_a/D_c	AC					V	Bid	Ask
1979											
	6/26	97.13[a]	131/181	2.90					100.03	(91.07)	
	8/15	96.31	1.00	4.00					100.31	91.93	92.02
	9/20	94.56	36/184	0.78	1.00	4.00			99.34	92.16	92.24
	10/ 5	93.00	51/184	1.11	1.00	4.00			98.11	92.37	92.46
	10/ 9	91.81	55/184	1.20	1.00	4.00			97.01	91.83	91.97
	11/16	89.34	93/184	2.02	1.01	4.04			95.40	92.78	92.88
	12/20	90.50	127/184	2.76	1.02	4.08			97.34	93.96	94.03
1980											
	2/15	85.03	1.00	4.00	1.04	4.16			93.19	95.36	95.42
	3/20	82.88	34/182	0.75	1.04	4.16	1.01	4.04	91.83	95.97	96.05
	3/24	80.69	38/182	0.84	1.04	4.16	1.01	4.04	89.73	95.90	96.04
	6/19	96.84	125/182	2.75	1.09	4.36	1.05	4.20	108.15	99.89	99.90
	6/24	96.41	130/182	2.86	1.09	4.36	1.05	4.20	107.83	(100)	

P = price of the 8s of 1985 to the nearest penny per \$100 face value
D_a/D_c = proportion of time expired in coupon period, assuming "cash" settlement
$AC = 4(D_a/D_c)$ = accrued interest
$p/p(\text{Aug.})$ = bid price of the 52-week bill as a proportion of its asked price on 8/15/79
$IC(\text{Aug.}) = 4[p/p(\text{Aug.})]$ = value of investment of the August coupon in the 52-week bill
$p/p(\text{Feb.})$ = bid price of the 52-week bill as a proportion of its asked price on 2/15/80
$IC(\text{Feb.}) = 4[p/p(\text{Feb.})]$ = value of investment of the February coupon in the 52-week bill
V = total value of the investment in the 8s of 1985 = $P + AC + IC(\text{Aug.}) + IC(\text{Feb.})$
p = bid and asked prices of the 52-week bill maturing 6/24/80; the numbers in parentheses indicate auction and redemption values

a The asked price; other prices are bid prices.

Source: Table 6.7.

total value of the investment, which is the sum of the price of the bond in column 1, accrued interest in column 3, and the values of coupon investments in bills in columns 5 and 7.

4. The final plan involves the purchase on 6/26/79 of the T bill maturing 9/20/79, reinvestments of the proceeds of this and successive 13-week bills at average auction prices on 9/20/79, 12/20/79, and 3/20/80, and finally the application of the accumulated value of the preceding bill investments to the purchase on 6/19/80 of the bill maturing 6/24/80. The value of this investment plan on 6/24/80 was

$$\$100 \times \frac{100}{97.38} \times \frac{100}{96.91} \times \frac{100}{96.20} \times \frac{100}{99.90} = \$110.26$$

The \$100 face value of the 9/20/79 bill was invested in the 12/20/79 bill, which cost \$97.38 per bill, enabling the investor to buy 100/97.38 = 1.0269 new bills. This process was repeated three times, finally giving the investor ownership of 1.1026 bills on 6/24/80. The end-of-period value of this plan was thus 110.26/97.92 = 112.60 percent of the initial investment, which means an annual return of 12.60(366/364) = 12.67 percent, as shown in Table 6.8.

INVESTMENT RETURNS. The fortunes of the four plans varied considerably. Yields had been rising since 1976 and the upward movement continued during the summer and early fall of 1979. Bill yields rose between one and two percentage points while long-term yields rose between one-half and a full percentage point between June 26 and October 5. Table 6.8 shows that investors in the 8s of 2001 lost more than 3.5 percent of their investments during this period, giving losses at a simple annual rate of 12.94 percent. Holders of the 1985 notes suffered less, purchasers of the long (52-week) bills were thankful for a positive—if small—return, and investors in short (13-week) bills were insufferable.

Then on Saturday, October 6, Chairman Paul Volcker of the Federal Reserve Board promised at a widely publicized news conference that he and his associates would start behaving themselves. In particular they would temper their inflationary policies by reducing the rate of growth of Fed credit in order to slow the rates of growth of bank credit and the money supply. The effect of this news on interest rates was dramatic. The markets were closed on Monday (Columbus Day), but on Tuesday the long-bill yield rose nearly a full percentage point above Friday's level (12.12 compared with 11.15), and the 8s of 2001 rose twenty-eight basis points to 9.67. The bid price of these bonds fell 2.5 percent (from 86.28 to 84.22, in thirty-seconds of a dollar; see Table 6.7) between Friday and Tuesday. The price of the long bill fell 0.58 percent (from 92.37 to 91.83; see Table 6.8).

These were large losses to have taken place between one business day and the next. But the sufferings of bondholders were not over. By the time yields stopped rising, on November 16, the bid price of the 22-year bond had fallen 8 percent from its October 5 level and 14 percent from that prevailing on June 26. An investor who had purchased this security on 10 percent margin during the summer would have seen his investment wiped out.[15] The reader with his own financial problems might not weep for these speculators, who would after all have made a killing if bond prices had risen as they had predicted. Nevertheless, investors should not be forced to operate under conditions such as these, whether they are speculators or widows and orphans in search of a reasonable and safe return. The world is sufficiently uncertain and interest rates are more than

---

15 Brokers commonly require 10 percent margin on long-term U.S. securities. That is, an investor is able to buy $100,000 worth of government securities with $10,000 of his own money and a $90,000 loan from his broker. Margin requirements and returns from investments on margin are discussed in Chapter 11.

sufficiently variable for the tastes of most people without the gyrations of an out-of-control central bank adding to their difficulties.

But they hadn't seen nothin' yet. After a period of stability between mid-November and mid-December, yields resumed their rise and, as they approached their peak, bond prices fell during the 4-day period March 20 to 24 even more than they had fallen between October 5 and October 9. The Fed had cut the annual rate of growth of the money supply in half between the third and fourth quarters of 1979, from 9.2 to 4.5 percent, and then, after a period of relaxation, monetary expansion was brought to a screeching halt in March and April. Investors unlucky enough to have bought 6-year or 22-year notes or bonds on 6/26/79 and held them until 3/24/80 would have suffered losses exceeding 13 and 30 percent at annual rates. (Please refer to Tables 6.7 to 6.9.)

Then yields fell nearly as precipitately as they had risen, probably because of the combined effects of recession and the resumption of early-1979 rates of monetary expansion by the Fed. Whatever the causes, bondholders now had something to cheer about although little cheering was reported in the financial press; for gains receive less publicity than losses. Bondholders had recouped their losses by June. But because long-term yields had not quite fallen back to the levels of a year before, long-term securities still did not perform so well as short-term investments during the 52 weeks between 6/26/79 and 6/24/80—as we see from the rates of return in the last line of Table 6.8.

CONCLUSION

The yield and return fluctuations reported in this chapter were due to a variety of causes. One of the most important of those causes, and certainly the one attracting the most attention from the financial press, was the vacillating behavior of the Fed. But other, less dramatic causes were also at work. The financial markets would probably be more stable in the absence of the Fed, but they would not be perfectly stable. Interest rates are also subject to disturbing influences from fluctuating spending and borrowing patterns of governments, firms, and, to a smaller extent, consumers. We hope that the student has developed sufficient interest in the concepts and events of Chapters 5 and 6 to want to learn how these influences interact to cause fluctuations in yields and rates of return. Much of this book is devoted to an investigation of these influences.

PROBLEMS

1. What were the bid and asked prices on August 11, 1983, of the T bill maturing September 29, 1983?
2. Confirm the yield of the bill maturing September 29, 1983, as reported in Table 6.2.

3. What was the simple annual yield on August 11, 1983, of the bill maturing January 12, 1984? (There is a small error in the yield reported in Table 6.2.)

4. Confirm the yield of the bill maturing February 23, 1984, as reported in Table 6.2.

5. What was the representative dealer bid price for the 14s of June 1985 in the midafternoon of August 10, 1983? For the 12s of August 2008 to 2013?

6. Using Equation (6.7), (a) calculate and (b) explain the approximate yield Y_a on the 8s of August 1986 on August 11, 1983.

7. Using methods 1, 2, and 3, calculate the yield on August 11, 1983, of the 8s of August 1986.

8. What is the price of a 10 percent bond that yields 10 percent midway between coupons?

9. What was the yield of the $9\frac{1}{4}$s of May 1984 on August 11, 1983? (The yield reported in Table 6.2 is incorrect.)

10. What was the yield of the 14s of July 1988 on August 11, 1983? (The yield reported in Table 6.2 is incorrect.)

11. You buy (a) a 1-year, 8 percent bond, (b) an 18-year, 8 percent bond, and (c) a perpetuity—all at yields of 8 percent. Now suppose the yields immediately rise to 10 percent. What proportion of each of these investments have you lost?

12. Calculate the simple annual rates of return for the periods and securities indicated (assume quotations are for cash settlement): (a) between 10/5/79 and 11/16/79 for the 52-week bill maturing 6/24/80, (b) between 11/16/79 and 2/15/80 for the 8s of 1985, (c) between 2/15/80 and 3/20/80 for the 8s of 1996 to 2001, (d) between 3/20/80 and 3/24/80 for the 13-week bill maturing 6/19/80.

13. The period 6/26/79 to 6/19/80 may be separated into four distinct subperiods of generally rising or falling yields: 6/26/79 to 11/16/79, 11/16/79 to 12/20/79, 12/20/79 to 3/24/80, and 3/24/80 to 6/19/80.

    (a) Identify the best investments, and calculate their rates of return during each of these subperiods. Given $100 on 6/26/79, how much would you have had on 6/19/80 if you had held the best investment during each of these subperiods?

    (b) Repeat (a) except substitute "worst" for "best." (Assume cash settlement.)

REFERENCES

Bruce D. Fielitz, "Calculating the Bond Equivalent Yield for T-bills," *Journal of Portfolio Management,* Spring 1983, pages 58–60.

Kenneth Garbade, *Securities Markets,* McGraw-Hill, New York, 1982.

Leo M. Loll and Julian G. Buckley, *The Over-the-counter Securities Markets,* 4th ed., Prentice-Hall, Englewood Cliffs, NJ, 1981.

6.A

DURATION AND IMMUNIZATION

Investors are interested in the effects of yield changes on security prices and rates of return. Except for a couple of footnotes the discussion in Chapters 5 and 6 presumed that the prices of securities with long terms to maturity are more sensitive to fluctuations in yields to maturity than are the prices of securities with shorter terms to maturity. This is always true of annuities and single-payment securities and is usually true of bonds. But not always. A generally correct statement is that the prices of long-*duration* securities are more sensitive to yield fluctuations than are the prices of those with shorter durations—where sensitivity is understood as the proportional change in price, and duration is a time-weighted average of a security's payments that will be defined precisely in the next section. The last section of this appendix shows how the concept of duration may be applied to portfolio *immunization*—by which is meant the selection of a portfolio with a rate of return that cannot be adversely affected by a change in yield .

DURATION

A definition and some examples

When two bonds are compared, one maturing in 20 years and the other maturing in 30 years, the latter is usually called the longer-term bond. This is true if we are thinking only of the time elapsed before the final payment is due. But it may not be true of the average length of time that we have to wait for our money, taking all of the payments (coupons and principal) into account. One measure of the average maturity of the future payments due to a bondholder is *duration*. Frederick Macaulay (1938, pages 44 to 51) introduced this concept in an effort to find a better summary measure of the time structure of a bond than term to maturity.[16] He defined the duration of an M-period security with face value F, coupon C, and yield to maturity Y, as follows:

$$(6.A.1) \qquad D_M = \frac{\displaystyle\sum_{t=1}^{M} \frac{tC}{(1 + Y)^t} + \frac{MF}{(1 + Y)^M}}{\displaystyle\sum_{t=1}^{M} \frac{C}{(1 + Y)^t} + \frac{F}{(1 + Y)^M}}$$

---

16 J. Hicks (1939, page 186) advanced the same concept shortly after Macaulay but called it "the *Average Period* of the stream" of payments; "for it is the *average length of time for which the various payments are deferred from the present, when the times of deferment are weighted by the discounted values of the payments*" (Hicks's emphasis).

Table 6.A.1   Durations of Two-period Bonds and a Three-period Annuity

Yield to Maturity	Two-Period Bonds Coupon Rates				Three-Period Annuity
	0.01	0.05	0.10	0.20	
0.0	1.9902	1.9545	1.9167	1.8571	2.0000
0.05	1.9897	1.9524	1.9129	1.8511	1.9675
0.10	1.9892	1.9502	1.9091	1.8451	1.9366
0.20	1.9883	1.9459	1.9016	1.8333	1.8791

Duration is the weighted average of the present values of the payments expressed as proportions of the price (total present value) of the security, where the weights are the numbers of time periods $(t = 1, 2, \ldots, M)$ before the payments are to be made.[17] For example, the duration of a two-period bond is

(6.A.2)

$$D_2 = \frac{\dfrac{(1)C}{1 + Y} + \dfrac{(2)C}{(1 + Y)^2} + \dfrac{(2)F}{(1 + Y)^2}}{\dfrac{C}{1 + Y} + \dfrac{C}{(1 + Y)^2} + \dfrac{F}{(1 + Y)^2}}$$

$$= \frac{\dfrac{C}{F}(1 + Y) + 2\left(\dfrac{C}{F} + 1\right)}{\dfrac{C}{F}(1 + Y) + \left(\dfrac{C}{F} + 1\right)}$$

Notice that $D_2 = 2$ when $C = 0$. The durations of single-payment securities are always the same as their terms to maturity. Duration falls as the coupon rate, C/F, rises because an increase in C relative to the final payment F means an increase in the relative size of early payments. This is illustrated for a two-period bond in Table 6.A.1, which shows, for example, that, if the yield to maturity is 5 percent, duration falls from $D_2 = 1.9897$ when $C/F = 0.01$ to $D_2 = 1.8511$ when $C/F = 0.20$.

For a given coupon rate duration declines as yield rises. This is because present values of payments in the distant future are reduced proportionally more by yield increases than are the present values of payments in the near future. This may be illustrated for a two-period,

17 The discussion in this appendix assumes coupons to be paid once per period. In the case of semiannual coupons Y is the semiannual yield, and $D_M/2$ is duration in years.

20 percent bond: When $Y = 0$, duration is

$$D_2 = \frac{20 + 2(120)}{20 + 120} = \frac{1}{7} + 2\frac{6}{7} = \frac{13}{7} = 1.8571$$

One-seventh of the total present value is paid at the end of one period, and six-sevenths is paid in two periods. On the other hand, when $Y = 0.20$, duration is

$$D_2 = \frac{\dfrac{20}{1.2} + \dfrac{2(120)}{(1.2)^2}}{\dfrac{20}{1.2} + \dfrac{120}{(1.2)^2}} = \frac{16.67 + 2(83.33)}{16.67 + 83.33} = \frac{1}{6} + 2\frac{5}{6} = \frac{11}{6} = 1.8333$$

A larger proportion (one-sixth) of total present value is now paid at the end of the first period. These results are listed in Table 6.A.1.

The duration of a three-period annuity is obtained from Equation (6.A.1) by letting $F = 0$ and $M = 3$:

$$\textbf{(6.A.3)} \qquad D_3 = \frac{\dfrac{(1)C}{1 + Y} + \dfrac{(2)C}{(1 + Y)^2} + \dfrac{(3)C}{(1 + Y)^3}}{\dfrac{C}{1 + Y} + \dfrac{C}{(1 + Y)^2} + \dfrac{C}{(1 + Y)^3}}$$

When $Y = 0$, $D_3 = (1 + 2 + 3)/3 = 2$. The duration of an M-period annuity is $D_M = (M + 1)/2$ when the yield is zero. As for the two-period bond discussed above, the duration of an annuity falls as Y rises. Some examples are shown in the last column of Table 6.A.1. Durations for different payment sizes, C, are not shown for the annuity in the table; as may be seen in Equation (6.A.3), C cancels out so that duration is independent of the size of the annuity as long as all of the payments are the same size.

We have shown that the duration of the two-period bond is inversely related to both yield and coupon rate.[18] The duration of the three-period annuity is also inversely related to yield, but in a more pronounced fashion because of the cubed terms in Equation (6.A.3) that do not appear in Equation (6.A.2).[19] This gives reason to suspect that there might be combinations of high yields and low coupon rates for which the duration of the two-period bond exceeds that of the three-period annuity; and this is indeed what we find when the

18 Some other properties of duration are the following: (1) for bonds priced at or above par D increases with maturity at a decreasing rate; (2) for a perpetuity $D = (1 + Y)/Y$; (3) for bonds selling below par duration increases with maturity up to a point and then declines. For statements of these and other properties, see Lawrence Fisher and Roman Weil (1971).

19 Compare the changes in duration in the last column of Table 6.A.1 with those in the other columns.

lower-left portion of Table 6.A.1 (demarcated by the dark line) is compared with the last column of that table. Securities with longer terms to maturity also usually have greater durations. But this is not always true, as the six examples in Table 6.A.1 demonstrate.

Duration is also a measure of the sensitivity of prices to yields

It can be shown that duration is equal to the negative of the elasticity of price with respect to $(1 + Y)$. Differentiating P, which is the denominator of Equation (6.A.1), with respect to $(1 + Y)$ gives

$$
\textbf{(6.A.4)} \quad \frac{dP}{d(1 + Y)} = - \sum_{t=1}^{M} \frac{tC(1 + Y)^{t-1}}{(1 + Y)^{2t}} - \frac{MF(1 + Y)^{M-1}}{(1 + Y)^{2M}}
$$

$$
= - \frac{1}{1 + Y} \left[\sum_{t=1}^{M} \frac{tC}{(1 + Y)^t} + \frac{MF}{(1 + Y)^M} \right]
$$

Multiplying Equation (6.A.4) by $-(1 + Y)/P$ gives

$$
-\frac{dP}{d(1 + Y)} \frac{1 + Y}{P} = - \frac{\dfrac{dP}{P}}{\dfrac{d(1 + Y)}{1 + Y}}
$$

$$
\textbf{(6.A.5)}
$$

$$
= \frac{\displaystyle\sum_{t=1}^{M} \frac{tC}{(1 + Y)^t} + \frac{MF}{(1 + Y)^M}}{\displaystyle\sum_{t=1}^{M} \frac{C}{(1 + Y)^t} + \frac{F}{(1 + Y)^M}} = D_M
$$

which is the definition of duration in Equation (6.A.1). Duration is thus seen to be minus the proportional change in P relative to the proportional change in $(1 + Y)$; that is, D is minus the elasticity of P with respect to $(1 + Y)$. Therefore we ought to say that the sensitivity of security prices to yields is a function not of maturity but of duration. This point is illustrated in Table 6.A.2. The columns headed P_3 and P_2 contain the prices of the three-period annuity and the two-period bond discussed above. The periodic payment by the annuity is assumed to be $36.72 so that its price is $100 when $Y = 0.05$ and proportional changes in P_3 may be easily compared with those in P_2. These changes are indicated in percentages by $\dot{P}_3$ and $\dot{P}_2$ in the table and are all negative because they correspond to *increases* in Y.[20] Equation (6.A.5) implies that, when two securities with different

---

20 For example, the value of $\dot{P}_2$ corresponding to an *increase* in Y from 0 to 0.01 is (107.88 − 110.00)/110.00 = −0.0193 = −1.93 percent. If we had shown percentage price changes in response to *decreases* in Y, all the entries in the last four columns would have been moved up one line and altered slightly. For example the value of $\dot{P}_2$ corresponding to a *decrease* in Y from 0.01 to 0 is (110.00 − 107.88)/107.88 = +1.97 percent.

Table 6.A.2   Durations and Price Changes of Long- and Short-term Securities

Y	P_{60}	P_{40}	P_3	P_2	D_{60}	D_{40}	D_3	D_2	$\dot{P}_{60}$	$\dot{P}_{40}$	$\dot{P}_3$	$\dot{P}_2$
0	340.00	140.00	110.16	110.00	39.18	34.43	2.000	1.955				
0.01	234.87	100.00	107.99	107.88	35.14	33.16	1.993	1.954	-30.92	-28.57	-1.97	-1.93
0.02	169.52	72.64	105.90	105.82	31.04	31.67	1.987	1.954	-27.82	-27.36	-1.94	-1.91
0.03	127.68	53.77	103.87	103.83	27.12	29.96	1.980	1.953	-24.68	-25.98	-1.92	-1.88
0.04	100.00	40.62	101.90	101.89	23.53	28.05	1.974	1.953	-21.68	-24.46	-1.90	-1.87
0.05	81.07	31.36	100.00	100.00	20.41	25.98	1.967	1.952	-18.93	-22.80	-1.86	-1.85
0.06	67.68	24.77	98.15	98.17	17.77	23.82	1.961	1.952	-16.52	-21.01	-1.85	-1.83
0.07	57.88	20.01	96.36	96.38	15.60	21.63	1.955	1.952	-14.48	-19.22	-1.82	-1.82
0.08	50.49	16.53	94.63	94.65	13.82	19.49	1.949	1.951	-12.77	-17.39	-1.80	-1.79
0.09	44.76	13.94	92.95	92.96	12.38	17.47	1.943	1.951	-11.35	-15.67	-1.78	-1.79
0.10	40.20	11.99	91.32	91.32	11.20	15.61	1.937	1.950	-10.19	-13.99	-1.75	-1.76

$P_{60}, D_{60}, \dot{P}_{60}$ = price, duration, and percentage change in price of a sixty-period, 4 percent bond
$P_{40}, D_{40}, \dot{P}_{40}$ = price, duration, and percentage change in price of a forty-period, 1 percent bond
$P_3, D_3, \dot{P}_3$ = price, duration, and percentage change in price of a three-period, $36.72 annuity
$P_2, D_2, \dot{P}_2$ = price, duration, and percentage change in price of a two-period, 5 percent bond
Y = yield to maturity

durations but the same yield undergo identical yield changes, the proportional price change will be greater for the security with the greater duration. For example the absolute value of $\dot{P}_2$ is less than that of $\dot{P}_3$ for low yields (when $D_2 < D_3$) but exceeds that of $\dot{P}_3$ for high yields (when $D_2 > D_3$). The same is true of a comparison of the forty- and sixty-period bonds except that D_{40} overtakes D_{60} much earlier than in the two- and three-period case. This relationship is depicted in Figure 6.A.1. In order that changes in the prices of these securities may be easily compared, we have multiplied P_{40} as shown in Table 6.A.2 by $100/40.62 = 2.4618$. This causes P_{60} and the adjusted P_{40} to be equal at $100 when $Y = 0.04$.[21] Percentage changes are not affected, and we see in the figure, as in the table, that the price of the shorter-term but lower-coupon bond falls proportionally more than that of the longer-term, higher-coupon bond as yield to maturity rises from 2 to 10 percent.[22]

A simpler expression and some special cases

The summations in Equations (6.A.1) and (6.A.5) may be taken[23] and rearranged to give

$$(6.A.6) \qquad D_M = \frac{1 + Y}{Y} - \frac{1 + Y + M(C/F - Y)}{(C/F)[(1 + Y)^M - 1] + Y}$$

---

21 This adjusted P_{40} would be the actual price of the forty-period security if the face value were $246.18 and the coupon continued to be 1 percent of the face value.

22 Other examples of the relations among coupon, yield, term to maturity, and duration are listed in Frederick Macaulay (1938, page 51) and Lawrence Fisher and Roman Weil (1971, Table 4).

23 Appendix A shows how to take the sum of a geometric series.

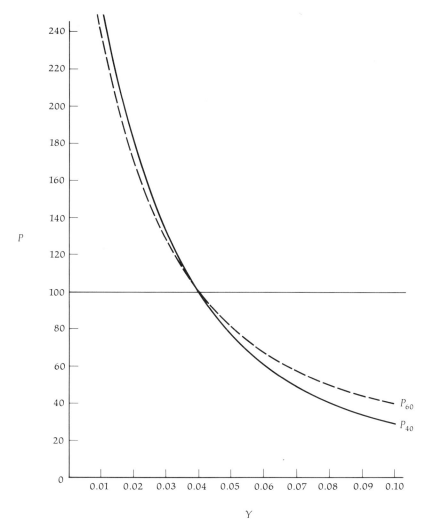

Figure 6.A.1   Yield sensitivities of the prices of a sixty-period, 4 percent bond and a forty-period, 1 percent bond.

The duration of an annuity is

(6.A.7)
$$D_M = \frac{1 + Y}{Y} - \frac{M}{(1 + Y)^M - 1}$$

Other special cases include

(6.A.8) $D_\infty \rightarrow \dfrac{1 + Y}{Y}$ for $M \rightarrow \infty$ (a perpetuity)

(6.A.9) $D_M = M$ for $C = 0$ (a single-payment security)

These and the other relations stated above will be found useful in the immunization problems presented below.

IMMUNIZATION
Immunized portfolios

Suppose an investor desires a portfolio for some holding period (H) that guarantees a rate of return (R) at least as large as the portfolio's yield to maturity (Y) at the beginning of the period. Such a portfolio is said to be *immunized*.

A bondholder's worries about yield movements may be summarized as follows: Suppose yields rise; the bad news is the fall in bond prices, and the good news is the rise in returns earned on coupons. On the other hand, if yields fall, bond prices rise (good news) and coupons are reinvested at lower rates (bad news). An immunized portfolio is one for which the good news at least offsets the bad news.

Necessary conditions for immunization

Unfortunately, immunized portfolios are possible only under very special conditions. This appendix presents an example of the simplest of those conditions. Specifically, we find an immunized portfolio when (1) the yield curve is flat[24] at the beginning of the holding period and (2) the investor has no idea which way yields will move in the future but is sure that (3) any movement will occur immediately (or at least before the first coupon is received), (4) there will be only one movement during the holding period, and (5) the movement will take the form of a parallel shift to another flat yield curve.

The duration of an immunized portfolio equals the holding period

We shall show that immunization can be achieved under the above conditions by choosing a portfolio consisting of a single bond with duration (D) equal to the holding period; that is, $D = H$. For a flat and constant yield curve at level Y, the value after H periods of the reinvestment of coupons from a bond is

(6.A.10)

$$C(Y, H) = C (1 + Y)^{H-1}$$
$$+ C(1 + Y)^{H-2} + \cdots + C(1 + Y)$$
$$+ C = \frac{C}{Y} [(1 + Y)^H - 1]$$

For example, if $H = 10$, the first coupon, which is received after one period, accumulates interest for nine periods, the second coupon for eight periods, and finally, the last coupon is received at the end of the holding period.

---

24 A flat yield curve is one for which all yields are the same.

If we buy an M-period bond with face value $F = 1$, its price after H periods is[25]

(6.A.11) $P(Y, H) = \dfrac{C}{Y}\left[1 - \dfrac{1}{(1 + Y)^{M-H}}\right] + \dfrac{1}{(1 + Y)^{M-H}}$

The value of this investment after H periods is thus

(6.A.12)

$$V(Y, H) = C(Y, H) + P(Y, H)$$

$$= \frac{C}{Y}(1 + Y)^H + \frac{1}{(1 + Y)^{M-H}}\left(1 - \frac{C}{Y}\right)$$

We are looking for an immunized bond, that is, a bond for which a change in Y does not reduce $V(Y, H)$. This means that the return on the bond investment takes its minimum value at the current Y. Such a bond satisfies the condition

(6.A.13)

$$\frac{\partial V(Y, H)}{\partial Y} = 0 = \frac{C}{Y} H (1 + Y)^{H-1} - \frac{C}{Y^2} (1 + Y)^H$$

$$+ \frac{1}{(1 + Y)^{M-H}}\frac{C}{Y^2} - \frac{(M - H)}{(1 + Y)^{M-H+1}}\left(1 - \frac{C}{Y}\right)$$

Solving Equation (6.A.13) for H gives

(6.A.14) $H = \dfrac{1 + Y}{Y} - \dfrac{1 + Y + M(C - Y)}{C[(1 + Y)^M - 1] + Y}$

But this is the definition of duration in Equation (6.A.6) for $F = 1$. That is, an immunized portfolio under the five conditions stated above is one for which duration equals the investor's holding period. We have chosen a particularly simple portfolio—one bond—to illustrate this result.

Examples of immunized and unimmunized investments when $H = 7$ and $Y = 0.04$

Table 6.A.3 presents the outcomes of five investments for a holding period of $H = 7$ and beginning yields of $Y = 0.04$ when yields (1) remain unchanged, (2) immediately rise to and then remain at 0.06, or (3) immediately fall to and then remain at 0.02.[26] Equation (6.A.14) tells us that, if the goal is immunization and our holding period is 7, we should choose a security or a portfolio of securities with duration of 7. There is an infinity of portfolios with $D = 7$, and we have chosen two

25 See Equation (6.4).

26 A similar table is presented in G. Bierwag, G. Kaufman, Robert Schweitzer, and Alden Toevs (1981).

Table 6.A.3   Effects of Changes in Y on Five Investment Strategies

Given: Flat Yield Curve, $Y = 0.04$; Holding Period, $H = 7$; Face Values, $F = \$100$	Rollover of One-Period Securities[a]	A Seven-Period, 4% Bond	A Seven-Period, Single-Payment Security	An Eight-Period, 4% Bond	A Perpetuity That Pays $4 Per Period
Maturity	1	7	7	8	∞
Coupon rate[b]	0	4%	0	4%	$4
Duration	1	6.2	7	7	26
Beginning price	$96.15	$100	$75.99	$100	$100
1. No Change in Y					
Price after seven periods	$126.53	$100	$100	$100	$100
Reinvestment of coupons[c]	—	$31.59	—	$31.59	$31.59
Total value of investment	$126.53	$131.59	$100	$131.59	$131.59
Rate of return[d]	4%	4%	4%	4%	4%
2. Immediate Rise to Y = 0.06					
Price after seven periods	$141.85	$100	$100	$98.11	$66.67
Reinvestment of coupons[c]	—	$33.58	—	$33.58	$33.58
Total value of investment	$141.85	$133.58	$100	$131.69	$100.25
Rate of return[d]	5.71%	4.22%	4%	4.01%	0.04%
3. Immediate Fall to Y = 0.02					
Price after seven periods	$112.62	$100	$100	$101.96	$200.00
Reinvestment of coupons[c]	—	$29.74	—	$29.74	$29.74
Total value of investment	$112.62	$129.74	$100	$131.70	$229.74
Rate of return[d]	2.28%	3.79%	4%	4.01%	12.62%

a The face value of the original purchase is $100, which is reinvested in another one-period security with face value of $100(1 + Y), and so on.

b Since $F = \$100$, all the coupon securities pay coupons of $4 per period.

c Calculated from Equation (6.A.10).

d Rate of return = (total value of investment/beginning price)$^{1/7}$ − 1.

one-security examples that apply when $Y = 0.04$. They are a seven-period, single-payment security and an eight-period, 4 percent coupon bond. We have also chosen two investments with durations less than 7: a series of one-period securities (that is, with $D = 1$) and a seven-period, 4 percent bond with $D = 6.2$. Finally, we have chosen a consol, with $D = 26$ when $Y = 0.04$.

Part 1 of Table 6.A.3 shows that all five investments earn 4 percent per period when yields remain unchanged at 4 percent. Parts 2 and 3 show that the two investments with $D < H = 7$ earn more than 4 percent when yields rise but earn less than 4 percent when yields fall, while the investment with $D > H$ earns less than 4 percent when yields rise but more than 4 percent when yields fall.

For long-term securities, which in the present context have a precise

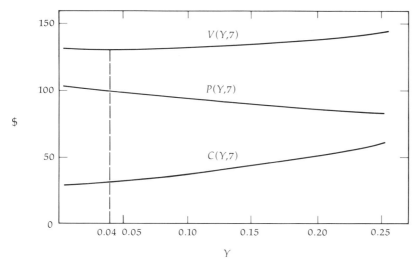

Figure 6.A.2   Value of an investment in an eight-period, 4 percent bond for seven periods (face value = $100).

meaning, that is, they have duration longer than the holding period, capital gains and losses due to yield changes dominate changes in the reinvestment values of coupons. The reverse is true of short-term securities, that is, for which $D < H$.

Now consider the two investments with $D = H$. First, the seven-period, single-payment security earns 4 percent during the holding period of the same length no matter what happens to yields. Second, the eight-period, 4 percent bond with $D = 7$ earns slightly more than 4 percent no matter whether yields rise or fall. Parts 2 and 3 of the table show a rate of return of 4.01 percent for this bond both when Y rises to 6 percent and when Y falls to 2 percent.

More information about the eight-period, 4 percent bond is provided in Figure 6.A.2, which shows that the value after seven periods of an investment in this bond is smallest when Y remains unchanged at 4 percent and rises as Y departs from 4 percent in either direction.

Examples of immunized and unimmunized investments when $H = 7$ and $Y = 1/6$

Figure 6.A.3 shows how the value of a consol investment responds to yield changes, rising as Y falls from 4 percent but falling as Y rises above 4 percent, as indicated in Table 6.A.3. But suppose Y had been 1/6 (about 16.67 percent) at the beginning of the holding period. Then, from Equations (6.A.6) and (6.A.8), the duration of the eight-period, 4 percent bond would have been 6.42 and the duration of the consol would have been 7. That is, for $H = 7$ and $Y = 1/6$, the consol is an immunized investment. This is confirmed by Figure 6.A.3, which shows the value of the consol investment to be at a minimum when $Y = 1/6$ and to rise as Y departs from 1/6 in either direction. On the

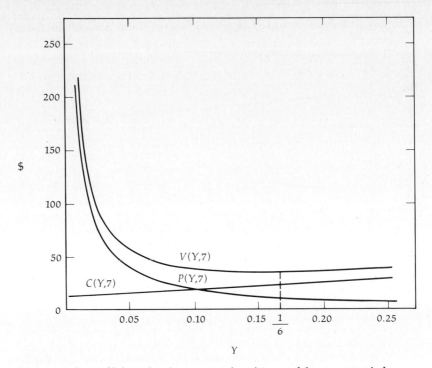

Figure 6.A.3   Value of an investment in a $4 consol for seven periods.

other hand an investment in the eight-period, 4 percent bond, with duration less than 7 when $Y = 1/6$, is not immunized under these conditions. It increases in value when Y rises above 1/6 and decreases in value when Y falls below 1/6. Figures 6.A.2 and 6.A.3 demonstrate that the choice of an immunized investment is sensitive to yields existing at the beginning of the holding period.

Conclusion: the possibility and desirability of immunization

An investment can be immunized against risk of loss under very special conditions that were listed above. Most important, the investment's duration must equal the holding period and there must occur at most one parallel shift in the yield curve during the holding period. It is unlikely that these conditions will be satisfied except for very short holding periods.[27] Therefore an immunization strategy has the most chance of being feasible for active portfolios.

---

27   More general immunization conditions, along with more general definitions of duration, have been developed by G. Bierwag (1977), who showed immunization to be possible for multiplicative as well as additive shifts of the yield curve and for more than one shift during the holding period. However, the investor must know the stochastic process that generates yield changes and, instead of the D in Equation (6.A.6), must apply an "immunizing duration" with weights that depend on the nature of the stochastic process.

But you might not wish an immunized portfolio even if one were possible. Your desire for gain might be sufficiently strong to induce you to accept some risk of loss. Under the conditions presented in Table 6.A.3, for example, a risk taker who thought yields were more likely to fall than to rise would have bought the perpetuity and, if yields had in fact fallen to 2 percent, would have earned an annual rate of return of 12.62 percent during his holding period of $H = 7$. This greatly exceeds the 4.01 percent return to the immunized investment. But there is a catch. If yields had risen to 6 percent, his rate of return would have been only 0.04 percent. An investor's desire for immunization depends on his willingness to accept risk in pursuit of gain, his confidence in his yield forecasts, and—perhaps most important—the size of transaction costs, which can quickly consume an active portfolio.

QUESTIONS

1. Explain the answers to problem 5 at the end of Chapter 5 in terms of duration.
2. Using the duration and immunization terminology of this appendix, explain why the rates of return in Exercises 5.7(b) and 5.8(b) exceeded the purchase yields.
3. Discuss Relationships 5.1 to 5.3 in Chapter 5 in terms of immunization and compare those relationships with the results in Table 6.A.3.
4. Explain the results in Table 6.8 in terms of duration and immunization.

PROBLEMS

1. Using Equation (6.A.1), calculate the duration of a four-period, 5 percent bond when the yield is (a) 0, (b) 5 percent, and (c) 10 percent.
2. Confirm your answers to problems 1(b) and 1(c), using Equation (6.A.6). [Equation (6.A.6) is undefined for $Y = 0$ and therefore cannot be used for problem 1(a).]
3. Confirm the durations in Table 6.A.1 for the yield of 10 percent.
4. Calculate the duration of a four-period annuity when the yield is (a) 0, (b) 5 percent, and (c) 10 percent.
5. Calculate the duration of a four-period, single-payment security when the yield is (a) 0, (b) 5 percent, and (c) 10 percent.
6. Add a line for $Y = 0.11$ to Table 6.A.2, and explain why the price of the forty-period bond fell proportionally more than that of the sixty-period bond and why the price of the two-period bond fell more than that of the three-period annuity when Y rose from 0.10 to 0.11.

The last three problems are based on the following information: Suppose the yield curve is currently flat at $Y = 0.125$ and you are considering the following investments, all of which are currently selling for $100, for a holding period of $H = 4$: (1) a series of one-period securities, (2) a four-period single-payment security, (3) a five-period bond that pays coupons of $12.50 per period, and (4) a perpetuity.

7. What is the duration of each investment?

8. Which investments are immunized or almost immunized?

9. Calculate the rate of return on each investment for **(a)** an unchanged yield curve and for single parallel shifts of the yield curve first to **(b)** 20 percent and then to **(c)** 5 percent. Please present your answers in the format of Table 6.A.3.

REFERENCES

G. O. Bierwag, "Immunization, Duration, and the Term Structure of Interest Rates," *Journal of Financial and Quantitative Analysis,* December 1977, pages 725–741.

G. O. Bierwag, George G. Kaufman, Robert Schweitzer, and Alden Toevs, "The Art of Risk Management in Bond Portfolios," *Journal of Portfolio Management,* Spring 1981, pages 27–36.

Lawrence Fisher and Roman L. Weil, "Coping with the Risk of Interest-rate Fluctuations:
Returns to Bondholders from Naive and Optimal Strategies," *Journal of Business,* October 1971, pages 408–431.

J. R. Hicks, *Value and Capital,* Oxford University Press, London, 1939.

Frederick R. Macaulay, *Some Theoretical Problems Suggested by the Movements of Interest Rates, Bond Yields and Stock Prices in the United States since 1856,* National Bureau of Economic Research, New York, 1938.

FOUR

Financial Instruments

"... when you have to turn into a chrysalis
—you will some day, you know
—and then after that into a butterfly,
I should think you'll feel it a little queer, won't you?"
"Not a bit," said the Caterpillar.

Lewis Carroll, *Alice's Adventures in Wonderland*, ch. 5

CHAPTER 7

CHARACTERISTICS OF SECURITIES AND THEIR MARKETS

As it is the power of exchanging that gives occasion to the division of labour, so the extent of this division must always be limited by the extent of that power, or, in other words, by the extent of the market.
Adam Smith, *An Inquiry into the Nature and Causes of the Wealth of Nations,* **bk. 1, ch. 3, 1776**

Chapters 8 to 12 contain discussions of the most important financial instruments, including stocks, bonds, financial futures contracts, money, and several short-term securities that are close substitutes for money. The present chapter serves as an introduction to the next five chapters by summarizing the principal characteristics of securities and their markets. The price that people are willing to pay for a security depends, as with other goods, on its characteristics. We discuss four of the most frequently mentioned security characteristics: *liquidity* may be viewed either as the speed with which the full market value of a security can be realized by its owner if she suddenly decides to sell it or as the proportion of full value that can be realized immediately; *divisibility* is inversely related to the price of a security relative to the amount of money an investor wishes to invest in that class of securities; *reversibility* is concerned with the turnaround transaction costs of buying and selling a security; *risk* is a measure or set of measures of the predictability of rate of return.

Security characteristics depend upon (and influence) the kinds of markets in which they are traded. We will discuss four types of markets (direct-search, brokered, dealer, and auction) and three market characteristics (breadth, depth, and resiliency). The final section includes a list of securities, along with the types of markets in which they are traded and the places in this book in which they may be found.

CHARACTERISTICS OF SECURITIES[1]

Liquidity[2]

Liquidity can be measured either in units of time or as a proportion of market value.

> **DEFINITION 7.1a.**   One measure of *liquidity* is the inverse of the amount of time $(1/t)$ that elapses between the decision to sell a security and the receipt of its full market value by the seller.

Securities that are traded continuously in large quantities in centralized markets provide almost perfect liquidity. A phone call to a Treasury bill (T bill) dealer, for example, usually results in the exchange of the bill for money by wire transfer on the same day.

By *full market value* in Definition 7.1a, we mean the proceeds that could be realized from the sale of a security if the holder had all the time in the world to look for the best price and market conditions did not change during the search. The full market values of T bills are obvious because the prices bid by dealers are well known and searches are conducted swiftly, requiring only the time to dial a phone, wait for one or two rings, and ask a short question.

But for many other securities and real assets full market values are less precise. As an extreme but important example consider houses. Most state legislatures, which consist mainly of lawyers, compel house buyers and sellers for their *protection*[3] to complete an expensive and time-consuming series of legal steps that just happen to require the services of lawyers. But houses would still be illiquid assets even if there were no lawyers. Unlike T bills houses are not homogeneous goods traded in a centralized market. This is true even of those in the same housing development. One T bill is for all practical purposes identical with other T bills of the same maturity. But house buyers must wend their weary way from house to house, inspecting and evaluating the peculiar characteristics of each. And in the meantime sellers, even energetic sellers, must wait and bite their nails. The full market value of a house on a particular date is an estimated average. It is an average of the prices for which similar houses in similar neighborhoods have, to the best of the house owner's knowledge, been selling in the recent past. Even under the best of conditions—in an active market with steady or steadily changing prices in a nearly homogeneous area—full market value remains an estimate.

---

1 Our discussion of the characteristics of securities owes much to an undated manuscript by James Tobin.

2 See Inglis Palgrave (1896) and Ray Westerfield (1933) for early discussions of the concept of liquidity presented here.

3 We use *protection* here and throughout this book in precisely the way it is used by Frank Nitti, of *Untouchables* fame.

DEFINITION 7.1b.   Liquidity may also be defined as the proportion of an asset's full market value that can be realized immediately once the decision to sell has been made.

The liquidity of houses is also low in terms of our second measure. Suppose lawyers vanish overnight, leaving buyers and sellers free to make trades as quickly or as slowly as they wish. The owner of a house with an estimated full market value of $100,000 might then, in the event of a sudden and desperate need for cash, be able to get $100,000 on the day following the decision to sell if he is very lucky or very ingenious. But such quick sales often bring considerably less than full market value.

Many students have been faced with the decision of how much time and trouble to take in their efforts to sell a bicycle or car for *what it was really worth,* that is, for full market value. This is the liquidity problem—not so serious as in the case of houses but more serious than for U.S. securities.

Now let us consider securities with less liquidity than T bills but more than houses. Municipal bonds are a good example. The bond obligations of many cities are held by only a few investors, especially banks. The banks often wish that matters had not developed this way. But when the mayor or one of his cronies tells the chairman of the First National Bank that the city wishes to place $50 million of new 20-year bonds, that the bank's share is 20 percent, that the city is reconsidering its decision to keep its deposits with First National, and that it is about time for the fire inspector to make his annual visit to the bank's ancient premises, the bank's options are limited.

So the bank finds itself the reluctant owner of $10 million of a rather special issue. Most municipal issues are not so special as most houses because similar issues have been sold by other cities and they are evaluated by rating services. Information about municipals is more widely dispersed and more reliable than is information about houses. But municipals are still inferior in these respects to U.S. securities, which are identical in their freedom from default risk, and are widely held and actively traded. U.S. securities are close substitutes for one another, with the result that dealers and portfolio managers are continuously shifting among them in response to changes in cash flows and in actual and expected returns. This is less true of municipal bonds, even those of large cities with good credit ratings. None of this matters if First National holds the city's bonds until maturity or if it sells small fractions of its holdings from time to time. But problems arise if the bank suffers a loss of deposits or is confronted with a large increase in the demand for loans by valued customers. Under either of these conditions First National must obtain funds quickly, perhaps by selling securities. An attempted quick sale of $5 million or $10 million of a single municipal issue—10 or 20 percent of the issue—is likely to involve some sacrifice. Unless the bank can find a dealer or portfolio manager who happens to be in need of just such an issue, the process of unloading the city's bonds may require several days (a lifetime in the money markets) unless the bank offers an attractive price, that is, a low price.

Figure 7.1 gives a rough indication of the relative liquidities of T bills, municipal bonds, and houses. The horizontal axis measures elapsed time (t) following the date (D day) of the decision to sell. The vertical axis shows the proportion of full market value realized. The almost vertical curve indicates that this value is realized very quickly for T bills while the curve with the gentlest slope shows that house sellers must be patient in order to collect full market value. The liquidities of bills, municipals, and houses are $(1/t_1) > (1/t_2) > (1/t_3)$. The same order is implied by our second measure of liquidity, the proportion of full market value realized immediately. If by *immediately* we mean the brief time (t_1) required to sell a T bill and collect the proceeds, the liquidities of bills, municipals, and houses are $1 > 0.25 > 0.10$. These values are intended to give only a rough idea of relative liquidities in normal circumstances. Actual liquidities vary over time and between investors.

So far the discussion has been limited to *individual liquidity* as distinct from *group liquidity*. The latter is nearly always less than the former. Individual liquidity refers to the speed with which the full market value of an asset can be realized by a single seller, assuming that she is acting *more or less independently* of others, that is, that she

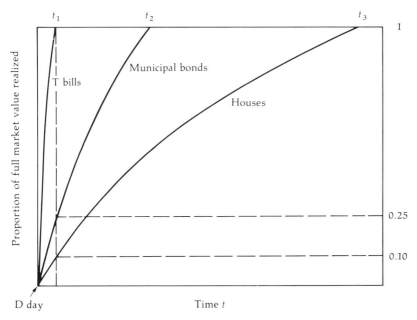

Figure 7.1   Liquidities of T bills, municipal bonds, and houses.

is not part of a general movement out of the asset. This assumption distinguishes individual from group liquidity.

Even U.S. government securities are illiquid in the presence of a widespread shortage of cash. For example suppose there is an outflow of reserves from the banking system, due to an unfavorable balance of payments or a restriction of credit by the Federal Reserve (the Fed), at a time when investors have borrowed heavily from banks and brokers because they expect yields to fall. The loss of bank reserves leads to cutbacks in bank lending and increases in interest rates. Banks call in the loans that can be called and do not renew those that mature. Investors are unable to borrow further to maintain their margins,[4] and their outstanding loans are coming due. The investors' only way to obtain the cash to pay their debts is to sell securities. But banks are also trying to sell securities in an effort to replenish their reserves. And brokers and dealers are trying to sell securities to raise cash to repay their bank loans. Everyone, it seems, is in debt to everyone else. All are trying to raise cash to satisfy insistent creditors. All want to sell, and no one wants to buy. This general scramble for cash, or *panic,* leads to precipitate price falls and market closings. Nothing except cash is liquid.

But panics are extreme and, nowadays, rare examples of group illiquidity. We have not had a panic worthy of the name since the early 1930s although the occasional "credit crunch" serves as a reminder of what could happen. Milder and more frequent examples of group illiquidity are the large-scale bank sales of municipal securities during periods of expanding economic activity and rising loan demands. These conditions have typically induced banks to sell securities in order to obtain funds for their loan customers. This causes greater losses on municipals for each bank than if it were the only seller. That is, the group liquidity of municipals is less than their individual liquidity. A bank's estimate of the former is the more appropriate measure for portfolio planning as long as its own fortunes and behavior are expected to move in concert with those of other banks.

Reversibility

Reversibility refers to the ability to move into and out of a security without the original investment's being consumed by transaction costs. We will use the following definition:

DEFINITION 7.2.   *Reversibility* is the proportion of an investment that remains after the purchase and sale of a security when

---

4 An investor is able to buy a bond selling for $100,000 with $10,000 of his own money and a $90,000 loan from his broker if the broker requires 10 percent margin. The broker holds the bond as collateral for the loan. If the price of the bond falls to $95,000, the investor's margin falls to $5,000, and the broker will require the customer to sell the bond or deposit additional funds, perhaps $4,500 if it is desired to maintain the margin at 10 percent. Margins are discussed further in Chapter 11.

the purchase and sale prices have not changed. It is unity less the transaction costs (T) of buying and selling a security expressed as a proportion of the purchase price (P):

$$\text{Reversibility} = \frac{P - T}{P} = 1 - \frac{T}{P}$$

For example we see from Table 6.2 that the U.S. 10s of 2005 to 2010, which on August 11, 1983, had bid and ask prices of $P_b = \$84.50$ and $P_a = \$84.75$ per \$100 face value, had reversibility of

$$1 - \frac{S}{P_a} = 1 - \frac{\$0.25}{\$84.75} = 0.997$$

where in this case the purchase price is the dealer's asked price, and transaction costs take the form of the dealer's spread (S).

Notice that most of the spreads on long-term bonds in Table 6.2 are \$0.25 per \$100 face value, whereas most of the spreads on short-term notes and bonds are \$0.125. These are normal spreads so that, on average, when bonds are selling at par, the reversibilities of short-term and long-term U.S. bonds are 0.99875 and 0.99750, respectively, as indicated in Table 7.1.

The reversibilities of T bills are even greater. Using the relationships in Table 6.1 and assuming quotations for immediate delivery, the reversibility on August 11, 1983, of the 63-day bill of October 13 was

$$1 - \frac{S}{P_a} = 1 - \frac{P_a - P_b}{P_a} = 1 - \frac{(\$98.3865 - \$98.3725)}{\$98.3865} = 0.99986$$

This value appears in Table 7.1, along with the reversibilities of the 175-day and 336-day bills maturing February 2 and July 12, 1984.

Reversibility tends to be inversely related to maturity. But there are exceptions, such as the "flower bonds" maturing in May 1985 (the 3¼s of 1985 and the 4¼s of 1975 to 1985), which had spreads of \$1 per \$100 face value on August 11, 1983. Flower bonds are U.S. Treasury bonds that may be used at face value plus accrued interest to satisfy federal estate-tax liabilities, which is why they have higher prices and lower yields than other securities with similar maturities. No flower bonds have been issued since 1971, and amounts outstanding have declined as existing issues have been used to meet estate taxes. Their small amounts outstanding relative to other Treasury issues may be seen in Table 6.4.

The highest reversibility in Table 7.1 is possessed by federal funds, which are principally overnight loans between commercial banks. A fed funds transaction is accomplished when the lending bank phones or wires its Federal Reserve Bank to transfer funds from its own

Table 7.1   Reversibilities of Federal Funds, U.S. Securities, Common
Stock, and Houses, 1983

Investment	Reversibility
Federal funds	0.999999
Treasury bills	
2-month	0.99986
6-month	0.99959
11-month	0.99918
Treasury notes and bonds	
Short-term	0.99875
Long-term	0.99750
Stock	0.970
A typical house	0.90

Sources: New York Stock Exchange *Fact Book*, 1983, *Federal Home Loan Bank Board Journal*,
and Table 6.1.

reserve account at the Fed to the account of the borrowing bank. If the
two banks have a regular working arrangement, there is no brokerage
fee. But if they locate each other through a fed funds broker there is
usually a fee of $1 per $1 million traded so that the reversibility of fed
funds is 0.999999.

Compared to fed funds, U.S. securities, and other investments
traded in other highly organized ways, the reversibility of houses is
low. This is mainly due to the 6 or 7 percent of house prices paid to real
estate brokers. Brokerage fees are payments by sellers for the dissemination of information to prospective buyers. These fees do not have to
be paid if an owner chooses to sell his house without the aid of a
broker. (The same is true of stocks and bonds.) But he must bear the
cost in other ways if he decides to undertake the brokerage function
himself. These costs are probably in most cases at least as large as
brokers' fees; most sellers, after comparing the costs of the alternatives, call in a broker. The principal transaction costs paid by house
buyers are loan-application fees and other up-front charges imposed
by lenders. In 1983 these were approximately 2 percent of the value of
house purchases financed by mortgages.[5] Title searches, recording
fees, and lawyers' fees can easily amount to another 1 or 2 percent of
the price of a house. The sum of these typical transaction costs arising
from the purchase and sale of a house is 10 or 11 percent of the price.
This suggests an average reversibility of $1 - 0.105 = 0.895$, which we
have changed to 0.90 in Table 7.1 in order not to convey a false sense of
precision.

5 From *Federal Home Loan Bank Board Journal*.

Most stock purchases involve two sets of transaction costs: the spread earned by the dealer (called the "specialist") on the floor of the stock exchange and the commission paid to the brokerage firm that trades with the specialist on your behalf.[6] The reversibility of stock is therefore

$$\text{Reversibility of stock} = 1 - \frac{(1+c)P_a - (1-c)P_b}{(1+c)P_a} = \frac{(1-c)P_b}{(1+c)P_a}$$

(7.1)

$$= \frac{(1-c)(P_a - S)}{(1+c)P_a} = \frac{1-c}{1+c}\left(1 - \frac{S}{P_a}\right)$$

where P_a and P_b are the specialist's bid and ask prices, his spread is $S = P_a - P_b$, and c is the broker's commission as a proportion of the stock's price. Specialists' spreads are normally about 1 percent of stock prices, and in 1983 discount brokers were charging commissions of about 1 percent, so that the reversibility of stock traded on exchanges was $(0.99)(0.99)/1.01 = 0.970$, although large investors were able to negotiate lower commissions.

The concept of reversibility has already, in our analysis of the demand for money in Chapter 3, played an important role in this book. People must have money in order to buy goods and discharge debts. But the amount of money that they hold depends on differences between rates of return on money and other investments and on costs of shifting between money and other investments, that is, reversibilities.

Divisibility

You may think T bills are a good investment; but their minimum denomination is $10,000, and you only have $5,000. This is an example of the indivisibility of a security for a particular investor. Divisibility may be defined as follows:

DEFINITION 7.3.   The divisibility of a security for an investor is the ratio of the amount of money that he wishes to invest in the security to the minimum denomination in which it is available.

If investors as small as the one described above dominated the financial markets, the minimum amounts in which many securities are now available might affect their yields. But the existence of large investors tends to make yields independent (or almost independent) of minimum denominations. For example, if the $10,000 minimum for T bills deters small investors, that by itself depresses bill prices and raises bill yields. But the higher yields are an incentive to large

---

6 Small transactions in U.S. securities must also be handled through brokers so that their reversibilities for small investors are less than those in Table 7.1.

investors to buy more bills, causing bill yields to approach the values that would prevail if no investors were excluded from the market. And just in case large investors are not sufficiently interested, money market funds offer bills in $1,000 (or smaller) pieces.

So it is unlikely that divisibility is an important direct influence on security prices. However, there is some evidence that divisibility may exert an indirect influence on security returns by affecting dealer spreads.[7] The willingness of dealers to take positions in (hold inventories of) a security depends on several factors, including the probability of large blocks suddenly being thrust on the market by large holders. If a security is widely held, which is more likely to be the case if it is available in small denominations, trading is likely to proceed fairly steadily in fairly small amounts so that dealers' risk will be small. Competition between dealers for this desirable issue will lead to narrow spreads.

An aside: the "moneyness" of securities

The reader may by now have gotten the idea that the characteristics of securities are mainly defined relative to money. For example, when liquidity is defined as the speed with which the full market value of an asset can be realized, we understand that "value" is measured in dollars and we are anxious about how soon we can get our grubby little paws on those dollars, sometimes in currency but usually in our checking accounts. Similarly, divisibility refers to the minimum number of dollars required for the purchase of a security, reversibility is a measure of the dollars lost in the process of moving from money to a security and back to money, and finally risk refers to measures of the predictability of rates of return on securities where rates of return are dollars earned as proportions of dollars invested.[8]

It is not absolutely necessary that these characteristics be defined relative to money. After all, money is merely a means to the ends of gaining control of production and consumption goods, and it would for many purposes be useful to define the characteristics of securities in terms of their abilities to command those goods. But money is a convenient standard not only by which to compare the values of goods but also for comparing the characteristics of securities. Furthermore, this is not the place to introduce a new terminology. So we shall follow others in thinking of the characteristics of securities in terms of their *moneyness*.

A security whose price is within the range of investors' pocketbooks and which can be converted quickly and at little cost into a reasonably predictable full monetary value—that is, which possesses high divisi-

---

7 Some of this evidence is presented below in Table 7.6.

8 This is *nominal* risk. We shall also discuss *real* risk and *real* returns, which are denominated in terms of goods, usually consumption goods.

bility, liquidity, and reversibility but low risk—is called a *money substitute* or a *money market instrument*. Substitutability between goods is nearly always a matter of degree, that is, a question of more or less rather than of yes or no. The moneyness of securities is a continuum so that distinctions between money market instruments and other securities have to be somewhat arbitrary. The conventional distinction, which may be as good as any, is between securities with maturities exceeding 1 year and those maturing in less than 1 year. This convention is reflected in Table 7.2. The money market rates in the left-hand portion of the table pertain to securities with maturities ranging from overnight in the case of fed funds to 1 year in the case of 52-week T bills. Some investors make a practice of always holding their certificates of deposit (in commercial banks) and/or T bills until maturity and then applying their redemption values to purchases of new rounds of the same securities. In these cases money market securities take on the character of long-term investments. But many other borrowers and lenders are almost continuously in the process of moving between these securities and money in response to the shifting cash flows arising from their operations. Temporary cash surpluses are applied to purchases of commercial paper, T bills, and other money market securities. Temporary cash shortages force sales of securities. High liquidity is usually associated with short maturity except in the event of panics or credit crunches, and even then short-term securities are likely to be no more illiquid than long-term securities. This is because the ownership of short-term securities tends to be more widely dispersed and they tend to be traded more actively than long-term securities. Even the Bank of America can count on unloading a large part of its T bill portfolio without affecting bill prices.

Yields on securities with maturities exceeding 1 year are called capital market rates in the right-hand portion of Table 7.2. This is because long-term securities are usually issued to finance long-term capital-investment projects. This means plant and equipment by firms and houses by individuals. It is possible to finance steel mills and office buildings by rolling over, say, eighty successive issues of 3-month commercial paper. This might even be desirable if the firm is confident that rates will decline during the next 20 years and the commercial paper market will never "dry up" in the sense that it will always be possible to find another buyer (lender) when each issue comes due. However, conservative opinion argues that "foolhardy" is a better description than "confident" of such a strategy. There is little doubt that financing long-term investments with short-term debt involves greater uncertainty than long-term debt.

Nominal (money) risk
Nominal risk refers to the unpredictability of cash flows accruing to an investment. There are so many reasonable definitions of unpredictability (or risk) that we shall not limit ourselves to one but merely

Table 7.2 Average Interest Rates (Percent per Annum) in Money and Capital Markets

Instrument	1980	1981	1982	Instrument	1980	1981	1982
MONEY MARKET RATES				**CAPITAL MARKET RATES**			
Federal funds[a]	13.36	16.38	12.26	U.S. Treasury notes and bonds[g]			
				Constant maturities[h]			
Commercial paper[b,c]				1-year	12.05	14.78	12.27
1-month	12.76	15.69	11.83	2-year	11.77	14.56	12.80
3-month	12.66	15.32	11.89	3-year	11.55	14.44	12.92
6-month	12.29	14.76	11.89	5-year	11.48	14.24	13.01
Finance paper, directly				7-year	11.43	14.06	13.06
placed[b,c]				10-year	11.46	13.91	13.00
1-month	12.44	15.30	11.64	20-year	11.39	13.72	12.92
3-month	11.49	14.08	11.23	30-year	11.30	13.44	12.76
6-month	11.28	13.73	11.20	Composite[i]			
				Over 10 years			
Bankers' acceptances[b,d]				(long-term)	10.81	12.87	12.23
3-month	12.72	15.32	11.89	State and local notes			
6-month	12.25	14.66	11.83	and bonds			
				Moody's series[j]			
Certificates of deposit,				Aaa	7.85	10.43	10.88
secondary market[e]				Baa	9.01	11.76	12.48
1-month	12.91	15.91	12.04	*Bond Buyer* series[k]	8.59	11.33	11.66
3-month	13.07	15.91	12.27				
6-month	12.99	15.77	12.57	Corporate bonds			
				Seasoned issues[l]			
Eurodollar deposits,				All industries	12.75	15.06	14.94
3-month	14.00	16.79	13.12	Aaa	11.94	14.17	13.79
				Aa	12.50	14.75	14.41
U.S. Treasury bills[b]				A	12.89	15.29	15.43
Secondary market[f]				Baa	13.67	16.04	16.11
3-month	11.43	14.03	10.61	Aaa utility bonds[m]			
6-month	11.37	13.80	11.07	New issue	12.74	15.56	14.41
1-year	10.89	13.14	11.07	Recently offered			
Auction average				issues	12.70	15.56	14.45
3-month	11.506	14.029	10.686				
6-month	11.374	13.776	11.084	Memo: Dividend/price			
1-year	10.748	13.159	11.099	ratio[n]			
				Preferred stocks	10.60	12.36	12.53
				Common stocks	5.26	5.20	5.81

a Average of rates weighted by the volume of transactions through fed funds brokers. All calendar days included, where the rate for a weekend or holiday is taken to be the rate prevailing on the preceding business day. (Rates on other securities apply to business days only and for all business days unless otherwise noted.)

b Quoted on a discount basis (other rates are yields to maturity).

c Unweighted average of offering rates quoted by at least five dealers (for commercial paper) or finance companies (for finance paper).

d Most representative dealer closing offered rate for the acceptances of top-rated (first-tier) banks.

e Unweighted average of offered rates quoted by at least five dealers early in the day.

f Unweighted average of closing bid rates quoted by at least five dealers.

g Based on closing bid prices of at least five dealers.

h Yields are read from a yield curve based on recently issued, actively traded securities (see Figure 19.1).

i Average of yields on all bonds not due or callable within 10 years, including several low-yielding flower bonds.

j Thursday figures from Moody's Investors Service.

k Bonds of mixed quality with 20 years to maturity issued by twenty state and local governments; Thursday figures.

l Daily figures from Moody's Investors Service; based on yields of selected long-term bonds.

m With maturities of 20 years or more. New issue yields are based on quotations on date of offering. Yields on recently offered issues are based on Friday closing quotations for first 4 weeks after the end of underwriters' stabilization.

n Standard & Poor's corporate series. Preferred stock ratio based on a sample of ten issues: four public utilities, four industrials, one financial, and one transportation. Common stock ratios on the 500 stocks in the price index.

Source: *Federal Reserve Bulletin*, December 1983, tab. 1.35.

mention in passing that the most popular definition of risk in the finance literature is the *variance* of cash flows.

Payments to the owner of a security may be uncertain for either or both of two reasons: The borrower may fail to make the promised payments on time, and the security's price is subject to variation because of fluctuations in market yields. These sources of risk are called, respectively, *default risk* and *interest rate risk*. Securities of the U.S. government are virtually free of default risk. The federal government cannot be forced into bankruptcy through an inability to fulfill its promises to pay dollars—because it prints the dollars. But we can never be sure that it will not repudiate some or all of its debt.[9] All other securities are subject to nonnegligible default risks, and all securities, including those of the U.S. government, are subject to interest rate risk.

It is impossible to give a generally applicable ranking of securities by risk because some securities may be viewed as highly risky by some investors but as almost free of risk by other investors. For example consider an investment firm that is anxious to secure a return of at least 10 percent on its portfolio over the next year. If 52-week T bills currently yield 10 percent, the firm is sure of earning that rate of return if it puts all its money into those bills. On the other hand, if the firm takes a chance with either a 20-year bond or four successive investments in 13-week bills, its return becomes imperfectly predictable and may either exceed or fall short of 10 percent during the next year. An investor in search of a predictable return should buy a single-payment (zero-coupon) 20-year bond if his investment horizon is 20 years but should buy a 13-week bill if his horizon is 13 weeks.[10] We shall find in succeeding chapters that life insurance companies and pension funds, with mainly long-term liabilities, hold predominantly long-term assets; commercial banks, with mainly short-term liabilities, hold short-term assets. The most serious transgressors against this principle—savings and loan associations (S&Ls), which hold mainly long-term assets (mortgages) even though their liabilities are almost entirely short-term deposits—suffered greatly when interest rates rose during the late 1970s and early 1980s.

Real (purchasing-power) risk

Inflation is repudiation.

Calvin Coolidge, speech in Chicago, 1922

But what good is money except as a means to the purchase of goods? Even Silas Marner had to eat. This suggests that the returns in which

---

9 The U.S. government has repudiated various debts, for example, when it refused to honor the gold clause in its bonds after the devaluation of 1934 and when it refused to honor its promise to convert foreign dollar holdings into gold after 1971.

10 More generally, he should match the duration of his investment with the length of his horizon, as shown in our discussion of immunization in Appendix 6.A.

we should be most interested are real returns and that the most meaningful concepts of risk are those relating to the predictability of the purchasing power of cash flows.

If we have earned $10 on an investment of $100, our nominal rate of return is 10 percent. But if the prices of the goods we buy have risen 6 percent, the investment has increased our purchasing power only 4 percent. This is our real rate of return. Eugene Fama and William Schwert calculated the monthly nominal and real rates of return on T bills, U.S. bonds, houses, and common stock during the 1953 to 1971 period of moderate inflation. The means and standard deviations of these rates of return, at annual rates, are shown in Table 7.3. The rates of change of the prices of goods and services (inflation) and of wages and salaries (labor income) are also shown. Stocks performed best, on average, during this period although they also carried the greatest risk

Table 7.3   Means and Standard Deviations of Real and Nominal Rates of Return and the Rate of Inflation, 1953 to 1971 (Percentages at Annual Rates)

Instrument[a]	Nominal Rates of Return		Real Rates of Return	
	Mean	Standard Deviation	Mean	Standard Deviation
Treasury bills				
1-month	3.17	1.57	0.87	2.43
2-month	3.54	1.69	1.24	2.43
3-month	3.78	1.81	1.48	2.43
U.S. government bonds				
1–2-year	3.78	5.41	1.48	5.79
2–3-year	3.78	8.21	1.48	8.47
3–4-year	3.54	10.03	1.24	10.43
4–5-year	3.17	12.15	0.87	12.55
Real estate	2.06	4.41	−0.24	4.16
Labor income	3.91	7.31	1.61	7.57
Common stock				
Equally weighted index	11.22	53.22	8.92	53.93
Value-weighted index	12.95	64.78	10.65	65.73
Inflation	2.30	2.80		

a The monthly returns to 1-, 2-, and 3-month *bills*, which pay no coupons, depend only on the change in prices from one month to the next. The returns to *bonds* are based on indexes of yields on bonds with from 1 to 2 years to maturity, from 2 to 3 years to maturity, and so on. The return to *real estate* is measured as the rate of inflation of the Home Purchase Price Component of the Consumer Price Index. The return to *labor income* is the rate of change of wages and salaries plus proprietors' income per capita of the labor force. The *common stock* returns are those on equally weighted and value-weighted portfolios of all New York Stock Exchange stocks. *Inflation* is the monthly rate of change of the Consumer Price Index.

Source: Eugene F. Fama and G. William Schwert, "Asset Returns and Inflation," *Journal of Financial Economics,* December 1977.

Table 7.4 Average Real and Nominal Rates of Return and the Rate of Inflation, 1971 to 1980 (Percentages at Annual Rates)

Instrument[a]	Average Nominal Rate of Return	Average Real Rate of Return
3-month T bills	7.08	−1.60
4-year U.S. government bonds	7.93	−0.75
Real estate	9.58	0.90
Labor income	7.76	−0.92
Common stock	7.30	−1.38
Savings accounts	4.95	−3.73
Checking accounts	0.0	−8.68
Inflation	8.68	

a The *inflation, labor income,* and *real estate* data are calculated in the same way as in the Fama-Schwert study. The *3-month T bill* data assume the rolling over of forty consecutive issues at the average auction rate. The index of 3- to 5-year U.S. yields as reported by the Fed was used as an approximation of the yield on *4-year U.S. bonds.* The *common stock* figures were based on the price and yield series of Standard & Poor's index of 500 stocks. The return to *savings accounts* is based on the maximum rate payable on passbook accounts at commercial banks.

Sources: *Federal Reserve Bulletin* and *Survey of Current Business.*

in the sense that their monthly returns were more variable and therefore probably less predictable.

The 1971 to 1980 story was different. Table 7.4 updates some of the Fama-Schwert average returns (but not standard deviations of returns) and adds rates of return on checking and savings accounts in commercial banks. The table shows that the average annual rate of inflation between 1971 and 1980 was 8.68 percent, compared with 2.30 percent between 1953 and 1971. All the investments in Table 7.3 except common stock performed better in nominal terms during 1971 to 1980 than during the preceding 18 years. But all performed badly in real terms during the 1970s, and only home owners managed to keep their heads above water. So much for stocks as an inflation hedge.

The interdependence of security characteristics

Liquidity, reversibility, and risk are interdependent.[11] High liquidity and reversibility go together. An active market in a security (and therefore high liquidity) will not exist if transaction costs are high. Greater competition between dealers, less regulation, or anything else that reduces transaction costs (that is, increases reversibility) will encourage more active trading and therefore greater liquidity.

Active trading also facilitates smooth price movements, which mean less risk. And in turn those securities with the least risk tend to be traded most actively so that low risk encourages greater liquidity.

11 The possible influence of divisibility on reversibility (and therefore, as we shall see as this discussion proceeds, on liquidity and risk) was mentioned above. But divisibility does not deserve equal billing with the other characteristics and will not be discussed further in this subsection.

Furthermore, low risk and high liquidity induce high reversibility because competing brokers, dealers, and exchanges are attracted by the commissions and spreads to be earned in active markets. Some empirical evidence of the interdependence of security characteristics—specifically, the effects of liquidity and risk on reversibility—is presented in the next section.

TYPES OF SECURITY MARKETS

Direct search

The shares of small firms are traded so seldom that there is no inducement for brokers and dealers to become involved. If you want to buy stock in the Littleville State Bank, it will do you no good to call your broker unless he owes you a personal favor. You will have to conduct your search for a seller without assistance. And even after a potential seller is found there is still the problem of determining a price because neither of you has the benefit of the information about prices that is available in more active markets.[12]

Brokered markets

Brokers bring buyers and sellers together. The costs to an investor of searching for a buyer or a seller would be substantial even for actively traded issues, involving many phone calls and newspaper ads, if there were no brokers, dealers, or exchanges. Brokers reduce search costs, that is, information costs, in two ways. Think of a brokerage office as a clearinghouse for two kinds of information: the identities of buyers and sellers, along with their bid and ask prices, and the prices of recent transactions. So the hopeful buyer makes only a few calls: first to Bob, his favorite broker, and then to a few of Bob's competitors just to keep him honest. One or more of these brokers will either have anxious sellers on their lists, or they will call around until they find a broker who does.

The most important brokered financial markets may be described as follows: We begin with the *retail market for state and local government bonds* (called *municipals*, for short). The bonds of small towns require direct search because they are not sufficiently active to attract brokers or dealers. On the other hand highly rated large issues are popular with banks and insurance companies and are traded in a dealer market because there is almost a continuous demand for them. Between these inactive direct search and continuously active dealer markets is a brokered market in medium-sized issues that is devoted primarily to transactions of less than $100,000 on behalf of individuals in high tax brackets.[13] These investors contact their brokers, who have

---

12 In the terminology of Definitions 7.1a and 7.1b neither of you is certain of the stock's full market value.

13 Municipal securities are exempt from federal income taxes. The advantages of these securities for high-income investors are discussed in Chapter 10.

Table 7.5   Selections from the "Blue List" of Current Municipal Offerings,[a] December 12, 1983

Amount	Security	Coupon	Maturity	Yield	Offered by
10	Agawam	8.00	6/1/93	8.75	Merrill-White (Boston)
5	Andover	9.60	5/1/86	6.50	Merrill-White (Boston)
10	Andover	4.60	12/15/86	6.50	Alex Brown (Boston)
90	Attleboro	11.40	1/15/86	7.25	Prudential-Bache (Boston)
10	Auburn	4.875	6/1/90	9.00	Prudential-Bache (Boston)
80	Billerica	6.00	4/1/86	7.00	Shawmut Bank of Boston
25	Billerica	5.125	4/1/92	9.40	Paine Webber (Boston)
100	Billerica	6.00	4/1/95	9.40	Alex Brown (Boston)
25	Blue Hills	6.90	8/1/85	5.75	Kidder, Peabody (Boston)
40	Boston	7.30	10/1/84	6.50	Shawmut Bank of Boston
20	Boston	6.10	4/1/86	7.00	Fleet National Bank
920	Boston	7.50	7/1/87	7.75	Kidder, Peabody (Boston)

a Published by the Blue List Publishing Company, a division of Standard & Poor's Corporation. The issue of December 12, 1983, had about 20,000 municipal offerings, about 1,300 corporate bond offerings, and a list of about 150 "offerings wanted." The bonds set forth in this list were offered at the close of business on the day before the date of this issue by the houses mentioned, subject to prior sale and change in price.

developed a variety of methods of exchanging information with other brokers. One of these methods is Standard & Poor's "Blue List." Each afternoon subscribing brokers place entries for their clients on this list, which is distributed to the same group of brokers the next morning. An excerpt from the "Blue List," which identifies the issue, the broker, and the terms of the offer, is shown in Table 7.5. A shortcoming of the "Blue List" is its lack of timeliness. Offers may have been withdrawn or their terms may have been altered between yesterday afternoon and this morning. The demand for up-to-date information has led Standard & Poor to introduce the "Blue List ticker," which is a video screen that shows bond offerings as they are received.

Term fed funds, which are interbank loans with maturities exceeding 1 day, are also traded in a brokered market. Overnight fed funds are traded in a continuous auction market. But trading in fed funds with a maturity of 30 days, for example, is not sufficiently steady and voluminous that a bank can count on its needs being met immediately from anyone's order book. There must be a search, mainly by phone, and fed funds brokers are willing to help.[14]

Large blocks of common stock are also traded through brokers. Most stock is traded in continuous auction markets on the floors of exchanges or through dealers in the over-the-counter market. But these procedures are unable to provide quick execution at a good price to an insurance company that wants to unload a million shares of the

14 See Kenneth Garbade (1982, pages 453–454) and Marcia Stigum (1983, pages 391–393) for discussions of the market for term federal funds.

XYZ Corporation. The growing importance of large institutions in the stock market has led the New York Stock Exchange (NYSE) and other exchanges to develop special, off-floor trading procedures for large blocks, that is, 10,000 or more shares.[15] The largest blocks are brokered by investment banking firms in much the way that they handle new issues.[16] Suppose the Peace of Mind Insurance Company wants to sell a million shares of XYZ and asks for bids from investment bankers large enough to handle this transaction. It accepts a bid of 40 by Goldman Sachs, which then places the issue among other large institutional investors. Peace of Mind pays a commission to Goldman Sachs for the certainty of getting $40 a share, and Goldman Sachs hopes that the price of XYZ will not fall before it sells the block.[17]

Dealer markets

Predictable immediacy is a rarity in human actions, and to approximate it requires that costs be borne by persons who specialize in standing ready and waiting to trade with the incoming orders of those who demand immediate servicing of their orders. The ask-bid spread is the markup that is paid for predictable immediacy of exchange in organized markets; in other markets, it is the inventory markup of retailer or wholesaler.

Harold Demsetz, "The Cost of Transacting,"
Quarterly Journal of Economics, February 1968

DEALERS AND THEIR SPREADS. A dealer is one who is continuously ready to buy or sell normal quantities of a security at stated prices. The advantage of a dealer market over a brokered market is that it provides facilities for the immediate execution of trades. Brokers earn their livings by charging commissions. Dealers effectively do the same by quoting different bid and ask prices: their spread.

Harold Demsetz called the dealer's spread the price of "predictable immediacy" and analyzed its determinants within the supply-and-demand framework in Figure 7.2. D and S are the sums of the desired purchases (demands) and sales (supplies) per unit of time of security X. Buyers and sellers would like their orders to be serviced immediately. If this were possible without transaction costs, D and S would be

---

15 See the 1942 entry in the chronology of the NYSE in Chapter 11 for a brief history of block-trading procedures.

16 See Frank Fabozzi and Frank Zarb (1981, pages 163 and 164) and Kenneth Garbade (1982, pages 457–459) for more about the mechanics of block trades. New issues are discussed below in Chapter 11.

17 Studies by Alan Kraus and Hans Stoll (1972) and others have demonstrated the very substantial efficiency of these block-trading procedures. A block trade initiated by a seller (buyer) tends to occur at a slightly lower (higher) price than that immediately preceding the block transaction, indicating some loss of liquidity by large investors. But these illiquidity effects are seldom sufficient to cover the transaction costs of investors wanting to take advantage of them and tend to vanish completely in a few minutes. See Kenneth Garbade (1982, pages 256–259, 459–460) for discussions of these results.

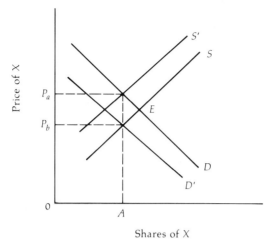

Figure 7.2   Determination of a dealer's spread.

conventional demand and supply curves, and the equilibrium quantity exchanged and price would occur at point E.

But someone wanting to buy shares of X at price E cannot always find a seller at that price *at a given moment*. Similarly, sellers cannot count on the continuous presence of buyers. Dealers, or "market makers," fill this gap by their continuous willingness to buy and sell at announced prices. But those who stand ready to sell, and are willing to wait before selling, must be compensated for the costs of waiting. This compensation is the distance between S and the dealers' supply curve, S'. The intersection of the dealers' supply curve and the demand curve, D, of those who wish to buy immediately determines the equilibrium ask price, P_a. The willingness to stand ready to buy immediately must also be compensated. Consequently, the dealers' demand curve (that is, the schedule of prices they are willing to pay), D', is lower than that of those who cannot or will not wait. The intersection of D' with the supply curve of those who wish to sell immediately gives the equilibrium bid price, P_b.

The existence of trading costs means that fewer securities will be exchanged than in the costless situation occurring at point E. For the demands and supplies in Figure 7.2, the number of shares traded per period is indicated by A.

The costs of standing ready to provide immediate purchases and sales ought to depend on the liquidity and risk of the securities involved. A dealer who keeps an inventory of X in order to provide immediate service to buyers and who accepts all the shares of X that are offered to him at his bid price will earn large profits if the value of his inventory rises. On the other hand he suffers losses if the price of X falls. His risk exposure is directly related to the variability of the price of X.

A dealer's risk is inversely related to the time rate of transactions. A rapid turnover of the security means that he can service buyers and sellers quickly without taking a substantial position in the security. At the extreme, if buy and sell orders arrive continuously, he can simply perform the broker's function of matching orders without an inventory and therefore without risk.

Consequently, we should expect dealers' spreads on a security to be positively related to the variation of the security's price over time and negatively related to the continuity and volume of transactions. Seha Tinic (1972) compared these expectations with data on eighty stocks traded by sixteen specialist units during March 1969.[18] Some of his results are shown in the regression equation in Table 7.6. Notice that spreads (S) tended to be significantly inversely correlated with the volume and continuity of trading (as measured by ln V and C) and positively related to the standard deviation of price (σ_p) although the last result was not statistically significant.

However, a significant coefficient was obtained for another possible indicator of risk: the number of institutional holders of the stock (I). If only a few institutions hold blocks of the stock, their purchases and sales might exert substantial short-term effects on its price. But as the number of institutional holders grows, their transactions may to some extent be offsetting since the owners of large blocks find it convenient to trade with each other, either directly or through brokers. Even small and temporary price movements are important to specialists because they are responsible for smoothing price movements, which means buying when prices are falling and selling when prices are rising.

The remaining coefficients in Table 7.6 may be explained as follows: The cost of financing an inventory of a stock varies directly with its price (P). The concentration index (M) is included because a dealer's spread is affected by competition as well as by costs. Many stocks are traded on several exchanges, and a small value of M means that trading in a stock is evenly distributed between exchanges—meaning greater competition and smaller spreads.[19] The positive influence of the number of stocks handled by a specialist unit (N) is consistent with the notion that there are economies of scale in managing stocks; that is, the dispersion of effort and resources among several issues may increase the costs of dealing in each. This scale effect apparently outweighs the favorable effect on risk that a diversified portfolio might bring. However, the capitalization of specialist units relative to the average daily transactions in their stocks (K/T) had no significant

---

18 A specialist is a dealer in a stock on an exchange and is usually a member of a specialist unit that makes markets in several stocks.

19 Thomas Ho and Hans Stoll (1983) presented a theoretical analysis in which, with three dealers, the equilibrium spread is $S_3 = \sigma^2 \rho Q/(1 + R)$, where R is the expected rate of return on the stock, σ^2 is the variance of the rate of return, Q is the fixed transaction size, and ρ is a coefficient of dealer risk aversion. The equilibrium spread is equal to or greater than S_3 when there are two dealers and is equal to or less than S_3 when there are more than three dealers.

Table 7.6   Determinants of Specialists' Spreads on Common Stock

$$S = 1.139 - 0.038 \ln V - 0.780C + 0.0002\sigma_p - 0.0002I + 0.005P + 0.131M$$
$$(6.07)\quad(5.75)\qquad(3.97)\qquad(0.24)\qquad(2.28)\qquad(12.22)\quad(2.30)$$

$$+ 0.001N - 0.000002(K/T)$$
$$(2.02)\qquad(0.51)$$

$$\bar{R}^2 = 0.84$$

Definitions

S = average bid-ask spread of a stock

V = average number of shares of the stock traded daily

C = trading continuity = number of days traded/number of days sampled

σ_p = standard deviation of stock's price

I = number of institutional investors holding the stock

P = average price of the stock

M = index of concentration of trading in the stock; $M = 1$ if traded in only one market, and $M = 1/n$ if traded equally in n markets. [See Seha Tinic (1972) for more detail.]

N = number of stocks handled by the specialist unit

K = capitalization of the specialist unit handling the stock

T = average daily number of transactions in the stock

$\bar{R}^2$ = coefficient of determination adjusted for degrees of freedom

Absolute values of t ratios shown in parentheses

The data

The results are based on eighty common stocks and sixteen specialist units during the 19 trading days in March 1969.

Source: Seha Tinic, "The Economics of Liquidity Services," *Quarterly Journal of Economics*, February 1972.

influence on their spreads. This suggests that a greater ability to take substantial positions in anticipation of increasing demands and rising prices has no significant effect on specialist profits; at least, any profits due to such an effect are not passed on to investors in the form of lower spreads.

Other studies of dealer spreads in both bond and stock markets have produced findings broadly consistent with those in Table 7.6.[20] Perhaps the three strongest results of these studies have been the positive relation between S and P, the negative relation between S and trading volume, and the positive relation between S and various indicators of

---

20 For reviews of this literature see Kenneth Garbade (1982, Chapter 24) and Kalman Cohen, Steven Maier, Robert Schwartz, and David Whitcomb (1979).

risk, such as the concentration of investor holdings of securities, recent price variation, and the maturity and duration of bonds.

SOME EXAMPLES OF DEALER MARKETS. Not surprisingly, the most highly developed dealer market is that in U.S. Treasury securities.[21] This market revolves around dealers who trade actively with each other as well as with hundreds of insurance companies, pension funds, banks, and other large investors. The number of dealers, the volume of trading, and the rapidity of price changes in this market are such that even the dealers make use of brokers. In addition to facilitating the search process, brokers provide anonymity to dealers who do not wish to show their hands. Before the early 1970s the telephone was the principal means by which dealers and brokers searched for the best prices. But they now have video screens that show the best quotations for actively traded issues. An example of such a *billboard screen* is presented in Table 7.7. Billboard screens do not preserve anonymity and have no capability for execution. If dealer X wants to sell some 8s of 1985, he calls dealer C or dealer D, who have quoted the highest bid price. These quotations are not binding, and X may or may not find upon contacting C that the 98.24 ask is still good. Conditions may have changed.

Another service introduced in the 1970s for active issues is the *execution screen,* which is anonymous and shows only the best bids and asks that have been submitted to the *screen broker* who operates the system. An example also appears in Table 7.7. The operators of billboard screens earn income by charging rent to subscribers. But the operators of execution screens charge commissions. If you like a quotation on the execution screen, you place an order through the broker. But you have to work fast. The quotations are firm for only 2 or 3 minutes. Dealer spreads became smaller after the introduction of screens because of the reduction in search costs. Only the best prices now have a chance of being accepted. Brokers' commissions also fell because the screen brokers attracted business by charging lower fees than their telephone competitors.

The dealer markets in *bankers' acceptances, certificates of deposit,* and *Eurodollars* are only a little less sophisticated than the market in Treasury securities. These securities are liabilities of commercial banks, and banks are among the principal dealers.[22] Bankers' acceptances are bank-guaranteed bills of exchange. CDs are negotiable time deposits in banks located in the United States. Eurodollars are negotiable time deposits that are also denominated in dollars but are held in banks outside the United States. In all three of these securities active dealer markets have arisen in the issues of the largest, most

21 The following discussion is based on Kenneth Garbade (1978; 1982, pages 430–435).

22 Several banks are also dealers in Treasury securities.

Table 7.7   Screen Brokers for U.S. Treasury Dealers

Pictured below are bid and offered discount rates for three T bills and bid and offered prices for seven Treasury coupon issues quoted by four dealers as they appeared on the video screen of a billboard system at about 2:30 P.M. on June 7, 1978. Prices for coupon issues are quoted in percentage of par value, with fractions of a percent expressed in thirty-seconds. The bid of 99.29+ by dealer A on the 8 percent note maturing in May 1980 means a bid of 99 plus 29½/32 percent of par value. The numbers to the right of the decimal point are in thirty-seconds, and the plus means an additional ½ of a thirty-second of a percent.

Billboard Screen

	Dealer A		Dealer B		Dealer C		Dealer D	
Issue	Bid	Ask	Bid	Ask	Bid	Ask	Bid	Ask
3-month bill[a]	6.64	6.62	6.64	6.62	6.64	6.62	6.64	6.62
6-month bill[b]	7.115	7.095	7.12	7.10	7.12	7.10	7.12	7.10
1-year bill[c]	7.36	7.34	7.36	7.34	7.36	7.34	7.36	7.34
8 percent, May 1980	99.29+	99.30+	99.29+	99.30+	99.29+	99.30+	99.29+	99.30+
8¼ percent, June 1982	100.3	100.5	100.4	100.5	100.4	100.5	100.4	100.5
7⅞ percent, May 1983	98.18	98.20	98.18+	98.20+	98.18+	98.20+	98.18	98.20
8 percent, February 1985	98.23	98.27	98.23	98.27	98.24	98.26	98.24	98.26
8¼ percent, May 1988	99.5	99.9	99.7	99.9	99.7	99.9	99.7	99.9
7⅞ percent, February 1993	95.8	95.10	95.8	95.10	95.8	95.10	95.7	95.11
8⅜ percent, August 2000	98.31	99.1	98.31	99.1	98.31+	99.1+	98.31	99.1

Video display screens for execution systems show only the highest bid and the lowest offer in each issue. If the same four dealers had entered the *same* bids and offers as those shown above into an execution system (which they need not have done), the video screen for that system would look like the representation below.

Execution Screen

Issue	Bid	Ask
3-month bill	6.64	6.62
6-month bill	7.115	7.10
1-year bill	7.36	7.34
8 percent, May 1980	99.29+	99.30+
8¼ percent, June 1982	100.4	100.5
7⅞ percent, May 1983	98.18+	98.20
8 percent, February 1985	98.24	98.26
8¼ percent, May 1988	99.7	99.9
7⅞ percent, February 1993	95.8	95.10
8⅜ percent, August 2000	98.31+	99.1

In contrast to billboard screens, bidders and offerers are not identified on execution screens. A transactor has to call a sponsor to complete a purchase or sale. The operational execution screens also show the size of a bid or offer, for example, $1 million of T bills, although this is omitted above.

a Bill maturing September 7, 1978.

b Bill maturing December 7, 1978.

c Bill maturing May 29, 1979.

Source: Adapted from Kenneth Garbade, "Electronic Quotation Systems and the Market for Government Securities," Federal Reserve Bank of New York *Quarterly Review,* Summer 1978, pages 13–20.

highly rated banks because of the issues' low risk, convenient sizes (usually $1 million blocks), and standardized maturities (such as 1 week, 30 days, and 60 days). The homogeneity of each of these groups of securities is not much less than that of T bills. The markets in bankers' acceptances and CDs are centered in New York, whereas

London is the center of Eurodollar activity. Brokers are active in these markets for the same reasons as for T bills—to speed communications between dealers and to preserve anonymity.[23]

The markets for *large issues of municipal and corporate bonds* may be called dealer markets although they are not so highly developed as those in the standardized short-term issues of large banks and the U.S. Treasury discussed above. Municipal and corporate bond dealers could just as well be described as brokers; for while they will quote prices upon request for a fairly wide range of issues, they can afford to take positions in only a few. However, they know where the others can be purchased or placed. So in many cases they provide "pretty quick" rather than "immediate" execution.[24]

A very large and dispersed dealer market is the *over-the-counter market in unlisted stocks,* that is, in stocks which are not listed on stock exchanges and which, therefore, in the days before the development of nationwide telegraph and telephone systems in the latter part of the nineteenth century, were traded "over the counters" of stock dealers. The most active of these stocks are quoted on a nationwide computer hookup of video terminals somewhat like the billboard screens used by brokers and dealers in Treasury securities. Dealers disseminate quotations on less active stock issues through the National Daily Quotation Service, which is similar to the "Blue List" of municipal bonds discussed earlier.[25]

About half of *commercial paper* is placed directly, without the assistance of brokers or dealers, by large finance companies that are in the market frequently enough and on a sufficient scale to justify their own sales staffs. These issues are called "direct" or "finance" paper. But nonfinancial corporations and smaller finance companies use the services of commercial paper "dealers," whose principal function in this market is in fact brokerage, that is, the bringing together of borrowers and lenders. There is little true dealer activity in commercial paper because of the heterogeneity of the issuers and their issues. A commercial paper note is a short-term, single-payment security almost identical in form with a bank CD. But the credit ratings of the more-than-1,200 issuers vary substantially, and the sizes and maturities of issues are frequently tailored to the specific desires of lenders. So dealer commercial paper could just as easily have been considered under the heading Brokered Markets. However, commercial paper dealers also reluctantly provide the dealer's service of standing ready, in a pinch, if the lender decides that he didn't really want the paper after all, to take the paper back at a fairly wide spread (about 1/8)

---

23 For further discussions of these markets, see Timothy Cook and Bruce Summers (1981) and Marcia Stigum (1983).

24 See Kenneth Garbade (1982, pages 436–438, 460) for a discussion of these markets.

25 The over-the-counter market in stocks is discussed further in Chapter 11.

above the market. Only 1 or 2 percent of dealer paper is in fact "dealt" in this manner.[26]

Auction markets

An *auction* is a public sale of property to the highest bidder. There are many types of auctions, and they can be classified in a variety of ways. The following discussion will emphasize the distinction between discrete and continuous auctions. Most of these markets will be considered in more detail in later chapters.

Discrete auctions. Nearly everyone has seen an auction at which a stock of items is shown, one at a time, by an auctioneer to a group of prospective buyers and onlookers: artistic pieces at Sotheby's, a mixture of art and more utilitarian objects at Farmer Brown's prior to his departure for Florida, or perhaps the autographs and old clothes of celebrities at a charity benefit. These are *open auctions,* in which hopeful buyers can set their bids in light of the bids of others. *Sealed-bid auctions* are common in government building and equipment contracts and also in *new issues of U.S. Treasury securities.* For example, when the Treasury wishes to sell $10 billion of a particular issue, it requests bids no later than a specified day and hour. The highest bidder gets the quantity for which he bid at his bid price, the next-highest bidder gets his desired quantity at his bid price, and so on until the issue is sold. Low bidders get nothing.[27]

The NYSE was for many of its early years a *call-auction market.* Only a few stocks and bonds were traded on the Exchange, and activity was much less than it is today. The Chairman called listed securities in turn, and the members declared their bids and offers. The principal difference between this call auction and the other discrete auctions mentioned above was that the trading in an issue at the NYSE was not limited to a fixed amount. Later, with the growth of corporations and government debt, the volume of trading required two sessions ("calls"), and then in 1871 the discrete call system gave way to a continuous auction.[28]

Continuous auctions. Most continuous auctions are conducted on *exchanges,* where members gather to buy and sell precisely defined contracts, either for themselves or for their clients, during hours and according to procedures established by the various exchanges. One of the most active continuous auctions takes place at the Chicago Board of Trade's *wheat pit,* within which hundreds of traders shout their bids and offers for the future delivery of wheat. This is a *two-way*

---

26 The commercial paper market is discussed further in Chapter 8. Also see Timothy Cook and Bruce Summers (1981) and Marcia Stigum (1983).

27 A T bill auction is described in more detail in Chapter 8.

28 The development of trading procedures and other aspects of the NYSE are discussed in Chapter 11.

(direct) continuous auction between the buyers and sellers in the pit.[29] By a combination of shouts and hand signals, primarily the latter, a trader indicates his bid, and someone in the crowd responds with an acceptance or a counteroffer. The principle of an exchange auction is that every bid or offer is announced clearly to the crowd so that every trade is the result of *open outcry*. Ideally, a trader with something to sell is able to get the highest price possible at a given time.

Futures exchanges in commodities such as wheat and corn have been active in the United States since the nineteenth century. Continuous auctions of *contracts for the future delivery of financial instruments* date only from the early 1970s but now include foreign currency, Treasury securities, Eurodollars, commercial paper, bank CDs, packages of government-guaranteed mortgages, and even indexes of stock prices. The largest financial futures exchanges are the Chicago Board of Trade, the Chicago Mercantile Exchange, and the New York Futures Exchange. *Stock options* are traded at the Chicago Board Options Exchange and other exchanges in much the same way that futures contracts are traded.

The NYSE and several other *stock exchanges* are also continuous two-way auctions, with the added feature that at least one dealer (the specialist) is assigned to make a market in each stock in order to assure the continuous availability of a "good market," meaning one with "depth," "breadth," and "resiliency." The specialist was discussed above, and these indicators of market performance will be considered in the next section.

Continuous auctions in these futures contracts, stock options, and exchange-listed stocks are made possible and, indeed, necessary by the public's tremendous interest in them. For example a daily average of about 70 million shares, worth about $2 billion, were traded at the NYSE during 1982. Since there were 2,225 listed stocks, this meant average daily trading per stock exceeding 30,000 shares worth nearly $1 million. Average daily trading of IBM, the most active stock, exceeded 700,000 shares. These are small numbers compared to trading volumes on futures exchanges. For example, $25 billion is a normal day for 90-day T bill futures on the Chicago Mercantile Exchange.

Daily transactions in *overnight fed funds* normally exceed $100 billion. These loans are not quite homogeneous, but enough well-known banks trade in this market in sufficient volume that several firms have found it worthwhile to operate *continuous brokered auctions*. Instead of overnight fed funds traders yelling and signaling at one another around a pit or a specialist's post, they communicate their bids and offers by phone through auctioneer-brokers. The system is centered on the auctioneers' order books, which list the bids and offers

---

29 Actually, they are standing on steps that form a shallow hexagonal pit.

of borrowing and lending banks. A borrower phones the auctioneer for his book's best offer, which might be $50 million at 12 percent. Suppose the borrower responds with a bid of 11⅞ for some or all of the $50 million. It might get the funds if this bid beats other outstanding bids and the lending bank is willing to come down from 12 percent. If a bargain is struck, the broker puts the borrower and lender in touch with one another and they arrange the transfer of funds. The auction-eers' order books in overnight fed funds are similar in their function to the execution screens operated by screen brokers in active Treasury securities—which suggests that the latter market could just as well be considered an auction as a brokered market. In fact, it is both.

CHARACTERISTICS OF SECURITY MARKETS
Depth, breadth, and resiliency

A market

. . . possesses depth when there are orders, either actual orders or orders that can be readily uncovered, both above and below the market. The market has breadth when these orders are in vol-ume and come from widely divergent investor groups. It is resil-ient when new orders pour promptly into the market to take ad-vantage of sharp and unexpected fluctuations in prices.[30]

Suppose overnight fed funds have been trading at 8 percent, and the books of broker-auctioneers contain several large orders at each of the following tight array of bids: 8, 7$\frac{15}{16}$, 7⅞, 7$\frac{13}{16}$, . . . , 7½. In addition there are several large offers at each of the rates 8$\frac{1}{16}$, 8⅛, ... The market is said to be *deep* because there are potential buyers and sellers over a wide range of rates above and below that at which the most recent transaction occurred. The market is said to be *broad* because these potential orders exist in substantial volume. A security traded in a market with depth and breadth obviously possesses great *liquidity*. A fed funds lender can easily dump a large amount on this market very quickly with very little, if any, effect on the market rate.[31]

Full order books are visible evidence of depth and breadth. But such formality is not necessary. All that is required is that there be many potential buyers and sellers above and below the current rate—which will be the case in a market with a large number of actual and

---

30 *Report of Ad Hoc Subcommittee on the Government Securities Market to the Federal Open Market Committee,* November 12, 1952, page 265; published in U.S. Congress Joint Committee on the Economic Report, Subcommittee on Economic Stabilization, *Hearings on United States Monetary Policy: Recent Thinking and Experience,* 83rd Cong., 2nd Sess., 1954, pages 257–286. For further discussions of these market characteristics, see Louise Ahearn and Janice Peskin (1971) and Kenneth Garbade (1982).

31 Markets without depth or breadth are said to be *thin.* See Kenneth Garbade (1982, Chapter 26) for a discussion of thinness.

prospective traders in close, but not perfect, agreement about what is a good deal. Stock-exchange specialists also maintain order books. But the continuity of prices in several other markets without such books and sometimes even without dealers, such as futures markets, is evidence of depth and breadth.

A market is said to possess *price continuity* when price changes are small. The fed funds market described above will have price continuity even if several large buyers or sellers suddenly come on the scene. But a stock market which lacks depth or breadth and which receives large orders sporadically may see successive prices of 30, 33, 28, 24, and who knows what next. A rapid succession of sell orders may cause prices of 26, 24, 21, 16, and 12. Such markets, without price continuity, are said to be *disorderly*. An exchange may temporarily close trading in a security under these conditions to give prospective buyers time to respond to the low prices and to give prospective sellers time to reconsider.

Even the deepest and broadest markets are occasionally subjected to large price changes and have a disorderly appearance. Even the best markets (in fact *especially* the best markets) respond quickly and completely to new information. Sharp increases in the price of an oil stock from 30 to 35 to 40 following announcements of drilling successes are not inconsistent with depth and breadth. But large price changes caused merely by the time sequence of orders will not occur in such a market.

When good information, specifically the rapid dissemination of transaction prices, is added to depth and breadth, we have *resiliency*. A resilient market is one in which potential buyers and sellers quickly learn of price changes so that, for example, price declines promptly bring forth buy orders. Resiliency is clearly important to the price continuity discussed above.

Indicators of market quality at the NYSE[32]

Two indicators of the breadth and depth of the markets at the NYSE are listed in Table 7.8. The column headed "price continuity" shows that 89.5 percent of trades in the average stock during 1982 occurred with no change or a change of only $0.125 from the preceding price. This impressive price continuity was not limited to small trades. The NYSE's indicator of "market depth" states that 85.2 percent of trades involving 1,000 or more shares occurred with no change or the minimum ($0.125) change in price.

The remaining columns of the table are concerned with the contributions of specialists to market performance. The last column, the "stabilization rate," indicates that specialists assisted price continuity by directing 88.9 percent of their purchases and sales against prevail-

---

32 See Louise Ahearn and Janice Peskin (1971) for an analysis of indicators of the quality of the U.S. government securities market.

Table 7.8 Indicators of Market Quality at the NYSE

The NYSE keeps track of three "key indicators of market quality": *Price continuity* refers to the size of the price variation, if any, from one trade to the next in the same stock; in 1982, 89.5 percent of all transactions occurred with no change or the minimum variation of ⅛ point. *Market depth* indicates the amount of buying and selling pressure a stock will withstand before its price changes significantly; in 1982 the average stock showed no price change or the minimum ⅛-point change on 82.5 percent of 1,000-share trades. The *quotation spread* is the difference in price between the bid and offer on a stock and was ¼ point or less in 65.1 percent of all quotations during 1982.

Specialists are expected to stabilize price movements by buying and selling from their own accounts against prevailing market trends. The *specialists' stabilization rate* is the percentage of purchases at prices below or sales at prices above the last different price and was 88.9 percent in 1982.

Market Quality and Specialists' Stabilization

	Price Continuity, %	Market Depth, %	Quotation Spreads, %	Stabilization Rate, %
1982	89.5	85.2	65.1	88.9
1981	87.2	81.6	60.4	90.2
1980	86.4	80.4	60.6	90.9
1979	90.6	84.9	71.1	90.0
1978	90.8	84.4	72.9	90.0

Source: Adapted from NYSE *Fact Book*, 1983, page 14.

ing price movements. In other words the Exchange's specialist system is a built-in source of resiliency.

Competition among dealers forces narrow spreads in markets with depth, breadth, and resiliency because the active trading and price continuity in such markets assures substantial and relatively safe dealer profits. And the narrow spreads in turn reinforce depth, breadth, and resiliency by encouraging transactions. Almost two-thirds of specialists' spreads on the NYSE during 1982 were $0.25 or less.

SUMMARY

Much of the above discussion is summarized in Table 7.9, which may also be used as a quick guide to the financial markets and to the location of their treatment in this book. The characteristics of securities and markets are not stated explicitly in the table, but in many cases characteristics may be inferred from the types of markets in which the securities are traded. Continuous auctions, for example, suggest substantial liquidity, reversibility, breadth, depth, resiliency, and, for short periods under normal conditions, low risk.

Several of the securities in Table 7.9 played important parts in earlier chapters (such as certificates of deposit and Eurodollars in the discussions of incentives to innovation and the demand for money in Chapters 2 and 3 and Treasury notes and bonds in the calculation of yields in Chapter 6) and will not be treated in detail again. Some of the others, especially the money market instruments, were discussed previously and will be treated in some detail again, either in extensive

Table 7.9   Securities and Their Markets

Security	Description of Security	Description of Market	Chapters
Money			
Currency and checking accounts	The medium of exchange, the generally accepted means of payment.	Money is one side of every transaction.	1–20, especially 3 and 4
Other Money Market Instruments (Maturities of 1 Year or Less)			
Overnight federal funds	Unsecured 1-day loans of Fed deposits between depository institutions, especially commercial banks.	Some banks (correspondents) maintain continuous direct relationships; and some of these and other banks act as brokers; but most trading is through a continuous auction operated by specialized fed funds brokers.	3, 4, 7, 9
Term federal funds	Unsecured loans, with maturities exceeding 1 day, of Fed deposits between depository institutions.	Trading is directly between correspondents or in a brokered market through specialized brokers or banks acting as brokers.	3, 4, 7, 9
Repurchase agreements (overnight and term)	Secured loans between depository institutions and by nonfinancial corporations and state and local governments to depository institutions and nonbank government securities dealers; accomplished, like fed funds, by immediate transfers between accounts at Fed Banks, but are unlike fed funds in being collateralized by U.S. securities.	Much like the market for term fed funds, with government securities dealers also serving as brokers and dealers in RPs.	3, 4, 9
Call loans	Secured loans, redeemable on demand, by banks to security brokers and dealers.	Direct, continuous relationships between broker-dealers and their banks. (Call loans were auctioned on the floor of the NYSE until 1946.)	9, 11, 16
T bills	Single-payment (discount) securities of U.S. Treasury, mostly maturing in 13, 26, or 52 weeks.	New issues sold through a discrete, sealed-bid auction. Secondary market is a broker-assisted dealer market, which, since the appearance of screen brokers, approximates a continuous auction.	3, 6, 7, 8, 18, 19
Bankers' acceptances	Bank-guaranteed bills of exchange, similar in form to T bills.	Originated much like other bank loans. However, with the guarantees ("acceptances") of well-known banks they are traded in an active broker-assisted dealer market. "Tiers" of bankers' acceptances, ranked according to the names of accepting banks, are treated as homogeneous securities, much like T bills.	3, 7, 8
Large CDs ($100,000 or more)	Negotiable bank deposits with specified terms to maturity.	Most CDs are originated like other deposits—by being continuously available (on tap) at stated terms. Large blocks are offered through investment bankers. Secondary market is similar to that for bankers' acceptances.	2, 3, 7
Eurodollars	Negotiable dollar-denominated certificates of deposit in banks outside the United States.	Market is similar to that for large CDs but is centered on London instead of New York.	3, 7
Dealer commercial paper	Unsecured notes issued mainly by large nonfinancial corporations with the best credit ratings or by smaller firms with the guarantees of large financial or nonfinancial firms.	Issued through underwriter-broker-dealers. Not much of a secondary market though dealers will sometimes, for a fee, take paper back before maturity.	3, 7, 8
Direct (finance) commercial paper	Unsecured notes issued by a few large finance companies and bank holding companies.	Placed directly by issuers. Not much of a secondary market though issuers will sometimes take paper back before maturity.	3, 7, 8

Table 7.9 (continued)

Security	Description of Security	Description of Market	Chapters
Capital Market Instruments (Maturities Greater Than 1 Year)			
Common stock	Shares of ownership in corporations, to which profits may be distributed in the form of dividends.	New issues are sold through investment bankers who perform underwriter, broker, and dealer functions. In the secondary market less active issues are traded in direct search and/or brokered markets; active issues are traded in dealer and/or continuous-auction (exchange) markets. Large blocks are traded in a manner similar to new issues.	7, 10, 11
Preferred stock	Shares of ownership in corporations, for which dividends are fixed in advance but are not legally binding except that they must be paid before common stock can receive dividends.	Same as common stock except that common issues tend to be larger and more actively traded than preferred issues.	7, 10, 11
Corporate notes and bonds	Secured (mortgage bonds) and unsecured (debentures) debt, usually with payments in the forms of semiannual coupons and a principal at maturity.	The most active issues are traded in a dealer market, less active issues in a brokered market. A few very active issues are traded by continuous auction on exchanges.	7, 10, 11
Treasury notes and bonds	Similar in form to corporate notes and bonds, but without mortgage security or other covenants for investor protection.	New issues are sold like T bills. Secondary market is a broker-assisted dealer market, with the most active issues traded (like T bills) through screen brokers.	6, 7
Federal agency securities	Notes and bonds (similar in form to Treasury notes and bonds) and certificates (similar to mortgages), issued by federal agencies that mainly serve as intermediaries between the capital markets and the farm and housing sectors.	New issues are sold mainly through fiscal agents that perform the advising and marketing functions, on a continuing basis, normally performed by investment bankers. Large new issues are sometimes placed through investment banking syndicates in the same manner as corporate bonds. The secondary market is similar to that for Treasury securities and active corporate and municipal securities.	
State and local government notes and bonds ("municipals," "tax exempts")	Similar in form to corporate notes and bonds, but coupons are exempt from federal income taxes.	A new issue is sold through the investment banking syndicate that has submitted the best bid. The secondary market is similar to that for corporate debt.	7, 10
Other Securities			
Foreign exchange	The money of other countries, traded either for spot (within 2 days) or forward (after 2 days) delivery.	Traded in a broker-assisted dealer market much like those in Treasury securities and fed funds.	12
Financial futures	Contracts for the future delivery, at stated prices, of several of the securities listed above, foreign exchange, or indexes of stock prices.	Continuous auctions on organized exchanges.	7, 12
Options	Options are contracts for the discretionary, or "optional," purchase or sale of an asset at a specified "exercise" price; available on gold futures and several of the securities listed above (including some financial futures).	Continuous auctions on organized exchanges.	7

accounts of their own characteristics and trading conditions in Chapters 8 and 9 or as supporting players in the development of other themes. Very little was said in Chapters 1 to 6 about capital market instruments other than Treasury issues or about futures contracts. These will be discussed in Chapters 10 to 12.

QUESTIONS

1. Discuss the characteristics of one of your investments, for example, a car or a bicycle. How, if at all, did these characteristics affect the price you were willing to pay?

2. Suppose you get a monthly allowance of $200 for living expenses. Where do you keep this money until you spend it, in a checking account, savings account, stocks, bonds, or some other form? Why?

   On the other hand suppose you are given custody of $200 million to disburse over the next month. Where do you keep these funds? Why?

3. Suppose a text that you have bought and are using this term is going to be used next term. The bookstore will buy it for one-half and sell it for three-quarters of the original price. If the bookstore's resale price is assumed to be the full market value, what is your estimate of the liquidity of this book in terms of both (a) the proportion of that value that can be realized immediately and (b) the time that is likely to elapse between your decision to sell (immediately after the final) and your ability to get the full value?

4. Is the bookstore's dealer spread exorbitant? On what calculations have you based your answer?

5. Why do long-term securities carry larger bid-ask spreads than short-term securities?

6. Why is the reversibility of a 10-year flower bond less than the reversibilities of other 10-year U.S. bonds?

7. Why should investments in common stock be a good hedge against inflation?

8. Under what conditions would T bills be a good hedge against inflation?

9. What was the average rate of return on demand deposits during 1953 to 1971?

10. The amounts bought and sold by the dealer in Figure 7.2 are identical. This will not be the case every day but is likely to be the case on the average. Why? Please use a diagram like Figure 7.2 in your answer, except that D' and S intersect at a different quantity than S' and D.

11. (a) How may a dealer market approximate an auction market?
    (b) How may a dealer market also be a brokered market?
    (c) How may an auction market be a brokered market?

12. The markets for consumer loans from (a) banks and (b) automobile finance companies were not discussed in Chapter 7. In what kinds of markets are these loans traded?

13. Explain the relative liquidities of T bills, municipals, and houses in Figure 7.1 in terms of the market concepts of breadth, depth, and resiliency.

14. Discuss the relative breadths, depths, and resiliencies of stocks *A* and *B* in problem 5.

15. Compare the markets for T bills, municipals, and houses in terms of the NYSE's indicators of market quality.

PROBLEMS

1. Confirm the values of P_a and P_b used in the derivation of the reversibility of the 63-day bill of October 13, 1983.

2. Confirm the reversibilities of the 6-month and 11-month T bills reported in Table 7.1.

3. Calculate, compare, and explain the reversibilities, on August 11, 1983, of the U.S. 3¼s and 14⅛s of May 1985.

4. Suppose the specialist in XYZ stock quotes 36 ask and 35 bid. Your broker charges a commission of 2 percent of the value of each transaction. What is the reversibility of an investment in this stock?

5. About 90,000 shares of stock *A* are traded daily in 100 transactions; *A* sells for an average of $30, with a day-to-day standard deviation of $1; it is held by three institutions, is traded about equally on two exchanges, and is one of four stocks handled by its specialist unit, which has a capitalization of $1 million. On the other hand about 50,000 shares of stock *B* are traded daily in 100 transactions; *B* sells for an average of $40, with a day-to-day standard deviation of $2; it is held by two institutions, is traded on only one exchange, and is one of five stocks handled by its specialist unit, which has a capitalization of $500,000. Which stock has the largest spread, and why?

REFERENCES

Louise Ahearn and Janice Peskin, "Market Performance as Reflected in Aggregative Indicators," in *Joint Treasury–Federal Reserve Study of the U.S. Government Securities Market,* Staff Studies, part 2, January 1971, pages 94–153.

Kalman J. Cohen, Steven F. Maier, Robert A. Schwartz, and David K. Whitcomb, "Market Makers and the Market Spread: A Review of Recent Literature," *Journal of Financial and Quantitative Analysis,* November 1979, pages 813–835.

Timothy Q. Cook and Bruce J. Summers (eds.), *Instruments of the Money Market,* 5th ed., Federal Reserve Bank of Richmond, Richmond, VA, 1981.

Harold Demsetz, "The Cost of Transacting," *Quarterly Journal of Economics,* February 1968, pages 33–53.

Frank J. Fabozzi and Frank G. Zarb (eds.), *Handbook of Financial Markets,* Dow Jones-Irwin, Homewood, IL, 1981.

Eugene F. Fama and G. William Schwert, "Asset Returns and Inflation," *Journal of Fi-*

nancial Economics, December 1977, pages 115–146.

Kenneth Garbade, "Electronic Quotation Systems and the Market for Government Securities," Federal Reserve Bank of New York *Quarterly Review,* Summer 1978, pages 13–20.

Kenneth Garbade, *Securities Markets,* McGraw-Hill, New York, 1982.

Thomas S. Y. Ho and Hans R. Stoll, "The Dynamics of Dealer Markets under Competition," *Journal of Finance,* September 1983, pages 1053–1074.

Alan Kraus and Hans R. Stoll, "Price Impacts of Block Trading on the New York Stock Ex-change," *Journal of Finance,* June 1972, pages 569–588.

R. H. Inglis Palgrave, "Liquid Assets," *Dictionary of Political Economy,* vol. 2, Macmillan, London, 1896.

Marcia Stigum, *The Money Market,* rev. ed., Dow Jones-Irwin, Homewood, IL, 1983.

Seha M. Tinic, "The Economics of Liquidity Services," *Quarterly Journal of Economics,* February 1972, pages 79–93.

James Tobin, "Properties of Assets," chap. 2, unpublished ms.

Ray B. Westerfield, "Liquidity," *Encyclopaedia of the Social Sciences,* vol. 9, Macmillan, New York, 1933, pages 491–495.

TRADITIONAL MONEY MARKET INSTRUMENTS

For I have bils for monie by exchange
From Florence, and must heere deliver them.
William Shakespeare, *The Taming of the Shrew*, act 4, sc. 2

Debt instruments are simply promises to pay specified sums of money on specified dates. The money market instruments considered in this and the next chapter are, next to money itself, the most elementary form of debt. Each is a promise to pay a *single* specified sum of money on a specified date, usually in the very near future. Most of them have "good characters" in the senses discussed in Chapter 7: low risk and high liquidity, divisibility, and reversibility. Several were encountered in the discussions of money substitutes and the payments system in Chapters 3 and 4. But money market instruments are not identical. Sometimes significant differences in their characteristics have evolved over time in response to a variety of needs. Most of them are still in the process of change. This chapter is concerned with the evolution, present state, and possible future direction of a few "traditional" money market instruments. By traditional we mean those that have been important in the money markets for at least 50 years.

Newspapers have made it easy to follow the adventures of money market instruments by reporting "money rates" in convenient formats, such as that of Table 8.1, which has been reproduced from the *Wall Street Journal*. One of the purposes of our discussion is to help the reader place newspaper accounts in perspective through an awareness of the evolution of money market instruments and rates. Another objective is to increase the understanding of those accounts by familiarity with some of the more important technical aspects of the money markets—the nature of each instrument and who trades it, how, and why. We begin with *bills of exchange* because this centuries-old instrument has served as the model for the later and now more important money market securities considered in the three subsequent sections: *bankers' acceptances, Treasury bills,* and *commercial paper.*

Table 8.1

Money Rates

Monday, October 24, 1983

The key U.S. and foreign annual interest rates below are a guide to general levels but don't always represent actual transactions.

PRIME RATE: 11%. The base rate on corporate loans at large U.S. money center commercial banks.

FEDERAL FUNDS: 9½% high, 9⅜% low, 9⅜% near closing bid, 9 7/16% offered. Reserves traded among commercial banks for overnight use in amounts of $1 million or more. Source: Mabon, Nugent & Co., N.Y.

DISCOUNT RATE: 8½%. The charge on loans to depository institutions by the New York Federal Reserve Bank.

CALL MONEY: 10% to 10½%. The charge on loans to brokers on stock exchange collateral.

COMMERCIAL PAPER placed directly by General Motors Acceptance Corp.: 9% 30 to 89 days; 8⅞% 90 to 179 days; 8¾% 180 to 270 days.

COMMERCIAL PAPER: High-grade unsecured notes sold through dealers by major corporations in multiples of $1,000: 9.20% 30 days; 9.15% 60 days; 9⅛% 90 days.

CERTIFICATES OF DEPOSIT: 9.15% one month; 9.15% two months; 9¼% three months; 9.30% six months; 9½% one year. Typical rates paid by major banks on new issues of negotiable C.D.s, usually on amounts of $1 million and more. The minimum unit is $100,000.

BANKERS ACCEPTANCES: 9.15% 30 days; 9.15% 60 days; 9.10% 90 days; 9.10% 120 days; 9.05% 150 days; 9.05% 180 days. Negotiable, bank-backed business credit instruments typically financing an import order.

LONDON LATE EURODOLLARS: 9⅝% to 9½% one month; 9⅝% to 9½% two months; 9¾% to 9⅝% three months; 9 13/16% to 9 11/16% four months; 9⅞% to 9¾% five months; 9⅞% to 9¾% six months.

LONDON INTERBANK OFFERED RATES (LIBOR): 9¾% three months; 9⅞% six months; 10⅛% one year. The average of interbank offered rates for dollar deposits in the London market based on quotations at five major banks.

FOREIGN PRIME RATES: Canada 11%; Germany 7.75%; Japan 6.3%; Switzerland 6%; Britain 9%. These rate indications aren't directly comparable; lending practices vary widely by location. Source: Morgan Guaranty Trust Co.

TREASURY BILLS: Results of the Monday, October 24, 1983, auction of short-term U.S. government bills, sold at a discount from face value in units of $10,000 to $1 million: 8.66%, 13 weeks; 8.91%, 26 weeks.

FEDERAL HOME LOAN MORTGAGE CORP. (Freddie Mac): Posted yields on 30-year mortgage commitments for delivery within 30 days. 13.270%, standard conventional fixed-rate mortgages; 12.15%, three-year adjustable rate mortgages.

MERRILL LYNCH READY ASSETS TRUST: 9.12%. Annualized average rate of return after expenses for the past 30 days; not a forecast of future returns.

Source: *Wall Street Journal,* October 25, 1983.

BILLS OF EXCHANGE

What are bills of exchange?

We begin with the legal definition:

> A bill of exchange is an unconditional order in writing addressed by one person to another, signed by the person giving it, requiring the person to whom it is addressed to pay on demand or at a fixed or determinable future time a sum certain in money to order or to bearer.
>
> Uniform Negotiable Instruments Act, Section 126[1]

1 The Uniform Negotiable Instruments Act dates from the early twentieth century. It has since been superseded by the Uniform Commercial Code, which has retained most of the provisions

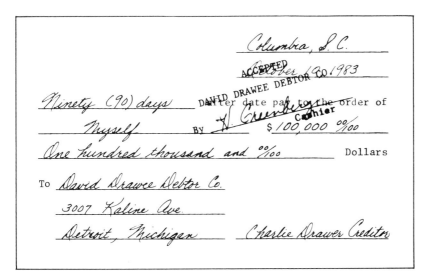

Columbia, S.C.

ACCEPTED *October 10, 1983*

DAVID DRAWEE DEBTOR

Ninety (90) days   DA̶ft̶er date pay to the order of

BY *L. Greenberg*   Cashier

Myself $ *100,000 00/100*

One hundred thousand and 00/100 _____ Dollars

To *David Drawee Debtor Co.*

   3007 Kaline Ave.

   Detroit, Michigan   *Charlie Drawer Creditor*

Figure 8.1   An accepted bill of exchange.

A bill of exchange is shown in Figure 8.1. Unlike a promissory note, which is an IOU, or *promise to pay,* a bill of exchange is an *order to pay.* The person who gives the order is called the drawer, and the person ordered to pay is the drawee. In the case in Figure 8.1 Charlie Creditor has ordered the David Drawee Debtor Co. to pay him (Creditor) $100,000 90 days after October 10, 1983. In many cases, the drawer will order the drawee to pay a third party, perhaps the drawer's agent or someone to whom the drawer is in debt. In such an event, the third party's name replaces "Myself" on the bill.

Bills of exchange are often called "drafts" and in this section we use the terms "bills," "bills of exchange," and "drafts" interchangeably.

Acceptances

Of course ordering someone to pay may be easier than getting him to pay. Let us see how the bill in Figure 8.1 was originated by the drawer and validated (accepted) by the drawee. Charlie Creditor of Columbia, South Carolina, operates a trucking company. On October 10 one of his trucks delivers an order of grits worth $98,000 to the David Drawee Debtor Co., a food wholesaler in Detroit. By prior arrangement Creditor does not demand payment on the spot but extends credit to the Debtor Co. for 90 days at a rate of interest slightly in excess of 8 percent per annum. The evidence of the latter's debt to the former is the *accepted* bill in Figure 8.1. Charlie instructed his driver not to unload the goods until an authorized official of the Debtor Co. had accepted the bill, that is, had agreed to make the ordered payment at

---

of the UNI, including the requirements that must be satisfied by a bill of exchange. See Jules Bogen (1964, page 24.1) and Article 3-104 of the UCC.

the specified time. Upon acceptance the bill effectively becomes a promissory note.

Bills of exchange are discount instruments

Although the rate of interest on this bill exceeds 8 percent annually, it is quoted at a discount rate of precisely 8 percent. As in the case of market quotations for Treasury bills discussed in Chapter 6, as well as most other money market instruments, bills of exchange are quoted at simple annual discounts. The Debtor Co. has in effect issued (sold) a 90-day, single-payment security with a face value of $100,000 payable on January 8, 1984. The bill has been sold to Charlie Creditor for $98,000, that is, at a 2 percent discount from its face value, which, following the money market's practice of quoting simple annual rates and its assumption that there are 360 days in a year, gives the quoted discount rate of 8 percent.

Rediscounting

Bills of exchange differ from ordinary trade credit in being negotiable. Creditor might not want to wait until January for Debtor's payment, in which case he *rediscounts* the bill. He may *endorse* the bill and sell it to a bank, bill dealer, or someone else at a price determined by current interest rates and the buyer's assessment of the creditworthiness of the Debtor Co. and Charlie. Yes, Charlie. Once he has signed his name on the back of the bill, he is liable for the Debtor Co.'s debt if the latter fails to pay the holder of the bill the full $100,000 on January 8.

Suppose Charlie holds the bill 30 days and then rediscounts it at the Carolina National Bank at a rate of 9 percent. Because the bill now has 60 days to maturity, he sells the bill for $98,500.[2] The bank itself might later endorse and sell (rediscount) the bill. Every time the bill changes hands (gains another endorsement) its creditworthiness is increased because every one of the endorsers stands surety in the event of default by the Debtor Co.[3]

Some special types of bills of exchange

It is interesting to note that a check is a "bill of exchange drawn on a bank payable on demand."[4] If the entry "Ninety (90) days after date" on the bill in Figure 8.1 were changed to "on demand" or "at sight"

---

2 $P = \$100,000 \ [1 - (60/360) \ (0.09)] = \$98,500.$

3 One of Charles Dickens's characters, Mr. Pancks, was not impressed by such evidences of security:

> It's no satisfaction to be done by two men instead of one. One's enough. A person who can't pay gets another person who can't pay to guarantee that he can pay.

> *Little Dorrit*, bk. 1, ch. 23

4 UCC, Article 3-104.

and if the Debtor Co.'s name were replaced by that of a bank, the bill would be simply an ordinary check written to "cash." Unless your checking account has insufficient funds, the bank "accepts" the check by making the ordered payment. Bills of exchange like those in Figure 8.1, which are payable on or after some specified date in the future, are often called "time drafts." Checks are often called "sight drafts." Another special case of bills of exchange is the banker's acceptance, which is considered next.

BANKERS' ACCEPTANCES (BAs)
A working definition
BAs are bank-guaranteed bills of exchange normally used to finance foreign trade. Under specified conditions and for a fee a bank may guarantee payment of a draft that has been drawn on it by an importer or an exporter by stamping "accepted" on the face of the draft (bill). These instruments, which were the principal means by which London became the world's leading financial center, make it possible for traders whose creditworthiness is unknown to each other to enter into virtually riskless transactions. BAs travel widely and experience interesting lives. The next section describes the origin and life of a typical BA.[5]

Creation and life of an acceptance
BAs are often supported by *letters of credit* (L/C). For example suppose Leather Goods, Inc., of Chicago wants to buy leather coats costing $100,000 from Fabricas Majorca, S.A., of Barcelona. Leather Goods contacts its loan officer at the First National Bank of Chicago (First Chicago) and applies for an L/C to be issued "on its behalf" and "in favor of" Fabricas Majorca.[6] The application is shown in Figure 8.2.[7] If the loan officer is satisfied with the terms proposed by Leather Goods, he will mail an L/C that conveys those terms to the beneficiary (Fabricas Majorca) through an "advising bank," which is usually the beneficiary's bank and in this case is Banco Español de Credito.

The L/C authorizes Fabricas Majorca to draw a draft for $100,000

---

5 There are many types of BAs not discussed below. For example BAs may be used to finance domestic rather than foreign trade, not all are initiated by letters of credit, not all are accompanied by shipping documents, and some, such as "dollar exchange" acceptances, are not based on specific transactions but are used to acquire foreign exchange for short periods. These and other BAs are discussed in the references at the end of this chapter.

6 This example has been taken from First National Bank of Chicago's publications of 1977 (Sy Banaitis) and 1981. Other examples are given in First Boston Corporation (1980), Jack Hervey (1976), and Timothy Cook and Bruce Summers (1981).

7 Most L/Cs, like that arising from the application in Figure 8.2 are "irrevocable." "A revocable credit, once established, can be modified or cancelled at any time without notice to or consent from the seller," although such "modification or cancellation . . . becomes effective only upon receipt of such notice." For obvious reasons, revocable L/Cs are not popular with sellers and are used largely between parent and subsidiary companies [First National Bank of Chicago (1981, page 20)].

APPLICATION FOR IRREVOCABLE COMMERCIAL LETTER OF CREDIT

The First National Bank of Chicago
International Banking Department/Import Letter of Credit Unit
Two First National Plaza, Chicago, Illinois 60670

F.N.B.C. No. GC 1234
(FOR BANK USE ONLY)

Date February 13, 198—

Please issue an irrevocable Letter of Credit substantially as set forth below and forward same to your correspondent by:

[X] Airmail   [ ] Airmail, with short preliminary cable advice   [ ] Full Cable, for delivery to the beneficiary

In issuing the credit you are expressly authorized to make such changes from the terms of this application as you, in your sole discretion, may deem advisable provided no such changes shall vary the principal terms hereof.

	FOR ACCOUNT OF (APPLICANT)
BANCO ESPANOL DE CREDITO BARCELONA, SPAIN	LEATHER GOODS INC. CHICAGO, ILLINOIS

IN FAVOR OF (BENEFICIARY)	AMOUNT
FABRICAS MAJORCA S.A. (COMPLETE ADDRESS)'	US$100,000.00 (ONE HUNDRED THOUSAND U.S. DOLLARS) Drafts must be presented for negotiation or presented to Drawee on or before (Expiry Date) August 12, 198—

Available by drafts ____180 days sight____ drawn, at your option, on you or your correspondent for ____100____ % of the Invoice value.

When accompanied by the following documents, as checked:

[X] Commercial Invoice (4)   [ ] Packing List
[X] Customs Invoice (4)
[ ] Marine and War Risk Insurance Policy and/or Certificate ____
[ ] Other ____
(If other insurance is required, please state risks)

[ ] Other documents ____

[ ] Air Waybill consigned to ____

[X] ON BOARD Original Ocean Bill of Lading (if more than one original has been issued all are required)
issued to order of: Shipper, blank endorsed
marked: NOTIFY ABC Forwarding Co., 38 S. Dearborn St., Chicago Freight: [ ] Collect [ ] Paid

COVERING: Merchandise described in the invoice as: (Mention commodity only in generic terms omitting details as to grade, quality, etc.)
2000 leather coats at $50.00 each

Check one: [ ] FAS   [ ] FOB   [X] C&F   [ ] CIF   [ ] C&I   Chicago, Illinois

Shipment from: Spain
To: Chicago, Illinois via the Great Lakes   [X] Partial Shipments Prohibited   [X] Transshipments Prohibited

[X] Documents must be presented to negotiating or paying bank within ____10____ days after the date of issuance of documents evidencing shipment or dispatch or taken in charge (shipping documents) but within validity of letter of credit.

[X] Insurance effected by applicant. Applicant agrees to keep insurance coverage in force until this transaction is completed.
Please instruct the negotiating or Drawee Bank to forward one set of negotiable documents to our Customs House Broker.
ABC Forwarding Co., 38 South Dearborn Street, Chicago, Illinois

Other Instructions: Discount charges are for [X] Applicant [ ] Beneficiary

Unless otherwise instructed, documents shall be forwarded to you in one airmail.

PLEASE DATE AND OFFICIALLY SIGN THIS AGREEMENT ON THE REVERSE SIDE OF THIS APPLICATION

FOR BANK USE ONLY: Liabilities outstanding:	Approved by:	COMMISSION
Contingent ____ Acceptances ____ Accept. not under L/C ____ Accept. by other banks ____ Standby ____ Loans ____ Total ____	AUTHORIZED SIGNATURE Group:	RATE ____ % MIN. ____ APPROVED ____

FORM 8270-7-AA (REV. 4-77)

The credit will be subject to the Uniform Customs and Practice for Documentary Credits of the International Chamber of Commerce, presently in effect.

Source: First National Bank of Chicago, *Collections, Letters of Credit, and Bankers' Acceptances,* Chicago, 1981.

Figure 8.2

against First Chicago. The term "180 days sight" means that First Chicago will pay the beneficiary (the seller) the face amount ($100,000) of the draft at sight, that is, immediately upon presentation of the draft, and expects to be repaid by the applicant (the buyer) within 180 days. The bank has thus extended credit (for 180 days) to Leather Goods by paying that company's debt to Fabricas Majorca.

L/Cs are not unconditional guarantees of payment. Payment will be made only after the terms of the letter have been fulfilled. In particular the shipping documents checked in Figure 8.2 must accompany the draft before it will be honored by First Chicago. The bank wants proof that the loan is secured, that is, that the coats were actually sent to Leather Goods.

Upon receipt of the L/C, Fabricas Majorca ships the coats, obtains the necessary shipping documents, draws a draft for $100,000 against First Chicago, and asks its bank to collect the money. Banco Español de Credito forwards the shipping documents and the draft shown at the top of Figure 8.3 to its correspondent in the United States, say, the Chase Bank of New York, with instructions to present the draft for acceptance at the originating (drawee) bank, First Chicago. If the documents conform to the agreement with Leather Goods (see Figure 8.2), First Chicago accepts the draft by stamping it ACCEPTED as indicated in Figure 8.3. By accepting this time draft, First Chicago promises to pay the draft amount of $100,000 at maturity.[8] The draft in Figure 8.3 is due 180 days from the date of acceptance, that is, on October 28, which is 180 days after May 1.

The cost of an acceptance

Although First Chicago pays the face amount ($100,000) of the draft immediately (on May 1) to the beneficiary (Fabricas Majorca), its loan to Leather Goods is less than $100,000. This is because BAs are discount instruments and the L/C specifies that the discount charges are for the account of Leather Goods (the "Applicant" in "Other Instructions"). For example suppose the market rate of discount on virtually risk-free BAs of the kind we have been discussing is 10.25 percent. The discount charge on a 180-day acceptance with face value of $100,000 will be

$$\frac{\$100,000(180)(0.1025)}{360} = \$5,125$$

---

8 The form in Figure 8.3 has been replaced by newer and more efficient drafts, which are accepted when an authorized official's name is signed in a space already provided on the form. Acceptance *stamps* are therefore no longer necessary. But we show a stamp for old times' sake so that, in years to come, people might realize why they still speak of stamping acceptances even though stamping no longer occurs.

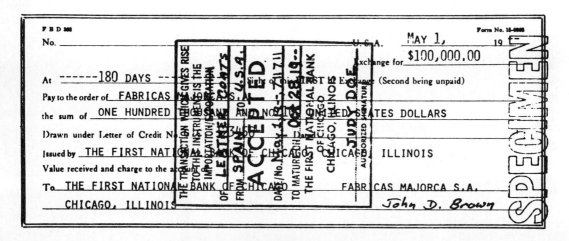

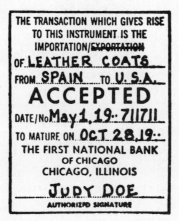

Source: Sy J. Banaitis, *International Letters of Credit*, First National Bank of Chicago, Chicago, 1977.

Figure 8.3   A banker's acceptance.

Discount charges have to be paid immediately so that the amount of the loan (before commission) is

(8.1)

$$L = \$100,000 \left[1 - \frac{Dd}{360} \right]$$

$$= \$100,000 \left[1 - \frac{180(0.1025)}{360} \right] = \$94,875$$

First Chicago also charges a commission, which may vary from 1.5 to 3 percent per annum, depending on Leather Goods' creditworthiness and competitive strength. Assuming a commission of 3 percent, we see from Table 8.2 that the effective cost to Leather Goods of financing its purchase of Spanish coats by means of a BA is 13.25 percent on a 360-day discount basis, or—more meaningfully—14.19 percent per annum on a simple interest basis. This is compared with the simple annual interest rate of 15.25 percent on a hypothetical prime loan.

Table 8.2   A Comparison of the Costs of Acceptance and Prime Loan Financing

180-day Acceptance, %		Prime Loan,[a] %	
Discount rate	10.25	Prime rate	12.20
Acceptance commission	3.00	Implicit cost of 20%	
Total cost on discount basis	13.25	compensating balance	3.05
Total cost on simple annual		Total cost on simple annual	
basis	14.19	basis	15.25

The acceptance is a liability of the Leather Goods Co. for $100,000, for which it received the face amount less the discount charge and commission and fees, that is

$$\$100,000 - \frac{0.1325(180)}{360} (\$100,000) = \$93,375$$

Therefore the simple annual interest rate on the acceptance, which for comparability with the prime rate will be quoted on a 360-day basis, is

$$R_a = \frac{\$6,625}{\$93,375} \times \frac{360}{180} = 14.19\%$$

Now consider the effective cost of a prime loan. With a 20% compensating balance Leather Goods must borrow $125,000 to obtain the use of $100,000. At a prime rate of 12.20% on a 360-day basis, or 6.10% on a 180-day basis, the effective simple annual rate of interest on the loan is

$$R_p = \frac{0.0610(\$125,000)}{\$100,000} \times \frac{360}{180} = 15.25\%$$

a The prime rate is quoted on a simple annual (not a discount) basis, assuming 360 days in a year.

Source: Patterned after Marcia Stigum, *The Money Market,* rev. ed., Dow Jones-Irwin, Homewood, IL, 1983, tab. 17.4.

The data in Table 8.2 do not account for all the costs of BAs and prime loans. Bank-customer relationships are often complicated and involve many costs and benefits to bank and borrower. Access to prime loans and also to BAs may be contingent upon the deposit record and the use of bank services by prospective borrowers. So we are unsure even in the present example which source of funds is cheaper for Leather Goods. But there is at least one important factor operating to make the cost of BAs less than that of prime loans: the liquidity of the former as an investment for First Chicago. The existence of a good secondary market for BAs makes it possible for investors in these securities to convert them quickly into cash. This feature is worth something to First Chicago and serves as an inducement to extend credit in the form of BAs somewhat more cheaply than through prime loans.

Acceptances as investments

Because they are guaranteed by the largest banks, BAs are considered relatively riskless and therefore earn low yields. Yields on BAs move closely with those on large certificates of deposit (CDs), which are also liabilities of large banks. Their low risk is indicated in Figure 8.4 by the close relationship between the discount rates quoted by dealers on 3-month BAs and 3-month Treasury bills—except just before and during recessions, when business failures tend to be greatest.[9] Apparently investors worry about the safety even of BAs during such periods although there has been no reported loss of principal on these investments since they were introduced to the United States in 1914. The courts have held that the accepting bank enters into or holds the L/C agreement "not for its own benefit or the benefit of its general creditors, but in trust for the holder of the acceptance."[10] That is, holders of BAs take precedence over other bank creditors. This may explain why BA yields are slightly lower than are those on CDs. Notice in Table 8.1 that representative discount rates on 3-month CDs, BAs, and Treasury bills were 9.25, 9.10, and 8.66 percent, respectively, on October 24, 1983.

Banks have found the sale of their acceptances a convenient way of attracting funds from foreign and domestic investors interested in safe, liquid, short-term assets—almost as good as Treasury bills and

---

9 The shaded areas in Figure 8.4 identify recessions as defined by the National Bureau of Economic Research (NBER). The beginning and ending months (peaks and troughs) of recessions are chosen by the NBER by necessarily nonrigorous finger-in-the-wind methods. Yet their dates are probably as reasonable as any and may in fact, as advertised, "mark the approximate dates when . . . aggregate economic activity reached its cyclical high or low levels" (*Business Conditions Digest*, any issue, page 1). Although the 1966 to 1967 "minirecession" has not been accorded official sanction by the NBER, some of their publications acknowledge such a recession, and we have used their dates [Solomon Fabricant (1971)].

10 First Boston Corporation (1980, page 192). Continuing to quote from this source: "The landmark decision on this subject [*Bank of the United States v. Seltzer*, App. Div. 225, 251 N.Y. Supp. 637 (1937)] involved the failure of the Bank of the United States in New York in December 1930, with 403 acceptances outstanding."

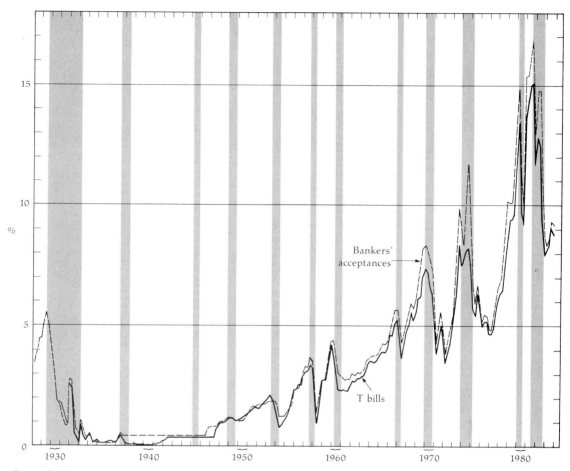

Source: *Banking and Monetary Statistics* and *Federal Reserve Bulletins*.

Figure 8.4   Discount rates on 3-month Treasury bills and bankers' acceptances, quarterly averages, 1928 to 1983.

with a higher yield. In 1983 only about 11 percent of BAs were held by the accepting banks, down from about 30 percent in the early 1970s.

The dealer market for BAs

The secondary market for BAs, like that for U.S. government securities, is an over-the-counter market. About twenty dealers, both separate firms and divisions of large banks, deal in BAs directly with other dealers, banks, insurance companies, corporations, and other large investors. Dealers quote bid and asked discount rates for BAs in the same manner as for Treasury bills (discussed in Chapter 6).

Because of the varying dollar amounts involved in international trade transactions, acceptances are available in a wide variety of principal amounts. Since the acceptance dealers carry a stock of

drafts purchased from the many prime commercial banks doing
an international business, acceptances are usually available in
principal amounts suitable for both large and small investments
and with a wide variety of maturity dates.

First Boston Corporation (1980, page 193)

Acceptance dealers have developed a *tier system,* by which banks
are ranked according to the quality of their BAs. The top tier contains
the ten largest U.S. banks. The "eligible" BAs of these banks are called
"prime" BAs and are traded anonymously by dealers in $5 million
blocks. The bank's name is not mentioned. All the BAs receive the
same rate, and dealers need only state that these BAs are "on the run"
(that is, in the top tier) and specify the number of days to maturity.
On-the-run BAs are the most homogeneous group of securities issued
by the private sector.

The second, third, and fourth tiers consist of U.S. banks that are
smaller or less active in the acceptance market than are banks in the
top tier. U.S. branches of foreign banks have separate tier systems.
The most important are Japanese banks, whose BAs (called—would
you believe it?—"Yankee BAs") now account for about half of those
outstanding in the U.S. There is an on-the-run dealer system for the
top eleven Japanese banks much like that for the top tier of U.S.
banks.

History and prospects

The framers of the Federal Reserve Act sought to encourage the
development of New York as an international financial center by
fostering the growth of an acceptance market in New York in competition with London. To this end the prohibition against American
banks' entering into acceptance agreements was repealed, and the
Federal Reserve (the Fed) was empowered to discount (buy) *eligible*
BAs, that is, short-term acceptances arising from shipments of goods.
The requirements for eligibility for discounting by the Fed were
essentially the same for BAs connected with foreign trade as for bills of
exchange used to finance domestic transactions.[11] The idea was that
banks and others would be more willing to invest in eligible BAs if they
knew that those investments could be rediscounted at the Fed. The
Federal Reserve Act was passed in December 1913, and in September
1914 the National City Bank of New York accepted the first draft.

The volume of BAs grew rapidly for a while. But the decline in
foreign trade in the 1930s and direct government financing of agricultural exports almost eliminated the acceptance market. The revival of
foreign trade after World War II meant a corresponding growth in

---

11 See Jack Hervey (1983) and William Melton and Jean Mahr (1981) for more detailed statements of the eligibility requirements for BAs.

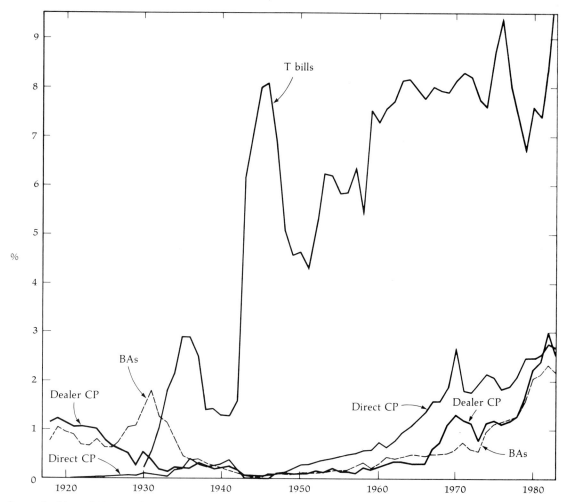

Source: *Banking and Monetary Statistics* and *Federal Reserve Bulletins.*

Figure 8.5   Treasury bills, bankers' acceptances, and commercial paper: midyear outstanding values as percentages of annual GNP, 1918 to 1983.

BAs, and by 1980 the volume of BAs outstanding relative to GNP had surpassed the previous high reached in 1931.

The outstanding values of BAs, commercial paper, and Treasury bills are shown in Figure 8.5 as proportions of annual GNP. The recent growth of BAs and commercial paper is impressive in view of the fact that the total debt of nonfinancial borrowers (households, governments, and nonfinancial businesses) has been quite a steady proportion of GNP since 1960, varying only within the range 1.39 to 1.45 between 1960 and 1980 after fluctuating widely between 1930 and 1960 and being fairly steady around 1.30 in the 1920s.[12]

---

12 Benjamin Friedman (1982, pages 92–97).

The largest part of the growth of BAs has been in *third-country bills,* which are to finance trade between countries other than the United States. Third-country bills have in recent years accounted for more than one-half of acceptances outstanding. Japan has been particularly active in using the American acceptance market to finance its trade.[13]

The Fed has almost dropped out of the market for BAs because the market is "well developed and efficient and no longer in need of support. . . ."[14] The Fed's participation is now confined to purchases on behalf of its foreign correspondents.[15]

The continued growth of BAs has been encouraged by several amendments to the Federal Reserve Act contained in the Export Trading Company Act of 1982. The most important of these amendments may turn out to be an increase in the ceiling on eligible BAs sold by an accepting bank from 100 percent to 200 percent of its capital and permission for institutions to participate in acceptances. The ceiling refers only to acceptances that may be classified as eligible by the Fed. BAs created and sold by a bank in excess of 200 percent of its capital are, along with BAs which are not tied to specific transactions or which have maturities exceeding 6 months, ineligible for discount at the Fed. So what! The Fed seldom buys acceptances anyway. The secondary market forms its own ideas about the liquidity and safety of securities and apparently treats all secured short-term BAs of highly rated banks in the way that they have always treated eligible BAs, whether or not they are now considered eligible for regulatory purposes. Investors and dealers used the Fed's classification scheme as long as it conveyed useful information concerning the security (secured by goods) and maturity (less than 6 months) of an acceptance and about the Fed's willingness to buy it. But investors no longer look askance at BAs classified as ineligible by the Fed. After all, banks have found many better ways of increasing their risk exposure than by guaranteeing BAs. Nevertheless, the Fed has taken steps to discourage ineligible BAs by subjecting them to reserve requirements at the same ratio as nonpersonal time deposits.[16]

TREASURY BILLS (T BILLS)

History and description

Nearly all government debt used to be long-term, with short-term securities issued only on special occasions, most commonly in anticipation of tax receipts. When the British Treasury began to issue

---

13 *Federal Reserve Bulletins* report the volumes of BAs arising from imports into the U.S., exports from the United States, and "all other." The third category gives a rough indication of the volume of third-country bills.

14 From a statement by the Federal Open Market Committee, March 1977, published in *Federal Reserve Bulletin,* May 1977, page 485.

15 See *Federal Reserve Bulletin,* April 1984, page 332.

16 See Gilbert Schwartz and Robert Ballen (1984) for an account of Fed regulation of BAs.

short-term securities on a regular basis in 1877, it chose an instrument for which there was already a well-developed market, bills of exchange. The only difference between Treasury and private bills was that the former needed no endorsement beyond the name of the original issuer. Since the Treasury prints money, its promises to pay money need no further guarantee.

The U.S. Treasury began to issue bills in 1929. Regular issues were for many years limited to 13-week maturities, but both 13- and 26-week bills are now issued every week, and 52-week bills are issued every fourth week. Other maturities, most often shorter-term "cash management" bills, are issued at irregular intervals. Like the private bills discussed earlier, T bills are sold at discounts from their face values. They are subject to federal income taxes, as are most other U.S. securities. The Internal Revenue Code treats price changes on T bills as ordinary income rather than as capital gains. In June 1983, T bills made up 25 percent of the federal debt: $334 billion of $1,318 billion.

T bill auctions

Following Monday auctions, 13-week and 26-week bills are issued on Thursdays. Prospective purchasers must submit bids by mail or in person at Federal Reserve Banks or their branches no later than 1:30 P.M. on the day of the auction. Bids may be *competitive* or *noncompetitive*. For competitive bids, prospective buyers specify the rates they are willing to pay. Purchasers submitting noncompetitive bids do not specify rates but instead agree to pay the average price of the competitive bids accepted by the Treasury. All noncompetitive bids are accepted in full up to the maximum of $1 million per bid.

The results of an auction are shown in Table 8.3. Expressing values to the nearest *million*, the Treasury wanted to sell $6,010 (face value) of 13-week bills. Bids worth $17,194 were received, of which $2,254 were noncompetitive—$1,109 by the public and $1,145 by the Fed.[17] This meant that competitive bids worth $3,756 were accepted and competitive bids worth $11,184 were unsuccessful. The happiest bidders were those who bid at or just below the highest accepted discount rate of 8.67 percent, that is, at or just above the lowest accepted price of $97.808 per $100 of face value.[18] (Bids must be submitted in percentage discount rates to no more than two decimal places.) There were two groups of unhappy bidders; those who bid low (at or near the lowest successful bid of 8.64 percent) and those who bid too high (above 8.67 percent). The yield to maturity ("coupon equivalent") corresponding to the average discount rate of accepted bids is also shown.

The distribution of bids is shown in Table 8.4.[19] Since the Treasury

---

17 The last figure is not reported in the financial press. See the footnote to Table 8.4.

18 Calculated according to the procedures in Table 6.1.

19 Obtained by communication with the U.S. Treasury.

Table 8.3 Results of the Treasury Bill Auction of October 24, 1983

> **Here are details of yesterday's auction of short-term Treasury bills:**
>
> Rates are determined by the difference between the purchase price and face value. Thus, higher bidding narrows the investor's return while lower bidding widens it. The percentage rates are calculated on a 360-day year, while the coupon equivalent yield is based on a 366-day year.
>
> | | 13-Week | 26-Week |
> |---|---|---|
> | Applications | $17,194,195,000 | $17,438,695,000 |
> | Accepted bids | $6,010,210,000 | $6,005,860,000 |
> | Accepted at low price | 63% | 80% |
> | Accepted noncompet'ly | $1,109,205,000 | $962,675,000 |
> | Average price (Rate) | 97.811 (8.66%) | 95.496 (8.91%) |
> | High price (Rate) | 97.816 (8.64%) | 95.501 (8.90%) |
> | Low price (Rate) | 97.808 (8.67%) | 95.496 (8.91%) |
> | Coupon equivalent | 9.00% | 9.48% |
>
> Both issues are dated Oct. 27, 1983. The 13-week bills mature Jan. 26, 1984, and the 26-week bills mature April 26, 1984.

Source: *Wall Street Journal*, October 25, 1983.

wanted to sell bills worth $6,010 million and was committed to accept all $2,254 million of the noncompetitive bids, it accepted all competitive bids below 8.67 percent and 63 percent of the bids at 8.67 percent.

The Treasury opens a new front in the war on the small saver

Figure 8.4 shows that T bill rates rose rapidly during the late 1960s. From a recession low of 3.46 percent on June 5, 1967, the average

Table 8.4 Distribution of Bids for the Auction of 13-week Bills, October 24, 1983

Bids		Millions of Dollars	
Rate	Price	Applications	Amounts Accepted
8.64	97.816	94	94
8.65	97.813	387	387
8.66	97.811	2,548	2,548
8.67	97.808	1,154	727 (63%)
Above 8.67	Below 97.808	10,757	0
Noncompetitive bids			
Fed[a]		1,145	1,145
Others		1,109	1,109
Total		17,194	6,010

a By Federal Reserve Banks for themselves or as agents for foreign or international monetary authorities. The Fed has not since 1981 had the authority to increase its holdings of Treasury securities except in the secondary market but may exchange bills that it holds for auctioned bills at the rate applicable to other noncompetitive bidders.

Sources: *Wall Street Journal*, October 25, 1983, and U.S. Treasury.

auction yield on 3-month bills rose to a peak of 8.38 percent on December 29, 1969. But Regulation Q ceilings on the rates payable on passbook savings accounts remained unchanged at 4 percent at commercial banks and 4.75 percent at most savings and loan associations (S&Ls). In response small savers used the noncompetitive bidding process to shift substantial sums from savings accounts to T bills. The value of public noncompetitive bids rose from $327 million on June 5, 1967, to $663 million on December 29, 1969, and then to a peak of $1,161 million on January 12, 1970. As a percentage of total accepted bids, public noncompetitive bids rose from 14 to 39 percent between these dates. In retaliation financial institutions persuaded the Treasury to shut out many potential purchasers of T bills by raising their minimum denomination from $1,000 to $10,000. The intended effect was achieved immediately. Public noncompetitive bids were cut in half, and the small saver's patriotic duty to lend to banks and S&Ls at below-market rates was fulfilled.

The public's noncompetitive bids have continued to rise and fall with T bill yields, as may be seen in Table 8.5. But the 39 percent noncompetitive submission of January 12, 1970, has not been repeated. The possible cost to the Treasury of its action against small savers may be illustrated as follows: Suppose 39 percent of the accepted bids for 13-week bills at the October 24, 1983, auction had been noncompetitive bids by the public. From Table 8.4 (again in millions) this would have meant $0.39($6,010) = $2,344$ instead of $1,109 of such bids, sales to the lowest $2,521 instead of the lowest $3,756 of competitive bids, an average discount rate of 8.658 percent instead of 8.660 percent, and an

Table 8.5   T Bill Yields and Public Noncompetitive Bids at Peaks and Troughs of 3-month Bill Yields

Auction Date	Total Bids Accepted[a]	Public Noncompetitive Bids Accepted[a]	Public Noncompetitive Bids as a Percentage of Total Accepted	Yield on 3-Month Bills	Passbook Ceiling Rates	
					Banks	S&Ls
6/5/67	2,301	327	14	3.46	4.00	4.75
12/29/69	3,004	663	22	8.38	4.00	4.75
3/8/71	3,302	338	10	3.38	4.50	5.00
9/2/74	4,811	873	18	9.51	5.00	5.25
12/20/76	5,213	351	7	4.38	5.00	5.25
3/24/80	6,808	1,814	27	17.49	5.25	5.50
6/9/80	5,616	1,083	19	6.70	5.25	5.50
12/15/80	8,299	1,593	19	17.64	5.25	5.50
11/30/81	9,437	1,432	15	10.83	5.25	5.50
2/15/82	10,052	2,282	23	15.52	5.25	5.50
10/12/82	11,202	2,045	18	7.68	5.25	5.50

a In millions of dollars. Only 3- and 6-month bills are included.

Sources: *Treasury Bulletin* and *Wall Street Journal*.

average yield of 8.999 percent instead of 9.002 percent.[20] If all bill auctions were affected similarly, the annual cost to the Treasury would be about $10 million (based on the $334 billion of outstanding bills mentioned earlier).

Maybe the Treasury believes that its campaign against the small saver is worth $10 million a year. On the other hand maybe the Treasury (or rather the taxpayer) has lost nothing by raising the minimum denomination of bills. If a reduction in noncompetitive bidding causes bill yields to rise and if there is no change in the risk, liquidity, or reversibility of bills relative to other securities, then investors for whom the $10,000 minimum is not a problem shift from other securities into bills. This tends to move the spreads between bills and other securities back toward the values that existed when the smallest bill was $1,000. It is not clear whether this offsetting effect is complete. Some writers have suggested that reductions in noncompetitive bids cause bill yields to rise relative to other yields.[21] But their interpretations of the data were put forth tentatively, and the question remains open. In any case, as indicated by our hypothetical illustration, the yield increases caused by reductions in noncompetitive bids are likely to be quite small even in the absence of offsetting effects. However, these increases are sensitive to the distribution of bids and might be greater during unsettled conditions in which bids are widely dispersed.[22]

It is likely that noncompetitive bids will in the future be less responsive to T bill yields as other investments yielding market rates become increasingly available to small investors. These investments now include money market mutual funds and small CDs, and when interest rate ceilings are lifted will include ordinary savings accounts.

Do Treasury auctions minimize financing costs?

The idea behind Treasury auctions is that price discrimination produces greater revenue and lower financing costs for the Treasury than would be obtained by a competitive procedure. For example suppose the offering of 3-month bills to competitive bidders is indicated by the SS line in Figure 8.6. Face values of quantities supplied and demanded are measured along the horizontal axis. S is the total offering less noncompetitive bids. Bid prices are measured along the vertical axis. The highest bid is P_H, and the amount bid at that price is indicated by the length of the line intersecting the price axis at the height P_H. The

20 Problem 5 at the end of the chapter asks the student to confirm the new average discount rate and yield.

21 See Edward Kane (1970, page 514) and Donald Mullineaux (1973, page 209).

22 To take an extreme example, suppose that the Treasury wants to issue (in *billions*) $10 of bills and that it receives $5 of noncompetitive bids and competitive bids of $5 at a rate of 8 percent and $5 at 9 percent. It accepts all competitive bids at the low rate and none at the high rate, and the average (and only) rate is 8 percent. But if there had been no noncompetitive bids, all competitive bids would have been accepted, giving an average rate of 8.50 percent.

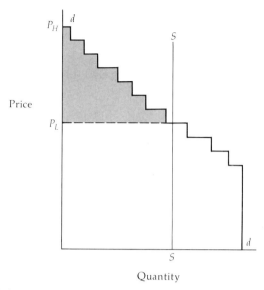

Source: Vernon L. Smith, "Bidding Theory and the Treasury Bill Auction: Does Price Discrimination Increase Bill Prices?," *Review of Economics and Statistics,* May 1966.

Figure 8.6   Discriminator's gain when discriminatory and competitive demands are the same.

array of competitive bids forms a stepwise demand function dd. The lowest accepted price is P_L.

Assuming that bids would be the same in a competitive situation as when the Treasury acts as a price discriminator by means of its present procedure, that is, assuming demand to be dd in both cases, the auction increases Treasury revenue by an amount equal to the shaded area. Total revenue under competition, in which all bills would be sold for the price, P_L, at which demand and supply were equal, would be SP_L. This corresponds to the area of the square under P_L and to the left of S. But by charging bidders the full amounts of their bids, the Treasury obtains revenue equal to the total area under dd to the left of S.

However, Vernon Smith (1966) pointed out that demand functions are not likely to be the same under competitive and discriminatory situations. For example, let DD in Figure 8.7 be an ordinary demand curve of the type familiar in price theory. That is, each of the prices indicated by DD is the maximum, or reservation, price that a particular group of investors will pay for a specified quantity of bills. Under competitive bidding, in which all accepted orders are filled at the same price, investors have no incentive to submit bids below their reservation prices. Under price discrimination, however, investors do have an incentive to bid lower than their reservation prices—because successful bids are filled at bid prices. The demand for bills under conditions of price discrimination, dd, will therefore be lower than the competitive demand, DD. In Figure 8.7 the discriminator's revenue is, as

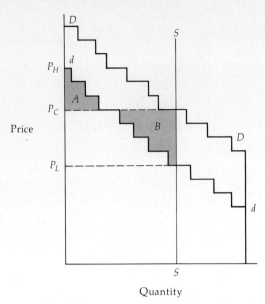

Source: Vernon L. Smith, "Bidding Theory and the Treasury Bill Auction: Does Price Discrimination Increase Bill Prices?," *Review of Economics and Statistics*, May 1966.

Figure 8.7   Discriminator's gain (or loss) when discriminatory demand is less than competitive demand.

before, the area under *dd* to the left of *S*. But the competitive revenue now corresponds to the square below the competitive price, P_c, and to the left of *S*. Consequently the Treasury may get either *more* or *less* revenue under the present system of price discrimination, depending upon whether area *A exceeds* or *is less than* area *B* in Figure 8.7.[23]

COMMERCIAL PAPER (CP)

Characteristics of CP[24]

CP is the name given to short-term unsecured notes sold by large corporations, usually on a discount basis, to dealers and other financial and nonfinancial firms.[25] A small amount of CP is coupon bearing. CP is as uniquely American as basketball. It is said that the baskets used by Dr. Naismith had contained peaches financed by the sale of CP in Boston when the Cousy Fruit and Vegetable Company was unable to obtain a good rate of interest from the banks in Springfield.

---

23 Steven Bolten (1973) estimated that under a competitive auction an increase in demand of only 1 percent would be sufficient to yield a higher revenue to the Treasury than does the present discriminatory procedure. For criticisms of Bolten's study see Robert Boatler (1975) and Henry Goldstein and George Kaufman (1975).

24 For more detail, see Peter Abken (1981), First Boston Corporation (1980), Evelyn Hurley (1982), and rating service publications, such as *Moody's Commercial Paper Record* (monthly).

25 We use the narrow, popular definition of CP. In the more general and much older sense CP refers to all short-term negotiable instruments (including notes, bills, and acceptances) arising from commercial transactions.

The Securities Act of 1933 exempted CP with maturities of 9 months or less from the registration procedures required of most securities offered to the public. The expense and delays of these procedures are such that the longest-term paper is 270 days. Maturities may be as short as 1 day, and some paper is payable on demand. The average maturity of CP is less than 30 days, most issues having maturities between 20 and 45 days.

Most CP is secured not by property or other collateral but only by a name, and the CP market has in the past been dominated by the issues of the largest, most creditworthy corporations. Even these firms are expected to support their CP with lines of credit at their banks. However, many smaller firms have recently gained access to the CP market by means of bank L/Cs and other guarantees by larger financial and nonfinancial firms. The number of firms issuing CP has grown from 335 in 1965 to well over 1,000 in the 1980s, and the number of issues is sufficiently great and their quality is sufficiently variable that many investors find CP ratings useful. The ratings of three services are compared in Table 8.6. The quality of a CP issue depends very much on the liquidity of the issuer, including the state of its line of credit. A firm's long-term prospects may be excellent; but if it wishes to sell 30-day notes, it had better have a more-than-fair expectation of being able to lay its hands on some cash at the end of

Table 8.6   Commercial Paper Ratings

Standard & Poor's[a]		Moody's	Fitch Investors Service	
A-1:	highest investment grade	Prime-1	F-1:	highest grade
A-2:	high investment grade	Prime-2	F-2:	investment grade
A-3:	medium investment grade	Prime-3	F-3:	good grade
B :	medium grade		F-4:	not recommended
C :	speculative			
D :	expected to default			

a Standard & Poor's CP rating schedule, which is "a current assessment of the likelihood of timely payment," is de.ined as follows:
  A: Issues assigned this highest rating are regarded as having the greatest capacity for timely payment and are further refined, as follows, to indicate the relative degree of safety:
  A-1: This designation indicates that the degree of safety regarding timely payment is very strong. A (+) sign indicates overwhelming safety.
  A-2: Capacity for timely payment on issues with this designation is strong. However, the relative degree of safety is not so overwhelming as for issues designated A-1.
  A-3: Issues carrying this designation have a satisfactory capacity for timely payment. They are, however, somewhat more vulnerable to the adverse effects of changes in circumstances than obligations carrying the higher designations.
  B: Issues rated B are regarded as having only an adequate capacity for timely payment. However, such capacity may be damaged by changing conditions or short-term adversities.
  C: This rating is assigned to short-term debt obligation with doubtful capacity for payment.
  D: This rating indicates that the issue is either in default or is expected to be in default upon maturity.

Sources: Adapted from David M. Darst, *The Complete Bond Book*, McGraw-Hill, New York, 1975, page 181, and *Standard & Poor's Rating Guide*, page 131.

the month. When L/Cs are used, the issue is given the rating of the guarantor.

CP is perhaps the least homogeneous of the major money market instruments partly because of the large number of issuing firms, with greater disparity in their creditworthiness than, for example, the large banks that dominate the market for BAs. But the heterogeneity of CP is also due to the frequent "tailoring" of issues to the specific needs of investors. Suppose the Treasurer of the Cousy Fruit and Vegetable Company calls Walter the Commercial Paper Dealer in Boston about the rate at which he can sell a 30-day, $100,000 issue to finance a shipment of peaches expected to arrive tomorrow. Walter says 30 days is not a good maturity. He knows no one looking for a 30-day investment in paper of the Cousy Company's grade at a rate that would appeal to Cousy. However, the Jones Shipping Company, with a temporary surplus of cash, is looking for an investment of $90,000 for 32 days, until some accounts payable come due. If the interest rate on CP is less than the cost of other sources of funds, Cousy is likely to tailor its issue to suit Jones and will get the other $10,000 somewhere else. Large issuers find it even more necessary to accommodate the desires of prospective lenders. An issue of $200 million, for example, may be broken down into several subissues of different sizes and maturities.

The cost of CP

The four main noninterest costs of CP may be described as follows:[26]

1. CP issuers must pay fees between $5,000 and $25,000 in order to obtain a rating from a rating service.
2. Fees must also be paid to the banks that act as agents and do the associated paper work for CP issuers.
3. The six major CP dealers usually charge ⅛ of 1 percent commission on the face value of the paper for their placement services.
4. CP is usually backed by standby loan commitments that enable the issuer to pay off the notes in the event the paper cannot be either rolled over at maturity or redeemed with funds from other sources. Banks do not give commitments away. Payment for standby commitments is sometimes in the form of compensating balances, often equal to 10 percent of the size of the commitment, and sometimes in the form of explicit fees between ¼ and ¾ of 1 percent of the commitment. L/Cs involve additional fees.

Table 8.7 compares the costs of a hypothetical issue of 180-day CP through a dealer with the cost of a prime loan. Using the loan data in Table 8.2, the prime rate is assumed to be 12.20 percent, with a

26 See Peter Abken (1981, pages 11–12) and Randall Merris (1978, pages 16–19).

Table 8.7   A Comparison of the Costs of Dealer CP and Prime Loan
Financing

180-day Dealer Paper, %		Prime Loan,[a] %	
Discount rate	11.10	Prime rate	12.20
Credit line fee	0.50	Implicit cost of 20%	
Dealer commission	0.25	compensating balance	3.05
Total cost on discount basis	11.85	Total cost on simple annual	
Total cost on simple annual		basis	15.25
basis	12.60		

a The prime loan cost calculations are explained near the bottom of Table 8.2.
   Only two notes of explanation are required for the cost of CP. First, the assumed credit line fee
of ¼ percent and dealer commission of ⅛ percent translate to annual rates of ½ percent and ¼ percent, respectively, for 180-day paper. Second, the last line converts the discount rate to simple annual interest on a 360-day basis in order to be comparable with the cost of the prime loan.
   For another comparison of the costs of bankers' acceptances, commercial paper, and bank
loans, see William Melton and Jean Mahr (1981, Table 1).

compensating balance requirement of 20 percent for prime loans so
that the total cost on a simple annual basis is 15.25 percent. Table 8.7
assumes a CP discount rate of 11.10 percent because 180-day dealer
CP rates have averaged somewhat more than 1 percent below the
prime rate. As in our comparison of the costs of BAs and prime loans,
Table 8.7 does not encompass all the costs of CP and prime loans. For
example the first two costs in the above list have been omitted.
Nevertheless, everything considered, CP is probably, during most
periods, a cheaper source of funds for large corporations than bank
loans. But these corporations still like to keep some bank loans
outstanding, along with CP, as part of their policy of maintaining a
variety of sources of credit in the event one or more "dries up."

Dealer and direct (finance) paper

About half of CP is placed directly by borrowing firms that use their
own sales staffs. Notice the entry in Table 8.1 for the directly placed
paper of the General Motors Acceptance Corporation. Since the large
finance companies initiated and have dominated the practice of
bypassing CP dealers, the terms "direct paper" and "finance paper"
are used interchangeably. Direct issuers often assure themselves of
steady supplies of funds by means of "master-note agreements."
"Under these agreements, the investor—usually a bank trust department—makes daily purchases of commercial paper, payable on
demand, up to some predetermined amount. Each day the trust
department tells the issuer the amount of paper it will take under the
master note."[27]
   Direct placement of securities is not common in the capital markets.

27 Evelyn Hurley (1982, page 328).

Even the largest companies do not issue stocks and bonds often enough to justify an in-house operation for the purpose of selling their issues. They deal with investment bankers, who are continuously in the capital markets and have the expertise and capacity to place stocks and bonds more cheaply than borrowers can do it for themselves. Although many borrowers sell CP much more frequently than stocks and bonds, they are still not continuously in the process of placing CP and therefore go to CP dealers for the same reasons that they use investment banks. The large finance companies are in a different league. They *are* in the market continuously and find it cheaper to run their own placement operations, with their own networks of customers built up over the years, than to pay the dealers' one-eighth. About 40 percent of total finance company debt was in the form of CP in 1983, and about 60 percent of their CP issues had been placed directly.[28]

Secondary market (not much)

Largely because of the heterogeneity of CP, there is no active secondary market. However, a purchaser of CP may sell its paper back to the dealer or direct issuer in the event of an unforeseen need for funds. This is not done very often partly because of the cost. Dealers usually buy back CP at $\frac{1}{8}$ of 1 percent above the current market rate. Estimates of the proportions of CP redeemed before maturity vary between 1 and 2 percent.[29]

History of CP

BEFORE 1920. "Bill brokers" and commercial banks dealt actively in CP as early as the eighteenth century. But most histories of CP begin in the 1840s with the formation of *commercial paper houses* in the Northeast. In contrast to brokers, who brought buyers and sellers together, CP houses (dealers) actually took possession of CP. Financing themselves with short-term loans from banks, CP houses bought paper in high-interest-rate areas and then sold it in low-interest-rate areas. These intermediaries in effect borrowed at low interest rates and lent at high interest rates. The potential gains to efficient CP houses were substantial because of the large differentials in the interest rates prevailing between different sections, and sometimes between nearby cities, of the United States. These differentials were made possible by banking regulations that prohibited interstate branching and limited intrastate branching. Thus the primary vehicle for the efficient geographical dispersion of funds in other countries was unavailable to Americans. The average discount rate on prime CP

---

28 The latter figure has fallen considerably in recent years. Ninety percent of finance company CP was directly placed in 1975. Data on finance company debt and the nature of their CP issues may be obtained from the Federal Reserve Board's quarterly and annual flow of funds accounts and the *Federal Reserve Bulletin.*

29 See Marcia Stigum (1983, page 614) and Peter Abken (1981, page 11).

during 1893 to 1897 was 3.83 percent in Boston, 4.60 in Hartford, 4.41 in New York, 6.01 in Buffalo, 5.74 in Chicago, 7.98 in Omaha, 6.22 in San Francisco, and 10.00 in Denver.[30]

CP dealers were as important to the winning of the West as the Colt 45 and the pickup truck. Lance Davis has argued that regional interest-rate differentials declined rapidly in the late-nineteenth and early-twentieth centuries and that a "region by region examination" shows that those declines were "closely associated with the entry of a commercial paper house into an area. . . . The 'festive note broker' may have been the bane of the midwestern banker's life (and certainly of his monopoly position), but he played a major role in the development of a national short-term capital market."[31]

The expansion was not only westward but also within regions from large cities to smaller cities and towns. Picture Professor Harold Hill, no longer selling trombones but carrying a carpetbag stuffed with CP. Making the rounds from his Omaha base to Des Moines, Dubuque, and Mason City, he heeded his own counsel that "you gotta know the territory." Banks were by far the largest purchasers of CP, and it was Professor Hill's business not to wait for them to request paper but to anticipate the availability of investment funds.[32] Low interest rates in a community attracted the special attention of Hill as he attempted to place paper at high prices. High interest rates invited offers from Hill to purchase CP.

Just as CP houses had accomplished their useful work of coordinating American short-term financial markets—of reducing interest-rate differentials by facilitating flows of funds from low- to high-interest-rate areas—they began to decline in importance. The development of communications and the growth of nationwide firms, with headquarters in the major financial centers, meant that most of the buying and selling of CP could be concentrated in a few dealers in those centers. Another reason was the development of direct placement in the 1920s.

THE 1920s. We consider three important changes in the CP market during the 1920s, the first temporary, the second persisting until the mid-1960s, and the third permanent (so far).

1. The tremendous increase in stock prices in the late twenties, combined with rising CP rates, induced many firms to turn to stock issues for short-term finance. Many inventories were financed by equity instead of by short-term debt. This explains at least part of the decline in dealer paper from $915 million to $265 million between

---

30 John James (1978, page 10).

31 Lance Davis (1975, pages 19–20).

32 See Roy Foulke (1931, Chapter 11) and Albert Greef (1938, Chapter 4) for interesting discussions of CP salesmen.

September 1924 and September 1929 in the face of mainly rising economic activity, which usually stimulates CP issues.[33]

2. The number of borrowers declined from 4,395 in 1920 to 1,653 in 1929. This downward trend continued at a more rapid rate during the Great Depression and then at a slower rate until the mid-1960s, when the number of borrowers reached a low of about 300.[34] The average amount of paper issued annually per borrower also declined between 1923 and 1932 but rose fairly steadily during the next 30 years as finance companies and the largest nonfinancial corporations increasingly dominated the market. The average amount of paper issued per borrower has continued to rise. However, as noted toward the beginning of our discussion of CP, the decline in the number of borrowers was reversed in the 1960s and had reached 1,300 by 1983.

3. The General Motors Acceptance Corporation began placing its own CP in 1920. It was joined by the Commercial Credit Company and the CIT Financial Corporation in 1934 and by the General Electric Credit Corporation in 1952.[35] The number of direct borrowers had grown to 11 in 1961 and was about 110 in 1983. Figure 8.5 shows that directly placed CP vanished during World War II along with the production of cars and other durable goods. However, the volume of direct paper exceeded that of dealer paper continuously between 1948 and 1980, usually by a substantial margin. Dealer paper gained rapidly in the early 1980s partly because of the growing number of smaller firms issuing CP through dealers and partly because of the decline in durable-goods purchases during the 1980 recession.

REGULATION Q AND THE CREDIT CRUNCHES OF 1966 AND 1969. Both direct and dealer paper increased fairly steadily during the prosperous years following World War II. However, as we see in Figure 8.5, the most dramatic expansions of the CP market came in the late 1960s and the late 1970s. We shall examine the earlier period first. Please look at Figure 8.4 and notice the sharp rise in market interest rates during 1966. This rise was part of a "credit crunch" caused by the Fed's about-face from an expansionary to a restrictive monetary policy. Bank CDs did not share in the increase in rates because they were still subject to interest ceilings under Regulation Q.[36] This restriction had important implications for the lending capacities of the money market banks because large negotiable CDs had grown rapidly since their introduction in 1961 to become an important source of funds for those

---

33 See Roy Foulke (1931, pages 34 and 35) for a discussion of this period. Standard & Poor's common stock index (1935 to 1939 = 100) rose from 79 to 238 and the 4- to 6-month prime CP rate rose from 3.13 to 6.25 between September 1924 and September 1929.

34 See Richard Selden (1963, Table 2) and Peter Abken (1981, page 11).

35 Richard Selden (1963, page 15).

36 See Figure 2.1.

banks.[37] Large CDs in large banks amounted to about $18 billion, or 9 percent of their total deposits, in mid-1966. One-sixth of these were lost by the end of the year as investors shifted to T bills and other securities paying unregulated market rates. The consequence was a credit squeeze and a scramble for funds by the large corporations that had relied on loans from the large banks. They turned to the CP market for funds, and dealer paper outstanding rose from $1.9 billion at the end of 1965 to $3.1 billion at the end of 1966 and $4.9 billion at the end of 1967.

The expansion of CP continued after the credit crunch had ended because firms were determined to maintain a presence in the open market in the event of recurrences of difficulties in obtaining bank loans.[38] By early 1969 the number of firms issuing CP had reached 500, compared with 335 in 1965, and dealer paper outstanding had risen to about $8 billion. And a good thing too, because the events of 1966 were repeated with even greater force in 1969, when large CDs in large banks fell from about $23 billion to $11 billion between January and December. Banks also turned to CP as a source of funds to make up for the loss of CDs,[39] and continued to issue large amounts of CP even after interest ceilings were relaxed. By mid-1983 bank-related paper amounted to $35 billion and made up nearly 40 percent of total direct paper (though only about 5 percent of dealer paper).

PENN CENTRAL. Only five CP defaults occurred during the 1960s, the largest being for $35 million. Then on June 21, 1970, Penn Central filed for bankruptcy. Among its liabilities was CP worth $82 million. This event was not entirely unexpected; Penn Central's difficulties had been widely reported for several months, their bond and CP ratings were low, and investors required high yields on the company's debt. They gambled and lost. Nevertheless, the actual default apparently conveyed some new information about the CP market to investors; for nonbank paper fell $3 billion, about 8 percent of the amount outstanding, during the next 3 weeks, and the spread between the prime 4- to 6-month CP rate and the 3-month T bill rate rose from about 1.5 percent to 2 percent. But the impact of Penn Central's failure on the cost of the best paper was short-lived, and the spread had returned to its pre-June 21 figure by early August.[40] The impact

---

37 The "large banks" in this discussion include 341 weekly reporting banks with deposits in excess of $100 million in 1966. The "large CDs" are those with minimum denominations of $100,000. The data are from the Federal Reserve Board's *Banking and Monetary Statistics, 1941–70.*

38 See John Judd (1979) for a discussion of the considerations affecting borrower choices between bank loans and CP.

39 And as a way of obtaining funds that were free of reserve requirements if the CP was issued through a holding company.

40 See Dwight Jaffee (1975) and David Kidwell and Charles Trzcinka (1979) for alternative views of the effects of the Penn Central failure on CP yields.

on the volume of CP may have been greater and more lasting. Total nonbank paper continued to decline until June 1971, by which time it had fallen 25 percent and did not return to its June 1970 level until October 1973.[41]

Recent developments in CP[42]

Barring a prolonged period of depression and low interest rates—which would be associated with a fall in consumer demands for durable goods, less borrowing by businesses, and probably a reversal of the recent tendency to substitute short-term for long-term debt—recent developments in all aspects of the CP market point to the continued growth of that market.

NEW BORROWERS. The largest addition to the borrowing side of the CP market has come from relatively small firms that have entered with the support of L/Cs and other guarantees from banks, insurance companies, and large nonfinancial corporations. This group is the most important reason for the growth of dealer relative to direct paper in recent years. At the end of 1983, about half of all CP issuers were supported by L/Cs and other guarantees. This does not count the many issues that were supported by working agreements, such as the pipeline issues supported by agreements with oil companies.

Perhaps next in importance is the growth of issues by foreign borrowers, which accounted for about 6 percent of CP outstanding in 1980.

State and local governments and a few not-for-profit organizations such as universities have begun to issue tax-exempt CP. These issues have grown at a rapid rate but still account for only about 1 percent of all CP.

Mutual savings banks and S&Ls have recently been granted permission to issue CP. But few have taken advantage of this opportunity because CP is classified as nonpersonal time deposits against which reserves of 3 percent must be held, and the low earnings of thrifts in recent years have made it difficult to obtain good credit ratings.

NEW LENDERS. CP makes up about one-third of the assets of money market mutual funds. The rapid growth of these funds was accompanied by a growth in their CP holdings from about $1 billion to $60 billion between 1977 and 1982. They accounted for half the growth of CP between 1977 and 1982 and two-thirds of that growth between 1978 and 1982.

---

41 The volume of CP was also adversely affected by a decline in economic activity and by interest ceilings on bank loans under the Nixon price-control package, which induced borrowers to substitute bank loans for CP. After controls were abandoned in late 1973, loan rates again rose above CP rates, and the volume of CP grew rapidly throughout 1974.

42 The data in the following discussion are from Peter Abken (1981), Evelyn Hurley (1982), *Moody's Commercial Paper Record* (November 1983), and *Federal Reserve Bulletins*.

NEW DEALERS. The Glass-Steagall Banking Act of 1933 attempted to separate the businesses of investment banking and commercial banking. It reflected "the unalterable and emphatic intention of Congress to divorce commercial banks from the business of underwriting and dealing securities."[43] But in the 1970s commercial banks began to place some CP issues for their customers and to extend lines of credit in support of other issues. These placement and financial-support activities are the essence of underwriting, and investment bankers complained to the Federal Reserve Board about the commercial-bank invasion of their turf. But the Fed said that commercial banks were not in violation of the law because CP is not a security. The Securities Industry Association and A. G. Becker contested this opinion in court, and the Fed was overruled in the district court but upheld by the U.S. Court of Appeals in 1982. The higher court stated that "We can find nothing in the language . . . that explicitly articulates a congressional intent to bar commercial banks from trading in commercial paper. The language and legislative history of the Glass-Steagall Act strongly suggest that commercial paper should be viewed as a loan rather than as a single 'security' for the purpose of the Act."[44]

QUESTIONS

1. Discuss the differences, for both borrower and lender, between bills of exchange, on the one hand, and credit cards and trade credit, on the other hand.
2. Discuss the relationships between drafts, bills, and checks.
3. Discuss the reasons for the existence of secondary markets in BAs and T bills but not CP.
4. What are the reasons for imposing reserve requirements on BAs?
5. How would you change the Treasury's auction procedure and why? (Surely you can think of *something*.)

PROBLEMS

1. Suppose Charlie had been able to rediscount the bill in Figure 8.1 after 30 days at 6 percent instead of 9 percent. What would his simple annual rate of return on this investment have been?
2. Using the method of Table 8.2, compare the costs of acceptance and prime loan financing when the prime rate is 10 percent, compensating balances on prime loans are 20 percent, the discount

---

43 *Baker, Watts & Co. v. Saxon (Controller of the Currency)*, Circuit Court of the District of Columbia, 1968. See Larry Mote (1979) for a history of the role of commercial banks in the securities industry.

44 Quoted from Edwin Cox (1983, page 35). Subsequent judicial opinions have reinforced this decision (although appeals to the U.S. Supreme Court are still pending) but have raised new problems; see Theresa Einhorn (1984).

rate on 180-day acceptances is 9 percent, and the acceptance commission is 3 percent.

3. Suppose the Treasury wants to sell $2 billion of 13-week bills. It receives noncompetitive bids totaling $1.1 billion and competitive bids of $200 million at each of the following ten discount rates: 8.00, 8.01, . . ., 8.09.

   Based on this information, construct a report like that for 13-week bills in Table 8.3.

4. What would the average price, discount rate, and yield on 13-week bills in problem 3 have been if noncompetitive bids had been 80 percent instead of 55 percent of accepted bids? In this, as in other problems, please show your work.

5. The average discount rate and yield on 13-week bills that would have prevailed on October 24, 1983, if the public's noncompetitive bids had been 39 percent instead of 18 percent of accepted bids were presented in the text. Please confirm these results.

6. Using the method of Table 8.7, compare the costs of CP and bank loan financing when the prime rate is 10 percent, compensating balance requirements on prime loans are 20 percent, the 180-day CP rate is 9 percent, the credit line fee is 0.5 percent, and the dealer commission is 0.25 percent.

REFERENCES

Peter A. Abken, "Commercial Paper," Federal Reserve Bank of Richmond *Economic Review,* March/April 1981, pages 11–21. Reprint in Timothy Q. Cook and Bruce J. Summers (eds.), *Instruments of the Money Market,* 5th ed., Federal Reserve Bank of Richmond, Richmond, VA, 1981.

Sy J. Banaitis, *International Letters of Credit,* First National Bank of Chicago, Chicago, 1977.

Robert W. Boatler, "Treasury Bill Auction Procedures: An Empirical Investigation: Comment," *Journal of Finance,* June 1975, pages 893–894.

Jules I. Bogen (ed.), *Financial Handbook,* 4th ed., Ronald Press, New York, 1964.

Steven Bolten, "Treasury Bill Auction Procedures: An Empirical Investigation," *Journal of Finance,* June 1973, pages 577–583.

Timothy Q. Cook and Bruce J. Summers (eds.), *Instruments of the Money Market,* 5th ed., Federal Reserve Bank of Richmond, Richmond, VA, 1981.

Edwin B. Cox, *Bankers Desk Reference,* Warren, Gorham & Lamont, New York, 1983.

David M. Darst, *The Complete Bond Book,* McGraw-Hill, New York, 1975.

Lance E. Davis, "The Evolution of the American Capital Market, 1860–1940: A Case Study in Institutional Change," in William L. Silber, *Financial Innovation,* Heath, Lexington, MA, 1975.

Theresa A. Einhorn, "National Banks' Discount Brokerage Services Are Permissable under Glass-Steagall Act, but an Office at Which Such Services Are Offered Constitutes a Branch," *Banking Law Journal,* May–June 1984, pages 349–361.

Solomon Fabricant, "Recent Economic Changes and the Agenda of Business Cycle Research," *National Bureau of Economic Research Report* Supplement, May 1971.

First Boston Corporation, *Handbook of Securities of the United States Government and Federal Agencies and Related Money Market Instruments,* New York, published biennially.

First National Bank of Chicago, *Collections, Letters of Credit, and Bankers' Acceptances,* Chicago, 1981.

Roy A. Foulke, *The Commercial Paper Market,* Bankers Publishing, Boston, 1931.

Benjamin M. Friedman, "Debt and Economic Activity in the United States," in B. M. Friedman (ed.), *The Changing Roles of Debt and Equity in Financing U.S. Capital Formation,* University of Chicago Press, Chicago, 1982.

Henry N. Goldstein and George G. Kauf-

man, "Treasury Bill Auction Procedures: Comment," *Journal of Finance,* June 1975, pages 895–899.

Albert O. Greef, *The Commercial Paper House in the United States,* Harvard University Press, Cambridge, MA, 1938.

Jack L. Hervey, "Bankers' Acceptances," Federal Reserve Bank of Chicago *Business Conditions,* May 1976, pages 3–11.

Jack L. Hervey, "Bankers' Acceptances Revisited," Federal Reserve Bank of Chicago *Economic Perspectives,* May/June 1983, pages 21–31.

Evelyn M. Hurley, "The Commercial Paper Market Since the Mid-seventies," *Federal Reserve Bulletin,* June 1982, pages 327–334.

Dwight M. Jaffee, "Cyclical Variations in the Risk Structure of Interest Rates," *Journal of Monetary Economics,* July 1975, pages 309–325.

John A. James, *Money and Capital Markets in Postbellum America,* Princeton University Press, Princeton, NJ, 1978.

John P. Judd, "Competition between the Commercial Paper Market and Commercial Banks," Federal Reserve Bank of San Francisco *Economic Review,* Winter 1979, pages 39–53.

Edward J. Kane, "Short-changing the Small Saver: Federal Government Discrimination against the Small Saver during the Vietnam War," *Journal of Money, Credit and Banking,* November 1970, pages 513–522.

David S. Kidwell and Charles A. Trzcinka, "The Risk Structure of Interest Rates and the Penn-Central Crisis," *Journal of Finance,* June 1979, pages 751–760.

William C. Melton and Jean M. Mahr, "Bankers' Acceptances," Federal Reserve Bank of New York *Quarterly Review,* Summer 1981, pages 39–55.

Randall C. Merris, "Loan Commitments and Facility Fees," Federal Reserve Bank of Chicago *Economic Perspectives,* March/April 1978, pages 14–21.

Larry R. Mote, "Banks and the Securities Markets: The Controversy," Federal Reserve Bank of Chicago *Economic Perspectives,* March/April 1979, pages 14–20.

Donald J. Mullineaux, "Deposit-rate Ceilings and Noncompetitive Bidding for U.S. Treasury Bills," *Journal of Money, Credit and Banking,* February 1973, pages 201–212.

Gilbert T. Schwartz and Robert G. Ballen, "Bankers' Acceptance Financing: The Expanding Opportunities," *Banking Law Journal,* May–June 1984, pages 331–347.

Richard T. Selden, *Trends and Cycles in Commercial Paper,* occas. pap. 85, National Bureau of Economic Research, Cambridge, MA, 1963.

Vernon L. Smith, "Bidding Theory and the Treasury Bill Auction: Does Price Discrimination Increase Bill Prices?," *Review of Economics and Statistics,* May 1966, pages 141–146.

Standard and Poor's Rating Guide, McGraw-Hill, New York, 1979.

Marcia Stigum, *The Money Market,* rev. ed., Dow Jones-Irwin, Homewood, IL, 1983.

Uniform Commercial Code, 3 vols., West Publishing, St. Paul, MN, 1968.

THE MONEY MARKETS AND THE MANAGEMENT OF BANK RESERVES

BOSTON MONEY MARKET
Boston special — The week opens with a decidedly firmer feeling in
the money market. Money between banks continues in sharp
demand, 5 and 6% being readily paid for loans this a.m. It is
possible that money will be brought over from New York to-night.
It is claimed by some that from this time on the clearing house
rate will stand 4% at least. The firmness of clearing house
money is reflected on the outside.

The banks are not loaning on call to-day less than 6% except in
the case of very favored borrowers. Business on time loans is at very
low ebb and rates are nominal[1] at 4 or 5%. Very little paper will be
offered until rates become more settled.
The Wall Street Journal, vol. 1, no. 1, Monday, July 8, 1889, page 1[2]

Most economic transactions in modern societies are accomplished by
exchanges of claims on banks, specifically by checks or wire transfers.
Bank reserves are therefore sensitive to changes in the directions of
flows of funds, both within the United States and between the United
States and other countries. For example a poor orange crop, which
means a net outflow of funds from Florida, necessitates reserve
adjustments by Florida banks. They will attempt to regain reserves by
selling securities, cutting back on loans, and/or borrowing reserves
from the Federal Reserve System (the Fed) and other banks. If loan
demand is strong and loan rates are high in Florida, these banks will be
willing to pay high interest rates for funds. If the loss of reserves was
sudden and severe and if they wish to avoid reducing their loans and

---

1 "Nominal" rates, meaning rates quoted but at which no trades occurred, were common during
rapidly changing conditions in pre-1914 financial markets, most spectacularly during panics.

2 "Published daily, except Sundays and Stock Exchange Holidays, at 3:15 p.m. Price two cents.
Subscription price $5 per annum."

investments, they will try to attract new reserves quickly, certainly by the end of the current reserve maintenance period. This chapter discusses three of the most convenient and least costly ways available to banks for rapid adjustments of their reserve positions: the Fed discount window, federal funds (fed funds), and repurchase agreements (RPs).

Fed discount rates are potentially important to the money markets and the process of money creation because they are the costs of bank reserves borrowed from the twelve district Federal Reserve Banks. But their importance falls short of their potential because Federal Reserve Banks often set these rates at levels that bear little relation to financial market conditions and then, when discount rates are below free-market rates, ration their lending by nonprice means. Rates of interest on fed funds, on the other hand, may be the key money market rates because they are free to reflect supplies and demands for bank reserves, which are in turn determined by public and private supplies and demands for credit throughout the economy.[3] Like other prices and interest rates, fed funds rates are causes as well as effects. They are the marginal costs of funds for most banks and therefore exert strong influences on the rates of interest required on bank assets. Fed funds rates take on added significance because of the crucial role assigned to them in the conduct of monetary policy. The last part of this chapter considers alternative operating procedures by which the Fed might carry out its responsibilities. We will see that both of the procedures that have been followed at different times in recent years have been based on fed funds rates.

It may not be too much to say that short-term events in the money and capital markets are dominated by commercial bank reserve adjustments and Fed responses to those adjustments as reflected in fed funds rates. These daily interactions between banks, the Fed, and other traders are the subject of this chapter. We begin with small potatoes, the discount window, and work up to the fed funds market.

THE DISCOUNT WINDOW

The original Federal Reserve Act

After a series of financial panics and depressions the Federal Reserve System was established in 1913 to provide the nation with an "elastic currency." This meant that the Fed was to supply reserves to commercial banks in a manner that in normal conditions permitted the money supply to vary in line with economic activity, that is, to "expand and contract as business needs expanded and contracted."[4] In addition the

---

3 This is not to say that the Fed does not influence fed funds rates. But it exerts that influence by supplying or withdrawing reserves instead of by administrative decree as in the case of its discount rates.

4 Henry Willis (1923, page 1521). Willis's book is the most complete source for the legislative history and early implementation of the Federal Reserve Act.

Fed was to act as "lender of last resort" to the banking system in order to avert financial panics.

Taken together, those two related functions are conducive to price stability. This may be demonstrated with the aid of the *equation of exchange* introduced in Chapter 3:

$$MV = PY \quad \text{or} \quad M = kPY$$

where $k = 1/V$; M is the average money supply during some period; V is the income velocity of money, that is, the number of times the average dollar is spent on final goods and services during the period; P is an index of prices of final goods and services; and Y is the output of final goods and services (that is, real GNP) during the period. The inverse of velocity, k, may be interpreted as the demand for money as a proportion of the nominal value of output, PY. If velocity is reasonably constant, a money supply that varies proportionally to Y produces a reasonably stable price level.

On the other hand financial panics are characterized by "rushes to liquidity" as investors seek to convert nonmoney assets into money. This means an increase in the demand for money as denoted by k. By supplying reserves to the banking system, that is, by exercising its lender-of-last-resort function, a central bank may be able to cause the supply of money to increase in line with the demand for money and so to moderate or prevent price declines.

The principal tool explicitly given by Congress to the Federal Reserve System to perform these functions was the power of the twelve district Federal Reserve Banks to create bank[5] reserves by discounting (buying) bills of exchange. Banks sometimes extended credit by discounting bills of exchange such as those discussed in Chapter 8. A bank in need of reserves and a member of the Federal Reserve System could sell bills to its district Federal Reserve Bank at discounts from their face values determined by the Fed's discount rate. The Fed paid for these bills by crediting the commercial bank's reserve account at the Fed. This was known as *going to the (discount) window*.[6]

Not all bills were eligible for discount at the Fed. *Eligible* bills were defined as those which had low default risk and short maturities (not more than 6 months for agricultural bills and not more than 90 days for others) and which, with an important exception to be noted below, arose from "actual commercial transactions."[7] The Fed was not to lend

---

5 As in other chapters references to "banks" indicate commercial banks or sometimes all depository institutions. When we mean "Federal Reserve Banks," we use the complete expression.

6 Federal Reserve Banks actually used to have discount windows, much like tellers' windows, through which pieces of paper (securities) were exchanged. Book-entry computer transfers of securities have made these windows obsolete, but the term remains.

7 Section 13 of the Federal Reserve Act; reprinted in Henry Willis (1923, pages 1667 to 1696).

on the basis of other private debt instruments, including long-term loans and "speculative" stock market loans.

This part of the Federal Reserve Act was founded on the "real-bills doctrine," or "commercial-loan theory," which maintains that price stability is enhanced if bank lending is tied dollar for dollar to the volume of trade so that M and Y in the equation of exchange rise and fall together. Unfortunately the real-bills doctrine has long been known to be fallacious on several grounds, not the least of which are the impossibilities of associating a unique number of dollars with a unit of goods or limiting the number of times that a good is sold. The first difficulty implies that the price level is indeterminate under the real-bills doctrine, and the second means that the same good may be financed in its travels by several bills and thus give rise to several additions to bank reserves.[8] So the Federal Reserve Act was self-contradictory, its real-bills operating procedure being inconsistent with its stable-price-level goal. However, the proponents and critics of the real-bills doctrine were not given a chance to see that theory applied because the Act also provided a home for an opposing doctrine, that a primary duty of a central bank is the financing of government, and accordingly declared that bills drawn for the purpose of trading or carrying U.S. government securities were also eligible for discounting by the Fed. This provision was very soon applied to the monetization of federal deficits during World War I.

Amendments in the 1930s

Another shortcoming of the Federal Reserve Act arose from its framers' ignorance of the markets that they presumed to control. Only a small and declining part of the nation's business was in fact financed by bills of exchange. Bank credit has from its earliest days in the United States taken the two principal forms in which it exists today: government securities and the nonnegotiable promissory notes of businesses and individuals (just like your own bank loan). The commercial-loan theory has always been recommended to banks, and they have usually paid it lip service. But nineteenth- and early-twentieth-century writers pointed out that little bank credit was extended through the discounting of real bills,[9] and post-1913 observ-

---

8 One of the earliest and most persuasive critics of the real-bills doctrine was Henry Thornton (1802, Chapters 8 to 10). But it must be admitted that the real-bills doctrine has had many supporters in addition to the framers of the Federal Reserve Act. For a history of the controversies related to this theory and to other theories of monetary control, see Lloyd Mints (1945) and Thomas Humphrey (1982).

   Even though the real-bills doctrine is invalid as a theory of price stability, a case can be made that an emphasis on real bills promotes secure and liquid bank assets. But the same case can be made for stock exchange loans or short-term obligations of the U.S. Treasury.

9 The inadequacy of the commercial-loan theory as a description of contemporary and previous American banking practice was the subject of Waldo Mitchell's 1925 book, *The Uses of Bank Funds.*

   The Bank of New York opened in 1784 with the announcement that it would discount notes and bills "at six per cent. per annum; but no discount will be made for longer than thirty days,

ers could only wonder at the Fed's early attempts to encourage real bills in order to "change the commercial credit practices of this country in directions thought to be an improvement."[10]

Eventually it was alleged that the lack of eligible paper interfered with monetary policy—specifically that the Fed's failure to halt the decline in money during the Great Depression was partly due to the inability to find eligible paper to be discounted at Federal Reserve Banks. This belief led Congress, in a pair of emergency measures in 1932 and 1933 and more permanently in the Banking Act of 1935, to give Federal Reserve Banks the power to lend to banks in the form of *advances*. The effect on bank reserves is the same as discounting, but there are procedural differences. In the case of discounting, a Federal Reserve Bank buys a marketable security from a bank at a discount from its face value, the bank's reserve account at the Fed is credited by an amount equal to the security's price, and upon maturity the Fed returns the security to the bank and deducts the face value from the bank's reserve account. An advance, on the other hand, is simply a loan obtained by presenting the bank's promissory note to the Fed, which credits the bank's reserve account by the amount of the note and upon the maturity of the loan deducts the amount of the note plus interest from the bank's reserve account.[11]

Virtually all discount window lending now takes the form of advances. The discounting of private securities in the manner envisioned by the Federal Reserve Act sometimes requires time-consuming checks for eligibility standards and is discouraged. Advances based on municipal or U.S. government securities as collateral are simpler.

The liberalization of the Fed's lending capabilities was not permitted to influence actual Fed lending during the 1930s because Fed discount rates were kept well above market rates. (See Figure 9.1.) No amount of eligible paper could have induced commercial banks to borrow from the Fed at high rates in order to lend at low rates.[12] In any case the issue of access to the discount window had become irrelevant to the conduct of monetary policy because by then the Fed knew that

---

nor will any note or bill be discounted to pay a former one." But we soon find the bank buying U.S. government bonds, extending and renewing loans to director Alexander Hamilton's Society for Establishing Useful Manufactures, and granting long-term loans to the State of New York. See Allan Nevins (1934, pages 15–25). Bray Hammond (1957, page 192) wrote that such practices were common in 1800 although "the tradition of short-term credit continued to be held in pious respect and bankers liked to pretend that they were faithful to it."

It is not enough merely to say that banks have never lived up (or down) to the commercial-loan theory. There has in fact never been any intention to do so. Early banks were chartered by national or state governments for the purpose of financing those governments, the most notable examples being the Bank of England (where the overdraft was also widely used) and the First and Second Banks of the United States.

10 Luther Harr and Carlton Harris (1936, page 433).

11 See Howard Hackley (1973, Chapter 8) for a more extensive discussion of discounts and advances.

12 There can be little doubt that the Fed *could* have "changed the credit practices of the country" toward a greater reliance on real bills by an offer to discount those bills at rates below the market.

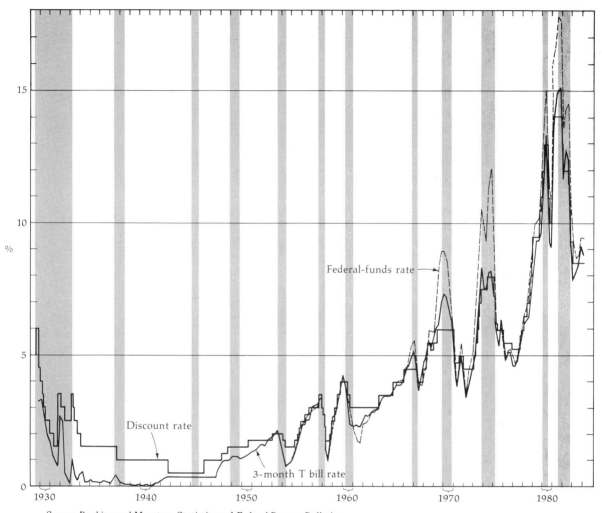

Source: *Banking and Monetary Statistics* and *Federal Reserve Bulletin*s.

Figure 9.1   Rates of interest on Federal Reserve lending, 3-month Treasury bills, and overnight federal funds.*

* The surcharge that was added to the discount rate for large, frequent borrowers during portions of 1980 and 1981 is not shown in this figure but is shown in Table 9.1 and Figure 9.2. The federal funds rate is shown only since data became available in 1954.

it had been given sufficient power to control bank reserves by its authority to buy and sell government securities directly in the open market.

The discount rate

Reported Federal Reserve Bank discount rates are no longer true discount rates and are not officially called such by the Fed. These rates have since 1971 been simple annual rates of interest, consistent with the above discussion of advances.[13] But the original term is still widely[14] used, and we shall conform.

We also normally adhere to the custom of referring to "the" discount rate. Each Federal Reserve Bank charges different rates for different types of loans, which will be discussed in the next section. It is sufficient for the present to know that most Federal Reserve Bank loans are called "short-term adjustment credit" and Federal Reserve Banks usually charge identical rates on these loans because the Federal Reserve Board usually exercises its power under the Federal Reserve Act to impose a uniform rate on the system for each type of loan. Whenever discount rates differ, our discussions, tables, and figures use the rate charged by the New York Fed on short-term adjustment credit.

The demand by a commercial bank for credit from its Federal Reserve Bank should be expected to respond to the difference between the Fed's discount rate and the costs of alternative sources of funds. A low discount rate encourages bank borrowing from the Fed and, because of the consequent increase in bank reserves, induces increases in bank lending and the money supply accompanied by declines in interest rates. Presumably, banks continue to borrow from the Fed rather than from other sources until rates on the latter have fallen to the level of the discount rate. A high discount rate, on the other hand, discourages bank borrowing from the Fed. The resulting decline in bank reserves induces reductions in bank lending and increases in interest rates.

This was approximately the way that the Bank of England influenced money, credit, and interest rates through its manipulation of Bank Rate. It would be too much to say that the Federal Reserve System was patterned after the Bank of England. Nevertheless, the structure and conduct of the best-known central bank of the day must have been in the minds of the framers of the Federal Reserve Act, and the Act's description of discounting is consistent with the functioning of Bank Rate.[15] All of this might lead one to suspect that Fed discount rates have (like Bank Rate in England) been the principal or at least an important instrument of monetary policy. But this has not been the case for two reasons: First, the Federal Reserve System has preferred open market operations (which are completely under the Fed's control) to lending through the discount window (which depends on bank responses and is difficult to predict).[16] Second, discount rates have frequently not been the principal means by which the Fed has

---

13 See the Federal Reserve Board's *Banking and Monetary Statistics, 1941–70*, page 635n.

14 But not universally; see the title of Table 9.1.

15 See the testimony of Bank of England officials to the National Monetary Commission (1910, pages 19–28). This commission, established by Congress, played an important role in the political controversies that eventually resulted in the Federal Reserve Act in 1913.

16 Such a preference has also been demonstrated by the Bank of England since the 1930s.

regulated lending through its discount windows. Notice the occasions in Figure 9.1 (in 1966, 1969 to 1970, 1973 to 1975, and 1979 to 1983) when the fed funds rate exceeded Fed discount rates by substantial margins. These circumstances could not have arisen in the presence of *meaningful* Fed discount rates, by which we mean rates at which the Fed is willing to lend to all legally qualified borrowers who meet the Fed's credit standards. Since credit standards are routinely satisfied by using U.S. securities as collateral, we may confidently surmise that some heretofore unconsidered factor limits bank borrowing from the Fed in unlimited amounts whenever the costs of other sources of reserves, such as fed funds, exceed the discount rate. That factor must, of course, be nonprice rationing, which Fed personnel like to call "administration of the discount window."

Administration of the discount window

The administration of the discount window refers to the determination and application of rules governing who may borrow from the Fed, when, and how much. These rules are set forth in *Regulation A: Extensions of Credit by Federal Reserve Banks*.[17] Regulation A describes three categories of credit: (1) "Short-term adjustment credit," which will be discussed below; (2) "Extended seasonal credit" to small depository institutions with regular seasonal reserve needs and without access to other sources of funds; and (3) "Other extended credit" in response to "exceptional circumstances," such as those "where an individual depository institution is experiencing financial strains arising from particular circumstances or practices affecting that institution—including sustained deposit drains, impaired access to money market funds, or sudden deterioration in loan repayment performance" and "where similar assistance is not reasonably available from other sources" (Regulation A, Section 201.3).

The rates applicable to these three categories on April 30, 1984, are listed in the top portion of Table 9.1. Note the uniformity of the rates charged by Federal Reserve Banks. Interest rates on short-term adjustment credit during 1974 to 1983 are shown in the lower half of the table, which indicates frequent but always short-lived occasions when discount rates differed. The remainder of our discussion of discount rates will concentrate on (1), short-term adjustment credit.

> Short-term adjustment credit . . . is available . . . , to the extent appropriate, in meeting temporary requirements for funds, or to cushion more persistent outflows of funds pending an orderly adjustment of the institution's assets and liabilities. Such credit

---

17 The most important change in Regulation A in recent years has been the extension of the borrowing privilege to all depository institutions (as part of the Depository Institutions Deregulation and Monetary Control Act of 1980) instead of its being limited, as previously, to commercial banks that are members of the Federal Reserve System.

Table 9.1   Federal Reserve Bank Interest Rates (Percent per Annum)

Current and previous levels

Federal Reserve Bank	Short-term adjustment credit and seasonal credit			Extended credit [a]						Effective date for current rates
				First 60 days of borrowing		Next 90 days of borrowing		After 150 days		
	Rate on 4/30/84	Effective date	Previous rate	Rate on 4/30/84	Previous rate	Rate on 4/30/84	Previous rate	Rate on 4/30/84	Previous rate	
Boston	9	4/9/84	8½	9	8½	10	9½	11	9½	4/9/84
New York		4/9/84								4/9/84
Philadelphia		4/9/84								4/9/84
Cleveland		4/10/84								4/10/84
Richmond		4/9/84								4/9/84
Atlanta		4/10/84								4/10/84
Chicago		4/9/84								4/9/84
St. Louis		4/9/84								4/9/84
Minneapolis		4/9/84								4/9/84
Kansas City		4/13/84								4/13/84
Dallas		4/9/84								4/9/84
San Francisco	9	4/13/84	8½	9	8½	10	9½	11	9½	4/13/84

Range of rates in recent years [b]

Effective date	Range (or level)—All F.R. Banks	F.R. Bank of N.Y.	Effective date	Range (or level)—All F.R. Banks	F.R. Bank of N.Y.	Effective date	Range (or level)—All F.R. Banks	F.R. Bank of N.Y.
In effect Dec. 31, 1973	7½	7½	1978— July 3	7-7¼	7¼	1981— May 5	13-14	14
1974— Apr. 25	7½-8	8	10	7¼	7¼	8	14	14
30	8	8	Aug. 21	7¾	7¾	Nov. 2	13-14	13
Dec. 9	7¾-8	7¾	Sept. 22	8	8	6	13	13
16	7¾	7¾	Oct. 16	8-8½	8½	Dec. 4	12	12
1975— Jan. 6	7¼-7¾	7¼	20	8½	8½	1982— July 20	11½-12	11½
10	7¼-7¾	7¼	Nov. 1	8½-9½	9½	23	11½	11½
24	7¼	7¼	3	9½	9½	Aug. 2	11-11½	11
Feb. 5	6¾-7¼	6¾	1979— July 20	10	10	3	11	11
7	6¾	6¾	Aug. 17	10-10½	10½	16	10½	10½
Mar. 10	6¼-6¾	6¼	20	10½	10½	27	10-10½	10
14	6¼	6¼	Sept. 19	10½-11	11	30	10	10
May 16	6-6¼	6	21	11	11	Oct. 12	9½-10	9½
23	6	6	Oct. 8	11-12	12	13	9½	9½
1976— Jan. 19	5½-6	5½	10	12	12	Nov. 22	9-9½	9
23	5½	5½	1980— Feb. 15	12-13	13	26	9	9
Nov. 22	5¼-5½	5¼	19	13	13	Dec. 14	8½-9	9
26	5¼	5¼	May 29	12-13	13	15	8½-9	8½
1977— Aug. 30	5¼-5¾	5¼	30	12	12	17	8½	8½
31	5¼-5¾	5¾	June 13	11-12	11	1984— Apr. 9	8½-9	9
Sept. 2	5¾	5¾	16	11	11			
Oct. 26	6	6	July 28	10-11	10			
1978— Jan. 9	6-6½	6½	29	10	10			
20	6½	6½	Sept. 26	11	11			
May 11	6½-7	7	Nov. 17	12	12			
12	7	7	Dec. 5	12-13	13	In effect Apr. 30, 1984	9	9
			8	13	13			

a Applicable to advances when exceptional circumstances or practices involve only a particular depository institution and to advances when an institution is under sustained liquidity pressures. See Section 201.3(b)(2) of Regulation A.

b Rates for short-term adjustment credit. For description and earlier data see the following publications of the Board of Governors: *Banking and Monetary Statistics, 1914–1941,* and *1941–1970; Annual Statistical Digest, 1970–1979, 1980, 1981,* and *1982.*

In 1980 and 1981 the Fed applied a surcharge to short-term adjustment credit borrowings by institutions with deposits of $500 million or more that had borrowed in successive weeks or in more than 4 weeks in a calendar quarter. A 3 percent surcharge was in effect from March 17, 1980, through May 7, 1980. There was no surcharge until November 17, 1980, when a 2 percent surcharge was adopted; the surcharge was subsequently raised to 3 percent on December 5, 1980, and to 4 percent on May 5, 1981. The surcharge was reduced to 3 percent effective September 22, 1981, and to 2 percent effective October 12. As of October 1, the formula for applying the surcharge was changed from a calendar quarter to a moving 13-week period. The surcharge was eliminated on November 17, 1981.

Source: *Federal Reserve Bulletin,* May 1984, tab. 1.14.

generally is available only after reasonable alternative sources of funds . . . have been fully used.

Regulation A, sec. 201.3

How much borrowing is "appropriate" has never been defined. Neither has "reasonable alternative sources of funds." Many complicated official explanations and procedures have been set forth. But the practical criteria by which the discount officers of the twelve Federal Reserve Banks administer their windows has not been stated. Nevertheless, the actual pattern of their behavior is unsurprising and easily understood. The most important borrowers have been large banks with the easiest access to alternative sources, and these banks have borrowed most when the discount rate is well below other interest rates, particularly the fed funds rate. That is, the actual administrations of discount windows have merely amounted to partial accommodations of bank profit motives, with little regard for what is appropriate for "orderly adjustment" and no regard at all for the availability of alternative sources.

The discount window as a subsidy

The Federal Reserve Act provided no guide to discount-rate policy beyond a statement in Section 14 that rates "shall be fixed with a view of accommodating commerce and business." There has apparently been a feeling in the Federal Reserve System that discount rates ought to vary more or less in line with market rates. However, the idea of a continuously close relationship, such as would be achieved either by a floating discount rate tied to some market rate or by the enforced conformity of market rates to the discount rate that would follow from a meaningful discount rate (that is, no rationing of borrowers with eligible paper), has been rejected.[18] The result has been, as we saw in Figure 9.1, that discount rates have sharply diverged from market rates. Figure 9.2 shows the strong positive relationship between bank borrowing from the Fed and the profitability of that borrowing as reflected in the spread between the fed funds rate and the discount rate.[19]

Is the discount rate an indicator of monetary policy?

Although the discount rate may not itself be an important instrument of policy, there is evidence that it has been used to announce shifts in monetary policy that are then implemented by open market operations, changes in reserve requirements, and more-or-less-stringent

---

18 See Clay Anderson (1971, pages 139, 157–161) and Lorraine Duro (1980) for histories of Fed views regarding discount rates.

19 This relationship has been documented by several statistical studies, including Stephen Goldfeld and Edward Kane (1966). Similar relationships, based on a variety of market rates, were presented by Robert Turner (1938) for the period between 1922 and 1936. Alton Gilbert (1979) calculated the values of the discount window subsidy to commercial banks of various sizes in the St. Louis district during the years 1974, 1975, 1976, and 1977. The largest banks borrowed the most (even in proportion to their sizes) and received the greatest subsidies.

   Gilbert's results are corroborated for the Federal Reserve System as a whole during 1963 to 1968 in the Federal Reserve Board's *Reappraisal of the Federal Reserve Discount Mechanism* (1971, i, pages 114 and 115).

   Another study of borrowing, reported in James Parthemos and Walter Varvel (1981), indicates that, although small banks borrow smaller amounts and less frequently than large banks, they tend to borrow for longer periods of time, averaging 4 or 5 consecutive weeks during 1979 and 1980 for banks with deposits less than $200 million, compared with 1 to 2 consecutive weeks for banks with deposits exceeding $3 billion.

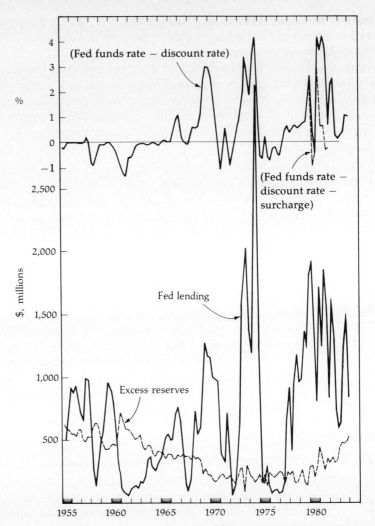

Source: *Banking and Monetary Statistics, Annual Statistical Digests,* and *Federal Reserve Bulletins.*

Figure 9.2   Member-bank excess reserves, Federal Reserve lending, and the difference between the federal funds rate and the Federal Reserve discount rate (quarterly averages of daily figures).*

* The applicable dates and values of the surcharge on Fed lending to "institutions with deposits of $500 million or more that had borrowed in successive weeks or more than 4 weeks in a calendar quarter" are given in the note to Table 9.1.

administration of discount windows. Some of this evidence is presented in Table 9.2, which shows the dates of discount rate changes (or the beginnings of sequences of changes) that were not reversed within 6 months, changes in the 3-month Treasury bill (T bill) rate and Fed lending 3 and 6 months before and after these dates, and percentage

changes in the adjusted monetary base (AMB) and the money supply
(M1) 3 and 6 months before and after the same dates.[20]

For example, consider the reduction in the discount rate from 14
percent to 13 percent on November 2, 1981. As may be seen from the
lower portion of Table 9.1, this began a series of reductions that
reached 8.5 percent in December 1982. However, our analysis is
limited to events 3 and 6 months immediately preceding and following
the initial change in November 1981. We see that on this occasion the
discount rate decrease did indeed presage a more expansionary monetary policy. On the basis of both 3-month and 6-month comparisons,
Fed lending was increased and both AMB and M1 grew more rapidly
after the increase in the discount rate. For example, Fed lending rose
(in *millions*) $1,018 between November 1981 and February 1982,
compared with a fall of $713 between August and November 1981; Fed
lending rose $410 between November 1981 and May 1982, compared
with a fall of $1,459 between May and November 1981. Furthermore,
AMB increased at an annual rate of 11.9 percent between November
1981 and February 1982, compared with an increase of only 0.5 percent
during the preceding 3 months; AMB rose at an annual rate of 10
percent between November 1981 and May 1982, compared with a 2.3
percent rise during the preceding 6 months. The money-supply figures
tell a similar story.

The lower portion of Table 9.2 confirms that, as in 1981, most
discount rate changes were honest indicators of the future course of
monetary policy. That is, compared with the periods immediately
preceding discount rate changes, most discount rate increases were
followed by greater declines or smaller rises in Fed lending and by
reductions in the rates of growth of AMB and M1; and most discount
rate decreases were followed by greater rises or smaller falls in Fed
lending and by increases in the rates of growth of AMB and M1. More
than three-quarters (93 of 120) of the shifts in speed or direction of
Fed lending, AMB, and M1 reported in the table might have been
correctly predicted by a model in which an increase (decrease) in the
Fed's discount rate is a precursor of a tighter (easier) monetary
policy.

Now consider the relationships between movements in the discount
rate and the T bill rate. The strongest relationship in Table 9.2 is the
tendency of the discount rate to follow the T bill rate—on all 20
occasions when 3-month movements in the T bill rate are considered
and on 18 of 20 occasions considering 6-month movements.[21] These

---

20 AMB is the monetary base adjusted for changes in reserve requirements. Since the monetary
    base consists of bank reserves and nonbank currency holdings and is largely determined by the
    Fed, AMB may be the best overall indicator of Fed influences on the money supply. AMB is cal-
    culated and published by the St. Louis Fed and is described by John Tatom (1980).

21 The last change in the discount rate shown in Table 9.1, the increase from 8.5 to 9 percent in
    April 1984, conformed to this tendency since the T bill rate had been rising since mid-October
    1983.

Table 9.2   The Discount Rate As an Indicator of Interest Rates and Monetary Policy

| | | 3-month Changes | | | | | | | |
| Date | Change in Discount Rate[a] | 3-month T Bill Rate,[b] Basis Points | | Change in Fed Lending,[d] Millions of $ | | AMB[d] % Change Annual Rate | | M1[d] % Change Annual Rate | |
		B[c]	A	B	A	B	A	B	A
1/12/48	1.00 to 1.25	12	3	16	38	0	− 6.2	1.8	− 3.9
8/21/50	1.50 to 1.75	10	11	56	− 27	2.1	2.1	4.7	3.2
1/16/53	1.75 to 2.00	30	19	279	− 188	5.9	0.0	1.9	3.2
2/ 5/54	2.00 to 1.75	− 37	− 24	− 186	− 136	−0.9	1.9	1.2	1.9
4/15/55	1.50 to 1.75	35	− 6	141	− 9	1.9	0.0	2.7	2.7
11/15/57	3.50 to 3.00	− 2	−169	− 200	− 568	0.0	6.7	− 2.4	− 0.3
9/12/58	1.75 to 2.00	154	45	334	88	−0.9	2.7	3.2	4.7
6/10/60	4.00 to 3.50	− 99	− 5	− 212	− 192	0.9	3.6	− 0.3	4.9
7/17/63	3.00 to 3.50	29	28	171	21	6.6	2.4	4.6	3.2
11/24/64	3.50 to 4.00	28	21	99	17	5.3	6.8	5.1	2.5
12/ 6/65	4.00 to 4.50	44	29	− 43	81	8.0	6.4	7.2	6.8
4/ 7/67	4.50 to 4.00	− 85	25	− 234	− 64	6.0	5.9	4.9	10.7
11/20/67	4.00 to 4.50	50	11	44	228	6.5	7.0	5.2	5.6
12/18/68	5.25 to 5.50	85	− 3	250	153	7.9	4.1	9.8	5.8
11/13/70	6.00 to 5.75	−105	−178	− 424	− 97	4.9	10.9	5.4	7.7
1/15/73	4.50 to 5.00	62	76	590	557	12.3	10.5	11.5	1.9
12/ 9/74	8.00 to 7.75	−186	−178	−2,584	− 597	11.7	3.8	5.4	3.7
8/31/77	5.25 to 5.75	53	48	871	− 231	10.4	8.1	6.4	9.8
9/26/80	10.00 to 11.00	303	417	931	306	11.3	7.5	18.2	3.7
11/ 2/81	14.00 to 13.00	−322	147	− 713	1,018	0.5	11.9	5.0	10.4

a Changes in the discount rate (on short-term adjustment credit by the Federal Reserve Bank of New York) are shown for dates on which changes (or sequences of changes) occurred (or began) that were not reversed within 6 months. Later changes in the same direction within 12 months are treated as part of the same sequence.

b Changes in the T bill rate are between weekly averages of daily figures.

c B and A denote changes during the 3- and 6-month periods immediately before (B) and after (A) changes in the discount rate.

d Changes in Fed lending, AMB (adjusted monetary base), and M1 (money supply) are between monthly averages of daily figures. Only AMB and M1 are seasonally adjusted. Changes are between averages of full calendar weeks or months regardless of when in a week or month a discount rate change occurred.

Sources: *Banking and Monetary Statistics, Annual Statistical Digests,* and Federal Reserve Bank of St. Louis *Review,* December 1980.

Table 9.2   (continued)

Date	Change in Discount Rate[a]	3-month T Bill Rate,[b] Basis Points		Change in Fed Lending,[d] Millions of $		AMB[d] % Change Annual Rate		M1[d] % Change Annual Rate	
		B^c	A	B	A	B	A	B	A
1/12/48	1.00 to 1.25	37	3	105	102	2.1	− 3.6	2.2	−2.1
8/21/50	1.50 to 1.75	14	10	− 6	158	−0.5	3.7	5.2	3.7
1/16/53	1.75 to 2.00	24	− 2	280	−944	4.9	2.4	3.2	2.1
2/ 5/54	2.00 to 1.75	−108	− 20	− 350	− 98	−0.5	0.9	0.6	2.5
4/15/55	1.50 to 1.75	65	63	331	310	0.9	0.9	3.7	2.0
11/15/57	3.50 to 3.00	40	−236	− 121	−691	0.0	3.7	− 1.0	1.8
9/12/58	1.75 to 2.00	98	48	337	144	0.0	1.8	4.4	5.2
6/10/60	4.00 to 3.50	−187	− 33	− 486	−331	0.0	2.2	− 0.7	2.0
7/17/63	3.00 to 3.50	29	35	221	− 33	6.2	5.2	4.2	3.3
11/24/64	3.50 to 4.00	31	10	177	87	5.7	5.2	5.8	2.2
12/ 6/65	4.00 to 4.50	53	24	− 53	195	6.5	4.9	6.8	4.7
4/ 7/67	4.50 to 4.00	−144	54	− 594	− 29	6.1	6.6	3.3	8.9
11/20/67	4.00 to 4.50	127	96	7	626	6.2	6.6	7.7	6.7
12/18/68	5.25 to 5.50	58	53	60	642	7.3	4.4	8.1	4.6
11/13/70	6.00 to 5.75	−132	−152	− 641	− 95	5.7	9.9	5.0	9.2
1/15/73	4.50 to 5.00	135	263	962	887	9.7	9.2	10.9	4.9
12/ 9/74	8.00 to 7.75	− 99	−224	−2,297	−432	9.4	6.3	4.0	6.4
8/31/77	5.25 to 5.75	90	83	992	−666	9.1	9.8	6.5	8.5
9/26/80	10.00 to 11.00	−510	246	−1,517	−307	8.7	5.6	7.8	6.9
11/ 2/81	14.00 to 13.00	−423	33	−1,459	410	2.3	10.0	3.4	7.0

Proportion of occasions that a change in the discount rate:	3 Months	6 Months
followed a movement in the T bill rate in the same direction	20/20	18/20
reinforced the movement in the T bill rate	5/20	4/18
preceded a change in the change of Fed lending in the opposite direction (exceptions boxed)	16/20	14/20
preceded a change in the percentage change of AMB in the opposite direction (exceptions boxed)	15/20	15/20
preceded a change in the percentage change of M1 in the opposite direction (exceptions boxed)	15/20	18/20

observations are consistent with the view that the discount rate is not itself an instrument of policy and that to an important extent its changes merely reflect a desire by the Fed that the discount rate not get too far out of line with market rates. But the apparent usefulness of the discount rate as an indicator of shifts in monetary policy means that these observations are also consistent with the view that monetary policy exacerbates economic fluctuations—by becoming tighter only after interest rates have been rising for some time and becoming easier long after interest rates have begun to fall.

Now let's look at what happens to the T bill rate *after* changes in the discount rate. Table 9.2 tells us that, in all but nine of the thirty-eight observations on changes in the discount rate following movements in the T bill rate in the same direction, increases in the discount rate preceded reductions or decelerations in the T bill rate and decreases in the discount rate preceded increases or accelerations in the T bill rate. There are at least two plausible explanations of this relationship, each of which may play a part. The first is consistent with the procyclical Fed behavior described above, by which the Fed worsens economic fluctuations by tightening credit just at the ends of economic expansions or even after the onset of recessions so that discount rate increases tend to occur in a weakening economy with declining credit demands that cause interest rates, including T bill rates, to fall.[22] This argument is symmetrical, claiming that monetary expansions tend to occur in the midst of, or immediately preceding, economic expansions. The second explanation is based on the concept of rational expectations, by which in the present case we mean that investors form expectations of future prices and interest rates partly on the basis of their observations of Fed actions. For example, if market participants believe that discount rate increases tend to precede contractions of Fed credit and the money supply, their inflationary expectations will be revised downward, putting downward pressure on interest rates. Whatever the reasons for the observed relationship between Fed discount and market rates, an investor conversant with history is not likely to bet that a change in the Fed discount rate will reinforce movements in market rates in the same direction.

FEDERAL FUNDS[23]

Early forms of interbank funds transfers

OUR SHACKLED BANKING SYSTEM. Nearly all the significant peculiarities of the American banking system were developed during the nineteenth century although some of the names have changed. The great contribution of a well-developed financial system is the efficient transfer of funds from savers to investors. Commercial banks are essential to this

---

22 See Milton Friedman (1961).

23 Portions of this section have been drawn from John Wood (1983).

process in the first instance because of their role as managers of the payments system. Borrowers and lenders, whether trading directly or through financial intermediaries, exchange funds by exchanging claims on banks. Banks also perform the intermediary function of borrowing from savers in order to lend to investors. The efficient performance of these functions is particularly challenging in the United States because of the size and diversity of the country. Possibly the most efficient means of transferring funds between national regions (and that used in most countries) is a system of national banks. But Americans, who are most in need of such a system, have by severe legal restrictions on branch banking—especially the prohibition of interstate branching—denied themselves the benefits of national banks.[24] Banks in surplus, low-interest-rate regions have not had branches in deficit, high-interest-rate regions to which to transfer funds.

BANKERS' BALANCES. But where there's a dollar there's a way. The nineteenth century saw the evolution of a competitive national banking system in spite of regulation. The system was based on correspondent banking and bankers' balances. Then as now, correspondent banks in New York, Chicago, San Francisco, and other financial centers managed the reserves and money market investments, cleared the checks, and performed other services for banks in smaller cities and rural areas. Bankers' balances, largely demand deposits held with their urban correspondents by smaller banks in outlying areas, were the principal form of interbank lending. Until interest on demand deposits was made illegal by the Glass-Steagall Banking Act of 1933, large banks competed for the balances of small banks by paying interest. A dozen of sixty members of the New York Clearing House paid interest on deposits in 1857, a practice continued by about half a dozen of thirty-eight national banks in that city in 1907.[25] These banks and their competitors in other cities held the bulk of interbank deposits and thus as a group held the country's reserve and served as the principal conduits through which funds flowed between and within regions.

Bankers' balances have long been an object of regulatory interference. The National Banking Act of 1863 allowed national banks in smaller cities and towns to keep a part of their required reserves in the form of deposits with banks in "central reserve" and "reserve" cities.[26] After the Federal Reserve Act of 1913, however, members of the Federal Reserve System, which included all federally chartered ("na-

---

24 A charter conferred by the Comptroller of the Currency under the National Banking Act of 1863 makes a bank "national" only in name.

25 O. Sprague (1910, pages 20 and 232).

26 In 1914, there were three central reserve cities (New York, Chicago, and St. Louis) and forty-nine reserve cities (ranging through the alphabet from Albany to Wichita).

tional") banks and those state-chartered banks that chose to be members, had to keep their required reserves with Federal Reserve Banks. The architects of the Federal Reserve Act hoped that the Act would discourage the use of bankers' balances.[27] But most state banks stayed outside the System and continued normal relations with their urban correspondents. Many national banks also continued to rely upon deposits with correspondents as a primary source of liquidity.

Banks in most cities colluded in attempts to "regulate" competition for deposits, that is, to fix rates at low levels. But most of these attempts failed because of the refusal of one or more banks to cooperate. Beginning about 1920, the Fed attempted to bolster these rate-fixing agreements.[28] For example the Federal Reserve Bank of New York arranged a scheme based on that of the London Clearing House banks, by which the rate on bankers' balances was tied to the central bank's lending rate.[29] But the fact that bankers' balances continued to flow to New York even though "agreed" New York deposit rates were less than elsewhere[30] suggests that, by some means or other (either by exceeding the clearinghouse maximum rate or by various forms of nonprice competition) at least a few New York banks evaded the Fed's anticompetitive restrictions. During the 1920s about 20 percent of the deposits of national banks in New York City were owed to other banks.

Bankers' balances persisted even after interest on demand deposits was made illegal in 1933 because borrowing banks have been as imaginative in evading regulations in order to attract the deposits of other banks as in competing for the funds of nonbank investors.[31] Urban correspondents have been willing to provide check clearing, assistance with loan participations, and other services to rural banks as payment for the use of their funds. As a result the contemporary interbank-deposit market has managed to contribute to financial efficiency almost as well recently as during the nineteenth century in spite of the efforts of legislators and regulators. The market continues to revolve around the large banks. For example Paul Jessup reported that in 1979 "about 175 large banks hold about 85 percent of all

---

27 See Leonard Watkins (1929, pages vii and 39). Public officials and bankers opposed interest competition for bankers' balances on several grounds, claiming (1) that the concentration of interest-sensitive deposits in the money centers promoted panics because banks in those centers were subject to losses of funds as the result of developments elsewhere, such as when deposits flowed out of New York to agricultural areas to finance crop movements in the fall [this controversial view has been discussed by Brian Gendreau (1979), C. Goodhart (1969), and John James (1978)], (2) that funds ought to stay home where they belong, and (3) that these payments reduced bank profits and thereby weakened the financial system (see the statements by Senator Glass early in Chapter 2).

28 For an early account of the Federal Reserve's support of collusive arrangements, see *Federal Reserve Bulletin*, February 1920, page 157.

29 The resulting agreed maximum rates are shown in James Boughton and Elmus Wicker (1979, Figure 1).

30 See Leonard Watkins (1929, page 264).

31 See lines 2 and 50 of Table 4.2.

correspondent deposits; and about 20 large banks in Chicago and New York account for almost 60 percent of all such deposits" (1980, pages 98 and 99).[32]

But the legislators and regulators have not given up. Interbank competition for funds was dealt another blow by the Depository Institutions Deregulation and Monetary Control Act of 1980, which imposed uniform reserve requirements on all depository institutions,[33] whether members of the Federal Reserve System or not. After a phase-in period, all required reserves must be held either as vault cash (currency and coin on the premises) or on deposit at Federal Reserve Banks.[34]

INTERBANK LOANS. The funds that banks in the interior lent to New York in the form of bankers' balances were in part sent back to the interior as loans by New York banks to banks in the South and West. But interbank borrowing was not exclusively between New York and other places. It was a common feature of relationships between city and country correspondents and was thus an effective means of transferring funds within regions. Country banks kept interest-earning deposits in city banks, which were channeled back to them and to other country banks in the form of interbank loans.

Lines of credit were common. Oliver Lockhart wrote that "General arrangements for borrowing are usually made at the time of opening correspondent relations. In recent years an investigation of the credit standing of the depositing bank is regularly made before the acceptance of the account. . . . The line of credit is adjusted to the average balance carried by the depositing bank, as is the practice in individual loans. In New York the balance was formerly expected to amount to one-fifth of the line of credit extended."[35] During the 1920s about 5 percent of the loans of New York City national banks were to other banks.[36]

CLEARINGHOUSE BALANCES. The closest early approximation to the modern fed funds market was the practice of borrowing and lending balances at clearinghouses. Originally, banks which were indebted to a clearinghouse in the morning in amounts too large to settle immediately without inconvenience but which expected inflows of funds (usually by calling loans) in the afternoon borrowed funds directly from other banks. Eventually, instead of going from bank to bank, the

---

32 Also see Robert Knight (1970, 1971).

33 Commercial banks, S&Ls, mutual savings banks, and credit unions.

34 A nonmember institution may hold some of its required reserves with another depository institution as long as the latter passes those deposits on to a Federal Reserve Bank.

35 Oliver Lockhart (1921, pages 156–157).

36 About 7 percent of the loans of large New York City banks were to other domestic banks at the end of 1982. About 6.5 percent of the loans of all large weekly reporting banks were to other domestic banks, 5 percent in the form of fed funds (see lines 19, 20, 23, and 31 of Table 4.2).

representatives of banks met at the clearinghouse to borrow and lend their balances. About 60 percent of balances at the Boston Clearing House were settled in this way in 1900. James Cannon wrote that "In practice, some banks habitually loan, but never borrow. Others habitually borrow, but seldom or never loan. The rate of interest on such loans corresponds very closely with the rate on call loans."[37]

FEDERAL FUNDS IN THE 1920s. Interbank borrowing and lending were extended to reserve balances at Federal Reserve Banks in the 1920s.[38] Hence the name "federal" funds. Most fed funds transactions were arranged by the discount (or acceptance) houses, which dealt in U.S. government securities, commercial paper (CP), bankers' acceptances (BAs), and other securities. These firms were the forerunners of modern securities dealers. They bought and sold fed funds, usually on a quarter-point spread, although "as interdistrict trading developed, the spread ran as high as one percentage point at times because of discount rate differentials between the East Coast and West Coast."[39] San Francisco relied heavily on eastern banks for funds. New York banks with excess reserves in the afternoon could send funds to San Francisco before the wires closed in the East at 2:30. These flows were especially large when the discount rate of the Federal Reserve Bank of San Francisco exceeded that of the New York Fed.[40]

Fed funds rates fell rapidly along with other rates between 1929 and 1933, and the fed funds market disappeared as interest rates remained low throughout the 1930s and banks chose to hold large quantities of excess reserves. The market experienced a small revival in 1941 as the war stimulated economic activity. But the Fed's wartime policy of supplying unlimited reserves at a T bill rate of 0.375 percent made the fed funds market unnecessary. Banks adjusted their reserves through purchases and sales of riskless T bills.

Table 9.3 indicates the relative importance of the fed funds market and other short-term markets in the 1920s and also shows the great increase in the relative importance of fed funds during the postwar period. All except the first item have already been discussed in this and earlier chapters. The first item consists mainly of "call," or "demand," loans, which for many years were the main vehicle for short-term bank-reserve adjustments. Banks are able in this market to lend funds to brokers and dealers, either directly or through their

---

37 James Cannon (1908, pages 235–236). Call loans are discussed below. Clearinghouse rates were reported regularly in the financial press (see the quotation at the beginning of this chapter).

38 See Parker Willis (1970) for a discussion of the early fed funds market.

39 Parker Willis (1970, page 7).

40 Federal Reserve Bank discount rates, though seldom differing by large amounts for long periods, were usually not uniform before 1942. See the Federal Reserve Board's *Banking and Monetary Statistics, 1914–41*, pages 439–442, and *1941–70*, page 667.

Table 9.3   Selected Money Market Instruments, 1922 to 1980
(Estimated Annual Averages, Millions of Dollars)

	1922	1928	1960	1970	1980
Brokers' and dealers' loans[a]	1,312	4,335	1,918	3,986	6,038
Bankers' balances[b]	932	1,004	5,507	11,755	22,251
Commercial paper	766	501	4,689	37,093	121,624
BAs	550	1,065	1,529	5,870	52,976
U.S. short-term securities[c]	4,336	2,626	72,700	107,125	273,205
Borrowing from the Fed	571	840	436	835	1,420
Federal funds and RPs	55	175	1,400	18,500	106,428

a The 1922 and 1928 values include loans by New York City banks both on their own account and
   for the accounts of correspondents. Since most broker and dealer loans at that time were made
   through New York City banks, these data are roughly comparable with postwar data, which include loans by all large weekly reporting banks.

b Balances owed to domestic banks by large New York City banks.

c U.S. marketable securities maturing in 1 year or less outstanding on June 30.

Sources: Federal Reserve Board's *Banking and Monetary Statistics, 1914–41, 1941–70, Annual
Statistical Digest*s, and *Federal Reserve Bulletin*s; *Annual Reports of the Secretary of the Treasury;* Parker B. Willis, *The Federal Funds Market . . .* , 4th ed., Federal Reserve Bank of Boston,
Boston, 1970, and Dorothy M. Nichols, *Trading in Federal Funds,* Federal Reserve Board, Washington, 1965.

correspondents, in the knowledge that the funds can be "called"
immediately when reserves are needed. The largest part of this market
used to be centralized, with loans arranged at the money desk of the
New York Stock Exchange (NYSE).[41] Most broker and dealer loans
arise from the extension of credit by stock brokers to customers for
whom they carry securities on margin. Stringent legal margin requirements on stock purchases and the growing use of fed funds and RPs by
brokers and dealers has retarded the growth of the call-loan market.
The NYSE's money desk closed during the easy-money, low-interest-
rate year of 1946 and has not reopened. However, although call loans
have lost their dominant position, they remain an important overnight
outlet for bank funds, with transactions now arranged directly
between banks and securities brokers and dealers.[42]

41 "Time loans," that is, those with specific maturities, were arranged directly between banks and
    borrowers away from the Exchange. The rise and fall of an organized money market at the
    NYSE is documented in Chapter 11 in the 1869, 1917, and 1946 entries in the chronology of the
    development of the NYSE. . . . The operation of that market during the 1920s and 1930s has
    been described as follows: "The loans to brokers who are not deposit customers with the bank
    may be made either through the agency of money brokers or through the agency of the various
    stock exchanges, where money tables are established for the purpose of bringing together the
    borrowing brokers and the lending banks. In some few cases the loans may be made by direct
    contact between the borrowing broker and the bank, but the former is the prevailing method.
    The brokers submit to the officials in charge of the money table at the exchanges their require-
    ments, and the banks furnish them with statements of the amounts available. These sums are
    allocated among the brokers who apply, and such loans are made at rates which are determined
    by the officials in charge of the money tables on the exchanges" [Luther Harr and Carlton Har-
    ris (1936, pages 176–178)].

42 In addition to the top line of Table 9.3, see line 35 of Table 4.2.

The modern fed funds market

ALTERNATIVE MEANINGS OF FED FUNDS. The term fed funds has four
more or less common meanings:

1. Sometimes it means simply "commercial bank deposits in Federal Reserve Banks."[43]

2. A more common meaning is "overnight borrowing and lending
between commercial banks by means of transfers of their deposits at
Federal Reserve Banks."

3. The broadest meaning and that used most often by money
market participants is "immediately available funds"—which are
usually wire transfers between bank reserve accounts at Federal Reserve Banks, either on their own behalf or for their customers.

4. Commercial banks and the Fed usually report all "transfers of
immediately available funds not subject to reserve requirements" under the heading of federal funds or sometimes federal funds and repurchase agreements,[44] as in Table 9.4.

Our discussion will for the most part use the fourth definition. But
we will from time to time, for simplicity, use the narrow second
definition, which, as we see in Table 9.4, accounts for about 40 percent
of the broader fourth definition ($57,614 million of $139,446 million
borrowed by large banks on December 29, 1982).

An understanding of the fourth definition requires that we know
which bank liabilities are subject to reserve requirements. Fed decisions concerning reserve requirements have greatly affected the
growth of the fed funds market. There is no reason for monetary-
control purposes to require reserves against interbank fed funds
because those transactions merely redistribute funds without affecting
required reserves or the banking system's potential for creating money
and credit. This is illustrated by steps 1 and 2 in Table 9.5, which
shows fed funds purchases by bank P from bank S. (Step 3 and firm X
will be considered later.) In market parlance borrowers are called
"purchasers" and lenders are called "sellers" of fed funds.

However, the Fed has lengthened its list of "immediately available
funds exempt from reserve requirements" in ways that affect money
and credit. In 1964 the Fed authorized member banks to borrow as fed
funds deposit balances held by other commercial banks—member or
nonmember—even when such borrowing did not involve transfers of
deposits with the Fed.[45] This effectively allowed correspondents to pay
interest on balances kept with them by other banks. Then in 1970 the

---

43 See Wesley Lindow (1972, page 13).

44 RPs were introduced in connection with the topic of new ways of paying interest on money in
    Chapter 3 and will be treated in more detail below.

45 This discussion of the effects of changing reserve requirements on federal funds only slightly
    paraphrases Thomas Simpson (1979, pages 1 and 2).

Table 9.4   Federal Funds and Repurchase Agreements of Large Member Banks[a]
(Averages of Daily Figures, Millions of Dollars)

By Maturity and Source	1982 and 1983. Week Ending Wednesday								
	12/29	1/5	1/12	1/19	1/26	2/2	2/9	2/16	2/23
One day and continuing contract									
1 Commercial banks in United States	57,614	63,310	69,120	66,138	60,143	59,405	63,549	60,970	61,055
2 Other depository institutions, foreign banks, foreign official institutions, and U.S. government agencies	22,007	21,949	25,588	28,792	29,051	26,980	27,928	29,014	30,612
3 Nonbank securities dealers	4,494	4,056	4,515	4,437	4,342	5,022	4,273	5,110	4,654
4 All other	20,707	22,302	25,995	25,279	25,232	26,054	24,697	24,468	24,727
All other maturities									
5 Commercial banks in United States	6,127	5,768	4,352	4,229	4,229	4,337	4,608	4,765	4,435
6 Other depository institutions, foreign banks, foreign official institutions, and U.S. government agencies	11,065	10,352	8,801	8,652	8,580	8,802	9,299	9,534	9,487
7 Nonbank securities dealers	3,866	4,072	3,439	4,270	4,809	4,914	4,986	4,898	5,010
8 All other	13,566	13,132	8,769	9,187	8,938	8,808	8,544	9,441	9,581
Memo: fed funds and resale-agreement loans in maturities of 1 day or continuing contract									
9 Commercial banks in United States	21,544	23,750	27,326	27,936	24,771	23,575	23,574	24,176	25,220
10 Nonbank securities dealers	5,115	4,848	5,328	4,641	3,968	4,749	4,638	4,137	3,897

a Banks with assets of $1 billion or more as of December 31, 1977. Lines 1 to 8 are borrowings (fed funds "purchases") and account for $139,446 million of "All other liabilities for borrowed money" on line 68 of Table 4.2. Lines 9 to 10 are loans (fed funds "sales"). Total fed funds loans by large banks on December 29, 1982 ($36,373 million) are shown on lines 20 to 22 of Table 4.2.

Source: *Federal Reserve Bulletin,* March 1983, page A6.

Fed extended the exemption from reserve requirements to fed funds borrowed from S&Ls, foreign banks, agencies of the federal government, and nonbank securities dealers. The Fed's action enabled these groups to transfer funds from bank deposit accounts to fed funds loans, thereby reducing bank reserve requirements and enabling the lenders to earn market rates of return on what were effectively demand deposits. Virtually the same opportunity had been extended in 1969 to other groups—including corporations, state and local governments, and wealthy individuals—by exempting funds from

Table 9.5   The Effects of Fed Funds and RP Transactions on Required Reserves

Step	Bank S				Bank P				Firm X	
1	R	65	500	D	R	115	1,000	D	D	100
	L	485	50	K	L	985	100	K		
2	R	60	500	D	R	120	1,000	D	D	100
	FF	5					5	FF		
	L	485	50	K	L	985	100	K		
3	R	60	500	D	R	120	900	D	RP	100
							100	RP		
	FF	5					5	FF		
	L	485	50	K	L	985	100	K		

Definitions. Let the required reserve ratio applicable to the only type of deposit (D) be 12 percent. R, K, RP, FF, and L denote reserves, equity, RPs, fed funds, and other loans, respectively.

An interbank fed funds transaction. Initially, in step 1, the large bank (P) is deficient in reserves by $5 and finds a bank (S) with excess reserves of $5. They agree on a fed funds loan by which, in step 2, S transfers $5 of its Fed deposits to P's account at the Fed. Both banks are now just "loaned up," with neither a deficiency nor an excess of reserves. Total required reserves have not been affected.

A bank-nonbank RP transaction. The fed funds transaction between S and P is continued to step 3. The conversion of X's deposit to an RP reduces P's required reserves to $0.12(900) = 108$.

reserve requirements that had been obtained by means of repurchase agreements involving Treasury or federal-agency securities. The following discussion illustrates the advantages to be gained from this opportunity by corporate cash managers and their banks.

RPs AND CORPORATE CASH MANAGEMENT. An RP may be used to evade the prohibition of interest on checking accounts, which, although it has been lifted for everyone else, still applies to corporations. Consider the situation of bank P at step 2 of Table 9.5. This bank is "loaned up," with $120 of reserves that are required to be held against its demand deposits of $1,000, no excess reserves, and earning assets of $985. Included among these demand deposits is the $100 account of firm X, shown as an asset in the incomplete balance sheets on the right-hand side of Table 9.5. This situation makes X's cash manager very unhappy, especially when interest rates are high. She is looking around for a way of getting a return on the $100 when her banker calls and says "Leave your money with us. At the end of the day we will sell you a government security for $100 and buy it back tomorrow morning for $100.025, that is, at an RP rate of 9 percent, calculated on a 360-day basis so that the overnight return is $100(0.09/360) = $0.025 or, if you prefer more realistic numbers, $250 for a $1,000,000 transaction. You will have use of the funds during the day and earn interest on them overnight. You can even write checks since the funds will be returned to your account first thing in the morning, before the checks clear. Furthermore, your possession of the security is security for the loan." (An RP is effectively a fed funds transaction with collateral.)

The cash manager agrees and at the end of the day her books show a government security (or, equivalently, a secured loan to the bank) in place of the deposit. For its part the bank has substituted an RP loan liability for the deposit liability. Since reserve requirements are based on end-of-day deposits and since RPs are not subject to reserve requirements, the bank's required reserves are reduced and its earning assets may be increased $12.[46]

Of course the banker would rather not pay the RP rate for the customer's funds and longs for the time when the zero-interest ceiling on demand deposits was effective. However, if he wants the funds in today's high-interest, competitive environment, he must pay for them. But the reduction in required reserves reduces the pain somewhat.[47]

Most RP arrangements are overnight, but many are continuing contract. One arrangement, much like the continuing contract, is particularly convenient for corporate cash managers: At the end of each business day all the funds in a firm's demand account in excess of some agreed amount are "swept" into RPs. The rate paid on these sweep accounts is usually tied to that prevailing in New York.

THE MECHANICS OF FED FUNDS TRANSACTIONS. Overnight fed funds are traded in a continuous auction market made possible by the tremendous volume of trading—over $100 billion daily, as we see in Table 9.4, compared with about $4 billion on the NYSE. This market is maintained by telephone by several firms, including Mabon Nugent, whose rates for October 24, 1983, were quoted in Table 8.1 and are reproduced on the next page.[48]

---

46 Norman Bowsher (1979) presents a similar example.

47 Suppose the bank's loan rate is 13 percent, the zero-interest ceiling is effective, and the costs of servicing demand deposits are just covered by service charges and other benefits received from customers. The contribution of the account to bank profits under these conditions is $0.13 \times \$88 = \$11.44$ at an annual rate. When a 9 percent RP rate must be paid for funds, the account's profitability is reduced to $(0.13 - 0.09)(\$100) = \$4$.

Funds obtained by means of RPs will be less profitable than costless demand deposits as long as

$$\frac{R_R}{R_A} > \frac{(k_D - k_R)}{(1 - k_R)}$$

where R_R and R_A are the rates of return on RPs and bank assets and k_D and k_R are reserve requirements on demand deposits and RPs. Unlike the above numerical example, we have allowed k_R to be nonzero because RPs have at times been subject to reserve requirements. The above inequality may be rearranged as follows when $k_R = 0$, $k_D = 0.12$, and $R_A = 0.13$:

$$R_R > k_D R_A = 0.12(0.13) = 0.0156$$

48 The characteristics of auction markets were described in Chapter 7. For more detail on the overnight fed funds market as an auction market see Kenneth Garbade (1982, Chapter 22). Other discussions of the fed funds market are presented by Charles Lucas, Marcos Jones, and Thom Thurston (1977), Seth Maerowitz (1981), Thomas Simpson (1979), Marcia Stigum (1983), and Parker Willis (1970).

FEDERAL FUNDS: 9½% high, 9⅜% low, 9⅜% near
closing bid, 9⁷⁄₁₆% offered. Reserves traded among commercial banks for overnight use in amounts of $1 million or
more. *Source:* Mabon Nugent & Co., N.Y.

The auctioneers keep order books of bids for funds and offerings of
funds called in by hundreds of banks each day. The nonbank auction-
eers do not take positions themselves. That is, they are not dealers but
brokers who put compatible borrowers and lenders in touch with one
another. In the case cited above, for example, Mabon Nugent had on
its books a best offer or offers from would-be fed funds sellers to lend
at 9⁷⁄₁₆ percent and a best bid or bids from hopeful fed funds buyers to
borrow at 9⅜ percent. Something has to give if there is to be any
trading. If the market "softens," that is, if few bids are forthcoming
but many banks have funds to sell, the latter will have to reduce their
offers if they hope to place their funds. And deals will be struck,
perhaps at 9⅜.

The first two rates listed above are the high and low rates actually
consummated through Mabon Nugent during the day. A widely used
rate is the "effective" fed funds rate calculated by the Federal Reserve
Bank of New York, which is an average of the rates on overnight fed
funds transactions arranged through brokers. The effective fed funds
rate on October 24, 1983, was 9.47 percent.[49] Many continuing arrangements between large banks and clients who trade too infrequently or
in amounts too small to justify going to the auction market are based
on the effective fed funds rate. These agreements specify that the
borrowing bank will take funds offered by their customers at a rate
tied to the day's effective rate.

RESERVE ACCOUNTING AND THE FED FUNDS MARKET. The discussion has
so far proceeded as if banks were continuously informed of their
reserve deficiencies or excesses. In fact reserve requirements are
computed on the basis of average deposits during 14-day "computation periods," and those requirements are met by average reserves
during an overlapping "maintenance period." A bank cannot be
certain of its reserve position until the end of the maintenance period.
It must therefore trade fed funds and other financial instruments in
anticipation of its reserve needs.

The present system of reserve accounting went into effect on
Groundhog Day, 1984, and is described by the 44-day calendar in
Table 9.6. Punxsutawney National Bank's required average reserve
balance at the Federal Reserve Bank of Cleveland during the reserve
maintenance period March 4 to 17 is equal to (1) 3 percent of average
nonpersonal time deposits during the 2-week reserve computation
period of February 2 to 15 for liabilities subject to reserve requirements other than transaction deposits, less (2) average vault cash

49 Federal Reserve Board Statistical Release H.15, October 31, 1983.

Table 9.6   An Example of Almost Contemporaneous Reserve Accounting (Millions of Dollars)

	February				March			
Date	2	15		2 4		15 17		

week 1   week 2   week 3   week 4   week 5   week 6
T W Th F S Su M T W Th F S Su M T W Th F S Su M T W Th F S Su M T W Th F S Su M T W Th F S Su M T W

Reserve Accounting for Liabilities

2-week computation period for all reservable liabilities other than transaction deposits

2-week computation period for transaction deposits

Accounting for Reserves

Average vault cash in this 2-week period counts as reserves in the maintenance period ending 30 days later

2-week reserve maintenance period

Average values February 2–15	Balance Sheet of Punxsutawney National	Average values March		
		2–3	4–15	16–17
14	Reserves at Fed	26	12	26
7	Vault cash	7	7	7
10	Fed funds and RPs	10	10	10
504	Other assets	504	504	504
125	Transaction accounts	125	125	125
200	Nonpersonal time deposits[a]	200	200	200
120	Fed funds and RPs	132	118	132
90	Other liabilities and equity[b]	90	90	90

Required reserves at Fed during maintenance period due to:[c]	
nonpersonal time deposits	$0.03(200) = 6$
vault cash	-7
transaction accounts	$0.12(125) = 15$

a Includes Eurodollar liabilities and approximately $25 million of transaction accounts, which are subject to 3 percent required reserve ratios.

b Includes approximately $2 million of deposits otherwise subject to a 3 percent required reserve ratio, but which were exempted from reserve requirements by the Depository Institutions Act of 1982.

c A reserve excess or deficiency not exceeding the greater of $25,000 or 2 percent of required reserves is carried forward to the next maintenance period. Any carryover not offset in the next period may not be carried forward to additional periods. For example, if Punxsutawney National had carried over no excess or deficiency from the Febrary 18 to March 3 maintenance period, it could have satisfied requirements during March 4 to 17 by an average balance of $14 million less $280,000, to be offset by an equal excess during March 18 to 31.

A Federal Reserve Bank may assess penalties for deficiencies at a rate of interest 2 percent per annum above its lowest loan rate in effect on the first of the month.

Sources: Federal Reserve Board's Regulation D and Alton Gilbert and Michael Trebing (1982, exhibit 1).

during February 2 to 15, plus (3) 12 percent of average transaction deposits during the 2-week computation period of March 2 to 15. That is, Punxsutawney National's required average balance (in *millions*) at the Cleveland Fed during March 4 to 17 is 0.03($200) − $7 + 0.12($125) = $14, which is just satisfied since the average balance is $12 for the 12 days March 4 to 15 and $26 for the 2 days March 16 and 17. All data pertain to the close of business, the required reserve ratios of 3 and 12 percent are subject to change by the Fed, computation periods always run from Tuesday through the Monday 13 days later, maintenance periods always run from Thursday through the Wednesday 13 days later and end 2 days after the second computation period, and computation and maintenance periods are the same for all banks (that is, all banks settle their reserve accounts on the same day).[50]

The Fed calls this "contemporaneous" reserve accounting to distinguish it from the fully lagged system used between 1968 and 1984, in which average balances required to be held at the Fed during a 7-day maintenance period were determined by deposits and vault cash during a 7-day computation period 2 weeks previously. The system in effect until 1968 computed the average balances required to be held at the Fed at the close of business during a 7-day settlement period on the basis of deposits and vault cash at the start of business during the same 7 days. Many bankers and Fed officials considered this system unsatisfactory because banks did not know early in the settlement week what their reserve targets were—because they did not know what their deposits would be later in the week. This led, it was argued, to unnecessarily large fluctuations in interest rates, especially at the ends of settlement periods, as banks attempted to rectify the effects of earlier forecasting errors by acquiring needed reserves or lending excess reserves.[51]

It was hoped that the lagged system introduced in 1968 would lessen these difficulties by enabling banks to know their required reserves at the beginning of reserve maintenance periods, thereby eliminating one of the sources of uncertainty in reserve management. But this system came under attack in its turn in 1980 when Fed officials claimed that their attempts to control the money supply were frustrated by bank lending and deposit creation (during reserve computation periods) in ignorance of the availability of the reserves necessitated by those decisions during later reserve maintenance periods. This claim was partly an attempt to divert criticism from the Fed by laying the blame for its erratic behavior at the door of an institutional defect (albeit instituted by the Fed itself). However, although the principal source of uncertainty was the week-to-week unpredictability of the Fed, the problem was compounded by lagged reserve accounting. It is desirable when extending loans that banks know the costs of funds (including fed funds) relative to the returns on loans. This is seldom fully achieved because, for example, the cost of a 90-day fixed-rate loan is the average cost of fed funds during the next 3 months. But at least in a system of contemporaneous reserve accounting a substantial increase

50 Except institutions with deposits less than $15 million, for which there is a single 1-week computation period each quarter and the maintenance period is a quarter in length.

51 The three reserve accounting systems considered here are discussed in more detail by Alton Gilbert (1980) and Alton Gilbert and Michael Trebing (1982).

in bank loans is accompanied during the same 7- or 14-day reserve maintenance period by an increased demand for reserves and, unless the Fed supplies the additional reserves, by an increase in their cost and probably reappraisals of bank lending policies.

The costs of loan expansions are felt less quickly under lagged reserve accounting, and a forecasting error by the banking system may force accommodation by the Fed. For example, if banks think that the Fed is going to pursue an easy-money, low-interest-rate policy in the future, they may increase loans and deposits this week without having to pay the price of the increase in required reserves until they begin to compete for reserves during the reserve maintenance period 2 weeks later—and the Fed has to supply those reserves, either voluntarily through the discount window and open-market operations or by accepting reserve deficiencies although it can, if it wishes, exact a high price.

So in 1984 the Fed adopted a reserve accounting system that was largely contemporaneous but retained some parts of the 1968 to 1984 lagged system that banks had found convenient, including a full knowledge of reserve requirements due to nontransaction liabilities at the beginning of the reserve maintenance period and a knowledge of all reserve requirements before (though only 2 days before) the end of the maintenance period. In addition, banks were given a 2-week maintenance period to arrange their reserves.

Now let us consider the fed funds plan of a reserve manager under the present system. Punxsutawney National wants its $14 (again in millions) average reserve balance during March 4 to 17 to be inexpensive, which means having more than $14 in Cleveland when reserves are cheap (that is, when interest rates are low) and less than $14 when reserves are expensive (when interest rates are high). The most flexible way of adjusting reserves is provided by the fed funds market. Punxsutawney National's fed funds plan requires three sets of forecasts: (1) average transaction deposits during the March 2 to 15 reserve computation period, which depend on the Fed's activities as well as the results of Punxsutawney National's efforts to attract transaction accounts; (2) other effects on the bank's reserves during the March 4 to 17 reserve maintenance period, including its loan policies and the success of its efforts to attract time and savings deposits; and (3) the pattern of fed funds rates during March 4 to 17. The first two sets of forecasts are included among the data in Table 9.6 and, together with the bank's desire to maintain average vault cash of $7, imply average net purchases of fed funds of $110 during the reserve maintenance period. That is, $[12(108) + 2(122)]/14 = 110$, where net purchases of fed funds are $118 − $10 = $108 during March 4 to 15 and $132 − $10 = $122 during March 16 and 17.

The fed funds plan is shown in detail in Table 9.7. The bank's money manager, Nostradamus Dixon, has noticed a pattern in the fed funds rate that he expects to be repeated in the future. Specifically, he

Table 9.7   A Fed Funds Plan

	Thursday	Friday	Saturday	Sunday	Monday	Tuesday	Wednesday
	4	5	6	7	8	9	10
R_f	0.1010	0.1030	...	...	0.1050	0.1070	0.1090
NFF	120	115	115	115	110	106	100
R	24	19	19	19	14	10	4
	11	12	13	14	15	16	17
R_f	0.1110	0.1080	...	...	0.1050	0.1020	0.0990
NFF	96	103	103	103	110	120	124
R	0	7	7	7	14	24	28

R_f = fed funds rate; NFF = net fed funds; R = reserves at the Fed

expects the fed funds rate to rise during the early part of the reserve maintenance period, from 0.1010 on March 4 to 0.1110 on March 11, and then to fall during the latter part of the period, reaching 0.0990 on March 17. He plans his net purchases of fed funds *(NFF)*, and therefore the bank's balances at the Fed *(R)*, to vary inversely with the fed funds rate (R_f) as shown in Table 9.7. Notice that no fed funds rate is quoted on Saturday or Sunday. Reserves outstanding at the close of business Friday also apply to Saturday and Sunday, and fed funds borrowed on Friday are 3-day loans that carry Friday's rate.

Patterns of R_f similar to that assumed in Table 9.7 have in fact been observed under a variety of conditions[52] and are consistent with risk-averse behavior on the parts of money managers. Unlike Nostradamus most of them do not claim to know the future course of R_f. Therefore, in developing their fed funds plans, they insure against the possibility of having to borrow at high rates later by accumulating excess reserves early in the period, bidding up R_f in the process. As a result they are often in a position to sell fed funds at the end of the period, causing R_f to fall.[53]

Of course things do not always turn out this way. There has been a large variance about the average pattern of R_f, especially at the end of the maintenance period. In fact the average last-day high has been

---

52 James Boughton (1972, page 42) found such a pattern both under the contemporaneous reserve accounting system used until 1968 and in the first year (September 1968 to September 1969) of the lagged accounting system. A similar pattern was observed by Robert Laurent (1974) for 1968 to 1971 and also by R. Hanna and Michael Vogt (1981), both during the 6 months preceding October 6, 1979, when the Fed pursued an interest-rate goal, and during the succeeding 6 months, when its announced goals were bank reserves and the money supply.

53 This argument assumes that risk-averse borrowers fear later high rates more than risk-averse lenders fear later low rates. This assumption may not be unreasonable if the end-of-period distribution of fed funds rates is skewed toward high rates (although no evidence on this point has been reported).

above the average highs earlier in the period.[54] Bank money managers
have been willing to pay a premium (by borrowing at higher *average*
rates early and in the middle of the period) to avoid the necessity of
having to borrow at the very high rates that *occasionally* occur later in
the period.

MONETARY POLICY, BANK RESERVES, AND THE FED FUNDS RATE

Interest-rate targets and money-supply targets

We shall not consider the relative merits and defects of alternative
monetary policies as ways of achieving the Fed's ultimate goals of full
employment, economic growth, and price stability. Our attention will
be limited to the short-term effects of those policies on the money
supply and interest rates. The Fed's short-term, money market goals
have alternated between interest rates and the money supply. That is,
it has sometimes sought to achieve its ultimate goals by manipulating
interest rates and sometimes by manipulating the money supply. Of
course, nearly all Fed actions affect both money and interest rates, and
the Fed almost always pays some attention to both. But it has
occasionally shifted its emphasis from one to the other with drastic
effects on the money markets. These policy shifts and their money
market effects are the principal concerns of the remainder of this
chapter.

Interest-rate targets in the 1970s

The Fed realizes that in this uncertain world its goals must be
specified in terms of ranges. For example, on September 18, 1979, the
Federal Open Market Committee (FOMC)[55] directed the Manager of
the Trading Desk (the Desk) at the Federal Reserve Bank of New York
to conduct open market purchases and/or sales of securities (open
market operations) in such a way as to keep the fed funds rate between
11.25 and 11.75 percent and the annual rate of growth of the money
supply (*M*1) between 3 and 8 percent. These ranges are indicated in
the FOMC Directive at the top of Table 9.8. The narrow interest range
and the wide money range suggest that interest was the principal
target, with only a secondary concern for money. In fact, FOMC
Directives before October 1979 suggest infinitely wide money ranges.
The fed funds rate was "to be raised or lowered in an orderly fashion
within its range" even at the cost of violating money ranges. The
evidence indicates that the Desk faithfully implemented these directives. A sample of this evidence is presented in Figure 9.3, which shows

---

54 Robert Laurent (1974, page 5) and R. Hanna and Michael Vogt (1981, page 18).

55 The FOMC consists of the seven members of the Board of Governors of the Federal Reserve
    System, the president of the Federal Reserve Bank of New York, and four of the other eleven
    bank presidents on a rotating basis. The chairman of the Board of Governors is also chairman of
    the FOMC.

Table 9.8 FOMC Directives Before and After October 1979

Meeting of September 18, 1979

Early in the period before the next regular meeting, System open market operations are to be directed at attaining a weekly average federal funds rate slightly above the current level. Subsequently, operations shall be directed at maintaining the weekly average federal funds rate within the range of 11.25 to 11.75 percent. In deciding on the specific objective for the federal funds rate, the Manager for Domestic Operations shall be guided mainly by the relationship between the latest estimates of annual rates of growth in the September-October period of M1 and M2 and the following ranges of tolerance: 3 to 8 percent for M1 and 6.5 to 10.5 percent for M2. If rates of growth of M1 and M2, given approximately equal weight, appear to be close to or beyond the upper or lower limits of the indicated ranges, the objective for the funds rate is to be raised or lowered in an orderly fashion within its range.

Meeting of April 22, 1980

In the short run, the Committee seeks expansion of reserve aggregates consistent with growth over the first half of 1980 at an annual rate of 4.5 percent for M1A and 5 percent for M1B,[a] or somewhat less, provided that in the period before the next regular meeting the weekly average federal funds rate remains within a range of 13 to 19 percent. . . .

If it appears during the period before the next meeting that the constraint on the federal funds rate is inconsistent with the objective for the expansion of reserves, the Manager for Domestic Operations is promptly to notify the Chairman who will then decide whether the situation calls for supplementary instructions from the Committee.

Meeting of March 28, 1983

For the short run, the Committee seeks to maintain generally the existing degree of restraint on reserve positions, anticipating that would be consistent with a slowing from March to June in growth of M2 and M3 to annual rates of about 9 and 8 percent, respectively. The Committee expects that M1 growth at an annual rate of about 6 to 7 percent would be consistent with its objectives for the broader aggregates. . . . The Chairman may call for Committee consultation if it appears to the Manager for Domestic Operations that pursuit of the monetary objectives and related reserve paths during the period before the next meeting is likely to be associated with a federal funds rate persistently outside a range of 6 to 10 percent.

a $M1B$ was approximately the current $M1$, currency and transaction accounts. $M1A$ was currency and only those transaction accounts in commercial banks and has not been reported since 1981.

Source: *Federal Reserve Bulletin,* November 1979, pages 912–913; June 1980, page 488; June 1983, pages 425–426. Also see Alton Gilbert and Michael Trebing (1981, page 8) for the first two Directives and a discussion of the significance of their differences.

that money targets were missed more frequently and by greater amounts than interest targets.

October 6, 1979

Unprecedented peacetime increases in the money supply during the 1970s were accompanied by record peacetime inflation. These movements, in combination with rising interest rates, indicate that the Fed caused inflation by financing borrowers' excess demands for credit, that the inflation led to increased credit demands, and that the Fed

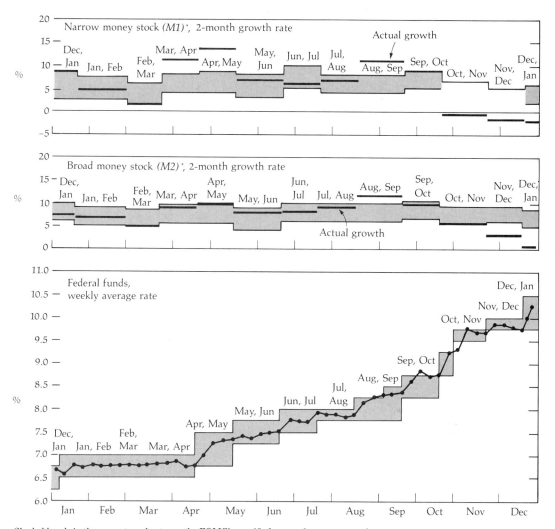

Shaded bands in the upper two charts are the FOMC's specified ranges for money-supply growth over the 2-month periods indicated. No lower bound was established for $M1$ at the October and November meetings. In the bottom chart the shaded bands are the specified ranges for fed funds rate variation. Actual growth rates in the upper two charts are based on data available at the time of the second FOMC meeting after the end of each period.

* Seasonally adjusted annual rates.

Source: Federal Reserve Bank of New York *Quarterly Review*, Spring 1979, page 60. See also Fred Levin and Ann-Marie Meulendyke (1979).

Figure 9.3   FOMC ranges for short-run monetary growth and the fed funds rate in 1978.

slowly responded to the effects of its low-interest-rate policy by raising its interest-rate targets. Suppose the rate of interest consistent with price stability is 4 percent, but the Fed pursues a stable-interest-rate target of 3 percent. In the absence of Fed security purchases, those who wish to spend more than their incomes must persuade others (savers) to spend less than their incomes by offering an attractive interest rate, specifically 4 percent. There is an excess demand for credit if the rate is only 3 percent. But now the Fed supplies the difference by effectively printing and lending all the money that people desire at 3 percent.

The problems caused by the Fed's accommodation of excess demands at low interest rates worsen with time because of the inflationary expectations induced by the Fed's inflationary policies. Current demands increase as people seek to buy goods now in order to protect themselves against, or take advantage of, future price rises. The rate of interest acquires an inflationary component, and if people expect annual inflation of 10 percent, the rate of interest necessary for equilibrium is no longer the 4 percent required in the presence of stable prices but is $4 + 10 = 14$ percent.

The Fed's desire for stable interest rates eventually leads to the opposite. Its concern for inflation during the 1970s led to increases in interest targets. But as long as rates were not allowed to rise to levels (including the rising inflationary component) consistent with the equality of desired aggregate borrowing and lending, the inflationary process was bound to continue. And interest rates climbed the inflationary staircase shown in Figure 9.3. Finally, in October 1979, the Fed declared its intention to stop inflation by bringing the money supply under control. Chairman Volcker of the Federal Reserve Board announced a "significant refocusing of monetary policy. The central bank will pay more attention to the amount of bank reserves and hence the money supply [and] less attention to fluctuations in a key interest rate—the rate on federal funds. . . ."[56]

The new Directive and its unexpected consequences

FOMC Directives have been very different in the 1980s from those issued before October 1979. Precise money targets are named, and the fed funds range is much wider, as indicated by the twelvefold increase between September 1979 and April 1980 (from 0.50 percent to 6 percent) stated in Table 9.8. Furthermore, the final sentences of post-1979 Directives suggest that the FOMC has been willing to consider fed funds rates outside their stated ranges in order to achieve the levels of bank reserves required for the now dominant money-growth targets.

One of the major consequences of the new monetary policy was an increase in the volatility of interest rates. This is illustrated in Figure 9.4 by daily percentage changes in short-term and long-term interest rates during the 12-month periods before and after October 6, 1979. This result of the new policy was expected and followed directly from

---

56 Robert Greenberger (1979). See Paul Volcker (1979) for an official explanation of the Fed's change in policy.

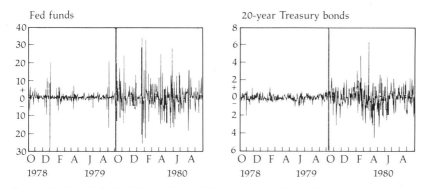

Source: Paul Kasriel, Federal Reserve Bank of Chicago *Economic Perspectives*, January/February 1981, page 11.

Figure 9.4   Daily percentage changes in selected interest rates in 1978 to 1980.

the Fed's abandonment of orderly fed funds rates—although people didn't expect rates to become *that* volatile.

However, the second major consequence of the new policy, the increased volatility of money, came as a surprise both to the Fed and to most Fed watchers. Figure 9.5 portrays the Fed's inability to keep money within desired limits in 1980 and 1982, and things were no better in 1981 and 1983. For example the right-hand panel of Figure 9.5 indicates that the FOMC's desired growth range of money between the fourth quarter of 1981 and the fourth quarter of 1982 was 2.5 to 5.5 percent. The actual growth rate was much higher, about 8.5 percent.

But annual *average* target misses caused the financial markets less trouble than did the short-run volatility of money. For example the quarterly rates of growth (at annual rates) in money between the fourth quarter of 1981 and the fourth quarter of 1982 were about 9, 5, 2, and 20 percent. Another way of looking at the increased volatility of money is provided by Table 9.9. The lower portion of this table lists the frequent turnarounds of money growth between October 1979 and January 1982.[57]

An understanding of these fluctuations requires that we be familiar with the short-term creation of money, which is the outcome of dynamic interactions among (1) the fed funds market, (2) the prevailing system of required-reserve accounting, and (3) the prevailing Fed operating procedure. The interactions of (1) and (2) will be considered next.

An advanced course in money creation

THE TRADITIONAL STABLE-MONEY-MULTIPLIER EXPLANATION OF MONEY. The process of money creation is traditionally explained in the following steps: (1) The Fed buys securities from dealers, payment

---

57 Movements in Table 9.9 during 1980 may be compared with the left-hand panel of Figure 9.5 and continued through 1982 by the right-hand panel.

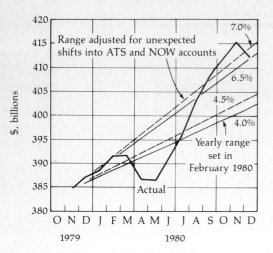
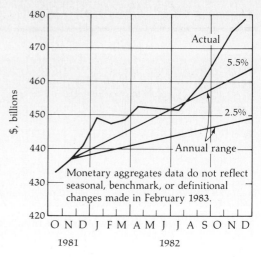

Sources: Federal Reserve Bank of New York *Quarterly Review*, Summer 1981, page 57, and Spring 1983, page 83. See also Fred Levin, Christopher McCurdy, and Betsy White (1981) and Christopher McCurdy and Kenneth Guentner (1983).

Figure 9.5   Targeted and actual growth of $M1$ in 1980 and 1982.

taking the form of credits to the reserve accounts of the dealers' banks; (2) this adds to bank reserves, and if the required reserve ratio is 10 percent and the Fed buys securities worth $100, the dealers' banks' required reserves rise $10 and their excess reserves rise $90; (3) under conditions of high interest rates and loan demands the banks take advantage of the opportunity to increase loans and deposits by the full amount of their excess reserves; (4) this leads to a loss of reserves by these banks and a gain of reserves by other banks amounting to $90; (5) the latter banks may now increase their loans and deposits by $81; (6) and so the process goes on until the total deposits of the banking system rise by $1,000 = $100/0.10. Leakages from bank reserves, due mainly to currency holdings, moderate the effects of Fed purchases and sales. But the essence of the story is unchanged: Open market operations cause changes in bank reserves, which filter through the banking system and lead to magnified changes in the money supply. The traditional explanation is usually summarized in the relation $M = mH$, where M is the money supply, H is the monetary base (or high-powered money) that is supplied principally by Fed security purchases and is held by banks as reserves and by the nonbank public as currency, and m is the money multiplier that determines the effect of H on M and depends mainly on bank reserve requirements and nonbank public currency demands. In the simple example presented above there was no currency and $H = \$100$, $m = 10$, and $M = \$1,000$.

The traditional story is correct as far as it goes. But it neglects significant details of the money-expansion process. Most important, many banks, especially large banks, do not sit back and wait for reserves and deposits to arrive. They aggressively seek reserves by

Table 9.9   Ups and Downs in Monetary Growth

Turning Point	Date	Interval in Weeks	Annualized Rate of Change in $M1$	Change in Rate of Change
Before October 6, 1979, Policy Change				
Peak	October 5, 1977			
Trough	March 15, 1978	23	6.7	
Peak	September 27, 1978	28	9.8	+ 3.1
Trough	March 14, 1979	24	5.8	− 4.0
Peak	October 3, 1979	29	9.5	+ 3.7
After October 6, 1979, Policy Change				
Trough	November 28, 1979	8	− 1.4	−10.9
Peak	February 20, 1980	12	+12.1	+13.5
Trough	April 30, 1980	10	−12.4	−24.5
Peak	November 26, 1980	30	+15.0	+27.4
Trough[a]	February 4, 1981	10	−13.1	−28.1
Peak	April 22, 1981	11	+23.8	+36.9
Trough	July 1, 1981	10	−10.6	−34.4
Peak	September 16, 1981	11	+ 7.2	+17.8
Trough	October 28, 1981	6	− 5.1	−12.3
Peak	January 13, 1982	11	+24.6	+29.7

a Roughly corrected for NOW accounts.

Source: Milton Friedman, "The Federal Reserve and Monetary Instability," *Wall Street Journal*, February 1, 1982, page 16.

expending resources up to the points at which the expected marginal costs of funds (deposits, fed funds, other liabilities, and equity) equal the expected marginal revenues from the assets purchased with those funds.[58] Competition for funds takes many forms, such as advertising, branches, and services for depositors. But interest rates constitute the most important form of competition, particularly in the fed funds market. We therefore treat the fed funds rate, R_f, as the marginal cost of bank reserves. This means that the expected marginal cost of a 90-day loan, for example, is an average of fed funds rates expected to prevail over the life of the loan. We refer to this expected average simply as R_f^e.

In a world of *continuous contemporaneous reserve accounting* (in which reserve requirements must be satisfied every day) banks compete for reserves and loans until the expected marginal cost of reserves, R_f^e, equals the expected marginal revenue from loans *subject to daily reserve requirements and the existing quantity of reserves as*

---

58 Models of this type of behavior are presented in Chapters 2 and 16. Risk aversion might cause spreads between expected marginal revenues and costs but would not alter any of the processes or results in the following discussion.

determined by Fed credit and the public's demand for currency. An increase in the demand for loans, that is, a willingness by firms and consumers to borrow more at higher interest rates, produces no effect, at least in the short run, on bank credit or the money supply. Higher loan rates, R_L, induce increased competition for reserves and therefore increases in current and, probably, expected fed funds rates. In any case, banks cannot borrow more reserves than are available so that reserve requirement ratios and the existing quantity of bank reserves set limits on bank loans and deposits.

Shifts in the demand for money also affect interest rates while leaving the money supply unchanged. Suppose that, because of financial innovation, people economize on their money holdings. The increased rapidity with which funds are transferred between bank accounts leaves total bank deposits and the money supply unaffected but depresses interest rates as people attempt to shift from money to interest-earning assets. If the fall in interest rates spreads to R_L, banks compete less vigorously for reserves so that R_f also falls. However, bank credit and the money supply are not changed. The long-term money-supply relation $M = mH$ applies continuously under continuous reserve accounting.

AVERAGE RESERVE ACCOUNTING. The tight link between money and bank reserves is loosened by average reserve accounting. For example, consider the first week of a 2-week reserve maintenance period under the present almost contemporaneous reserve accounting system. The reserve losses caused by a bank's loans do not have to be made up until next week although the bank might borrow fed funds this week, depending on the expected course of the fed funds rate. The point is that there is no legal limit to the extension of loans and creation of deposits this week because reserve requirements do not have to be satisfied until later.

But the day of reckoning will come, when the fed funds rate will depend on bank reserve needs relative to the quantity of reserves made available by the Fed. If banks lent large amounts early in the reserve maintenance period, expecting to borrow reserves at low fed funds rates late in the period and the Fed does not supply the reserves implied by the additional deposits, the banks are in trouble. And so is the Fed. The fed funds rate will rise sharply as banks fight over the insufficient reserves, and there will be either a forced contraction of loans and deposits or widespread reserve deficiencies. Of such things are panics made, and the Fed is forced to come to the aid of the system after all—by supplying at least a portion of the reserves in the second week made necessary by bank lending in the first week.

This experience is likely to be followed by a reaction as banks revise their expectations of future fed funds rates. Current high rates probably lead to expectations of future high rates, a reduction in lending, and possibly very low fed funds rates at the end of the next reserve maintenance period.

An obvious way to dampen these swings in money and fed funds rates would be for the Fed to announce a steady credit policy in advance so that banks and others could plan their affairs accordingly. But the Fed refuses to be specific about its intentions. Directives are not made public until after they have been superseded by later Directives.

The swings tended to be larger and longer under the lagged reserve accounting system prevailing before February 1984, in which deposits created one week did not lead to required reserves until 2 weeks later, than under the present almost contemporaneous system. When the normal lags in commercial bank and Fed adjustments to changes in each other's behavior under the post-1979 operating procedure were compounded by lagged reserve accounting, the consequence was the instability of money that is shown in the lower portion of Table 9.9 and was described by Professor Friedman as a "ten-week yo-yo." But the lags in any average reserve accounting system, even the present system, raise problems for monetary control and promote instability in the financial markets when the Fed's future actions are unknown. The problems and effects of alternative approaches to monetary policy under the present reserve accounting system are analyzed in the next section.

The problems and effects of alternative monetary policies under average reserve accounting

INTEREST-RATE TARGETS. The Desk's ability to hit an interest-rate target, for example the fed funds rate R_f^*, is virtually complete and is independent of the reserve accounting scheme. All that it has to do is buy securities when R_f is above R_f^* and sell securities when R_f is below R_f^*. This was essentially the procedure before October 1979.

THE POST-1979 RESERVE TARGETING PROCEDURE. Matters became more complicated when the FOMC began to aim at money targets through bank reserves. The new procedure may be described within the framework of the six-equation system in Table 9.10. We begin by explaining the key policy Equation (9.1) in somewhat more detail than is provided in the table. Let us denote borrowed reserves (through the discount window) and unborrowed reserves (mainly through Fed open-market operations) as A_b and A_u, respectively. We have let A stand for reserves to avoid confusion with interest rates, R. Equation (9.1) states that today's fed funds rate, R_f, is an inverse function of $A_b + A_u - kD_-$, where $A_b + A_u$ is today's total reserves and kD_- denotes the required reserves implied by average deposits up to the present date of the currently applicable reserve computation period. For example, in the present almost contemporaneous system, if the

Table 9.10   A Framework for the Analysis of Federal Reserve Operating Procedures

Equations

(9.1) $R_f = R_f(A_b + A_u - kD_-)$ The fed funds rate responds inversely to the quantity of excess reserves implied by available reserves and required reserves accumulated to date.

(9.2) $R_f^e = R_f^e(R_f)$ The expected fed funds rate responds positively to the current fed funds rate.

(9.3) $\Delta L = L^s(R_L - R_f^e)$ The supply of bank loans responds positively to the difference between the loan rate and expected marginal costs of funds.

(9.4) $\Delta L = L^d(R_L)$ The demand for loans is a negative function of the loan rate.

(9.5) $\Delta L = \Delta D$ Deposits are created in the process of making loans

(9.6) $A_b = A_b(R_f - R_D)$ Bank borrowing from the Fed responds positively to the difference between the fed funds and discount rates.

Definitions of Variables (All Pertaining to the Current Reserve Week unless Otherwise Specified)

R_f = fed funds rate
A_b = bank borrowing from the Fed (borrowed reserves)
A_u = unborrowed reserves (determined by open market operations)
$A_b + A_u$ = total bank reserves
k = required reserve ratio
D_- = average deposits during the reserve computation period to date
kD_- = required reserves implied by D_-
$A_b + A_u - kD_-$ = excess reserves implied by available reserves and D_-
R_f^e = an average of the fed funds rates expected to prevail over the lives of
    the new loans
ΔL = change in bank loans during the week
ΔD = change in deposits during the week
R_L = rate of interest on bank loans
R_D = Fed discount rate

Source: This model has been adapted from Robert Laurent (1981, 1982), who developed it in relation to lagged reserve accounting.

reserve maintenance period is June 3 to 16 so that the relevant computation period is June 1 to 14 and if today is June 10, then D_- is average deposits during June 1 to 10. If total reserves are currently far in excess of the requirements implied by deposits to date, that is, if $A_b + A_u - kD_-$ is positive and large, then, unless banks in general have a strong desire to satisfy the bulk of their reserve requirements early in the period, the abundance of reserves will cause R_f to be low. Whatever the preferences of banks regarding the time pattern of reserve holdings, a reduction in the quantity of available reserves $(A_b + A_u)$ relative to the requirements accumulated to date (kD_-) will force an increase in R_f.

The FOMC meets approximately at 6-week intervals, whereas the Desk is continuously trying to move unborrowed reserves in a manner consistent with the money growth specified in the latest Directive, perhaps as modified during daily conference calls. The Desk must work through the following steps before selecting the path of unborrowed reserves that it hopes will produce desired money growth ΔM^* during some period, say, the first week of a 2-week reserve maintenance period.

1. The Desk first forecasts the change in currency demand, ΔC, which gives the desired growth in bank deposits, $\Delta D^* = \Delta M^* - \Delta C$. Fixing ΔD at ΔD^* in Equation (9.5) completes the six-equation system in the unknowns R_f, R_f^e, R_L, ΔL, A_b, and A_u. The Desk's remaining task is the solution of this system for the A_u consistent with ΔD^*.[59]

2. The Desk next forecasts the loan demand and supply Equations (9.3) and (9.4), in order to obtain an estimate of the expected fed funds rate, R_f^e, consistent with ΔD^*. The steps in the solution of R_f^e are to observe from Equation (9.5) that $\Delta L = \Delta D^*$, then to use this result to solve Equation (9.4) for R_L, and finally to use ΔL and R_L to solve Equation (9.3) for R_f^e.

3. The Desk must also guess the influence of the current fed funds rate on expectations of future rates. That guess is embodied in Equation (9.2).

4. Then, if it knows the nature of the dependence of the current fed funds rate on excess reserves as stated in Equation (9.1), the Desk is in a position to choose the total quantity of bank reserves, $A_b + A_u$, necessary to achieve the desired R_f. (Remember that we have already assumed a correct forecast of ΔC so that the FOMC knows the change in Fed credit necessary to produce the desired change in bank reserves.)

5. But the Desk is still not home free because it controls only the portion A_u of total bank reserves and must therefore forecast bank borrowing (A_b) from the district Federal Reserve Banks.[60] Only then

---

59 An unborrowed-reserves operating procedure based on predictions of borrowed reserves and currency is equivalent to a high-powered-money operating procedure because $A_u + A_b + C = H$.

60 This may be the Desk's most difficult task. The relationship between A_b and $R_f - R_D$ is volatile and largely unpredictable, at least partly because of the way in which discount windows are administered. Limitations on the size and frequency of borrowing cause A_b to depend in a complicated way on past borrowing and expected future spreads, $R_f - R_D$. This point is developed by Marvin Goodfriend (1983).

does it know the volume of open market purchases or sales necessary to achieve ΔD^*.

The path by which A_u determines ΔD may be followed by retracing the steps of the Fed's decision process: Given the forecast of A_b, it selects the A_u that determines the R_f that leads to the R_f^e that induces banks to extend the quantity of loans, ΔL, consistent with ΔD^*. The Desk shoots for ΔD^* through the fed funds market. The new operating procedure is a circuitous version of a straight interest-rate operating procedure. The latter procedure would require the Fed to choose the R_f that is consistent with the R_f^e that, given Equations (9.3) to (9.5), produces the desired ΔD^*. Even this would be a difficult and uncertain task. But it would eliminate steps 4 and 5 of the present procedure and therefore the uncertainties associated with Equations (9.1) and (9.6). Small wonder that ΔD and ΔM have been more volatile since 1979 than before.

CONCLUSION: THE PROSPECTS FOR BANK RESERVE MANAGEMENT AND MONETARY POLICY

Interbank lending will continue to be one of the most important ways of sending funds from surplus to deficit areas as long as the present severe restrictions on branch banking continue. Whether these transfers will be called fed funds or bankers' balances is unimportant. But they will probably increasingly be called fed funds because of the great increase in the regulation of bank reserves under the Depository Institutions Deregulation and Monetary Control Act of 1980—which, by extending reserve requirements to all depository institutions, has diverted bankers' balances to Federal Reserve Banks.

The future of the discount window is more difficult to predict. Its economic function, except to provide a subsidy to banks wishing to avoid the implicit or explicit market rates that must be paid for bankers' balances and fed funds, has never been clear. Its main role seems to have been political: to assist the Fed in its pursuit of greater regulatory control by serving as an inducement to banks to join the Federal Reserve System. But that role has been superseded by the Fed's achievement of control over all depository institutions in the Act of 1980. We should not be surprised if the traditional use of the discount window as a source of short-term adjustment credit becomes insignificant while political pressure to use the window for other extended credit in exceptional circumstances, that is, to bail out failing banks, continues to grow.

The only thing predictable about monetary policy is its unpredictability. The Fed will continue to fluctuate between money and interest targets, between reserve accounting schemes, and between the wish for price stability and the accommodation of federal deficits at low interest rates.

QUESTIONS

1. What is meant by an "elastic" currency? Is the discount window necessary to an elastic currency? How about the fed funds market?

2. What useful functions does the discount window perform in the presence of an efficient fed funds market?

3. Suppose Federal Reserve Banks make their discount rates "honest" in the sense that they stand ready to lend without limit, subject to acceptable collateral, at their announced rates. Suppose all twelve discount rates are 8 percent.

    What will be the rates on **(a)** federal funds, **(b)** T bills, and **(c)** prime loans? Describe the market processes by which these rates will be achieved.

4. The Fed's discount rates exceeded 10 percent throughout 1980 and 1981. Were they "high"?

5. Why do banks borrow from the Fed?

6. The purpose of this question is to get you to look at Table 9.2. Discuss the evidence for and against the view that changes in the discount rate are accurate indicators of the future course of monetary policy.

7. How would the fed funds market be affected by the removal of restrictions on branch banking?

8. Which definition of fed funds do *you* prefer and why?

9. Discuss the meanings of the terms "bid" and "offered" as used by fed funds brokers, and compare those meanings with "bid" and "asked" as used by dealers.

10. What would happen to the fed funds market if all restrictions on interest rates were lifted? As part of your answer, please discuss the ways in which the transactions in Table 9.5 would be affected. Would the dollar transfers be affected or would only the names of the transfers be changed?

11. For what range of interest rates would a banker rather attract funds through RPs than through corporate demand deposits when the reserve requirement ratio on those deposits is 12 percent? When it is 30 percent? Please explain the difference between your answers.

12. Suppose Punxsutawney National's average balance sheet for February 2 to 15 was changed such that its vault cash was $10, transaction accounts were $108, and nonpersonal time deposits were $220. Suppose these values continue unchanged through March 17.

    (a) What are the bank's average required balances with the Fed during March 4 to 17?

    (b) Suppose the bank's average balances with the Fed during March 4 to 15 were $12. What are its required balances during March 16 and 17? Should the reserve manager be promoted or fired?

13. Given the average pattern of fed funds rates in Table 9.7, how would you as a reserve manager plan your weekly fed funds purchases and sales? State your assumptions about expected flows of funds from other sources.

14. What reserve accounting procedure do *you* prefer from the standpoint of (a) the individual bank that wishes as much information as possible in planning its reserve positions and other activities and (b) the Fed when it wants to control the money supply?

15. What would Figure 9.3 have looked like if post-1979 Directives had been in force in 1978?

16. (a) Describe the swings in interest rates and money that are likely to follow from a mistaken commercial bank belief in the first week of a reserve maintenance period that the Fed is going to tighten up next period.

    (b) How long will these swings continue, and what kinds of responses by banks and the Fed determine this length?

    (c) How would your answer be affected if the old lagged reserve accounting system were brought back?

REFERENCES

Clay J. Anderson, "Evolution of the Role and the Functioning of the Discount Mechanism," in Federal Reserve Board, *Reappraisal of the Federal Reserve Discount Mechanism,* Washington, 1971.

James M. Boughton, *Monetary Policy and the Federal Funds Market,* Duke University Press, Durham, NC, 1972.

James M. Boughton and Elmus R. Wicker, "The Behavior of the Currency-Deposit Ratio during the Great Depression," *Journal of Money, Credit and Banking,* November 1979, pages 405–418.

Norman N. Bowsher, "Repurchase Agreements," Federal Reserve Bank of St. Louis *Review,* September 1979, pages 17–22. Partial reprint in Timothy Q. Cook and Bruce J. Summers (eds.), *Instruments of the Money Market,* 5th ed., Federal Reserve Bank of Richmond, Richmond, VA, 1981.

James G. Cannon, *Clearing Houses: Their History, Methods and Administration,* Appleton, New York, 1908.

Timothy Q. Cook and Bruce J. Summers (eds.), *Instruments of the Money Market,* 5th

ed., Federal Reserve Bank of Richmond, Richmond, VA, 1981.

Lorraine E. Duro, "The Federal Reserve Discount Mechanism," Federal Reserve Bank of Cleveland *Economic Review,* April 1980, pages 1–9.

Federal Reserve Board, *Reappraisal of the Federal Reserve Discount Mechanism,* 3 vols., Washington, 1971.

Federal Reserve Board, *The Federal Reserve System: Purposes and Functions,* 6th ed., Washington, 1974.

Milton Friedman, "The Lag in Effect of Monetary Policy," *Journal of Political Economy,* October 1961, pages 447–466.

Milton Friedman, "The Federal Reserve and Monetary Instability," *Wall Street Journal,* February 1, 1982, page 16.

Kenneth Garbade, *Securities Markets,* McGraw-Hill, New York, 1982.

Brian C. Gendreau, "Bankers' Balances, Demand Deposit Interest, and Agricultural Credit before the Banking Act of 1933," *Journal of Money, Credit and Banking,* November 1979, pages 506–514.

R. Alton Gilbert, "Benefits of Borrowing from the Federal Reserve When the Discount Rate Is below Market Interest Rates," Federal Reserve Bank of St. Louis *Review,* March 1979, pages 25–32.

R. Alton Gilbert, "Lagged Reserve Requirements: Implications for Monetary Control and Bank Reserve Management," Federal Reserve Bank of St. Louis *Review,* May 1980, pages 7–20.

R. Alton Gilbert and Michael E. Trebing, "The FOMC in 1980: A Year of Reserve Targeting," Federal Reserve Bank of St. Louis *Review,* August/September 1981, pages 2–22.

R. Alton Gilbert and Michael E. Trebing, "The New System of Contemporaneous Reserve Requirements," Federal Reserve Bank of St. Louis *Review,* December 1982, pages 3–7.

Stephen M. Goldfeld and Edward J. Kane, "The Determinants of Member-bank Borrowing: An Econometric Study," *Journal of Finance,* September 1966, pages 499–521.

Marvin Goodfriend, "Discount Window Borrowing, Monetary Policy, and the Post-October 6, 1979, Federal Reserve Operating Procedure," *Journal of Monetary Economics,* September 1983, pages 343–356.

C. A. E. Goodhart, *The New York Money Market and the Finance of Trade, 1900–1913,* Harvard University Press, Cambridge, MA, 1969.

Robert S. Greenberger, "Fed Takes Strong Steps to Restrain Inflation, Shifts Monetary Tactic," *Wall Street Journal,* October 8, 1979, page 1.

Howard H. Hackley, *Lending Functions of the Federal Reserve Banks: A History,* Federal Reserve Board of Governors, Washington, 1973.

Bray Hammond, *Banks and Politics in America from the Revolution to the Civil War,* Princeton University Press, Princeton, NJ, 1957.

R. S. Hanna and Michael G. Vogt, "Variations in the Rate of Interest on Federal Funds under the Federal Reserve's New Operating Procedure," presented to the Midwest Economics Association, Eastern Michigan University, April 1981.

Luther Harr and W. Carlton Harris, *Banking Theory and Practice,* 2nd ed., McGraw-Hill, New York, 1936.

Thomas M. Humphrey, "The Real Bills Doctrine," Federal Reserve Bank of Richmond *Economic Review,* September/October 1982, pages 3–12.

John A. James, *Money and Capital Markets in Postbellum America,* Princeton University Press, Princeton, NJ, 1978.

Paul F. Jessup, *Modern Bank Management,* West Publishing, St. Paul, MN, 1980.

Paul L. Kasriel, "Interest Rate Volatility in 1980," Federal Reserve Bank of Chicago *Economic Perspectives,* January/February 1981, pages 8–17.

Robert E. Knight, "Correspondent Banking," Federal Reserve Bank of Kansas City *Monthly Review,* November 1970, pages 3–14, December 1970, pages 12–24, and December 1971, pages 3–17.

Robert D. Laurent, "Interbank Lending—an Essential Function," Federal Reserve Bank of Chicago *Business Conditions,* November 1974, pages 3–7.

Robert D. Laurent, "A Critique of the Federal Reserve's New Operating Procedure," Occasional Paper 81–4, Federal Reserve Bank of Chicago, April 1981.

Robert D. Laurent, "Lagged Reserve Accounting and the Fed's New Operating Procedure," Federal Reserve Bank of Chicago *Economic Perspectives,* Midyear 1982, pages 32–43.

Fred J. Levin and Ann-Marie Meulendyke, "Monetary Policy and Open Market Operations in 1978," Federal Reserve Bank of New York *Quarterly Review,* Spring 1979, pages 53–66.

Fred J. Levin, Christopher J. McCurdy, and Betsy B. White, "Monetary Policy and Open Market Operations in 1980," Federal Reserve Bank of New York *Quarterly Review,* Summer 1981, pages 56–75.

Wesley Lindow, *Inside the Money Market,* Random House, New York, 1972.

Oliver C. Lockhart, "The Development of Interbank Borrowing in the National System, 1869–1914," *Journal of Political Economy,* February and March 1921, pp. 138–160, 222–240.

Charles M. Lucas, Marcos T. Jones, and Thom B. Thurston, "Federal Funds and Repurchase Agreements," Federal Reserve Bank of New York *Quarterly Review,* Summer 1977, pp. 33–48.

Seth P. Maerowitz, "The Market for Federal Funds," Federal Reserve Bank of Richmond *Economic Review,* July/August 1981, pp. 3–7. Reprint in Timothy Q. Cook and Bruce J. Summers (eds.), *Instruments of the Money Market,* 5th ed., Federal Reserve Bank of Richmond, Richmond, VA, 1981.

Christopher J. McCurdy and Kenneth J. Guentner, "Monetary Policy and Open Market Operations in 1982," Federal Reserve Bank of New York *Quarterly Review,* Spring 1983, pages 37–54.

Lloyd W. Mints, *A History of Banking Theory,* University of Chicago Press, Chicago, 1945.

Waldo F. Mitchell, *The Uses of Bank Funds,* University of Chicago Press, Chicago, 1925.

National Monetary Commission, *Interviews on the Banking and Currency Systems of England, Scotland, France, Germany, Switzerland, and Italy,* U.S. Government Printing Office, Washington, 1910.

Allan Nevins, *History of the Bank of New York and Trust Company,* Bank of New York and Trust Company, New York, 1934.

Dorothy M. Nichols, *Trading in Federal Funds,* Federal Reserve Board, Washington, 1965.

James Parthemos and Walter Varvel, "The Discount Window," in Timothy Q. Cook and Bruce J. Summers (eds.), *Instruments of the Money Market,* 5th ed., Federal Reserve Bank of Richmond, Richmond, VA, 1981.

Thomas D. Simpson, "The Market for Federal Funds and Repurchase Agreements," Federal Reserve Board Staff Study 106, July 1979.

O. M. W. Sprague, *History of Crises under the National Banking System,* U.S. Government Printing Office, Washington, 1910.

Marcia Stigum, *The Money Market,* rev. ed., Dow Jones-Irwin, Homewood, IL, 1983.

John A. Tatom, "Issues in Measuring an Adjusted Monetary Base," Federal Reserve Bank of St. Louis *Review,* December 1980, pages 11–29.

Henry Thornton, *An Enquiry into the Nature and Effects of the Paper Credit of Great Britain,* Hatchard, London, 1802.

Robert C. Turner, *Member-bank Borrowing,* Ohio State University Press, Columbus, OH, 1938.

Paul A. Volcker, "Statement before the Joint Economic Committee of the U.S. Congress," October 17, 1979, *Federal Reserve Bulletin,* November 1979, pp. 888–890.

Leonard L. Watkins, *Bankers' Balances,* Shaw, Chicago, 1929.

Henry Parker Willis, *The Federal Reserve System,* Ronald Press, New York, 1923.

Parker B. Willis, *The Federal Funds Market: Its Origin and Development,* 4th ed., Federal Reserve Bank of Boston, Boston, 1970.

John H. Wood, "Familiar Developments in Bank Loan Markets," Federal Reserve Bank of Dallas *Economic Review,* November 1983, pages 1–13.

CAPITAL MARKET
INSTRUMENTS

*October. This is one of the peculiarly dangerous months to speculate
in stocks in. The others are July, January, September, April,
November, May, March, June, December, August, and February.*

Mark Twain, *Pudd'nhead Wilson's Calendar*

This chapter is about stocks and bonds. These long-term financial
claims are issued by businesses and governments to obtain the funds
with which to undertake capital projects, such as roads, plant, and
machinery, that are expected to yield private or public returns over
long periods. We begin with detailed descriptions of the principal
types of corporate stocks and bonds and show how to follow their
fortunes in the financial press. The prices of these securities depend
not only on general market conditions and investor beliefs about the
future earnings of firms but also on the special terms and conditions of
each security. We shall pay particular attention to three categories of
the terms and conditions of bonds and preferred stock: call features,
convertibility, and restrictive covenants. A callable security is one that
a firm has the option to redeem (call) at specified prices on specified
dates. This option is worth something and must be paid for in the form
of lower prices (higher yields) on callable issues. Convertibility and
restrictive covenants are explained as resolutions of owner-creditor
conflicts within an analytic framework that combines the theories of
finance and agency and is most closely associated with the names
Michael Jensen and William Meckling. The last section considers
state and local government bonds ("municipals") and describes alternative theories of the equilibrium relationship between corporate and
municipal yields.[1]

---

1 This chapter does not consider the bill, note, or bond issues of the U.S. Treasury, which were
discussed in Chapters 6 to 8. Nor do we explicitly consider the issues of agencies of the federal
government, which, except for their ambiguous security (will the federal government bail out
the Federal Deposit Insurance Corporation after it has bailed out the Continental Bank?), are
similar to Treasury issues.

CORPORATE SECURITIES

Corporations[2]

A corporation is a group of persons authorized by law to act as a unit. It may be an educational institution, labor union, or charitable foundation although in the United States the term is normally reserved for business enterprises. Roman law regarded the corporation as a person in law, distinct from its members, and this idea was carried over to canon law and the English common law.[3] The fictitious legal person represented by the corporation may sue, be sued, and hold and transfer property. Since the corporation holds its property distinct from that of its members, it follows that the property of members cannot be taken to pay the debts of the corporation, and vice versa. This is *limited liability,* by which, in the event of the corporation's bankruptcy, the members may lose their stake in the corporation but the remainder of their property is protected.

Until the nineteenth century, business corporations (or "chartered companies") were authorized by governments for more or less specific public purposes. Their charters gave them certain rights and privileges and bound them to certain obligations. The earliest English chartered companies were the medieval merchant adventurers, who were granted monopolies by the crown (for a price) in certain areas of manufacture and trade. Whether these royal grants improved the realm by providing incentives for groups to risk their capital in publicly desirable enterprises or whether they merely represented the sale of publicly harmful monopolies with no beneficiaries except the monarch and the monopolists was a hotly debated question and has remained so although the monarch's role has been taken over by others.

The origins of the modern business corporation may be found in the seventeenth century, when the scale and risk of overseas ventures led to the joint-stock form of organization, in which capital was provided by shareholders who then participated in the profits of the joint enterprise. One of the earliest and largest was the East India Company, which was established in 1600 to promote trade with the East Indies and was given an English monopoly of eastern trade. The Hudson's Bay Company was formed in 1670 with an English monopoly of trade in that area and the obligation to seek the northwest passage.[4]

---

2 Excellent discussions related to the development of limited-liability corporations are presented in the *Encyclopaedia Britannica* under the headings "Chartered Company," "Company," "Corporation," and "Merchant Adventurers."

3 In the case of *Santa Clara County v. Southern Pacific R.R.*, 1886, the U.S. Supreme Court expressly recognized corporations to be "persons" within the meaning of the Fourteenth Amendment, which therefore could not be deprived of "life, liberty, or property without due process of law." However, "Corporations cannot commit treason, nor be outlawed, or excommunicated, for they have no souls" (Sir Edward Coke in the case of Sutton's Hospital, 1612)—except U.S. Steel [Arundel Cotter (1921)].

4 Of course these "monopolies" were valuable only to the extent that the English companies could overcome French and Dutch competition. The English were successful in India and Canada, but

Domestic ventures also grew in scale and number, and the Bank of England was organized in 1694 with a monopoly of joint-stock banking in London and the obligation to serve as the government's banker.

Business corporations in the American colonies were small in size and few in number. Aside from William Penn's Free Society of Traders, a mutual fire insurance society in Philadelphia, and the New London trading society, corporations for the most part carried on activities that are now performed by local governments or public utilities, such as wharf operators in New Haven and Boston and three small water companies in Rhode Island.

This situation changed rapidly during the last two decades of the eighteenth century, partly because of the end of British restrictions but also because of the expanding needs of a rapidly growing and increasingly dispersed population. More than 300 business corporations were chartered by state governments between 1783 and 1801. Two-thirds of these were transportation companies, principally for inland navigation, turnpikes, and toll bridges. Most of the others were commercial banks, fire and marine insurance companies, water companies, and a few companies to build and operate docks.

Incorporation had become easier, but it was not yet automatic. Limited-liability joint-stock companies were still considered quasi-public agencies of the state and were largely reserved to "publicly beneficial" activities upon which certain exclusive privileges were bestowed. These privileges included explicit monopoly rights of way, the right of eminent domain, and tax exemptions. But in many cases the most important benefit arose from an understanding that the number of enterprises in a particular sphere of activity would be limited.

Opposition to privileged corporations grew with profit opportunities and the number of aspiring new enterprises. New York and Connecticut passed general laws in 1811 and 1817 that permitted manufacturing concerns satisfying certain standard requirements to obtain corporate charters by direct application to the secretary of state. In other states, however, special acts of the legislature were required for incorporation until the late 1830s, when a Massachusetts bridge company could still claim with apparent seriousness that simply the

---

the government's grant of a monopoly of trade with South America and the Pacific to the new South Sea Company in 1711 was less profitable. Nevertheless, this company led the tremendous rise and decline of stock prices during the South Sea Bubble of 1720. The South Sea Company's shares rose from £128 in January to over £1,000 in July and August, before falling to £175 in September and £124 in December. Other stocks behaved similarly. Many speculative schemes were advanced during the market's rise, the most famous being one in which an unnamed person circulated a prospectus seeking funds for "A company for carrying on an undertaking of great advantage, but nobody to know what it is." The required capital was stated to be 5,000 shares of £100 each, subscribers to deposit £2 per share. He sold 1,000 shares in 1 day and that evening left for the Continent [Charles Mackay (1841, page 55)].

In as much of a panic as investors, Parliament responded with the hastily conceived and vaguely worded Bubble Act of 1720, which continued to raise questions about the legality of joint-stock companies and hindered the finance of industry until its repeal in 1825.

existence of a corporate charter implied monopoly rights. Specifically the owners of the Charles River Bridge argued that the state's grant of a corporate charter to build a toll bridge implied that the state could do nothing to impair the value of that charter—such as the construction of a free bridge paralleling the toll bridge. In the case of *Charles River Bridge v. Warren Bridge*, 1837, the Supreme Court upheld the right of the state to build the new bridge and declared that a corporation possessed only such exclusive privileges as might be expressly granted by its charter.

In the 1840s several states passed general incorporation laws (often to implement constitutional amendments), and by the 1870s special charters had almost everywhere become unnecessary in most fields of endeavor. Monopolistic charters have remained important, however, in transportation, in public utilities, and, after a brief period of free banking following the Charles River Bridge decision, in banking.

By the end of the nineteenth century American business was dominated by corporations (86 percent of the activity of mining and other extractive industries, 67 percent of manufacturing output, and nearly 100 percent of public utilities and railroads),[5] and their importance has continued to grow in the twentieth century. In 1979, although only 16 percent of businesses were incorporated, corporations accounted for 88 percent of business receipts. Corporations took in 89 percent of mining receipts, 99 percent of manufacturing receipts, and 95 percent of transportation and public utility receipts.[6]

Common stock

COMMON STOCK (EQUITY) REPRESENTS OWNERSHIP. Holders of common stock may vote for the firm's directors and are entitled to receive dividends declared by the directors in proportion to their ownership of the total common stock outstanding. For example we see in the balance sheet in Table 10.1 that the owners of International Telephone & Telegraph (ITT) held about 130 million[7] shares of its common stock at the end of 1981. Each share is carried on ITT's books at a "par value" of $1. The description of ITT's common stock in Table 10.3 indicates that the directors had been authorized by the shareholder-owners to issue up to 200 million shares. Common stockholders often have *preemptive rights,* which give them first chance to purchase new common stock in the same proportion as that of their existing ownership in the company.

The $1 par value of ITT's common stock is an arbitrary number

5 These estimates are from Adolf Berle and Gardiner Means (1932, Chapter 2).

6. Data for 1979 are from Bureau of the Census, *Statistical Abstract of the U.S., 1982–83,* pages 528–529. For earlier data, beginning in 1939, see Bureau of the Census, *Historical Statistics of the United States: Colonial Times to 1970,* vol. 2, page 911, Washington, 1971.

7 The difference between this number and the number of "outstanding" common shares shown in Table 10.2 represents about 17 million shares of "treasury stock" that had been repurchased by the company.

Table 10.1   Balance Sheet of International Telephone and Telegraph, December 31, 1981 (Millions of Dollars)

Assets			Liabilities and Capital		
Current assets		581	Current liabilities		844
Cash	12		Short-term debt	246	
Accounts receivable	160		Accounts payable	109	
Inventories	383		Accrued taxes and liabilities	489	
Other current assets	26		Unfunded pension reserves		86
Plant, property, and equipment		406	Other deferred liabilities		93
Subsidiaries		4,104	Long-term debt		1,788
Other assets		276	Preferred stock[a]		497
Total assets		5,367	Common stock[b]		130
			Capital surplus[c]		989
			Retained earnings		940
			Total liabilities and capital		5,367

a No par; carried on the books at liquidation values. See Table 10.3 for an example.

b Represented by $1 par shares.

c Credits to capital surplus include excess over par received for stock options, stock issued for companies acquired, and conversions of debt and preferred stock. Debits include excess of cost of treasury stock (stock repurchased by the company) over par value of common stock.

Source: *Moody's Industrial Manual*, 1982, page 1611.

bearing no relation to the stock's value (price), which we see from Table 10.4 was $37.625 at the close of trading March 25, 1983. The value of a share is what people will pay for it, which in turn depends on expected company earnings and dividends. Bond par values have meaning because they refer to promised final (or "principal" or "maturity") payments to bondholders. Holders of common stock are not creditors and possess no such contractual claim on the company. Their receipts depend solely upon the company's profits (if any) and upon the directors' willingness (if any) to pay dividends. Declarations of stock par values have not been required in most states since early this century, and most companies either declare no par value or par values so low that they cannot possibly be confused with the actual value (price) of the stock—and also because some states do not allow shares to be sold below par value. The popular choices are "no par" and a par value of $1, each representing about one-third of all stocks.[8] The difference between the price at which new shares are sold and their stated par value must be accounted for in some way on the company's books, such as by "capital surplus" (as in Table 10.1) or some other name that distinguishes it from par value.[9]

8 *Moody's Handbook of Common Stocks*, published quarterly, is a convenient source of data relating to common stocks, including their par and recent market values.

9 One of the financial abuses alleged in support of the capital market regulations of the 1930s was the issuance of "watered stock," which is a pejorative but empty reference to an excess of the sale price of newly issued stock over its par (or book) value. Fraudulent practices existed (and still exist), but discrepancies between par and market values, that is, watered stock, cannot be

Table 10.2 ITT's Capital Structure, December 31, 1981

Long Term Debt Issue	Rating	[2] Amount outstanding	Interest Dates		Call Price
1. S.F. debenture 8.90s, 1995	A2	$ 93,878,000	A & O	1	[1] 104.005
2. S.f. deb. 10s, 2000	A2	75,000,000	J & D	1	[1] 106.094
3. 9⅛% notes, 1983	A2	75,000,000	J & D	1	100
4. S.F. debenture, 12⅝s, 1991–05	A2	150,000,000	J & J	15	[1] 111.138
5. S.F. deb. 4.90s, 1987	A2	15,669,000	A & O	1	[1] 101.50
6. Deb. 6½s, 2001	A2	150,000,000	J & J	1	100
7. Deb. 7½s, 2011	A2	150,000,000	J & J	1	100
8. 14¾% notes, 1991	A2	150,000,000	M & N	15	100
* 9. Conv. subord. deb. 8⅝s, 2000	A3	61,084,000	J & D	1	[1] 106.037
*10. Conv. sub. deb. 4¾s, 1987	—	50,000,000	Oct.	1	[1] 100
11. 8¾% notes, 1989	—	50,000,000	—		—
12. French Franc deb. 8.50s, 1988	—	44,243,000	—		—
13. 8.65% senior notes, 1983–97	—	60,000,000	—		—
14. 8.31-9% notes, 1982	—	15,400,000	—		—
15. 4⅞% notes, 1984	—	22,500,000	—		—
16. 7½–17.1% L.t. bank loans, due 1983	—	471,500,000	—		—
17. 8% prom. notes 1983	—	28,400,000	—		—
18. 5½% Sterling 1 Dollar Conv. Ln. Stk.	—	15,048,000	—		—
19. Other	—	20,676,000	—		—
20. Consolidated Subsidiaries	—	1,877,533,000	—		—

Capital Stock Issue	Par Value	Amount Outstanding	Divs. per Sh. 1981	Divs. per Sh. 1980	Call Price
* 1. $4 cum. conv. pfd., ser. H.	No par	165,163 shs.	$4.00	$4.00	100
* 2. $4.50 cum. conv. pfd., ser. I	No par	1,695,056 shs.	4.50	4.50	100
* 3. $4 cum. conv. pfd., ser. J	No par	384,584 shs.	4.00	4.00	[1] 100.75
* 4. $4 cum. conv. pfd., ser. K	No par	6,481,496 shs.	4.00	4.00	100
* 5. $2.25 series N	No par	1,632,966 shs.	2.25	2.25	85.00
* 6. $5 series O	No par	999,990 shs.	5.00	5.00	[1] 102.30
7. Common	$1	147,184,000 shs.	2.60	2.40	. . .

[1] Subject to change; see Table 10.3 for examples.

[2] Except for debt issued in 1981, values outstanding refer to December 31, 1979.

* Conversion ratios: debt convertible into common at (9) $25⅜ and (10) $56⅛ per share; preferred convertible into (1) 1.8734, (2) 1.6880, (3) 1.6810, (4) 1.6155, (5) 1.2560, and (6) 1.4364 common shares.

Source: *Moody's Industrial Manual*, 1982, page 1606.

THE VALUATION OF COMMON STOCK. Now let's examine the determinants of stock prices in the simplest possible situation, in which there is neither uncertainty nor taxes.[10] Although payments to bondholders are fixed by contract while payments to stockholders are not, stocks

---

counted among them. Perhaps the most frequently cited example is that of U.S. Steel, whose stock sold for much more than the book value of the firms that were combined to form that corporation. Nevertheless, as George Stigler (1965) has pointed out, during the first two decades of its existence U.S. Steel stock earned twice the average rate of return of other steel stocks.

10 The combined effects of taxes, inflation, and accounting procedures on stock valuation are examined in Chapter 18.

and bonds are valued in the same manner. The price of each is the present value of its future receipts: coupons and principal for a bond, dividends for a share of stock. Let R be the (assumed constant) rate of return on an alternative investment (perhaps a corporate bond), let $\overline{D}_t$ be dividends paid by a firm in the tth future period, and let N be the number of shares outstanding. Then the present value of all the firm's shares, S_0, and the price of one of those shares, P_0, are[11]

(10.1)
$$S_0 = \sum_{t=1}^{\infty} \frac{\overline{D}_t}{(1+R)^t} \quad \text{and}$$
$$P_0 = \frac{S_0}{N} = \sum_{t=1}^{\infty} \frac{\overline{D}_t/N}{(1+R)^t} = \sum_{t=1}^{\infty} \frac{D_t}{(1+R)^t}$$

where D_t is the dividend per share paid at time t. Suppose the dividend per share is expected to be forever constant at D. Then the price of a share is[12]

(10.2)
$$P_0 = \sum_{t=1}^{\infty} \frac{D}{(1+R)^t} = \frac{D}{R}$$

INTERPRETATION OF REPORTED DIVIDEND YIELDS AND PRICE/EARNINGS RATIOS. The price of the certain, constant-dividend stock in Equation (10.2) is precisely analogous to the price of the default-free, constant-coupon, perpetual bond in Equation (5.26). This is the context in which the highly publicized price/dividend (P/D) and price/earnings (P/E) ratios *may* be meaningful. We see from Equation (10.2) that the price/dividend ratio is $P_0/D = 1/R$, which turned upside down is $R = D/P_0$. Under certainty the rate of return from holding stocks must equal the rate of return (R) on the alternative investment. For example, if dividends are expected to be constant, we should observe D/P_0 equal to the yield on a high-grade corporate bond, where D is represented by dividends paid during the preceding year, or during the preceding quarter and converted to an annual rate. Price/earnings ratios (P/E) may be constructed and interpreted in similar ways.

Now let's look at stock prices and D/P and P/E ratios as reported in the financial press. Table 10.4 is a partial reproduction of stock transactions reported on the consolidated tape that since the mid-1970s has included trades on the New York Stock Exchange (NYSE), five regional exchanges, the over-the-counter (OTC) market reported by the National Association of Securities Dealers Automated Quotations (NASDAQ) System, and Instinet, which is a computer-linked

---

11 See John Williams (1938, pages 56–77) for an early presentation of statements equivalent to Equations (10.1) and (10.2).

12 See the method for calculating the sum of a geometric series in Appendix A.

Table 10.3   Descriptions of Selected ITT Debt and Stock Issues

Long Term Debt

1. International Telephone & Telegraph Corp. sinking fund debenture 8.90s due 1995:

Rating—A2

AUTH.—$100,000,000; outstg., Dec. 31, 1979, $93,878,000.
DATED—Oct. 1, 1970. DUE—Oct. 1, 1995.
INTEREST—A&O1 by mail to holders registered on 15th day of preceding month.
TRUSTEE—Bankers Trust Co., NYC.
DENOMINATION—Fully registered, $1,000 and authorized multiples thereof. Transferable or exchangeable without service charge.
CALLABLE—As a whole or in part, on at least 30 days' notice to each Sept. 30, incl. as follows:

1980	104.895	1981	104.450
1982	104.005	1983	103.560
1984	103.115	1985	102.670
1986	102.225	1987	101.780
1988	101.335	1989	100.890
1990	100.445	1995	100.000

Also callable for sinking fund (which see) at par.
SINKING FUND—Annually, on or before Oct. 1, 1980–94, to retire debs., cash (or debs.) equal to $6,000,000; plus similar optional payments. Payments calculated to retire 90% of issue prior to maturity.
SECURITY—Not secured. Co. may not create debt secured by lien on property without securing debs. equally, except for (a) purchase money mtges. or title retention agreements, provided that debt secured thereby shall not exceed 66⅔% of cost or fair value of property and provided that aggregate amount of all such debt does not exceed 3% of consolidated net worth; (b) any mtge. or other lien on property existing at time it is acquired by merger, consolidation or acquisition of substantially all assets of another corporation, provided that debt secured thereby shall not exceed 66⅔% of fair value of such other Co.'s assets; (c) pledges or deposits to secure payment of workmen's compensation or insurance premiums, or relating to tenders, bids, contracts (ex-

cept contracts for payment of money) or leases, or deposits to secure statutory obligations or surety or appeal bonds; (d) pledges or liens in connection with tax assessments or other governmental charges; (e) pledges or liens to secure a stay of process in proceedings to enforce a contested liability, or deposits with a governmental agency entitling Co. or a domestic subsidiary to maintain self-insurance or to participate in other specified insurance arrangements; (f) mechanics', carriers', workmen's and other like liens; (g) pledges of moneys due under contracts with or originating from the U.S. Govt.; (h) encumbrances in favor of the U.S. Govt. to secure progress or advance payments; (i) mtges. securing debt incurred to finance, refinance or hold, or arising from discount or sale with guaranty or endorsement of Co. or any subsidiary of, any note or other instrument arising from sale of products; (j) mtges. securing debt incurred to finance cost of property leased to the U.S. Govt. at a rental sufficient to pay the principal of and interest on such debt; and (k) renewals and extensions thereof.
DIVIDEND RESTRICTION—Co. may not pay cash divs. on or acquire capital stock in excess of consolidated net income after Jan. 1, 1970 plus $200,000,000.
OTHER PROVISIONS—Same as deb. 4.90s, due 1987.
LISTED—On New York Stock Exchange.
PURPOSE—Proceeds to reduce bank debt and for construction.
OFFERED—($100,000,000) at 100 (proceeds to Co., 99.125) on Sept. 30, 1970 thru Kuhn, Loeb & Co. and Lazard Freres & Co. and associates.

5. International Telephone & Telegraph Corp. debenture 4.90s, due 1987:

Rating—A2

AUTHORIZED—$50,000,000; outstanding, Dec. 31, 1979, $15,669,000.
DATED—Apr. 1, 1962.
MATURITY—Apr. 1, 1987.
INTEREST—A&O 1 at company's office, 320 Park Ave., New York.

TRUSTEE—Morgan Guaranty Trust Co., New York.
DENOMINATION—Coupon, $1,000; registerable as to principal; fully registered, $1,000 and multiples. C&R interchangeable.
CALLABLE—As a whole or in part, on at least 30 days' notice at any time to each Mar. 31, incl., as follows (as amended by indenture modification approved by bondholders Dec. 28, 1966):

1982	101.75	1983	101.50
1984	101.25	1985	101.00
1986	100.75	1987	100.50

Also callable at 100 for sinking fund (which see).
SINKING FUND—Each Apr. 1, 1967–86, cash (or debentures) to retire $2,000,000 debentures at sinking fund redemption price, plus similar optional amounts. Payments estimated to retire 80% of issue before maturity.
SECURITY—Not secured.
CREATION OF ADDITIONAL DEBT—Company or any consolidated subsidiary may not (except for certain refundings) incur additional funded debt or issue subsidiary preferred unless consolidated net tangible assets equal at least 233⅓% of consolidated funded debt and subsidiary preferred.
DIVIDEND RESTRICTIONS—(as amended; see callable, above). Company may not pay cash dividends on or acquire capital stock in excess of consolidated net income after Dec. 31, 1965 plus $45,000,000.
RIGHTS ON DEFAULT—Trustee or 25% of debentures may declare principal due and payable (60 days' grace for payment of interest or sinking fund installment).
INDENTURE MODIFICATION—Indenture may be modified, except as provided, with consent of 66⅔% of debentures.
LISTED—On New York Stock Exchange.
PURPOSE—Proceeds to pay $32,500,000 bank loans and for construction.
OFFERED—($50,000,000) at 100 (proceeds to company, 98⅞) on Mar. 28, 1962 by Kuhn, Loeb & Co., Inc., New York, and associates.

system by which subscribers, mainly large institutional investors, trade directly with each other.[13] Table 10.4 lists D/P and P/E ratios corresponding to closing prices on March 25, 1983 (P), the latest quarterly or semiannual dividends converted to annual rates (D), and earnings for the most recent four quarters (E).[14] For example we see from the report for AAR (the AAR Corporation, formerly Allen Aircraft Radio, Inc.) that $P/E = \$11.25/E = 27$ so that AAR's earnings during the preceding four quarters were approximately $E = \$11.25/27 = \$0.42$ per share. AAR's D/P ratio is shown in the yield column of Table 10.4 as 3.9 percent, which is an approximation of $\$0.44/\$11.25 = 0.0391$.

In a world of certainty with constant earnings and dividends D/P

13 These trading systems are discussed in Chapter 11.

14 See the Explanatory Notes to Table 10.4 and James Greenleaf, Ruth Foster, and Robert Prinsky (1982, page 6).

Table 10.3   (continued)

Long Term Debt

9. International Telephone & Telegraph Corp. convertible subordinated debenture 8⅝s, due 2000:
Rating—A3
AUTH.—$100,000,000; outstg., Dec. 31, 1979, $61,084,000.
DATED—June 1, 1975. DUE—June 1, 2000.
INTEREST—J&D 1 by mail, to holders registered M&N 15.
TRUSTEE—Chase Manhattan Bank (N.A.), NYC.
DENOMINATION—Fully registered, $1,000 and any integral multiple thereof. Transferable and exchangeable without service charge.
CALLABLE—As a whole or in part at any time on at least 30 but not more than 60 days' notice to each May 31, as follows:

1982	106.037	1983	105.606
1984	105.175	1985	104.744
1986	104.312	1987	103.881
1988	103.450	1989	103.019
1990	102.587	1991	102.156
1992	101.725	1993	101.294
1994	100.862	1995	100.431

thereafter at 100.
    Also callable for sinking fund (which see) at 100.
SINKING FUND—Annually, prior to each June 1, 1986–99, cash (or debs.) to retire 6⅔% of the aggregate principal amount of debs. outstg. on June 1, 1985; plus similar optional payments. Sinking fund designed to retire 93% of issue prior to maturity.
SECURITY—Not secured; subordinated to all senior debt.
CONVERTIBLE—Into com. on or before June 1, 2000 (unless previously redeemed) at $25⅜ per sh. No adjustment for interest or divs. Cash paid in lieu of fractional shs. Conversion privilege protected against dilution.
RIGHTS ON DEFAULT—Trustee, or 25% of debs. outstg., may declare principal due and payable (60 days' grace for payment of interest or sinking fund installment).
INDENTURE MODIFICATION—Indenture may be modified, except as provided, with consent of 66⅔% of debs. outstg.
LISTED—On New York Stock Exchange.
PURPOSE—Proceeds to reduce short-term debt originally incurred for advances to and investments in domestic subsidiaries, increases in working capital, plant construction and expansion of facilities.

OFFERED—($100,000,000) at 100 (proceeds to Co., 98.875) on June 5, 1975 thru Kuhn, Loeb & Co. and Lazard Freres & Co. and associates.

Capital Stock

1. International Telephone & Telegraph Corp. $4 cumulative convertible preferred, series H; no par:
AUTH.—All series, 50,000,000 shs.; outstanding series H, Dec. 31, 1981, 165,163 shs.; no par.
PREFERENCES—Has equal preference with other series for assets and divs.
DIVIDEND RIGHTS—Entitled to cum. cash divs. of $4 annually, payable quarterly on last days of Feb., etc.
DIVIDEND RESTRICTIONS—See Long Term Debt.
LIQUIDATION RIGHTS—$100 a sh. if involuntary; redemption price if voluntary; plus divs. in either case.
VOTING RIGHTS—Has one vote per share, also, on default of 6 quarterly dividends on all preferreds, holders of preferreds of all classes, entitled to elect two additional directors. Consent of 66⅔% of preferreds of all classes required to create prior stock or increase authorized amount of prior stock or change terms of preferreds adversely. Consent of majority of preferreds of all classes required to increase authorized preferred, create parity stock or voluntarily dissolve. Consent of 66⅔% of preferred of any series required to change terms of such series adversely.
CALLABLE—To Aug. 31 1980, $100.50; thereafter, $100.00 (per share plus accrued dividends).
SINKING FUND—None provided.
PREEMPTIVE RIGHTS—None.
CONVERTIBLE—Each pfd. sh. convertible at any time (if called, on or before 5th business day before redemption date) into 1.8734 com. shs.; no adj. for divs.; cash for fractions. Has anti-dilution clause.
PURPOSE—(375,000 shs.) in Aug. 1967 acq. of Alfred Teves G.m.b.H.; (11,241 shs.) in Jan. 1868 acq. of Jasper Blackburn Corp.; (181,148 shs.) in Jan. 1968 exchange of former cum. conv. pref. (participating) stock of I.T.&T.
TRANSFER AGENT—Company's office.
REGISTRAR—Citibank, N.A., NYC.
LISTED—On NYSE (Symbol: ITT Pr H).

7. International Telephone & Telegraph Corp. common; par $1:
AUTHORIZED—200,000,000 shares; outstg., Dec. 31, 1981, 130,200,493 shares; par $1.
    Note: At Dec. 31, 1981, 25,103,000 shares reserved as follows: 17,775,000 for conversion of cumulative preferred stock; $3,145,000 conversion of $148,725,000 principal amounts of debt; $4,183,000 for stock option and incentive plans; and other.
    Par changed from $100 to no par in May, 1929, by 3-for-1 split; no par shares split 2-for-1 Feb. 5, 1959; 2-for-1 split effected Mar. 7, 1968 (record date Jan. 26, 1968) and par changed to $5; par changed to $1, sh. for sh., upon change from Md. to Del. Corp. on Jan. 31, 1968.
VOTING RIGHTS—Has one vote per share.
PREEMPTIVE RIGHTS—Eliminated in 1968 upon change from Md. to Del. Corp.
DIVIDENDS PAID—
    Dividends payable quarterly, Jan. 1, etc. to stock of record about Nov. 23, etc.
DIVIDEND REINVESTMENT PLAN—Company offers its holders of common stock the opportunity to buy additional shares of common stock through an Automatic Dividend Reinvestment and Optional Cash Payment Plan. Participating share-owners may invest each month from $10.00 to $1,000 in addition to their dividend, at their option. The Plan is administered by Citibank, N.A., NYC.
DIVIDEND LIMITATION—See long term debt and preferred above.
TRANSFER AGENTS—Company's office, New York; Dresdner Bank A.G. Frankfurt-am-Main, Germany.
REGISTRARS—Citibank, N.A., NYC; Citibank, N.A., Frankfurt-am-Main, Germany.
LISTED—On NYSE (Symbol: ITT); also listed on London, Paris, Basle, Bern, Geneva, Lausanne, Brussels, Antwerp, Frankfurt, Tokyo, Vienna and Zurich (Switzerland) Stock Exchanges. Unlisted trading on all U.S. exchanges.
Stock Options held by employees of corporation and subsidiaries at Dec. 31, 1980 on 2,650,512 com. shs. at prices from $14.88 to $64.88 a share (aggregate $83,093,000).

Source: *Moody's Industrial Manual*, 1982, pages 1614–1617.

and *E/P* ratios will be identical across firms. However, Table 10.4 shows that these ratios vary widely between firms. The reader will not be surprised at this; for you never really believed that our assumptions of constancy and certainty were even approximately realistic, did you? Two stocks, A and B, with identical recent earnings and dividends may show very different current prices for at least two reasons: First, investors may believe that A's earnings and dividends will continue on average to be the same as B's but that, since firm A is in a volatile industry, A's earnings and dividends will be more *variable* than B's.

Table 10.4

Friday's Volume
89,067,720 Shares; 410,900 Warrants

TRADING BY MARKETS

	Shares	Warrants
New York Exchange	77,330,000	409,000
Midwest Exchange	4,914,000	....
Pacific Exchange	2,957,400	....
Nat'l Assoc. of Securities Dealers	1,763,420	1,900
Philadelphia Exchange	1,346,500	....
Boston Exchange	522,100	....
Cincinnati Exchange	221,000	....
Instinet System	13,300	....

NYSE – Composite

Volume since Jan. 1:	1983	1982	1981
Total shares	5,910,448,614	3,582,219,643	3,213,529,521
Total warrants	31,465,800	9,592,600	9,542,100

New York Stock Exchange

Volume since Jan. 1:	1983	1982	1981
Total shares	5,074,983,999	3,086,385,283	3,053,989,191
Total warrants	31,350,200	9,582,100	10,326,400

MOST ACTIVE STOCKS

	Open	High	Low	Close	Chg.	Volume
PhillipsPet	31¼	31⅜	30¼	30½	− ⅞	1,205,500
NtMedCare	15½	15½	13⅞	14½	−1⅜	1,044,700
Sony Corp	15¼	15¼	14⅞	14⅞	− ⅝	1,010,700
RCA	26⅛	26⅞	26	26⅝	+ ⅝	988,700
Amer T&T	66⅝	66¾	65½	65⅞	−1	975,300
Southland s	27	28¾	27	28½	+1⅞	938,200
ContIllCp	23⅛	23⅛	22⅞	23	....	908,100
DowChem	28½	28½	27½	27⅝	− ⅞	861,100
INCO Ltd	12⅞	13⅜	12⅞	13⅛	+ ⅛	847,100
MesaPtr n	10½	10¾	10⅜	10¾	....	777,100
SoumrkCp pf	10⅜	10⅞	10	10⅞	+ ½	726,800
NatMedEnt	35⅜	36¾	35⅜	36½	+1⅞	691,900
HouseIntl	23⅞	24⅝	23⅞	24¼	+ ¼	689,900
IBM	102½	103¼	101¾	102⅛	− ⅛	653,200
WasteMgt	47¾	48½	47	47¾	+1	608,200

52 Weeks High	Low	Stock	Div.	Yld %	P-E Ratio	Sales 100s	High	low	Close	Net Chg.
		– A–A–A –								
12⅝	5¾	AAR	.44	3.9	27	37	11⅞	11¼	11¼	− ½
38	27½	ACF	2.76	8.5	9	139	32⅝	32¼	32½	....
20	12¼	AMF	1.36	8.1	32	376	17⅛	16⅝	16¾	− ¼
28⅝	13	AMR Cp		..	..	3836	28⅜	27¼	27½	− ¾
14⅞	4	AMR wt		..	..	1178	14¾	13⅝	13⅞	− ¾
18¼	12⅞	AMR	pf2.18	13.	..	29	17¼	17	17⅛	+ ⅛
32⅝	24⅞	AMR	pf2.13	6.8	..	122	32⅛	31⅛	31⅛	−1
6⅝	2½	APL		..	..	41	5⅝	5½	5⅝	+ ⅛
47½	24⅝	ARA	2	4.3	14	286	47¼	46⅜	46½	....
79⅞	24½	ASA	3a	5.3	..	531	57½	56½	57⅛	+ ⅝
27⅝	13⅞	AVX	.32	1.2	34	520	26	24¼	25⅝	+1⅝
44⅝	27⅝	AbtLab	1	2.3	18	962	44¼	43½	43¾	....
		AccoW	n.12e	.4	20	198	27¼	26¾	26⅞	....
22½	15⅝	AcmeC	.40	2.2	20	435	18⅛	17⅞	18	+ ⅛
12⅝	5¾	AcmeE	.32b	2.9	29	42	11⅜	11	11⅛	− ⅛
13⅞	4½	AdmDg	.04	.3	12	149	u14	13⅝	13¾	− ⅛
17⅞	12½	AdaEx	1.73e	11.	..	89	16	15¾	16	+ ¼
9¾	4⅝	AdmMI	.20e	2.3	12	241	9	8⅞	8⅞	− ⅛
22⅝	12⅝	Advest	s .16	.7	14	202	u22¾	22⅛	22¼	....
39¼	13	AMD s	•	..	54	526	36¼	35	35½	+ ⅜
48¼	32⅞	AetnLf	2.64	6.8	8	1046	39¾	38⅞	39	− ⅝
37⅝	8	Ahmns	.60	1.9	..	1522	32⅜	31¾	31⅞	+ ⅛
4	2⅝	Aileen		..	..	196	3⅜	3⅜	3⅜	....
48⅛	23⅝	AirPrd	.80	1.9	12	1008	43½	41⅞	42⅛	−1¼
24¼	8½	AirbFrt	.60	2.7	29	109	22½	22	22	− ½
3	2	AlMoa n		..	4	64	2⅝	2⅝	2⅝	....
31¾	24½	AlaP	pfA3.92	13.	..	18	31	30¾	30¾	+ ⅛
7¼	5⅝	AlaP	dpf.87	12.	..	13	7⅛	7	7⅛	....
71	54½	AlaP	pf 9	13.	..	z220	69½	69¼	69½	− ½
65½	50¼	AlaP	pf 8.16	13.	..	z130	64½	63	63	−1
17½	13	Alagsco	1.60	9.4	6	6	17	17	17	....
15½	4⅞	AlskAir	.12	.9	11	759	13⅞	13	13¼	− ⅜
35⅝	23⅛	Albany	1.40	4.5	13	6	31	30¾	31	+ ¼
24⅛	10¾	Alberto	.54	3.0	12	18	18	17¾	17¾	− ¼
49½	26¾	Albtsn	1.20	2.5	13	235	48½	48	48	+ ½
33	15⅞	Alcan	.90	3.0	..	415	30¾	30⅜	30⅜	− ½
32⅛	18	AlcoStd	1.12	3.9	10	439	28⅞	28	28⅜	− ¼
30⅝	18⅝	AlexAlx	1	4.5	37	648	22¾	21⅝	22	+ ⅜
13⅞	7½	Alexdr		..	19	102	13⅞	13⅝	13⅞	+ ⅜
60½	35⅝	AllgCp	1.08	1.8	10	43	60⅜	60⅛	60⅜	+ ¼
25⅞	18⅞	AlgCp	pf2.86	11.	..	2	25½	25½	25½	+ ¼
32¼	16⅜	AlgInt	1.40	4.7	141	146	29⅝	29⅛	29⅝	+ ½
21⅛	14	AlgIn	pf2.19	10.	.	38	20⅞	20⅝	20⅞	+ ⅛
88⅝	68	AlgI	pfC11.25	13.	..	41	87⅞	87¾	87¾	− ¼
25⅝	18	AllgPw	2.40	10.	7	601	23½	23⅛	23⅛	− ⅛
18⅛	12⅛	AllenG	.40b	2.2	.	98	u18¼	17⅝	17⅞	− ¼
43⅝	28¾	AlldCp	2.40	5.5	7	3371	u43½	43	43⅜	+ ⅜
63¾	46¼	AldCp	pf6.74	10.		44	u65½	64¼	65⅛	+1⅜
105½	84⅛	AldCp	pf 12	11.	..	6	u106½	106	106¼	+ ¾
110¼	99¾	AldCp	pf1.78e	1.8		68	100	99¾	100	...

NYSE-Composite Transactions

Friday, March 25, 1983

Quotations include trades on the Midwest, Pacific, Philadelphia, Boston and Cincinnati stock exchanges and reported by the National Association of Securities Dealers and Instinet

52 Weeks High	Low	Stock	Div.	Yld %	P-E Ratio	Sales 100s	High	low	Close	Net Chg.
40¾	18½	Ethyl	1.70	4.5	8	210	38¼	38	38	....
20⅜	9¼	Ethyl wi		..	..	2	19¾	19¾	19¾	+ ¼
15⅞	4⅞	EvanP		..	..	178	15½	14⅞	15	− ½
11½	6⅝	Evan	pf1.40	13.	..	4	10⅝	10⅝	10⅝	....
15⅞	10	Evan	pf2.10	14.	..	3	15¼	15¼	15¼	− ⅛
30	19¼	ExCelo	1.60	5.4	9	61	30	29⅝	29¾	− ¼
16⅞	13⅜	Exclsr	1.87e	11.	..	32	16½	16⅜	16½	+ ¼
32¼	24⅞	Exxon	3	10.	6	5479	30¼	29¾	29⅞	− ¼
		– F–F–F –								
38⅛	23¾	FMC	1.80	4.9	8	242	36⅞	36½	36½	− ¼
47	30	FMC	pf 2.25	5.0	..	2	45⅜	45	45	+ ⅜
22¼	13	Fabrge	.48	2.4	18	236	20½	19½	20⅛	+ ⅞
22¾	8¾	FabCt	s .28	1.4	13	59	20½	20⅛	20⅜	− ⅛
11	4⅞	Facet		..	25	72	9⅞	9¾	9¾	− ¼
19⅝	12⅛	Fairchd	.80	4.1	10	1119	u20½	19¾	19¾	+ ¼
38	26½	Fairc	pf3.60	9.3	..	179	u39½	38⅛	38¾	+ ¾
30⅞	9⅛	FamDl	s .27	.9	25	30	30⅝	30⅛	30⅛	....
16	5¾	FrWstF		..	..	126	u16½	16	16⅜	+ ⅜
18⅜	5	Farah	.11	.6	10	104	18⅛	17¾	17¾	− ⅛
24⅜	3¼	FayDrg	s.20	.9	23	82	22⅜	22	22⅛	− ⅛
5⅞	2¾	Feders		..	..	1555	5⅞	5	5⅞	+ ⅞
30¼	19	FedlCo	1.44	5.1	10	42	28½	28	28¼	− ¼
85⅝	41½	FdExp		..	21	605	82⅜	80¾	81¼	....
30½	18	FdMog	1.32	4.5	13	19	29⅞	29½	29⅝	+ ⅛
27¼	7¾	FedNM	.16	.7	..	2036	23⅞	23½	23⅞	− ⅜
34¾	17¾	FedPB	1.20	3.5	13	x53	34⅝	34¼	34½	+ ⅞
22½	12½	FdSgnl	.88b	4.4	13	54	19⅞	19⅝	19⅞	....
60	36⅛	FedDSt	2.10	3.7	12	1466	58¾	56⅜	56⅞	−2⅛
33⅝	18½	Ferro	1.20	3.7	24	112	33	32¼	32¼	....
31¾	21½	FidUni	2.80	8.9	68	35	31⅝	31⅜	31⅜	....
34⅞	17⅛	Fldcst	2	5.8	13	142	34¾	34¼	34⅜	− ⅜
26⅛	15⅛	Figgie	.68	2.9	6	41	23⅛	23	23⅛	+ ¼
36	7	FnCpA	s .68	2.0	14	1031	34⅛	33½	33⅝	....
9¼	2½	FnSBar		..	.	561	u 9⅜	8⅛	8⅜	− ¾
40½	11⅞	FinlFed		..	271	317	u40¾	40½	40⅝	+ ⅛
20¼	9⅞	Firestn	.60	3.2	52	1331	19⅛	18¾	18¾	....
24¾	14	FtAtlan	1	4.1	7	29	24¾	24½	24½	....
57	51¼	FtAtl	pf1.44e	2.7	..	10	53⅞	53⅞	53⅞	−1⅝
24¾	15¾	FBkFla	1.08	4.7	10	1	22¾	22¾	22¾	+ ¼
25⅛	7⅝	FtChrt	.80	3.2	..	5267	25	24⅝	24⅝	− ⅛
23⅛	13½	FstChic	1.20	5.5	6	2496	22⅛	21⅝	21⅝	− ⅛
29⅞	15⅝	FtBTex	1.30	6.2	6	125	21⅛	20¾	20⅞	− ⅛
8⅛	3¼	FtCity		..	..	170	7⅝	7½	7½	− ⅛
39	21⅝	Fintste	2.14	5.8	7	84	37½	37⅛	37⅛	− ⅜
12⅝	6	FtMiss	.24	2.0	15	x1090	12⅝	12	12⅛	− ⅛
41¼	21⅜	FNBos	s2.12	5.2	6	273	u41⅜	40½	40½	− ⅝
34⅞	21½	FNStB	2.40	7.0	5	74	34½	34⅛	34⅛	....
5½	2½	FstPa		..	..	244	5	4¾	4¾	− ¼
13-16	⅛	FstPa wt		..	..	18	5-32	5-32	5-32	....
24	13⅜	FtUnRl	1.32	5.6	13	x95	23⅞	23	23⅜	− ¼
15¾	7	FtVaBk	.68	4.5	8	x241	15⅜	14¾	15⅛	....
35	21	FtWisc	2.10	5.9	5	57	u35⅞	35	35⅝	+ ⅝
53⅛	30¼	Fischb	2.40	5.0	6	149	49	47¾	48⅜	− ⅜
13⅞	7⅜	FishFd		..	..	160	10	9⅞	10	....
40	20½	FltFinG	2.20	5.7	6	19	39¼	38¾	38¾	− ¼
47½	40	FltFn pf		..	..	2	41½	41½	41½	+ ½
55½	11¾	FleetEn	.52	1.0	26	158	50⅛	49⅜	49⅞	− ⅜
27¾	5⅞	FletE wi		..	..	12	25⅛	25	25	....
55⅝	23¾	Flemng	1.32	2.4	14	67	u55⅞	55½	55½	+ ⅛
28½	11⅞	Flmng wi		..	..	2	28	28	28	....
25¾	14⅛	FlexiV	.80	3.5	7	18	23⅜	23	23⅛	− ⅜
12½	9⅜	Flexi	pf1.61	13.	..	1	12⅜	12⅜	12⅜	− ⅛
31½	22	Flexi	pf2.75	9.1	..	14	30½	30⅜	30⅜	− ⅛
34	16	FligtSf	.16	.5	20	16	30	29¾	29⅞	− ⅛
38⅜	16	FloatPt		.	28	140	36	35¾	35¾	− ¼
26⅜	14	FlaEC	.10	.4	18	15	24¾	24⅜	24¾	+ ⅛

52 Weeks High	Low	Stock	Div.	Yld %	P-E Ratio	Sales 100s	High	low	Close	Net Chg.
61¼	41⅝	HoInt	pf6.25	11.	..	x7	58⅝	58	58⅝	+1
21⅝	17½	HouInd	2.16	10.	13	1091	20⅝	20½	20⅝	....
41	24⅜	HouNG	1.82	5.2	6	381	35¼	34⅝	35⅛	+ ½
21½	14¾	HouOR	2.41e	14.	..	67	17⅛	16⅞	16⅞	− ⅛
13	6⅝	Howell	.40	3.6	24	2	11¼	11	11¼	+ ¼
20¼	8⅝	HowPt	.40	2.3	13	5	17½	17½	17½	− ⅛
21⅞	14½	Hubbrd	2.20	9.7	12	119	u22¾	21⅞	22¾	+ ⅞
19¼	10¼	HudM g		..	..	30	14½	14½	14½	....
15	8⅝	Huffy	.30	2.2	..	60	13⅞	13⅜	13½	− ⅛
31⅛	14⅜	HughTl	.84	5.1	6	680	16½	16⅛	16⅜	− ⅛
35½	16⅛	Human	s.60	1.6	21	5584	u37⅜	35¾	36⅞	+1⅞
23⅛	17½	Huma	pf2.50	11.	..	14	23	22⅞	23	− ⅛
19	8⅝	HuntCh	.50	2.8	19	42	18⅛	18	18⅛	+ ⅛
48⅞	21⅞	HuttEF	.80	1.7	11	1293	48⅜	46⅝	46¾	−1
22½	15⅝	Hydral	1.84	8.4	9	20	22	22	22	....
		– I–I–I –								
41¼	24⅝	IC Ind	2.28	5.9	19	714	39⅝	38⅝	38⅞	− ⅞
61	38	IC In	pf 3.50	6.0	.	15	59½	57⅞	57⅞	−1⅝
10½	4¾	ICN		..	34	231	9¾	9½	9⅝	− ⅛
18⅛	13⅝	INAIn	1.92a	11.	..	28	17⅜	17⅜	17⅜	− ⅛
19¾	10⅝	IU Int	1.15	6.4	13	634	18⅛	17⅞	18	....
31¼	21¼	IdahoP	2.88	9.4	7	139	30⅞	30½	30¾	+ ⅛
23¼	11¾	IdealB	.60	2.6	.	77	23⅛	22½	22⅞	....
24⅛	18⅞	IllPowr	2.48	10.	8	509	23⅞	23⅝	23¾	− ⅛
20	13¾	IlPow	pf2.13	11.	..	z460	u20⅛	20⅛	20⅛	+ ⅝
45½	24¾	ITW	1.16	2.7	13	16	42¾	42½	42¾	− ¼
16	4¾	ImplCp		..	..	33	13	12¾	12¾	− ¼
14	7⅞	INCO	.20	1.5	..	8471	13⅜	12⅞	13⅛	+ ⅛
101	79¼	IndiM	pf 12	13.	..	z50	95	95	95	....
18¼	13½	IndiM	pf2.25	13.	..	1	17⅜	17⅜	17⅜	....
29⅞	22¾	IndiM	pf3.63	13.	..	57	29⅛	28⅞	29	+ ⅛
29	22⅛	IndiGas	3.04	11.	9	14	27½	27¼	27¼	− ¼
29⅝	22	IndiPL	2.76	10.	8	236	26¾	26½	26⅝	− ⅛
17⅜	6⅜	Inexco	.14	1.7	11	x1531	8¼	7¾	8¼	+ ⅛
30	9½	Infmtc n		..	19	66	29¾	28¼	28¼	−1¼
51½	35½	IngerR	2.60	5.7	19	92	46½	45¼	45½	− ¾
33⅝	23½	IngR	pf 2.35	7.6	..	8	31¼	31	31	− ¼
33	18⅛	InldStl	.50	1.6	..	394	30⅝	30⅜	30⅜	− ⅛
25¼	12¼	Insilco	1b	4.2	26	156	24	23⅝	23¾	− ⅜
1⅞	½	InstInv		..	..	38	1¼	1⅛	1¼	....
45⅝	14	IntegRs		..	13	722	u46½	44⅝	46¼	+1⅝
30¼	9¼	IntgR wi		..	..	1	u31	31	31	+ ¾
36⅛	23½	IntgR	pf3.03	8.9	.	15	34	33¾	34	+ ⅜
27⅛	12⅜	IntRFn	2.95t	13.	23	84	22¼	21½	21⅞	− ½
19⅜	15	ItcpSe	2.10a	11.	..	x60	18⅝	18¼	18⅝	+ ¼
70½	35½	Interco	2.88	4.1	13	57	u70⅞	69¾	70⅞	+1⅛
30⅛	16⅝	Intrfst	1.20	6.5	5	2842	18¾	18¼	18½	− ⅛
38	22½	Intrlk	2.60	7.5	38	83	35	34½	34¾	+ ¼
21½	8½	IntAlu	.60	3.1	17	33	19⅜	19	19¼	+ ¼
103⅜	57½	IBM	3.44	3.4	14	6532	103¼	101¾	102⅛	− ⅛
30	17½	IntFlav	1.04	3.6	17	180	29½	28¾	28¾	− ½
7½	2¾	IntHarv		..	..	1348	6⅞	6½	6⅝	− ⅛
4	1	IntHr wt		..	..	1232	3½	3¼	3¼	− ⅛
15½	6¼	IntHr pf		..	..	35	15¼	14⅝	14⅝	− ⅜
25⅝	20½	IntHr	pf 3	13.	..	20	24½	24	24	....
40⅞	23½	IntMin	2.60	6.5	14	1935	40¼	39¾	39¾	− ⅜
37	29	IntMn	pf 4	12.	..	3	34	34	34	− ½
34¾	21½	IntMult	1.58e	4.6	8	56	34¾	34	34	− ½
58⅜	32¾	IntPapr	2.40	4.5	20	1046	54⅜	53¼	53¼	− ⅞
15¾	7⅜	IntRect		..	..	11	14	13⅞	14	− ⅛
37¼	22⅜	IntTT	2.76	7.3	8	5792	u37⅞	37	37⅝	+ ½
60½	37½	ITT	pfJ 4	6.5	.	1	u61½	61½	61½	+1½
59½	35¾	ITT	pfK 4	6.6	.	32	u60½	59½	60⅜	+ ⅞
56¾	39	ITT	pfO 5	8.6	.	10	u58	57	58	+1¼
45½	28	IntTT	pf2.25	4.8	.	3	u46½	45¾	46½	+1
62	38	IntTT	pf4.50	7.2	..	4	u62½	62	62½	+1

EXPLANATORY NOTES

(For New York and American Exchange listed issues)

Sales figures are unofficial.

The 52-Week High and Low columns show the highest and the lowest price of the stock in consolidated trading during the preceding 52 weeks plus the current week, but not the current trading day.

u–Indicates a new 52-week high. d–Indicates a new 52-week low.

g–Dividend or earnings in Canadian money. Stock trades in U.S. dollars. No yield or PE shown unless stated in U.S. money. n–New issue in the past 52 weeks. The high-low range begins with the start of trading and does not cover the entire 52 week period. s–Split or stock dividend of 25 per cent or more in the past 52 weeks. The high-low range is adjusted from the old stock. Dividend begins with the date of split or stock dividend. v–Trading halted on primary market.

Unless otherwise noted, rates of dividends in the foregoing table are annual disbursements based on the last quarterly or semi-annual declaration. Special or extra dividends or payments not designated as regular are identified in the following footnotes.

a–Also extra or extras. b–Annual rate plus stock dividend. c–Liquidating dividend. e–Declared or paid in preceding 12 months. i–Declared or paid after stock dividend or split up. j–Paid this year, dividend omitted, deferred or no action taken at last dividend meeting. k–Declared or paid this year, an accumulative issue with dividends in arrears. r–Declared or paid in preceding 12 months plus stock dividend. t–Paid in stock in preceding 12 months, estimated cash value on ex-dividend or ex-distribution date.

x–Ex-dividend or ex-rights. y–Ex-dividend and sales in full. z–Sales in full.

wd–When distributed. wi–When issued. ww–With warrants. xw–Without warrants.

vj–In bankruptcy or receivership or being reorganized under the Bankruptcy Act, or securities assumed by such companies.

Source: *Wall Street Journal*, March 28, 1983.

Consequently, investors will pay more for B than for the risky A, meaning that B's D/P and E/P ratios will be less than A's. Second, B's ratios may currently be less than A's because investors expect B's *average* profits to rise relative to A's and so are willing to pay more for B than for A. These considerations suggest that it is not possible merely by looking at D/P, E/P, and P/E ratios to say that they are either too high or too low. These ratios are less useful as measures of current returns on stocks than as indicators of expected future earnings and dividends. Firms that are expected to grow fastest, with the least risk, will have the highest prices and the lowest D/P and E/P ratios.

STOCK PRICES AND INTEREST RATES. It is sometimes said that increases in interest rates cause stock prices to fall. And indeed this is so if nothing else affecting stock prices is altered; for an increase in the discount rate that is applied to a dividend stream must reduce the present value of that stream. In the case presented in Equation (10.2), for example, a stock that pays a constant once-a-year dividend of $D = \$1$ will fetch a price $P_0 = \$20$ if the rate of interest is $R = 0.05$ but is worth only $P_0 = \$10$ if $R = 0.10$.

However, earnings and dividends do not in general remain unchanged in the face of fluctuations in interest rates because corporate profits tend to rise and fall with general economic activity and therefore with interest rates. In fact fluctuations in profits and expected profits *cause* fluctuations in interest rates as firms borrow more or less in response to the growth or decline of perceived profit opportunities. The following analysis will demonstrate that, under conditions of certainty and no taxes, stock prices must at any point in time be independent of interest rates.[15]

We begin by considering a typical firm that consists simply of M machines that each period, net of replacement and other costs, produce the equivalent of rM new machines. The real rate of return of this firm (and of all other firms because in a certain world all investments must earn the same rate of return) is r.

Let P_0 be the current price of a machine. The current value of our firm, S_0, is the value of its equipment, MP_0, which in turn is the present value of the net revenues, rMP_t, to be generated by that equipment:

$$(10.3) \qquad S_0 = MP_0 = \sum_{t=1}^{\infty} \frac{rMP_t}{(1 + R)^t}$$

where P_t is the price of a machine in the tth period and R is still the constant nominal rate of return on a bond. The price of a share of stock is S_0 divided by the number of shares outstanding. We assume for

---

15 These assumptions are relaxed in Chapter 18, which considers variations in inflation, interest rates, and stock prices in the presence of taxes.

simplicity that all net revenues, or earnings, are paid out as dividends.

We now consider the connections between r, P_t, and R. Suppose that all prices, including the firm's costs and the price of its output (machines), are expected to rise forever at the rate p per period (or to fall if p is negative). This means that the firm's tth-period earnings in the numerator of Equation (10.3) are $rMP_0(1 + p)^t$. But we must also adjust the denominator to take account of the dependence of the nominal rate of interest, R, on the real rate of interest, r, and the rate of inflation, p:[16]

(10.4) $$1 + R = (1 + r)(1 + p)$$

This is an equilibrium relationship in our constant, certain, no-tax nirvana because it implies the equality of returns to financial and real investments and, therefore, investor indifference between these investments. For example suppose the nominal rate of return on a typical bond, which promises coupons and a principal that are fixed in dollars, is $R = 0.0920$. Now suppose that a machine produces the equivalent of $r = 0.04$ new machines (net of costs) each period and that the price of machines rises at the rate $p = 0.05$. The return on an investment in this machine (or in the group of machines that constitutes our firm) is therefore $(1 + r)(1 + p) - 1 = (1.04)(1.05) - 1 = 0.0920$, and Equation (10.4) is satisfied. If that equation is not satisfied—if, for example, $1 + R = 1.08 < 1.0920 = (1 + r)(1 + p)$ —investors will attempt to sell bonds and buy machines (or claims on the earnings of machines, for example, shares of stock) until the price of bonds falls relative to the price of machines sufficiently to bring the rates of return on the two investments to equality.

Substituting Equation (10.4) into the denominator of Equation (10.3), remembering that the numerator is $rMP_0(1 + p)^t$, and calculating the sum give

(10.5)
$$S_0 = MP_0 = \sum_{t=1}^{\infty} \frac{rMP_0(1 + p)^t}{(1 + r)^t(1 + p)^t}$$

$$= rMP_0 \sum_{t=1}^{\infty} \frac{1}{(1 + r)^t} = rMP_0 \frac{1}{r} = MP_0$$

Equation (10.5) seems circular, but its apparent circularity merely illustrates two facts: the value of a real asset (such as a machine or a firm) is the present value of the profits from that asset, and the appropriate rate of discount is the rate of profit (because it equals the real rate of interest). As a consequence we cannot determine the

---

16 Equation (10.4) forms the basis of the discussion of interest rates and inflation in Chapters 18 to 20.

nominal value of a machine (P_0) or of the firm (S_0) by this equation alone. The real value of the firm, S_0/P_0, is its stock of machines, M. But nominal values depend upon prices in the economy, including P_0, as determined by the supply and demand for money.[17]

Equation (10.5) provides the following interesting insights: First, note that changes in the anticipated real rate of return, r, and/or rate of inflation, p, do not affect the value of the firm, S_0. Real and/or nominal increases in the rate of profit, $r(1 + p)$, are associated with increases in the rate of interest and therefore in the discount factor, $(1 + r)(1 + p)$, leaving the present value of profits (the value of the firm) unchanged. That is, once we take account of the connection between the anticipated rate of profit and the rate of interest, we see that stock prices are at any point in time unaffected by variations in the rate of interest.

We also see from Equation (10.5) that the nominal value of the firm changes over time at the same rate as the rate of inflation so that the real value of the firm remains constant.[18] This may be shown as follows, where $P_t = P_0(1 + p)^t$ and S_t are, respectively, the price of a machine and the value of the firm at time t. The firm's nominal value at time t is

(10.6) $$S_t = MP_t = MP_0(1 + p)^t$$

so that its real value is

(10.7) $$\frac{S_t}{P_0(1 + p)^t} = M = \text{constant}$$

Finally we may confirm that returns to stocks and bonds are equal. The nominal rate of return to a stockholder between times t and $t + 1$ is the sum of the appreciation in the stock's price, $S_{t+1} - S_t$, and the dividend, rMP_{t+1}, divided by the value of the stock at time t:

(10.8)

$$\frac{S_{t+1} - S_t + rMP_{t+1}}{S_t}$$

$$= \frac{MP_0(1 + p)^{t+1} - MP_0(1 + p)^t + rMP_0(1 + p)^{t+1}}{MP_0(1 + p)^t}$$

$$= (1 + p)(1 + r) - 1$$

---

17 And therefore require a complete macroeconomic model of money, prices, and interest rates, such as that presented in Chapter 20. The dependence of the value of capital on profits has important (destructive) implications for the regulatory pretense that utility rates can be set such that profits represent a fair return on a given value of capital.

18 The points of this and the preceding paragraph were made by John Williams (1938, pages 103 and 104) in the following way: "Because inflation itself makes stocks go up, most people think that the mere prospect of inflation should do so too. Yet this is not true, . . . [for] how can stocks be a hedge against inflation, protecting their owners during inflation, if they go up before inflation? They cannot discount the same event twice. No, they should respond but once to inflation, and that *during* inflation, step by step, dollar for dollar, with the rise in general prices."

Table 10.5

CORPORATION BONDS
Volume, $36,750,000

Bonds	Cur Yld	Vol	High	Low	Close	Net Chg
AMF 10s85	10.	33	99	98¾	98¾	...
AlaP 7⅞s02	12.	10	66¼	66¼	66¼	⅛
AlaP 7¾s02	12.	2	66⅜	66⅜	66⅜	+ ⅛
AlaP 8¼s03	12.	27	68½	67¾	67¾	– 2⅛
AlaP 9¾s04	12.	19	78⅞	78⅞	78⅞	– ⅛
AlaP 10⅞s05	12.	12	87⅞	87½	87½	+ ¾
AlaP 10½05	12.	20	84¼	83½	84¼	+ ¼
AlaP 9½08	12.	16	77¼	76⅜	76⅜	– ⅛
AlaP 9⅝08	12.	30	77½	77⅛	77⅛	– ⅜
AlaP 12⅝10	13	38	99	99	99	....
AlaP 15¼10	14.	58	111¾	111⅛	111¼	⅝
AlaP 14¾91	14.	3	109	109	109	+ 2
AlaP 17⅜11	15.	31	118	117½	117½	– ½
AlaP 18¼89	15.	8	120	120	120	– 2
AlskH 16¼94	14.	20	115½	115½	115½	+ 1½
AlskH 18⅜01	15.	5	124	124	124	– 3
AlskH 15s92	14.	15	108¼	108¼	108¼	– ¾
Allgl 9s89	11.	1	83¾	83¾	83¾	+ 1⅝
AlldC 9s2000	12.	1	76½	76½	76½	....
AlldC zr92		5	35½	35½	35½	– ⅜
AlldC zr96s	..	77	24¼	24¼	24¼	– ⅜
AlldC zr98s	..	38	21	21	21	.....
AlldC zr2000s	..	218	15	14¾	15	.....
AlldC 6s88	7.8	134	77½	76¾	76⅞	– ⅛
AlldSt 9½07	cv	5	118	118	118	.....
AlsCha 10.35s99	14.	8	75⅛	75⅛	75⅛	+ ⅜
AlsCha 16s91	16.	78	102	100¾	101⅛	+ 1⅛
AllstF 7⅞s87	8.6	16	91⅛	91	91⅛	+ ¼
AllstF 9⅝s86	9.9	5	97⅝	97⅝	97⅝	– ⅞
Alcoa 6s92	8.5	28	71	71	71	+ ½
Alcoa 9s95	11.	5	83¼	83¼	83¼	– 2¼
AMAX 8s86	9.0	3	88¾	88¾	88¾	....
AMAX 8½84	8.7	50	98½	98⅛	98⅛	– 5-32
Amax 14¼90	14.	2	105	105	105	+ ½
AFoP 4.8s87	6.2	5	77¼	77¼	77¼	– ¾
AAirl 11s88	12.	15	96½	95⅛	95⅛	– 1⅞
AAirl 10s89	11.	10	94½	94½	94½	+ 2⅜
ACan 13¼93	13.	37	105	104⅜	105	+ ⅝
AExC 8½s85	8.9	12	95⅜	95⅜	95⅜	– ⅞
AExC 8½s86	9.0	11	94⅜	94⅜	94⅜	+ ⅜
AmGn 11s07	cv	83	130½	130	130½	+ ½
AmGn 11s08	cv	186	130¾	129½	130¾	+ 2¼
AInvt 8¾s89	11.	15	79½	79½	79½	+ 2⅜
AmMed 8s00	cv	20	220	220	220	+ 14½
AmMot 6s88	cv	69	81	78½	81	+ 4
AmStr 12s90	12.	10	100¼	100¼	100¼	– ¾
ATT 3¼s84	3.5	95	92⅞	92⅝	92⅝	– ⅜
ATT 4⅜s85	4.8	95	92	91⅝	91⅝	– ⅝
ATT 2⅝s86	3.1	122	85¼	84⅜	84⅜	– ½
ATT 2⅞s87	3.5	30	83	82⅝	82⅝	– ⅜
ATT 3⅞s90	5.3	67	72½	72	72½	+ ¼
ATT 8¾00	11.	396	81½	80⅞	80⅞	– ⅜
ATT 7s01	10.	127	68⅛	67½	67⅞	– ½
ATT 7⅛s03	10.	156	68½	67¾	68	– ⅛
ATT 8.80s05	11.	789	80⅞	79¾	80⅜	+ ⅜
ATT 8⅝s07	11.	198	78¾	78	78	– ⅜
ATT 10⅜90	11.	468	98⅜	98⅛	98⅛	– ½
ATT 13¼91	12.	163	107⅜	107	107¼	– ⅜
Ames 10s95	13.	5	78⅝	78⅝	78⅝	+ ⅛
Amfac 5¼94	cv	4	73½	73½	73½	+ ½
Ampx 5½94	cv	31	94	93¼	93¼	– 1¼
Ancp 13⅞02	cv	26	145	143	145	+ 2
Anhr 11⅞12	12.	10	97¼	97¼	97¼	– 2¼
Anxtr 8¼03	cv	5	115	115	115	+ 4
Arco 8s84	8.1	10	98 25-32	98¾	98¾	...
ArizP 10⅜00	12.	5	90	90	90	+ 1
ArizP 12⅛09	12.	46	99½	99½	99½	...
ArmS 4.35s84	4.6	10	94½	94½	94½	– 2
ArmS 8.7s95	11.	10	79	77	79	+ 3½
AsCp 8.2s87	8.9	25	92½	91	92½	+ 3
Atchsn 4s95	7.3	24	55	54⅞	55	+ 2⅞
Atchn 4s95r	7.7	24	52¼	52¼	52¼	....
ARich 7.7s00	11.	35	72⅜	72⅜	72⅜	– 1⅛
Augat 8¼05	cv	30	126	126	126	+ 1
AvcoC 5½93	cv	102	74½	73	74	+ ⅞
AvcoC 7½93	11.	5	69⅝	69⅝	69⅝	....
AvcoF 7⅝97	11.	5	69	69	69	+ ⅛
AvcoF 8½s84	8.6	10	98⅜	98⅜	98⅜	....

EXPLANATORY NOTES
(For New York and American Bonds)

Yield is current yield. cv–Convertible. ct-Certificates. d-Deep discount. f-Dealt in flat. m–Matured bonds, negotiability impaired by maturity. na–No accrual. r–Registered. st–Stamped. wd–When distributed. ww–With warrants. x–Ex interest. xw–Without warrants. zr–Zero coupon.

vi–In bankruptcy or receivership or being reorganized under the Bankruptcy Act, or securities assumed by such companies.

Yearly highs and lows reflect the previous 52 weeks plus the current week but not the latest trading.

New York Exchange Bonds

Friday, March 25, 1983

Total Volume $37,190,000

SALES SINCE JANUARY 1

1983	1982	1981
$2,153,997,000	$1,249,180,000	$1,029,942,000

	Domestic Fri.	Domestic Thu.	All Issues Fri.	All Issues Thu.
Issues traded	1070	1061	1080	1075
Advances	440	579	443	587
Declines	434	292	439	295
Unchanged	196	190	198	193
New highs	124	144	125	149
New lows	1	2	1	2

Dow Jones Bond Averages

–1981– High	–1981– Low	–1982– High	–1982– Low	–1983– High	–1983– Low		Friday –1983–		Friday –1982–		Friday –1981–	
65.78	54.99	71.52	55.67	74.06	70.78	20 Bonds	74.06	+ .17	58.28	– .18	61.83	– .33
66.18	53.61	72.71	53.80	73.39	69.62	10 Utilities	73.32	+ .04	57.00	– .41	61.30	– .21
66.15	56.32	71.23	57.36	74.81	71.51	10 Industrial	74.81	+ .30	59.56	+ .05	62.37	– .44

Bonds	Cur Yld	Vol	High	Low	Close	Net Chg
CnNG 8⅝99	11.	13	79⅜	79⅜	79⅜	+ 2¾
CnPw 4½88	6.4	6	70⅝	70⅝	70⅝	+ 1
CnPw 4⅝89	6.7	1	69	69	69	– 1
CnPw 5⅞96	10.	40	56½	56	56	– ¾
CnPw 6⅞98	11.	1	61⅛	61⅛	61⅛	+ 1⅞
CnPw 6⅝98	11.	18	57¾	57½	57¾	+ ⅜
CnPw 8⅛01	12.	1	66	66	66	+ ½
CnPw 7½02J	12.	3	62⅝	62⅝	62⅝	+ 1⅝
CnPw 7½02O	13.	29	62	59¾	59¾	– ⅜
CnPw 8⅝03	12.	42	69¾	69¼	69⅝	+ ⅞
CnPw 11⅜94	13.	3	91	89⅛	89⅛	– 1⅞
CnPw 9s06	13.	5	72	72	72	.....
CnPw 8⅞07	13.	15	69½	69½	69½	+ ⅛
CnPw 9s08	12.	7	72⅝	71	72⅝	+ 3⅜
CtlAir 3½92	cv	49	48	47½	47½	– 1⅛
Ct IC 8½85	9.1	3	93⅜	93⅜	93⅜	+ ⅛
Ct IC 9.20s87	9.6	10	95¾	95¾	95¾	+ ⅜
CrnPd 5¾92	8.5	5	67⅞	67⅞	67⅞	....
Crane 7s93	10.	5	67	67	67	....
Crane 7s94	11.	9	63⅜	63⅛	63⅛	+ ⅛
CrdF 8.2s87	9.2	27	89	89	89	– ¼
CrdF 10¼89	11.	5	91¾	91¾	91¾	– 1¼
CrdF zr90s	..	25	41¾	41¾	41¾	+ 1¾
CrwnZ 8⅞00	12.	9	73	73	73	....
Dana d5⅞06	cv	56	64½	64	64	– ½
Dart 4¼97	cv	29	86⅜	85½	85½	– ½
Datpnt 8⅞06	cv	81	74½	74⅛	74½	.....
Dayc 5¾94	cv	36	63	63	63	.....
Dayc 6s94	cv	22	67½	67½	67½	.....
DaytP 8s03	12.	30	68⅜	67⅜	67⅜	+ 1¾
Deere 10½85	11.	20	99⅝	99⅝	99⅝	– ⅞
DeerCr 8s84	8.2	25	97⅛	97⅛	97⅛	– ½
DelPw 6⅜97	10.	5	64	64	64	...
Denny 9½07	cv	10	113	113	113	– 1
DetEd 9s99	12.	130	74½	74⅛	74¼	+ ½
DetEd 9.15s00	12.	40	74¾	73¾	74¾	+ 1
DetEd 8⅛01	12.	1	67¼	67¼	67¼	+ ¼
DetEd 7⅜01	12.	60	60⅝	60⅜	60⅜	– 1⅜
DetEd 7½03	12.	15	61⅞	61¼	61⅞	+ ¼
DetEd 9⅞04	13.	39	78	77⅝	77⅝	– ¼
DetEd 11⅞00	13.	26	94⅞	93	94⅞	+ 1⅞
DetEd 10⅝06	13.	18	84	82½	84	.....
Dow 6.70s98	10.	20	64⅝	64⅝	64⅝	+ ⅛
Dow 8⅞2000	11.	9	78⅛	78	78⅛	– ⅞
Dow 8½s05	11.	53	75⅜	74⅞	74⅞	+ ⅜
Dow 8⅝08	11.	131	75⅞	75	75⅞	+ ¾
Dresr 8.65s85	9.0	2	96½	96⅜	96⅜	+ ⅜
duPnt 8.45s04	11.	30	76⅜	76⅜	76⅜	+ ¼
duPnt 8½06	11.	25	77	76⅛	77	+ ⅛
duPnt 14s91	12.	5	112¼	112¼	112¼	+ ¼
duPnt d6s01	10.	5	58½	58½	58½	+ ⅛
DukeP 7⅜02	11.	10	64¾	64¾	64¾	.....
DukeP 7¾03	11.	20	68¾	67½	67½	– 1¼
DukeP 8⅛03	12.	7	71	70½	70½	– ½
DukeP 9½05	12.	17	80½	80⅜	80⅜	+ ⅝
DukeP 8⅜06	12.	68	72⅜	72¼	72¼	– ⅛
DukeP 8⅛07	12.	90	70½	70	70½	+ 2⅛
DukeP 9⅝08	12.	10	80⅜	80	80⅜	+ 1¾
DukeP 10⅞09	12.	10	89⅜	89⅜	89⅜	– ⅝
DukeP 14⅜87	13.	5	110	110	110	+ ⅞
DukeP 13⅛10	13.	2	104⅝	104⅝	104⅝	+ 2⅜
DuqL 8¾00	12.	15	73⅜	73⅜	73⅜	– 1⅛
DuqL 10⅛09	12.	10	82	82	82	+ 1⅝
EasAir 5s92	cv	16	50¾	50½	50¾	+ ¼
EasAir 4¾93	cv	98	50	50	50	+ 1½
GlfWn 7s03A	12.	200	60⅛	59½	60⅛	+ ⅞
GlfWn 7s03B	12.	23	59½	59¼	59½	+ ½
GlfMO 4s44	7.4	29	53¾	50	53¾	– ¼
GlfOil 10.80s09	11.	32	97	96½	97	– ½
GlfRes 12½04	13.	20	93½	93½	93½	.....
Hallb 9¼00	11.	63	85½	85¼	85¼	– ¾
Hallb 16s88	14.	60	113¾	113	113	+ ½
HartH 8s05	cv	1	115½	115½	115½	+ 2
Hawn 11¼04	12.	10	90⅝	90⅝	90⅝	.....
Hellr 7¾92	11.	15	73⅛	73⅛	73⅛	– 1⅜
Hellr 8.1s87	9.2	1	88¼	88¼	88¼	– ¾
Hercul 6½99	cv	29	106	105	105½	+ 1
Heubn 4½97	cv	25	82	82	82	.....
HoCp 8½08	cv	55	119	114	119	+ 8
HousF 9s00	12.	10	78	78	78	+ 1⅞
HouF 8.45s97	11.	15	75⅛	75⅛	75⅛	– ⅝
HousF 8.2s07	12.	7	71⅛	71⅛	71⅛	+ 1⅝
HousL 5½85	cv	25	94	93⅞	94	.....
HugheT 9s08	12.	5	77⅝	77⅝	77⅝	+ 1⅝
HugheT 9½06	cv	115	87½	87⅛	87½	+ ¼
Humn 11.7s98	12.	69	96	95⅝	95⅝	.....
HuntIR 9⅞04	15.	10	64⅜	63¾	64⅜	+ ⅝
Hutton 12s05	13.	64	95	94⅛	94⅛	– ⅞
Hutton 9½05	cv	52	139⅝	136½	136½	– 1½
IBM Cr 14⅜86	13.	25	110⅞	110¼	110¾	– ¼
ICI 8⅞03	12.	5	74	74	74	– 1
ITTF 10½95	12.	10	89	89	89	– 4
ITTF 11¼85	11.	33	101½	101½	101½	– ⅛
ITTF 11s88	11.	1	102	102	102	+ ½
IllBel 7⅝06	11.	1	67⅞	67⅞	67⅞	– ⅜
IllBel 8s04	11.	5	71⅜	71⅜	71⅜	+ ⅜
IllBel 8¼16	11.	1	71⅞	71⅞	71⅞	+ ½
IllPw 8⅞08	12.	37	75⅛	75	75	+ ⅜
IllPw 11⅜87	11.	10	103⅞	101¼	103⅞	+ 3⅜
Inco 12⅜10	13.	14	93⅞	92½	92½	– 1⅜
InMic 11s83	11.	10	100⅛	100⅛	100⅛	.....
InMic 13⅞87	13.	3	105	105	105	.....
IndBel 8⅛11	11.	22	71⅜	70⅜	71⅜	+ ½
IndBel 8⅛17	11.	10	71	71	71	– 2½
Inexc 8½00	cv	63	68	67½	67⅝	– ⅜
IngR 8¾s85	9.0	35	97	97	97	+ 1⅝
InldStl 4½89	6.6	89	68	67	68	+ ¾
InldStl 9½00	13.	5	76	76	76	+ 3
InldStl 11¼90	12.	1	96¾	96¾	96¾	+ 2¾
Intrfst 9s83	9.1	110	99 19-32	98¾	98¾	– 29-32
Intrfst 7¾05	cv	77	89	87½	87½	– ½
IBM 9½86	9.7	123	98⅛	97¾	97⅞	.....
IBM 9⅜04	11.	217	88½	87¾	87¾	– ½
IntHrv 4⅝88	8.7	25	53	53	53	+ 2⅞
IntHrv 4.8s91	11.	2	45	45	45	+ 2½
IntHrv 6¼98	14.	2	44¼	44	44¼	.....
IntHrv 8⅝95	17.	171	52	51¼	51⅞	– 1
IntHrv 9s04	17.	151	52¾	52	52⅛	+ ⅛
IntHrv 18s02	21.	303	87¼	86	86⅝	+ ⅝
InHvC 8⅝91	15.	5	59	59	59	– ½
InHvC 7⅝93	14.	20	53⅜	53	53⅜	+ 1½
InHvC 7½94	14.	27	52	50⅞	52	+ ⅛
InHvC 9s84	10.	192	90⅛	90	90⅛	.....
InHvC 8.35s86	12.	139	69½	68⅞	69¼	+ ¼
InHvC 13½88	17.	169	79½	77⅛	79	+ 1½
IPap 8.85s95	10.	55	84⅝	84⅜	84⅝	– ⅜
IPap 4¼96	cv	10	161½	161½	161½	.....
IntTT 4.9s87	5.9	14	82⅞	82⅞	82⅞	+ 2
IntTT 8.9s95	10.	2	84⅞	84⅞	84⅞	+ 1⅞
IntTT 8⅝00	cv	26	145	144	145	+ 3⅛

Source: *Wall Street Journal*, March 28, 1983.

which is seen from Equation (10.4) to be equal to the rate of return, R, earned by bondholders.

A corollary to these results is that stocks are a perfect inflation hedge. This may be seen from Equation (10.8) by deflating end-of-period values (S_{t+1} and rMP_{t+1}) by $1 + p$ to give a real rate of return on stocks equal to r, which is the real rate of return on the firm's equipment and, in a world of certainty and no taxes, is independent of the rate of inflation.

All these results are contingent on the assumptions of certainty and no taxes. The latter assumption is relaxed in Chapter 18, where we consider the conditions under which stock may not be an inflation hedge.

Bonds

BONDS ARE LONG-TERM OBLIGATIONS TO PAY SPECIFIC AMOUNTS AT SPECIFIC TIMES. The promises of most corporate bonds are similar to those of the U.S. Treasury bonds discussed in Chapter 6. Each promises a series of relatively small semiannual (coupon) payments and a final large (principal) payment upon maturity. For example, ITT's 8.9s of 1995 (the first issue in Table 10.2) represent promises to pay $44.50 each April 1 and October 1 until 1995, with a final principal payment of $1,000 on October 1, 1995, to the owner of one of these bonds with a "face value" of $1,000. The owner of a bond with a $10,000 face value receives $445 coupons and a $10,000 principal. As with stocks, there is an active secondary market in the bonds of large firms. Part of this market is conducted in the Bond Room of the NYSE. We see from Table 10.5 that on March 25, 1983, the closing price of ITT's 8.9s of 1995 was $84.875 per $100 face value. Corporate bonds, like U.S. Treasury bonds, are quoted as percentages of face value.

BOND INDENTURES. A bond is defined by its indenture, which is a contract between the debtor, the bondholders, and a trustee, who is entrusted with the tasks of receiving payments into the sinking fund, making payments to bondholders, and attempting to ensure that the company performs its part of the bargain. The most common provisions of corporate bond indentures are summarized below, as far as possible in relation to the selections from Moody's report of ITT's capital structure in Tables 10.2 and 10.3.

1. Most bonds are *callable,* at the company's discretion, on dates and at prices stipulated in the indenture.[19] For example, ITT may

---

19 Many U.S. Treasury bonds are also callable (all at par), as indicated by the ranges of dates (from first call to maturity) in Tables 6.2 and 6.4. The daily financial press does not indicate call dates for corporate bonds. A convenient reference for call dates and other information about bonds is *Moody's Bond Record.*

redeem as many of its 8.9s of 1995 as it wishes, with 30 days' notice, on September 30, 1985, for $102.67 (plus accrued interest) per $100 face value. The excess of the call price over the face value is the *call premium,* and is $2.67 on September 30, 1985, for the 8.9s of 1995.

Suppose yields fall between 1983 and 1985 such that 10-year bonds in the same risk class (rated A2 by Moody's) are yielding 7 percent at the end of August 1985. The company decides to call $10,000,000 (in face value) of its 8.9s on September 30, to be paid for with funds raised by issuing $10,267,000 of 10-year, 7 percent bonds at par.[20] The annual coupon bill on the redeemed 8.9s would have been $10,000,000 (0.089) = $890,000, compared with that on the new 7s of $10,267,000 (0.07) = $718,690. Neglecting underwriting and other costs of the new issue, the substitution of the 7s of 1995 for the 8.9s of 1995 has reduced the company's annual interest cost by $171,310.

It may be shown[21] that the price of an 8.9 percent, 10-year, noncallable bond with a 7 percent yield to maturity is 113.50 (as a percentage of face value). But ITT's callable issue will not fetch this price unless you can find someone to pay $113.50 for a bond that is likely to be called next month at $102.67 (plus accrued interest of $4.45).[22] A callable bond is like the familiar fixed-rate home mortgage in the sense that the borrower may refinance his debt when interest rates fall below the rate at which he originally borrowed.[23] This places the lender (bondholder or financial institution) at a disadvantage and reduces the value of his investment. If the Friendly Savings and Loan lends to Mr. and Mrs. John Q. Public at 8.9 percent in the form of a 25-year mortgage or if Mr. Bondholder lends to a corporation at 8.9 percent by buying a bond due in 25 years, neither can count on earning 8.9 percent for the full 25 years because in both cases the borrower may refinance his debt at a lower rate whenever rates fall. But if rates rise, the mortgage borrower and the corporation will find it advantageous to keep their 8.9 percent debt outstanding as long as possible. The advantages conferred by callable securities upon borrowers and the disadvantages imposed on lenders mean that fixed-

---

20 See Edwin Elton and Martin Gruber (1971) for an application of dynamic programming to the firm's decision of when to call bonds based on its expectations of future yields.

21 And *will* be shown if the student does problem 1 at the end of this chapter. The relations between the prices and yields to maturity of corporate bonds are identical with those for U.S. bonds presented in Chapter 6 except that 30-day months are assumed for corporate bonds. Corporate bond yields to maturity are not reported in the financial press. The *current yields* reported for these bonds are the annual coupons as percentages of the most recent closing prices, for example, 10/98.75 = 10 percent to the nearest percentage point for AMF's 10s of 1985 at the top of Table 10.5.

22 Problem 2 at the end of the chapter asks the student to calculate the price of this bond on August 31, 1985, when the yield curve is flat at 7 percent per annum (about 0.6 percent per month).

23 The call features of these securities usually differ in detail, one being specified by the bond indenture whereas the mortgage may be called any time at par (that is, by paying the present value of future payments using the contract rate as the rate of discount). Prepayment penalties on mortgages are analogous to call premiums on bonds.

rate mortgages and callable bonds must pay higher yields than otherwise identical noncallable securities.[24]

Empirical studies of the value of call provisions have been hindered by the scarcity of noncallable bonds. However, Frank Jen and James Wert (1966, 1968)[25] found that new issues subject to immediate call tended to pay higher yields than bonds of the same quality with deferred call features—such as ITT's 8.9s of 1995, which were issued in 1970 with first call in 1980. This differential tends to be greatest during periods of high yields, when investors apparently place a high probability on the chance that yields will fall, that is, that market prices will rise, perhaps above call prices, inducing companies to redeem their immediately callable bonds. The excess yield on immediately callable new issues tends to be near zero when yields are low so that investors expect prices to fall. Simple examples of these tendencies are presented in Table 10.6.[26]

2. Most long-term corporate bonds have *sinking funds*. This means that, usually after an initial grace period, the company is obligated to retire a debt issue according to a sinking-fund schedule specified in the indenture. For example at least $6 million of ITT's 8.9s of 1995 must be retired each year during 1980 to 1994, leaving no more than $10 million to be redeemed at maturity. The company may meet the sinking-fund schedule either by buying bonds in the market (which it will do when the market price is less than 100) or by calling randomly selected bonds at par (when the market price exceeds 100). The phrase "plus similar optional payments" in the sinking-fund indentures in Table 10.3 means that the company may, if it chooses, call double the required amount at par.

Sinking funds appeal to the holders of risky issues, who are thereby given some assurance that the firm will retire its debt gradually instead of having to pay a very large amount at maturity. Of large, long-

---

24 A few bonds have *reverse* call features. For example, Beneficial Corporation's 8s of 2001, which were issued in 1976, could not be called by the company and provided that the "holder of any deb. may irrevocably elect to have his deb. mature on June 15, 1983 or any June 15 thereafter thru June 15, 2000 by giving notice and surrendering such deb. to Co. between Feb. 15 and Mar. 15 of such year" (*Moody's Bank & Finance Manual,* 1982, page 2540).

25 See James Van Horne (1978, Chapter 7) for a discussion of these and other studies of the influence of callability. More recent studies by Timothy Cook and Patric Hendershott (1978) and William Marshall and Jess Yawitz (1981) have tended to confirm the results of Jen and Wert.

26 Tildes denote random variables, and the expectations operator is indicated by E. More realistic (and more complicated) examples have been presented by Arleigh Hess and Willis Winn (1962), Gordon Pye (1966), and Jess Yawitz, Kevin Maloney, and William Marshall (1983). The examples in Table 10.6 derive conditions in which both borrowers and lenders are indifferent between callable and noncallable bonds. But William Marshall and Jess Yawitz (1980) have argued that the "tax laws [ignored in our examples] create a bias in favor of the inclusion of call provisions on corporate bonds. Since call premiums are deductible from ordinary income as an expense of the borrower, but are treated by the lender as a capital gain, the exercise of the call provision results in a reduction in the aggregate tax liability. . . . Borrower and lender determine and divide the net value of the call provision through choices over the terms of the call." Marshall and Yawitz present examples of optimal call provisions in a variety of circumstances.

Table 10.6   Simple Examples of the Value of Call Provisions

A. Yields Are Expected with Certainty to Fall

Assume two newly issued 2-year bonds. Each has a face value of $100 and pays one annual $10 coupon at the end of each year. One bond is not callable, and the other is callable at par at the end of the first year. Assume that the noncallable bond initially sells at par, $P_n = \$100$, so that its yield to maturity is $Y_n = 0.10$:

(10.9)
$$P_n = \frac{C}{1 + Y_n} + \frac{C + F}{(1 + Y_n)^2} = \frac{\$10}{1.10} + \frac{\$110}{(1.10)^2} = \$100$$

Suppose 1-year yields are expected at the end of 1 year to be $Y_1 = 0.05$. The issuer of the callable bond will exercise his call option because he can redeem the outstanding promise to pay $110 in the second year with $100 raised by issuing a promise to pay $105.

Assuming that all investors reinvest their first-year receipts at $Y_1 = 0.05$, the terminal values of investments in callable and noncallable bonds are $T_c = \$110(1.05) = \$115.50$, and $T_n = \$10(1.05) + \$110 = \$120.50$.

The price of the callable bond at issue, P_c, will be such that the two-period returns on callable and noncallable bonds are equal, that is, such that

$$\frac{T_c}{P_c} = \frac{T_n}{P_n} \qquad \text{or} \qquad \frac{\$115.50}{P_c} = \frac{\$120.50}{\$100} \qquad \text{or} \qquad P_c = \$95.85$$

which, substituting P_c for P_n in Equation (10.9) and remembering that $C = \$10$ and $F = \$100$, implies a yield to maturity of $Y_c = 0.1247$. The value of the call provision is $4.15 (in dollars), or 2.47 percent (in yield).

B. Yields Are Expected with Certainty to Rise

Suppose that 1-year yields are expected at the end of 1 year to be $Y_1 = 0.15$. The call option will not be exercised because the issuer will not exchange a debt of $110 for a debt of $115. The callable bond has the same expected (with certainty) return as the noncallable bond and will therefore sell for the same price and yield. The call provision has no value.

C. Uncertainty: Yields May Either Rise or Fall

Suppose that Y_1 may with equal probabilities be either 0.05 or 0.15. The expected terminal values of the two bonds are

$$E\tilde{T}_c = 0.5[\$110(1.05)] + 0.5[\$10(1.15) + \$110] = \$118.50$$

and

$$E\tilde{T}_n = 0.5[\$10(1.05) + \$110] + 0.5[\$10(1.15) + \$110] = \$121$$

Assume that (risk-neutral) investors are indifferent between the two bonds only when their expected two-period returns are the same so that the initial price of the callable bond is such that

$$\frac{E\tilde{T}_c}{P_c} = \frac{E\tilde{T}_n}{P_n} \qquad \text{or} \qquad \frac{\$118.50}{P_c} = \frac{\$121}{\$100} \qquad \text{or} \qquad P_c = \$97.93$$

which implies a yield to maturity of $Y_c = 0.1121$, and the value of the call provision is $2.07 (in dollars), or 1.21 percent (in yield).

term debt issues[27] in 1981 about 85 percent of industrial issues, 30 percent of utility issues, and no U.S. Treasury issues were bound by sinking-fund provisions.

3. The greatest part of most bond indentures is devoted to the *security* of bondholders' claims. A common form of security is provided by *mortgage bonds,* which are secured by mortgages on all or specified parts of the company's property. Unsecured bonds are called *debentures.* Most utility bonds are secured by mortgages although ITT's bonds are debentures. But notice that the 8.9s of 1995 are protected by the provision that they become mortgage bonds if (with certain exceptions) ITT acquires any mortgage indebtedness. Many bond indentures also limit the company's freedom to "sell and lease-back" its property.[28]

The security of bonds also depends on their *seniority,* that is, on their place in line for the company's funds in the event of bankruptcy. For example the claims of *subordinated debentures,* such as ITT's 8⅝s of 2000, are junior to the claims of other debentures, such as the 8.9s of 1995.[29] A similar ranking also exists among mortgage bonds. For example *junior (second) mortgage* bonds are secured by claims on whatever is left of the proceeds from the sale of property after the claims of senior (or first) mortgages have been satisfied.

RISKY ACTIVITIES, LEVERAGE, AND BOND SECURITY. Indentures attempt to provide security for bondholders by means of *covenants* entered into by the firm that, for example, require it to keep mortgaged property insured and in good repair, to pay its taxes, and to maintain working capital at or above specified dollar amounts or proportions of long-term debt. Restrictions may also be imposed on the firm's freedom to create senior or equal claims, to dispose of its property, to pay dividends beyond specified amounts relative to earnings and capital,[30] or to accumulate total liabilities beyond certain proportions of total assets.[31] Nevertheless, in spite of these and other attempts to secure debt, there may be, in the absence of a covenant that transfers control

27 Exceeding $5 million and 10 years. The percentages for private issues are based on Drexel Burnham Lambert's *Public Offerings of Corporate Securities,* 1981.
   Thomas Ho and Ronald Singer (1984) have pointed out that sinking funds exert opposing effects on yields. First, the amortization feature shortens a bond issue's average maturity and therefore reduces risk, which lowers the required yield. Second, the firm's options to retire bonds either at the market price or at par and to choose the amounts retired reduce bondholder expected returns and therefore raise the required yield for the same reason that callable issues require higher yields.

28 An example is ITT's 10s of 2000 (*Moody's Industrial Manual,* 1982, pages 1615 and 1616).

29 Notice from Table 10.3 that the 8.9s have a higher rating (A2) than the 8⅝s (A3).

30 See the "Dividend Restrictions" in Table 10.3. Also see Avner Kalay (1982) for a discussion of dividend constraints and their probable effects on corporate behavior. He found that all of a random sample of 150 firms in *Moody's Industrial Manual* in fact paid fewer dividends than permitted by their indentures.

31 See Jules Bogen (1964, Chapter 14) for more detail regarding bond covenants. Clifford Smith and Jerold Warner (1979) discuss possible rationales of popular covenants.

Table 10.7   Returns to Debt and Equity from a Risky Venture

Definitions and Assumptions

$\tilde{R}_a$, $\tilde{R}_s$, $\tilde{R}_b$ = uncertain rates of return on assets, equity, and debt
C_b = contract rate of interest on debt
S, B, A (= $S + B$) = initial values of equity, debt, and assets
$\tilde{S}_1$, $\tilde{B}_1$ = end-of-period values of equity and debt
Tildes denote uncertain (random) variables.

The firm's assets are sold after one period, and the proceeds are paid first to the creditors and then to the owners.

Leverage and the Returns to Debt and Equity

The end-of-period value of equity is the greater of the value of the assets less debt or zero, where the latter value applies if asset value is not sufficient to repay the debt:

(10.10) $$\tilde{S}_1 = \max[(1 + \tilde{R}_a)A - (1 + C_b)B, \quad 0]$$

Substituting $S + B$ for A and rearranging, the rate of return on equity is

(10.11) $$\tilde{R}_s = \max\left[\frac{\tilde{S}_1 - S}{S}, -1\right] = \max\left[\tilde{R}_a + \frac{(\tilde{R}_a - C_b)B}{S}, -1\right]$$

The end-of-period value of debt is the smaller of the promised payment of principal and interest or the value of assets (in the event of default):

(10.12) $$\tilde{B}_1 = \min[(1 + C_b)B, \quad (1 + \tilde{R}_a)A]$$

The rate of return to creditors is therefore

(10.13) $$\tilde{R}_b = \min\left[C_b, \quad \tilde{R}_a + \frac{(1 + \tilde{R}_a)S}{B}\right]$$

of the firm from stockholders to creditors, no limit to the risk that a company might impose on its creditors. This is a serious problem for creditors because there are usually strong incentives for the stockholders to increase the risk of existing debt.

Consider a simple one-period case in which a group forms a corporation by putting up $1 of their own money and borrowing $9 at 10 percent from credulous investors.[32] The funds are applied to the purchase of assets costing $10. The stockholders have two ventures under consideration: One is a safe project that will bring a certain return of $1, or 10 percent, on their assets and will enable them to repay their debt in full and at the same time earn 10 percent on their equity; they also have an opportunity to engage in a risky venture with a fifty-fifty chance of increasing the value of their assets by 120 percent or losing everything. In the event of success, the value of assets is $22, the creditors are paid $9.90, and the remaining $12.10 is kept by

---

32 See Eugene Fama and Merton Miller (1972, pages 179 and 180) for another numerical example.

Table 10.7   (continued)

Consider two cases: In both, $S = \$1$, $B = \$9$, and there is a fifty-fifty chance that $\tilde{R}_a$ will be $+1.20$ or -1; the only difference in initial conditions is that $C_b = 0.10$ in case A and $C_b = 1.20$ in case B:

Case A.

$$S = \$1, B = \$9, C_b = 0.10$$

Outcome 1. $\tilde{R}_a = 1.20$.

$$\tilde{S}_1 = \$22 - \$9.90 = \$12.10; \quad \tilde{R}_s = \frac{\$12.10 - \$1}{\$1} = 11.10; \quad \tilde{R}_b = \frac{\$9.90 - \$9}{\$9} = 0.10$$

Outcome 2. $\tilde{R}_a = -1$.

$$\tilde{S}_1 = 0; \quad \tilde{R}_s = \frac{0 - \$1}{\$1} = -1; \quad \tilde{R}_b = \frac{0 - \$9}{\$9} = -1$$

Expected outcome

$$E\tilde{R}_a = \frac{1.20 - 1}{2} = 0.10; \quad E\tilde{R}_s = \frac{11.10 - 1}{2} = 5.05; \quad E\tilde{R}_b = \frac{0.10 - 1}{2} = -0.45$$

Case B.

$$S = \$1, B = \$9, C_b = 1.20$$

Outcome 1. $\tilde{R}_a = 1.20$.

$$\tilde{S}_1 = \$22 - \$19.80 = \$2.20; \quad \tilde{R}_s = \frac{\$2.2 - \$1}{\$1} = 1.20; \quad \tilde{R}_b = \frac{\$19.8 - \$9}{\$9} = 1.20$$

Outcome 2. $\tilde{R}_a = -1$.

$$\tilde{S}_1 = 0; \quad \tilde{R}_s = \tilde{R}_b = -1$$

Expected outcome

$$E\tilde{R}_a = E\tilde{R}_s = E\tilde{R}_b = \frac{1.2 - 1}{2} = 0.10$$

the owners, who have gained $11.10 on an investment of $1. In the event of failure, the assets are worth nothing, the creditors lose their $9, and the owners lose their $1. The expected returns to equity and debt from the 120-percent-or-nothing venture are 505 and -45 percent, respectively. These results are shown in case A of Table 10.7.

Most of the results in Table 10.7 follow from Equation (10.11), which shows that the rate of return on equity ($\tilde{R}_s$) responds positively to the excess of the rate of return on assets over the contract rate of interest on debt ($\tilde{R}_a - C_b$) and the firm's leverage as measured by its debt/equity (B/S) ratio—that is, by the proportion of the firm's activities that the owners can persuade creditors to finance at a rate less than at least some of the possible rates of return on assets.

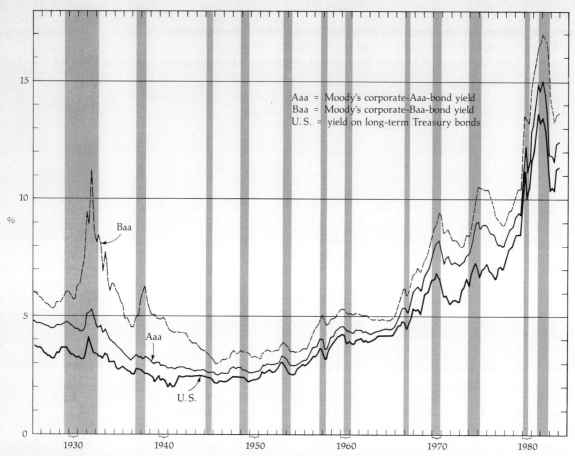

Sources: Federal Reserve Board's *Banking and Monetary Statistics, 1914–41 and 1941–70* and *Federal Reserve Bulletins*; Moody's *Industrial Manual* (and other *Manuals*).

Figure 10.1   Yields on U.S. Treasury and high- and medium-grade corporate bonds (quarterly averages, 1926 to 1983).

"Now *wait* a minute," say the prospective creditors, who upon reflection have become less trusting. If the ventures available to the firm are generally known, the owners will be able to borrow only if they issue debt with an indenture that restricts them to the riskless venture or agree to a debt contract that allows the creditors a share in the returns commensurate with the risk to which they are likely to be exposed by the firm's owners. In the latter case, the creditors' prospects become identical with those of the owners if the contract rate on debt is set equal to the rate of return on assets in the event the risky venture is undertaken and is successful, that is, 120 percent. This is case *B* in Table 10.7, in which creditors and owners share equally in the good and bad outcomes of the risky venture.

It is interesting that the creditors' suspicion that the owners will expose them to as much risk as possible in fact forces the owners to

Table 10.8   Defaults and Default Premiums on Medium- and High-Grade Corporate Bonds, 1920 to 1939 and 1950 to 1983

Period	Annual Average of Numbers of Defaults as Percentages of Large Issues Outstanding				Default Premiums: Spreads Between Yields on Corporate and U.S. Bonds			
	Aaa	Aa	A	Baa	Aaa	Aa	A	Baa
1920–1929	0.12	0.17	0.20	0.80	0.98	1.34	1.80	2.58
1930–1939	0.42	0.44	1.94	3.78	0.92	1.34	2.04	3.34
1950–1959	0	0	0	0	0.31	0.42	0.57	0.94
1960–1969	0	0	0	0	0.50	0.64	0.79	1.14
1970–1979	0	0	0	0	1.36	1.64	1.92	2.44
1980–1983	0	0	0.03	0.14	1.30	1.83	2.49	3.15

Sources: *Yields* on corporate bonds rated Aaa, Aa, A, and Baa by Moody's are available in *Moody's Industrial Manual* (and other manuals). They are also available, along with U.S. long-term yields, in the Federal Reserve Board's *Banking and Monetary Statistics, 1914–41* and *1941–70* and *Federal Reserve Bulletins.*

The 1920 to 1939 *default data* were calculated by Gordon Pye (1974) from data in Braddock Hickman (1960), who reported defaults by large issues classified by their ratings two years prior to default. The 1950 to 1959, 1960 to 1969, 1970 to 1979, and 1980 to 1983 default percentages are based on all corporate bonds as classified by Moody's in January 1950, 1960, 1970, and 1980, respectively.

pursue the risky course of action.[33] If the creditors expect the risky course and so require a contract rate of 120 percent, the owners are certain to lose all their investment if they undertake the venture that yields a certain 10 percent, for which the end-of-period values of assets and debt are $11 and $19.80, respectively.

The extreme nature of these results is due to the firm's short horizon. The results are modified considerably if firms desire to remain in operation for long periods, which they may be able to accomplish only by limiting their exposure to risk and maintaining an ability to borrow at relatively low rates, which in turn requires repayment of maturing claims.

BOND RATINGS. Various private organizations rate corporate bonds in terms of their "probabilities of timely payment of interest and principal."[34] The largest rating agencies are Moody's Investors Service and Standard & Poor's Corporation. These firms also report average yields

---

33 See Michael Jensen and William Meckling (1976, Section 4) for a more general discussion of owner incentives produced by debt and the roles of bond indentures in altering those incentives.

34 *Standard & Poor's Ratings Guide* (1979, page xxiii). Standard & Poor's ratings apply to bonds for which the capacity to pay interest and principal are "extremely strong" (AAA), "very strong" (AA), "strong" (A), and "adequate" (BBB). Bonds rated BB, B, CCC, and CC are "speculative." Moody's ratings are described in their *Industrial Manual* and other manuals.

Table 10.9   Derivation of a Default Premium

Consider a simple case in which yields to maturity on all default-free bonds are expected to be equal and constant so that the rate of return between dates t and $t + 1$ on any of these bonds is equal to its yield and may be written

(10.14)
$$Y = \frac{C + P_{t+1} - P_t}{P_t}$$

where C is the coupon paid at the end of each period and P_t is the bond's price at time t. The rate of return in the event of default is

(10.15)
$$-L = \frac{V_{t+1} - P_t}{P_t}$$

where L is the loss rate (that is, the negative rate of return) and V_{t+1} is the present value at time $t + 1$ of payments expected subsequent to default.

Let d be the probability of default for a bond that has not defaulted. The expected return on such a bond is

(10.16)
$$(1 - d)\frac{C + P_{t+1} - P_t}{P_t} + d(-L) = Y + \Pi$$

where Π is the premium in excess of the return on the riskless bond required by risk-averse investors as compensation for the variability of return on the default-prone bond. Solving for P_t gives

(10.17)
$$P_t = \frac{C + P_{t+1}}{1 + \rho} \quad \text{where} \quad \rho = \frac{Y + \Pi + dL}{1 - d}$$

This relation must hold in every period. Therefore, letting T be the term to maturity and P_T be the the face value of the bond,

$$P_{T-1} = \frac{C + P_T}{1 + \rho}, \quad P_{T-2} = \frac{C + P_{T-1}}{1 + \rho} = \frac{C}{1 + \rho} + \frac{C + P_T}{(1 + \rho)^2}$$

and finally

(10.18)
$$P_t = \frac{C}{1 + \rho} + \frac{C}{(1 + \rho)^2} + \cdots + \frac{C + P_T}{(1 + \rho)^T}$$

which is merely the present-value expression for the price of the bond when the yield is ρ. Therefore, the bond must be priced to yield

(10.19)
$$\rho = \frac{Y + \Pi + dL}{1 - d}$$

and the yield spread between default-prone and default-free bonds is

(10.20)
$$\text{Default premium} = \rho - Y = \Pi + \frac{d(L + Y + \Pi)}{1 - d}$$

Source: Based on Gordon Pye, "Gauging the Default Premium," *Financial Analysts Journal*, January/February 1974, pages 49–52.

on medium-grade (Baa or BBB) to high-grade (Aaa or AAA) bonds. Quarterly averages of yields on corporate bonds rated Aaa and Baa by Moody's are shown for the period 1926 to 1983 in Figure 10.1, where they are compared with yields on default-free long-term U.S. securities.[35] Yields are an increasing function of default risk. Baa yields have exceeded Aaa yields, which have exceeded U.S. yields. These spreads usually widen during declines in economic activity, when falling profits and the rising frequency of business failures lead to increased investor fears of default, especially by lower-quality bonds. This tendency is seen most strikingly in Figure 10.1 during the Great Depression of 1929 to 1933 and the severe recession of 1937 and 1938 and somewhat less strikingly during the two most severe post-World War II recessions of 1973 to 1975 and 1981 to 1982.[36]

Empirical and theoretical connections between default experience and default premiums on corporate bonds with different ratings. Some empirical connections are summarized in Table 10.8. The left-hand side of the table lists average annual percentages of large issues not previously in default that missed all or part of at least one coupon or principal payment. The right-hand side of the table lists *default premiums,* that is, the premiums over the average U.S. Treasury long-term bond yield required by investors as compensation for default risk. Table 10.8 indicates that default premiums were closely related to default experience until the 1970s. For example the average annual percentage of large Baa issues defaulting rose from 0.80 percent in the 1920s to 3.78 percent in the 1930s, before falling to zero throughout the 1950s and 1960s; the average Baa default premium rose from 2.58 percent in the 1920s to 3.34 percent in the 1930s and then fell to an average of 1.04 percent during 1950 to 1969. However, the substantial increases in the Baa and other default premiums during the 1970s and 1980s have not been accompanied by even remotely corresponding increases in default experience. The severe recessions of these years, reminiscent of the volatile world that existed before World War II, have apparently revived investor fears of widespread corporate failures. But these fears have not been realized.

A theoretical default premium is derived in Table 10.9 for the

---

35 Moody's corporate yield series are unweighted averages of market yields to maturity on about thirty long-term nonconvertible seasoned bonds (about ten industrials, ten railroads, and ten public utilities), with an average maturity of about 20 years, for each of four rating classes: Aaa, Aa, A, and Baa. Only the Aaa and Baa average yields are shown in Figure 10.1.

The U.S. series is an unweighted average of yields to maturity on bonds selling at or below par, or yields to next call on bonds selling above par, for Treasury bonds due or callable after periods ranging from 8 to 15 years (after 10 years since 1953). Interest (but not capital gains) on direct "obligations of the United States" are exempt from state and local taxes (except estate and inheritance taxes) but have not since 1941 been exempt from federal taxes.

36 Based on National Bureau of Economic Research turning points (including the 1966 to 1967 minirecession) in Figure 10.1, the spread between Baa and Aaa yields has widened during contractions on ten of thirteen occasions since 1926 and has narrowed during expansions on seven of twelve occasions since that time. Identical figures apply to the spread between Aaa and U.S. yields. For a more detailed analysis of cyclical variations in the spreads between Baa and higher-grade yields between 1954 and 1969, see Dwight Jaffee (1975).

simple case in which yields and the probability of default are expected to remain constant. A close approximation of Equation (10.20) when d, Y, and Π are small is

(10.20a)   Default premium $= \rho - Y = \Pi + dL$

where Y is the yield on a default-free bond and ρ is the yield on a default-prone bond that has an annual probability of default equal to d and an expected loss rate of L in the event of default; dL is the part of the default premium that is due directly to the expected loss through default. The other portion of the premium, Π, is required by risk-averse investors as compensation for the greater variability of the rate of return on the default-prone than on the default-free bond.

W. B. Hickman (1958) reported an average loss rate on defaulted corporate bonds of approximately $L = 0.40$ between 1900 and 1943.[37] Using this value of L in Equation (10.20a) and ignoring Π for the moment, the data in Table 10.8 suggest that the default premiums required by investors consistently exceeded actual default experience even before 1970.[38] During 1930 to 1939, for example, estimated losses on Aaa, Aa, A, and Baa bonds were $dL = 0.42(0.4) = 0.17$, $0.44(0.4) = 0.18$, $1.94(0.4) = 0.78$, and $3.78(0.4) = 1.51$ percent, respectively, falling far short of their default premiums of 0.92, 1.34, 2.04, and 3.34 percent. These differences may be due to the risk premium (Π) component of the default premium[39] although, as always, we must not dismiss the possibility that our simple model has omitted important explanatory variables.

Do default premiums lead or follow bond ratings? There is considerable evidence that variations in yield spreads anticipate rating revisions. How could it be otherwise? The rating services are not the only people to devote time and effort to estimating probabilities of default and expected losses. Their sources of information are widely available, and researchers have shown that ratings may be explained by applying standard statistical methods to published data on the income, leverage, and dividends of companies and to the seniority and

37 In Table 22 of *Corporate Bond Quality and Investor Experience* (1958), Braddock Hickman reported average prices of large issues at the time of default and also the average present values of their receipts after default, using both 3 percent and 6 percent discount rates. Our estimated loss rate of $L = 0.40$ uses an approximate average of these two average present values and the assumption that the average price of default-free bonds between 1900 and 1943 was equal to par.

38 This is true for annual data as well as for the decennial and other averages in Table 10.8.

39 Such an explanation would be consistent with Braddock Hickman's (1958, Chapter 2) finding that bond prices on default dates tended to be much less than the present values of future payments on those bonds, suggesting a risk-averse, bird-in-hand strategy by investors. In the most extreme case, for bonds defaulting between 1930 and 1943, defaulting bonds yielded about -4 percent per annum between their issue and the date of default and yielded about 29 percent per annum between default and "extinguishment," when all the claims that could be paid had been paid. (Our estimate of the loss rate if we had used the average price at default would have been $L = 0.57$.)

other security characteristics of issues.[40] Furthermore, since the rating agencies do not have the resources necessary for the continuous analysis of rated issues, their periodic rating reviews and revisions must almost necessarily lag behind the information causing those revisions and the market's use of that information. Mark Weinstein (1977) found for a sample of 100 rating-revision announcements during 1962 to 1974 that bond prices tended to precede those announcements by 7 to 18 months.[41]

Preferred stock

PREFERRED STOCK HAS SOME OF THE FEATURES OF BOTH COMMON STOCK AND BONDS. Preferred is like common in the sense that its dividends are paid only at the discretion of the firm's directors in light of past and expected earnings. Unlike the repayment of debt there is no contractual obligation to pay dividends on either preferred or common stock. But preferred stock is more like debt than common stock in several ways, of which the most important may be summarized as follows:

1. Preferred dividends are specified in the preferred indenture and are therefore similar to bond coupons. An example is ITT's $4 preferred, which, as we see from Table 10.3, pays quarterly dividends of $1.00. Although there is no contractual obligation to pay preferred dividends (unlike bond coupons), no dividends may be paid on common stock until preferred dividends have been satisfied. Most preferred stock (including ITT's) is *cumulative,* which means that dividend claims accumulate; missed preferred dividends must be made up before any common dividends may be paid.

2. Preferred stock may be callable, as in the case of ITT's issues, and/or contain a sinking-fund provision.

3. Preferred stock also has meaningful face values in the form of call and liquidation values. (The claims of preferred stock precede those of common stock in the event of bankruptcy although preferred stock takes a back seat to other claims.)

4. Preferred stock indentures are intended to ensure the payment of preferred stock dividends in the same manner that bond indentures attempt to provide security for bondholders. These indentures most often take the form of limits on dividends to common stock. The idea is to prevent the company's owners, that is, the common stockholders, from borrowing or from selling the company's assets in order to pay large dividends to themselves currently and thereby impairing their capacity to pay preferred stock dividends (as well as debt obligations) in the future.

---

40 For example see the application of multiple discriminant analysis to corporate bond ratings by George Pinches and Kent Mingo (1973). For a similar study of municipal bond ratings see Paul Farnham and George Cluff (1982).

41 George Pinches and Clay Singleton (1978) found that *stock* prices also tend to anticipate bond-rating revisions.

5. Most preferred stock is also like debt but unlike common stock in conferring *neither preemptive rights nor full voting rights.*[42] However, the consent of two-thirds of the preferred stock is usually required on matters affecting the seniority of their claim, such as the issue of senior preferred stock. In addition, preferred stock normally acquires limited voting rights if preferred dividends are missed. A typical indenture states that, whenever dividends are in arrears in an aggregate amounting to the equivalent of at least (say) six quarterly dividends, preferred shareholders may elect two directors until all arrears have been paid.

6. Not all preferred stock has the same seniority. Junior preferred stock is often termed *preference stock* and is indicated by "pr" instead of "pf" in stock market reports although none of these appears in Table 10.4.

THE DECLINE OF PREFERRED STOCK. Like dividends on common stock but unlike interest on debt, preferred dividends may not be treated as tax-deductible expenses for the issuing corporation. The consequence has been a decline in the use of preferred stock as corporate profits taxes rose from zero in 1913 to 52 percent in 1951 and subsequently have remained near 50 percent. The market value of outstanding preferred stock as a proportion of total stock outstanding fell from about 13 percent in 1930 to about 5 percent in 1970.[43] Most preferred stock is issued by regulated public utilities, whose taxes are counted as costs in rate negotiations. The tax bill due to an issue of preferred stock instead of debt is passed on to utility customers.

Although the tax structure discourages the *supply* of preferred stock (except by public utilities), corporations have been given an important tax incentive to *demand* preferred stock (as well as common stock). Corporations may exclude 85 percent of dividend earnings from their taxable income. Given the corporate profits tax rate of 46 percent, this means an effective tax rate on dividend income of $0.46(0.15) = 6.9$ percent, compared with the full profits tax rate of 46 percent on interest income. This explains why most preferred stock is held by corporations.

In view of the order of claims on a company's funds—debt before preferred stock before common stock—we should, if investors are averse to risk, expect average returns on preferred stock to exceed those on bonds of similar quality but to be less than those on common

---

42 Table 10.3 shows that ITT's preferred does not have preemptive rights but is unusual in possessing all the voting rights of common stock (plus some voting rights special to preferred).

43 Robert Soldofsky and Dale Max (1978, page 18). Annual issues of preferred and common stock since 1919 are listed in *Historical Statistics of the United States: Colonial Times to 1970* (vol. 2, pages 1005 and 1006) and in the *Statistical Abstract of the United States,* both published by the U.S. Department of Commerce. Preferred amounted to 39 percent of all stock issues during the 1920s but only 22 percent during 1950 to 1981. These figures overstate the contribution of preferred to total stock outstanding since most preferred has call and sinking-fund provisions.

stock. And in fact this ranking was observed until the great rise in income taxes during the 1940s, and it probably still holds for *after-tax* returns. But the tax advantages of preferred have caused its average *before-tax* returns to be less than those on corporate bonds since the 1950s.[44]

Convertible securities

A *convertible security* is one that the holder may at his option exchange for other securities of the firm at the times and on the terms stated in the convertible security's indenture. The most common examples are debentures and preferred stock that may be converted into common stock, such as ITT's 8⅝ percent bonds and $4 (series H) preferred stock described in Table 10.3.[45]

Exercise dates are sometimes restricted, and conversion ratios sometimes vary, but ITT's convertibles may be exchanged at any time (before maturity or call) at a fixed ratio. One share of series H preferred may be exchanged for 1.8734 common shares. Bond conversion ratios are seldom stated directly but are expressed as the number of dollars of face value that must be given up for a share of common stock. The $25.375 conversion value of common stock stated in ITT's convertible bond indenture means that a bond with $100 face value may be exchanged for $100/25.375 = 3.941$ shares, a bond with $1,000 face value may be exchanged for 39.41 shares, and so on. There is a cash payment when the conversion involves a fractional number of shares. In the second case, for example, the bondholder would receive 39 shares plus 41 percent of the value of a share in cash. Convertible securities are usually protected against *dilution,* which means, for example, that in the event of a two-for-one split of common stock the series H preferred conversion ratio increases to 3.7468.

Abstracting from transaction costs and accrued interest and dividends, the price of a convertible security must be at least as great as the maximum of its *straight investment value,* which is the price of an otherwise identical nonconvertible security (that is, a "straight" bond or share of preferred stock with the same maturity, call schedule, risk, and tax liability), and its *conversion value:*

(10.21)   Price of a convertible security

$$\geq \max [\text{straight investment value, conversion value}]$$

44 Average annual rates of return on samples of U.S. bonds and various grades of corporate bonds and preferred and common stocks are presented for the periods 1910 to 1976, 1910 to 1938, 1939 to 1953, and 1954 to 1976 by Robert Soldofsky and Dale Max (1978, page 33).

45 Common stock may also be convertible when a firm has more than one class of common stock outstanding. Occasionally, in an effort to retain control of the company while engaging in equity financing, firms issue nonvoting common stock or stock with deferred dividend rights. Another type of convertible security is the *warrant,* which is attached to bonds or preferred stock and may, upon payment of an *exercise price,* be detached from the accompanying security and converted into the company's common stock.

Let us see whether the price quoted on ITT's $2.25 preferred stock at the close of trading on March 25, 1983, conformed to this relation. We first note that its price greatly exceeded its value as straight preferred stock because $46.50 was much higher than the prices paid for other high-grade but nonconvertible preferred issues with approximately the same dividend rate, such as the Indiana & Michigan Electric Company's (IndiM) $2.25 issue, which closed at $17.375 and at that price would have paid a simple annual yield of about 2.25/17.375 = 0.1295, more in line with prevailing yields than the 2.25/46.50 = 0.0484 yield implied by the price of ITT's issue. The high price of this issue is explained by its 1.256 conversion ratio and the $37.625 price of ITT's common stock,[46] which together imply a conversion value of 1.256($37.625) = $47.257. If there had been no transaction costs, you could have earned an arbitrage profit of $0.757 per share[47] by buying preferred for $46.50 and converting it into common worth $47.257. But even the 1 percent commission available from discount brokers entails costs of nearly $1 for each purchase of a preferred share and sale of the acquired common shares—0.01 ($46.50 + $47.257) = $0.93757—more than consuming the profits of the purchase, conversion, and sale.

The same procedure is applied in Exercise 10.1 to ITT's 8⅝ percent convertible bonds. Further exercises are requested in problems 7 and 8 at the end of the chapter, including one for which the investment value exceeds the conversion value.

EXERCISE 10.1.   Does the price of ITT's convertible 8⅝s of 2000 at the close of trading on March 25, 1983, conform to relation (10.21)?

We first examine the bond's *investment value.* Similar straight bonds were paying yields above 12 percent in May 1983, which implies investment values less than 100 on bonds with coupon rates less than 12 percent.

Second, the *conversion value of the bond* is

$$\text{(Conversion ratio)} \times \text{(stock price)} = \frac{100}{25.375} \times 37.625 = 148.276$$

The *cost of the bond* (price plus accrued interest with settlement on April 1, as indicated in Definition 6.1, and assuming

46 See Tables 10.2 and 10.4.

47 There is no need to take account of dividends in our calculations because, unlike the practice of adding accrued interest to the cost of bonds, it is not normal market practice to add accrued dividends on common stock (which of course is uncertain) or preferred stock to the costs of these securities.

30-day months, as indicated in footnote 21 of this chapter) is

$$P + AC = \$145 + \frac{\$8.625}{2}\frac{120}{180} = \$147.875$$

This is about $0.40 less than its conversion value so that arbitrage profits are not possible in the presence of transaction costs.

But the price of a convertible security may exceed both its investment and conversion values. Such a case, in which the inequality in relation (10.21) holds, is described in Table 10.10. The current price of a nonconvertible 1-year pure discount bond that pays $110 in 1 year is $100 under the conditions assumed in the table, in which expected returns are 10 percent on all investments. The convertible bond's conversion value is also $100 because the price of common stock is

Table 10.10   A Simple Example of the Price of a Convertible Bond

Definitions and Assumptions

Assume a world of risk-neutral investors in which the expected return on every asset is 10 percent per annum.

The ABC Company's common stock is currently (January 1) selling for $100 a share and with certainty pays an annual dividend of $10 each December 31 to holders of the stock on that date. The stock's price may with equal probabilities either increase or decrease by the amount σ between now and the end of the year. Hence the expected return on stock is

$$E\tilde{R}_s = \frac{0.5(\$110 + \sigma) + 0.5(\$110 - \sigma) - \$100}{\$100} = 0.10$$

Each of ABC's pure-discount 1-year bonds pays a certain $110 on December 31 and may at any time be exchanged for one share of common stock.

The Price of the Bond on January 1

Bondholders will keep the bond until maturity if the stock's price falls but will exercise their conversion privilege if the stock's price rises. Therefore, the expected terminal value (on December 31) of the convertible bond is

$$E\tilde{T}_B = 0.5(\$110) + 0.5(\$110 + \sigma) = \$110 + 0.5\sigma$$

and given 10 percent expected returns on all investments, the price of the bond (P_B) on January 1 is

$$P_B = \frac{E\tilde{T}_B}{1.10} = \frac{\$110 + 0.5\sigma}{1.10} = \$100 + \frac{0.5\sigma}{1.10}$$

In this example the price of the convertible bond equals its investment and conversion values, which are both $100, plus the present value of the expected *rise* (not the expected *change*, which is zero) in the stock's price.

currently $100 and the conversion ratio is one for one. But suppose there is a fifty-fifty chance that the stock's price will be $90 or $110 by the end of the year.[48] Assuming a certain annual dividend of $10 to be paid at the end of the year, the expected rate of return on stock is $0.5(0) + 0.5(0.20) = 0.10$. But the holder of a convertible bond has the best of both worlds: If the price of stock falls, she keeps the bond and collects $110; if stock rises, she converts the bond into stock and collects $120. But she must pay for the privilege; for the convertible's price under these conditions is $104.545, giving the familiar expected rate of return of $0.5(0.0522) + 0.5(0.1478) = 0.10$.

Why do firms issue convertible securities? There are reasons for not doing so, perhaps the most important being that such issues transfer portions of windfalls from owners to creditors. On the other hand, convertibility may reduce the cost of debt by providing a guarantee to creditors that they will not suffer from risk-increasing owner decisions like the one described in Table 10.7. Referring to that table, we are reminded that, if the firm, which is financed 90 percent by debt, undertakes a riskless venture with a certain 10 percent return on assets, the returns to equity (R_s) and debt (R_b) are both certain to be 10 percent. But if the owners choose a risky venture with a fifty-fifty chance of 120 percent or -100 percent return on assets, the stockholders have a fifty-fifty chance of earning 1,110 percent or losing their investment in the firm (giving them an expected return of 505 percent), whereas the exploited creditors have a fifty-fifty chance of earning 10 percent or losing everything. If the creditors believe the risky venture will be chosen, they will require a contract yield of 120 percent, which gives them the same distribution of returns (120 percent or -100 percent) as the owners.

Table 10.11 shows that the owner-creditor conflict may be resolved by issuing convertible bonds, which enable bondholders to escape the disproportionate risk imposed on debt by the firm's choice of the risky venture.[49] Convertible bonds are especially useful to the owners if they are not indifferent to risk. By issuing convertible bonds and thus guaranteeing the bondholders an equal share in the firm's profits, they will be able to borrow at 10 percent and earn a certain 10 percent return on equity by pursuing the riskless venture instead of being forced into the risky venture by a contract yield of 120 percent demanded by suspicious creditors.

The above discussion suggests that a firm should be more likely to

---

48 This example assumes σ in Table 10.10 to be $10. For a more general example, in which the stock's price is allowed to vary continuously over some interval, see William Baumol, Burton Malkiel, and Richard Quandt (1966). It may be shown, for example, that when the stock's price is distributed uniformly between $100 - \alpha$ and $100 + \alpha$, the price of the convertible bond in Table 10.10 becomes $P_0 = \$100 + 0.25\alpha/1.10$.

49 See Michael Jensen and William Meckling (1976) and Clifford Smith and Jerold Warner (1979) for more general discussions of the use of convertible debt to resolve stockholder-bondholder conflicts of interest.

Table 10.11   Convertible Bonds As a Guarantee to Bondholders That They Will Share the Firm's Fortunes Equally with the Owners

Definitions and assumptions are the same as in Table 10.7, with one addition: Each bond, which has a face value of $1.10, is convertible at any time into one share of stock newly issued for that purpose.

Returns to Debt and Equity

If the riskless venture is chosen and $C_b = 0.10$, the initial $10 value of assets rises to $11, the nine bonds are redeemed for $9.90, and the single share of common stock receives the remaining $1.10. Each bondholder and stockholder earns 10 percent on his $1 investment.

If $C_b = 0.10$ and the risky venture is chosen, the price of bonds immediately falls such that, if investors are indifferent to risk, the expected return on bonds is the 10 percent required on riskless investments; that is,

$$P_B = \frac{E\tilde{T}_B}{1.10} = \frac{0.5(\$1.10 + 0)}{1.10} = \$0.50$$

where $E\tilde{T}_B$ is the expected terminal value of the bonds (a fifty-fifty chance of full payment or complete default) and P_B is the price of a bond at the beginning of the investment period, when the firm's choice of activity first becomes known. The price of the share of stock rises to

$$P_s = \frac{E\tilde{T}_s}{1.10} = \frac{0.5(\$22 - \$9.90) + 0.5(0)}{1.10} = \$5.50$$

The bondholders lose no time in exchanging bonds worth $0.50 for stock worth $5.50. The firm's debt is eliminated, the number of shares increases to 10, the payoff to each share will be $2.20 or 0, and the price of a share is now

$$P_s = \frac{E\tilde{T}_s}{1.10} = \frac{0.5(\$2.20 + 0)}{1.10} = \$1.00$$

include the convertibility privilege in its bonds the greater the firm's debt/equity ratio and the greater the dispersion of possible returns to available projects—because the potential transfer of wealth from bondholders to stockholders and therefore the potential benefits of convertibility to bondholders are positively related to these characteristics of the firm. Wayne Mikkelson (1980) has presented evidence that the firms most strongly possessing these risky characteristics are in fact the most likely to issue convertible bonds. In a later study, Mikkelson (1981) found common stock prices to be unaffected by conversions of preferred stock.[50] The failure of conversions to transfer wealth from stockholders to the owners of convertible securities is consistent with the view that convertibility privileges have been effective in removing incentives for owners to make decisions that benefit common stock at the expense of convertible preferred stock and debt.

---

50 Mikkelson argued that the negative effects of bond conversions on common stock prices were probably due to increased corporate taxes caused by the reductions in tax-deductible interest payments.

MUNICIPALS
Distinguishing characteristics: security and tax status

The obligations of states and their political subdivisions are as a group simply called "municipals." Municipal bonds are similar in form to the corporate bonds discussed above. Most are callable, promise semiannual coupons and par values payable at maturity, and are redeemed according to serial or sinking-fund schedules.[51] The two main differences between corporate and municipal bonds concern the nature of their security and the liability of their interest payments to the federal income tax.

The security of a corporate bond depends on the firm's earnings.[52] The security of a municipal bond depends on whether it is a *general obligation bond* or a *revenue bond*. General obligation bonds are paid from tax receipts and are secured by a government's power (and willingness) to tax. Revenue bonds are like corporate bonds in the sense that they are secured by the revenues (and sometimes by the property) of specific activities.[53] Most of the bonds in Table 10.12, which lists municipal issues that were actively traded on October 24, 1983, are revenuc bonds.[54] The list includes several issues of the ill-fated Washington Public Power Supply System ("Whoops") which were intended to be redeemed by revenues from electric power facilities but which defaulted in 1983.[55] General obligation bonds are also subject to default, most often when tax receipts decline during economic downturns. About two-thirds of all municipal defaults since 1839, when the first was recorded, occurred between 1929 and 1937. At one time or another during that period more than 4,700 government units were reported in arrears in payment of principal or interest. The debt of these units amounted to about 16 percent of all state and local debt. However, most creditors eventually got their money, and the total loss of principal and interest due to these defaults amounted only to about 0.5 percent of state and local debt outstanding at the beginning of the period.[56]

---

51 Municipal bonds are either *serial* or *term*. A serial issue consists of many different maturities designed to meet investor preferences. For example a serial bond (we should really say "bonds") issued in 1985 may be arranged to mature serially in twenty annual installments between 1990 and 2009. A term bond has a single specified maturity date but, like corporate bonds, usually includes sinking-fund provisions. For more detail regarding municipal bonds see Gordon Calvert (1972) and Frank Fabozzi and Frank Zarb (1981, Chapter 17).

52 Mortgage bonds are also backed by claims on the firm's property.

53 *Special-tax bonds* possess some of the characteristics of both general obligation and revenue bonds because they are secured by the receipts from a special tax, such as highway bonds financed by a gasoline tax, rather than by the government's general taxing authority.

54 These bonds are quoted like the U.S. Treasury bonds in Table 6.2, and their yields to maturity are calculated, also like Treasury bonds, according to the relationships in Table 6.6 except, like corporate bonds, with the modification that all months are assumed to have 30 days. The broker and dealer markets in small and large municipal issues were discussed in Chapter 7.

55 The issues of the canceled Power Plants 4 and 5 were trading "flat," that is, without accrued interest, as is customary for bonds failing to meet coupon obligations.

56 These data are from George Hempel (1971, pages 19–24).

Table 10.12

Tax-Exempt Bonds

Monday, October 24, 1983

Here are current prices of several active tax-exempt revenue bonds issued by toll roads and other public authorities.

Agency	Coupon	Mat	Bid	Asked	Chg.
Alabama G.O.	8⅜s	'01	90	92	– 1
Bat Park City Auth NY	6⅜s	'14	62	66	....
Chelan Cnty PU Dist	5s	'13	62	64	– ½
Clark Cnty Arpt Rev	10½s	'07	97½	99½	– 1
Columbia St Pwr Exch	3⅞s	'03	67½	69½	– ½
Dela River Port Auth	6½s	'11	69½	71½	– ½
Douglas Cnty PU Dist	4s	'18	42½	44½	– ½
Ga Mun El Auth Pwr Rev	8s	'15	80	84	....
Intermountain Pwr	7½s	'18	72	76	– ½
Intermountain Pwr	10½s	'18	96½	98½	– 1
Intermountain Pwr	14s	'21	119½	123½	....
Jacksonville Elec Rev	9¼s	'13	90	93	– 1½
Loop	6½s	'08	66	69	+ ½
MAC	7½s	'92	88½	92½	– ½
MAC	7½s	'95	85½	89½	– ½
MAC	8s	'86	99	103	....
MAC	8s	'91	97½	101½	....
MAC	9.7s	'08	96	100	– ½
MAC	9¾s	'92	100½	104½	....
MAC	10¼s	'93	109½	113½	....
Mass Port Auth Rev	6s	'11	68	71	....
Massachusetts G.O.	6½s	'00	73	76	....
Mass Wholesale	6⅜s	'15	55	58	....
Mass Wholesale	13⅜s	'17	106	109	....
Metro Transit Auth	9¼s	'15	92	95	....
Michigan Public Pwr	10⅝s	'18	99½	101½	– 1
Nebraska Pub Pwr Dist	7.1s	'17	70	74	– ½
NJ Turnpike Auth	4¾s	'06	62	64	– 1
NJ Turnpike Auth	5.7s	'13	67	70	– 1
NJ Turnpike Auth	6s	'14	71	73	– ½
NY Mtge Agency Rev	9¾s	'13	97½	99½	– 1½
NY State Pwr Escr	5½s	'10	61½	65½	....
NY State Pwr	6⅝s	'10	71	74	....
NY State Pwr Escr	9½s	'01	103	105	....
NY State Pwr	9⅞s	'20	98½	101½	....
NY State Thruway Rev	3.1s	'94	68	71	+ ½
NY State Urban Dev Corp	6s	'13	60	64	+ 2
NY State Urban Dev Corp	7s	'14	70	74	....
NC East Mun Pwr Agcy	11¼s	'18	102	105	....
Okla Tpke Auth Rev	4.7s	'06	65	68	....
Port of NY & NJ	4¾s	'03	59	61	....
Port of NY & NJ	6s	'06	67	70	....
Port of NY & NJ	7s	'11	77	80	....
Port of NY-Delta	10½s	'08	105	107	....
Salt River-Arizona	9¼s	'20	93	96	– ½
SC Pub Svc Auth	10¼s	'20	98½	101½	– ½
Texas Munic Pwr Agcy	9½s	'12	91½	94½	– ½
Valdez (Exxon)	5½s	'07	64	67	– ½
Valdez (Sohio)	6s	'07	64	67	– ½
Wshngtn PPSS #4-5	f6s	'15	15	18	– 1
Wshngtn PPSS #4-5	f7¾s	'18	15	18	– 1
Wshngtn PPSS #4-5	f9⅞s	'12	16	19	– 1
Wshngtn PPSS #4-5	f12½	'10	19	22	– 1
Wshngtn PPSS #2	6s	'12	41	45	– 1
Wshngtn PPSS #1	7¾s	'17	49	53	– 1
Wshngtn PPSS #2	9¼s	'11	60½	64½	– 1
Wshngtn PPSS #3	13⅞s	'18	76	79	– 2½
Wshngtn PPSS #2	14¾s	'12	84	87	– ½
Wshngtn PPSS #1	15s	'17	83½	86½	– 1

f-Trades flat without payment of current interest.

Source: *Wall Street Journal*, October 25, 1983.

There has been a shift in recent years from general obligation bonds to revenue bonds partly because of growing taxpayer reluctance to vote for bond issues to be financed by tax increases[57] and partly because of growing local government involvement in a wide variety of activities that are expected to pay their own way. For example,

57 The most famous expression of this attitude is California's Proposition 13, adopted in 1978, which was designed to cut existing property taxes as well as to limit future tax increases.

mortgage or *loan-backed bonds* provide low-interest home mortgages or student loans, *lease-rental bonds* finance the construction of public housing projects, hospitals, and other facilities that are leased to not-for-profit organizations, *pollution control revenue bonds* finance pollution-control facilities that are leased or sold to private users, and *industrial development revenue bonds* finance the construction of manufacturing or commercial facilities that are leased or sold to private users.[58] These bonds are secured by loan repayments, revenues from public facilities, or, as in the last two cases, the credit of the private users. All are devices by which private individuals or firms are enabled to benefit from the tax-exempt interest rates available to state and local governments. However, the benefits must usually be shared with the governments concerned, as indicated in the last sentence of the following report of an issue of La Plata County, Colorado:

> The Durango Ski Corporation will have the use of $7.5 million next week for the first phase of a planned three-year expansion of Purgatory Ski Resort following the scheduled issuance of Industrial Development Revenue Bonds.
>
> A bond resolution which refers to the financing agreement was signed Tuesday by R. T. Scott, chairman of the La Plata County Commissioners, and a closing for the bond issuance is scheduled Aug. 4 in Denver.
>
> The money will be used this summer to fund the planning necessary for the expansion, according to Bob Hill, Director of Finance and Administration for Durango Ski Corp., and will pay for land preparation for the eventual installation of snow making equipment. A snow vehicle and heavy equipment will also be purchased.
>
> During the subsequent construction seasons, the expansion will include the snow making equipment, a new restaurant, the construction of a beginners' ski area, and expanded trails. . . .
>
> La Plata County will receive an estimated $56,250 for lending its name to the initial bond issuance in order to qualify it for tax-exempt interest status.
>
> *Durango Herald,* July 29, 1981

The most important distinguishing feature of municipal securities is the exemption of their interest (that is, coupon) income from federal income taxes.[59] Let the marginal federal income-tax rate of the *i*th

---

58 See Frank Fabozzi and Frank Zarb (1981, Chapter 17) for more detail.

59 The exemption of municipals from the federal income tax is based on the doctrine of "reciprocal immunity," the origins of which may be traced to Chief Justice Marshall's opinion for the majority in the case of *McCulloch v. Maryland*, 1819. Marshall argued that, since "the power to tax involves the power to destroy," the ability of the State of Maryland to tax the activities of an agency of the federal government, specifically the note issues of the Second Bank of the United States, would amount to an abridgment of the constitutional separation of the powers of the states and the federal government. By the same token the federal government could not tax the

investor be τ_i, and suppose that the yield to maturity of a high-grade (and taxable) corporate bond is Y_c. Then in the simple case in which both bonds are selling at par the investor will be indifferent between the corporate bond and an otherwise identical tax-exempt municipal bond when

$$(10.22) \qquad\qquad Y_m = (1 - \tau_i)\, Y_c$$

where Y_m is the municipal bond yield. Equation (10.22) may be illustrated as follows: Suppose that both bonds are selling at a par of $100, the corporate bond pays an annual coupon of $10, and $\tau_i = 0.50$. We know that the corporate yield equals the coupon rate when the bond sells at par; that is, $Y_c = \$10/\$100 = 0.10$. But the investor gets only $\$10(1 - \tau_i) = \$5$ after taxes. He will therefore be indifferent between the corporate bond and a municipal bond that pays a tax-exempt coupon of $5, which, since the bond is selling at par, means a yield of $Y_m = 0.05$. Both securities yield after-tax annual rates of return of 5 percent.

The equation of indifference between municipal and corporate bonds becomes more complicated when the bonds are not selling at par, primarily because capital gains on municipals are taxable at the same rate as capital gains on corporates. This means that Y_m will normally be greater relative to Y_c than is indicated in Equation (10.22). In situations in which prospective capital gains are very large relative to coupons, for example, Y_m will be almost as large as Y_c because most of the earnings on both securities will be taxed at the same rate.

Returning to the par-value case of Equation (10.22) and also assuming for simplicity that the corporate yield is fixed at 10 percent and the maximum marginal income tax rate is 50 percent, the demand for municipal bonds may be indicated by the line DMB in Figure 10.2. The distance DM represents the investible funds of investors in the 50 percent tax bracket. Any value of Y_m above 5 percent attracts all of these funds to municipals. The rising portion (MB) of the curve indicates that investors in lower and lower tax brackets are attracted by higher and higher values of Y_m. At the equilibrium value of $Y_m^e = 0.07$, determined by the intersection of DMB with the supply curve SS, investors in tax brackets above 30 percent are attracted to municipals. Equation (10.22) can be used to solve for the marginal tax rate, τ^*, of investors who are indifferent between the two securities in equilibri-

activities of states. As with all legal doctrines there have been many disagreements regarding the proper application of reciprocal immunity, and it has been argued from time to time, most vigorously by the Department of Justice in 1938 and the Bureau of Internal Revenue in 1941, that federal taxation of municipal bonds is constitutional. But Congress and the courts have consistently sided with state and local governments on this issue, and the tax-exempt status of municipals appears relatively secure. For more detail regarding the legal history of the tax-exempt status of municipals see Gordon Calvert (1972, Chapter 8).

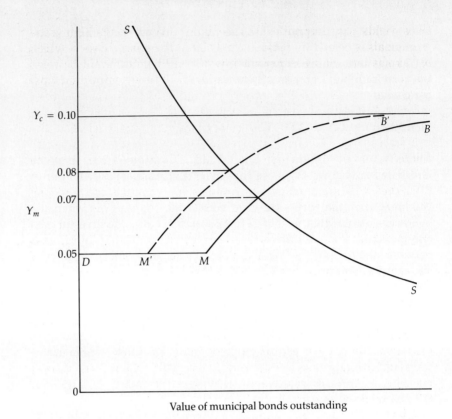

Figure 10.2   The institutional-demand theory of municipal bond yields.

um. Given Y_c and Y_m^e, τ^* is such that

(10.23) $Y_m^e = (1 - \tau^*) Y_c$ or $\tau^* = \dfrac{Y_c - Y_m^e}{Y_c} = 0.30$

when $Y_c = 0.10$ and $Y_m^e = 0.07$.

The tax exemption on municipal bonds conveys no direct benefit in our example to investors in marginal tax brackets of 30 percent or below. The gainers are state and local governments, who are enabled to borrow more cheaply than are issuers of taxable securities, and investors in tax brackets above 30 percent. For example an investor in the 50 percent bracket can earn 7 percent free of taxes on municipals, compared with 5 percent after taxes on corporates.

Two theories of municipal yields[60]

The *institutional-demand theory* is based on the assumption that security supplies are unresponsive to interest rates with the result that

---

60 This discussion is based on Charles Trzcinka (1982).

their yields are determined by demand. About one-third[61] of all municipals is owned by commercial banks, which use these securities as tax shelters. Some researchers have argued that the relationship between municipal and corporate yields depends on commercial bank purchases and sales of municipals in response to fluctuations in their incomes. For example a decline in bank profits causes a reduction in bank purchases of municipals, and municipal yields must rise in order to attract investors in lower tax brackets. Such an event is depicted by the leftward shift of the demand curve in Figure 10.2 from DMB to $DM'B'$, which means an increase in the equilibrium municipal yield to 8 percent and a reduction in the marginal tax rate of municipal investors to 20 percent.

We have so far assumed the corporate yield to be determined independently of the municipal yield. But Merton Miller (1977) has set forth a *tax-arbitrage theory* that takes account of the response of the supply of taxable debt to the relative yields of taxable and tax-exempt bonds. With τ_c denoting the tax rate on corporate profits, corporations have an incentive to issue debt as long as the after-tax cost of their debt, $(1 - \tau_c)Y_c$, is less than their tax-free return on municipals, Y_m. If $\tau_c = 0.50$, $Y_c = 0.10$, and $Y_m = 0.07$, for example, corporations will issue taxable debt in order to purchase tax-free debt, causing Y_c to rise and/or Y_m to fall until the following condition is reached, at which tax arbitrage is no longer profitable:[62]

(10.24) $$Y_m^e = (1 - \tau_c)Y_c^e$$

The e superscripts denote equilibrium yields and emphasize that municipal and corporate yields are interdependent.

Most of the support for a belief in this tax-arbitrage relation comes from the activities of commercial banks, which issue many kinds of taxable securities (such as bonds, certificates of deposit, federal funds, and interest-bearing checking accounts) and are free to invest the funds so acquired in either taxable (loans or U.S. securities) or tax-exempt (municipal) forms. Empirical tests of the tax-arbitrage and institutional-demand theories have been inconclusive, primarily because of the difficulties involved in identifying taxable and tax-exempt securities that are identical in every respect (especially risk) except tax status.[63] The tendency for municipal yields to vary between 70 and 80 percent of yields on corporate bonds with the same maturities and credit ratings lends support to the institutional-

---

61 This proportion applies to 1983. It has been falling since its peak of about one-half in 1971.

62 The tax-arbitrage argument is applied below, in Figure 15.7, to the determination of corporate debt/equity ratios.

63 Municipal yields are subject to many influences, including call provisions, coupon rates, nature of security, size of issue, stage of the business cycle, and changes in tax laws. See Timothy Cook (1982) for a survey of empirical investigations of the relative importance of these and other influences.

demand theory, but some writers[64] have claimed that the data are consistent with the tax-arbitrage theory when risk is properly measured.

QUESTIONS

1. Suppose corporations are deprived of limited liability. What will happen to bond yields? What will happen to stock prices? Why?

2. (a) What were ACF's and AMF's earnings per share during the four quarters preceding March 25, 1983?

   (b) Discuss the possible explanations for ACF's greater E/P ratio.

3. In a world of certainty and no taxes what happens to stock prices when inflationary expectations are revised upward? Distinguish between the situations in which (a) interest rates fully reflect inflationary expectations, as assumed in the section on stock prices and interest rates, and (b) interest rates are pegged to a constant level by the central bank.

4. (a) Discuss some possible reasons for the existence of call premiums.

   (b) What is the relationship between (i) the value of the call provision and (ii) the size of the call premium? (*Hint.* See your answers to problems 4 and 5.)

   (c) Please try to guess why consumer groups have opposed call premiums on mortgages but not on bonds.

   (d) What form does the call premium on a mortgage take?

5. Choose a large industrial corporation, a large public utility, a large airline, and a large bank. Look up their bonds and preferred stock in *Moody's Manuals* and summarize the principal differences in the security indentures of the four firms. Give possible explanations for those differences. Also discuss the possible reasons for the different ratings assigned by Moody's to these securities.

6. Based on your reading of Figure 10.1, calculate the default premiums on Aaa and Baa bonds at cyclical peaks and troughs. Present the premiums in a table, and (a) describe any regularities, or patterns, that you are able to discern and (b) present possible explanations of those patterns (including references to both d and Π in Table 10.9).

7. Politicians and executives are often heard to complain of the higher borrowing costs imposed on their governments and firms by downward revisions in their bond ratings. Comment.

8. A large body of finance literature suggests that the value of a firm is independent of its capital structure (its debt/equity ratio)

---

64 Especially Charles Trzcinka (1982). Also see this article for references to empirical studies that have supported the institutional-demand theory.

when there is no profits tax but that in the presence of such a tax the firm's value is increased by the substitution of debt for equity since interest payments are tax deductible. This has led Michael Jensen and William Meckling (1976, page 334) to ask, "Why don't we observe large corporations individually owned with a tiny fraction of the capital supplied by the entrepreneur in return for 100 percent of the equity and the rest simply borrowed? We believe there are a number of reasons," which include "the incentive effects associated with highly leveraged firms" and "the monitoring costs these incentive effects engender."

Please give some examples of (a) these incentive effects and (b) arrangements between owners and creditors that reduce these effects without incurring substantial monitoring costs.

9. Average annual percentage rates of return on samples of the highest-grade corporate bonds and preferred stock as rated by Moody's and reported by Robert Soldofsky and Dale Max (1978, page 33) were:

	1910–1938	1939–1953	1954–1976
Aaa bonds	4.92	2.80	3.01
High-grade preferred	6.29	3.91	2.95

Give at least one reason for the decline of returns on preferred stock relative to bonds.

10. Suppose you want to open a ski resort and the bank will lend you the necessary $5 million dollars at 12 percent. But you have a talk with your friendly county commissioners. What interest rate will you actually have to pay?

11. Compare and explain the bid-asked spreads in Tables 6.2 and 10.12. Please base your explanation on the security and market characteristics discussed in Chapter 7.

PROBLEMS

1. What is the price of an 8.9 percent, 10-year bond with a 7 percent yield to maturity? Please show your calculations, as always. [*Hint*. See Equation (6.5).]

2. Assume a flat, 7 percent yield curve, and consider an 8.9 percent bond that can be called in 1 month at 102.67 (plus the coupon). What is the current market price of this bond?

3. Confirm the yields Y_c in Table 10.6.

4. Refer to Table 10.6: What is the value of the call option if the call price is $102 (a) when 1-year yields at the end of 1 year are expected with certainty to be $Y_1 = 0.05$ and (b) when there is a fifty-fifty chance that 1-year yields at the end of 1 year will be 0.05 or 0.15?

5. Refer to Table 10.6: What is the value of the call option if the call price is $105 (a) when 1-year yields at the end of 1 year are

expected with certainty to be $Y_1 = 0.05$ and **(b)** when there is a fifty-fifty chance that 1-year yields at the end of 1 year will be 0.05 or 0.15?

6. Assume the data in case A of Table 10.7, except that assets are financed by equal amounts of debt and equity.

   (a) What are the returns to debt and equity if the firm undertakes the risky venture? Calculate expected returns as well as the returns from each outcome.

   (b) What contract rate of interest on debt would produce the same returns for debt and equity?

   (c) Which of the two ventures, the risky venture or the one with a certain 10 percent rate of return on assets, will the owners select when $C_b = 0.10$? Why?

   (d) Which of the two ventures will the owners select if the contract rate of interest is your answer to (b)?

7. The conversion ratios of ITT's preferred stock traded on March 25, 1983, are:

Issue	Conversion ratios
$4 preferred, series J	1.6810
$4 preferred, series K	1.6155
$5 preferred	1.4364
$2.25 preferred	1.2560
$4.50 preferred	1.6880

   Did any arbitrage profits exist on March 25, 1983? Please show your calculations.

8. American Medical's 8s of 2000 and Dayco's 6s of 1994 are convertible into common at $14.15 per share and $20.92 per share, respectively. American Medical's and Dayco's common stock sold for 32⅛ and 10⅞, respectively, at the close of trading on March 25, 1983. Referring to Table 10.5, were the prices of these two bonds consistent with relation (10.21) on that date? (Assume no accrual of interest on the bonds.)

9. **(a)** In terms of the situation described in Table 10.10, what is the price of the convertible bond if there is a fifty-fifty chance that the end-of-year stock price will be $50 or $150?

   (b) Assuming no risk of default, discuss why P_B is directly related to σ.

10. **(a)** Consider the situation in Table 10.11, except that the firm's assets of $10 are financed on January 1 by issuing five shares of stock and five straight 1-year bonds. Each of the bonds has a face value of $1.10. Furthermore, investors are aware of the existence only of the riskless project promising a 1-year rate of return of 10 percent. We assume that investors require a 10 percent expected rate of return on every asset. What is the price of a share of stock on January 1? What is the price of a bond?

    (b) What happens to the prices of shares and bonds on January 2, when the availability of the risky project becomes known and it is generally believed that the firm will undertake the risky project? Assume nonconvertible bonds.

(c) What happens to stock and bond prices on January 2 if each bond is convertible into one share of stock?

11. Consider the following three groups of investors: (1) financial intermediaries, all in the 50 percent income-tax bracket, with $300 billion available for investments in corporate and municipal bonds; (2) individuals in the 40 percent bracket, with $100 billion available for investments in corporates and municipals; and (3) individuals in the 30 percent bracket, with $100 billion available for investments in corporates and municipals. Assume that the yield on corporates is fixed at 10 percent and that outstanding municipals, all perpetuities (so that you can easily calculate the relationship between value and yield), pay coupons totalling $15 billion annually.

(a) What is the equilibrium yield on municipals?

(b) Now suppose there is an outflow of funds from intermediaries such that they have only $240 billion available for municipal and corporate bonds. The investible funds of investors in the 30 and 40 percent tax brackets remain the same. What will be the equilibrium yield on municipals (*i*) according to the institutional-demand theory and (*ii*) according to the tax-arbitrage theory?

REFERENCES

William J. Baumol, Burton G. Malkiel, and Richard E. Quandt, "The Valuation of Convertible Securities," *Quarterly Journal of Economics,* February 1966, pages 48–59.

Adolf A. Berle and Gardiner C. Means, *The Modern Corporation and Private Property,* Macmillan, New York, 1932.

Jules I. Bogen (ed.), *Financial Handbook,* 4th ed., Wiley, New York, 1964.

Gordon C. Calvert (ed.), *Fundamentals of Municipal Bonds,* 9th ed., Securities Industry Association, New York, 1972.

Timothy Q. Cook, "Determinants of Individual Tax-exempt Bond Yields: A Survey of the Evidence," Federal Reserve Bank of Richmond *Economic Review,* May/June 1982, pages 14–39.

Timothy Q. Cook and Patric H. Hendershott, "The Impact of Taxes, Risk, and Relative Security Supplies on Interest Rate Differentials," *Journal of Finance,* September 1978, pages 1173–1186.

Arundel Cotter, *United States Steel: A Corporation with a Soul,* Doubleday, Garden City, NY, 1921.

Edwin J. Elton and Martin J. Gruber, "Dy-

namic Programming Applications in Finance," *Journal of Finance,* May 1971, pages 475–505.

Frank J. Fabozzi and Frank Zarb (eds.), *Handbook of Financial Markets,* Dow Jones-Irwin, Homewood, IL, 1981.

Eugene F. Fama and Merton H. Miller, *The Theory of Finance,* Holt, Rinehart & Winston, New York, 1972.

Paul G. Farnham and George S. Cluff, "Municipal Bond Ratings: New Results, New Directions," *Public Finance Quarterly,* October 1982, pages 403–455.

James Greenleaf, Ruth Foster, and Robert Prinsky, *Understanding Financial Data in the Wall Street Journal,* Dow Jones, Princeton, NJ, 1982.

George H. Hempel, *The Postwar Quality of State and Local Debt,* National Bureau of Economic Research, New York, 1971.

Arleigh P. Hess and Willis J. Winn, *The Value of the Call Privilege,* University of Pennsylvania Press, Philadelphia, 1962.

W. Braddock Hickman, *Corporate Bond Quality and Investor Experience,* Princeton University Press, Princeton, NJ, 1958.

W. Braddock Hickman, *Statistical Measures of Corporate Bond Financing since 1900,* Princeton University Press, Princeton, NJ, 1960.

Thomas Ho and Ronald F. Singer, "The Value of Corporate Debt with a Sinking-fund Provision," *Journal of Business,* July 1984, pages 315–336.

Dwight M. Jaffee, "Cyclical Variations in the Risk Structure of Interest Rates," *Journal of Monetary Economics,* July 1975, pages 309–325.

Frank C. Jen and James C. Wert, "The Value of the Deferred Call Privilege," *National Banking Review,* March 1966, pages 369–378.

Frank C. Jen and James C. Wert, "The Deferred Call Provision and Corporate Bond Yields," *Journal of Financial and Quantitative Analysis,* June 1968, pages 157–169.

Michael C. Jensen and William H. Meckling, "Theory of the Firm: Managerial Behavior, Agency Costs and Ownership Structure," *Journal of Financial Economics,* October 1976, pages 305–360.

Avner Kalay, "Stockholder-Bondholder Conflict and Dividend Constraints," *Journal of Financial Economics,* July 1982, pages 211–233.

Charles Mackay, *Extraordinary Popular Delusions and the Madness of Crowds,* Bentley, London, 1841.

William J. Marshall and Jess B. Yawitz, "Optimal Terms of the Call Provision on a Corporate Bond," *Journal of Financial Research,* Summer 1980, pages 203–211.

William J. Marshall and Jess B. Yawitz, "Measuring the Effect of Callability on Bond Yields," *Journal of Money, Credit and Banking,* February 1981, pages 60–71.

Wayne H. Mikkelson, "Convertible Debt and Warrant Financing: A Study of the Agency Cost Motivation and the Wealth Effects of Calls of Convertible Securities," Managerial Economics Research Center Monograph and Theses Series 80–03, University of Rochester, Rochester, NY, 1980.

Wayne H. Mikkelson, "Convertible Calls and Security Returns," *Journal of Financial Economics,* September 1981, pages 237–264.

Merton Miller, "Debt and Taxes," *Journal of Finance,* May 1977, pages 261–275.

George E. Pinches and Kent A. Mingo, "A Multivariate Analysis of Industrial Bond Ratings," *Journal of Finance,* March 1973, pages 1–32.

George E. Pinches and J. Clay Singleton, "The Adjustment of Stock Prices to Bond Rating Changes," *Journal of Finance,* March 1978, pages 29–44.

Gordon Pye, "The Value of the Call Option on a Bond," *Journal of Political Economy,* April 1966, pages 200–205.

Gordon Pye, "Gauging the Default Premium," *Financial Analysts Journal,* January/February 1974, pages 49–52.

Clifford W. Smith and Jerold B. Warner, "On Financial Contracting: An Analysis of Bond Covenants," *Journal of Financial Economics,* June 1979, pages 117–161.

Robert M. Soldofsky and Dale F. Max, *Holding Period Yields and Risk-premium Curves for Long-term Marketable Securities: 1910–1976,* New York University Graduate School of Business Administration, New York, 1978.

Standard & Poor's Ratings Guide, McGraw-Hill, New York, 1979.

George J. Stigler, "The Dominant Firm and the Inverted Umbrella," *Journal of Law and Economics,* October 1965, pages 167–172.

Charles Trzcinka, "The Pricing of Tax-exempt Bonds and the Miller Hypothesis," *Journal of Finance,* September 1982, pages 907–923.

Mark Twain, *Pudd'nhead Wilson,* American Publishing, Hartford, CT, 1894.

James C. Van Horne, *Financial Market Rates and Flows,* Prentice-Hall, Englewood Cliffs, NJ, 1978.

Mark I. Weinstein, "The Effect of a Rating Change Announcement on Bond Price," *Journal of Financial Economics,* December 1977, pages 329–350.

John B. Williams, *The Theory of Investment Value,* Harvard University Press, Cambridge, MA, 1938.

Jess B. Yawitz, Kevin J. Maloney, and William J. Marshall, "The Term Structure and Callable Bond Yield Spreads," *Journal of Portfolio Management,* Winter 1983, pages 57–63.

TRADING CAPITAL MARKET INSTRUMENTS[1]

Cotton is good, corn is good, real estate is very good; but none of these has the beautiful qualities of 3 per cent British consols or United States 5-20s. Commodore Vanderbilt can convert the bulk of his vast property into money in a day. There is no similar market ready to perform a like service for William B. Astor.[2] . . . The clergyman whose ten years' faithful ministry has resulted in the painful saving of a thousand dollars is very much at the mercy of his parish if his money is in land, and quite his own master if it be locked up in bonds or shares, merchantable at once in the great city which lies an hour's distance from his village. . . .
Nor is the proverbial sensitiveness of paper values any considerable bar to their popularity. Over all the rumor of fraud, of "street" artifices, of the perils of open market, and of whirlwind crises, is the mighty fact that the main bulk of securities in the great stock boards bear annual fruitage in interest, and are assured of instant sale at current prices.

James K. Medbury, *Men and Mysteries of Wall Street*, 1870

In view of its advanced technology, which permits the almost instantaneous communication of information and execution of trades, and its high degree of organization, which enables thousands of diverse financial instruments to be traded over a wide geographical area in what is essentially a single market, the American capital market must be considered the world's most sophisticated trading system. And it has consistently held first place since the mid-nineteenth century. Such a diverse yet integrated market could not exist except in a large, rich, industrially competitive, and politically stable free trade area, that is, an area with a wide variety of large and attractive (profitable

---

1 With emphasis on corporate stocks and bonds. Procedures for trading other securities were discussed in Chapters 6 to 9.

2 Vanderbilt's wealth consisted mainly of railroad shares; Astor's was in real estate.

and relatively safe) security issues. But equally necessary is a competitive financial system. Firms issue stocks and bonds to acquire funds for profitable ventures. Brokers and dealers in stocks and bonds quote prices, offer services, and execute trades in pursuit of similar profit-seeking goals. In addition, also like other entrepreneurs, brokers and dealers try to structure their environment to their own advantage. One of their most successful innovations to this end has been the formation of limited-membership "exchanges" for the more efficient exchanges of information and securities and for the purposes of excluding competition and fixing commissions. The early exchanges thrived. But their collusive practices and limited capacities, in combination with the growth of the nation's business, stimulated the growth of rival exchanges and advances in off-exchange trading practices—until we now have a system in which people who wish to invest in securities, and firms that wish their securities to be widely available, are presented with a variety of competing alternatives. These include several exchanges, an electronic quotation system among thousands of video-screen computer terminals in broker and dealer offices, and less sophisticated search processes for inactively traded securities. Take your choice. To the extent permitted by government regulations, brokers and dealers in all these closely linked trading alternatives are busily engaged in trying to develop more immediate and less costly means of acquiring information and executing trades that will attract your business on terms that are profitable to them.

The present competitive financial system is not merely the result of price and service competition among brokers, dealers, and others within a succession of given institutional and technological environments. Each environment has itself been determined by competitive forces. This chapter describes the evolution and present state of the American capital market. The future of this system is more than usually difficult to predict, not only because of our inability to forecast technological developments and entrepreneurial responses to those developments but also because of increasing government interference. Congress and the regulators are presently engaged in a substantial effort to force the capital market into a narrow government-controlled system. We already know from our study of the Federal Reserve's attempts (through interest rate ceilings and barriers to entry) to suppress competition in commercial banking that the principal result of such attempts is the development of new financial instruments, institutions, and trading arrangements to avoid the effects of regulation.

STOCK EXCHANGES
A definition

DEFINITION 11.1.   An *exchange* is defined by two features: a place and a set of rules. A *securities exchange* is a location where traders come together for the purpose of buying and selling securities according to procedures laid down by the governing body of the exchange.

Since an efficient market is one in which prices reflect values, market efficiency is possible only if all buyers and sellers are confronted by the same (or nearly the same) prices. This means low transaction costs, that is, small brokers' commissions and narrow dealer spreads between buying and selling prices, and in a world of rapidly changing prices, continuous communication between potential buyers and sellers. Brokers, dealers, and others in search of the lowest available buying prices and the highest available selling prices have an incentive to promote the rapid exchange of information, especially price information, and thereby to promote market efficiency. Before the teletype and telephone the continuous exchange of information and the execution of trades based on that information could be achieved only by physical proximity—often in an exchange. Traders continue to find securities exchanges useful even in the presence of today's electronic communications systems. Whether exchanges will continue to flourish as communications systems become more sophisticated and more widely available is yet to be determined.

The development of the New York Stock Exchange (NYSE) and its connections with other parts of the capital market

Stock certificates originated with the development of joint-stock companies in the early seventeenth century. By the end of that century shares were being actively traded, and terms such as "bears," "bulls," and "puts" had become familiar. For nearly a century, stock trading in London took place in an informal "curb market" on the street and in the coffeehouses of 'Change Alley. Finally an indoor location and rules of procedure were settled, and the London Stock Exchange was formed in 1773. The Paris *Bourse* had been founded in 1726. Organized securities trading in the United States, as in France and England, had to wait for the appearance of large firms and a substantial government debt, that is, for the appearance of securities sufficient in quantity and attractiveness to justify the costs of formal trading arrangements. A stock exchange existed in Philadelphia in 1754, and the present Philadelphia Stock Exchange was established in 1790. Wall Street had also by the 1790s become a center for securities trading. The beginnings of the NYSE may be traced to the following agreement signed by twenty-four securities brokers who had been trading under a buttonwood tree on Wall Street:

> We the Subscribers, Brokers for the Purchase and Sale of Public Stock, do hereby solemnly promise and pledge ourselves to each other, that we will not buy or sell from this day for any person whatsoever, any kind of Public Stock, at less than one quarter of one per cent Commission on the Specie value and that we will

Table 11.1   Average Daily Volume and Value of Stock Transactions on U.S. Exchanges, 1982

Exchange	Shares, Millions	% of Total	Value, Millions $	% of Total	% of Total Value in 1950
New York	71.9	81.0	2,031.9	85.1	86.0
American	6.3	7.1	81.9	3.4	6.8
Midwest (Chicago)	4.5	5.1	138.9	5.8	2.4
Pacific[a]	3.2	3.6	72.8	3.1	2.2
Philadelphia	1.9	2.1	37.9	1.6	0.9
Boston	0.4	0.5	12.1	0.5	1.1
Cincinnati	0.4	0.5	11.2	0.5	0.1
Others[b]	0.1	0.1	0.1	c	0.5
	88.7	100.0	2,386.8	100.0	100.0

a The Los Angeles and San Francisco Stock Exchanges in 1950.

b Intermountain (Salt Lake City) and Spokane in 1982; Colorado Springs, Detroit, Honolulu, New Orleans, Pittsburgh, Richmond, St. Louis, Spokane, and Wheeling in 1950.

c Less than one-twentieth of 1 percent.

Sources: 1950 data from James E. Walter, *The Role of Regional Security Exchanges,* University of California Press, Berkeley, 1957, page 128; 1982 data from *SEC Monthly Statistical Review,* February 1983, tab. A-110.

give preference to each other in our Negotiations. In Testimony whereof we have set our hands this 17th day of May at New York, 1792.

The remainder of this history is concerned primarily with the NYSE. But most of the events that we discuss were equally important to the development of trading on other exchanges and other parts of the capital market. (Some idea of the relative importance of the NYSE and other exchanges in 1950 and 1982 may be gained from Table 11.1.)

1793. Each of the "buttonwood brokers" subscribed $200 toward the construction of the Tontine Coffee House,[3] which served both business and social needs until 1820. Memberships soon began to be called "seats" because members transacted business from more or less regular seats in the coffeehouse.

1817. All the requisites for a genuine exchange were achieved when the Tontine Coffee House members adopted a name—the New York Stock and Exchange Board—and a constitution that specified

---

3 A *tontine* (after the seventeenth-century Italian banker Lorenzo Tonti) is an insurance or other financial arrangement among a group of contributors to a fund such that, upon the death or default of a member, his share is distributed among the remaining members until, upon the death of all but one or at the end of an agreed period, the entire fund goes to those remaining. Tontine is also the name for a share in the arrangement.

formal trading rules. A "call" system of trading was adopted, whereby the chairman called the listed stocks in turn, beginning at 11:30 A.M., and the twenty-eight members declared their bids and offers. Business had to be over by 2:15 P.M., but trading usually ended before 1:00.

The initiation fee was $25. Three negative votes constituted a blackball.

1820. The membership was thirty-eight, the initiation fee was raised to $40, new quarters were secured, and the constitution was revised. There were daily calls from two lists: first from the regular list, which included market leaders, and then from a free list, to which any broker might submit names. A list of broker commissions for trades in stocks, bonds, mortgage loans, and domestic and foreign currency was adopted. Fictitious (or "wash") sales were prohibited. A wash sale is one in which two brokers report a pretended transaction in order to give a stock a fictitious quotation. For example a fictitious quotation below the "true" market price for an inactive stock might enable the conspirators to buy that stock at a lower price than otherwise if sellers treat the quoted price as the market's judgment of the worth of the stock. The Exchange desires that every trade be a "genuine transaction."

1825. Completion of the Erie Canal improved communications with the West and reinforced the growing commercial and financial supremacy of New York over Philadelphia.

1830. The first public steam railway, built by George Stephenson between Stockton and Darlington, opened in 1825. In 1829 Stephenson's *Rocket* demonstrated the superiority of steam over horses. In 1830 the first American railroad (the Baltimore & Ohio) began operation, and the first railroad stock (the Mohawk and Hudson) was placed on the Exchange's list. By 1835 trading in railroad stocks led all others, continuing to do so until they were overtaken by industrials during World War I.

1835. Regular market reports began to appear in the papers. An example appears in Figure 11.1.

1844. The first land telegraph line was constructed between Washington and Baltimore. By 1846 New York was connected with Boston, Buffalo, Philadelphia, Baltimore, and Washington. On March 3, 1846, the *New York Herald* complained that "certain parties in New York and Philadelphia were employing the telegraph for speculating in stocks."[4] By 1852 there were over 23,000 miles of wire connecting nearly all medium- and large-size cities east of the Mississippi. The East was linked to the already advanced California system in 1861. The telegraph was the greatest single influence on the devel-

---

4 Robert Thompson (1947, page 47).

Stocks—Yesterday the fancy stocks took a tumble of from 2 to 4 per cent. on some descriptions, the railroads especially. Money is beginning to get scarce, and there is some fear that the banks mean to curtail. This impression does not prevail generally.

SALES AT THE STOCK EXCHANGE

110 shares	East River Insurance		99
25 "	Manhattan Gas Company		$129\frac{3}{4}$
50 "	" " " on time		100
150 "	Mohawk Railroad Company		126
500 "	Utica and Schenectady, opening		128
350 "	" " " "		$128\frac{1}{4}$
250 "	Jamaica Railroad		189
25 "	United States Bank		$112\frac{1}{4}$
160 "	Union Bank		122
40 "	" "		$121\frac{3}{4}$
100 "	Delaware and Hudson		$112\frac{1}{4}$
450 "	" " "		$112\frac{1}{4}$
200 "	" " "		$112\frac{1}{4}$
310 "	Harlem Railroad		106
550 "	" " "		$105\frac{3}{4}$
100 "	" " "		$105\frac{1}{4}$
200 "	" " "		$105\frac{1}{4}$
51 "	Dry Dock Bank		150
50 "	" " "		$149\frac{3}{4}$

Source: Sereno S. Pratt, *The Work of Wall Street,* Appleton, New York, 1921, page 11.

Figure 11.1   An early stock market report from the *New York Herald,* May 13, 1835.

opment of American financial markets. By providing an immediate link between Wall Street and investors throughout the United States, it has enabled New York to remain the country's financial center despite the westward movement of population and industry.

1853. The New York Clearing House was formed, allowing banks to settle their net indebtedness with other banks by debits and credits to balances with the Clearing House instead of by actual exchanges of cash between pairs of banks.[5] The Clearing House was to have an important beneficial influence on the stock market. Settlement between banks was now daily, rather than weekly, and banks were in a better position to control their cash flows and therefore to be a steadier source of credit to the stock market. (See the discussion of call loans in the 1869 entry). In addition, the Clearing House attempted to provide some of the stabilizing influence of a lender of last resort that ideally would have been provided by a central bank. In the face of drains of gold from New York in 1857, 1860, 1873, 1884, 1893, and 1907, either to the interior or overseas, the banks agreed to expand their loans, and Clearing House certificates were issued to serve in place of gold in the settlement of interbank indebtedness.

5 See the discussion of clearinghouses in Chapter 4.

The U.S. Treasury also helped on some of these occasions either by making an effort to sell bonds overseas instead of at home or by purchasing bonds through brokerage houses (open-market purchases).[6]

1857.   The *New York Times* declared that "the New York Stock Exchange as at present managed is little more than an enormous gambling establishment"[7]—a time, in short, like all other times.

1858.   The state of New York's 1812 ban on short selling was lifted. "No contract, written or verbal, hereafter made for the sale of any share in the stock of any incorporated company shall be voidable because the vendor, at the time of making such contract, is not the owner of such share."[8]

1863.   The Exchange's name was changed to the New York Stock Exchange.

1866.   Completion of the Atlantic cable permitted instant communication between American and European markets. Before the English Channel cable was laid in 1851, London and Paris brokers had often communicated by carrier pigeon.

The Exchange had begun to request financial information from listed companies. The requests were not binding, however, and one company treasurer responded that "The Delaware, Lackawanna & Western R.R. makes no reports and publishes no statements—and has not done anything of the kind for the past five years."[9] But disclosure of company earnings, debt, and other information was eventually made mandatory, and information requirements have become more stringent over time, first according to rules laid down by the NYSE[10] and since the 1930s to conform with federal securities legislation as administered by the Securities and Exchange Commission (SEC).

1867.   Edward Calahan developed a printing machine, which he called the "Gold and Stock Ticker, to hook up to a telegraph line. A telegrapher stationed at the New York Stock Exchange tapped out the latest gold and stock trading prices as they were reported, and the information was instantly printed on tickers in the offices of [subscribing] brokers."[11] The ticker was improved in 1870 by Thomas Edison, who in 1883 further increased the speed of the system and introduced the famous glass-domed ticker, which was used for over half a century.

---

6 See Margaret Myers (1931) for a history of the New York money market before 1913.

7 Sereno Pratt (1921, page 17).

8 Peter Wyckoff (1972, page 15).

9 John Neumark (1960, page 44). For an even greater aversion to disclosure, see the discussion of the South Sea Bubble in footnote 4 in Chapter 10.

10 See Edward Meeker (1930, pages 549–584) for a statement of the NYSE's listing requirements in 1930 and Richard Teweles and Edward Bradley (1982, Chapter 6) for a history of those requirements.

11 Frank Zarb and Gabriel Kerekes (1970, page 216).

1869. Two sessions (calls) were instituted: 10:30 A.M. to 12 noon and 1 to 2 P.M. Memberships were made salable. The New York Stock and Exchange Board had been a relatively small, closed group. There were less than 100 members in 1860, each with his own seat in the Board Room. Election to membership was made difficult by active use of the blackball. The large volume of trading during the Civil War stimulated increases in the number and importance of competing exchanges and curbstone brokers.[12] In 1869 the NYSE (then with 533 members) took in the 354 members of the Open Board of Brokers and the 173 members of the Government Bond Department, raising its membership to 1,060. Memberships (seats) could be bought and sold, subject to the approval of the governing board. The number of seats has been 1,366 since 1953. In 1982, thirty-four seats were sold at prices ranging from $190,000 to $340,000. The high and low prices since World War II were $515,000 in 1968 and 1969 and $35,000 in 1949 and 1977.

The *money post* was established. Brokers borrowed from banks and from other firms and individuals by means of *time loans* (that is, loans of fixed maturities exceeding 1 day) or *call (demand) loans,* which could be terminated by either party at any time.[13] Most of these loans were arranged directly between brokers and lenders (or by New York banks for out-of-town lenders on the basis of cabled or wired instructions from Europe or the American interior). But a significant portion of call loans was negotiated at the NYSE. Some members acted for one or more banks in negotiating loans with other brokers. In addition brokers often borrowed and lent funds for their own accounts. Money was bought and sold, just like stocks, through a process of bids and offers between members. Eventually, in 1869, the brokers who specialized in lending money were assigned a separate post on the floor of the Exchange.[14]

1871. The old call system had become unable to accommodate the volume and continuity of trading desired by members, and the present *two-way auction* trading system was established whereby buyers and sellers may continuously bid against each other on any stock during trading hours.

1873. The NYSE was closed from September 18 through September 29 because of panic caused by the failure of Jay Cooke & Co.

---

12 See the 1921 entry below for a discussion of trading "on the curb."

13 The nineteenth-century time loan market was similar to the present term RP market discussed in Chapter 9. Also see Chapter 9 for a discussion of the importance of the call loan market to the management of bank reserves before 1930. Current methods of financing brokers and dealers are discussed later in the present chapter.

14 For discussions of the brokers' loan market, including procedures for money lending at the NYSE, see Margaret Myers (1931, Chapters 7 and 13), R. Schabacker (1930, Chapter 11), Charles Dice and Wilford Eiteman (1941, Chapter 25), and the Federal Reserve Board's *Banking and Monetary Statistics, 1914–41,* pages 432–438. The last reference also contains data on amounts and rates of brokers' loans.

and others. The only trading was "on the curb." Other panic closings occurred in 1914 (for 19 weeks at the outbreak of World War I) and 1933 (for 1 week during the bank holiday).

1874. Odd-lot trading, which had been abolished with the adoption of the auction system in 1871, was resumed when some members offered to handle transactions of fewer than 100 shares at prices based on round-lot sales. Odd-lot trading has declined in importance in recent years largely because of the growth of institutional investors. The number of shares traded in odd lots was less in 1982 than in 1965. The proportion of shares traded in odd lots fell from 17 percent in 1960 to 1.2 percent in 1982.

1875. The *specialist* system began when (so the story goes), because of a broken leg, James Boyd was forced to handle all his business from one spot on the floor and decided to limit his trading to a single active stock, Western Union. Word spread that brokers could always find a market for Western Union at Boyd's "post," his business and profits increased, and imitators applied Boyd's practices to other stocks.[15]

Brokers began to leave *limit orders* (that is, at prices above or below the current market) with Boyd and other specialists.

1876. Alexander Graham Bell developed the first successful telephone. Telephones began to be used on the NYSE in 1878.

1892. The specialist system was encouraged by the assignment of some stocks to specific posts. By 1910, 123 of 1100 members were specialists; 406 of 1,366 members were specialists in 1981.[16]

The NYSE Clearing House was formed. The first successful stock clearing system was started in Frankfort in 1867, followed by Berlin, Hamburg, Vienna, London, and in 1892 New York. A complete stock clearing facility operates much like a bank clearinghouse except that the former clears both stocks and money. It greatly reduces the number of transactions and the need for bank credit. Instead of the exchange of stock certificates and money in connection with every transaction, members receive or deliver only their *net* claims or obligations of certificates and money. For example suppose that Adcock & Co. sells 200 shares of Xerox at 40 to Bruton, who sells the same amount to Crandall at 41. Adcock then buys 100 shares from Dittmer at 39. Adcock and Dittmer each deliver 100 shares to the clearing facility, which delivers the 200 shares to Crandall. Crandall pays $8,200 to the clearing facility, which pays $4,100 to Adcock, $200 to Bruton, and $3,900 to Dittmer, net of clearing fees and transfer

---

15 This story is told in many places. Robert Sobel (1977, page 29) presents a more prosaic and probably more reliable account of the development of the specialist system, according to which some traders continuously stationed themselves at the centers of crowds trading in the various stocks as early as 1866 at the Open Board of Brokers.

16 Alfred Bernheim and Margaret Schneider (1935, page 406) and NYSE, *Report of the Quality of Markets Committee* (1982).

taxes. In fact the Clearing House established in 1892 cleared only stock certificates. The clearing of money had to wait for the Stock Clearing Corporation formed in 1920.[17]

1915. Stock prices began to be quoted on the NYSE in dollars instead of percentage of par value. Newspapers had already begun to report quotations in dollars.

1917. The *money desk* replaced the money post. The post was a place where the "money crowd" gathered. The desk added a clerical establishment to communicate the borrowing and lending desires of members to each other. Member brokers acting for banks informed the desk of their lendable funds, and brokers who wished to borrow communicated their needs to the desk. The desk kept borrowers and lenders informed of each others' identities and of the amounts desired to be borrowed or lent. The desk was informed of transactions, and after its formation in 1920 the Stock Clearing Corporation transferred money and collateral between the parties concerned.

1920. The Stock Clearing Corporation, with a clearing fund provided by members, was established to assume and expand the functions performed by the Stock Clearing House formed in 1892. The new Clearing Corporation cleared money as well as stocks. Previously, if Adcock sold stock to Bruton and wanted to buy stock from Crandall, he either waited for payment from Bruton or arranged a bank loan before he could complete his purchase from Crandall. After 1920 Adcock was required to increase his borrowing only if his purchases exceeded his sales.

1921. The New York Curb Market moved indoors. Trading on the curb had existed since colonial days, when dealers left their offices during active trading periods to meet with customers outdoors. Curb trading was described by one writer as follows:

> In the street a jostling mass of human beings, fantastically garbed, wearing many-colored caps like jockeys or pantaloons, their heads thrown back, their arms extended high as if in prayer to some heathen deity, their fingers working with frantic symbols, their voices crying an agonized frenzy, and at a hundred windows in the great buildings on either side of the street little groups of men and women gesticulated back as wildly to the mob below. It is the outside market of Mammon.
>
> A. G. Gardiner, *New Republic,* August 18, 1920.[18]

---

17 See Sereno Pratt (1921) and R. Schabacker (1930) for discussions of the development of clearing procedures at the NYSE.

18 Quoted from Charles Dice and Wilford Eiteman (1941, page 100). Also see the descriptions in Robert Sobel (1970, Chapter 5) and the American Stock Exchange's 1980 *Annual Report.*

Despite its appearance curb trading had been formalized in 1911 with the formation of the New York Curb Market Association, which established trading rules, regular hours of trading, and procedures for record keeping and the listing of stocks and bonds admitted to trading. Its name was changed to the New York Curb Exchange in 1929 and the American Stock Exchange in 1953.

1925. The Trans-Lux Daylight Movie Corporation introduced a projected display of Edison's "ticker tape on a frosted screen, which could be installed on the wall of a brokerage office. This enabled many people in each office to see the ticker simultaneously, instead of having to huddle around the glass-domed machine, passing the tape greedily from hand to hand. The Trans-Lux display, moving from right to left, became universal in most successful brokerage offices, and generations of 'tape watchers' have become familiar with it."[19]

1929. A central quotation system for reporting bid and ask prices at trading posts was introduced.

The Dow Jones Industrial (DJI) Stock Index rose from 202 at the end of 1927 to 300 at the end of 1928 to a high of 381 on September 3, 1929. The ensuing decline became a panic on October 23. The biggest loss (38) occurred on October 28, and the year's low of 199 was reached on November 13. After reaching 294 on April 17, 1930, the DJI fell to 158 on December 16, 1930, and finally to its twentieth-century low of 41 on July 8, 1932.

Daily average trading volume (in millions of shares) rose from 1.0 in 1924 to 2.1 in 1927, 3.4 in 1928, and 4.3 in 1929 (16.4 on October 29), before falling to 3.0 in 1930, 2.1 in 1931, and 1.5 in 1932. Brokers' loans from banks and others rose (in billions of dollars at the end of the month) from $3.2 in September 1926 to $8.5 in September 1929, before falling to $0.4 in September 1932.

The stock market panic was aggravated by the withdrawal of credit by the Federal Reserve System (the Fed). Fed credit was reduced by 41 percent between the end of October 1929 to the end of October 1930, from $1,680 million to $985 million. This action more than off-set a $148 million gold inflow and an attempt by New York banks to absorb panic selling with a $250 million bankers' pool.

1933. Congress passed the Securities Act of 1933, later supple-mented by the Securities Exchange Act of 1934 (which established the SEC), the Investment Company and Investment Advisers Acts of 1940, and the Securities Acts Amendments of 1975. The most impor-tant effect of this legislation as administered by the SEC has been to increase new financing costs. But the main effect on secondary mar-kets has been the SEC's interference with competition, most notably by supporting the NYSE's attempts to preserve the buttonwood

---

19 Frank Zarb and Gabriel Kerekes (1970, page 216).

agreement and, consistent with the policy of supporting collusion between existing brokers and dealers, by attempting to limit entry into the securities business. The principle of self-regulation embodied in much of the legislation of the 1930s, according to which price fixing and other collusive arrangements were given the force of law, may have delayed the *de facto* breakdown and certainly delayed the *de jure* abandonment of the NYSE's rules that all members shall charge the same commission and trade only with each other in listed stocks.

As an example of its attitude toward entry the first and most frequent complaint registered by the SEC in its *Report of Special Study of Securities Markets* in 1963 was directed at the "notable ease of entry" into the over-the-counter (OTC) securities business. "The ease with which anyone can start his own securities firm and deal with the public has permitted many an amateur to embark on the deep waters of broker-dealer entrepreneurship." The SEC drew a sharp contrast between the swimming abilities required of OTC broker-dealers and the "significant standards of character, competence, and minimum capital" required by the "major exchanges." "If the public is to be protected from the perils of incompetent and irresponsible broker-dealers, there should be erected uniform minimum standards of competence, experience, character, and capital which are applicable to the entire securities industry."[20] The SEC's second recommendation was that uniform selling and investment advisory practices should be imposed by the industry (through its self-regulatory powers) on its members.

1938. Although specialists had long been growing in numbers and importance, they were not officially recognized by the NYSE until 1938, when they were required to register and submit to supervision.

1942. Special procedures were adopted for sales of "large blocks" that could not be handled in the regular auction market within a reasonable time: (1) Subject to the approval of the Exchange, a specialist may buy a block outside the regular auction market if this is necessary for the maintenance of an orderly market. (2) A member firm receiving a large sell order may solicit purchase orders through its own organization and other members and member firms; the buy and sell orders thus obtained are then "crossed" on the floor in the auction market at a price between the bid and ask prices prevailing at the time, thus conforming to the NYSE's desire that trades be made public knowledge through open outcry. (3) However, unusually large blocks are exchanged in an after-hours meeting between members and, perhaps, nonmembers.[21] Large block transactions (10,000 or more shares) accounted for 41 percent of all shares

---

20 SEC (1963, Volume 1, page V, and Volume 5, pages 39–40).

21 Paraphrased from NYSE *Fact Books.*

traded on the NYSE in 1982, compared with 17 percent in 1975 and 3 percent in 1965. The largest transaction in the NYSE's history (through 1982) involved the transfer of 6,290,700 shares of the Federal National Mortgage Association on September 10, 1982.

1946. The prolonged period of low interest rates, easily available bank credit, and slow stock trading led to the closing of the money desk in 1946. Call loans have since been arranged directly between banks and brokers. Most broker credit now takes the form of repurchase agreements, either directly with banks and other borrowers or through fed funds brokers.

1949. The merger of the Chicago, Cleveland, Minneapolis, and St. Louis Stock Exchanges into the Midwest Stock Exchange permitted direct and continuous contact between the floor in Chicago and members in the branch cities as well as in other cities such as New York and Dallas. The Midwest Exchange originated clearing by mail, which allowed firms in other cities to transact business on the Exchange without a Chicago office.

The Philadelphia and Baltimore Stock Exchanges also merged in 1949, and Washington joined in 1953 to form the PBW Exchange. The trading floor remained in Philadelphia, and the name of this exchange has since reverted to the original Philadelphia Stock Exchange.

In 1957 the San Francisco and Los Angeles Exchanges merged to form the Pacific Stock Exchange.

Most of the following entries are concerned with the causes and effects of new technology in two areas: (1) the breakdown of the buttonwood agreement, that is, the growth of competition between NYSE members in the commissions they charge and in the ways they execute trades as electronic quotation systems and other technological developments have enabled the OTC market and some of the more aggressive regional exchanges to draw business away from the NYSE; and (2) the installation of new technology by the NYSE in efforts to meet the competition and to keep up with the great rise in trading volume indicated in Table 11.2.[22]

1962. The ticker fell 143 minutes behind trades on May 23, the longest lag in the NYSE's history with the exception of the 160-minute lag on October 24, 1929. The ticker ran late 124 days in 1966. Some information (volume of transactions) began to be omitted from the ticker when it fell behind. From June to December 1968 the major exchanges closed on Wednesdays in order to catch up on paperwork. Wednesday trading resumed in January 1969 but with sessions

---

22 As we saw in Table 11.1, the NYSE has held its own against other exchanges (actually growing in importance since 1968 after declining between 1950 and 1968). But it has lost ground to the OTC market.

Table 11.2   Daily Trading Volume on the NYSE, 1920 to 1980 (Millions of Shares)

	1920	1930	1940	1950	1960	1970	1980
Annual average	0.8	3.0	0.8	2.0	3.0	11.6	44.9
High day	2.0	8.3	3.9	4.9	5.3	21.3	84.3

Source: NYSE, *Fact Book*, New York, 1982, page 64.

cut to four hours, 10 to 2; 3:30 closings were resumed in May 1970, and in October 1974 the trading day was extended to 4 P.M.

1963.   The failure of Ira Haupt & Co. as a result of the "Great Salad Oil Swindle"[23] led the NYSE to develop a customer-assistance program by which members' customers were in most cases protected from loss. The number of member firms (partnerships and corporations that hold two or more seats on the exchange) fell from a high of 681 in 1961 to 473 in 1977, fewer than the 521 member firms existing in 1899. Most of the attrition was due to failure or mergers to avert failure during the volatile 1968 to 1974 period, when Standard & Poor's 500 index fell 30 percent between December 1968 and June 1970, then rose 60 percent by January 1973, and fell 45 percent by December 1974. The Exchange intervened in the affairs of about 200 firms experiencing difficulties, often arranging mergers, and by 1981 had disbursed $95 million dollars to the customers of those firms.

The Exchange's protection has been supplemented since 1971 by a government insurance scheme under the Securities Investor Protection Act, which established the Securities Investor Protection Corporation (SIPC). The SIPC protects the customers of failed brokers and dealers up to amounts that have been raised from time to time—$500,000 per customer in 1980. The SIPC's funds are raised by assessments on registered broker-dealers and members of national securities exchanges up to 1 percent of gross income. If the fund should prove inadequate, the SEC is authorized to lend $1 billion (borrowed from the U.S. Treasury) to the SIPC. The securities industry is expected to repay such a loan by means of future assessments.

1964.   A new ticker, capable of 900 characters a minute, replaced the 500-characters-a-minute ticker introduced in 1930. The ticker was linked directly to trading posts in 1966.

---

23 During the early 1960s, Anthony De Angelis borrowed hundreds of millions of dollars from banks, brokerage firms, and others in order to buy commodity futures, using warehouse receipts attesting to salad oil in storage tanks as collateral. Unfortunately, futures prices fell, De Angelis was unable to meet margin calls, and the creditors found the tanks filled with—you guessed it— water. The shortage of oil amounted to 1.9 billion pounds and $175 million, and the subsidiary of American Express that had issued the warehouse receipts (thus guaranteeing the oil's existence) declared bankruptcy. For a thorough account see Norman Miller (1965).

1965. In its first application of the computer the NYSE provided direct links between the Exchange floor and member firm offices, over which subscribers received the most recent quotations, last sales, and other trading information.

1966. Under pressure from members and with the approval of the SEC the NYSE's governing board "with great reluctance" relaxed "a practice that has been one of the foundation stones of the Exchange ever since 1792" by amending Rule 394 to allow members to conduct transactions in listed stocks with nonmembers if, "after making a diligent effort," they had been unable "to obtain a satisfactory execution on the Floor of the Exchange. . . . Eleven nonmember firms registered with the SEC as market makers in a total of 340 issues."[24] This break in the buttonwood agreement was one of the consequences of the NYSE's attempts to maintain a flat commission rate on all transactions, even the block trades of large institutions. The commission on a 10,000-share block was 100 times that on 100 shares even though the costs to brokerage firms of executing large trades were only slightly greater than for small trades. The excessive charges to nonmembers for doing business at the NYSE led pension funds, mutual funds, and insurance companies (who were forbidden memberships on the Exchange) to trade NYSE-listed stocks at lower commissions with nonmember brokers away from the NYSE on other exchanges and over the counter.

Rule 394 was the twentieth-century successor to the second part of the buttonwood agreement and had required members to execute all orders for listed stocks on the exchange, thereby costing compliant members a share of the profitable and rapidly increasing institutional business. Procedures under the amended Rule 394 were too cumbersome to permit any significant change, and between 1969 and 1971, for example, "only 44 inquiries were made by members attempting to consummate trades off board [that is, off the NYSE] and only 30 transactions were executed wholly or partly off board in compliance with the amended rule."[25] (We shall see, however, that members were ingenious in circumventing the rule). A more meaningful change was adopted in 1976 in the form of Rule 390, which allowed members to execute orders in listed stocks off the floor whenever they could get a better price.

1967. Brokerage firms began to move from New York to avoid the state's *stock transfer tax*. All the proceeds of the tax were turned over to New York City beginning in 1965; in 1966 the mayor proposed a 50 percent increase, which became 25 percent after the NYSE

---

24 NYSE *Annual Report*, New York, 1966, page 4.

25 Carter Geyer (1978). This article recounts the histories of Rule 394 and its successor, Rule 390.

threatened to move. After several years of controversy the tax was eliminated in a series of steps between 1978 and 1981.

1968. The NYSE's minimum commission schedule was altered to permit reduced rates on transactions of more than 1,000 shares. During the 1960s NYSE members had increasingly found the evasion of both parts of the buttonwood agreement necessary to secure institutional business—through "free" investment advisory services, kickbacks, and *give-ups*.[26] *Give-up* is the term applied to a method of splitting a commission between two or more brokerage firms that share the costs of a transaction. Many small and out-of-town Exchange members who do not clear their own transactions arrange for the necessary paperwork to be handled by a clearing member and in return "give up" the name of the clearing member to receive a share of the commission received from the customer. Most NYSE stocks were also listed on at least one regional exchange,[27] and give-ups began to be used to reduce effective commissions by arranging for transactions to be conducted on regional exchanges so that NYSE member firms could give up shares of their commissions to nonmember brokers, who would treat those payments as commissions for other transactions handled for the customer. The rapid increase in regional trading owed much to these give-up schemes, which enabled NYSE member firms to retain their institutional business by charging effective commissions below those required by the Exchange.[28]

These developments caused unhappiness in the SEC and the NYSE's Board of Governors. In its 1963 *Special Study* the SEC had pronounced the NYSE's commission schedule "far too complex . . . to be the subject of specific recommendations" but noticed that the "absence of block or volume discount" had caused "the establishment of a variety of ad hoc practices designed to temper the rigidity of the schedule without violating the letter of the NYSE's rule." After referring to the "questionable consequences" of these competitive practices, the SEC recommended the continuation of a collusive (although, of course, "reasonable") commission structure but made more effective by legal sanctions accompanying SEC "rate reviews" similar to those carried out by public utility commissions. These legally binding commission rates were to be based on the costs of providing brokerage services and would include appropriate discounts intended to eliminate the need for any of the evasive and "questionable" forms of price and nonprice competition then in existence.[29]

26 These and other competitive practices are discussed by Chris Welles (1975).

27 But not on the American Stock Exchange, for SEC rules do not permit a stock to be listed on more than one exchange in the same city. "Regional" (as in "provincial") exchanges are those outside New York City.

28 The market value of shares traded on regional exchanges, as a percentage of NYSE trades, rose from about 8 percent in 1955 to 15 percent in 1972, before falling to 11 percent in 1980 (NYSE *Fact Books*).

29 SEC (1963, Volume 5, pages 102–107).

There was little difference between the positions of regulator and regulated, and the NYSE's next request (or notice) to the SEC that minimum commission rates be increased, in January 1968, was accompanied by recommendations for the establishment of a volume discount and restrictions on give-ups. However, this request turned out to be less routine than the usual NYSE notice to the SEC because the U.S. Department of Justice entered the scene with a brief to the SEC questioning not only the proposed increase but the legality under the antitrust laws of any system of fixed commission rates.[30] The NYSE's January proposals were adopted with slight modifications in October. But the Justice Department's action prodded the SEC to conduct an inquiry into the propriety of fixed commission rates that, assisted by events, led to the introduction of competitive commissions in the 1970s.

1970. Direct trading between institutions increased during the 1960s, and in 1970 the Instinet system enabled subscribers to communicate bids and offers and execute trades via a private, anonymous computer network. Instinet is included in the composite report of transactions in NYSE-listed stocks in Table 10.4 and is part of the "fourth market," which is discussed below in the section on the over-the-counter market. Instinet has not grown as much as expected. It was a consequence of fixed commission rates at the NYSE and then a cause and finally a victim of negotiated commissions.

1971. The National Association of Securities Dealers Automated Quotations (NASDAQ) System began operation. NASDAQ is a nationwide hookup of computer terminals that allows the instant communication of bid and ask quotations between OTC dealers and brokers. NASDAQ was the most important advance in securities trading since the telephone, and its daily trading volume has grown to rival and sometimes exceed that of the NYSE.

Commissions on trades exceeding $500,000 became negotiable. The SEC had begun an inquiry into the necessity of fixed commission rates in 1968 under pressure from the Justice Department's threat of an antitrust suit. The SEC's newly discovered aggressiveness, combined with the NYSE Board's inability to produce an effective defense, resulted in the SEC's imposition of freely negotiated rates beginning with the largest trades in April 1971 and eventually extending to all trades in May 1975. During the following 18 months, from May 1975 to November 1976, commissions as a percentage of the value of trades charged by NYSE members fell 38 percent for institutions and 8 percent for individuals.[31]

---

30 U.S. Department of Justice (1968).

31 SEC (1977). For trends in commission rates charged to institutions and individuals by order size between April 1975 and December 1978 see Seha Tinic and Richard West (1980). Commissions on orders exceeding 10,000 shares fell 46 percent for institutions and 37 percent for individuals during this period.

The history of price fixing in the securities business since 1934 has been almost perfectly analogous to that of depository institutions during the same period. In both cases private collusion was protected by official bodies, the SEC for fixed minimum commissions and the Fed for fixed maximum deposit rates. In both cases the regulators acted to reinforce existing monopoly positions by obstructing the entry of new brokers, exchanges, and banks. In both cases collusive arrangements have been relaxed by agreement of regulator and regulated under the pressure of outside competition, from regional exchanges and the OTC market that competed for the NYSE's institutional business and from rising interest rates on money market instruments that drew funds away from money center banks.

1973. The Depository Trust Company was established to hold stock certificates and to transfer them by bookkeeping (computer) entry instead of physical delivery. This service was supplemented in 1974 by a system of continuous clearance and settlement that replaced the old daily balance procedure.

1974. A pilot of the *consolidated tape* began to report transactions in fifteen stocks traded on the NYSE and at least one of the three participating regional exchanges or in the OTC market. In 1975, the NYSE ticker began to report transactions in all NYSE-listed stocks in nine markets. (These are the "NYSE-composite transactions" in Table 10.4).

1975. The Securities Acts Amendments, the most far-reaching securities legislation since the 1930s, provided for increased surveillance and enforcement powers by the SEC in its attempts to secure uniform standards in the securities business, gave legal sanction to the refusal of the NYSE and most other exchanges to admit institutions or their broker affiliates to membership, and in order to eliminate existing "market fragmentation," directed the SEC to facilitate the development of a National Market System. The trend toward more closely linked financial markets which has persisted almost continuously since colonial times and which began to accelerate in the 1960s has not slowed since 1975. But no system has yet been found that is sufficiently uniform to satisfy Congress and the SEC.

1976. A new data line with a capacity of 36,000 characters a minute was installed.

The Designated Order Turnaround (DOT) System was introduced, by which orders from brokers' offices could be communicated directly to trading posts on the floor of the Exchange. Ninety percent of DOT orders are filled within 5 minutes.

1977. The National Securities Clearing Corporation (NSCC) combined the previously separate clearing operations of the NYSE's Stock Clearing Corporation (see the 1892 and 1920 entries), the American Stock Exchange's Clearing Corporation, and NASD's National Clearing Corporation, which cleared a large proportion of OTC trades. Ownership of the NSCC is distributed equally between the NYSE, the American Stock Exchange, and NASD.

1978. The Intermarket Trading System (ITS) was introduced, permitting trades between dealers and brokers on the floors of different exchanges.

The Multiple Dealer Trading System (MDT) was introduced on the Cincinnati Stock Exchange. The system is a computer operation that receives and stores orders and matches them for execution. Users of this system may observe the flow of orders and executions on screens. The display screens present what amounts to an open limit-order book, as opposed to the specialist's private book in Figure 11.2 below.

1980. The SEC ruled that exchange members were allowed, beginning in June 1980, to make markets over the counter in stocks newly listed on their exchanges after April 1979. The purpose of this move was to divert business from specialists toward a centrally controlled National Market System.

1981. The NYSE achieved an estimated capability of handling a "peak one-day volume of 150,000 trades—or about 150 million shares at current average trade size—and 80,000–90,000 trades a day for sustained periods of two weeks or more."[32] On August 3, 1984, 236 million shares were handled without difficulty.

1982. Exchanges were linked to the OTC market by the Computer Assisted Execution System (CAES) connecting NASDAQ and ITS (see the 1971 and 1978 entries above). However, only stocks newly listed on exchanges (after April 26, 1979)[33] are traded through this system.

1983. Merrill Lynch announced that it will "stop making markets in exchange-listed securities because it is finding the off-board trading experiment cumbersome and unprofitable." "The decision generally is considered a victory for the New York Stock Exchange market makers, or specialists, against whom Merrill Lynch and a handful of other big member firms are competing."[34] Merrill Lynch was one of the firms that accepted the SEC's invitation in 1980 to compete with specialists (see the 1980 entry). After some initial but costly successes these firms began to reduce their off-floor activities until, in March 1983, of 487 eligible stocks NYSE members made markets in only 88 away from the exchange and accounted for only 10

---

32 NYSE, *Annual Report,* New York, 1981, page 9.

33 These are called Rule 19c-3 stocks after the SEC's rule that exchange members must without restriction be allowed to continue over-the-counter trading of stocks listed on their exchange after April 26, 1979.

34 *Wall Street Journal,* March 22, 1983, page 12.

percent of the trading in those 88 stocks. Merrill Lynch's involvement had fallen from 30 stocks in 1981 to 11 in March 1983.

Listing requirements on the NYSE

With the exception of closely held companies most corporations like their stock to be listed and traded on exchanges. The ease of buying and selling securities on exchanges, where specialists and other dealers make continuous markets, reduces transaction costs and improves the liquidity of those securities. The result is a reduction in the cost of capital for listed corporations.

But listing is not automatic.[35] Exchanges impose certain minimum qualifications on corporations before their stock may be listed. The general nature and reasons for these requirements may be summarized as follows: Most important, we must recognize that an exchange is operated for the benefit of its members, for whom memberships are investments. We must also take into consideration the fact that, at any point in time, an exchange's capacity is limited. These two considerations suggest that a stock exchange wishes to attract those stocks most likely to produce the highest profits, with the least risk, for its members.[36] Such stocks should ideally have the following characteristics:

1. Listed stocks should be actively traded. This means high profits and low risk for market makers and other member brokers and dealers. Remember that the main function of an exchange is to provide a continuous market for securities, which of course is possible only with active trading. Consequently, exchanges prefer large, widely held companies. This means many relatively small investors. Corporations owned by a few large institutions are undesirable because they may not generate many commissions and because the sale of large blocks may induce large price changes and therefore high risk.

2. Listed stocks should be attractive to investors. Most important, they should offer high expected returns relative to risk. Exchanges cannot guarantee high returns. But they try to offer stocks which have in the past, at least occasionally, shown good earnings and about which there is abundant information so that investors can evaluate prospective returns. This means that a corporation must provide substantial information to the exchange and to investors about its past and current financial affairs in order to obtain listing, and con-

---

35 Nor is it free. For a small, 2-million-share company, for example, the initial fee to gain listing is $20,000, followed by an annual fee of $10,000. The initial and annual fees for a 100-million-share company are $250,000 and $50,000, respectively. (From NYSE, *Company Manual*, Section B-4.)

36 No such competition between exchanges for listings is envisaged by the Securities Acts Amendments of 1975, which authorized the SEC to determine which securities will be traded in the projected National Market System.

Table 11.3   Listing Requirements of the New York Stock Exchange

To be listed on the NYSE, a company is expected to meet certain qualifications and to be willing to keep the investing public informed on the progress of its affairs. The company must be a going concern or be the successor to a going concern. In determining eligibility for listing, particular attention is given to such qualifications as: (1) the degree of national interest in the company, (2) its relative position and stability in the industry, and (3) whether it is engaged in an expanding industry, with prospects of at least maintaining its relative position.

Initial listing

While each case is decided on its own merits, the Exchange generally requires the following as a minimum:
1. Demonstrated earning power under competitive conditions of $2.5 million before Federal income taxes for the most recent year and $2 million pretax for each of the preceding 2 years.
2. Net tangible assets of $16 million, but greater emphasis is placed on the aggregate market value of the common stock.
3. Market value of publicly held shares, subject to adjustment depending on market conditions, within the following limits: maximum, $16 million; minimum, $8 million; present (May 1, 1982), $16 million. [The market-value requirement is subject to adjustment, based on the NYSE Index of Common Stock Prices. The base in effect as of May 1, 1982, is the Index on July 15, 1971 (55.06). The Index as of January 15 and July 15 of each year (if lower than the base) is divided by the base, and the resulting percentage is multiplied by $16 million to produce the adjusted market-value standard.]
4. A total of 1 million common shares publicly held.
5. 2,000 holders of 100 shares or more.

Listing agreement

The listing agreement between the company and the Exchange is designed to provide timely disclosure to the public of earnings statements, dividend notices, and other information that might reasonably be expected materially to affect the market for securities. The Exchange requires actively operating companies to agree to solicit proxies for all meetings of stockholders.

Source: NYSE, *Fact Book,* New York, 1982, pages 29–30. This source also gives the somewhat less stringent requirements for continued listing.

tinued financial reporting is required to preserve that listing. Long before the disclosures required by the Securities Act of 1933, exchanges increasingly competed for the business of investors by requiring that as much information as possible be made available to them, without at the same time making those requirements so burdensome that desirable companies left their lists.

The membership

Some members of the NYSE are retired or are executives of brokerage firms and do little or no floor trading. But most members operate on the floor of the exchange in one or more of the following capacities:

About half of all brokers are *commission house brokers,* who are affiliated with member organizations that do business with the public.[37] These are the most active people on the floor, running from teletype machines and telephones, where they receive buy and sell orders from their firms, to trading posts to execute those orders. They also communicate information about market conditions to their firms.

There are about 400 *specialists,* who make markets in one or more stocks by standing ready to trade with other members at stated bid and ask prices. Specialists perform both broker and dealer functions and "place their own capital at risk to maintain fair, orderly and continuous markets and a competitive trading environment for the stocks in which they are registered."[38]

There are about 200 *independent floor brokers,* who execute trades for other members, firms whose members are unavailable, and firms who do not employ commission brokers of their own. These people are called "two-dollar brokers" because they used to charge a commission of $2 per 100 shares.

There are about 70 *competitive traders* who deal principally for their own accounts. They have little or no contact with the public and generally do not execute trades for other members. Paying no commissions and maintaining no office staffs, these traders have few overheads and contribute to market efficiency by being willing to buy and sell within narrow spreads.

There are about 30 *registered competitive market makers,* who usually behave like competitive traders "but who also have particular obligations imposed on them by the [Exchange]. When called upon, they must make a bid or offer that will narrow the existing quote spread or improve the depth of an existing quote."[39]

Making markets on the floor

THE SPECIALIST UNIT.[40] The typical specialist unit is a relatively small firm with six or seven partners or stockholders who are members of the Exchange and who make markets in a total of about twenty-five stocks. Specialists may be old or young although all must have the physical and mental endurance to stand at their posts, in the midst of jostling, shouting crowds, taking orders, buying and selling, and adjusting bids and asks to changing conditions, for 6 hours a day. Some specialists bring their own money to units for the purchase of their

---

37 See the NYSE's *Report of the Quality of Markets Committee* (1982) for the numbers of the different categories of floor traders at the end of 1981. See Leonard Sloane (1980) for an interesting description of their activities.

38 NYSE (1982).

39 Leonard Sloane (1980, page 8). See the discussion of depth, breadth, and resiliency in Chapter 7.

40 See Michael Zahorchak (1974), Leonard Sloane (1980), Louis Engel and Brendan Boyd (1982), and Richard Teweles and Edward Bradley (1982) for interesting discussions of the work of specialists on the American Stock Exchange and the NYSE.

seats and contributions to their firms' capital; some buy their seats with money borrowed from their firms.

Stocks are allocated to specialist units (rather than to individual specialists) by the Exchange's Allocation Committee, which is composed mainly of commission house brokers, the people most interested in effective performance by specialists. Stocks may be reallocated if performance is unsatisfactory. The primary criterion used in the allocation of new listings and the reallocation of old listings is the Specialist Performance Evaluation Questionnaire, which is completed quarterly by commission brokers and "measures the degree of specialist participation as principal to ensure price continuity and depth; effectiveness in bringing buyers and sellers together; leadership of active crowds; and efficiency in handling administrative details such as the confirmation of open orders, the issuing of timely and accurate status and execution reports and the resolution of questioned trades and errors."[41]

The NYSE has promised to maintain "fair and orderly" markets in its listed stocks. This means continuous markets, narrow spreads between buying and selling prices, and frequent small changes rather than occasional large changes in prices. They have not guaranteed that you will make money. But they attempt, usually with success, to give you the chance to buy or sell at any time, with small turnaround costs (that is, a small take by the house), at a price that is not very different from that at which the last trade was executed.[42] A specialist is expected to buy or sell for his own account in order to moderate price movements or when there is a wide disparity between the lowest selling price and the highest buying price at which other brokers have offered to trade his stock. He keeps an inventory of stock and may have to sell shares that he does not own (that is, sell short) with the intention of acquiring them later.

THE SPECIALIST'S BOOK. Mark Spector is the specialist responsible for two common stocks, Powdermilk Biscuit and Bob's Bank, although he sometimes helps other members of his specialist unit with their stocks when they are busy and his own stocks are inactive. Spector buys and sells in two capacities: As a broker, he executes orders for other brokers and earns commissions; as a dealer, or market maker, he buys and sells for his own account, again earning commissions but also making or losing money as the stocks in his inventory rise or fall in price. His customers are limited to other members. He does not, as a specialist, do business directly with the public.

Spector receives several types of orders. We will consider three:

---

41 NYSE, *Annual Report*, New York, 1977, page 8.

42 The Exchange's record in this area was summarized by the "key indicators of market quality" in Table 7.8.

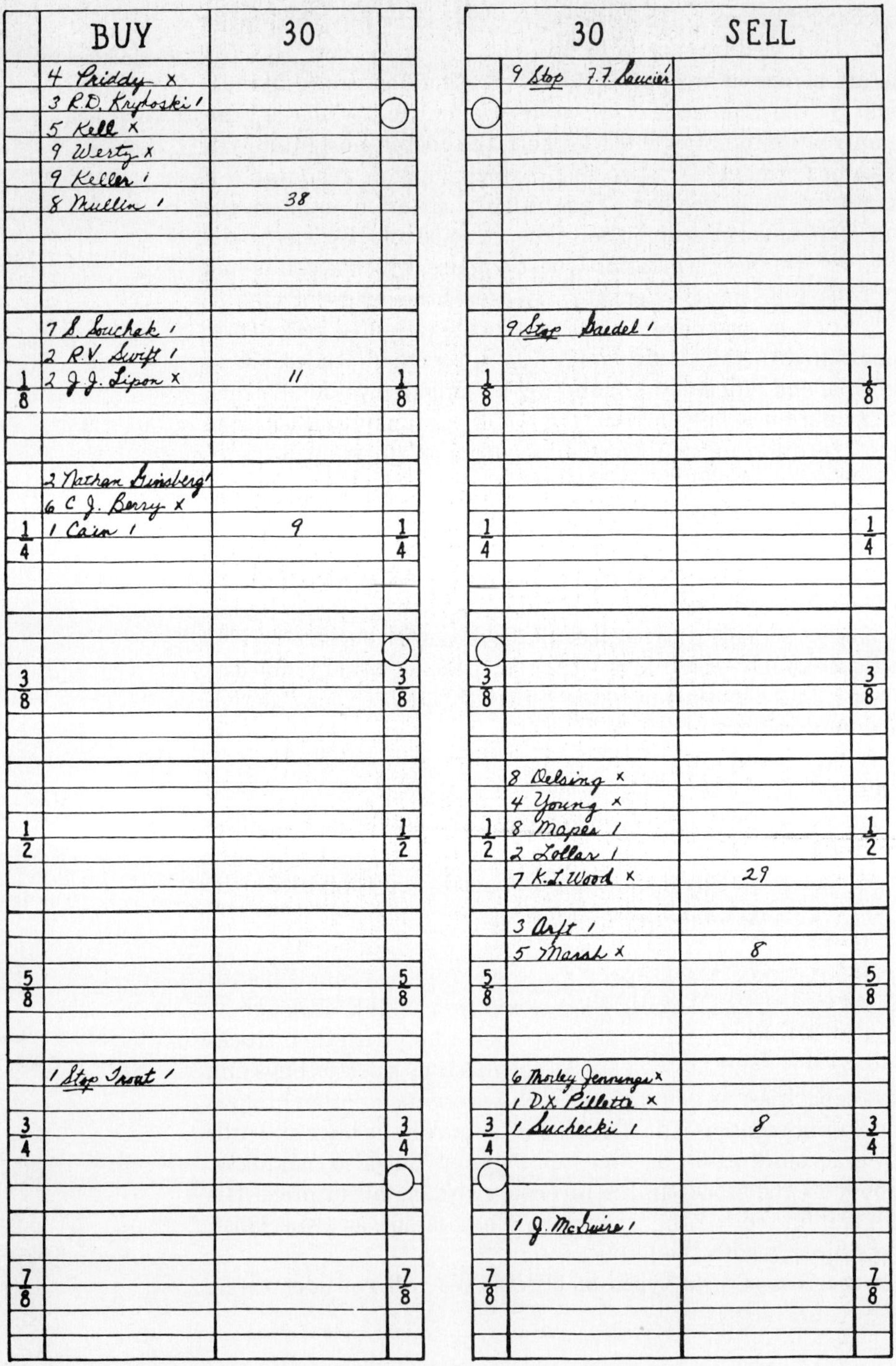

	BUY	30			30	SELL	
	4 Priddy x				9 Stop 7.7 Laucier		
	3 R.D. Kryloski /		○	○			
	5 Kell x						
	9 Werty x						
	9 Keller /						
	8 Mullin /	38					
	7 S. Souchak /				9 Stop Daedel /		
	2 R.V. Swift /						
1/8	2 J.J. Lipon x	11	1/8	1/8			1/8
	2 Nathan Ginsberg/						
	6 C.J. Berry x						
1/4	1 Cain /	9	1/4	1/4			1/4
3/8			○ / 3/8	○ / 3/8			3/8
					8 Delsing x		
					4 Young x		
1/2			1/2	1/2	8 Mapes /		1/2
					2 Lollar /		
					7 K.L. Wood x	29	
					3 Arft /		
5/8			5/8	5/8	5 Marsh x	8	5/8
	1 Stop Trout /				6 Morley Jennings x		
					1 D.X. Pillette x		
3/4			3/4	3/4	1 Suchecki /	8	3/4
			○	○			
					1 J. McGuire /		
7/8			7/8	7/8			7/8

Source: Based on a similar example in Richard Teweles and Edward Bradley (1982, page 150), with discussions from Louis Engel and Brendan Boyd (1982), Leonard Sloane (1980), and Michael Zahorchak (1974).

Figure 11.2   Two pages from the Powdermilk specialist's book.

market, limit, and stop orders.[43] Most transactions on the Exchange are *market orders* placed by commission house brokers who seek to buy and sell stock at the best available prices for their firm's customers as soon as their orders reach the floor. Market orders may also be executed by independent floor brokers or by competitive traders or registered competitive market makers dealing for their own accounts. Suppose you learn from your broker, who works for G. Priddy & Co., that the specialist (Spector) is quoting $30\frac{1}{2}$ asked and $30\frac{1}{4}$ bid for Powdermilk. You decide to place a market order to buy 400 shares. Within a few minutes one of Priddy's floor brokers is at Spector's post, asking, "How's Powdermilk?," without indicating whether he is buying or selling. If conditions haven't changed, the specialist (or perhaps another broker in the Powdermilk crowd) answers, "One–half to one-quarter," the 30 being understood. Priddy's man may then execute your order at $30\frac{1}{2}$, or he may wait a few seconds before tipping his hand if he believes that he can get the stock for less than $30\frac{1}{2}$. Suppose he waits and then shouts, "Three-eighths for four hundred." If he gets no response, he may offer "one-half for four hundred," and if the market hasn't moved up, you become the proud owner of 400 shares of Powdermilk at $30.50 a share.

The next-most-important type of order is the *limit order,* which is to be filled only at or better than a specified price. Suppose you think you can do better than the current price by waiting, and you may also be skeptical of Priddy's ability to get you the best possible price. Powdermilk has been fluctuating between $29\frac{1}{2}$ and 32 the past few days, and you think it will soon fall again to 30. So you place a limit order with Priddy to buy 400 at 30. Priddy's floor broker immediately tries to execute the order at 30 or less, and if that is not possible, he leaves the order with the specialist for entry in his "book." You may indicate that your limit order is to be kept open for a day, a week, or a month or until canceled. Suppose yours is an open (or GTC, "good 'til canceled") limit order and that tomorrow broker A asks 30 for 400. The specialist calls out "Sold!" and allocates the sale to the first order in his book at that price, the order that you placed through Priddy. The specialist gives up Priddy's name to broker A and reports the execution to Priddy. You are happy that you placed a limit order for 30 instead of a market order at $30\frac{1}{2}$. You would not have been so happy if, instead of falling from $30\frac{1}{2}$, Powdermilk had begun a steady rise, never to see $30\frac{1}{2}$ again.

Many people would pay substantial sums to see the specialist's book, which lists all currently outstanding buy and sell orders that have been placed with the specialist. But he may not show it to other traders, and he is subjected to a great many regulations and surprise

---

43 See Richard Teweles and Edward Bradley (1982, Chapter 7) and Frank Zarb and Gabriel Kerekes (1970, Chapter 42) for more complete lists of orders and their uses.

inspections that attempt to ensure that he does not take advantage of his special information at the public's expense. The style of these books varies among specialists according to their particular needs and preferences. Two pages from a hypothetical book are presented in Figure 11.2. These pages contain limit and stop orders at prices from 30 to 30⅞. The most unrealistic aspect of this sample book is its neatness. Normally, many orders that have been filled or canceled will be crossed out.

The position of your limit order at the top left of the book indicates that it is the oldest buy order at that price and will be the first to be filled when Powdermilk falls to 30. The number to the left of your broker (Priddy) indicates that the order is for four round lots (400 shares). The x indicates an open order. The mark ($/$) indicates a day limit order. Specialists may not accept week or month limit orders. The market buy order discussed above would have been allocated to Delsing, who is at the top of the list of brokers offering to sell at 30½.

A *stop order* (or stop-loss order) is a conditional, or *suspended,* market order and is executed only if a stock reaches a specified price. Suppose one of F. F. Saucier's clients bought Powdermilk at 25 some time ago and thinks that the price is going to rise above its present selling price of 30½. But he is not sure of this and wants to lock in a certain minimum profit just in case the price begins to fall. His stop order to sell becomes a market order if the price falls to 30. On the other hand one of Trout's clients thinks the price will fall but, just in case it rises, has placed a stop order to buy at 30¾.

All the specialist's work so far has been gravy. It has consisted simply of acting as a broker for other brokers who cannot afford to hang around the Powdermilk post indefinitely, waiting for the right moment to execute your limit order. Much more interesting is the specialist's function as a market maker, particularly his contribution to an orderly market for Powdermilk. Suppose Powdermilk's price begins a rapid and potentially erratic rise. Market and limit buy orders at 30⅜, 30½, and up flow in as the crowd around the Powdermilk post becomes larger and more unruly. Sell orders at 30½ and then 30⅝ are filled or withdrawn. Prices move above 31 and sometimes, in this uncertain situation, the spread between the highest buy order (say, 31¼) and lowest sell order (say, 32) in the specialist's book or from the floor is ¾. Spector is not doing his job if he allows this spread to persist because the Exchange's perception of an orderly market is one in which spreads are no greater than ½, preferably ¼. Furthermore, Spector is supposed to buy and sell for his own account in order to moderate the speed of price movements and to ensure that price changes between successive trades do not exceed ⅛ (see Table 7.8).[44] In

---

[44] The specialist is subject to many regulations designed to promote market quality and avoid conflicts of interest. For example he may not buy or sell for his own account at prices at which he has unexecuted orders. Nor may he buy or sell for his own account when such transactions

our example, these obligations require Spector to quote a narrower spread than the one given by the market and to buy Powdermilk. If the last trade in this volatile market was at 31¼, he might offer to buy at 31⅜ and to sell at 31⅝. If Powdermilk's rise continues, with more buyers than sellers, Spector will buy at 31⅜, 31½, ... If the market continues to rise for a while and then settles down, he will be able to sell off later at a profit. If it suddenly turns down, he loses. About 10 percent of all trades at the NYSE are executed by specialists for their own accounts.

Specialist and other dealer systems are popular with investors. But they have long been regarded with deep suspicion by the protectors of the public welfare. One of the principal objectives of the projected federally controlled National Market System is the elimination of market makers in order that investors may (and must) trade directly with each other without paying the tolls of these evil middlemen. It will be interesting to see whether the dealer function, that is, the provision of the "predictable immediacy" discussed in Chapter 7, will survive this regulatory attack. Our own guess is that the specialist system and other dealer markets will survive in something close to their present form because there seems to be no private demand for their replacement.

BOND EXCHANGES

Volume

Most stock exchanges also trade bonds although in every case the volume of bond trading is now small relative to stock transactions. The NYSE is by far the most important bond exchange, accounting for about 90 percent of the value of all exchange bond transactions.[45] In 1983 about 3,300 bonds and 2,200 stocks were listed on the NYSE although the total market value of these bond issues was only about 40 percent of that of the stock issues, and exchange trading of bonds is much less active than for stocks. For example we see from Table 10.5 that only about one-third (1,080) of NYSE-listed bonds were traded on March 25, 1983. This compares with trading in almost 90 percent (1,957) of listed stocks.[46] Of the traded bond issues the average par value amount that changed hands at the NYSE was \$37,190,000/1,080 = \$34,435, or about 34 bonds each with a par value of \$1,000.[47] On the other hand, referring to Table 10.4 and assuming an average stock price of \$40, we find that the average value of transactions

---

would widen the spread; for example the sale of 900 shares to the market orders of 30¼ would widen the spread in Spector's book from ¼ to ⅜. A useful discussion of specialist regulations is presented by Richard Teweles and Edward Bradley (1982, pages 153–161).

45 The American Stock Exchange accounts for most of the remainder. Except where noted the data in this section are from SEC *Annual Reports* and NYSE *Fact Books*.

46 From the "Market Diary," *Wall Street Journal*, March 28, 1983.

47 The trading volumes in Table 10.5 are in thousands of dollars of par value.

in each NYSE stock issue on that date was approximately $40(77,330,000)/1,957 = $1,580,583. The par value of NYSE bond transactions on March 25, 1983, was approximately $37,190,000/ $40(77,330,000) = 1.2 percent of the market value of NYSE stock transactions: normal for the 1980s but down from the 4 percent figure that prevailed during most of the 1960s and 1970s.

The Bond Room

Bonds are traded at the NYSE in a separate room below the main (stock) trading floor. Bond trading differs from stock trading principally in being conducted without specialists. Most bond transactions are effected through the *Automated Bond System* (ABS), by which bid and asked prices and order quantities for nonconvertible bonds are displayed on video terminals located around the 5,600-square-foot Bond Room. Members execute trades by punching their buy and sell orders into the terminals.

The ABS, which is a localized version of the nationwide OTC system for trading stocks, is a convenient arrangement for trading the large number of inactive issues that make up the bulk of NYSE bonds. But a few hundred active issues (mainly volatile convertibles) are traded by the *free crowd* in a manner much like commodities. A broker who wishes to execute an order for a *free bond* steps inside an octagonal brass railing, or "ring," that serves the same purpose as the Chicago Board of Trade's wheat pit. He announces his bid or offer, thereby inviting other brokers to step into the ring with counteroffers or an acceptance of his original offer.

Most bonds, even most NYSE-listed bonds, are traded over the counter. This is especially true of large orders by institutions. But the NYSE's Rule 396, called the "Nine Bond Rule," states that members receiving orders for nine or fewer (that is, $9,000 or less in par value) listed bonds must with certain exceptions[48] send those orders to the Bond Room for execution unless the customer directs otherwise. The idea is that small orders should be given the benefit of public auction and open outcry, in addition to the bid and asked prices available over the counter, in order that they be assured of the best available price.

THE OVER-THE-COUNTER MARKET
Origins

A substantial proportion of stock trades, the great majority of bond trades, and all mortgage trades have always been executed away from exchanges. During colonial times and the early years of independence the old merchant houses and the new state-chartered banks dealt in

---

48 See Leo Loll and Julian Buckley (1981, page 202) and Frank Zarb and Gabriel Kerekes (1970, pages 111–112) for the exceptions. Also see Richard Teweles and Edward Bradley (1982, pages 161–162) and Leonard Sloane (1980, pages 178–179) for discussions of the NYSE bond market.

securities on their premises. But the term "over the counter" seems to have originated somewhat later in connection with private banks that specialized in trading and underwriting securities.[49] These firms, which were the forerunners of investment banks and modern securities dealers, negotiated terms and exchanged securities and money over the counters in their offices. "Hence, purchases and sales transacted by these institutions came to be known as transactions 'over the counters' to distinguish them from those effected by public auction on the 'stock and exchange boards' as exchanges were then called."[50]

The National Daily Quotation Service (NDQS)

More than 40 years ago, observers of the OTC market wrote, "By means of the telephone, telegraph and teletype, investment dealers and brokers in all parts of the country are linked together in one immense securities market."[51] "The speed with which traders find markets and negotiate transactions, particularly for large blocks of securities, frequently astonishes those who are not familiar with how the market operates."[52] Typical transactions might have been initiated by Mr. Aaron of Mobile, Alabama, who informs his broker, McCovey & Co., also in Mobile, that he wants to buy 100 shares of the actively traded stock of Windy City Inc., as well as ten U.S. Treasury bonds, specifically, the 3s of 1946. After "checking the market" for the best available prices, beginning with dealers in Chicago and New York, who are known to make markets in these securities, McCovey reports to Aaron that Cavaretta & Co. of Chicago is asking 16½ for Windy City and Neun & Co. of New York is asking 103 for the 3s of 1946. Aaron directs McCovey to accept these prices, the transactions are confirmed by phone, and the securities and payment are exchanged either by registered mail directly between the brokers or through their banks.

This system worked well for actively traded securities, such as federal government bonds and the common stock of large corporations. But the search for competing bids on inactive issues or those traded principally in distant locations could be expensive in time and phone bills. The search process has been greatly assisted by the National Quotation Bureau, a private firm that on a daily basis since 1913 has disseminated bid and asked prices on a wide range of securities to broker and dealer subscribers throughout the country.

---

49 "Private banks" are partnerships or individual proprietorships, as distinguished from incorporated banks. Until 1933 private "banking houses" combined commercial banking (that is, the acceptance of demand and time deposits) with their investment banking activities as underwriters, brokers, and dealers in securities. But the Banking Act of 1933 decreed that investment banking and commercial banking functions may not be performed by the same firm and also that commercial banks must be incorporated.

50 John Loeser (1940, page 7).

51 Charles Dice and Wilford Eiteman (1941, page 107).

52 John Loeser (1940, page 52).

Subscribers send quotations by messenger, phone, wire, or mail to the Bureau's offices in New York, Chicago, and San Francisco, where they are assembled and printed in the early evening for distribution throughout the country in time for business the next morning. Conditions can change overnight and the quotations are not always good the next day. But this service has for many years been the best guide to the search for inactive issues; for more than 10,000 stock issues are not quoted at all, and many more are quoted infrequently on the electronic NASDAQ system. The NDQS quotes about 30,000 stock issues each year.[53]

National Association of Securities Dealers (NASD)

Even before the 1930s the Federal Trade Commission had promoted "self-regulation" by industries in the form of "codes of fair practice" to be administered by trade associations—in order to correct situations in which "competition forced the low standards of the unethical minority upon all who wished to survive."[54] This attitude achieved its postfeudal nadir in the National Industrial Recovery Act (NIRA) of 1933. The NIRA suspended the antitrust laws to allow industry representatives to meet with the head of the specially created National Recovery Administration (NRA) to negotiate codes of fair practice, which upon the President's approval would have the force of law. The OTC securities business was to be self-regulated by a Code Committee formed to administer the Investment Bankers' Code.

The NRA codes were invalidated in 1935 by the U.S. Supreme Court's ruling in *Schechter Poultry Corp. v. U.S.* that they were unconstitutional delegations of legislative power to the President. But Congress salvaged much of the NRA program in subsequent legislation, including the Connolly Act of 1935 to regulate the "overproduction" of oil, the Walsh-Healy Act of 1936 to regulate wages and hours of workers employed on federal contracts, the Robinson-Patman Act of 1936 to outlaw volume discounts and rebates to large buyers, and the Miller-Tydings Act of 1937 to support state price-fixing ("fair-trade") laws. The Investment Bankers' Code Committee was kept together after 1935, at the request of the SEC, as the Investment Bankers' Conference and was succeeded in 1939 by NASD. NASD was authorized by the Maloney Act of 1938 to act for the securities industry in negotiating "rules of fair practice" with the SEC.

NASD is the only association registered under the Maloney Act and has been allowed to adopt legally binding rules that effectively require membership of every broker and dealer. Members may not deal with nonmembers except on the same terms that they deal with the investing public: "Only association members have the advantage of

---

53 Leo Loll and Julian Buckley (1981, page 180).

54 Cornelius Gillam (1970, page 472).

price concessions, discounts, and similar allowances."[55] NASD must approve all advertisements and solicitations by securities dealers "to insure fair dealing and prevent misleading or exaggerated statements."[56] It has also adopted a "5% markup policy" on securities sales as a "general guide" for members. Markups may under certain conditions deviate from 5 percent. But "the markup must not be unfair. Section 4, Article III of the NASD's Rules of Fair Practice indicates that securities will be bought from or sold to customers at prices that are fair."[57]

The National Association of Securities Dealers Automated Quotations System (NASDAQ)

NASDAQ was introduced in 1971 as a nationwide hookup of computer terminals among brokers, dealers, and large investors. Dealers send quotations on the stocks in which they make markets to the central computer complex in Trumbull, Connecticut, where the information is arranged by issue and disseminated to more than 100,000 desk-top terminals with video screens in broker, dealer, and investor offices. A key figure in this system is the *registered market maker,* who is in some respects similar to a stock exchange specialist. Each performs both broker and dealer functions and each must stand behind his quotes. But neither registered market makers nor anyone else in the OTC market bears the responsibilities for the continuity and stabilization of prices that exchanges impose on specialists.

The NASDAQ system does not yet permit the execution of trades via computer.[58] Purchases and sales must still be arranged over the phone.[59] Nevertheless, the more rapid and complete dissemination of information made possible by NASDAQ has contributed substantially to the efficiency of the OTC market. James Hamilton (1978) estimated that in its first year of operation NASDAQ caused a 15 percent reduction in the average OTC dealer spread.

Stocks achieve NASDAQ "authorization" according to the same principle that determines exchange "listing"—which means the admission of those stocks to the substantial but not unlimited NASDAQ facilities that are most likely to be profitable to securities dealers.[60] The specific criteria for NASDAQ authorization are less stringent because they are directed at smaller companies, but they are similar in form to those for NYSE listing, with one important addition:

---

55 Leo Loll and Julian Buckley (1981, page 411).

56 NASD (1983, page 114).

57 See Adam Smith's comment at the beginning of Chapter 1.

58 Unlike the system provided by U.S. Treasury security "screen brokers," described in Chapter 7 (see Table 7.7).

59 Although most transactions must be reported through the NASDAQ Transactions Reporting System within 90 seconds of execution.

60 See NASD (1983, paragraph 1653A). Also see this paragraph for NASDAQ's "issuer quotation" (that is, listing) fees.

Table 11.4

Over-the-Counter Markets

4:00 p.m. Eastern Standard Time Prices, Friday, March 25, 1983

Volume, All Issues, 57,490,000

SINCE JANUARY 1

	1983	1982	1981
Total sales	3,451,942,897	1,596,186,394	1,828,850,695

MARKET DIARY

	Fri	Thur	Wed	Tues	Mon
Issues traded	3,383	3,380	3,379	3,378	3,372
Advances	732	816	855	757	658
Declines	577	503	481	499	610
Unchanged	2,074	2,061	2,043	2,122	2,104
xNew highs	180	196	196	170	159
xNew lows	16	11	14	14	23

x-Based on 4 p.m. Eastern time bid quote.

ACTIVE STOCKS

	Dollar Volume	4:00 Bid	Chg.
Glaxo Holdings ADR	$37,671,000	12⅛	+ 1⅛
MCI Communications	22,135,000	46¼	....
Masstor Systems	15,025,000	18¼	....
Convergent Tech	14,233,000	30⅞	+ ⅜
Graphic Scanning	12,095,000	24¾	+ 3⅝
Service Merchandise	12,064,000	34½	+ ⅛
F M I Financial Cp	11,681,000	7½	+ ½
Apple Computer	11,145,000	43	− ⅛
Intergraph	8,975,000	29¾	+ 1
Tandem Computers	7,177,000	27⅛	+ ⅛

Nasdaq National Market

1983 High	1983 Low	Stock	Sales (hds)	High	Low	Last	Net Chg.
24¼	19	Academy Insu	162	22⅞	22½	22½	− ¼
27⅜	18	Adac Labs	337	23¾	23⅝	23¾	+ ⅛
(H)	28½	Alex Bald 1.80	131	37¼	36⅛	36⅜	− ¼
25⅞	20⅞	AlliedBcsh .80	739	23	22⅝	22⅞	+ ¼
28½	20	Altos Comptr	1456	22¾	22	22¾	+ ¼
2⅞	1¼	qAmarexInc p	195	1½	1⅜	1⅜	...
14⅝	10¼	ABnkrs Ins .50	315	13¼	12⅞	13⅛	+ ⅛
23½	17⅜	AmGreetg .34	2312	21⅜	20⅝	20⅞	− ½
29⅜	21⅝	Am Income Lf	184	26½	26⅛	26⅜	+ ⅛
(H)	65⅝	AmIntlGrp .48	504	91½	90	90⅜	+ ⅜
19⅝	15	AmNatlIns .84	93	19⅛	18⅞	19	...
41½	33½	Andrew Corpn	165	38¾	38½	38¾	...
48⅝	27¼	Apple Comptr	2580	43⅞	43	43⅛	...
33½	21¾	Applied Matrl	627	32¾	32½	32⅝	+ ⅛
13	10¼	Astrosystms	146	12½	12¼	12⅜	...
49½	35½	Atl Research	8	46	45¼	45½	+ ½
25⅝	20	Avantek Inc	693	24¼	23¼	24	+ ½
39	32¾	BancOne 1.36	50	37¾	37½	37½	− ¼
(H)	26⅛	BayBanks 2	86	34⅝	34⅛	34⅝	+ ¾
17¾	14½	Bekins Co .60	204	17⅜	17⅛	17⅜	+ ¼
39¾	32¾	Betz Labs .88	63	39¼	39	39	− ½
40¾	9⅞	Bliss AT Co	808	13½	12¾	13¼	+ ¼
29¼	25⅛	Bob Evan .30g	52	26½	26	26	...
22¼	14¾	C Cor Electrn	414	16¾	15¾	16¾	+ ¾
31¼	21	Cal Mcrowave	508	30⅜	30	30	− ¼
25½	20¾	Carl Karcher	57	24¼	23¾	23¾	− ½
16⅝	11⅝	Cetus Corptn	406	15¾	15⅜	15½	...
(H)	13⅜	Char Shops .22	724	20	19⅜	19⅞	+ ⅞
(H)	20⅝	ChartHous .60	1614	27¼	26⅜	27⅛	+ ½
27¼	22⅛	ChiChis Incrp	598	23⅝	22¾	22¾	− ⅞
28	22⅜	Liebert Corp	49	25¾	25⅜	25¾	...
39¾	31¾	Lin Broadcast	455	37	36¾	36¾	− ¼
28	19¾	LngviewF 1.20	65	26	25¼	26	+ ¾
21¼	17	Manitowoc .80	106	19	18¾	18¾	− ¼
11¼	7½	May Petrolm	141	8	7¾	7⅞	− ⅛
46⅞	33⅝	MCI Communi	4786	46¾	45¾	46¼	...
29⅛	24⅜	McCormk .88a	474	28¾	28½	28¾	+ ⅛
11⅛	6⅞	McCorm OlGs	169	8⅝	8¼	8⅜	+ ⅛
14½	9	McRaeCn Oil	137	11½	11¼	11¼	...
14½	11⅛	MDC Corp .16	266	13¼	13⅛	13⅛	− ⅛
37½	24⅞	Micom Systm	99	36¾	36	36½	− ¼
15⅞	10¾	Microdyne .06	633	13⅜	13⅛	13⅜	...
19¼	14⅜	Midway Airln	295	17	16⅝	17	+ ⅜
33½	26½	MilliporeCp .36	87	29⅜	29⅛	29⅛	− ⅜
32	23¾	MonrchCp 1.36	44	30¼	30	30¼	+ ¼
29⅛	18¼	Monlithc Mem	553	29⅛	28¾	28⅞	...
20¼	16¾	Morrison .36	371	20⅛	19¾	19¾	− ⅜
23⅞	17	Natl Data .36	70	20⅝	20½	20⅝	...
22⅝	16⅜	Nat Microntcs	377	20½	20¼	20⅜	− ⅛
44	33⅝	Netwrk Systm	364	38½	37¾	38⅛	+ ⅛
6	4	Nicklos Oil Gs	257	4⅝	4¼	4¼	− ¼
23¾	15⅛	Nike Inc B	2242	16⅜	15¾	16⅛	+ ¼
64	45¾	Nordstrom .56	43	61¾	61½	61½	...
12¾	11⅛	NowstNG 1.28	142	12½	12⅛	12⅛	− ¼
16¾	11⅞	Nuclear Phar	1124	15⅛	14¾	15	...
16⅝	10⅛	Oceanrg Intl	231	11⅛	10¾	10⅞	− ⅜
12	9¼	Onyx IMI	300	10	9¾	9⅞	− ⅛
10¾	7¾	OXOCO Inc	104	9	8¾	8¾	− ⅛
(H)	20⅝	Pabst Brw .40	1272	51	47½	50¼	+ 1¼
(H)	22⅛	PandickPr .20	214	31⅝	31	31⅝	+ ½

(H)-New 1983 high. (L)-New 1983 low.

Stock & Div.	Sales 100s	Bid	Asked	Net Chg.
--A A--				
Aaron Rents	13	23¾	24½	...
Abrmsind .32g	10	6¾	7¾	...
Acapulco Rest	7	5½	5¾	...
AcclrtnCp .05d	35	7	7¼	...
AccurayCp .14	82	16⅞	17⅛	...
AcetoChem 3i	1	21½	22	...
ACMAT Corp	5	9½	10	...
Acme Genl .20	x10	14½	15	+ ⅛
Adage Incorp	37	45½	46½	...
AddWesley .50	79	19	19½	− ¼
Advance Ross	95	4½	4⅝	...
AdvSemi Mat	120	17½	18	...
Advn Syst .15f	70	22	22¾	...
AEC Inc .40	8	7	7½	+ ¼
AEICOR Inc	976	13-16	⅞	...
Aero Syst Inc	472	6⅞	7	...
AffilBkCp 1.56	2	26½	29	+ ½
AffilBkshrs 1	11	19	19½	...
A F G Indust	24	26½	27	...
Agnico Eagle	100	12⅛	12¼	+ ⅛
AGS Computr	237	19¼	19¾	+ 1
AirCargo Eqp	87	5¾	6	− ⅛
Air Fla Sys p	987	2⅜	2 7-16	− ⅛
Air Wisconsin	157	14	14¾	+ ½
Alamo Sv .10b	95	31½	33	− 2
AlBkCmrc 10i	z31	9½	11½	...
AlaskPcB .20e	20	18	19	...
AlaTennRes 4	3	58	60	...
Alexndr Enrg	13	3	3¼	...
Algorex Corp	29	23	23¾	− ¾
Allico Incp .30	2	45	49	...
Allegh Bev .40	474	17⅜	17⅝	+ ⅝
Allegh LndMn	543	3	3⅛	...
AllghWstn En	105	5⅜	5⅝	...
Allen Org .48a	30	34½	37	...
AlliedCaptl 1a	5	21¾	22¾	...
Alo SchererH	4	7¾	8¼	...
Alpha Micrsys	37	14⅜	14⅝	...
Altair Corp	6	6¾	7¼	...
AM Cable TV	141	6¾	7	...
Ambass Gr .28	x84	7¾	8¼	− ⅛
Ameribanc	20	21	22¼	+ ¼
AmAggregat 1	9	20	22	...
AmApraisl .36	52	8½	9½	...
AmBcpPa 1.10	43	12⅝	12¾	...

Stock & Div.	Sales 100s	Bid	Asked	Net Chg.
BnkMontS 2.40	113	29⅛	30	...
BkNwEng 2.60	x160	49⅜	49⅝	+ 1½
Bankers Note	186	8	8⅛	...
Bankrs Tr 1.60	142	31¾	32¼	− ¾
BankIowa 1.52	z33	42	43½	...
BnkSecur .25d	3	8½	9¼	...
BantaGeor .88	241	37	37½	+ 1
Barber Green	14	16½	16¾	...
Barden Corp 1	7	31	34	+ ½
BarringerRs p	2	4⅞	5⅛	...
Barris Indust	425	5¼	5⅜	− ¼
Barton Valve	140	6	6¼	...
BaseTnA .15g	163	13½	14	+ ½
Basic EarthSc	304	2 9-16	2 11-16	...
BasicResr Intl	378	1⅜	1 7-16	...
BassFurn .80a	112	53¼	53¾	+ 1¼
BassWlkr .61b	30	38¾	39¼	− ¼
Baylss Mkt .60	14	14¾	15¾	− ¼
BaylyCp .32	52	36½	37¾	+ 1
Bayswatr Rlty	10	13½	14	...
BBDOIntl 1.80	66	42	42½	+ ½
BearCreek .36	13	22¼	22¾	...
Beck Arnley	18	9¼	9⅞	...
Bedford Cmpt	6	10¾	11¼	...
BeelineInc .35	z10	7⅛	7½	...
BegleyDrg .68	3	15	16	...
Belknap .80	11	13¼	13⅜	...
BellPetrol Svc	10	2⅞	3¼	− ⅛
Bell&W Co 5i	11	12½	13	...
Bell Natl Corp	43	24,	24½	+ ½
Belo Corp .72	172	40¾	41	+ 1
BerkleyW .32g	44	11½	12	...
BerklineCp .50	1	12¼	12⅝	...

Stock & Div.	Sales 100s	Bid	Asked	Net Chg.
Centocor	170	18¾	19	...
CentrlBcp 1.95	18	25	25¼	+ ¼
CnBkgSys .40g	x22	20	20½	− ⅛
CenBcsSo 1.20	38	17	17¼	...
CnCar Bt 1.12	x2	28	29	+ 1⅜
CenFidBk 1.36	10	24½	24⅞	...
CenJerBT 1.10	3	14⅝	15½	− ⅛
CentrlPac .64	x19	10	10½	+ ½
CPennNt 1.40a	10	21½	21⅝	...
Centran Cp .40	x45	16¾	17¼	− ⅛
Cenvill Devl	92	17⅝	17⅞	+ ¼
CFS Cont .52	11	32⅜	32⅝	...
CGA Assc Inc	222	13¾	14	...
Champ Pt .07d	63	9⅜	9½	− ⅛
Chapparl Res	25	1½	1⅝	...
CharlesRiv .48	x107	40½	41¼	+ ⅞
ChartrCp 1.88	z5	28	28¾	...
Chathm Mf .60	15	14¾	15¼	...
Chattem .48	25	20½	21	...
Checkpnt Syst	47	16⅜	16⅝	− ¼
ChezmDv .10f	9	8⅞	9⅛	...
Chefs Intl Inc	429	1 11-16	1⅞	+ 1-16
Chemlawn .40	x61	47¾	48¼	+ 1⅝
Chemtrnc Inc	37	26	27	+ 1¼
Cherry El .06b	3	17½	18	...
ChesapkUtil 2	90	19¾	20¾	...
Childrn World	97	9⅛	9¼	...
Chittenden 1g	7	19	19¾	...
Chomerics Inc	81	14½	15	...
ChurchDwt .72	2	19¾	20½	+ ¼
ChyronCp .10b	41	27½	27¾	+ ¼
CinciFincl 2	18	60½	61	...
CircIIncm 1.44	11	13⅜	13⅝	− ⅛

EXPLANATORY NOTES

z-Sales in full.

a-Annual rate, also extra or extras. b-Paid so far in 1983, no regular rate. c-Payment of accumulated dividends. d-Paid in 1982. e-Cash plus stock paid in 1982. f-Cash plus stock paid in 1983. g-Annual rate plus stock dividend. h-Paid in 1983, latest dividend omitted. i-Percent in stock paid in 1982. j-Percent in stock paid in 1983, latest dividend omitted. k-Percent in stock paid in 1983. n-Asked price not applicable. p-Granted temporary exception from Nasdaq qualifications. q-In bankruptcy proceedings. t-Liquidating dividend. ut-Units. wt-Warrants. x-Ex-dividend, ex-rights or ex-distribution.

Source: *Wall Street Journal*, March 28, 1983.

An authorized stock must have at least two market makers. This means that, understandably, there must already exist public interest in an issue before it may be admitted to NASDAQ.

OTC issues with the greatest trading volume are carried on NAS-DAQ's *National List,* of which a selection is reported in Table 11.4. In addition more than 120 Local Quotations Committees supply lists of quotations to the media for securities in which there is particular local interest. In connection with its encouragement of a "national market system," the SEC has separated the National List into two parts. Effective May 1, 1982, the forty-five most active NASDAQ stocks were designated "national market system (NMS) securities," in which transactions were to be reported continuously in the manner practiced on exchanges. Additional issues are being added to this list, and the *Wall Street Journal* reported trading in about 180 NMS stocks on March 25, 1983, some of which are shown in the upper portion of Table 11.4. Notice the similarity between the data reported for NMS stocks in Table 11.4 and NYSE stocks in Table 10.4. The lower portion of Table 11.4 shows the highest bid and lowest offer through NASDAQ for a selection of non-NMS stocks on the National List at 4:00 P.M. Eastern Time on March 25, 1983.

The number of NASDAQ listings has grown rapidly. Of the more than 30,000 stocks not listed on exchanges, we see from Table 11.4 that 57,490,000 shares in 3,383 issues were traded with the assistance of NASDAQ. NASDAQ's volume (79,750,000 shares) exceeded trading on the NYSE (76,290,000 shares) for the first time on May 27, 1983. Five years previously, in 1978, about 2,500 issues were listed on NASDAQ, and volume was only one-third of the NYSE's.[61]

The third market

OTC trading of exchange-listed shares is called the "third market."[62] Most trades in the third market are initiated by institutions in a few active stocks. At the peak of its importance in the early 1970s the third market's fifty most active stocks each quarter accounted for about 40 percent of its total trading volume.[63] The number of NYSE-listed shares traded on the third market, as a proportion of total shares traded on the NYSE, rose from 2.6 percent in 1966 to a peak of 7.3 percent in 1972,[64] before falling in response to the decline in commission rates on the NYSE to 2.3 percent on March 25, 1983. (This may be calculated from Table 10.4.)

61 SEC, *Annual Report,* Washington, 1979, page 106.

62 The NYSE and the American Stock Exchange have preempted "first" and "second" in this enumeration of markets.

63 NYSE, *Fact Book,* New York, 1976, page 17.

64 From the SEC *Monthly Statistical Bulletin*s, summarized and discussed in Frank Fabozzi and Frank Zarb (1981, page 150).

The fourth market

Direct trading of stocks between two parties without broker interme- diation is called the "fourth market." Large institutional investors with active portfolios have an incentive to deal with each other in order to avoid brokers' commissions. Several private fourth-market organizations provide teletype or private phone hookups between institutional subscribers. One of these, Instinet, has since 1970 pro- vided a computer network through which subscribers may quote bids and offers and execute trades.[65] Because of the fourth market's dispersed, largely informal, and confidential nature, there are no good estimates of its size. But Instinet is included on the NYSE consoli- dated tape, which enables us to determine from Table 10.4 that 13,300 NYSE shares were traded through Instinet on March 25, 1983, compared with 77,330,000 shares traded at the NYSE. Since about 30 percent of shares traded at the NYSE are in blocks of 10,000 or more, we may conclude that the search and execution facilities of the exchange are worth their cost even for large traders.

A GOVERNMENT-CONTROLLED NATIONAL MARKET SYSTEM?

The Securities Acts Amendments of 1975

In the Securities Acts Amendments of 1975 Congress declared that "the securities markets are an important national asset which must be preserved and strengthened"[66]—meaning, of course, greater regula- tion. Congress envisioned a nationwide computer link between exchanges and the OTC market that would ensure that customers' orders were executed in the "best market," if possible "without the participation of a dealer." The SEC was directed, "therefore, having due regard for the public interest [etc.], to use its authority under this [act] to facilitate a national market system for securities. . . ." In the furtherance of this directive the SEC was authorized "by rule or order, to authorize or require self-regulatory organizations to act jointly . . . in planning, developing, operating, or regulating a national market system," and to appoint a National Market Advisory Board, which would make recommendations to the SEC about the steps that should be taken to facilitate the national system and also to inquire into the possible need for a National Regulatory Board to regulate the National Market System.

Evolution of a competitive national market system

The history of the NYSE and other aspects of the capital markets presented in this chapter has been a story of the development of an

---

65 See Robert Sobel (1977) and Chris Welles (1975) for discussions of Instinet's early history.

66 This and the following quotations are from Section 11A of the Securities Exchange Act of 1934 as amended by the Securities Acts Amendments of 1975.

efficient national market, by means of innovations in technology and organization, in spite of government-imposed or government-protected monopolistic impediments. The most visible innovations have been the organization of exchanges in the late eighteenth and early nineteenth centuries, the telegraph in 1844, the stock ticker and the continuous auction system on exchanges shortly after the Civil War, the telephone in 1876, NDQS and NASDAQ for the OTC market in 1913 and 1971, the consolidated tape in 1974, high-speed ticker and trade execution and clearing equipment on exchanges during the 1970s and 1980s, a national clearing system for exchanges and the OTC market in 1977, the ITS system permitting trades between dealers and brokers on the floors of different exchanges in 1978, and the CAES link between NASDAQ and ITS in 1982.

Kenneth Garbade and William Silber (1978) examined the contributions of three of these innovations to the integration of financial markets. Specifically, they looked at price spreads between American cities before and after telegraph service, between New York and London before and after the Atlantic cable, and between the NYSE and regional stock exchanges before and after the consolidated tape. They found that the "first two innovations . . . led to significant and rapid narrowing of inter-market price differentials . . . as market participants appear to have quickly appreciated the usefulness and profit opportunities of the new technologies for financial investment and arbitrage." But they found little evidence that the consolidated tape narrowed price differentials between the NYSE and regional exchanges. The most obvious reason for this difference is that the "telegraph and the cable were innovated by the private sector, in response to perceived profit opportunities. The consolidated tape, on the other hand, owes its existence to the regulatory authority of the [SEC]. We conjecture that the tape would not have been innovated by private sector initiative. . . . The already advanced state of communications . . . made the consolidated tape unnecessary, and its measurable economic benefits minimal."

What next?

In view of the history of American financial markets one might have thought that legislators and regulators genuinely interested in promoting efficient markets would have been content to refrain from imposing or encouraging monopolistic obstacles. But such has not been the case. In 1978 the SEC suggested a program that to an unusual degree reflected traditional bureaucratic antagonisms toward change, diversity, competition, and privacy. Its proposed *Central Limit Order File (CLOF)* would have consisted of a network of computer terminals between all "qualified" brokers and dealers, like NASDAQ on a larger scale and meant to display not only the bid and ask prices of market makers who wished to participate but *all* quotations (for no other means of information exchange would be allowed; see Table 11.5 for an

Table 11.5   The SEC's Authority Over Quotations and Transactions

No self-regulatory organization, member thereof, securities information processor, broker, or dealer shall make use of the mails or any means or instrumentality of interstate commerce to collect, process, distribute, publish, or prepare for distribution or publication any information with respect to quotations for or transactions in any security other than an exempted security, to assist, participate in, or coordinate the distribution or publication of such information, or to effect any transaction in, or to induce or attempt to induce the purchase or sale of, any such security in contravention of such rules and regulations as the Commission shall prescribe as necessary or appropriate in the public interest . . . .

Source: Section 11A(c)(1) of the Securities Exchange Act of 1934, as amended by the Securities Amendments Acts of 1975.

existing SEC regulation) and all customer limit orders and their time of submission. The specialist's private book was to be eliminated, and market and limit orders were to be filled automatically in the order of their submission.[67]

CLOF might—or might not—have satisfied the "best execution," "orderly markets," and other "in the public interest" criteria of Congress. There is no way to tell because not enough is known about the functioning of markets, even in the absence of technological change, to be able to predict with confidence the degree of success or failure of a completely new market system imposed on an industry.[68] Progress in the securities industry, as in other industries, has taken the form of innovations by entrepreneurs in search of an advantage. Some innovations have turned out to be useful and have been retained. Others have been discarded. Dominant groups, such as the NYSE, have often resisted change and, with the government's help, have stifled competition. No one knows what the future holds for innovations in financial instruments and their methods of exchange. The efficiency of these markets requires free entry into the securities business and the unrestricted freedom, subject to the laws of fraud (so that information is correct), to introduce new types of securities and new ways of trading them.

The SEC's proposal was withdrawn in 1979 under strong opposition from the securities business. This was partly due to its incomplete form and the failure to convince specialists and other market makers that markets function "automatically." But more important, brokers and dealers apparently prefer a more complex, less uniform, and often less impersonal and less automatic system, by which trades may be executed, as they see fit, in a variety of ways: on exchanges, through

67 CLOF was meant to be a nationwide version of the Multiple Dealer Trading System introduced on the Cincinnati Stock Exchange in 1978.

68 The behavior of competitive markets under different organizations has been the subject of many experimental and theoretical studies by scholars interested in *how* and *how well* the invisible hand works. These studies include Haim Mendelson (1982) and the references cited therein.

NASDAQ, or by other means that they may develop from time to time in their efforts to gain a competitive advantage. (Regulators refer to this apparent lack of system as "market fragmentation.") The NYSE is pursuing the development of the Intermarket Trading System, which communicates bid and ask prices between exchanges, so that members at one exchange can have orders executed on other exchanges, but does not diminish the importance of floor trading as it presently exists, including the specialist's book and his responsibility for price continuity.[69] Some large brokerage firms have developed their own electronic systems that automatically route a customer's orders to the best market. But no execution system can be completely automatic. It is inconceivable even in a national system in which all bid and ask prices and all limit orders are on display, even with the capability of instant execution of trades, that no one will perceive a possible advantage to be gained from direct negotiation—either over the phone or on the floor of an exchange.

It may eventually be possible, in this electronic age, for all prices to be quoted and all trades to be executed between offices without the benefit of exchange floors. Nevertheless, exchanges appear to have a future. There is apparently something about the physical proximity of groups of buyers and sellers that leads brokers and dealers to believe that they can be best informed about market conditions in such a system. Or maybe haggling on the floor is more fun than punching keys in an office; it would be nice to believe that great organizational decisions are made on such grounds. In any event, for whatever reasons, exchanges have thrived—not only the old exchanges interested in their own preservation but also the new and rapidly growing futures and options exchanges initiated by traders free to choose any trading system they liked.

Congress has criticized the SEC for failing to proceed more rapidly toward a national market system, and as early as 1979 the Government Accounting Office "charged that the absence of an explicit plan for the development of the NMS was resulting in unnecessary time delays and excessive costs."[70] This is because "substantial disagreement continues to exist, both in the securities industry and in the [SEC], concerning what the ultimate NMS configuration should be."[71] Such disagreement is inevitable because Congress has posed an insoluble problem; it is impossible that there should be an *ultimate* national-market-system configuration except in a police state. Let us hope that the following Congressional nightmare is not realized:

> Despite the diversity of views with respect to the practical details of a national market system, all current proposals appear to

---

69 See discussions of ITS in NYSE, *Annual Reports*, New York, 1977, 1979.

70 Frank Fabozzi and Frank Zarb (1981, page 186).

71 Frank Fabozzi and Frank Zarb (1981, page 186).

assume that there will be an exclusive processor or service bureau to which the exchanges and the NASD will transmit data and which in turn will make transactions and quotation information available to vendors of such information. . . . The Committee believes that if such a central facility is to be utilized, the importance of the manner of its regulation cannot be overestimated. An exclusive processor of this sort will play a key role in deter-

Table 11.6   The Fantastic Returns (and Losses) to Margin Trading

---

Definitions

P_0 = initial price of stock

P_1 = end-of-period price of stock

m = margin (customer's investment) as a proportion of P_0

R_s = one-period rate of return on stock

R_{mp} = one-period rate of return on a margin purchase

R_{ss} = one-period rate of return on a short sale

R_b = one-period rate of interest on a broker's loan

A Margin Purchase

$$R_{mp} = \frac{[P_1 - (1 + R_b)(1 - m)P_0] - mP_0}{mP_0} = \frac{P_1 - P_0 - R_b(1 - m)P_0}{mP_0}$$

(11.1)
$$= \frac{R_s - (1 - m)R_b}{m}$$

Notice that

(11.2) $R_{mp} = \begin{cases} \dfrac{R_s}{m} & \text{if} \quad R_b = 0 \\[2ex] 0.40 & \text{if} \quad m = 0.5, R_b = 0.10, R_s = 0.25 \\ & \qquad \text{(as in the discussion of XYZ stock)} \\[2ex] -0.843 & \text{if} \quad m = 0.5, R_b = 0.01, R_s = \dfrac{-25}{60} \text{ (as in Table 11.7)} \end{cases}$

A Short Sale

(11.3)
$$R_{ss} = \frac{(P_0 + mP_0 - P_1) - mP_0}{mP_0} = -\frac{R_s}{m}$$

Notice that

(11.4) $R_{ss} = 0.833$ if $m = 0.5, R_s = \dfrac{-25}{60}$ (as in Table 11.7)

mining how information about transactions in securities will reach the public. Its decisions as to who may report transactions through its facilities and in what manner will influence the extent and nature of competition among market facilities. . . .

Any exclusive processor is, in effect, a public utility, and thus it must function in a manner which is absolutely neutral with respect to all market centers, all market makers, and all private firms. . . . Therefore, in order to foster efficient market development and operation and to provide a first line of defense against anti-competitive practices, Sections 11A(b) and (c)(1) would grant the SEC broad powers over any exclusive processor and impose on that agency a responsibility to assure the processor's neutrality and the reasonableness of its charges in practice as well as in concept.

Senate Committee Report 94-75 (1975), pages 11 and 12

FINANCING THE CAPITAL MARKETS
Customer financing: trading on margin

There are two kinds of margin transactions: margin buying and short sales. In the first case the customer buys securities with money borrowed from a broker or other lender in the hope that prices will rise. In the second case the customer sells borrowed securities in the hope that he can repay the loan with securities purchased at lower prices in the future. In both transactions regulations limit the customer's leverage by requiring him to deposit with the lender a specified amount of money, called the *customer's margin.*

MARGIN BUYING. You purchase 100 shares of XYZ stock for $4,000 because you believe its price will rise. And lo and behold, the price rises to 50 and you have earned $1,000 (less commissions) on an investment of $4,000. But how much nicer if you could have earned $1,000 on an investment of $2,000, or less, freeing the remainder of your $4,000 for other uses. You can do this by borrowing to buy the stock, using the stock as collateral for the loan.

For example suppose you put up $2,000 of your own money (your "margin") and borrow the remainder of the $4,000 cost of the shares from your broker at a rate of interest of 10 percent per annum. Abstracting from commissions and assuming you sell the stock for $5,000 after 1 year, the annual rate of return on your investment is 40 percent, which is the increase in the value of the stock less the interest on the broker's loan ($1,000 − $200) divided by your original investment, or margin, of $2,000. If you had been able to increase your leverage by depositing a margin of only 25 percent of the purchase, your rate of return would have been ($1,000 − $300)/$1,000 = 70 percent. These rates of return and their sensitivity to margins may be confirmed by Equation (11.1) in Table 11.6. Notice that the term in brackets in Equation (11.1) is your net receipts at the end of the year:

Table 11.7   The Fortunes and Misfortunes of Bulls and Bears: A Numerical Example

Bull's Margin Purchase

Date	Price of ABC, $	Market Value of 100 Shares, $	Customer's Debit Balance, $	Customer's Equity, $	Interest on Broker's Loan, $	Margin Call, $	Customer's Net Gain,[a] $
1/2	60	6,000	3,000	3,000			
1/9	66	6,600	3,000	3,600			600
1/16	50	5,000	3,000	2,000			− 1,000
1/23	40	4,000	3,000	1,000			− 2,000
1/30	35	3,500	3,000	500			− 2,500
1/30	35	3,500	3,030	470	30		− 2,530
1/30	35	3,500	1,750	1,750		1,280	− 2,530
2/6	60	6,000	1,750	4,250			− 30
2/13	72	7,200	1,750	5,450			1,170
2/13	72	7,200					
2/20	500	50,000	1,750	48,250			43,970

Bear's Short Sale

Date	Price of ABC, $	Market Value of 100 Shares, $	Customer's Credit Balance, $	Customer's Equity, $	Margin Call, $	Customer's Net Gain,[b] $
1/2	60	6,000	9,000	3,000		
1/9	66	6,600	9,000	2,400		− 600
1/16	50	5,000	9,000	4,000		1,000
1/23	40	4,000	9,000	5,000		2,000
1/30	35	3,500	9,000	5,500		2,500
1/30						
1/30						
2/6	60	6,000	9,000	3,000		0
2/13	72	7,200	9,000	1,800		− 1,200
2/13	72	7,200	10,800	3,600	1,800	− 1,200
2/20	500	50,000	10,800	− 39,200		− 44,000

a Bull's net gain = increase in equity − margin calls = increase in value of stock − interest on loan.

b Bear's net gain = increase in equity − margin calls = decrease in value of stock.

the sale price of the stock less the principal and interest on the broker's loan.

But what if the price of XYZ falls, say, to 20? Your broker is no less worried by this possibility than you are—for in such an event the collateral that he holds may be worth less than his loan to you. If you had deposited an original margin of 50 percent ($2,000 of $4,000), a fall in the value of the collateral to $2,000 still covers the loan's principal. But if you had put up only 25 percent margin and the price of XYZ falls to 20, the collateral is worth only two-thirds of the value of the loan, and the broker begins to worry about your ability to repay the loan, especially if XYZ continues its decline. He asks you to reestablish your margin, and if you do not he sells the stock to recover as much of the loan as he can.

Because purchases on less than 100 percent margin are the rule in securities transactions, it is conceivable that significant declines in securities prices might force sales that cause further declines, which, if they proceed far enough, lead to bankruptcies among investors, brokers, and their banks; and these events should be more likely to occur, the smaller are the margins (collateral) required by brokers and other lenders. The extent to which inadequate margins (compared to, for example, the drastic withdrawal of credit by the Fed) contributed to the 1929 Crash is unknown. Nevertheless, the Crash and the Great Depression reinforced traditional public and official hostilities toward speculation, and the Securities Exchange Act of 1934 directed the Federal Reserve Board to impose regulations "for the purpose of preventing the excessive use of credit for the purchase or carrying of securities." Fed initial margin requirements on approved[72] stocks and convertible bonds have fluctuated between 25 and 100 percent and have been 50 percent since 1974. Exchanges and the NASD also require minimum maintenance margins, usually 25 percent, in addition to the Fed's initial margin requirements.[73] Brokerage firms often have "house rules" greater than 25 percent.

An example of a margin purchase is presented in Table 11.7. Mr. Bull believes that the price of ABC stock will rise from its present $60 per share, and on January 2 he buys 100 shares with $3,000 of his own money and $3,000 borrowed from his broker at a rate of interest of 12 percent per annum. Thus his initial debit balance (the amount owed to the broker) is $3,000. His equity (margin) is the difference between the value of the stock that he has purchased (but which is held by the

---

72 Approved "margin stocks" were initially restricted to those traded on "national" (that is, New York) exchanges. In 1969 the regulations were amended to include other stocks deemed acceptable by the Fed.

73 There are no Fed margin requirements on government or nonconvertible corporate bonds. But NYSE members must require the following minimum maintenance margins: 5 percent of the par value of U.S. Treasury and most U.S. agency bonds, the lesser of 15 percent of the par value or 25 percent of the market value of municipal bonds, and 25 percent of the market value of corporate bonds.

broker as collateral) and the broker's loan. The price of ABC rises to 66 during the next week so that Bull's equity rises to $3,600. Thus on January 9 Bull's equity exceeds the legal requirement by $3,600 − 0.50($6,600) = $300. He may, if he likes and if the broker has no more stringent house margin requirements, withdraw this $300 in the form of a loan from the broker or use it to purchase additional securities. But we shall assume that he leaves the cash on deposit with the broker—and a good thing too, because ABC promptly takes a nose-dive, eventually falling to 35 on January 30. The value of the stock is now $3,500, and Bull owes the broker $3,030 in principal and interest, leaving him an equity of $470. Bull's margin is only $470/$3,500 = 13 percent, less than the 25 percent minimum maintenance margin required by the exchange, and he gets a *margin call* from his broker. Table 11.7 assumes that the broker asks Bull for an additional deposit of $1,280 to bring his equity up to 50 percent of the stock's value and that Bull complies (instead of cutting his losses at $2,530 by asking the broker to sell the stock and pay him the remaining $470).

SHORT SALES.

DEFINITION 11.2.   A *short sale* represents a debt contracted in goods, services, or securities instead of in money.[74]

We are used to speaking of debts as if they were obligations to pay money. But many credit transactions involve the receipt of money in exchange for promises to deliver goods. This is true of retail stores' layaway plans and of builders who receive partial or full payment before beginning construction. The store and the builder are "long money" and "short goods"; that is, they own money but owe goods.

In Chapter 12 we shall consider short sales of obligations to deliver securities and foreign exchange represented by contracts traded on futures exchanges. The following discussion is concerned with the simpler and less formal arrangement between a broker and his customer by which the latter borrows securities from the former. An example of this kind of short sale is presented in Table 11.7. Mr. Bear[75] believes that the price of ABC stock will fall and on January 2 borrows 100 shares from his broker in order to sell them for $6,000. Mr. Bear actually sees neither the securities nor (until he closes his account with the broker, and then only if he realizes a profit) the money. The broker probably borrows 100 shares of ABC from the account of another

74 This brief but comprehensive definition was suggested by Edward Meeker (1930, page 1), who also presents an extensive history of short sales.

75 It has been said that bears derived their name from the proverb of "selling the skin before you have got the bear." Or maybe it is a corruption of the statement "to be *bare* of stock." "Bear" used to be reserved for those who sold stock short but now is often applied to anyone who thinks that stock prices will fall. The early use of bear and other terms on the London Stock Exchange is discussed by Charles Duguid (1901, Chapter 2).

customer (perhaps Mr. Bull, who has given the broker permission to do so in the standard broker-customer agreement), sells the stock, and keeps the proceeds in Bear's credit balance. Bear's hopes for the future include watching ABC fall to 35, "covering" his short position by restoring the borrowed securities with 100 shares purchased for $3,500, withdrawing his $6,000 credit balance from the broker, and spending his $2,500 profit[76] on a weekend in Philadelphia. But what if ABC rises to 90? The repayment of Bear's securities debt would be $9,000 and, if he is unable to come up with the extra $3,000, the broker is stuck with a bad loan. So margins are required on short sales as protection against price increases, just as they are required on security purchases as protection against price declines. Minimum initial margins are the same for short sales as for purchases (50 percent of the value of the securities), and Bear must deposit $3,000 with the broker, which, when added to the value of the securities that have been sold on his behalf, brings his credit balance to $9,000.

Bear's hopes are realized during the first 4 weeks of the venture. But he doesn't take his profits,[77] the fall in ABC is reversed, and on February 13, when the price has risen to 72, Bear's equity is only $1,800. His credit balance is unchanged at $9,000, but $7,200 is now required to repay his debt. Bear's equity on February 13 is 25 percent ($1,800/$7,200) of the value of the securities, which would just satisfy the minimum maintenance margin on a stock purchase. But the NYSE requires a higher maintenance margin (30 percent) on short sales because of their greater risk. The possible loss on a purchase is limited because the price cannot fall below zero. For example Bull could not have lost more than $6,000 (plus interest) on his purchase of 100 shares of ABC at 60; nor could his broker have lost more than $3,000 even if Bull had not maintained his margin and the price fell suddenly to zero. But there is no limit to the potential loss on a short sale because there is no upper limit to a stock's price.

Returning to Bear: The equity in his account falls below the 30 percent trigger on February 13, and he gets a margin call from his broker for $1,800 to bring his equity up to 50 percent of the value of the securities. The last entry (February 20) in Table 11.7 has been included for dramatic effect: to illustrate the possible losses arising from a short sale.

Short sales normally account for about 8 percent of all transactions on the NYSE.[78] During 1981 about 84 percent of short sales were conducted by members of the Exchange, half of that amount by specialists attempting to maintain orderly markets in the face of large

---

76 Bear pays no interest to the broker because he has borrowed no money.

77 An 83.3 percent rate of return between January 2 and January 30, consistent with Equations (11.3) and (11.4) in Table 11.6.

78 The proportions in this paragraph are based on data in NYSE, *Fact Book,* New York, 1982, pages 46, 67, 71, 73.

inflows of buy orders. Although only 16 percent of short sales were by public customers, most of the *short interest* is owed by this group. The "short interest" at a given time is the total of all shares sold short and not covered (bought back). The average short interest during 1981 was about two-tenths of 1 percent of all NYSE-listed shares outstanding.

RAIDS AND CORNERS. A *bear raid* is a concerted attempt by a group of investors to force the price of a stock down by means of short sales, hoping to realize large profits by covering their short positions with stock purchased at low prices. A *corner* is a bear trap laid by speculators who buy all or nearly all of the stock, for which they can demand high prices from the bears who must obtain the stock to cover their short positions. Several famous raids and corners occurred between the Civil War and 1920.[79] Some of the corners were caused unintentionally by groups competing for control of a company. The groups would bid up the price of a stock in their efforts to acquire as much of the issue as possible, which induced some investors to sell the stock short because they perceived it to be overvalued. On a few occasions, as in the Northern Pacific Corner of 1901, more stock was borrowed and sold short than was outstanding. The price of Northern Pacific shares rose from 101 on April 22 to 1,000 on May 9 as the two competing groups (James J. Hill of the Northern Pacific, backed by J. P. Morgan & Co., and E. H. Harriman of the Union Pacific, backed by Kuhn, Loeb & Co.) and the desperate bears attempted to acquire stock. The call money rate rose to 70 percent and the market crashed as speculators sold stock to raise cash. However, the corner was unintentional and Morgan and Kuhn Loeb set the bears free by accepting $150 per share from those who had sold stock short to them and could not deliver and by lending stock to others who had sold short.

The last successful intentional corner was the Stutz Corner of 1920, engineered by Allan A. Ryan of the NYSE firm of the same name. The price of Stutz rose from 100 at the beginning of the year to 134 on February 2. Short selling forced the price to near 100 in early March. But loans of $12 million from the Chase National Bank and Guaranty Trust enabled Ryan to buy at higher and higher prices, finally reaching 391 on March 31. At the end of the game Ryan owned 80,000 shares outright and had contracts for the delivery of 110,000 shares to himself and his associates—more than the 100,000 shares of Stutz stock in existence. He offered to settle with the bears for $750 a share. Ryan had violated no rules of the day, written or unwritten, and no innocent parties had been harmed. He had bet that he could raise the funds necessary to corner the bears, who had bet that he could not. But the NYSE's Governing Board (which, according to Ryan, contained

79 See Edward Meeker (1932, Appendix 14) and Richard Teweles and Edward Bradley (1982, Chapter 17).

several Stutz bears) defeated Ryan by changing the rules. They suspended trading and delayed delivery of Stutz stock. Pressed by the banks for repayment of their loans and unable to collect on his contracts, Ryan was forced to sell the stock off the NYSE at low prices and was eventually forced into bankruptcy.[80]

In 1925 the NYSE adopted rules directed at corners by which the Exchange may postpone deliveries and suspend trading in stocks that "cannot be obtained for delivery on existing contracts except at prices and on terms arbitrarily dictated by" a group that has acquired control of the stock.[81] The Exchange may also set a "fair settlement price" on those contracts.

Broker and dealer financing

SOURCES OF FUNDS. Brokers and dealers used to obtain most of their funds by means of *call loans* (payable on demand) or *time loans* (with specified maturities) from banks.[82] The first item on the liability side of the balance sheet in Table 11.8 indicates that this source is still important. Brokers and dealers borrow from banks on the basis of security collateral and, like their customers, are subject to the Fed's margin regulations. Regulation U prohibits banks from extending credit to brokers and dealers in amounts exceeding the maximum loan value of the collateral, meaning at present 50 percent on stocks and 100 percent on nonconvertible U.S. and private bonds; the NYSE and other exchanges impose further requirements on their members.

Additional sources of funds include loans from other brokers and dealers, customers' margin accounts and deposits in excess of margin requirements, and proceeds from sales of borrowed securities (short positions). But the most important form of broker and dealer financing is the *repurchase agreement* (RP), by which the borrower sells securities to another party subject to an agreement to repurchase those securities at a specified price at a later date. The repurchase price is the sale price plus the agreed interest charge.[83] In recent years more than half of the bank funds obtained by brokers and dealers have been through RPs,[84] and even larger amounts have been borrowed from corporations and state and local governments in this form.

Brokers and dealers, like many other financial firms, manage highly leveraged portfolios. Table 11.8 shows that only $6.7/121.0 = 5.5$ percent of broker and dealer assets were financed by partner or stockholder *equity*. This is far less than the approximately 50 percent

---

80 See John Brooks (1969, pages 26–40) for an interesting account of the Stutz Corner and its aftermath.

81 Edward Meeker (1932, page 204).

82 The rise and fall of the call loan market at the NYSE was described in the 1869, 1917, and 1946 entries in the chronology earlier in this chapter.

83 RPs were discussed in connection with the federal funds market in Chapter 9.

84 For example, see lines 21 and 35 of Table 4.2.

Table 11.8   Balance Sheet of NYSE Member Firms Doing Business with the Public,[a] December 31, 1981 (Billions of Dollars)

Assets		Liabilities and Owners' Equity	
Currency and bank deposits	2.3	Borrowings on securities (bank loans)	10.2
Receivable from other brokers and dealers	12.0	Securities sold under repurchase agreements	51.7
Receivable from customers and partners	21.8	Payable to other brokers and dealers	11.1
Long positions in securities and commodities[b]	79.9	Payable to customers and partners	13.3
Exchange memberships	0.2	Short positions in securities and commodities	17.3
Land, equipment, and other assets	4.8	Other accrued expenses and accounts payable	9.2
Total assets	121.0	Long-term subordinated debt	1.5
		Owners' equity	6.7
		Total liabilities and owners' equity	121.0

a Of the 604 member organizations of the NYSE at the end of 1981, 390 dealt with the public.

b Including $42.4 billion of securities acquired under agreements to resell.

Source: NYSE, *Fact Book*, New York, 1982 pages 55 and 56.

average for nonfinancial corporations[85] but is comparable to the equity/asset ratio of 5.8 percent for all U.S. commercial banks at the end of 1981.[86] The riskiness of leveraged portfolios was pointed out in our discussion of margin transactions. But that discussion was limited to unhedged positions, specifically those of Mr. Bull, who was long securities and short cash, and of Mr. Bear, who was short securities and long cash. A combined Bull-Bear portfolio would be riskless and similar to the combined broker-dealer portfolio in Table 11.8, in which the assets are roughly like the liabilities. But brokers and dealers are not perfectly hedged; that is, their assets and liabilities are not identical. They go short in securities whose prices are expected to fall and long in securities whose prices are expected to rise.[87] Severely unmatched assets and liabilities, when combined with incorrect forecasts, can cause losses and even failure.

---

85 See Figure 15.6 in the chapter on nonfinancial firms.

86 See Samuel Talley (1983, page 2).

87 See Marcia Stigum (1983, Chapters 9, 11, and 12) for discussions of broker and dealer portfolio management. For reasons of data availability most empirical studies of dealer portfolio behavior have been limited to the large government securities dealers that do business with the Fed. These studies include Allan Meltzer and Gert von der Linde (1960), Ira Scott (1965), William Colby (1973), and P. Tinsley, Bonnie Garrett, and M. Friar (1978).

USES OF FUNDS. We have already discussed most of the assets in Table 11.8, including loans between brokers and dealers, loans to customers, and long positions in securities. Somewhat more than half of the last item consists of lending in the form of RPs. These RPs may be held for any of several reasons: For example some dealers make markets in RPs by borrowing and lending at stated bid and offer rates in the hope of making a profit on the spread. Brokers and dealers also speculate in RPs, for example, by borrowing in the form of overnight RPs at low rates and investing in term RPs at higher rates (and hoping that interest rates don't rise). Finally, brokers and dealers, in common with nonfinancial corporations and state and local governments, have worked out arrangements with their banks that in effect allow them to earn interest on demand deposits.[88] A typical arrangement is one by which every afternoon the bank applies all of a checking account's funds above some agreed amount to the overnight purchase of a security. The bank restores the checking account the next morning by repurchasing the security at a price such that the depositor earns the going RP rate.

New issues

INVESTMENT BANKERS.[89] This chapter has so far been devoted entirely to the *secondary market,* that is, the market for previously issued securities. We now consider the *primary market,* in which new securities are traded. Financial intermediaries in the primary market for securities are called *investment banks,* which are firms that help other firms (and governments) raise money through new issues. Most investment banking in the United States is done by securities firms that are also active brokers and dealers in the secondary market, and we shall see below that some secondary market intervention during the early life of an issue is part of the investment banking function. Investment bankers provide three services to security issuers: (1) advice, (2) underwriting, and (3) distribution.[90]

---

88 These arrangements were discussed earlier in connection with the demand for money (Chapter 3) and the management of bank reserves (Chapter 9).

89 See Irwin Friend et al. (1967) for an extensive study of investment banking and the new issues market. For a history of the development of investment banking in the United States see Vincent Carosso (1970). Detailed discussions of practices and regulations in the new issues market are given in Jules Bogen (1964, Chapters 9, 10, and 14). More recent discussions are presented by Leo Loll and Julian Buckley (1981, Chapter 8) and Richard Teweles and Edward Bradley (1982, Chapter 16).

90 The following discussion is limited to *negotiated public offerings,* that is, to issues offered to the general public by investment bankers on terms negotiated with the issuers. These make up the bulk of new issues, but *competitive bidding* and *private placements* are also important. The investment banker's functions are the same in competitive bids as in negotiated deals except that in the former case underwriting contracts are awarded on the basis of prices submitted in sealed bids. A private placement is one in which the entire issue is sold to one or a few large investors, most often life insurance companies or pension funds.

1. Suppose the Jettison Brothers Salvage Co. has decided to buy $55 million worth of new demolition equipment with funds raised by issuing long-term debt. But what kind of debt? The financial vice-president, J. Sam Jettison, Jr., knows something of the financial markets, including current yields, but he wants to make sure the company borrows on the best terms possible. For this, he needs an expert, an investment banker. After discussions with a few investment bankers Jettison negotiates what seem to be the best available terms with Jay Cooke & Co., which advises Jettison that the market is likely to be receptive to a $60 million, 10 percent, 20-year debenture that has standard indenture provisions[91] and is priced at 99.15 to yield 10.10 percent.[92] If all goes as Cooke expects (based on interest rate forecasts, discussions with potential purchasers, and an awareness of competing issues), the proceeds to the company will be $0.9915(\$60,000,000) = \$59,490,000$ less underwriting, management, and selling charges of $1,800,000.

2. The investment banker's insurance function is called *underwriting.* Cooke guarantees $57,690,000 to Jettison and earns a nice profit if the issue sells quickly at 99.15. Bad news about Jettison or an unexpected general increase in yields may force the selling price below 99.15, in which case Cooke earns a smaller profit and may even suffer a loss. But Jettison is sure of $57,690,000 (unless Cooke fails).[93]

3. Cooke uses its contacts with other securities firms and institutional investors to distribute Jettison's issue. Investment bankers' charges for the easily placed bonds of well-known, highly rated companies may under favorable conditions be less than 1 percent. Other firms may under volatile conditions pay more than 6 percent.[94] The difference (as a percentage of face value) between the expected sale price of an issue and the amount promised to the issuer is called the *underwriter's spread* and is about 3 percent in Jettison's case.

---

91 Bond indentures are discussed in Chapter 10.

92 The investment banker also helps to prepare the expensive and time-consuming "full disclosure" statement required of most new issues by the Securities Act of 1933. These burdens weigh most heavily on small companies. The cost of registering a stock issue exceeds $200,000. There is little evidence that these deterrents to investment have been offset by any advantages to investors. For example see George Benston (1973).

93 This is a *firm commitment contract,* in which the underwriter guarantees a minimum amount of funds to the issuer. Other arrangements include the *best efforts contract,* in which the investment banker makes his best efforts to sell as much of the issue for as much as he can as soon as he can, and the *standby contract,* in which the investment banker takes all the securities, at a specified price, that the issuer is unable to sell on his own. The investment banker bears all the risk in the first case, the issuer bears all the risk in the second case, and the risk is shared in the third case. Gershon Mandelker and Artur Raviv (1977) and David Baron (1982) have analyzed some of the conditions under which each of these contracts is optimal. In general the optimal underwriting contract depends on the predictability of the issue's price and the attitudes of the parties toward risk.

94 Table 10.3 describes three ITT bond issues for which the charges ranged from 0.875 percent (for a $100 million straight debenture issue) to 1.125 percent (for a $50 million straight debenture issue and a $100 million subordinated convertible issue). Louis Ederington (1975) has reported that underwriters' spreads vary directly with uncertainty about the price at which an issue can be sold and inversely with the issue's credit rating, size, and call protection.

Spreads tend to be greater for stock issues, which are more widely
held than bonds and therefore often require extensive selling cam-
paigns. The spread for a stock issue of a little-known firm may exceed
20 percent.

SYNDICATES. A single investment banker will not take on all the
underwriting risk and distribution responsibility of a large issue.
Cooke may organize a syndicate of a dozen or more investment
bankers for the Jettison issue. The syndicate members sign an agreement that sets the fee for Cooke as manager of the issue, authorizes
Cooke to negotiate terms with Jettison, and establishes the proportions of the underwriting risk and distribution responsibility to be
accepted by each member.[95] Syndicate members are listed, with the
manager at the top, on a "tombstone ad" that publicizes the issue and
tells prospective investors whom they may contact for more information—though many investors will already have been made aware of the
issue. An example of a tombstone is shown in Figure 11.3 for a pair of
large IBM issues that had comanagers. Tombstones may have been
named for their simple, tombstonelike appearance or perhaps because
little information is given beyond an issue's name, parentage, and
dates of its birth and death.

STABILIZATION. In most cases, when syndicate members have been able
to interest prospective buyers in the issue and market conditions have
been steady, the sale is completed in a day or two, the syndicate's
books are closed, and the proceeds are distributed. But some support
of the price is required even in the best of circumstances. Even when
an issue is quickly sold, some of it will immediately find its way to the
secondary market because some purchasers have changed their minds
and some may have bought with the intention of selling quickly in
anticipation of a rapid price increase. The SEC allows an exception to
the prohibitions against price manipulation by permitting syndicate
members to engage in limited stabilizing purchases in order to maintain a new issue's price in the secondary market at its offering price
until the issue has been sold. In the Jettison case Cooke and associates
quote bids of 99.15 until the sale is completed or until, by the terms of
their agreement, they have purchased a certain proportion (usually 10
to 15 percent) of the issue. If there is strong downward pressure on the
price because of a miscalculation or changing market conditions, the
syndicate will be forced to let the price go to the level dictated by the

---

95 See Kenneth Garbade (1982, page 43) for an example of underwriting allotments. Underwriting
and other fees, and total spreads, are listed weekly in the *Investment Dealers Digest.* Leo Loll
and Julian Buckley (1981, page 161) give an example in which a spread of $6.25 per $100 face
value consists of a $1 management fee, $3.60 selling commission, $1.05 to underwriters, and
$0.60 in miscellaneous expenses.

This announcement is neither an offer to sell nor a solicitation of an offer to buy these securities.
The offer is made only by the Prospectus.

New Issues / October 5, 1979

$1,000,000,000

International Business Machines Corporation

$500,000,000

9½% Notes Due 1986

Price 99.40% and accrued interest, if any, from October 16, 1979

$500,000,000

9⅜% Debentures Due 2004

Price 99.625% and accrued interest, if any, from October 16, 1979

Copies of the Prospectus may be obtained in any State in which this announcement is circulated only from such of the undersigned as may legally offer these securities in such State.

Salomon Brothers

Merrill Lynch White Weld Capital Markets Group
Merrill Lynch, Pierce, Fenner & Smith Incorporated

Morgan Stanley & Co. Incorporated

The First Boston Corporation

Goldman, Sachs & Co.

Bache Halsey Stuart Shields Incorporated

Bear, Stearns & Co.

Blyth Eastman Dillon & Co. Incorporated

Dillon, Read & Co. Inc.

Donaldson, Lufkin & Jenrette Securities Corporation

Drexel Burnham Lambert Incorporated

E. F. Hutton & Company Inc.

Kidder, Peabody & Co. Incorporated

Lazard Frères & Co.

Lehman Brothers Kuhn Loeb Incorporated

Paine, Webber, Jackson & Curtis Incorporated

L. F. Rothschild, Unterberg, Towbin

Shearson Hayden Stone Inc.

Smith Barney, Harris Upham & Co. Incorporated

Warburg Paribas Becker A. G. Becker

Wertheim & Co., Inc.

Dean Witter Reynolds Inc.

Source: Courtesy of IBM.

Figure 11.3 A tombstone.

market. The syndicate will be closed and the members freed to sell their holdings for whatever they can get.

AN EXAMPLE OF UNDERWRITERS' RISK. In October 1979, in the largest debt offering up to that time, IBM issued $1 billion of notes and bonds through a syndicate comanaged by Salomon Brothers and Merrill Lynch (Figure 11.3). The issues had originally been scheduled for late October, perhaps in the hope that September's high yields would come down. But when the upward trend in yields accelerated, it was announced on October 2 that the issues would be brought to market on Thursday, October 4. Too late. Bond prices continued to drop, the issues met "surprisingly stubborn investor resistance," and they were only 75 percent sold on the first day.[96] Friday was even worse, and on Saturday the Fed raised the discount rate and announced a new anti-inflationary, high-interest-rate policy. Monday was a holiday, but Tuesday opened with 25-year bond prices down 2 points from their Friday close, which had been 2 points below the beginning of the week. By Wednesday afternoon, the syndicate, now in possession of 40 percent of the issues, abandoned its stabilization efforts and left the members to dispose of the securities as best they could. Both issues dropped about 5 points, to 94½, and the underwriters suffered losses estimated between $15 million and $30 million.

QUESTIONS

1. What do you think the securities business will look like in 1990? Will it look like the National Market System envisioned by Congress? Or something like the present diverse but interconnected system of exchange floors, NASDAQ, and independent OTC trades? Or something quite different from either of these? Please describe your prediction in detail and give the reasons why you expect the system to develop in such a manner.

2. We are told that some day we shall be able to do our banking from home by means of our own computer terminals, for example, by directing that funds be paid from our account to another account. Why shouldn't this procedure be extended to securities trading? And if so, what is the future (if any) of professional brokers and dealers? What role would be played by specialists and other market makers in such a system? What role would be played by the SEC? (For example what would have to happen to regulations such as the one in Table 11.5?)

3. The SEC has complained of the "notable ease" with which "many an amateur" may become a broker or dealer. Please explain, if

---

96 *Wall Street Journal*, October 5, 1979, page 35.

you can, why this is a more serious social problem than the unrestricted entry into, for example, the restaurant business.

4. Why should the communication of information about securities by securities dealers be more severely restricted by government regulation than is the communication of information about, for example, prices and other characteristics of food by restaurants and supermarkets?

5. How are the NYSE's listing requirements in Table 11.3 conducive to good market quality as indicated in Table 7.8?

6. Describe the conditions under which you would place a market order instead of a limit order, and vice versa.

7. A broker's office with a screen and record of the consolidated tape is just around the corner from your office. Discuss how you can evaluate your broker's performance.

8. Discuss how you, as a specialist, might apply the privileged information in the book in Figure 11.2 to your own advantage. Be specific about price quotations and trades. How would your actions (a) violate the rules directed at specialists and (b) detract from market quality as indicated in Table 7.8?

9. Why are exchanges much less important (relative to the OTC market) for bonds than for stocks?

10. Please describe (a) the differences between the quotations at the top and bottom of Table 11.4 and (b) the reasons for these differences.

11. Suppose you buy XYZ stock at $40 a share on 50 percent margin and the price during the next month changes to (a) $50, (b) $65, (c) $30, or (d) $15. The rate of interest on brokers' loans is 1 percent per month. Show the changes in your position by means of formats similar to Table 11.7, and calculate the rates of return on your investment. Compare your results with the statements in Table 11.6.

12. Respond to question 11 in the case in which you sell XYZ short on 50 percent margin when its price is $40.

13. Broker-dealer balance sheets are highly leveraged. Are they risky? Why or why not?

14. Discuss the possible reasons for the differences in the underwriters' spreads on the ITT bond issues in Table 10.3.

REFERENCES

David P. Baron, "A Model of the Demand for Investment Banking and Advising and Distribution Services for New Issues," *Journal of Finance,* September 1982, pages 955–976.

George J. Benston, "Required Disclosure and the Stock Market: An Evaluation of the Securities Exchange Act of 1934," *American Economic Review,* March 1973, pages 132–155.

Alfred L. Bernheim and Margaret G. Schneider (eds.), *The Security Markets,* Twentieth Century Fund, New York, 1935.

Jules I. Bogen (ed.), *Financial Handbook,* 4th ed., Wiley, New York, 1964.

John Brooks, *Once in Golconda,* Harper & Row, New York, 1969.

Vincent P. Carosso, *Investment Banking in America,* Harvard University Press, Cambridge, MA, 1970.

William G. Colby, "Dealer Profits and Capital Availability in the U.S. Government Securities Industry, 1955–65," in *Joint Treasury–Federal Reserve Study of the U.S. Government Securities Market,* Staff Studies, pt. 3, Washington, 1973.

Charles A. Dice and Wilford J. Eiteman, *The Stock Market,* 2nd ed., McGraw-Hill, New York, 1941.

Charles Duguid, *The Story of the Stock Exchange,* Richards, London, 1901.

Louis H. Ederington, "Uncertainty, Competition, and Costs in Corporate Bond Underwriting," *Journal of Financial Economics,* March 1975, pages 71–94.

Louis Engel and Brendan Boyd, *How to Buy Stocks,* 7th ed., Little, Brown, Boston, 1982.

Frank J. Fabozzi and Frank G. Zarb (eds.), *Handbook of Financial Markets,* Dow Jones-Irwin, Homewood, IL, 1981.

Irwin Friend, James R. Longstreet, Morris Mendelson, Ervin Miller, and Arleigh P. Hess, *Investment Banking and the New Issues Market,* World, Cleveland, 1967.

Kenneth Garbade, *Securities Markets,* McGraw-Hill, New York, 1982.

Kenneth Garbade and William L. Silber, "Technology, Communication and the Performance of Financial Markets: 1840–1975," *Journal of Finance,* June 1978, pages 819–832.

Carter T. Geyer, "The Abrogation of Rule 390," *Financial Analysts Journal,* January/February 1978, pages 22–30.

Cornelius W. Gillam, "Business Codes," *Encyclopaedia Britannica,* vol. 4, 1970, page 472.

James L. Hamilton, "Marketplace Organization and Marketability: NASDAQ, the Stock Exchange, and the National Market System," *Journal of Finance,* May 1978, pages 487–503.

George L. Leffler and Loring C. Farwell, *The Stock Market,* 3rd ed., Ronald Press, New York, 1963.

John C. Loeser, *The Over-the-counter Securities Market,* National Quotation Bureau, New York, 1940.

Leo M. Loll and Julian G. Buckley, *The Over-the-counter Securities Markets,* 4th ed., Prentice-Hall, Englewood Cliffs, NJ, 1981.

Gershon Mandelker and Artur Raviv, "Investment Banking: An Economic Analysis of Optimal Underwriting Contracts," *Journal of Finance,* June 1977, pages 683–694.

James K. Medbury, *Men and Mysteries of Wall Street,* Fields, Osgood, New York, 1870. Reprint Greenwood Press, New York, 1968.

J. Edward Meeker, *Short Selling,* Harper, New York, 1932.

J. Edward Meeker, *The Work of the Stock Exchange,* rev. ed., Ronald Press, New York, 1930.

Allan H. Meltzer and Gert von der Linde, *A Study of the Dealer Market for Federal Government Securities,* report for the Joint Economic Committee of the U.S. Congress, U.S. Government Printing Office, Washington, 1960.

Haim Mendelson, "Market Behavior in a Clearing House," *Econometrica,* November 1982, pages 1505–1524.

Norman C. Miller, *The Great Salad Oil Swindle,* Coward McCann, New York, 1965.

Margaret G. Myers, *The New York Money Market,* vol. 1: *Origins and Development,* Columbia University Press, New York, 1931.

National Association of Securities Dealers, *Securities Dealers Manual,* Commerce Clearing House, Chicago, 1983.

John A. Neumark (ed.), *Wall Street, 20th Century,* Investment Association of New York, New York, 1960.

New York Stock Exchange, *Company Manual,* New York, 1976.

New York Stock Exchange, *Report of the Quality of Markets Committee,* New York, 1982.

Sereno S. Pratt, *The Work of Wall Street,* Appleton, New York, 1921.

R. W. Schabacker, *Stock Market Theory and Practice,* Forbes, New York, 1930.

Ira O. Scott, *Government Securities Market,* McGraw-Hill, New York, 1965.

Securities and Exchange Commission, *The Effects of the Absence of Fixed Rates of Commissions,* fourth report to the U.S. Congress, Washington, 1977.

Securities and Exchange Commission, *Report of Special Study of Securities Markets,* to the U.S. Congress, referred to the Committee on Interstate and Foreign Commerce, 5 vols., U.S. Government Printing Office, Washington, 1963.

Leonard Sloane, *The Anatomy of the Floor: The Trillion-dollar Market at the New York Stock Exchange,* Doubleday, Garden City, NY, 1980.

Robert Sobel, *The Curbstone Brokers: The Origins of the American Stock Exchange,* Macmillan, New York, 1970.

Robert Sobel, *Inside Wall Street,* Norton, New York, 1977.

Marcia Stigum, *The Money Market,* rev. ed., Dow Jones-Irwin, Homewood, IL, 1983.

Samuel H. Talley, *Bank Capital Trends and Financing,* Federal Reserve Board Staff Study, February 1983.

Richard J. Teweles and Edward S. Bradley, *The Stock Market,* 4th ed., Wiley, New York, 1982.

Robert L. Thompson, *Wiring a Continent: The History of the Telegraph Industry in the United States, 1832–1866,* Princeton University Press, Princeton, NJ, 1947.

Seha M. Tinic and Richard R. West, "The Securities Industry under Negotiated Brokerage Commissions: Changes in the Structure and Performance of New York Stock Exchange Firms," *Bell Journal of Economics,* Spring 1980, pages 29–41.

P. A. Tinsley, Bonnie Garrett, and M. E. Friar, *The Measurement of Money Demand,* Federal Reserve Board Special Studies Paper 133, 1978.

U.S. Department of Justice, *Inquiry into Proposal to Modify the Commission Rate Structure of the NYSE,* SEC Release 8239, 1968.

James E. Walter, *The Role of Regional Security Exchanges,* University of California Press, Berkeley, 1957.

Chris Welles, *The Last Days of the Club,* Dutton, New York, 1975.

Peter Wyckoff, *Wall Street and the Stock Markets: A Chronology, 1644–1971,* Chilton, Philadelphia, 1972.

Michael G. Zahorchak, *Favorable Executions: The Wall Street Specialist and the Auction Market,* Van Nostrand Reinhold, New York, 1974.

Frank G. Zarb and Gabriel T. Kerekes (eds.), *The Stock Market Handbook,* Dow Jones-Irwin, Homewood, IL, 1970.

CHAPTER 12

FORWARD AND FUTURES MARKETS

*To prophesy is extremely difficult, especially
with respect to the future.*

Chinese Proverb

People have long been interested in ways of protecting themselves against, and speculating on, fluctuations in prices and interest rates. Forward and futures markets in agricultural commodities and foreign exchange are the oldest institutional arrangements for the pursuit of these hedging and speculative objectives. The greatly increased volatility of interest rates since 1970 has caused financial instruments to be added to the list. Our primary objectives in this chapter are to describe the institutional arrangements and trading procedures of the principal forward and futures markets in foreign exchange and other financial instruments, to show how these markets can be used for hedging and speculative purposes, and to evaluate their efficiency.

We begin with an analysis of one of the main determinants of exchange rates, interest rate discrepancies between countries, and then describe the functions and trading procedures of forward and futures markets in a world of volatile exchange rates. Most of our discussion of trading procedures on futures exchanges is in the context of foreign currencies. But that discussion applies equally to futures markets in interest-bearing financial instruments. The section on interest rate futures concentrates on 90-day Treasury bills (T bills). Since the procedures and uses of the various interest rate futures markets are similar, we can most efficiently begin to understand all of them by a thorough examination of one.

SPOT AND FORWARD MARKETS IN FOREIGN EXCHANGE

Interest rate parity

Suppose you wish to invest $100 for 3 months and desire the security that offers the greatest expected return. The securities under consideration have been narrowed to a choice between American and British 3-month T bills. The value of an investment in American bills after 3 months is

(12.1) $V_a = \$100(1 + R_a)$

where R_a is the 3-month yield on 3-month U.S. T bills.[1]

An investment in British bills requires three transactions: two foreign exchange transactions and a securities transaction. Let E_0 be the dollar/pound exchange rate at the time of the investment. For example $E_0 = 2$ if the pound is worth two dollars, that is, if £1 = \$2. Suppose E_1^e is the exchange rate expected to prevail in 3 months. Then the dollar value of an investment in British bills is expected to be

(12.2) $V_b = \dfrac{\$100}{E_0}(1 + R_b)E_1^e$

where R_b is the 3-month yield on 3-month U.K. T bills.

For example suppose $E_0 = 2.00$, $E_1^e = 2.02$, and $R_b = 0.04$ (which is a 3-month yield so that the simple annual yield is 16 percent). Then

$$\frac{\$100}{E_0}(1 + R_b)E_1^e = \frac{\$100}{2.00}(1.04)\,(2.02) = \$105.04$$

and the total expected dollar rate of return on these security and foreign exchange transactions is 5.04 percent. The investor first buys £50 from a foreign exchange dealer and then buys £50 worth of British bills yielding 4 percent per quarter with the expectation of selling the £50(1.04) = £52 received upon the maturity of those bills to a foreign exchange dealer for £52(\$2.02 per pound) = \$105.04.

You expect to earn 4 percent in pounds from U.K. T bills and an additional 1 percent in dollars from the investment in pounds since the pound is expected to appreciate (0.02/2.00) = 1 percent relative to the dollar during the next 3 months. The total dollar rate of return is therefore (1.04)(1.01) − 1 = 0.0504, as indicated above. Consequently you will be indifferent between American and British bills if and only if $R_a = 0.0504$. A higher value of R_a attracts you to American bills; a value of R_a less than 0.0504 sends you to the London money market.

In general the investor is indifferent between American and British bills when $V_a = V_b$, that is, when

(12.3) $1 + R_a = (1 + R_b)\dfrac{E_1^e}{E_0}$

or $1 + R_a = (1 + R_b)\,(1 + \dot{E}^e)$

---

1 We know from Chapter 5 that the rate of return, R, on a single-payment security that is held to maturity equals its yield to maturity, Y, at the time of purchase.

where

(12.4)
$$\dot{E}^e = \frac{E_1^e - E_0}{E_0}$$

is the expected rate of change of the exchange rate (which was 1 percent in the above example).

The lower version of Equation (12.3) is called the *interest rate parity (IRP) equation* and expresses the relationship between interest rates and the expected change in the exchange rate such that investors are indifferent between the securities of two countries. An often-used *linear approximation of the IRP equation* is

(12.5) $R_a = R_b + \dot{E}^e$ or $R_a - R_b = \dot{E}^e$

Using the values $R_b = 0.04$ and $\dot{E} = 0.01$ from our numerical example, we see that this approximation gives $R_a = 0.05$, compared with the exact value $R_a = 0.0504$.

The IRP theory asserts that interest rate differences between countries tend to be approximately equal to expected rates of change in exchange rates. For example, if $R_a = 0.08$ while $R_b = 0.04$ and $\dot{E}^e = 0.01$, then British, American, and other investors will shift from U.K. to U.S. securities, putting downward pressure on R_a and upward pressure on R_b until the IRP equation is satisfied. In addition this shift from pounds to dollars causes a decline in E_0 (as the pound becomes less valuable relative to the dollar). Given the expected exchange rate[2] of $E_1^e = 2.02$, this means an increase in $\dot{E}^e = (E_1^e - E_0)/E_0$. The IRP theory does not say what the equilibrium values of R_a, R_b, and $\dot{E}^e$ will be—only that they will conform to Equation (12.3). One of an infinity of equilibria is $R_a = 0.0710$, $R_b = 0.05$, and $\dot{E}^e = 0.02$, which conforms to Equation (12.3) because $1.0710 = (1.05)(1.02)$.

The interbank market in foreign exchange

Now let's look at the mechanics of trading foreign exchange. Since commercial banks manage domestic money, it is natural that they should also handle exchanges between domestic and foreign currencies.[3] After all, foreign exchange is part of the payments system. Hundreds of banks in New York and other financial centers around the world make markets in foreign exchange by standing ready to buy

---

2 It is of course conceivable that falls in E lead to expectations of further falls such that E^e is revised downward. This raises the possibility of destabilizing movements in exchange rates, preventing the attainment of the equilibrium Equation (12.3). For example suppose that $\dot{E}^e$, instead of rising to 0.02, falls to -0.01. In this case the difference between the rates of return on U.S. and U.K. T bills increases from $0.08 - (0.04 + 0.01) = 0.03$ to $0.0710 - (0.05 - 0.01) = 0.0310$, which is a move away from equilibrium.

3 We follow common practice in discussions of international finance by referring to domestic and foreign money as "currencies" even though most foreign exchange transactions involve bank deposits.

Table 12.1 Spot and Forward Exchange Rates and Eurocurrency Interest Rates, London, February 17, 1982

The Dollar Spot and Forward

Feb. 17	Day's Spread	Close	One Month	% p.a.	Three Months	% p.a.
UK†	1.8340–1.8420	1.8350–1.8360	0.30–0.40c dis	−2.29	0.92–1.02 dis	−2.11
Ireland†	1.4735–1.4765	1.4735–1.4755	0.21–0.11c pm	1.30	0.70–0.55 pm	1.69
Canada	1.2154–1.2182	1.2177–1.2182	0.16–0.13c pm	1.43	0.33–0.29 pm	1.02
Nethlnd.	2.6130–2.6290	2.6260–2.6290	1.35–1.25c pm	5.96	4.09–3.99 pm	6.18
Belgium	40.65–40.81	40.79–40.81	2–5c dis	−1.03	18–20 dis	−1.87
Denmark	7.8175–7.8650	7.8450–7.8550	0.85–0.70ore pm	1.19	0.75–0.45 pm	0.31
W. Ger.	2.3830–2.4000	2.3985–2.3995	1.20–1.15pf pm	5.88	3.64–3.59 pm	6.03
Portugal	69.25–69.75	69.30–69.50	15–75c dis	−7.79	50–185 dis	−6.78
Spain	100.95–101.30	101.20–101.25	15–5c pm	1.18	10 pm–5 dis	0.10
Italy	1272½–1278	1276–1278	3½–4¼lire dis	−3.65	14–15½ dis	−4.63
Norway	5.9780–6.0050	5.9850–5.9950	1.85–1.75ore pm	3.61	3.65–3.45 pm	2.37
France	6.0550–6.0915	6.0865–6.0915	1.20–1.05c pm	2.23	1.90–1.65 pm	1.17
Sweden	5.7950–5.8225	5.8050–5.8150	0.85–0.70ore pm	1.60	4.00–3.85 pm	2.71
Japan	238.75–240.55	240.45–240.55	1.95–1.80y pm	9.35	5.85–5.70 pm	9.60
Austria	16.728–16.77½	16.76–16.77	11–10gro pm	7.52	30–27 pm	6.80
Switz.	1.9030–1.9160	1.9145–1.9155	1.35–1.25c pm	8.15	3.80–3.70 pm	7.83

Feb. 17	Sterling	U.S. Dollar	Canadian Dollar	Dutch Guilder	Swiss Franc
Euro-Currency Interest Rates (market closing rates)					
Short term	14¼–14½	16⅜–16⅝	13–14	10⅛–10¼	2½–2¾
7 days' notice	14¼–14½	16⅜–16⅝	13–14	10⅛–10¼	2¾–3¼
Month	14 7/16–14 9/16	16½–16¾	15–15⅜	10⅛–10¼	7½–7⅝
Three months	14⅝–14¾	16½–16¾	15½–15⅞	10 3/16–10 5/16	8⅛–8¼
Six months	14¾–14⅞	16½–16¾	16–16⅜	10 3/16–10 5/16	8⅝–8¾
One Year	14¾–14⅞	16¼–16½	16⅜–16¾	10 5/16–10 7/16	8⅜–8½

†UK and Ireland are quoted in U.S. currency. Forward premiums and discounts apply to the U.S. dollar and not to the individual currency.

Source: *Financial Times*, February 18, 1982.

and sell at stated bid and offer rates. At the close of business on February 17, 1982, for example, London banks were quoting spot sterling[4] at $1.8350–60, meaning that they bid (would buy) pounds at $1.8350 and offered (would sell) pounds at $1.8360. These rates may be

4 It was customary in England in the Middle Ages to coin a pound of silver of a specified degree of fineness into 240 pennies, which together were referred to as "a pound." "Early in the twelfth century the penny was called a 'sterling.' The origin of the word remains doubtful, but the coins very soon gained a wide reputation on the continent for their consistent fineness and 'sterling silver' ultimately became the silver of commerce in a great part of the world" [A. Feavearyear (1931, page 8)]. The pound sterling was detached from silver when Great Britain went to the gold standard in the nineteenth century and from gold when it went to a paper standard in 1931, and it has consisted of 100 pennies since decimalization in 1971. But it is still called sterling.

Table 12.1 (continued)

The Pound Spot and Forward

Feb. 17	Day's Spread	Close	One Month	% p.a.	Three Months	% p.a.
U.S.	1.8340–1.8420	1.8350–1.8360	0.30–0.40c dis	−2.29	0.92–1.02dis	−2.11
Canada	2.2310–2.2380	2.2350–2.2360	0.07–0.17c dis	−0.64	0.55–0.70dis	−1.12
Nethlnd.	4.80½–4.83½	4.82¼–4.83¼	1⅝–1⅛c pm	3.42	5–4¼ pm	3.83
Belgium	74.85–75.00	74.35–74.95	18–38c dis	−4.48	70–90 dis	−4.27
Denmark	14.36–14.43	14.41½–14.42½	½–1¾ ore dis	−0.94	5½–7¼ dis	−1.77
Ireland	1.2435–1.2510	1.2485–1.2505	0.30–0.42p dis	−3.46	1.10–1.27dis	−3.79
W. Ger.	4.38–4.41	4.40–4.41	1⅝–1⅛pf pm	3.74	4¾–4¼ pm	4.09
Portugal	127.00–128.75	127.15–127.45	45–160c dis	−9.66	155–410 dis	−8.88
Spain	185.40–186.20	185.70–185.90	5c pm–20 dis	−0.48	65–95 dis	−1.72
Italy	2337–2345	2343–2345	11–14lire dis	−6.40	39–42 dis	−6.91
Norway	10.98–11.03	11.00–11.01	2–1ore pm	1.63	1 pm–par	0.18
France	11.13–11.18	11.17–11.18	¼c pm–¾ dis	−0.27	2½–3½ dis	−1.07
Sweden	10.65–10.68	10.66¼–10.67¼	par-¾ore dis	−0.42	2½–1¾ pm	0.80
Japan	438–443	441–442	2.85–2.55y pm	7.34	8.60–8.25 pm	7.63
Austria	30.72–30.87	30.80–30.85	15–12gro pm	5.25	39–32½ pm	4.64
Switz.	3.49½–3.52½	3.51¼–3.52¼	1⅞–1⅜c pm	5.54	5⅜–4⅞ pm	5.83

Feb. 17	West German Mark	French Franc	Italian Lira	Belgian Franc Convertible	Japanese Yen
Euro-Currency Interest Rates (market closing rates)					
Short term	9⅝–9¾	13¾–14¼	17½–19½	13–15	5½–5¾
7 days' notice	9⅞–10	13¾–14¼	19–21	15–17	5⅞–6
Month	10⅛–10¼	14–14½	20⅝–21⅝	17½–18½	6⅛–6¼
Three months	10¼–10⅜	15–15½	21⅝–22¼	18¼–19¼	6⅜–6½
Six months	10¼–10⅜	16–16½	22–22⅝	18¼–19¼	6¾–6⅞
One Year	10⅛–10¼	16⅝–17⅛	22½–23⅜	17–18	7–7⅛

Belgian rate is for convertible francs. Financial franc 83.10–83.20. Six-month forward dollar 1.70–1.80c dis. 12-month 3.05–3.20c dis.

seen at the top of the second column of numbers in Table 12.1. The first column of numbers lists the ranges of rates at which trades occurred during the day.

Foreign exchange markets are similar to those in federal funds and U.S. Treasury securities. In all three, banks and other dealers may trade directly with each other or through brokers. American banks usually trade with banks in other countries directly by telephone or telex.[5] But they usually trade with each other through brokers. The most active New York foreign exchange brokers have direct telephone

5 "Telex" is short for "telegraph exchange," which is a worldwide telegraph system.

Table 12.2   Foreign Exchange Futures, International Monetary Market, Chicago, February 17, 1982
(Open Interest Reflects Previous Trading Day)

	Open	High	Low	Settle	Change	Lifetime High	Lifetime Low	Open Interest
British Pound (IMM) — 25,000 pounds; $ per pound								
Mar	1.8430	1.8445	1.8330	1.8395	−.0025	2.2570	1.7790	13,590
June	1.8510	1.8530	1.8420	1.8480	−.0025	1.9580	1.8055	4,954
Sept	1.8570	1.8570	1.8525	1.8545	−.0045	1.9580	1.8475	263
Dec	...	...	...	1.8605	−.0045	1.9350	1.8590	84
		Est vol 5,120; vol Tue 6,075; open int 18,891, −7.						
Canadian Dollar (IMM) — 100,000 dlrs.; $ per Can$								
Mar	.8230	.8239	.8210	.8222	−.0014	.8500	.7912	7,476
June	.8235	.8245	.8222	.8232	−.0012	.8427	.7901	3,601
Sept	.8235	.8235	.8216	.8225	−.0008	.8380	.7890	379
Dec	.8225	.8231	.8208	.8220	−.0004	.8350	.8120	118
		Est vol 1,891; vol Tue 2,215; open int 11,574, +433.						
Japanese Yen (IMM) — 12.5 million yen; cents per yen								
Mar	.4212	.4215	.4184	.4202	−.0001	.4820	.4175	10,930
June	.4320	.4320	.4288	.4304	−.0006	.4830	.4275	1,287
Sept	.4415	.4415	.4385	.4394	−.0008	.4775	.4370	77
		Est vol 3,968; vol Tue 2,935; open int 12,294, −8.						
Swiss Franc (IMM) — 125,000 francs; $ per franc								
Mar	.5281	.5284	.5245	.5265	−.0011	.6680	.4755	10,688
June	.5380	.5380	.5342	.5364	−.0011	.5840	.4865	1,852
Sept	.5455	.5460	.5440	.5460	+.0004	.5815	.4975	37
Dec	.5550	.5550	.5545	.5545	−.0005	.5920	.5545	7
		Est vol 6,480; vol Tue 6,314; open int 12,564, +959.						
W. German Mark (IMM) — 125,000 marks; $ per mark								
Mar	.4209	.4214	.4181	.4196	−.0011	.4735	.4010	11,628
June	.4270	.4272	.4244	.4259	−.0012	.4720	.4135	1,562
Sept	.4332	.4332	.4308	.4325	−.0008	.4775	.4308	279
Dec	...	...	...	.4438	...	.4675	.4430	3
		Est vol 5,619; vol Tue 4,234; open int 13,472, +34.						

Notes. *Open interest* is the number of contracts outstanding; *volume* is the number of contracts traded in a day; *settle* is the day's closing, or settlement, price.

Source: *Wall Street Journal*, February 18, 1982.

lines with more than 100 banks for the purpose of taking bids and offers, and their commissions for connecting buyers and sellers are about $25 per $1 million traded. The operations of foreign exchange brokers have been described as follows.

> In simplified form, a typical trade in the brokers market might start with Bank A, which wants to buy spot sterling, calling a broker on its direct telephone line and bidding for £1 million at a rate of $1.7440. Bank B, which wants to sell spot sterling, might call the same broker and make an offer of £2 million at a rate of $1.7442. The bid and offer are valid until explicitly canceled by the bank making them. If any other bank calls and asks the broker, "What is sterling?" the broker will respond "40–42, one by two." This is shorthand for a bid for £1 million at $1.7440 and an offer of £2 million at $1.7442. The $1.74 is understood.
>
> What happens depends upon how eager Banks A and B are to buy and sell, as well as on the potential actions of any other bank which deals through the same broker. The main possibilities are these:
>
> - Bank A's bid may be "hit." That is, another bank, perhaps even Bank B, may agree to sell £1 million to A at the rate A wants to pay.
> - Bank B's offer may be "taken." Another bank, perhaps even Bank A, may agree to buy £2 million from B at the rate B wants to receive.
> - The broker may be able to work out a compromise satisfactory to Banks A and B at a rate between $1.7440 and $1.7442.
> - Nothing may happen. The broker continues to show the bid and offer to the market until A or B decides to change its rate or cancel its order, or until a new and better bid or offer is made by a third bank.
>
>   Roger Kubarych (1983, page 15)

The standard settlement date, or *value date* as it is known in foreign exchange, is 2 business days following the day on which the trade is agreed. Trades are often for "next-day" value and some are for "cash" (payment on the date of the agreement) although cash transactions are rare for U.S. dollar–European currency trades in New York because of time zone differences.

In an example of a typical spot transaction, on September 19, Bank A buys one million German marks from Bank B for dollars, at a rate of DM2.50 per dollar for value September 21. On that value date, B will pay DM1 million for credit to A's account at a bank in Germany, while A will pay $400,000 for credit to B's account at a bank in the U.S. The two payments complete the transaction.

                                      Roger Kubarych (1983, page 9)

Whether dealing directly or through a broker, a bank's purchase of foreign exchange, if not for its own account, will be for a customer who probably wants the funds transferred immediately to a foreign bank as payment for goods or securities purchased abroad.

Forward rates

The discussion has so far been limited to *spot* transactions, that is, to currency trades for delivery within 2 days. But *forward* transactions, for which value (settlement) dates are more than 2 days in the future, constitute nearly one-half of all trades in the foreign exchange markets. The mechanics of the interbank forward market are identical with those of the spot market described above. Brokers and dealers quote bid and offer rates for future delivery (forward rates) as well as for delivery within 2 days (spot rates). The most convenient sources of foreign exchange quotations are *The Times* and the *Financial Times,* both published in London. There is no systematic reporting of forward rates in the popular American press.[6] This is the most important reason why Table 12.1, which shows spot and forward rates on the pound and the dollar on February 17, 1982, has been taken from the *Financial Times.* Other reasons for using London rates will become clear later.

It is customary to quote U.S./U.K. and U.S./Ireland exchange rates as the numbers of dollars at which the British and Irish pounds are valued. We have already noted that banks in London were bidding $1.8350 for a British pound at the close of trading on February 17, 1982. Other dollar exchange rates are quoted as the numbers of units of foreign currencies at which the dollar is valued. For example the closing spot bid and offer quotations for West German marks (or DM for *Deutsche Mark*) mean that dealers were willing to pay DM2.3985 for $1 and to accept DM2.3995 for $1, which is equivalent to selling marks for ($1/2.3985) = $0.41693 and buying marks for ($1/2.3995) = $0.41675.

A forward rate is quoted as a premium (pm) on, or a discount (dis) from, the spot rate. *Premium* means *dearer* so that it is deducted from the spot rate. For example, if the forward mark is quoted at a premium on the dollar, this means the forward dollar is worth fewer marks than

---

6 The best American source of exchange rate and foreign interest rate data is probably the weekly *Business International Money Report.*

Table 12.3   Calculation of Forward Rates and Annualized Forward Premiums

	Bid, DM	Offer, DM
Spot rate	2.3985	2.3995
− 1-month premium	−0.0120	−0.0115
= 1-month forward rate	2.3865	2.3880
Spot rate	2.3985	2.3995
− 3-month premium	−0.0364	−0.0359
= 3-month forward rate	2.3621	2.3636

The 1-month and 3-month premiums in simple annual percentages are

1-month: $(12) \dfrac{(0.0120 + 0.0115)/2}{2.3990} = 12(0.00490) = 0.0588 = 5.88$ percent

3-month: $(4)\dfrac{(0.0364 + 0.0359)/2}{2.3990} = 4(0.01507) = 0.0603 = 6.03$ percent

Source: Table 12.1, patterned after a table in D. Whiting, *Finance of Foreign Trade and Foreign Exchange,* 2nd ed., MacDonald and Evans, London, 1973, page 147.

the spot dollar. An illustration is given in Table 12.3. (Table 12.2 will be discussed later.) Notice from Table 12.1 that the 1-month forward dollar/mark quotation is

1.20–1.15pf pm

which means a forward premium on the mark of 1.20 to 1.15 pfennigs. (The pfennig is the hundredth part of a mark.) The first forward quote, 1.20 pf = 0.0120 marks, is deducted from the spot bid, and the second forward quote is deducted from the spot offer to obtain the 1-month forward bid and offer rates of 2.3865 and 2.3880 at the top of Table 12.3. An identical procedure gives 3-month forward rates.

The forward premium or discount is also usually expressed as a simple annualized percentage change from the spot rate. Using midpoints of spot and forward quotations, the lower portion of Table 12.3 shows that March 17 and May 17 marks were quoted at 0.490 percent and 1.507 percent premiums relative to the dollar. We see in the columns headed "% p.a." in Table 12.1 that these figures have been converted to the simple annual rates of 5.88 percent and 6.03 percent. In mid-February 1982 traders in foreign exchange apparently expected the dollar to fall relative to the mark at an annual rate near 6 percent during the next 3 months.

Forward discounts may be used to calculate forward bid and offer rates by the same method as in Table 12.3 except that discounts are *added* to spot rates. Notice in Table 12.1[7] that forward discount spreads list the smaller number first. This means that forward rate spreads always are wider than spot rate spreads.

A check on IRP: covered interest arbitrage

Covered interest arbitrage is the process of taking advantage of an interest differential between two currencies that exceeds the foreign exchange premium or discount. The arbitrageur seeks to take advantage of interest differentials between countries while hedging, or covering, his currency risk by taking an opposite position in the foreign exchange market, for example, by buying 3-month Italian securities and simultaneously entering into a 3-month forward contract to sell lire. Suppose the simple annual rates of interest on 3-month dollar and lire investments are 16 and 20 percent, respectively, and the 3-month forward lire is quoted at a 0.25 percent discount (1 percent at a simple annual rate), say 1,200 lire per dollar spot and 1,203 lire per dollar 3 months forward.[8] An arbitrageur who sells $1 million from his holdings of U.S. securities to buy lire with which to invest in Italian securities and at the same time sells his future lire receipts forward for dollars can count on a riskless (arbitrage) gain of

$$(12.6) \qquad \$1,000,000 \left[\frac{1.05(1,200)}{1,203} - 1.04 \right] = \$7,382$$

This hypothetical arbitrage profit was made possible by the failure of IRP, specifically by the fact that, at simple annual rates, 3-month Italian investments were earning 4 percent more than similar American investments while the 3-month forward lira was selling at only a 1 percent discount relative to the dollar. Such easy pickings are not plentiful. Table 12.4 represents a search for arbitrage profits in the forward currency market on February 17, 1982, as reported in Table 12.1. Table 12.4 is also a check on IRP since in the presence of forward markets the IRP theory is an assertion that no arbitrage profits are possible. The IRP theory gains strength from forward markets because these markets enable us to replace Equation (12.3) by

$$(12.7) \qquad 1 + R_a = (1 + R_b)(1 + \dot{E}^f)$$

where the forward premium or discount, $\dot{E}^f$, is substituted for the expected rate of change in the spot rate, $\dot{E}^e$. Forward dealers quote $\dot{E}^f$ on the basis of their expectations of future spot rates, but we no longer

---

7 If you wish to repeat the exercise in Table 12.3 for U.S. dollars and either British or Irish pounds, remember that pounds are quoted upside down under "The dollar spot and forward" in Table 12.1 and are merely repeated from the top two lines of "The pound spot and forward."

8 Except for the small forward discount on the lira these data are not much different from those in Table 12.1. We shall see that the arbitrage profit earned in this hypothetical example vanishes when the actual data, including the larger actual discount, are used in Exercise 12.1.

Table 12.4   Covered Interest Arbitrage, Eurocurrency Investments,
February 17, 1982 (Percentages at Annual Rates)

	E^f		$\dfrac{1 + R_a}{1 + R_o} - 1$	
	Forward Premium (+) or Discount (−) against the Dollar		Forward Premium or Discount Implied by IRP	
	1-month	3-month	1-month	3-month
U.K.	2.29	2.11	1.86	1.69
Canada	1.43	1.02	1.25	0.81
Netherlands	5.96	6.18	5.84	5.78
Switzerland	8.15	7.83	8.43	7.80
West Germany	5.88	6.03	5.84	5.72
France	2.23	1.17	2.08	1.19
Italy	−3.65	−4.63	−3.72	−4.36
Belgium	−1.03	−1.87	−1.17	−1.79
Japan	9.35	9.60	9.83	9.57

	$R_a - R_o$		$R_o + \dot{E}^f$	
	Eurodollar Rate of Interest Less Other Eurocurrency Rates		Covered Eurocurrency Returns[a]	
	1-month	3-month	1-month	3-month
U.K.	2.1250	1.9375	16.7900	16.7975
Canada	1.4375	0.9375	16.6175	16.7075
Netherlands	6.4375	6.3750	16.1475	16.4300
Switzerland	9.0625	8.4375	15.7125	16.0175
West Germany	6.4375	6.3125	16.0675	16.3425
France	2.3750	1.3750	16.4800	16.4200
Italy	−4.5000	−5.3125	17.4750	17.3075
Belgium	−1.3750	−2.1250	16.9700	16.8800
Japan	10.4375	10.1875	15.5375	16.0375

a Compared to the 1-month and 3-month Eurodollar rate of 16.625 percent.

Source: Table 12.1.

have to guess those expectations. Given observations of interest rates on investments in different currencies, R_a and R_b, the existence of forward currency quotations allows us to check the validity of the IRP theory.

Our check on IRP is also aided by the London Eurocurrency market, which enables us to use interest rates that are all quoted by the same or similar banks (and which therefore have the same or similar risk) within a small area and a highly competitive, relatively unregulated environment (so that information is good and trades can be executed quickly and at low cost). The assumptions of the IRP theory probably come closest to being satisfied in the London Eurocurrency and foreign exchange markets.

We will now explain the first line of 1-month numbers in Table 12.4. The 1-month forward premium on the pound relative to the dollar is 2.29 percent (which the British like to quote as a discount on the dollar), as shown in Table 12.1. Continuing to use midpoints of spreads, we also see from Table 12.1 that 1-month sterling and U.S. dollar rates of interest in London were $R_b = 0.14500$ and $R_a = 0.16625$, respectively. Therefore, using Equation (12.7), IRP implied a 1-month forward premium on the pound of

$$\frac{1 + R_a}{1 + R_o} - 1 = \frac{1.16625}{1.14500} - 1 = 1.86 \text{ percent}$$

as shown in the third column of Table 12.4, where R_a indicates the U.S. rate (as before) and R_o indicates "other" rates. The linear approximation

$$R_a - R_o = 16.625 - 14.500 = 2.125 \text{ percent}$$

is given in the fifth column.[9] The seventh column is a linear approximation of the annualized dollar rate of return on an investment in pounds, which is the 1-month Eurosterling rate (using the midpoint of the dealer spread) plus the forward sterling premium against the dollar:

$$R_o + \dot{E}^f = 14.50 + 2.29 = 16.79 \text{ percent}$$

This return may also be described as the Eurosterling return "covered" by the sale of pounds. We have used a linear approximation in order to conform with market reporting practices. Notice that the differences between the covered Eurocurrency returns and the Eurodollar interest rate of 16.625 percent (for example, 16.79 − 16.625) are the forward premiums against the dollar less the excesses of the dollar rate of interest over the interest rates of the various currencies (for example, 2.29 − 2.125).

What do these differences suggest about the possibility of arbitrage profits or, what amounts to the same thing, the validity of IRP? Comparing the first and third columns in Table 12.4, the largest discrepancy between the actual and theoretical forward premiums and discounts (and therefore the largest discrepancy between returns on dollar and other investments) was 0.48 percent in the case of the yen.

9 The linear approximation 2.125 is in this case closer to the observed 2.29 than is the theoretically "exact" 1.86. This happens in seven of the eighteen cases shown in the table.

Dividing this annual rate by 12 gives a monthly discrepancy of 0.04 percent. A comparison of the second and fourth columns shows the largest quarterly discrepancy (for the pound) to be 0.42/4 = 0.105 percent. Estimates of transaction costs in these markets have ranged from about 0.125 percent of investment values during the period of tranquil foreign exchange markets in the mid-1960s to about 1.030 percent during the turbulent mid-1970s.[10] The failure of any of the discrepancies in Table 12.4 to exceed transaction costs lends support to IRP. No arbitrage opportunities existed; the divergences of actual forward premiums and discounts from those implied by the theory were less than the costs of exploiting those divergences.

An arbitrage opportunity would have existed if the 3-month forward discount on the lira had been only 1 percent at an annual rate as assumed in the example of successful covered interest arbitrage in Equation (12.6). But we see in Table 12.4 that the discount was in fact 4.63 percent.[11] Exercise 12.1 demonstrates that there was no 3-month dollar-lira arbitrage opportunity in London even if we consider only that part of transaction costs implicit in dealer spreads.[12]

EXERCISE 12.1.   (a) Show that an American (or anyone else with a 3-month dollar deposit in London on February 17, 1982) would have been better off staying with that dollar deposit than shifting to lire. (b) Show that an Italian (or anyone else with a 3-month Eurolira deposit on the same date) would have been better off staying with lire than shifting to dollars.

(a) We assume that our investors earn the interest rates offered by dealers so that an American with an investment of $1 million will after 3 months have

$$\$1,000,000\left(1 + \frac{0.1650}{4}\right) = \$1,041,250$$

---

10 Jacob Frenkel and Richard Levich (1977, page 1215). Foreign exchange dealers require wider spreads as compensation for greater risk during periods of volatile exchange rates.

11 Even this number, which is based on midpoints of dealer quotations, understates the lira discount that is in fact available to investors who sell lire forward. Using midpoints of the quotations in Table 12.1 and following the procedure of Table 12.3, the 3-month forward discount on the lira at a simple annual rate was 4(14.75/1,277) = 4.62 percent (which differs slightly from the 4.63 percent reported in Table 12.1). But the lira discount available to someone who sells spot dollars at the dealer's bid of 1,276 lire and sells lire 3 months forward at the dealer's bid of 1,293.5 lire per dollar is 4(17.5/1,276) = 5.49 percent at a simple annual rate.

12 Problem 6 at the end of the chapter requests similar demonstrations for the British pound and the Dutch guilder, which had the largest discrepancies between actual and theoretical 3-month premiums in Table 12.4.

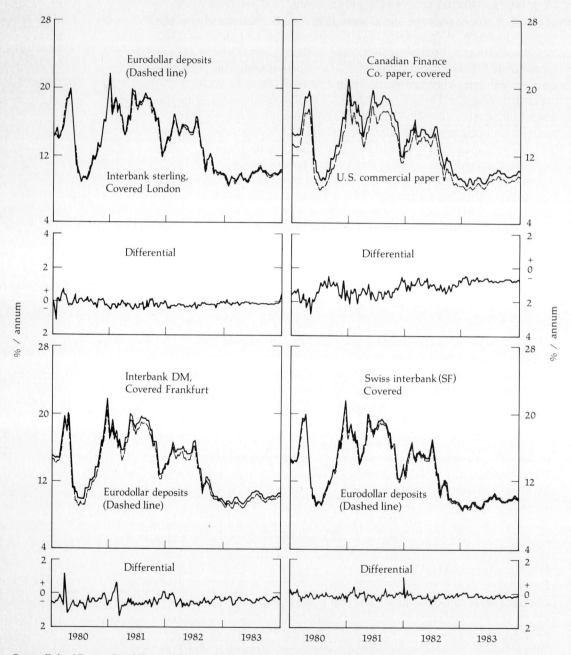

Source: Federal Reserve Board Financial Markets Section, *Selected Interest and Exchange Rates* (weekly), January 3, 1984, cht. 8.

Figure 12.1   Interest arbitrage, 3-month funds. "Covered" returns on foreign investments are foreign interest rates plus or minus forward premiums or discounts (as in the last two columns of Table 12.4).

if he stays in dollars, compared with

$$\frac{\$1,000,000\ (1,276)\left(1 + \dfrac{0.21625}{4}\right)}{1,293.5} = \$1,039,802$$

if he buys lire at the (1,276 lire per dollar) spot closing price on February 17, invests those lire at the simple annual interest rate of 21.625 percent, and simultaneously sells 3-month lire forward for 1,278 + 15.5 lire per dollar.

(b) An Italian with an investment of L1 million will after 3 months have

$$\text{L}1,000,000\left(1 + \frac{0.21625}{4}\right) = \text{L}1,054,063$$

if he stays in lire, compared with

$$\frac{\text{L}1,000,000}{1,278}\left(1 + \frac{0.1650}{4}\right)(1,290) = \text{L}1,051,027$$

if he converts lire to dollars at the spot closing price of 1,278 lire per dollar on February 17, invests those dollars at the simple annual interest rate of 16.50 percent, and simultaneously sells 3-month dollars forward at 1,276 + 14 lire per dollar.

Table 12.4 shows results for only one date, and IRP does not work perfectly all the time.[13] However, there is much evidence suggesting that it works very well most of the time.[14] Further examples of the empirical validity of IRP are provided by weekly data from 1980 to 1983 in Figure 12.1. The dashed curves in the graph are yields on dollar investments, all but one on 3-month Eurodollars as in Table 12.1. The darker solid curves are covered rates of return on investments in other currencies, for example, investments in pounds (at the London interbank rate) covered by a pound-dollar exchange in the forward market. The graph is based on the linear approximation of covered returns used in the last two columns of Table 12.4. For example the comparable covered 3-month Eurosterling return on February 17, 1982, was 14.6875 + 2.11 = 16.7975 percent, and the "differential," that is, the excess of the covered return over the dollar rate of interest was 16.7975 − 16.6250 = 0.1725 percent.

---

13 For example, see Michael Dooley and Peter Isard (1980) for a discussion of deviations from IRP in West German markets during the period of official controls on capital flows into Germany during the period 1970 to 1974.

14 See Jacob Frenkel and Richard Levich (1977) and Mark Eaker (1980).

Hedging foreign exchange risk in the forward market

The forward currency market can be used to hedge foreign exchange risk under a variety of conditions.[15] One of the more common situations is described in Exercise 12.2. The use of the futures market as a hedge in the same situation is described later in Exercise 12.3.[16]

EXERCISE 12.2.   Suppose that on February 17 the Colorado Cheese Company arranges to take delivery of 20,000 kilograms of limburger cheese on March 17 and agrees to pay the German exporter DM500,000 upon delivery. Show how Colorado Cheese can use the forward market in foreign exchange to lock in a certain dollar price of the limburger.

The financial vice-president of Colorado Cheese calls his bank in Denver and arranges a forward contract by which, consistent with Table 12.3, he will exchange dollars for marks on March 17 at the rate $2.3985 - 0.0120 = 2.3865$ marks per dollar; or, what is the same thing, $1/2.3865 = 0.4190$ dollar per mark. He thus guarantees that no matter what happens to exchange rates between February 17 and March 17 he will pay $\$0.4190(500,000) = \$209,500$ (or, more precisely, $500,000/2.3865 = \$209,512$) for the cheese.

If the mark appreciates in value relative to the dollar, say, to $\$0.44$ on March 17, our financial officer will be pleased with his hedge. For if he had waited until receipt of the goods to buy the necessary marks in the spot market, the cheese would have cost $\$0.44(500,000) = \$220,000$.

He would not have been so self-satisfied, however, if the mark had fallen to $\$0.40$ on March 17; for in that case he could have bought the cheese for $\$0.40(500,000) = \$200,000$ obtained in the spot market.

Efficiency of the foreign exchange market: forward rates as predictors of spot rates

An inefficient market is one in which prices do not reflect all available information so that people with access to more information than is

---

15 See Heinz Riehl and Rita Rodriguez (1977) for several examples.

16 We can be confident that these hedges will reduce risk only if we are certain that the hedged foreign currency cash receipt or payment will actually take place. (The same reservation applies to the interest rate futures hedges discussed later in this chapter.) For example, if Colorado Cheese's order in Exercise 12.2 is canceled or delayed, the company finds itself with a speculative forward contract in German marks. A better hedging instrument in such cases is the right but not the obligation to buy or sell a specified quantity of foreign currency at a specified price. Such rights are provided by *foreign exchange options,* which have long been offered to their customers by banks and are now traded on the Philadelphia Exchange. See Ian Giddy (1983) for a discussion of these options.

available to others can systematically earn greater-than-normal profits. They can beat the market because current prices do not fully
reflect the values of investments.

Any test of market efficiency must be conducted jointly with a
hypothesis of equilibrium prices because there must be a specification
of the prices that would be achieved if a market were indeed efficient,
that is, if all available information were fully utilized.[17] Most tests of
the efficiency of the foreign exchange market have jointly tested the
hypothesis that the market is dominated by expected-profit-maximiz-
ing investors who are always ready to trade whenever one asset has a
greater expected return than another. These investors rest, and the
market is in equilibrium, when the structure of prices is such that all
assets have the same expected return.

Market efficiency in a world of expected-profit maximizers implies,
for example, that the one-period forward rate at time $t-1$, which we
denote F_{t-1}, equals the spot rate expected at time $t-1$ to prevail at
time t, which is denoted S_t^e. At this point expected profits from trades
in foreign exchange are zero. If the equality does not hold (for example
if the one-period forward rate on pounds is $F_{t-1} = \$2$ while the spot
rate expected to prevail next period is $S_t^e = \$2.10$), we can at time $t-1$
enter into a contract to buy pounds for \$2 at time t with the
expectation of selling those pounds for \$2.10 immediately upon
receipt. However, if our expectations are shared by others, the price of
forward pounds will be bid up to $F_{t-1} = S_t^e = \$2.10$, the forward rate
will be an unbiased predictor of the spot rate, and currency trades will
offer no expected profit.

The joint hypotheses of market efficiency and expected-profit
maximizers, which we shall call the ME-EPM hypotheses, may be
examined within the framework provided by the following equations:

(12.8) $S_t = A(F_{t-1})^b U_t$ or $\ln S_t = a + b \ln F_{t-1} + u_t$

where S_t is the spot rate at time t, F_{t-1} is the one-period forward rate at
time $t-1$, U_t is a residual that encompasses all influences on the spot
rate not reflected in the forward rate, $a = \ln A$, and $u_t = \ln U_t$.

If expected profit is the goal of investors and the foreign exchange
market is efficient, we should observe $A = b = 1$ and U_t serially
uncorrelated with a mean of unity—so that the forward rate is an
unbiased predictor of the spot rate. For example, if $A = 1.05$ or $b = 1.07$
so that

$$S_t = 1.05(F_{t-1})U_t \qquad \text{or} \qquad S_t = (F_{t-1})^{1.07} U_t$$

we should, if U_t is serially uncorrelated with a mean of unity, expect S_t

---

17 Other tests of market efficiency are discussed later in this chapter and in Chapters 18 and 19.

to be $2.10 whenever F_{t-1} is $2. This situation is inconsistent with an efficient market because it leaves open the opportunity for increasing expected profits by buying pounds forward for $2 and then selling them spot for $2.10 as in the example given above.

On the other hand, if U_t is serially correlated, that is, if it is systematically dependent on its own past values such that, for example,

$$U_t = (U_{t-1})^c e_t \qquad \text{so that} \qquad S_t = (F_{t-1})(U_{t-1})^c e_t$$

our observation of U_{t-1} provides information about S_t beyond that contained in F_{t-1}. For example, if $U_{t-1} = 1.10$, $c = 0.50$, and e_t is a serially uncorrelated random variable with a mean of unity, we can expect $S_t = \$2.10$ if $F_{t-1} = \$2$.

Jacob Frenkel (1981) estimated the logarithmic form of Equation (12.8) for three exchange rates and, as in so many tests of the efficient markets hypothesis, obtained results consistent with *almost efficient markets*. Some of his results are presented in Table 12.5. First consider Equation (12.11), which shows that (1) the estimate of a is not

Table 12.5   Efficiency of Foreign Exchange Markets, Monthly Data, June 1973 to July 1979

Dependent Variable $\ln S_t$	Constant	$\ln F_{t-1}$	$\ln F_{t-2}$	R^2	D-W
Dollar/pound:					
(12.9)	0.033 (0.017)	0.956 (0.024)	—	0.96	1.72
(12.9a)	0.031 (0.018)	1.047 (0.116)	−0.088 (0.113)	0.96	1.94
Dollar/franc:					
(12.10)	−0.237 (0.078)	0.843 (0.051)	—	0.79	2.23
(12.10a)	−0.225 (0.082)	0.706 (0.117)	0.146 (0.117)	0.79	1.90
Dollar/mark:					
(12.11)	−0.023 (0.027)	0.971 (0.032)	—	0.93	2.12
(12.11a)	−0.019 (0.028)	0.913 (0.119)	0.063 (0.122)	0.93	1.96

Notes: The standard errors of the regression coefficients are shown in parentheses; R^2 is the coefficient of determination; D-W is the Durbin-Watson statistic.

Source: Adapted from Jacob A. Frenkel, "Flexible Exchange Rates, Prices, and the Role of 'News': Lessons from the 1970s," *Journal of Political Economy*, August 1981, tab. 1.

significantly different from zero,[18] (2) the estimate of b is not significantly different from unity, and (3) the Durbin-Watson (D-W) statistic is consistent with the absence of serial correlation in u_t. We saw
above that these three results are implied by the ME-EPM hypotheses. We do not reject the hypothesis that the 1-month dollar/mark
forward rate was an unbiased predictor of the spot rate even in the
midst of the highly volatile conditions that prevailed between 1973
and 1979.

The dollar-pound results in Equation (12.9) are marginally consistent with ME-EPM, but the individualistic French have as usual gone
their own way. The estimates of a and b in the dollar-franc Equation
(12.10) differ significantly from (are more than two standard errors
away from) zero and unity, respectively.

So much for Equations (12.9) to (12.11). The results of further tests
are presented in Equations (12.9a) to (12.11a). The ME-EPM hypotheses imply that no other information available to investors at time
$t-1$ could have improved the forward rate's prediction of the spot
rate. Candidates for the "other information available" are limitless,
but the usual nominees have been past spot and/or forward rates in the
belief that, if forward rates are inadequate predictors of spot rates, it is
because traders have fallen behind events.[19] Frenkel tried several
variations of this approach, with the simplest variation appearing in
Equations (12.9a) to (12.11a). As implied by ME-EPM, the addition of
$\ln F_{t-2}$ as an explanatory variable neither produces a coefficient
significantly different from zero nor improves the equation's fit. These
results were essentially unchanged when lagged spot rates and additional lagged forward rates were added as explanatory variables.[20]

The results in Table 12.5 are fairly representative of tests of the
efficiency of the foreign exchange markets. Most tests have found
those markets to be efficient or almost efficient.[21] However, Richard

---

18 Our significance tests are at the 95 percent confidence level.

19 A simple example of an inefficient market is one in which investors naively expect the current
spot rate to be repeated next period so that $F_{t-1} = S_{t-1}$, but the spot rate is systematically related to past spot rates such that

$$S_t = (1 + g)S_{t-1} U_t$$

where g is the average rate of change of S_t. Investors have not yet perceived g to be nonzero.
Substituting F_{t-1} for S_{t-1} gives

$$S_t = (1 + g)F_{t-1} U_t$$

so that the market is inefficient, and you can make some money if you are one of the first to
learn the true value of g.

20 These are known as "weak form" tests of market efficiency because they take account only of
the information contained in historical prices and neglect other types of information.

21 For a survey of empirical work on the efficiency of the foreign exchange market see Laurent
Jacque (1978, pages 69–75), who concluded that the evidence supports the efficiency hypothesis
except perhaps in periods of "dirty floats," that is, when central banks have "managed" or
"smoothed" exchange rate fluctuations.

Levich (1975) found that forward rates tend to underpredict spot rates when rates are rising and to overpredict spot rates when rates are falling. It apparently takes some time for investors to identify new trends in exchange rates.[22]

FUTURES MARKETS IN FOREIGN EXCHANGE
Differences between forward and futures markets

Spot and forward markets in foreign currencies are primarily over-the-counter broker or dealer markets much like those in U.S. Treasury securities, federal funds, or the shares of medium-sized corporations. For convenience most transactions are conducted according to well-understood routine procedures. But hedgers, speculators, brokers, and dealers are free to deviate from those procedures whenever they find it in their interests to do so. Special arrangements are common in transactions between banks and their deposit and loan customers. A bank may quote a smaller spread to important customers than to others. Furthermore, the contract between the parties may be a standard verbal or written agreement, or it may be unique to the particular transaction.

Currency futures, on the other hand, are traded in continuous two-way auctions on the floors of exchanges. The large groups and the rapidity of transactions in these markets require complete agreement about trading rules and the contracts being traded. In fact a *futures market* is defined by the standardized futures contract and the rules for trading that contract laid down by the exchange. The following passage was written with commodities such as wheat and soybeans in mind. But it applies equally to futures contracts in securities and foreign exchange.

Regardless of whether the user of the futures contract is a hedger or speculator, the common bond is the nature of the contract itself. That contract is a firm legal agreement between a buyer (or seller) and an established commodity exchange or its clearing house in which the trader agrees to deliver or accept

---

22 Levich's results have been summarized by Gunter Dufey and Ian Giddy (1978, page 69). Other tests of the efficiency of the foreign exchange markets, with mixed results, have been reported by John Geweke and Edgar Feige (1979), Lars Hansen and Robert Hodrick (1980), Craig Hakkio (1981), and Richard Baillie, Robert Lippens, and Patrick McMahon (1983). Hakkio's paper includes an interesting discussion of why researchers who have assumed constant equilibrium prices have sometimes found evidence of market inefficiency in the form of serially correlated prediction errors (U_t in the above analysis): "Consider, for example, a permanent shock such as the oil crisis. People initially interpreted this as a temporary shock, and only over time was it perceived to be a permanent shock. It is only over time, while people accumulated new information, that the exchange rate (gradually) attained its new equilibrium level. Consequently, looking at a time series we observe serial correlation. However, this serial correlation simply reflects people eliminating their initial confusion of whether the oil shock was permanent or transitory..." [Craig Hakkio (1981, page 676)].

during a designated period a specified amount of a certain commodity that adheres to the particular quality and delivery conditions prescribed by the commodity exchange on which that commodity is traded. The contract, if allowed to run to its termination, is fulfilled by a cash payment on the delivery date based on
the settlement price for that day in return for the delivery of the
commodity.

Richard Teweles, Charles Harlow, and Herbert Stone
(1974, pages 22 and 23)

Further differences between forward and futures markets are listed
in Table 12.6. Some of the items in the table may become clear only
upon reading The Mechanics of Futures Trading, which comes after
the following historical section.

Some historical background to modern forward and futures markets[23]

EARLY FORWARD MARKETS: MEDIEVAL FAIRS. Most stories about forward
markets, like those about the origins of other financial markets, begin
with Renaissance Italy. Consider a Florentine merchant who sold cloth
in Cologne in return for a bill of exchange drawn on the German buyer
ordering the latter to pay x marks 3 months later. To avoid exchange
risk, it was not unusual for our Florentine merchant either to sell the
bill for florins immediately or to arrange to sell the bill at a later date
at a florin/mark exchange rate agreed in advance with another
merchant or a banker dealing in spot and forward foreign exchange.
Both spot and forward foreign exchange markets have developed over
the centuries more or less in line with trade and the improvements in
communication that have contributed to the growth of other financial
markets.[24] But forward currency markets have been most active during
two periods of particularly volatile exchange rates: the period between
the end of World War I and the reestablishment of the gold standard
in 1925 and the current period of floating exchange rates that began in
the early 1970s.

Forward markets in commodities have also been important. As with
currencies, forward markets in commodities developed in conjunction
with spot markets. The centers of trade in medieval Europe were the
market fairs held several times a year in the principal cities of
northern Italy and Flanders. Many traders brought their merchandise
to the fairs and exchanged goods for cash on the spot. But many

---

23 This section is based on Henry Bakken (1966, pages 1–15), Thomas Hieronymus (1977, pages
    10–13), Richard Teweles, Charles Harlow, and Herbert Stone (1974, pages 7–10), and the Chi-
    cago Board of Trade's *Commodity Trading Manual* (1980, pages 1–4).

24 See Paul Einzig's *The History of Foreign Exchange* (1962).

Table 12.6   Comparison of Forward Market and Futures Market

	Forward	Futures
Size of contract	Tailored to individual needs	Standardized
Delivery date	Tailored to individual needs	Standardized
Method of transaction	Established by the bank or broker via telephone contact with limited number of buyers and sellers	Determined by open auction among many buyers and sellers on the exchange floor
Accessibility	Limited to very large customers who deal in foreign trade	Open to anyone who needs hedge facilities or has risk capital with which to speculate
Commissions	Set by "spread" between bank's buy and sell price	Published small brokerage fee and negotiated rates on block trades
Security deposit	None as such, but compensating bank balances required	Published small security deposit required
Clearing operation (financial integrity)	Handling contingent on individual banks and brokers; no separate clearinghouse function	Handled by exchange clearinghouse; daily settlements to the market
Marketplace	Over the telephone worldwide	Central exchange floor with worldwide communications
Regulation	Self-regulating	Regulated under the Commodity Futures Trading Commission
Frequency of delivery	More than 90% settled by actual delivery	Theoretically, no deliveries in a perfect market; in reality less than 1%
Price fluctuations	No daily limit	Daily limit imposed by the exchange
Market liquidity	Forward positions are not as easily offset or transferred to other participants	All positions, whether long or short, can be liquidated easily

Source: Based on a table in *International Monetary Market, Understanding Futures in Foreign Exchange*, Chicago, 1977.

transactions made use of forward contracts that provided for the delivery of goods on specified future dates. These contracts often included a forward pricing provision, by which the price to be paid upon delivery of the goods was determined in advance.

THE ROYAL EXCHANGE. The English extended the concept of the market fair by setting up permanent trading facilities that were open throughout the year. These trading locations were called exchanges, and the

Royal Exchange, which opened in London in 1570, is still in operation.[25]

Dealers soon began acting in the London commodity exchanges as middlemen willing to absorb price risks that the merchants wished to avoid in return for the opportunity to profit in forward transactions. Although spot, or cash, trades remained the essential part of the market, increasingly large numbers of traders took advantage of the forward contracts.
Richard Teweles, Charles Harlow, and Herbert Stone
(1974, page 7)

THE OSAKA RICE MARKET AND THE FIRST FUTURES CONTRACT. The earliest known futures market along the lines of those existing today was the rice market established at Osaka, Japan, in 1697. This market grew up in response to the desire by farmers to secure reliable revenues in the face of fluctuating prices. The rules of the Osaka rice market were strikingly similar to the rules of modern American futures trading:

1. Contract term duration was limited.
2. All contracts within any term were standardized.
3. A basic grade for any contract period was agreed on beforehand.
4. No contract could be carried over into a new contract period.
5. All trades had to be cleared through a clearinghouse.
6. Every trader had to establish a line of credit with the clearinghouse of his choice.[26]

THE CHICAGO BOARD OF TRADE (CBT). Chicago's situation on water and rail routes between the agricultural regions of the West and the population centers of the East had made it the principal trading center for commodities by the 1830s. Forward contracting existed at least as early as 1833, but no permanent trading location existed until the organization of the Chicago Board of Trade in 1848. Trading procedures and contracts progressively became more uniform until the first futures contracts of the modern standardized form, in corn and wheat, were adopted by the CBT in 1865. The modern procedures were thus essentially in place, and the most important developments since then have been the extension of futures contracts to other commodities and, in the 1970s, to financial instruments (including foreign

---

25 The Royal Exchange has been separated into several specialized exchanges now known collectively as the London Commodity Exchange. For a list of the world's commodity exchanges see Ethel de Keyser (1979).

26 Quoted from Richard Teweles, Charles Harlow, and Herbert Stone (1974, pages 8–9). For more detail on the Osaka futures market see Henry Bakken (1966, pages 8–12).

Table 12.7   International Monetary Market Contract Specifications

(1)	(2)	(3)	(4)	(5)	(6)
Contract	Size	Hours[a]	Months	Minimum Fluctuation in Price	Equals Contract
Pound sterling	25,000	7:30[d] 1:24 (9:20)	Jan., Mar., Apr., Jun., Jul., Sep., Oct., Dec., spot mo.	0.0005 (5 pt.) ($2.50/pt.)	$12.50
Canadian dollar	100,000	7:30[d] 1:22 (9:19)	Jan., Mar., Apr., Jun., Jul., Sep., Oct., Dec., spot mo.	0.0001 (1 pt.) ($10/pt.)	$10.00
Dutch guilder	125,000	7:30[d] 1:30 (9:23)	Jan., Mar., Apr., Jun., Jul., Sep., Oct., Dec., spot mo.	0.0001 (1 pt.) ($12.50/pt.)	$12.50
German mark	125,000	7:30[d] 1:20 (9:18)	Jan., Mar., Apr., Jun., Jul., Sep., Oct., Dec., spot mo.	0.0001 (1 pt.) ($12.50/pt.)	$12.50
Japanese yen	12,500,000	7:30[d] 1:26 (9:21)	Jan., Mar., Apr., Jun., Jul., Sep., Oct., Dec., spot mo.	0.000001 (1 pt.) ($12.50/pt.)	$12.50
Mexican peso	1,000,000	7:30[d] 1:18 (9:17)	Jan., Mar., Apr., Jun., Jul., Sep., Oct., Dec., spot mo.	0.00001 (1 pt.) ($10/pt.)	$10.00
Swiss franc	125,000	7:30[d] 1:16 (9:16)	Jan., Mar., Apr., Jun., Jul., Sep., Oct., Dec., spot mo.	0.0001 (1 pt.) ($12.50/pt.)	$12.50
French franc	250,000	7:30[d] 1:28 (9:22)	Jan., Mar., Apr., Jun., Jul., Sep., Oct., Dec., spot mo.	0.00005 (5 pt.) ($2.50/pt.)	$12.50
90-day U.S. T bill	$1,000,000	8:00 2:00 (10:00)	Jan., Mar., Apr., Jun., Jul., Sep., Oct., Dec.	0.01 (1 basis pt.) ($25/pt.)	$25.00
Domestic CD	$1,000,000	7:30 2:00 (11:00)	Mar., Jun., Sep., Dec.	0.01 (1 basis pt.) ($25/pt.)	$25.00
Eurodollar time deposit	$1,000,000	7:30 2:00 (9:30)	Mar., Jun., Sep., Dec., spot mo.	0.01 (1 basis pt.) ($25/pt.)	$25.00

a Times in parentheses indicate close on last day of trading.

b I refers to initial margins; M refers to maintenance margins.

c Margin on intercommodity spreads: The margin on all intercommodity spreads is the higher nonspread margin of the two commodities. Allowable IMM intercommodity spreads are gold vs. Swiss franc, domestic CDs vs. 90-day T bill, Eurodollar time deposit vs. domestic CDs, Eurodollar time deposit vs. 90-day T bill, and spreads between British pound, Dutch guilder, German mark, Swiss franc and French franc. Exception: domestic CDs vs. 90-day T bill is $500 (I), $400 (M), Eurodollar time deposit vs. domestic CDs is $500 (I), $400 (M), and Eurodollar time deposit vs. 90-day T bill is $700 (I), $600 (M). Dutch guilder vs. German mark nondelivery month spread is $500, Swiss franc vs. German mark spread rate is $1,000 (I), $700 (M). Delivery month spread margins apply to spreads involving the lead month.

d Central Time. On the last day of trading, currency contracts close in rotation starting at 9:16 A.M. Currency contracts open on call with Swiss franc opening at 7:30 A.M.

e Spot month to start trading without limits on the last trading day of the previous month; for example, February '81 would start trading without limits on the last trading day of the January '81 contract.

f Spot month margins start on the last trading day of the prior contract month.

Source: *International Monetary Market,* January 1982.

Table 12.7   (continued)

(7) Limit	(8) Last Day Trading	(9) Delivery Date	(10) Minimum Margin[b]	(11) Spread Margin[c]	(12) Delivery Month Margin	(13) Delivery Month Spread Margin
0.05[e] (500 pt.) ($1,250)	2 bus. days bef. 3rd Wed.	3rd Wed.	I $1,500 M $1,000	Market	I $2,200[f] M $1,500	I $1,000[f] M $ 700
0.0075[e] (75 pt.) ($750)	2 bus. days bef. 3rd Wed.	3rd Wed.	I $ 900 M $ 700	Market	I $1,200[f] M $ 900	I $1,000[f] M $ 700
0.0100[e] (100 pt.) ($1,250)	2 bus. days bef. 3rd Wed.	3rd Wed.	I $1,200 M $ 900	Market	I $2,200[f] M $1,500	I $1,000[f] M $ 700
0.0100[e] (100 pt.) ($1,250)	2 bus. days bef. 3rd Wed.	3rd Wed.	I $1,500 M $1,000	Market	I $2,200[f] M $1,500	I $1,000[f] M $ 700
0.000100[e] (100 pt.) ($1,250)	2 bus. days bef. 3rd Wed.	3rd Wed.	I $1,500 M $1,000	Market	I $2,200[f] M $1,500	I $1,000[f] M $ 700
0.00150[e] (150 pt.) ($1,500)	2 bus. days bef. 3rd Wed.	3rd Wed.	I $5,000 M $4,000	I $5,000 M $4,000	I $5,000[f] M $4,000	I $5,000[f] M $4,000
0.0150[e] (150 pt.) ($1,875)	2 bus. days bef. 3rd Wed.	3rd Wed.	I $2,000 M $1,500	Market	I $3,000[f] M $2,000	I $1,500[f] M $1,000
0.00500[e] (500 pt.) ($1,250)	2 bus. days bef. 3rd Wed.	3rd Wed.	I $1,200 M $ 900	Market	I $2,200[f] M $1,500	I $1,000[f] M $ 700
0.60 (60 pt.) ($1,500)	2nd day following 3rd weekly T bill auc- tion in del. mo.	1st Thurs. aft. 3rd weekly bill auction in del. mo.	I $2,000 M $1,500	I $ 400 M $ 200	I $2,000 M $1,500	I $ 400 M $ 200
0.80 (80 pt.) ($2,000)	Bus. day prior to last del. day	From 1st bus. day after 14th to end mo.	I $2,000 M $1,500	I $ 400 M $ 200	I $2,000 M $1,500	I $ 400 M $ 200
1.00 (100 pt.) ($2,500)	2nd London bus. day bef. 3rd Wed.	Last day of trading	I $2,000 M $1,500	I $ 400 M $ 200	I $2,000 M $1,500	I $ 400 M $ 200

exchange). The commodities traded on the CBT and the other dozen or so American futures exchanges now include wheat, corn, soybeans, oats, rye, barley, cattle, hogs, pork bellies, iced broilers, eggs, Maine potatoes, Idaho potatoes, sugar, coffee, cocoa, orange juice, cotton, wool, plywood, copper, silver, platinum, and gold.[27]

CURRENCY AND INTEREST RATE FUTURES. The breakdown of the Bretton Woods fixed exchange rate system led to the introduction of foreign exchange futures on the International Monetary Market (IMM) in 1972 as some people sought a way[28] to hedge against, and others sought a way to speculate on, exchange rate fluctuations. Similar forces (specifically the increased volatility of interest rates) led to the introduction of futures contracts in government-insured mortgages (GNMAs) at the CBT in 1975 and 3-month T bills at the IMM in 1976. Other interest rate futures have since been introduced on these and other exchanges.[29]

The mechanics of futures trading

THE CONTRACT. Specifications of the currency and interest rate contracts traded on the IMM are listed in Table 12.7. Let's discuss the *pound sterling* contract (1), column by column. (2) The *size* entry indicates that there are 25,000 pounds in the pound sterling contract. All currencies are quoted on the IMM in terms of the dollar so that, if the price of a pound is $2, the contract's value is $50,000. Contract sizes are also normally listed in newspaper quotations, such as Table 12.2, which has been placed near Table 12.1 for ease of comparison of forward and futures exchange rates. (3) The pound is traded between the *hours* of 7:30 A.M. and 1:24 P.M. (Chicago time) except on the last day of trading, when the pound sterling contract closes at 9:20 A.M. (4) The *months* column indicates that as many as eight or nine pound sterling contracts may be traded on a given day although Table 12.2 reports only four. (5) The *minimum fluctuation,* or "tick," in the pound's price is $0.0005, which (6) *equals* a minimum change of 0.0005(25,000) = $12.50 per *contract.* (7) The maximum change, or *limit move,* in the pound during a day (from the previous day's close, or "settlement") is $0.05, or $1,250 per contract. Limits on price fluctuations are imposed to prevent overreactions to news. A limit move, for example a rise on February 18 in the price of the March pound (see Table 12.2) from 1.8395 to 1.8895, would not stop trading but it would prohibit trades at prices above 1.8895 (and below 1.7895).

---

27 Consult the financial section of your newspaper for a more complete list of futures contracts and for the exchanges on which they are traded.

28 Another way to hedge foreign exchange risk is, as we have seen, the forward market, although this market is normally available only to large firms.

29 See Tables 12.2, 12.7, and 12.10 for lists of foreign currency and interest rate futures contracts.

(8) The *last day of trading* of, for example, January BP contracts is the second business day before the third Wednesday in January and (9) the *delivery date* for pounds is the third Wednesday. The last four columns of Table 12.7 will be discussed under the next and later headings.

MARGINS AND THE CUSTOMER'S AGREEMENT. If you want to trade futures, you must contact a brokerage firm with a membership on the exchange in which you are interested. After finding a firm and a broker that you like, you open an account by signing a *customer's agreement* and writing a check to the firm for at least its minimum required deposit. This deposit will be available for *margin* when you begin trading. The most important part of the customer's agreement, or "customer security deposit statement," binds you to make up any losses incurred during the course of trading.

Futures margins are different from stock margins. A stock margin is a partial payment for the purchase of stock, the difference between the margin and the cost of the stock being a loan from your broker on which you pay interest. Futures margins are simply good-faith deposits to protect the broker against adverse price moves. If there are no adverse price moves, it is unlikely that any payments beyond the margin will be made since it is unlikely that delivery of the commodity or financial instrument will be taken. Minimum stock margins are set by the Fed and typically range from 50 to 90 percent of the values of stock purchases. Futures margins, which are regulated by the Commodities Futures Trading Commission (CFTC), are much smaller, often less than 5 percent and seldom exceeding 10 percent of the values of futures contracts.

THE CLEARINGHOUSE. Every exchange operates a clearinghouse that keeps track of purchases and sales between members and settles member accounts at the end of each trading day. The most important function of the clearinghouse from the standpoint of customers is that it takes the opposite side of every transaction. For example the sale of a pound sterling contract by A to B becomes a sale (by A) *to* the clearinghouse and a purchase (by B) *from* the clearinghouse. "By severing the direct relationship between buyer and seller, each is subsequently free to buy and sell independently of the other. For example, a buyer who wishes to sell his futures contract a day, a week, or a month after purchasing it need have no concern for whether the original seller desires to buy it back."[30] The clearinghouse thus greatly enhances the liquidity of futures contracts. In addition, as "a party to every trade," it guarantees the opposite side of every transaction.

---

30 Chicago Board of Trade (1981, page 14).

Table 12.8   Margin Account for the Purchase of 25,000 (One Contract) British Pounds

Day	Transaction	Price, $	Initial Margin, $	Maintenance Margin, $	Position Value, $	Capital, $	Equity, $
1	Buy 25,000 June BP	1.8480	1,500	1,000	0	1,500	1,500
2	—	1.8600	1,500	1,000	+300	1,500	1,800
3	—	1.8400	1,500	1,000	−200	1,500	1,300
4	—	1.8200	1,500	1,000	−700	1,500	800
5	Margin call of $700	1.8200	1,500	1,000	−700	2,200	1,500
6	Sell 25,000 June BP	1.8100	1,500	1,000	−950	2,200	1,250

Patterned after a table in Thomas Hieronymus, *Economics of Futures Trading for Commercial and Personal Profit,* 2nd ed., Commodity Research Bureau, NY, 1977, page 65.

There has been no customer loss because of default on a CBT futures contract since the formation of its clearinghouse in 1925.[31]

THE LIFE OF A CONTRACT. The role of margins in futures markets is illustrated in Table 12.8. You think the pound will rise, and on day 1 (February 17) you go to the local office of a brokerage firm that deals in futures and tell a broker that you wish to buy one June BP contract. He informs you that in your case the initial margin required by the firm is the minimum required by the regulators and the exchange. We see from column 10 in Table 12.7 that the initial (I) margin is $1,500. You write a check to the broker for this amount and sign a customer's agreement. Your broker phones or wires your order to his firm's communications desk on the floor of the IMM, and it is taken by a runner to a floor broker at the BP pit. Suppose the floor broker executes your order toward the end of day 1 at the settlement price of $1.8480. You have made a contract to buy 25,000 British pounds deliverable on the third Wednesday in June. If the pound rises between February and June (or whenever you choose to sell your contract) you will earn a profit equal to the difference between the purchase and sale prices, less the broker's commission.

Notice that the margin is $1,500/($1.8480)(25,000) = $1,500/ $46,200 = 3.25 percent of the value of the contract although for some customers and under some conditions the broker may require more than the minimum margin.

We see in Table 12.8 that things look good initially because at the end of day 2 the pound has risen to $1.8600 and you have earned $0.0120(25,000) = $300, which is now the value of your position. You have put up capital of $1,500 and the equity in your account is $1,800. But matters soon take a turn for the worse. On day 3 the price falls to $1.8400, a loss of $0.0200(25,000) = $500, and your position is now worth $-\$200$ instead of $+\$300$. The price falls to $1.8200 on day 4, reducing your position value to $-\$700$ and your equity with the broker to $800. This is less than the $1,000 minimum required to be maintained with the broker for each BP contract, the minimum maintenance (M) margin indicated in column 10 of Table 12.7, and he asks you for $700 to bring your account back up to $1,500 and your position value to zero. He might have asked for something less than (or more than) $700, depending upon his view of your creditworthiness and the likely future course of the pound. For example, in the most pessimistic case of a downward limit move of the pound, your position will fall by $0.05(25,000) = \$1,250$ and your equity to $\$800 - \$1,250 = -\$450$, which the broker will be stuck with if you skip town. And this assumes he can sell the contract at the "limit down" price. He will lose much more than $450 if the pound takes a series of limit down moves with no trading.

However, we will suppose the pound's price remains at $1.8200 on day 5 and then falls to $1.8100 on day 6. So far, you have paid $2,200 to the broker and have lost $0.0380(25,000) = \$950$ so that the equity of your account is $1,250. You decide to cut your losses and advise the broker to sell the contract, which (we assume) he is able to do at the end of day 6 for $1.8100.

Hedging foreign exchange risk in the futures market

The following exercise illustrates how the futures market may be used to hedge exchange rate risk in the circumstances considered in Exercise 12.2 for the forward market.[32]

EXERCISE 12.3.   Suppose as before that the Colorado Cheese Company has agreed (on February 17) to pay 500,000 marks on March 17 to a German exporter. Show how Colorado Cheese can use the futures market to lock in a certain expenditure of dollars.

The company's financial officer places an order to buy 500,000 March marks, which we see from Tables 12.2 and 12.7 is four contracts and requires an initial margin of 4($1,500) = \$6,000$. We assume that the purchase comes at the end of the day, when, as Table 12.2 shows, marks are selling for $0.4196. That is, 500,000 March marks cost $209,800 on February 17 although Colorado Cheese has to put up only $6,000.

The delivery date for currency futures is the third Wednesday of the month, which in March 1982 was St. Patrick's Day. The last trading date for March marks is therefore March 15, and we

---

32 Other types of foreign exchange futures hedges are described in the International Monetary Market's *Understanding Futures in Foreign Exchange* (1977).

assume Colorado Cheese gets out of the futures market on that date by selling 500,000 March marks.

Table 12.1 shows that spot marks were selling for $1/2.3985 = $0.4169 on February 17. The table at the end of this exercise shows how the cheese company can use the futures market to lock in a net cost of $0.4169 per mark to be paid in March. In case 1 the spot mark falls from $0.4169 on February 17 to $0.4000 on March 15, when Colorado Cheese closes out its futures contract and, at the same time, buys spot marks. The *basis* is the difference between the spot and futures prices of the mark. These prices normally move closely together so that changes in the basis tend to be small although the basis usually becomes smaller as the futures contract approaches its delivery date. For simplicity we assume in this exercise that the basis remains constant at $0.4196 − $0.4169 = $0.0027, which permits a perfect hedge. Given the constant basis, the price of March mark futures on March 15 is $0.4000 + $0.0027 = $0.4027 so that 500,000 March marks are sold on that date for $201,350. This means a loss of $8,450 on the futures transactions, which, when added to the cost of spot marks on March 15, gives a total cost of $0.4169 per mark, which was the cost of spot marks on February 17.

Case 2 considers a rise in the value of the spot mark to $0.44 and the March futures mark to $0.4427, both on March 15. This means a profit of $11,550 on the futures transactions, which, when deducted from the cost of spot marks, again gives a net cost of $0.4169 per mark.

Date	Cash Market	Futures Market	Basis
Case 1: Spot mark falls to $0.40			
Feb. 17		Buys 500,000 March marks at $0.4196 for $209,800	$0.0027
Mar. 15	Buys 500,000 spot marks at $0.40 for $200,000	Sells 500,000 March marks at $0.4027 for $201,350	$0.0027
		A loss of $8,450	
	Total cost: $208,450, or $0.4169 per mark		
Case 2: Spot mark rises to $0.44			
Feb. 17		Buys 500,000 March marks at $0.4196 for $209,800	$0.0027
Mar. 15	Buys 500,000 spot marks at $0.44 for $220,000	Sells 500,000 March marks at $0.4427 for $221,350	$0.0027
		A profit of $11,550	
	Total cost: $208,450, or $0.4169 per mark		

The constant basis has made possible a perfect hedge. Neglecting commissions, Colorado Cheese has been able to guarantee
itself a net cost of marks on March 15 identical with the price of
spot marks on February 17.

The basis

The basis is the difference between the cash (spot) price of a commodity (or financial instrument) and the price of that commodity in the
futures market. Cash[33] and futures prices normally rise and fall
together because they are affected by the same events. Increased fears
of American inflation, for example, will cause declines in the dollar's
value in both spot and futures markets. Cash and futures prices tend
to converge (that is, the basis tends to zero) as the delivery date of the
futures contract approaches. We should not expect the price of cash
marks on March 15 (the last trading day of March mark futures) to
differ very much from the price of March futures, for which the
delivery date is March 17. For example, if the cash and futures prices
on March 15 were $0.40 and $0.41, respectively, traders could earn
certain (arbitrage) returns by buying spot marks on the Ides of March
at $0.40 and delivering them on St. Patrick's Day for $0.41. Similar
though less pronounced considerations apply to dates close to, but not
coincident with, the last trading day. Except in the face of highly
volatile markets and fears of large and sudden changes we should not
expect cash marks to trade on March 14 or March 13 at prices very
different from March futures prices.

Now let's consider how changes in the basis might have affected the
hedge in Exercise 12.3. Colorado Cheese achieved a perfect hedge in
that exercise because of the assumption of a constant basis. But in
general, hedging is speculation on the basis because future differences
between cash and futures prices are unknown.[34] Nevertheless, speculation on the basis is usually less risky than not hedging at all because
variations in the basis are usually less than variations in cash prices.
Suppose the March mark basis in Exercise 12.3 had fallen from
$0.0027 on February 17 to $0.0007 on March 15 (instead of remaining
constant at $0.0027). Referring to the table at the end of the exercise,
this means that in case 1 the Colorado Cheese Company sold 500,000
March marks on March 15 at $0.4007 per mark for $200,350. It incurs a
loss of $9,450 (instead of $8,450) on the futures transactions and a total
cost of $209,450 for 500,000 marks, or $0.4189 per mark (instead of
$0.4169). In case 2 a basis of $0.0007 on March 15 means a sale of

---

33 We use "cash" in place of "spot" in the following discussion in order to be consistent with the
     terminology of futures traders.

34 Thomas Hieronymus has written, "The essence of hedging is speculation in basis" (1977, page
     151).

Table 12.9   An Interdelivery (Intracommodity) Spread

Date	Actions	
Feb. 17	Bought one contract June marks at $0.4259	Sold one contract December marks at $0.4438
May 10	Sold one contract June marks at $0.4500	Bought one contract December marks at $0.4600
Result	Gain on June marks of $0.0241(125,000) = $3,012.50	Loss on December marks of $0.0162(125,000) = $2,025

Patterned after a table in George Angell, *Winning in the Commodities Market,* Doubleday, Garden City, NY, 1979, page 77.

500,000 March marks at $0.4407 for $220,350. This means a gain of $10,550 (instead of $11,550) on futures transactions and again a total cost of $209,450 for 500,000 marks.[35]

Although Colorado Cheese lost $1,000 on its hedge in both case 1 and case 2 owing to the fall in the basis, the hedge was still valuable because it locked in a mark price close to the February 17 spot price of $0.4169. The basis change resulted in a mark cost of $0.4189, but the hedge insured the importer against the risk of having to pay $0.44, as in case 2, or perhaps even higher.[36]

Spreads (straddles)

Spreads are futures transactions in which the trader's profit or loss arises not from the rise or fall of a single price but from the price *difference* between two futures contracts.[37] Traders use spreads (which are also called "straddles") as a way of speculating—but not too much.

> When you *place,* or *put on,* a spread, you buy one contract while simultaneously selling another. Thus you are long and short in two related commodity futures at the same time. The relative changes between the two prices at which you purchased and sold your two contracts will determine your profit or loss. For example, you might spread corn and wheat by buying one contract of December wheat and simultaneously selling a contract of December corn. This is known as an *intercommodity spread,* in which

---

35 See the International Monetary Markets' *Understanding Futures in Foreign Exchange* for more examples of hedging gains and losses because of changes in the basis.

36 Problem 9 at the end of this chapter asks the student to examine the outcomes of Colorado Cheese's hedge in the face of a different change in the basis.

37 This discussion is based on George Angell (1979, pages 67–97) and the Chicago Board of Trade's *Commodity Trading Manual* (1980, pages 115–126).

different commodities on the same exchange are bought and sold in the same contract month.

George Angell (1979, page 67)

Traders usually put on spreads when they believe that price differences are abnormal.[38] In the example just quoted, the trader apparently believed that the price of December wheat would rise relative to the price of December corn. Since corn and wheat prices normally move in the same direction, this spread is considered less risky than speculation in single commodities. Consequently, spread margins are often less than those on single contracts.

Another type of spread is the *interdelivery (or intracommodity) spread,* in which "futures contracts for the same commodity traded on the same exchange are spread between two different delivery months."[39] This is the most common type of spread and is illustrated in Table 12.9 for June and December German marks at the IMM. Suppose you buy (undertake to receive) one contract (125,000) of June marks at the close of trading on February 17 at $0.4259 and simultaneously sell (undertake to deliver) one contract of December marks at $0.4438 (see Table 12.2). You did this because, along with other investors, you expected the U.S. dollar to weaken (that is, the mark price to rise) but also thought that the December mark price exaggerated the likely fall in the dollar, that is, that it was out of line with other contracts. You expected June marks to rise more than December marks, and therefore, by buying June marks and selling December marks, you expected to profit from a narrowing of the difference between the prices of the two contracts.

Your dreams came true, and by May 10, when you liquidated your spread, June and December marks had risen $0.0241 and $0.0162, respectively, providing a net profit of $987.50 less commissions. You would have been better off, of course, if you had not engaged in the spread. If you had only bought (and not sold) marks, you would have made a profit of $3,012.50 instead of $987.50. But you were betting on price *differences,* specifically on a narrowing of June and December marks. If you had been wrong about the direction of mark price movements but right about the June-December difference, for example, if June and December marks had fallen to $0.39 and $0.40, respectively, you would have lost $4,487.50 on your purchase of the

---

38 Much time and effort are devoted to the development and uses of data concerning historical, or "normal," futures price differences. For discussions of some of this research, see George Angell (1979, pages 86–91), Thomas Hieronymus (1977, pages 151–172), and the Chicago Board of Trade's *Commodity Trading Manual* (1980, pages 117–124).

39 CBT, *Commodity Trading Manual* (1980, page 116). Other types of spreads are the *intermarket spread,* in which "contracts for the same commodity deliverable in the same month are spread between two different commodity exchanges," for example, New York silver and London silver, and the *commodity-product spread,* in which contracts in a "commodity and the product or products derived from it . . . are traded on the same exchange," for example, between soybeans and soybean oil at the CBT.

June contract but gained $5,475 on your sale of the December contract—a net gain of $987.50 on the spread.[40] We hardly need add that it is possible to predict price differences incorrectly so that you may lose your shirt on spreads almost as easily as on other speculations.[41]

Spread margins[42]

Column 11 of Table 12.7 lists the margins on *intracommodity* spreads. "Market" in this context means that the initial margin is zero and the financial relation between customer and broker is one of *mark to market,* that is, the day-to-day adjustment of the account to reflect profits and losses. Notice that, because of the extreme price volatility of the Mexican peso, the intracommodity spread margin on this currency was as high as on unspread transactions. *Intercommodity* spread margins are listed in the notes at the bottom of Table 12.7.

Delivery

In none of the examples presented thus far have we allowed delivery to take place. Purchases of contracts have been offset by sales, and sales have been offset by purchases before delivery dates. This is consistent with market practice, for actual delivery of the commodities and financial instruments specified in futures contracts seldom occurs. This is not surprising because speculators trade futures contracts in order to profit from price movements (as in Table 12.9) and hedgers trade them in order to offset movements in spot prices (as in Exercise 12.3). Both speculation and hedging can be fully accomplished by buying and then selling or by selling and then buying contracts. Neither requires delivery. If your objective is the actual purchase or sale of soybeans or pesos, it is normally easier and cheaper to go directly to the appropriate spot market without incurring the commission charges of futures brokers.[43]

TREASURY BILL FUTURES

Interest rate futures

A partial list of interest rate futures is presented in Table 12.10: fourteen contracts in pooled mortgage certificates guaranteed by the

---

40 Problem 10 at the end of this chapter asks you to confirm these results.

41 See Michael Adler (1983) for further discussion of spread strategies in foreign exchange futures.

42 Notice the higher margins in columns 12 and 13 of Table 12.7 (on spreads as well as other transactions) during delivery months because of the increasing volatility of futures prices as contracts approach expiration. See Thomas Hieronymus (1977, page 172) for a discussion of the dangers of delivery month transactions.

43 Delivery does occasionally take place, however. For discussions of the delivery process see Edward Schwarz (1979), Thomas Hieronymus (1977), and the CBT's *Understanding the Delivery Process in Financial Futures* (1980). According to the last reference, "less than one-half of one percent of all financial futures traded at the CBT from 1975 through 1979 resulted in delivery. . ." (page 1).

Table 12.10   Financial Cash and Futures Markets, New York and Chicago, Thursday, March 25, 1982

T Bills

U.S. Treas. Bills

Mat. date 1982	Bid Discount	Asked	Yield
4/1	12.24	11.82	12.00
4/8	12.58	12.32	12.53
4/15	12.61	12.39	12.64
4/22	12.74	12.54	12.82
4/29	12.42	12.24	12.54
5/6	12.52	12.26	12.59
5/13	12.59	12.33	12.70
5/20	12.57	12.31	12.71
5/27	12.55	12.33	12.76
6/3	12.60	12.44	12.91
6/10	12.69	12.47	12.97
6/17	12.76	12.58	13.12
6/24	12.75	12.69	13.27
7/1	12.79	12.65	13.26
7/8	12.82	12.68	13.33
7/15	12.85	12.71	13.40
7/22	12.85	12.71	13.43
7/29	12.85	12.71	13.47
8/5	12.89	12.75	13.55
8/12	12.90	12.76	13.59
8/19	12.90	12.76	13.63
8/26	12.90	12.76	13.63
9/2	12.89	12.69	13.62
9/9	12.89	12.71	13.68
9/16	12.88	12.76	13.77
9/23	12.80	12.74	13.79
10/7	12.74	12.58	13.63
11/4	12.74	12.58	13.66
12/2	12.67	12.51	13.63
12/30	12.67	12.51	13.71
1983			
1/27	12.52	12.36	13.62
2/24	12.53	12.37	13.73
3/24	12.50	12.44	13.93

Financial Futures

GNMA 8% (CBT)—$100,000 prncpl; pts., 32nds of 100%

	Open	High	Low	Settle	Chg	Yield Settle	Chg	Open Interest
Mar	—	—	—	—	—	—	—	796
June	61-18	61-27	61-13	61-22	+2	15.185	-.017	17,166
Sept	61-11	61-17	61-04	61-11	—	15.279	—	7.707
Dec	61-00	61-09	60-30	61-04	—	15.338	—	8,129
Mar83	61-00	61-05	60-25	60-31	—	15.381	—	6.708
June	60-28	60-31	60-24	60-27	—	15.415	—	6,292
Sept	60-22	60-26	60-22	60-24	—	15.441	—	4,549
Dec	60-20	60-23	60-18	60-22	—	15.459	—	2,896
Mar84	60-26	60-26	60-18	60-20	—	15.476	—	3,505
June	—	—	—	60-19	—	15.484	—	1,490
Sept	—	—	—	60-18	—	15.493	—	1,115
Dec	—	—	—	60-17	—	15.502	—	697
Mar85	—	—	—	60-16	—	15.510	—	75
June	—	—	—	60-15	—	15.519	—	13

Est. vol 8,500; vol Wed 5,680; open int 61,138, +89.

Treasury Bonds (CBT)—$100,000; pts. 32nds of 100%

	Open	High	Low	Settle	Chg	Yield Settle	Chg	Open Interest
Mar	—	—	—	—	—	—	—	3,666
June	62-26	62-30	62-12	62-23	+3	13.399	-.020	67,989
Sept	63-02	63-06	62-21	63-01	+3	13.332	-.020	21,776
Dec	63-12	63-17	63-00	63-11	+3	13.266	-.020	15,996
Mar83	63-21	63-25	63-12	63-21	+3	13.201	-.020	15,767
June	63-28	64-01	63-22	63-31	+3	13.136	-.020	11,502
Sept	64-10	64-10	64-01	64-08	+3	13.079	-.019	16,304
Dec	64-15	64-20	64-08	64-17	+3	13.021	-.019	12,271
Mar84	64-23	64-26	64-18	64-25	+3	12.971	-.019	10,090
June	—	—	—	65-01	+3	12.920	-.019	5,416
Sept	65-09	65-09	65-01	65-08	+3	12.877	-.018	2,057
Dec	—	—	—	65-15	+3	12.833	-.019	1,001

Est vol 59,000; vol Wed 57,452; open int 183,835, +675.

Treasury Bills (IMM)—$1 mil.; pts. of 100%

	Open	High	Low	Settle	Chg	Discount Settle	Chg	Open Interest
June	87.38	87.43	87.17	87.26	-.10	12.74	+.10	21,405
Sept.	87.15	87.19	87.02	87.08	-.08	12.92	+.08	6,843
Dec	87.08	87.09	86.90	86.94	-.10	13.06	+.10	3,286
Mar83	87.02	87.05	86.89	86.90	-.12	13.10	+.12	1,964
June	87.00	87.01	86.86	86.88	-.13	13.12	+.13	1,029
Sept	—	—	—	86.94	-.10	13.06	+.10	154
Dec	86.99	86.99	86.99	86.99	-.11	13.01	+.11	59
Mar84	86.99	87.00	86.99	87.00	-.14	13.00	+.14	13

Est vol 22,174; vol Wed 24,771; open int 34,753, -992.

Banks CDs (IMM)—$1 mil.; pts. of 100%

	Open	High	Low	Settle	Chg	Settle	Chg	Open Interest
Mar	—	—	—	85.72	-.08	14.28	+.08	232
June	85.23	85.38	85.17	85.25	-.08	14.75	+.08	6,530
Sept	85.28	85.31	85.18	85.22	-.11	14.78	+.11	1,520
Dec	85.27	85.41	85.27	85.30	-.13	14.70	+.13	186

Est vol 5,141; vol Wed 6,743; open int 8,468, +180.

Source: *Wall Street Journal*, March 26, 1982.

Government National Mortgage Association, twelve contracts in U.S. Treasury bonds, eight contracts in 90-day T bills, and four contracts in commercial bank certificates of deposit—traded at the CBT and the IMM. Several more interest rate futures are traded on these and other exchanges,[44] but our interest in the remainder of this chapter is limited to 90-day T bills.

---

44 For example, a Eurodollar contract is specified in Table 12.7. For discussions of interest rate futures contracts see Marcelle Arak and Christopher McCurdy (1979–1980), Edward Schwarz (1979), Allan Loosigian (1980), Mark Powers and David Vogel (1981), the CBT's *An Introduction to Financial Futures* (1981) and *Financial Instruments Markets: Cash-Futures Relationships* (1980), and the IMM's *Treasury Bill Futures* (1980).

The 90-day T bill contract

Most of the specifications of this contract are stated in Table 12.7. But it is also worth noting that the 90-day T bill contract calls for delivery of bills with face value of $1 million and maturity of 90, 91, or 92 days. Most deliveries are made in 91-day bills.

Now let's look at the method used in quoting the prices of these contracts. The T bill prices in Table 12.10 are not percentages of face value as in the cash and futures markets for coupon bonds. Instead the closing price of 87.26 on the June T bill contract implies a discount (in annual percentage terms) of $100 - 87.26 = 12.74$, as shown in the table. This contrasts sharply with cash market procedures. To take a simple example, consider a discount of 8 percent on a 90-day bill. In the cash market this means a price (as a percentage of face value) of [45]

$$P = 100\left(1 - \frac{Dd}{360}\right) = 100\left[1 - \frac{90(0.08)}{360}\right] = 98.00$$

But the quoted futures price corresponding to a discount of 8 percent is

$$P = 100 - 8 = 92.00$$

Returning to the June T bill contract in Table 12.10, the cash price of a 90-day T bill with a discount of 12.74 percent is

$$P = 100\left[1 - \frac{90(0.1274)}{360}\right] = 96.815$$

instead of 87.26 as shown in the table. That is, the actual delivery price of the 90-day June T bill contract is $96.815 per $100 face value.

Using T bill futures to hedge interest rate risk

The following exercise illustrates how financial futures may be used to hedge interest rate risk.[46]

EXERCISE 12.4. The Cousy Fruit and Vegetable Company places an order on March 25 for produce to be delivered June 1, payment of $950,000 due on delivery. Cousy expects to finance this purchase by issuing 90-day commercial paper (CP) with face value of $1 million. The current annual discount rate on 90-day CP issued by firms with Cousy's credit rating is 13.60 percent. That is, the revenue on March 25 from such an issue would be

---

45 See Table 6.1.

46 Other types of financial futures hedges are presented in the references in footnote 44.

$$\$1,000,000\left[1 - \frac{90(0.1360)}{360}\right] = \$966,000$$

Interest rates might fall between March 25 and June 1, when Cousy will want to sell the CP. On the other hand, interest rates might rise. Show how Cousy can use the T bill futures market to reduce interest rate risk.

The procedure is set forth in the table at the end of this exercise. Assume that Cousy sells (undertakes to deliver) one June 90-day T bill contract (with face, or delivery, value of $1 million) at the settlement discount of 12.74 shown in Table 12.10. The value of this contract on March 25 is

$$\$1,000,000\left[1 - \frac{90(0.1274)}{360}\right] = \$968,150$$

Now suppose (and this is an important assumption) that the rates on T bill futures and cash CP rise by equal amounts, say, 1.26 percent, between March 25 and June 1. In such an event (case 1 in the table), the futures contract may be liquidated (bought) for

$$\$1,000,000\left[1 - \frac{90(0.14)}{360}\right] = \$965,000$$

giving a profit of $968,150 − $965,000 = $3,150 in the futures market.

Cousy's sale of 90-day CP on June 1 brings

$$\$1,000,000\left[1 - \frac{90(0.1486)}{360}\right] = \$962,850$$

which, when added to the futures profit, gives a total revenue of $966,000. As we saw at the beginning of the exercise, this is the revenue obtained from a sale of $1 million face value of 90-day CP with a discount of 13.60, which was the rate prevailing on March 25.

Cousy has secured a perfect hedge against the rise in interest rates; that is, the firm has locked in a borrowing rate of 13.60. Case 2 in the following table shows that Cousy's effective borrowing rate also remains at 13.60 when rates fall—under the assumption that T bill futures and cash CP rates fall by the same amount.[47]

---

47 Problem 12 at the end of this chapter asks the student to confirm the numbers in case 2.

Date	Cash Market		Futures Market	
Mar. 25	Anticipated selling $1 million face value of 90-day CP on June 1; current discount 13.60% and revenue $966,000		Sold 1 June T bill contract at a discount of 12.74%	
			Value	$968,150

Case 1: 90-day CP and T bill rates rise 1.26 percent

Jun. 1	Sold $1 million of 90-day CP at 14.86%		Bought (offset) 1 T bill contract at 14.00%	
	CP revenue	$962,850	Value	$965,000
	+ Hedge profit	3,150	Profit from futures	$ 3,150
	Total revenue	$966,000		

Case 2: 90-day CP and T bill rates fall 0.74 percent

Jun. 1	Sold $1 million of 90-day CP at 12.86%		Bought (offset) 1 T bill contract at 12.00%	
	CP revenue	$967,850	Value	$970,000
	− Hedge loss	1,850	Loss from futures	$ 1,850
	Total revenue	$966,000		

The hedge in Exercise 12.4 was perfect—that is, it locked in the March 25 borrowing rate for June 1—because T bill futures and CP cash rates moved equally. This will not in general be the case. There will almost always be some gain or loss due to movements in the basis. Nevertheless, hedges of this kind will normally reduce interest rate risk as long as CP and T bill cash rates vary together and so do T bill cash and futures rates.[48]

The efficiency of the T bill futures market

A COMPARISON OF RETURNS TO INVESTMENTS IN THE CASH AND FUTURES MARKETS. The T bill cash and futures markets offer alternative ways of earning near-certain returns.[49] We should therefore expect the rates of return on cash and futures investments with identical maturities to be very similar. The following discussion checks this expectation for 3- and 6-month T bill investments on March 25, 1982.

Consider the following courses of action, both free of risk and both executed on March 25: (1) the purchase of a 6-month bill to be held until maturity on September 23 and (2) the purchase of a 3-month bill to be held until maturity on June 24 and the simultaneous purchase of

---

48 Some writers have argued that banks and other firms planning to issue certificates of deposit or CP are well advised to use "cross hedges" with T bill futures rather than "straight hedges" with CD or CP futures because of the much greater activity, and therefore liquidity, of the T bill futures market. See Bradford Cornell (1981) and Andrew Senchack and John Easterwood (1983).

49 Interest rate uncertainty causes these returns to be uncertain, even when the cash securities and the futures contracts are held to maturity, by causing fluctuations in margin requirements.

a June 90-day T bill futures contract with a June 24 delivery date. Except for taxes and transaction costs all the data necessary to evaluate the certain outcomes of these two courses are contained in Table 12.10. For ease of comparison the basic period in the following calculations is 3 months, and yields are expressed in quarterly rather than annual terms. We know from Chapter 6 that precise comparisons between rates of return on T bills require the conversion of quoted discount rates either to compound annual yields or, as below, to quarterly yields.

1. The price of the 6-month (two-period) bill asked by dealers is[50]

$$P_2 = 100\left[1 - \frac{182(0.1274)}{360}\right] = 93.55922$$

with quarterly yield Y_2 such that

$$(1 + Y_2)^2 = \frac{100}{93.55922} = 1.06884$$

so that

$$Y_2 = (1.06884)^{1/2} - 1 = 0.03385$$

That is, the rate of return on the 6-month bill will be 3.385 percent at a quarterly rate or 6.884 at a semiannual rate if held to maturity.

2. The price of the 3-month bill is

$$P_1 = 100\left[1 - \frac{91(0.1269)}{360}\right] = 96.79225$$

with quarterly yield Y_1 such that

$$1 + Y_1 = \frac{100}{96.79225} = 1.03314 \qquad \text{so that} \qquad Y_1 = 0.03314$$

The 90-day T bill futures contract deliverable in June may be secured for the price

$$_1P_1^f = 100\left[1 - \frac{91(0.1274)}{360}\right] = 96.77961$$

where $_1P_1^f$ denotes the price of a one-period (that is, one-quarter) T bill futures contract deliverable one period in the future. The quar-

---

50 We assume cash delivery (that is, on March 25) of the cash bills bought on March 25.

terly yield on this contract is

$$1 + {}_1Y_1^f = \frac{100}{96.77961} = 1.03328 \qquad \text{so that} \qquad {}_1Y_1^f = 0.03328$$

Notice that ${}_1P_1^f$ and ${}_1Y_1^f$ are the futures price and yield quoted March 25 on 3-month bills originating (to be delivered) June 24.[51]

Now let's compare the outcomes of these two courses of action. The 6-month rate of return to the successive 3-month bills obtained in the cash and futures markets is

$$(1 + Y_1)(1 + {}_1Y_1^f) - 1 = (1.03314)(1.03328) - 1 = 0.06752$$

compared with the 6-month rate of return of 0.06884 on the 6-month cash bill.

FORWARD AND FUTURES RATES. Another way of comparing the returns to the two investment plans is by comparing the June futures yield to the June forward yield implicit in the spot term structure of yields. We now solve for this forward yield by showing that an investor who simultaneously sells a one-period bill and buys a two-period bill secures a one-period investment to begin one period in the future, with a yield implied by the current spot yield curve.[52]

We continue to assume the spot one-period and two-period yields, Y_1 and Y_2, that were used above. Therefore, if the one-period bill has a face value of $100, our investor receives the following amount from its sale:

$$\frac{\$100}{1 + Y_1} = \frac{\$100}{1.03314} = \$96.792$$

Immediately investing the proceeds in (perfectly divisible) two-period bills, she receives the following amount when they mature two periods later:

$$\frac{\$100}{1 + Y_1}(1 + Y_2)^2 = \frac{\$100}{1.03314}(1.06884) = \$103.455$$

The investor has given up a claim on $100 after one period in exchange for a claim on $103.455 after two periods. This is equivalent

---

51 The 91-day bill used in this example differs from the 90-day bill assumed in Exercise 12.4. Remember that 90-, 91-, or 92-day bills may be delivered in satisfaction of the 90-day T bill contract, 91-day bills being most common.

52 These implicit forward yields are an important part of the analysis of the term structure of interest rates presented in Chapter 19.

to a one-period forward loan one period in the future, on which she has locked in the yield

(12.12)

$$_1F_1 = \frac{[\$100/(1 + Y_1)] (1 + Y_2)^2 - \$100}{\$100} = \frac{\$103.455 - \$100}{\$100}$$

$$= \frac{(1 + Y_2)^2}{1 + Y_1} - 1 = \frac{1.06884}{1.03314} - 1 = 0.03455$$

The two-period yield on a two-period bill is thus equivalent to the outcome of successive investments in one-period bills at the yields Y_1 and $_1F_1$:

(12.13)

$$(1 + Y_2)^2 = (1 + Y_1) (1 + {}_1F_1)$$

$$= (1.03314) (1.03455) = 1.06884$$

This may be compared with the outcome of the investments in spot and futures bills in the second course of action discussed above:

(12.14) $(1 + Y_1) (1 + {}_1Y_1^f) = (1.03314) (1.03328) = 1.06752$

We have found the quarterly forward and futures yields to be $_1F_1 = 0.03455$ and $_1Y_1^f = 0.03328$, which may be converted to the compound annual rates of 14.55 percent and 13.99 percent, respectively. Most (perhaps all) of this difference is due to the favorable tax treatment given to T bill futures.[53] The returns on cash T bills are taxed as ordinary income, but 60 percent of the returns on T bill futures are treated as capital gains. The differences between forward and futures T bill rates between the inception of the T bill futures market in 1976 and the introduction of tax differences in 1978 were much smaller than those prevailing since 1979.[54] In a study of the 1976 to 1978 period, Richard Rendleman and Christopher Carabini (1979) found the differences between T bill forward and futures rates to be too small for profitable arbitrage opportunities net of transaction costs.[55]

---

53 Some of the difference may also be due to the different cash flows associated with forward and futures contracts. The contract price of a forward contract is fixed throughout its life (even in the case of implicit forward contracts, such as the one considered here, in which a claim on $100 after one period has been exchanged for a claim on $103.455 after two periods). But the price of a futures contract changes continuously; the futures contract is effectively settled every day and rewritten at the new price. Fischer Black (1976) showed that forward and futures contracts are essentially equivalent in the presence of a constant interest rate. But John Cox, Jonathan Ingersoll, and Stephen Ross (1981) and Robert Jarrow and George Oldfield (1981) have shown that in the presence of uncertainty forward and futures rates will in general be different even in the absence of taxes and transaction costs. However, Richard Rendleman and Christopher Carabini (1979, page 897n) tried a wide range of parameters of the Cox-Ingersoll-Ross model (available in a working paper in 1977) and were unable to find significant differences between forward and futures yields ("generally less than one basis point").

54 Examples are presented by Marcelle Arak (1983, Table IV).

55 Also see Richard Rendleman and Christopher Carabini for a useful review of studies of the efficiency of the T bill futures market.

CONCLUSION: THE PROSPECTS
FOR FINANCIAL FUTURES MARKETS

Brilliant prospects . . .

Commodity forward and futures markets are very old, and so are forward markets in foreign exchange. But markets in financial futures contracts on organized exchanges date only from the great increase in the volatility of interest rates and exchange rates in the 1970s. Many of these contracts have been highly successful. They have been popular with both hedgers and speculators, and their future seems assured. Forward and futures markets in foreign exchange will continue to be useful until the unlikely return of the gold standard or some other system of fixed exchange rates. It is difficult to envision any circumstances in which interest rate futures might vanish, except possibly the recurrence of another prolonged period of low and stable interest rates like that prevailing during the 1930s and 1940s. Now that the start-up costs of these markets have been incurred, they will probably continue to be popular even if monetary and fiscal policies settle into more stable patterns and interest rate volatility returns to the less extreme and possibly more normal behavior of the years between the Civil War and 1930.

. . . with a cloud or two

The discussion in this chapter has emphasized the usefulness of forward and futures markets in securing risk-reducing hedges. But these markets have costs as well as benefits, and they are not meant for everyone. So it is appropriate that we conclude the chapter by calling attention to a few circumstances in which managers and other investors should not enter into forward or futures contracts. A proper understanding of these circumstances requires an awareness that (1) forward and futures contracts are negative-sum games for investors and (2) these markets are approximately efficient. With regard to (1) the parties to these contracts are betting against each other on price movements. What one gains the other loses. And the house takes its cut from both. Playing the futures game is very different from playing the stock market. Stocks have traditionally produced aggregate net gains to investors and will continue to do so as long as most corporations earn profits. Similarly, investors can buy bonds and other debt instruments with the reasonable expectation of positive returns. But expected returns from forward and futures investments are negative when transaction costs are taken into account. With regard to (2) the efficiency of these markets means that their negative expected returns are borne by all investors. The tendency for forward and futures prices to be approximately unbiased predictors of spot prices means that there is no easy way, no formula, by which an investor may convert expected losses into expected gains.

We shall now consider three broad sets of circumstances in which forward and futures contracts may not be appropriate. First, you might as well place your money on the tables at Las Vegas as in a forward or futures contract that is not part of a hedge. Few investments are not gambles in some degree. But most investments in the money and capital markets, excluding forward and futures contracts, are more likely to win than lose.

Second, we begin with the observation that for a speculator the expected losses on forward and futures contracts are the house's take, but for a hedger they are insurance premiums. However, it is often a mistake to pay for insurance against losses that have inconsequential effects on one's wealth. A case is easily made for paying $200 a year for fire insurance on a house worth $100,000 even though there is only one chance in a thousand that it will be destroyed by fire so that there is an expected loss of $200 − 0.001($100,000) = $100 on the insurance contract. Better a certain payment of $200 a year than even one chance in a thousand of financial ruin. However, there is much less reason for a well-to-do person to pay an annual premium of $200 for theft insurance on a $200 bicycle that has a 50 percent chance of being stolen during the year (so that the expected loss on the insurance contract is $100). The bicycle's theft is a loss that the person can easily bear and *will* bear unless he is so averse to risk that he buys insurance against every conceivable adverse event, however insignificant, until all his wealth has been transferred to insurers. By the same token it is unlikely to be in the interests of a manager to enter into forward or futures contracts in order to hedge interest rate or foreign exchange risks that can easily be borne by his firm.

Finally, although we have illustrated the hedging (insurance) uses of forward and futures contracts, it must be emphasized that these are not the only hedging devices available to firms and individuals. For example, in the case of the Colorado Cheese Company, which is obligated to pay 500,000 marks at the end of the month, the desirability of an offsetting forward or futures contract depends not only on the size of this particular risk relative to the scale of the firm and on management's attitude toward risk but also on other parts of the firm's operation. Colorado Cheese may expect to receive and deliver a variety of foreign currencies during the next month according to a schedule such that the risks of these transactions are offsetting. Overall foreign exchange risk may be unimportant so that special hedges may be unnecessary.[56] Similarly, commercial banks have in the new volatile environment increasingly hedged their interest rate risks by matching the maturities of their assets and liabilities. Much has been written about the potential usefulness of futures contracts to commercial banks; but many have remarked on the reluctance of

---

[56] See Andreas Prindl (1975, Chapter 7) for a discussion of several internal hedging methods available to companies engaged in international business. These methods include flexibility in the currencies in which bills are stated and in which loans are negotiated and, for multinational companies, intrafirm transfers of funds.

banks to enter into these contracts. The explanation probably lies in the already-hedged nature of bank operations.[57] The real usefulness of futures markets lies in insurance against very large relative losses to firms and individuals whose operations are essentially unhedged and for whom less costly forms of insurance are not available—such as insurance against a low price for a farmer's only crop or against a fall in the value of a dollar when an importer is obligated to pay for a very large shipment in a foreign currency or against a rise in interest rates when a nonfinancial firm is planning a large bond issue.

QUESTIONS

1. Suppose that the current (simple annual) yields on 3-month U.S. and U.K. T bills are 16 percent and 8 percent, respectively, and that the dollar value of the pound is expected to rise 1 percent during the next 3 months. How might the British and American T bill and foreign exchange markets adjust to this situation? Present an equilibrium consistent with IRP and discuss the processes by which this equilibrium might be achieved.

2. Considering Exercise 12.2, suppose the Colorado Cheese Company believes the foreign exchange market to be efficient. What should it have done in that market on February 17? Why?

3. You have contracted to make a payment in German marks in 3 months, and you notice that the 3-month forward rate has underpredicted the spot rate in each of the past two periods. Should you use the forward market to hedge exchange risk? Why or why not?

4. Suppose we observe that the one-period dollar/pound forward exchange rate at time $t-1$ (F_{t-1}) bears the following relationship to the spot rate at time t (S_t): $S_t = 1.01 F_{t-1}$.
   What are the implications of this observation for market efficiency? How can you make money in this market?

5. Governments frequently buy and sell foreign exchange for the purpose of smoothing fluctuations in exchange rates. Describe how these actions might interfere with the efficient allocation of resources by causing forward rates to be biased predictors of spot rates.

6. Under what conditions are hedges perfect in futures markets? In forward markets?

7. Discuss the importance of clearinghouses to the liquidity of futures contracts.

8. Were the 1-month forward and futures prices of the German mark on February 17, 1983, consistent with market efficiency?

57 See Familiar Developments in Bank Loan Markets in Chapter 16.

9. Discuss why spreads are normally less risky than other futures transactions. Under what conditions are spreads as risky as other futures transactions?

10. Considering Exercise 12.4, suppose the Cousy Company believes the T bill futures market is efficient. What should it have done in that market on March 25? Why?

PROBLEMS

1. Suppose that the current (simple annual) yields on 3-month U.S. and U.K. T bills are 16 percent and 8 percent, respectively, and that the dollar value of the pound is expected to rise 1 percent during the next 3 months.
   (a) Should you buy U.S. or U.K. bills?
   (b) Given the U.K. T bill yield and the expected change in the exchange rate, at what U.S. T bill yield would you be indifferent between U.S. and U.K. T bills?

2. Using the method of Table 12.3, please confirm the forward percentage premiums on the Canadian dollar in the top-left portion of Table 12.1.

3. Using the method of Table 12.3, please check the forward percentage discounts on the Belgian franc (relative to the dollar) reported in Table 12.1 (c here stands for centime, which is the hundredth part of a franc). (There is a small error in one of the percentages in the table.)

4. Eurocurrency interest rates on Spanish pesos are not shown in Table 12.1. What do you think the 1-month and 3-month Euro-peso rates were?

5. We saw that the lira discount was 5.49 percent at an annual rate for someone who converted dollars to lire in the spot market on February 17, 1982, and simultaneously sold 3-month forward lire for dollars. What was the lira discount (or dollar premium) for someone who held dollars during this period, that is, for someone who converted lire to dollars in the spot market and sold 3-month forward dollars for lire on February 17, 1982?

6. Using the method of Exercise 12.1, find whether there were any arbitrage opportunities through spot and 3-month forward transactions on February 17, 1982, in (a) U.S. dollars and Dutch guilders and (b) U.S. dollars and British pounds.

7. Referring to Table 12.7, what are the minimum initial and maintenance margins as percentages of contract values for (a) the pound sterling when pounds are selling for $2, (b) the Canadian dollar when it is selling for $1, and (c) 90-day T bills? Why do you suppose margins on Canadian dollars are smaller than those on British pounds?

8. Referring to Exercise 12.3, (a) show Colorado Cheese's profit or loss on its futures transactions if spot marks had been selling for

$0.50 on March 15 (and the basis had remained at $0.0027), and (b) show that the company's net cost of marks would have remained at $0.4169 per mark.

Please present your answer in the format used at the end of Exercise 12.3.

9. After reading the section on The Basis, calculate the outcomes of Colorado Cheese's hedge in cases 1 and 2 when the basis falls from $0.0027 on February 17 to 0 on March 15.

    Please use the format of Exercise 12.3 for your answer.

10. Referring to Table 12.9, what would the profit or loss on your spread have been if June and December marks had fallen to $0.39 and $0.40, respectively, on May 10?

    Please present your answer in the format of Table 12.9.

11. Suppose a 90-day T bill futures contract is quoted at 88.00. What are (a) the discount rate, (b) the delivery price, and (c) the yield to maturity on this bill?

12. Confirm the data in case 2 of Exercise 12.4.

13. Suppose the current quarterly yields on 3- and 6-month T bills are 2 and 3 percent, respectively.

    (a) In perfectly efficient markets, what yield should you expect to see on a 3-month T bill futures contract deliverable in 3 months?

    (b) Show that for the futures yield calculated in (a) the 6-month returns on (i) a 6-month cash bill and (ii) 3-month cash and futures bills are the same.

REFERENCES

Michael Adler, "Designing Spreads in Foreign Exchange Contracts and Foreign Exchange Futures," *Journal of Futures Markets,* Winter 1983, pages 355–368.

George Angell, *Winning in the Commodities Market,* Doubleday, Garden City, NY, 1979.

Marcelle Arak, "The Effect of the Tax Treatment of Treasury-bill Futures on Their Rates," *Journal of Futures Markets,* Spring 1983, pages 65–75.

Marcelle Arak and Christopher J. McCurdy, "Interest Rate Futures," Federal Reserve Bank of New York *Quarterly Review,* Winter 1979–1980, pages 33–46.

Richard T. Baillie, Robert E. Lippens, and Patrick C. McMahon, "Testing Rational Expectations and Efficiency in the Foreign Exchange Market," *Econometrica,* May 1983, pages 553–563.

Henry H. Bakken, "Futures Trading—Origin, Development and Present Economic Status," in Erwin A. Gaumitz (ed.), *Futures Trading Seminar,* vol. 3, Mimir, Madison, WI, 1966.

Fischer Black, "The Pricing of Commodity Contracts," *Journal of Financial Economics,* January/March 1976, pages 167–179.

Chicago Board of Trade, *Commodity Trading Manual,* Chicago, 1980.

Chicago Board of Trade, *Financial Instruments Markets: Cash-Futures Relationships,* Chicago, 1980.

Chicago Board of Trade, *Understanding the Delivery Process in Financial Futures,* Chicago, 1980.

Chicago Board of Trade, *An Introduction to Financial Futures,* Chicago, 1981.

Bradford Cornell, "The Relationship between Volume and Price Variability in Futures Markets," *Journal of Futures Markets,* Fall 1981, pages 303–316.

John C. Cox, Jonathan E. Ingersoll, Jr., and Stephen A. Ross, "The Relation between Forward Prices and Futures Prices," *Journal of Financial Economics,* December 1981, pages 321–346.

Ethel de Keyser (ed.), *Guide to World Commodity Markets,* Nichols, NY, 1979.

Michael P. Dooley and Peter Isard, "Capital Controls, Political Risk, and Deviations from Interest-rate Parity," *Journal of Political Economy,* April 1980, pages 370–384.

Gunter Dufey and Ian H. Giddy, *The International Money Market,* Prentice-Hall, Englewood Cliffs, NJ, 1978.

Mark R. Eaker, "Covered Interest Arbitrage: New Measurement and Empirical Results," *Journal of Economics and Business,* Spring/Summer 1980, pages 249–253.

Franklin R. Edwards, "The Clearing Association in Futures Markets: Guarantor and Regulator," *Journal of Futures Markets,* Winter 1983, pages 369–392.

Paul Einzig, *The History of Foreign Exchange,* Macmillan, London, 1962.

A. E. Feavearyear, *The Pound Sterling,* Oxford University Press, Oxford, 1931.

Jacob A. Frenkel, "Flexible Exchange Rates, Prices, and the Role of 'News': Lessons from the 1970s," *Journal of Political Economy,* August 1981, pages 665–705.

Jacob A. Frenkel and Richard M. Levich, "Transaction Costs and Interest Arbitrage: Tranquil versus Turbulent Periods," *Journal of Political Economy,* December 1977, pages 1209–1226.

John Geweke and Edgar Feige, "Some Joint Tests of the Efficiency of Markets for Forward Foreign Exchange," *Review of Economics and Statistics,* August 1979, pages 334–341.

Ian H. Giddy, "Foreign Exchange Options," *Journal of Futures Markets,* Summer 1983, pages 143–166.

Craig S. Hakkio, "Expectations and the Forward Exchange Rate," *International Economic Review,* October 1981, pages 663–678.

Lars P. Hansen and Robert J. Hodrick, "Forward Exchange Rates As Optimal Predictors of Future Spot Rates: An Econometric Analysis," *Journal of Political Economy,* October 1980, pages 829–853.

Thomas A. Hieronymus, *Economics of Futures Trading for Commercial and Personal Profit,* 2nd ed., Commodity Research Bureau, NY, 1977.

International Monetary Market, *Understanding Futures in Foreign Exchange,* Chicago, 1977.

International Monetary Market, *Treasury Bill Futures,* Chicago, 1980.

Laurent L. Jacque, *Management of Foreign Exchange Risk,* Heath, Lexington, MA, 1978.

Robert A. Jarrow and George S. Oldfield, "Forward Contracts and Futures Contracts," *Journal of Financial Economics,* December 1981, pages 373–382.

Roger M. Kubarych, *Foreign Exchange Markets in the United States,* rev. ed., Federal Reserve Bank of New York, New York, 1983.

Richard M. Levich, "Tests of Foreign Exchange Forecasting Models and Market Efficiency," New York University Business School Working Paper 75–88, November 1975.

Allan M. Loosigian, *Interest Rate Futures,* Dow Jones, Princeton, NJ, 1980.

Mark Powers and David Vogel, *Inside the Financial Futures Markets,* Wiley, NY, 1981.

Andreas R. Prindl, *Foreign Exchange Risk,* Wiley, London, 1975.

Richard J. Rendleman and Christopher E. Carabini, "The Efficiency of the Treasury Bill Futures Market," *Journal of Finance,* September 1979, pages 895–914.

Heinz Riehl and Rita M. Rodriguez, *Foreign Exchange Markets: A Guide to Foreign Currency Operations,* McGraw-Hill, NY, 1977.

Edward W. Schwarz, *How to Use Interest Rate Futures Contracts,* Dow Jones-Irwin, Homewood, IL, 1979.

Andrew J. Senchack, Jr., and John C. Easterwood, "Cross Hedging CDs with Treasury Bill Futures," *Journal of Futures Markets,* Winter 1983, pages 429–438.

Richard J. Teweles, Charles V. Harlow, and Herbert L. Stone, *The Commodity Futures Game,* McGraw-Hill, NY, 1974.

D. P. Whiting, *Finance of Foreign Trade and Foreign Exchange,* 2nd ed., MacDonald and Evans, London, 1973.

FIVE

Decision Makers

*"No room! No room!" they cried out
when they saw Alice coming.
"There's plenty of room!" said Alice indignantly,
and she sat down in a large arm-chair
at one end of the table.*

Lewis Carroll, *Alice's Adventures in Wonderland*, ch. 7

AN OVERVIEW OF BORROWERS AND LENDERS: THE NATIONAL INCOME AND FLOW OF FUNDS ACCOUNTS

Saving equals investment.
George Jaszi[1]

Borrowing equals lending.
Stephen P. Taylor[2]

Chapters 14 to 17 describe the saving, investment, borrowing, and lending behavior of the principal private groups that trade the financial instruments discussed in preceding chapters. Governments are considered later, in Chapter 20. The present chapter describes how these groups fit together. The discussion will be framed in terms of the national income and product accounts, which show how households, businesses, and governments acquire and spend income, and the flow of funds accounts, which show where deficit and surplus units borrow and lend. The early portions of the chapter use simple hypothetical accounts to emphasize basic principles and to illustrate the usefulness of the accounts in economic analysis and forecasting. Then, after a look at the borrowing and lending records of households, firms, and governments, actual national income and flow of funds accounts are described in detail to help those engaged in empirical research.

---

1 Director, Bureau of Economic Analysis (U.S. Department of Commerce), the agency responsible for the compilation of the U.S. national income and product accounts.

2 Chief, Flow of Funds Section (Board of Governors of the Federal Reserve System).

SAVING EQUALS INVESTMENT: PRINCIPLES OF NATIONAL INCOME ACCOUNTING

Income consists of payments to factors of production: wages and salaries to labor, rent to land, and interest and profits to capital. The sum of these factor payments is the national income. The national *product,* on the other hand, is the net value of the goods and services produced in the economy during some period of time. The national product equals national income because contributions to output are remunerated to the factors of production. The total value of output must accrue in some proportion or other to those factors; that is, factor payments exhaust the national product. This is an accounting statement, not a theoretical proposition. Regardless of how relative factor payments (the distribution of income) are determined—whether, like Karl Marx you believe that labor gets less than its fair share, like J. P. Morgan you believe that capitalists are exploited, or, as has come to be generally accepted, you believe that college professors are underpaid—the value of output is paid to *someone.*

Saving is income that is not consumed. Since income, or product, consists solely of consumption and investment goods, investment also equals unconsumed income. *Investment* takes the forms of additions to fixed capital and the accumulation of inventories; it is the increase in society's wealth. In the absence of government and foreign sectors these two definitions may be expressed as follows, where S is saving, I is investment, and Y is national income, or product:

(13.1) $$S = Y - C$$

(13.2) $$Y = C + I$$

We see from (13.1) and (13.2) that

(13.3) $$S = I$$

Equation (13.3) is an identity, a truism that follows from definitions (13.1) and (13.2). There is no way that investment can increase unless saving increases by an equal amount. Some people or organizations must save more of their incomes if investment is to be increased. Such a rise in saving may be accomplished, for example, by a reduction in consumption out of a fixed level of income or by an increase in income that exceeds the increase in consumption.

Saving does not have to equal investment for every sector of the economy. But the sum of the savings of all sectors must equal total investment in the economy. This will be shown for an economy that consists of the following four sectors: households, corporations, government, and foreigners. The value of aggregate output, Y, equals the sum of household consumption, C, household investment (mainly houses), I_h, corporate investment (plant, equipment, and inventory accumulation), I_c, government purchases of goods and services, G, and exports, X, less imports, M:

(13.4) $$Y = C + I_h + I_c + G + X - M$$

Equation (13.4) may be rewritten as

(13.5) $$Y + M = C + I_h + I_c + G + X$$

which states that all goods produced or imported into the economy are consumed by households, invested by households and corporations, purchased by the government, or exported.

The value of output, or national income, goes to workers and capitalists as wages and salaries (hereafter simply called "wages"), W, profits, Π, rent, R, and interest, i:[3]

(13.6) $$Y = W + \Pi + R + i$$

The variables in Equation (13.6) are payments to factors of production, that is, remunerations for contributions to output. But we must also take account of two other kinds of money exchanges: *taxes* paid by households and corporations (which we will denote T_h and T_c) and *transfer payments*. Transfers are payments other than taxes that are not in return for contributions to production. Examples of transfers are gifts and welfare payments. We denote the transfer payments in our example as follows (the numbers in parentheses are the dollar values assumed in the numerical example given below):

Net government transfers to households, A_{gh} (290)
Net government transfers to foreigners, A_{gf} (5)
Net household transfers to foreigners, A_{hf} (1)

Any of these values may in principle be negative (for example if gifts from foreigners to U.S. households exceeded those from U.S. house-

---

3 We shall see in Table 13.4 that national income is less than total expenditure mainly because some of society's capital is used up in the production process. These "capital consumption allowances" must be deducted from total expenditures (which equal "gross" product) to obtain income. We abstract from capital consumption allowances and the other differences between gross national product (GNP) and national income in the present simplified example. But we shall see in our discussion of the actual national income and product accounts that capital consumption allowances and other complications do not alter the equality of saving and investment.

holds to foreigners, in which case A_{hf} would be negative), but they have in practice usually been positive.

Now let us calculate the saving of each sector while referring to the numerical example in Table 13.1. We first have to calculate *household disposable income* (Y_h), which is wage, rent, and interest income plus corporate dividends (D) plus transfers received from the government less taxes. (All numbers in Tables 13.1 and 13.2 are billions of dollars.)

(13.7)
$$Y_h = W + R + i + D + A_{gh} - T_h$$
$$= 1{,}820 + 60 + 50 + 60 + 290 - 460 = 1{,}820$$

Y_h is called "disposable personal income" in Table 13.1.

Household saving (S_h) is disposable income less outlays, which in our example consists of consumption expenditures and transfers to foreigners:[4]

(13.8) $S_h = Y_h - C - A_{hf} = 1{,}820 - 1{,}719 - 1 = 100$

Corporate saving (S_c) is simply undistributed profits, that is, profits less taxes less dividends:

(13.9) $S_c = \Pi - T_c - D = 230 - 110 - 60 = 60$

The saving, or surplus, of government (S_g) is tax receipts less government purchases of goods and services less transfers to households and foreigners:

(13.10)
$$S_g = T_h + T_c - G - A_{gh} - A_{gf}$$
$$= 460 + 110 - 305 - 290 - 5 = -30$$

The saving, or current account surplus, of foreigners (S_f) in their dealings with the U.S. is the current account balance of the U.S. with the sign reversed. It is foreign sales to the U.S. (American imports) plus U.S. transfers to foreigners less U.S. sales (exports) to foreigners:

(13.11) $S_f = M - X + A_{hf} + A_{gf} = 320 - 340 + 1 + 5 = -14$

The sum of the savings of our four sectors equals aggregate investment. Substituting Equation (13.7) into Equation (13.8) and adding

---

4 We abstract from interest paid by consumers, shown in the real-world Table 13.4.

Table 13.1 Simplified Hypothetical National Income and Product Accounts, with Net Financial Investment (Billions of Dollars)

Product or Expenditure

Gross national product $(Y)^a$			2,160
Personal consumption expenditures (C)			1,719
Gross private domestic investment $(I)^a$			116
Fixed investment		119	
Nonresidential	79		
Residential	40		
Change in business inventories		-3	
Net exports of goods and services			20
Exports (X)		340	
Imports (M)		320	
Government purchases of goods and services (G)			305

Income

National income $(Y)^a$		2,160
Wages and salaries (W)		1,820
Rental income of persons (R)		60
Corporate profits before tax (Π)		230
Profits tax (T_c)	110	
Profits after tax	120	
Dividends (D)	60	
Undistributed profits (S_c)	60	
Net interest $(i)^b$		50

Relation of National Income and Personal Income

National income (Y)		2,160
Less corporate profits (Π)		230
Plus		
Government transfer payments to persons (A_{gh})		290
Dividends (D)		60
Equals personal income		2,280
Less personal taxes (T_h)		460
Equals disposable personal income (Y_h)		1,820
Less personal outlays		1,720
Personal consumption expenditures (C)	1,719	
Net personal transfer payments to foreigners (A_{hf})	1	
Equals: Personal saving (S_h)		100

Net Financial Investment

	Saving	−	Investment	=	Net financial investment	
Households	100	−	40	=	60	$S_h - I_h = N_h$
Corporations	60	−	76	=	-16	$S_c - I_c = N_c$
Government	-30			=	-30	$S_g \quad\ = N_g$
Foreigners	-14			=	-14	$S_f \quad\ = N_f$
	116	−	116	=	0	$S\ -\ I\ = 0$

a Gross national product equals national income, and gross investment equals net investment, in this example, because we have abstracted from capital consumption allowances, indirect business taxes, business transfer payments, the statistical discrepancy, and subsidies less surplus of government enterprises. This may be seen by comparing Tables 13.1 and 13.4.

b We have assumed net interest to equal personal interest income (so that these two terms in Table 13.4 cancel) and have abstracted from interest paid by consumers in personal outlays.

the result to Equations (13.9) to (13.11) gives

$$
\begin{aligned}
S &= S_h + S_c + S_g + S_f = 100 + 60 - 30 - 14 = 116 \\
&= W + R + i + D + A_{gh} - T_h - C - A_{hf} + \Pi - T_c - D \\
&\quad + T_h + T_c - G - A_{gh} - A_{gf} + M - X + A_{hf} + A_{gf} \\
&= (W + R + \Pi + i) - [C + G + (X - M)] \\
&= Y - (Y - I) = I = 76 + 40 = 116
\end{aligned}
$$

(13.12)

where S and I are aggregate saving and investment. We know from Equations (13.4) and (13.6) that the left-hand term on the next-to-last line of Equation (13.12) is income, Y, and the right-hand term is product less investment, $Y - I$.

ONLY A SLIGHT DIGRESSION: TWO CONCEPTS ESSENTIAL TO THE UNDERSTANDING AND USE OF THE NATIONAL INCOME AND PRODUCT ACCOUNTS (NIPA)

The distinction between accounting identities and equilibrium conditions

Aggregate saving equals aggregate investment at every instant of time. There is no way for this not to be true. The value of output (income) that is not consumed is saved. But the value of output that is not consumed is added to society's wealth as new houses, plant and equipment, and additions to inventories, that is, as investment. However, *desired* saving and investment may not be equal. For example households might surprise businessmen by reducing consumption, that is, by increasing saving. Businessmen may not have planned an increase in investment, but the accumulation of inventories as production runs ahead of consumption represents an unintended increase in investment to match the increase in saving.

Equilibrium requires that desired saving and investment be equal, that the plans of savers be consistent with the plans of investors. Suppose, given the level and distribution of income, that desired saving (S^d) responds positively and desired investment (I^d) responds negatively to interest rates as shown in Figure 13.1. If "the" interest rate is 6 percent, desired saving and investment are equal. But if the rate of interest is 3 percent, desired investment exceeds desired saving. Investors want to borrow more to finance investment projects than savers want to lend. There is an excess demand for funds. There is also an excess demand for goods. In terms of the simple case in Equation (13.1)

(13.13) $S^d = Y - C^d < I^d$ or $I^d + C^d > Y$

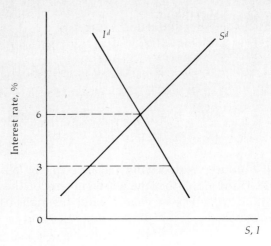

Figure 13.1   Desired saving and investment.

That is, an excess of desired investment over desired saving implies an excess demand for goods; people want to buy more goods ($I^d + C^d$) than are being produced (Y).

Although desires are consistent only in equilibrium, actual saving and investment are always equal. The NIPA numbers reported in the *Survey of Current Business* do not know the difference between planned and unplanned saving and investment. They merely tell us that the quantity of goods bought equals the quantity of goods sold, that actual $C + I$ equals actual Y.[5] Figure 13.1 does not tell us what this quantity will be, but realized $S = I$ should fall somewhere between I^d and S^d as the excess demands for credit and goods lead to credit rationing, queues, back-orders, and unexpected price increases that cause actual purchases of consumption and investment goods to be less than planned.

The distinction between stocks and flows

Flows are variables that change at various rates per unit of time. *Stocks* are without time dimension. Income and product accounts report flows. Income is earned over time. That is, when you tell us that your income is $1,000 we do not know whether you are doing well or badly—reasonably well if the unit of time is 1 week, on the edge of starvation at today's prices if the unit of time is a month. Balance sheets report stocks. When you say you have $1,000 in a checking account or that you owe $300 to Mastercard, you need not specify a unit of time such as "per week" or "per month."[6]

Consider the stock of capital goods, which includes existing industrial plant and equipment, and the flow of investment goods, which

5 Or in the unsimplified case that actual $C + I + G + X - M$ equals actual GNP.

6 See Don Patinkin (1965, pages 515–523) for a review of the literature on stocks and flows.

includes additions to industrial plant and equipment. To say that the American steel industry has 200 blast furnaces is to make a statement about the stock of blast furnaces. But to say that the number of blast furnaces is increasing at the *rate* of 5 per year is to make a statement about the flow of investment in blast furnaces, that is, about additions to the stock of capital goods.[7]

Your wealth, that is, the value of your assets less the value of your liabilities, is a stock. But your saving (or more likely your "dissaving" if you are a student) is a flow. Saving (or dissaving) is the rate at which you add to (or consume) your stock of wealth. Suppose that on August 25, after a profitable summer job and a stake from your parents, you have net wealth (all in a bank account) of $6,000. Between August 25 and May 15 you receive income from a few odd jobs and a few transfers from home at the rate of $1,000 per school year and spend money at the rate of $7,500 per school year. You have saved at the rate of $-$6,500 per school year, and your wealth has fallen from $6,000 to $-$500. Your dissaving has been financed by selling assets (done simply by writing checks when the asset is a checking account) and incurring liabilities, for example, a student loan of $500.

BORROWING EQUALS LENDING: PRINCIPLES OF FLOW OF FUNDS (FOF) ACCOUNTING

THE FOF ACCOUNTS SHOW CHANGES IN BALANCE SHEETS. We know from the preceding section that changes in balance sheet items and other stocks are flows. The FOF accounts show the relationships between the income and expenditure flows in the NIP accounts, on the one hand, and financial flows, on the other hand. They tell us how savings are disposed of (by additions to assets and/or reductions in liabilities) and how dissaving is financed (by reductions in assets and/or increases in liabilities).

We start with *net financial investment* (N) at the bottom of Table 13.1, which is the connecting link between the NIP and FOF accounts. We see in our example that, although households have consumed or given away $100 (in billions) less than their disposable income, they have only $60 available for financial investments because they have spent $40 on investment in residential housing.

Note that, when we write "investment," we mean "real" investment, that is, additions to inventories and the capital stock—houses and plant and equipment. When we mean "financial" investment, that is, the acquisition of pieces of paper, we shall say so.

Moving to corporations, although their saving (undistributed profit) was $60, they have had to scrape together $16 by selling financial

---

7 If we were good monetary economists and therefore fond of metaphors, we might tell a story about the stock of water in a lake augmented by the flow of water from a stream. But you would learn only about lakes and streams, whereas we want you to understand capital and investment.

Table 13.2   Simplified Hypothetical Flow of Funds Accounts (Billions of Dollars)

	House-holds		Nonfinancial Corporations		Govern-ment		Rest of the World		Financial Institu-tions	
	U	S	U	S	U	S	U	S	U	S
1. Saving		100		60		−30		−14		0
2. Real and net financial investment (3 + 7)	100		60		−30		−14		0	
3. Private capital expenditures[a]	40		76							
4. Residential construction	40									
5. Plant and equipment			79							
6. Inventory change			− 3							
7. Net financial investment (8 − 9)	60		−16		−30		−14		0	
8. Financial uses	161		26		3		7		177	
9. Financial sources		101		42		33		21		177
10. Deposits in financial institutions	84		14		3		1			102
11. Money market fund shares	20									20
12. Insurance and pension reserves	55									55
13. Domestic corporate bonds and equities	−8			− 5			3			
14. Foreign bonds and equities	5		8					21	8	
15. Government securities	5		1			33	3		24	
16. Loans from financial institutions		98	47						145	
17. Consumer credit		3	3							

a We have followed the NIPA instead of the FOF practice of not including consumer durables in investment. Also, all residential construction is assumed to be done by households.

assets or issuing financial liabilities because they have spent $76 on plant, equipment, and inventories.

The NIP and FOF accounts treat government saving and net financial investment as synonymous. All government purchases—buildings and roads as well as pencils and paper—are treated as consumption, and none is treated as investment. Similarly, the entire net balance of U.S. transactions with foreigners is assumed to be financial (and none to be real) investment or disinvestment.

Table 13.2 shows one of an infinity of FOF accounts consistent with the NIP accounts in Table 13.1. Just as Table 13.1 is a simplified version of the complete set of NIP accounts presented below in Tables 13.3 to 13.8, Table 13.2 is a simplified version of the complete set of FOF accounts in Table 13.9. The financial markets were called upon to deal with the following problem: Corporations spent $16 more than they took in. The government also ran a deficit of $30, and foreigners were in the red in their dealings with Americans to the extent of $14. These sectors borrow from and lend to each other, but mainly they borrow from households.

However, most household lending is not done directly. We see in the not-far-from-realistic[8] data of Table 13.2 that the preponderance of household lending (159 of 161) to domestic corporations, government, and foreigners was channeled through financial intermediaries, now mentioned for the first time in this chapter. The corporate sector of Table 13.1 has been separated into financial and nonfinancial firms in Table 13.2. The flow-of-funds story told in Table 13.2 is a simple one. Households made money available to other sectors by increasing their deposits in depository institutions (84), buying money market mutual fund shares (20), and paying into life insurance policies and pension funds (55). These financial institutions lent their funds partly to government by buying government securities (24) and partly in loans to nonfinancial businesses (47), but mainly in loans (principally mortgages) back to households (98). For simplicity we have made our financial intermediaries just what the name suggests; they merely receive and hand out money, earning no surplus or deficit and undertaking no real investment.

The sum of the net financial investments of the various sectors is zero. Since net financial investment is net lending (lending less borrowing), this is merely another way of saying that total borrowing equals total lending. Referring to lines 8 and 9 of Table 13.2, we see that the sum of financial uses (lending) equals the sum of financial sources (borrowing). The same point is made by the connection between the FOF and NIP accounts shown at the bottom of Table 13.1. Since net financial investment equals saving minus investment, the equality of aggregate saving and investment implies that aggregate net financial investment is zero.

USES OF THE NATIONAL INCOME AND FLOW OF FUNDS ACCOUNTS

Macroeconomic analysis

Macroeconomic models include two kinds of statements: (1) behavioral and technical relationships, such as consumption and production functions, which describe the responses of households, firms, and governments to changes in incomes, prices, and technical conditions;

---

8 See Table 13.9.

and (2) accounting relationships, pertaining both to particular groups and to the economy as a whole, which impose the conditions that each sector's sources and uses of funds must be equal, that the economy's total saving must equal its investment, and that total borrowing must equal lending. The national income and FOF accounts provide most of the data (nearly all the quantities but not the prices) for both kinds of statements, conveniently in the form of the second. This chapter thus provides the framework of a macroeconomic model, that is, of an explanation of aggregate economic movements and the interrelationships between sectors.[9] The following chapters will complete the system by providing the behavioral and technical relationships of the various sectors.

Forecasting

The national income and FOF accounts are essential to forecasting. They require the forecasts of individual sectors and markets to be consistent. If a financial analyst believes that the federal deficit is going to increase from $30 billion this year to $40 billion next year and wants an idea of how this will affect interest rates and spending by other sectors, he goes to work on a FOF matrix similar to Table 13.2. Where is the money coming from? Households? Businesses? Foreigners? Maybe he thinks that the rise in interest rates due to the increased government borrowing will have the greatest impact on the demand for houses and a somewhat smaller impact on business inventories, meaning that households and businesses buy fewer houses and materials and more government securities. The rise in interest rates may also attract foreign funds to government and private securities in the United States.[10]

Estimated behavioral relationships, such as housing and inventory demand functions, are needed at this point to obtain forecasts of the distribution of impacts on private spending. If residential construction is more sensitive than inventories to interest rates, cutbacks in the former will be a more important source of government receipts than the latter. If private spending in general is highly sensitive to interest rates, only a small rise in rates will be needed to divert funds from private to government uses.

Whatever the sources of funds—reduced spending on houses, inventories, and other goods and securities here and abroad—they must add up to their uses. Events in the various markets and sectors are not independent. The FOF accounts impose the discipline that the forecast of next year's numbers in Table 13.2 will be consistent, that the net financial investments of the sectors sum to zero. The national

---

9 See Patric Hendershott (1977) for the use of the FOF accounts in a macroeconomic model.

10 For the use of the FOF accounts in forecasting see Arnold Sametz and Paul Wachtel (1977) and the annual forecasts of Goldman Sachs and Salomon Brothers.

income accounts are used in a similar fashion to ensure that forecasts of total saving and investment are equal.

BORROWERS AND LENDERS: THE RECORD

We saw in the hypothetical example presented above and will see in the actual case below that the main surplus (lending) sector is households and the main deficit (borrowing) sectors are business and government. Figures 13.2 to 13.5 indicate that this case is typical.

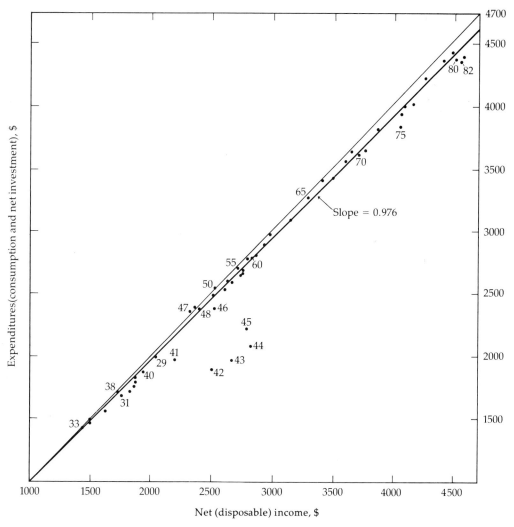

Sources: *National Income and Product Accounts of the U.S., 1929–74* and *Survey of Current Business.*

Figure 13.2   Household real per capita net income and expenditure in 1972 dollars.

Figure 13.2 shows the relationship between annual real per capita household disposable income and expenditure from 1929 to 1982. The thin line between the corners of the chart has a slope of 1; a point on this line means that expenditure equals income. Since expenditure includes both consumption and investment, the distance of a point below the thin line measures household net financial investment in real per capita terms. For example net financial investment in the year indicated by the lowest point, 1933, was close to zero. Household net financial investment during World War II, with high incomes, rationing, and little production of durable goods, was very large.

Apart from World War II the most striking characteristic of household net financial investment has been its stability. The dark line with a slope of 0.976 corresponds to median household expenditures as a proportion of income since 1950. That is, the net financial investment of households as a proportion of disposable income has typically been 2.4 percent since 1950. Variations around this line have been small. More evidence and some reasons for this stability are presented in Chapter 14.

Household spending behavior may be contrasted with the behavior of business and the federal government in Figures 13.3 and 13.4. The line with slope 1.355 in Figure 13.3 corresponds to median annual corporate net investment as a proportion of undistributed profits since 1950. That is, corporations have tended to finance about three-quarters of investment through retained earnings and about one-quarter (0.355/1.355) by sales of stock and increases in debt (mainly borrowing from households either directly or indirectly through financial intermediaries). But these proportions have been volatile. Points to the left of the vertical line correspond to negative retained earnings, which occurred only during 1930 to 1938. Points below the horizontal line indicate negative net investment, that is, most of the 1930s and World War II, when new investment was so small that it was exceeded by the depreciation of plant and equipment.

After very large deficits during World War II and then substantial surpluses immediately after the war, we see from Figure 13.4 that the federal government's spending was a fairly steady proportion of its net income until the mid-1970s. Government net income is total tax and nontax receipts less transfer and interest payments and subsidies plus the surplus of government enterprises. This enables us to compare government purchases of goods and services (G) with what may be considered the government's disposable (or net) income. Notice that in one year, 1931, federal government net income by this definition was negative. [In the example in Equation (13.10) government net income was $275 and expenditure was $305.] Table 13.5 shows federal government and state and local government income and expenditure data separately. The net income and expenditure of the federal government in 1980 were, respectively, $136.7 billion and $198.9

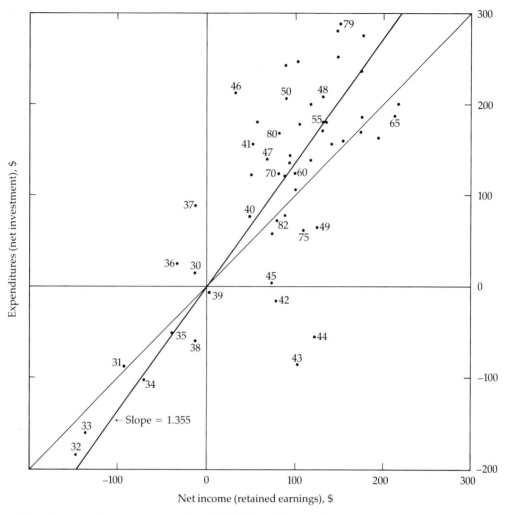

Sources: *National Income and Product Accounts of the U.S., 1929–74* and *Survey of Current Business.*

Figure 13.3   Corporate real per capita net income and expenditure in 1972 dollars.

billion and those of state and local governments were $364.6 billion and $335.7 billion. The ratio of expenditure to net income of 198.9/ 136.7 = 1.455 for the federal government was greater than the median of 1.091 since 1950 but less than the ratios for 1975 to 1976 and 1982. Figures 13.2 to 13.5 differ from the accounts in Tables 13.3 to 13.9 by being in real per capita terms instead of total dollar values, but ratios of spending to income are the same in both cases.

We see from Figure 13.5 that during the 1950s and 1960s the stability of state and local government income-spending behavior was

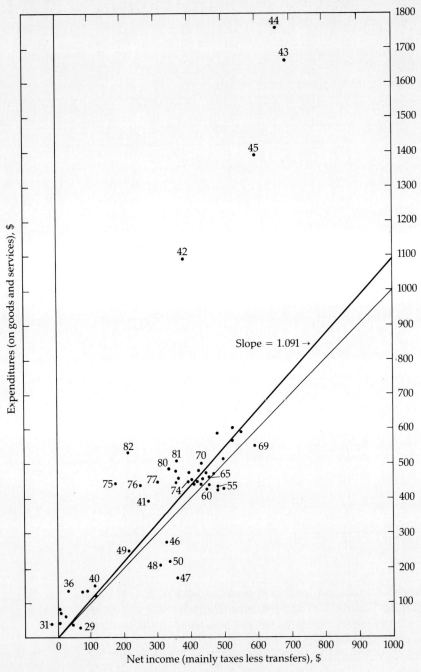

Sources: *National Income and Product Accounts of the U.S., 1929–74* and *Survey of Current Business.*

Figure 13.4   Federal government real per capita net income and expenditure in 1972 dollars.

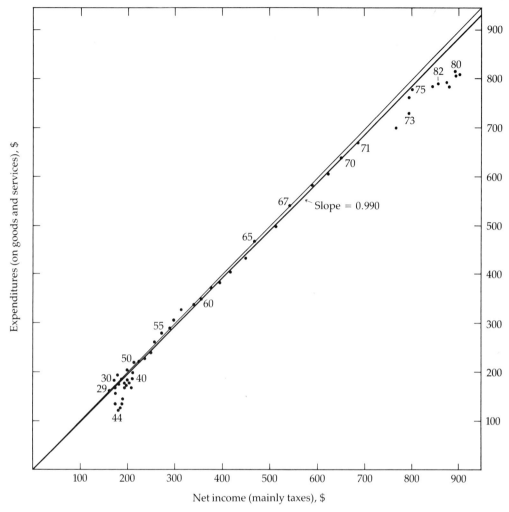

Sources: *National Income and Product Accounts of the U.S., 1929–74* and *Survey of Current Business.*

Figure 13.5   State and local government real per capita net income and expenditure in 1972 dollars.

similar to that of households. But there has been a marked increase in state and local government saving and net financial investment since 1971. That is, state and local governments have joined households as important lenders to the deficit sectors, business and the federal government. This does not mean that state and local governments are as a group in an enviable financial position, however, because most of their current saving, sometimes more than their current saving, has to be placed in employee retirement funds (which are invested in business and government securities).

Table 13.3   National Income and Product, 1980 (Billions of Dollars)

Product or Expenditure

Gross national product			2,626.5
Personal consumption expenditures			1,672.3
Durable goods		211.9	
Nondurable goods and services		1,460.5	
Gross private domestic investment			395.4
Fixed investment		400.8	
Nonresidential	295.4		
Residential	105.3		
Change in business inventories		− 5.3	
Net exports of goods and services			24.2
Exports		340.1	
Imports		315.9	
Government purchases of goods and services			534.6
Federal		198.9	
State and local		335.7	

Income

National income			2,119.5
Wages, salaries, and supplements			1,596.5
Proprietors' income with IVA and CCAdj			130.7
Proprietors' income with IVA		139.4	
CCAdj		− 8.8	
Rental income of persons with CCAdj			31.8
Rental income of persons		64.9	
CCAdj		− 33.1	
Corporate profits with IVA and CCAdj			180.7
Corporate profits with IVA		197.9	
Profits before tax	241.8		
Profits tax	80.7		
Profits after tax	161.1		
Dividends	56.0		
Undistributed profits	105.1		
IVA	− 43.9		
CCAdj	− 17.2		
Net interest			179.9

Note. Components may not sum to totals in Tables 13.3 to 13.9 because of rounding.

Source: *Survey of Current Business,* February 1981, tabs. 1.1, 1.11.

A DETAILED LOOK AT THE NATIONAL INCOME AND PRODUCT ACCOUNTS[11]

The simple hypothetical NIP and FOF accounts presented above are sufficient for an understanding of the general principles of those accounts. But their use in the analysis of actual economic events

11 Based on Richard Ruggles and Nancy Ruggles (1956, 1983) and the publications of the U.S. Department of Commerce listed in the references at the end of the chapter.

requires a more detailed knowledge of the reporting practices of the Department of Commerce and the Federal Reserve (the Fed). The following discussion supplies that detail. It is intended to serve as a reference for those who want to analyze financial flows and their relationships with incomes.

Our discussion of the NIP accounts is directed toward Tables 13.3 to 13.7, which are based on similar tables in the *Survey of Current Business.* We shall encounter a few complications that were excluded previously for reasons of simplicity, such as noncorporate businesses, indirect business taxes, capital consumption allowances, and inventory valuation adjustments. Now to the accounts.

TABLE 13.3, NATIONAL INCOME AND PRODUCT. The product (expenditure) side is self-explanatory and, if GNP were equal to national income, would be virtually identical with the expenditure account in the hypothetical example in Table 13.1. However, the income accruing to factors of production (national income) is significantly less than the value of goods and services produced (GNP). The reasons for this will be discussed in connection with Table 13.4. For the present we are concerned with the lower half of Table 13.3, which lists the components of national income. Some of these components require explanation.

Supplements to wages and salaries are mainly employer contributions for social security, workman's compensation, unemployment insurance, and private pension funds.

Proprietors' income consists of the monetary earnings and income in kind of partnerships and sole proprietorships.

Inventory valuation adjustment (IVA) is the change in inventories valued at current market prices less the change in inventories reported by business (book value). During periods of inflation prevailing historical-cost accounting procedures understate costs and overstate profits by valuing goods sold at acquisition costs rather than current market values. The IVA is required for consistency of the NIP accounts, which try to express all forms of income and product in current value terms.

Capital consumption allowances (CCA) are depreciation charges and damages to fixed capital. They are the charges made by business for the current consumption of capital goods. We shall not run into CCA until Table 13.4. But we must know the meaning of CCA in order to appreciate its adjustment, CCAdj.

Capital consumption adjustment (CCAdj) is the difference between CCA, which is based on tax returns, and the Commerce Department's estimate of true capital consumption, which is based on estimates of economic service lives and replacement costs. During periods of inflation, depreciation allowances based on historical costs understate replacement costs and therefore overstate profits. The

Table 13.4   Relationship of Gross National Product, National Income, and Personal Income, 1980 (Billions of Dollars)

Gross National Product		2,626.5
Less		
Capital consumption allowance		287.3
Indirect business taxes		212.2
Business transfer payments		10.5
Statistical discrepancy		1.7
Plus subsidies less surplus of government enterprises		4.6
Equals national income		2,119.5
Less		
Corporate profits with IVA and CCAdj		180.7
Net interest		179.9
Contributions for social insurance		203.7
Plus		
Government transfer payments to persons		283.8
Personal interest income		256.2
Personal dividend income		54.4
Business transfer payments		10.5
Equals personal income		2,160.2
Less personal taxes		338.6
Equals disposable personal income		1,821.6
Less		
Personal outlays		1,719.8
Personal consumption expenditures	1,672.3	
Interest paid by consumers	46.4	
Net personal transfer payments to foreigners	1.1	
Equals net personal saving		101.8

Source: *Survey of Current Business,* February 1981, tabs. 1.7, 2.1.

main purpose of CCAdj is to do for fixed capital what IVA does for inventories, that is, to express all quantities in current market values.

Rental income of persons with CCAdj includes (1) the monetary earnings of persons from the rental of property, except the income of persons primarily engaged in the real estate business (which is included in proprietors' income or corporate profits), (2) the imputed net rental income of owner-occupants of nonfarm dwellings, and (3) royalties received by persons from patents, copyrights, and rights to natural resources. Item (2) may be explained as follows: Some units of fixed capital (blast furnaces, for example) produce streams of output (iron) that are part of GNP and generate income for workers and owners. Other units of fixed capital, such as houses, produce streams of services (shelter) for which people are willing to pay rent. Rent is also part of the national income. Since owner-occupied houses produce services that may be considered income to their owners, the Department of Commerce counts the estimated rental value of these dwellings as part of national income.

If IVA and CCAdj were zero, all that we should need to know about *corporate profits* would be the reported amount (241.8), which is allocated to three uses: *profits taxes* (80.7), *dividends* (56.0), and *undistributed profits,* or retained earnings (105.1). However, because of IVA (−43.9) and CCAdj (−17.2), corporate profits in current market values are 180.7.

Net interest is the excess of interest payments of domestic and foreign businesses over their interest receipts and therefore represents claims on product not already included in wages, rent, and profits.

We are interested in the saving, investment, and financial behavior of each sector of the economy. Let's begin with the saving of the largest group, households. The derivation of household, or personal, saving is normally set forth in the NIP accounts in the format of Table 13.4, which we now discuss.

TABLE 13.4, RELATIONSHIP OF GROSS NATIONAL PRODUCT, NATIONAL INCOME, AND PERSONAL INCOME. *Gross national product (GNP)* is the market value of goods and services produced in the economy during some period. *National income,* on the other hand, is the cost of employing labor and other factors of production. The national product is allocated to the factors of production as wages and salaries, profits, rent, and interest. But total expenditures on goods (GNP) differ from total payments to factors of production for four reasons: (1) Some of the economy's capital stock deteriorates or is used up. This deprecia- tion of capital (CCA) must be deducted from GNP in order to arrive at the net product available to the factors of production.[12] (2) *Indirect business taxes* consist mainly of sales and excise taxes. They include all business taxes except corporate profits taxes. Since these taxes contribute to the costs of goods and therefore to GNP but are not paid to factors of production, they must be deducted from GNP in the process of deriving national income. (3) *Business transfer payments* are mainly corporate gifts to nonprofit institutions and deductions for consumer bad debts. These are not payments to factors of production and must therefore be deducted from business receipts to obtain national income. (4) *Government subsidies* are contributions to income that are not part of the costs of producing goods. Consequently these subsidies must be *added* to GNP to obtain national income. Surpluses of *government enterprises* operate in the opposite direction by withdrawing income from the private sector. These two items are reported in the NIP accounts as the difference shown in Table 13.4—subsidies less current surplus of government enterprises.

The four items in the preceding paragraph exhaust the *conceptual* differences between GNP and national income. But there is a fifth difference between the *reported* values of these variables. GNP is estimated in two different ways: first by adding up estimated expend- itures and second by adding up estimated payments to factors of production and then adjusting for items 1 to 4 described above. It

---

12 An often-used concept not shown in Table 13.4 is *net national product*, NNP = GNP − CCA = 2,339.2.

Table 13.5   Government Receipts and Expenditures, 1980

	Federal	State and Local	Total Government
Receipts	539.4	383.7	923.1
Personal tax and nontax receipts	257.8	80.7	338.5
Corporate profits taxes	68.7	11.9	80.7
Indirect business taxes	40.6	171.6	212.2
Social insurance contributions	172.2	31.5	203.7
Grants in aid from federal government	—	87.9	87.9
Expenditures	601.6	354.8	956.4
Purchases of goods and services	198.9	335.7	534.6
Transfer payments	249.4	38.9	288.3
To persons	244.9	38.9	283.8
To foreigners	4.5	0	4.5
Grants in aid to state and local governments	87.9	—	87.9
Net interest paid	53.4	− 12.4	41.0
Subsidies less current surplus of government enterprises	12.0	− 7.4	4.6
Surplus or deficit (−)	− 62.3	28.8	− 33.4

Source: *Survey of Current Business,* February 1981, tabs. 3.2, 3.3.

would be surprising if the two methods of estimation gave identical results. The *statistical discrepancy* is the difference between them.

Now let us derive *personal income* from national income. First deduct corporate profits (180.7), and add the dividends paid to persons (54.4). Then replace net interest paid by domestic and foreign business (179.9) with the interest income accruing to persons (256.2). Finally deduct social security taxes (203.7), and add government and business transfer payments (283.8 + 10.5) to persons. This gives personal income, which may also be expressed as the following sum based on data from Tables 13.3 and 13.4:

Wages, salaries, and supplements	1,596.5
+ Proprietors' income with IVA and CCAdj	+ 130.7
+ Rental income of persons with CCAdj	+ 31.8
+ Personal dividend income	+ 54.4
+ Interest income of persons	+ 256.2
+ Transfer payments to persons	+ 294.3
− Contributions for social insurance	− 203.7
= Personal income	=2,160.2

Net personal saving is obtained from personal income by first deducting *personal taxes* to get *disposable personal income* and then subtracting *personal outlays,* which consist mainly of personal consumption expenditures.

Table 13.6   Foreign Transactions, 1980 (Billions of Dollars)

Receipts from foreigners		341.3
Exports of goods and services	340.1	
Capital grants received by U.S. (net)	1.1	
Payments to foreigners		334.3
Imports of goods and services	315.9	
Transfer payments (net)	5.6	
From persons (net)	1.1	
From government (net)	4.5	
Interest paid by government to foreigners	12.7	
Net foreign investment		7.0

Source: *Survey of Current Business,* February 1981, tab. 4.1.

Net corporate saving may be derived from Table 13.3 and is undistributed profits less IVA and CCAdj: 105.1 − 43.9 − 17.2 = 44.0.

THE SAVINGS OF GOVERNMENT AND FOREIGNERS (IN THEIR DEALINGS WITH THE U.S.) ARE SHOWN IN TABLES 13.5 AND 13.6. The NIP accounts show government saving simply as the government surplus, which is the excess of receipts over expenditures. In a similar fashion, foreign saving with respect to the U.S. is the excess of the receipts of foreigners from Americans (334.3) less their payments to Americans (341.3) and is therefore the negative of U.S. net foreign investment (−7.0).

TABLE 13.7, GROSS SAVING AND INVESTMENT. The savings of the private and government sectors are added up in Table 13.7 to give *gross*

Table 13.7   Gross Saving and Investment (NIPA), 1980 (Billions of Dollars)

Gross saving			400.7
Gross private saving			433.1
Net personal saving		101.8	
Undistributed corporate profits with IVA and CCAdj		44.0	
Undistributed profits	105.1		
IVA	− 43.9		
CCAdj	− 17.2		
Corporate CCA with CCAdj		175.4	
Noncorporate CCA with CCAdj		111.8	
Government surplus or deficit (−)			− 33.4
Capital grants received by U.S. (net)			1.1
Gross investment			402.5
Gross private domestic investment			395.4
Net foreign investment			7.0
Statistical discrepancy			1.7

Source: *Survey of Current Business,* February 1981, tab. 5.1.

Table 13.8   Gross Saving (FOF), 1980: Reconciliation of the NIP and FOF Accounts (Billions of Dollars)

From NIPA Personal to FOF Household	
Net personal saving (NIPA)	101.8
Government insurance credits	30.7
Capital gains dividends	1.4
Net durables in consumption	33.8
CCA (NIPA) (housing)	52.7
CCA (FOF) (durables)	178.1
Gross household saving (FOF)	398.5

Government	
Surplus (NIPA)	−33.4
Less insurance credits	−30.7
Plus surplus of government agencies	+ 0.9
Gross saving (FOF)	−63.1

Foreign	
Less U.S. net foreign investment	−7.0
Plus net capital grants	1.1
Gross saving by foreigners (FOF)	−5.9

From NIPA Corporate to FOF Business	
Undistributed corporate profits with IVA and CCAdj	44.0
Corporate CCA	175.4
Noncorporate business CCA	59.1
Gross business saving (FOF)	278.5
Nonfinancial business	259.5
Commercial banks and monetary authorities	5.0
Nonbank financial institutions	14.0

Source: Federal Reserve Board, *Flow of Funds Accounts,* February 1981.

saving, which is the difference between the gross output of the economy (GNP) and the current consumption of persons and governments. Gross saving is the sum of net personal saving (101.8), net corporate saving (44.0), adjusted capital consumption allowances (175.4 + 111.8),[13] the government surplus (−33.4), and net capital grants (1.1). The last item consists of allocations to the U.S. of special drawing rights (SDRs) created and distributed by the International Monetary Fund. *Gross investment* is the sum of gross private domestic investment (395.4) and the accumulation of claims against foreigners, that is, net foreign investment (7.0). Gross saving and investment are

13 Net saving and investment are obtained by deducting adjusted capital consumption allowances from gross saving and investment.

conceptually equal. The difference between their estimated values (1.7) is the same statistical discrepancy that appeared in Table 13.4 and is the difference between estimates of the income and product sides of the NIP accounts.

In summary we see from the actual NIP accounts that (except for the statistical discrepancy) saving still equals investment. But there is a difference between Table 13.7 and our previous simplified example, which treated the negative of U.S. net foreign investment as foreign saving. According to that approach, the estimated gross saving in Table 13.7 is $400.7 - 7.0 = 393.7$, and estimated gross investment is 395.4.

A DETAILED LOOK AT THE FLOW OF FUNDS ACCOUNTS[14]

Before analyzing flows of funds we must take account of the adjustments made by the FOF people to the savings measures reported in the NIP accounts. The most important difference between the NIP and FOF accounts is the treatment of consumer durables. Expenditures on consumer durables are treated as consumption in the NIP accounts but as investment in the FOF accounts. The top portion of Table 13.8 shows that the FOF accounts add consumer purchases of durable goods (211.9) to the NIPA measure of consumer saving; 178.1 of this amount is allocated to the capital consumption of consumer durables, and 33.8 represents the net increase in the stock of consumer durables.

Also notice that *noncorporate CCA* (111.8) in the NIPA Table 13.7 has been allocated between households for the depreciation of houses (52.7) and noncorporate business for the *depreciation of plant and equipment* (59.1).[15]

Another large item is the accumulation of household claims against government life insurance and retirement funds. Unlike the NIP accounts, the FOF accounts treat this item, called *government insurance credits* in Table 13.8, as a household asset and a government liability. The final adjustment to household saving is the addition of *capital gains dividends* of open-end investment companies, which is treated in the FOF accounts as a dividend component of personal income.

Government saving in the FOF accounts is obtained from the surplus reported in Table 13.5 (-33.4) by subtracting the household insurance credits (-30.7) discussed above and adding the *surplus of federal government credit agencies* (0.9).

---

14 Based on Federal Reserve Board (1980).

15 Deducting CCA for housing and durables, net household saving in the FOF accounts is 167.7, compared with 101.8 in the NIP accounts.

Table 13.9   Summary of FOF Accounts, 1980 (Billions of Dollars)

	Sector							
	House-holds		Non-Financial Business		Govern-ment		Rest of the World	
Transaction Category	U	S	U	S	U	S	U	S
1. Gross saving		398.5		259.5		− 63.1		− 5.9
2. Capital consumption		230.8		225.0				
3. Net saving		167.7		34.5		− 63.1		− 5.9
4. Real and net financial investment (5 + 11)	456.1		228.1		−71.9		−42.1	
5. Private capital expenditures	305.4		299.1		− 6.5			
6. Consumer durables	211.9							
7. Residential construction	86.1		19.4					
8. Plant and equipment	7.4		278.5					
9. Inventory change			− 5.3					
10. Mineral rights			6.5		− 6.5			
11. Net financial investment (12 − 13)	150.7		− 71.0		−65.4		−42.1	
12. Financial uses	259.4		67.1		97.9		22.2	
13. Financial sources		108.8		138.1		163.3		64.3
14. Gold and official foreign exchange					4.3		1.1	8.0
15. Treasury currency						1.3		
16. Demand deposits and currency								
17. Private domestic	1.9		4.8		− 0.2			
18. Foreign							0.5	
19. U.S. government					− 3.3			
20. Time and savings accounts								
21. At commercial banks	70.5		5.4		− 0.2		1.3	
22. At savings institutions	56.2							
23. Fed funds and security RPs			3.6		3.0			
24. Money market fund shares	29.2							
25. Life insurance reserves	12.0					0.5		
26. Pension fund reserves	73.7					8.7		
27. Net interbank claims							−21.8	
28. Corporate equities	− 7.0			11.4			5.3	2.2
29. Credit market instruments								
30. U.S. Treasury securities	15.7		0.4		10.6	79.8	9.4	
31. Federal agency securities	3.0		0.5		9.1	47.1		
32. State and local government securities	− 1.8		− 0.3	2.5	0.2	19.8		
33. Corporate and foreign bonds	5.4			27.6			2.9	0.8
34. Mortgages	12.9	84.1		41.7	49.3	− 0.1		
35. Consumer credit		3.1	1.9					
36. Bank loans		5.1		32.8				11.8
37. Open-market paper	− 10.3		7.9	5.8			4.4	10.1
38. Other loans		8.5		11.0	25.8	1.0		5.0
39. Security credit	3.7	5.1						
40. Trade credit		1.4	16.4	17.5	3.4	3.4	2.5	1.8
41. Taxes payable				− 7.3	− 5.2			
42. Equity in noncorporate business	− 13.9			− 13.9				
43. Miscellaneous	8.3	1.5	26.5	9.1	1.1	1.8	16.6	24.6
44. Sector discrepancies (1 − 4)	− 57.6		31.4		8.8		36.2	

Source: Federal Reserve Board, *Flow of Funds Accounts*, February 1981.

Table 13.9   (continued)

	Commercial Banks and Monetary Authorities		Nonbank Financial Institutions		All Sectors		Discrepancy
Transaction Category	U	S	U	S	U	S	U
1. Gross saving		5.0		14.0		608.0	
2. Capital consumption		4.3		5.3		465.4	
3. Net saving		0.7		8.7		142.6	
4. Real and net financial investment (5 + 11)	14.6		12.7		597.5		10.6
5. Private capital expenditures	6.1		3.2		607.3		0.8
6. Consumer durables					211.9		
7. Residential construction			− 0.2		105.3		
8. Plant and equipment	6.1		3.4		295.4		
9. Inventory change					− 5.3		
10. Mineral rights							
11. Net financial investment (12 − 13)	8.5		9.5				9.8
12. Financial uses	114.8		217.2		778.7		
13. Financial sources		106.3		207.7		788.5	
14. Gold and official foreign exchange	2.6				8.0	8.0	
15. Treasury currency	1.1				1.1	1.3	0.2
16. Demand deposits and currency							
17. Private domestic	0.6	10.9	2.5		9.6	10.9	1.3
18. Foreign		0.6			0.5	0.6	0.1
19. U.S. government		− 3.1			− 3.3	− 3.1	0.2
20. Time and savings accounts							
21. At commercial banks		97.8	20.8		97.8	97.8	
22. At savings institutions			− 0.8	55.4	55.4	55.4	
23. Fed funds and security RPs		10.9	0.7	2.4	7.3	13.3	6.0
24. Money market fund shares				29.2	29.2	29.2	
25. Life insurance reserves				11.5	12.0	12.0	
26. Pension fund reserves				65.0	73.7	73.7	
27. Net interbank claims	− 2.4	− 26.0			− 24.2	− 26.0	− 1.8
28. Corporate equities		0.4	18.7	3.1	17.0	17.0	
29. Credit market instruments							
30. U.S. Treasury securities	20.9		22.9		79.8	79.8	
31. Federal agency securities	8.3		26.2		47.1	47.1	
32. State and local government securities	15.5		8.5		22.2	22.2	
33. Corporate and foreign bonds	1.0	0.2	26.3	7.0	35.6	35.6	
34. Mortgages	19.4		43.2	− 0.9	124.8	124.8	
35. Consumer credit	− 9.7		10.9		3.1	3.1	
36. Bank loans	50.7			1.0	50.7	50.7	
37. Open-market paper	1.8	5.6	17.5	− 0.2	21.4	21.4	
38. Other loans			6.7	7.1	32.5	32.5	
39. Security credit	− 0.1		5.0	3.6	8.7	8.7	
40. Trade credit			1.8		24.1	24.1	
41. Taxes payable		0.5		3.1	− 5.2	− 3.7	1.5
42. Equity in noncorporate business					− 13.9	− 13.9	
43. Miscellaneous	5.1	8.8	6.3	20.3	63.8	66.0	2.2
44. Sector discrepancies (1 − 4)	− 9.6		1.4		10.6		10.6

Table 13.10   Explanation of Selected Categories in Table 13.9

Sector Categories

Households also include personal trusts and nonprofit organizations.

Nonfinancial business is the sum of three categories reported in the FOF accounts: farm business, nonfarm noncorporate business, and corporate nonfinancial business.

Government includes state and local government general funds, the federal government, and federally sponsored credit agencies and mortgage pools.

Rest of the world shows the international transactions of the U.S.

Commercial banks include all banks that have head offices in the fifty states (domestic banks), domestic affiliates of banks (mainly holding-company parents), foreign banking offices in the U.S., and banks in U.S. territories and possessions. *Monetary authorities* include the Fed and certain monetary (gold, silver, and currency) accounts of the U.S. Treasury.

Nonbank financial institutions include savings and loan associations, mutual savings banks, credit unions, life insurance companies, private pension funds, state and local government employee retirement funds, other (such as fire and casualty) insurance companies, finance companies, real estate investment trusts, open-end investment companies (mutual funds), money market funds, and security brokers and dealers.

Financial Transaction Categories

Real and net financial investment (item 4), which is the sum of *private capital expenditures* (5) and *net financial investment* (11), is called "gross investment" in the FOF accounts. We have renamed it to avoid confusion with gross investment as used in the NIP accounts, which is identical to private capital expenditures less consumer durables.

Private domestic demand deposits and currency (17) has a discrepancy that is mainly mail float, that is, checks that have not yet entered the banking system's clearing process.

Fed funds and security RPs (23) contain a discrepancy because the net borrowing by banks is larger than the lending reported by nonbanks.

State and local government securities (32) show an item owed by nonfinancial business, which consists of tax-exempt issues by state and local government agencies that finance projects for corporations, with payment guaranteed by the corporations.

Mortgages (34) include nonfinancial business liabilities for home mortgages, which are construction loans on work in process; the nonbank financial liability is loans in process in savings and loan balance sheets, which is an offset against mortgages in their assets that have not yet been disbursed.

Open-market paper (37) is commercial paper and bankers' acceptances.

Other loans (38) to nonbank financial institutions are Federal Home Loan Bank advances to savings and loans.

Security credit (39) consists mainly of loans by brokers and dealers to their customers and customer balances with brokers and dealers.

Miscellaneous financial claims (43) include direct foreign investment by nonfinancial business and direct investment in the United States by foreigners.

Source: Federal Reserve Board (1980).

The saving of foreigners in their dealings with the U.S. (-5.9) is their net accumulation of claims against Americans. This is shown in the FOF accounts as the negative of U.S. net foreign investment (-7.0) from Table 13.6 plus the International Monetary Fund's allocation of SDRs (1.1) to the U.S.

We now, at long last, arrive at our destination, the FOF accounts in

Table 13.9. The reader should refer to Table 13.10 for explanations of the items that may not be clear from the brief listings in Table 13.9. The following discussion is limited to a summary of the principal financial flows—sources (S) and uses (U) of funds—in 1980.

We see from line 11 of Table 13.9 that household net financial investment, in billions of dollars, was 150.7, which was the difference (with a rounding error) between household increases in assets and liabilities of 259.4 and 108.8. The main asset increases were accounts in depository institutions (1.9 + 70.5 + 56.2 = 128.6), life insurance and pension funds (12.0 + 73.7 = 85.7), money market fund shares (29.2), and government securities (15.7 + 3.0 − 1.8 = 16.9). Households reduced their holdings of corporate stock (−7.0), interests in noncorporate business (−13.9), and open-market paper, that is, commercial paper and bankers' acceptances (−10.3). By far the largest increase in household liabilities was mortgages (84.1).

Household lending to banks and other financial institutions (remember the lending to depository institutions, life insurance companies, pension funds, and money market funds totaling 243.5, to which we should add the 3.7 of "security credit," that is, balances with brokers and dealers) enabled those institutions to be the main sources of credit to the deficit sectors: for example, 20.9 + 8.3 + 22.9 + 26.2 = 78.3 in purchases of federal government securities, 32.8 in bank loans to business, and 11.8 in bank loans to foreigners.

SUMMARY: THE DOMINANT CHARACTERISTICS OF AMERICAN FINANCIAL MARKETS

1. The principal savers and lenders are households and state and local governments. These sectors are also the most stable in their behavior. The saving and lending of state and local governments are mainly in the interests of employee pension funds.

2. The main dissavers and borrowers are business and the federal government. These sectors are also the most volatile in their behavior.

3. Most of the funds supplied by surplus units (households and state and local governments) to deficit units (business and the federal government) are channeled through financial institutions. This was illustrated by the hypothetical case in Table 13.2, in which 159/161 of the increase in household assets was directed to financial institutions, and in the actual case in Table 13.9, in which the analogous ratio was 247.2/259.4.

4. Governments, especially the federal government, are also important financial intermediaries, as shown in Table 13.9 by the large volumes of mortgages (49.3) and "other loans" (25.8) extended by governments.

QUESTIONS

1. The Department of Commerce (NIPA) counts purchases of consumer durables (toasters and cars) as consumption along with food and clothing. But the Fed (FOF) likes to count consumer durables as investment along with houses and blast furnaces. Which approach, in your opinion, is better?
2. Are transfer payments part of national income? Why or why not?
3. Suppose corporations and the federal government ran surpluses. How, in detail, might this affect the asset and liability accumulations of households in Table 13.2? (There are many possible answers. But all correct answers must "add up"; that is, $S = I$, and $N = 0$.)
4. Are actual saving and investment in Figure 13.1 likely to be closer to I^d or to S^d when the interest rate is 3 percent? Why?
5. Which of the following variables are stocks and which are flows: investment, rent, transfer payments, demand deposits, and net financial investment? Explain your answers.
6. Discuss the long-term changes in the total borrowing and lending of households, business, and the federal and state and local governments.

The following questions ask the student to apply the material learned in previous chapters to the analysis of the FOF accounts in Table 13.9:

7. As ceilings on interest rates payable on accounts at depository institutions are phased out, what is likely to happen to the variables on lines 17 and 18, 21 to 24, and 37 in Table 13.9? (See Chapters 2, 3, and 9.)
8. Notice **(a)** the net change in the open-market paper liabilities of U.S. nonfinancial business in Table 13.9 and **(b)** the change in inventories in Table 13.3 (also line 9 of Table 13.9) during the recession year of 1980. Is there a connection between (a) and (b)? (See Chapter 8.)

PROBLEMS

1. Using the same income, expenditure, asset, and liability items that were used in the hypothetical example of Tables 13.1 and 13.2, construct a set of FOF accounts without financial institutions that is consistent with the following income and expenditure flows (see the hint at the end of question 3). Discuss your flows of funds.

$C = 200$	$M = 32$	$\Pi = 20$	$T_c = 8$
$I_h = 6$	$G = 22$	$i = 4$	$A_{gh} = 30$
$I_c = 14$	$W = 210$	$D = 5$	$A_{gf} = 2$
$X = 30$	$R = 6$	$T_h = 40$	$A_{hf} = -1$

2. Using the data in problem 1, construct and discuss a set of FOF accounts in which financial institutions are important.

3. Suppose there is a large federal tax cut and small changes in federal expenditures such that $T_h = 30$, $A_{gh} = 28$, and $A_{gf} = 1$. Other data are identical with those in problem 1. Starting with the FOF accounts constructed for problem 2, show and discuss how flows of funds might be affected by these changes in federal revenues and expenditures.

REFERENCES

Federal Reserve Board, *Introduction to Flow of Funds,* June 1980.

Goldman Sachs, *The Pocket Chartroom,* New York, bimonthly.

Patric H. Hendershott, *Understanding Capital Markets,* vol. 1: *A Flow-of-funds Financial Model,* Heath, Lexington, MA, 1977.

Don Patinkin, *Money, Interest, and Prices,* 2nd ed., Harper & Row, New York, 1965.

Richard Ruggles and Nancy D. Ruggles, *An Introduction to National Income and Income Analysis,* 2nd ed., McGraw-Hill, New York, 1956.

Richard Ruggles and Nancy D. Ruggles, "The United States National Income Accounts, 1947–1977: Their Conceptual Basis and Evolution," in Murray F. Foss (ed.), *The U.S. National Income and Product Accounts: Selected Topics,* University of Chicago Press, Chicago, 1983.

Salomon Brothers, *Prospects for the Credit Markets,* New York, annual.

Arnold W. Sametz and Paul Wachtel (eds.), *Understanding Capital Markets,* vol. 2: *The Financial Environment and the Flow of Funds in the Next Decade,* Heath, Lexington, MA, 1977.

U.S. Department of Commerce, *National Income,* Washington, 1954.

U.S. Department of Commerce, *Business Statistics,* Washington, 1979.

HOUSEHOLDS

It may be observed in general, that the future is purchased by the present. It is not possible to secure distant or permanent happiness but by the forbearance of some immediate gratification.
Samuel Johnson, *The Rambler,* no. 178

This chapter begins our analyses of the main borrowing and lending groups in the U.S. economy. We start with the largest sector, households, because it is the easiest to understand. The spending behavior of households is quite stable and appears to be rational and otherwise consistent with traditional economic theory. Consequently households provide a convenient vehicle for the development of the theoretical tools that will also prove useful in the analysis of other sectors. The most important of those tools is the principle of constrained maximization. Most households strive to forecast their future income streams and to formulate reasonably steady consumption plans that will give them the greatest possible enjoyment over their lifetimes subject to the constraint imposed by their often highly variable incomes.

The chapter is laid out as follows: We present a theory of household consumption, borrowing, and lending decisions and then show how those decisions interact to determine the real rate of interest. Finally the empirical implications of our simple theory are compared with observed household behavior.

THE CONSUMPTION, SAVING, AND BORROWING (OR LENDING) PLAN

Assumptions

We shall examine household decisions within a framework that is simple but captures the essential elements of those decisions. The framework is made manageable by the following simplifying assumptions:

1. The household's plan considers only two points in time, the present date t_1 and a future date t_2. We refer to the interval between t_1 and t_2 as a period.

2. The household receives income and buys consumption goods on both dates but buys or sells bonds only on the first date. All securities have one-period maturities.

3. Decisions affecting income have already been made. Household income earners have jobs that pay wages or salaries in amounts that are known for both the current and the future dates.

4. Households spend income in only two ways: on consumption goods and bonds. Consumption goods are quickly used up so that goods bought at t_1 cannot serve as investments.

5. All current and future values affecting the plan are known with certainty, including the income stream, prices of consumption goods, and the rate of return on bonds.

6. There are no taxes, and borrowing and lending rates are equal. Households can borrow (issue bonds) as well as lend (buy bonds) at the rate of interest R.

The set of consumption opportunities (the budget constraint)

The household looks ahead only one period and knows its current and future dollar incomes, Y_1 and Y_2, and the rate of return on bonds, R. We need no time subscript on R because we consider bond purchases on only one date, the beginning of the period. The household is interested in current consumption and future consumption, which in dollar values are C_1 and C_2. Since t_2 is the end of the planning horizon, the household plans to consume all the resources available to it at that time. Its consumption expenditures at time t_2 are therefore

(14.1) $$C_2 = (Y_1 - C_1)(1 + R) + Y_2$$

For example suppose after-tax incomes are $Y_1 = Y_2 = \$1,000$, R is 1 percent per period, and the household spends $C_1 = \$900$ on consumption goods at time t_1. This means that

$$C_2 = (\$1,000 - \$900)(1.01) + \$1,000 = \$1,101$$

is available for consumption at t_2—$\$1,000$ from income at t_2 and $\$101$ from the investment of the saving at t_1 in bonds yielding 1 percent.

If the household had spent more than its income on the first date, say, $\$1,100$, it would have had

$$C_2 = (\$1,000 - \$1,100)(1.01) + \$1,000 = \$899$$

available for consumption at t_2—$\$1,000$ from income at t_2 less the repayment of $\$101$ principal and interest.

We must make an adjustment to Equation (14.1) because consumers are interested not in dollar values of consumption but in *quantities* of goods consumed. Let those quantities be expressed by lower-case letters, c_1 and c_2, and let the prices of a unit of consumption on the two dates be P_1 and P_2. Therefore $C_1 = P_1 c_1$ and $C_2 = P_2 c_2$. If the household consumes only one commodity, for example, potatoes as in Ireland before the famine, then P_1 and P_2 are the prices per unit (say, a bushel) of potatoes on the two dates. Alternatively we could assume that the household consumes goods in baskets whose contents do not change over time and that P_1 and P_2 are the prices per basket on dates t_1 and t_2.

Using these prices, the real income stream is $y_1 = Y_1/P_1$ and $y_2 = Y_2/P_2$. For example, if $Y_1 = Y_2 = \$1,000$, $P_1 = \$1$, and $P_2 = \$1.25$, real incomes are $y_1 = 1,000$ and $y_2 = 800$. That is, household dollar (nominal) incomes are worth, in real terms, 1,000 units and 800 units on dates t_1 and t_2.

Using these relations between real and money consumption and income, the *household's budget constraint* may be written

(14.2) $$P_2 c_2 = (P_1 y_1 - P_1 c_1)(1 + R) + P_2 y_2$$

or, dividing through by P_2 and rearranging,

(14.3) $$c_2 = (y_1 - c_1)\frac{P_1}{P_2}(1 + R) + y_2$$

Equation (14.3) shows that, given the rate of interest and the real income stream, the relationship between current and future real consumption depends not on the absolute prices P_1 and P_2 but on their ratio P_1/P_2. This ratio may be expressed in terms of the rate of inflation, p, which is the rate of change of prices between t_1 and t_2:

(14.4) $$p = \frac{P_2 - P_1}{P_1} = \frac{P_2}{P_1} - 1 \quad \text{or} \quad 1 + p = \frac{P_2}{P_1}$$

Substituting (14.4) into (14.3) gives

(14.5) $$c_2 = (y_1 - c_1)\frac{1 + R}{1 + p} + y_2$$

or

(14.6) $$c_2 = (y_1 - c_1)(1 + r) + y_2$$

where r is the real rate of interest, which is defined such that

(14.7) $$1 + r = \frac{1 + R}{1 + p} \quad \text{or} \quad r = \frac{R - p}{1 + p}$$

The relation between c_2 and c_1 stated in Equation (14.6) has been drawn in Figure 14.1. The diagonal line with slope $-(1 + r)$ is the

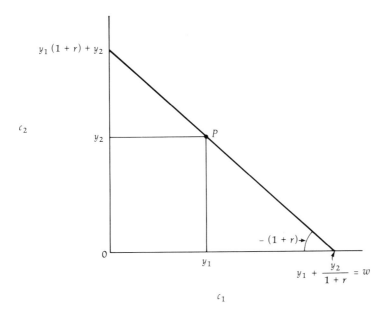

Figure 14.1   The set of consumption opportunities (the budget constraint).

household's budget constraint. It describes the consumption opportunities available to the household. The household may choose simply to consume its income on each date, in which case $c_1 = y_1$ and $c_2 = y_2$, and the consumption plan occurs at point P.

If the household desires to consume more than y_1, it must forgo c_2 at a rate determined by the slope of the budget constraint, that is, $-(1 + r)$. The negative of this slope is the *opportunity cost (or price) of current consumption*. It is the amount of future consumption that must be forgone in order to increase current consumption by one unit. For example suppose $P_1 = P_2 = \$1$ and $R = 0.01$ so that $1 + r = 1 + R = 1.01$. An increase in c_1 by 100 units under these conditions means a present increase in borrowing or reduction in lending of \$100, a future increase of \$101 in interest and principal to be paid or reduction of \$101 to be received, and therefore a reduction of c_2 by 101 units.

The extremes of the household's consumption opportunities are indicated by the intercepts of the budget constraint in Figure 14.1. An unnaturally thrifty household might choose to maximize future consumption by consuming nothing now and, if they do not all starve to death, consuming $c_2 = y_1(1 + r) + y_2 = 2{,}010$ at time t_2 if $Y_1 = Y_2 = \$1{,}000$, $P_1 = P_2 = \$1$, and $R = 0.01$. At the opposite extreme is the profligate family that borrows all it can against future income so that $c_1 = y_1 + y_2/(1 + r) = 1{,}990.10$. This family borrows $\$1{,}000/(1 + R) = \$1{,}000/(1.01) = \$990.10$ at time t_1 and devotes all of Y_2 to the repayment of the interest and principal amounting to $(1.01)(\$990.10) = \$1{,}000$. We can think of the present value of the household's real income stream as its real wealth, w:

(14.8) $w = y_1 + \dfrac{y_2}{1 + r}$ = household real wealth

The profligate household consumed all its wealth at time t_1.

Sets of consumption preferences (the utility function)

Now that we have seen what households *are able* to consume, let's look at what they *would like* to consume. Consumer preferences are often described by utility functions such as the following:

(14.9) $U = U(c_1, c_2)$

The household's utility depends on its current and future consumption. Naturally the household would always like to have more of both. But since this is not possible, it is convenient to rank levels of utility using *indifference curves* such as those in Figure 14.2. Each of the indifference curves in the figure corresponds to a specific value of U. The slopes of the curves indicate the rates at which the consumer is willing to give up consumption on one date in order to increase consumption at another time while preserving an unchanged level of utility. For example consider the consumption set (c_1', c_2') indicated by point B. According to the indifference curve U^1, a reduction in c_2 to c_2'' that is accompanied by an increase in c_1 to c_1'' leaves the household's utility unchanged. This is also true of the decrease in c_2 to c_2''' if it is accompanied by an increase in c_1 to c_1'''. Notice that the indifference

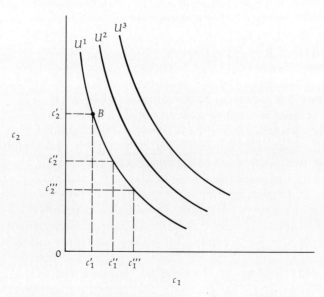

Figure 14.2   Sets of consumption preferences (the utility function).

curves have been drawn such that an unchanged level of household happiness, U^1, requires smaller and smaller reductions in c_2 in return for equal increases in c_1. As current consumption, c_1, becomes greater, the household is willing to relinquish less and less of c_2 for given increases in c_1. Even shortsighted households become less willing to forgo the future for the present as their stomachs approach capacity.

The optimal plan

The household wants to achieve the highest utility possible. It would rather have a consumption set (c_1, c_2) on U^2 than on U^1 because it is possible to have more of c_2 for a given amount of c_1 and more of c_1 for given c_2. U^3 would be even nicer than U^2. But the household's income stream may not permit U^3 or even U^2. As in other economic and noneconomic situations, the household is confronted by a constrained maximization problem. It wants to maximize utility subject to the limitations imposed by the budget constraint. That is, it wants to reach the highest indifference curve in Figure 14.2 allowed by the budget constraint in Figure 14.1. The problem is solved by combining the two diagrams, as we have done in Figure 14.3.

The optimal consumption plan in Figure 14.3 is (c_1^*, c_2^*). This is the point at which the budget constraint touches the highest possible indifference curve. This indifference curve, U^2, and the budget constraint are tangent at the optimum point, E. At this point the rate at which the household is willing to exchange c_1 and c_2 while remaining on the same level of utility (the slope of U^2) equals the rate at which c_1

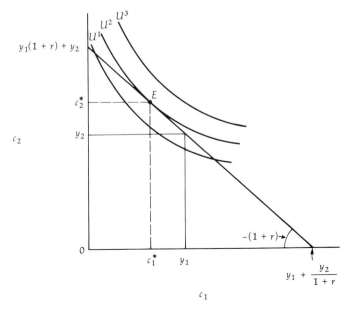

Figure 14.3   The consumption plan of a saver (lender).

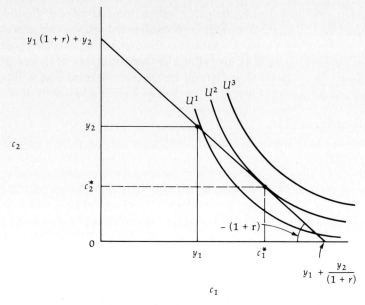

Figure 14.4   The consumption plan of a dissaver (borrower).

and c_2 must be exchanged in the marketplace, which is dictated by the slope of the budget constraint.

The slope of an indifference curve is $-U_1/U_2$, where U_1 and U_2 are the marginal utilities of c_1 and c_2, that is, the changes in utility due to changes in c_1 and c_2. We already know that the slope of the budget constraint is $-(1 + r)$. Therefore the optimal consumption plan must occur at a point such that[1]

(14.10)
$$\frac{U_1}{U_2} = 1 + r$$

The household consumes c_1 and c_2 up to the point at which the marginal utility of c_1 relative to that of c_2, U_1/U_2, equals the cost of c_1 relative to c_2, $P_1 (1 + R)/P_2 = 1 + r$.

The household in Figure 14.3 is a saver at t_1 in the amount $y_1 - c_1^*$ in real terms and $P_1(y_1 - c_1^*)$ in dollars. The household in Figure 14.4 has a different utility function. The indifference curves of the latter household lie farther to the right than those in Figure 14.3. This means a greater preference for current consumption relative to future consumption and, given the same income stream and r, more c_1 and less c_2 than in Figure 14.3. The household in Figure 14.4 dissaves (borrows against future income) by the amount $c_1^* - y_1$ in real terms.

---

1 Equation (14.10) is derived in Appendix 14.A.

THE EQUILIBRIUM REAL RATE OF INTEREST

If the economy consists entirely of households like those in Figures 14.3 and 14.4 and if the amount that the first group wishes to lend equals the amount that the second group wishes to borrow at the existing real interest rate, r^e, then r^e is the equilibrium rate and will not change. But suppose the economy consists entirely of the thrifty folk of Figure 14.3. In that case everyone wants to lend (buy bonds) and no one wants to borrow (sell bonds) at the existing real rate, say, $r \doteq 4$ percent. The price of bonds will be bid up, that is, r will be bid down, until desired borrowing and lending are equal, that is, until desired saving is in total equal to zero. The budget constraints facing households will rotate counterclockwise, from the solid line in Figure 14.5 with slope -1.04 to the dashed line with slope, say, -1.03.

The fall in r reduces the cost of current consumption, that is, reduces the return to saving and lending, so that the consumer increases c_1 from c_1^* to $c_1^{**} = y_1$ and reduces c_2 from c_2^* to $c_2^{**} = y_2$. In an economy in which all households are alike (identical preferences and income streams) there will be no borrowing. But there will be an equilibrium r, which is the real rate of interest at which total desired borrowing equals total desired lending—which for identical households means neither borrowing nor lending.

The determinants of the equilibrium real rate of interest may be illustrated by the following algebraic example, which begins with an optimal consumption plan based on an explicit utility function and

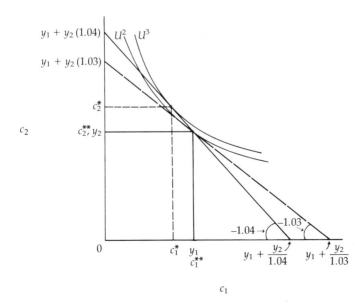

Figure 14.5   Causes and consequences of changes in the equilibrium real rate of interest.

then combines households to derive the equilibrium value of r. Let the utility function (14.9) take the following explicit form:

(14.11) $$U = U(c_1, c_2) = c_1^a c_2^b$$

The exponents a and b indicate the relative strengths of household preferences for current and future consumption. A high value of a relative to b means a preference for current consumption, as indicated by indifference curves like those of the dissavers in Figure 14.4. A high value of b relative to a means a preference for future consumption as indicated by the indifference curves of the savers in Figure 14.3.

Maximizing the utility function (14.11) subject to the budget constraint (14.6) and solving for c_1 and c_2 gives[2]

(14.12) $$c_1^* = \frac{a}{a+b}\left(y_1 + \frac{y_2}{1+r}\right) = \frac{a}{a+b}w$$

(14.13) $$c_2^* = \frac{b}{a+b}(1+r)\left(y_1 + \frac{y_2}{1+r}\right) = \frac{b}{a+b}(1+r)w$$

Optimal current consumption is the proportion $a/(a+b)$ of the present value of the household's income stream (that is, the household's wealth). As expected, current consumption is positively related to a and negatively related to b and r. The opposite is true of planned future consumption. Notice that the ratio of current to future consumption is

(14.14) $$\frac{c_1^*}{c_2^*} = \frac{a}{b(1+r)}$$

The household's optimal real saving, s^*, and therefore its optimal real demand for bonds, is the difference between current real income and consumption:

(14.15) $$s^* = y_1 - c_1^* = y_1 - \frac{a}{a+b}\left(y_1 + \frac{y_2}{1+r}\right)$$
$$= \frac{b}{a+b}y_1 - \frac{a}{a+b}\left(\frac{y_2}{1+r}\right)$$

There is no time subscript on s because in our two-date model the household saves (or dissaves) only on the first date. The results in Equations (14.12) to (14.15) are illustrated by Exercise 14.1.

---

2 Equations (14.12) and (14.13) are derived in Appendix 14.A.

EXERCISE 14.1.   Suppose that current and expected real incomes are $y_1 = 500$ and $y_2 = 816$, the current real rate of interest
is $r = 0.02$, and the household's utility is described by Equation
(14.11) with equal desires for current and future consumption so
that $a = b$. Solve for the optimal consumption-saving plan.

Substituting the above values into Equations (14.12), (14.13),
and (14.15) gives

$$c_1^* = \frac{1}{2}\left(500 + \frac{816}{1.02}\right) = 650 \qquad c_2^* = \frac{1}{2}\left(500 + \frac{816}{1.02}\right)1.02 = 663$$

$$s^* = \frac{1}{2}(500) - \frac{1}{2}\left(\frac{816}{1.02}\right) = -150$$

As a check we see that the household borrows $c_1^* - y_1 =$
$650 - 500 = 150 = -s^*$ in the first period. After repaying the
principal and interest of the loan, amounting to $150(1.02) = 153$,
it consumes $y_2 + s_1^*(1 + r) = 816 - 150(1.02) = 663 = c_2^*$ in the
second period.

Notice from Equation (14.12) that current consumption responds
positively to both current and future income. Equation (14.15) shows
that current saving responds positively to current income but negatively to future income. The effect of future income on current
consumption and saving is understated in our myopic one-period
model. For most of us the bulk of our income stream is yet to come.
Consequently future income is usually more important than current
income in determining current consumption and saving. This explains
why rising incomes are often associated with increasing demands for
funds and, therefore, rising interest rates. Increases in current incomes
cause people to make upward revisions in their expected income
streams and to borrow against those future incomes. A promotion for a
household's breadwinner often leads to a decision to live more expen-
sively—nicer clothes, better food, and a bigger house—which means
borrowing to be repaid from the forthcoming increase in income.

Equations (14.12) and (14.15) also illustrate the negative influence
of r on c_1^* and the positive influence of r on s^*. These equations are
consistent with the previous discussion, in which we emphasized the
role of the real rate of interest as the cost of current consumption and
the return to current saving. The saving-interest relation is illustrated
in Figure 14.6 for a given income stream, y_1 and y_2, and consumer
preferences, a and b.

We shall now derive the equilibrium real rate, r^e, which is the value
of r for which total desired saving equals total desired borrowing.
Continuing the example of identical households depicted in Figure

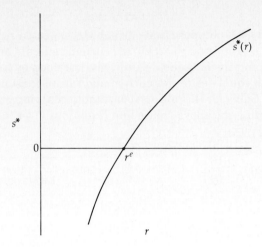

Figure 14.6   Optimal saving as a positive function of the real rate of interest.

14.5, the equilibrium real rate is the rate for which the desired saving of every household is zero. This is indicated by r^e in Figure 14.6. Setting s^* in Equation (14.15) equal to zero and solving for the equilibrium r give

(14.16) $$1 + r^e = \frac{a}{b} \frac{y_2}{y_1} = \frac{a}{b} (1 + g)$$

where $g = (y_2 - y_1)/y_1 =$ the rate of change of real income.

The rate of interest is sometimes said to be determined by *productivity and thrift* although Irving Fisher, the foremost developer of the ideas presented in this chapter, preferred *opportunity and impatience*.[3] Either way, the two main determinants of r are represented in Equation (14.16). First, for a given income stream, the real rate of interest will be higher in a spendthrift, impatient society—that is, one in which the preference for current consumption as measured by a is great relative to the preference for future consumption as measured by b—than in a society consisting mainly of thrifty, patient people. In the former society the urge to consume today means a large demand for credit and a high real rate of interest. Consequently r is positively related to a/b.

Second, the rate of growth of household real incomes, g, reflects society's productivity. An expected increase in productivity and therefore an upward revision of expected real incomes lead households to borrow against those future incomes. This in turn puts upward pressure on r.

---

3 See "Preface" to *The Theory of Interest.*

THE LIFE CYCLE OF INCOME, CONSUMPTION, AND SAVING

Life is badly arranged. One of the many imperfections of our existence on this mortal coil is that income, like the police, is seldom at hand when most needed. Young families have many needs and little income. Not until the kids have finished college, the teeth are no longer up to a steak, and the taste buds have disappeared do many couples, at last and too late, begin to earn the income for which they would have been so thankful a few years before. But maybe it's not too late, for the capital markets provide a means by which future income may be converted to present consumption. Exercise 14.1 gave a hypothetical example of this. A more extensive real-world example is presented in Figure 14.7, which shows how American households use the capital markets to make their lifetime consumption patterns smoother than their income streams. The chart shows that young families borrow against future income, middle-aged families repay earlier debt and accumulate savings for their old age, and elderly families live off their savings.[4]

THE PERMANENT-INCOME HYPOTHESIS AND THE STABILITY OF CONSUMER BEHAVIOR

Now let's look at the aggregate consumption-income relation as it has behaved historically in the United States. The steady spending performance of households has exerted a stabilizing influence on the American economy. We saw in Figure 13.2 that total household expenditures, including both investment and consumption, have been almost a constant proportion of household disposable income. This is also true of consumption expenditures alone, which are shown in Figure 14.8. The middle line in the lower-left portion of the chart has a slope of 0.835, which was the median consumption/income ratio during 1897 to 1928 based on data reported by Raymond Goldsmith in his *Study of Saving*. The data beginning in 1929 are those of the Department of Commerce and are not strictly comparable with Goldsmith's data. The middle line in the upper-right portion of the chart has a slope of 0.781, which was the median consumption/income ratio during 1951 to 1983 based on the Commerce Department's data. The consumption data in Figure 14.8 include only expenditures on nondurable goods and services and exclude housing and other durables.

The behavior of household consumption reported in Figure 14.8 is implied by the theory of consumption developed by Irving Fisher (1930) and summarized in previous sections of this chapter. Fisher

---

4 Young families typically borrow much more than is indicated in Figure 14.7. But most of that borrowing takes the form of home mortgages, that is, for investment in houses rather than the current consumption expenditures shown in the chart.

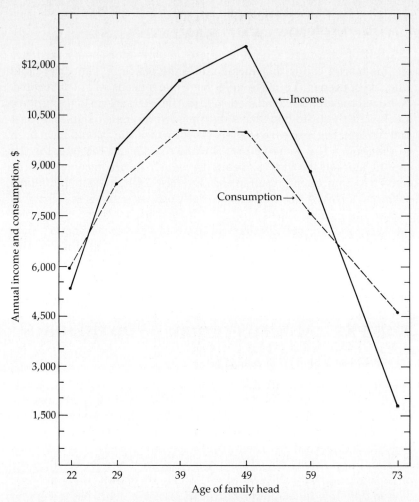

Income is after-tax wage, salary, and self-employment income, that is, excluding social security, welfare, and pension benefits.
Consumption is current consumption expenditures, excluding personal insurance, gifts, and contributions.

Source: Bureau of Labor Statistics, *Annual Expenditures and Sources of Income Cross-classified by Family Characteristics, 1972–1973,* bull. 1985, Washington, 1978.

Figure 14.7   The typical life cycle of income and consumption.

pointed out that the current and planned consumption of households in well-functioning financial markets ought to depend on the present value of household income streams, which in the simple model presented above was $w = y_1 + y_2/(1 + r)$. Much useful theoretical and empirical research on consumption behavior has been conducted since Fisher, most notably by Franco Modigliani and Richard Brumberg (1955), Milton Friedman (1957), Albert Ando and Franco Modigliani

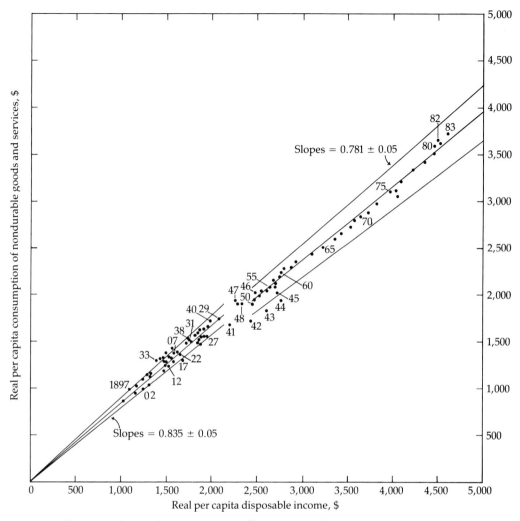

Note that the median consumption/income ratio during 1897 to 1928, using Goldsmith's data, was 0.835 and the median ratio during 1951 to 1979, using Department of Commerce data, was 0.781.

Sources: *National Income and Product Accounts of the U.S., 1929–74, Survey of Current Business,* and Raymond W. Goldsmith, *A Study of Saving in the United States,* Princeton University Press, Princeton, NJ, 1955, 1956.

Figure 14.8   Household real per capita income and consumption in 1972 dollars.

(1963), and Robert Hall (1978). Friedman has called Fisher's model the "permanent-income" hypothesis while Modigliani and his collaborators have called it the "life-cycle" hypothesis of consumption (or saving). But the essential characteristics of Fisher's theory have been retained. The most important empirical implications of that theory are consistent with the data, which have shown the following tendencies:

EMPIRICAL TENDENCY 14.1.   Per capita consumption is over long periods quite a stable proportion of income. That is, changes in income are normally accompanied by changes in consumption in the same proportion.

EMPIRICAL TENDENCY 14.2.   However, large or temporary changes in income are often accompanied by less than proportional changes in consumption.

EMPIRICAL TENDENCY 14.3.   Consumption at time $t - 1$ is a good predictor of consumption at time t.

These tendencies may be explained within Fisher's theoretical framework by long-run and short-run consumption functions that will be derived by extending our analysis to allow planning horizons to be any length and letting investor expectations of future income be related to current income. We shall find that the short-run relationship between consumption and income depends upon whether changes in income are expected to be permanent or transitory.

Letting a typical household's planning horizon be n future dates instead of one future date as in our previous example and assuming a constant expected real rate of interest, r, real consumption at time t is

$$(14.17) \quad c_t = \beta w_t = \beta \left[y_t + \frac{y_{t+1}}{1 + r} + \frac{y_{t+2}}{(1 + r)^2} + \cdots + \frac{y_{t+n}}{(1 + r)^n} \right]$$

where the ys are current and expected real incomes, w_t is the present value of that income stream, and β is the proportion of w_t that is allocated to consumption at time t.[5] When $n = 1$, Equation (14.17) reduces to Equation (14.12), and $\beta = a/(a + b)$. If the household has equal preferences for consumption on all $n + 1$ dates under consideration, $\beta = 1/(n + 1)$.

Now let us examine the impact of a change in current income, Δy_t, on current consumption. The change in current consumption, Δc_t, due to Δy_t depends largely upon whether the change in current income leads to revisions of expectations of future incomes. We use α_i to denote the household's revision of its expected income in period

5 The analysis is easily extended to take account of assets and liabilities carried over from the past (which are included in the first date's receipts, y_t) and desired wealth at the end of the planning horizon (which is included in the final date's consumption, c_{t+n}).

$t + i$ as a proportion of a change in its income in period t:

(14.18)
$$\alpha_i = \frac{\Delta y_{t+i}/y_{t+i}}{\Delta y_t/y_t}$$

For example, if a 10 percent increase in y_t leads to an upward revision of income in the next period, y_{t+1}, of 8 percent, then $\alpha_1 = 0.08/0.10 = 0.80$. The αs are *elasticities of income expectations*.

Using Equations (14.17) and (14.18), the impact of Δy_t on Δc_t is

(14.19)
$$\Delta c_t = \beta \left[\Delta y_t + \frac{\Delta y_{t+1}}{1+r} + \cdots + \frac{\Delta y_{t+n}}{(1+r)^n} \right]$$
$$= \beta \left[\Delta y_t + \frac{\alpha_1}{1+r} \left(\frac{y_{t+1}}{y_t} \right) \Delta y_t + \cdots + \frac{\alpha_n}{(1+r)^n} \frac{y_{t+n}}{y_t} \Delta y_t \right]$$

since we see from Equation (14.18) that

$$\Delta y_{t+i} = \alpha_i \frac{y_{t+i}}{y_t} \Delta y_t$$

Factoring out Δy_t, Equation (14.19) may be written

(14.20) $\Delta c_t = \beta \left[1 + \dfrac{\alpha_1}{1+r} \left(\dfrac{y_{t+1}}{y_t} \right) + \cdots + \dfrac{\alpha_n}{(1+r)^n} \dfrac{y_{t+n}}{y_t} \right] \Delta y_t$

The expected future income stream of a typical American household was shown in Figure 14.7. That chart showed the consumption-income behavior of families of different ages observed during a particular year. We now wish to analyze the aggregate behavior of households over time. We shall assume a simple case in which the average household expects its income to grow at the constant rate, g, so that Equation (14.20) may be written

(14.21) $\Delta c_t = \beta \left[1 + \alpha_1 \dfrac{1+g}{1+r} + \cdots + \alpha_n \dfrac{(1+g)^n}{(1+r)^n} \right] \Delta y_t$

Most young families expect their income to grow faster than g, and most elderly families expect the opposite. It is helpful to think of g as the per capita rate of growth of the nation's output. Equation (14.21) presents a situation in which Δc_t is a constant proportion of Δy_t. Of course g and r are not constant so that $\Delta c_t/\Delta y_t$ will vary over time. However, the stability of $\Delta c_t/\Delta y_t$ in Figure 14.8 suggests that Equation (14.21) is a reasonable working hypothesis.

Equation (14.21) can be made even simpler if we assume the

expected rate of growth of real income to equal the real rate of interest so that

(14.22) $\Delta c_t = \beta(1 + \alpha_1 + \cdots + \alpha_n)\Delta y_t$

If all increases in income are expected to be *permanent,* that is, if proportional changes in current income lead to revisions of all expected future incomes in the same proportion so that $\alpha_1 = \alpha_2 = \cdots = \alpha_n = 1$, then our consumption-income relation reduces still further to

(14.23) $\Delta c_t = \beta(n + 1)\Delta y_t$

Finally, if consumption preferences are equal over the entire planning horizon so that $\beta = 1/(n + 1)$, Equation (14.23) reduces to[6]

(14.24) $\Delta c_t = \dfrac{n + 1}{n + 1}\Delta y_t = \Delta y_t$

It may be useful at this point to review the assumptions leading to Equation (14.24). We have assumed that (1) the elasticities of income expectations (the αs) are all unity, (2) income is expected to grow at a constant rate equal to the real rate of interest, and (3) consumption preferences are equal over the planning horizon. These assumptions and Equation (14.24) are consistent with the equilibrium defined in Equation (14.16). They are also consistent with a simple form of Empirical Tendency 14.1, in which c_t and y_t are equal and therefore change in the same proportion. Furthermore they are consistent with Empirical Tendency 14.3. If c_t and y_t both change in the proportion g, Equation (14.24) may be written

(14.25) $\dfrac{c_t - c_{t-1}}{c_{t-1}} = g$ or $c_t = (1 + g)c_{t-1}$

and c_{t-1} is a perfect predictor of c_t.

The world is not this simple, of course. The simplicity and precision of our results are due to the extreme nature of our assumptions. Nevertheless, several aspects of these results conform closely to observed behavior. We have already seen in Figure 14.8 the tendency for c_t and y_t to change in the same proportion. And Robert Hall (1978) has demonstrated that Equation (14.25) was a close approximation of

---

6 This result follows from the assumption of our simple model that all income is consumed, that is, that borrowing and lending are solely for the purpose of purchasing consumption goods (now or in the future). The ratio $\Delta c_t/\Delta y_t$ would be less than unity in a model in which part of output is invested.

the actual time path of consumption during 1948 to 1977.[7] This behavior (that is, Empirical Tendency 14.3) is consistent with the permanent-income–life-cycle hypothesis in a rational expectations world in which the consumption plan $c_t, c_{t+1}, c_{t+2}, \ldots$ incorporates all available information. Unless new information that causes an alteration in that plan becomes available at time $t + 1$, c_{t+1} will be a function of the same information as c_t. Specifically c_{t+1} and c_t will both be fractions of consumer wealth and therefore perfectly correlated.

But what constitutes new information? For example which unusually large increases in income are regarded as evidence of permanent increases in the rate of growth of income and therefore as bases for upward revisions in the consumption plan; which are viewed as merely transitory deviations from the already-known permanent trend and therefore almost or entirely irrelevant to the consumption plan; and which are considered partly permanent and partly transitory? We will see that changes viewed in the second and third ways give rise to Empirical Tendency 14.2.

A possible example of a perceived transitory change in income was the income tax surcharge of 1968. The administration wanted to expand the war in Vietnam without the inflationary consequences of a growing federal deficit. The optimal way to achieve both objectives was an increase in taxes. But the war was not popular with taxpayers or their Congressmen, and a compromise was arranged whereby Congress passed a temporary (1-year) tax surcharge. Several writers have argued that the anti-inflationary impact of the surcharge was less than hoped by the administration because, as with other transitory changes in income, consumer demand was only slightly affected.[8] However, the policy was stoutly defended by its architects, who argued that the impact of the surcharge on consumption was as much as that of a permanent tax. These government advisors believed that private behavior was myopic and irrational and that the capital markets were highly imperfect so that people formed no opinions of the future, wouldn't use those opinions in a consistent manner anyway, and even if they did, based current consumption largely on current income because they were unable to reallocate income across time. A similar controversy surrounded the impact—or lack thereof—of the temporary tax cut in 1975.

These controversies cannot completely resolve the dispute about the relative impacts of permanent and transitory income changes on consumption because we do not know for sure which changes in

---

7 Hall's regression of c_t on c_{t-1}, c_{t-2}, and c_{t-3} produced a coefficient of determination of $R^2 = 0.9988$, a highly statistically significant coefficient on c_{t-1}, insignificant coefficients on the other variables, and an insignificant constant term. The addition of lagged values of y_t as explanatory variables produced insignificant coefficients on the y_{t-i} and failed to improve upon the predictive power of c_{t-1}.

8 See Robert Eisner (1969), William Springer (1975), and Alan Blinder (1981).

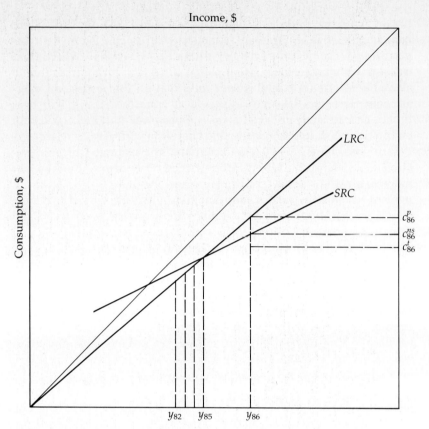

Figure 14.9   The range of possible consumption responses to a larger-than-usual increase in income.

income are permanent and which are transitory. It is unlikely that consumers give much credence to promises about the temporary nature of tax changes. The 1968 surcharge and the 1975 reduction were in fact extended. Consequently we might expect the consumption effect of so-called temporary tax changes to lie between the strong impact of a permanent change in income illustrated by Equation (14.24) and the near-zero impact of a transitory change.[9]

These considerations also apply to changes in income due to other causes. Is a recent substantial rise in the rate of growth of income during an economic expansion likely to be continued? Your guess is as good as ours—and as good as the average household's. Consider the situation in Figure 14.9, which shows consumption as ordinarily a constant proportion of income on the long-run consumption (LRC) function. The line above LRC, between the corners of the box, is the

---

9 This is roughly the conclusion of Walter Dolde (1979) and Alan Blinder (1981).

45-degree line for which consumption equals income. The figure shows three normal increases in consumption, on the LRC line, between 1982 and 1985 in response to normal increases in income (from y_{82} to y_{85}). Now suppose that income rises by an extraordinarily large amount between 1985 and 1986. Figure 14.9 shows three possible responses of consumption:

1. If households regard the rate of increase in income from y_{85} to y_{86} as "permanent" and expectations of future incomes are revised upward accordingly, consumption in 1986 will rise in the same proportion as income. This is indicated by c_{86}^p, which lies on the LRC function.

2. If the rate of increase in income is regarded as "transitory" so that expectations of future incomes are not revised, consumption in 1986 will rise only to c_{86}^t, about as much as if the rate of increase in income between 1985 and 1986 had been the average of past experience.

3. Perhaps the most likely short-run consumption response to the large jump in income is somewhere between c_{86}^p and c_{86}^t. Such a response is indicated by c_{86}^{ns}, when households are "not sure" whether the change in income is permanent or transitory and may suspect that some of it is permanent and some only transitory.[10]

Partial short-run responses like the third case generate short-run consumption functions like SRC. Such SRC functions are consistent with Empirical Tendency 14.2, which is illustrated further in Figure 14.10. This chart is identical with Figure 14.8 except that per capita real consumption and disposable income are plotted only for selected years. Four apparent SRC functions are shown, corresponding to the large falls and succeeding rises in income during 1929 to 1936 and 1937 to 1940 and the smaller changes during 1952 to 1956 and 1972 to 1975, periods during which there was substantial uncertainty regarding the permanence of income changes.

CONCLUSION

Households are the economy's most important savers, and their desire to consume their wealth in a relatively steady manner means that they are a stable source of funds for other sectors. Fluctuations in interest rates are due mainly to the often erratic demands for funds by the nonhousehold sectors, especially business and government. The production and financial decisions of nonfinancial firms are discussed in the next chapter.

---

10 See Franco Modigliani and Richard Brumberg (1955, pages 406–418) for an early discussion of partial short-run consumption responses to large changes in income.

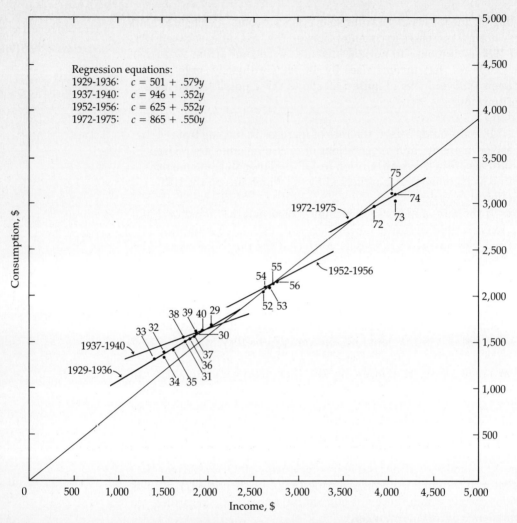

Figure 14.10   Four short-run consumption functions (from Figure 14.8).

QUESTIONS

1. What is meant by "the rate of inflation"?
2. Who is likely to borrow more, low-income or high-income households? Why?
3. Which group of students do you think has the highest standard of living, medical students or philosophy students? Why? What kinds of capital market imperfections might change your answer?
4. In which economy will the real rate of interest be higher: **(a)** one consisting of hard-working (productive), thrifty people or **(b)** one consisting of lazy spendthrifts?
5. Describe how Figures 14.7 to 14.10 illustrate Empirical Tendencies 14.1 to 14.3.

PROBLEMS

1. Suppose the current nominal rate of interest, R, on a one-period investment is 10 percent and the expected rate of inflation during the next period is 5 percent.
   (a) What is the expected one-period real rate of interest, r?
   (b) What is the price of current consumption, c_1, in terms of forgone future consumption, c_2?

2. Figure 14.5 shows how the real rate of interest responds to an excess of saving (lending). Draw a figure that shows the response of r to a deficiency of saving, that is, an excess demand for credit.

3. Do Exercise 14.1 when the nominal rate of interest is $R = 4.04$ percent and the expected rate of inflation, p, is (a) zero, (b) 2 percent, and (c) 4.04 percent.

4. Do Exercise 14.1 when the pattern of the income stream is reversed, that is, when $y_1 = 816$ and $y_2 = 500$.

5. Exercise 14.1 assumed a real rate of interest of 2 percent. Drop that assumption and solve for the equilibrium value of r when the income stream and preferences of the household in the exercise are shared by all households.

6. Suppose that a household expects its real income to grow at a rate equal to the real rate of interest, has a planning horizon of 25 years, and has equal consumption preferences for all of those years. What will be the household's consumption response to an increase in income when the increase is expected to be (a) permanent, (b) transitory, and (c) half permanent and half transitory?

REFERENCES

Albert Ando and Franco Modigliani, "The 'Life Cycle' Hypothesis of Saving: Aggregate Implications and Tests," *American Economic Review,* March 1963, pages 55–84.

Alan S. Blinder, "Temporary Income Taxes and Consumer Spending," *Journal of Political Economy,* February 1981, pages 26–53.

Walter Doide, "Temporary Taxes as Macroeconomic Stabilizers," *American Economic Review,* May 1979, pages 81–85.

Robert Eisner, "Fiscal and Monetary Policy Reconsidered," *American Economic Review,* December 1969, pages 897–905.

Irving Fisher, *The Theory of Interest,* Macmillan, New York, 1930.

Milton Friedman, *A Theory of the Consumption Function,* Princeton University Press, Princeton, NJ, 1957.

Raymond W. Goldsmith, *A Study of Saving in the United States,* 3 vols., Princeton University Press, Princeton, NJ, 1955, 1956.

Robert Hall, "Stochastic Implications of the Life Cycle—Permanent Income Hypothesis: Theory and Evidence," *Journal of Political Economy,* December 1978, pages 971–987.

Samuel Johnson, *The Rambler,* 4 vols., Rivington, London, 1789.

Franco Modigliani and Richard Brumberg, "Utility Analysis and the Consumption Function: An Interpretation of Cross-section Data," in Kenneth K. Kurihara (ed.), *Post-Keynesian Economics,* Allen & Unwin, London, 1955.

William L. Springer, "Did the 1968 Surcharge Really Work?" *American Economic Review,* September 1975, pages 644–659.

APPENDIX
14.A
DERIVATION OF THE OPTIMAL CONSUMPTION PLAN

This appendix mathematically derives the optimal consumption plans stated in Equations (14.10) and (14.12) and shown graphically in Figure 14.3.

Derivation of Equation (14.10)

The household's problem is to choose the combination of c_1 and c_2 that maximizes utility,

$$\text{(14.A.1)} \qquad U = U(c_1, c_2)$$

subject to the budget constraint,

$$\text{(14.A.2)} \qquad c_2 = (y_1 - c_1)(1 + r) + y_2$$

where Equations (14.A.1) and (14.A.2) are identical with Equations (14.9) and (14.6).

Totally differentiating Equation (14.A.1), the change in utility due to changes in c_1 and c_2 is

$$\text{(14.A.3)} \qquad dU = U_1 dc_1 + U_2 dc_2$$

where U_1 and U_2 are the *marginal utilities* of c_1 and c_2 obtained by partially differentiating U with respect to c_1 and c_2.

Since by definition an indifference curve shows all the combinations of c_1 and c_2 that give the same utility, that is, for which $dU = 0$, we obtain the slopes of the indifference curves by setting dU in Equation (14.A.3) equal to zero and rearranging to obtain

$$\text{(14.A.4)} \qquad \frac{dc_2}{dc_1} = -\frac{U_1}{U_2} = \text{slopes of indifference curves}$$

The slope of the budget constraint is obtained by differentiating c_2 with respect to c_1 in Equation (14.A.2):

$$\text{(14.A.5)} \qquad \frac{dc_2}{dc_1} = -(1 + r) = \text{slope of budget constraint}$$

We see in Figure 14.3 that the optimal consumption plan occurs when the slope of the highest attainable indifference curve equals the slope of the budget constraint. Equating the right-hand sides of

Equations (14.A.4) and (14.A.5), this means that

(14.A.6)
$$\frac{U_1}{U_2} = 1 + r$$

which is identical with Equation (14.10).

Derivation of Equations (14.12) and (14.13)

Suppose we are given the specific utility function (14.A.7) in place of the general function (14.A.1). The problem now is to choose c_1 and c_2 in such a way as to maximize

(14.A.7)
$$U = c_1^a c_2^b$$

subject to Equation (14.A.2). If we substitute the right-hand side of Equation (14.A.2) for c_2 in the utility function, utility is expressed as a function of only one decision variable, c_1:

(14.A.8)
$$U = c_1^a [(y_1 - c_1)(1 + r) + y_2]^b$$

Setting the derivative of U with respect to c_1 equal to zero and solving for c_1 give optimal current consumption, c_1^*:

$$\frac{dU}{dc_1} = c_1^a b [(y_1 - c_1)(1 + r) + y_2]^{b-1} [-(1 + r)]$$

$$+ a c_1^{a-1} [(y_1 - c_1)(1 + r) + y_2]^b = 0$$

The solution for c_1 is

(14.A.9)
$$c_1^* = \frac{a}{a + b} \left(y_1 + \frac{y_2}{1 + r} \right)$$

which is identical with Equation (14.12). Substituting the solution for c_1^* into the budget constraint (14.A.2) and solving for c_2 give optimal second-period consumption:

(14.A.10)
$$c_2^* = \frac{b}{a + b} (1 + r) \left(y_1 + \frac{y_2}{1 + r} \right)$$

NONFINANCIAL FIRMS

*There are few ways in which a man can be more
innocently employed than in getting money.*
Samuel Johnson (in Boswell's *Life*), March 27, 1775

After considering the largest source of savings (households) in Chapter 14, we now introduce the most important group of investors: nonfinancial firms. In the first two sections we examine the theoretical effects of interest rates and inflation on the production and financial decisions of firms in perfect capital markets with no taxes. Then tax effects are considered, and finally, in the concluding section, actual business decisions are compared with the theory.

THE PRODUCTION DECISION

We want the simplest possible model that permits us to analyze the influence of interest rates on the production and financial decisions of firms. Such a model is one in which the firm buys inputs in the quantity x at time 1 and converts those inputs through its production process into a quantity of output z to be sold at time 2. Inputs cost P_1 per unit at time 1, and the unit price of output at time 2 is P_2. The firm's profit for the period is

(15.1) $\Pi = P_2 z - (1 + R)P_1 x = P_2 f(x) - (1 + R)P_1 x$

where R is the nominal rate of interest, and $z = f(x)$ is the production function. If the firm borrows the amount $P_1 x$ in order to buy inputs at time 1, it must repay $(1 + R)P_1 x$ at time 2. Even if the firm does not borrow but rather purchases inputs with its own funds, we must still count $(1 + R)P_1 x$ as an expense. In this case the quantity $RP_1 x$ is an opportunity cost that would have been earned if the firm had invested the amount $P_1 x$ in securities paying the rate of return R.

The firm's production function is pictured in Figure 15.1. The positive but decreasing slope of $f(x)$ means that output z increases at a decreasing rate as more inputs x are applied to the production process.

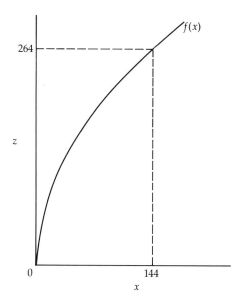

Figure 15.1   The firm's production function.

We shall find it convenient to express the slope of the production function as

(15.2)
$$\frac{dz}{dx} = f'(x) > 0$$

That is, $f'(x)$ is the change in output (dz) due to a change in the quantity of inputs (dx).

Suppose the firm has available at time 1 an investment fund F made up of retained earnings and/or new sales of common stock. There are two ways in which it can transform these current dollars into future dollars, and these ways are depicted by the *production opportunities curve* and the *financial opportunities line* in Figure 15.2:[1]

1. The production opportunities curve, which is the dark curve connecting points F and $P_2 f(F/P_1)$ in Figure 15.2, describes the rate at which current dollars generate dollars through the firm's production process. The steepness of this curve and therefore the attractiveness of this course of action depend upon the firm's production function, $z = f(x)$, and also upon the input and output prices P_1 and P_2. Specifically a firm that is **(a)** highly productive (that is, has a steep production function as shown in Figure 15.1), **(b)** buys inputs cheaply, and **(c)** sells output dearly is able to transform current into future

---

1 The following discussion is based on Irving Fisher (1930, Chapter 11) and J. Hirshleifer (1970, Chapter 3).

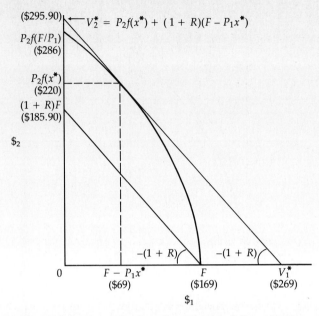

Figure 15.2   The firm's optimal production plan (all equity financing).

dollars at a rapid rate. The importance of these three factors are illustrated in the following exercise:

EXERCISE 15.1.   Suppose the firm has $F = \$169$ at time 1, inputs cost $P_1 = \$1$ each, output is expected to sell for $P_2 = \$1$ per unit, and the production function is $z = 22\sqrt{x}$. The production opportunities curve is shown in Figure 15.2. The intercept on the horizontal axis is F, at which point the firm leaves all the \$169 in the bank so that input costs and therefore output revenues are zero. The intercept on the vertical axis corresponds to the decision to spend all of F on inputs to obtain 169 units of x in order to produce $z = 22\sqrt{169} = 286$ units of output to be sold for $P_2 z = P_2 f(F/P_1) = P_2 f(169) = \$286$.

To obtain an intermediate point on the curve, suppose the firm spends \$100 in inputs. This leaves \$69 for other uses at time 1 and produces revenue of $P_2 f(\$100/P_1) = P_2 f(100) = P_2 22\sqrt{100} = \$220$ at time 2, as shown at the point of intersection of the dashed lines in Figure 15.2.

The student may complete the exercise by showing, when F remains \$169, how the production opportunities curve is improved by the following changes, one at a time: **(a)** The production function rises to $z = 24\sqrt{x}$; **(b)** P_1 falls to \$0.81; **(c)** P_2 rises to \$1.10.

The slope of the production opportunities curve may be derived as follows: Time 2 dollars depend on the firm's choice of x such that $\$_2 = P_2 z = P_2 f(x)$. We know from Equation (15.2) that the change in z resulting from a change in x is $dz/dx = f'(x)$. Therefore the change in time 2 dollars relative to a change in x is $d\$_2/dx = P_2 f'(x)$. Now consider the impact of x on time 1 dollars. The funds remaining after purchasing inputs is $\$_1 = F - P_1 x$. Therefore the change in time 1 dollars relative to a change in x is $d\$_1/dx = -P_1$. Combining these results the change in time 2 dollars relative to a change in time 1 dollars via the production process is

$$\textbf{(15.3)} \qquad \frac{d\$_2}{d\$_1} = \frac{d\$_2/dx}{d\$_1/dx} = -\frac{P_2 f'(x)}{P_1}$$

This is the slope of the production opportunities curve. That is, current dollars devoted to the production process generate future dollars at the rate $P_2 f'(x)/P_1$, a rate that accelerates with increases in $f'(x)$ and P_2 and diminishes with increases in P_1.

2. The other means available to the firm for transforming current dollars into future dollars is the purchase of securities yielding the nominal rate of return R. If all its funds are devoted to the purchase of securities yielding $R = 10$ percent, the firm ends up with the principal and interest of $(1 + R)F = \$185.90$ shown in Figure 15.2. The slope of this financial opportunities line is $d\$_2/d\$_1 = -(1 + R)$.

But the firm is not committed exclusively to either of these courses. The firm's managers are entrusted with the goal of maximizing the wealth of their employers, the firm's owners. The way to maximize owners' wealth is to maximize the present value of the firm's stream of future profits. Referring to Equation (15.1), the firm's contribution to owners' wealth in our two-date example is

$$\textbf{(15.4)} \qquad \begin{aligned} V_1 &= \frac{\Pi}{1 + R} + F = \frac{P_2 f(x) - (1 + R) P_1 x}{1 + R} + F \\ &= \frac{P_2 f(x)}{1 + R} + (F - P_1 x) \end{aligned}$$

The firm spends $P_1 x$ on inputs and generates revenue of $P_2 f(x)$ from sales. The remainder of its funds, $F - P_1 x$, is invested in securities, which at time 2 are worth $(1 + R)(F - P_1 x)$. The sum of the revenues from these two activities is $P_2 f(x) + (1 + R)(F - P_1 x)$, which has a present value of V_1 as defined in Equation (15.4).

The crucial decision variable to be selected by the firm is x. The firm spends money on x as long as the rate of transformation of current dollars into future dollars through the production process exceeds the rate of transformation offered by the securities market. That is, the firm devotes available funds, F, to the purchase of x as long as the production opportunities curve in Figure 15.2 is steeper than the financial opportunities line, that is, as long as $P_2 f'(x)/P_1$ exceeds $1 + R$. This means that the optimal value of x, which we call x^*, occurs at the point at which the financial opportunities line is tangent to the production opportunities curve. Beyond this point the financial opportunities line is steeper than the production opportunities curve, and the best policy is to devote the funds remaining after buying x^* inputs to the purchase of securities. This procedure enables the firm to maximize its future payout, which is $V_2^* = P_2 f(x^*) + (1 + R)(F - P_1 x^*)$ as shown in Figure 15.2.

Equating the slope of the production opportunities curve as shown in Equation (15.3) with the slope of the financial opportunities line, $-(1 + R)$, we see that the optimal production decision, $f(x^*)$, is that for which

(15.5)
$$-\frac{P_2 f'(x)}{P_1} = -(1 + R)$$

$$\text{or} \quad f'(x) = \frac{P_1(1 + R)}{P_2} = \frac{1 + R}{1 + p} = 1 + r$$

where $1 + r = P_1(1 + R)/P_2 = (1 + R)/(1 + p)$ is unity plus the real rate of interest, and $1 + p$ is the ratio of the expected output price, P_2, to the current input price P_1. One firm's output is another's input. That is, output at time 1 supplies the input necessary to output at time 2 so that, for the economy at large, P_1 and P_2 are price indexes for the same goods on different dates, and we may think of $p = (P_2 - P_1)/P_1$ for the average firm as an index of the expected rate of inflation in the economy.

These principles are illustrated by Exercise 15.2 in a numerical example suggested by Figure 15.2.

EXERCISE 15.2.   As in Exercise 15.1 assume $F = \$169$, $P_1 = P_2 = \$1$, and $f(x) = 22\sqrt{x}$ so that $f'(x) = 11/\sqrt{x}$. Also assume $R = 0.10$. What are the firm's **(a)** optimal purchase of inputs, **(b)** optimal investment in securities, and **(c)** maximum contribution to owners' wealth?

   (a) From Equation (15.5),

$$f'(x) = \frac{11}{\sqrt{x}} = \frac{P_1(1 + R)}{P_2} = 1.10 \qquad \text{so that} \qquad x^* = 100$$

   (b) The amount left for securities is

$$F - P_1 x^* = \$169 - \$100 = \$69$$

(c) The firm's contribution to owners' wealth when $x = 100$ is, from Equation (15.4),

$$V_1^* = \frac{P_2 f(x^*)}{1 + R} + (F - P_1 x^*) = \frac{\$22 \sqrt{100}}{1.10} + (\$169 - \$100) = \$269$$

which is the present value, $\$295.90/1.10$, of the firm's payout at time 2 as shown in Figure 15.2.

In closing this section, it may be worthwhile to point out that we may also think of the production opportunities curve as a continuous approximation to the returns from discrete productive activities ranked in decreasing order of rates of return. According to this interpretation, the slope of the curve is $-(1 + \text{IRR})$, where IRR denotes *internal rate of return,* and the optimal production plan in Equation (15.5) is that for which

(15.6) $-(1 + \text{IRR}) = -(1 + R)$ or $\text{IRR} = R$

that is, for which the internal rate of return equals the market rate of interest.

FINANCIAL DECISIONS
Irrelevance theorems
The following two theorems concerning the irrelevance of the firm's financial decisions are among the best-known results of modern finance.[2] We begin with the crucial assumptions underlying these theorems.

ASSUMPTION 15.1.   Future prices and the outcomes of production processes and security investments—$P_2, f(x)$, and R in our example—are known with certainty.

ASSUMPTION 15.2.   Capital markets are perfect in the senses that there are perfect competition and no transaction costs so that borrowing and lending rates of interest are equal and individual firms and households may borrow or lend as much as they like without affecting the single, prevailing rate of interest, R.

ASSUMPTION 15.3.   There are no taxes.

---

2 The analysis of this section, like nearly all other work in corporate finance during the past 25 years, is based on the pathbreaking work of Franco Modigliani and Merton Miller (1958).

ASSUMPTION 15.4.   The firm's managers operate in the best interests of the owner-shareholders, that is, consistent with the utility-maximizing objectives of the owners.

The following theorems are implied by the above assumptions:

THEOREM 15.1.   The optimal production plan and the utility and wealth of the owners are independent of the firm's capital structure, that is, the debt/equity ratio of the firm.

THEOREM 15.2.   The optimal production plan and the utility and wealth of the owners are independent of the dividend decision.

THEOREM 15.2a.   Maximization of owners' wealth is sufficient for maximization of owners' utilities.

Theorems 15.1 and 15.2 assert that the firm's borrowing, lending, stock-issue, and dividend decisions are irrelevant to the owners' welfare—always subject, of course, to the condition that the firm retains or raises sufficient funds to implement its optimal production plan. Theorem 15.2a is another way of stating Theorem 15.2. Both imply that the timing of the firm's payments (dividends) to the owners is irrelevant. The managers' task is to maximize the present value of those payments. The owners are capable of arranging their receipts and payments over time (by borrowing and lending and by buying and selling the firm's stock) in the manner dictated by their consumption preferences regardless of the dividend schedule and capital structure selected by the managers.

Illustrations of the irrelevance theorems

Consider Figure 15.3, in which $F = 0$ and the firm borrows funds at the rate of interest R. Instead of no debt, as in Figure 15.2, inputs are now financed entirely by debt. But the production decision is not altered. The firm borrows money to buy inputs as long as the net revenue generated by those inputs exceeds the cost of borrowing, that is, as long as the slope of the production opportunities curve exceeds that of the financial opportunities line. Figure 15.3 is identical with Figure 15.2 except that now $F = 0$ instead of \$169, which has shifted the origin of the production opportunities curve from \$169 to 0. However, nothing has happened to change the slope of that curve so that the firm continues to spend $P_1 x = \$100$ on inputs at time 1 to produce output to be sold for $P_2 f(x^*) = \$220$ at time 2, that is, to produce up to the point at which $f'(x) = 1 + r$, as stated in Equation (15.5). This course of action maximizes owners' wealth regardless of the dividend

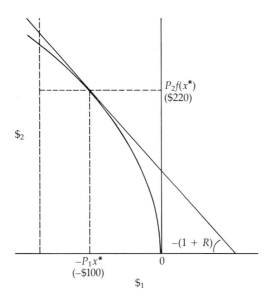

Figure 15.3   The firm's optimal production plan (all debt financing).

and capital structure decisions of the firm, as will be demonstrated
during the course of the following exercise:

EXERCISE 15.3.   Assuming as in Exercises 15.1 and 15.2 that
$F = \$169$, inputs cost $P_1 = \$1$ each, output sells for $P_2 = \$1$ per
unit, the nominal rate of interest is $R = 0.10$, and the production
function is $z = 22\sqrt{x}$, show that the owners' wealth is independent of the firm's borrowing, lending, dividend, and capital
structure decisions.

We denote dividends by D while B and L are bond issues and
purchases (borrowing and lending, each with a one-period maturity) by the firm. The initial number of the firm's shares outstanding is $S_0 = 100$. The number of shares may be changed to S_1
as the firm issues new shares or retires existing shares. The price
of each of the S_1 shares is P_s.

Six cases are presented in the following table. The firm has
three sources of funds at time 1: (a) its stake of $F = \$169$,
(b) debt issues of B, and (c) new stock issues of $(S_1 - S_0)P_s$,
where $S_1 - S_0$ is the number of new shares (if $S_1 > S_0$) and P_s is
the price of those shares. The last source is negative if existing
shares are retired, that is, if $S_1 < S_0$.

The funds raised from these sources may be allocated to three
uses: (a) purchase of the optimal quantity of inputs, costing
$P_1 x = \$100$; (b) dividends, D; and (c) bond purchases (lending), L.

Case	Sources of Funds = Uses of Funds		Present Value of Owners' Claims
	$F + B + (S_1 - S_0)P_s$ =	$P_1 x + D + L$	$S_0 P_s + D = V_1$
1.	$169 + \$ 0 + \$ 0$ =	$\$100 + \$ 0 + \$69$	$\$269 + \$ 0 = \$269$
2.	$169 + 0 + 0$ =	$100 + 30 + 39$	$239 + 30 = 269$
3.	$169 + 0 + 0$ =	$100 + 69 + 0$	$200 + 69 = 269$
4.	$169 + 100 + 0$ =	$100 + 169 + 0$	$100 + 169 = 269$
5.	$169 + 0 + 100$ =	$100 + 169 + 0$	$100 + 169 = 269$
6.	$169 + 150 - 50$ =	$100 + 169 + 0$	$100 + 169 = 269$

Case	Price of Shares $P_s = \dfrac{1}{S_1}\left[\dfrac{P_2 f(x)}{1 + R} + L - B\right]$	Value of Firm's Shares $S_1 P_s$	Net Value of Firm's Debt $B - L$	Value of the Firm $S_1 P_s + B - L = \dfrac{P_2 f(x)}{1 + R}$
1.	$\$2.69$	$\$269$	$-\$ 69$	$\$200$
2.	2.39	239	$- 39$	200
3.	2.00	200	0	200
4.	1.00	100	100	200
5.	1.00	200	0	200
6.	1.00	50	150	200

The first three rows of the table correspond to Figure 15.2, in which the firm borrows no money, spends $100 of F on inputs, and divides the remaining $69 between dividends and lending. The top right-hand side of the table shows that all three of these cases produce the same outcome for the owners: stock and dividends worth $269. The owners do not care whether (a) the firm pays dividends at time 1, which the owners can invest at the rate of interest R, or (b) the firm retains those funds, invests them on behalf of the owners at the rate of interest R, and pays the interest and principal to the owners at time 2.

The price of shares, P_s, is shown at the bottom-left portion of the table and is the present value of the firm's payout in period 2 divided by the number of shares, which is $S_0 = S_1 = 100$ in cases 1 to 4.

Case 4 shows that, even if the firm borrows in order to pay dividends, owners' wealth is not affected. With identical borrowing and lending rates borrowing by the firm to lend (or to pay dividends so that the owners may lend) leaves V_1 unaffected. This case corresponds to Figure 15.3, in which the firm's inputs were financed entirely by borrowing.

In case 5 the firm raises funds by issuing $S_1 - S_0 = 200 - 100 = 100$ new shares. The present value, or price, of each of these 200 shares when $L = B = 0$ is

$$P_s = \frac{1}{200} \frac{\$220}{1.10} = \$1.00$$

The difference between cases 4 and 5 is that, in the latter, dividends are financed by the sale of stock instead of bonds. Given that stock and bonds earn the same rate of return, R, owners' wealth is not affected by the choice between debt and equity financing. (This *equal rate of return principle* will be discussed further below.)

In case 6 the firm increases its debt issues to $150 in order to retire 50 shares of stock, which fetch the price

$$P_s = \frac{1}{50} \left(\frac{\$220}{1.10} - 150 \right) = \$1.00$$

Notice that in case 6, as in the previous cases, the value of the owners' shares at the beginning of time 1 is $S_0 P_s = 100 P_s$ because they have the option of selling those shares, either on their own account or, as in case 6, through the firm's equity retirement program.

The last three columns show that the value of the firm, that is, the sum of the present values of equity $(S_1 P_s)$ and net debt $(B - L)$ claims on the firm, is independent of the firm's choices of S_1, B, and L. This is an illustration of Modigliani and Miller's "Proposition I," according to which, given Assumptions 15.1 to 15.4, the value of a firm is independent of its capital structure and is the net present value of the firm's future operating cash flows—simply $P_2 f(x)/(1 + R)$ in the present example.

The irrelevance results in Exercise 15.3 may be presented in more general form as follows: We first solve the sources-and-uses equation for D and substitute the result into the definition of V_1 to obtain

(15.7) $V_1 = S_0 P_s + F + B + (S_1 - S_0) P_s - P_1 x - L$

Canceling terms and using the definition of P_s in Exercise 15.3 give

(15.8)
$$V_1 = F + B + S_1 \frac{1}{S_1} \left[\frac{P_2 f(x)}{1 + R} + L - B \right] - P_1 x - L$$
$$= \frac{P_2 f(x)}{1 + R} + F - P_1 x$$

which is identical with Equation (15.4). These equations show that the firm's borrowing, lending, equity, and dividend decisions—B, L, S, and D, which do not appear in Equations (15.4) or (15.8)—have no effect on owners' wealth, as asserted by Theorems 15.1 and 15.2.

These results have made use of the equal rate of return principle, which under certainty and perfect capital markets requires rates of return on all securities to be the same. Since (1) the rate of return on bonds is R, (2) the payout of the firm at time 2 is $P_2 f(x) + L(1 + R) - B(1 + R)$, and (3) the value of the firm's shares at time 1 is $S_1 P_s$, the rate of return on shares must be

(15.9) $$R = \frac{[P_2 f(x) + L(1 + R) - B(1 + R)] - S_1 P_s}{S_1 P_s}$$

Solving for the value of the firm's shares gives

(15.10) $$S_1 P_s = \frac{P_2 f(x)}{1 + R} + L - B$$

as indicated in Exercise 15.3.[3]

To complete our illustrations of Theorems 15.1 and 15.2, we show that utilities are independent of the firm's dividend policy. This is done by Figure 15.4, which represents one shareholder's interest in the firm. If no dividends are paid at time 1, V_{1i} is the current value of the shares of the ith owner and V_{2i} is the future payout to those shares. In the numerical example in case 1 of Exercise 15.3 the ith owner's shares are worth $26.90 if he owns one-tenth of the firm (ten shares).

What if this owner has a high preference for current consumption, as indicated by his indifference curves U_{1i} and U_{2i}, but the managers declare no dividend? No matter. The owner may obtain the desired funds by selling stock. A thrifty household, on the other hand, can invest unwanted dividends. In either case owners are indifferent to the managers' financial decisions and are free to reallocate their wealth between time 1 and time 2 in the manner dictated by their consumption preferences.

THE INFLUENCE OF TAXES ON FINANCIAL AND PRODUCTION DECISIONS

The introduction of income and capital gains taxes usually—but not always—invalidates the irrelevance theorems. Our results will be developed slowly as we proceed from simple to more complicated cases. As before, we assume a single input. In this section that input (x) is entirely used up during the single production period. In the next

---

3 A more general statement of the equal rate of return principle is given in Eugene Fama and Merton Miller (1972, pages 79–80).

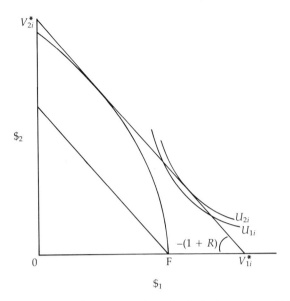

Figure 15.4   An owner's consumption plan is independent of the firm's dividend and other financial decisions.

section the input will be a capital good (K) that is only partially used up in one period.

The classical one-date model

Knut Wicksell (1896) showed for the case of instantaneous production usually considered in microeconomics texts, from which time and interest rates are absent, that the production decision is not affected by an income tax. First consider the decision of a competitive firm that wishes to maximize

(15.11) $\Pi = Pf(x) - Wx$

where Π is profit, P and W are the unit prices of the input x and the output z, and $z = f(x)$ is the production function. Profit is maximized when

(15.12) $\dfrac{d\Pi}{dx} = Pf'(x) - W = 0$ that is, when $f'(x) = \dfrac{W}{P}$

The optimal production decision is that for which the marginal product of x, $f'(x)$, equals the ratio of input and output prices. When x is labor and W is the wage rate, we can say that the firm hires labor to the point at which the marginal product of labor, $f'(x)$, equals the real wage, W/P.

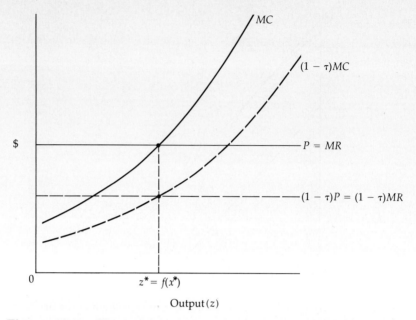

Figure 15.5   The instantaneous production plan is independent of a profits tax.

Now assume a profits tax τ. The firm's objective becomes the maximization of after-tax profit,

$$(15.13) \qquad (1 - \tau)\Pi = (1 - \tau)[Pf(x) - Wx]$$

The optimal production decision in this case is

$$(15.14) \qquad \frac{d(1 - \tau)\Pi}{dx} = (1 - \tau)[Pf'(x) - W] = 0 \qquad \text{or} \qquad f'(x) = \frac{W}{P}$$

The production plan that maximizes before-tax profit is identical with the plan that maximizes after-tax profit.[4] This result is illustrated in Figure 15.5, which depicts the familiar case of a competitive firm maximizing profit by producing output $z^* = f(x^*)$ such that marginal cost, MC, equals price (or marginal revenue, MR). The imposition of a profits tax τ reduces the after-tax value of marginal revenue to $(1 - \tau)MR$, but it also reduces after-tax marginal cost to $(1 - \tau)MC$. If $\tau = 0.50$, the government takes 50 percent of revenue but also bears 50 percent of the costs of inputs, which are tax deductible.

---

4 We have chosen the simple case of a constant proportional tax rate. But the same result is obtained if the profits tax is progressive or regressive. Wicksell also obtained the same result for a monopoly firm, that is, when P is inversely related to the quantity of output.

Production requires time[5]

Now let us resume our analysis of the two-date model considered earlier, with the added complication of three constant-proportion tax rates:

$$\tau_c = \text{tax rate on corporate profits}$$

$$\tau_p = \text{tax rate on personal income}$$

$$\tau_g = \text{tax rate on personal capital gains}$$

The task of the firm's managers at time 1 is to maximize owners' wealth, which means maximizing the value of the sum of their shares in the firm, $S_0 P_s$, and the after-tax dividend payment at time 1, $(1 - \tau_p)D$:

(15.15)
$$V_1 = S_0 P_s + (1 - \tau_p)D$$

Our analysis makes use of three more statements. First, the sources-and-uses equation is

(15.16)
$$F + B + (S_1 - S_0)P_s = P_1 x + D$$

where, as before, F is the firm's initial endowment of funds, B is borrowing, S_0 is the number of shares outstanding immediately preceding time 1, and $(S_1 - S_0)$ is the number of shares newly issued at time 1. We have dispensed with L, the firm's lending, considered previously. Lending is adequately covered by negative values of B.

Second, the value of the firm's shares at time 1 is

(15.17) $$S_1 P_s = S = \frac{V_2 - \tau_g(V_2 - S)}{1 + (1 - \tau_p)R} \quad \text{or} \quad S = \frac{(1 - \tau_g)V_2}{(1 - \tau_g) + (1 - \tau_p)R}$$

The first equation in (15.17) states that the value of shares at time 1 is the present value of the firm's second-period payout, V_2, less the tax on the capital gains, $V_2 - S$, accruing to shareholders. In our simple two-date model the firm ceases to exist at time 2, either being "taken over" or otherwise distributing its net worth, V_2, to its owners. The second-period payout is discounted by the after-tax return on personal bond investments. This is an application of the equal rate of return principle, in this case between the after-tax returns on stocks and bonds.

---

5 The model presented in this subsection and the next section is in most respects a special one-period case of the more general model developed by Joseph Stiglitz (1973) and Mervyn King (1975).

The right-hand equation in (15.17) is the solution of the left-hand equation for S. We see that S is positively related to τ_p. This is because an increase in the personal tax rate, which reduces the after-tax rate of return on bonds, induces investors to shift to stock. We also see that an increase in τ_g, which means a decrease in $1 - \tau_g$ that reduces the numerator of (15.17) proportionately more than the denominator, causes S to fall. An increase in the capital gains tax makes stock less attractive.

Third, the firm's second-period payout is[6]

$$
\begin{aligned}
V_2 &= P_2 f(x) - (1 + R)[P_1 x + D - F - (S_1 - S_0)P_s] \\
&\quad - \tau_c \{ P_2 f(x) - P_1 x - R[P_1 x + D - F - (S_1 - S_0)P_s] \} \\
&= [P_2 f(x) - (1 + R)P_1 x](1 - \tau_c) \\
&\quad - [1 + (1 - \tau_c)R][D - F - (S_1 - S_0)P_s]
\end{aligned}
$$

(15.18)

The first two terms of the first equation in (15.18) is the before-tax payout: output revenue less principal and interest on the amount borrowed at time 1. We see from Equation (15.16) that the expression in brackets in the first equation of (15.18) represents borrowing (B). The expression in braces in (15.18) is profit, which is output revenue less input and interest costs. Interest is revenue instead of cost if B is negative. The second equation in (15.18) is the result of combining terms in the first equation. Substituting this expression into Equation (15.17) and solving for S give

(15.19)
$$
S = \frac{\begin{aligned} S_1(1 - \tau_g)\{ [P_2 f(x) - (1 + R)P_1 x](1 - \tau_c) \\ + [1 + (1 - \tau_c)R](F - D) \} \end{aligned}}{\begin{aligned} S_1[(1 - \tau_p) - (1 - \tau_g)(1 - \tau_c)]R \\ + (1 - \tau_g)[1 + (1 - \tau_c)R]S_0 \end{aligned}}
$$

We have now come to the point at which we can analyze the influence of taxes on financial and production decisions. Noting that $S_0 P_s = S_0(S/S_1)$ and substituting (15.19) into (15.15), we have

$$
V_1 = \frac{S_0}{S_1} S + (1 - \tau_p)D
$$

(15.20)
$$
= \frac{\begin{aligned} S_0(1 - \tau_g)\{ [P_2 f(x) - (1 + R)P_1 x](1 - \tau_c) \\ + [1 + (1 - \tau_c)R](F - D) \} \end{aligned}}{\begin{aligned} S_1[(1 - \tau_p) - (1 - \tau_g)(1 - \tau_c)]R \\ + (1 - \tau_g)[1 + (1 - \tau_c)R]S_0 \end{aligned}} + (1 - \tau_p)D
$$

6 Assuming positive profits. Otherwise, τ_c times the expression in braces is omitted.

The implications of Equation (15.20) for the firm's (1) production, (2) capital structure, and (3) dividend decisions are as follows:

1. The rate of production that maximizes owner wealth is the value of x that maximizes the expression in the first square brackets in the numerator of Equation (15.20), $[P_2 f(x) - (1 + R)P_1 x]$. This is the expression that was to be maximized in the no-tax case in Equation (15.1). The optimal production decision is independent of taxes and is unchanged from that in Equation (15.5).

2. The coefficient of S_1 in the denominator of Equation (15.20) shows that owner wealth is reduced by a substitution of equity for debt if[7]

(15.21) $(1 - \tau_p) > (1 - \tau_g)(1 - \tau_c)$ or $\tau_p < \tau_c + \tau_g - \tau_c \tau_g$

If the firm finances production by issuing stock, it must do so at a price P_s such that the new (as well as existing) stockholders earn a rate of return equal to the after-tax rate of return on bonds, that is, $(1 - \tau_p)R$. On the other hand, if the firm borrows, it must pay bond-holders the before-tax rate R; the after-tax cost of debt to the firm is $(1 - \tau_c)R$ and to the owners is $(1 - \tau_g)(1 - \tau_c)R$. For example, if $\tau_c = 0.40$, $\tau_g = 0.20$, and the firm borrows $B = \$1,000$ at $R = 0.10$, the after-corporate-profits-tax cost to the firm is $(1 - \tau_c)RB = \$60$, and the after-capital-gains-tax cost to the owners is $(1 - \tau_g)(1 - \tau_c)RB = \$48$. This is less than the cost of issuing new stock if $\$48 < (1 - \tau_p)RB$, that is, if $0.48 < (1 - \tau_p)$, or $\tau_p < 0.52$.

3. In the case in which there is no new issue or retirement of stock, that is, $S_1 = S_0$, the response of owner wealth to dividends is seen from Equation (15.20) to be

$$\frac{dV_1}{dD} = -\frac{(1 - \tau_g)[1 + (1 - \tau_c)R]}{(1 - \tau_g) + (1 - \tau_p)R} + (1 - \tau_p)$$

(15.22)
$$= \begin{cases} -\tau_p & \text{if } \tau_c = \tau_p \text{ and } \tau_g = 0 \\[2mm] \dfrac{\tau_c R - \tau_p(1 + R)}{1 + R} & \text{if } \tau_g = \tau_p \\[2mm] -0.386 & \text{if } \tau_p = \tau_c = 0.40, \\ & \quad \tau_g = 0.20, R = 0.10 \end{cases}$$

Equation (15.22) suggests that dividends will not be paid in the presence of a wide range of tax rates, three of which are shown below the equation. In the first case the firm's owners are all in the same marginal tax bracket, τ_p, which is assumed to be the same as the corpo-

---

7 This is Joseph Stiglitz's result (a) (1973, page 17).

rate income tax, τ_c. Furthermore, the owners pay no capital gains taxes (that is, $\tau_g = 0$), possibly because of offsetting capital losses elsewhere. Under these conditions the owners prefer the firm to retain earnings rather than paying them out as dividends. This is also true in the second case unless τ_p is small relative to τ_c, specifically unless $\tau_p < \tau_c R/(1 + R)$. The third case gives a fairly realistic numerical example. In general the owners would rather not receive dividends unless the personal income tax rate, τ_p, is small relative to τ_c and τ_g.

Summarizing, in the case of an input that is used up during a one-period production process, the introduction of taxes affects the firm's financial decisions in ways that depend upon the specific tax rates to which the firm and its owners are subject but leaves the production decision unaffected regardless of the specific tax rates assumed. These results are illustrated in Exercise 15.4.

EXERCISE 15.4.   Assume as in Exercises 15.1 to 15.3 that $P_1 = P_2 = \$1$, $R = 0.10$, and $f(x) = 22\sqrt{x}$. We know that optimal production is given by $f'(x) = 11/\sqrt{x} = 1.10$, or $x^* = 100$, and $[P_2 f(x^*) - (1 + R)P_1 x^*] = \$110$. Assume $F = 0$ so that production must be financed by borrowing and/or stock issues. Let the tax rates be $\tau_g = 0.20$ and $\tau_c = \tau_p = 0.40$. The initial number of shares is $S_0 = 100$.

(a) Under these conditions, what are the value of shares (S), the price of shares (P_s), and owners' wealth (V_1) as functions of S_1 and D? What are S, P_s, V_1, V_2, $S_0 P_s$, and B when (b) $S_1 = S_0 = 100$ and $D = 0$, (c) dividends are increased to $D = \$10$, (d) D is again zero but the firm issues fifty new shares as a partial substitute for debt, and (e) D is still zero and the firm issues debt in order to reduce the number of shares to $S_1 = 1$?

(a) It is convenient to begin with Equations (15.15) to (15.20), which may now be written

(15.15)′ $$V_1 = 100P_s + 0.6D$$

(15.16)′ $$B + (S_1 - 100)P_s = \$100 + D$$

(15.17)′ $$S_1 P_s = S = \frac{0.80}{0.86} V_2$$

(15.18)′ $$V_2 = \$66 + 1.06[(S_1 - 100)P_s - D]$$

(15.19)′ $$S = \frac{(52.8 - 0.848D)S_1}{0.012S_1 + 84.8}$$

(15.20)' $V_1 = 100P_s + 0.6D = \dfrac{5{,}280 - 84.8D}{0.012S_1 + 84.8} + 0.6D$

Equations (15.19)' and (15.20)' show S and V_1 as functions of S_1 and D. Dividing Equation (15.19)' by S_1 gives $P_s = S/S_1$.

(b) The results for $S_1 = 100$ and $D = 0$ are shown in the first line of the table at the end of this exercise.

(c) A dividend of $10 reduces owner wealth by $61.40 − $57.53 = $3.87. The reduction in the present value of shares, S, is slightly less (by $0.13) than the increase in borrowing (from $100 to $110) necessary to finance the dividends because of the tax deductibility of interest. But this advantage is more than offset by the $(1 - \tau_p)D = \$4$ personal income tax on dividends.

(d) A stock issue increases the value of shares by reducing debt and thereby increasing the future payout, V_2, to the owners (old and new). But the wealth of the original owners is reduced because, referring to inequality (15.21) above,

$$1 - \tau_p = 0.6 > 0.48 = (1 - \tau_g)(1 - \tau_c)$$

(e) If debt is so beneficial, why don't we (the owners) direct the firm to borrow in order to buy all but one share of our stock? We can sell our shares to the firm at a higher price than they would previously have fetched ($0.6226 compared with $0.6140) because future payouts to the remaining shares (or, in this case, share) benefit from the tax deductibility of the interest on the debt issued to buy the stock.

| | Assumptions | | | Results | | | | |
	S_1	D	V_2	S	P_s	S_0P_s	V_1	B
(b)	100	$ 0	$66.00	$61.40	$0.6140	$61.40	$61.40	$100.00
(c)	100	10	55.40	51.53	0.5153	51.53	57.53	110.00
(d)	150	0	98.31	91.45	0.6097	60.97	60.97	69.52
(e)	1	0	0.67	0.62	0.6226	62.26	62.26	161.63

THE INFLUENCE OF TAXES ON INVESTMENT

We now assume that production depends on a single capital input purchased at a cost of P_1 per unit at time 1 and with a resale value of $(1 - \delta)P_2$ per unit at time 2, where δ is the rate of depreciation $(0 \le \delta \le 1)$. Financial decisions are unchanged from those shown above and will not be considered in this section. Our concern will be limited to how, given those financial decisions, the optimal investment-production plan is affected by taxes.

Instead of Equation (15.18) the firm's second-period payout is now

$$
\begin{aligned}
V_2 = \; & P_2 f(K) + (1 - \delta) P_2 K \\
& - (1 + R)[P_1 K + D - F - (S_1 - S_0) P_s] \\
& - \tau_c \{ P_2 f(K) - \delta P_1 K - R[P_1 K + D - F - (S_1 - S_0) P_s] \} \\
& - q \tau_c [P_2 (1 - \delta) K - P_1 (1 - \delta) K] \\
= \; & P_2 \left\{ [f(K) - (r + \delta) K](1 - \tau_c) + \frac{\tau_c (1 - q)(1 - \delta) K p}{1 + p} \right\} \\
& - [1 + (1 - \tau_c) R][D - F - (S_1 - S_0) P_s]
\end{aligned}
$$

(15.23)

The first three terms of (15.23) are the firm's before-tax second-period payout, consisting of revenues from the sale of output and the sale of the K units of the capital good purchased in the first period, less the repayment of debt plus interest. The amount of borrowing is expressed as before except that K has replaced x. The next expression deducts the tax on profit, where profit is revenue from output less depreciation and interest. Depreciation for tax purposes is assumed equal to true economic depreciation. The last expression in the first equation of (15.23) deducts capital gains taxes on the difference between the proceeds of the sale of capital goods and the cost net of depreciation. The term q takes account of the lower tax rate on capital gains than on ordinary income. Since corporate capital gains are taxed at 60 percent of ordinary corporate income, $q = 0.60$. Our discussion assumes inflation ($P_2 > P_1$) so that this term affects V_2 negatively.

The second equation in (15.23) is the result of rearrangement of the first equation. Now consider the optimal investment decision in the absence of corporate taxes. The firm invests up to the point at which

(15.24) $f'(K) = r + \delta$ or $f'(K) - \delta = r$

At the optimum the marginal product of capital, $f'(K)$, equals the real rate of interest, r, plus the rate of depreciation of capital, δ. The second equation in (15.24) states that at the optimum the *net* marginal product of capital, that is, the marginal contribution of capital to output less the rate at which capital is used up, equals the real rate of interest. If the rate of depreciation is 100 percent, Equation (15.24) is identical with Equation (15.5), which stated that $f'(x) = 1 + r$ when the input was entirely used up during the one-period production process.

Now introduce corporate taxes τ_c and q. If capital gains are taxed at the same rate as ordinary income, that is, if $q = 1$, the optimum investment decision with taxes is identical with that without taxes shown in Equation (15.24). This result is analogous to those discussed above, in which production decisions were independent of taxes. Taxes are also irrelevant to the investment decision if the rate of depreciation is 100 percent ($\delta = 1$) and/or there is no inflation ($p = 0$) so that there are no capital gains to be taxed. In other circumstances, however, when the term in τ_c does not vanish, optimal investment requires that

(15.25) $$f'(K) = r + \delta - \frac{\tau_c(1 - q)(1 - \delta)p}{(1 - \tau_c)(1 + p)} = k$$

The terms to the right of the first equal sign make up the *cost of capital, k.* Given positive inflation ($p > 0$) and $0 < \tau_c, q, \delta < 1$, an increase in τ_c causes a reduction in the cost of capital and therefore in $f'(K)$. With declining marginal product, as shown in Figure 15.1, a fall in marginal product means an increase in K. The surprising result that an increase in the corporate tax rate stimulates investment and production is due to the greater effect of τ_c on cost than on revenue— because the increase in the value of capital goods is taxed at a lower rate than expenses. In terms of Figure 15.5 the after-tax marginal revenue line has fallen proportionately less than the after-tax marginal cost curve so that their after-tax point of intersection lies to the right of the before-tax optimal output, z^*. This result is reversed during deflationary periods, when an increase in τ_c retards investment and production.

THE EVIDENCE

We conclude this chapter by confronting the theoretical implications of the models presented above with the evidence. How well does the theory of corporate finance explain corporate behavior? We shall see that the theory is reasonably consistent with real investment decisions and helps to explain some aspects of financial decisions, but much remains to be explained.

Investment and the cost of capital

Equation (15.25) indicates that a firm's *optimal* stock of capital, the amount of plant and equipment that it would *like* to have on hand, during any production period is an inverse function of the current cost of capital. But desired and actual stocks of capital are seldom equal because foresight is imperfect and plants and machines cannot be chosen, ordered, and installed overnight. Current investment is largely the result of past decisions and therefore of costs of capital (and other variables) observed in the past:

(15.26) $K_t - K_{t-1} = I_t = f(k_t, k_{t-1}, \ldots, k_{t-n}, a_t, a_{t-1}, \ldots, a_{t-n})$

Investment is defined as additions to the capital stock, and the a's indicate variables other than the cost of capital that affect investment.

These include technological developments, wage rates, and fluctuations in aggregate demand. Investment may in some degree be affected by present as well as past observations (projects can be *stopped* at a moment's notice), hence the inclusion of k_t and a_t.

Most recent empirical studies have found the response of investment to lagged distributions of the cost of capital to be statistically significant. These studies have differed substantially in length of lags, that is, the size of n in Equation (15.24), variables other than k entering the investment equation, and definitions of the cost of capital, that is, in the ways in which taxes, inflation, depreciation, accounting procedures, bond yields, and equity yields enter k.[8] Apparently the negative influence of k on I is sufficiently strong, as suggested by the theory, that substantial variations in the specification of the investment equation do not alter the direction of that influence.

This does not mean that k's influence is strong enough to survive *any* specification. Several studies conducted during the 1940s and 1950s found the relationship between investment (I_t) and the cost of capital defined simply as the current rate of interest ($k_t = R_t$) to be statistically insignificant. This result is not surprising in view of the nearly constant rate of interest and the great fluctuations in the neglected inflation and tax determinants of the cost of capital during the sample period.

Capital structure[9]

Research on the capital structure of firms has proceeded in three stages. First, Irrelevance Theorem 15.1 states that, in perfect capital markets with no taxes, owners of firms are indifferent to capital structure, that is, to debt/equity ratios. Second, the introduction of taxes into the analysis causes capital structure to matter. Inequality (15.21) implies that firms will have capital structures consisting of either all equity or (almost)[10] all debt, depending on corporate and

---

8 See Walter Elliott (1980) and Robert Chirinko and Robert Eisner (1983) for discussions of some of these results.

9 Unfortunately, "capital" is widely used in two senses: to indicate capital equipment, as above, and to indicate sources of finance, specifically debt and equity, as below.

10 There must be at least one share of stock; *someone* must own the firm.

Theorem 15.1 and inequality (15.21) both abstract from *bankruptcy costs*. The arguments that capital structure is indeterminate in the absence of taxes and should be almost entirely debt in the presence of taxes (for certain tax structures, such as those considered above) depend upon the assumption that expected earnings are independent of the capital structure. This is not true if bankruptcy is possible and if there are administrative, legal, and other costs associated with bankruptcy because the expected value of these costs must be deducted from the expected earnings stream in calculating the value of the firm. Since the probability of bankruptcy (that is, the inability to service debt) rises with leverage, there may be a unique optimal capital structure, with a limited amount of debt, even in the presence of taxes. This occurs at the point at which the increase in expected bankruptcy costs due to the issue of another dollar of debt equals the expected gain due to the tax deductibility of interest on debt. See Nevins Baxter (1967) for an early and readable contribution to this literature and James Scott (1976) and Wayne Lee and Henry Barker (1977) for examples of formal models of optimal capital structure that take bankruptcy costs into account. James Ang, Jess Chua, and John McConnell (1982)

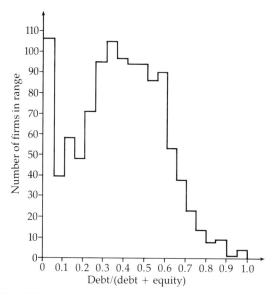

Source: E. Han Kim, Wilbur G. Lewellen, and John J. McConnell, "Financial Leverage Clienteles: Theory and Evidence," *Journal of Financial Economics,* March 1979, pages 83–109.

Figure 15.6   The distribution of capital structures of a sample of 1,140 firms.

personal tax rates. Furthermore, given prevailing tax rates, we should expect the latter capital structure to dominate. This is not the case, however, as is illustrated by the distribution of debt/(debt + equity) ratios in Figure 15.6. Inequality (15.21) asserts that the distribution of such ratios should be bimodal, with large numbers of observations at zero and near unity. The sample reported in the chart is indeed bimodal, with one mode at zero. But the other mode is not pronounced and, at 0.30, cannot be considered "high." Furthermore, about 60 percent of the firms in the sample are almost evenly distributed between debt/(debt + equity) ratios of 0.25 and 0.60.

The third stage was introduced by Merton Miller, who attempted to explain observations such as those in Figure 15.6 in terms of *clientele effects,* while at the same time reconciling them with the Modigliani-Miller Irrelevance Theorem 15.1. Miller's analysis in "Debt and Taxes" (1977) was presented within the framework of Figure 15.7. Assume for simplicity that the capital gains tax, τ_g, is zero, and suppose that R_0 is the equilibrium rate of interest on the fully tax-exempt bonds of state and local governments. Corporations must pay interest rates higher than R_0 in order to induce investors to hold their bonds: If $R_0 = 0.05$, for example, corporations must pay at least $R_0/(1 - \tau_p) = 0.05/(1 - 0.2) = 0.0625$ to induce investors in the 20

present estimates of the administrative costs of bankruptcy and a useful bibliography of theoretical and empirical work on this problem.

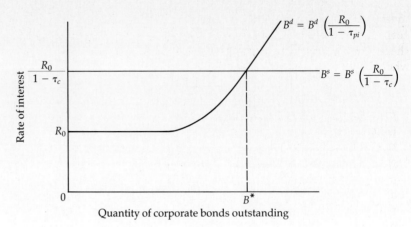

Figure 15.7   The equilibrium amount of corporate debt.

percent tax bracket to hold their bonds and at least $0.05/(1 - 0.5) = 0.10$ to induce investors in the 50 percent tax bracket to hold their bonds. The rising curve, B^d, in Figure 15.7 shows the aggregate demand for corporate bonds to be an increasing function of the rate on corporate bonds. The flat portion of the curve at the level of R_0 is the demand for taxable corporate bonds by tax-exempt investors. Tax-exempt individuals and organizations, such as universities and other charities, would be the only holders of corporate bonds if the yield on these bonds were R_0. Taxable investors would prefer tax-exempt bonds. The rising portion of the bond demand curve is the result of investors in successively higher tax brackets (τ_{pi}) being attracted away from tax-exempt bonds by increases in the corporate bond rate.

The market equilibrium for corporate debt occurs at the rate of interest $R_0/(1 - \tau_c)$, where τ_c is the corporate tax rate. Referring to inequality (15.21), letting τ_{pi} be the personal tax rate of investors in the ith tax bracket, and assuming $\tau_g = 0$, *corporations prefer debt over equity financing as long as*[11]

(15.27) $(1 - \tau_c) < (1 - \tau_{pi})$ that is, as long as $\dfrac{R_0}{1 - \tau_c} > \dfrac{R_0}{1 - \tau_{pi}}$

The horizontal line, B^s, at the level $R_0/(1 - \tau_c)$ is a perfectly elastic corporate bond supply curve. It will be to the advantage of corporations to issue bonds as long as there are investors who can be attracted by rates of interest less than $R_0/(1 - \tau_c)$, that is, as long as there are

---

11   The relaxation of the simplifying assumption that $\tau_g = 0$ does not affect the substance of Miller's analysis. Letting $\tau_g > 0$, equilibrium in the corporate bond market is achieved at the B^* for which, referring to inequality (15.21),

$$\frac{R_0}{1 - \tau_c} = \frac{R_0}{(1 - \tau_p)/(1 - \tau_g)}$$

investors in tax brackets τ_{pi} less than τ_c. The equilibrium amount of corporate debt, in the aggregate, is therefore B^*. This means that there is "an equilibrium debt-equity ratio for the corporate sector as a whole."

But there would be no optimum debt ratio for any individual firm. Companies following a no-leverage or low leverage strategy (like I.B.M. or Kodak) would find a market among investors in the high tax brackets; those opting for a high leverage strategy (like the electric utilities) would find the natural clientele for their securities at the other end of the scale. But one clientele is as good as the other. And in this important sense it would still be true that the value of any firm, in equilibrium, would be independent of its capital structure, despite the deductibility of interest payments in computing corporate income taxes.

Merton Miller (1977)

John Harris, Rodney Roenfeldt, and Philip Cooley (1983) found some evidence of a clientele effect based on estimated marginal income tax rates.[12] They arranged a sample of 316 firms in quintiles from the lowest to the highest debt/(debt + equity) ratios. The average ratio for each quintile is shown in the second column of Table 15.1, and the third column shows the estimated average marginal income tax rates of stockholders in the five groups. The results are roughly consistent with Miller's prediction that investors in low tax brackets should be expected to substitute corporate for personal leverage. Specifically the most highly leveraged firms, with an average debt ratio of 0.73, attract investors from the lowest tax brackets, whereas firms with the least leverage attract investors from the highest tax brackets. So the extreme observations are consistent with a clientele effect. But the intervening observations (quintiles 2 to 4)

---

12 Edwin Elton and Martin Gruber (1970) estimated marginal income tax rates of marginal investors in individual firms from changes in the prices of stock going *ex dividend*. For example, if a firm declares a dividend on May 15 payable June 30 to stockholders of record on June 15, an investor must buy the firm's stock at least by June 8 in order to receive the dividend because stockholders are recorded on the firm's books 5 business days after their purchases. Shares purchased after June 8 do not earn the June 30 dividend. They are ex (without) dividend. An investor who buys the stock with dividend on June 8 rather than ex dividend on June 9 adds $(1 - \tau_p)D$ to his after-tax income, where D is the amount of the dividend and τ_p is his marginal income tax rate. If he buys the stock on June 9, he saves on the earlier purchase price but incurs an additional capital gains tax so that the present value of his after-tax gain is $(P_o - P_e)[1 - \tau_g/(1 + R)^n]$, where P_o is the with-dividend price on June 8, P_e is the ex dividend price on June 9, τ_g is the investor's marginal capital gains tax rate, R is the investor's required rate of return, and n is the number of years that he intends to hold the stock, that is, the number of years for which the capital gains tax will be deferred. If n is large so that $\tau_g/(1 + R)^n \approx 0$, the investor is indifferent between purchases on June 8 and June 9 if

$$(1 - \tau_p)D = P_o - P_e \qquad \text{or} \qquad \tau_p = 1 - (P_o - P_e)/D$$

John Harris, Rodney Roenfeldt, and Philip Cooley estimated τ_p from price and dividend data for the years 1968, 1970, 1972, 1974, and 1976 for 316 firms stratified into the quintiles in Table 15.1.

Table 15.1   Corporate Debt Ratios and Estimated Investor Marginal Income Tax Rates

Leverage Quintile	Average Debt Ratio	Estimated Average Investor Marginal Tax Rate
1	0.18	0.65
2	0.36	0.23
3	0.48	0.37
4	0.60	0.19
5	0.73	0.16

Source: From John Harris, Rodney Roenfeldt, and Philip Cooley, "Evidence of Financial Leverage Clienteles," *Journal of Finance,* September 1983, tab. 1.

indicate that the clientele effect is not sensitive to small variations in the debt ratio. This result was anticipated by Robert Taggart (1980), who suggested that Miller's conclusions are likely to be modified by costs of issuing debt that Miller did not consider, such as expected bankruptcy costs (which increase with leverage)[13] and efforts to avoid conflicts of interest between stockholders and bondholders.[14] These nontax considerations interfere with the perfect inverse relationship between personal tax rates and corporate debt ratios implied by Miller's analysis. Apparently this relationship can be counted upon only between extremes, such as between the first and fifth quintiles of Table 15.1.

Dividends

Existing theory and evidence related to dividends resemble the theory and evidence discussed above in connection with debt/equity ratios. This is not surprising because dividend decisions form one part of the overall capital structure decision. Irrelevance Theorem 15.2 states that in perfect capital markets with no taxes owners of firms are indifferent to dividend decisions. The introduction of taxes implies, according to Equation (15.22), that investors in high tax brackets prefer to own the stock of firms that pay low dividends while investors in low tax brackets prefer to own firms that pay high dividends. However, clear evidence of such a clientele effect is lacking. Several alternative explanations of observed dividend policies have been offered, but none has gained widespread acceptance.[15]

13 See footnote 10, above.

14 These conflicts were discussed in Chapter 10 in connection with bond covenants and convertible bonds.

15 For example see the discussion by Fischer Black (1976) and some recent attempted partial explanations in the May 1982 *Journal of Finance* by Nils Hakansson, Patrick Hess, Kose John and Avner Kalay, and Robert Litzenberger and Krishna Ramaswamy.

QUESTIONS

1. Discuss in your own words, without using technical jargon, the two principal ways in which firms earn profits. Illustrate your answers with figures.
2. Discuss the factors affecting the profitability of the production process and illustrate your answers with figures.
3. Discuss the relation between the internal rate of return and the market rate of interest (or cost of capital).
4. Briefly what is the meaning of Exercise 15.3?
5. Discuss the connections between the equal rate of return principle, the rate of interest, and the price of shares.
6. How should bankruptcy costs affect dividends?
7. Discuss the connections between Figure 15.6, Figure 15.7, and Table 15.1. Do they tell consistent stories? Why or why not?
8. Firm X has declared a dividend of $2 a share on March 25 payable April 30 to stockholders of record on April 10. The stock sells for $50 on April 3 and $49 on April 4. What is the marginal income tax rate of the marginal investors in firm X? What assumptions have you made and why? What do we mean by the *marginal* income tax rate of the *marginal* investor? Confirm your result by showing that stock purchasers on April 3 and April 4 earn the same returns.

PROBLEMS

1. Draw the production opportunities curves implied by (a), (b), and (c) at the end of Exercise 15.1. Show the calculations underlying these curves.
2. Do Exercise 15.2 when $F = \$169$, $P_1 = \$1$, $P_2 = \$1.10$, $R = 0.21$, and $f(x) = 26.4\sqrt{x}$ so that $f'(x) = 13.2/\sqrt{x}$.
3. How are the production and securities decisions in problem 2 affected by an increase in the rate of inflation from 10 to 21 percent with P_1, R, F, and the production function remaining unchanged?
4. Do Exercise 15.3 when $F = 0$ and the difference is made up by borrowing. Please present your results in the format of the table in Exercise 15.3, and explain them.
5. Calculate the contribution of the firm, V_1, to owners' wealth when (a) $F = 0$, $P_1 = P_2 = \$1$, $R = 0.21$, $f(x) = 22\sqrt{x}$, $\tau_c = \tau_p = 0.40$, $\tau_g = 0.20$, and no new shares are issued or old shares retired, (b) $P_2 = \$1.10$ and all the other values in (a) are unchanged, and (c) $\tau_c = 0.30$ and all the other values in (b) are unchanged. Explain the similarities and differences between (a), (b), and (c).
6. Following the procedure of Exercise 15.4 and assuming $P_1 = P_2 = \$1$, $R = 0.10$, $f(x) = 22\sqrt{x}$ so that $x^* = 100$, $F = 0$, $\tau_g = 0.20$, $\tau_c = \tau_p = 0.40$, and $S_0 = 100$, show what happens to S, P_s, V_1, V_2, $S_0 P_s$, and B when (a) $S_1 = 100$ and $D = \$20$ and (b) $S_1 = 200$ and $D = 0$. Present

your results in a table like that in Exercise 15.4 (also show your calculations), and compare them with the results in Exercise 15.4.

7. Referring to the section entitled The Influence of Taxes on Investment, calculate the optimal investment decision, K^*, when **(a)** $P_1 = P_2 = \$1$, $R = \delta = 0.05$, $f(K) = 22\sqrt{K}$, $F = \$169$, $q = 0.60$, and no taxes, **(b)** we assume the same values as (a) except $\tau_c = \tau_p = 0.24$ and $\tau_g = 0.12$, and **(c)** we assume the same values as (b) except $P_2 = \$1.25$ and $R = 0.3125$. **(d)** Explain your results. **(e)** Which of the data given in (a) to (c) are irrelevant and why?

REFERENCES

James S. Ang, Jess H. Chua, and John J. McConnell, "The Administrative Costs of Corporate Bankruptcy: A Note," *Journal of Finance,* March 1982, pages 219–226.

Nevins D. Baxter, "Leverage, Risk of Ruin and the Cost of Capital," *Journal of Finance,* September 1967, pages 395–403.

Fischer Black, "The Dividend Puzzle," *Journal of Portfolio Management,* Winter 1976, pages 5–8.

Robert S. Chirinko and Robert Eisner, "Tax Policy and Investment in Major U.S. Macroeconomic Econometric Models," *Journal of Public Economics,* March 1983, pages 139–166.

J. Walter Elliott, "The Cost of Capital and U.S. Capital Investment: A Test of Alternative Concepts," *Journal of Finance,* September 1980, pages 981–999.

Edwin J. Elton and Martin J. Gruber, "Marginal Stockholder Tax Rates and the Clientele Effect," *Review of Economics and Statistics,* February 1970, pages 68–74.

Eugene F. Fama and Merton H. Miller, *The Theory of Finance,* Holt, Rinehart & Winston, New York, 1972.

Irving Fisher, *The Theory of Interest,* Macmillan, New York, 1930.

Nils H. Hakansson, "To Pay or Not to Pay Dividends," *Journal of Finance,* May 1982, pages 415–428.

John M. Harris, Rodney L. Roenfeldt, and Philip L. Cooley, "Evidence of Financial Leverage Clienteles," *Journal of Finance,* September 1983, pages 1125–1132.

Patrick Hess, "The Ex-dividend Day Behavior of Stock Returns: Further Evidence on Tax Effects," *Journal of Finance,* May 1982, pages 445–456.

J. Hirshleifer, *Investment, Interest, and Capital,* Prentice-Hall, Englewood Cliffs, NJ, 1970.

Kose John and Avner Kalay, "Costly Contracting and Optimal Payout Constraints," *Journal of Finance,* May 1982, pages 457–469.

E. Han Kim, Wilbur G. Lewellen, and John J. McConnell, "Financial Leverage Clienteles: Theory and Evidence," *Journal of Financial Economics,* March 1979, pages 83–109.

Mervyn A. King, "Taxation, Corporate Financial Policy, and the Cost of Capital: Comment," *Journal of Public Economics,* August 1975, pages 271–279.

Wayne Y. Lee and Henry H. Barker, "Bankruptcy Costs and the Firm's Optimal Debt Capacity: A Positive Theory of Capital Structure," *Southern Economic Journal,* April 1977, pages 1453–1465.

Robert H. Litzenberger and Krishna Ramaswamy, "The Effects of Dividends on Common Stock Prices: Tax Effects or Information Effects?" *Journal of Finance,* May 1982, pages 429–444.

Merton H. Miller, "Debt and Taxes," *Journal of Finance,* May 1977, pages 261–275.

Franco Modigliani and Merton H. Miller, "The Cost of Capital, Corporation Finance, and the Theory of Investment," *American Economic Review,* June 1958, pages 261–297.

James H. Scott, "A Theory of Optimal Capital Structure," *Bell Journal of Economics,* Spring 1976, pages 33–54.

Joseph E. Stiglitz, "Taxation, Corporate Financial Policy, and the Cost of Capital," *Journal of Public Economics,* February 1973, pages 1–34.

Robert A. Taggart, "Taxes and Corporate Capital Structure in an Incomplete Market," *Journal of Finance,* June 1980, pages 645–659.

Knut Wicksell, "Taxation in the Monopoly Case," first published in Swedish, 1896. Richard A. Musgrave (tr.), in Richard A. Musgrave and Carl S. Schoup, *Readings in the Economics of Taxation,* Irwin, Homewood, IL, 1959.

COMMERCIAL BANK LOAN AND INVESTMENT BEHAVIOR

Bankers are just like anybody else, except richer.

Ogden Nash

This is the third chapter in which commercial banks have played the leading role. Chapters 4 and 9 dealt with the distinctive functions of banks in creating and handling money. But not all bank activities are peculiar: In some respects banks are "just like anybody else." In common with other capitalists, bank owners borrow and put up some of their own money and apply these funds to the purchase of assets in the hope of earning profits. Banks hold their assets in three main forms: reserves, loans, and government securities. The last category is often referred to as "investments." The reserve decision was discussed in Chapter 9. The present chapter is concerned with the allocation of earning assets between loans and investments.

In this as in other chapters we relate theory and practice. In particular we wish to understand the causes of recent changes in bank loan markets as reflected in the shortening of average loan maturities and the increase of the volatility of bank loan rates relative to other interest rates. Three possible explanations of these events, which represent a return to banking practices of the 1920s, will be considered: the weakening of incentives to engage in nonprice *credit rationing,* the weakening of long-term *customer relationships,* and the strengthening of incentives to avoid interest rate risk by *matching the maturities and/or interest rate flexibilities of assets and liabilities.* The next section explains the recent familiar developments in bank loan markets in terms of the interplay of all three of these forces. The following sections take closer looks at the influences of customer relationships and credit rationing on bank loan rates and the allocation of bank assets.

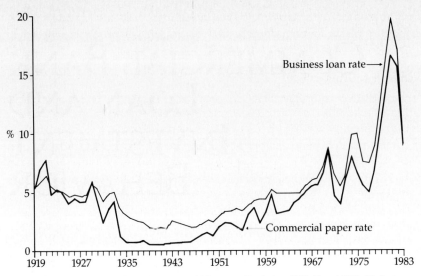

Sources: Federal Reserve Board, *Banking and Monetary Statistics, 1914–41 and 1941–70, Annual Statistical Digests,* and *Federal Reserve Bulletins;* the data are described in Table 16.2

Figure 16.1   Interest rates (on first-quarter loan survey dates) on short-term business loans and commercial paper, 1919 to 1983.

FAMILIAR DEVELOPMENTS IN BANK LOAN MARKETS[1]

An overview

Bank loan rates used to be described as "sticky" because they appeared to be relatively insensitive to conditions affecting other interest rates. No longer. The volatility of loan rates has increased dramatically in recent years, not only absolutely but in comparison with other rates. The main theme of the following discussion is that this development is part of a return to the conditions and practices that characterized bank loan markets before 1930. Hence the title "Familiar developments . . . ."

A supporting theme contends that the differences in bank loan practices between three more or less distinct periods (before 1930, the mid-1930s to the mid-1960s, and the late 1960s to the present) may be explained by differences in the volatility of interest rates between those periods. An average short-term business loan rate and the 4- to 6-month prime commercial paper rate during 1919 to 1983 are shown in Figure 16.1. Notice the low and (more important for the present discussion) relatively steady rates during the middle period, extending from the mid-1930s to the mid-1960s, between two periods of higher and more volatile rates, although you might want to replace "mid-1960s" by either "late 1950s" or "early 1970s," depending on your idea

---

1 This section is drawn from John Wood (1983).

of volatility. We shall now look at bank loan practices during each of these periods in turn. You already know the punch line: The third period represents a return to the first.

Bank loans in the 1920s

A substantial proportion of the liabilities of the large money center banks paid interest that varied more or less in line with money market rates during the 1920s. The most interest-sensitive liabilities were interbank deposits, which made up about 20 percent of the total deposits of New York City and Chicago banks. The more aggressive banks also paid interest on large nonbank demand deposits. Furthermore, 20 to 25 percent of deposits consisted of interest-bearing savings and time deposits, including certificates of deposit.

The top portion of Table 16.1 shows how these funds were distributed among various loan categories in the fifty or sixty largest cities.[2] A small but important category was loans to correspondent banks, most of which had maturities between 60 and 90 days and paid rates close to that on prime commercial paper.[3] The largest item was "unsecured [time] paper with one or more individual or firm names." These were predominantly business loans of the kind that dominate the modern "commercial, industrial, and agricultural production" category in the lower portion of the table. Although nearly all these loans were formally short term (3 months or less), their liquidity was doubtful because they were repeatedly renewed (and expected to be renewed) as part of long-term customer relationships.

The often-renewed commercial call loans also lacked genuine liquidity. However, the short-term contractual nature of business loans, which permitted the frequent adjustment of loan rates (daily in the case of call loans, whether renewed or not), allowed rates of return on assets to vary with the rates on their volatile managed liabilities and thus protected banks against the interest rate risk that arises from

---

2 The upper and lower portions of Table 16.1 differ because the best loan data for large banks (which correspond roughly to banks in large cities) in the 1920s and before were reported by the Comptroller of the Currency for "reserve cities" and "central reserve city" banks but more recently by the Federal Reserve for "large weekly reporting banks." The former classification may be explained as follows: The National Banking Act of 1863 required federally chartered banks to hold specified minimum cash reserves except that, recognizing existing correspondent banking practices, "country" banks could satisfy three-fifths of their reserve requirements by deposits with reserve city banks, which in turn could keep half their required reserves as deposits with central reserve city banks. Reserve requirements were 15 percent of deposits for country banks and 25 percent of deposits for others. The Federal Reserve Act required national banks (and others that chose to join the Federal Reserve System) to keep their reserves with Federal Reserve Banks but retained the National Banking Act's classification of country, reserve city, and central reserve city banks for purposes of reserve requirements. In 1914 there were three central reserve cities (New York, Chicago, and St. Louis) and forty-nine reserve cities. By 1928, because of reclassifications, there were two central reserve cities (New York and Chicago) and sixty-four reserve cities. (See the Federal Reserve Board's *Banking and Monetary Statistics, 1914–41*, page 401.)

The reporting dates in Table 16.1 were chosen for comparability of season and stage of the cycle (expansion but not peak).

3 These loans are discussed by Leonard Watkins (1929, pages 191–192).

Table 16.1   Percentage Distributions of Loans of Selected Banks: End of June 1922, 1928, 1969, 1981

National Banks in Central Reserve and Reserve Cities	1922	1928
Demand (call) loans		
Unsecured paper with one or more individual or firm names	4.6	4.5
Secured by stocks and bonds	17.5	21.6
Secured by other personal securities, including merchandise and warehouse receipts	3.2	3.2
Time (fixed maturity) loans		
Unsecured paper with one or more individual or firm names	48.5	37.3
Secured by stocks and bonds	15.4	19.3
Secured by other personal securities, including merchandise and warehouse receipts	8.2	6.2
Secured by real estate	0.9	6.1
Bankers' acceptances	1.7	1.7
Memo: loans to banks	a	3.2
by New York City banks	a	5.5

Large Weekly Reporting Banks	1969	1981
Loans by type of borrower		
Brokers, dealers, and others for purchasing and carrying securities (including fed funds)	4.6	3.4
Banks (including fed funds)	4.0	7.5
Other fed funds	b	0.6
Bankers' acceptances and commercial paper	0.3	1.0
Commercial, industrial, and agricultural production	45.7	38.6
Real estate	19.0	25.2
Consumer	11.2	15.2
Nonbank financial	6.5	5.5
Other	8.6	3.0

a Unavailable

b Less than 0.5 percent.

Sources: Comptroller of the Currency, *Annual Reports* and *Federal Reserve Bulletins*.

unmatched asset and liability maturities. The real estate loans in Table 16.1 were also short term, national banks before 1927 being limited to maturities of no more than 1 year on these loans.[4] The rise in real estate loans between 1922 and 1928 occurred almost entirely after the McFadden Act of 1927 extended the maximum maturity to 5 years and in other ways lessened official interference with national bank lending on real estate.[5]

4 The liquidity of real estate mortgages was increased by the practice, especially in the case of large loans, of placing the mortgage "as security in trust and issuing real estate bonds against the mortgage in convenient denominations," usually to depositors [Rollin Thomas (1937, page 138)].

5 See Ralph Young (1932, page 98). Rollin Thomas (1937, page 137) reports that state banks held

But the most liquid form of bank investment was the stock exchange call loan. Nearly all the demand loans secured by stocks and bonds in Table 16.1 went to brokers and dealers for the purpose of carrying securities. These loans "are made by banks to brokers who keep no deposit account with the bank. There being no deposit relationship, the bank feels at perfect liberty to call such loans whenever the need arises, and those loans are the first to be called if the bank must entrench."[6] About half of the time loans secured by stocks and bonds also went to brokers and dealers.[7] Most stock market loans were made by New York City banks. But substantial amounts were extended directly to brokers and dealers by banks in the interior and also by nonfinancial businesses.[8]

In summary substantial parts of bank assets and liabilities paid returns and incurred costs that varied with other short-term rates. Banks were nicely hedged against interest rate risk. But no one was protected against, nor could anyone have foreseen, the withdrawal of 40 percent of Federal Reserve credit between October 1929 and October 1930, the currency drains and bank panics of 1931 and 1933, the failure of half the banks between 1929 and 1933, and the loss of 37 percent of bank deposits and 55 percent of bank loans during the same period.

Changes in bank loan practices during the 1930s and 1940s

Davis Dewey and Martin Shugrue (1922, pages 177 and 178) wrote as follows about business call loans:

It is not unusual for loans of this kind to run for 6 months or a year or even longer. There is usually a mutual understanding (not a written agreement) between the bank and its customer that demand for payment of the note will not be made until some time which is convenient to the borrower. . . . A large commercial bank in Boston states that during its fifty years of existence it has not served a single notice on a borrower for payment of a demand loan and this case is probably by no means exceptional.

Not so during the Great Depression as banks and other creditors pressed for the repayment of debt with no thought of customer relationships or of anything else except survival. The effects of this

more than three times the real estate loans of national banks, expressed as proportions of total loans and investments.

6 Luther Harr and Carlton Harris (1936, page 176). The operations of the call loan market were discussed in connection with Table 9.3, and its history was included in the chronology of the development of the New York Stock Exchange in Chapter 11.

7 The estimated proportions of loans secured by stocks and bonds that went to brokers and dealers are based on estimates in Rollin Thomas (1937, page 116) and Ray Westerfield (1938, page 325).

8 See Margaret Meyers (1931, pages 266–269).

trauma on bank loan contracts lasted 40 years. One of the earliest effects was the increased use of explicit long-term loans, which borrowers wanted in order to make sure of funds for the full periods for which they were needed, having learned not to count on renewals,[9] and which banks were willing to supply because they had turned to new sources of liquidity, having learned that call loans are not in fact callable during general liquidity crises.[10]

Banks accumulated substantial excess reserves both because of their low opportunity costs during the low-interest-rate decades of the 1930s and 1940s and in fear of another attack on bank reserve positions by the Federal Reserve.[11] Banks also attempted to improve their liquidity by shifting from loans to marketable government securities until the former had declined as a proportion of earning assets from about 70 percent in 1929 to 40 percent in 1940. Excess reserves rose from 2 to 91 percent of required reserves during the same period.

Banks extended few loans, but their liquid cash and security positions made them willing to extend a higher proportion of long-term loans than in the 1920s. There were also more strings attached. Banks imposed covenants on long-term loans similar to those required by bondholders, including restrictions on dividend payments, minimum working capital requirements, liens on property, limits on other debt, limits on pledges of property to secure other debt, and the greater use of security in the forms of warehouse receipts and the assignment of accounts receivable.[12]

Banks also required implicit or explicit long-term deposit commitments from both short-term and long-term borrowers in order to achieve stability in their reserve positions and lending capabilities and also as part of a policy of competition for deposits through preferential loan terms, a practice that became more important after the prohibition of interest on demand deposits in 1933. All these developments acted to restore, with greater strength than ever, the customer relationships that had been interrupted by the Great Depression. Banks increasingly provided insurance against the premature loss of

---

9 The increased demand for long-term bank loans as a proportion of long-term debt has also been partly attributed to the increased costs of issuing bonds following the Securities Exchange Acts of 1933 and 1934. The combination of long-term loans and loan participations also enabled banks and their customers to evade the 1933 Banking Act's prohibition against bank underwriting of securities. See Neil Jacoby and Raymond Saulnier (1942, Chapter 1; 1947, Chapter 5) and George Moore (1959). Loan participations have grown over time, with groups of commercial banks operating very much like the syndicates of investment banks discussed in Chapter 11.

10   GLENDOWER. I can call Spirits from the vastie Deepe.
      HOTSPUR. Why so can I, or so can any man:
         But will they come, when you doe call for them?

         William Shakespeare, *Henry IV*, pt. 1, act 3, sc. 1

11 This fear proved justified when the Fed doubled reserve requirement ratios in three steps between August 1936 and May 1937.

12 For a discussion of protective provisions in long-term loans see Neil Jacoby and Raymond Saulnier (1947, Chapters 5 and 6) and George Moore (1959).

financing to borrowers who in exchange insured banks against bad loans and the loss of deposits until business loans with maturities of 1 year or more (term loans) had risen from almost nothing in 1929 to nearly one-third of business loans in 1940.[13]

These mutual insurance arrangements begun in response to the catastrophic events of 1929 to 1933 were strengthened by the stable conditions that prevailed during the dozen or so years following World War II, even when interest rates rose and excess reserves and security holdings declined. Relatively steady economic growth, combined with relatively steady monetary and fiscal policies, meant a stable interest rate and bank reserve environment in which banks could safely extend long-term fixed-rate loans.

Familiar developments...

The tendency of commercial bank loan rates to be less variable than other short-term (or "money market") rates has been rationalized in a variety of ways: First, it might be in the interests of a well-diversified bank and a borrower engaged in repeated short-term ventures (such as the purchase and sale of goods) for the bank to offer insurance against "excessive" (as measured by money market rates) fluctuations in the future cost of funds. That is, there may be an understanding between bank and borrower that the loan rate will be higher (the insurance premium) but less variable than in the case of borrowers with no such implicit contract.[14] Such understandings might apply to medium- and long-term as well as to short-term loans, and all raise the possibility of credit rationing (that is, the nonprice allocation of funds) during periods of rising interest rates if the slower increase in bank loan rates leads to excess demands for bank funds.

Second, the bank-customer relationships implied by repeated loan renewals suggest that the current accommodation of prospective borrowers by a bank influences the bank's future deposits and loan demands. These effects are due both to the costs to banks of acquiring information about borrowers and to the search costs and other borrower costs of shifting from one source of funds to another. This in turn implies that increases in loan demands that are expected to be continued into the future will induce smaller increases in loan rates than would occur in the absence of customer relationships because future loan demands and deposit supplies are strengthened by current loan supplies.[15] The intertemporal effects of customer relationships on

---

13 Neil Jacoby and Raymond Saulnier (1942, page 1).

14 This argument has been made by Joel Fried and Peter Howitt (1980). Davis Dewey and Martin Shugrue (1922, page 178) earlier pointed out in connection with call loans, "When there is a mutual understanding between the borrower and lender that the loan will not be called until it is convenient for the borrower, the rates usually do not vary much from those on time loans. [Time loan rates were less variable than call loan rates.] When no such understanding exists, however, as in the case of brokers and traders in the produce and stock exchanges, a bank will generally make a call loan at a lower rate of interest than is charged for a time loan."

15 These aspects of customer relationships are analyzed in the following section.

Table 16.2   Commercial Bank Loans and Investments, Loan Rates, and Money Market Rates: At Loan Rate Peaks and Troughs, 1919 to 1929 and 1953 to 1983

	Month	L	S	$\dfrac{L}{L+S}$	R_{BL}	R_{CF}	R_{CP}	ΔR_{BL}	ΔR_{CF}	ΔR_{CP}
T	5/19	9.9	5.0	.664	5.65	5.26	5.38			
P	2/21	12.9	3.2	.801	6.94	7.05	8.42	1.29	1.79	3.04
T	9/22	11.1	4.4	.716	5.21	4.26	4.20	−1.73	−2.79	−4.22
P	9/23	12.0	4.4	.732	5.61	5.14	5.50	0.40	0.88	1.30
T	8/24	12.6	4.9	.720	4.78	2.00	3.17	−0.83	−3.14	−2.33
P	10/26	14.6	5.2	.737	5.19	4.86	4.72	0.41	2.86	1.55
T	11/27	15.3	5.8	.725	4.87	3.50	4.07	−0.32	−1.36	−0.65
P	10/29	17.3	5.4	.762	6.21	5.96	6.42	1.34	2.46	2.35
P	12/53	40.3	40.2	.501	3.65	a	2.78			
T	3/55	41.8	43.4	.491	3.43	1.34	1.32	−0.22		−1.46
P	12/57	55.2	33.4	.623	4.74	2.98	4.07	1.31	1.64	2.75
T	6/58	54.5	40.4	.574	4.06	1.02	1.60	−0.68	−1.96	−2.47
P	12/59	68.5	38.4	.641	5.25	3.99	4.98	1.19	2.97	3.38
T	12/61	73.2	45.8	.615	4.85	1.93	2.97	−0.40	−2.06	−2.01
P	12/66	135.0	50.2	.729	6.20	5.48	6.15	1.35	3.55	3.18
T	5/67	136.7	56.1	.709	5.79	3.92	4.83	−0.41	−1.56	−1.32
P	2/70	174.3	57.2	.753	8.70	9.20	8.90	2.91	5.28	4.07
T	2/72	200.5	80.3	.714	5.52	3.24	4.06	−3.18	−5.96	−4.84
P	8/74	313.1	83.5	.789	12.40	12.13	12.02	6.88	8.89	7.96
T	5/76	285.5	101.0	.739	7.44	5.03	5.32	−4.96	−7.10	−6.70
P	5/80	408.0	108.8	.789	17.75	12.98	13.68	10.31 b	7.95	8.36
T	8/80	410.8	116.4	.779	11.56	9.23	9.22	−6.19 b	−3.75	−4.46
P	8/81	466.7	119.8	.796	21.11	18.25	18.68	9.55 b	9.02	9.46
T	2/83	527.0	129.6	.803	10.20	8.50	8.47	−10.91 b	−9.75	−10.21

a Not available.

b The box indicates greater change in loan rate than commercial paper rate.

P, T = peak and trough dates of R_{BL}

R_{BL} = average rate on short-term business loans. (Data have been adjusted for changes in the Federal Reserve's Quarterly Survey to make rates comparable over time.)

R_{CF} = average rate on stock exchange call loans (1919 to 1929) and fed funds (1955 to 1983)

R_{CP} = average rate on 4- to 6-month prime commercial paper (average of 3- and 6-month commercial paper rates after 1979), converted to a 360-day yield basis to be comparable with R_{BL} and R_{CF}

R_{BL} was reported for the 15th of each month during 1919 to 1929, the first half of 1 month in each quarter during 1953 to 1976, and the first business week in the middle month of each quarter during 1977 to 1983. The other rates apply to approximately the same dates as R_{BL} except that R_{CP} is reported for its own peaks and troughs based on reporting dates for R_{BL}.

Sources: Federal Reserve Board, *Banking and Monetary Statistics, 1914–41* and *1941–70, Annual Statistical Digests*, and *Federal Reserve Bulletins*.

current loan rate policies are strengthened by interest rate ceilings that restrict bank abilities to attract funds by other means. These arguments are supported by the suggestion that the current accommodation of long-term, steady customers reduces the variances of future deposits, loan demands, and bank profits.[16]

Finally the possibilities of "adverse selection" and "moral hazard"

---

16 Edward Kane and Burton Malkiel (1965) have stressed these effects of customer relationships.

suggest that increased loan rates in the presence of uncertainty might reduce the bank's expected profits either by screening out the least risky borrowers or by providing an incentive for existing borrowers to undertake riskier projects—thereby inducing banks to rely on means other than interest rates to ration credit.[17]

The events intended to be explained by these theories are summarized in Table 16.2 for 1919 to 1929 and 1953 to 1983. These periods were chosen because bank loan rate data first became available on a regular basis in 1919 and there were no significant cyclical fluctuations in interest rates between 1929 and 1953, these years being dominated first by a strong downward trend in rates until early in World War II and then by a Federal Reserve bond support program until 1953. The first two columns of the table indicate the peak (P) and trough (T) dates of short-term business loan rates. The next two columns list total bank loans (L) and investments (S) on those dates. The ratio of loans to earning assets, $L/(L + S)$, will be an important part of our analysis of the customer relationship. The columns headed R_{BL} and R_{CF} list an average short-term business loan rate and the rate on the primary source of short-term bank reserve adjustments (call loans during 1919 to 1929 and fed funds during 1953 to 1983) at the peaks and troughs of R_{BL}. The R_{CP} column lists the 4- to 6-month prime commercial paper rate at the peaks and troughs of that rate, which are not shown but have usually led the turning points of R_{BL} listed in the table.

We begin our examination of these data by considering relative movements in interest rates during the period 1919 to 1929. Notice that the average short-term business loan rate always moved less than other short-term rates, which is consistent with the customer relationship and credit rationing theories mentioned above. Nevertheless, banks were well hedged against interest rate risk because the rate of return on their large investments in stock exchange call loans varied with other money market rates, including the costs of bankers' balances and other bank liabilities.

The lower portion of Table 16.2 shows that business loan rates continued to vary less than other short-term rates in the 1950s and 1960s. However, instead of R_{BL} being an understatement of the variability of returns on bank assets, as in the 1920s when call loans were important, it had become an overstatement because of the continued growth of long-term loans (consumer and real estate loans as well as business term loans) that had begun in the 1930s. Nevertheless, the maturity mismatch of bank assets and liabilities was not dangerous so long as interest rates were fairly steady. Furthermore, bank liabilities were concentrated in demand and time deposits with constant or slowly changing interest rate ceilings.

---

17 These effects were discussed in connection with bond covenants and convertible securities in Chapter 10 and will be considered in connection with the Stiglitz-Weiss theory of credit rationing near the end of this chapter.

Table 16.3 Commercial and Industrial Loans: Average Maturities and Percentages with Floating Rate, 1977 to 1983[a]

	1977	1978	1979	1980	1981	1982	1983
Short-term loans							
Amount, billion $	24.7	30.6	31.8	47.8	83.9	143.6	144.1
Average maturity, months	2.2	1.9	2.1	1.8	1.5	1.1	1.1
Percent with floating rate	45	41	47	45	39	29	33
Long-term loans							
Amount, billion $	4.6	5.2	6.1	8.2	12.1	15.2	15.0
Average maturity, months	44.1	45.1	47.3	44.9	48.9	48.4	54.2
Percent with floating rate	49	53	57	65	73	70	73

a From the Federal Reserve's "Survey of Terms of Bank Lending," which is based on loans during the first full business week of the middle month of each quarter at the 48 largest banks and about 300 banks selected at random. Reported loan volumes are estimates of all lending in each category by U.S. commercial banks during the survey period based on the loans of the surveyed banks relative to all banks as shown on call reports. (See *Federal Reserve Bulletin*, May 1977, pages 442–455, for a description.) The average maturities in this table differ from those reported in the survey by taking account of zero-maturity demand loans.

Source: *Federal Reserve Bulletin*.

But the growth of fed funds, repurchase agreements, and short-term time deposits (especially certificates of deposit) that are free of interest regulation means that the preponderance of bank liabilities once again, as in the 1920s, pay money market rates. This in turn means that, with the return (with a vengeance) to the pre-1930 world of volatile interest rates, banks now have greater incentive to achieve asset returns that vary with money market rates than during the period of tranquil interest rates existing between the 1930s and the 1960s. But how? For banks, even money center banks, are much less important lenders directly to the money market now than before 1930. Table 16.1 indicates that in 1969 only about 7 percent[18] of the loans of the largest banks were 1-day loans to the money market. This had grown to 9 percent in 1981 but was still much less than the 17.5 percent of 1922 and 21.6 percent of 1928 for roughly comparable banks. Other factors tending to reduce the flexibility of asset returns compared with the 1920s were large increases in the volume and maturities of real estate loans, the growth of consumer installment loans, and the growing importance of term loans.

There were two ways in which banks might have made asset rates of return vary with those on liabilities. First, they might have shifted from business, real estate, and consumer loans toward money market loans. The lower portion of Table 16.1 indicates that there may have been a small shift in this direction although its effects on asset return flexibility were offset to the extent that the increase in real estate loans took the form of fixed-rate mortgages. In fact a substantial

18 This assumes that 80 percent of fed funds and other loans to banks and brokers were for 1 day or had rates that changed daily.

adjustment along these lines was never in the cards because the traditional vehicle for bank asset return flexibility—stock exchange call loans—was one of the casualties of Congress's attack on the capital markets in the 1930s (not dead, but severely wounded). Second, banks might have continued to lend to the same people for the same purposes but for shorter terms and/or at rates of interest tied to money market rates. That is what they have done, especially for business loans— specifically, as shown in Table 16.3, by increasing the proportion of short-term loans (with maturities less than 1 year), reducing the maturity of short-term loans, and increasing the proportion of long-term loans with floating rates.[19]

These changes are reflected in Figure 16.1, which shows that loan rates, after remaining fairly steady in the face of increasingly volatile money market rates, began in the late 1960s to vary nearly as much as, and then in the late 1970s to vary more than, the latter. The same story is told in Table 16.2, where the boxed entries correspond to periods during which bank loan rates have varied more than the rate on commercial paper. Banks took a while to adjust to the new environment, but they have decided that they will no longer bear the risk of interest rate fluctuations for their business customers. Furthermore, the end of Regulation Q's effectiveness has reduced incentives to compete for deposits by means of steady loan-rate policies.

Summary

The above discussion was separated into three periods determined by differences in the volatility of interest rates and the effects of those differences on bank loan contracts: (1) The volatile world that existed before the 1930s saw vigorous bank competition for liabilities whose costs varied closely with money market rates. Banks avoided interest rate risk in that environment by investing primarily in short-term business loans and, most important, stock exchange call loans. (2) The interruption of loan renewals and the large-scale (though often futile) loan calls during the Great Depression led to the growth of long-term fixed-rate loans and the reestablishment and strengthening of customer relationships as banks and their borrowers sought to insure themselves against future losses of finance. A relatively stable interest rate and bank reserve environment enabled these mutual insurance arrangements to survive through the 1960s. (3) In recent years the

19 These data are available only from the inception in 1977 of the Federal Reserve's "Survey of Terms of Bank Lending" in its present form. For a discussion of changing bank loan practices during the 1970s, especially the growing importance of floating rates, which "have probably been the most important innovation in bank lending since the advent of the term loan," see Randall Merris (1979).

    The selection of assets and liabilities with a view toward their relative maturities and interest-rate sensitivities is sometimes called *gap management,* which in its simplest form has been defined as "the difference between the dollar amounts of rate-sensitive assets and rate-sensitive liabilities" [Alden Toevs (1983)]. Toevs discusses gap models of varying degrees of complexity and sophistication. The immunization model in Appendix 6.A is a form of gap model that uses the more sophisticated concept of duration in place of maturity.

return of volatile interest rates has led to the restoration of bank liability management and to bank loan contracts providing for asset returns that vary with the costs of money market liabilities. The main difference between the 1920s and the 1980s is that the principal methods by which banks hedge interest rate risk are now short-term and variable-rate commercial and industrial loans instead of stock exchange call loans as in the earlier period.

The remainder of this chapter is devoted to more precise statements of two of the theories of bank loan rate behavior mentioned above—bank-customer relationships and credit rationing—with applications of these theories to explanations of observed bank behavior.

THE CUSTOMER RELATIONSHIP
A broad definition

> DEFINITION 16.1.   A *bank-customer relationship,* which is usually abbreviated to *customer relationship* by those who, like ourselves in the present chapter, are interested in the relationship primarily from the bank's standpoint, is a relationship *over time* and is said to exist when future arrangements between the bank and a customer are likely to be affected by their current arrangements.

The preceding section told of the shock that has recently been dealt customer relationships by the increase in interest rate volatility so that banks, without substantial short-term assets of other kinds, have become less able or willing to guarantee loan renewals and relatively steady interest rates to their business borrowers. Additional and perhaps more telling blows to customer relationships were the "credit crunches" of 1966, 1975, 1979, and 1980, which reminded banks and their customers that the Federal Reserve System of 1929 was still around and that they could not count on a stable monetary environment with the predictable bank reserves necessary for reliable loan renewals. But customer relationships were important in the volatile-interest-rate and uncertain-reserve environment of the nineteenth and early twentieth centuries and are likely to continue in the similar environment of the 1980s, even if less strongly than between the 1930s and the 1970s. Borrower-lender and buyer-seller relationships will always exist as long as information is costly and past experience shared by two parties provides information about each other that can be used in the future.

The influence of customer relationships
on bank portfolios and loan rates

The customer relationships described above in connection with the 1920s (and before), 1930s, and 1940s have continued to be documented in the 1950s,[20] 1960s,[21] 1970s,[22] and 1980s.[23] Based on a study of bank lending practices during 1967 to 1970, for example, Duane Harris (1973) concluded that, especially during periods of tight money, banks gave preference to established customers since the "customer relationship promises some sort of continued loan and deposit activity in future periods. Also, established customers offer a banking history so that lenders may make some judgment concerning probability of default on the basis of past repayment records."

These considerations have important implications for bank loan rate policies because they suggest that current loan rates, which determine the numbers of new borrowers gained and old borrowers retained, influence future loan demands and deposit supplies faced by the bank. Customer relationships are less relevant to a bank's purchases of securities; for the profitability of future security transactions is not altered by the bank's failure to buy another bond today.[24] However, by a decision not to accommodate a prospective private borrower on favorable terms, not only does a bank forgo the current revenue from that loan but the dissatisfied borrower may take his business elsewhere in the future. The bank has missed an opportunity to strengthen future loan demands and deposit supplies.

Suppose the bank faces a downward-sloping loan demand function in the current period (period 1) such as that described by the line L_1A_1 in Figure 16.2(a). The corresponding marginal revenue line is L_1M_1. We thus assume the bank to be an imperfect competitor in the market for loans: As it raises the loan rate, the bank will lose some, but not all, of its customers. But the bank is assumed to be a perfect competitor in the securities market. That is, it can buy all the securities it wishes at the yield y_1. There are thus two differences between loans and securities as viewed by the bank: (1) The bank is an imperfect competitor in the loan market, and (2) loans extended today encourage loan demands and deposit supplies in the future.

Now let's see how these considerations affect bank behavior. We

20 The Federal Reserve Bank of Cleveland (1956) found from a survey of bank loans that "the majority of business loans, although nominally of short maturities, have been converted into longer-term credit in effect through the practice of continuous renewals."

21 Donald Hodgman's (1961, 1963) discussions of the customer relationship were based on interviews with bankers.

22 Donald Hester (1979) found from a Federal Reserve Board update of the Cleveland survey that loan rates were significantly influenced by the size of deposit accounts, the age of accounts, and the profitability of past connections.

23 The *American Banker* reported on August 10, 1981, page 1, that "when Citibank recently announced increases in consumer loans and mortgages, it established two separate rates for depositors and noncustomers": 21 percent for customers who did not have an account at the bank and 19 percent for customers with "full relationships," that is, with both checking and savings accounts.

24 Except on those occasions when state and local government deposits are directed toward buyers of their securities.

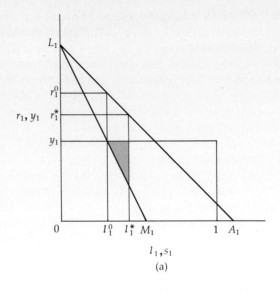

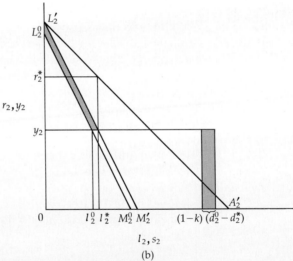

Figure 16.2   The customer relationship.

begin by ignoring item 2, the intertemporal customer relationship, and assume the bank to be concerned with only the current period. If the rate of return on securities is y_1 as indicated in Figure 16.2(a), the bank maximizes profit in period 1 by setting the loan rate at r_1^0 so that loans (as a proportion of earning assets) are l_1^0, that is, such that the marginal revenue from loans (indicated by $L_1 M_1$) equals the constant marginal revenue y_1 from securities.[25]

---

25 This decision is identical with those depicted on the left-hand sides of Figures 2.2 to 2.5.

All the loan, security, and deposit values in Figures 16.2 and 16.3 are expressed as proportions of total first-period earning assets. For example $l_1 = L_1/(L_1 + S_1)$ and $s_1 = S_1/(L_1 + S_1)$ denote first-period loans and investments as proportions of their sum. Referring to Figure 16.2(a), this means that the quantity of first-period bank investments

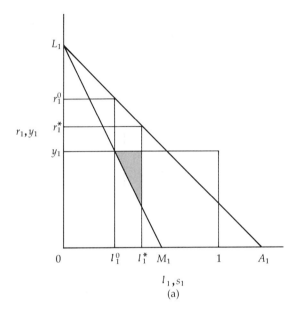

(a)

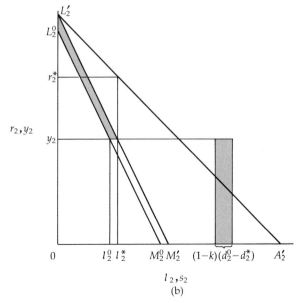

(b)

Figure 16.3   Bank response to increased credit demands under the customer relationship.

(security holdings) consistent with first-period profit maximization is $s_1^0 = 1 - l_1^0$.

We use y_t and r_t in this section to denote the one-period expected rates of return on bank security holdings and a group of homogeneous loans, respectively, for economy of notation and also to avoid confusion with the notation of the next (credit rationing) section. We also assume for simplicity that the length of a period is 3 months, y_t is the certain return on 3-month Treasury bills, and the loans are thought to be riskless (say, to firms whose debentures are rated Aaa by Moody's) so that the loan rate is also the certain expected return on these loans. The customer relationship operates in this simple case through the search costs saved and the convenience gained by borrowers who repeatedly do business with the same bank and also by the implicit promise that the bank will give them preference during credit crunches. A richer (and more complicated) model of the customer relationship would allow the bank to be less certain of the characteristics of new borrowers so that the learning process would also lead to improved estimates of default probabilities.[26]

We now introduce the customer relationship into the model in Figure 16.2 by supposing the bank to be interested in future as well as current profits and by allowing the future loan demands and deposit supplies facing the bank to be influenced by the bank's current lending policy. We assume the two-period case described by Figure 16.2; that is, the bank looks only one period into the future. Based on its observation of the current rate of return on securities (y_1), its estimate of current loan demand (L_1A_1), and its (certain) expectations of the second-period rate of return on securities (y_2) and loan demand (L_2A_2), it chooses a current loan rate (r_1^*) and plans a second-period loan rate (r_2^*) to maximize the present value of the sum of first- and second-period profits.

The introduction of the customer relationship and a concern for future profits induce the bank to lower the loan rate from r_1^0 to r_1^* in order to increase loans to l_1^*, beyond the point at which first-period profit is maximized. Given the funds available, this means a simultaneous reduction in investments to $s_1^* = 1 - l_1^*$. Since loans in excess of l_1^0 earn marginal revenues (L_1M_1) less than the marginal revenue from securities (y_1), first-period profit is reduced below its maximum by the amount indicated by the shaded area in Figure 16.2(a), that is, by the area of the triangle between the marginal revenues from loans and securities with base equal to the distance between l_1^0 and l_1^*.

But the reduction in first-period profit is more than offset by second-period gains. The loan demand facing the bank in the second period is L_2A_2, and the corresponding marginal revenue curve is L_2M_2. If the bank had maximized first-period profit by choosing r_1^0 and l_1^0,

_____

26 As indicated in the above quotation from Harris.

second-period marginal revenue would have been $L_2^0 M_2^0$, as shown in Figure 16.2(b). (The corresponding demand curve $L_2^0 A_2^0$ is not shown.) But the lower first-period loan rate ($r_1^* < r_1^0$) and greater first-period loans ($l_1^* > l_1^0$) have kept and/or attracted customers so that the second-period loan demand due to r_1^* and l_1^* is $L_2' A_2'$, with the corresponding marginal revenue curve $L_2' M_2'$. The added revenue from second-period loans due to the customer relationship is the shaded area above the second-period rate of return on securities (y_2) plus the rectangle with height $0y_2$ and base $l_2^0 l_2^*$, that is, the area under the higher marginal revenue curve as far as l_2^* less the area under the lower marginal revenue curve as far as l_2^0. Since the increase in second-period loans reduces second-period investments by the distance $l_2^0 l_2^*$ and therefore investment revenues by an amount equal to the area of the rectangle with height $0y_2$ and base $l_2^0 l_2^*$, the *net* additional revenue from second-period loans due to the customer relationship is the shaded area above y_2 in Figure 16.2(b).

In addition to its impact on the net revenue from second-period loans the customer relationship adds to bank revenue through its contribution to future deposits. The increase in second-period funds available for the purchase of earning assets due to the customer relationship is $(1 - k)(d_2^0 - d_2^*)$, where d_2^0 and d_2^* are the second-period deposits resulting from the loan quantities l_1^0 and l_1^*, respectively, and k is the required reserve ratio so that the proportion $(1 - k)$ of the additional deposits can be invested. The revenue generated by these funds, which is used to purchase securities earning the rate of return y_2, is represented by the rectangular shaded area at the right of Figure 16.2(b).

The starred (*) values of r_1 and l_1 in Figure 16.2(a) thus describe a lending policy such that the bank currently extends more loans than are consistent with short-term profits in order to encourage future loan demands and deposit supplies that will generate increases in future profits. The profit-maximizing bank lowers r_1 and raises l_1 as long as the increase in the present value of additional future profits (the shaded areas in Figure 16.2(b) reduced by the appropriate discount factor) exceeds the reduction of current profits (the shaded area in Figure 16.2(a)).[27]

Notice that the bank's plan for r_2^* and l_2^*, at which second-period marginal revenues from loans and securities are equal, implies a policy of maximizing second-period revenue without regard for the more distant future. This is due to our assumption that the bank is concerned only with profits earned this and next period. A longer

---

27 The accumulation of loan demands through the customer relationship eventually leads to a higher loan rate (r^*) than in the absence of the customer relationship (r^0) [see John Wood, (1975, pages 24–27)]. The difference ($r^* - r^0$) between these long-run values may be interpreted as a premium paid by established customers for reductions in search costs and guaranteed financing during credit crunches or, following Joel Fried and Peter Howitt (1980), for the guarantee of less variable loan rates.

planning horizon would mean more loans in both the first and second periods and some profit forgone in the second period in order to increase profits in later periods.

The customer relationship and the cyclical behavior of loan rates and bank portfolios

This section applies the customer relationship to an explanation of the data in Figure 16.1 and Table 16.2, that is, to an explanation of why business loan rates have usually been less volatile than other short-term rates while bank portfolios have been strikingly volatile. Figure 16.2 showed the influence of the customer relationship on loans and loan rates for a given level of economic activity. Figure 16.3 extends Figure 16.2 by showing how the customer relationship affects the responses of loans and loan rates to fluctuations in economic activity.

Assume an expansion of economic activity that is associated with increases in loan demand $(L_1 A_1)$ and short-term market rates (y_1) from those in Figure 16.2 to those in Figure 16.3. In the absence of the customer relationship the bank will raise its loan rate and increase its loans from r_1^0 and l_1^0 in Figure 16.2(a) to the values of r_1^0 and l_1^0 shown in Figure 16.3(a), possibly as shown in the upper portion of Table 16.4.

Introduction of the customer relationship moderates the rise in r_1 relative to y_1 and accentuates the rise in l_1, possibly as shown in the lower portion of Table 16.4. This is because the rise in economic activity between Figures 16.2 and 16.3 has confronted the bank with increased loan demands from present and prospective customers. As a result each increase in the loan rate means more disappointed borrowers than formerly and, therefore, a greater opportunity cost to the bank in the form of weaker future loan demands than might have been achieved by a more liberal lending policy. This effect is greater, the

Table 16.4   An Example of the Effects of an Economic Expansion with and without the Customer Relationship[a]

	Before the Expansion (Figure 16.2)	After the Expansion (Figure 16.3)	Change	Relationship
y_1	0.0500	0.0600	0.0100	—
r_1^0	0.0800	0.0928	0.0128	No
$r_1^0 - y_1$	0.0300	0.0328	0.0028	customer
l_1^0	0.300	0.328	0.028	relationship
r_1^*	0.0663	0.0754	0.0091	A strong
$r_1^* - y_1$	0.0163	0.0154	−0.0009	customer
l_1^*	0.437	0.502	0.065	relationship

a This example is based on the linear two-period model in John H. Wood, *Commercial Bank Loan and Investment Behaviour*, pages 10–20, Wiley, London, 1975.

greater the bank's inclination to extrapolate recent developments into the future.

Extrapolative expectations are important to these results. Regressive expectations, that is, a tendency by banks to believe that recent increases in loan demands will soon reverse themselves, produce results opposite to those in Figure 16.3. Banks will not forgo current profits to accommodate the increased loan demands of customers who they believe will soon be depressed and willing to borrow only at low rates, if at all, and to supply deposits that can be invested only at low market rates of interest. The increases in expected future loan demands and market interest rates between Figures 16.2(b) and 16.3(b) are based on extrapolative expectations.

The opposite movements in $r_1 - y_1$ and l_1 in the strong-customer-relationship case in Table 16.4 were characteristic of observed behavior until the late 1970s. Referring to Table 16.2 and substituting r_1 for R_{BL}, y_1 for R_{CF} or R_{CP}, and $L/(L + S)$ for l_1, we see that $r_1 - y_1$ and l_1 moved oppositely during every movement in interest rates during 1919 to 1929 and 1953 to 1976 shown in the table (which means every pronounced movement in interest rates during those periods). But recent experience suggests that we now live in a world between the opposite hypothetical cases of Table 16.4, that is, between a world in which customer relationships dominate bank decisions and the complete absence of customer relationships that would be made possible by free information and no transaction costs and therefore without gains from continuing connections between borrowers and lenders or buyers and sellers. Significant intertemporal connections will continue to affect decisions by banks and their customers, but those relationships will be less important in a volatile world in which banks are less able to guarantee steady supplies of funds at relatively steady loan rates.

CREDIT RATIONING

A definition

FirstBanc of Peoria is advertising small business loans at 10 percent. So the hopeful restaurateur applies for a $35,000 loan, which, when added to his own $5,000, is expected to cover remodeling and equipment costs of $25,000, an initial $3,000 payment on the lease, and an expected loss of $12,000 during the first 6 months of operation, until Ethelred's Eatery develops a profitable clientele. The loan request is denied, and Ethelred asks, "Why?" Many words are spoken, but the simple message is that his Personal Banker doubts Ethelred's ability to repay the loan. Ethelred offers 15 percent with no effect, and an offer of 20 is followed by an embarrassing silence. We have observed an instance of "credit rationing," which may be defined as follows.

DEFINITION 16.2.   *Credit rationing* exists when a prospective borrower cannot obtain as large a loan as he would like even if he agrees to all of the lender's advertised terms for borrowers of his description or even if he more than agrees to meet those terms, including the payment of a higher rate of interest than asked by the lender.

Why does credit rationing exist? What is the optimal amount of credit rationing? The following discussion describes some steps toward answers to these questions.[28] We begin with an early model in which interest rates and other loan terms are given so that the existence of credit rationing is *assumed*. The second model explains credit rationing as the result of uniform loan rates. Finally we reach a model that demonstrates the possible existence of credit rationing in the presence of freely variable loan rates and other loan terms.

Credit rationing when loan rates are fixed

It is useful to begin with the analysis of Marshall Freimer and Myron Gordon (1965) because their model has served as the basis for later developments. Their assumptions may be stated as follows:

1. A borrower has decided to invest in a risky one-period venture of fixed size,[29] that is, costing a predetermined amount of money, C, and wishes to borrow as much of C as possible from the bank because the bank's contract loan rate, R_c, is less than rates on other sources of funds available to the borrower.

2. The bank treats both the loan rate and the certain rate of return (R_b) on alternative investments, say, Treasury bills, as given.

3. The bank wishes to grant a loan of a size that maximizes its expected one-period profit.

Now suppose that the proceeds, $\tilde{x}$, from the borrower's venture may (in the bank's view) take any value between q and Q with the probabilities indicated by the bell-shaped curve in Figure 16.4. If the amount of the loan is L, the borrower owes the bank $(1 + R_c)L$ at the end of the period. If the venture generates less than the principal and interest of the loan, that is, if $\tilde{x} < (1 + R_c)L$, the borrower is in at least partial default. The probability of default is the shaded area in Figure 16.4. The actual payment to the bank, which is limited to the venture's proceeds, is the smaller of $\tilde{x}$ and $(1 + R_c)L$. That is, if the venture's proceeds are $\tilde{x} \geq (1 + R_c)L$, the bank is paid in full, and the borrower keeps the remainder. But the bank gets all of $\tilde{x}$ if $\tilde{x} \leq (1 + R_c)L$.

---

28 See Ernst Baltensperger (1978) for a more complete survey of the credit rationing literature.

29 The assumption of a project with size independent of the loan rate was previously used by Donald Hodgman (1960). We shall make use of this assumption for simplicity of exposition, but Dwight Jaffee (1971, pages 57–62) and Vernon Smith (1972) have shown that the principal results stated below are also consistent with a variable project size.

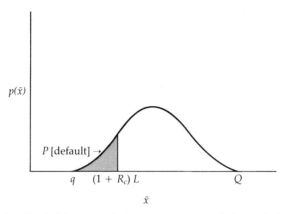

Figure 16.4   Probable proceeds from a venture and the probability of default.

The loan size that maximizes the bank's expected profit under these conditions is such that[30]

(16.1) $$P[\text{default}] = P[\tilde{x} < (1 + R_c)L] = \frac{R_c - R_b}{1 + R_c}$$

That is, the optimal loan size is the amount for which the probability of default equals the present value of the excess of the loan rate over the opportunity cost of the loan. For example values of $R_c = 0.10$ and $R_b = 0.05$ induce the bank to extend a loan such that $P[\text{default}] = 0.045$. An increase in the potential reward to $R_c = 0.20$ induces the bank to accept a probability of default of 0.125.

The optimal loan size is expressed as a function of the loan rate by the loan offer function, $L = S(R_c)$, in Figure 16.5. [Please ignore the downward-sloping demand function $D(R_c)$ for the moment.] The loan offer function has the following properties:[31]

1. $L = 0$ when $R_c < R_b$ because the bank will extend no risky loans at a contract rate less than the certain return on Treasury bills.

2. If $R_c = R_b$, then $0 \leq L \leq q/(1 + R_b)$. The bank is indifferent between a loan size in this range and a purchase of Treasury bills when the loan rate equals the Treasury bill rate because the loan is certain to be repaid when $L(1 + R_c) \leq q$. Notice from Equation (16.1) that the bank restricts the loan to a size for which the probability of default is zero when $R_c = R_b$.

3. The bank will not extend a loan beyond an amount such that

---

30 This result is derived in Appendix 16.A.

31 These properties were first fully expounded by Dwight Jaffee and Franco Modigliani (1969) and are illustrated in Appendix 16.A for the special case in which $\tilde{x}$ is uniformly distributed.

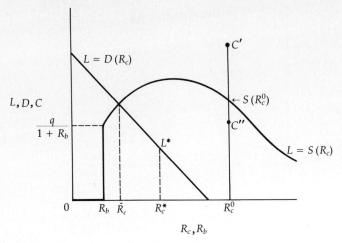

Figure 16.5   Loan-demand and loan-offer curves.

the contracted payment exceeds the maximum possible proceeds from the project, that is, $(1 + R_c)L \leqq Q$.

4. *L* approaches zero as R_c goes to infinity. This follows from property 3 and implies that, as R_c increases beyond some point, the optimal loan size does not rise and eventually declines, as shown in Figure 16.5. The lender is happiest when R_c is infinitely large and *L* is infinitesimally small so that he gets all the project's proceeds with little or no risk. Notice from Equation (16.1) that the probability of default, that is, the probability that the borrower will not be able to come up with all the repayment $(1 + R_c)L$, goes to unity as R_c goes to infinity.

5. For given R_c expected profit decreases monotonically as the loan deviates from its optimal size; that is, it pays the lender to extend a loan as close in size to the offer curve as possible.

6. Finally expected profit increases along the offer curve for successively higher R_c. We see from the shape of the offer curve in Figure 16.5 that, as R_c rises above R_b, the bank increases *L* so that expected profit increases due to increases in both R_c and *L*. However, as the contracted payment $(1 + R_c)L$ approaches the upper limit (Q) of the project's proceeds, the bank prefers to increase R_c while reducing *L*, for the reasons given in property 4. (We shall see that property 6 is crucial to the results of Jaffee and Modigliani and that its absence is crucial to the results of Stiglitz and Weiss.)

The model presented to this point explains credit rationing *for a given loan rate,* say, R_c^0, as follows: Suppose that the cost of the borrower's project is C', as indicated in Figure 16.5. Rationing occurs in this case because the bank will not grant a loan greater than $S(R_c^0)$. The borrower must go elsewhere for the remaining $C' - S(R_c^0)$. On the other hand rationing does not occur if the cost of the project is equal to, or less than, $S(R_c^0)$, say, C''.

But the bank's refusal to lend all of C' begs the essential question of credit rationing, which is: Why doesn't it raise the loan rate when confronted by an excess demand, $C' - S(R_c^0)$, at the existing rate, R_c^0? One answer to this question—the one implied by the properties of the loan-offer curve discussed above—is that the bank should charge an infinitely high loan rate. But this immediately raises another question: How will the borrower respond to higher loan rates? An answer to the second question requires an explicit loan-demand function, which is introduced next.

Credit rationing when loan rates are uniform

Let a customer's demand for loans be inversely related to the loan rate according to the function $L = D(R_c)$ in Figure 16.5. The customer will be rationed if the loan rate is less than $\hat{R}_c$ because in such a case the bank's optimum loan offer is less than the customer's demand. But rationing will not occur if there are no restrictions on the loan rate; for we know from property 6 that the bank's expected profit increases along the loan-offer curve for successively higher R_c. Therefore, the optimal loan rate is at least as high as $\hat{R}_c$. The bank would like to move farther to the right on the offer curve but cannot since the customer's demand lies below the bank's offer for rates beyond $\hat{R}_c$. The optimal loan rate, say, R_c^*, will exceed $\hat{R}_c$ by an amount that depends on the elasticities of the offer and demand functions. The loan size is L^* when the loan rate is R_c^* because property 5 implies that for a given loan rate the bank will extend a loan as close in size to the offer curve as possible, which means all the customer wants at that rate.

Now suppose that the bank's customers are assigned to a limited number of classes and that each class is charged a uniform loan rate. Dwight Jaffee and Franco Modigliani argued that "usury ceilings, the pressure of legal restrictions and considerations of good will and social mores" as well as rate-fixing agreements among banks keep the number of rate classes small and "make it inadvisable if not impossible for the banker to charge widely different rates to different customers" (1969, pages 851 and 861). We shall show that credit rationing may exist under these conditions.

Consider a rate class that consists of two customers, and let expected profits ($E\Pi_1$ and $E\Pi_2$) from those customers be the functions of their loan rates (R_{c1} and R_{c2}) shown in Figure 16.6.[32] The bank maximizes total expected profits from these customers by charging the

---

32 The 1 and 2 subscripts in this section apply to heterogeneous borrowers in the same period, unlike their application in the preceding section to homogeneous borrowers in different time periods. The credit rationing models in this section are more restrictive than the customer relationship model discussed above in their limitation to a single period but are less restrictive than the customer relationship model in their explicit analysis of uncertainty.

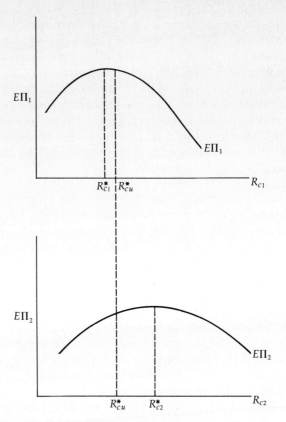

Figure 16.6   The optimal uniform loan rate.

separate rates R_{c1}^* and R_{c2}^*. If the bank is constrained to charge the same rate to both customers, that rate will lie between R_{c1}^* and R_{c2}^*. If the bank charged a uniform rate less than R_{c1}^*, it would find that expected profits from both customers could be increased by charging a higher rate. If the uniform rate were greater than R_{c2}^*, expected profits from both customers could be increased by charging a lower rate. The optimal uniform rate (R_{cu}^*) occurs between R_{c1}^* and R_{c2}^* at the point at which the absolute values of the slopes of $E\Pi_1$ and $E\Pi_2$ are equal. The fall in $E\Pi_1$ due to an increase in R_{cu} would exceed the rise in $E\Pi_2$; and the fall in $E\Pi_2$ due to a decrease in R_{cu} would exceed the rise in $E\Pi_1$.

Now suppose that Figure 16.5 pertains to the second customer so that R_c^* and $\hat{R}_c$ in that figure should be read R_{c2}^* and $\hat{R}_{c2}$. This customer is rationed if $R_{cu}^* < \hat{R}_{c2}$. Those customers are most likely to suffer credit rationing who are riskiest and have the least elastic loan demands. These are the customers who in the absence of a uniform rate policy pay the highest rates.

Notice that the uniform-rate credit-rationing model does not imply sticky loan rates if the profit functions $E\Pi_1$ and $E\Pi_2$ in Figure 16.6 retain their relative positions over time so that R_{c1}^*, R_{c2}^*, and R_{cu}^* rise and fall together. This might be the case if customers' loan demands are highly correlated over time. On the other hand, if variations in R_{c1}^* and R_{c2}^* are to some extent offsetting, the observed uniform rate under credit rationing might be less variable than the separate rates that would be observed in the absence of credit rationing. The latter case suggests a further explanation of increases in the relative volatility of loan rates during the 1970s when we realize that a uniform loan rate policy imposes costs upon banks, costs that become increasingly burdensome in a volatile world in which there are frequent sharp divergences between the rates that would optimally be charged to different customers. Eventually, rate-fixing agreements such as the prime rate convention are abandoned along with "considerations of good will and social mores," and banks charge the freely variable rate appropriate to each customer.[33]

Credit rationing when loan rates are freely variable

Jaffee and Modigliani explained credit rationing as the result of a uniform loan rate charged to borrowers with different characteristics even though the bank was fully informed of the characteristics of each customer. Joseph Stiglitz and Andrew Weiss (1981) also analyzed a case in which the rate was the same for different types of borrowers. But rate uniformity in their analysis arises from the bank's inability to distinguish high-risk from low-risk borrowers. Consider a class of borrowers, say, small businesses, which the bank knows from past experience consists half and half of risky and riskless ventures. In current economic conditions the bank believes that half will earn a certain 10 percent return on assets, whereas the others have a fifty-fifty chance of earning 75 percent or losing 55 percent on their assets. The expected return is 10 percent for both groups, and every borrower wants to buy $10 worth of assets financed with $5 of equity and a $5 loan from FirstBanc. Each borrower knows his own chances of profit and loss, but the bank does not and is not helped by every borrower's assurance that his loan is perfectly safe. Finally we assume the certain rate of return on Treasury bills to be 5 percent.

The first column in Table 16.5 lists alternative contract loan rates (R_c) charged to small businesses. The second and third columns list rates of return to the entrepreneurs (R_{s1}) and the bank (R_{L1}) from a riskless venture. The actual rate of return to the bank equals the contract rate as long as the latter does not exceed 120 percent, that is,

---

33 The "prime rate convention" was the name given to the commercial bank practice of charging a uniform loan rate to prime business borrowers. This convention was introduced in December 1933, and the agreed rate was not changed until 1947. It was changed only nineteen times in the next 18 years. This price-fixing agreement broke down during the 1970s, when banks began to tie rates on large loans to market rates. The so-called prime rate now applies only to small borrowers without access to low-cost substitutes. In February 1984, 89 percent of the short-term business loans of the forty-eight largest banks were made at rates below prime (from "Federal Reserve Statistical Release E.2," March 23, 1984).

Table 16.5   Returns on a Portfolio of Loans to Equal Numbers of Indistinguishable Risky and Riskless Borrowers

Loan Rate	Riskless Borrowers		Risky Borrowers				The Loan Portfolio	
R_c	R_{s1}	R_{L1}	$E\tilde{R}_{s2}$	$\sigma(\tilde{R}_{s2})$	$E\tilde{R}_{L2}$	$\sigma(\tilde{R}_{L2})$	$E\tilde{R}_L$	$\sigma(\tilde{R}_L)$
			Returns to Loans and Borrowers' Equity $(L = S = \$5)$					
0.0	0.20	0.0	0.250	1.250	−0.0500	0.0500	−0.0250	0.0250
0.05	0.15	0.05	0.225	1.225	−0.0250	0.0750	0.0125	0.0375
0.10	0.10	0.10	0.200	1.200	0.0	0.1000	0.0500	0.0500
0.15	0.05	0.15	0.175	1.175	0.0250	0.1250	0.0875	0.0625
0.16	—	—	0.170	1.170	0.0300	0.1300	0.0300	0.1300
0.20	—	—	0.150	1.150	0.0500	0.1500	0.0500	0.1500
0.25	—	—	0.125	1.125	0.0750	0.1750	0.0750	0.1750
0.30	—	—	0.100	1.100	0.1000	0.2000	0.1000	0.2000
0.35	—	—	0.075	1.075	0.1250	0.2250	0.1250	0.2250
0.40	—	—	0.050	1.050	0.1500	0.2500	0.1500	0.2500
			$L = \$4.50, \quad S = \$5.50$					
0.15	—	—	0.120	1.120	0.0750	0.0750	0.0750	0.0750
			$L = \$4, \quad S = \$6$					
0.15	—	—	0.075	1.075	0.1375	0.0125	0.1375	0.0125

Definitions and assumptions:

$S, \tilde{S}$ = initial and end-of-period borrower's equity
$L, \tilde{L}$ = initial and end-of-period value of loan
$A = L + S$ = initial value of borrower's assets
R_c = contract loan rate
$\tilde{R}_a, \tilde{R}_s, \tilde{R}_L$ = rates of return on assets, borrower's equity, and the bank loan

(16.2) $\tilde{S} = \max[(1 + \tilde{R}_a)A - (1 + R_c)L, \quad 0]$ **(16.3)** $\tilde{L} = \min[(1 + R_c)L, \quad (1 + \tilde{R}_a)A]$

(16.4) $\tilde{R}_s = \max[\tilde{R}_a + (\tilde{R}_a - R_c)L/S, \quad -1]$ **(16.5)** $\tilde{R}_L = \min[R_c, \quad \tilde{R}_a + (1 + \tilde{R}_a)S/L]$

Now add subscripts 1 and 2 to the above variables to denote the riskless and risky borrowers, respectively, and assume that $L = S = \$5$, $R_{a1} = 0.10$ with certainty, and $\tilde{R}_{a2} = 0.75$ or -0.55 with equal probabilities. Therefore,

$$R_{s1} = R_{a1} + (R_{a1} - R_c)L/S = 0.20 - R_c \quad \text{and} \quad R_{L1} = R_c \quad \text{for } R_c \leq 1.20$$
$$\tilde{R}_{s2} = \max[\tilde{R}_{a2} + (\tilde{R}_{a2} - R_c)L/S, -1] = 1.50 - R_c \quad \text{or} \quad -1$$

with equal probabilities so that $E\tilde{R}_{s2} = 0.25 - 0.5\,R_c$.

$$\tilde{R}_{L2} = \min[R_c, \quad \tilde{R}_{a2} + (1 + \tilde{R}_{a2})S/L] = R_c \quad \text{or} \quad -0.10$$

with equal probabilities so that $E\tilde{R}_{L2} = 0.5\,R_c - 0.05$.

$E\tilde{R}_L = 0.5\,R_{L1} + 0.5\,E\tilde{R}_{L2} = 0.75\,R_c - 0.025$ = expected rate of return on the loan portfolio if risky and riskless borrowers occur with equal probabilities.

The variances (V) and standard deviations (σ) of the rates of return to risky equity and loans and to the loan portfolio are

$$V(\tilde{R}_{s2}) = E[\tilde{R}_{s2} - E\tilde{R}_{s2}]^2 = (1.25 - 0.5\,R_c)^2; \quad \sigma(\tilde{R}_{s2}) = 1.25 - 0.5\,R_c \quad \text{for } R_c \leq 2.50$$

$$V(\tilde{R}_{L2}) = E[\tilde{R}_{L2} - E\tilde{R}_{L2}]^2 = (0.05 + 0.5\,R_c)^2; \quad \sigma(\tilde{R}_{L2}) = 0.05 + 0.5\,R_c$$

$$V(\tilde{R}_L) = E[\tilde{R}_L - E\tilde{R}_L]^2 = (0.025 + 0.25\,R_c)^2; \quad \sigma(\tilde{R}_L) = 0.025 + 0.25\,R_c = 0.5\sigma(\tilde{R}_{L2})$$

if risky and riskless borrowers occur with equal probabilities.

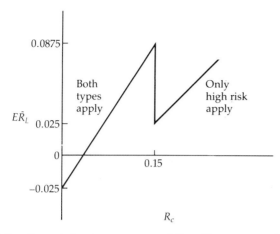

Figure 16.7   Expected returns on a portfolio of loans to equal numbers of indistinguishable risky and riskless borrowers.

as long as the principal and interest on the loan, $L(1 + R_c)$ = $\$5(1 + R_c)$, does not exceed the end-of-period value of assets, $A(1 + R_a) = \$10(1.10) = \$11$. But these riskless borrowers will borrow only at loan rates of 15 percent or less. Higher loan rates cause the return to equity to fall below the certain 5 percent return on Treasury bills. Outcomes of loans to riskless borrowers at rates above 15 percent have therefore been omitted from Table 16.5 as irrelevant.

The end-of-period value of assets of a risky venture is either $\$17.50$ or $\$4.50$, with equal probabilities. The rate of return to the bank on a $\$5$ loan to this firm is therefore either the contract rate R_c or -10 percent; for the bank claims all the firm's assets in the event of default. A contract rate of $R_c = 0.10$ therefore produces an expected return of $E\tilde{R}_{L2} = 0$ from the risky borrowers and $E\tilde{R}_L = 0.05$ from all borrowers. These results are presented in Table 16.5 and Figure 16.7, which also show an expected return on loans of 8.75 percent when the contract rate is 15 percent.

But the expected return on loans drops sharply when the contract rate is raised above 15 percent because riskless borrowers drop out while risky borrowers remain. So a risk-averse bank prefers a 15 percent rate on small business loans to higher rates because it does not want to exclude the riskless group. The bank will set the contract rate just below 15 percent (say, 14.9 percent so that the riskless borrowers will prefer their business ventures to Treasury bills) and refuse applications in excess of the amount allocated to small business loans.[34] Credit rationing is clearly possible in this situation because the bank does not respond to excess demands by raising the loan rate

---

34 It is helpful to think of a bank portfolio of various classes of loans and securities based on their expected return and risk characteristics and on the cost of funds. Unless the bank is indifferent to risk, its desired allocation of funds to any category is limited.

above 14.9 percent.[35] The loan officer will not only refuse your offer to pay a higher rate but will interpret such an offer as evidence of high risk and therefore prejudicial to your chances of obtaining a loan at any rate even if more funds become available or other applicants withdraw.[36]

The possibility of credit rationing is ruled out of our example only if the bank is willing to undertake substantial risks. Such a bank might be willing to accept the risk arising from the exclusion of riskless borrowers if it is compensated by a high expected return, such as the 10 percent expected return associated with a loan rate of 30 percent. But a risk-averse bank would rather ration credit than drive riskless borrowers away with high interest rates.

Credit rationing when all loan terms are freely variable

But the contract rate of interest is not the only decision variable by which the bank may attempt to increase its profits. The loans discussed above consisted of two terms: the contract rate, R_c, which was assumed to be variable, and the borrower's equity in the project, which was assumed to be fixed at 50 percent. The borrower's equity serves as collateral for the loan. Suppose that, instead of raising R_c above 15 percent, the bank attempts to increase its expected return by requiring borrowers to put up more equity. But this immediately eliminates the riskless borrowers, who would not have borrowed at 15 percent in order to invest in assets returning 10 percent if they had been able to put up more money of their own.[37] And small increases in collateral requirements may not reduce the riskiness of risky loans sufficiently to make up for the loss of the riskless loans. For example the next-to-last row in Table 16.5 shows that an increase in required equity from 50 to 55 percent of a project causes a reduction in the expected return (from 0.0875 to 0.0750) and an increase in the standard deviation of return (from 0.0625 to 0.0750) on the bank's small business loans. More stringent equity requirements would improve the risk-return characteristics of loans although perhaps at the cost of severely reducing loan applications. The last line of Table 16.5 indicates that an increase in required equity to 60 percent reduces the expected return on risky equity to 0.0750. This may not be sufficient reward to induce potential risky borrowers to undertake

---

35 In a similar analysis of "honest" and "dishonest" borrowers Dwight Jaffee and Thomas Russell (1976) pointed out that the borrowers who are least likely to default prefer a situation with low interest rates and credit rationing to one with high interest rates and no credit rationing, whereas those most likely to default prefer the latter situation.

36 We have assumed that each borrower has access to only one project. But if some borrowers are free to choose risky or riskless ventures, increases in the loan rate may encourage the selection of risky ventures, giving the bank further incentive to ration credit instead of raising R_c. (An example of risk-taking actions promoted by high borrowing rates was presented in connection with bond covenants in Table 10.7.)

37 For example the return to equity in a riskless venture when $R_c = 0.15$, $S = \$6$, and $L = \$4$ is $R_{s1} = 0.10 + (0.10 - 0.15)\,(2/3) = 0.0667$, compared with 0.05 in Table 16.5 for $S = L = \$5$.

their projects. Thus instead of the pleasant problem of an excess demand for small business loans at a 15 percent loan rate and a 50 percent equity requirement the bank might now be presented with only a few safe 60 percent equity loans that have high expected returns (0.1375) but are not sufficient in quantity to compensate for the loss of a large quantity of loans with expected returns of 0.0875. The bank might prefer to keep the loan rate and equity requirement at 15 and 50 percent, respectively, and ration credit by some arbitrary means, say, by refusing every fifth application.

Concluding note: other examples of adverse selection

Adverse selection in loan markets refers to the tendency of the riskiest borrowers to borrow the most. Stiglitz and Weiss explained credit rationing as an attempt by lenders to avoid the increased adverse selection that might be caused by higher loan rates and collateral requirements. Adverse selection also exists in other markets. In the used-car market, for example, the worst cars are most likely to be brought to market while the best cars are most likely to be kept by their owners, who in the absence of perfect buyer information know that their cars are imperfectly distinguishable from inferior cars and cannot, therefore, be sold for their true worth.[38]

The insurance market is also characterized by adverse selection. The least healthy have an incentive to buy the most medical and life insurance. Insurers try to distinguish different risk classes by age and estimates of health based on medical examinations. But their information is imperfect, and the low-risk purchasers of insurance often subsidize high-risk purchasers (just as the riskless borrowers subsidized the risky borrowers in the loan market discussed above) because different risks are often asked to pay the same premium.

Recent regulations have worsened the problems of adverse selection in two ways: First, lenders are prohibited by the Consumer Credit Protection Act from acquiring certain kinds of information that might enable them to ascertain the riskiness of borrowers in the personal loan market, with the result that the less risky borrowers must pay loan rates based at least in part on the default experience of risky groups.[39] Second, insurance companies have been prevented from incorporating available information in their rate structure. In Canada and increasingly in the United States insurance companies may not charge different rates to men and women in spite of their markedly different mortality, sickness, and accident propensities. In perhaps

---

38 See George Akerlof (1970) for a seminal article that deals with this and other examples of adverse selection.

39 Clifford Smith (1980) pointed out that "consumer-protection" legislation has harmed borrowers more than lenders because it is the borrowers who benefit most from well-informed lenders and provisions in loan contracts that protect lenders. Good information enables low-risk borrowers to obtain low interest rates, and its absence means that all borrowers are asked to pay the high rates that well-informed lenders would ask only of risky borrowers.

the most extreme regulatory promotion of adverse selection young men and women must in many places be charged the same rates for automobile accident insurance even though the former are more accident prone.[40] The result of this public policy is clear: The high-risk people will buy the most insurance, insurance companies will charge rates based on the accident record of the high-risk group, and the low-risk group will subsidize the high-risk group, do without insurance, or circumvent the regulations by developing efficient insurance contracts (that is, contracts with premiums that accurately reflect expected losses). We should expect to see a rapid growth in group accident and medical insurance for secretaries and nurses.

QUESTIONS

1. Discuss the similarities (if any) and the differences (if any) between the markets for (*i*) interbank deposits (bankers' balances) in the 1920s and (*ii*) fed funds in the 1980s.

2. Discuss the similarities (if any) and the differences (if any) between the benefits provided to commercial banks by the markets for (*i*) stock market loans in the 1920s and (*ii*) fed funds in the 1980s.

3. (a) Discuss why the maturities of bank loans (*i*) increased during the 1930s and 1940s and (*ii*) have decreased during the 1970s and early 1980s.

   (b) Under what conditions are the maturities of bank loans likely to (*i*) increase or (*ii*) decrease in the future?

4. (a) Based on Table 16.1, discuss the principal differences *and their causes* between bank asset portfolios in the 1920s and the 1980s.

   (b) Based on Table 16.1 and your knowledge of bank liabilities during 1919 to 1929 and 1976 to 1983, explain the differences between movements in business loan rates in the two periods.

5. Customer relationships and long-term, fixed-rate loans are ways by which banks can provide insurance to their customers.

   (a) Insurance against what?

   (b) What are the costs of this insurance and in what forms are the premiums paid?

6. Customer relationships are ways by which customers can provide insurance to their banks.

   (a) Insurance against what?

---

40 The most common rationale for the bill "To prohibit discrimination in insurance on the basis of race, color, religion, sex, or national origin," introduced in the U.S. House of Representatives in 1983, is that people should not be penalized for something over which they have no control. Illogically but sanely age and no-fault illnesses were not included. Otherwise we should all expect to pay the life insurance rates of 90-year-old cancer patients.

    (b) What are the costs of this insurance and in what forms are the premiums paid?

7. Without referring to bank loan markets, give an example of **(a)** a market in which customer relationships are likely to be strong and **(b)** a market in which customer relationships are likely to be weak. Finally **(c)** describe the similarities and differences between bank loan markets and each of your examples.

8. How might the results in Figures 16.2 and 16.3 be affected by deregulation, especially the elimination of ceilings on deposit rates?

9. Explain the real-world data in Table 16.2 in terms of the hypothetical cases summarized in Figures 16.2 and 16.3 and Table 16.4.

10. List the principal differences, and discuss the reasons for those differences, between the results of the credit-rationing models of Freimer and Gordon, Jaffee and Modigliani, and Stiglitz and Weiss.

11. **(a)** Under what conditions would credit rationing not exist?
    (b) What would Ethelred have to do to avoid being rationed?

12. A person favors no invasion of privacy, no discrimination on the basis of the characteristics of borrowers and insurance purchasers, and other consumer protection legislation.

    Do you think he is a good or a bad lending or insurance risk? Explain why, and give an example.

13. Suppose that FirstBanc acquires more information about the two groups of borrowers in Table 16.5. How will the riskless and risky borrowers be affected in terms of **(a)** the interest rates they have to pay **(b)** their ability to borrow, and **(c)** their collateral requirements?

PROBLEMS

1. Figure 16.3 shows the effects of an increase in economic activity in the presence of strong customer relationships. Depict a similar situation when customer relationships are weak (but still present).

2. Using the Freimer-Gordon framework, suppose that the Treasury bill rate is 5 percent and the contract loan rate is **(a)** 8 percent and **(b)** 16 percent. What are the probabilities of default in these two cases? Illustrate your results with a diagram similar to Figure 16.4.

3. Figure 16.5 shows a case in which borrowers with loan demand $D(R_c)$ are not rationed. (They pay the rate R_c^* and get all the loans, L^*, they want at that rate.) Present a diagram similar to Figure 16.5 for a group of borrowers who must also pay the uniform rate R_c^* and are rationed. Why is the latter group rationed; that is, what are

the reasons for the differences between the $D(R_c)$ and $L(R_c)$ of this group and those described by Figure 16.5?

4. (a) Present a list of results in the format of Table 16.5 for the situation in which the expected returns on all investments are twice those shown in Table 16.5, specifically, for which the Treasury bill rate is 10 percent, the return on riskless assets is 20 percent, and the risky assets have a fifty–fifty chance of earning 85 percent or losing 45 percent. Each $10 investment is financed with $5 of equity and a $5 bank loan.

(b) Show the bank's expected return on loans as a function of the contract loan rate in a diagram like Figure 16.7.

(c) What is the bank's optimal loan rate? Will rationing occur at this rate?

(d) Based on the results in (a), would you say that Stiglitz-Weiss credit rationing implies sticky loan rates?

REFERENCES

George A. Akerlof, "The Market for 'Lemons': Quality Uncertainty and the Market Mechanism," *Quarterly Journal of Economics,* August 1970, pages 488–500.

Ernst Baltensperger, "Credit Rationing: Issues and Questions," *Journal of Money, Credit and Banking,* May 1978, pages 170–183.

Davis R. Dewey and Martin J. Shugrue, *Banking and Credit,* Ronald Press, 1922.

Federal Reserve Bank of Cleveland, "Continuous Borrowing through 'Short-term' Bank Loans," *Monthly Business Review,* September 1956, pages 6–18.

Marshall Freimer and Myron J. Gordon, "Why Bankers Ration Credit," *Quarterly Journal of Economics,* August 1965, pages 397–410.

Joel Fried and Peter Howitt, "Credit Rationing and Implicit Contract Theory," *Journal of Money, Credit and Banking,* August 1980, pages 471–487.

Luther Harr and W. Carlton Harris, *Banking Theory and Practice,* 2nd ed., McGraw-Hill, New York, 1936.

Duane G. Harris, "Some Evidence on Differential Lending Practices at Commercial Banks," *Journal of Finance,* December 1973, pages 1303–1311.

Donald D. Hester, "Customer Relationships and Terms of Loans: Evidence from a Pilot Survey," *Journal of Money, Credit and Banking,* August 1979, pages 349–357.

Donald R. Hodgman, "Credit Risk and Credit Rationing," *Quarterly Journal of Economics,* May 1960, pages 258–278.

Donald R. Hodgman, "The Deposit Relationship and Commercial Bank Investment Behavior," *Review of Economics and Statistics,* August 1961, pages 257–268.

Donald R. Hodgman, *Commercial Bank Loan and Investment Policy,* University of Illinois Bureau of Business and Economic Research, Champaign, IL, 1963.

Neil H. Jacoby and Raymond J. Saulnier, *Term Lending to Business,* National Bureau of Economic Research, New York, 1942.

Neil H. Jacoby and Raymond J. Saulnier, *Business Finance and Banking,* National Bureau of Economic Research, New York, 1947.

Dwight M. Jaffee, *Credit Rationing and the Commercial Loan Market,* Wiley, New York, 1971.

Dwight M. Jaffee and Franco Modigliani, "A Theory and Test of Credit Rationing," *American Economic Review,* December 1969, pages 850–872.

Dwight M. Jaffee and Thomas Russell, "Imperfect Information and Credit Rationing," *Quarterly Journal of Economics,* November 1976, pages 651–666.

Edward J. Kane and Burton G. Malkiel, "Bank Portfolio Allocation, Deposit Variability, and the Availability Doctrine," *Quarterly Journal of Economics,* February 1965, pages 113–134.

Randall C. Merris, "Business Loans at Large Commercial Banks: Policies and Practices," Federal Reserve Bank of Chicago *Economic Perspectives,* November/December 1979, pages 15–23.

Margaret G. Meyers, *The New York Money Market: Origins and Development,* Columbia University Press, New York, 1931.

George S. Moore, "Term Loans and Interim Financing," in Benjamin H. Beckhart, *Business Loans of American Commercial Banks,* Ronald Press, New York, 1959.

Ogden Nash, "Bankers Are Just Like Anybody Else, Except Richer," in *I'm a Stranger Here Myself,* Little, Brown, Boston, 1938.

Clifford W. Smith, "On the Theory of Financial Contracting: The Personal Loan Market," *Journal of Monetary Economics,* July 1980, pages 333–357.

Vernon L. Smith, "A Theory and Test of Credit Rationing: Some Generalizations," *American Economic Review,* June 1972, pages 477–483.

Joseph E. Stiglitz and Andrew Weiss, "Credit Rationing in Markets with Imperfect Information," *American Economic Review,* June 1981, pages 393–410.

Rollin G. Thomas, *Modern Banking,* Prentice-Hall, New York, 1937.

Alden L. Toevs, "Gap Management: Managing Interest Rate Risk in Banks and Thrifts," Federal Reserve Bank of San Francisco *Economic Review,* Spring 1983, pages 20–35.

Leonard L. Watkins, *Bankers' Balances,* Shaw, Chicago, 1929.

Ray B. Westerfield, *Money, Credit and Banking,* Ronald Press, New York, 1938.

John H. Wood, *Commercial Bank Loan and Investment Behaviour,* Wiley, London, 1975.

John H. Wood, "Familiar Developments in Bank Loan Markets," Federal Reserve Bank of Dallas *Economic Review,* November 1983, pages 1–13.

Ralph A. Young, *The Banking Situation in the United States,* National Industrial Conference Board, New York, 1932.

APPENDIX
16.A
DERIVATION AND EXAMPLE OF THE FREIMER-GORDON LOAN-OFFER CURVE, EQUATION (16.1)

Derivation

Consider a borrower who wishes to finance as much of a venture's cost as possible by means of a bank loan, L, at the bank's predetermined rate, R_c. Principal and interest on the loan are due at the end of one period. The proceeds $\tilde{x}$ from the venture are uncertain and may take any value between q and Q, with probabilities described by the density function $p(\tilde{x})$, for example, as in Figure 16.4. Repayment to the bank is limited to the venture's proceeds and is the smaller of $\tilde{x}$ and $(1 + R_c)L$.

The bank's expected profit from the loan is

$$
\begin{aligned}
E\Pi = &\int_q^{(1+R_c)L} \tilde{x}p(\tilde{x})d\tilde{x} \\
&+ (1 + R_c)L \int_{(1+R_c)L}^Q p(\tilde{x})d\tilde{x} - (1 + R_b)L
\end{aligned}
$$

(16.A.1)

The first term in Equation (16.A.1) is the expected repayment if the proceeds of the venture fall short of the contracted repayment (for example the expected value of $\tilde{x}$ in the shaded interval in Figure 16.4 or in Figure 16.A.1), in which case the bank receives the entire outcome $\tilde{x}$. The second term is the contracted repayment times the probability that the venture's proceeds will be sufficient to repay the loan in full. The last term is the opportunity cost of the loan to the lender, where R_b is the certain rate of return on Treasury bills. The following analysis is relevant only if $R_b \leq R_c$. Otherwise $L = 0$. The bank will not assume a certain cost R_b in order to extend a risky loan with a maximum return $R_c < R_b$.

The optimal loan size is obtained by setting the derivative of $E\Pi$ with respect to L equal to zero:[41]

$$
\begin{aligned}
\frac{d(E\Pi)}{dL} = &(1 + R_c)[(1 + R_c)Lp((1 + R_c)L)] \\
&+ (1 + R_c)L[-(1 + R_c)p((1 + R_c)L)] \\
&+ (1 + R_c)\int_{(1+R_c)L}^Q p(\tilde{x})d\tilde{x} - (1 + R_b) = 0
\end{aligned}
$$

(16.A.2)

---

41 For the rule for differentiating an integral with respect to a parameter when the parameter enters the limits see, for example, Richard Courant (1936, Volume 2, page 220).

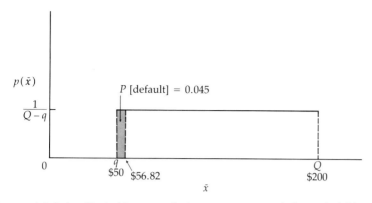

Figure 16.A.1 Probable proceeds from a venture and the probability of default: a uniform distribution.

Rearranging gives

(16.A.3) $\dfrac{1 + R_b}{1 + R_c} = \displaystyle\int_{(1+R_c)L}^{Q} p(\tilde{x})d\tilde{x} = 1 - \int_{q}^{(1+R_c)L} p(\tilde{x})d\tilde{x}$

and

(16.A.4) $\displaystyle\int_{q}^{(1+R_c)L} p(\tilde{x})d\tilde{x} = \dfrac{R_c - R_b}{1 + R_c} = P[\text{default}]$

Taking the second derivative of $E\Pi$ with respect to L gives

$$\dfrac{d^2(E\Pi)}{dL^2} = -(1 + R_c)^2 p[(1 + R_c)L]$$

(16.A.5)

$$\begin{cases} < 0 & \text{for } q \le (1 + R_c)L \le Q \\ = 0 & \text{otherwise} \end{cases}$$

which means that Equations (16.A.2) and (16.A.3) are consistent with a profit maximum for all values of L between $q/(1 + R_c)$ and $Q/(1 + R_c)$.

An example: the venture's proceeds are uniformly distributed

Suppose the lender believes $\tilde{x}$ to be uniformly distributed between q and Q as in Figure 16.A.1. That is,

(16.A.6) $p(\tilde{x}) = \begin{cases} \dfrac{1}{Q - q} & \text{for } q \le \tilde{x} \le Q \\[2ex] 0 & \text{elsewhere} \end{cases}$

and Equation (16.A.4) becomes

(16.A.7)
$$\int_{q}^{(1+R_c)L} \frac{1}{Q-q}\,d\tilde{x} = \frac{(1+R_c)L - q}{Q-q} = \frac{R_c - R_b}{1 + R_c}$$

$$= P[\text{default}]$$

Rearranging gives the loan-offer function:

(16.A.8) $$L = S(R_c) = \frac{q}{1+R_c} + \frac{(Q-q)(R_c - R_b)}{(1+R_c)^2} \quad \text{for } R_c \geq R_b$$

This loan-offer function illustrates the six properties attributed in Chapter 16 to Figure 16.5: (1) $L = 0$ when $R_c < R_b$; (2) L lies between 0 and $q/(1 + R_b)$ when $R_c = R_b$; (3) Equation (16.A.8) may be rearranged to show that $L(1 + R_c) < Q$; (4) notice that L goes to zero as R_c becomes infinitely large; (5) the second-order condition in Equation (16.A.5) shows that expected profit decreases monotonically as L deviates from its optimal size; (6) substituting the optimal loan decision in Equation (16.A.8) into Equation (16.A.1) gives the maximum expected profit, which, when differentiated with respect to R_c, shows that expected profit increases monotonically with the loan rate.[42]

PROBLEMS

1. Construct a loan-offer curve for $q = \$50$, $Q = \$250$, and $R_b = 0.05$. Show your calculations for selected points between $R_c = 0.05$ and 2.00.
2. Assuming $R_b = 0.05$ and a uniform distribution with $Q = \$200$ and $q = \$50$, what are the optimal values of L and the corresponding probabilities of default when $R_c = 0.02, 0.05, 0.20$, and 1.00?

REFERENCES

R. Courant, *Differential and Integral Calculus,* 2 vols., trans. by E. J. McShane, Interscience, New York, 1936.

Marshall Freimer and Myron J. Gordon, "Why Bankers Ration Credit," *Quarterly Journal of Economics,* August 1965, pages 397–410.

[42] For the uniform distribution in Equation (16.A.6) expected profit in Equation (16.A.1) is

$$E\Pi = \frac{2Q(1 + R_c)L - (1 + R_c)^2 L^2 - q^2}{2(Q - q)} - (1 + R_b)L$$

Substituting the optimal loan offer from Equation (16.A.8) into $E\Pi$ gives the maximum expected return,

$$(E\Pi)^0 = \frac{(R_c - R_b)[Q(R_c - R_b) + q(2 + R_c + R_b)]}{2(1 + R_c)^2}$$

Differentiating $(E\Pi)^0$ with respect to R_c gives

$$\frac{d(E\Pi)^0}{dR_c} = \frac{(1 + R_b)[Q(R_c - R_b) + q(1 + R_b)]}{(1 + R_c)^3} > 0 \qquad \text{for all } R_c > R_b$$

NONBANK FINANCIAL INTERMEDIARIES

Business? It's quite simple. It's other people's money.

Alexander Dumas the Younger,
La Question d'Argent, **vol. 2, p. vii, 1857**

THE GROWTH OF FINANCIAL INTERMEDIARIES SINCE 1950

Most Americans save most of their money in the form of loans to nonbank financial intermediaries (NBFIs). In 1980, for example, 66 percent of household financial investment went to deposits at nonbank savings institutions, premiums and contributions to insurance companies and pension funds, and shares in money market funds.[1] By comparison 27 percent went to commercial banks, and 6 percent took the form of direct purchases of business and government stocks and bonds. Most business and government deficits are financed by households through financial intermediaries, especially NBFIs.

Financial intermediaries are similar to one another in most important respects, especially in their desires to borrow as cheaply and to lend as dearly as possible. However, there are a few differences between the ways in which they borrow and lend. This chapter describes some of the most important of these similarities and differences. The emphasis is on how NBFIs have changed in recent years and how they are likely to change in the near future. Like nearly everyone else NBFIs have been affected by, and have reacted to, inflation and regulation. Some groups, like life insurance companies and savings and loan associations (S&Ls), have been hard hit by rising and volatile interest rates. Others have benefited, some, like money market funds, even owing their existence to the combination of high market interest rates and interest ceilings on other investments.

---

1 The first column of Table 13.9 shows that, of household financial investment of 259.4 (in billions of dollars), 56.2 went to deposits at savings institutions, 29.2 to money market fund shares, 12 to life insurance companies, and 73.7 to pension funds.

The list of financial institutions in Table 17.1 is based on the classification scheme of the Federal Reserve's flow of funds accounts. The table compares the growth of these institutions since 1950 with the growth of the nation's annual gross national product (GNP). All these groups have grown in nominal (dollar) values during the postwar period. But much of their growth has been due to inflation. A better understanding of the sometimes increasing, sometimes decreasing roles of the various financial intermediaries is achieved by comparing their rates of growth with that of GNP. Looking at the right-hand side of Table 17.1, we see that commercial banks have grown closely in line with GNP since 1950, but most NBFIs have grown more rapidly than GNP.

Figure 17.1 tells a story similar to that of Table 17.1. The figure groups the institutions in the table into four categories: (1) commercial banks, (2) NBFIs with liabilities consisting mainly of short-term savings accounts (S&Ls, mutual savings banks, and credit unions), (3) those with predominantly long-term liabilities (life insurance companies and pension and retirement funds), and (4) all others, that is, the last six intermediaries in Table 17.1. All three of these NBFI groups grew fairly steadily relative to GNP and relative to commercial

Table 17.1   Financial Assets of Commercial Banks and Nonbank Financial Intermediaries and Gross National Product, 1950 to 1983 (Billions of Dollars)

	End-of-Year Values					Average Annual Rates of Change	
	1950	1960	1970	1980	1983	1950–1970	1970–1983
Commercial banks	150	228	505	1,391	1,757	6	10
All NBFIs	143	369	823	2,368	3,306	9	11
Savings and loan associations	17	71	173	622	822	12	13
Mutual savings banks	22	41	79	172	192	7	7
Credit unions	1	6	18	72	103	16	14
Life insurance companies	63	116	201	464	637	6	9
Private pension funds	7	38	110	287	409	15	11
State and local government retirement funds	5	20	60	198	314	13	14
Other insurance companies	12	26	50	174	228	7	12
Finance companies	9	28	64	199	253	10	11
Real estate investment trusts	0	0	4	6	8	—	5
Mutual funds	3	17	47	64	129	15	8
Money market funds	0	0	0	74	163	—	—
Security brokers and dealers	4	7	16	36	49	7	9
GNP	287	507	993	2,632	3,311	6	10

Sources: Federal Reserve flow of funds accounts and *Survey of Current Business.*

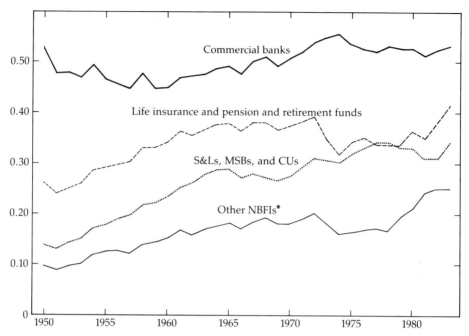

*The last six intermediaries listed in Table 17.1.

Sources: Federal Reserve flow of funds accounts and *Survey of Current Business.*

Figure 17.1   Financial assets of financial intermediaries relative to GNP, 1950 to 1983.

banks until about 1965 and then leveled off until the early 1970s. Since that time their fortunes have been erratic. The most noteworthy developments affecting NBFIs in the 1970s and 1980s may be summarized as follows:

1. The sharp fall of life insurance and pension and retirement funds in 1973 and 1974 was caused by the stock market losses of private pension funds. The recovery of this group has been due mainly to the growth of state and local government retirement funds, but there has been a general increase in pension and retirement funds of all kinds because of the deferred-tax advantages of saving in this form.

2. Moving to the short-term savings (or depository) institutions, the rapid growth of credit unions was more than offset between 1977 and 1981 by the slow growth of S&Ls, which was caused by interest ceilings on small savings accounts and the reluctance of S&Ls to compete for less-regulated accounts during a period of rapidly rising market interest rates. The relaxation of these ceilings, in combination with falling market rates, has allowed S&Ls to resume their former rapid growth.

3. Changes in the course of other NBFIs have been dominated by stock mutual funds and money market funds. The dramatic rise in the latter was the big story of the money markets between 1979 and 1982. Their decline in 1983 as a consequence of the introduction of taxpayer-insured competing instruments in depository institutions was offset by the public's renewed interest in stock mutual funds in response to the increase in stock prices. The fall in stock prices during 1973 and 1974 was responsible for the decline in mutual funds, and in "Other NBFIs" generally, seen in Figure 17.1.

Instead of giving more or less equal treatment to all the NBFIs in Table 17.1, we concentrate on those that have undergone the greatest changes and that present the most interesting problems of analysis. We are especially interested in the problems arising from the interactions of inflation, regulation, and taxation: the near failure of the S&L industry as a result of severely restricted portfolios (short-term liabilities and long-term assets) and interest rate ceilings during a period of rapidly rising interest rates, the difficulties of life insurance company short-term financial management caused by rising and increasingly volatile interest rates, and the encouragement given to pension and retirement funds by rising inflation, interest rates, and taxation.[2]

SAVINGS AND LOAN ASSOCIATIONS (S&Ls)
A brief description

S&Ls are among the simplest of financial organizations. Historically their activities have been almost completely described as borrowing in the form of short-term deposits (passbook savings accounts) and lending in the form of long-term mortgages. This plain balance sheet dates from the earliest S&Ls formed in the nineteenth century. In 1831 a group of thirty-seven residents of Frankford, Pennsylvania,

> subscribed to shares toward which monthly payments were made. When the sum of $500 was available for a loan, members would submit bids for that amount. The money was alloted as a loan and repaid in monthly payments over a 10-year period. This process continued until all members had purchased a home.
>
> Ronald Auerbach (1978, page 6)

Associations like the one in Frankford were called "terminating societies" because they ceased to exist once all the members had bought homes. Permanent associations much like those existing today,

---

2 Some other important developments affecting NBFIs were discussed earlier: Chapter 3 dealt with the effects of interest ceilings, rising interest rates, and financial innovation on the growth of credit unions and money market funds; finance companies were treated in connection with commercial paper in Chapter 8; and security brokers and dealers were discussed in Chapter 11.

Table 17.2 Savings and Loan Associations: End-of-Year Financial Assets and Liabilities, 1950 to 1983 (Billions of Dollars)

	1950	1960	1970	1980	1983
Total financial assets	16.9	71.5	173.1	621.9	821.7
Mortgages	13.7	60.1	146.7	494.4	526.3
Consumer credit	0.4	1.6	3.4	17.4	26.6
Other assets	2.8	9.8	23.0	110.2	268.8
Demand deposits and currency	0.7	1.7	1.2	2.6	9.1
Time deposits	0.0	0.0	0.6	7.5	15.2
Fed funds and RPs	0.0	0.0	0.0	10.8	21.1
U.S. government securities	1.5	5.2	11.0	48.4	130.2
State and local government securities	0.0	0.0	0.1	1.2	0.9
Open-market paper	0.0	0.0	1.8	4.9	12.5
Miscellaneous assets	0.6	2.9	8.2	34.8	79.9
Total liabilities	15.6	66.5	161.1	588.6	794.7
Deposits (savings shares)	14.0	62.1	146.4	511.8	678.0
Fed funds and RPs	0.0	0.0	0.0	8.5	25.2
Credit market instruments	0.9	2.2	11.0	57.8	71.6
Corporate bonds	0.0	0.0	0.0	3.7	3.5
Commercial bank loans	0.1	0.2	0.4	5.1	9.2
Federal Home Loan Bank loans	0.8	2.0	10.6	49.0	59.0
Miscellaneous liabilities	0.7	2.1	3.7	10.6	19.9

Source: Federal Reserve flow of funds accounts.

which accepted deposits from, and made loans to, the general public, grew rapidly after 1880 and by 1900 held 13 percent of nonfarm residential mortgages in the United States. More than 90 percent of their assets were in home mortgages.[3] The balance sheet data in Table 17.2 show that S&Ls have not changed a great deal since 1900. Most assets and liabilities are still in mortgages and deposits. S&Ls have been granted tax exemptions on condition that a certain high proportion of their revenues comes from mortgages. These are manifestations of the old and strongly felt desire by legislators and regulators, as well as by S&L executives, that S&Ls should lead the way in making it possible for every American family to own its home. Mortgages had fallen during the Great Depression and World War II from more than 90 percent of S&L assets in the 1920s to 63 percent in 1945. But they rose steadily during the early postwar years, reaching 85 percent in 1963, remaining at about that level until 1975, and not falling below 80 percent until 1980. However, we shall see below that S&L balance sheets have recently begun to undergo substantial changes.

We now take a detailed look at the responses of S&Ls to the inflationary and high interest rate conditions prevailing since 1965,

3 Ronald Auerbach (1978, page 14).

and we shall try to understand why those responses were too little and too late to maintain the profitability of the S&L industry. It will help to begin with a description of the regulatory environment in which S&Ls operate.

The Federal Home Loan Bank System

An understanding of the problems of the S&L industry requires a knowledge of the conduct of its regulator-protector, the FHLB System. This agency was founded in the 1930s with functions and a structure much like the Federal Reserve System. At its head is the Federal Home Loan Bank Board (FHLBB), with three members appointed to 4-year terms by the President subject to the consent of the Senate. Twelve Federal Home Loan Banks (FHL Banks) carry out many of the supervisory functions of the FHLB System but their most important job is the extension of loans (called "advances") to S&Ls. These advances have tended to be highest during periods of high interest rates as the FHL Banks have sought to offset S&L losses of funds when investors have shifted from S&L deposits to money market instruments because of the low interest ceilings on the former.[4] The regulator has been forced into action B as an antidote for the ill effects of action A. The major difference between FHL Banks and Federal Reserve Banks is that the former cannot create money. The FHLB System must go to the capital markets for funds, and the interest rates paid by S&Ls for advances are connected to market rates.

The FHLBB is the chartering and chief regulatory authority for federal S&Ls. All federally chartered S&Ls must belong to the FHLB System. State-chartered S&Ls and mutual savings banks may also choose to become members. The FHLBB has exercised its regulatory powers even more rigorously than have other financial regulators. For example commercial banks, which were already possessed of wider powers than S&Ls to attract and invest funds, were not prevented from offering adjustable-rate loans in response to increasing interest-rate volatility in the late 1960s and early 1970s. Federally chartered S&Ls, on the other hand, were prohibited from offering variable-rate mortgages until 1979, and even since then the FHLBB has imposed so many restrictions on their use that their development has been severely retarded except at state-chartered S&Ls. This is unfortunate because the need for protection against interest-rate fluctuations is much greater for S&Ls, with predominantly long-term assets and short-term liabilities, than it is for commercial banks, with predominantly short-term assets to go with their short-term liabilities. Variable-rate mortgages did not make up half of new mortgage loans until

---

4 Notice in column 4 of Table 17.3 that "Other borrowing" by S&Ls, which is predominantly FHLB advances, increased sharply during 1973 to 1975 and 1978 to 1982 as market rates rose above deposit rate ceilings. These rates are compared in Figure 2.1.

late in 1983, after both the level and the volatility of market interest rates had fallen from their 1980 and 1981 peaks.[5]

We cannot be sure of the reasons for the risk-increasing exercise of its regulatory authority by the FHLBB. We can say, however, that their actions have resembled the anticompetitive behavior of many regulators and trade associations. Their resistance to competition between S&Ls for mortgage business by means of product development has been consistent with their opposition to interest-rate competition for deposits.

A sorry tale

The fundamental defect of the savings and loan industry is that it borrows short from its depositors and then freezes those funds into very long-term assets whose yield is also frozen for a long period of time. ...

What has saved this industry so far is the fact that the periods of very hard money have tended to be short in duration. Let us make no mistake about it: If the economy were to move into a new era in which rates of return like 8 percent persisted permanently, then most of our financial intermediaries whose assets consist of mortgages frozen into returns of 4, 5, 6, and 7 percent would be technically insolvent. If the institution had to pay 8 percent to hold its deposits, it would run large annual deficits that would have to be financed out of principal. In the end, someone would be left holding the bag: Either the depositors or the government agency which had insured those deposits.

Paul Samuelson (1969, pages 1584 to 1585)

Reasonably steady interest rates are essential to the survival of S&Ls as their portfolios are presently constituted. A person might think that in a world of volatile interest rates S&Ls come out even in the long run because losses during periods of high interest rates are offset by gains during periods of low interest rates—when all deposits earn low rates while the mortgage loans previously extended at high rates are still generating large revenues. That person would be wrong, for the relationships of borrowers to lenders in the mortgage market, as well as in other financial markets, are like the relationships of football coaches with long-term contracts to universities. Universities are bound by these contracts and continue to perform their financial obligations even when coaches are fired. The coaches, on the other hand, may sever those contracts without penalty. Similarly the standard fixed-rate mortgage binds an S&L to specific terms (a fixed monthly payment for, say, 20 years) while the borrower may escape the loan's terms any time by paying it off early. This means that, if you

[5] The proportions of new fixed-rate and adjustable-rate mortgage loans are listed in Table S.5.1 of the *Federal Home Loan Bank Board Journal.*

take out a 20-year mortgage at 5 percent, and then mortgage rates rise to 15 percent, you may still enjoy your low monthly payment based on the lower interest rate. Furthermore, if you secure a 20-year mortgage at 15 percent, and then mortgage rates fall to 5 percent, you are free to secure a loan at 5 percent from a mortgage lender and use the proceeds to repay the high-rate mortgage. S&Ls sometimes impose early-payment penalties, but these are small and do not prevent the loss of high-yielding mortgages during periods of falling rates. Early payment was so prevalent between 1970 and 1972, when average annual effective mortgage rates on new houses fell from 8.45 percent to 7.60 percent,[6] that, instead of taking the trouble and expense of renegotiating mortgage terms with existing borrowers individually, many S&Ls simply scaled all old rates down to the new levels and informed their borrowers accordingly. On the other hand repayment rates fell sharply as interest rates rose between 1972 and 1974 and between 1977 and 1981.[7] A person with a 9 percent mortgage taken out in 1977 would have been better off (in both liquidity and expected wealth) investing a $10,000 inheritance received in 1981 in a long-term government bond yielding 14 percent than in redeeming part of her mortgage.

So S&Ls are in an unenviable position. They hold largely unhedged portfolios and as a result are exposed to greater risk than any other group of financial institutions, without the expected return supposed to be associated with that risk. You may wonder how S&L managers have attempted to alter their position. Broadly speaking, there are two courses: (1) The first is to strive for more diversified portfolios, with shorter-term lending and longer-term borrowing, partly by persuading the legislators and the regulators to give them more freedom of action and partly by pushing against existing constraints.[8] (2) The other is to hide and hope that government will pile constraints upon other sectors of society sufficient to protect S&Ls as they have been constituted. Unfortunately most S&L executives, assisted by their regulators, for a long time chose the latter course. This is made clear by listing some of the options under each of the two courses:

COURSE 1. S&L managers might have devoted their lobbying efforts to gain permission to extend more short-term consumer and commercial loans and to follow the lead of other countries in being able to tie mortgage payments to current interest rates.[9] They might also have made greater use of their limited existing powers to lend and invest at short term. (This is not Monday-morning quarterbacking. The quota-

---

6 See Table 17.3.

7 See Figure 17.2.

8 The incentives to innovation by commercial banks described in Chapter 2, especially in Figures 2.2 to 2.5, have also existed, in greater degree, for S&Ls.

9 For example like British Building Societies.

tion from Paul Samuelson at the beginning of this section and statements of many other observers demonstrate that the problems encountered by S&Ls in the late 1970s and early 1980s were widely foreseen in the 1960s.) But fixed-rate mortgages continued their dominance until the 1980s. Only in California did S&Ls begin to offer mortgage loans with variable rates on a significant scale in the 1970s.[10] California borrowers and lenders were able to make these arrangements because their S&Ls were predominantly state chartered and were therefore subject to fewer federal restrictions. Moving to the liability side of the balance sheet, an obvious way to avoid risk in the presence of predominantly long-term fixed-rate assets would have been to issue long-term bonds.

COURSE 2. But S&Ls chose to go as far as they could by relying on short-term debt in the form of passbook savings—with the substantial but eventually insufficient help of government ceilings on the rates payable on those deposits. The political influence of the S&L industry was concentrated on using the federal government to take away the ability of small savers to invest their funds except at the low rates allowed on S&L deposits. When some S&Ls began to compete vigorously for deposits as market rates rose, Congress imposed ceilings on S&L deposit rates in 1966 as it had done on commercial bank deposit rates in the 1930s. The ceiling on passbook saving rates had been raised only to 5.50 percent by the early 1980s even though money market rates often exceeded 15 percent. When S&L depositors shifted to Treasury bills, the minimum denomination of bills was raised from $1,000 to $10,000.[11] Almost everything was tried short of forcing investors at gunpoint to lend to S&Ls at below-market rates. But people persisted in seeking the best available rates, and S&Ls were forced, step by step, to offer higher rates to interest-sensitive investors. The resulting discriminatory rate structure is listed in Table 2.2. By 1980 a few S&Ls outside California had begun to pursue less coercive and more socially desirable ways of improving their portfolios. But most S&Ls continued to use Congress and their regulators in the old ways. The new Chairman of the Federal Home Loan Bank Board testified during his Senate confirmation hearings in 1981 "that the rapid growth of money market funds may have to be checked through temporary Federal restraints [because] MMFs are adding to the financial difficulties being experienced by S&Ls by depleting association deposits."[12]

---

10 See George Kaufman (1976).

11 See the section on Treasury bills in Chapter 8 for a discussion of some of the effects of this attempt by the Treasury to protect S&Ls by putting market rates of interest beyond the reach of small investors.

12 *Federal Home Loan Bank Board Journal*, May 1981, page 3.

Table 17.3   The S&L Story, 1965 to 1983: Major Income, Expense, and Balance Sheet Items
(Billions of Dollars and Percentages)

	(1) Mort-gages[a]		(2) Other Assets[a]		(3) Deposits[b]		(4) Other Borrow-ing[b]		(5) Other Liabili-ties[b]		(6) Net Worth[b]	
Year	$	%	$	%	$	%	$	%	$	%	$	%
1965	106	85	18	15	106	85	6	5	4	3	8	6
1970	145	86	24	14	141	83	10	6	6	4	12	7
1971	162	85	29	15	160	84	10	5	8	4	13	7
1972	190	85	34	15	190	85	9	4	10	4	14	6
1973	219	85	39	15	217	84	13	5	11	4	16	6
1974	241	85	43	15	235	83	21	7	10	4	18	6
1975	264	83	53	17	264	83	23	7	11	3	19	6
1976	301	82	64	18	311	85	20	5	13	4	21	6
1977	352	83	73	17	361	85	23	5	17	4	24	6
1978	407	83	84	17	409	83	35	7	20	4	27	5
1979	454	82	97	18	450	82	49	9	21	4	31	6
1980	489	81	115	19	491	81	60	10	21	3	33	5
1981	511	79	137	21	518	80	77	12	21	3	31	5
1982	500	73	185	27	546	80	93	14	19	3	27	4
1983	487	66	251	34	599	81	95	13	15	2	28	4

a Average amounts outstanding in billions of dollars and percentages of total assets.

b Average amounts outstanding in billions of dollars and percentages of total liabilities and net worth.

c Contract rates on conventional loans for new houses adjusted for points and loan application fees.

d Interest income on mortgages as a percentage of average mortgages outstanding.

e Operating income consists mainly of loan fees and interest on mortgages and investments.

f Operating expenses consist mainly of wages, employee benefits, office occupancy, and advertising.

g Interest paid on deposits and other borrowing as a percentage of average deposits and other borrowing.

h Before taxes.

i Based on data for the first half of 1983 from *Federal Home Loan Bank Board Journal,* January 1984, pages 25, 41, 42.

Sources: *Federal Home Loan Bank Board Journals, Savings and Loan Fact Books,* and *Savings and Loan Sourcebooks.*

The recent history of S&Ls is summarized in Table 17.3. Columns 1
to 6 describe S&L balance sheets. Especially notice that mortgages
have begun to give way to other investments, falling to 66% of total
assets in 1983. But our main interests in the table are the fluctuations
in the spread between mortgage rates and the cost of funds and the
implications of those fluctuations for S&L profits. Let's concentrate
on the period of volatile and generally rising interest rates between
1976 and 1981. Column 8 shows that the effective rate on *new*
mortgages rose from 8.99 percent to 14.70 percent between 1976 and
1981. But the rate of return on *all* mortgages, including those extended
in previous years at lower rates, grew much more slowly, from 7.73 to
9.74 percent, as indicated in column 9. Columns 13 and 15 show that
during the same period the cost of deposits (including the long-term,

Table 17.3   (continued)

Year	(7) New Mortgages,[a] $	(8) Effective Rate on New Mortgages,[c] %	(9) Return on Mortgages,[d] %	(10) Operating Income[e]/ Assets, %	(11) Operating Expense[f]/ Assets, %	(12) Net Operating Income/ Assets, %
1965	26	5.81	5.81	5.69	1.10	4.59
1970	25	8.45	6.41	6.53	1.16	5.37
1971	46	7.74	6.65	6.84	1.14	5.70
1972	61	7.60	6.83	6.93	1.12	5.81
1973	55	7.95	7.13	7.26	1.18	6.08
1974	44	8.92	7.33	7.57	1.23	6.34
1975	62	9.01	7.48	7.63	1.26	6.37
1976	90	8.99	7.73	7.91	1.28	6.63
1977	120	9.01	7.95	8.14	1.28	6.86
1978	119	9.54	8.13	8.43	1.28	7.15
1979	111	10.77	8.60	8.99	1.31	7.68
1980	84	12.66	9.03	9.46	1.33	8.13
1981	63	14.70	9.74	10.25	1.41	8.84
1982	77	15.14	10.41	10.70	1.53	9.17
1983	178	12.57	11.04[i]	10.54[i]	1.62[i]	8.92[i]

Year	(13) Cost of Deposits,[g] %	(14) Cost of Other Borrowing,[g] %	(15) Cost of Borrowing,[g] %	(16) Net Income[h]/ Assets, %	(17) Net Income/ Net Worth, %
1965	4.23	4.10	4.22	0.79	11.78
1970	5.10	7.61	5.27	0.69	9.59
1971	5.37	6.26	5.42	0.91	13.38
1972	5.39	5.25	5.38	1.06	16.50
1973	5.54	6.99	5.62	1.06	16.90
1974	5.96	8.25	6.15	0.78	12.47
1975	6.21	7.22	6.29	0.67	11.17
1976	6.29	7.18	6.34	0.90	15.77
1977	6.37	6.56	6.39	1.11	19.97
1978	6.49	7.69	6.59	1.19	21.50
1979	7.28	8.93	7.44	0.96	17.18
1980	8.64	10.00	8.79	0.20	3.68
1981	10.65	12.19	10.85	−0.97	−20.23
1982	10.99	12.83	11.26	−0.88	−21.46
1983	9.68[i]	10.62[i]	9.81[i]	0.36[i]	9.68[i]

high-yield certificates listed in Table 2.2) increased from 6.29 to 10.65 percent while the average cost of funds from all sources (including FHLB advances) rose from 6.34 to 10.85 percent. That is, the rate of return on the mortgage portfolio increased between 1976 and 1981 by 2.01 percent (7.73 to 9.74), compared with an increase of 4.51 percent (6.34 to 10.85) in the cost of funds. (These movements are shown in Figure 17.2.) You don't have to be a financial wizard to realize that this train of events could not continue for long. Columns 10 to 12, 16, and

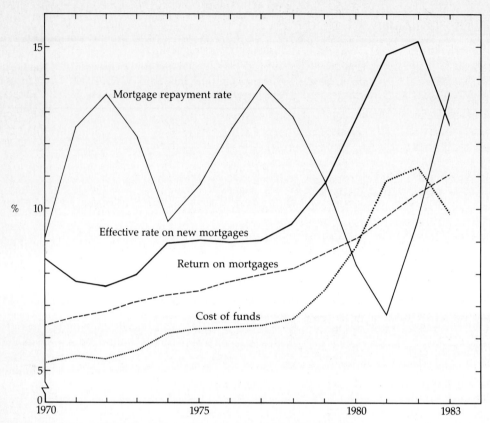

Sources: Table 17.3, *Savings and Loan Fact Books*, and *Savings and Loan Sourcebooks* and suggested by Michael Moran, "Thrift Institutions in Recent Years," *Federal Reserve Bulletin*, December 1982, Figs. 1 and 2.

Figure 17.2   Repayment rates on mortgages and mortgage returns and
costs at S&Ls, 1970 to 1983 (percentages at annual rates).

17 complete the story by taking other sources of income and expense
into account. But the conclusion implied by the comparison of mortgage returns and the cost of funds is not altered; net income fell
drastically, both as a proportion of assets and as a proportion of net
worth.[13]

The inability of the S&L industry to deal with the events of the
1970s and 1980s in an effective manner came as no surprise to those
familiar with their choice of course 2, that is, their reliance on
government, described above. Edward Kane (1978, pages 9 and 10)
forecast the losses of the 1980s in the following interesting manner:

"Differential" deposit-rate ceilings for banks and S&Ls can be
likened to a back brace. Wearing a back brace alleviates pain and

13 Other discussions of S&L problems during this period may be found in Daniel Vrabac (1982),
Michael Moran (1982), and Andrew Carron (1983).

allows the wearer to function in the short run, but if worn month after month, it weakens supporting abdominal muscles and aggravates the underlying condition it is designed to treat.

Deposit-rate ceilings can also be likened to the sedan chair on which the Swiss Guard carried Pope Paul during public audiences and other formal appearances. The regulatory sedan chair bears S&Ls on the backs of small savers, lifting them above the hurly-burly of funds competition. Unlike the Pope, who moved under his own power at least within the Vatican, many S&Ls have ridden in the regulatory sedan chair for twelve long years. As a result, their competitive muscles have atrophied noticeably. If authorities can't coax them out of their chair soon, a good portion of them could eventually become true basket cases.

Alternative mortgage instruments (AMIs)

S&Ls have recently begun to respond to inflation and volatile interest rates by investing in more short-term, nonmortgage instruments[14] and by offering a wider variety of mortgages. The traditional fixed-rate, fixed-payment mortgage continues to be an important form of S&L lending, but AMIs have been growing in importance. The availability of a variety of plans is beneficial to both borrowers and lenders, who are enabled to negotiate terms suited to their needs. Four of the responses to the inflationary environment of the 1970s and 1980s are briefly discussed below, after which we present a more detailed example of the most popular AMI, the variable-rate mortgage.[15]

VARIABLE-RATE MORTGAGE (VRM). The interest rate on a VRM is tied to some market rate or index of market rates. For example most California VRMs are linked to the average cost of funds of California S&Ls. An interest rate change may be reflected in a change in the size of the monthly payment with the maturity of the mortgage unaffected, an unchanged monthly payment but an adjustment in maturity, or adjustments in both payment size and maturity. The mortgage contract specifies the minimum period between interest rate changes and the minimum and maximum percentages by which the interest rate may be altered each change, each year, and during the life of the mortgage. A typical contract is one that provides for interest rate changes no more frequently than 6 months, a minimum change of 0.10 percent per change, a maximum change of 0.50 percent per year, and a maximum change of 2.50 percent during the life of the mortgage. In view of the great interest rate volatility of recent years, these are severe limitations on the usefulness of VRMs. But their flexibility continues to be severely restricted by regulation.

---

14 See Table 17.2.

15 Further information on these and other AMIs may be obtained from Donald Kaplan (1977), George Kaufman and Eleanor Erdevig (1981), Joseph McKenzie (1982), and Marcos Jones (1982).

RENEGOTIABLE-RATE (OR ROLLOVER) MORTGAGE (RRM OR ROM). This is a variation of the VRM in which the mortgage is extended at a fixed interest rate for a specified period, usually 5 years, although the payments are of a size that would repay the mortgage in 20, 25, or 30 years. The mortgage is renewable after 5 years at the rate set by the S&L according to current market conditions (although the original contract may set limits on the new interest rate). If the rate is not acceptable to the borrower, he must refinance the outstanding value of the mortgage from another source, perhaps by selling the property.

PRICE-LEVEL-ADJUSTED MORTGAGE (PLAM). Suppose both interest rates and home-buyer incomes vary closely with inflation. VRMs and RRMs are good hedges against inflation for borrowers under these circumstances because mortgage payments vary with incomes. The correspondence between payments and incomes is especially close during the early years of a mortgage, when payments consist mainly of interest. But a better hedge against inflation is the PLAM, which is directly linked to inflation. Since the balance and monthly payment on a PLAM are tied to the rate of inflation, the initial interest rate on a PLAM is a "real" interest rate without an inflationary premium.[16] Assume the real rate of interest to be 3 percent and the expected rate of inflation to be 9 percent, both at annual rates. This implies an interest rate of about 12 percent on fixed-rate mortgages and, on a $60,000 loan for 30 years, a monthly payment of $617.17.[17] The appropriate initial interest rate and monthly payment for a PLAM would be 3 percent and $252.96. At the end of the first year the balance of this PLAM is adjusted upward 9 percent, if that has been the actual rate of inflation. Payments are then recomputed on the basis of the new balance, and the second year's monthly payment is $275.73, which is 9 percent higher than the initial payment. The real value of the payments remains nearly constant; we say "nearly" because the payment size adjusts to inflation with an average lag of 6 months. Monthly payments in the thirtieth year, after 29 years of inflation, will be $(\$252.96)(1.09)^{29} = \$3,079.08$. But if house prices have also risen 9 percent per annum, the value of a house costing $75,000 (we assume a down payment of 20 percent) will after 30 years be $995,076. You will be a millionaire. However, the real values of both your mortgage payments and your house will have remained the same. The PLAM provides a hedge against inflation for mortgage lenders and, because of

---

16 This discussion paraphrases Joseph McKenzie (1982, page 19).

17 See Chapter 18 for a discussion of the equilibrium relations between real and nominal rates of interest and the rate of inflation. The monthly payment on the mortgage may be confirmed by Equation (5.24), which defines the present value of an annuity. In terms of that equation the loan (that is, the present value of the mortgage payments) is $A_n = \$60,000$, the monthly interest rate is $Y = 0.01$, and the number of payments is $n = 360$. Solving for the monthly payment gives $C = \$617.17$.

the low initial payment, may make home ownership in an inflationary environment more accessible to young families.

GRADUATED-PAYMENT MORTGAGE (GPM). The GPM has a fixed interest rate (unlike the three instruments considered above) but the payments start at a lower level than on the standard fixed-rate mortgage and rise according to a formula during the early years of the loan. For example the payments may increase by 7.5 percent each year during the first 5 years of the loan. Sometimes the early payments are less than accrued interest so that the balance of the loan rises for a while and the home buyer's equity in the property declines correspondingly (unless the value of the property increases). Sometimes the features of the GPM and the VRM are combined in a single instrument, giving a graduated-payment-adjustable mortgage (GPAM).

THE EQUILIBRIUM RELATION BETWEEN RATES ON TWO-PERIOD FIXED-RATE AND VARIABLE-RATE MORTGAGES. We now take a closer look at VRMs. We begin with a fixed-rate loan of $M = \$1,000$, which is used to finance the construction of a new doghouse for your St. Bernard (or for yourself if you don't do better on the next exam). Two equal payments (P_f) are to be made, one at the end of each of the next 2 years. These payments are just sufficient to retire the loan if

(17.1) $[M(1 + F) - P_f](1 + F) - P_f = 0 \quad \text{or} \quad P_f = M\dfrac{(1 + F)^2}{2 + F}$

where F is the rate of interest on the FRM.[18] For example, if $F = 0.10$, then $P_f = \$576.19$. After the first payment the owner owes $\$1,000(1.10) - \$576.19 = \$523.81$. This amount plus interest comes to $\$523.81(1.10) = \$576.19$ at the end of the second year, which not coincidentally is the payment due at that time.

Now consider a VRM, also for $M = \$1,000$. Payments on VRMs are constructed exactly like those on FRMs. That is, both VRM and FRM payments are the constant periodic payments that, given the rate of interest existing at the time of the calculation, retire loans at maturity. Therefore, using Equation (17.1), the first payment on the VRM is

(17.2) $$P_1 = M\frac{(1 + V_1)^2}{2 + V_1}$$

---

18 This example is identical with Exercise 5.6. Notice that Equation (17.1) may be rewritten such that

$$M = \frac{P_f}{1 + F} + \frac{P_f}{(1 + F)^2}$$

That is, the loan is the present value of the payments.

where V_1 is the interest rate on the VRM in the first period. Subscripts are used to denote dates of VRM interest rates and payments but are unnecessary for the constant FRM interest rates and payments.

The second payment, P_2, is the same as P_1 if V_2 equals V_1. But in general P_2 must satisfy

(17.3) $$[M(1 + V_1) - P_1](1 + V_2) - P_2 = 0$$

Substituting the solution for P_1 from Equation (17.2) into Equation (17.3) gives

(17.4)
$$P_2 = M(1 + V_1)(1 + V_2) - M\frac{(1 + V_1)^2}{2 + V_1}(1 + V_2)$$
$$= M\frac{(1 + V_1)(1 + V_2)}{2 + V_1}$$

Notice that $P_1 = P_2 = P_f$ if the rate of interest on the VRM is constant and equal to that on the FRM, that is, if $V_1 = V_2 = F$.

To illustrate the difference between FRMs and VRMs, suppose $F = 0.10$ and $P_f = \$576.19$ as above and further suppose $V_1 = 0.10$ and $V_2 = 0.12$. Using Equation (17.2), this means that $P_1 = P_f = \$576.19$. Then using Equation (17.4), we see that $P_2 = \$586.67$, which is about 2 percent more than P_1 and P_f.[19] You may use Equation (17.3) to confirm that these values of P_1 and P_2 actually pay off the mortgage.

Now let's derive the conditions under which the borrower and lender are indifferent between an FRM and a VRM. The *terminal value of the FRM* (that is, the accumulated payments plus interest earned on them) is

(17.5) $$T_f = P_f(1 + V_2) + P_f = M\frac{(1 + F)^2}{2 + F}(2 + V_2)$$

where we have used the solution of P_f from Equation (17.1) and have assumed the first payment to be reinvested at the variable rate V_2. That is, the variable rate is tied to (in fact is equal to) a money market rate at which the lender can reinvest his receipts. We also make the less realistic assumption that there is no regulatory restriction on the flexibility of variable rates.

Following the same procedure, the *terminal value of the VRM* is

(17.6) $$T_v = P_1(1 + V_2) + P_2 = M(1 + V_1)(1 + V_2)$$

where we have used the solutions for P_1 and P_2 from Equations (17.2)

---

19 More precisely, $P_2/P_1 = (1 + V_2)/(1 + V_1) = (1.12)/(1.10) = 1.018$ when $V_2 = 0.12$ and $V_1 = 0.10$.

and (17.4) and have again assumed first-period receipts to be rein-vested at the money market rate prevailing in the second period.

Both lender and borrower are indifferent between the FRM and the VRM when the terminal values of their receipts (payments) are the same. That is, setting T_f equal to T_v defines the equilibrium relation-ship between the (long-term) fixed rate F and current and expected (short-term) variable rates V_t:

(17.7)
$$\frac{(1 + F)^2}{2 + F} (2 + V_2) = (1 + V_1)(1 + V_2)$$

or $\quad \dfrac{(1 + F)^2}{2 + F} = \dfrac{(1 + V_1)(1 + V_2)}{2 + V_2}$

Our understanding of this equilibrium relation may be helped by the following linear approximation. First rewrite the second equation in Equation (17.7) as

$$\frac{(1 + F)^2}{2\left(1 + \dfrac{1}{2} F\right)} = \frac{(1 + V_1)(1 + V_2)}{2\left(1 + \dfrac{1}{2} V_2\right)}$$

Then taking natural logarithms of both sides of this equation and using the approximation $\ln(1 + x) = x$ when x is small, we have

$$2F - \frac{1}{2} F = V_1 + V_2 - \frac{1}{2} V_2$$

which is solved for F to obtain

(17.7a)
$$F = \frac{2V_1 + V_2}{3}$$

That is, in equilibrium the (long-term) fixed rate is approximately a weighted average of current and expected (short-term) variable rates, with higher weights for variable rates currently and in the near future.[20] The following exercise illustrates the equivalence of an FRM and a VRM when Equation (17.7a) is approximately satisfied.

---

20 The equilibrium relation between the rate (F) on an N-period FRM and current and expected rates $(V_1, V_2, \ldots, V_N)$ on a VRM may (as a linear approximation) be written

$$F = \frac{NV_1 + (N - 1)V_2 + \ldots + V_N}{1 + 2 + \ldots + N}$$

EXERCISE 17.1.   Suppose the current short-term rate of interest is $V_1 = 0.08$ and the short-term rate expected next period is $V_2 = 0.14$. Derive the equilibrium rate (F) on a two-period FRM, and show that for this rate the terminal values of the FRM and VRM are the same.

We know from Equation (17.7a) that F is approximately $[2(0.08) + 0.14]/3 = 0.10$. But we want an exact value for F, which may be obtained from Equation (17.7) by trial and error or directly by use of the quadratic formula. Equation (17.7) may be rearranged such that

$$AX^2 + BX + C = 0$$

where $X = 1 + F$, $A = 1$, and $B = C = -(1 + V_1)(1 + V_2)/(2 + V_2) = -0.57533$ since $V_1 = 0.08$ and $V_2 = 0.14$. Using the positive root of the quadratic formula gives

$$1 + F = X = \frac{-B + \sqrt{B^2 - 4AC}}{2A} = 1.0989$$

Thus the equilibrium F is 0.0989.

The payment on the FRM is, using Equation (17.1) and again letting $M = \$1{,}000$, $P_f = \$575.34$. The terminal value of an investment in this mortgage is

$$T_f = \$575.34(1.14) + \$575.34 = \$1{,}231.23$$

where we again assume the first payment to be invested at the short rate ($V_2 = 0.14$) prevailing in the second period.

Using Equations (17.2) and (17.4), the first- and second-period payments on the VRM are $P_1 = \$560.77$ and $P_2 = \$591.92$. Therefore, the terminal value of the VRM is

$$T_v = \$560.77(1.14) + \$591.92 = \$1{,}231.20$$

which differs slightly from our solution of T_f because of rounding errors.

SOME OF THE BENEFITS OF THE SIMULTANEOUS AVAILABILITY OF VRMs AND FRMs. The above discussion assumed a world of certainty, specifically a certain knowledge of the future short rate V_2. But the existence of a choice between VRMs and FRMs is most useful in the presence of uncertainty. Consider two prospective house buyers: (1) A young schoolteacher who expects his income to remain steady, that is, to be unresponsive to inflation, and (2) a retiree who expects his social security and other benefits to be tied to the price level. Suppose each wishes to insure against the possibility that his future mortgage payments will outstrip his income.

We are interested in the preferences of these people when confronted by the situation posed in Exercise 17.1—$F = 0.0989$, $V_1 = 0.08$, and expected $V_2 = 0.14$—except that now no one knows for sure what V_2 will be. The risk-averse schoolteacher will choose the FRM in order to ensure a constant $P_f = \$575.34$ to go with his fixed income. On the other hand the risk-averse retiree will choose the VRM in order to ensure that his monthly payment will fall in line with his income if prices and interest rates should fall.[21]

AN EXAMPLE OF THE HARM DONE TO CONSUMERS BY CONSUMER GROUPS: THE IMPOSSIBILITY OF THE SIMULTANEOUS AVAILABILITY OF VRMs AND FRMs IN THE ABSENCE OF EARLY-PAYMENT PENALTIES. Unfortunately the regulators have limited the usefulness of VRMs by restricting the size and frequency of rate adjustments. But even if this were not so, another form of regulation—the prohibition of early-payment penalties—would tend to reduce the range of mortgage instruments available and thereby to increase the risk exposure of borrowers and lenders. This will be illustrated within the framework of our two-period example.

The equilibrium relation (17.7) assumes the borrower, like the lender, to be bound to the contract until maturity. Suppose that this is not the case and that the borrower may refinance the mortgage at any time. Consider the case in which short rates are expected to fall such that $V_1 = 0.14$ and $V_2 = 0.08$. We see from Equation (17.7a) that in such an event the rate of interest on the FRM is approximately 0.12, or more precisely, using the quadratic formula in Exercise 17.1, $F = 0.1203$. The borrower's optimal strategy under these conditions is to take out an FRM at 12.03 percent in the first period and then to refinance the second year of the mortgage at $V_2 = 0.08$, in which case the terminal value of his payments on this combination FRM-VRM will be

(17.8) $$T_{fv} = P_f(1 + V_2) + [M(1 + F) - P_f](1 + V_2)$$

where the first term on the right-hand side of the equation is the first-period payment on the FRM plus its reinvestment value and the second term is the outstanding balance at the end of the first-period multiplied by unity plus the rate of interest (V_2) on the loan in the

---

21 Based on our previous discussion of AMIs, the retiree would in these circumstances be even
    more favorably disposed to a PLAM than to a VRM. For more general discussions of borrower
    choices between FRMs and VRMs based on the difference between the rates on the two mort-
    gages and the covariance between the borrower's income and the rate of inflation, see Jerome
    Baesel and Nahum Biger (1980) and Meir Statman (1982).

second period. Equation (17.8) reduces to

(17.8)′ $T_{fv} = M(1 + F)(1 + V_2)$

The FRM becomes a VRM at the borrower's discretion, which he will exercise whenever $V_2 < F$. That is, the borrower stays with the FRM if interest rates rise but switches to a VRM (or to a new FRM at a lower rate) if interest rates fall.

But the lender will be reluctant to play this game. He will not extend FRMs at $F = 0.1203$ rather than VRMs at $V_1 = 0.14$ unless he is allowed to charge an early-payment penalty sufficient to bring the expected revenue from the FRM-VRM strategy up to the expected revenues from loans to borrowers who stay with FRMs or VRMs for the full lives of these loans. Comparing Equations (17.8)′ and (17.6), when $V_2 < F$ the lender will charge an early-payment penalty to those who wish to refinance their FRMs such that

(17.9)
$$T_{fv} = M(1 + F)(1 + V_2) + \text{penalty}$$
$$= M(1 + V_1)(1 + V_2) = T_v$$

that is, such that

(17.9)′
$$\text{Penalty} = M(V_1 - F)(1 + V_2)$$
$$= \$1,000(0.1400 - 0.1203)(1.08) = \$21.28$$

The numerical values on the right-hand side of Equation (17.9)′ show the size of the penalty in the present example, that is, for $M = \$1,000$, $V_1 = 0.14$, $V_2 = 0.08$, and $F = 0.1203$. We see from Equation (17.1) that $P_f = \$591.93$ and from the last term in Equation (17.8) that the second-period payment of the sharpie who switches from an FRM to a VRM is

$$[\$1,000(1.1203) - \$591.93](1.08) = \$570.64$$

Adding the early-payment penalty of \$21.28 gives, except for a rounding error of a penny, the original FRM contract payment of $P_f = \$591.93$.[22]

Now suppose consumer advocates persuade legislatures to outlaw early-payment penalties, as they have done in several states.[23] Given

---

22 Because mortgages may be redeemed at the option of borrowers, they are like the callable bonds discussed in Chapter 10. Early-payment penalties are analogous to call premiums on bonds. Both are payments by borrowers for the exercise of their call options.

23 "If I knew for a certainty that a man was coming to my house with the conscious design of doing me good, I should run for my life" (Henry Thoreau, *Walden*, pages 66 and 67).

V_1 and V_2, lenders will respond by raising F such that

(17.10) $T_{fv} = M(1 + F)(1 + V_2) = M(1 + V_1)(1 + V_2) = T_v = T_f$

or $F = V_1 = 0.14$ instead of $F = 0.12$, and under these conditions the effect of the legislation is to reduce choice by eliminating one form of mortgage, the FRM, by making FRMs effectively identical with VRMs.[24]

LIFE INSURANCE COMPANIES

Life insurance companies as financial intermediaries

Life insurance is an investment much like other investments, and life insurance companies are financial intermediaries much like other financial intermediaries. You (the "insured," or "policyholder") invest in a life insurance contract (policy) by making regular payments (premiums), and the life insurance company invests your money in real estate and securities and hopes to profit from the spread between the rate of return on its investment portfolio and the rate of return it pays you. The difference between life insurance and other investments arises from the conditions under which you can retrieve your money, that is, the conditional nature of your return. You may withdraw funds from your S&L account anytime during working hours that you have 45 minutes to spare to watch the teller play with one of their new "labor-saving" machines. You may retrieve your investment (plus or minus a capital gain or loss) in a bond by selling it. The dividend on an investment in a share of common stock is conditional on company profits. Of course rates of return on investments in debt instruments such as bonds, S&L deposits, and life insurance policies are also conditional on the solvency of the borrowers. But the rate of return on your life policy is in addition conditional on the date of your death. This is typical of insurance policies, which promise to pay only upon the occurrence of specified events, for example, a dented fender or a broken leg for car or medical insurance.

Life insurance company assets and liabilities

LIABILITIES (LIFE INSURANCE AND PENSION FUND RESERVES). We should expect most life insurance company liabilities to be promises to pay funds in the event of death. These liabilities are indicated by "Life insurance reserves" in Table 17.4. We see from the table that life insurance reserves have become a decreasing proportion of life company liabilities in recent years as the industry has moved into health

---

24 S&Ls and other mortgage lenders have striven to preserve early-payment penalties in the face of these attempts at consumer protection, for example, under the name "renegotiation fees." See Patric Hendershott, Sheng Hu, and Kevin Villani (1982) for a general statement of the up-front charges and/or higher rates on FRMs required to compensate lenders for the expected losses arising from borrower options to terminate mortgages.

Table 17.4   Life Insurance Companies: End-of-Year Financial Assets and Liabilities, 1950 to 1983 (Billions of Dollars)

	1950	1960	1970	1980	1983
Total financial assets	62.6	115.8	200.9	464.2	636.5
Demand deposits and currency	1.0	1.3	1.8	3.2	4.6
Corporate equities	2.1	5.0	15.4	47.4	65.1
Credit market instruments	57.9	105.6	174.6	385.1	514.6
U.S. government securities	13.5	6.5	4.6	17.0	49.0
State and local government securities	1.2	3.6	3.3	6.7	10.7
Corporate and foreign bonds	24.8	48.1	74.1	178.8	221.0
Mortgages	16.1	41.8	74.4	131.1	150.2
Open-market paper	0.0	0.3	2.1	10.1	29.3
Policy loans	2.4	5.2	16.1	41.4	54.5
Miscellaneous assets	1.6	3.9	9.2	28.5	52.1
Total liabilities	59.2	108.5	187.7	438.4	604.4
Life insurance reserves	49.1	78.8	123.1	213.5	253.0
Pension fund reserves	5.6	18.9	41.2	165.8	270.6
Miscellaneous liabilities	4.6	10.9	23.4	59.1	80.8

Source: Federal Reserve flow of funds accounts.

insurance and the management of pension funds. Life insurance reserves made up 83 percent of total life company liabilities in 1950, compared with 66 percent in 1970 and 42 percent in 1983. Pension fund reserves grew from 9 to 22 to 45 percent of total liabilities in 1950, 1970, and 1983.

LIFE INSURANCE COMPANY ASSETS ARE MAINLY LONG TERM. Turning to the asset side of the balance sheet, policyholder and pension fund reserves are invested principally in long-term mortgages and corporate bonds. This is standard risk-averse behavior for investors with long-term liabilities. A life company that has sold no policies since 1920 will have only short-term liabilities on its books. If it wants to be sure of meeting these imminent claims it should hold high-grade short-term securities maturing on the dates that, according to its mortality tables, the claims are likely to fall due. But most life insurance companies, even though they have not grown so rapidly as other financial institutions, have sold most of their policies fairly recently to relatively young people.[25]

FORWARD COMMITMENTS. Life companies are very large, and their investments must be arranged well in advance. The Prudential Insurance Company, for example, has an average daily cash inflow of about

---

25 Three-fifths of ordinary life insurance purchased in 1981 was for people between the ages of 15 and 34, and life insurance ownership is most common in households with children and in which the head is between 30 and 34 (*Life Insurance Fact Book,* 1983, pages 11 and 33).

$40 million. Most of these funds are committed to specific future investments based on forecasts of the company's cash flow and yields on alternative investments. These forward commitments take the form of contracts to buy mortgages on large projects, such as office buildings, and private placements of corporate bonds. Private placements are security issues sold to one or a few investors instead of to the general public.[26]

POLICY LOANS. A small but interesting part of life company assets consists of policy loans. These are loans to policyholders secured by the values of their policies. Investors in "whole" life insurance policies accumulate savings, or "cash value," in those policies, which they can borrow back from life companies at rates of interest stated in the policies. For many years the standard policy loan rate was 5 percent and during the period of low interest rates extending from the early 1930s to the mid-1960s was high enough to discourage most policyholders from exercising their borrowing option. Policy loans fell from 15 percent of life company assets in 1935 to less than 4 percent during the 1950s.[27]

Figure 17.3 shows that policy loans began to rise with interest rates during the late 1950s as policyholders found it profitable to borrow against their policies to obtain funds for investments paying more than 5 percent. The increased level and volatility of interest rates beginning in the 1960s was more than matched by the increased level and volatility of policy loans. For example growth in policy loans accounted for 17, 27, 16, 18, and 17 percent of new life company investable funds during the high-interest-rate years 1966, 1969, 1974, 1980, and 1981. The comparable percentages for the lower-interest-rate years 1971, 1972, 1975, and 1976 were 8, 7, 8, and 5. Even the latter figures were greater than those prevailing between 1935 and 1960. By the end of 1981, policy loans made up more than 9.6 percent of life company financial assets before falling back to 8.6 percent in 1983.

Life insurance companies as savings as well as insurance institutions

The two principal types of life insurance are "term" and "whole life." *Term insurance* is "pure" life insurance obtained for a limited period, perhaps 5 years (although most policies contain renewal options), with increasing premiums as the policyholder grows older. If you expire before your policy, you (or rather your beneficiaries) earn a good return. But if you obstinately survive your policy, your rate of return is

26 See Robert Rennie (1977) and Eli Shapiro (1977) for discussions of the life company forward commitment decision process. See David Cummins (1975), James Pesando (1974), and William Silber (1970) for econometric studies of life company investments.

27 *Life Insurance Fact Book* (1981, page 69). Policy loans were actually less in dollar value in 1955 than in 1935.

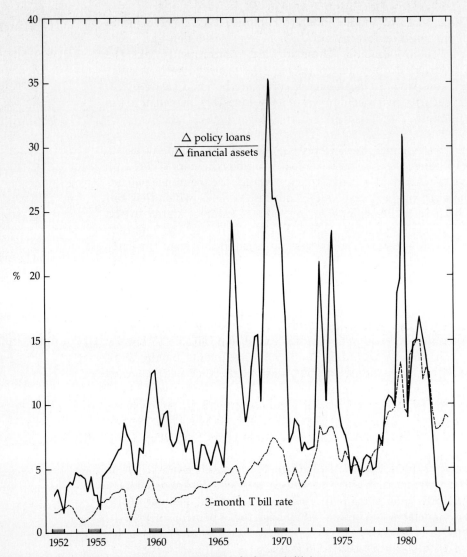

$$\frac{\Delta \text{ policy loans}}{\Delta \text{ financial assets}}$$

3-month T bill rate

Quarterly changes in policy loans are shown as percentages of quarterly changes in life insurance
company financial assets. Treasury bill rates are quarterly averages of daily figures.

Sources: Federal Reserve flow of funds accounts and *Federal Reserve Bulletins*.

Figure 17.3   Interest rates and policy loans, 1952 to 1983.

zero—except peace of mind for you and your dependent beneficiaries,
which of course is worth something. Car insurance and medical
insurance also possess these features. But *whole life insurance* adds a
savings feature. Whole life is a combination of term insurance and a
savings account to which you contribute regularly. It differs from term
insurance in two ways: by providing for a payment upon the death of
the insured whenever it occurs, instead of being limited to a specific
term, and by providing for a constant, or "level," premium either

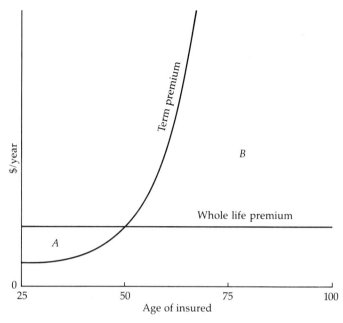

Figure 17.4   An increasing term premium and a level whole life premium.

throughout the insured's lifetime or for a limited period, often until age 65.

Suppose two 25-year-old men, T and W, each insures his life for $50,000. T buys a term policy with an option to renew until he reaches 65, whereas W buys a whole life policy with premiums to be paid throughout his lifetime. For representative policies[28] T's annual premium starts at $200 and rises to $1,600 as he approaches 65 while W's premium is constant at $650. T's premiums reflect the true cost of life insurance, based on the probability of death during the years in which premiums are paid.[29] W's early payments in excess of T's are savings that together with interest are used by the insurance company to defray the increasing cost of insurance as the policyholder ages. Figure 17.4 presents an illustration of the relationship between an increasing term premium and a level whole life premium for someone who wishes to maintain a constant death benefit beginning at age 25.[30] Area A

---

28 As selected by Consumers Union (1972, page 69).

29 By "true cost of insurance" we mean the insurance company's expected (in a statistical sense) payout to a policyholder in light of his age and the size of his policy. For example, if 0.20 percent of 25-year-old American males do not make it to 26, which is approximately the statistic in the mortality tables of life insurance companies, the expected payment to T during the year following his first premium payment of $195 is 0.0020($50,000)=$100. The difference between the $100 cost and the $195 premium (plus the company's return on its investment of the premium) is taken up by company profits, taxes, and expenses.

30 Figures 17.4 and 17.5 are based on Figures 2 and 3 in Janice Greider and William Beadles (1964, pages 32 and 33).

represents the excess premium paid by W during the early years of the policy; area *B* represents the amounts by which the premium falls short of costs in later years. Area *B* is made possible by *A* and exceeds *A* because of the returns expected by the company on the early excess premiums. The accelerating term premiums reflect accelerating mortality rates as the policyholder ages.

By paying premiums in excess of the true cost of insurance, W accumulates equity, or cash value, in his whole life policy. Such an accumulated cash value is illustrated in Figure 17.5. The difference between the cash value, which is due to the savings portion of W's premium, and the $50,000 face value of the policy is pure insurance. It is the amount that from the company's point of view is "at risk." So W's whole life policy is a combination savings plan and decreasing term insurance. Most policies are written such that the insured collects the full face value on his hundredth birthday.

W may leave all the cash value with the company, as assumed above, to be collected by himself at age 100 or to be paid along with the pure insurance to his beneficiaries if he dies before then. Or he may withdraw some or all of this cash value in the form of policy loans, on which the policyholder-investor pays interest to the company at a rate specified in the policy. He can withdraw all his accumulated savings by cashing in the policy. This terminates the insurance.

Life insurance company responses to inflation

The following discussion considers life company responses to two of the many ways in which inflation has affected the life insurance industry: the diminished attractiveness of life insurance as an outlet for savings and the increased volatility of policy loans.

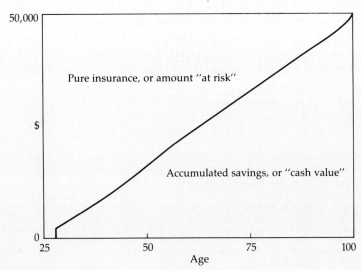

Figure 17.5   Accumulation of cash value in a $50,000 whole life insurance policy issued at age 25.

THE DECREASING IMPORTANCE OF LIFE COMPANIES AS SAVINGS INSTITU-
TIONS. Rates of return on the savings portions of whole life insurance
have not kept up with market rates of interest, so that life insurance as
a form of savings has become less attractive. Term insurance rose from
41 percent of life insurance sales in 1970 to 59 percent in 1981.[31] This
reduction in the use of life insurance companies as savings institutions
is largely responsible for their decline in importance relative to other
financial institutions.[32] Although life companies have maintained their
position as insurance institutions by shifting into health insurance, we
see in Table 17.1 that no group of financial institutions other than
mutual savings banks has grown more slowly since 1950. Their
financial assets fell from 22 percent to 13 percent of the financial
assets of all financial institutions between 1950 and 1983 and from 44
percent to 19 percent of the total financial assets of NBFIs.

Life companies have tried to arrest the relative decline of whole life
insurance by tying rates of return to the rate of inflation. *Variable
annuities,* in which policy cash values and future benefits are linked to
portfolios of market securities, have been around for a long time.[33] But
they have become increasingly important since the mid-1960s, and in
recent years companies have begun to market both term and whole life
policies with benefits tied directly to the Consumer Price Index.[34] Of
course premiums on these policies must be high enough to account for
expected inflation. It is too early to tell whether variable premium and
pay-out policies will reverse the declining fortunes of life insurance
companies.

POLICY LOANS AND FORWARD COMMITMENTS. High and volatile inflation
and interest rates have also affected the ways in which life companies
manage their assets. We noted early in our discussion of life companies
that (1) they commit their funds to mortgages and the private
placement of corporate bonds well before the receipt of those funds,
but that (2) policy loans, which the companies cannot control, have
represented a growing and volatile claim on their investable funds.
The inability of company investment managers to forecast (2) has
made the management of (1) more difficult. Because of the unpredictability of policy loans and therefore of the funds available for other
investments, companies have had to reduce their forward commitments. At the same time they have increased the flexibility of their
portfolios by allocating more funds to short-term securities. Table 17.4
shows that open-market paper (commercial paper and bankers accep-

31 *Life Insurance Fact Book* (1983, page 12).

32 Mark Warshawsky (1982) argues that more than 60 percent of the decline in life insurance savings as a proportion of personal disposable income can be explained by the widening of the differential between the rate of return on saving through life insurance and the after-tax rate of return on market portfolios of similar risk.

33 The first variable annuity was the College Retirement Equities Fund established in 1952.

34 See Mary Greenebaum (1980) for the details of some of these policies.

tances) rose from 1.0 to 4.6 percent of life company assets between 1970 and 1983. Sales of short-term assets may with little risk of loss be used to fulfill forward commitments when policy loans exceed predictions and to provide funds for spot purchases of mortgages and bonds when desired.

In addition to these measures life companies have taken steps to reduce the variability and/or average level of policy loans in the future by raising policy loan rates or linking them to market rates. This is likely to reduce the uncertainty of life company cash flows, but it also reduces the attractiveness of life insurance as an investment.[35]

PENSION AND RETIREMENT FUNDS

Pension and retirement plans (we use these terms interchangeably) consist of funds set aside by employers, unions, or individuals for the purpose of providing income to workers during retirement. About 50 percent of private workers and nearly all government workers participate in pension plans in addition to social security.

The management of pension funds

Employer and employee contributions to private pension plans are either used to buy group annuity policies from life insurance companies or are paid into the custody of trustees, usually trust departments of large commercial banks. In the former case pension contributors pay premiums now and insurance companies pay benefits to retired employees later. Most pension plans use the trustee system, which allows more flexibility in the size and timing of contributions (especially by employers) and more control over how those contributions are invested. Under both systems, to qualify for employer income tax deductions, pension fund contributions must be separated from those of the employer and be managed (by an insurance company or a trustee) for the exclusive benefit of the participants (employees) and their beneficiaries.

The top line of Table 17.5 and the next-to-last line of Table 17.4 show that in 1983 the financial assets of trustee plans were $409.3 billion while the contribution of pension funds to life insurance company portfolios was $270.6 billion. Insurance companies have recently increased their competition for pension funds by offering a wider variety of plans, and their share of pension fund assets has increased from a post-World War II low of 25 percent in 1972 to 40 percent at the end of 1983.

The investment principles that we discussed in connection with life insurance companies also apply to pension funds. The two groups are confronted by similar actuarial problems, have predominantly long-

---

35 See David Cummins (1975, pages 168–175) for an examination of the likely effects of alternative fixed and variable policy loan rates on policy loans.

Table 17.5 Pension and Retirement Funds End-of-Year Financial Assets, 1950 to 1983 (Billions of Dollars)

Private Pension Funds

	1950	1960	1970	1980	1983
Total financial assets	7.1	38.1	110.4	286.8	409.3
Demand deposits and currency	0.3	0.5	1.1	1.9	2.2
Time deposits	0.0	0.0	0.7	10.3	7.0
Corporate equities	1.1	16.5	67.1	175.8	250.7
Credit market instruments	5.3	19.7	36.6	92.6	142.0
U.S. government securities	2.3	2.7	3.0	30.9	68.6
Corporate and foreign bonds	2.8	15.7	29.4	58.1	68.2
Mortgages	0.1	1.3	4.2	3.7	5.2
Miscellaneous assets	0.4	1.4	4.9	6.2	7.4

State and Local Government Employee Retirement Funds

	1950	1960	1970	1980	1983
Total financial assets	4.9	19.7	60.3	198.1	313.7
Demand deposits and currency	0.1	0.2	0.6	4.3	6.0
Corporate equities	0.0	0.6	10.1	44.3	88.1
Credit market instruments	4.7	18.9	49.6	149.5	219.6
U.S. government securities	2.5	5.9	6.6	40.0	85.5
State and local government securities	1.5	4.4	2.0	4.1	3.0
Corporate and foreign bonds	0.6	7.1	35.1	94.5	116.6
Mortgages	0.1	1.5	5.9	10.9	14.5

Source: Federal Reserve flow of funds accounts.

term liabilities, and invest their receipts principally in long-term high-grade securities. The main difference, again comparing Tables 17.4 and 17.5, is that trustee pension funds hold mainly corporate equities whereas insurance companies hold mainly corporate bonds. Studies of pension fund investment performance have produced results similar to performance studies of other institutions: that they do about as well, or as badly, as the average investor.[36] Pension fund equity holdings have performed in line with the S&P index.

State and local government pension funds, like private funds, are operated as distinct entities. Unlike the trustee and insurance company private funds, however, government pension funds are self-administered. They used to be heavily invested in state and local government securities, these securities making up 31 percent of their assets in 1950. This is not wise policy for pension funds. The largely tax-free state and local government securities are good buys for investors in high tax brackets but not for institutions like pension funds, whose earnings are tax exempt or tax deferred. Table 17.5 shows that by the end of 1983 state and local government securities

---

36 See, for example, Martin Schwimmer and Edward Malca (1976) and G. Beebower and G. Bergstrom (1977).

had fallen below 1 percent of the financial assets of state and local government pension funds.

Tax advantages of pension funds

Pension fund beneficiaries gain two important tax advantages. First, they may defer taxes on contributions made by them or on their behalf until retirement benefits are actually received, when they have often moved to a lower tax bracket. Second, taxes on pension fund investment income are also deferred until the receipt of retirement benefits. These tax advantages of pension plans are illustrated by the following example, in which a middle-aged worker whose marginal tax bracket is expected to be $\tau_w = 0.25$ during the remainder of her working life is trying to decide whether to urge her union to negotiate a wage increase of $V = \$1,000$ per annum or an increase of $1,000 per annum in the employer's payment into her pension plan. She expects an annual rate of return of $R = 0.08$ on both her own investments and those of the pension fund. She expects her marginal tax bracket to be $\tau_r = 0.15$ during retirement, beginning $n = 20$ years in the future. The after-tax value of $1,000 received in wages now and invested at 8 percent for 20 years will be

(17.11) $V(1 - \tau_w)[1 + R(1 - \tau_w)]^n$

$$= \$1,000(1 - 0.25)[1 + 0.08(1 - 0.25)]^{20} = \$2,405$$

compared with the after-tax value of an equal pension fund contribution amounting to

(17.12) $V(1 + R)^n(1 - \tau_r) = \$1,000(1.08)^{20}(1 - 0.15) = \$3,962$

If her tax bracket remains unchanged so that $\tau_r = \tau_w = 0.25$, her pension fund contribution will after 20 years be worth

(17.13) $V(1 + R)^n(1 - \tau_w) = \$1,000(1.08)^{20}(1 - 0.25) = \$3,496$

Remuneration in the form of a pension fund contribution rather than directly in wages results in a gain of $3,496 - $2,405 = $1,091 because of the ability to reinvest interest earnings that otherwise would have gone to the tax man, and an additional gain of $3,962 - $3,496 = $466 if her retirement tax bracket is 10 percent less than during her working years.

But what if Ms. Smith doesn't want to wait until she is 65 before enjoying the things that a $1,000 pay raise can buy? The optimal policy even under these conditions may be to arrange for her pay raise to be paid into a pension fund and then to *finance current expenditures by borrowing against the fund*. Some of the conditions under which such a policy is optimal are illustrated by Exercise 17.2.

EXERCISE 17.2.   A 45-year-old worker in the 25 percent tax bracket has a $1,000 annual pay raise contributed to her pension fund instead of $750 added to her pay envelope. Show that she can still increase current spending by $750 a year by borrowing against her pension *and have money left in the fund at age 65.* First, **(a)** assume that Ms. Smith can borrow at the rate earned on pension fund investments (8 percent per annum), and then **(b)** let her borrowing rate exceed the fund's lending rate and calculate the borrowing rate such that she is indifferent between being paid directly and through pension fund contributions.

(a) We assume that Ms. Smith receives the raise, in one form or another, at the beginning of the year, that is, on her 45th, 46th, . . . , 64th birthdays. If the money is paid into her pension fund, she immediately, at age 45, borrows $750 at 8 percent. She owes, principal and interest, $750(1.08) = $810 at age 46. But 25 percent of the interest is tax deductible so that her interest expense is effectively 6 percent. She then refinances the original loan plus interest and obtains $750 for consumption in the next year by borrowing $750(1.06) + $750 = $1,545. This process is repeated at age 47 by means of a loan of $1,545(1.06) + $750 = $2,387.70. By borrowing $750 at ages 45, 46, . . . , 64, Ms. Smith accumulates a debt that on her 65th birthday amounts to

$$\$750[1.06 + (1.06)^2 + \cdots + (1.06)^{20}]$$

$$= \$795[1 + 1.06 + \cdots + (1.06)^{19}]$$

$$= 795[\text{terminal value of an annuity of} \\ \$1 \text{ per year for 20 years at 6 percent}]$$

$$= 795(\$36.786) = \$29,245$$

where the value 36.786 is read from Table C.4 in Appendix C.
But this debt may be paid from her pension fund, which has earned 8 percent per annum and at age 65 has an after-tax value of

$$\$1,000[1.08 + (1.08)^2 + \cdots + (1.08)^{20}](1 - \tau_r)$$

$$= \$1,080[1 + 1.08 + \cdots + (1.08)^{19}](0.75)$$

$$= 810[\text{terminal value of an annuity of} \\ \$1 \text{ per year for 20 years at 8 percent}]$$

$$= 810(\$45.762) = \$37,067$$

where we have assumed retirement and working tax brackets to be equal at $\tau_w = \tau_r = 0.25$.

So Ms. Smith enjoys $750 each year for current consumption and has $37,067 − $29,245 = $7,822 left at the end.

(b) If Ms. Smith's working and retirement tax rates are equal at 25 percent and if she wishes to spend her $750 after-tax wage increase currently, she will be indifferent between receiving the $1,000 pay raise directly or through a pension fund when the after-tax rate of interest at which she borrows equals the rate earned by the pension fund, that is, if $R(1 − 0.25) = 0.08$, or $R = 0.1067$, where R is her before-tax borrowing rate. She prefers to be paid through the pension fund whenever she can borrow at a rate less than 0.1067.

The above exercise demonstrated the tax advantages of being paid in the form of pension fund contributions—even if the worker wishes to consume currently by borrowing against the fund and even if her borrowing rate substantially exceeds the pension fund's lending rate. But in fact these advantages may not be diluted by an excess of the borrowing rate over the lending rate. This is partly because the worker can sometimes finance current consumption by the sale of existing security holdings, in which case the lending rate becomes the opportunity cost of borrowing, and partly because many pension funds lend to participants at rates equal to those earned by the fund.[37]

The growth of pension and retirement funds

We can calculate from Table 17.1 that trustee private pension funds and state and local government retirement funds grew at more rapid rates between 1950 and 1983 (13.1 and 13.4 percent per annum) than any other group of financial intermediaries existing in 1950 except credit unions. Insurance company pension reserves grew at an average annual rate of 12.5 percent during the same period. Some of this growth may have been due to inflation, which increases the gain from pension fund contributions relative to other forms of saving *if interest rates keep pace with inflation.*[38] This may be demonstrated by means of Equations (17.11) and (17.13) as modified to show the *real,* or purchasing power, advantages of pension funds. Assume a constant rate of inflation p and a constant real before-tax rate of interest r such that[39]

37 All these results depend upon the employer's actually performing his part of the bargain by making the agreed contribution to the fund. Ms. Smith would probably be unable to borrow against promised future retirement benefits that were not properly funded. The failure of employers to fund pension plans was declared a matter of public policy by the Employee Retirement Income Security Act of 1974, in which Congress obligated the American taxpayer to guarantee all private pension promises. The problems raised by this Act have been discussed in many places, including Alicia Munnell (1982).

38 This point has been made by Martin Feldstein (1981).

39 The real rate r was seen in Chapters 14 and 15 to be an important determinant of the decisions of households and firms, specifically in Equations (14.10) and (15.5). Equation (17.14) will be

(17.14) $1 + R = (1 + r)(1 + p)$

The following numerical examples use $r = 0.04$ and initially $p = 0.05$ so that $R = 0.0920$. We also assume that both working and retirement marginal tax rates are $\tau = 0.25$. Then the after-tax real value of a $V = \$1,000$ pension contribution will after 20 years be

(17.15) $\dfrac{V(1 + R)^n (1 - \tau)}{(1 + p)^n} = V(1 - \tau)(1 + r)^n$

$$= \$1,000(0.75)(1.04)^{20} = \$1,643$$

On the other hand the after-tax real value of a \$1,000 direct wage increase will be

(17.16) $\dfrac{V(1 - \tau)[1 + R(1 - \tau)]^n}{(1 + p)^n} = V(1 - \tau)(1 + r)^n \dfrac{[1 + R(1 - \tau)]^n}{(1 + R)^n}$

$$= \$1,074$$

where this result has used Equation (17.14) to substitute $(1 + R)/(1 + r)$ for $1 + p$. Comparing Equations (17.15) and (17.16), we see that the real value of the direct wage is less than that of the pension contribution whenever the marginal tax rate, τ, is positive. We will now show that this difference increases with the rate of inflation. Again using Equation (17.14) to substitute $(1 + r)(1 + p) - 1$ for R in the second statement of Equation (17.16) and then rearranging, the real value of the direct wage is

(17.16)' $V(1 - \tau)(1 + r)^n \left[(1 - \tau) + \dfrac{\tau}{(1 + r)(1 + p)} \right]^n$

$$= \begin{cases} \$1,074 & \text{for } p = 0.05 \\ \$\ \ 867 & \text{for } p = 0.10 \end{cases}$$

For $V = \$1,000$, $\tau = 0.25$, $r = 0.04$, and $n = 20$ an increase in the rate of inflation from 5 percent to 10 percent per annum reduces the real value of the wage increase after 20 years from \$1,074 to \$867. This result follows from the depressing effect of inflation on the real after-tax rate of return on nonpension-fund investments. When $\tau = 0.25$, $r = 0.04$, and $p = 0.05$, the nominal rate of interest is $R = 0.0920$, the after-tax nominal rate of return is $(1 - \tau)R = 0.0690$, and the after-tax real rate of return used in Equation (17.16) is

shown in the derivation of Equation (18.28) to be an equilibrium relationship under conditions of certainty with or without taxes if incomes from real and financial assets are taxed at the same rate.

$(1.0690/1.05) - 1 = 0.0181$. When p increases to 0.10, we see from Equation (17.14) that R rises by 0.0520 to 0.1440, but $(1 - \tau)R$ rises by only three-quarters of this amount, to 0.1080, so that the real after-tax rate of return falls to $(1.1080/1.10) - 1 = 0.0073$. This contrasts with the unchanged real rate of return on pension fund investments in Equation (17.15).

We offer this only as a possible explanation of why unions and individuals have increasingly desired to be paid in the form of pension fund contributions, because interest rates have not always fully reflected inflation. We shall see in Chapter 18 that movements in interest rates corresponded closely to movements in inflation during 1953 to 1971 but that this correspondence has been weak since 1971, as it was before 1953.

QUESTIONS

1. What will Figure 17.1 look like during the next 10 years if inflation accelerates? Please pay special attention to the possible effects of inflation on S&Ls, life insurance companies, pension and retirement funds, and money market funds.

2. Using Table 17.2, list individual S&L financial assets and liabilities as proportions of their total financial assets and liabilities in 1980 and 1983. Discuss the reasons for the principal changes between 1980 and 1983. What will these statements (still expressed in proportions) look like in 1990? How will S&Ls differ from commercial banks?

3. "Reasonably steady interest rates are essential to the survival of S&Ls as their portfolios are presently constituted." Do you think this statement will be true in the year 2000? How might your answer be changed if the Congressmen who advocate the elimination of VRMs (whenever interest rates rise) get their way?

4. Extend Figure 17.2 under the assumption that interest rates rise sharply during the next 3 years. How would your picture have been changed if most S&L mortgages had been VRMs?

5. Given the entries in columns 1 to 8 of Table 17.3, what would the 1978 to 1981 entries in columns 9 to 17 have been if most mortgages had been VRMs?

6. What type of mortgage do you think you will prefer when you buy your next house? Why?

7. (a) What are the similarities, if any, between life insurance companies and other financial intermediaries?
   (b) What are the differences, if any, between life insurance companies and other financial intermediaries?

8. Using Table 17.4, list individual life insurance company financial assets and liabilities as proportions of their total financial assets and liabilities in 1980 and 1983. Discuss the reasons for the

principal changes between 1980 and 1983. What will these statements look like in 1990? Why?

9. Present a rough sketch of what Figure 17.3 would have looked like if policy loan rates had been tied to market rates.

10. There has recently been a strong tendency for financial intermediaries to become more similar. For example commercial banks now underwrite securities, and securities dealers service checking accounts; S&Ls and CUs have also become more like commercial banks by offering checking accounts; and S&Ls have begun to follow banks into short-term and variable-rate loans. But life insurance companies are an exception to this tendency: They have become less like other savings institutions. Explain how and why this has happened.

11. Suppose you have two job offers. Employer A pays a slightly lower current salary than B but has a "good" pension plan. How will you go about evaluating the relative financial advantages of these two jobs?

12. (a) Suppose you are given control of government fiscal (including tax) policies, and you want to reduce the importance of pension funds. What will you do?

    (b) Suppose you are given control of the Federal Reserve, and you want to reduce the importance of pension funds. What will you do?

PROBLEMS

1. Consider two borrowers, Frank and Vera, who arrange a two-period $1,000 FRM and a two-period $1,000 VRM, respectively. Current and expected short rates are $V_1 = 0.10$ and $V_2 = 0.07$. Assume that mortgages may not be paid off before maturity.

    (a) What is the equilibrium rate on the fixed-rate mortgage?

    (b) What are Frank's and Vera's payments?

    (c) Show that the terminal values of their payments are the same.

2. Now suppose mortgages may be repaid early without penalty.

    (a) What is the optimal borrowing strategy for Frank and Vera, given the data in problem 1(a)?

    (b) But the S&L will not put up with this. How will the rate on its FRM be altered in light of expected early payment?

3. (a) Referring to Table 17.3, please calculate the average "effective rate on new mortgages" for the 10-year periods 1970 to 1979, 1971 to 1980, 1972 to 1981, and 1973 to 1982. These averages ought to be rough approximations of the "Return on mortgages" in 1979, 1980, 1981, and 1982. Are they?

    (b) Suppose the "Effective rate on new mortgages" and the "Cost of borrowing" both increased 2 percent between 1983 and 1984. What are the entries for 1984 in columns 6, 16, and 17?

(*Note.* There is no unique answer. You will have to make assumptions about, for example, "Operating income/assets" and "Operating expense/assets.")

4. Suppose you are going to retire in 10 years, your working and retirement tax brackets are expected to be equal at $\tau_w = \tau_r = 0.20$, and the market rate of return available both to you and to your pension fund is $R = 0.10$. You want to allocate a $1,000 bonus to retirement. Calculate the gain from having the bonus paid into your pension fund rather than directly to you.

5. Please do Exercise 17.2 for $\tau_w = \tau_r = 0.20$ and $R = 0.10$. That is, show how much money Ms. Smith will have at age 65 if she receives a $1,000 annual pay raise, beginning at age 45, in the form of an employer pension fund contribution and each year borrows (and spends) the after-tax value—$1,000(1 - \tau_w) = 800—of that pay raise.

6. Using the method of Equations (17.14) to (17.16), show the real gain after 20 years from having a $1,000 bonus paid into a pension fund rather than directly when the before-tax real rate of interest is $r = 0.05$, the rate of inflation is $p = 0.06$, and both working and retirement marginal tax rates are $\tau = 0.20$. Show the real gain if the rate of inflation is 10 percent.

7. Calculate the *real* gain in problem 4 when the before-tax real rate of interest is 4 percent.

REFERENCES

Ronald P. Auerbach, *Historical Overview of Financial Institutions in the United States,* Federal Deposit Insurance Corporation, Washington, 1978.

Jerome B. Baesel and Nahum Biger, "The Allocation of Risk: Some Implications of Fixed versus Index-linked Mortgages," *Journal of Financial and Quantitative Analysis,* June 1980, pages 457–468.

G. L. Beebower and G. L. Bergstrom, "A Performance Analysis of Pension and Profit-Sharing Portfolios: 1966–75," *Financial Analysts Journal,* May/June 1977, pages 31–41.

Andrew S. Carron, *The Rescue of the Thrift Industry,* The Brookings Institution, Washington, 1983.

Consumers Union, *The Consumers Union Report on Life Insurance,* rev. ed., Grossman, New York, 1972; 4th ed., Holt, Rinehart & Winston, New York, 1980.

J. David Cummins, *An Econometric Model of the Life Insurance Sector of the U.S. Economy,* Heath, Lexington, MA, 1975.

Martin Feldstein, "Private Pensions and Inflation," *American Economic Review,* May 1981, pages 424–428.

Irwin Friend (ed.), *Study of the Savings and Loan Industry,* 4 vols., Federal Home Loan Bank Board, Washington, 1969.

Mary Greenebaum, "Cost-of-living Insurance Costs Too Much," *Fortune,* June 16, 1980, pages 205–208.

Janice E. Greider and William T. Beadles, *Principles of Life Insurance,* vol. 1, Irwin, Homewood, IL, 1964.

Patric H. Hendershott, Sheng Hu, and Kevin E. Villani, "The Economics of Mortgage Terminations: Implications for Mortgage Lenders and Mortgage Terms," National Bureau of Economic Research Working Paper 918, June 1982.

Marcos T. Jones, "Mortgage Designs, Inflation, and Real Interest Rates," Federal Reserve Bank of New York *Quarterly Review,* Spring 1982, pages 20–29.

Edward J. Kane, "Inflation, Disintermediation, and the Housing Market," *Financial Institutions in the 1980s: The Public Policy Issues,*

Western Michigan University Economics Lecture Series, October 1978.

Donald M. Kaplan, *Alternative Mortgage Instruments Research Study,* 3 vols., Federal Home Loan Bank Board, Washington, 1977.

George G. Kaufman, "Variable Rate Residential Mortgages: The Early Experience from California," Federal Reserve Bank of San Francisco *Economic Review,* Summer 1976, pages 5–16.

George G. Kaufman and Eleanor Erdevig, "Improving Housing Finance in an Inflationary Environment: Alternative Residential Mortgage Instruments," Federal Reserve Bank of Chicago *Economic Perspectives,* July/August 1981, pages 3–23.

Joseph A. McKenzie, "Borrower's Guide to Alternative Mortgage Instruments," *Federal Home Loan Bank Board Journal,* January 1982, pages 16–22.

Michael J. Moran, "Thrift Institutions in Recent Years," *Federal Reserve Bulletin,* December 1982, pages 725–738.

Alicia H. Munnell, "Guaranteeing Private Pension Benefits: A Potentially Expensive Business," Federal Reserve Bank of Boston *New England Economic Review,* March/April 1982, pages 24–47.

James E. Pesando, "The Interest Sensitivity of the Flow of Funds through Life Insurance Companies: An Econometric Analysis," *Journal of Finance,* September 1974, pages 1105–1121.

Robert A. Rennie, "Investment Strategy for the Life Insurance Company," in J. David Cummins (ed.), *Investment Activities of Life Insurance Companies,* Irwin, Homewood, IL, 1977.

Paul A. Samuelson, "An Analytic Evaluation of Interest Rate Ceilings for Savings and Loan Associations and Competitive Institutions," in Irwin Friend (ed.), *Study of the Savings and Loan Industry,* 4 vols., Federal Home Loan Bank Board, Washington, 1969.

Martin J. Schwimmer and Edward Malca, *Pension and Institutional Portfolio Management,* Praeger, New York, 1976.

Eli Shapiro, "Developments in the Private Placement Market: The Changing Role of the Life Insurance Industry," in J. David Cummins (ed.), *Investment Activities of Life Insurance Companies,* Irwin, Homewood, IL, 1977.

William L. Silber, *Portfolio Behavior of Financial Institutions,* Holt, Rinehart & Winston, New York, 1970.

Meir Statman, "Fixed Rate or Index-linked Mortgages from the Borrower's Point of View: A Note," *Journal of Financial and Quantitative Analysis,* September 1982, pages 451–457.

Henry David Thoreau, *Walden and Other Writings,* Modern Library, New York, 1937.

Daniel J. Vrabac, "Savings and Loan Associations: An Analysis of the Recent Decline in Profitability," Federal Reserve Bank of Kansas City *Economic Review,* July/August 1982, pages 3–19.

Mark Warshawsky, "Life Insurance Savings and the After-tax Life Insurance Rate of Return," National Bureau of Economic Research Working Paper 1040, December 1982.

SIX

Inflation and the Financial Markets

She went on growing, and growing,
and very soon had to kneel on the floor:
in another minute there was not even room
for this, and she tried the effect of lying
down with one elbow against the door,
and the other arm curled round her head.
Still she went on growing,
and, as a last resource,
she put one arm out the window
and one foot up the chimney,
and said to herself "Now I can do
no more, whatever happens.
What will become of me?"

Lewis Carroll, *Alice's Adventures in Wonderland*, ch. 4

INFLATION, INTEREST RATES, AND STOCK PRICES

It was material to observe that there had, since the beginning of the war, been a continual fall in the value of money [at the rate of] 2 or 3 per cent. per annum: it followed ... that if, for example, a man borrowed of the Bank £1000 in 1800, and paid it back in 1810, ... he paid back that which had become worth less by 20 or 30 per cent. than it was worth when he first received it .... [H]e would find that he had borrowed at 2 or 3 per cent., and not at 5 per cent. as he appeared to do.... Accordingly, in countries in which the currency was in a rapid course of depreciation, supposing that there were no usury laws, the current rate of interest was often ... proportionably augmented. Thus, for example, at Petersburgh, at this time, the current interest was 20 or 25 per cent., which he conceived to be partly compensation for an expected increase of depreciation of the currency.

Henry Thornton (from *Hansard*'s account),
speech in the House of Commons, May 7, 1811

INTRODUCTION: THE FISHER RELATION AND RECENT EVENTS

The Fisher relation and expected rates of return

The *equal rate of return principle* tells us that under conditions of certainty the rates of return on financial and real assets must be the same. For example suppose that R_t^e is the nominal (dollar) rate of return expected from an investment in a fixed-income security (perhaps a Treasury bill) between dates t and $t + 1$, r_t^e is the real rate of return expected from a physical asset (such as a machine) or collection of physical assets (such as a farm or a factory) during the same period, and p_t^e is the expected rate of change in the prices of all goods (including the prices of physical assets) between t and $t + 1$. Then real and nominal expected rates of return must conform to the following relation when all expectations are held with certainty:[1]

(18.1) $$1 + R_t^e = (1 + r_t^e)(1 + p_t^e)$$

A numerical example may help convey the meaning of this relation:[2] Suppose that a firm's production process is expected to yield goods worth 5 percent (net of costs) of the firm's real assets, where production requires the interval of time t to $t + 1$ and both output and assets are valued as of date t. If the firm's real assets are worth \$100 on date t and it expects to sell output on date $t + 1$ that will be worth \$5 (net of costs and valued at date t prices), its expected real rate of return is $r_t^e = 0.05$. Now suppose that the prices of all goods (including plant and equipment) are expected to increase at the rate $p_t^e = 0.10$ between t and $t + 1$. This means that the firm expects to have assets and output worth

$$\$100(1 + r_t^e)(1 + p_t^e) = \$100(1.05)(1.10) = \$115.50$$

on date $t + 1$. The expected nominal rate of return on the firm's real assets is 15.5 percent, and investors will be indifferent between shares in the firm and Treasury bills if and only if the expected nominal rate of return on the latter is the same, that is, if and only if

$$R_t^e = (1 + r_t^e)(1 + p_t^e) - 1 = (1.05)(1.10) - 1 = 0.155$$

as required by relation (18.1).

This relation has been well known at least since the eighteenth century, but we will call it *the Fisher relation* after its most famous expositor, Irving Fisher.[3] A close linear approximation of the Fisher

---

1 Adjustments to take account of uncertainty are presented below in Table 18.3. We have already seen relation (18.1) in Chapters 10, 14, and 15. It was used in Equation (10.4) to state the assumption of equal rates of return on stocks (real investments) and bonds (financial investments) and served as the basis for a demonstration that under conditions of certainty variations in interest rates do not affect stock prices. It appeared as Equation (14.7) in connection with a demonstration that households arrange their consumption plans such that their ratios of marginal utilities of consumption on dates 1 and 2 are equal to the real rate of return on investments during the same interval; specifically $1 + r$ is the price of consumption on date 1 in terms of forgone consumption on date 2. It was also used in Equation (15.5) to represent the production decision of a value-maximizing firm; the firm produced up to the point at which the real marginal rate of return from production was equal to the real rate of return on securities.

In every case the expression has represented equal expected rates of return, whether on investments in stocks and bonds, on consumption now and in the future, or on the allocation of funds to production or to financial assets.

2 This example is based on one used by Alfred Marshall (1887, page 190; 1920, page 594; and other places).

3 The first book devoted primarily to relation (18.1) was Fisher's *Appreciation and Interest* (1896), so entitled because the value of money had been appreciating during the preceding quarter century. The relation had previously been stated by several writers, including William Douglass (1740, pages 324 and 335–337) and, as we have seen, Thornton and Marshall. Fisher described early contributions to this literature in 1896 (pages 3–5). A more recent summary may be found in Thomas Humphrey (1983).

relation when r_t^e and p_t^e are small is

(18.1a) $$R_t^e \doteq r_t^e + p_t^e$$

For example R_t^e is approximately 0.150 when $r_t^e = 0.05$ and $p_t^e = 0.10$, compared with the exact value of 0.155 derived above. The approximation improves when r_t^e and p_t^e are reduced, as may be illustrated by the case in which $r_t^e = p_t^e = 0.01$, $R_t^e = (1.01)^2 - 1 = 0.0201$, and $R_t^e \doteq 0.0200$.

Realized real rates of return on financial assets

The Fisher relation explains equilibrium expected rates of return on financial assets when expectations are held with certainty. If expectations are correct, realized real rates of return on financial and real assets will be equal. But what if the naive certainty of these investors, who have listened too much to their brokers, is unfounded? The actual real rate of return on a financial asset, r_{ft}, may be defined as follows, where we have dropped the e superscripts in order to denote realized, as distinct from expected, values: The real rate of return during the interval t to $t + 1$ on a nominally riskless security[4] that promises a nominal rate of return R_t on date t is

(18.2)
$$r_{ft} = \frac{[(1 + R_t)V_t/P_{t+1}] - (V_t/P_t)}{V_t/P_t}$$

$$= (1 + R_t)\frac{P_t}{P_{t+1}} - 1 \quad \text{or} \quad 1 + r_{ft} = \frac{1 + R_t}{1 + p_t}$$

where V_t is the amount of money invested on date t, P_t is the price index applicable to investor purchases of goods, and $p_t = (P_{t+1} - P_t)/P_t$ is the rate of inflation between t and $t + 1$.

For example consider a student who lives exclusively on Big Macs, which now, on date t, cost \$2. His decision whether to use a \$200 windfall to increase his present consumption or to invest the money in a certificate of deposit (CD) to be able to consume more next year depends on the number of Big Macs gained next year relative to the number relinquished now, that is, on the real (hamburger) rate of return on his investment. Suppose the 1-year CD promises a yield of $R_t = 15.5$ percent, payable 1 year from now, on date $t + 1$. If the rate of inflation (that is, the rate of increase in the price of Big Macs) between t and $t + 1$ turns out to be $p_t = 10$ percent so that Big Macs cost \$2.20

---

4 A "nominally riskless" security is one with a certain dollar rate of return during a specified interval, for example, a 3-month, default-free, single-payment security when the investment period is 3 months. A 3-month Treasury bill is such a security.

on date $t + 1$, the hamburger rate of return on the CD investment is

(18.3)

$$r_{ft} = \frac{\dfrac{1.155(\$200)}{\$2.20/\text{Big Mac}} - \dfrac{\$200}{\$2/\text{Big Mac}}}{\dfrac{\$200}{\$2/\text{Big Mac}}}$$

$$= \frac{105 \text{ Big Macs} - 100 \text{ Big Macs}}{100 \text{ Big Macs}} = 0.05$$

The student gave up $\$200/\$2 = 100$ hamburgers on date t in exchange for $\$231/\$2.20 = 105$ hamburgers on date $t + 1$. But what if the rate of inflation had turned out to be $p_t = 20$ percent so that Big Macs cost \$2.40 on date $t + 1$? The student will be able to buy only $\$231/\$2.40 = 96.25$ Big Macs (sharing one with three friends) and his real rate of return is

$$r_{ft} = \frac{1 + R_t}{1 + p_t} - 1 = \frac{1.155}{1.200} - 1 = -3.75 \text{ percent}$$

He has gained dollars (at the rate of 15.5 percent per annum) but lost hamburgers (at the rate of -3.75 percent per annum) because the rate of interest failed to anticipate inflation in this uncertain world. We shall see below that his disappointment has been shared by many.

Recent events

Suppose that expected real rates of return on real assets (r_t^e) are fairly steady and investors' expectations of inflation (p_t^e) are unbiased so that p_t^e is on average equal to actual inflation (p_t). Then the Fisher relation implies that observed yields on nominally riskless securities (for which $R_t^e = R_t$) are good predictors of inflation. In terms of the linear approximation (18.1a), for example, if r_t^e is constant at 3.4 percent, a rise in inflation from 1.6 percent to 12.6 percent ought to be accompanied, on average, by a rise in R_t from about 5 percent to about 16 percent. But the world does not work this way. Interest rates tend to adjust slowly and incompletely to changes in the rate of inflation, a tendency that has received a great deal of attention in recent years. The top two lines of Table 18.1 show that the 11 percent increase in the rate of change of the Consumer Price Index (CPI) between August 1971 and May 1974 was accompanied by only a 3.6 percent increase in the yield on 3-month Treasury bills. The consequence was a 6.9 percent decrease in the realized real rate of return on Treasury bills, calculated according to the exact relation (18.2). The lower portion of the table shows the failure of R_t to fall as fast as the rate of inflation between 1979 and 1982. Notice that R_t continued to rise for quite some

Table 18.1   Treasury Bill Yield (R_t), Rate of Change of the Consumer Price Index (p_t), and the Realized Real Rate of Return on Treasury Bills (r_{ft})[a] (3-month rates converted to annual percentages)

Month (t)	R_t	p_t	r_{ft}
August 1971	5.15	1.65	3.44
May 1974	8.77	12.66	− 3.45
November 1979	12.87	16.59	− 3.19
August 1981	17.35	5.76	10.96
November 1982	8.59	− 1.22	9.93

a R_t is the average yield on Treasury bills during the month shown, p_t is the rate of change of the CPI between the month shown and 3 months later, and r_{ft} has been calculated according to Equation (18.2).

Sources: *Federal Reserve Bulletin* and *Survey of Current Business*.

time after the rate of inflation had begun to descend from its peak in late 1979.

Table 18.1 describes only two experiences. But we shall see that these events are typical of the reluctance of interest rates to keep pace with changes in inflation—no matter whether the story is told in terms of Treasury bills and the CPI or is based on a different financial asset and another price index. This historical perspective, or awareness of experience, undermines any attractions that many popular explanations of the data in Table 18.1 might otherwise have had. The fall in realized real rates of return (r_{ft}) in the early 1970s was attributed to the rise in oil prices, which presumably constituted a "supply shock," causing declines in expected real rates of return on real assets. And the rise in r_{ft} in the early 1980s was said to be due to the increase in government borrowing made necessary by the federal deficit. But those aware of the history of interest rates and inflation know that, for reasons not yet fully understood, r_{ft} *always* varies inversely with changes in the rate of inflation when those changes are large and have done so regardless of the directions of movements of deficits and import prices.

Coming attractions

So nominal interest rates have not been good predictors of inflation when inflation has been volatile, and the 1970s and 1980s have in this respect been normal. This means that investors are not good forecasters of inflation, the Fisher relation is not generally valid, and/or expected real rates of return have been incredibly volatile—and we mean "incredibly" because expected real returns cannot be negative in the presence of nonperishable real investments such as paintings, land, houses, mineral reserves, wine, and baseball cards. The remainder of this chapter is devoted to a closer examination of the history of relative movements of interest rates and inflation and to alternative explanations of those movements. The next section develops the history of "the Gibson relation," which is the name of the high correlation between interest rates and the price *level* (R_t and P_t), as distinct from the low correlation between interest rates and the rate of price *changes* (R_t and p_t). The final section considers the influence of the tax structure on the relative rates of return to various assets, particularly stocks, bonds, and houses, in an attempt to explain why stocks have not been good hedges against inflation in our uncertain and heavily taxed environment.

THE GIBSON RELATION: OBSERVATIONS AND EXPLANATIONS

The Gibson nonparadox

Economists and others sometimes describe the following hypothetical sequence of events: An increase in the quantity of money induces a reduction in interest rates and an increase in the demand for goods. This increased demand for goods, which is financed by the new money, produces a rise in prices, an increased transactions demand for money due to the higher costs of goods, and therefore a reversal of the decline in interest rates. The idea that increases in money and decreases in interest rates go together has a strong hold on those who have not examined the data. There is nothing *theoretically* wrong with this story. But it just does not fit the facts. In practice, interest rates, money, and inflation tend to rise and fall together. These connections, in combination with the tendency of investment to be positively related to interest rates, suggest that fluctuations in the demand for investment goods—not money—have been the principal initiating cause of economic disturbances. For example increases in investment demands induce increases in interest rates, prices, bank loans, and money. The effects on loans and money are accentuated if the central bank supplies bank reserves to moderate the rise in interest rates.

These empirical relationships were already well known in the nineteenth century, and the two most famous contributions to monetary thought in that century, by Henry Thornton in 1802 and Knut Wicksell in 1898, were motivated by the authors' desires to explain why money, interest, and prices were positively correlated. But the positive correlation between interest and prices had to wait until 1930 for a name. In *The Bankers' Magazine* in 1923 A. H. Gibson presented a chart showing a positive relationship between the yield on British consols and a wholesale commodity price index during the period 1820 to 1922. Figure 18.1(a) reproduces the Gibson relation for a longer period, 1729 to 1974, from a paper by Robert Shiller and Jeremy Siegel (1977), and Figure 18.1(b) shows a similar though less highly correlated relationship between the price index and a short-term rate of interest. The Shiller–Siegel charts differ from Gibson's in their use of

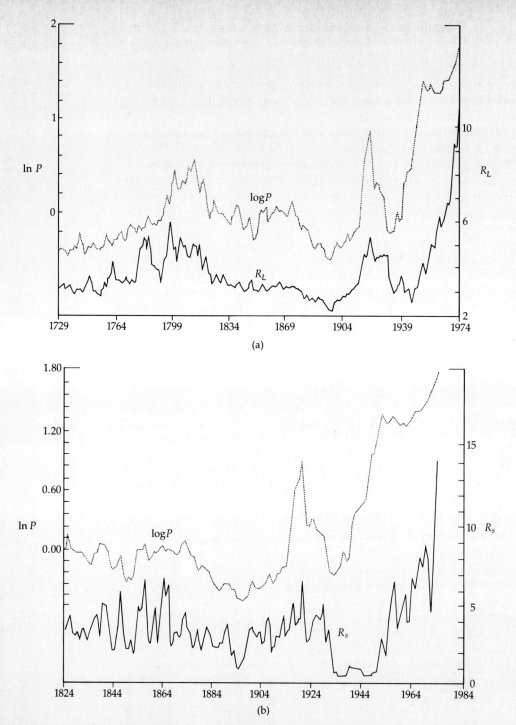

Correlation (ln P, R_L) = 0.743; correlation (Δ ln P, R_L) $\doteq$ correlation (p, R_L) = 0.045; correlation (ln P, R_s) = 0.421; correlation (Δ ln P, R_s) $\doteq$ −0.01. Notice that Δ ln P_{t+1} =ln P_{t+1} − ln P_t = ln (P_{t+1}/P_t) = ln (1 + p_t) $\doteq$ p_t, where the approximation follows from the use of natural logarithms and p_t is the rate of inflation between t and $t+1$.

Source: Robert J. Shiller and Jeremy J. Siegel, "The Gibson Paradox and Historical Movements in Real Interest Rates," *Journal of Political Economy*, October 1977, pages 891–907.

Figure 18.1 Natural logarithm of a price index (ln P) and (a) a long-term rate of interest (R_L) in Great Britain and (b) a short-term rate of interest (R_s) in Great Britain.

the natural logarithm of the price index. Charts that represent price levels between the 1930s and the present must use some compressed form if they are to be of manageable size. None of the story is lost when logarithms are used, and we shall see below that they offer some analytical advantages.

The significant positive correlations between the natural log of the price level and security yields may be contrasted with the very low correlations between these yields and the rate of inflation. That is, changes in yields tend to accompany long-term price movements but are not closely associated with short-term variations in the price level.

J. M. Keynes (1930, volume 2, page 198) gave the literature on inflation and interest rates a name by referring to Gibson's observations as "the Gibson paradox," perhaps because he had earlier (pages 148 to 163) presented a series of historical examples in which price increases were assumed to have been initiated by monetary rather than by real disturbances so that he expected interest rates and prices to be inversely related. Or perhaps Keynes thought the data paradoxical because they appeared to contradict Fisher's "well-known theorem" that the rate of interest ought to anticipate price movements. In either case, in view of Thornton's and Wicksell's explanation of these data and many similar explanations by early-twentieth-century business cycle theorists,[5] the paradox label cannot be taken seriously. We refer to the observed correlation between interest rates and the price *level* as *the Gibson relation* in order to distinguish it from the theoretical and usually unobserved correlation between interest rates and price *changes* implied by the Fisher relation.

Some authors have followed Gibson and Keynes in studying the relation between prices and long-term yields. But most have concentrated on short-term yields because these provide the ideal basis for the simultaneous study of the Fisher and Gibson relations. We saw in Equation (18.1) that the Fisher relation includes a nominal expected rate of return, R_t^e. Nominally riskless single-payment securities with maturities equal to the period of observation (for example, 3-month Treasury bills and quarterly observations) provide direct observations on $R_t^e = R_t$. Furthermore, these short-term securities avoid the problems of predicting the future prices of long-term securities and real rates of interest and rates of inflation over the lives of long-term securities. We shall as far as possible concentrate on high-grade short-term securities because they offer the Fisher relation its best

---

5 In "a statement of the nature of the phenomena for which an explanation needs to be found" F. Lavington (1925, page 13) indicated that prices, production, investment, profits, wages, and interest rates all tended to vary procyclically, with the last two variables being less volatile than the others and tending to lag the general movement. The explanations of these phenomena by Lavington, D. Robertson (1915), R. Hawtrey (1913), A. Pigou (1912) and W. Mitchell (1913) differed in many details, but all argued that price movements were initiated by real disturbances, with interest rates adjusting slowly to changes in inflation and credit demands.

chance of success—because expected nominal rates are known and investors are required to forecast real rates of interest and rates of inflation only for short periods. If the Fisher relation fails under these conditions, it is unlikely to be valid when nominal returns are uncertain and expectations of the distant future are required.

Gibson and Fisher

The most extensive tests of the Fisher and Gibson relations were reported by Fisher in 1930 in *The Theory of Interest*. He began with the linear approximation of the Fisher relation stated in Equation (18.1a). Since Fisher realized that this relation was theoretically valid only under conditions of certainty, it was natural that he began his investigations with an examination of the correlation between the rate on a short-term high-grade security and the actual rate of change (approximately)[6] of a price index during the life of that security. Consistent with British experience during the period 1824 to 1974 depicted in Figure 18.1(b), Fisher's correlations between the rate of inflation and the commercial paper rate in New York were low, in fact negative, during both of his sample periods, 1890 to 1914 and 1915 to 1927 (as may be seen in Figure 18.2 for $i = 0$). Since for a nominally riskless security the Fisher relation states that $R_t \doteq r_t^e + p_t^e$, these results mean that (1) expected real rates of interest were strongly inversely correlated with inflation (that is, R did not anticipate p because of more than offsetting movements in r^e), (2) price expectations lagged behind changes in rates of inflation, and/or (3) nominal interest rates were slow to adjust to changes in inflationary expectations. Explanation (1) is not consistent with the tendency of investment to be positively correlated with inflation.[7] Explanations (2) and (3) are more promising.

Fisher next tried correlations between the rate of interest and various leads and lags of inflation, again without success. (See Figure 18.2.) The relation between the commercial paper rate and future (as well as past) single rates of inflation was weak. His final step was to see whether the influence of inflation on interest rates might be *"distributed in time*—as, in fact, must evidently be true of any influence." Figure 18.3 shows correlations between the commercial paper rate (R) and weighted averages (distributed lags) of past rates of inflation ($\bar{P}'$) for lags (n) up to 120 quarters. These correlations are higher than those in Figure 18.2 and for 1915 to 1927 improved monotonically with the length of the lag until Fisher had exhausted his data set.

---

6 Fisher's approximation, P', of the rate of inflation, p, is defined in Table 18.2.

7 We shall see in a later section of this chapter (Taxes, Inflation, and Stock Prices) that, for given productivity of capital, there is a tendency under the present tax system for anticipated inflation to depress stock prices and discourage investment. That is, in a world in which inflationary disturbances spring from exogenous changes in M and inflation is anticipated by R, investment ought to be negatively related to p. This gives us further reason to believe that the common procyclical tendencies of investment, money, and prices arise from variations in the expected profitability of new investment.

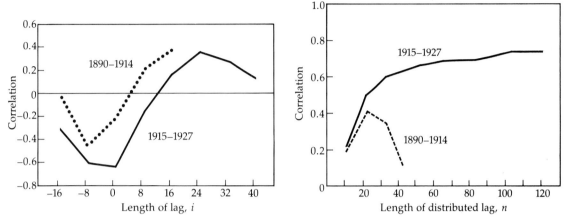

Fisher's correlations between the commercial paper rate
(R), inflation (P'), and distributed lags of inflation ($\overline{P}_n'$).
(quarterly data)

Source: Irving Fisher, *The Theory of Interest,* Macmillan, New York, 1930, charts 50 and 51.

Figure 18.2
Correlations between R_t and P'_{t-i}

Figure 18.3
Correlations between R_t and $\overline{P}'_{n,t}$

We now turn to Fisher's interpretation of these results. It is important to recognize that lags in the formation of price expectations were for Fisher only one of many reasons why interest rates adjusted slowly to changes in the rate of inflation.[8] That is, his distributed lag of past inflation rates was interpreted by Fisher to contain much more than an adaptive expectations mechanism. In fact there was little in a dynamic economy characterized by imperfect foresight and costly adjustments that such a distributed lag might not contain (1930, pages 428 and 429):

> It seems fantastic, at first glance, to ascribe to events which occurred last century any influence affecting the rate of interest today. And yet that is what the correlations with distributed effects of P′ show. A little thought should convince the reader that the effects of bumper wheat crops, revolutionary discoveries and inventions, Japanese earthquakes, Mississippi floods, and similar events project their influence over prices and interest rates over many years even after the original causal event has been forgotten. The skeptical reader need only be reminded that the economic effects on the farmer of the deflation of 1920 are now, in 1929, sufficiently acute to make farm relief a pressing political problem and that these economic effects may be expected to per-

---

8 This point was emphasized by John Rutledge (1974, page 21).

sist for many years to come. A further probable explanation of the surprising length of time by which the rate of interest lags behind price change is that between price changes and interest rates a third factor intervenes. This is business, as exemplified or measured by the volume of trade. It is influenced by price change and influences in turn the rate of interest.

Fisher went on to reconcile the theoretical Fisher relation with the observed Gibson relation (1930, pages 440 to 442):

> . . . it seems impossible to interpret [the positive correlation between interest rates and the price *level*] as representing an independent relationship with any rational theoretical basis. It certainly stands to reason that *in the long run* a high level of prices due to previous monetary and credit inflation ought not to be associated with any higher rate of interest than the low level before the inflation took place. It is inconceivable that, for instance, the rate of interest in France and Italy should tend to be permanently higher because of the depreciation of the franc and the lira, or that a billion-fold inflation as in Germany or Russia would, after stabilization, permanently elevate interest accordingly. This would be as absurd as it would be to suppose that the rate of interest in the United States would be put on a higher level if we were to call a cent a dollar and thereby raise the price level a hundredfold. The price level as such can evidently have no permanent influence on the rate of interest except as a matter of transition from one level or plateau to another.
>
> The *transition* from one price level to another may and does work havoc as we have seen, and the havoc follows with a lag which is widely distributed. The result is that during a period of inflation the interest rate is raised *cumulatively,* so that at the end of this period when the price level is high, the interest rate is also high. It would doubtless in time revert to normal if the new high level were maintained, but this seldom happens. Usually prices reach a peak and then fall. During this fall the interest rate is subject to a cumulative downward pressure so that it becomes subnormal at or near the end of the fall of prices. Thus, at the peak of prices, interest is high, not because the price level is high, but because it has been rising and, at the valley of prices, interest is low, not because the price level is low, but because it has been falling. . . .
>
> Such considerations seem to be sufficient to explain the otherwise puzzling and apparently irrational coincidence which we have so often found to exist between high and low prices and high and low interest rates.

Table 18.2   Fisher's Distributed Lag of Inflation

Fisher's "price change," P', is an approximate two-period moving average of inflation rates:

$$(18.4) \qquad P'_t = 2\left(\frac{P_{t+1} - P_{t-1}}{P_t}\right) \doteq 2(p_t + p_{t-1})$$

where P_t is the commodity price level at time t, $p_t = (P_{t+1} - P_t)/P_t$ is the quarterly inflation rate, and P'_t is a moving average of quarterly inflation rates converted to a simple annual rate. For example, if inflation is a constant 2 percent per quarter, that is, if $p_t = p_{t-1} = 0.02$ so that $P_{t-1} = 100$, $P_t = 102$, and $P_{t+1} = 104.04$, Fisher's approximate annual inflation rate is $P'_t = 0.0792$.

Fisher's distributed lags are defined

$$(18.5) \qquad \overline{P}_{n,t} = \frac{(n-1)P'_{t-1} + (n-2)P'_{t-2} + \cdots + P'_{t-(n-1)}}{1 + 2 + \cdots + (n-1)} = \frac{\sum\limits_{i=1}^{n-1}(n-i)P'_{t-i}}{\sum\limits_{i=1}^{n-1}i}$$

Substituting the approximation (18.4) into Equation (18.5) gives

$$(18.6) \qquad \overline{P}'_{n,t} \doteq \frac{4[(n-1)p_{t-1} + \sum\limits_{i=2}^{n}(2n+1-2i)p_{t-i}]}{n(n-1)}$$

where $\overline{P}'$ is a distributed lag of quarterly inflation rates converted to a simple annual rate. The sum of coefficients in Equation (18.6) is 4 so that, for example, a constant quarterly rate of inflation $p_{t-1} = p_{t-2} = \cdots = p_{t-n} = p$ implies $\overline{P}'_{n,t} = 4p$.

We now show that Fisher's highest correlations amount virtually to a restatement of the Gibson relation. The precise form of Fisher's distribution is shown in Table 18.2. Its simple and inflexible form, which could be varied only in the length of the lag, was dictated by the high computation costs of that preelectronic era. Suppose the lag is $n = 5$. Then the weights associated with $p_{t-1}, \ldots, p_{t-5}$ are $4[0.20, 0.35, 0.25, 0.15, 0.05]$, with the first weight being smaller than the second weight because p_{t-1} enters the distribution only once (in P'_{t-1}) while the other p_{t-i} (except p_{t-n}) enter two P'_{t-i}. For Fisher's longest lag $n = 120$ and the weights are $4[0.0083, 0.0166, 0.0165, 0.0163, 0.0162, \ldots]$, with the ratio of the median weight to the next higher weight being about 0.98.

So Fisher's best correlation (for $n = 120$) was between R_t and a virtual unweighted average (beginning with p_{t-2}) of past inflation rates. But the Gibson relation is expressed in terms of the current price level, P_t, or, as we saw in Figures 18.1(a) and 18.1(b), in terms of $\ln P_t$. The connection between the price level and past inflation is

$$(18.7) \qquad P_t = (1 + p_{t-1})(1 + p_{t-2}) \cdots (1 + p_{t-n})P_{t-n}$$

so that, for $P_{t-n} = 1$,

(18.8) $$\ln P_t = \sum_{i=1}^{n} \ln (1 + p_{t-i}) \doteq \sum_{i=1}^{n} p_{t-i}$$

which for large n (for example, $n = 120$) is not much different from
Fisher's distribution (18.6).

Some more Gibson and Fisher

The modern computer enables researchers to estimate quickly and
cheaply a wider variety of distributed lags than Fisher could have
examined in a lifetime with all the resources of the National Science
Foundation at his disposal.[9] But the results obtained since 1930 have
given us no reason to revise in any significant way the data summary
contained in the Gibson relation and restated in Fisher's distributed
lags. The contributions of the new methods have been limited to the
endorsement and reinforcement of Fisher's results in two respects:
First, interest rates tend to be correlated with the price level and also
with past inflation rates no matter what estimation procedure, sample
period, observation frequency, interest rate, and price index are
chosen. Prewar and postwar data, quarterly and annual observations,
short-term and long-term interest rates, and consumer and wholesale
prices are all consistent with Fisher.[10] Second, the results are highly
unstable. That is, the estimated weights, lengths of lags, and correlation coefficients vary greatly between sample periods.[11] This is also
consistent with Fisher, as may be seen in the differences between 1890
to 1914 and 1915 to 1927 in Figure 18.3.

The Fisher relation under uncertainty

The symbols r_t^e and p_t^e were used in Equation (18.1) to denote *certain*
expectations. But in the following discussion we use Er_t and Ep_t to
denote the mathematical expectations (or "means" or "expected
values") of r_t and p_t when they are random variables. We now show
that the original Fisher relation (18.1) is not valid in the presence of
uncertainty. Referring to Equation (18.2), the equalization of expected
returns on a real asset and a nominally riskless asset (so that R_t is
certain) requires that

(18.9) $$E(1 + r_t) = E(1 + r_{ft}) = (1 + R_t) E\left(\frac{1}{1 + p_t}\right) \geq \frac{1 + R_t}{E(1 + p_t)}$$

---

9 These methods of estimating distributed lags have included regressions of a nominal interest
rate on past inflation rates with no constraints on the estimated weights of the distributed lag
[as in William Gibson (1970)] or the constrained estimation of the weights by Almon [as in William Yohe and Denis Karnosky (1969)] or Koyck [as in Thomas Sargent (1969)] procedures.

10 Fisher himself conducted many variations on the work that we have described and presented
charts similar to Figures 18.2 and 18.3 based on long-term interest rates in Great Britain (for
1820 to 1924) and the United States (for 1900 to 1927).

11 This has been emphasized by Thomas Cargill and Robert Meyer (1977).

where the inequality holds under uncertainty.[12] For example suppose that p_t may with equal probabilities take the values -0.20 and $+0.20$. Then

$$
(18.10) \quad E\left(\frac{1}{1+p_t}\right) = 0.5\left(\frac{1}{0.8}\right) + 0.5\left(\frac{1}{1.2}\right) = 0.5\,(1.25 + 0.833)
$$

$$
= 1.042 > \frac{1}{E(1+p_t)} = 1
$$

Rearranging Equation (18.9) and remembering that $E(1 + x) = 1 + Ex$, we have

$$
(18.11) \quad 1 + R_t = \frac{1 + Er_t}{E[1/(1+p_t)]} \leq (1 + Er_t)\,(1 + Ep_t)
$$

where again the inequality holds under uncertainty. We see that the equilibrium nominal rate of interest implied by the equalization of expected returns is less in the presence of uncertainty than would be given by the Fisher relation (18.1) if r_t^e and p_t^e were replaced by Er_t and Ep_t. For example, if $Er_t = 0.10$ and we again assume a fifty–fifty chance that p_t will be -0.20 or $+0.20$, the statements in Equation (18.11) become

$$
(18.12) \quad 1 + R_t = \frac{1.10}{1.042} = 1.056 \leq (1.10)\,(1.0) = 1.10
$$

This result follows from the nonlinear effect of inflation on the purchasing power of the financial asset. Consider an investment of \$100 on date t in a riskless nominal asset that promises the rate $R_t = 0.10$. If there is a fifty–fifty chance that the rate of inflation will be -0.20 or $+0.20$ between t and $t+1$, the expected real value of the \$110 to be received at $t+1$ is

$$
0.5\left(\frac{1.10}{0.8} + \frac{1.10}{1.20}\right) = 0.5\,(1.375 + 0.917) = 1.146
$$

---

12 This is an example of *Jensen's inequality*, which states that, for a random variable x and a convex function $g(x)$, $E[g(x)] \geq g[E(x)]$. Jensen's inequality follows directly from the definition of a *convex function*, $g(x)$, which is a function such that between any two points x_1 and x_2

$$
g[\alpha x_1 + (1 - \alpha)x_2] \leq \alpha g(x_1) + (1 - \alpha)g(x_2)
$$

For example, if $x = 1 + p_t$, $g(x) = 1/x$, $\alpha = 0.5$, $x_1 = 0.8$, and $x_2 = 1.2$, as in the case considered above, this inequality becomes

$$
\frac{1}{0.5(0.8) + 0.5(1.2)} = \frac{1}{E\,(1+p_t)} = \frac{1}{1} < 0.5\left(\frac{1}{0.8}\right) + 0.5\left(\frac{1}{1.2}\right) = E\left(\frac{1}{1+p_t}\right) \doteq 1.042
$$

That is, the expected real rate of return on the financial asset is $Er_{ft} = 0.146$, compared with $r_{ft}^e = 0.10$ when inflation is certain to be zero. This is because a reduction in inflation from zero to $p_t = -0.20$ causes r_{ft} to rise from 0.10 to 0.375, whereas a rise in inflation to $p_t = 0.20$ causes r_{ft} to fall only to -0.083.

If the expected real rate of return on the real asset is $Er_t = 0.10$ and if investors desire to maximize their expected wealth, they will attempt to shift from the real asset to the financial asset. They will bid up the price of the latter relative to the former until, if Er_t remains 10 percent, R_t falls to 5.60 percent.[13] Another numerical example is presented in Table 18.3.

Some of these complications can be avoided by working with the purchasing power of a dollar, $1/P_t$, instead of its inverse, the price level. The rate of change in the purchasing power of money between dates t and $t + 1$ is

(18.13)
$$\Delta_t = \frac{1/P_{t+1} - 1/P_t}{1/P_t} \quad \text{so that}$$

$$1 + \Delta_t = \frac{P_t}{P_{t+1}} = \frac{1}{1 + p_t}$$

We see from Equations (18.2) and (18.9) that the expected returns on our real and financial assets are equal when

(18.14)
$$E(1 + r_t) = E(1 + r_{ft}) = (1 + R_t)\,[E(1 + \Delta_t)] \quad \text{or}$$

$$1 + R_t = \frac{1 + Er_t}{1 + E\Delta_t}$$

This result checks with the numerical example discussed above because

(18.15)
$$1 + R_t = 1.056 = \frac{1.10}{1.042} = \frac{1 + Er_t}{1 + E\Delta_t}$$

where Equation (18.10) shows that $E\Delta_t = 0.5(0.25) + 0.5(-0.167) = 0.042$. Equation (18.15) is equivalent to Equation (18.12). Equation

---

13 Problem 3 at the end of the chapter asks for a proof that $Er_{ft} = 0.10$ under these conditions.
    As we have indicated, our results apply to risk-neutral investors, that is, those desiring to maximize expected wealth without regard to its variability. Vijay Bawa and Stephen Smith (1981) have considered risk-averse investors in the context of a lifetime consumption model. One of their results—for a nominally riskless security paying a nominal rate R and a security that is riskless in real terms and earns the real rate r—may be expressed approximately as

$$R \doteq r + Ep - 0.5\,\text{Var}\,(p) - \lambda\,\text{Cov}\,(g, p)$$

where g is the rate of growth of consumption and λ is an index of risk aversion. Thus in the presence of risk aversion R may be either greater or less than implied by the Fisher relation $(R \doteq r + p)$, depending on the value of λ and the sign and size of the covariance of g and p relative to the variance of p.

Table 18.3   Probably the Simplest Possible Expression of the Fisher Relation under Uncertainty

Let the rate of inflation p_t be a random variable with mean $\bar{p}_t$ and a fifty–fifty chance that $p_t = \bar{p}_t \pm \sigma_t$. Then from Equation (18.9)

$$1 + Er_t = (1 + R_t)\left[0.5\left(\frac{1}{1 + \bar{p}_t + \sigma_t}\right) + 0.5\left(\frac{1}{1 + \bar{p}_t - \sigma_t}\right)\right]$$

(18.16)

$$= \frac{1 + R_t}{(1 + \bar{p}_t) - \sigma_t^2/(1 + \bar{p}_t)}$$

Rearranging gives

(18.17) $1 + R_t = (1 + Er_t)[(1 + \bar{p}_t) - \sigma_t^2/(1 + \bar{p}_t)] \leq (1 + Er_t)(1 + Ep_t)$

Now suppose that $Er_t = 0.10$ and there is a fifty–fifty chance that p_t will be 0 or 0.20 so that $\bar{p}_t = \sigma_t = 0.10$. Then

(18.18) $1 + R_t = (1.10)(1.10 - 0.01/1.10) = 1.20$

and $R_t = 0.20$ under uncertainty, compared with $R_t = 0.21$ if p_t were expected with certainty to be $p_t^e = 0.10$.

We see from Equation (18.13) that

(18.19) $1 + E\Delta_t = 0.5\left(\dfrac{1}{1 + \bar{p}_t + \sigma_t} + \dfrac{1}{1 + \bar{p}_t - \sigma_t}\right) = 0.5\left(\dfrac{1}{1.2} + \dfrac{1}{1}\right) = \dfrac{1.1}{1.2}$

so that, from Equation (18.14),

(18.20) $1 + R_t = (1 + Er_t)/(1 + E\Delta_t) = (1.10)/(1.1/1.2) = 1.20$

which agrees with Equation (18.18).

(18.14) gives the same result as Equation (18.11) and is simpler because it expresses R_t solely in terms of expected values. As we see in Table 18.3, which summarizes and extends these results, the use of p_t instead of Δ_t requires that the variance of p_t be taken explicitly into account.

A constant expected real rate?

The best known study of interest rates and inflation since Fisher's was that of Eugene Fama (1975), who set out to test the joint hypotheses that (1) the Treasury bill (T bill) market is efficient and (2) the expected real rate of return is constant. We shall discuss the implications of these hypotheses in turn.

1. Efficiency in this context means that observed T bill rates (R_t) reflect all available information, including all information that might be useful in forecasting rates of change in the purchasing power of money (Δ_t). But we must be specific about the manner in which R_t reflects information. A test of *whether* the T bill market uses available information must be accompanied by an explicit hypothesis of *how* that information is used by investors. Fama hypothesized that investors maximize expected returns so that the Fisher relation adjusted to account for uncertainty, that is, Equation (18.14), is empirically valid. We henceforth refer to this equation as *the* Fisher relation, and we know that it holds under both certainty and uncertainty, whereas Equation (18.1) is valid only under certainty. A close approximation of Equation (18.14) for small Er_t and $E\Delta_t$ is

(18.14a) $$R_t \doteq Er_t - E\Delta_t$$

The approximate real rate of return actually realized on a T bill is

(18.21) $$r_{ft} \doteq R_t + \Delta_t$$

Combining Equations (18.14a) and (18.21) gives

(18.22) $$r_{ft} \doteq Er_t + (\Delta_t - E\Delta_t)$$

The realized real rate of return on a T bill is positively related to the actual rate of change in the purchasing power of money, Δ_t, relative to the expected rate of change $E\Delta_t$. Suppose that $Er_t = 0.10$ and $E\Delta_t = 0.04$ so that, from Equation (18.14a),

$$R_t \doteq 0.10 - 0.04 = 0.06 \quad \text{and} \quad Er_{ft} \doteq R_t + E\Delta_t = 0.06 + 0.04 = 0.10$$

But suppose that the actual rise in the purchasing power of the investor's dollar receipts from his T bill investment is greater than his expectation, for example, $\Delta_t = 0.25$. Then we see from Equations (18.21) and (18.22) that

$$r_{ft} \doteq 0.06 + 0.25 = 0.31 = 0.10 + (0.25 - 0.04)$$

A minimum requirement for efficiency is that the forecasting errors, $\Delta_t - E\Delta_t$, not be serially correlated. Mistakes will happen and may be very large. The existence of market efficiency does not imply that investors are good at predicting the future. Inflation may be highly volatile and extremely difficult to predict. Market efficiency implies that mistakes will not be *systematic*. If past errors contain information about future rates of return, investors will take account of that information, causing prices to adjust such that expected future forecasting errors are zero and uncorrelated with past errors. An example of investor behavior in the presence of serially correlated forecasting errors is presented in Exercise 18.1.

EXERCISE 18.1.   Let the forecasting errors in Equation (18.22) be denoted e_t and be serially correlated such that

$$\Delta_t - E\Delta_t = e_t = \rho e_{t-1} + u_t$$

where u_t is a random disturbance that has a mean of zero and is not serially correlated. Show that an investor who is aware of the time pattern of forecasting errors can beat the market.

Substituting the above error structure into Equation (18.22) gives

$$r_{ft} = Er_t + \rho e_{t-1} + u_t$$

The expected real rate of return on the T bill is therefore

$$Er_{ft} = Er_t + \rho e_{t-1}$$

For example, if $\rho = 0.5$ and last period's forecasting error was $e_{t-1} = 0.02$, the rate of return expected on the T bill is 1 percent greater than that expected on the real asset, and the investor buys the T bill. He would have bought the real asset if e_{t-1} had been negative.

This market is not efficient. It becomes efficient when many investors catch on to the systematic variation in forecasting errors and they cause prices and interest rates to change accordingly. In the example discussed above, where $e_{t-1} = 0.02$, the price of T bills is bid up until R_t falls sufficiently to equalize the expected rates of return on T bills and real assets. The expected value of the forecasting error, $e_t = \Delta_t - E\Delta_t$, becomes zero and is no longer serially correlated.

---

2. If the expected real rate of return is constant, that is, if it can be expressed as $Er_t = Er$, Equation (18.22) may be written

(18.23) $$r_{ft} = Er + (\Delta_t - E\Delta_t)$$

Fama's joint hypotheses imply a world in which disturbances spring entirely from the money market and have no real effects because investors instantly perceive the pattern of each inflationary or deflationary movement. Prices instantly and correctly reflect changes in the purchasing power of money so that real rates of return on both financial and real assets are, on the average, unaffected by monetary disturbances. In terms of Equation (18.23), $Er_{ft} = Er$ because expected forecasting errors are zero.

We now look at Fama's tests. If (1) investors use all available information in a well-understood world so that there are no systematic errors in predicting the rate of change of the purchasing power of money, that is, $\Delta_t - E\Delta_t = e_t$ is not serially correlated, and (2) the expected real rate of return on real assets is constant, then the realized real rate of return on T bills, which may be written

(18.24) $r_{ft} = Er + e_t$

will not be serially correlated. That is, the serial correlations (or "autocorrelations," as they are usually called) between r_{ft} and $r_{f, t-j}$ ($j = 1, 2, \ldots$) will be zero. As an example of nonzero autocorrelation, substitute the error term in Exercise 18.1 into Equation (18.24) to get

(18.25) $r_{ft} = Er + \rho e_{t-1} + u_t$ and $r_{f, t-1} = Er + e_{t-1}$

The first-order ($j = 1$) autocorrelation of r_{ft} in this case (that is, the correlation between r_{ft} and $r_{f, t-1}$) is ρ. Although Equations (18.22) to (18.24) have been derived from the approximations (18.14a) and (18.21), the autocorrelations of r_{ft} reported below are based on the exact expression $1 + r_{ft} = (1 + R_t)(1 + \Delta_t)$.

The insignificant autocorrelations of r_{ft} in Table 18.4(a) are consistent with Fama's joint hypotheses. Fama also reported higher-order autocorrelations. But we show only first-order autocorrelations because in both Fama's case and in the cases to be presented later nearly all higher-order autocorrelations of r_{ft} are not significantly different from zero at the 95 percent confidence level.

Notice the significant autocorrelations of 1- and 3-month rates of change in purchasing power during January 1953 to July 1971 shown in Table 18.4(a). These seem to be due to the high autocorrelations of Δ_t during August 1964 to July 1971 reported by Fama (but not shown here) because those during January 1953 to February 1959 and March 1959 to July 1964 were not statistically significant. But in every subperiod, whatever the autocorrelation structure of Δ_t, T bill rates anticipated Δ_t so that realized real rates of return on T bills were not autocorrelated.

Some more of Fama's tests are reported in Table 18.4(b). The regression equations are derived from Equation (18.14a), where a_0 represents the constant expected real rate and the residual e_t is the random deviation of Δ_t from the market's expectation (as reflected in R_t). As implied by the model, the coefficients of R_t do not differ significantly from -1, and the prediction errors are uncorrelated.

If R_t incorporates all available information about Δ_t, then the addition of explanatory variables readily available to investors, such as past values of Δ_t, cannot improve R_t's prediction of Δ_t. The insignificant coefficients of Δ_{t-1} in the regressions reported in Table 18.4(c) thus lend further support to Fama's hypotheses.

Table 18.4   Selections from Fama's Tests of the Efficiency of the
Treasury Bill Market, 1/53 to 7/71: 1- and 3-Month Rates of Change in
Purchasing Power and Rates of Return on Treasury Bills

(a) First-order autocorrelations of Δ_t and r_{ft}:

| | Autocorrelations | | | |
	Δ_t	r_{ft}	σ	$T-1$
1-month intervals	0.36*	0.09	0.07	222
3-month intervals	0.53*	0.00	0.12	73

$T-1$ is the number of observations used to compute the autocorrelations of Δ and r, and $\sigma = 1/\sqrt{T-1}$ is the approximate standard error of the estimated autocorrelations under the hypothesis that the true autocorrelation is zero.

(b) Regressions without lagged Δ_t:

$$\Delta_t = a_0 + a_1 R_t + e_t$$

	a_0	$s(a_0)$	a_1	$s(a_1)$	R^2	$\hat{\rho}_1(e)$
1-month bills	0.0007*	0.0003	-0.98*	0.10	0.29	0.09
3-month bills	0.0023*	0.0011	-0.92*	0.11	0.48	0.00

(c) Regressions with lagged Δ_t:

$$\Delta_t = a_0 + a_1 R_t + a_2 \Delta_{t-1} + e_t$$

	a_0	$s(a_0)$	a_1	$s(a_1)$	a_2	$s(a_2)$	R^2	$\hat{\rho}_1(e)$
1-month bills	0.0006*	0.0003	-0.87*	0.12	0.11	0.07	0.30	-0.05
3-month bills	0.0017	0.0011	-0.79*	0.15	0.11	0.12	0.48	-0.06

* Statistically different from zero at the 0.95 confidence level. $s(a_i)$ is the standard error of the regression coefficient a_i. R^2 is the coefficient of determination. $\hat{\rho}_1(e)$ is the first-order autocorrelation of the residual.

Source: Eugene Fama, "Short-term Interest Rates as Predictors of Inflation," *American Economic Review*, June 1975, pages 269–282.

Fisher again

Fama's paper prompted responses by several writers, who found Fama's 1953 to 1971 data to possess essentially the same characteristics, although in smaller degrees, as those which Fisher had found in 1890 to 1927 data. In particular the regressions in Table 18.4(c) could not validly be compared with Fisher's results because Fisher used many past rates of inflation, not one. We saw from Figure 18.3 that one or a few past rates of inflation contributed little to Fisher's correlations. The Gibson relation requires a long history of inflation, and

Table 18.5   Nelson and Schwert's Regressions of Inflation on the Yield on
1-Month Treasury Bills, 2/53 to 7/71

$$p_t = -0.0008 + 0.97R_t; \quad \overline{R}^2 = 0.292; \quad DW = 1.81$$
$$\quad (0.0004) \quad (0.10)$$

$$p_t = -0.0006 + 0.65R_t + 0.38\hat{p}_t; \quad \overline{R}^2 = 0.310; \quad DW = 1.93$$
$$\quad (0.0004) \quad (0.17) \quad (0.16)$$

where

$$\hat{p}_t = \sum_{i=0}^{\infty} (0.11)(0.89)^i p_{t-1-i}$$

Standard errors of the regression coefficients are in parentheses. DW is the Durbin-
Watson statistic. $\overline{R}^2$ is the coefficient of determination adjusted for degrees of freedom.

Source: Charles R. Nelson and G. William Schwert, "Short-term Interest Rates as Predictors of Inflation: On Testing the Hypothesis That the Real Rate of Interest Is Constant," *American Economic Review*, June 1977, pages 478–486.

Charles Nelson and William Schwert (1977) showed that a Fisher-type
distributed lag of past inflation in fact made a small but statistically
significant improvement upon the nominal interest rate's prediction of
inflation. Nelson and Schwert's results, which are based on the rate of
inflation instead of the rate of change of purchasing power, are shown
in Table 18.5: Fama + Nelson and Schwert = Fisher.

Fama's hypotheses are rejected even more forcefully as soon as we
depart from the stable 1953 to 1971 period. The special nature of his
sample is seen clearly in Figure 18.4, which shows the rate of change of
the Wholesale Price Index (WPI) and real and nominal rates of return
on 4- to 6-month prime commercial paper beginning in June 1894,
when 4- to 6-month prime commercial paper rates began to be
reported on a regular basis. Observations are monthly averages at
5-month intervals expressed in percentages at annual rates.[14]

One of the most striking features of this figure is the stability of
inflation in Fama's 1953 to 1971 sample, compared with the large
fluctuations before 1953 and after 1971. Also notice the fairly long
periods when realized real rates r_f (indicated by the dashed lines) were
very high because R repeatedly failed to anticipate reductions in
inflation and also when realized real rates were low because R did not
keep pace with increases in inflation. A similar story would be told by a
figure based on the data used by Fama—that is, T bill rates and the
CPI—beginning with the introduction of T bills in 1929. We have
presented the data used by Fisher (commercial paper and the WPI)
because they allow a longer period of observation. In either case runs

---

14 Fisher also used commercial paper rates and the WPI although Figures 18.2 and 18.3 are based
    on quarterly averages and the interest rates are for 60- to 90-day choice double-name commer-
    cial paper until February 1924 and 4- to 6-month prime commercial paper thereafter.

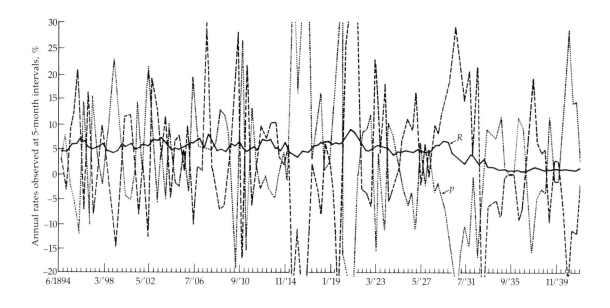

Source: Scott Ulman and John H. Wood, "Fisher to Fama to Fisher: Inflation and Interest Rates, 1890–1981," Federal Reserve Bank of Dallas Research Paper 8204, November 1982.

Figure 18.4   Inflation and real and nominal interest rates.

of high and low r_f outside the 1953 to 1971 period suggest significant autocorrelations, which are reported in Tables 18.6 and 18.7.

   The results in these tables indicate that insignificant real rate autocorrelations may be peculiar to 1953 to 1971. This conclusion is quite robust. It is independent of the choice of price indexes (CPI or WPI), short-term interest rates (T bill or commercial paper rates), and

Table 18.6   First-order Autocorrelations of Real Rates of Return on 3-Month Treasury Bills for Selected Time Periods, Data Sets, and Price Indexes

(a) Autocorrelations based on the CPI and (1) Fama's data from Salomon Brothers' quote sheets (last day of the month) and (2) Federal Reserve Board monthly averages, both for 1/53 to 7/71:

	$\hat{\rho}_1(r_f)$
1. Fama	0.00
2. Federal Reserve Board	0.03
$T-1,\ \ \sigma$	73, 0.12

(b) Autocorrelations based on Federal Reserve Board monthly averages of yields:

		1/34–10/52	1/53–4/71[a]	4/74–10/81
$\hat{\rho}_1(r_f)$	CPI	0.52*	0.03	0.40*
	WPI	0.60*	0.01	0.48*
$T-1,\ \ \sigma$		75, 0.12	73, 0.12	30, 0.18

a   The 7/71 observation was omitted in order to avoid the use of the CPI in 10/71, after price controls had been instituted.

*   Statistically different from zero at the 0.95 confidence level.

Source: Same as that for Figure 18.4.

the frequency of interest-rate observations (once a month or monthly averages). Fama had good reasons for choosing January 1953 to July 1971 as his sample period, which was delimited by the end of the Federal Reserve's bond-support program in early 1953 and the beginning of price controls in August 1971. The Fed interfered with market efficiency during 1942 to 1952 by preventing interest rates from reflecting inflationary expectations, and price controls during World War II and August 1971 to April 1974 prevented stated prices from reflecting the true costs (including side payments and gas queues) of

Table 18.7   First-order Autocorrelations of 5-Month Real Rates on 4- to 6-Month Prime Commercial Paper Based on the Wholesale Price Index

	8/94–3/29	8/29–12/52	2/53–6/71	5/53–9/81
$\hat{\rho}_1(r_f)$	0.43*	0.60*	0.10	0.49*
$T-1,\ \ \sigma$	83, 0.11	56, 0.13	44, 0.15	68, 0.12

*   Statistically different from zero at the 0.95 confidence level.

Source: Same as that for Figure 18.4.

Table 18.8   Regressions on 1-Month Treasury Bills, 1953 to 1971 and 1974 to 1981[a]

$$\Delta_t = a_0 + a_1 R_t + a_2 \Delta_{t-1} + e_t$$

Period	a_0	$s(a_0)$	a_1	$s(a_1)$	a_2	$s(a_2)$	R^2	$\hat{\rho}_1(e)$
1/53–7/71	0.0006*	0.0003	−0.843*	0.111	0.092	0.064	0.309	0.005
4/74–9/81	−0.0023*	0.0008	−0.247*	0.122	0.468*	0.106	0.371	−0.043

a These results differ slightly from Fama's in Table 18.4 for 1953 to 1971 because of the omission of the 7/71 observation, which requires the price index in 8/71, after price controls had been instituted.

* Statistically different from zero at the 0.95 confidence level.

Source: Same as that for Figure 18.4.

goods to consumers. Nevertheless, his results carry no implications for the behavior of financial markets outside his tranquil sample period.

Table 18.6(a) shows that the first-order autocorrelation of the real rate of return on T bills during January 1953 to July 1971 was not altered significantly by the use of the monthly average T bill rates reported in the *Federal Reserve Bulletin* instead of the end-of-the-month quotations used by Fama.[15] The middle column of Table 18.6(b) shows that the autocorrelations are relatively unaffected by the price index used to calculate rates of change in purchasing power. However, notice the significant autocorrelation of r_f when we move outside the 1953 to 1971 sample.

Table 18.7 presents similar results for commercial paper and the WPI, that is, an insignificant autocorrelation of the real rate during 1953 to 1971 and highly significant autocorrelations at other times.

Finally, let us apply Fama's regression on 1-month bills (in Table 18.4(c)) to the period since the end of price controls in 1974. The results are reported in Table 18.8, which also shows the results for 1953 to 1971. For consistency with Fama we use the CPI and once-a-month yield quotations. We see that R_t has not been an efficient predictor of Δ_t in recent years. Unlike the 1953 to 1971 period, the addition of Δ_{t-1} as an explanatory variable adds significantly to the predictive power of R_t during 1974 to 1981.

In summary Fama's joint hypotheses appear reasonably consistent with experience during the uniquely stable 1953 to 1971 period. If we ever want to find a period during which expected real rates of return were constant and investors fully anticipated monetary disturbances, we should look first at 1953 to 1971—although Nelson and Schwert

15 Since data for the CPI are collected throughout the month and therefore the CPI is something of a monthly average, a case can be made that consistency requires the use of monthly average interest rates in Fama's tests, which would then pertain to monthly average real rates of return. But as we see, it makes little difference whether monthly average or once-a-month data are used.

have shown that Fama's hypotheses cannot bear very careful scrutiny even during these years. More important, Fama's joint hypotheses are strongly rejected for the years before 1953 (as Fisher and others had already demonstrated) and after 1971. The 1970s and 1980s have generated observations like those observed by Gibson and Fisher and are consistent with an explanation in which macroeconomic disturbances originate from fluctuations in expected real rates of return on investment goods that induce rapid and large increases in money and prices followed by moderate increases in nominal interest rates.

TAXES, INFLATION, AND STOCK PRICES

A uniform tax rate

Suppose the constant tax rate on nominal income and capital gains from both real and financial assets is τ. Then the real after-tax rate of return on a real asset is

$$\textbf{(18.26)} \quad r_t^a = \frac{\dfrac{P_{t+1}(1 + r_t)v_t - \tau[P_{t+1}(1 + r_t)v_t - P_t v_t]}{P_{t+1}} - \dfrac{P_t v_t}{P_t}}{\dfrac{P_t v_t}{P_t}}$$

For example suppose that a firm buys $v_t = 100$ units of goods at time t for $P_t = \$1$ each, the real rate of return on these goods is $r_t = 0.10$, and the price of goods at time $t + 1$ is $P_{t+1} = \$1.10$. Then the firm's receipts are $P_{t+1}(1 + r_t)v_t = \$1.10(1.10)(100) = \$121$, its before-tax profit is $\$121 - \$100 = \$21$, which is the term in brackets in Equation (18.26), and its after-tax profit is $\$10.50$ if $\tau = 0.50$. This is a nominal after-tax rate of return of $\$10.50/\$100 = 0.105$. But the after-tax receipts at time $t + 1$ can buy only $(\$121 - \$10.50)/\$1.10 = 100.45$ units of goods so that the real after-tax rate of return is $r_t^a = 0.0045$.

Now consider a one-period security that costs $V_t = \$100$ and promises a nominal rate of return of $R_t = 0.21$. The real after-tax rate of return on this financial asset is

$$\textbf{(18.27)} \quad r_{ft}^a = \frac{\dfrac{(1 + R_t)V_t - \tau[(1 + R_t)V_t - V_t]}{P_{t+1}} - \dfrac{V_t}{P_t}}{\dfrac{V_t}{P_t}}$$

The nominal profit on this investment is $R_t V_t = \$21$ so that the after-tax nominal return is $\$10.50/\$100 = 0.105$. The real after-tax rate of return is $r_{ft}^a = 0.0045$.

Notice that the assumed relation between $R_t = 0.21$, $r_t = 0.10$, and $p_t = 0.10$ is consistent with the no-tax Fisher relation because $1 + R_t = (1 + r_t)(1 + p_t) = 1.21$. Also notice that the after-tax real rates of return, r_t^a and r_{ft}^a, are equal under these conditions. That is, the introduction of a uniform tax rate does not alter the connections between R_t, r_t, p_t, and r_{ft} implied by the Fisher relation. This may be shown more generally as follows: First rearrange Equations (18.26) and (18.27) to give

(18.26)'
$$1 + r_t^a = (1 + r_t)(1 - \tau) + \frac{\tau}{1 + p_t}$$

and

(18.27)'
$$1 + r_{ft}^a = \frac{(1 + R_t)(1 - \tau) + \tau}{1 + p_t}$$

Equating the right-hand sides of Equations (18.26)' and (18.27)', we see that $r_t^a = r_{ft}^a$ when

(18.28)
$$1 + R_t = (1 + r_t)(1 + p_t)$$

It is easy to show that Equations (18.26)', (18.27)', and (18.28) conform to the numerical values used in the example above, that is, $r_t = p_t = 0.10$, $\tau = 0.50$, and $R_t = 0.21$:

$$1 + r_t^a = (1.10)(0.50) + \frac{0.50}{1.10} = 1 + r_{ft}^a = \frac{(1.21)(0.50) + 0.50}{1.10} = 1.0045$$

and

$$1 + R_t = (1 + r_t)(1 + p_t) = (1.10)(1.10) = 1.21$$

Thus we see that the Fisher relation is unaffected by a uniform tax rate.[16]

Discriminatory taxes, inflation, and stock prices

But tax rates are not the same for all assets.[17] The most extreme illustration of this statement is probably the great difference between the heavily taxed corporate sector and the virtually untaxed[18] owner-

---

16 This point has been made by Milton Ezrati (1982) and Arthur Gandolfi (1982).

17 A simple example of the effects of differential tax rates under certainty may be seen from Equations (18.26)' and (18.27)' when the tax rate on income from real assets is η and the tax rate on income from financial assets continues to be τ. Then real after-tax rates of return are equal when

$$1 + \frac{1 - \tau}{1 - \eta} R_t = (1 + r_t)(1 + p_t)$$

There have been many discussions, for example Michael Darby (1975), of the case in which income from real assets is not taxed, that is, $\eta = 0$.

18 Except for property taxes, which are paid by both sectors.

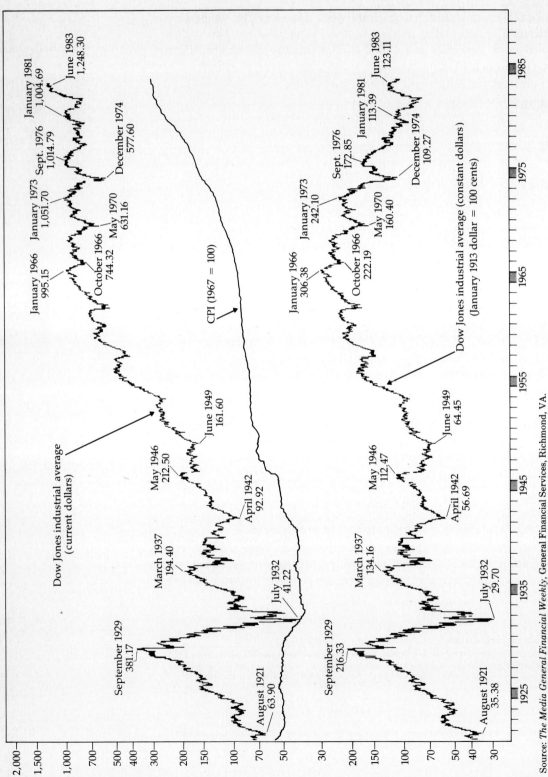

Source: *The Media General Financial Weekly*, General Financial Services, Richmond, VA.

Figure 18.5   The "constant-dollar Dow."

occupied residential housing sector. This difference is magnified by
inflation.

> Inflation dramatically alters the relative tax treatment of cor-
> porate and noncorporate capital. The effective tax rate on corpo-
> rate capital income is increased because of nonneutralities at
> both the corporate and individual level. At the corporate level,
> taxable profits are overstated because of historic cost deprecia-
> tion and FIFO inventory accounting. At the individual level, the
> taxation of nominal as well as real capital gains significantly
> increases effective tax rates. An additional minor effect is the in-
> crease in marginal tax rates which occurs as inflation pushes tax-
> payers into higher brackets.
>
> None of these features impact on the taxation of owner-
> occupied housing. The imputed rent is untaxed, and capital gains
> on real estate largely escape taxation because of roll over provi-
> sions, deferral, and the exemption for those over 55.
>
> Lawrence Summers (1981)

Several researchers have argued that the nearly 75 percent fall in
the real value of stock prices between 1966 and 1982, when stock prices
were virtually unchanged while the CPI more than tripled, as may be
seen in Figure 18.5,[19] was due largely to these combined tax and
inflation effects. Patric Hendershott (1979) wrote as follows:

> With a neutral tax system an increase in observed and antic-
> ipated inflation would not be expected to alter either real after-
> tax yields on bonds and equities or the ratio of the market value
> of equities to the replacement cost of corporate real capital. In
> the real world, however, declines in real after-tax bond yields and
> the relative value of shares have been observed. . . .
>
> The decline in share values can be attributed to many factors,
> but the most important is probably the favorable taxation of in-
> come from owner-occupied housing (no taxation of either im-
> plicit rents or real capital gains). As a result housing has become
> more attractive with the acceleration of inflation, and house-
> holds have substituted housing for equity shares.

We shall present a model that shows two of the ways in which an
acceleration of anticipated inflation may depress real stock prices:
first, by increasing the real tax burden of corporate income taxes
because real depreciation expenses, which are based on historical

---

19 Notice the vertical logarithmic scale. Similar charts, accompanied by a discussion of the historical performance of stock prices relative to the CPI, may be found in Douglas Pearce (1982).

prices, are reduced and, second, by imposing a real tax burden on nominal capital gains.[20]

Tax effects may be best understood by beginning with a situation in which there are no taxes. Consider an all-equity firm that has a constant physical capital stock (K) and pays out all its profits as dividends (D) so that shareholders earn no real capital gains. We are interested in the value of the firm's shares at time t (S_t), which under certainty is the present value of the future stream of dividends, D_{t+1}, $D_{t+2}, \ldots$. With no taxes and a rate of economic depreciation δ, the payout at time $t + i$ is

(18.29) $D_{t+i} = P_{t+i}f(K) - P_{t+i}\delta K = P_t(1 + p)^i[f(K) - \delta K]$

where $f(K)$ is the constant number of units of output per period, K is the constant number of units of capital (measured in the same units as output), P_{t+i} is the dollar price per unit of goods (both output and capital) at time $t + i$, and p is the assumed constant rate of change of this price. $P_{t+i}f(K)$ is the firm's receipts, and $P_{t+i}\delta K$ is the replacement cost of capital.

Let R be the constant nominal rate of return on an alternative investment, where $1 + R = (1 + r)(1 + p)$. We assume the Fisher relation to hold so that our analysis is most appropriate for comparisons between long-run, steady-state equilibria in which all adjustments to changes in expected r and p have been made.[21] The value of the firm's shares at time t under these conditions is

(18.30)
$$S_t = \sum_{i=1}^{\infty} \frac{D_{t+i}}{(1 + R)^i}$$
$$= \sum_{i=1}^{\infty} \frac{P_t(1 + p)^i[f(K) - \delta K]}{(1 + r)^i(1 + p)^i} = \frac{P_t[f(K) - \delta K]}{r}$$

Changes in the anticipated rate of inflation do not affect the value of the firm at time t.[22] Furthermore, the real value of the firm is

(18.31)
$$\frac{S_t}{P_t} = s_t = \frac{f(K) - \delta K}{r} = s = \text{constant}$$

---

20 This model is similar to the one represented by Equation (15.23). It differs from the earlier model principally by assuming an infinite (instead of a one-period) horizon and an all-equity (instead of a debtor) firm. Neither of these differences affects the qualitative nature of the results obtained below.

21 The failure of nominal interest rates to anticipate inflation during periods of rapidly changing inflation rates tends to raise the real rates of return on real assets during periods of rising inflation but may not significantly affect the relative prices of corporate and home ownership.

22 This point was also made for the no-tax case in connection with Equation (10.5).

There is no real capital gain. But there is a nominal capital gain between periods $t + i$ and $t + i + 1$ equal to

(18.32) $S_{t+i+1} - S_{t+i} = (P_{t+i+1} - P_{t+i})s = P_t(1 + p)^i ps$

Nominal capital gains occur at the rate

(18.33) $$\frac{S_{t+i+1} - S_{t+i}}{S_{t+i}} = \frac{P_t(1 + p)^i ps}{P_t(1 + p)^i s} = p$$

We now introduce taxes in the form of a profits tax τ_c, and we assume that capital is depreciated for tax purposes in a straight-line fashion at the rate δ' over $n = 1/\delta'$ periods.[23] The payout falls to

(18.34)

$$D_{t+i} = P_{t+i}f(K) - P_{t+i}\,\delta K - \tau_c[P_{t+i}f(K) - \sum_{j=1}^{n} \delta\delta' P_{t+i-j}\,K]$$

$$= P_t(1 + p)^i[(1 - \tau_c)f(K) - \delta K + \tau_c\,\delta\delta' K \sum_{j=1}^{n}(1 + p)^{-j}]$$

The last term in this equation is the reported depreciation expense and may be illustrated as follows: Suppose there are $K = 100$ machines, of which $\delta K = 0.20(100) = 20$ must be replaced each period. If $P_t = \$1$, the nominal economic depreciation expense at time $t + 1$ is $P_{t+1}\,\delta K = P_t(1 + p)\delta K = \$20$ if $p = 0$ and \$22 if $p = 0.10$. Now suppose the tax accountants depreciate the machines over $n = 5$ periods at the rate $\delta' = 1/n = 20$ percent of the purchase price of each machine each period. Since $\delta K = 20$ machines are purchased each period, machines bought at time t are written off at time $t + 1$ in the dollar amount $\delta'\delta K P_t = (0.20)(0.20)(100)(\$1) = \$4$; machines bought at time $t - 1$ are written off at time $t + 1$ in the amount $\delta'\delta K P_{t-1} = \$4/(1 + p) = \$4$ if $p = 0$ or \$3.64 if $p = 0.10, \ldots$; and machines bought at time $t - 4$ are written off in the amount $\$4/(1 + p)^4 = \$4$ if $p = 0$ or \$2.73 if $p = 0.10$.

---

23 The tax code actually permits accelerated depreciation but continues to be based on historical costs. Several writers, including Martin Feldstein (1980, page 841), have pointed out, "When there is no inflation, the various methods of 'accelerated depreciation' that are allowed for tax purposes may cause tax depreciation to exceed the economic depreciation for some assets. [However], accelerated depreciation does not change the conclusion that inflation reduces the real value of depreciation."

For discussions of the historical development of tax depreciation up to the mid-1970s and the relationships between various methods of economic and tax depreciation, see John Shoven and Jeremy Bulow (1975).

The total reported depreciation expense per unit of capital at time $t + i$ is[24]

$$(18.35) \quad W_{t+i} = \delta\delta' P_t(1 + p)^i \sum_{j=1}^{n} (1 + p)^{-j}$$

$$= \begin{cases} \delta P_t & \text{if } p = 0 \\ \delta\delta' P_t(1 + p)^i \dfrac{[1 - (1 + p)^{-n}]}{p} & \text{if } p \neq 0 \end{cases}$$

If $\delta = \delta' = 0.2$, $K = 100$, $P_t = \$1$, $i = 1$, and $n = 5$, the depreciation write-off is $\$24.97$ if $p = -0.10$, $\$20$ if $p = 0$, and $\$16.68$ if $p = 0.10$. The write-off is negatively related to the rate of inflation.

Dividing W_{t+i} by P_{t+i} gives the real value, w, of the depreciation expense per unit of capital:

$$(18.36) \quad \frac{W_{t+i}}{P_{t+i}} = w = \delta\delta' \sum_{j=1}^{n} (1 + p)^{-j}$$

$$= \begin{cases} \delta & \text{if } p = 0 \\ \delta\delta' \dfrac{[1 - (1 + p)^{-n}]}{p} & \text{if } p \neq 0 \end{cases}$$

The real depreciation expense is negatively related to the rate of inflation. "In other words, the U.S. tax laws make the depreciation tax shield a nominal contract between the firm and the government, so that higher inflation reduces the real value of the tax shield to the firm."[25] Combining Equations (18.34) and (18.36) gives the pay-out stream

$$(18.37) \quad D_{t+i} = P_t(1 + p)^i[(1 - \tau_c)f(K) - \delta K + \tau_c w(p)K]$$

where we have written the real depreciation expense per unit of capital as $w(p)$ to remind ourselves that w is a (negative) function of p.

We now introduce a personal income tax, which is paid at the fixed rate τ_p. The real value of the firm at time t is the real present value of

---

24 The simple expression for the depreciation expense when $p = 0$ follows from $n = 1/\delta'$.

25 Kenneth French, Richard Ruback, and William Schwert (1983).

dividend payments net of taxes:

$$\frac{S_t}{P_t} = s = \sum_{i=1}^{\infty} \frac{(1-\tau_p)D_{t+i}/P_t}{(1+R)^i}$$

(18.38)
$$= \sum_{i=1}^{\infty} \frac{(1-\tau_p)(1+p)^i[(1-\tau_c)f(K) - \delta K + \tau_c w(p)K]}{(1+r)^i(1+p)^i}$$

$$= \frac{(1-\tau_p)[(1-\tau_c)f(K) - \delta K + \tau_c w(p)K]}{r}$$

The real value of the firm is adversely affected by a rise in p when there is a profits tax and tax depreciation is based on historical prices. A key assumption underlying this result is the unchanged real rate of return, r, on the alternative asset. We assume this asset to be housing, which is effectively free of income (and capital gains) taxes. If the implicit returns to owner-occupied housing were taxed, with expenses being allowed for depreciation based on historical costs, r would also be a negative function of p and the effects of changes in anticipated inflation on real stock values, that is, on s, would be ambiguous.

Now suppose that, in addition to the corporate and personal income taxes discussed above, individuals must pay taxes on capital gains at the rate τ_g. This means that owners' receipts from the firm at time $t + i$, net of taxes, are[26]

$$(1 - \tau_p)D_{t+i} - \tau_g(S_{t+i} - S_{t+i-1})$$

where $S_{t+i} - S_{t+i-1}$ is the increase in the value of the firm's stock between $t + i - 1$ and $t + i$. We see from Equation (18.32) that this term may be written

$$S_{t+i} - S_{t+i-1} = (1 + p)^i S_t - (1 + p)^{i-1} S_t = p(1 + p)^{i-1} S_t$$

Therefore, the present value of the owners' after-tax receipts is

(18.39)
$$S_t = \sum_{i=1}^{\infty} \frac{(1 - \tau_p)D_{t+i} - \tau_g p(1 + p)^{i-1} S_t}{(1 + R)^i}$$

Substituting the right-hand side of Equation (18.37) for D_{t+i}, continuing to let $1 + R = (1 + r)(1 + p)$, solving Equation (18.39) for S_t, and dividing by P_t give

(18.40)
$$\frac{S_t}{P_t} = s = \frac{(1 - \tau_p)[(1 - \tau_c)f(K) - \delta K + \tau_c w(p)K]}{r + \tau_g g(p)}$$

---

26 We assume for simplicity that capital gains are taxed each period regardless of whether they are realized.

The difference between this expression and Equation (18.38) is $\tau_g g(p)$ in the denominator, where $g(p) = p/(1 + p)$ is a positive function of p. Thus the taxation of nominal capital gains on corporate stock (but not on houses) provides an additional negative effect of inflation on stock prices. Exercise 18.2 gives some numerical examples of these effects.

EXERCISE 18.2.   Suppose $K = 100, f(K) = 40, \delta = 0.20$, and $r = 0.10$. Calculate the real value of the firm's shares (s) in all four combinations of the following circumstances: no inflation and $p = 10$ percent; no taxes and tax rates of $\tau_c = 0.50, \tau_p = 0.40$, and $\tau_g = 0.20$, with the depreciation rule indicated in Equation (18.36) when $\delta' = 0.20$ and $n = 5$.

The results are presented in the following table. We had to calculate $w(p)$ from Equation (18.36) and $g(p) = p/(1 + p)$ before using Equation (18.40) to obtain s.

	No Taxes		Taxes	
	$p=0$	$p=0.10$	$p=0$	$p=0.10$
$w(p)$	0.20	0.152	0.20	0.152
$g(p)$	0	0.091	0	0.091
s	200	200	60	38.58[27]

The greatest impact on the value of the firm is due to the introduction of double taxation—first taking away 50 percent in profits taxes and then taking 40 percent of the remainder in personal income taxes—even in the absence of inflation. Then inflation adds some taxes of its own by reducing the real value of the nominal depreciation write-off and by confiscating some of the nominal capital gains.

SUMMARY OF EMPIRICAL TENDENCIES AND THEIR POSSIBLE EXPLANATIONS

1. Money, prices, profits, investment, production, and interest rates all tend to rise during economic expansions and to fall during

---

27 This fall in the real value of the firm is for a given capital stock and will not be quite as much as is indicated here because the firm will make some adjustments. The reduction in the real depreciation expense increases the cost of capital and reduces the optimal value of K. The capital decision in the presence of taxes and inflation was discussed in connection with Equation (15.25). For further discussions of the possible depressing effects of inflation on investment see Patric Hendershott and Sheng Hu (1981) and James Kau and Donald Keenan (1983).

contractions. That is, they are all procyclical. In the terminology of
W. C. Mitchell, they exhibit a high degree of "conformity." But their
conformity is not perfect, for money, prices, profits, and investment
tend to lead cyclical turning points in general economic activity (and
are highly volatile), whereas interest rates tend to lag behind the general movement (and are less volatile). These covariations were noticed by many observers during the nineteenth and early twentieth
centuries, they were carefully documented by Arthur Burns and
Wesley Mitchell (1946), and they have been confirmed for the postwar period.[28]

The tendency of interest rates to respond slowly and weakly to
changes in the rate of inflation means that the real rates of return
realized on nominal assets vary countercyclically. They are virtually
the mirror image of the rate of inflation. The failure of nominal interest rates to anticipate significant changes in the rate of inflation re-
futes the Fisher relation, at least during volatile periods. The correlation of interest rates with the price level over long periods is termed
the Gibson relation, which has not yet been satisfactorily explained
but has at various times been ascribed to slow adjustment of inflationary expectations to actual inflation, excess commercial bank reserves in the early stages of economic expansions, and central bank
resistance to interest rate movements (although the Gibson relation
prevailed in the United States even before the formation of the Federal Reserve System). A theory of causation that is *not* consistent
with these data is one in which economic fluctuations are caused in
the first instance by exogenous changes in the quantity of money—
which implies countercyclical variations in interest rates. The most
promising explanation of the data (or rather the beginnings of an explanation) is one in which cyclical movements are initiated by variations in the expected profitability of new or expanded investment
projects so that prices and eventually interest rates are bid up by the
increased demands for investment goods and the money and credit
needed to finance those goods.

2. Real stock prices have fallen drastically since 1966. But they
have continued to rise during the early stages of economic expansions. The most common explanation of their long-term decline stems
from the impact of inflation on the real value of depreciation write-
offs and other corporate tax deductions. An additional burden of inflation on stock prices arises from the taxation of nominal capital
gains on corporate shares but not (effectively) on houses. These opposing short-term and long-term relations between stock prices and
inflation are consistent with the story told above, in which economic

---

28 See Robert Lucas (1977), Christopher Sims (1980), and Robert Litterman and Laurence Weiss
(1983). The best summary of these and other cyclical tendencies is found in *Business Conditions Digest,* a monthly publication of the U.S. Department of Commerce, whose staff continues
the business cycle measurement work begun by Mitchell under the auspices of the National Bureau of Economic Research.

expansions are initiated by increases in the expected productivity of capital so that, for short periods, while the expected profitability of investment goods is rising, share values rise faster than the prices of goods. These short-run increases in real stock prices are also helped, until interest rates catch up, by decreases in the real costs of funds.

QUESTIONS

1. **(a)** The high realized real rates of return on financial investments during the early 1980s (when nominal interest rates did not fall as fast as the rate of inflation) have been blamed on large federal deficits. Why?
   (b) The low realized real rates of return on financial investments during the mid-1970s (when nominal interest rates did not rise as fast as the rate of inflation) have been blamed on high oil prices. Why?
   (c) Referring to Figure 18.4, we see that there have been many occasions when realized real rates were higher than in the 1980s or lower than in the 1970s and that these occasions were largely independent of the occurrence of large federal deficits or high oil (or other import) prices. What has been the dominant characteristic of periods of (i) low realized real rates and (ii) high realized rates?
   (d) Please give your own explanation of the relationship between p_t and r_{ft} described in your answer to (c).
2. Discuss the implications of the correlations of Figures 18.1(a) and 18.1(b) for the Fisher and Gibson relations.
3. What is paradoxical about the Gibson paradox?
4. Elaborate on each of the following explanations of why interest rates are less variable than inflation:
   (a) Expectations adjust slowly to changes in inflation.
   (b) The central bank causes inflation by injecting reserves into the banking system through open-market purchases.
   (c) Business profits and real rates of return are adversely affected by inflation.
5. Slow adaptation of inflationary expectations to inflation may be one cause of autocorrelation in observed real rates of interest. Discuss other possible causes.
6. Discuss the similarities and differences **(a)** between the results of Fisher and Fama and **(b)** between those of Fisher and Nelson and Schwert.
7. Referring to Figure 18.4, identify and discuss the principal periods of **(a)** inflation, **(b)** deflation, and **(c)** relative price stability during the past 90 years—and relate your discussions to Tables 18.4 to 18.8.

8. Compare movements in the CPI and any stock price index since the termination of the data in Figure 18.5. Give an explanation of the causes of these movements. Is your explanation consistent with that in the section Taxes, Inflation, and Stock Prices? (Good data sources include *Business Conditions Digest* and *Survey of Current Business,* both published monthly by the U.S. Department of Commerce.)

PROBLEMS

1. Suppose the price of Big Macs is expected with certainty to rise from $2 to $2.25 between dates t and $t + 1$ and the nominally riskless rate of return on a bank deposit during the same period is 17 percent. What is the real rate of return on the deposit for someone on a strict hamburger diet?

2. Let's change the situation in problem 1 to allow uncertainty. Specifically assume a fifty–fifty chance that the price of a Big Mac will be $2 or $2.40 at time $t + 1$. What is the investor-consumer's expected real rate of return on the bank deposit?

3. Show that $Er_{ft} = 0.10$ when p_t is -0.20 or $+0.20$ with equal probabilities and $R_t = 0.0560$.

4. (a) Why is the difference between R_t with and without inflation uncertainty less in Table 18.3 (where $\sigma = 0.10$) than in the example presented in Equations (18.11) to (18.15) (where $\sigma = 0.20$)?

   (b) Suppose that the expected rate of return on the real asset is $Er_t = 0.10$ and there is a fifty–fifty chance that p_t will be -0.30 or $+0.30$. Using the Fisher relation under uncertainty in Table 18.3, what is the equilibrium value of R_t? Show that $Er_{ft} = Er_t$.

   (c) Suppose that $Er_t = 0.10$ and p_t may with equal probabilities be -0.30, 0, or $+0.30$. What is the equilibrium value of R_t? Show that $Er_{ft} = Er_t$. [*Hint for (c).* It is necessary to go directly to Equation (18.9) for this problem. Equation (18.17) does not apply to this case.]

5. Referring to (b) and (c) in problem 4, calculate Δ_t and solve for the equilibrium R_t in each case. Your answers should be the same as for problem 4.

6. (a) Suppose the T bill market is efficient but the expected real rate of return on real assets (Er_t) is serially correlated. Referring to Equation (18.22), what do these assumptions imply for Er_{ft} and Fama's autocorrelations in Table 18.4(a)?

   (b) Suppose Er_t is constant but the T bill market is not efficient. What do these assumptions imply for Er_{ft} and Fama's autocorrelations in Table 18.4(a)? [*Hint for (b).* You will have to specify the nature of the inefficiency. An example was given in Exercise 18.1.]

7. How would the regression equations in Table 18.4 be stated if (a) the expected real rate of interest were a constant one-eighth of 1 percent per month and (b) the T bill market were perfectly efficient?

8. Given the values assumed in Exercise 18.2—specifically $K = 100$, $f(K) = 40$, $\delta = 0.20$, and $r = 0.10$—calculate the real value of the firm's shares in all four combinations of the following circumstances: deflation of $p = -0.20$ and inflation of $p = 0.20$; no taxes and tax rates of $\tau_c = 0.50$, $\tau_p = 0.40$, and $\tau_g = 0.20$, with the depreciation rule indicated in Equation (18.36) when $\delta' = 0.20$ and $n = 5$. (Assume for simplicity that capital losses can be deducted from capital gains on other investments so that the rate τ_g applies to losses as well as to gains.) Please present your results in the format of the table in Exercise 18.2.

9. Please do Exercise 18.2 with one change in the assumed conditions: Assume an accelerated depreciation write-off such that *all* capital purchased at time t is written off profits during the period between t and $t + 1$. Please present your results in the format of the table in Exercise 18.2.

Why is the firm harmed less by inflation in this problem than in Exercise 18.2?

REFERENCES

Vijay S. Bawa and Stephen D. Smith, "The Impact of Inflation on Asset Returns: Theory and Testable Implications," Graduate School of Business, Working Paper 81/82-2-7, University of Texas, Austin, 1981.

Arthur F. Burns and Wesley C. Mitchell, *Measuring Business Cycles,* National Bureau of Economic Research, New York, 1946.

Thomas F. Cargill and Robert A. Meyer, "Intertemporal Stability of the Relationship between Interest Rates and Price Changes," *Journal of Finance,* September 1977, pages 1001–1015.

Michael R. Darby, "The Financial and Tax Effects of Monetary Policy on Interest Rates," *Economic Inquiry,* June 1975, pages 266–276.

William Douglass, *A Discourse Concerning the Currencies of the British Plantations in America,* Kneeland and Green, Boston, 1740. Reprint Macmillan for the American Economic Association, New York, 1897.

Milton Ezrati, "Inflationary Expectations, Economic Activity, Taxes, and Interest Rates: Comment," *American Economic Review,* September 1982, pages 854–857.

Eugene F. Fama, "Short-Term Interest Rates as Predictors of Inflation," *American Economic Review,* June 1975, pages 269–282.

Martin Feldstein, "Inflation and the Stock Market," *American Economic Review,* December 1980, pages 839–847.

Irving Fisher, *Appreciation and Interest,* Publications of the American Economic Association, vol. 11, no. 4, Macmillan, New York, 1896.

Irving Fisher, *The Theory of Interest,* Macmillan, New York, 1930.

Kenneth R. French, Richard S. Ruback, and G. William Schwert, "Effects of Nominal Contracting on Stock Returns," *Journal of Political Economy,* February 1983, pages 70–96.

Arthur E. Gandolfi, "Inflation, Taxation, and Interest Rates," *Journal of Finance,* June 1982, pages 797–808.

A. H. Gibson, "The Future Course of High-class Investment Values," *The Bankers' Magazine* (London), January 1923, pages 15–34.

William E. Gibson, "Price-expectations Effects on Interest Rates," *Journal of Finance,* March 1970, pages 19–34.

R. G. Hawtrey, *Good and Bad Trade,* Constable, London, 1913.

Patric H. Hendershott, "The Decline in Aggregate Share Values: Inflation and Taxation of the Returns from Equities and Owner-occupied Housing," National Bureau of Economic Research Working Paper 370, June 1979.

Patric H. Hendershott and Sheng Cheng Hu, "Inflation and Extraordinary Returns on Owner-occupied Housing: Some Implications for Capital Allocation and Productivity Growth," *Journal of Macroeconomics,* Spring 1981, pages 177–203.

Thomas M. Humphrey, "The Early History of the Real/Nominal Interest Rate Relationship," Federal Reserve Bank of Richmond *Economic Review,* May/June 1983, pages 2–10.

James B. Kau and Donald Keenan, "Inflation, Taxes and Housing: A Theoretical Analysis," *Journal of Public Economics,* June 1983, pages 93–104.

J. M. Keynes, *A Treatise on Money,* Macmillan, London, 1930.

F. Lavington, *The Trade Cycle,* King, London, 1925.

Robert B. Litterman and Laurence Weiss, "Money, Real Interest Rates and Output: A Reinterpretation of Postwar U.S. Data," NBER Working Paper 1077, February 1983.

Robert E. Lucas, Jr., "Understanding Business Cycles," in Karl Brunner and Allan H. Meltzer (eds.), *Stabilization of the Domestic and International Economy,* Carnegie-Rochester Conference Series on Public Policy, North-Holland Publishing, Amsterdam, 1977, pages 7–30.

Alfred Marshall, "Remedies for Fluctuations of General Prices," *Contemporary Review,* March 1887. Reprint A. C. Pigou (ed.), *Memorials of Alfred Marshall,* Macmillan, London, 1925, pages 188–221.

Alfred Marshall, *Principles of Economics,* 8th ed., Macmillan, London, 1920.

W. C. Mitchell, *Business Cycles,* University of California Press, Berkeley, 1913.

Charles R. Nelson and G. William Schwert, "Short-Term Interest Rates as Predictors of Inflation: On Testing the Hypothesis That the Real Rate of Interest Is Constant," *American Economic Review,* June 1977, pages 478–486.

Douglas K. Pearce, "The Impact of Inflation on Stock Prices," Federal Reserve Bank of Kansas City *Economic Review,* March 1982, pages 3–18.

A. C. Pigou, *Wealth and Welfare,* Macmillan, London, 1912.

D. H. Robertson, *A Study of Industrial Fluctuation,* King, London, 1915.

John Rutledge, *A Monetarist Model of Inflationary Expectations,* Heath, Lexington, MA, 1974.

Salomon Brothers Hutzler, *Yield Book,* New York, 1981.

Thomas J. Sargent, "Commodity Price Expectations and the Interest Rate," *Quarterly Journal of Economics,* February 1969, pages 127–140.

Thomas J. Sargent, "Interest Rates and Expected Inflation: A Selective Summary of Recent Research," *Explorations in Economic Research,* Summer 1976, pages 303–325.

Robert J. Shiller and Jeremy J. Siegel, "The Gibson Paradox and Historical Movements in Real Interest Rates," *Journal of Political Economy,* October 1977, pages 891–907.

John B. Shoven and Jeremy I. Bulow, "Inflation Accounting and Nonfinancial Corporate Profits: Physical Assets," *Brookings Papers on Economic Activity,* 3, 1975, pages 557–598.

Christopher Sims, "Comparison of Interwar and Postwar Business Cycles: Monetarism Reconsidered," *American Economic Review,* May 1980, pages 250–257.

Lawrence H. Summers, "Inflation, the Stock Market, and Owner-occupied Housing," *American Economic Review,* May 1981, pages 429–434.

Henry Thornton, *An Enquiry into the Nature and Effects of the Paper Credit of Great Britain,* Hatchard and Rivington, London, 1802. Reprint with an introduction by F. A. Hayek and three appendixes containing some of Thornton's Parliamentary evidence and speeches on monetary affairs, Allen & Unwin, London, 1939.

Scott Ulman and John H. Wood, "Fisher to Fama to Fisher: Inflation and Interest Rates, 1890–1981," Federal Reserve Bank of Dallas Research Paper 8204, November 1982.

Knut Wicksell, *Interest and Prices,* Fischer, Jena, 1898. Translated from Swedish by R. F. Kahn and published by the Royal Economic Society, 1936.

William P. Yohe and Denis S. Karnosky, "Interest Rates and Price Level Changes, 1952–69," Federal Reserve Bank of St. Louis *Review,* December 1969, pages 18–38.

THE TERM STRUCTURE OF INTEREST RATES

To morrow, and to morrow, and to morrow,
Creepes in this petty pace from day to day,
To the last Syllable of Recorded time . . .
Shakespeare, *Macbeth,* **act 5, sc. 5**

YIELD CURVES

The "term structure of interest rates" is the name given to the configuration of yields to maturity on securities that are free of default risk and are otherwise identical except in their terms to maturity. The term structure is usually expressed in the form of *yield curves* such as the one in Figure 19.1.[1] We see that on September 30, 1981, the yield on the shortest-term Treasury security shown (3-month bills) was about 15.05 percent. Yields on that date tended to rise with maturity until, reading from the curve, they peaked at about 16.70 percent for bonds maturing after about 20 months, that is, in May 1983. After this hump the yield curve fell steadily, and the yield on the longest-term Treasury security, maturing in mid-2011, was about 15.20 percent. (See the inset in Figure 19.1.)

This yield curve is a rough approximation of a true yield curve because even Treasury securities, although free of default risk, differ in many respects in addition to term to maturity. The U.S. tax code is the most important source of these differences. The yields in Figure 19.1 and in the figures to follow are before-tax yields, which even for the same maturity often differ because coupons and capital gains are taxed at different rates and because of special tax features on various issues.

---

1 Precisely the same type of yield curve could be constructed for August 11, 1983, from the yields in Table 6.2.

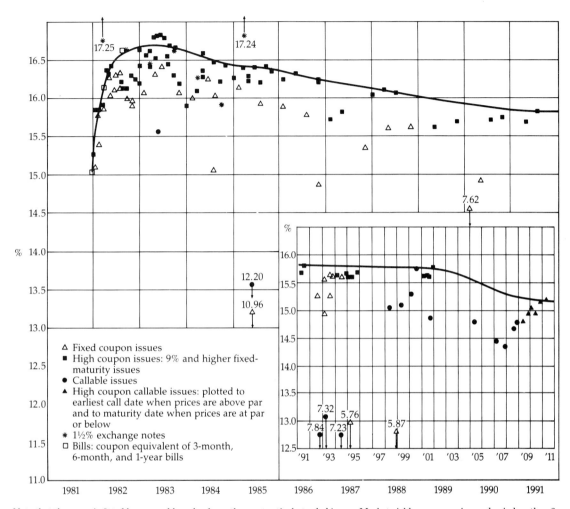

Note that the curve is fitted by eye and based only on the most actively traded issues. Market yields on coupon issues due in less than 3 months are excluded.

Source: *Treasury Bulletin*, October 1981.

Figure 19.1   Yields of Treasury securities, September 30, 1981, based on closing bid quotations.

The discussion of yield curves in this chapter is arranged as follows: We begin with a summary of the principal characteristics of yield curves. We then describe the three best-known attempts to explain the slopes of yield curves: the traditional expectations, term preference, and market segmentation theories. Several empirical investigations and policy uses of these theories are presented, and in the concluding section we summarize their usefulness as explanations of the behavior of yield curves.

This chapter does not present a complete theory of interest rates. Theories of the yield curve take the general *level* of interest rates as given and attempt to explain the *slope* of the yield curve, given that level. That approach is followed in the present chapter. A complete explanation of interest rates requires that a theory of the slope of the yield curve (from this chapter) be combined with a theory of the determination of the level of interest rates (based on inflationary expectations and other factors), which was the principal concern of Chapter 18 and will be considered again in Chapter 20.

THE DATA TO BE EXPLAINED

Most empirical generalizations are subject to qualification. This is especially true of generalizations about yield curves because of the data's shortcomings. Except possibly for Treasury bills (which will form the basis of much of our discussion) there exist no securities that are identical in all respects except term to maturity—not even, as we have seen, coupon issues of the U.S. Treasury. But even with this caveat in mind it is difficult not to be impressed by the regularities that have been observed in American yield curves during the past 120 years. These regularities may be summarized as follows:

EMPIRICAL TENDENCY 19.1.   Yield curves tend to have positive slopes when yields are low and to have negative slopes when yields are high.

EMPIRICAL TENDENCY 19.1a.   A necessary supplement to the first tendency is a statement about which yields may be considered "high" and which may be considered "low." Yields have been higher under paper money standards (1862 to 1878 and since 1971) than under the gold standard (1879 to 1970) so that many yields that were considered high during the period 1879 to 1970 are now thought to be low.

EMPIRICAL TENDENCY 19.2.   Yield curves tend to become level as maturity increases regardless of their slopes in early maturities; steep slopes occur only in early maturities. (See Figure 19.1, although most yield curves are flatter at the long end than the one observed on September 30, 1981.)

EMPIRICAL TENDENCY 19.3.   Yield curves tend to be upward sloping in the very early maturities regardless of their slopes in later maturities, often producing humps as in Figure 19.1.

We now go to the most popular explanations of these tendencies.

THE TRADITIONAL EXPECTATIONS THEORY

The traditional expectations (TE) theory, which asserts that long-term yields are averages of current and expected short-term yields, has long been the dominant theory of the term structure of interest rates.[2] Its appeal has been due both to its simplicity and, on many occasions, its apparent correspondence with observed yield curves. In most cases even advocates of the principal competing theories accept the main theme of the TE theory (that is, the paramount importance of expectations of future yields) and express their theories as variations on that theme. It is therefore worthwhile to develop the TE theory in detail. We begin with some definitions:

Y_n = the current yield (or spot rate) on an n-period security

$_iY_k^e$ = the yield currently expected to prevail on a k-period security i periods in the future

$_iF_k$ = the forward yield (or forward rate) that is implied by the current term structure on a k-period security i periods in the future

For simplicity and exactness, most of our discussion of the TE theory is limited to single-payment securities, mainly Treasury bills (T bills). T bills are the only group of securities that completely satisfy the requirements of the term structure specified at the beginning of this chapter. They are free of default risk, are subject to federal income (but not capital gains) taxes, and are identical except for term to maturity.

Expectations and decisions: the two-period case

Consider an investor who wishes to invest an amount V in such a way that his wealth after two periods is maximized. Suppose the choice lies between a two-period and successive one-period, single-payment securities. If he buys the two-period security, the value of his investment after two periods is

$$V(1 + Y_2)^2$$

If he buys a one-period security now and reinvests the proceeds in another one-period security next period, he expects to have, at the end of two periods,

$$V(1 + Y_1)(1 + {_1Y_1^e})$$

---

2 The development of the expectations theory is due mainly to Irving Fisher (1896, pages 23–29 and 88–92; 1930, page 70).

Note from our definitions that Y_1 and Y_2 are yields on one-period and two-period securities observed currently (on the date of the formulation and implementation of the investment plan), whereas $_1Y_1^e$ is the yield on a one-period security expected to prevail at the beginning of the next period.

According to the traditional expectations theory the investor is indifferent between the two courses of action, that is, between one-period and two-period securities, if and only if

(19.1) $(1 + Y_2)^2 = (1 + Y_1)(1 + {}_1Y_1^e)$ or

$$1 + Y_2 = [(1 + Y_1)(1 + {}_1Y_1^e)]^{1/2}$$

If Equation (19.1) is not satisfied, the investor prefers one of the securities. For example suppose $Y_2 = 0.15$, $Y_1 = 0.05$, and $_1Y_1^e = 0.08$ so that an investment of $V = \$100$ in the two-period security gives $\$100(1.15)^2 = \$132.25$ after two periods, compared with $\$100(1.05)(1.08) = \$113.40$ from successive one-period investments. Our investor and other investors with (we assume) the same objectives and expectations will shift from the one-period to the two-period security, inducing a fall in the price of the former and a rise in the price of the latter. We do not know what the final, equilibrium configuration of current and expected yields will be. But this process will proceed until Y_1 has risen and Y_2 has fallen (expectations may also be affected) sufficiently to cause Equation (19.1) to be satisfied, at which point investors will be indifferent between the two investment plans. One of an infinite number of possible equilibria is $Y_2 = 0.1049$, $Y_1 = 0.09$, and $_1Y_1^e = 0.12$ so that $\$100(1.1049)^2 = \$100(1.09)(1.12) = \$122.08$.

Investors are not bound to hold securities until maturity. Equilibrium condition (19.1) implies that an investor may expect the same return from alternative investment plans regardless of the length of his investment horizon. For example suppose the purchaser of a two-period security plans to sell it after one period. His expected rate of return is[3]

(19.2)
$$_1R_2^e = \frac{_1P_1^e - P_2}{P_2} = \frac{[\$100/(1 + {}_1Y_1^e)] - [\$100/(1 + Y_2)^2]}{[\$100/(1 + Y_2)^2]}$$

$$= \frac{(1 + Y_2)^2}{1 + {}_1Y_1^e} - 1 = Y_1$$

---

3 Chapter 5 dealt with the distinction between *yield to maturity* (Y), which is the rate at which a security's future payments must be discounted to give its present value (price), and *rate of return* (R), which is the change in an investment's value during some period as a proportion of its value at the beginning of the period.

Equation (19.2) holds when expectations are held with certainty. Uncertainty is considered later in the chapter.

where the face value is $100 and the prices, which correspond to the yields defined above, are

P_n = the current price of an n-period security
$_iP_k^e$ = the price currently expected to prevail on a k-period security i periods in the future

and furthermore

$_iR_k^e$ = the average rate of return expected on a k-period security that is purchased now and held for i periods

The final statement in Equation (19.2), that is, the equality of $_1R_2^e$ and Y_1, follows from Equation (19.1).

The expected one-period rate of return on a default-free one-period security is simply its yield at the beginning of the period:

(19.3) $$_1R_1^e = \frac{\$100 - [\$100/(1 + Y_1)]}{[\$100/(1 + Y_1)]} = Y_1$$

Comparing Equations (19.2) and (19.3), we see that in equilibrium the one-period rates of return expected on one- and two-period securities are identical and equal to the yield on the one-period security:

(19.4) $$_1R_2^e = {}_1R_1^e = Y_1 \qquad (\text{In equilibrium})$$

These results are illustrated in Exercise 19.1.

EXERCISE 19.1.   Show that expected one-period and two-period returns on investments in one-period and two-period securities are identical when Equation (19.1) is satisfied, specifically when $Y_1 = 0.09$, $Y_2 = 0.1049$, and $_1Y_1^e = 0.12$.

Using face values of $100 (though the results are independent of face values), the two-period security is purchased for $P_2 = \$100/(1.1049)^2 = \$81.91$, giving it a two-period expected rate of return of

$$\frac{\$100 - [\$100/(1.1049)^2]}{\$100/(1.1049)^2} = \frac{\$100 - \$81.91}{\$81.91} = 0.2208$$

or an average expected rate of return $_2R_2^e$ such that

$$(1 + {}_2R_2^e)^2 = (1.1049)^2 = 1.2208 \qquad \text{or} \qquad {}_2R_2^e = 0.1049$$

If an investor buys a one-period security with face value of $100 for $P_1 = \$100/(1 + Y_1) = \$100/1.09 = \$91.74$ and reinvests the face value next period, he expects to have, at the end of two periods,

$$\$100(1 + {}_1Y_1^e) = \$100(1.12) = \$112$$

and a two-period rate of return of

$$\frac{\$100\,(1 + {}_1Y_1^e) - [\$100/(1 + Y_1)]}{\$100/(1 + Y_1)} = \frac{\$112 - \$91.74}{\$91.74}$$

$$= 0.2208 = (1 + Y_1)(1 + {}_1Y_1^e) - 1$$

which is identical to that on the two-period security.

The expected one-period rate of return on the two-period security is, from Equation (19.2),

$${}_1R_2^e = \frac{{}_1P_1^e - P_2}{P_2} = \frac{(\$100/1.12) - [\$100/(1.1049)^2]}{\$100/(1.1049)^2} = 0.09$$

which is equal to Y_1 and ${}_1R_1^e$. Like successive one-period investments the two-period security earns 9 percent in the first period and 12 percent in the second period.

Exercise 19.1 and the preceding discussion have illustrated the *two most important theoretical implications* of the TE theory:

1. Long-term yields are geometric averages of current and expected short-term yields.
2. All expected holding-period rates of return are equal regardless of the securities purchased or the lengths of holding periods.

These implications follow from the *two most important assumptions* of the TE theory:

1. People prefer more wealth to less.
2. Expectations are held with certainty.

The liquidity preference and market segmentation theories discussed below take some notice of uncertainty, and a rigorous treatment of the term structure under uncertainty is set forth toward the end of the chapter. In the meantime we shall see that the simpler certainty theory is often quite consistent with the data. We will now consider some more general (*n*-period) implications of the traditional theory.

n periods

Equation (19.1) and its implications may be extended to any number of periods. For example, expected-value-maximizing investors with identical expectations are indifferent between an n-period security and n successive one-period securities if and only if

(19.5) $1 + Y_n = [(1 + Y_1)(1 + {_1}Y_1^e) \cdots (1 + {_{n-1}}Y_1^e)]^{1/n}$

Suppose, for example, that current and expected one-period yields (up to $n = 4$) are $Y_1 = 0.06$, ${_1}Y_1^e = 0.08$, ${_2}Y_1^e = 0.10$, and ${_3}Y_1^e = 0.07$. That is, yields are expected to rise and then fall. Using Equation (19.5), we see that in equilibrium these expectations imply a humpbacked yield curve, as indicated by, along with $Y_1 = 0.06$, the following longer-term rates:

$$Y_2 = [(1.06)(1.08)]^{1/2} - 1 = 0.06995$$

$$Y_3 = [(1.06)(1.08)(1.10)]^{1/3} - 1 = 0.07988$$

$$Y_4 = [(1.06)(1.08)(1.10)(1.07)]^{1/4} - 1 = 0.07740$$

Exercise 19.2 shows that the expected one-period rates of return on all these securities are the same.

EXERCISE 19.2.   Given $Y_1 = 0.06$, ${_1}Y_1^e = 0.08$, ${_2}Y_1^e = 0.10$, ${_3}Y_1^e = 0.07$, and Equation (19.5), show that expected one-period rates of return on two-, three-, and four-period securities equal ${_1}R_1^e = Y_1 = 0.06$.

We need the expected prices for next period's one-, two-, and three-period securities. This in turn requires the expected yields on these securities, which, given the expected one-period yields stated above, are such that

$$1 + {_1}Y_1^e = 1.08$$

$$1 + {_1}Y_2^e = [(1 + {_1}Y_1^e)(1 + {_2}Y_1^e)]^{1/2} = 1.08995$$

$$1 + {_1}Y_3^e = [(1 + {_1}Y_1^e)(1 + {_2}Y_1^e)(1 + {_3}Y_1^e)]^{1/3} = 1.08326$$

If the one-period yields expected one, two, and three periods in the future are 0.08, 0.10, and 0.07, then the two- and three-period yields expected one period in the future are 0.08995 and 0.08326.

The expected one-period rates of return on two-, three-, and four-period securities are therefore, using the current long-term

current price.

yields calculated prior to this exercise,

$$_1R_2^e = \frac{_1P_1^e - P_2}{P_2} = \frac{(\$100/1.08) - [\$100/(1.06995)^2]}{\$100/(1.06995)^2} = 0.06$$

$$_1R_3^e = \frac{_1P_2^e - P_3}{P_3} = \frac{[\$100/(1.08995)^2] - [\$100/(1.07988)^3]}{\$100/(1.07988)^3} = 0.06$$

$$_1R_4^e = \frac{_1P_3^e - P_4}{P_4} = \frac{[\$100/(1.08326)^3] - [\$100/(1.0774)^4]}{\$100/(1.0774)^4} = 0.06$$

Expected rates and forward rates

Suppose the TE theory is not valid. That is, suppose investors do not behave in the manner described above so that long-term yields are not geometric averages of current and expected short-term yields as asserted in Equation (19.5). Even under these conditions the term structure contains useful information because current yields imply a set of forward rates that may be secured now by simultaneously buying and selling securities of different maturities. These forward rates are defined by Equation (19.6), which is obtained by substituting $_iF_1$ for the $_iY_1^e$ used in Equation (19.5). Unlike Equation (19.5), which is dependent on the validity of the expectations theory, Equation (19.6) is true by definition.

(19.6) $(1 + Y_n)^n = (1 + Y_1)(1 + {}_1F_1) \cdot \cdot \cdot (1 + {}_{n-1}F_1)$

The forward yields (usually called "forward rates") on one-period securities i periods in the future, $_iF_1$, are defined such that Equation (19.6) is satisfied. We now give an example of the meaning of forward rates: An investor who simultaneously sells a one-period security and buys a two-period single-payment security secures a one-period investment to begin one period hence at a rate of interest implied by the current yield curve.[4] Suppose current one-period and two-period market yields are $Y_1 = 0.09$ and $Y_2 = 0.1049$. Then if the one-period security has a face value of $100, our investor currently receives

$$\frac{\$100}{1 + Y_1} = \frac{\$100}{1.09} = \$91.74$$

---

4 See Charles Nelson (1972, pages 6–9) for an excellent discussion, with examples, of the "futures market implicit in the term structure."

from its sale. Investing the proceeds in a two-period security, she receives

$$\frac{\$100}{1 + Y_1} (1 + Y_2)^2 = \frac{\$100}{1.09} (1.1049)^2 = \$112.00$$

after two periods. Summarizing, the investor has promised to pay $100 after one period and has been promised $112 after two periods. She has thus locked in a yield of

(19.7)
$$_1F_1 = \frac{[\$100/(1 + Y_1)] (1 + Y_2)^2 - \$100}{\$100}$$

$$= \frac{(1 + Y_2)^2}{1 + Y_1} - 1 = \frac{(1.1049)^2}{1.09} - 1 = 0.12$$

on a forward loan one period in the future.

Equation (19.7) shows that the term structure implies a forward rate, $_1F_1$, on a one-period investment one period in the future such that

$$1 + {_1F_1} = \frac{(1 + Y_2)^2}{1 + Y_1} \qquad \text{or} \qquad (1 + Y_2)^2 = (1 + Y_1)(1 + {_1F_1})$$

which is Equation (19.6) when $n = 2$.

Now consider a one-period implicit forward contract $n - 1$ periods in the future. Rewrite Equation (19.6) such that

(19.8)
$$(1 + Y_n)^n = [(1 + Y_1)(1 + {_1F_1}) \cdots (1 + {_{n-2}F_1})](1 + {_{n-1}F_1})$$
$$= (1 + Y_{n-1})^{n-1} (1 + {_{n-1}F_1})$$

Equation (19.8) states that an n-period investment may be viewed as equivalent to n successive one-period investments or an $(n - 1)$-period investment plus a forward one-period investment. For example suppose our investor sells an $(n - 1)$-period security for

$$\frac{\$100}{(1 + Y_{n-1})^{n-1}}$$

and uses the proceeds to buy an n-period security that pays

$$\frac{\$100}{(1 + Y_{n-1})^{n-1}} (1 + Y_n)^n$$

n periods in the future. By these actions she has locked in a one-period rate of return of

(19.9)
$$_{n-1}F_1 = \frac{[\$100/(1 + Y_{n-1})^{n-1}] (1 + Y_n)^n - \$100}{\$100}$$

$$= \frac{(1 + Y_n)^n}{(1 + Y_{n-1})^{n-1}} - 1$$

$(n - 1)$ periods in the future. This is the forward rate implied by Equation (19.8).

We do not have to restrict ourselves to one-period forward rates. Break up Equation (19.6) in a more general way such that

(19.10)
$$(1 + Y_n)^n = [(1 + Y_1)(1 + {}_1F_1)$$
$$\cdots (1 + {}_{i-1}F_1)][(1 + {}_iF_1) \cdots (1 + {}_{n-1}F_1)]$$
$$= (1 + Y_i)^i (1 + {}_iF_{n-i})^{n-i}$$

Equation (19.10) expresses a current n-period investment as equivalent to a current i-period investment and an $(n - i)$-period investment beginning in the ith period. As in the previous examples we can show that a forward yield is implicit in the term structure; the only difference is that the forward yield in this case is on an $(n - i)$-period security instead of on a one-period security. Suppose the investor sells an i-period security for

$$\frac{\$100}{(1 + Y_i)^i}$$

and uses the proceeds to buy an n-period security that pays

$$\frac{\$100}{(1 + Y_i)^i} (1 + Y_n)^n$$

after n periods. She has thus locked in an implicit $(n - i)$-period loan in the ith period with a yield over $(n - i)$ periods totaling

$$\frac{[\$100/(1 + Y_i)^i] (1 + Y_n)^n - \$100}{\$100} = \frac{(1 + Y_n)^n}{(1 + Y_i)^i} - 1$$

and a per-period yield of ${}_iF_{n-i}$, where

(19.11)
$$(1 + {}_iF_{n-i})^{n-i} = \frac{(1 + Y_n)^n}{(1 + Y_i)^i}$$

as implied by Equation (19.10).

We have assumed that investors are able to borrow and lend at the same yields. This assumption becomes plausible when we realize that it may be satisfied not only by issuing securities but also by selling securities from one's portfolio.

Summarizing the above discussion, the yield curve implies a set of forward rates that exist regardless of expectations. The TE theory amounts to an assertion that these forward rates are in fact the market's expectations of future rates, that Equations (19.5) and (19.6) are equivalent.

A good linear approximation

Equations (19.5) and (19.6) state that long rates are geometric averages of forward or expected short rates. Using the forward rate notation of Equation (19.6), the following arithmetic average is normally a close approximation of the exact relation:[5]

$$\textbf{(19.6a)} \qquad Y_n \doteq \frac{Y_1 + {}_1F_1 + \cdots + {}_{n-1}F_1}{n}$$

This approximation is especially good when current and expected yields are close, as we shall see in Table 19.1.

A numerical example based on actual T bill rates

We now apply the above equations to actual data and assume the TE theory to be valid so that forward and expected rates are equivalent. The top-left portion of Table 19.1 reports T bill discount rates for February 23, 1984. The top-right portion of the table shows days to maturity (D), dealer asked prices (P_a) calculated according to Relationship 6.2 in Table 6.1 (assuming cash delivery), and yields (Y) expressed, like the discount rates, in percentages. Unlike the discount rates, however, these yields are expressed on a 12-week basis. Conversion of Y to a compound annual basis would raise all the results in the lower-left portion of the table by the power 366/84. These results are the expected one-period yields implied by the term structure Equation (19.5). To their right are approximations based on Equation (19.6a), with expected yields substituted for forward rates because the example assumes the validity of the TE theory. The approximations are all exact to one-tenth of a basis point because the differences between current and expected yields are very small.

We see from the top-right portion of Table 19.1 that the T bill yield

---

5 This approximation is obtained by taking natural logarithms of both sides of Equation (19.6) and noting that $\ln(1 + x) \doteq x$ for small x.

Table 19.1   The Term Structure of 12-week Treasury Bill Yields, February 23, 1984; Quotations Assumed for Cash (Same-day) Delivery

Dealer Quotations						Further Data on Selected Issues			

U.S. Treas. Bills Mat. date	Bid	Asked	Yield Discount	Mat. date	Bid	Asked	Yield Discount	Maturity Date	D	P_a	Y
-1984-				6-21	9.26	9.20	9.64	*1984*			
3- 1	8.66	8.56	8.71	6-28	9.27	9.21	9.67	5/17	84	97.856	2.191
3- 8	8.78	8.68	8.85	7- 5	9.33	9.27	9.75	8/9	168	95.632	2.258
3-15	8.70	8.60	8.78	7-12	9.35	9.31	9.81	11/1	252	93.448	2.285
3-22	8.90	8.86	9.06	7-19	9.35	9.29	9.81	*1985*			
3-29	8.80	8.74	8.95	7-26	9.36	9.32	9.86	1/24	336	91.320	2.296
4- 5	8.95	8.89	9.12	8- 2	9.38	9.32	9.88				
4-12	9.00	8.92	9.17	8- 9	9.40	9.36	9.94				
4-19	9.14	9.08	9.35	8-16	9.39	9.35	9.95				
4-26	9.11	9.07	9.36	8-23	9.40	9.38	10.00				
5- 3	9.19	9.13	9.44	9- 6	9.37	9.31	9.94				
5-10	9.18	9.12	9.45	10- 4	9.40	9.34	9.99				
5-17	9.25	9.19	9.54	11- 1	9.42	9.36	10.04				
5-24	9.26	9.24	9.61	11-29	9.42	9.36	10.08				
5-31	9.26	9.22	9.61	12-27	9.38	9.34	10.11				
6- 7	9.24	9.18	9.58	-1985-							
6-14	9.26	9.20	9.62	1-24	9.36	9.30	10.11				
				2-21	9.42	9.40	10.29				

12-week Expected Yields   ·   **Linear Approximations**

$$1 + {}_1Y_1^e = \frac{(1+Y_2)^2}{1+Y_1} = \frac{(1.02258)^2}{1.02191} = 1.02325$$

$$2(0.02258) - 0.02191 = 0.02325$$

$$1 + {}_2Y_1^e = \frac{(1+Y_3)^3}{(1+Y_2)^2} = \frac{(1.02285)^3}{(1.02258)^2} = 1.02339$$

$$3(0.02285) - 2(0.02258) = 0.02339$$

$$1 + {}_3Y_1^e = \frac{(1+Y_4)^4}{(1+Y_3)^3} = \frac{(1.02296)^4}{(1.02285)^3} = 1.02329$$

$$4(0.02296) - 3(0.02285) = 0.02329$$

Check:

$$(1 + Y_1)(1 + {}_1Y_1^e)\,(1 + {}_2Y_1^e)(1 + {}_3Y_1^e) = (1.02296)^4 = (1 + Y_4)^4$$

Current market yields were calculated as follows:

$$P_1 = 97.856 = 100/(1 + Y_1); \quad P_2 = 95.632 = 100/(1 + Y_2)^2; \quad P_3 = 93.448 = 100/(1 + Y_3)^3;$$
$$P_4 = 91.320 = 100/(1 + Y_4)^4$$

where the P_i and Y_i were current market asked prices and 12-week yields on bills maturing in 12, 24, 36, and 48 weeks.

Source: *Wall Street Journal*, February 24, 1984.

curve had a gentle upward slope on February 23, 1984, with 12-, 24-, 36-, and 48-week bills having yields of 2.191, 2.258, 2.285, and 2.296 percent. According to the TE theory these observed yields implied expected 12-week yields of 2.325, 2.339, and 2.329 percent 12, 24, and 36 weeks in the future.[6]

---

6 On a compound annual basis the observed yields are (in percentages) $Y_1 = 9.90$, $Y_2 = 10.22$, $Y_3 = 10.34$, and $Y_4 = 10.40$, and the implied expected yields are ${}_1Y_1^e = 10.53$, ${}_2Y_1^e = 10.60$, and ${}_3Y_1^e = 10.55$.

  Notice that a continuously upward-sloping yield curve does not imply continuously rising expected yields. Observed long-term yields are averages of current and expected short-term yields, and we may think of these short-term yields as marginal contributions to that average. The av-

TWO MORE TRADITIONAL THEORIES OF THE TERM STRUCTURE

Term preference

The term preference (TP) theory of the term structure extends the TE theory by taking account of uncertainty and risk aversion. The TP theory accepts the TE theory's assertion that expectations of future yields are strong influences on the shape of the yield curve but contends that the relative riskiness of returns to securities of different maturities is also important. The TP theory is commonly expressed in the form of Equation (19.5) with the addition of term premiums, L_i:[7]

(19.12) $1 + Y_n$

$$= [(1 + Y_1)(1 + {}_1Y_1^e + L_1) \cdots (1 + {}_{n-1}Y_1^e + L_{n-1})]^{1/n}$$

The standard argument for the TP theory points out that, since prices of long-term securities are more volatile than those of short-term securities, investors require premiums as compensation for investing in the former. That is, $L_1, \ldots, L_{n-1}$ are usually treated as positive and increasing with maturity because of the assumption that risk-averting lenders prefer to invest short term and risk-averting borrowers prefer to borrow long term. The latter are willing to pay premiums to induce the former to hold long-term debt. The existence of term premiums means that the forward rates discussed above cannot be expectations of future rates as asserted by the TE theory. Specifically

(19.13) $_iF_1 = {}_iY_1^e + L_i$

---

erage rises (falls) if the marginal contribution is above (below) the average even if it is below (above) the preceding marginal contribution. Substituting an expected yield for the forward rate in Equation (19.8) and rearranging, we see that

$$\left(\frac{1 + Y_n}{1 + Y_{n-1}}\right)^n = \frac{1 + {}_{n-1}Y_1^e}{1 + Y_{n-1}} \gtreqless 1 \quad \text{as} \quad {}_{n-1}Y_1^e \gtreqless Y_{n-1}$$

In terms of the example above, $Y_4 = 10.40 > Y_3 = 10.34$ because $_3Y_1^e = 10.55 > Y_3$ even though $_3Y_1^e < {}_2Y_1^e$.

7 These premiums are denoted L_i for consistency with common usage. This notation corresponds to the theory's popular name, "liquidity preference," in which the L_i are called "liquidity premiums." These names are unfortunate because the theory is concerned with risk due to price volatility rather than liquidity, which measures the ability to realize the full-market value of a security quickly. (See Chapter 7 for discussions of the distinctions, as well as the connections, between liquidity and risk.) Since most recent empirical work on this theory has used T bills and differences in the liquidity of bills of different maturities are small or nonexistent, the use of the word liquidity in connection with this theory has become particularly inappropriate. So we follow Charles Nelson (1972, page 40) in using the names term preference and term premiums. It is interesting that the theory's originator, J. Hicks (1946, pages 146–147), referred to "risk premiums."

and we cannot infer expectations of future rates as we did in Table 19.1 without knowing the L_i.

Now let's look at the implications of the TP theory for expected returns on long-term investments. Using the method of Equation (19.2) and Exercise 19.2, the expected one-period rate of return on an n-period single-payment security with face value of $100 is

$$_1R_n^e = \frac{_1P_{n-1}^e - P_n}{P_n}$$

(19.14)
$$= \frac{[\$100/(1 + {_1Y_{n-1}^e})^{n-1}] - [\$100/(1 + Y_n)^n]}{\$100/(1 + Y_n)^n}$$

$$= \frac{(1 + Y_n)^n}{(1 + {_1Y_{n-1}^e})^{n-1}} - 1$$

Adding unity to both sides of this equation and using Equation (19.12) give

(19.15) $$1 + {_1R_n^e} = \frac{(1 + Y_1)(1 + {_1Y_1^e} + L_1) \cdots (1 + {_{n-1}Y_1^e} + L_{n-1})}{(1 + {_1Y_1^e})(1 + {_2Y_1^e} + L_1) \cdots (1 + {_{n-1}Y_1^e} + L_{n-2})}$$

A good linear approximation of this result is

(19.15a) $$_1R_n^e \doteq Y_1 + L_{n-1}$$

The TP theory implies that investors may expect a rate of return from the n-period security in excess of that on the one-period security by the amount of a term premium, L_{n-1}.

We have thus far assumed term premiums to be positive. But this is not necessarily the case even under the assumptions of the TP theory, for many risk-averse investors prefer long-term securities. Consider a

Table 19.2   Estimates of Term Premiums, 1951 to 1966 (In Percentages at Annual Rates)

	Months					Years						
Maturity (m)	1	2	3	6	9	1	2	3	5	10	20	30
Estimate	0.17	0.28	0.34	0.41	0.43	0.43	0.43	0.43	0.43	0.43	0.43	0.43
Standard error of estimate	0.02	0.03	0.04	0.06	0.07	0.07	0.07	0.07	0.07	0.07	0.07	0.07

The above estimates were constrained to vary according to the smooth exponential function

Term premium $= b(1 - e^{-am})$

Free-form estimates also rose rapidly and then leveled off, but the estimates for maturities exceeding 9 months were not statistically significant.

Source: J. Huston McCulloch, "An Estimate of the Liquidity Premium," *Journal of Political Economy*, January/February 1975, pages 95–119.

life insurance company with a preponderance of youthful policy-holders. Most of the company's liabilities (future policy claims) are long term. The best way to hedge these future payments, that is, the best way to avoid risk, is to invest in long-term securities. A $100 payment due in 30 years is assured by the purchase of a 30-year default-free bond that pays $100 in 30 years.[8] On the other hand the outcome of thirty successive investments in 1-year securities is uncertain. Pension funds and individuals concerned about the safety of their retirement incomes might also prefer long-term securities when the expected returns from long-term and short-term securities are equal. These investors are likely to require compensation for investing short term, thus putting upward pressure on the short end of the yield curve and perhaps even causing term premiums to be negative. Whether term preference produces upward or downward bias in the yield curve, that is, whether term premiums tend to be positive or negative, depends on the relative importance of investors with opposing term preferences. The empirical evidence produced to date supports the view that term premiums are positive although probably reaching a peak at very short maturities. J. H. McCulloch's (1975) estimates of term premiums are shown in Table 19.2. These estimates rise rapidly at first, from 0.17 percent on 1-month securities to 0.41 percent on 6-month securities, before leveling off at 0.43 percent on all remaining maturities.

Market segmentation

The market segmentation (MS) theory is an extreme form of the TP theory. Whereas the TE theory asserts that default-free securities of different maturities are perfect substitutes and the TP theory asserts that they are imperfect substitutes, the MS theory asserts that the markets for securities of different maturities are so tightly compartmentalized that maturity groups are nonsubstitutable and the yield curve is broken up into distinct, independent segments. Given the relative sizes of investor groups with different maturity preferences, the shape of the yield curve is determined completely by the relative supplies of different maturities outstanding and not at all by expectations of future yields. An illustration of the empirical implications of the MS theory for the shape of the yield curve is presented later in connection with "Operation Twist." According to the MS theory an increase in the supply of short-term relative to long-term debt reduces the slope of the yield curve.[9] This contrasts with the implication of the TE theory that relative supplies are irrelevant to the yield curve's slope.

---

8 Appendix 6.A presents the conditions under which returns may be immunized against risk by the choice of portfolios with durations equal to investor holding periods.

9 See John Culbertson (1957) for an early statement of the MS theory.

The tendency of different groups to concentrate their security holdings in well-defined and fairly stable maturity ranges has been offered as supporting evidence for the MS theory.[10] The preferences of nonfinancial firms for very short maturities, commercial banks for slightly longer maturities, and pension funds and life insurance companies for long maturities have been widely noticed and, as we saw above, serve as the foundation for the TP as well as for the MS theory. But these observations are not sufficient to demonstrate the validity of either of these theories. There is no contradiction between the TE theory, according to which short-term and long-term securities are treated by the market as perfect substitutes, and the fact that individual investors prefer specific maturities. This point was developed by David Meiselman (1962, page 53):

> There appear to be a great many overlapping areas of the yield curve in which important transactors tend to specialize. At the shortest end are the commercial banks; somewhat longer are savings banks and savings and loan associations, and at the very longest end of the yield curve are life insurance companies. The market is given even more continuity by security dealers and professional short-period traders. In addition, there are also speculators who trade in commodity futures or the equity markets on a non-professional or non-specialized basis. Taken together, the transactors who specialize in coping with uncertainty in one part of the yield curve and act to reduce the variance of expected returns, plus others who need not have such preferences or restraints imposed by legal and institutional requirements, give the market a continuity that is not apparent from observing the narrow range of choice of any one large transactor group.

In fact all that the TE theory requires is one group of well-financed, expected-wealth-maximizing speculators with identical and confidently held expectations. Under these conditions the theory implies (continuing to quote Meiselman, page 57)

> that market excess demand schedules of securities of given maturities tend to be infinitely elastic at rates consistent with current and expected short-term rates. Of course, it is not necessary that all transactors have infinitely elastic schedules in order that the market schedules be infinitely elastic. It is only necessary that one class of adequately financed transactors have an infinitely elastic excess demand schedule. . . . Speculators with given expectations adjust quantities of securities taken from or sup-

---

10 See James Van Horne (1978, pages 103–109) for a survey of tests of the MS theory.

plied to the market in order to maintain the structure of rates consistent with expectations.

We now turn to empirical investigations of the abilities of the TE, TP, and MS theories to explain observed yield curves.

EMPIRICAL STUDIES OF THE TERM STRUCTURE

The traditional expectations–regressive expectations (TERE) theory[11]

THE THEORY AND THE DATA, 1900 TO 1970. The TERE theory embodies two hypotheses, one about how expectations of future yields are formed and one about how those expectations are used by investors:

> HYPOTHESIS 19.1.   Expectations of future yields are based largely on the conviction that yields regress toward some "normal" range so that yields are expected to rise when they are "low" and are expected to fall when they are "high."[12]

> HYPOTHESIS 19.2.   The traditional expectations theory holds; that is, the regressively formed expectations of Hypothesis 19.1 are combined such that observed long-term yields are geometric averages of observed and expected short-term yields.

Now let us confront these hypotheses with the data. The longest available series of yield curves is for high-grade corporate bonds and is depicted in Figure 19.2. This series was begun by David Durand and has been continued by Scudder, Stevens and Clark.[13] As Durand emphasized, his yield curves are even rougher approximations of true yield curves than are those for Treasury securities. This is because corporate bonds have different risks of default and also because they differ more widely than Treasury bonds in their terms and conditions. Nevertheless, the slopes of corporate yield curves have been seen to correspond closely to those of Treasury yield curves since data became available on the latter in 1953.[14]

Durand's yield curves for 1900 to 1929 are shown in Figure 19.2(a). Those for 1930 to 1982 are shown in Figure 19.2(b). Curves since 1966 have been identified by year of occurrence. Perhaps the most striking

---

11 This theory was first discussed at length by F. A. Lutz (1940). The following discussion is based on John Wood (1983).

12 The idea of a normal range of rates was emphasized by J. M. Keynes (1936, Chapter 15).

13 Durand's original curves (for 1900 to 1942) were reported in David Durand (1942) and were updated by David Durand and Willis Winn (1947), by David Durand (1958), and since 1959 by the investment firm of Scudder, Stevens and Clark. Selected data are available for 1900 to 1970 in U.S. Department of Commerce, *Historical Statistics of the United States,* vol. 2, page 1004, and more recently in the annual *Statistical Abstract of the United States.*

14 Table 19.5 compares the slopes of Treasury and corporate yield curves between 1959 and 1982.

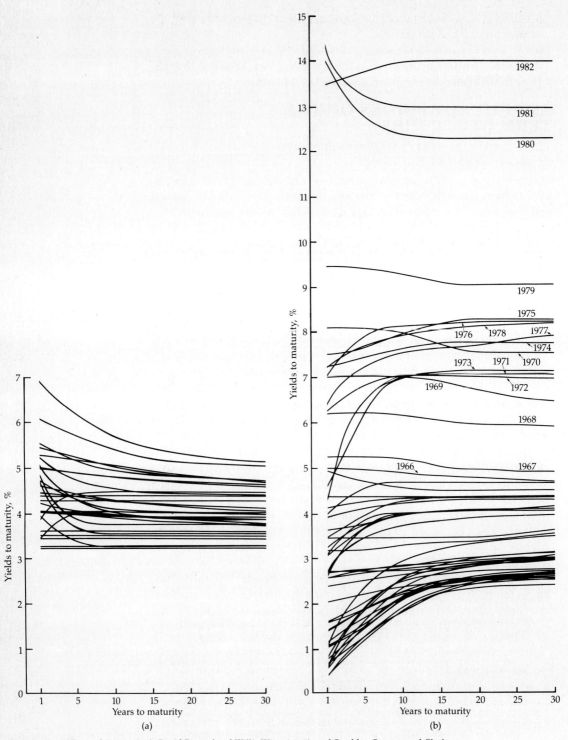

Sources: David Durand (1942, 1958), David Durand and Willis Winn (1947), and Scudder, Stevens and Clark.

Figure 19.2   Yield curves for high-grade corporate bonds, (a) 1900 to 1929 and (b) 1930 to 1982.

Table 19.3   Frequencies of Rising, Flat, and Falling Yield Curves, 1900 to 1982

1-year Corporate Bond Yield (percent per annum)	Slope of Yield Curve		
	Positive	Flat	Negative
1900–1970			
Above 4.40	0	0	20
3.25–4.40	10	10	5
Below 3.25	26	0	0
1971–1982			
Above 8.00	1	0	3
Below 8.00	8	0	0

Source: Figure 19.2.

feature of these yield curves has been their tendency, at least until the 1970s, to be positively sloped when yields were "low" and negatively sloped when yields were "high." Suppose, for example, that, between 1900 and 1970, 1-year yields above 4.40 percent were considered high while yields below 3.25 percent were thought to be low. The upper portion of Table 19.3 shows that, when high and low are distinguished in this manner, all yield curves had negative slopes when short-term yields were high and all yield curves had positive slopes when short-term yields were low.

Exercises 19.3 and 19.4 demonstrate that these observations are consistent with the TERE theory, that is, with the TE theory based on regressive expectations, and are not consistent with the TE theory based on extrapolative expectations. These exercises also illustrate the effects of changes in investors' views of the normal yield.

EXERCISE 19.3.   The yield on 1-year, single-payment securities on Mars, which has no trees and therefore no paper money, has fallen from 5 percent in 1982 to 3 and 2 percent in 1983 and 1984, respectively. Martians view a 4 percent yield as normal and in 1984 expected the 1-year yield to reverse its downward movement—specifically to climb half the distance between the normal yield and the yield at the beginning of the year during each of the next several years. That is, the 1-year yields expected to prevail 1, 2, and 3 years in the future were 3.00, 3.50, and 3.75 percent, as indicated in the following table. Since the Martian money markets conform to the assumptions of the TE theory, yields on 2-, 3-, and 4-year securities in 1984 were—using the linear approximation (19.6a)—2.500, 2.833, and 3.063, as shown in the left-hand portion of the table and also by the yield curve labeled $1984R$ in Figure 19.3.[15]

Observed and Expected Yields on Mars in 1984

n, i	Regressive Expectations		Extrapolative Expectations	
	Y_n	$_iY_1^e$	Y_n	$_iY_1^e$
1, —	2.000	—	2.000	—
2, 1	2.500	3.000	1.750	1.500
3, 2	2.833	3.500	1.583	1.250
4, 3	3.063	3.750	1.469	1.125

The yield curve presented in the right-hand portion of the table and by the curve $1984X$ in Figure 19.3 corresponds to extrapolative expectations such that the change in the 1-year yield is expected to be half that of the preceding year. This curve is unlike any observed this century in the United States when observed yields were less than 4 percent.

Now suppose that Earthlings establish a base on Mars, complete with central bank. One of the consequences is described in Exercise 19.4.

EXERCISE 19.4.   The Martian yield on 1-year, single-payment securities rises from 5 percent in 1999 to 7 and 8 percent in 2000 and 2001, respectively. In the new monetary regime Martians think of 6 percent as the normal yield and in 2001 expect the 1-year yield to reverse its upward movement—specifically to fall half the distance between the normal yield and the yield at the

15 A formal expression of this model is one in which expected one-period yields are $_iY_1^e = \overline{Y} - (1 - a)^i(\overline{Y} - Y_1)$, where $\overline{Y}$ is the normal yield and a governs the speed with which future short yields are expected to approach $\overline{Y}$. If $a = 1$, $_iY_1^e = \overline{Y}$ and the adjustment is instantaneous; if $a = 0$, $_iY_1^e = Y_1$ and there is no adjustment; if $a = 0.5$, $\overline{Y} = 0.04$, and $Y_1 = 0.02$, then $_1Y_1^e = 0.0300$, $_2Y_1^e = 0.0350$, and $_3Y_1^e = 0.0375$ as in the exercise. Substituting the above expression into the linear approximation of Y_n gives

$$Y_n = \frac{Y_1 + \sum_{i=1}^{n-1} {_iY_1^e}}{n} = \frac{Y_1 + \sum_{i=1}^{n-1} [\overline{Y} - (1 - a)^i(\overline{Y} - Y_1)]}{n}$$

$$= \frac{Y_1 + (n - 1)\overline{Y} - (\overline{Y} - Y_1)[(1 - a) - (1 - a)^n]/a}{n}$$

This expression gives the results in the exercise when $Y_1 = 0.02$, $\overline{Y} = 0.04$, and $a = 0.5$. Notice that Y_n approaches $\overline{Y}$ as n becomes large.

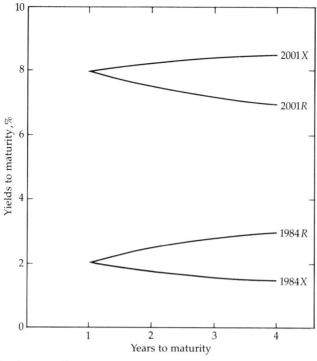

Sources: Exercises 20.3 and 20.4.

Figure 19.3   Martian yield curves, 1984 and 2001.

beginning of the year during each of the next several years. That is, the 1-year yields expected to prevail in 2002, 2003, and 2004 are 7.00, 6.50, and 6.25 percent, as indicated in the accompanying table. Consequently approximate yields on 2-, 3-, and 4-year securities prevailing in 2001 are 7.500, 7.167, and 6.938, as shown in the table and the yield curve labeled $2001R$ in Figure 19.3.

Observed and Expected Yields on Mars in 2001

n, i	Regressive Expectations		Extrapolative Expectations	
	Y_n	$_iY_1^e$	Y_n	$_iY_1^e$
1, —	8.000	—	8.000	—
2, 1	7.500	7.000	8.250	8.500
3, 2	7.167	6.500	8.417	8.750
4, 3	6.938	6.250	8.531	8.875

The yield curve labeled $2001X$ in Figure 19.3 corresponds to extrapolative expectations, specifically where the 1-year yield is expected to continue its climb, with each year's rise expected to be half that of the preceding year.

AN UPWARD REVISION OF EXPECTATIONS IN THE 1970s? Unfortunately Martians are not the only subjects of monetary experiments. Notice the high and upward-sloping yield curves for 1971 to 1978 and 1982 in Figure 19.2(b). These deviations from the earlier tendency for yield curves of this height to be downward sloping may be explained in a variety of ways. Two possible explanations may be stated as follows: (1) Perhaps the TERE theory that was so consistent with experience during the period 1900 to 1970 has failed recently either because investors no longer behave according to the tenets of the TE theory (the failure of Hypothesis 19.2) or because they no longer form expectations regressively (the failure of Hypothesis 19.1) or both. (2) On the other hand perhaps the TERE theory has remained consistent with the data but investors have revised their estimates of the normal yield.

An extrapolative expectations version of the TE theory (as in curve 2001X in Figure 19.3) is broadly consistent with the generally rising yields and positively sloped yield curves of 1971 to 1978. But its appeal is diminished by the yield curves of 1979 to 1981, which had negative slopes during a period of rapidly rising yields. So let us see how far we can go with alternative (2) of the preceding paragraph. This alternative requires an additional hypothesis, one that supplies a rule by which investors revise their estimates of the normal yield. However, such a rule, whatever it is, cannot be subjected to any kind of test based on the data considered so far because the only unambiguous twentieth-century revision or revisions of the normal yield have

Table 19.4   Frequencies of Rising and Falling Yield Curves, 1862 to 1929

Commercial Paper Yield (percent per annum)	Slope of Yield Curve	
	Positive	Negative
1862–1878		
Above 7.57	0	5
Below 7.56	12	0
1879–1929		
Above 5.40	0	16
4.21–5.40	4	17
Below 4.21	14	0

Source: Frederick Macaulay, *Some Theoretical Problems Suggested by the Movements of Interest Rates, Bond Yields and Stock Prices in the United States since 1856*, tab. 10, National Bureau of Economic Research, New York, 1938.

occurred since about 1970. At least one more observation is essential, and for that we must go to the nineteenth century.

THE NINETEENTH AND TWENTIETH CENTURIES COMPARED. Complete yield curves like those in Figure 19.2 are unavailable for the nineteenth century. However, the slopes of yield curves may be inferred from data on the prime commercial paper rate (the short-term yield) and Frederick Macaulay's railroad bond yield index (the long-term yield).[16] The signs of these slopes are summarized in Table 19.4, which indicates that between 1862 and 1878 all short-term yields below 7.56 percent were associated with rising yield curves, while between 1879 and 1929 all short-term yields above 5.40 percent were associated with falling yield curves. This table thus tells a story similar to that in Table 19.3 and Figure 19.2, that yield curves tended to be positively sloped when yields were low and negatively sloped when yields were high and that there was apparently a revision of the notions of high and low. However, instead of an upward revision as in the early 1970s, the data suggest a downward revision in the late 1870s. What events triggered these upward and downward revisions of investors' expectations of normal yields? The history of U.S. monetary standards since 1862 suggests an answer.

THE MONETARY STANDARD AND THE YIELD CURVE. The American monetary standard has undergone the following changes since early in the Civil War. The gold standard was abandoned when banks suspended convertibility in December 1861. In February 1862 Congress authorized the first of several issues of legal tender currency (the famous greenbacks). After a period of monetary expansion and depreciation of the dollar, followed by prolonged monetary controversy, a bill for the resumption of the gold standard at the prewar exchange rate was approved in January 1875. Resumption was achieved on the target date of January 1, 1879, although success was not assured until late in 1878.[17] The monetary standard remained unchanged until banks were legally prohibited from paying out gold in March 1933. The *international* gold standard was resumed in January 1934[18] although the gold value of the dollar was reduced to 59 percent of that prevailing between 1879 and 1933. Finally, in August 1971, the United States suspended the international convertibility of the dollar and embarked on a paper standard identical in all important respects with that of the greenback era of 1862 to 1878.

The following line of reasoning suggests that the monetary standard should be an important, perhaps the dominant, influence on the

16 See Frederick Macaulay (1938, Table 10).

17 See Davis Dewey (1936, pages 372–382) and Milton Friedman and Anna Schwartz (1963, Chapter 2) for discussions of this period.

18 The *domestic* circulation of gold was ended by the Gold Reserve Act of 1933.

normal yield. First, define the normal yield as the yield expected to prevail in the long run. Second, the evidence suggests that interest rates are in the long run dependent on inflationary expectations, which in turn depend on actual inflation. Finally inflation has for centuries been highly correlated (and generally believed to be highly correlated) with the choice of the monetary standard.[19]

These arguments are supported by the data summarized above that suggest a downward revision in the 1870s and an upward revision in the 1970s of investor estimates of normal yields. The rising 1982 yield curve suggests that the latter revision may not yet be complete. It is not clear from the data whether another revision followed the devaluation of 1934 because the steeply rising yield curves of that decade (and of the 1940s and 1950s) were, in view of the record low yields prevailing at the time, consistent with normal yields based on experience of both gold and paper standards.[20]

The story is not yet finished. We still have much to learn. But as a preliminary conclusion we may say that American yield curves since 1862 have been at least roughly consistent with the TE theory supplemented by regressive expectations *where the normal yield is a function of the monetary standard.*

RATIONAL EXPECTATIONS? Someone's expectations are "rational" if they are consistent with his view of how the world works. The concept of rational expectations extends the notion of economic rationality to the formation of expectations. The reader may be familiar with the notion of rationality as it is applied to preferences. For example, if a person prefers A to B and also prefers B to C, then he must prefer A to C. Otherwise, his preferences conflict. A rational person does not prefer A to B and at the same time prefer B to A. By the same token a rational person does not hold conflicting beliefs about the future. For example, referring to the case presented in Exercise 19.3, suppose that in 1984 the Martian central bank announces its intention to peg all future 1-year yields at the prevailing yield of 2 percent. Furthermore, either because Martians are more naive than Earthlings or because their central bank is more credible, they believe that the announced policy will be implemented. Under these conditions rational Martians abandon their former belief that yields will regress toward 4 percent.

Returning to Earth, if there is no indication of a central bank peg and if Earthlings believe that the principal determinant of yields is the rate of inflation, the average rate of inflation (and therefore average

---

19 See Michael Bordo (1981) and Alan Reynolds (1983) for discussions of actual and expected inflation under gold and paper standards.

20 In annual averages American commercial paper yields have not, except during the period 1935 to 1946, been less than 1 percent and have not, except during 1931 to 1958, been less than 3 percent. They were continuously less than 1 percent during 1935 to 1946 and continuously less than 3 percent during 1931 to 1955. These statements are based on data available since 1819 in Sidney Homer (1977).

yields) depends on the monetary standard, and cyclical deviations from these average (or normal) yields tend to be reversed in a fairly smooth fashion, then the TERE theory presented above, in which the expected normal yield is higher in the presence of a paper standard than a gold standard, may also be described as a rational expectations theory. But it is important to remember that people may be *rational* in the sense of using available information in a consistent manner and at the same time be *ignorant* in the sense of not having very much information. It is too early to tell (and we may never be able to predict with confidence) how the central bank will adjust to the new green-back standard.[21] Experience so far indicates that the rates of growth of money and prices under the post-1970 paper standard can be expected to be more like those observed under the 1862 to 1878 paper standard than during the intervening gold standard years. This still leaves a great deal unanswered, however. It seems a safe bet that future yields will on average exceed the normal 3.25 to 4.40 percent range of 1900 to 1970. But is 5 to 10 percent a good guess? How about 20 to 30 percent? It is extremely difficult under these conditions to forecast the levels and slopes of future yield curves. And yet that is what investors and managers must do. The next section indicates that they may not have done too badly in the past, at least until the volatile late 1970s and early 1980s.

Efficient markets and term preference

Efficient markets are those in which prices and interest rates correctly reflect available information. Tests of efficient markets usually hypothesize not only that investors' expectations are rational but also that investors know how the economy "really" works and are able to make use of what they know. These hypotheses imply that expectations are on average correct and that transaction costs are insignificant. Most tests of the efficiency of the T bill market begin with the assertion of the TE theory that the forward yields ($_iF_k$) implicit in the term structure are expected yields ($_iY_k^e$). This means that in the two-period case

(19.16)
$$\frac{(1 + Y_2)^2}{1 + Y_1} = 1 + {}_1F_1 = 1 + {}_1Y_1^e$$

---

21 Axel Leijonhufvud (1983) points out that the concept of " 'monetary regime' [which used to be called 'monetary standard'] figures prominently in the recent rational expectations literature" and defines "a monetary regime [as] a system of expectations that governs the behavior of the public and that is sustained by the consistent behavior of the policy-making authorities." We know how governments have behaved under paper standards in the past (see Bordo and Reynolds), and experience since 1970 has given us no reason to temper our pessimism. But we do not yet know for sure what the "consistent [or erratic] behavior of the policy-making authorities" will be. Our best hope is that we will never know and that the electorate will become disillusioned with and reject the latest paper standard as it did the Colonial, Continental, and greenback standards of the past.

For example, if $Y_1 = 0.09$, $Y_2 = 0.1049$, the TE theory is valid, and the T bill market is efficient, the market's prediction of next period's one-period yield is $_1F_1 = {_1}Y_1^e = 0.12$. Predictions are almost always wrong, of course, but efficient predictions are randomly wrong. That is, they are unbiased. They are not systematically too high or too low. Therefore an obvious joint test of market efficiency and the TE theory is the estimation of the following regression equation:

(19.17) $$Y_{1,t+1} = a + b\,{_1}F_{1t} + cX_t + e_{t+1}$$

where $_1F_{1t}$ is the one-period forward yield implied for time $t + 1$ by the term structure at time t and $Y_{1,t+1}$ is the one-period yield actually realized at time $t + 1$. The constant term a and X_t represent all information available at time t other than that incorporated in $_1F_{1t}$. Put anything in X_t you like—GNP, lagged interest rates, recent price changes, or George Brett's batting average. If that information is useful in beating the market's predictions of interest rates, you can make some money. Unless you are uninterested in money, you will make use of this information on a scale sufficient to affect prices until X_t is incorporated in $_1F_{1t}$ and exerts no separate influence. The last term in Equation (19.17), e_{t+1}, is a serially uncorrelated error term, that is, a list of forecasting mistakes systematically neither too high nor too low. Taken together, the efficient markets and traditional expectations theories (the EM-TE hypotheses) imply $b = 1$ and $a = c = 0$.

Nearly all tests of the EM-TE hypotheses have rejected these joint hypotheses.[22] It is not clear whether the tests imply the rejection of the TE theory, market efficiency, or both. But researchers have preferred to interpret nonzero values of a as consistent with the joint occurrence of constant term premiums and market efficiency. They have interpreted nonzero values of c as consistent with variable term premiums and market efficiency. For example significant explanatory power of inflation on $Y_{1,t+1}$ beyond that already incorporated in $_1F_{1t}$ has been interpreted to imply both market efficiency and term premiums that are responsive to inflation.[23] This interpretation may be correct. But we fear that it admits no possibility of the rejection of the EM hypothesis and is therefore not a valid test of that hypothesis.

Nevertheless it must be admitted that there is a great deal of evidence of short-term upward bias in yield curves, which, although inconsistent with the joint EM-TE hypotheses, is consistent with the joint EM-TP hypotheses, that is, with the joint hypotheses of efficient

22 An exception is Soo-Bin Park (1982), who found forward yields to be unbiased predictors of future spot yields in the Canadian T bill market during 1962 to 1979. Studies that have found positive term premiums include those of Richard Roll (1970), Michael Hamburger and Elliott Platt (1975), and Eugene Fama (June and October 1976).

23 Eugene Fama (June 1976).

markets and term preference. Some of this evidence was presented in Table 19.2 for the period 1951 to 1966. Additional evidence is presented in Table 19.5. The right side of the table shows 3- and 6-month T bill yields beginning in 1959, when 6-month bills were first issued on a regular basis. Average yields during February are shown for comparability with Durand's long-term private yields. Notice that ten of twenty-six government yield curves sloped downward on the long end (from 1 to 20 years), but only two of twenty-six were negatively sloped on the short end (3 to 6 months). Approximately one-third of these yield curves were humpbacked more or less like the curve in Figure 19.1.

Government yield curves have been reported only since 1953, and T bills have existed only since 1929. Therefore studies of earlier yield curves must rely on private securities.[24] The left side of Table 19.5 compares average yields on 3- and 6-month broker and dealer time loans in New York with Durand's 1- and 20-year corporate bond yields during the period 1900 to 1919.[25] Only one yield curve had a positive slope between 1 and 20 years to maturity, but eighteen of the curves had positive slopes between 3 and 6 months. Eleven of the twenty curves are humpbacked. Positive term preference has apparently exerted a strong and long-lived influence on the short ends of yield curves but has had little if any influence on the relative yields of securities with more than 1 year to maturity.

Market segmentation: evidence and implications for policy

THE EVIDENCE. The MS theory implies that permanent exogenous changes in the maturity distribution of outstanding debt have permanent effects on the slope of the yield curve. For example a substantial shift by the U.S. Treasury from short-term to long-term issues should, according to this theory, cause short-term yields to fall relative to long-term yields because of the reduction in the supply of short terms relative to long terms. However, the evidence indicates that such effects have been temporary, leading most researchers to reject the MS theory. Several studies have been conducted within the framework of the following yield-curve equation, in which Y_{Lt} and Y_{St} are long-term and short-term yields at time t, a is a constant term, $f(_iY_t^e)$ represents the influence of expected yields on the current term structure, $(S/L)_t$ is U.S. short-term debt relative to U.S. long-term debt outstanding and not held by U.S. government agencies or the Federal Reserve at

---

24   The lower-right portion of Table 19.5 indicates that the relationships discussed in this chapter are probably not significantly affected by the use of corporate instead of government yield curves. Their slopes had the same sign on twenty-three of twenty-four occasions between 1959 and 1982.

25   This period was determined by the first Durand curve in 1900 and the end of the *Financial Review's* convenient reporting of money market rates by term to maturity in 1919.

Table 19.5 Yields on Short-term and Long-term (3-month and 6-month) Money Market Securities and Short-term and Long-term (1-year and 20-year) Bonds, 1900 to 1919 and 1959 to 1984

First Quarter[a]	Private Yield Curves				Slopes of the Private Yield Curve	
	3 Month	6 Month	1 Year	20 Year	3–6 Months	1–20 Years
1900	4.65	4.93	3.97	3.30	+	−
1901	3.53	3.89	3.25	3.25	+	0
1902	4.30	4.67	3.30	3.30	+	0
1903	5.21	5.27	3.45	3.45	+	0
1904	3.69	4.36	3.60	3.60	+	0
1905	3.14	3.43	3.50	3.50	+	0
1906	5.32	5.28	4.75	3.55	−	−
1907	5.91	5.99	4.87	3.80	+	−
1908	4.67	5.02	5.10	3.95	+	−
1909	2.75	3.17	4.03	3.82	+	−
1910	4.41	4.27	4.25	3.87	−	−
1911	3.21	3.67	4.09	3.94	+	−
1912	3.17	3.51	4.04	3.91	+	−
1913	4.82	4.92	4.74	4.02	+	−
1914	3.35	3.82	4.64	4.16	+	−
1915	3.03	3.46	4.47	4.20	+	−
1916	2.32	3.09	3.48	4.05	+	+
1917	3.71	4.27	4.05	4.05	+	0
1918	5.99	6.17	5.48	4.82	+	−
1919	5.51	5.68	5.58	4.81	+	−

Definitions and sources of the data
Private yields pertain to 3- and 6-month broker and dealer time loans in New York; bond equivalent yields calculated from discount rates reported in the annually published *Financial Review* [weekly ranges of rates for 1890 to 1909 also available in National Monetary Commission (1910)]; 1- and 20-year high-grade corporate bonds calculated by David Durand and Willis Winn (1947) and Scudder, Stevens and Clark (see footnote 13 for sources).

Treasury yields pertain to: 3- and 6-month T bills; bond equivalent yields calculated from dealer bid rates reported in *Federal Reserve Bulletins*. 1- and 20-year Treasury bond yields and other "constant maturity" yields "are obtained by constructing a yield curve each day based on the closing market bid yields of actively traded Treasury securities. Yield values are then read from the yield curve at fixed maturities" (Federal Reserve Board *Annual Statistical Digest, 1972–76*, page 368); data for April 1953 to December 1976 are reported on pages 117 and 118 of this publication; later data may be found in *Federal Reserve Bulletins*.

a Quarterly averages of 3- and 6-month yields were used during 1900 to 1919 for comparison with Durand's bond yields, which until 1950 were based on monthly high and low prices during the first 3 months of the year. Since 1951 these yields have been based on February data only.

b Not yet available.

time t, and $\Delta(S/L)_t$ is the change in S/L between $t-1$ and t:

$$(19.18) \qquad Y_{Lt} - Y_{St} = a + f(_iY_t^e) + b(S/L)_t + c\Delta(S/L)_t$$

Regression estimates of equations of this type have shown highly significant effects of a wide variety of specifications of $f(_iY_t^e)$, which indicate that expectations are the dominant influence on the yield curve, positive values of a, which suggest positive term preference, values of b that are insignificantly different from zero, and signifi-

Table 19.5   (continued)

February[a]	Treasury Yields				Slopes of the Treasury Yield Curve		Long-term Private Yields		Slope of the Private Long-term Yield Curve
	3 Month	6 Month	1 Year	20 Year	3–6 Months	1–20 Years	1 Year	20 Year	
1959	2.76	3.21	3.54	3.96	+	+	3.67	4.10	+
1960	4.06	4.46	4.66	4.28	+	−	4.95	4.55	−
1961	2.47	2.67	2.93	3.84	+	+	3.10	4.12	+
1962	2.79	3.01	3.28	4.12	+	+	3.50	4.40	+
1963	2.98	3.07	3.01	3.97	+	+	3.25	4.10	+
1964	3.61	3.79	3.78	4.17	+	+	4.00	4.33	+
1965	4.02	4.14	4.03	4.21	+	+	4.15	4.35	+
1966	4.77	5.01	4.94	4.71	+	−	5.00	4.80	−
1967	4.68	4.76	4.71	4.61	+	−	5.29	5.00	−
1968	5.11	5.38	5.42	5.38	+	−	6.24	6.00	−
1969	6.30	6.60	6.41	6.11	+	−	7.05	6.77	−
1970	7.36	7.59	7.59	6.67	+	−	8.15	7.60	−
1971	3.79	3.91	3.89	6.15	+	+	4.60	7.12	+
1972	3.27	3.75	4.27	6.06	+	+	4.25	7.05	+
1973	5.76	6.09	6.19	6.88	+	+	6.25	7.20	+
1974	7.35	7.31	6.88	7.46	−	+	7.26	7.80	+
1975	5.65	5.86	5.98	7.71	+	+	7.55	8.35	+
1976	5.01	5.41	5.91	8.03	+	+	7.05	8.30	+
1977	4.79	5.09	5.47	7.64	+	+	6.35	7.75	+
1978	6.65	7.07	7.34	8.22	+	+	7.25	8.20	+
1979	9.67	10.01	10.24	9.03	+	−	9.48	9.08	−
1980	13.47	13.93	12.06	10.65	+	−	14.00	12.30	−
1981	15.57	15.32	14.57	12.98	−	−	14.50	13.00	−
1982	14.14	14.81	14.73	14.48	+	−	13.50	14.00	+
1983	8.39	8.70	8.92	11.03	+	+	b	b	
1984	9.43	9.76	10.04	12.00	+	+	b	b	

cantly negative values of c.[26] The last result suggests, for example, that a large Treasury issue of short-term securities exerts an immediate negative influence on the difference between long-term and short-term yields. Apparently, an increase in Y_S relative to Y_L is required to induce dealers and other market participants to accept the new

---

26 This is essentially a summary of the results of Frank de Leeuw (1965) and Franco Modigliani and Richard Sutch (1966).

short-term securities. But the insignificance of b suggests that this influence is short lived.[27] Temporary deviations from the equilibrium structure of yields implied by expectations are quickly erased as investors adjust their portfolios.

OPERATION TWIST. The weakness of the MS theory as an explanation of the term structure has naturally led to its use as a guide to official policy. The United States was faced in the early 1960s by domestic recession and balance of payments deficits. In his Economic Message of February 2, 1961, the President emphasized the importance of "increasing the flow of credit into the capital markets at declining long-term rates of interest to promote domestic recovery," while "checking declines in the short-term rates that directly affect the balance of payments."[28] That is, domestic expansion was to be assisted by encouraging private investment through low long-term yields, and the balance of payments was to be improved through high short-term yields that were expected to attract short-term funds from foreign financial centers.

Easier said than done—unless one believes, consistent with the MS theory, that relative yields to maturity are determined by relative maturities outstanding. By this line of reasoning all that the Treasury and the Federal Reserve had to do to twist the yield curve in the desired manner was to increase the supply of short-term securities available to the public while reducing the supply of long-terms. The plan is illustrated in Figure 19.4, which shows the demands for short terms and long terms (D_S and D_L) to be relatively inelastic positive functions of short-term and long-term yields (Y_S and Y_L). For given numbers of short-term and long-term securities outstanding their dollar values (S_S and S_L) are negative functions of their yields. Beginning with the supply functions S_S^o and S_L^o, initial yields are Y_S^o and Y_L^o. Operation Twist meant that the Treasury was to issue short-term debt to finance deficits and to replace maturing long-term debt and that Federal Reserve open market operations were to emphasize long-term purchases and short-term sales. The intended consequences were an increase in short-term debt (to S_S') and a decrease in long-term debt (to S_L') available to the public, thereby inducing an increase in Y_S to Y_S' and a decrease in Y_L to Y_L'.

Although long-term yields did not fall during the period 1961 to 1964, when Operation Twist was the White House's proclaimed policy, the yield curve did twist in the desired direction, as shown by the Treasury yield curves for January of 1961 to 1965 in Figure 19.5. The Council of Economic Advisors was pleased by the success of its policy

27 G.O. Bierwag and M.A. Grove (1971) also reported that the relative quantities of short-term and long-term debt outstanding had no perceptible effect on the yield curve and concluded that their results, in combination with those of de Leeuw and Modigliani and Sutch, "strengthen the contention that price adjustments in the markets for securities are very rapid."
28 *Economic Report of the President*, January 1962, page 86.

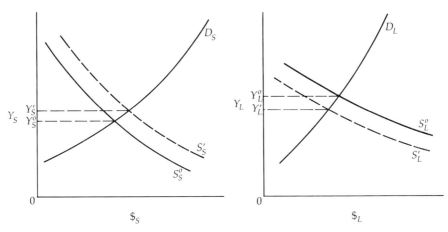

Figure 19.4   Goals of Operation Twist.

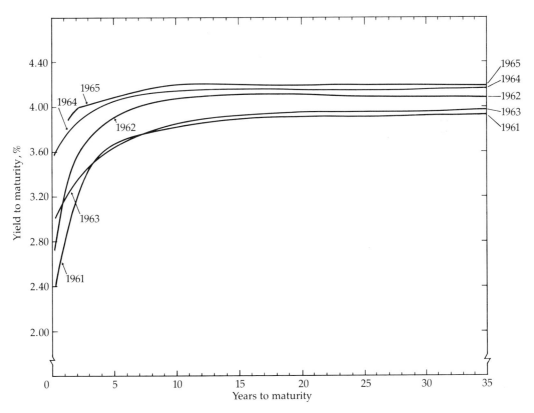

Source: *Treasury Bulletin*, March 1961, February 1962–1965.

Figure 19.5   Operation Twist: Treasury yield curves: end of January 1961 to 1965.

and pointed to the "remarkable stability" of long-term yields during a period of generally rising yields.[29]

Others were unimpressed, for it was common knowledge outside the White House and the Executive Office Building that increases in short-term yields normally exceed those in long-term yields. Franco Modigliani and Richard Sutch (1967), for example, reported that regressive expectations models explained yield curve movements during 1961 to 1964 as well as they had during earlier periods. They need not have bothered, however, for Operation Twist had not in fact been tried. Federal Reserve efforts were half-hearted,[30] and the Treasury acted contrary to declared policy by issuing more long-term than short-term debt. "As a result . . . the maturity of the debt in public hands [was] in fact lengthened appreciably, instead of shortened as the policy would require."[31]

AN INCONSISTENT PEG. The Federal Reserve made a more serious effort to control the term structure during and immediately after World War II. The overriding goal of the Fed's wartime policy was to enable the government to borrow at low interest rates. Specifically the Fed sought to prevent discount rates on T bills from rising above 0.375 percent and to keep yields on long-term government bonds below 2.50 percent.[32] The failure of the United States to recover from the Great Depression, the weakness of private demands throughout the 1930s and into the 1940s, had kept yields at very low levels. But the great increases in government spending and borrowing during the war put strong upward pressures on yields so that the Fed was soon forced to buy all the T bills offered to it at a discount rate of 0.00375, that is, at a price of $99.90625 per $100 face value for 90-day bills.

The large increases in the money supply that resulted from the Fed's open market purchases of bills and other short-term securities kept interest rates generally from fully reflecting inflationary expectations, and long-term government bond yields stayed between 2 and 2.50 percent without direct intervention by the Fed in that end of the market. Investors can never be sure of the duration of any government policy. But for 5 years, between June 1942 and June 1947, the rate of return on T bills was 0.38 percent and investors could be fairly confident of rates of return on long-term bonds above 2 percent in view of the Fed's commitment to prevent significant capital losses on these securities by seeing that their yields did not rise above 2.50 percent. So

---

29 *Economic Report of the President,* January 1966, page 50.

30 Notwithstanding the protestations in their *Annual Reports* for 1963 (pages 12–13) and 1964 (pages 12–13).

31 Harry Johnson (1963, page 286). For other accounts of Operation Twist, see Burton Malkiel (1966, pages 232–237) and Jacob Michaelson (1973, pages 148–149). Best of all, examine the data yourself in the Federal Reserve's *Banking and Monetary Statistics, 1941–70,* pages 884–887.

32 Elmus Wicker (1969) has discussed the formulation and implementation of this policy.

how many T bills do you think the public bought? And what proportion ended up with the Fed? The only surprising consequence of this effort to control more than one price is that the Fed did not end up with all the bills. Private and Fed holdings of T bills and long-term governments in June 1942 and June 1947 are shown in Table 19.6. The proportion of outstanding bills held by the Fed increased from 8 to 92 percent between these dates, with the small and declining amount in private hands being held mainly by commercial banks. These results are broadly consistent with the TE theory,[33] according to which a significant portion of investors (perhaps as many as 92 percent) maximize expected returns, and are highly inconsistent with the MS theory, according to which all investors have pronounced preferences for specific maturities. The MS theory implies a strong tendency for long-term yields to rise relative to the yield on T bills between 1942 and 1947 as a result of the increase in the supply of the former relative to the latter so that the Fed should have had to buy long terms (rather than T bills) to prevent the yield ceilings from being violated.[34]

UNCERTAINTY AND THE TERM STRUCTURE

Uncertainty and the traditional expectations theory

We shall now show how the TE theory must be modified in the presence of uncertainty. The TE theory's statement that long-term yields are averages of current and expected short-term yields depends on the assumption that future yields are known with certainty. The following analysis abandons that assumption and develops a theory of the equilibrium term structure when future yields are uncertain. The analysis proceeds in two stages, the first destructive and the second constructive. We first demonstrate that the TE equation breaks down under uncertainty, and then in the following section we develop and present some simple examples of the modern expectations theory, which is logically valid under both certainty and uncertainty.

The TE theory asserts that all expected holding-period rates of return are equal, regardless of the securities purchased or the lengths of holding periods. This statement cannot be true except under conditions of certainty, as we now illustrate in terms of the simple case considered earlier in Exercise 19.1. The expected one-period rate of return on a two-period single-payment security ($_1R_2^e$) is equal to the

---

33 These results are also consistent with a version of the TP theory in which the required term premium between 3-month and 10-year securities is about 2 percent.

34 However, a believer in the MS theory *and* rational expectations might explain these data as follows: Suppose that all investors are strongly risk averse and that they normally avoid risk by investing in assets that match the maturities of their liabilities. Now suppose that the Fed guarantees rates of return of 2.50 percent on long-term bonds and 0.38 percent on T bills. Both of these securities are now riskless, and all our risk-averse investors, who prefer more return to less, will prefer the bonds. Even if the MS theory explained the yield curve under ordinary conditions, it could not be used as the basis for a policy to control the yield curve, for such a policy removes one of the underpinnings of the theory by altering risk differences between securities.

Table 19.6   Yields and Ownership of Selected U.S. Government
Securities, June 1942 and June 1947

Ownership (billion \$)[a]	T Bills		Long-term Bonds[b]	
	6/42	6/47	6/42	6/47
Private holders	2.3	1.3	12.1	54.7
Federal Reserve	0.2	14.5	0.4	0.1
% held by Fed	8.0	91.8	3.2	0.2
Yields, %[c]	0.38	0.38	2.43	2.22

a End of month.

b More than 10 years to first call.

c Monthly averages of daily figures, on a bond equivalent basis. Bill yields pertain to bills maturing in 3 months.

Source: Federal Reserve Board, *Banking and Monetary Statistics, 1941–1970*, pages 693–694, 720–
721, 884–887.

certain one-period rate of return on a one-period security ($_1R_1^e = Y_1$) if

$$(1 + {}_1R_2^e) = E \frac{{}_1\tilde{P}_1}{P_2} = \frac{E\left(\dfrac{\$100}{1 + {}_1\tilde{Y}_1}\right)}{\dfrac{\$100}{(1 + Y_2)^2}}$$

(19.19)

$$= (1 + Y_2)^2 E\left(\frac{1}{1 + {}_1\tilde{Y}_1}\right) = 1 + Y_1$$

where P_2 and Y_2 are the current price and yield to maturity on the
two-period security and $_1\tilde{P}_1$ and $_1\tilde{Y}_1$ are the price and yield on a
one-period security one period in the future. The tildes ($\sim$) on the last
two variables indicate that they are uncertain. E is the expectations
operator.

Now let us look at two-period returns. The two-period rate of return
on successive one-period securities equals the certain two-period
return on a two-period security if

(19.20) $$(1 + Y_1)\, E(1 + {}_1\tilde{Y}_1) = (1 + Y_2)^2$$

But Equations (19.19) and (19.20) cannot in general both be
true—that is, expected one- and two-period rates of return cannot in
general both be equal for one- and two-period securities—because

(19.21) $$E\frac{1}{(1 + {}_1\tilde{Y}_1)} \geqq \frac{1}{E(1 + {}_1\tilde{Y}_1)}$$

where the equality holds only under certainty.[35] For example suppose $_1\tilde{Y}_1$ is described by a simple probability distribution such that it has a fifty–fifty chance of taking the value 0.05 or 0.15. Then

$$E\left(\frac{1}{1 + {}_1\tilde{Y}_1}\right) = 0.5\left(\frac{1}{1.05}\right) + 0.5\left(\frac{1}{1.15}\right) = \frac{1.10}{(1.05)(1.15)}$$

(19.22)

$$= 0.9110 > 0.9091 = \frac{1}{1.10} = \frac{1}{E(1 + {}_1\tilde{Y}_1)}$$

An intuitive understanding of this inequality is developed below in connection with the modern expectations theory.

The modern expectations (ME) theory

The contradiction inherent in the TE theory in the presence of uncertainty "can be avoided if it is postulated that expected holding period returns are equal only for one specific holding period. The natural choice of holding period is the next basic (i.e., 'shortest') interval."[36] Furthermore, Cox, Ingersoll, and Ross have shown that only this choice of holding period is consistent with equilibrium when trading is continuous and future yields are uncertain. The following discrete example of the Cox-Ingersoll-Ross ME theory will not do full justice to that theory, which is based on infinitely short holding periods. But the qualitative nature of our discrete results are consistent with the precise, continuous-time expression of the theory.

Rearranging Equation (19.19), we see that the expected one-period rates of return on one- and two-period securities are equal (as required by the ME theory) when

(19.23) $$(1 + Y_2)^2 = \frac{(1 + Y_1)}{E\left(\dfrac{1}{1 + {}_1\tilde{Y}_1}\right)} \leq (1 + Y_1)E(1 + {}_1\tilde{Y}_1)$$

where the inequality on the right-hand side of Equation (19.23) indicates that the value of Y_2 implied by the ME theory under uncertainty is less than that implied by the TE theory. Suppose as before that $_1\tilde{Y}_1$ may with equal probabilities be 0.05 or 0.15, and also let $Y_1 = 0.10$. Then the TE theory implies

(19.24) $(1 + Y_2)^2 = (1.10)(1.10) = 1.21$ and $Y_2 = 0.10$

---

35 This is an example of Jensen's inequality, which states that for a random variable x, $E(1/x) \geq 1/Ex$, the equality holding only under certainty. Jensen's inequality was discussed earlier in footnote 12 of Chapter 18.

36 John Cox, Jonathan Ingersoll, and Stephen Ross (1981, page 775).

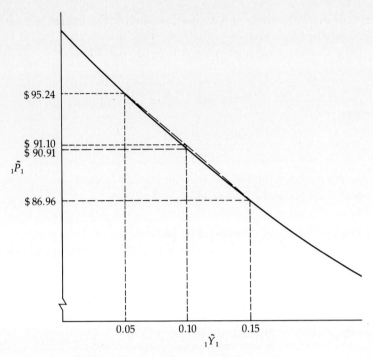

Figure 19.6   Yields and prices of a one-period security.

while the ME theory implies, referring to Equation (19.22),

(19.25)
$$(1 + Y_2)^2 = \frac{1.10}{(1.10)/(1.05)(1.15)}$$

$$= (1.05)(1.15) = 1.2075 \quad \text{and} \quad Y_2 = 0.0989$$

Risk-neutral investors are indifferent between one- and two-period securities under these conditions, according to the ME theory, only if Y_2 is less than the average of current and expected short-term yields. This result may be explained in terms of Figure 19.6, in which the curved line shows the relationship between the price and yield of a one-period security. The fifty–fifty chance of $_1\tilde{Y}_1$ being 0.05 or 0.15 implies a fifty–fifty chance of $_1\tilde{P}_1$ being \$86.96 or \$95.24, with an expected value of $E(_1\tilde{P}_1)$ = \$91.10, which is indicated by the midpoint of the straight line drawn between the two possible values of $_1\tilde{P}_1$ on the function relating $_1\tilde{P}_1$ and $_1\tilde{Y}_1$. On the other hand the certain price of a one-period security with certain yield of $_1Y_1$ = 0.10 is $_1P_1$ = \$90.91.[37] An expected-return maximizer will pay more for a two-period security with a fifty–fifty chance that its price next period will be \$86.96 or

---

[37] Problem 11 at the end of the chapter asks the student to prove that the expected one-period rates of return are 10 percent in both the certain and the uncertain cases presented here.

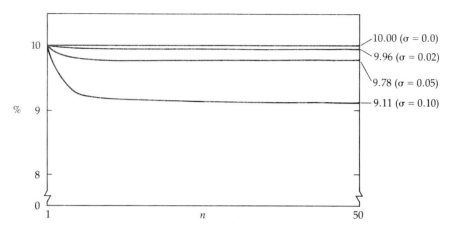

Figure 19.7   Yield curves implied by the ME theory under different degrees of uncertainty when all current and expected one-period yields are 10 percent (the σs are standard deviations of future one-period yields).

$95.24 than for a two-period security with a certain future price of $90.91. That is, current P_2 is more and Y_2 is less in the presence of uncertainty than when future yields are certain. The security is valued more highly under uncertainty than under certainty (if the expected uncertain yield is identical with the certain yield) because the nonlinear relation between yield and price means that upward deviations of $_1\tilde{Y}_1$ from its mean reduce $_1\hat{P}_1$ less than downward deviations of $_1\tilde{Y}_1$ raise $_1\tilde{P}_1$.

Figure 19.7 extends this sample case to equilibrium yields on securities with more than two periods to maturity. The curve denoted $\sigma = 0.05$ exactly corresponds to our example, in which there was a fifty–fifty chance that $_1\tilde{Y}_1$ would deviate from its mean of 0.10 by $+0.05$ or -0.05, that is, take the values 0.15 or 0.05. We see that the yield curve's slope becomes increasingly negative as uncertainty (σ) increases. This is because the expected-return advantages to deviations in future yields increase with the diversity of possible outcomes.[38]

To summarize, in the case in which the current and all expected one-period yields are 10 percent, the yield curve is flat at 10 percent under certainty but slopes downward under uncertainty, the downward slope becoming more pronounced as uncertainty increases.[39] The ME theory thus implies a downward bias in the yield curve. However, this downward bias may be offset or reversed if risk-averse investors

---

38 This may be demonstrated by the answer to problem 12.

39 Figure 19.7 is based on very simple discrete time-independent probability distributions. But Uri Dothan (1978) obtained essentially the same results for a variety of continuous interest rate processes.

with short holding periods require expected-return premiums on long-term securities. In fact the long ends of yield curves have sloped downward about 40 percent of the time during the past 120 years. They have sloped downward about 50 percent of the time if we exclude the continuously rising curves of 1930 to 1960, when yields were at record low levels and investors probably expected yields to rise.[40] So it appears that the downward bias implied by the ME theory and the opposite effect implied by risk aversion and short holding periods have approximately offset each other in the long ends of yield curves. The greatest impact of risk aversion appears to be felt on the short ends of yield curves, which usually slope upward over the first 6 or 12 months to maturity.

A REVIEW OF THE DATA IN LIGHT OF ALTERNATIVE THEORIES OF THE TERM STRUCTURE OF INTEREST RATES

The theories presented above suggest the following explanations of the empirical tendencies listed near the beginning of the chapter.

EMPIRICAL TENDENCY 19.1.   The tendency of yield curves to be upward sloping when yields are low and downward sloping when yields are high is consistent with both the traditional and modern expectations theories in combination with regressive expectations, that is, with TERE and MERE.[41] (This explanation suggests that the ME theory's implied downward bias to the yield curve is offset by expectations of rising yields when yields are low.)

EMPIRICAL TENDENCY 19.1a.   The upward shift of yield curves since the late 1960s is consistent with both TERE and MERE and a rational upward revision of expectations of future yields in response to the return to a paper standard similar to those which on previous occasions have meant increased inflation.

EMPIRICAL TENDENCY 19.2.   The tendency of yield curves to become flat with increasing maturities is also consistent with the TERE and MERE theories. (See Figures 19.3 and 19.7.) This explanation suggests that, although views concerning short-term movements in yields may vary from time to time, people are

---

40 These statements are based on Table 19.4 (for 1862 to 1929) and Figure 19.2 (for 1930 to 1982).

41 The ME theory is logically superior to the TE theory, but the empirical implications of the TE theory—that is to say, that there is no upward or downward bias in the yield curve—may be approximately correct, particularly when uncertainty regarding future yields (for example σ in Figure 19.7) is small.

usually confident that yields will eventually regress to their normal range.[42]

EMPIRICAL TENDENCY 19.3.   The tendency of even high and predominantly downward-sloping yield curves to have positive slopes for short maturities is consistent with the term preference theory when term premiums rise over short maturities but quickly level off.

In conclusion it should be said that the recent behavior of the yield curve has many historical precedents. In particular the short ends of yield curves tend to slope upward as implied by term preferences, whereas long-term yields have been consistent with the traditional and modern expectations theories when yields are expected to regress toward a normal range and the normal range depends on the monetary standard. Unfortunately this still leaves much to be explained because we do not know the full implications of the present standard—and will not know until some sort of consistent government adaptation to its new freedom is perceived by investors.

QUESTIONS

1. Draw a yield curve like that in Figure 19.1, except based on the data in Table 6.2.
2. Which of the Empirical Tendencies 19.1 to 19.3 are illustrated by **(a)** Figure 19.1 and **(b)** Figure 19.2? Please explain.
3. What are the differences between forward and expected yields under the **(a)** TE, **(b)** TP, and **(c)** MS theories?
4. Compare the yield curve in problem 6 to historical yield curves, and discuss the expectations implied by that yield curve.
5. Suppose the TE theory is valid. Are the yield curves in Figures 19.1 and 19.2 consistent with **(a)** extrapolative expectations, **(b)** regressive expectations, or **(c)** both extrapolative and regressive expectations? Please explain.
6. Are regressive expectations rational?

---

42 Unfortunately the tendency for *coupon* yield curves to become flat at long maturities is consistent with *any* pattern of expected yields, and data on long-term yields are almost entirely limited to coupon bonds as in, for example, Figures 19.1 and 19.2. Miles Livingston and Suresh Jain (1982) have demonstrated that coupon bond yield curves become flat with increasing maturities even when future yields are expected to rise without limit. This result is due to "coupon bias," which is the name given to the tendency for coupon yield curves to be flatter than the theoretical discount yield curves discussed in this chapter. Coupon bias arises because coupon bonds are equivalent to bundles of discount bonds so that coupon yields are averages of discount yields. Examples of coupon bias have been presented by Kenneth Garbade (1982, pages 293–299).
   The problem of coupon bias means that an explanation of Empirical Tendency 19.2 requires either more observations on long-term discount bonds (which may in the future be possible if the recent interest in these bonds continues) or a model based on available coupon bonds that is able to disentangle the expectations and coupon bias influences in order to permit the computation of implied discount yield curves.

7. Estimates of Equation (19.17) have usually found significant values of a and have often found significant values of c. Are these results consistent with market efficiency?

8. Estimates of Equation (19.18) have found significant values of c and insignificant values of b. Are these results consistent with market efficiency?

9. Have forward rates been good predictors of future spot rates? What does your answer suggest for market efficiency?

10. Suppose the Treasury decides to refinance maturing short-term debt with long-term debt. How will the shape of the Treasury yield curve be affected by this policy according to the MS, TE, and TP theories?

11. What do you expect the typical yield curve to look like during the next few years? What does your answer suggest for the importance of risk aversion, market segmentation, and the way expectations are formed?

PROBLEMS

1. Suppose $Y_1 = 0.10$ and $_1Y_1^e = 0.05$.
   (a) According to the TE theory what is Y_2?
   (b) Show that expected first-period rates of return are the same for one-period and two-period securities.

2. Suppose the current one-period yield is 2 percent and is expected to rise 1 percent per year during the next 5 years to $_1Y_1^e = 3$ percent, $_2Y_1^e = 4$ percent, ..., $_5Y_1^e = 7$ percent.
   (a) According to the TE theory, what are Y_3 and Y_6?
   (b) Show that expected three-period rates of return are the same for the three-period and six-period securities.

3. Suppose $Y_1 = 0.10$ and $Y_2 = 0.0747$. What is the one-period yield that can be locked in now for next period?

4. Suppose $Y_3 = 0.03$ and $Y_6 = 0.05$. What is the yield on a three-period investment that can be locked in now beginning three periods in the future?

5. Do problems 1(a) and 2(a) using the linear approximation (19.6a).

6. Suppose the dealer asked discounts reported in the paper for 12-, 24-, 36-, and 48-week bills are 8, 9, 8, and 7 percent, respectively. Calculate the 12-week yields expected to prevail 12, 24, and 36 weeks in the future. Give both exact expected yields and linear approximations.

7. T bill discount rates quoted on March 22, 1984, are shown in the accompanying table. Assuming cash delivery, calculate the 12-week yields expected (according to the TE theory) to prevail 12,

24, and 36 weeks in the future. Please present your results in a format like Table 19.1.

U.S. Treas. Bills Mat. date	Bid	Asked	Yield Discount	Mat. date	Bid	Asked	Yield Discount
-1984-				7-26	9.87	9.83	10.31
3-29	8.71	8.57	8.70	8- 2	9.90	9.84	10.34
4- 5	9.04	8.88	9.03	8- 9	9.91	9.85	10.37
4-12	9.22	9.10	9.27	8-16	9.90	9.84	10.38
4-19	9.42	9.36	9.55	8-23	9.90	9.84	10.40
4-26	9.36	9.30	9.51	8-30	9.90	9.86	10.45
5- 3	9.57	9.51	9.74	9- 6	9.92	9.88	10.49
5-10	9.65	9.57	9.82	9-13	9.93	9.89	10.52
5-17	9.69	9.61	9.88	10- 4	9.96	9.90	10.57
5-24	9.67	9.61	9.90	11- 1	9.98	9.92	10.61
5-31	9.66	9.60	9.91	11-29	9.98	9.92	10.65
6- 7	9.70	9.62	9.95	12-27	9.96	9.90	10.67
6-14	9.76	9.72	10.07	-1985-			
6-21	9.79	9.77	10.15	1-24	9.73	9.69	10.48
6-28	9.82	9.76	10.15	2-21	9.93	9.85	10.73
7- 5	9.84	9.80	10.22	3-21	9.95	9.93	10.89
7-12	9.85	9.81	10.25				
7-19	9.86	9.82	10.28				

8. Suppose the "correct" theory of the term structure is the TP theory as stated in Equations (19.12) and (19.13). Using the estimates of term premiums in Table 19.2 and assuming 12, 24, and 36 weeks are "close enough" to 3, 6, and 9 months, what are the correct expected short-term yields implied by the observed yields in problem 6?

9. Referring to Exercise 19.3, suppose Martians expect 1-year yields to change three-fifths of the distance between the normal yield and the yield at the beginning of the year.
   (a) What are the 1-year yields expected to prevail in 1985, 1986, and 1987?
   (b) What are the yields on 2-, 3-, and 4-year securities in 1984?

10. Referring to Exercise 19.4, suppose Martians expect 1-year yields to change three-fifths of the distance between the normal yield and the yield at the beginning of the year.
   (a) What are the 1-year yields expected to prevail in 2002, 2003, and 2004?
   (b) What are the yields on 2-, 3-, and 4-year securities in 2001?

11. Prove that expected one-period rates of return are 10 percent in both the certain and the uncertain cases discussed in connection with Figure 19.6. (*Hint.* The first step is to derive current P_2 in the certain and uncertain cases.)

12. Suppose the ME example discussed in connection with Figure 19.6 had specified $Y_1 = 0.10$ (as before) and possible values for $_1\tilde{Y}_1$ of 0 and 0.20, with equal probabilities.
   (a) According to the ME theory what is the equilibrium Y_2 corresponding to these data?
   (b) Why is the equilibrium Y_2 less in this problem than in the example presented in the text?
   (c) Show that the expected one-period rates of return on the one- and two-period securities are equal.

REFERENCES

G. O. Bierwag and M. A. Grove, "A Model of the Structure of Prices of Marketable U.S. Treasury Securities," *Journal of Money, Credit and Banking,* August 1971, pages 605–629.

Michael D. Bordo, "The Classical Gold Standard: Some Lessons for Today," Federal Reserve Bank of St. Louis *Review,* May 1981, pages 2–17.

John C. Cox, Jonathan E. Ingersoll, and Stephen A. Ross, "A Reexamination of Traditional Hypotheses about the Term Structure of Interest Rates," *Journal of Finance,* September 1981, pages 769–799.

John M. Culbertson, "The Term Structure of Interest Rates," *Quarterly Journal of Economics,* November 1957, pages 485–517.

Frank de Leeuw, "A Model of Financial Behavior," in J. S. Duesenberry *et al.* (eds.), *The Brookings Quarterly Econometric Model of the United States,* Rand McNally, Chicago, 1965, pages 464–530.

Davis R. Dewey, *Financial History of the United States,* 12th ed., Longmans, Green, and Co., New York, 1936.

L. Uri Dothan, "On the Term Structure of Interest Rates," *Journal of Financial Economics,* March 1978, pages 59–69.

David Durand, *Basic Yields of Corporate Bonds, 1900–1942,* National Bureau of Economic Research Technical Paper 3, Washington, 1942.

David Durand, "A Quarterly Series of Corporate Bond Yields, 1952–1957, and Some Attendant Reservations," *Journal of Finance,* September 1958, pages 348–356.

David Durand and Willis J. Winn, *Basic Yields of Bonds, 1926–1947: Their Measurement and Pattern,* National Bureau of Economic Research Technical Paper 6, Washington, 1947.

Eugene F. Fama, "Inflation Uncertainty and Expected Returns on Treasury Bills," *Journal of Political Economy,* June 1976, pages 427–448.

Eugene F. Fama, "Forward Rates as Predictors of Future Spot Rates," *Journal of Financial Economics,* October 1976, pages 361–377.

Irving Fisher, "Appreciation and Interest," *Publications of the American Economic Association,* vol. 11, August 1896.

Irving Fisher, *The Theory of Interest,* Macmillan, New York, 1930.

Milton Friedman and Anna J. Schwartz, *A Monetary History of the United States, 1867–1960,* Princeton University Press, Princeton, NJ, 1963.

Kenneth Garbade, *Securities Markets,* McGraw-Hill, New York, 1982.

Michael J. Hamburger and Elliott N. Platt, "The Expectations Hypothesis and the Efficiency of the Treasury Bill Market," *Review of Economics and Statistics,* May 1975, pages 190–199.

J. R. Hicks, *Value and Capital,* 2nd ed., Clarendon Press, Oxford, 1946.

Sidney Homer, *A History of Interest Rates,* 2nd ed., Rutgers University Press, New Brunswick, NJ, 1977.

Harry G. Johnson, "An Overview of Price Levels, Employment, and the U.S. Balance of Payments," *Journal of Business,* July 1963, pages 279–289.

J. M. Keynes, *The General Theory of Employment, Interest and Money,* Harcourt Brace, New York, 1936.

Miles Livingston and Suresh Jain, "Flattening of Bond Yield Curves for Long Maturities," *Journal of Finance,* March 1982, pages 157–167.

Axel Leijonhufvud, "Rational Expectations and Monetary Institutions," UCLA Department of Economics, Working Paper 302, September 1983.

F. A. Lutz, "The Structure of Interest Rates," *Quarterly Journal of Economics,* November 1940, pages 36–63.

Frederick R. Macaulay, *Some Theoretical Problems Suggested by the Movements of Interest Rates, Bond Yields and Stock Prices in the United States since 1856,* National Bureau of Economic Research, New York, 1938.

Burton G. Malkiel, *The Term Structure of Interest Rates,* Princeton University Press, Princeton, NJ, 1966.

J. Huston McCulloch, "An Estimate of the Liquidity Premium," *Journal of Political Economy,* February 1975, pages 95–119.

David Meiselman, *The Term Structure of Interest Rates,* Prentice-Hall, Englewood Cliffs, NJ, 1962.

Jacob B. Michaelson, *The Term Structure of Interest Rates,* Intext Educational Publishers, New York, 1973.

Franco Modigliani and Richard C. Sutch, "Innovations in Interest Rate Policy," *American Economic Review,* May 1966, pages 178–197.

Franco Modigliani and Richard C. Sutch, "Debt Management and the Term Structure of Interest Rates: An Empirical Analysis of Recent Experience," *Journal of Political Economy,* August 1967, pages 569–589.

National Monetary Commission, *Statistics for the U.S., 1867–1909,* Government Printing Office, Washington, 1910.

Charles R. Nelson, *The Term Structure of Interest Rates,* Basic Books, New York, 1972.

Soo-Bin Park, "Spot and Forward Rates in the Canadian Treasury Bill Market," *Journal of Financial Economics,* March 1982, pages 107–114.

Alan Reynolds, "Why Gold?," *Cato Journal,* Spring 1983, pages 211–232.

Richard Roll, *The Behavior of Interest Rates: An Application of the Efficient Market Model to U.S. Treasury Bills,* Basic Books, New York, 1970.

James C. Van Horne, *Financial Market Rates and Flows,* Prentice-Hall, Englewood Cliffs, NJ, 1978.

Elmus R. Wicker, "The World War II Policy of Fixing a Pattern of Interest Rates," *Journal of Finance,* June 1969, pages 447–458.

John H. Wood, "Are Yield Curves Normally Upward Sloping? The Term Structure of Interest Rates, 1862–1982," Federal Reserve Bank of Chicago *Economic Perspectives,* July/August 1983, pages 17–23.

A MACROECONOMIC MODEL OF INTEREST RATES AND INFLATION

The emitting of paper money by the authority of the government is wisely prohibited to the individual States by the National Constitution; and the spirit of that prohibition ought not to be disregarded by the Government of the United States. Though paper emissions, under a general authority, might have some advantages not applicable, and be free from some disadvantages which are applicable, to the like emissions by the States, separately, yet they are of a nature so liable to abuse—and, it may even be affirmed, so certain of being abused,—that the wisdom of the government will be shown in never trusting itself with the use of so seducing and dangerous an expedient. In times of tranquillity it might have no ill consequence,—it might even perhaps be managed in a way to be productive of good; but in great and trying emergencies there is almost a moral certainty of its becoming mischievous. The stamping of paper is an operation so much easier than the laying of taxes, that a government in the practice of paper emissions would rarely fail, in any such emergency, to indulge itself too far in the employment of that resource, to avoid, as much as possible, one less auspicious to present popularity.

Alexander Hamilton, *Report on a National Bank*, 1790

THE DETERMINANTS OF INTEREST RATES AND INFLATION

This chapter brings together within a unified framework the factors affecting interest rates and inflation that we have considered so far. These factors, the chapters in which they were introduced, and the symbols used to identify them in this chapter are listed in Table 20.1. Real rates of interest are determined by the spending and saving decisions of households, firms, and governments. The decisions of households and nonfinancial firms, including their responses to real rates of interest, were discussed in Chapters 14 and 15 after we saw in the national income and flow of funds accounts of Chapter 13 how these sectors are related to each other and to other market participants. No model of government behavior was presented because none that satisfactorily accounts for the several important government influences on real interest rates—including the governments' countercyclical monetary and fiscal policies, its role as provider of goods and services, its enforcement of redistributions of income, and its tax policies to induce the reallocation of resources—has appeared. The best we can do is describe what government has done and attempt to understand and explain the effects it has had. The latter portions of this chapter are devoted to these tasks.

But there is more to the story than real interest rates. To explain nominal interest rates, we must add inflationary expectations, which

Table 20.1   Factors Determining Interest Rates Brought Together in This Chapter

Chapters	Symbols	Factors Determining Real Interest Rates (r)
13	$S + T = I + G$ $S + T + \Delta M = I + G + \Delta L$	The national income and flow of funds accounts showed that supplies and demands for goods must add up (i.e., $S + T = I + G$), and so must supplies and demands for funds (i.e., $S + T + \Delta M = I + G + \Delta L$). We abstract from the foreign sector in this chapter and so have not shown exports and imports.
14	S	Saving, especially by households.
15	I	Investment, especially by firms.
20	T, G	Government taxes and spending.

Chapters	Symbols	Factors Determining Inflation (p) and Nominal Interest Rates (R)[a]
3	L	The demand for money by households and firms.
9	M	The supply of money as determined by interactions among the Federal Reserve, commercial banks, nonbank depository institutions, households, firms, and governments.
18, 19	$R = r + p$	Inflationary expectations. The equilibrium nominal interest rate (R) is approximately the sum of the expected real rate of return (r) and the expected rate of inflation (p).

a In addition to those listed in the top portion of the table.

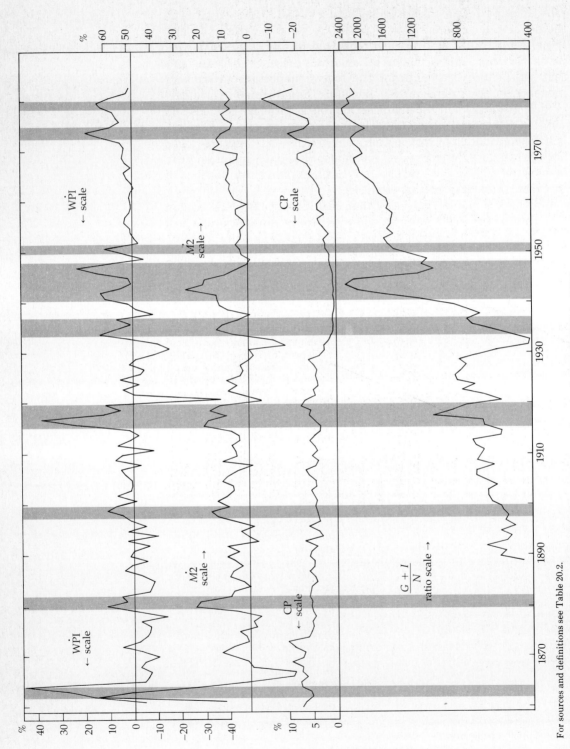

For sources and definitions see Table 20.2.

Figure 20.1   Money, prices, interest rates, and fluctuations in demand, 1860 to 1983.

were discussed in Chapters 18 and 19. Finally the model is completed by the principal determinants of inflation—the supply and demand for money—which were discussed in Chapters 3 and 9.

Most of the discussion in this book has been *micro*economic in the sense that decision makers have made choices given the prices and interest rates with which they were confronted. Households decided between current and future consumption, and firms decided how much investment to undertake partly on the basis of expected real rates of interest that they *individually* were unable to influence. This chapter is *macro*economic in the sense that it shows how individual (micro) units combine to determine prices and interest rates. We want to present a model that is consistent with American experience. Therefore it will be useful to begin by describing the patterns of inflation and interest rates as they have been observed in the United States.

MONEY, PRICES, INTEREST RATES, DEFICITS, AND DEMANDS, 1860 TO 1983

Using the symbols in Table 20.1 and adding $\dot{M}$ and $\dot{D}$ to represent rates of change of money and the federal debt, several strong and long-lived relationships may be described as follows:

> **EMPIRICAL TENDENCY 20.1.** $\dot{M}$, p, and G and/or I tend to rise and fall together.

> **EMPIRICAL TENDENCY 20.2.** R responds slowly and incompletely to p so that realized r varies inversely with p, and the correlation of R with the price level P (the "Gibson relation") is higher than the correlation of R with the rate of inflation p (the "Fisher relation").

> **EMPIRICAL TENDENCY 20.3.** $\dot{M}$ and $\dot{D}$ have a substantial positive correlation.

Some of these tendencies are depicted in Figure 20.1, which measures inflation by the rate of change of the Wholesale Price Index (WPI), the rate of change of money by the rate of change of the "broad" money stock ($M2$),[1] interest rates by the yield on high-grade commercial paper (CP), and I and G by private investment and government purchases of goods and services in 1972 dollars. N is population so that spending is expressed in real per capita terms.

---

1 We have used the Federal Reserve's pre-1979 definition of $M2$, that is, currency and all commercial bank deposits owned by the nonbank public, because data on the "narrow" money supply, $M1$, that is, currency and checking accounts, is not available before 1915. We have used $M2$ in all parts of Figure 20.1 and Table 20.2 for consistency, but the results based on $M1$ after 1915 are not substantially different from those shown for $M2$.

Estimates of I and G are available on an annual basis only as far back as 1889, and we have had to express $(G + I)/N$ in logarithms in order to keep the space required for this series within reasonable bounds.

Correlations between these and other variables are listed in Table 20.2. The first matrix in the table shows correlations between the variables for which there are data as far back as 1860. The rate of change of the federal deficit, $\dot{D}$, is not shown in Figure 20.1, but it was high during all but two of the shaded (that is, high inflation) portions of the figure, the exceptions being the periods 1880 to 1882 and 1950 and 1951. A long-term yield, RR, has also been added to the table.

We now discuss a few of the interesting features of Figure 20.1 and Table 20.2.

Table 20.2   Correlations between Money, Prices, Interest Rates, Deficits, and Demands, 1860 to 1983 (Annual Data)

	WPI	$\dot{\text{WPI}}$	$\dot{M}2$	RR	CP	$\dot{D}$
WPI	1					
$\dot{\text{WPI}}$	0.27	1				
$\dot{M}2$	0.07	0.57	1			
RR	0.54	0.04	0.01	1		
CP	0.40	0.06	−0.02	0.87	1	
$\dot{D}$	0.08	0.38	0.58	0.11	0.00	1

1860–1983

	WPI	$\dot{\text{WPI}}$	$\dot{M}2$	RR	CP	$\dot{D}$	$(G + I)/N$	I/N	
WPI	1	*0.59*	*0.47*	*0.95*	*0.86*	*0.77*	*0.73*	*0.73*	
$\dot{\text{WPI}}$	0.26	1	*0.45*	*0.58*	*0.70*	*0.23*	*0.64*	*0.68*	
$\dot{M}2$	0.16	0.55	1	*0.52*	*0.43*	*0.48*	*0.74*	*0.74*	
RR	0.69	0.13	0.08	1	*0.93*	*0.70*	*0.80*	*0.76*	
CP	0.51	0.12	0.04	0.88	1	*0.45*	*0.77*	*0.76*	**1953–1983**
$\dot{D}$	0.11	0.28	0.33	0.07	−0.01	1	*0.54*	*0.50*	
$(G + I)/N$	0.88	0.26	0.34	0.44	0.29	0.13	1	*0.70*	
I/N	0.66	0.25	0.23	0.51	0.58	0.27	0.62	1	

1889–1983

WPI, Wholesale Price Index

$\dot{\text{WPI}}$, rate of change of the Wholesale Price Index

$\dot{M}2$, rate of change of the "broad money supply": currency and all commercial bank deposits owned by the nonbank public

RR, yield on high-grade railroad bonds until 1930; Moody's Aaa corporate bond yield beginning in 1931

CP, yield on 3- to 6-month commercial paper

$\dot{D}$, rate of change of the gross federal debt held by the public

$(G + I)/N$, the sum of real per capita government purchases of goods and services and gross private domestic investment

I/N, real per capita gross private domestic investment

All data except RR and CP are logarithms or changes in logarithms.

Sources: *Historical Statistics of the United States; Long-term Economic Growth; National Income and Product Accounts of the United States, 1929–76; Survey of Current Business; Federal Reserve Bulletin;* Milton Friedman and Anna Schwartz, *Monetary Statistics of the United States,* National Bureau of Economic Research, New York, 1970.

$\dot{M}$ AND p. The high correlation between the rates of change of money and prices has for hundreds of years been one of the most reliable empirical economic relations. Table 20.2 shows this correlation to be 0.57 during the period 1860 to 1983. The most striking inflationary periods in the chart are the Civil War, World Wars I and II and the succeeding 2 or 3 years, and the 1970s and 1980s. The jagged price experience of 1941 to 1948 may have been due to the growing effectiveness of rationing and price controls during 1943 to 1945 and then to their removal following the war. Other substantial inflations occurred during: 1880 to 1882, when the United States experienced large balance-of-trade surpluses and inflows of gold due to "accidents of weather that produced two successive years of bumper crops in the United States and unusually short crops elsewhere";[2] 1898 and 1899, during and immediately following the Spanish-American War; 1934 and 1935, during the abortive recovery from the Great Depression; and 1950 and 1951, during the Korean War. These inflationary periods have been shaded on the chart. All rapid inflations have been accompanied by substantial monetary growth, $(\dot{M}2)$. Furthermore, severe deflations have been accompanied by marked declines in $(\dot{M}2)$. That is, there has been a very strong positive correlation between *large* variations in $(\dot{WPI})$ and $(\dot{M}2)$. Small changes in $(\dot{M}2)$ and $(\dot{WPI})$ are a different story. The relations between money and prices, even in the absence of rationing and price controls, are not sufficiently firm and rapid that small variations in money always produce immediate responses in prices. For example, during the period of greatest monetary and price stability in American history, 1953 to 1970, the correlation between $(\dot{M}2)$ and $(\dot{WPI})$ was -0.01. (The 1953 to 1970 period is not shown separately in Table 20.2.)

R, P, p, AND r. Figure 20.1 and Table 20.2 repeat part of the story told in Chapter 18. Specifically interest rates have tended to be less volatile than inflation so that their contemporaneous correlations have usually been small. For example notice the correlations of 0.06 and 0.12 between CP and $(\dot{WPI})$ during 1860 to 1983 and 1889 to 1983. However, notice that the correlations between $(\dot{WPI})$ and interest rates were much higher during 1953 to 1983 (0.58 and 0.70 for long and short rates, respectively). These correlations were very much influenced by the stable 1953 to 1970 period, during which interest rates were able to keep pace with inflation. Notice that interest rates were strongly correlated with the price *level*, WPI, in every case. This is the *Gibson relation,* which is consistent with a slow response of interest rates to changes in the rate of inflation.[3]

---

2 Milton Friedman and Anna Schwartz (1963, page 98).

3 Pictures of the Gibson relation in Great Britain for a long rate since 1729 and for a short rate since 1824 may be seen in Figure 18.1. The equivalence of this relation with a process in which interest rates adjust slowly to changes in the rate of inflation was demonstrated by Equation (18.8).

I/N AND *(G + I)/N*. We saw in Chapters 13 to 15 that federal government expenditures *(G)* and private investment *(I)* were the most volatile components of aggregate demand. Private consumption and state and local government spending have been remarkably stable proportions of the incomes of those sectors. Since increases in *G* and *I* are nearly always associated with increases in government and business borrowing, we should expect both inflation and interest rates to be positively correlated with *G + I*. Table 20.2 shows these correlations when *G* and *I* are measured in real per capita terms. As expected, the correlations are positive and, during 1953 to 1983, quite high. Because changes in *G* often dominate those in the sum of *G* and *I*, especially in wartime, it might be thought that correlations with *(G + I)/N* are in effect correlations with *G/N*. However, the correlations of *I/N* in Table 20.2 are in most cases similar to those for *(G + I)/N*.

$\dot{M}$ AND $\dot{D}$. All the correlations between government deficits and rates of change of the money stock are substantial. What can we add in explanation to what Alexander Hamilton and many others have already said?

The following sections develop a macroeconomic framework within which the causes of Empirical Tendencies 20.1 to 20.3 may be explained.

A MODEL OF PRICES AND INTEREST RATES[4]

Consider a system with markets for

1. Labor
2. Commodities
3. Money
4. Nonmoney financial instruments

---

4 The graphical approach used here, which has been adapted from Don Patinkin (1965) and George Horwich (1957, 1966), is less popular than the *IS-LM* exposition of J. R. Hicks. But we believe that the use of two diagrams permits us to analyze separate events in the commodity and money markets, as well as interrelationships between these markets, more clearly than is possible with *IS* and *LM* "loci of equilibria." Furthermore, our approach allows us to observe and distinguish between equilibria and disequilibria more easily than is possible with *IS-LM* models, which are usually limited to hybrid temporary equilibria. It is just not possible to be clear about the inflationary process, which is bound up with the interrelationships between the commodity and money markets, in an *IS-LM* framework.

Our framework might be called a "two-diagram loanable funds" model, in which the supplies and demands for funds arising from savings and investment are shown in one diagram and those arising from shifts in the supply and demand for money are shown in the other diagram. This approach permits us to determine the price level in addition to the rate of interest and the equilibrium quantity of lending that are determined in loanable funds models.

We shall handle these markets in the following ways:

The labor market

In order to be able to concentrate on prices and interest rates, we assume the labor market to be continuously in equilibrium at the *natural level of employment,* which is consistent with the *natural rate of aggregate output, Y.* These "natural" values of employment and output are modern names for what used to be called "long-run equilibrium" values. The system only *tends* toward these natural, or long-run equilibrium, values. But for simplicity we shall assume that in the cases of labor and output these values are maintained continuously. This allows us to isolate the direct impacts of events in the other three markets on prices and interest rates.

The commodity market

The commodity market is depicted in Figure 20.2(a). The demand for investment goods, $I^d = I(r, Y)$, is shown as an inverse function of the real rate of interest, r. Desired saving, $S^d = S(r, Y)$, is shown as a positive function of r. These functions are conditional upon the fixed rate of output, Y. If Y were to change, the S and I functions would shift, causing a change in the equilibrium real rate of interest.

In a later section of this chapter government expenditures and taxes will be added to the commodity market. But for the present, in Figure 20.2(a), the commodity market is in equilibrium when the aggregate private demand for investment and consumption goods and services

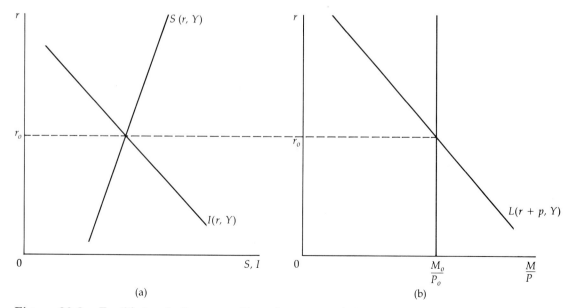

Figure 20.2   Equilibrium in the commodity and money markets.

(called "commodities" for short) equals the total supply of commodities, that is, equals total output, Y. Let the demands for consumption and investment goods be written

(20.1) $C^d = C(r, Y)$ and $I^d = I(r, Y)$

Aggregate demand equals aggregate supply when

(20.2) $C^d + I^d = Y$

Subtracting C^d from both sides of Equation (20.2) and remembering that saving is unconsumed income and aggregate income equals aggregate output, we have

(20.3) $I^d = S^d$ or $I(r, Y) = S(r, Y)$ because $S^d = Y - C^d$

We know from our discussion of the national income accounts in Chapter 13 that *actual* saving and investment are by definition always equal.[5] But equilibrium exists only when *desired* values equal actual values. This happens, according to Equation (20.3), when desired investment equals desired saving, where "desired" saving and investment are merely ways of referring to the "demands" for saving and investment. For a given rate of output, Y, the equilibrium real rate of interest is the value of r for which desired saving and investment are equal. The equilibrium real rate in Figure 20.2 is r_o.

The money market

The money market is depicted in Figure 20.2(b). The real demand for money, $(M/P)^d$, is shown as an inverse function, $L(r + p, Y)$, of the nominal rate of interest, $R = r + p$. The real demand for money is a positive function of Y although, as stated above, Y is held fixed in our analysis.[6] All the analyses of inflation in this chapter start from positions of stable prices and zero inflationary expectations, $p = 0$, for which $R = r$. The real demand for money in Figure 20.2 has been drawn as a function of the real rate of interest with such a position in mind. However, once inflationary or deflationary processes get underway, we

---

5 Equations (20.2) and (20.3) are equivalent to Equations (13.2) and (13.3) except that the former are in real terms and describe *desired* consumption and investment whereas the latter are in nominal (money) terms and represent *actual* consumption and investment.

6 There are two differences between $L(r + p, Y)$ in Figure 20.2(b) and the demand-for-money functions in Chapter 3. First, instead of the nonlinear square-root curves in Chapter 3, we have made the artist's life a bit easier by using a straight-line demand function. Second, instead of showing the demand for money as a function of the difference between the nominal rates of interest on money substitutes and money, $R_s - R_m$, as in Chapter 3, it is shown in Figure 20.2(b) as a function of a single nominal rate of interest, $R = r + p$. We have assumed that the rate of interest on money is zero and that nominal interest rates on all other financial instruments can be summarized by a single index rate, "the" rate of interest, R.

shall have to take account of shifts in the demand for money caused by changes in p.

The supply of money in real terms is indicated by the vertical line in Figure 20.2(b). The nominal money supply is

$$(20.4) \qquad\qquad M = mH$$

where m is the money multiplier and H is high-powered money. We assume m to be constant and H to be controlled by the Federal Reserve, principally through open market operations.[7]

Although the Federal Reserve determines the nominal supply of money, M, the public is interested in its real money holdings, M/P. That is, the demand for money is in real terms so that the dimensions of the horizontal axis in Figure 20.2(b) must be in real money balances and we must express the supply of money in real terms. This means that changes in both M and P cause shifts in the vertical line.

Given the price level, P, and rates of output, Y, and inflationary expectations, p, the intersection of the real demand, $L(r + p, Y)$, and supply, M/P, of money determine the real rate of interest consistent with equilibrium in the money market. (Given p and equilibrium r, we have equilibrium $R = r + p$.) This is shown as r_o in Figure 20.2(b), assuming $Y =$ the constant natural rate of output, $p = 0$, $M = M_o$, and $P = P_o$. *General equilibrium* prevails when the same real rate of interest equilibrates both the commodity and money markets. Figure 20.2 depicts a position of general equilibrium.

The bond market

The market for nonmoney financial instruments, which for brevity we call the "bond market," is not shown explicitly in Figure 20.2. But the bond market is implicit in the commodity and money markets as shown in Figure 20.2 and our assumption of continuous equilibrium in the labor market. For example, if an increase (upward shift) in the demand for investment goods, $I(r, Y)$,[8] is not accompanied by any other shift in the commodity or money markets (that is, in the saving schedule or in the supply or demand for money), that shift must be matched by an equivalent shift in the bond market because we have assumed no disturbances in the labor market. Describing this example another way, if an increase in the demand for investment goods is not financed by a decrease in the demand for consumption goods (that is, by an increase in desired saving), a reduction in the demand for money, an increase in the supply of money, an increase in the supply of

7 The money supply is independent of interest rates and therefore is a vertical function as shown in Figure 20.2(b) if the Fed does not respond to interest rates in determining H and the money multiplier is not responsive to interest rates. The former assumption will be modified below when we consider monetary policy.

8 Such a shift is shown in Figure 20.5.

labor, or a decrease in the demand for labor, then it must be financed in the bond market—by either an increase in the supply of bonds or a reduction in the demand for bonds. This is merely an application of the point stressed in Chapter 13 that total funds obtained must equal total funds supplied. Net financial investments must sum to zero.

We shall analyze the effects of several disturbances (shifts) in the commodity and money markets. All these disturbances will be accompanied by shifts in the bond market, which therefore forms an integral part of our analysis even though it has not been given a picture of its own.

THE WORKINGS OF THE MODEL: DISTURBANCES IN THE MONEY MARKET

Starting with a stable-price situation in which inflationary expectations are zero, the general equilibrium of our system is achieved when the following equations are satisfied:

(20.5) $$S(r, Y) = I(r, Y)$$

(20.6) $$\frac{M}{P} = L(r, Y)$$

Equations (20.5) and (20.6) describe the conditions of stable-price equilibrium in the commodity and money markets, respectively. Our system of two equations may be solved for the two unknowns, r and P, subject to the "givens" imposed on the system. These givens are the saving (S), investment (I), and money-demand (L) functions, the money supply (M), and the natural rate of output (Y). The workings of the model will be illustrated by analyses of the effects of shifts in I, L, and M. This section is concerned with the last two, that is, with shifts in the demand and supply of money.

Disturbance A: a Federal Reserve open market purchase

We start from an initial position of general equilibrium such as that depicted by Figure 20.2 or by the solid lines in Figure 20.3, in which the same real rate of interest, r_o, is consistent with equilibrium in both the commodity and money markets. Now suppose the Federal Reserve engages in an open market purchase that augments bank reserves and, through the money multiplier, the quantity of money. The result is a once-and-for-all increase in the money supply from the initial value of M_o to M'. We assume no further change in the money supply and proceed to examine the effects of this open market purchase on r and P.

In executing its open market purchase, the Federal Reserve Bank of New York bids bond prices up, that is, bids interest rates down.

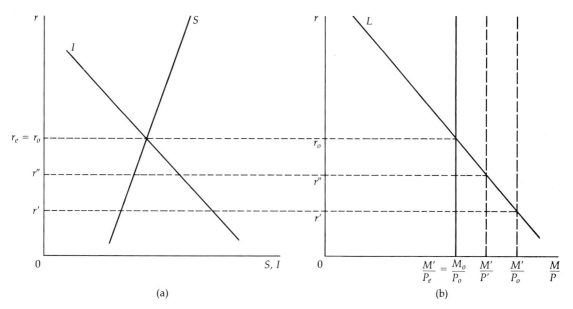

Figure 20.3   Disturbance *A*: an increase in the money supply.

Interest rates are further reduced as banks compete to lend their newly acquired excess reserves. Assuming, at first, no change in the price level, P_o, or in the expected rate of inflation, $p = 0$, the real rate of interest that equilibrates the money market falls from r_o to r'. This is the point at which the real demand for money, L, equals the new real supply of money, M'/P_o.

We now come to the most crucial assumption underlying our dynamic analysis of the system's adjustments to disturbances: We assume that, *although r is in the long run determined in the commodity market, it is dominated in the short run by events in the money market.* In the long run r is determined by productivity and thrift—by the productivity of investments in steel mills in Pittsburgh, hog farms in Iowa, cotton fields in Mississippi, and lumber mills in Oregon and by the willingness, or unwillingness, of people to save in order to lend to those seeking funds for investment projects. Southern Manhattan and other money centers exist chiefly to facilitate the movement of money from savers to investors. Dealers in these centers cannot for long combat the real forces of productivity and thrift in Pittsburgh and Oregon that cause equilibrium real rates to rise or fall. However, short-term movements in interest rates are dominated by fluctuations in the supply and demand for money, that is, by shifts— often very large, rapid, and highly publicized shifts—between money and other financial instruments.

In terms of the notation of Figures 20.2 and 20.3, r is determined in the long run by S and I but in the short run by L and M/P. The difference between short-run effects can be explained by the relative sizes of the money and commodity markets. The money market is in the main a market for the exchange of existing financial assets. The current value of these exceeds $20 trillion. Saving and investment, on the other hand, amount to "only" about $500 billion annually.[9] That is, new financial instruments coming onto the financial markets as the result of productivity and thrift amount over the course of a year to only about 2 percent of existing financial instruments. During an average week the ratio is about one-twentieth of 1 percent. In short, although fluctuations in productivity and thrift exert substantial influences on market rates of interest, those influences are often, even usually, in the short run dwarfed by fluctuations in the money supply and shifts by bulls and bears between existing assets.

Now let's return to the immediate impact of the open market operation shown in Figure 20.3(b). The new money market equilibrium occurs at the rate r', at which the real demand for money equals the new real supply of money. But this is only a *temporary money market equilibrium* because r' is not consistent with equilibrium in the commodity market. Nothing has happened to alter the S and I functions; so the real rate that equilibrates this market remains at r_o. The process by which r returns to r_o may be described as follows.

Notice that at r' desired investment exceeds desired saving. This means an excess demand for commodities, which causes dwindling inventories, unfilled orders, and rising prices. Suppose the price level rises from P_o to P' so that real money balances fall from M'/P_o to M'/P'. We now have an excess demand for money. That is, L exceeds M'/P' at r'. At the higher price level, P', people require more money to finance transactions. In their efforts to shift from bonds to money they bid bond prices down and interest rates up until a new temporary equilibrium is reached at r'', at which the real demand for money equals the new real supply, M'/P'. Again the rate of interest is determined in the money market. But again this is only a temporary equilibrium, for r'' is still below r_o.

At r'' there is still an excess demand for goods, although less than at r'. Prices continue to rise, causing further reductions in real money balances until we reach the point at which M'/P_e equals the real demand for money at the equilibrium real rate of interest, r_e. This is the rate at which desired saving equals desired investment and there is no further inducement for prices to rise. This new equilibrium is in real terms equivalent to the equilibrium existing before the Fed's open market purchase. The new equilibrium real rate of interest, r_e, is identical with the initial equilibrium rate, r_o. And the new level of real money balances, M'/P_e, is identical with that with which we started. The price level has risen in the same proportion as the money supply, causing M/P to be the same in the new as in the original equilibrium.

---

9 These data are based on the Federal Reserve's flow of funds accounts.

The chain of events in the adjustment process may be summarized as follows:

$$(20.7) \qquad \uparrow M \rightarrow \downarrow r \rightarrow \uparrow(I - S) \rightarrow \uparrow P \rightarrow \downarrow \frac{M}{P} \rightarrow \uparrow r$$

That is, the increase in M caused a decline in r, an increase in desired investment relative to desired saving, rising prices, and falling real money balances, which reversed the decline in r. (For simplicity we refer to desired investment and saving simply as I and S.) The Fed's action caused M/P to rise and r to fall for a while. But the public had its way eventually. The Fed's only lasting impact was on the price level. The public's attitudes toward saving, investing, and the demand for money ultimately determined the real rate of interest and the real supply of money. Since in our example the public's preferences did not change, equilibrium real values were not altered.

We have so far neglected the effects of inflationary expectations, p, on the adjustment process. If p responds positively to rises in the price level, inflation will accelerate, but the return of r to its equilibrium value, r_o, may be slowed. We know that an increase in p (which for given r means an increase in the nominal rate of interest, $R = r + p$) causes a reduction in the real demand for money. This would be reflected in Figure 20.3 by a leftward shift in L. We have not drawn the shift in order to keep the figure simple. But a reduction in L slows the upward movement of r and therefore slows the elimination of excess commodity demands. None of this affects the final outcome. Rising prices eventually cause M/P to fall sufficiently and r to rise sufficiently to eliminate the excess demand for commodities. The new stable-price equilibrium is that in Figure 20.3, for which $r = r_o = r_e$ and $P = P_e$.

Disturbance B: an increase in the demand for money

Suppose that for some reason people wish to hold greater average real money balances relative to transactions. This change in behavior is reflected in the rightward shift of L from L_o to L' in Figure 20.4. The increased demand for money might have been caused, for example, by new regulations that add to the costs of shifting between money and money substitutes.

The immediate impact of this disturbance is a rise in r from the initial equilibrium value of r_o to a new temporary equilibrium value of r', at which the increased real demand for money equals the real supply of money. The rise in r is caused by the efforts of bondholders to acquire money by selling bonds. We see from Figure 20.4(a) that desired saving exceeds desired investment when the real rate of interest is r'. This means an excess supply of commodities, growing inventories, and a fall in the price level to, say, P'. The fall in P causes an increase in real money balances to M_o/P' and a fall in r from r' to r'',

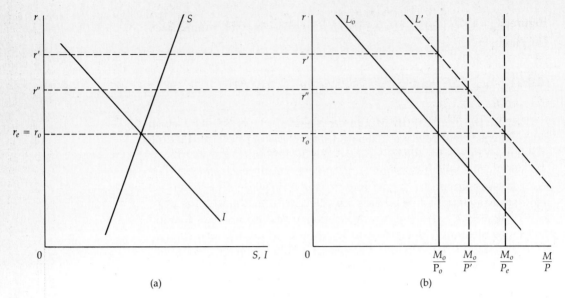

Figure 20.4   Disturbance B: an increase in the demand for money.

which is the rate at which the new real demand for money equals the new real supply of money.

But desired saving still exceeds desired investment at r'' so that P continues to fall—until real balances reach the level, M_o/P_e, at which the intersection of the real supply and demand for money occurs at the rate of interest that equilibrates the commodity market. The new equilibrium rate of interest, r_e, is identical with the initial equilibrium rate, r_o. We have described the following chain of events:

$$(20.8) \qquad \uparrow L \to \uparrow r \to \downarrow (I - S) \to \downarrow P \to \uparrow \frac{M}{P} \to \downarrow r$$

Again a disturbance in the money market (this time a shift in the demand for money instead of in the supply of money, as in disturbance A), has affected r only temporarily. The only long-run effect of a one-time shift in the demand for money (as in the supply of money) is on the price level. We see again that in the long run the real rate of interest is determined in the commodity market—by productivity and thrift.

THE WORKINGS OF THE MODEL: DISTURBANCES IN THE COMMODITY MARKET

Disturbance C: an increase in the demand for investment goods

Suppose, because of technological advances, that there is a permanent increase in the demand for investment goods from I_o to I', as shown in

Figure 20.5(a). We now have an excess demand for goods and therefore rising prices at the existing real rate of interest, r_o. Firms attempt to raise funds in the capital markets, causing r to rise. The increase in P adds to the upward pressure on r because of the fall in real balances from M_o/P_o to, say, M_o/P'. The new temporary equilibrium r, at which the supply and demand for real balances are equal, is r'. But desired investment, I', still exceeds desired saving, S, at this rate. Therefore P and r continue to rise until general equilibrium is attained at the price level P_e, the real rate of interest, r_e, and the real money supply, M_o/P_e. The chain of events has been

$$\text{(20.9)} \qquad \uparrow I \rightarrow \uparrow r, P \rightarrow \downarrow \frac{M}{P} \rightarrow \uparrow r$$

If the investment function remains permanently at I', the equilibrium real rate of interest stays at r_e. Unlike the money market disturbances considered in the preceding section, a commodity market disturbance has caused a change in the long-run equilibrium value of r. We see again that in the long run the money market conforms to the commodity market.

Disturbance D: an increase in thrift
Suppose households become more thrifty and decide to consume less (save more) of their incomes. This means a rightward shift in the

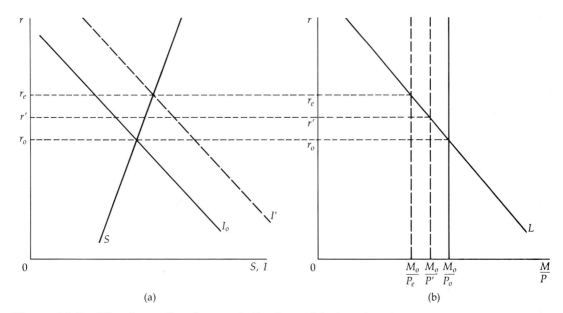

(a)   (b)

Figure 20.5   Disturbance C: an increase in the demand for investment goods.

saving function. It will be left as an exercise for the student to show how this disturbance causes r and P to fall.

THE EFFECTS OF GOVERNMENT SPENDING ON INTEREST RATES AND THE PRICE LEVEL

Introduction of the government

The preceding sections were concerned only with the spending, saving, borrowing, and lending of the private sector. But governments also spend, save, borrow, and lend. Taking account of government, aggregate demand equals aggregate supply when

$$(20.10) \qquad C^d + I^d + G^d = Y$$

Output is allocated between private consumption, private investment, and government purchases of goods and services. Now let T^d be the real value of tax receipts desired by the government. Given tax payments of T^d, desired private saving is disposable income $(Y - T^d)$ less desired consumption:

$$(20.11) \qquad S^d = Y - T^d - C^d$$

Desired real government saving, S_g^d, equals desired real government receipts less expenditures:

$$(20.12) \qquad S_g^d = T^d - G^d$$

Government demands, like private demands, often go unfulfilled because of order backlogs and unexpected price increases. Actual real tax receipts, T, also normally differ from desired, or planned, receipts, T^d.

The commodity market is equilibrated when total desired saving, $S^d + S_g^d$, equals desired investment, I^d. Applying the above equations, the equality of desired saving and investment may be expressed as follows:

$$(20.13) \quad I^d = S^d + S_g^d = S^d + T^d - G^d \quad \text{or} \quad I^d + G^d = S^d + T^d$$

Equilibrium occurs at the real rate of interest, r_o, for which $I + G = S + T$ as shown in Figure 20.6(a). I and G comprise those portions of income not devoted to private consumption, that is, the portion taken by the Internal Revenue Service (T) and the portion saved voluntarily (S).

The inflationary impact of an increase in government spending depends on how the spending is financed. There are three avenues by

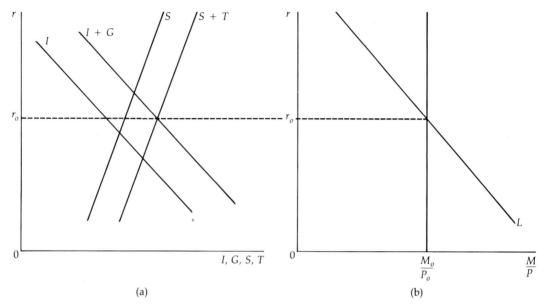

Figure 20.6   Introduction of government.

which the federal government obtains funds:

1. Borrowing from the private sector
2. Increased taxes
3. Borrowing from the central bank, which is equivalent to printing money

We consider all three avenues below. The first will be seen to involve some inflation of limited duration, the second is the least inflationary, and the third causes severe inflations that may be unlimited in either magnitude or duration.

An increase in government expenditures financed by borrowing from the public

We shall work with diagrams that show the sums of $I + G$ and $S + T$ instead of all four of these functions separately, as in Figure 20.6. We can do this because prices and interest rates are determined by *total* (government and private) excess demand and *total* net borrowing. Figure 20.7(a) shows the increase in aggregate demand due to a permanent increase in desired real government expenditures from G to G'. We assume that in this case all the increase in G is financed by selling securities to the public. The effects of this change are identical with those of disturbance C: An Increase in the Demand for Investment Goods. In disturbance C private firms borrowed to finance increased expenditures. We now assume the government to follow the

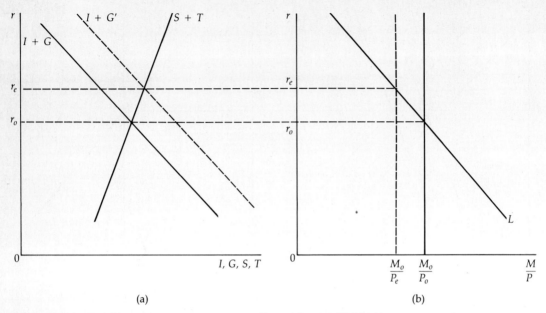

Figure 20.7   An increase in government expenditures financed by borrowing from the public.

same route by going to the financial markets and competing with other borrowers for the funds needed to finance its deficit.

The rise in G produces, at the initial equilibrium rate of interest, r_o, an excess demand for commodities that in turn leads to an increase in P, a reduction in M/P, and an increase in r. These movements proceed until the system reaches a new general equilibrium at P_e and r_e. There is some inflation, financed by the more rapid turnover of money balances in response to the increased rate of interest. However, as long as the money supply is not increased, the rise in P is limited to P_e, where the rate of interest that equilibrates the money market is also consistent with equilibrium in the commodity market.[10]

An increase in government expenditures financed by an equal increase in taxes

Figure 20.8 shows a permanent rise in desired government expenditures financed by an equal increase in desired tax receipts. That is, the shift $G' - G$ equals the shift $T' - T$ and is measured by the distance ac in Figure 20.8(a). If private consumption fell by an amount precisely

---

10 If the private sector reduces its consumption as a result of the reduction in its wealth caused by the future taxes implied by the government's borrowing, there will be a rightward shift in S and smaller increases in r and P than in Figure 20.7. The possible effects of future taxes on current spending will be considered in the section Do Government Deficits Really Matter?

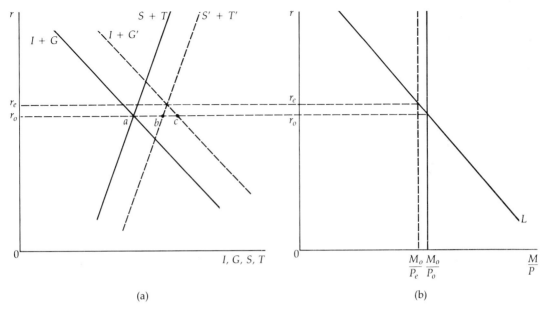

Figure 20.8   An increase in government expenditures financed by taxes.

equal to the increase in T, then S would be unchanged and there would be equal rightward shifts in $I + G$ and $S + T$. These lines would intersect at point c and the new equilibrium real rate of interest would be the same as the initial equilibrium rate, r_o.

However, changes in consumption are usually less than changes in disposable income, $Y - T$. This means that desired saving, $S^d = Y - T^d - C^d$, falls when T^d rises. This is the meaning of the reduction in the saving function from S to S' in Figure 20.8. Although the increases in G and T are equal, the reduction in S causes the rise in $S + T$ to be less than that in $I + G$. The increase in the public's borrowing, because C^d has fallen less than disposable income, has caused a rise in r to the new equilibrium r_e.

This result may be illustrated by the following numerical example. Let output and equilibrium taxes, expenditures, and private saving take the following real values when the real rate of interest is r_o:

$$Y = 5,000, \quad G = T = 1,000, \quad S = I = 400$$

Suppose households consume 90 percent of their disposable income so that

$$C = 0.9(Y - T) = 0.9(5,000 - 1,000) = 3,600$$

Now suppose actual G and T both increase by 100 units to $G' = T' = 1,100$. If households continue to consume 90 percent of disposable income, we have

$$C^d = 0.9(Y - T') = 0.9(5{,}000 - 1{,}100) = 3{,}510$$

Desired private saving has fallen from $4{,}000 - 3{,}600 = 400$ to $3{,}900 - 3{,}510 = 390$ so that $S + T$ has risen from $400 + 1{,}000 = 1{,}400$ to $390 + 1{,}100 = 1{,}490$. But $I + G$ has increased from $400 + 1{,}000 = 1{,}400$ to $400 + 1{,}100 = 1{,}500$. There is an excess demand for commodities of $1{,}500 - 1{,}490$ (indicated by the distance bc in Figure 20.8) at the real rate of interest r_o. This puts upward pressure on r and P until these variables rise to their new equilibrium values of r_e and P_e shown in Figure 20.8.

    This situation, in which government expenditures and taxes rise by equal amounts, in theory causes only a small and probably short-lived inflation. But there is no historical evidence of such a chain of events because no substantial increase in G has ever been accompanied by a similar rise in T. For that matter, no large increase in G has been accompanied by a similar increase in borrowing from the private sector. Governments have never been willing to accept the unpopularity associated with either of these measures, sufficiently high taxes to fully cover expenditures in the former case and sufficiently high interest rates to crowd out private expenditures in the latter case. All large increases in government expenditures have relied on monetary expansions. Some consequences of these policies are considered next.

An increase in government expenditures financed by the Federal Reserve

Figure 20.9 shows the initial stages of an inflation caused by a permanent increase in government expenditures with no change in taxes and accompanied by continuous increases in the money supply. If the rightward shift in G were to occur with no change in either T or M, we should be in the same situation as that in which the government deficit was financed by borrowing from the public; r and P would rise to r_e and P_e, as shown in Figure 20.7, and the system would settle down to a situation of stable prices.

    However, suppose the Federal Reserve resists the rise in interest rates. The Fed does this by buying securities, which generates bank reserves and leads to increases in M. Consider the extreme case in which the Fed uses its power to peg the nominal rate of interest, $R = r + p$, at its initial level, $R_o = r_o$. (Remember that we start from a situation of stable prices and therefore no inflationary expectations; that is, $p = 0$). As long as the Fed prevents R from rising and as long as $p = 0$, the excess demand for commodities in the amount ac shown in Figure 20.9(a) will be perpetuated. P will increase, but because M rises in the same proportion as P, the real supply of money, M/P, remains constant and r_o remains fixed at the level shown in the figure (because R_o is pegged and we have assumed $p = 0$). This is the meaning of the

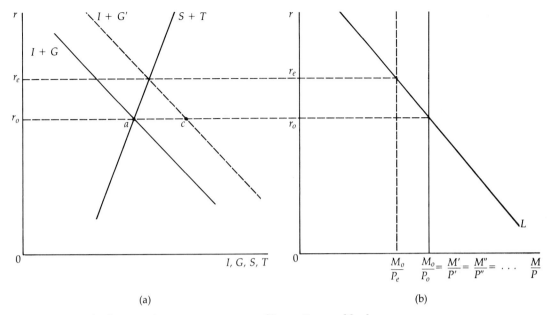

(a) (b)

Figure 20.9 An increase in government expenditures financed by borrowing from the central bank.

successively higher values of M and P (M_o, M', M'', . . . and P_o, P', P'', . . .) and constant M/P in Figure 20.9(b).

But this is just the beginning of the inflationary process caused by the Fed's monetization of government debt. The public will not for long remain unaware of the Fed's behavior. That is, p will become positive as past inflation leads to expectations of future inflation. Given the real rate r_o in Figure 20.9, this means upward pressure on the nominal rate, R_o. However, the Fed prevents R from rising above R_o, which means that increases in p cause r to fall *below* r_o and excess demands exceed the amount ac shown in Figure 20.9.

The Fed's resistance to interest rate increases causes inflation even in the absence of inflationary expectations. But these expectations accelerate the inflationary process. As long as nominal interest rates are prevented from rising while inflation continues at high levels, people will want to borrow in order to buy goods now before prices rise still further. *For a fixed nominal rate of interest, R_o,* the chain of events due to an increase in the government's deficit appears as follows:

(20.14) $\uparrow G \rightarrow \uparrow [(I + G) - (S + T)] \rightarrow \uparrow M, P \rightarrow \uparrow p \rightarrow \downarrow r \rightarrow$

$\uparrow\uparrow [(I + G) - (S + T)] \rightarrow \uparrow\uparrow M, P \rightarrow \uparrow\uparrow p \rightarrow \downarrow\downarrow r \rightarrow$

$\uparrow\uparrow\uparrow [(I + G) - (S + T)] \rightarrow \ldots$

The same sequence would result from any increase in the demand for commodities, whether due to a tax cut ($\downarrow T$), an increase in private investment ($\uparrow I$), a reduction in private saving ($\downarrow S$), or, as above, an increase in government expenditures ($\uparrow G$)—as long as the Federal Reserve met the increased demand for funds with increases in money at the existing rate of interest. Referring to the above chain of events, the initial excess demand for funds puts upward pressure on P and R. But the Fed prevents R from rising by causing M to rise proportionally to P. These events lead to inflationary expectations ($\uparrow p$), reductions in the real rate of interest ($\downarrow r$), and the heightened excess demand indicated by the double arrows. Excess demands, inflation, and inflationary expectations grow at ever-increasing rates, requiring the Fed to increase M at ever-increasing rates in order to maintain a constant R.

An increase in G financed partly by borrowing from the public, partly by taxes, and partly by increases in money

The extreme hypothetical example discussed above has never quite been realized in the United States. First, increases in G are usually partly financed by increases in T. Second, except for World War II the Federal Reserve has never pegged interest rates for a long period, and inflation was limited during those years because increases in G were partially offset by increases in S due to rationing. During most periods *resist* has been a better word than *peg* as a description of the Fed's attitude toward interest rates. Although the Fed has tended to purchase securities during periods of rising credit demands, those purchases have usually moderated rather than prevented rising interest rates. Not all the increased demands for funds, whether by government or the private sector, have been financed by increases in M. Part has been financed by increases in private lending induced by rising interest rates. The results have been less extreme than those in Figure 20.9 and the chain of events (20.14).

A common sequence of events is described below in (20.15). First, an increase in desired investment or government expenditures causes an excess demand for commodities and puts upward pressure on interest rates. But the rise in R is moderated by Federal Reserve open market purchases. Hence the small arrow in front of R. These purchases cause M to increase and reinforce the rise in P induced by the original commodity excess demands. The rise in P leads to inflationary expectations, $\uparrow p$, and, given the small increase in R, a falling real rate of interest, $\downarrow r$. This leads to another, and more extreme, round of excess demands and rising money and prices. Again the Fed grudgingly allows some increase in R.

Eventually the public's fear of inflation overcomes its fear of the disruptions caused by stopping inflation, and a reassessment of monetary policy is forced on the Fed. The result is a reduction in the rate of growth of, or perhaps even a fall in, M. Given the now very high inflationary expectations, p, the Fed's retreat from its battle against rising interest rates allows R to rise to very high levels. The Fed's desire for low interest rates has in the end led to higher rates than would have occurred if it had not resisted increases in R.

(20.15) $\uparrow I$ or $G \rightarrow \uparrow[(I + G) - (S + T)] \rightarrow \uparrow R, \uparrow M, P \rightarrow \uparrow p \rightarrow \downarrow r \rightarrow$

$\uparrow\uparrow[(I + G) - (S + T)] \rightarrow \uparrow R, \uparrow\uparrow M, P \rightarrow \uparrow\uparrow p \rightarrow \downarrow\downarrow r \rightarrow$

reassessment of monetary policy $\rightarrow \downarrow M, \uparrow R \rightarrow$?

The sequence of events following the turnaround in monetary policy is uncertain and depends on the course of inflationary expectations and the real effects of reducing the rates of growth of money and prices. First, we do not know how p will respond in the short run to the Fed's new anti-inflationary measures. Whether or not the public will revise its inflationary expectations depends on the Fed's credibility, which can only be proved by performance, probably over a long period of time. Second, there are likely to be unpleasant real effects of sudden cutbacks in monetary expansion and inflation. A great many households and firms have borrowed heavily in order to invest in houses, plant and equipment, and other real assets in the expectation of rising prices. If these price rises are not forthcoming, losses instead of profits will be realized, and many borrowers will not be able to repay their debts. Plant closings, unemployment, and mortgage foreclosures will be the order of the day. The occurrence of economic recession does not even require that M and P actually fall. It is enough that they rise less than anticipated.

DO GOVERNMENT DEFICITS REALLY MATTER?

The above analysis showed prices and interest rates to be positively affected by increases in government deficits no matter whether the deficits were caused by increases in government spending or by reductions in taxation.[11] But this is a controversial issue. Critics of tax cuts argue that the increased government borrowing made necessary by reduced taxes crowds out private investment by forcing up interest rates. The resources that might have been allocated to investment goods are directed toward current consumption because of the increased demand for the latter that is induced by the increase in disposable income, $Y - T$. These conclusions are consistent with the results obtained above. But government supply-siders, who believe that tax cuts encourage investment and growth, deny these effects. In

---

11 The effects of an increase in spending (G) with no increase in taxes (T) are shown in Figure 20.7. The effects of a reduction in T with no change in G may be seen by comparing Figures 20.7 and 20.8.

this section we develop the conditions under which each of these contradictory conclusions is correct.

We also examine a closely related issue, which concerns the role of the Federal Reserve in the face of rising deficits. Specifically, is it necessary for the Fed to buy government securities (and thereby to monetize deficits) in order to prevent rising interest rates from crowding out private investment? If such actions are necessary—or thought by the Fed to be necessary—then government deficits are inflationary. But if deficits do not put upward pressure on interest rates, no accommodation by the Fed is necessary and government deficits are not inflationary.

In summary, the following discussion is concerned with two related questions: Do government deficits crowd out private investment? Are government deficits inflationary?

Crowding out with a balanced budget

We answer the above questions within the framework of a steady-growth economy in which aggregate consumption, C, is a constant proportion, c, of aggregate wealth, W, which is the present value of perceived future income. If there is no government spending or taxation, output (or income) to be received at the end of the current period is Y, the rate of growth of income is g, and the real rate of interest is $r > g$, wealth is

$$(20.16) \quad W = \frac{Y}{1 + r} + \frac{(1 + g)Y}{(1 + r)^2} + \frac{(1 + g)^2 Y}{(1 + r)^3} + \ldots = \frac{Y}{r - g}$$

Now introduce a government that consumes the quantity G of this period's output and grows at the same rate as the economy. The government's budget is initially in balance so that the real value of its tax receipts, T, always equals G. Then private wealth is[12]

$$(20.17) \qquad\qquad W = \frac{Y - G}{r - g}$$

---

12 We make the following simplifying assumptions: (1) Either consumers are infinitely lived or they care about the utility of their descendants so that their horizon is infinitely long. (2) If the government transfers income between consumers, both groups have the same propensity to consume, c. Otherwise these transfers would affect the aggregate demand for consumption goods and cause changes in interest rates and investment. T is defined net of subsidies and includes only those taxes raised to finance purchases of goods, G. (3) G includes only those goods consumed in the conduct of government, such as defense and the administration of justice. It does not include goods that would otherwise be purchased by private consumers and investors, which are not deductions from private wealth. Complications arising from the relaxation of these assumptions are considered in a large and growing literature, including Martin Bailey (1971), Robert Barro (1979), John Bryant (1983, 1984), and Merton Miller and Charles Upton (1974). A useful taxonomy of the various types of crowding out may be found in Willem Buiter (1977).

and private consumption is

(20.18) $\quad C = cW = c\left(\dfrac{Y - G}{r - g}\right) = k(Y - G) \qquad$ where $k = c/(r - g) < 1$

We assume positive private investment, which requires that private consumption be less than the output not consumed by government. This is the meaning of the consumption/disposable-income ratio $C/(Y - G) = k < 1$.

Now assume increases in government spending and taxes to $G' = T' > G = T$. The total increase in government and private commodity demands is

(20.19) $\quad \Delta C + \Delta G = [k(Y - G') - k(Y - G)] + (G' - G)$

$$= (1 - k)(G' - G) > 0$$

The increased demand for goods puts upward pressure on interest rates. Suppose $k = 0.90$ and $G' - G = 100$ units of goods. Ninety percent of the desired increase in G is diverted to the government by means of the equal increase in taxes, $T' - T = 100$, because the public reduces its consumption by $0.9(100) = 90$ units. But ten more units must be bid away from the private sector. Attempts by consumers to borrow (or to reduce their lending) as the result of the greater decline in their disposable income than in their consumption (100 compared with 90) cause interest rates to rise until 10 more units of goods that would have been applied to private consumption or investment purposes are released to the government. Figure 20.8 presents an illustration of this effect.

A deficit due to an increase in government spending

Now assume a temporary, one-period excess of government spending above the normal path indicated in Equation (20.17). Denote this excess by ΔG, and assume that T remains on its normal path. The public's wealth is now

(20.20) $$W = \dfrac{Y - G}{r - g} - \Delta G$$

This equation may be explained as follows: The public's exchange of money for government bonds does not affect its wealth. But its wealth is reduced by the future taxes that will be required to repay the debt. Suppose that goods cost $1 each and ΔG is financed by B bonds, each of which represents a claim on $1 per period in perpetuity. Assuming no inflation so that real and nominal interest rates are equal, the present value of these bonds (that is, the sum of their current market prices) is

$$B\frac{\$1}{r} = \$\Delta G$$

But the present value of the taxes needed to service these bonds is also

$$\frac{\$B}{1+r} + \frac{\$B}{(1+r)^2} + \ldots = \frac{\$B}{r} = \$\Delta G$$

so that the public's real wealth, that is, the present value of its real disposable income, is given by Equation (20.20).

What if the increase in spending had been financed by taxes so that $\Delta T = \Delta G$? The result would have been the same. Equation (20.20) would still apply. This is David Ricardo's "equivalence theorem," according to which bonds and taxes are equivalent ways of financing government expenditures.[13] What difference does it make whether a person gives up $20 in taxes now, on which he might have earned $1 a year at an interest rate of 5 percent, or is obligated by a government deficit to pay $1 more in taxes every year in the future? In either case the real burden borne by society is the reduction in its wealth by ΔG this period. That burden cannot be shifted to future periods.

But maybe some citizens can be made to bear more than others. Equation (20.20) is sometimes expressed as follows:

(20.21) $$W = \frac{Y-G}{r-g} - \alpha\Delta G \qquad 0 \le \alpha \le 1$$

A value of α less than unity means that the public perceives its tax burden to be less than ΔG. Ricardo (1820, pages 186 and 187), in arguing that the conditions necessary to the equivalence theorem were not likely to be realized, explained the probably low value of α as follows:[14]

> But the people who pay the taxes never so estimate them, and therefore do not manage their private affairs accordingly. We are too apt to think, that the war is burdensome only in proportion to what we are at the moment called to pay for it in taxes, without reflecting on the probable duration of such taxes. It would be

---

13 See David Ricardo (1817, pages 244–245; 1820, pages 185–188).

14 See Gerald O'Driscoll (1977) for a discussion of Ricardo's statement and qualifications of the equivalence theorem. Modern discussions of this theorem often begin with the question "Are government bonds net wealth?" and include papers by Robert Barro (1974), Bennett McCallum (1984), and many others. A useful survey of theoretical and empirical work in this area may be found in the August 1982 issue of the Federal Reserve Bank of Atlanta's *Economic Review*.

difficult to convince a man possessed of 20,000 *l.*, or any other sum, that a perpetual payment of 50 *l.* per annum was equally burdensome with a single tax of 1000 *l.*

However, what at first appears to be an irrationally low perception of future tax burdens might more reasonably be regarded as a definite intention not to bear those burdens and a rational belief, based on experience, that they will not be borne. Ricardo (1817, pages 247 and 248) pointed out that in a "country which has accumulated a large debt,"

> . . . it becomes the interest of every contributor to withdraw his shoulder from the burthen, and to shift this payment from himself to another; and the temptation to remove himself and his capital to another country, where he will be exempted from such burthens, becomes at last irresistible, and overcomes the natural reluctance which every man feels to quit the place of his birth, and the scene of his early associations.

But repudiation is easier than emigration. The last 200 years have given no cause to revise Adam Smith's (1776) observations on the honesty of governments:

> When national debts have once been accumulated to a certain degree, there is scarce, I believe, a single instance of their having been fairly and completely paid. The liberation of the public revenue, if it has ever been brought about at all, has always been brought about by a bankruptcy; sometimes by an avowed one, but always by a real one, though frequently by a pretended payment.

The most common method of repudiation is inflation. Suppose the government manages a 50 percent reduction in the purchasing power of the pound [Adam Smith (1776, Book 5, Chapter 3)]:

> A national debt of about a hundred and twenty-eight millions . . . might in this manner be paid with about sixty-four millions of our present money. It would indeed be a pretended payment only, and the creditors of the public would really be defrauded of ten shillings in the pound of what was due to them. The calamity too would extend much further than to the creditors of the public, and those of every private person would suffer a proportionable loss. . . . A pretended payment of this kind, therefore, instead of alleviating, aggravates in most cases the loss of the creditors of the public; and without any advantage to the public, extends the calamity to a great number of other innocent people. . . . When it becomes necessary for a state to declare itself

bankrupt, in the same manner as when it becomes necessary for an individual to do so, a fair, open, and avowed bankruptcy is always the measure which is both least dishonourable to the debtor, and least hurtful to the creditor. The honour of a state is surely very poorly provided for, when, in order to cover the disgrace of a real bankruptcy, it has recourse to a juggling trick of this kind, so easily seen through, and at the same time so extremely pernicious.[15]

Now let's look at the short-run interest rate effects of a bond-financed increase in government spending when apparent future tax liabilities may not be fully reflected in present appraisals of wealth.[16] Using Equation (20.21), the total increase in government and private consumption demands is

(20.22) $\Delta C + \Delta G = k\Delta W + \Delta G = -k\alpha\Delta G + \Delta G = (1 - k\alpha)\Delta G$

If $\alpha = 1$, that is, if future tax liabilities due to ΔG are fully reflected in current wealth, the increase in demand is $(1 - k)\Delta G$, and we have a situation like that in Equation (20.19) and Figure 20.8, when spending was financed by current taxes. At the other extreme, if future taxes due to ΔG are completely ignored so that $\alpha = 0$, the increase in demand implied by Equation (20.22) is simply ΔG because the public perceives no change in its wealth and therefore does not alter its consumption plan until the excess demand causes interest rates to rise. This is the case depicted in Figure 20.7.[17]

A deficit due to reduced taxes

A rise in G necessarily means crowding out of private consumption and/or investment in a fully employed economy. But what about a

---

15 Herbert Stein (1984, page 22) recently pointed out that the United States offers no exception to Smith's observations and suggests, perhaps tongue in cheek, that we follow the less dishonorable of the methods of repudiation discussed by Smith.

> In 1946, after the end of World War II, the federal debt was $242 billion. Since then, Washington has run a total budget deficit of nearly $800 billion. But the federal debt today, in 1946 prices, is $232 billion. The real value of the debt is smaller today, despite the cumulative deficit.
> This magic has been performed by inflation. We have gradually but effectively repudiated all of the postwar debt by inflation. . . .
> Pursuing this line of thought led me to the conclusion that we should do in a straightforward, aboveboard way what we have been doing surreptitiously all these years. . . .
> The government should announce that, from this moment, it will not pay interest or principal on the debt now outstanding.

16 We still have not explained why savers are willing to buy the bonds of dishonest governments or why, having bought them, they do not revise their wealth downward to account for the probability of repudiation more or less equally with the upward revision of taxpayers' wealth. But these questions have not received the attention that they deserve, and we will not speculate on the answers here.

17 The present discussion differs somewhat from our earlier discussions of Figures 20.7 and 20.8, which assumed permanent changes in G and T. The present discussion is limited to temporary changes in G and/or T because we wish to allow for the possibility that the government's debt is expected to be redeemed, that is, $\alpha = 1$.

reduction in current taxation with no change in G? The public's perceived wealth in such a case is

(20.23)
$$W = \frac{Y - G}{r - g} + (1 - \alpha)D$$

where $D = -\Delta T$ is the deficit caused by the partial financing of current G by means of bonds rather than taxes. The public's wealth is increased by the substitution of government bonds for tax payments. But that wealth is reduced by the public's perception of the future taxes implied by these bonds. The increase in desired consumption due to the bond issue, that is, due to the substitution of future taxes for current taxes, is

(20.24)
$$\Delta C = k\Delta W = k(1 - \alpha)D$$

The tax cut induces an increase in consumption demand, upward pressure on interest rates, and some crowding out of private investment if taxpayers expect to evade at least a portion of their obligations and/or they do not fully take account of future tax payments in making their present consumption decisions, that is, if $\alpha < 1$. Those who favor tax cuts as a way of encouraging investment and growth would find their position strengthened by a stand against inflation so that taxpayers might bear the full burden of their government's borrowing. This might cause α to approach unity and reduce the expansive effects of tax cuts on current consumption.

Does the Federal Reserve monetize federal deficits?

The answer was indicated early in this chapter by Empirical Tendency 20.3 and is a resounding yes. Further evidence is presented below, evidence that also supports the view that government deficits crowd out private expenditures. We begin with the observation that the public has been reluctant (or has been perceived by politicians to be reluctant) to be taxed for the costs of government.

Table 20.3 lists federal government receipts and expenditures during the periods since 1860 in which government spending has grown most rapidly. Defense spending is shown separately. In all but two of these periods, 1933 to 1940 and 1970 to 1980, spending increases were primarily for military purposes. The 1933 to 1945 period has been divided between 1933 to 1940, when most of the rise in spending was nonmilitary, and 1941 to 1945, when the opposite was true. The data correspond to fiscal years ending on June 30 of the years listed in the table. As Alexander Hamilton predicted, Congressmen have been less anxious to vote for tax increases than for more spending. The columns headed $\Delta R/\Delta E$ in Table 20.3 show the extent to which increases in spending have been covered by increases in tax and other revenues. For example total spending during the fiscal years 1862 to 1865

Table 20.3   Federal Receipts and Expenditures during Periods of Rapidly Increasing Expenditures (Millions of Dollars)

Year	Receipts	Expenditures	Defense	$\Delta R/\Delta E$
1861	42	67	35	
1862	52	475	437	
1863	113	715	663	0.19
1864	265	865	777	
1865	334	1,298	1,154	
1897	348	366	84	
1898	405	443	151	0.71
1899	516	605	294	
1916	761	713	337	
1917	1,101	1,954	618	0.25
1918	3,645	12,677	6,149	
1919	5,130	18,493	11,011	
1933	1,997	4,598	784	
1934	3,015	6,645	706	
1935	3,706	6,497	924	
1936	3,997	8,422	1,147	
1937	4,956	7,733	1,185	0.88
1938	5,588	6,745	1,240	
1939	4,979	8,841	1,368	
1940	6,879	9,055	1,799	
1941	9,204	13,255	6,252	
1942	15,104	34,037	22,905	
1943	25,097	79,368	63,414	0.40
1944	47,818	94,986	75,976	
1945	50,162	98,303	80,537	
1950	40,940	39,544	13,440	
1951	53,390	43,970	20,857	1.08
1952	68,011	65,303	40,536	
1953	71,495	74,120	44,014	
1965	116,833	118,430	47,179	
1966	130,856	134,652	55,445	0.72
1967	149,552	158,254	68,763	
1968	153,671	178,833	78,673	
1970	193,743	194,460	77,150	
1971	188,392	211,425	74,546	
1972	208,649	231,876	75,150	
1973	232,225	246,526	73,297	
1974	264,932	268,392	77,625	
1975	280,997	326,105	85,420	
1976	299,197	365,648	88,036	0.78
1977	347,280	393,110	93,416	
1978	385,623	438,482	100,731	
1979	452,868	483,766	111,533	
1980	504,828	553,016	128,809	
1981	580,521	640,186	148,968	
1982	624,250	707,791	176,319	
1983	592,668	787,324	200,263	

Receipts, total expenditures, and defense expenditures are for the 12 months ending June 30 of the years shown. $\Delta R/\Delta E$ is the total rise in receipts as a proportion of the total rise in expenditures above the first year of each period. For example during 1897 to 1899

$$\Delta R/\Delta E = [(405 - 348) + (516 - 348)]/[(443 - 366) + (605 - 366)] = 225/316 = 0.71$$

Sources: *Historical Statistics of the United States, Business Statistics,* and *Survey of Current Business.*

exceeded the $67 million spent during 1861 by $3,085 million. But total receipts during 1862 to 1865 exceeded the $42 million received during 1861 by only $596 million, or 596/3,085 = 19 percent of the total rise in spending.[18] During only one of the eight periods, the Korean War years of 1951 to 1953, did revenues rise more than expenditures.

There is a close correspondence between the periods shown in Table 20.3 and the shaded periods in Figure 20.1. Except for 1880 to 1882 severe inflations since 1860 have been accompanied by large increases in government spending. And large increases in government spending have, except during 1965 to 1968, been accompanied by severe inflations. Contemporaries deplored the rising inflation associated with the Vietnam escalation. But this inflation cannot be called "severe" by historical standards.

Government deficits have been financed partly by borrowing from the public and partly by monetary expansions. During the Civil War the government issued paper money in large quantities. Monetization of deficits was made more efficient by the formation of the Federal Reserve System in 1913. When receipts fall behind expenditures, the Fed buys government securities, thereby creating bank reserves that serve as the base for increased bank lending and monetary expansion. This is the story told in the last example of the effects of increases in government spending: "An increase in G financed partly by borrowing from the public, partly by taxes, and partly by increases in money." The theoretical results presented there are consistent with the data in Table 20.4.

The first three columns of Table 20.4 show the federal debt, the broad money supply, and the WPI in the years beginning and ending each of the eight periods in Table 20.3. The last three columns show average annual rates of change in these three variables during and between the eight periods of rapid government expansion. The close associations between the rates of change in Table 20.4 are consistent with the significant positive correlations between the same three variables in Table 20.2.

The continued close association of the federal debt and the money supply in the 1970s and 1980s lends support to the view that federal deficits induce increased consumption demands and therefore crowd out private investment. This point can be developed in three steps. First, the recent expansion of government expenditures is of a very different kind from that which the United States has previously experienced. Only a small proportion (about one-seventh) has been devoted to government purchases of goods and services.[19] Most has been dispensed in various kinds of grants, subsidies, and transfer

---

18 A more detailed example of the calculation of $\Delta R/\Delta E$, for 1898 and 1899, is given below the table.

19 Using the GNP price deflator to estimate real values, only 14.5 percent of the real increase in federal expenditures was on goods and services between 1970 and 1983.

Table 20.4   Money, Prices, and the Federal Debt, 1860 to 1983

	Millions of Dollars			Average Annual Percentage Rates of Change		
	Debt	Money	WPI	$\dot{D}$	$\dot{M}$	$\dot{WPI}$
1861	91	640	31.4			
				133	31	20
1865	2,678	1,910	65.2			
				− 2	3	− 3
1897	1,227	4,640	24.0			
				8	15	6
1899	1,437	6,090	26.9			
				− 1	8	3
1916	1,225	20,850	44.1			
				175	14	17
1919	25,485	31,010	71.4			
				− 1	0	− 5
1933	22,539	32,220	34.0			
				10	8	3
1940	42,968	55,200	40.5			
				12	13	11
1941	48,223	62,510	45.1			
				49	19	5
1945	235,182	126,830	54.6			
				− 1	4	8
1950	219,023	150,810	81.8			
				0	4	2
1953	218,383	171,190	87.4			
				2	5	1
1965	261,614	304,680	96.6			
				4	8	2
1968	290,629	387,380	102.5			
				− 1	4	4
1970	284,880	422,720	110.4			
				11	10	8
1983	1,093,930	1,425,800	303.1			

     Debt is the gross outstanding federal debt in the hands of the public and the Federal Reserve (that is, not held in government accounts) on June 30.
     Money is the old broad money supply (*M*2), which is currency in the hands of the nonbank public plus total nonbank deposits in commercial banks.
     WPI is the Wholesale Price Index, 1967 = 100. Warren and Pearson's series to 1890 was connected with the Bureau of Labor Statistics series beginning in 1890. (See *Historical Statistics of the United States,* vol. i, pages 200–201.)

Sources: *Historical Statistics of the United States, Survey of Current Business,* and Federal Reserve money supply releases.

payments. Federal deficits now consist largely of bond issues to raise funds to be given away. Second, Federal Reserve behavior has been similar to that in periods during which federal deficits were due to purchases of goods and services. There has been much talk since 1979 of tight monetary policy. But the 8 percent average annual rate of increase of the money supply between mid-1979 and mid-1984 was still very high by historical standards. High federal deficits, whatever their cause, continue to be accommodated by the Federal Reserve. Third, the first two steps suggest that increases in the federal debt may be perceived as increases in private wealth as stated by Equation (20.23). These increases in perceived wealth lead to increases in consumption demand and upward pressures on interest rates, which are resisted by Federal Reserve open market purchases.[20] High federal deficits continue to mean high inflation even when the deficits are due to increased transfers and reduced taxes rather than to increased spending on goods and services.

A REVIEW OF THE FACTS IN LIGHT OF THE MODEL

Empirical Tendencies 20.1 and 20.2, Table 20.2, and Figure 20.1 highlighted the strong positive correlations between money, prices, interest rates, and private investment demands and government spending. These correlations are long lived, existing at least since 1860, but they have been especially strong during the last 30 years. We presented a theoretical framework within which these events were shown to be consistent with a world in which economic disturbances stem principally from fluctuations in government spending and private investment demands. Furthermore, these correlations in combination with the tendency of interest rates to adjust slowly to changes in the rate of inflation are consistent with an inclination on the part of the government to finance excess demands by money creation. This inclination is verified most strongly by the positive correlation between money and government deficits, but the positive correlation between money and private investment suggests that the central bank's resistance to interest rate movements also leads it to finance portions of private excess demands by money creation. This myopic desire for interest rate stability exacerbates price movements and eventually magnifies fluctuations in interest rates. Finally we saw that money and prices respond positively to government deficits even when

---

20 This traditional pattern of Fed behavior in the face of rising commodity demands was illustrated for 1978 in the lower portion of Figure 9.3. A substantial empirical literature has been concerned with the possible effects of government deficits on the money supply and includes contributions by William Niskanen (1978), Michael Hamburger and Burton Zwick (1981), Dennis Hoffman, Stuart Low, and Hubert Reineberg (1983), and Stuart Allen and Michael Smith (1983). These studies have been limited to the post-World War II period and report mixed results. The estimated effect or lack of effect of deficits on money has been sensitive to the choice of sample period. The instability of these estimates may be due to a pattern of Federal Reserve behavior that is concerned primarily with the stability of interest rates so that money displays a clear connection with government deficits only when changes in the deficit are large. Many factors, especially fluctuations in private investment demands, affect interest rates. During periods when government borrowing is fairly steady the effects of deficits on Federal Reserve actions and the money supply may be swamped by other factors. The clearest evidence of a strong relation between deficits and money is obtained from comparisons of high-deficit and low-deficit periods such as those in Table 20.4.

those deficits are not due to increased government purchases of goods and services, suggesting that tax reductions induce increased private consumption demands, upward pressures on interest rates, and the crowding out of private investment.

QUESTIONS

1. Who was Alexander Hamilton?
2. (a) Choose three of the empirical relationships indicated by the correlations in Table 20.2, and describe how those relationships are illustrated in Figure 20.1.

   (b) Using the model presented in this chapter, explain the causes of the relationships described in (a).
3. Discuss how the data in Table 20.4 help to explain some of the relationships in (a) Figure 20.1 and (b) Table 20.2.
4. Show how an increase in thrift causes r and P to fall. (This is disturbance D, which we promised to leave as an exercise for the student.)

Questions 5 to 8 ask the student to consider disturbances just the opposite of some of those discussed in the chapter.

5. Show graphically and discuss the long-run equilibrium effects of a Federal Reserve open market sale.
6. Show graphically and discuss the long-run equilibrium effects of a decrease in the demand for money.
7. Show graphically and discuss the long-run equilibrium effects of a decrease in the demand for investment goods.
8. Show graphically and discuss the long-run equilibrium effects of a decrease in thrift.
9. Suppose economic disturbances stem principally from fluctuations in the demand for money. What does this imply for relative movements in money, prices, interest rates, and investment? Are these theoretical relationships consistent with the data?
10. Suppose economic disturbances stem principally from fluctuations in household consumption demands. What does this imply for relative movements in money, prices, interest rates, and investment? Are these theoretical relationships consistent with the data?
11. Suppose economic disturbances are initiated by the Federal Reserve. What does this imply for relative movements in money, prices, interest rates, and investment? Are these theoretical relationships consistent with the data?
12. What are the differences between relative movements in money, prices, interest rates, and inflation when disturbances are initiated by the Federal Reserve (as in question 11) and when the

Fed attempts to moderate interest rate movements caused by disturbances in the demand for investment goods? Which results correspond most closely to the facts?

13. What are the effects of an increase in government spending that is financed by an equal increase in taxes? What have you assumed about the behavior of the Federal Reserve?

14. What are the effects of an increase in government spending unaccompanied by an equal increase in taxes? What have you assumed about the public's perception of the burden of future taxes? About the behavior of the Federal Reserve?

15. What are the effects of a tax cut? What have you assumed about the public's perception of the burden of future taxes? About the behavior of the Federal Reserve?

16. Classify and discuss the possible effects of government deficits on **(a)** the rate of inflation and **(b)** private investment.

REFERENCES

Stuart D. Allen and Michael D. Smith, "Government Borrowing and Monetary Accommodation," *Journal of Monetary Economics,* November 1983, pages 605–616.

Martin Bailey, *National Income and the Price Level,* 2nd ed., McGraw-Hill, New York, 1971.

Robert J. Barro, "Are Government Bonds Net Wealth?," *Journal of Political Economy,* November/December 1974, pages 1095–1117.

Robert J. Barro, "On the Determination of the Public Debt," *Journal of Political Economy,* October 1979, pages 940–971.

John Bryant, "Government Irrelevance Results: A Simple Exposition," *American Economic Review,* September 1983, pages 758–761.

John Bryant, "How Fiscal Policy Matters," Federal Reserve Bank of Dallas *Economic Review,* January 1984, pages 15–20.

Willem Buiter, " 'Crowding Out' and the Effectiveness of Fiscal Policy," *Journal of Public Economics,* June 1977, pages 309–328.

Milton Friedman and Anna J. Schwartz, *A Monetary History of the United States, 1867–1960,* Princeton University Press, Princeton, NJ, 1963.

Milton Friedman and Anna J. Schwartz, *Monetary Statistics of the United States,* National Bureau of Economic Research, New York, 1970.

Michael J. Hamburger and Burton Zwick, "Deficits, Money and Inflation," *Journal of Monetary Economics,* July 1981, pages 141–150.

Alexander Hamilton, *Report on a National Bank* (1790), in Henry Cabot Lodge (ed.), *The Works of Alexander Hamilton,* vol. 3, Putnams, New York, 1885.

J. R. Hicks, "Mr. Keynes and the 'Classics,' " *Econometrica,* April 1937, pages 147–159.

Dennis L. Hoffman, Stuart A. Low, and Hubert H. Reineberg, "Recent Evidence on the Relationship between Money Growth and Budget Deficits," *Journal of Macroeconomics,* Spring 1983, pages 223–231.

George Horwich, "Money, Prices and the Theory of Interest Determination," *Economic Journal,* December 1957, pages 625–643.

George Horwich, "Tight Money, Monetary Restraint, and the Price Level," *Journal of Finance,* March 1966, pages 15–33.

Bennett T. McCallum, "Are Bond-financed Deficits Inflationary? A Ricardian Analysis," *Journal of Political Economy,* February 1984, pages 123–135.

Merton H. Miller and Charles W. Upton, *Macroeconomics: A Neoclassical Introduction,* Irwin, Homewood, IL, 1974.

William Niskanen, "Deficits, Government Spending, and Inflation: What Is the Evidence?," *Journal of Monetary Economics,* April 1978, pages 591–602.

Gerald P. O'Driscoll, Jr., "The Ricardian Nonequivalence Theorem," *Journal of Political Economy,* February 1977, pages 207–210.

Don Patinkin, *Money, Interest, and Prices,* 2nd ed., Harper & Row, New York, 1965.

David Ricardo, *On the Principles of Political*

Economy and Taxation, Murray, London, 1817.
Reprint Piero Sraffa (ed.), *The Works and Correspondence of David Ricardo,* vol. 1, Cambridge University Press, Cambridge, 1951.

David Ricardo, "Funding System," in *Supplement to the Fourth, Fifth and Sixth Editions of the Encyclopaedia Britannica,* 1820. Reprint Piero Sraffa (ed.), *The Works and Correspon-dence of David Ricardo,* vol. 4, Cambridge University Press, Cambridge, 1951.

Adam Smith, *An Inquiry into the Nature and Causes of the Wealth of Nations,* Strahan and Cadell, London, 1776.

Herbert Stein, "Throw Away the National Debt," *Wall Street Journal,* March 30, 1984.

APPENDIXES

The Sum of a Geometric Series, Natural Logarithms, and Present and Terminal Values

APPENDIX A
The Sum of a Geometric Series

This appendix derives the sum of a geometric series, which is used to calculate the price of an annuity in Equation (5.24), the price of a bond in Equation (6.4), and the price of stock in Equation (10.2).

Let S be a sum such that

(A.1)
$$S = \sum_{i=1}^{n} g^i = g + g^2 + \cdots + g^n$$

Multiply S by g and subtract the result from (A.1):

(A.2)
$$S - gS = (g + g^2 + \cdots + g^n) - (g^2 + g^3 + \cdots + g^{n+1})$$

If $g \neq 1$, this equation may be solved for S to obtain

(A.3)
$$S = \frac{g - g^{n+1}}{1 - g}$$

If $g = 1/(1 + Y)$, S is

(A.4)
$$S = \frac{1 - \left(\dfrac{1}{1 + Y}\right)^n}{Y}$$

APPENDIX B
Natural Logarithms

N	0	1	2	3	4	5	6	7	8	9
1.0	0.00000	0.00995	0.01980	0.02956	0.03922	0.04879	0.05827	0.06766	0.07696	0.08618
1.1	0.09531	0.10436	0.11333	0.12222	0.13103	0.13976	0.14842	0.15700	0.16551	0.17395
1.2	0.18232	0.19062	0.19885	0.20701	0.21511	0.22314	0.23111	0.23902	0.24686	0.25464
1.3	0.26236	0.27003	0.27763	0.28518	0.29267	0.30010	0.30748	0.31481	0.32208	0.32930
1.4	0.33647	0.34359	0.35066	0.35767	0.36464	0.37156	0.37844	0.38526	0.39204	0.39878
1.5	0.40547	0.41211	0.41871	0.42527	0.43178	0.43825	0.44469	0.45108	0.45742	0.46373
1.6	0.47000	0.47623	0.48243	0.48858	0.49470	0.50078	0.50682	0.51282	0.51879	0.52473
1.7	0.53063	0.53649	0.54232	0.54812	0.55389	0.55962	0.56531	0.57098	0.57661	0.58222
1.8	0.58779	0.59333	0.59884	0.60432	0.60977	0.61519	0.62058	0.62594	0.63127	0.63658
1.9	0.64185	0.64710	0.65233	0.65752	0.66269	0.66783	0.67294	0.67803	0.68310	0.68813
2.0	0.69315	0.69813	0.70310	0.70804	0.71295	0.71784	0.72271	0.72755	0.73237	0.73716

APPENDIX C
Present and Terminal Values

Table C.1 Present Value of $1 to Be Paid n Periods in the Future

Periods n	Rate of Discount, %							
	1	2	3	4	5	6	7	8
1	0.99010	0.98039	0.97087	0.96154	0.95238	0.94340	0.93458	0.92593
2	0.98030	0.96117	0.94260	0.92456	0.90703	0.89000	0.87344	0.85734
3	0.97059	0.94232	0.91514	0.88900	0.86384	0.83962	0.81630	0.79383
4	0.96098	0.92385	0.88849	0.85480	0.82270	0.79209	0.76290	0.73503
5	0.95147	0.90573	0.86261	0.82193	0.78353	0.74726	0.71299	0.68058
6	0.94205	0.88797	0.83748	0.79031	0.74622	0.70496	0.66634	0.63017
7	0.93272	0.87056	0.81309	0.75992	0.71068	0.66506	0.62275	0.58349
8	0.92348	0.85349	0.78941	0.73069	0.67684	0.62741	0.58201	0.54027
9	0.91434	0.83676	0.76642	0.70259	0.64461	0.59190	0.54393	0.50025
10	0.90529	0.82035	0.74409	0.67556	0.61391	0.55839	0.50835	0.46319
11	0.89632	0.80426	0.72242	0.64958	0.58468	0.52679	0.47509	0.42888
12	0.88745	0.78849	0.70138	0.62460	0.55684	0.49697	0.44401	0.39711
13	0.87866	0.77303	0.68095	0.60057	0.53032	0.46884	0.41496	0.36770
14	0.86996	0.75788	0.66112	0.57748	0.50507	0.44230	0.38782	0.34046
15	0.86135	0.74301	0.64186	0.55526	0.48102	0.41727	0.36245	0.31524
16	0.85282	0.72845	0.62317	0.53391	0.45811	0.39365	0.33873	0.29189
17	0.84438	0.71416	0.60502	0.51337	0.43630	0.37136	0.31657	0.27027
18	0.83602	0.70016	0.58739	0.49363	0.41552	0.35034	0.29586	0.25025
19	0.82774	0.68643	0.57029	0.47464	0.39573	0.33051	0.27651	0.23171
20	0.81954	0.67297	0.55368	0.45639	0.37689	0.31180	0.25842	0.21455
21	0.81143	0.65978	0.53755	0.43883	0.35894	0.29416	0.24151	0.19866
22	0.80340	0.64684	0.52189	0.42196	0.34185	0.27751	0.22571	0.18394
23	0.79544	0.63416	0.50669	0.40573	0.32557	0.26180	0.21095	0.17032
24	0.78757	0.62172	0.49193	0.39012	0.31007	0.24698	0.19715	0.15770
25	0.77977	0.60953	0.47761	0.37512	0.29530	0.23300	0.18425	0.14602
26	0.77205	0.59758	0.46369	0.36069	0.28124	0.21981	0.17220	0.13520
27	0.76440	0.58586	0.45019	0.34682	0.26785	0.20737	0.16093	0.12519
28	0.75684	0.57437	0.43708	0.33348	0.25509	0.19563	0.15040	0.11591
29	0.74934	0.56311	0.42435	0.32065	0.24295	0.18456	0.14056	0.10733
30	0.74192	0.55207	0.41199	0.30832	0.23138	0.17411	0.13137	0.09938
31	0.73458	0.54125	0.39999	0.29646	0.22036	0.16425	0.12277	0.09202
32	0.72730	0.53063	0.38834	0.28506	0.20987	0.15496	0.11474	0.08520
33	0.72010	0.52023	0.37703	0.27409	0.19987	0.14619	0.10723	0.07889
34	0.71297	0.51003	0.36604	0.26355	0.19035	0.13791	0.10022	0.07305
35	0.70591	0.50003	0.35538	0.25342	0.18129	0.13011	0.09366	0.06763
36	0.69892	0.49022	0.34503	0.24367	0.17266	0.12274	0.08754	0.06262
37	0.69200	0.48061	0.33498	0.23430	0.16444	0.11579	0.08181	0.05799
38	0.68515	0.47119	0.32523	0.22529	0.15661	0.10924	0.07646	0.05369
39	0.67837	0.46195	0.31575	0.21662	0.14915	0.10306	0.07146	0.04971
40	0.67165	0.45289	0.30656	0.20829	0.14205	0.09722	0.06678	0.04603
41	0.66500	0.44401	0.29763	0.20028	0.13528	0.09172	0.06241	0.04262
42	0.65842	0.43530	0.28896	0.19257	0.12884	0.08653	0.05833	0.03946
43	0.65190	0.42677	0.28054	0.18517	0.12270	0.08163	0.05451	0.03654
44	0.64545	0.41840	0.27237	0.17805	0.11686	0.07701	0.05095	0.03383
45	0.63905	0.41020	0.26444	0.17120	0.11130	0.07265	0.04761	0.03133
46	0.63273	0.40215	0.25674	0.16461	0.10600	0.06854	0.04450	0.02901
47	0.62646	0.39427	0.24926	0.15828	0.10095	0.06466	0.04159	0.02686
48	0.62026	0.38654	0.24200	0.15219	0.09614	0.06100	0.03887	0.02487
49	0.61412	0.37896	0.23495	0.14634	0.09156	0.05755	0.03632	0.02303
50	0.60804	0.37153	0.22811	0.14071	0.08720	0.05429	0.03395	0.02132

Table C.1   (continued)

Periods n	Rate of Discount, %							
	9	10	12	14	16	18	20	25
1	0.91743	0.90909	0.89286	0.87719	0.86207	0.84746	0.83333	0.80000
2	0.84168	0.82645	0.79719	0.76947	0.74316	0.71818	0.69444	0.64000
3	0.77218	0.75131	0.71178	0.67497	0.64066	0.60863	0.57870	0.51200
4	0.70843	0.68301	0.63552	0.59208	0.55229	0.51579	0.48225	0.40960
5	0.64993	0.62092	0.56743	0.51937	0.47611	0.43711	0.40188	0.32768
6	0.59627	0.56447	0.50663	0.45559	0.41044	0.37043	0.33490	0.26214
7	0.54703	0.51316	0.45235	0.39964	0.35383	0.31393	0.27908	0.20972
8	0.50187	0.46651	0.40388	0.35056	0.30503	0.26604	0.23257	0.16777
9	0.46043	0.42410	0.36061	0.30751	0.26295	0.22546	0.19381	0.13422
10	0.42241	0.38554	0.32197	0.26974	0.22668	0.19106	0.16151	0.10737
11	0.38753	0.35049	0.28748	0.23662	0.19542	0.16192	0.13459	0.08590
12	0.35553	0.31863	0.25668	0.20756	0.16846	0.13722	0.11216	0.06872
13	0.32618	0.28966	0.22917	0.18207	0.14523	0.11629	0.09346	0.05498
14	0.29925	0.26333	0.20462	0.15971	0.12520	0.09855	0.07789	0.04398
15	0.27454	0.23939	0.18270	0.14010	0.10793	0.08352	0.06491	0.03518
16	0.25187	0.21763	0.16312	0.12289	0.09304	0.07078	0.05409	0.02815
17	0.23107	0.19784	0.14564	0.10780	0.08021	0.05998	0.04507	0.02252
18	0.21199	0.17986	0.13004	0.09456	0.06914	0.05083	0.03756	0.01801
19	0.19449	0.16351	0.11611	0.08295	0.05961	0.04308	0.03130	0.01441
20	0.17843	0.14864	0.10367	0.07276	0.05139	0.03651	0.02608	0.01153
21	0.16370	0.13513	0.09256	0.06383	0.04430	0.03094	0.02174	0.00922
22	0.15018	0.12285	0.08264	0.05599	0.03819	0.02622	0.01811	0.00738
23	0.13778	0.11168	0.07379	0.04911	0.03292	0.02222	0.01509	0.00590
24	0.12640	0.10153	0.06588	0.04308	0.02838	0.01883	0.01258	0.00472
25	0.11597	0.09230	0.05882	0.03779	0.02447	0.01596	0.01048	0.00378
26	0.10639	0.08391	0.05252	0.03315	0.02109	0.01352	0.00874	0.00302
27	0.09761	0.07628	0.04689	0.02908	0.01818	0.01146	0.00728	0.00242
28	0.08955	0.06934	0.04187	0.02551	0.01567	0.00971	0.00607	0.00193
29	0.08215	0.06304	0.03738	0.02237	0.01351	0.00823	0.00506	0.00155
30	0.07537	0.05731	0.03338	0.01963	0.01165	0.00697	0.00421	0.00124
31	0.06915	0.05210	0.02980	0.01722	0.01004	0.00591	0.00351	0.00099
32	0.06344	0.04736	0.02661	0.01510	0.00866	0.00501	0.00293	0.00079
33	0.05820	0.04306	0.02376	0.01325	0.00746	0.00425	0.00244	0.00063
34	0.05339	0.03914	0.02121	0.01162	0.00643	0.00360	0.00203	0.00051
35	0.04899	0.03558	0.01894	0.01019	0.00555	0.00305	0.00169	0.00041
36	0.04494	0.03235	0.01691	0.00894	0.00478	0.00258	0.00141	0.00032
37	0.04123	0.02941	0.01510	0.00784	0.00412	0.00219	0.00118	0.00026
38	0.03783	0.02673	0.01348	0.00688	0.00355	0.00186	0.00098	0.00021
39	0.03470	0.02430	0.01204	0.00604	0.00306	0.00157	0.00082	0.00017
40	0.03184	0.02209	0.01075	0.00529	0.00264	0.00133	0.00068	0.00013
41	0.02921	0.02009	0.00960	0.00464	0.00228	0.00113	0.00057	0.00011
42	0.02680	0.01826	0.00857	0.00407	0.00196	0.00096	0.00047	0.00009
43	0.02458	0.01660	0.00765	0.00357	0.00169	0.00081	0.00039	0.00007
44	0.02255	0.01509	0.00683	0.00313	0.00146	0.00069	0.00033	0.00005
45	0.02069	0.01372	0.00610	0.00275	0.00126	0.00058	0.00027	0.00004
46	0.01898	0.01247	0.00544	0.00241	0.00108	0.00049	0.00023	0.00003
47	0.01742	0.01134	0.00486	0.00212	0.00093	0.00042	0.00019	0.00003
48	0.01598	0.01031	0.00434	0.00186	0.00081	0.00035	0.00016	0.00002
49	0.01466	0.00937	0.00388	0.00163	0.00069	0.00030	0.00013	0.00002
50	0.01345	0.00852	0.00346	0.00143	0.00060	0.00025	0.00011	0.00001

Table C.2 Present Value of $1 per Period for n Periods

Periods n	Rate of Discount, %							
	1	2	3	4	5	6	7	8
1	0.990	0.980	0.971	0.962	0.952	0.943	0.935	0.926
2	1.970	1.942	1.913	1.886	1.859	1.833	1.808	1.783
3	2.941	2.884	2.829	2.775	2.723	2.673	2.624	2.577
4	3.902	3.808	3.717	3.630	3.546	3.465	3.387	3.312
5	4.853	4.713	4.580	4.452	4.329	4.212	4.100	3.993
6	5.795	5.601	5.417	5.242	5.076	4.917	4.767	4.623
7	6.728	6.472	6.230	6.002	5.786	5.582	5.389	5.206
8	7.652	7.325	7.020	6.733	6.463	6.210	5.971	5.747
9	8.566	8.162	7.786	7.435	7.108	6.802	6.515	6.247
10	9.471	8.983	8.530	8.111	7.722	7.360	7.024	6.710
11	10.368	9.787	9.253	8.760	8.306	7.887	7.499	7.139
12	11.255	10.575	9.954	9.385	8.863	8.384	7.943	7.536
13	12.134	11.348	10.635	9.986	9.394	8.853	8.358	7.904
14	13.004	12.106	11.296	10.563	9.899	9.295	8.745	8.244
15	13.865	12.849	11.938	11.118	10.380	9.712	9.108	8.559
16	14.718	13.578	12.561	11.652	10.838	10.106	9.447	8.851
17	15.562	14.292	13.166	12.166	11.274	10.477	9.763	9.122
18	16.398	14.992	13.754	12.659	11.690	10.828	10.059	9.372
19	17.226	15.678	14.324	13.134	12.085	11.158	10.336	9.604
20	18.046	16.351	14.877	13.590	12.462	11.470	10.594	9.818
21	18.857	17.011	15.415	14.029	12.821	11.764	10.836	10.017
22	19.660	17.658	15.937	14.451	13.163	12.042	11.061	10.201
23	20.456	18.292	16.444	14.857	13.489	12.303	11.272	10.371
24	21.243	18.914	16.936	15.247	13.799	12.550	11.469	10.529
25	22.023	19.523	17.413	15.622	14.094	12.783	11.654	10.675
26	22.795	20.121	17.877	15.983	14.375	13.003	11.826	10.810
27	23.560	20.707	18.327	16.330	14.643	13.211	11.987	10.935
28	24.316	21.281	18.764	16.663	14.898	13.406	12.137	11.051
29	25.066	21.844	19.188	16.984	15.141	13.591	12.278	11.158
30	25.808	22.396	19.600	17.292	15.372	13.765	12.409	11.258
31	26.542	22.938	20.000	17.588	15.593	13.929	12.532	11.350
32	27.270	23.468	20.389	17.874	15.803	14.084	12.647	11.435
33	27.990	23.989	20.766	18.148	16.003	14.230	12.754	11.514
34	28.703	24.499	21.132	18.411	16.193	14.368	12.854	11.587
35	29.409	24.999	21.487	18.665	16.374	14.498	12.948	11.655
36	30.108	25.489	21.832	18.908	16.547	14.621	13.035	11.717
37	30.800	25.969	22.167	19.143	16.711	14.737	13.117	11.775
38	31.485	26.441	22.492	19.368	16.868	14.846	13.193	11.829
39	32.163	26.903	22.808	19.584	17.017	14.949	13.265	11.879
40	32.835	27.355	23.115	19.793	17.159	15.046	13.332	11.925
41	33.500	27.799	23.412	19.993	17.294	15.138	13.394	11.967
42	34.158	28.235	23.701	20.186	17.423	15.225	13.452	12.007
43	34.810	28.662	23.982	20.371	17.546	15.306	13.507	12.043
44	35.455	29.080	24.254	20.549	17.663	15.383	13.558	12.077
45	36.095	29.490	24.519	20.720	17.774	15.456	13.606	12.108
46	36.727	29.892	24.775	20.885	17.880	15.524	13.650	12.137
47	37.354	30.287	25.025	21.043	17.981	15.589	13.692	12.164
48	37.974	30.673	25.267	21.195	18.077	15.650	13.730	12.189
49	38.588	31.052	25.502	21.341	18.169	15.708	13.767	12.212
50	39.196	31.424	25.730	21.482	18.256	15.762	13.801	12.233

Table C.2   (continued)

Periods n	Rate of Discount, %							
	9	10	12	14	16	18	20	25
1	0.917	0.909	0.893	0.877	0.862	0.847	0.833	0.800
2	1.759	1.736	1.690	1.647	1.605	1.566	1.528	1.440
3	2.531	2.487	2.402	2.322	2.246	2.174	2.106	1.952
4	3.240	3.170	3.037	2.914	2.798	2.690	2.589	2.362
5	3.890	3.791	3.605	3.433	3.274	3.127	2.991	2.689
6	4.486	4.355	4.111	3.889	3.685	3.498	3.326	2.951
7	5.033	4.868	4.564	4.288	4.039	3.812	3.605	3.161
8	5.535	5.335	4.968	4.639	4.344	4.078	3.837	3.329
9	5.995	5.759	5.328	4.946	4.607	4.303	4.031	3.463
10	6.418	6.145	5.650	5.216	4.833	4.494	4.192	3.571
11	6.805	6.495	5.938	5.453	5.029	4.656	4.327	3.656
12	7.161	6.814	6.194	5.660	5.197	4.793	4.439	3.725
13	7.487	7.103	6.424	5.842	5.342	4.910	4.533	3.780
14	7.786	7.367	6.628	6.002	5.468	5.008	4.611	3.824
15	8.061	7.606	6.811	6.142	5.575	5.092	4.675	3.859
16	8.313	7.824	6.974	6.265	5.668	5.162	4.730	3.887
17	8.544	8.022	7.120	6.373	5.749	5.222	4.775	3.910
18	8.756	8.201	7.250	6.467	5.818	5.273	4.812	3.928
19	8.950	8.365	7.366	6.550	5.877	5.316	4.843	3.942
20	9.129	8.514	7.469	6.623	5.929	5.353	4.870	3.954
21	9.292	8.649	7.562	6.687	5.973	5.384	4.891	3.963
22	9.442	8.772	7.645	6.743	6.011	5.410	4.909	3.970
23	9.580	8.883	7.718	6.792	6.044	5.432	4.925	3.976
24	9.707	8.985	7.784	6.835	6.073	5.451	4.937	3.981
25	9.823	9.077	7.843	6.873	6.097	5.467	4.948	3.985
26	9.929	9.161	7.896	6.906	6.118	5.480	4.956	3.988
27	10.027	9.237	7.943	6.935	6.136	5.492	4.964	3.990
28	10.116	9.307	7.984	6.961	6.152	5.502	4.970	3.992
29	10.198	9.370	8.022	6.983	6.166	5.510	4.975	3.994
30	10.274	9.427	8.055	7.003	6.177	5.517	4.979	3.995
31	10.343	9.479	8.085	7.020	6.187	5.523	4.982	3.996
32	10.406	9.526	8.112	7.035	6.196	5.528	4.985	3.997
33	10.464	9.569	8.135	7.048	6.203	5.532	4.988	3.997
34	10.518	9.609	8.157	7.060	6.210	5.536	4.990	3.998
35	10.567	9.644	8.176	7.070	6.215	5.539	4.992	3.998
36	10.612	9.677	8.192	7.079	6.220	5.541	4.993	3.999
37	10.653	9.706	8.208	7.087	6.224	5.543	4.994	3.999
38	10.691	9.733	8.221	7.094	6.228	5.545	4.995	3.999
39	10.726	9.757	8.233	7.100	6.231	5.547	4.996	3.999
40	10.757	9.779	8.244	7.105	6.233	5.548	4.997	3.999
41	10.787	9.799	8.253	7.110	6.236	5.549	4.997	4.000
42	10.813	9.817	8.262	7.114	6.238	5.550	4.998	4.000
43	10.838	9.834	8.270	7.117	6.239	5.551	4.998	4.000
44	10.861	9.849	8.276	7.120	6.241	5.552	4.998	4.000
45	10.881	9.863	8.283	7.123	6.242	5.552	4.999	4.000
46	10.900	9.875	8.288	7.126	6.243	5.553	4.999	4.000
47	10.918	9.887	8.293	7.128	6.244	5.553	4.999	4.000
48	10.934	9.897	8.297	7.130	6.245	5.554	4.999	4.000
49	10.948	9.906	8.301	7.131	6.246	5.554	4.999	4.000
50	10.962	9.915	8.304	7.133	6.246	5.554	4.999	4.000

Table C.3   Terminal Value of $1 after n Periods

Periods n	Rate of Discount, %							
	1	2	3	4	5	6	7	8
1	1.010	1.020	1.030	1.040	1.050	1.060	1.070	1.080
2	1.020	1.040	1.061	1.082	1.103	1.124	1.145	1.166
3	1.030	1.061	1.093	1.125	1.158	1.191	1.225	1.260
4	1.041	1.082	1.126	1.170	1.216	1.262	1.311	1.360
5	1.051	1.104	1.159	1.217	1.276	1.338	1.403	1.469
6	1.062	1.126	1.194	1.265	1.340	1.419	1.501	1.587
7	1.072	1.149	1.230	1.316	1.407	1.504	1.606	1.714
8	1.083	1.172	1.267	1.369	1.477	1.594	1.718	1.851
9	1.094	1.195	1.305	1.423	1.551	1.689	1.838	1.999
10	1.105	1.219	1.344	1.480	1.629	1.791	1.967	2.159
11	1.116	1.243	1.384	1.539	1.710	1.898	2.105	2.332
12	1.127	1.268	1.426	1.601	1.796	2.012	2.252	2.518
13	1.138	1.294	1.469	1.665	1.886	2.133	2.410	2.720
14	1.149	1.319	1.513	1.732	1.980	2.261	2.579	2.937
15	1.161	1.346	1.558	1.801	2.079	2.397	2.759	3.172
16	1.173	1.373	1.605	1.873	2.183	2.540	2.952	3.426
17	1.184	1.400	1.653	1.948	2.292	2.693	3.159	3.700
18	1.196	1.428	1.702	2.026	2.407	2.854	3.380	3.996
19	1.208	1.457	1.754	2.107	2.527	3.026	3.617	4.316
20	1.220	1.486	1.806	2.191	2.653	3.207	3.870	4.661
21	1.232	1.516	1.860	2.279	2.786	3.400	4.141	5.034
22	1.245	1.546	1.916	2.370	2.925	3.604	4.430	5.437
23	1.257	1.577	1.974	2.465	3.072	3.820	4.741	5.871
24	1.270	1.608	2.033	2.563	3.225	4.049	5.072	6.341
25	1.282	1.641	2.094	2.666	3.386	4.292	5.427	6.848
26	1.295	1.673	2.157	2.772	3.556	4.549	5.807	7.396
27	1.308	1.707	2.221	2.883	3.733	4.822	6.214	7.988
28	1.321	1.741	2.288	2.999	3.920	5.112	6.649	8.627
29	1.335	1.776	2.357	3.119	4.116	5.418	7.114	9.317
30	1.348	1.811	2.427	3.243	4.322	5.743	7.612	10.063
31	1.361	1.848	2.500	3.373	4.538	6.088	8.145	10.868
32	1.375	1.885	2.575	3.508	4.765	6.453	8.715	11.737
33	1.389	1.922	2.652	3.648	5.003	6.841	9.325	12.676
34	1.403	1.961	2.732	3.794	5.253	7.251	9.978	13.690
35	1.417	2.000	2.814	3.946	5.516	7.686	10.677	14.785
36	1.431	2.040	2.898	4.104	5.792	8.147	11.424	15.968
37	1.445	2.081	2.985	4.268	6.081	8.636	12.224	17.246
38	1.460	2.122	3.075	4.439	6.385	9.154	13.079	18.625
39	1.474	2.165	3.167	4.616	6.705	9.704	13.995	20.115
40	1.489	2.208	3.262	4.801	7.040	10.286	14.974	21.725
41	1.504	2.252	3.360	4.993	7.392	10.903	16.023	23.462
42	1.519	2.297	3.461	5.193	7.762	11.557	17.144	25.339
43	1.534	2.343	3.565	5.400	8.150	12.250	18.344	27.367
44	1.549	2.390	3.671	5.617	8.557	12.985	19.628	29.556
45	1.565	2.438	3.782	5.841	8.985	13.765	21.002	31.920
46	1.580	2.487	3.895	6.075	9.434	14.590	22.473	34.474
47	1.596	2.536	4.012	6.318	9.906	15.466	24.046	37.232
48	1.612	2.587	4.132	6.571	10.401	16.394	25.729	40.211
49	1.628	2.639	4.256	6.833	10.921	17.378	27.530	43.427
50	1.645	2.692	4.384	7.107	11.467	18.420	29.457	46.902

Table C.3 (continued)

Periods	Rate of Discount, %							
n	9	10	12	14	16	18	20	25
1	1.090	1.100	1.120	1.140	1.160	1.180	1.200	1.250
2	1.188	1.210	1.254	1.300	1.346	1.392	1.440	1.563
3	1.295	1.331	1.405	1.482	1.561	1.643	1.728	1.953
4	1.412	1.464	1.574	1.689	1.811	1.939	2.074	2.441
5	1.539	1.611	1.762	1.925	2.100	2.288	2.488	3.052
6	1.677	1.772	1.974	2.195	2.436	2.700	2.986	3.815
7	1.828	1.949	2.211	2.502	2.826	3.185	3.583	4.768
8	1.993	2.144	2.476	2.853	3.278	3.759	4.300	5.960
9	2.172	2.358	2.773	3.252	3.803	4.435	5.160	7.451
10	2.367	2.594	3.106	3.707	4.411	5.234	6.192	9.313
11	2.580	2.853	3.479	4.226	5.117	6.176	7.430	11.642
12	2.813	3.138	3.896	4.818	5.936	7.288	8.916	14.552
13	3.066	3.452	4.363	5.492	6.886	8.599	10.699	18.190
14	3.342	3.797	4.887	6.261	7.988	10.147	12.839	22.737
15	3.642	4.177	5.474	7.138	9.266	11.974	15.407	28.422
16	3.970	4.595	6.130	8.137	10.748	14.129	18.488	35.527
17	4.328	5.054	6.866	9.276	12.468	16.672	22.186	44.409
18	4.717	5.560	7.690	10.575	14.463	19.673	26.623	55.511
19	5.142	6.116	8.613	12.056	16.777	23.214	31.948	69.389
20	5.604	6.727	9.646	13.743	19.461	27.393	38.338	86.736
21	6.109	7.400	10.804	15.668	22.574	32.324	46.005	108.420
22	6.659	8.140	12.100	17.861	26.186	38.142	55.206	135.525
23	7.258	8.954	13.552	20.362	30.376	45.008	66.247	169.407
24	7.911	9.850	15.179	23.212	35.236	53.109	79.497	211.758
25	8.623	10.835	17.000	26.462	40.874	62.669	95.396	264.698
26	9.399	11.918	19.040	30.167	47.414	73.949	114.475	330.872
27	10.245	13.110	21.325	34.390	55.000	87.260	137.371	413.590
28	11.167	14.421	23.884	39.204	63.800	102.967	164.845	516.988
29	12.172	15.863	26.750	44.693	74.009	121.501	197.814	646.235
30	13.268	17.449	29.960	50.950	85.850	143.371	237.376	807.794
31	14.462	19.194	33.555	58.083	99.586	169.177	284.852	1,009.742
32	15.763	21.114	37.582	66.215	115.520	199.629	341.822	1,262.177
33	17.182	23.225	42.092	75.485	134.003	235.563	410.186	1,577.722
34	18.728	25.548	47.143	86.053	155.443	277.964	492.224	1,972.152
35	20.414	28.102	52.800	98.100	180.314	327.997	590.668	2,465.190
36	22.251	30.913	59.136	111.834	209.164	387.037	708.802	3,081.488
37	24.254	34.004	66.232	127.491	242.631	456.703	850.562	3,851.860
38	26.437	37.404	74.180	145.340	281.452	538.910	1,020.675	4,814.825
39	28.816	41.145	83.081	165.687	326.484	635.914	1,224.810	6,018.531
40	31.409	45.259	93.051	188.884	378.721	750.378	1,469.772	7,523.164
41	34.236	49.785	104.217	215.327	439.317	885.446	1,763.726	9,403.955
42	37.318	54.764	116.723	245.473	509.607	1,044.827	2,116.471	11,754.944
43	40.676	60.240	130.730	279.839	591.144	1,232.896	2,539.765	14,693.679
44	44.337	66.264	146.418	319.017	685.727	1,454.817	3,047.718	18,367.099
45	48.327	72.890	163.988	363.679	795.444	1,716.684	3,657.262	22,958.874
46	52.677	80.180	183.666	414.594	922.715	2,025.687	4,388.714	28,698.593
47	57.418	88.197	205.706	472.637	1,070.349	2,390.311	5,266.457	35,873.241
48	62.585	97.017	230.391	538.807	1,241.605	2,820.567	6,319.749	44,841.551
49	68.218	106.719	258.038	614.239	1,440.262	3,328.269	7,583.698	56,051.939
50	74.358	117.391	289.002	700.233	1,670.704	3,927.357	9,100.438	70,064.923

Table C.4   Terminal Value of $1 per Period for n Periods

Periods n	Rate of Discount, %							
	1	2	3	4	5	6	7	8
1	1.000	1.000	1.000	1.000	1.000	1.000	1.000	1.000
2	2.010	2.020	2.030	2.040	2.050	2.060	2.070	2.080
3	3.030	3.060	3.091	3.122	3.153	3.184	3.215	3.246
4	4.060	4.122	4.184	4.246	4.310	4.375	4.440	4.506
5	5.101	5.204	5.309	5.416	5.526	5.637	5.751	5.867
6	6.152	6.308	6.468	6.633	6.802	6.975	7.153	7.336
7	7.214	7.434	7.662	7.898	8.142	8.394	8.654	8.923
8	8.286	8.583	8.892	9.214	9.549	9.897	10.260	10.637
9	9.369	9.755	10.159	10.583	11.027	11.491	11.978	12.488
10	10.462	10.950	11.464	12.006	12.578	13.181	13.816	14.487
11	11.567	12.169	12.808	13.486	14.207	14.972	15.784	16.645
12	12.683	13.412	14.192	15.026	15.917	16.870	17.888	18.977
13	13.809	14.680	15.618	16.627	17.713	18.882	20.141	21.495
14	14.947	15.974	17.086	18.292	19.599	21.015	22.550	24.215
15	16.097	17.293	18.599	20.024	21.579	23.276	25.129	27.152
16	17.258	18.639	20.157	21.825	23.657	25.673	27.888	30.324
17	18.430	20.012	21.762	23.698	25.840	28.213	30.840	33.750
18	19.615	21.412	23.414	25.645	28.132	30.906	33.999	37.450
19	20.811	22.841	25.117	27.671	30.539	33.760	37.379	41.446
20	22.019	24.297	26.870	29.778	33.066	36.786	40.995	45.762
21	23.239	25.783	28.676	31.969	35.719	39.993	44.865	50.423
22	24.472	27.299	30.537	34.248	38.505	43.392	49.006	55.457
23	25.716	28.845	32.453	36.618	41.430	46.996	53.436	60.893
24	26.973	30.422	34.426	39.083	44.502	50.816	58.177	66.765
25	28.243	32.030	36.459	41.646	47.727	54.865	63.249	73.106
26	29.526	33.671	38.553	44.312	51.113	59.156	68.676	79.954
27	30.821	35.344	40.710	47.084	54.669	63.706	74.484	87.351
28	32.129	37.051	42.931	49.968	58.403	68.528	80.698	95.339
29	33.450	38.792	45.219	52.966	62.323	73.640	87.347	103.966
30	34.785	40.568	47.575	56.085	66.439	79.058	94.461	113.283
31	36.133	42.379	50.003	59.328	70.761	84.802	102.073	123.346
32	37.494	44.227	52.503	62.701	75.299	90.890	110.218	134.214
33	38.869	46.112	55.078	66.210	80.064	97.343	118.933	145.951
34	40.258	48.034	57.730	69.858	85.067	104.184	128.259	158.627
35	41.660	49.994	60.462	73.652	90.320	111.435	138.237	172.317
36	43.077	51.994	63.276	77.598	95.836	119.121	148.913	187.102
37	44.508	54.034	66.174	81.702	101.628	127.268	160.337	203.070
38	45.953	56.115	69.159	85.970	107.710	135.904	172.561	220.316
39	47.412	58.237	72.234	90.409	114.095	145.058	185.640	238.941
40	48.886	60.402	75.401	95.026	120.800	154.762	199.635	259.057
41	50.375	62.610	78.663	99.827	127.840	165.048	214.610	280.781
42	51.879	64.862	82.023	104.820	135.232	175.951	230.632	304.244
43	53.398	67.159	85.484	110.012	142.993	187.508	247.776	329.583
44	54.932	69.503	89.048	115.413	151.143	199.758	266.121	356.950
45	56.481	71.893	92.720	121.029	159.700	212.744	285.749	386.506
46	58.046	74.331	96.501	126.871	168.685	226.508	306.752	418.426
47	59.626	76.817	100.397	132.945	178.119	241.099	329.224	452.900
48	61.223	79.354	104.408	139.263	188.025	256.565	353.270	490.132
49	62.835	81.941	108.541	145.834	198.427	272.958	378.999	530.343
50	64.463	84.579	112.797	152.667	209.348	290.336	406.529	573.770

Table C.4   (continued)

Periods	Rate of Discount, %							
n	9	10	12	14	16	18	20	25
1	1.000	1.000	1.000	1.000	1.000	1.000	1.000	1.000
2	2.090	2.100	2.120	2.140	2.160	2.180	2.200	2.250
3	3.278	3.310	3.374	3.440	3.506	3.572	3.640	3.813
4	4.573	4.641	4.779	4.921	5.066	5.215	5.368	5.766
5	5.985	6.105	6.353	6.610	6.877	7.154	7.442	8.207
6	7.523	7.716	8.115	8.536	8.977	9.442	9.930	11.259
7	9.200	9.487	10.089	10.730	11.414	12.142	12.916	15.073
8	11.028	11.436	12.300	13.233	14.240	15.327	16.499	19.842
9	13.021	13.579	14.776	16.085	17.519	19.086	20.799	25.802
10	15.193	15.937	17.549	19.337	21.321	23.521	25.959	33.253
11	17.560	18.531	20.655	23.045	25.733	28.755	32.150	42.566
12	20.141	21.384	24.133	27.271	30.850	34.931	39.581	54.208
13	22.953	24.523	28.029	32.089	36.786	42.219	48.497	68.760
14	26.019	27.975	32.393	37.581	43.672	50.818	59.196	86.949
15	29.361	31.772	37.280	43.842	51.660	60.965	72.035	109.687
16	33.003	35.950	42.753	50.980	60.925	72.939	87.442	138.109
17	36.974	40.545	48.884	59.118	71.673	87.068	105.931	173.636
18	41.301	45.599	55.750	68.394	84.141	103.740	128.117	218.045
19	46.018	51.159	63.440	78.969	98.603	123.414	154.740	273.556
20	51.160	57.275	72.052	91.025	115.380	146.628	186.688	342.945
21	56.765	64.002	81.699	104.768	134.841	174.021	225.026	429.681
22	62.873	71.403	92.503	120.436	157.415	206.345	271.031	538.101
23	69.532	79.543	104.603	138.297	183.601	244.487	326.237	673.626
24	76.790	88.497	118.155	158.659	213.978	289.494	392.484	843.033
25	84.701	98.347	133.334	181.871	249.214	342.603	471.981	1,054.791
26	93.324	109.182	150.334	208.333	290.088	405.272	567.377	1,319.489
27	102.723	121.100	169.374	238.499	337.502	479.221	681.853	1,650.361
28	112.968	134.210	190.699	272.889	392.503	566.481	819.223	2,063.952
29	124.135	148.631	214.583	312.094	456.303	669.447	984.068	2,580.939
30	136.308	164.494	241.333	356.787	530.312	790.948	1,181.882	3,227.174
31	149.575	181.943	271.293	407.737	616.162	934.319	1,419.258	4,034.968
32	164.037	201.138	304.848	465.820	715.747	1,103.496	1,704.109	5,044.710
33	179.800	222.252	342.429	532.035	831.267	1,303.125	2,045.931	6,306.887
34	196.982	245.477	384.521	607.520	965.270	1,538.688	2,456.118	7,884.609
35	215.711	271.024	431.663	693.573	1,120.713	1,816.652	2,948.341	9,856.761
36	236.125	299.127	484.463	791.673	1,301.027	2,144.649	3,539.009	12,321.952
37	258.376	330.039	543.599	903.507	1,510.191	2,531.686	4,247.811	15,403.440
38	282.630	364.043	609.831	1,030.998	1,752.822	2,988.389	5,098.373	19,255.299
39	309.066	401.448	684.010	1,176.338	2,034.273	3,527.299	6,119.048	24,070.124
40	337.882	442.593	767.091	1,342.025	2,360.757	4,163.213	7,343.858	30,088.655
41	369.292	487.852	860.142	1,530.909	2,739.478	4,913.591	8,813.629	37,611.819
42	403.528	537.637	964.359	1,746.236	3,178.795	5,799.038	10,577.355	47,015.774
43	440.846	592.401	1,081.083	1,991.709	3,688.402	6,843.865	12,693.826	58,770.718
44	481.522	652.641	1,211.813	2,271.548	4,279.546	8,076.760	15,233.592	73,464.397
45	525.859	718.905	1,358.230	2,590.565	4,965.274	9,531.577	18,281.310	91,831.496
46	574.186	791.795	1,522.218	2,954.244	5,760.718	11,248.261	21,938.572	114,790.370
47	626.863	871.975	1,705.884	3,368.838	6,683.433	13,273.948	26,327.286	143,488.963
48	684.280	960.172	1,911.590	3,841.475	7,753.782	15,664.259	31,593.744	179,362.203
49	746.866	1,057.190	2,141.981	4,380.282	8,995.387	18,484.825	37,913.492	224,203.754
50	815.084	1,163.909	2,400.018	4,994.521	10,435.649	21,813.094	45,497.191	280,255.693

Illustration Credits

Author Index

Subject Index